In Their Words

A Genealogist's Translation Guide to Polish, German, Latin, and Russian Documents

Volume Two: Russian

by

Jonathan D. Shea, A. G.

and

William F. Hoffman

Language & Lineage Press

2002

Tír gan teanga, tír gan anam.
"A country without a language is a country without a soul" – Irish proverb
Thanks, RKE

Cover: this ornate document, which certifies that a soldier had completed a particular military training course, is examined in greater detail as Document VI-35 on page 303.

Published by **Language & Lineage Press**
8 Lyle Rd., New Britain CT 06053-2104
http://www.langline.com

Printed and bound in the United States of America.

ISBN 0-9631579-4-9

TABLE OF CONTENTS

Introduction viii
I. Phonetics and Spelling 1
A. The Cyrillic Alphabet 1
1. The Archaic Characters 2
2. Other Characters Needing Special Attention 3
3. Consonants 4
4. Vowels 5
5. Phonetic Miscellanea 6
6. Devoicing and Assimilation 7
B. Orthography 8
C. Handwriting: Cyrillic Script 9
D. Russian Forms of Proper Names 10
1. Transliteration vs. Translation 10
2. Transliterating Russian Names into the Roman Alphabet 12
3. Transliterating German Names from the Cyrillic Alphabet 14
4. Transliterating Jewish Names from the Cyrillic Alphabet 16
Phonetic Values of the Yiddish and Cyrillic Alphabets, with Observations on Names 18
5. Transliterating Lithuanian Names from the Cyrillic Alphabet 21
6. Transliterating Polish Names from the Cyrillic Alphabet 23
7. Conclusion: Sleepless in Shidlovo 27
E. Russian Alphabetical Order 30
F. Linguistic Interference from Other Languages 32
II. Structure of Russian 33
A. Grammar 33
Nouns and Adjectives 33
Sample Paradigms 35
Other Forms of These Endings 37
The "Chopping Block" 38
Pronouns 42
Verbs 43
Past Tense 44
Present Tense 44
Participles 44
B. Date and Time Expressions 45
Numbers 45
Months 47
Dates 47
Dates Using the Old Church Slavonic Alphabet 48
Days of the Week 49
Time 49
Hour 49
Time of Day 50
Age 50
C. Familial Relationships 51
D. Sample List of Occupations 52
III. Locating Records in America That Lead Back to Europe 73
A. Church Records 73
B. Civil Vital Records 73
C. Naturalization Records 74
D. Passenger Lists 75
E. Social Security 77

F. Probate Records....77
G. Polish Fraternal Organizations....77
H. Parish & Organizational Histories....78
I. Obituaries and Cemetery Inscriptions....78
J. Passports and Consular Records....78
K. Insurance and Fraternal Organization Death Claim Records....78
IV. Russian-Language Records Originating in America....80
A. Church Records....80
Document IV-1: A Church Registry Extract....80
Main Administrative Subdivisions of the Russian Empire....83
B. Obituaries....85
Document IV-2....85
Document IV-3....86
Document IV-4....87
Document IV-5....87
Document IV-6....88
Document IV-7....88
C. Cemetery Inscriptions....88
D. Terms Often Found in Obituaries and Gravestone Inscriptions....90
E. Russian Consular Records....94
1. Document IV-8: Notarized Attestation for Obtaining Traveling Papers....94
2. Document IV-9: A Questionnaire (Passport Application)....97
3. Document IV-10: A Handwritten Passport Application....103
4. Document IV-11: A Seaman's Certificate....106
5. Document IV-12: A Request for Exemption from Military Service....108
6. Document IV-13: A Certificate for Travel (in Place of a Passport)....111
7. Document IV-14: A Statement Regarding Previous Employment....114
V. Finding Your Ancestral Home and Its Records....115
A. "I've Found It ... But Where Is It?"....115
B. Basic Geography, and the Problems of Place Names....116
European Russia....116
Asiatic Russia....117
Russian Names of Provincial Capitals, Selected County Seats, and Other Localities....118
1. Kingdom of Poland (Королевство Польское *or* Царство Польское)....118
Map V-1: The Russian Partition in the mid-19th century....119
2. Finland (Великое Княжество Финляндское *or* Финляндія)....121
3. Baltic Provinces of the Russian Empire (not including Lithuania)....122
4. Lithuania (Великое Княжество Литовское *or* Литва)....123
Map V-2: Counties of Vil'na Province....123
Modern Kaliningrad Oblast', Russia....124
5. Belarus (old name Бѣлоруссія, now Беларусь)....125
Map V-3: Counties of Grodna Province....125
6. Ukraine (Украина)....127
Territory Formerly in the Austrian Partition (Eastern Galicia), Later in the Soviet Union....127
Map V-4: Galicia as of the mid-19th century....129
Ukrainian Territories in "Little Russia," "South Russia," and Western Russia....130
Map V-5: The Pale of Settlement as of the late 19th century....131
7. Great Russia....135
8. South Russia, or "New" Russia....135
9. The Region of Kazan'....135
10. The Region of Astrakhan'....135
Map V-6: The Western Russian Empire as of the End of the 19th Century....136
11. Asiatic Russia....137

The *Gubernias* and Districts of *Кавказ*, the Caucasus 137
The *Gubernias* and Regions of *Сибирь*, Siberia 137
The Districts of Central Asia 137
Map V-7: Western Russia as of 2001 138
Map V-8: Eastern Russia as of 2001 139
12. Other Russian Geographical Names You May Encounter 139
C. Gazetteers for the Russian Empire 140
Document V-1: Sample from a Russian Provincial Gazetteer 141
Document V-2: Sample page from *Географическо-статистическій словарь Россійской имперіи* 142
German-Language Works 143
English-Language Works 143
Belarus' 144
Document V-3: Sample from *Краткий тонономический словарь Белоруссии* 144
Document V-4: Sample from *Слоўнік назваў … воблацi* 146
Document V-5: Sample from *Список населенных мест Б.С.С.Р.* 148
Lithuania 149
Document V-6: sample from *Indeks alfabetyczny miejscowości dawnego Wielkiego Księstwa Litewskiego* 180
Ukraine 152
D. Gazetteers for the Regions of Poland Once Ruled by Russia 153
Document V-7: The 1934 *Skorowidz miejscowości* 153
Document V-8: Sample from the 1967 *Spis miejscowości PRL* 154
Document V-9: *Wykaz urzędowcyh nazw miejscowości w Polsce* 155
The *Słownik Geograficzny Królestwa Polskiego* 155
A Sampling of Abbreviations and Vocabulary in the *Słownik Geograficzny* 156
Document V-10: Sample *Słownik Geograficzny* Entry 160
Other Polish-Language Sources 161
Document V-11: The 1921 Polish Census 161
Document V-12: Bigo's Gazetteer of Galicia 162
Document V-13: *Alphabetisches Orts- und Gemeindelexikon … Warschau* 163
Document V-14: *Nazwy Miejscowe Polski–Historia–Pochodzenie* 163
Document V-15: Guidebook for Jedwabne 164
Document V-16: Sample Church Directory 165
Gazetteers for Former Austrian Territory 165
Document V-17: Sample from *Genealogical Gazetteer of Galicia* 166
What Does All This Have to Do with RUSSIA? 166
Map V-9: "Poland" (The Commonwealth of Poland and Lithuania) in 1634 and 1815 ... 167
Map V-10: Poland, 1921-1939 168
E. Dealing with Repositories of Records in the Former Russian Empire 169
1. Russia 169
Guide to Writing Letters in Russian 170
2. Lithuania 174
Guide to Writing Letters in Lithuanian 175
3. Belarus 179
4. Ukraine 180
Guide to Writing Letters in Ukrainian 183
5. Poland 187
VI. Russian-Language Records Originating in Europe 193
A. Indexes to Vital Records Registers 193
Document VI-1: Index to 1870 Births in Bargłów Kościelny, Poland 193
Document VI-2: Index to 1882 Marriage Register in Sadlno Parish, near Konin, Poland 194
Document VI-3: Index of 1882 Deaths from Sadlno Parish, near Konin, Poland 195
Document VI-4: Register Title from Białystok, Poland 196

B. Records of Birth, Baptism, or Circumcision 197
1. Components of a Paragraph-Form Birth/Baptismal Record 197
2. Document VI-5: A Paragraph-Form Catholic Birth Record from the Kingdom of Poland 198
3. Document VI-6: Example of a Marginal Notation in a Birth Record 205
4. Document VI-7: Another Example of a Marginal Notation in a Birth Record 207
5. Document VI-8: A Jewish Birth Record from Russian Poland 209
6. Document VI-9: A Written Transcript of a Catholic Birth Record from Lithuania 212
7. Document VI-10: A Written Transcript of a Jewish Birth Record from Russian Poland 217
8. Document VI-11: A Written Attestation of Determination of Age 221
9. Document VI-12: A Russian Orthodox Columnar Baptismal Record 225
10. Document VI-13: A Catholic Columnar Baptismal Record from Russian Poland 228
Document VI-14: A Catholic Columnar Baptismal Record from Lithuania 230
11. Document VI-15: A Jewish Columnar Birth Record 233
Document VI-16, Another Jewish Birth Record, from Białystok, Poland, 1880 238
12. Document VI-17, A Short-Form Birth Certificate 240
C. Records of Marriage 242
1. Documents VI-18 and VI-19: Premarital Examination 242
2. Document VI-20: A Paragraph-Form Marriage Record from Russian Poland 247
3. Document VI-21: A Paragraph-Form Jewish Marriage Record from Russian Poland 254
4. Document VI-22: A Russian Orthodox Columnar Marriage Register 260
5. Document VI-23: A Roman Catholic Columnar Marriage Register from Poland 263
Document VI-24: A Roman Catholic Marriage Register from Lithuania 267
6. Document VI-25: A Jewish Columnar Marriage Register from Russian Poland 270
7. Document VI-26: A Short-Form Certificate from Russian Poland 272
D. Death Records 274
1. Document VI-27: A Paragraph-Form Death Record from Russian Poland 274
2. Document VI-28: A Jewish Paragraph-Form Death Record from Russian Poland 278
3. Document VI-29: A Russian Orthodox Columnar Death Record 281
4. Document VI-30: A Catholic Columnar Death Record from Russian Poland 283
5. Document VI-31: A Jewish Columnar Death Record from Russian Poland 284
6. Terms Often Seen as Causes of Death or in Death Records 286
E. Miscellaneous Records 290
1. Document VI-32: A Jewish Divorce Record from Białystok 290
2. Military Records: Document VI-33: Conscription Lists 292
Document VI-34: A List of Draftable Males from a Population Register 299
Document VI-35: Certificate of Completing Training 303
Document VI-36: Certificate of Having Reported for Conscription 305
Document VI-37: Military Discharge Booklet 306
Document VI-38: Details from Another Discharge Booklet 311
Document VI-39: A "Militia Ticket" 313
3. Document VI-40: *Revizskie Skazki* (Revision Lists) 317
4. Returns from the 1897 Russian National Census 320
Document VI-41: Census Form A 322
Document VI-42: Census Return for Form A 324
Document VI-43: Military Census Form 326
Document VI-44: Questionnaire for Military Census Form 328
5. Document VI-45: A Легитимаціонная Книжка (Identification Booklet) 330
6. Notarial Documents – Document VI-46: A Notarized Deed of Sale 332
Document VI-47: A Bilingual Notarized Document 334
7. Document VI-48: A Catholic Church's Register of Easter Communicants 336
8. Document VI-49: A Population Register 338
9. Passports – Document VI-50: Long-Form Passport Booklet 342
Document VI-51: Sample of the "Short-Form" Booklet Passport 346
Document VI-52: A Single-Sheet Russian Passport 348

Document VI-53: Another Example of a Single-Sheet Russian Passport 350
Document VI-54: A 28-Day Identification Document 351
10. Document VI-55: A Guild Membership Certificate 352
11. Document VI-56: A Certificate of Nobility 354
12. Document VI-57: A Personal Letter 356
13. Other Documents 357
VII. Vocabulary 358
Symbols and Abbreviations 359
A List of Terms Frequently Encountered in Records 360
VIII. An Index of First Names 437
Feminine Forms 437
Linguistic and Ethnic Origins 437
Name Equivalents 438
Name Days 438
Name Variants, Diminutives, Alternate Forms, etc. 439
Alphabetical Order 440
Summary 440
Abbreviations and Symbols 440
Alphabetical List of Selected First Names 441
IX. Acknowledgements and Bibliography 467
X. Index 470

INTRODUCTION

There's no question about it—this is a big book! Maybe too big. But if your family history leads to the lands formerly ruled by the Russian Empire, you will probably need quite a bit of assistance. **If you're going to buy only one book to help you, we want this to be the one!**

So we've given you a lot here—better too much than too little. The idea is to provide everything you need to become as proficient as you want to be. If you only want to achieve modest skill at reading the records you find while doing genealogical research, this book should help you. On the other hand, if you'd like to grow really good at it, we think there's enough to get you off to an excellent start. Of course, true fluency in any language can come only through extensive practice with native speakers. But one can hope to read documents well even without developing any great fluency in speaking the language in question.

Actually this book began as update of Jonathan D. Shea's *Russian Language Documents from Russian Poland,* a 76-page translation manual published in 1989 by Genun Publishers. The fact that this book is so much bigger can be explained by the much, much greater amount of material now available to researchers.

Like that work, this one uses primarily sample documents from the regions that once comprised the western part of the Russian Empire, and are now the independent nations of Poland, Lithuania, Belarus', and Ukraine. That's because most researchers we've dealt with came from those areas; relatively few were natives of Russia itself. But we have tried to include information that will help researchers with roots in any part of the Empire. As time passes, more descendants of ethnic Russians become interested in tracing their roots, and more genealogically-relevant material from Russia itself becomes available, we hope this book will continue to help researchers use it.

To trace your family back to the old country, you **must** have these three pieces of information for each line you trace:

- **The name of your ancestor who emigrated – not an Anglicized version, but the original name he or she went by in the old country**
- **The date of that ancestor's birth**
- **The place of that ancestor's birth**

In preparing this book we asked a simple question: what information do we wish we'd had available years ago, when we first started working with Russian-language documents? What information, if readily available, would have saved us a lot of trouble? In this book we attempt to present that information, complete with sample documents that serve to illustrate it. We also provide pointers that can assist you with finding documents in the first place, a quest that can prove extremely frustrating.

Since the book is rather long, it seems needless to write a long introduction. But there are two points we really hope you'll remember as you study this material.

➢ **Use the Index**! (pages 470-486). We compiled it carefully, and it can assist you greatly in bypassing information you don't need, to focus on the exact issue troubling you. If, for instance, you have a lot of trouble reading the handwriting in the records you've found, look under "handwriting, samples printed for better legibility." There you will find the numbers of pages on which we have reprinted the text of chosen documents, line-by-line, in a more legible cursive or in italics, which you can compare with the original and use to decipher it. Or if you want to know about the Revision Lists drawn up in the Russian Empire for tax purposes, the Index will take you directly to pages 317-320, where we analyze a sample. We hope the Index will make this book much easier to use.

- **Don't be overwhelmed!** There is an enormous amount of information here, and one could easily be daunted at the prospect of trying to absorb it all. But you don't have to absorb it all! Our guiding principle was to give as much information as we had room for, so that readers who want details will have them. But if all you want is the big picture, concentrate on that. With some documents, for instance, we provide rather detailed analysis of the grammar, because we know some researchers value such analysis. If you aren't interested in the fine points of grammar, just read the translations and skip the rest. Or better yet, read the translations and focus only on specific points that baffle you.

You will notice from the Index that many topics are addressed repeatedly in different places in the text. We considered it unlikely that anyone's going to start at page 1 and read all the way through to the end. So we repeated certain key points in different places, or provide cross-references to discussions elsewhere in the text, for the convenience of readers who jump from one section to another and thus might miss something.

Having said that, we should point out that there is a kind of progression from one document to the next. You may benefit from studying whole sections as they appear. But the choice is yours: proceed methodically through each section, or jump from place to place, using the Index to find what you need. Either way, we've tried to accommodate you.

We considered the advisability of discussing the numerous and constantly proliferating sites on the Internet (primarily the World Wide Web) that provide information on Russian genealogy, history, culture—almost any Russian-related topic one can think of. But we decided against it, not because the subject does not deserve mention, but because things on the Internet change far too rapidly for any printed source to keep up with. Some of these sites—such as that of the LDS Family History Library, at **www.familysearch.org**—will surely be around for a long time; and we have included the addresses of some of those sites. Still, if we printed a long list of Web addresses that are simply priceless today, by the time this book is printed some of them will already have changed. The wiser course of action, it seemed, was to mention the potential value of information available on the Web, mention a few sites that seem likely to last, and let you find other material yourself with a good Internet search engine.

One word of advice: the Internet can be a big help, but don't make the mistake of thinking it can do it all for you. Successful genealogical research still relies, and always will rely, on the persistence and curiosity of the individual researcher. Others can help you enormously—but in the final analysis, success in research is still up to you.

Please realize, also, that what's true of change on the Internet is true of the physical addresses of brick-and-mortar institutions, as well as of their policies and procedures. As we go to press, the addresses and other information given in this book are accurate. But that will inevitably change, and any experienced researcher knows never to take **anything** as Gospel until it has been checked and verified. That includes information in books by "experts."

Finally, please forgive us if that one document you need help with is not discussed in this book. As it is, the book runs nearly 500 bindery pages, and we had to draw the line somewhere. But in our translating work and efforts on behalf of various genealogical organizations, we see a pretty good sampling of what's available. From what our experience tells us, this book deals with those documents you are most likely to find and need translated.

We hope you find it helpful, and wish you the best of luck with your research.

Jonathan D. Shea
William F. Hoffman
November, 2002

I. PHONETICS & SPELLING

A. THE CYRILLIC ALPHABET

Printed	*Cursive*	*English*	*Polish*	*Lith.*
А а	*А а*	*a*	*a*	*a, ą*
Б б	*Б б*	*b*	*b*	*b*
В в	*В в*	*v*	*w*	*v*
Г г	*Г г*	*g, h*	*g, h*	*g*
Д д	*Д д*	*d*	*d*	*d*
Е е	*Е е*	*(y)e*	*e, ie, je*	*[i]e, ę, ė*
Ё ё	*Ё ё*	*(y)o*	*o, io, jo*	*[i]o*
Ж ж	*Ж ж*	*zh*	*ż*	*ž*
З з	*З з*	*z*	*z*	*z*
И и	*И и*	*i*	*i*	*y, į*
Й й	*Й й*	*y*	*j*	*j, i*
К к	*К к*	*k*	*k*	*k*
Л л	*Л л*	*l*	*l*	*l*
М м	*М м*	*m*	*m*	*m*
Н н	*Н н*	*n*	*n*	*n*
О о	*О о*	*o*	*o*	*o*
П п	*П п*	*p*	*p*	*p*
Р р	*Р р*	*r*	*r*	*r*
С с	*С с*	*s*	*s*	*s*

Printed	*Cursive*	*English*	*Polish*	*Lith.*
Т т	*Т т*	*t*	*t*	*t*
У у	*У у*	*u*	*u*	*u, ų, ū*
Ф ф	*Ф ф*	*f*	*f*	*f*
Х х	*Х х*	*h, kh*	*ch, h*	*ch, h*
Ц ц	*Ц ц*	*ts*	*c*	*c*
Ч ч	*Ч ч*	*ch*	*cz*	*č*
Ш ш	*Ш ш*	*sh*	*sz*	*š*
Щ щ	*Щ щ*	*shch*	*szcz*	*šč*
Ъ ъ	*Ъ ъ*	—	—	—
Ы ы	*Ы ы*	*y*	*y*	*i*
Ь ь	*Ь ь*	*'*	—	—
Э э	*Э э*	*e*	*e*	*e*
Ю ю	*Ю ю*	*yu, yoo*	*u, iu, ju*	*iu, ju*
Я я	*Я я*	*ya, ia*	*a, ia, ja*	*ia, ja*

Archaic Characters				
Ѣ ѣ	*Ѣ ѣ*	*(i)e*	*e, ie, je*	*(i)e*
І і	*І і*	*i*	*i*	*y, i*
Ѵ ѵ	*Ѵ ѵ*	*i, y*	*i*	*y, i*
Ѳ ѳ	*Ѳ ѳ*	*f*	*f*	*f*

The Russian language is written in the Cyrillic alphabet, as are a number of other Slavic languages, including Bulgarian, Belarusian, Ukrainian, Serbian, and Macedonian. This alphabet differs markedly from the Roman alphabet used in most western European languages, including English, Polish, etc. Shown above is the version of Cyrillic used in modern Russian, including several archaic characters not used since the Russian Revolution, with approximate equivalents in English, Polish, and Lithuanian. Please understand from the start that these "equivalents" are **very approximate**—a fact which will shortly be discussed at greater length (page 4).

The Cyrillic alphabet is named after St. Cyril, 827-869, a Christian missionary; he and his brother St. Methodius (825-885) are regarded as the Apostles to the Slavs because they were the first to convert Slavs to Christianity, in Moravia. Traditionally St. Cyril is credited with creating this alphabet, adapted to Slavic phonetics, so that he could produce a written translation of the Scriptures into Old Church Slavonic. The brothers were clergymen of the Eastern Church, in which Greek was the language of the liturgy, and the characters of the Cyrillic alphabet were drawn largely from the Greek alphabet. Special characters were created for sounds typical of the Slavic languages but absent in Greek—**ш** and **ц** are said to have been modeled after Hebrew **ש** and **צ**, respectively. The Cyrillic alphabet has been modified considerably since then, and different Slavic languages use slightly different versions; thus reference to the "Russian" alphabet is to the version used by that language, as opposed to the version used in Belarusian or Ukrainian, for instance.

Where does the term "Cyrillic" come from?

Note that there are 33 characters in the modern Russian alphabet. Before orthographic reforms introduced after the Russian Revolution in 1917, there were 37. The four characters no longer used are marked separately in the chart on page 1. They still appear in records from before 1917, and thus will be seen in many of the records of interest to genealogical researchers. Modern dictionaries seldom feature them, thus they require some attention.

1. The Archaic Characters

Ѣ ѣ *Ѣ ѣ*

This symbol has been replaced in modern Russian by **Е**. Originally the sound represented by **Ѣ** was distinct from **Е**, but during the course of the language's development they both came to be pronounced in a like manner. Note the following examples:

Old Orthography	*Present Orthography*	*English Phonetics*
*л**ѣ**тъ*	*л**е**т*	*l**ye**t*
*н**ѣ**тъ*	*н**е**т*	*n**ye**t*

I i *I i*

This symbol had the same sound value as the letter **И**, by which it was replaced. The **I** occurred primarily before another vowel, and infrequently in other linguistic environments. The following examples are commonly used lexical items in vital records:

Old Orthography	*Present Orthography*	*English Phonetics*
*присутств**і**и*	*присутств**и**и*	*prisutstv**i**i*
*крещен**і**е*	*крещен**и**е*	*kreshchen**i**e*

We often see this symbol in records, in surnames ending in ***-ski*** or ***-sky*** or ***-skiy:***

*Адамск**і**й*	*Адамск**и**й*	*Adamskiy*
*Ольшевск**і**й*	*Ольшевск**и**й*	*Ol'shevskiy*

The other two archaic characters are less likely to be encountered in the course of genealogical research—one tends to see them mainly in theological contexts—but are offered here for reference purposes:

Ѳ ѳ *Ѳ ѳ*

An equivalent of Russian **Ф** (the sound of *f*), this symbol appeared in words borrowed from Greek. Incidentally, perhaps you're saying "I thought Greek Θ represented a *th* sound, and Φ was a *ph* sound." Exactly so, in classical Greek. But by Cyril's time some of the phonetic values of Greek had changed from their classical values; and since then there has been enough time for further alteration. It's no surprise some letters have come to be sounded differently.

Ѵ ѵ *Ѵ ѵ*

Deriving from the Greek letter **υ**, *upsilon*, this symbol had the same sound value as **И**.

2. Other Characters Needing Special Attention

Ъ ъ *Ъ ъ*

One final aspect of the spelling reforms we should note is the modification of the use of the symbol **ъ**, known as the "hard sign" (in Russian *твердый знак*). This symbol, formerly a vowel, gradually lost its sound value and was used most frequently after consonants in final word position to indicate they were pronounced as hard consonants rather than soft. This particular function of the symbol was eliminated by the post-Revolution spelling reforms.

Old Orthography	*Present Orthography*
Адамъ	*Адам*
паспортъ	*паспорт*

This symbol continues to be used in modern Russian, but appears infrequently; when it does appear, it usually follows verbal prefixes, e. g. *объявлять*.

Ь ь *Ь ь*

The "soft sign" **ь** (*мягкий знак*) likewise symbolized a vowel sound at one point, but in modern Russian it indicates palatalization (see page 4) of the consonant it follows.

Ы ы *Ы ы*

This symbol still retains its vowel quality. It is difficult to describe in print, but can best be summarized as a short *ĭ* sound, somewhat as in English "ship." It always follows a hard, i. e., non-palatalized, consonant. In Polish it is roughly comparable to the sound of the vowel *y*.

Note that the characters **ъ**, **ь**, and **ы** never begin words, and thus their uppercase forms are encountered only when a word is printed in all uppercase forms, for emphasis. The symbols **ъ** and **ь** do not really correspond to any letter in the Roman alphabet as used in English; when Russian words are transliterated into English, those symbols are usually disregarded. In academic usage the soft sign **ь** is often represented with an apostrophe, i. e., мать may be rendered as *mat'*.

3. Consonants

In the lists below, when we compare the various sounds in the Russian language to those of English, we are providing **approximations** of these sounds. You should read these sounds aloud, to get a better "feel" for the language's sound system and to begin to break the habit of pronouncing Russian names and geographical designations "in English." Never forget that almost every Russian consonant is pronounced at least slightly differently from its English counterpart. Whenever possible, listen to and imitate native speakers.

The basic sound values of Russian consonants—shown here in their standard printed forms, followed by their italic forms—are as follows:

б *б* similar to the *b* in English "*b*ook," but with no aspiration (no "h" sound after it)
в *в* similar to the *v* in English "*v*ow"
г *г* usually much like the *g* in English "*g*oose"; at the end of words devoices to the sound of *k* in English "lo*ck*"; in the declensional endings *–его* and *–ого*, and archaic *–аго* and *-яго*, like the sound of *v* in English "*v*ow"
д *д* (also seen in the italic form *g*) similar to the *d* in English "*d*ust," but without aspiration, and the tongue is placed behind the front teeth
ж *ж* similar to the *s* in English "plea*s*ure"
з *з* similar to the *z* in English "*z*one"
й *й* similar to the *y* in English "*y*es"
к *к* similar to the *k* in English "*k*ind"
л *л* similar to the *l* in English "*l*itter"
м *м* similar to the *m* in English "co*m*e"
н *н* similar to the *n* in English "*n*urse"
п *п* similar to the *p* in English "*p*it," but with no aspiration
р *р* trilled *r* as in Spanish or Polish, does not resemble the English *r*
с *с* similar to the *s* in English "*s*aw"
т *т* similar to the *t* in English "*t*ake," but without aspiration and with the tongue behind the front teeth
ф *ф* similar to the *f* in English "*f*ork"
х *х* no equivalent in English, somewhat resembles the *ch* sound in German "Ba*ch*"
ц *ц* similar to the *ts* in English "ca*ts*"
ч *ч* similar to the *ch* in English "*ch*air"
ш *ш* similar to the *sh* in English "*sh*ake"
щ *щ* the sound of **ш** followed by the sound of **ч**, like a combination of *shch* in English (or *szcz* in Polish), as heard in the phrase "fresh cheese"

What is "Palatalization"?

No discussion of Russian consonants is complete, however, without discussion of **palatalization**. A consonant is said to be palatalized or "soft" when its enunciation is shifted upward in the mouth, with more of the tongue approaching or touching the hard palate. In most cases the consonant is pronounced with a slight "y" sound after it. An example is the word spelled *нет* in Russian but pronounced "nyet"—the *n* is palatalized. Palatalization is an extremely pervasive and important feature of the Slavic languages in general, and Russian is no exception. (Poles are familiar with it: it's the difference between *c* and *ć*, *s* and *ś*, *z* and *ź*, etc.)

We do something similar in English, too; we're just not so aware of it. Consider the expression "Gotcha!" It started out as "Got you," but we tend to run the final *-t* of "Got" together with the initial *y-* of "you" and combine them into the sound of *ch*. Russians don't do that, exactly; a palatalized **т** does not become a *ch* sound—it is recognizably a *t*, but a softened one.

It is virtually impossible to describe this aspect of pronunciation accurately in print—you must listen to native speakers. In any case, you don't really need to master this phenomenon to decipher documents. You only need to grasp that palatalization affects spelling in certain ways.

4. Vowels

Russian is unusual to our way of thinking because it seems to have not 5 vowels, but 10. In fact, there are only 5 vowels. The way they are written differs, however, depending on whether or not the consonants preceding them are palatalized—that's how palatalization affects spelling. You could say the hardness or softness of the preceding consonant determines whether the vowel following it comes from the "hard" set or the "soft" set:

"hard," after non-palatalized consonants	**а**	**э**	**ы**	**о**	**у**
"soft," after palatalized consonants	**я**	**е**	**и**	**ё**	**ю**

These vowels do not always follow consonants, however. They can appear initially in words, or follow other vowels. In such cases the distinction is that the "soft" ones, except for **и**, have a slight "y" sound before the vowel itself. Thus, as mentioned before, the Russian word *нет* is pronounced "nyet"; the name *Елена* is pronounced "Yelena"; and there's a difference between *Аня*, "Anya," and *Анна*, "Anna." A Russian trying to spell our name "Ellen" would write it *Элен*, because that initial short *ĕ* is not preceded by a slight "y" sound, so he would have to spell it with **э** instead of **е**.

The pronunciation of these vowels in accented syllables is roughly as follows:

а much like the sound of *a* in English "f*a*ther"
я the same sound after palatalized consonants; initially or after another vowel, it is pronounced roughly like *ya* in English "*ya*cht"

э similar to the short *ĕ* in English "n*e*t"
е the same sound after palatalized consonants; initially or after another vowel, it is pronounced roughly like *ye* in the English word "*ye*t"

ы similar to the short *ĭ* in English "b*i*t"—there is no exact English equivalent
и similar to the long *ē* sound in English "tr*ee*" and "sh*ee*t"; even initially or after another vowel it does ***not*** have the slight *y* heard before **я** and **е** and **ю**

о similar to the sound in English "b*o*re," but shorter and with no lengthening
ё the same sound after palatalized consonants; initially or after another vowel, it resembles *yo* in English "*yo*del"; **ё** appears only in accented syllables

у similar to the sounds in English "t*oo*" and "gl*ue*," but much crisper and with no lengthening
ю the same sound after palatalized consonants; initially or after another vowel, it is pronounced roughly like the English word "*you*"

Note that before giving that that list we specified "The pronunciation of these vowels in accented syllables..." It is a feature of normal Russian speech that most words have only one accented syllable, and only the vowel in that syllable is given the pronunciation as described above. The farther a vowel is from the accented syllable, the less distinctly it is pronounced.

This is particularly noticeable with the vowel **о**. Thus the word for "milk," *молоко*, is accented on the final syllable. Only the final **о** is pronounced as an **о**; the middle one sounds more like Russian **а** than **о**; and the first one, farthest from the accent, sounds almost like the nondescript vowel sound we hear in the first syllable of English "along" or "upon"—linguists call this sound "schwa" and use the symbol ə for it. The vowels **е**, **э**, and **я** also sound different in unstressed syllables, more like Russian **и**, or like a brief *ee* as in English "feet." The vowels **а**, **и**, **ы**, **у** and **ю** are least affected, or not affected at all, by this phenomenon.

As with other features of the language, this subtlety cannot be described adequately in print; you must listen closely to native speakers' pronunciation to grasp it. It is mentioned here because it can affect the spelling of names, especially in terms of confusion between **о** and **а**.

5. Phonetic Miscellanea

One feature of Russian that can puzzle English-speakers is the lack of the sound we spell *h*. When a word with that sound is brought from another language into Russian, the *h* has historically been rendered with the letter **г**, the hard *g* as in "goose." Thus Russians call the German author Herman Hesse *Герман Гессе*, "German Gesse"; Hitler is *Гитлер*, "Gitler."

Suppose a name of, say, Polish or German origin has an *h*, but was written in Russian-language records. The *h* was rendered **г**, as a matter of course. Now when you go to read the Russian record, you may have no way of knowing whether that **г** originally stood for an actual *g* sound, or for a Russified *h*. Thus if a Huster is looking for ancestors in Russian records, and finds an entry for *Густер*, "Guster," he may or may not have reason to rejoice. *Guster* and *Huster* are both legitimate German names; there's no way to tell which one the Russian entry represents without examining the record in the context of results from other sources!

To add to the confusion, in Polish the letter *h* and the combination *ch* are pronounced the same, like the guttural sound represented in Russian by **х**. Thus the Polish surname *Chojnacki*, which can also be spelled *Hojnacki*, would typically be spelled *Хойнацки* by Russians. So we can't even say an *h* in another language is always rendered **г** in Russian; in some circumstances it might be spelled **х**, especially when dealing with names of Polish origin. (In fact in contemporary Russian there is a trend toward using **х**, not **г**, to represent the *h* sound in foreign words; but the records you study will almost certainly predate that trend.)

What's more, the guttural sound of Russian **х** is spelled *ch* in languages such as German (e. g., Ba*ch*) and English (e. g., the Scottish word lo*ch*). This *ch* could easily be confused with the *ch* in English "*ch*ur*ch*"—a sound represented in Russian with the letter **ч**. Here we see a compelling reason to become thoroughly familiar with the Cyrillic alphabet: if you can read the original spelling and sound out the words, you bypass the confusion and ambiguity that inevitably arise from attempts to render Russian sounds phonetically in our alphabet.

Remember that in records predating the Russian Revolution you will encounter the archaic characters **ѣ** and **і**. Simply replace them with their modern equivalents **е** and **и**, respectively. Thus *Гнѣзно* is an archaic Russian spelling for the modern spelling *Гнезно*, the name of the Polish town of Gniezno; *Россія* is archaic for modern *Россия*, "Russia."

6. Devoicing and Assimilation

In addition to the basic sound values enumerated in the previous section, two other important linguistic phenomena can alter pronunciation, thus inviting incorrect orthographic rendering of the spoken word. These two phenomena are devoicing and assimilation.

Devoicing of Consonants in Final Position

Some Russian consonants can be regarded as existing in pairs. The essential difference between the two members of each pair is that one member is voiced—meaning the vocal cords vibrate when the sound is uttered—and the other is voiceless, indicating that vibration of the vocal cords is absent. The table below lists the voiced/voiceless consonant pairs present in Russian, with indication in brackets of each sound's closest English equivalent:

Voiced:	**б** *[b]*	**в** *[v]*	**д** *[d]*	**з** *[z]*	**ж** *[zh]*	**г** *[g]*
Voiceless:	**п** *[p]*	**ф** *[f]*	**т** *[t]*	**с** *[s]*	**ш** *[sh]*	**к** *[k]*

When a voiced sound appears at the end of a word, it automatically devoices in most versions of modern spoken Russian. The spelling doesn't change, just the sound. The following examples illustrate the point.

Written	***Pronounced***
Гри*б*	Gri*p*
Льво*в*	L'vo*f*
Новгоро*д*	Novgoro*t*
Санкт-Петербург	Sankt-Peterbur*k*

Regressive Assimilation

Another linguistic phenomenon in Russian which may cause spelling errors is called **regressive assimilation**. In this process the *last* member of a cluster of consonants affects the pronunciation of those that precede it. The consonants all become either voiced or voiceless, depending on whether the last member of the cluster is voiced or voiceless.

	spelled		pronounced	
Examples:	*также* (voiceless / voiced)	→	ta**gzh**e (voiced / voiced)	*Here voiced* **ж**, *the last member of the cluster, causes the voiceless* **к** *to be pronounced like a voiced* **г** *[g].*
	водка (voiced / voiceless)		vo**tk**a (voiceless / voiceless)	*Here the voiceless* **к** *causes the voiced* **д** *to devoice to the sound of* **т** *[t].*

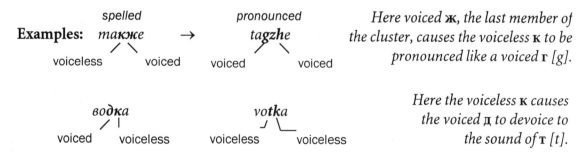

These phenomena affect researchers because they can cause confusion in the Roman-alphabet forms of Russian names. The reason is simple: they cause the way a name or word is pronounced to differ from the way it is spelled. When Russian words are rendered in our alphabet, the rendering is sometimes letter-for-letter, sometimes phonetic. When the spelling and the pronunciation don't match, the discrepancy can generate confusion.

B. ORTHOGRAPHY

There are several general observations that can be made on the subject of Russian orthography and may assist researchers in deciphering Russian words.

- Note that the characters **ъ**, **ь**, and the vowel **ы** never begin words, and thus are not capitalized except in words appearing in all uppercase letters for emphasis.
- The letter **ё** occurs only in stressed syllables; when you see it, you know that syllable is the one accented. Unfortunately you seldom see it. In most printed material (except for children's or beginners' books) Russians leave the diacritical marks off the **ё**, unless it is necessary to avoid ambiguity—to distinguish, say, *все*, "all," from *всё*, "everything." They assume any adult who can read Russian knows when the vowel is **е** and when it's **ё**. This is distinctly inconvenient for us; fortunately **ё** is not used all that often in words.
- The letter **э** almost never follows a consonant, except in words of foreign origin. It usually appears at the beginning of word, mainly in words of foreign origin. The only common native Russian words beginning with **э** are forms of the demonstrative *этот*, "this, that."
- Researchers who compare Russian spellings seen in documents with those in modern dictionaries will note several differences in addition to those connected with use of the archaic letters **ѣ**, **i**, **ѳ**, and **v** (see pages 2-3). For instance, the declensional endings ***-яго*** and ***-аго*** were used where modern Russian uses ***-его*** and ***–ого***, respectively. Also neuter nouns with the modern ending ***–ние*** were sometimes seen spelled ***–нье*** or ***–нiе***, e. g., *крещенье* or *крещенiе* is now *крещение*, "christening, baptism." Replacing the archaic spelling with the modern form will usually allow you to find it in the Vocabulary (page 358) or in a dictionary.
- There are certain combinations of letters that Russian does not allow, at least not in words of native origin (foreign words rendered phonetically in Russian may sometimes have these combinations; for examples, see pages 31-32). We cite this rule here because it may help you decipher handwritten Russian. If you know, for instance, that the letter **г** cannot be followed by the letter **я**, that may help you discern what the letter in question is:

  — the vowels **ы** and **э** never appear after the following characters: **ж ш ч щ г к х** — only **и** and **е** can follow those letters
  — the vowels **я** and **ю** never appear after the following characters: **ж ш ч щ г к х ц**— only **а** and **у**, respectively, can follow those letters
  — the vowel **ё** never appears after the following characters: **г х ц** (the combination ***кё*** appears in one verb form; otherwise it, too, is not used)

- Recall that the Russian Empire—and after it the Soviet Union—was a multicultural and multilingual entity. The Russian language was imposed by the government as the language of law and commerce, but many parts of the Empire were populated by non-Russians whose languages and orthographies had developed on their own terms. Thus Russian-language records from the westernmost parts of the Empire may feature names of Polish or Lithuanian origin; records from the southern regions often have names of Turkish or Persian or Arabic origin; and so on. Record keepers generally attempted to render such names phonetically, using the Cyrillic letters or letter combinations that came closest to matching the way the names sounded. These non-Russian names often included combinations of letters and sounds that don't occur naturally in Russian, so the Cyrillic spellings may include those combinations.

C. HANDWRITING: CYRILLIC SCRIPT

Handwritten Russian often puzzles English-speaking researchers because some of the letters look just familiar enough to confuse you. Familiarity with the printed form of the Russian alphabet helps one recognize the letters that are similar in Russian and English, such as *А а, Е е, І, і, К к,* as well as those Cyrillic letters with handwritten forms recognizable by their resemblance to the print forms: *З з, Ф ф, Ц ц, Ч ч, Э э, Ю ю, Я я*. Below are letters that can be deceptive or difficult for English-speakers to get used to:

Б б	Б б	the distinguishing feature of the lowercase form is the ascending stroke that rises, then breaks off to the right
В в	В в	confusing because it looks just like our letter *b* but represents the sound of our *v*
Г г	Г г	confusing because the uppercase form looks like our cursive *T*, and the lowercase form looks like our lowercase *r*
Д д д	Д д	the lowercase forms *д* and *д* are both used; the standard italic form is *д*; obviously the *д* can confuse us by its resemblance to our script *g*
Ж ж ж	Ж ж	if written legibly, this letter is easy to distinguish; but record keepers didn't always write it legibly! The form *ж* is less common, but you will see it in records.
З з з	З з	we see two lowercase forms, one a small version of the uppercase form, the other much like our lowercase *з*
И и	И и	confusing because of the similarity to our letter *U, u*
Й й	Й й	always distinguished by the little curve above the letter
Л л	Л л	the written form should always begin with a slight "hook" at the lower left, e. g., *село*, *село*, "village, settlement"
М м	М м	the written form should always begin with a slight "hook" at the lower left, e. g., *там*, *там*, "there"
Н н	Н н	confusing because of the similarity to our letter *H h*
П п	П п	the lowercase form is confusing because of its similarity to our lowercase *n;* it is often written with a horizontal line over it (*п̄*) to distinguish it from *т̄* and *ш̲*
Р р	Р р	confusing because of the similarity to our letter *P p*
С с	С с	confusing because of the similarity to our letter *C c*
Т т т	Т т	confusing because the script form is so different from the printed form, and the lowercase form looks like our lowercase *m;* some write this letter with a horizontal line over it (*т̄*), and we also see an alternate form *т* that looks somewhat like our lowercase *f*
У у	У у	confusing because of the similarity to our letter *Y y*
Х х х	Х х	confusing because of the similarity to our letter *X x; х* is a variant seen in records, easily confused with *т*, the alternate form of **Т т**.
Ц ц	Ц ц	confusing because it is distinguished from *И и* only by the little hook at lower right
Ч ч	Ч ч	confusing because the lowercase form looks a lot like our lowercase *r*
Ш ш	Ш ш	confusing because of the similarity to our letter *W w;* often written with a horizontal line under it (*ш̲*) to distinguish it from *т̄* and *п̄*
Щ щ	Щ щ	confusing because it differs from *ш* only by the little hook at lower right
Ъ ъ	Ъ ъ	confusing because it is distinguished from *Ь ь* only by the hook at the upper left
Ы ы	Ы ы	confusing because it could be construed as a combination of the letters *ь* and *і* — you must recall those two letters cannot come together in Russian
Ѣ ѣ	Ѣ ѣ	confusing because the script form is so different from the printed form
Я я	Я я	the written form should always begin with a slight "hook," e. g., *пять*, пять, "five"

Note that in instances where the "italic" form of a Russian letter differs substantially from its printed form, it is taken from the cursive form. Thus the italic form of lowercase **т** is ***т***, modeled after the cursive form *т*, and the italic form of **и** is ***и***, compare *и*, etc. In the sections where we analyze documents, we often give a rendition of the document in italics because those letters resemble cursive forms, yet are a bit easier to read and distinguish. For comparison's sake, here are a few place names in standard printed form, italic form, and cursive, followed by the form of the name as usually rendered in the Roman alphabet:

Printed	*Italic*	*Cursive*	*English*
Варшава	*Варшава*	*Варшава*	Warsaw (from Polish *Warszawa*)
Вильна	*Вильна*	*Вильна*	Vil'na (Wilno, Vilnius)
Волга	*Волга*	*Волга*	Volga
Крым	*Крым*	*Крым*	Krym (Crimea)
Ленинград	*Ленинград*	*Ленинград*	Leningrad
Москва	*Москва*	*Москва*	Moskva (Moscow)
Одесса	*Одесса*	*Одесса*	Odessa
Польша	*Польша*	*Польша*	Pol'sha (Poland)
Сибирь	*Сибирь*	*Сибирь*	Sibir' (Siberia)
Украина	*Украина*	*Украина*	Ukraina (Ukraine)
Чёрное море	*Чёрное море*	*Чёрное Море*	Chyornoye More (Black Sea)
Ялта	*Ялта*	*Ялта*	Yalta

D. RUSSIAN FORMS OF PROPER NAMES

Since we don't grow up speaking Russian, we have to come to terms both with the way sounds are represented in its version of the Cyrillic alphabet, and with the way Russian words are translated into English. The rest of this book deals with translation; let us devote some space here to the concept of transliteration—it will be well worth the effort.

1. Translation vs. Transliteration

When English-speakers deal with any language written in an alphabet other than the Roman alphabet used in English, it is important to distinguish between the concepts of translation and transliteration.

Translation refers to the process of changing a text, word, or idea from the way it is expressed in one language to the way it is expressed in another. It is complex and challenging skill, one you can spend a lifetime learning and still never really master all there is to know.

Transliteration merely involves the process of changing the characters or symbols of one alphabet into their closest equivalents in another. We see the results of transliteration daily in our local newspapers when we read of Riyadh, the capital city of Saudi Arabia, or of a Chinese city such as Beijing (which used to be called "Peking" in English, until *Beijing* was adopted as a more accurate way of representing the Chinese name). We are looking at transliterated forms of the words *Riyadh or Beijing*, which employ Arabic script or Chinese characters, respectively, in the languages from which they come. Transliteration is often challenging, but requires dealing with a finite set of alternatives, and can be learned adequately in a few hours at most.

When Russian records dealt with persons bearing names of Russian linguistic origin, it was a comparatively simple matter for the individual who had the responsibility of maintaining vital records to write down their names. But when those records dealt with persons of, say, Lithuanian or Polish or German or Armenian descent—languages using other alphabets—the individual keeping those records had to transliterate those names in the Russian alphabet. In fact the Russian government issued a series of directives for record keepers as to precisely how this was to be done. Not all record keepers followed those directives consistently, however.

Thus the text of the document was **translated** into Russian, but much more often than not, the names of the persons mentioned in the record, as well as names of the geographical locations, were **transliterated**. For example, the Polish first name *Jan* was supposed to be written *Янъ*, and should not have been translated into *Иванъ* (Ivan), the Russian equivalent of that name—although in fact some clerks did translate first names.

If all the sounds that are present in one language were present in all other languages, pronounced exactly the same way, transliteration would be a straightforward and simple task—one a computer could easily be programmed to do. Unfortunately, that is not the case. As an example, the following Polish sounds have no true equivalent in Russian: *ć, dź, ś, ź, ą, ę*. How, then, does one render them in the Cyrillic alphabet? Likewise, what was the vital records keeper to do with sounds that can be written more than one way in Polish but have only one form in the Cyrillic alphabet (such as *ó = u, rz = ż*)?

One can approach transliteration *mechanically* or *phonetically*.

Record keepers who recorded names of non-Russian origin in Russian spellings could take two different approaches, and we must consider these when we render Russian forms in our alphabet. One might be termed the "mechanical" approach; let us call the other the "phonetic" approach. The ***mechanical*** approach is one a machine might do: taking a word letter-by-letter, for each letter you consult a list of equivalents, and use its counterpart in the other alphabet, whatever it is. Thus a mechanical transliteration would note that our equivalent of Russian **с** is *s;* so whenever **с** appears in Russian, render it as *s* in English. The ***phonetic*** approach involves noting the pronunciation of the whole word, taking into account special values for certain characters or combinations, and then choosing for each the closest phonetic match available.

The mechanical approach is the easier, since it requires no creative thinking, no knowledge of the languages involved. It can produce poor results, however, because sometimes you **have** to take into account special characters or combinations; many letters can be pronounced more than one way, so you can't just exchange one for the other. A mechanical transliteration of German *Schultz* into Russian, for instance, would produce the letter-by-letter form *Сцгультз*, which would be pronounced "stsgul'tz" and would thoroughly baffle any Russian who saw it. The phonetic approach is more difficult, but is more likely to produce an accurate rendering. It would require one to note that German *sch* is pronounced the same as Cyrillic **ш**, and therefore that's the letter you should use to render it in Russian. The phonetic approach would produce *Шульц*—which is, in fact, the form this name most often takes in Russian.

Practically speaking, very few record keepers ever used a purely mechanical approach to transliteration; the resulting absurdities were too obvious. **Most** record keepers (not all!) knew enough, or had received enough training, to recognize the most common troublemakers involved in transliterating from one language to another and to deal with them. In other words, they all transliterated phonetically, to some extent. When we characterize a transliteration as mechanical or phonetic, the distinction is usually one of degree: a mechanical transliteration deals with the most obvious complications, but misses subtler ones.

As it happens, in turning Russian spellings into English ones, the mechanical approach works reasonably well; Russian spelling is highly phonetic. Some issues and problems arise, and we discuss them in Section 2. The complications become more troublesome when we encounter names of non-Russian origin in Russian records, and have to figure out how those names were spelled before they were Russified, so that we can tell whether these names are the ones we're looking for, or just similar ones. In these cases a mechanical approach simply is not adequate. Even a really good phonetic approach sometimes yields disappointing results, simply because most languages have at least a few distinctive sound combinations.

We will begin by looking at the process of rendering Russian names in our alphabet. Presumably most of the non-Russian researchers who use this book will be of German, Jewish, Lithuanian, or Polish heritage, so we will then consider issues involved in transliterating names identified with those ethnic and religious groups.

2. Transliterating Russian Names into the Roman Alphabet

Let us begin by examining how Russian names are rendered in our version of the Roman alphabet. Once English-speaking readers are familiar with that process, it is somewhat easier for them to deal with the distinctions that arise in transliterating the Cyrillic versions of German or Lithuanian or Polish names.

> If you have the English spelling of a name and want to use the chart on page 1 to generate its Russian spelling, convert the sounds in this order: *shch* to **щ**, *sh* to **ш**, *ch* to **ч**, *ya* or *ia* to **я**, *ye* or *ie* to **е**, *yu* or *iu* to **ю**, *kh* to **х**, *ts* or *tz* to **ц**, and *zh* to **ж**, and then the rest, letter-by-letter. This isn't foolproof, but it tends to work.

The third column of the chart on page 1 provides a reasonably good overview of how Russian letters are rendered mechanically in terms of the English version of the Roman alphabet. A few comments, followed by some examples of transliteration, should familiarize readers with this process and enable them to make phonetically accurate transliterations.

- As discussed on pages 6-7, the letter **г** in Russian usually sounds like the hard *g* in English "*g*oose." At the end of words, or before an unvoiced consonant, it sounds more like *k*, and that may affect how it is rendered. (The letter **г** is pronounced like Russian **в**, or our *v*, in the declensional endings *–ого* and *–его,* and in the word *сегодня*, "today." When **г** precedes the letter **к** , as in the word *мягкий*, it is pronounced like **х**, or somewhat like the guttural sound of *ch* in German Ba*ch*. But practically speaking, those pronunciations seldom show up in transliterating names.)
- The Russian vowels **е** , **ё** , **ю** and **я** are generally preceded by a slight *y*-sound, and this has complicated attempts to represent Russian pronunciation accurately by English phonetic values. The letters **ю** and **я** can usually be rendered either *yu* or *iu* and *ya* or *ia,* respectively. The Cyrillic **е**, however, is a problem. If it is mechanically rendered as *ye,* we soon find ourselves drowning in *ye*'s: the first name *Елевтерия* comes out *Yelyevtyeriya!* Some scholars find it better to use *i,* instead of *y,* to stand for that initial sound, but is *Ielievtieriia* really an improvement? Noting that the letter **э** is actually quite rare in Russian, and that the sound of

the vowel **e** is almost always associated with a palatalized consonant, most sane people choose to render Russian **e** as simply *e* in English, reserving *ye* or *ie* to stand for the vowel only when not preceded by a palatalized consonant. Thus that Russian first name *Елевтерия* is rendered either *Elevteriya* or *Yelevteriya*, which is at least tolerable. Incidentally, note that in that name the **в** is usually transliterated *v*, but in Russian it is actually pronounced *f* (it devoices due to regressive assimilation, see page 7). Thus one may sometimes see *Elefteriya* or *Yelefteriya*.

- The Cyrillic letter **ж** is often rendered in English as the rather exotic-looking *zh*. In fact English has a similar sound—not exactly the same, but very similar—represented by the *s* in the word "pleasure." There is no concise way to indicate that in spelling Russian names, however, except as *zh*. Most of us have heard of the movie "Doctor Zhivago," and can recognize the sound from that name. Those familiar with Polish can associate **ж** with the sound of *rz* or *ż*, and those familiar with Lithuanian can think of it as comparable to *ž*.
- The Cyrillic letter **x** has no exact equivalent in English. It sounds somewhat like *ch* as pronounced in German (e. g., in the name Ba*ch*), so by analogy some use *ch* for Russian **x**. The difficulty with that choice is that it's ambiguous: in English the combination *ch* is generally pronounced as in "*ch*ur*ch*," a sound represented in Russian by **ч**. The potential for confusion causes many to prefer using the combination *kh* to stand for Cyrillic **x**; that combination may look odd to English-speakers, but at least it can't be confused with the sound of "*ch*ur*ch*."
- The combination of *sh* and *ch* sounds represented by the Cyrillic letter **щ** often perplexes English-speakers because we're not used to seeing those letters in one word. But in fact we can pronounce this combination; we would have no trouble saying "fresh cheese," for instance. So while this letter may take a little getting used to, it need not present us any insuperable difficulties.

Let us conclude by comparing the way certain well-known Russian surnames are usually rendered in English, at the left; the vowel **ё** is shown here when it occurs, but remember that in most Russian-language sources it would be given as simple **e**. Just for fun, let's also examine how certain well-known English-language names are usually rendered in Russian, at the right:

Брежнев	*Brezhnev*	*Brown*	*Браун*
Горбачёв	*Gorbachev*	*Faulkner*	*Фолкнер*
Достоевский	*Dostoyevsky*	*Hemingway*	*Хемингуэй*
Ельцин	*Yeltsin*	*Kennedy*	*Кеннеди*
Живаго	*Zhivago*	*Meredith*	*Мередит*
Менделеев	*Mendeleyev*	*Shakespeare*	*Шекспир*
Скрябин	*Skriabin*	*Thackeray*	*Теккерей*
Солженицын	*Solzhenitsyn*	*Twain*	*Твен*
Хрущёв	*Khrushchev*	*Wilde*	*Уайльд*
Чайковский	*Tchaikovsky*	*Wordsworth*	*Вордсворт*
Чехов	*Chekhov*	*Yates*	*Йейтс*

Note that Russians have as much trouble spelling our names in Cyrillic as we have spelling theirs in English! Also, a glance at the original Russian forms of Russian names often clears up confusion resulting from complications in transliteration. Why, for instance, do some people insist on pronouncing the name of the former Soviet leader "Gorbachev" as if it were "Gor-ba-choff´"? Because that's how it's actually pronounced by Russians; the vowel **ё** indicates that the final syllable is accented, and at the end of words **в** devoices to an *f*-sound. But the subtleties of pronunciation and stress involved with the vowel **ё**—and the fact that in most Russian-language texts that letter isn't distinguished from plain **е** (see page 8)—made "Gorbachev" the most practical and least confusing way to render the name in English. That spelling, in turn, led many Americans to mispronounce the name.

3. Transliterating German Names from the Cyrillic Alphabet

Anyone even slightly familiar with the history of Eastern Europe knows why one might find Polish and Lithuanian names in Russian forms: Lithuania and much of Poland were forcibly incorporated into the Russian Empire during the Partitions of the Commonwealth, and after insurrections in the 1860s the Russian language was mandated in all records. Less obvious, perhaps, is why so many names of German origin appear in Russian records.

Actually, what is now Germany only became a nation in the 19th century. For centuries before that, it was a very loose conglomeration of city-states, tiny principalities, and the like. There were lengthy periods of internecine warfare, economic distress, religious persecution, and so forth. Large waves of ethnic Germans fled their homeland to settle to the east among Slavs. Often they were invited by nobles who wanted them to settle on their estates, hoping Germans' skills as craftsmen and farmers would increase revenue from their lands. Thus one finds German names all over Poland, Ukraine, Belarus, Lithuania, and Russia itself, and eventually those names came to be spelled in Russian forms.

As different as the German and Russian languages are, most German names were actually not too difficult to Russify. Sometimes record keepers would simply render German names letter by letter with the nearest Cyrillic equivalent; sometimes they pronounced the names correctly (more or less) and then spelled them phonetically. So every German name does not necessarily have one and only one Russian rendering. Still, familiarity with a few traits of Russian spelling make German names fairly easy to recognize and reconstruct.

- **devoiced consonants**: one source of possible confusion, the devoicing of voiced consonants (see page 7), is less of a problem in Russian than one might think, because German and Russian both deal with devoicing in much the same way. Thus a Russian might spell a German name like *Todt* letter for letter as *Тодт;* but then again he might spell it as it was pronounced, as if it were *Tot* = *Тот;* any German familiar with the name would not find that form difficult to recognize, once he had converted the Cyrillic letters to Roman equivalents.
- ***h* vs. *g*:** as we have discussed before, Russian does not have the sound of *h*, and usually it was converted it to a hard g, spelled **г**. Thus *Hoch* would often become *Гох*, "Gokh." However, some Russians found that *h*-sound similar to the guttural spelled **х** in Russian, and thus rendered *Hoch* as *Хох*. Note, however, that when *h* appeared in consonant combinations such as *ch, sch, th,* and *tsch,* these combinations were rarely transliterated letter by letter; *ch* became **х**, *sch* became **ш**, *tsch* became **ч**, and *th* became simply **т**. In German *h* also follows vowels sometimes as a sign of lengthening, as in *Ehrenburg*—the *h* simply indicates that the initial *E* is long—and in such cases Russians usually omitted the *h: Эренбург*.
- **diphthongs *ai, ei* and *eu*:** Germans and students who speak *Hochdeutsch*, the modern, standard form of the language, will find Russian renderings of the diphthongs *ai, äu, ei,* and *eu* odd. More often than not, for instance, the *eu,* which is pronounced like "oy" in standard *Hochdeutsch,* is rendered in Russian as if it were *ej*, that is, **ей**, or sometimes as if it were *aj*, **ай**.

The odd behavior of these diphthongs is actually not so hard to explain. As a rule the Germans who resettled in Slavic lands came from areas of Germany where these sounds were pronounced differently in the local dialect. For instance, Prussians pronounce *Preuß*, a surname meaning "Prussian," as "proiss," rhyming with "voice"; but in many parts of Germany they pronounce it as we pronounce "price." The Russian spellings tend to reflect the way these Germans actually pronounced their names. A mechanical, letter-for-letter rendering of *Preuß* in Russian would be *Преусс*, but you more often see it as *Прайс* or *Прейс*, because of the dialect tendencies. As a rule the values given in the chart below reflect those you'll actually see in records, even if they don't conform to "correct" German pronunciation norms.

- **umlauted vowels**: the German vowels with umlaut—*ä, ö,* and *ü,* also spelled *ae, oe,* and *ue*—puzzled Russians, as they had nothing remotely similar in their language. The *ä* was not too big a problem, it was generally pronounced like German *e,* so Russians rendered it as they did that vowel, either as **е** or **э**. The pronunciation of *ö* varies somewhat in different dialects of German, and that may be why we see it rendered in Russian sometimes as **е**, sometimes as **ё**. The *ü* was also rendered inconsistently, sometimes as **ю**, sometimes as **и** (rarely as **ы**).
- **rendering *j:*** when the sound Germans spell as *j* (we would write it as *y*) comes after a vowel, it is almost always rendered as **й** in Russian, e. g., **ай**, **ей**. When it comes before a vowel, it is generally rendered with the corresponding soft vowel; *ja, je,* and *ju* are especially likely to be rendered that way, as **я**, **е**, and **ю**, respectively. The combination *ji* is virtually unheard of in standard German, so that's a problem that doesn't arise. The combination *jo* is trickier. In theory Russian could use **ё** for it, and in fact we do sometimes see this usage; but that letter is used sparingly in Russian, so other methods were employed. The vowel **i**, abolished after the Russian Revolution, was used before other vowels, so it was a reasonable option: we often see *Іоанн* or *Іоганн* for German *Johann,* and even *Іакоб* for *Jakob* (even though **я-** worked as well, and was often used). We sometimes see **и** and even **й** used to represent that German *j*; thus *Иоанн* is not unheard of.
- **the different pronunciations of German *s:*** finally, the German *s* can be pronounced several different ways—as simple s, like our "sh," like our "z"—so Russian may render it several ways. You may see a straightforward replacement of *s* with **с**, or a more phonetic approach, replacing *s* with **с**, **з**, or **ш** according to its sound in German. None of these usages should present any problem to persons familiar with German pronunciation.

We could go into further details, but these main points should suffice to give you some assistance with Russian forms of German names, especially if you refer to the following table:

Cyrillic	German	Examples, Comments
ай	***ai, ay, ei, eu***	*Майнц* = German *Mainz, Айзенштейн* = *Eisenstein*
в	***w***	*Вайнтраубе* = *Weintraube, Левенберг* = *Löwenberg*
г	***g, h***	*Гёте* = *Goethe, Гейнрих Гейне* = *Heinrich Heine, Гох* = *Hoch*
е	***ä, e, eh, ö, oe***	*Гельд* = *Geld, Кениг* = *König* or *Koenig*
ей	***ai, ay, ei, eu***	*Байрейт* = *Bayreuth, Дейч* = *Deitsch* or *Deutsch*
ё	***ö, oe***	*Гёте* = *Goethe, Гёльдерлин* = *Hölderlin*

з	*s*	*Зальцбург* = *Salzburg, Дрезден* = *Dresden*
и	*i, ie, j, ü*	*Литке* = *Litke* or *Lütke, Либер* = *Liber* or *Lieber, Глик* = *Glück, Иозеф or Иосеф* = *Joseph, Иоахим* = *Joachim*
й	*i, j*	see also **ай** and **ей**
к	*k, ck*	*Бекер* = *Bäcker* or *Becker*
л	*l*	*ла, ля* = *la*, e. g., *Лауфер, Ляуфер* = *Laufer; лу, лю* = *lu*, e. g., *Луфт or Люфт* = *Luft*
т	*d, dt, t, th*	*Таубе* = *Taube, Гельт* = *Geld, Гёте* = *Goethe*
ф	*f, ff, v*	*Фатер* = *Vater, Шиф* = *Schiff, Штифель* = *Stiefel*
х	*ch, h*	*Мюнхен* = *München* (Munich), *Хох* or *Гох* = *Hoch*
ц	*c, tz, z*	*Цюрих* = *Zürich, Грильпарцер* = *Grillparzer, Шварц* = *Schwarz, Schwartz*
ч	*tsch*	*Дайч* = *Daitsch, Дейч* = *Deitsch* or *Deutsch*
ш	*sch, s*	German *sch, Буш* = *Busch;* can also stand for German *s* when it is pronounced like "sh," e. g. *Шпрингер* = *Springer, Шторм* = *Storm*
ъ	—	may appear in Cyrillic spellings of German names, but would normally have no phonetic equivalent in German
ы	*i, ü*	*Зыгмунт* = *Sigmund*
ь	—	may appear in Cyrillic spellings of German names, but would normally have no phonetic equivalent in German
э	*ä, äh, e, eh*	*Карлсруэ* = *Karlsruhe, Эбер* = *Eber, Эренбург* = *Ehrenburg*
эй	*äi, äu, ei, eu*	*Эйхендорф* = *Eichendorf, Эйлер* = *Euler*
ю	*ju, ü*	*Юнг* = *Jung, Мюнхен* = *München*
я	*a, ja*	*Якоб* = *Jakob, Ляуфер* = *Laufer*

4. Transliterating Jewish Names from the Cyrillic Alphabet

Jewish names can come from a variety of linguistic environments, among them ancient Hebrew, ancient Greek, Latin, Arabic, and Yiddish. If you wish to read material that deals with the subject in greater depth than is possible here, the following books are worth a look:

Alexander Beider. *A Dictionary of Jewish Surnames from the Russian Empire.* Avotaynu, Inc. Teaneck, NJ: 1993. LCCN 92-46252, ISBN 0-9626373-3-5

Alexander Beider. *A Dictionary of Ashkenazic Given Names : Their Origins, Structure, Pronunciation, and Migrations.* Avotaynu, Inc. Teaneck, NJ: 2001. ISBN 1-886223-12-2

Boris Feldblyum. *Russian-Jewish Given Names: Their Origins and Variants.* Avotaynu, Inc. Teaneck NJ: 1998. ISBN 1-886223-07-6, CIP 97-49485.

Beider's books deal with surnames and first names. Feldblyum's is based largely on a 1911 work by Iser Kulisher designed to help Russian officials deal with the complexities of accurately transliterating Russian Jews' given names.

Practically speaking, the notes just given on transliterating German names help a great deal with Jewish names, as well. This is not surprising, because the names of Eastern European Jews often resembled German names, either directly through German or indirectly through Yiddish, which was originally based on a medieval dialect of German. If you are familiar with the usual Roman-alphabet spellings of Jewish names, and apply those notes on German, you will be able to recognize the Cyrillic forms of many Jewish names as well. The following points are particularly worthy of note:

- **rendering *h* as г *(g)*:** the sound of the consonant *h* is prominent in many, many Jewish names, and as we have already seen, Russian usually converts that sound into a hard *g*, spelled with the letter **г**. Thus the name *Hillel* was usually rendered *Гилель, Gilel'*, and *Hershko* became *Гершко*, *Gershko*—the latter could easily be confused with other distinct names such as *Hirsh* (*Гирш*) and *Gershon* (*Гершон*), and with nicknames and affectionate short forms deriving from those names. Please note that *h* was rendered as **г** only when it was not combined with other consonants; the combinations represented in the Roman alphabet as *sh, ch, kh,* etc., were transliterated as **ш, ч, х**, and so on.
- ***ay, ey, oy:*** the Yiddish diphthongs ײַ [ay], ײ [ey], and וי [oy] have straightforward equivalents in Russian: **ай, ей**, and **ой**, respectively. In practice, however, the equivalents were not always used mechanically, due to variations in pronunciation. Thus a name like *Faynshteyn* in Yiddish [*Feinstein* in German] might be rendered as *Файнштейн [Faynshteyn]* in Russian, but it might also be written *Фейнштейн [Feynshteyn]* or *Фойнштейн [Foynshteyn]*. Similarly, the Yiddish name פֿויגל *Foygl* can appear not only in the form expected, *Фойгель [Foygel']*, but also as *Файгель [Faygel']* or *Фейгель [Feygel']*, or even *Фогель [Fogel']*. If the name you're interested in has one of these diphthongs, keep an eye open for spellings with either of the other two.
- **the sound of *y*:** as mentioned under the notes on German names, the sound we spell as *y*, and Germans spell as *j*, presents some complications. When it follows a vowel, it almost always appears as **й** in Russian, as we just saw. When it precedes a vowel, it is generally rendered with the corresponding soft vowel; *ya, ye,* and *yu* are especially likely to be rendered that way, as **я, е**, and **ю**, respectively. The combination *yi,* not uncommon in Jewish names, is usually simplified to **и**, e. g., *Израиль, Izrail'* (Yisra'el). The combination *io* or *jo* may sometimes be rendered **ё**, but that letter is used sparingly in Russian. More common is use of the vowel **i** (replaced after the Russian Revolution by **и**), since it was used before other vowels anyway: *Iохель* is *Iokhel', Iосифъ* is *Iosif,* etc. You may sometimes see **и** and even **й** used to represent that sound, so that *Иохель* and *Иосиф* are not unheard of. In fact, **i** (and later **и**) can appear with **a** or **y** instead of **я** and **ю**, and **ie** is sometimes used instead of just **e**: one may see *Iакоб* instead of *Якоб* (Jacob), or *Iегуда [Ieguda]* or *Егуда [Yeguda]* for *Yehuda* (Judah).

Here are a few examples of standard Russian spellings of Jewish first and last names:

Абрамович = Abramovich	*Ашкеназы = Ashkenazy*	*Барух = Baruch*
Лейбович = Leibovich	*Мендельсон = Mendelssohn*	*Москович = Moskovich*
Хацкель = Chatskel (Ezechiel)	*Эфроим = Ephraim*	*Янкель = Yankel*

Phonetic Values of the Yiddish and Cyrillic Alphabets, with Observations on Names

Yiddish Printed	Yiddish Cursive	English	Polish	Cyrillic	Yiddish Printed	Yiddish Cursive	English	Polish	Cyrillic
א	א	—	—	—	ם	ם	final m	m	м
ב	ב	b	b	б	נ	נ	n	n	н
בֿ	בֿ	v	w	в	ן	ן	final n	n	н
ג	ג	g	g	г	ס	ס	s	s	с
ד	ד	d	d	д	ע	ע	e	e	е
ה	ה	h	h	г/х	פּ	פּ	p	p	п
ו	ו	u	ó/u	у	פֿ	פֿ	f	f	ф
ז	ז	z	z	з	ף	ף	final f	f	ф
ח	ח	kh	ch	х	צ	צ	ts	c	ц
ט	ט	t	t	т	ץ	ץ	final ts	c	ц
י	י	y/i	j/i/y	й/и/ы	ק	ק	k	k	к
כּ	כּ	k	k	к	ר	ר	r	r	р
כ	כ	kh	k/ch	х	ש	ש	sh	sz	ш
ך	ך	final kh	k/ch	х	שׂ	שׂ	s	s	с
ל	ל	l	l/ł	л	תּ	תּ	t	t	т
מ	מ	m	m	м	ת	ת	s	s	с
Variants & Combinations									
אַ	אַ	a	a	а	יִ	יִ	i	i	и/ий
אָ	אָ	o	o	о	ײ	ײ	ey	ej	ей
וּ	וּ	u	u	у	ײַ	ײַ	ay	aj	ай
וו	וו	v	w	в	זש	זש	zh	ż	ж
וי	וי	oy	oj	ой	דזש	דזש	dzh	dż	дж
					טש	טש	ch	cz	ч

As a rule, parties to legal transactions, declarants and witnesses to birth, marriage, and death records—in short, all involved in drawing up a document—were supposed to sign their names to the official record. In fact this was often impossible because many of the inhabitants of the Russian Empire could not read and write. Records involving Jews often included at least one person who knew how to sign his name, but only in Yiddish, which uses a modified form of the Hebrew alphabet. It is not uncommon to find at the bottom of a document a signature in the cursive form of that alphabet, alongside its equivalent in the Cyrillic alphabet. The registrar was to make sure everything matched, so there was no possible misidentification.

The quality of handwritten script can vary dramatically, and sometimes it seems the people paid to fill out documents were the very ones most certain to scribble illegibly. In some cases the Cyrillic version of a Jew's name, as provided by the registrar, may be very hard to make out, but the witness's actual signature in Hebrew characters is quite legible. So familiarity with the phonetics of the Hebrew alphabet vis-à-vis those of Russian Cyrillic could prove helpful. When you can't tell whether a specific Cyrillic letter is ***и*** or ***ш***, examining the signature may enable you to tell whether the corresponding Yiddish letter is ' or ש, and thus settle the matter.

The chart given on page 18 is meant to provide general insights into how Yiddish and Cyrillic characters usually match up phonetically. It is adapted from information provided by Zachary M. Baker and Jeffrey Salant in Miriam Weiner's *Jewish Roots in Ukraine and Moldova.* Unfortunately, as with any aspect of language study, there are always exceptions; the chart is unquestionably oversimplified. But if you refer to it, and practice a little with the names given below, you may learn just enough to enable you one day to decipher that one letter in that one name on that one document—and that, in itself, may justify buying this book!

Note that certain letters in the Hebrew alphabet—specifically כ כ מ מ נ נ פ פ and צ צ — take different forms when appearing at the end of a word: ך ך ם ם ן ן ף ף and ץ ץ respectively. Since Russian and English don't distinguish final forms, those differences are not reflected in Russian and English spelling. But when you're trying to decipher a name, recognizing these final forms can help by indicating where one word ends and another begins.

(Incidentally, in Weiner's *Jewish Roots in Ukraine and Moldova,* Zachary M. Baker explains that in the 1920s Soviet Yiddish orthography eliminated the letters בֿ *[v]*, ח *[kh]*, כּ *[k]*, שׂ *[s]*, תּ *[t]*, ת *[s]* and spelled words of Hebrew/Aramaic origin phonetically. He adds that the distinctive final forms of כ מ נ and פ were often eliminated in Soviet Yiddish as well.)

Don't be surprised if in signatures a Yiddish first name is replaced by its formal Hebrew counterpart. Thus a man called *Yankl* in everyday life might sign his name יעקב *Yakov.* Jewish men generally had a "sacred name," in Hebrew *shem ha-kodesh,* by which they were called in synagogue to read the Torah, as well as a vernacular or "popular" name for everyday use, called *kinnui* in Hebrew. The sacred names, such as *Yakov,* were from the Bible or Talmud, from Hebrew or Aramaic; they were names of antiquity and tradition, reserved for use on formal, serious occasions such as worship. The *kinnuim* were less ancient and less formal, and could come from non-sacred languages such as German or Polish, or affectionate nicknames that began as modifications of sacred names, as *Yankl* came from *Yakov.* This is not to say a Jew never signed a document with his *kinnui;* but if all he knew how to write was his name, the "sacred" name, in its Hebrew form, would normally be the one he'd know how to spell.

For that reason, those sacred names were generally spelled with their traditional Biblical Hebrew spellings rather than by Yiddish phonetic values. Thus *Yakov* is written יעקב even though a Yiddish transliteration of that would be *Yeqv,* not *Yakov.* Male Jews were taught enough Hebrew to read from the Torah, and were familiarized with the Hebrew spellings of their names, even when the ancient Hebrew spellings of the names were inconsistent with

Yiddish phonetic values. So don't be surprised if you see a surname spelled exactly as the chart on page 18 suggests, but the corresponding first name is nothing like the Cyrillic version written alongside. That Cyrillic version, e. g., *Янкель, Yankel'*, has probably been replaced with the corresponding sacred name, e. g., יעקב *Yakov*.

Women's signatures appear less frequently on a document, but it can still be valuable to acquaint yourself with the spellings of female names. There are bilingual records, in Russian and Yiddish, and female names may be written in the body of the record, mentioned as wives and mothers. In such cases it may prove handy to compare the Russian and Yiddish spellings.

Below is a sampling of various first and last names in cursive Yiddish forms taken from real documents, and therefore in some cases not spelled "correctly"—for instance, without the diacritical marks that distinguish some letters in standard Yiddish. Each is followed by the same spelling in the more familiar "square" letters. Next is the standard Cyrillic spelling, and finally the phonetic spelling by English values. You may find you have to be able to deal with any or all of these forms, so we might as well give them all:

Yiddish Cursive	*Yiddish Printed*	*Cyrillic*	*English*	*Kind of name*
אליהו	אליהו	*Элія*	Eliya[hu]	*masc. first name*
הלל	הלל	*Гилель*	Hil[l]el'	*masc. first name*
וואלף	וואלף	*Вульфъ*	Vol'f, Vul'f	*masc. first name*
זעליק	זעליק	*Зеликъ*	Zelik	*masc. first name*
חיים	חיים	*Хаимъ*	Chaim	*masc. first name*
יעקב	יעקב	*Яковъ*	Yakov	*masc. first name*
ישראל	ישראל	*Сруль* or *Израиль*	Izrael'	*masc. first name*
מאיר	מאיר	*Мееръ*	Meir, Meyer	*masc. first name*
משה	משה	*Мовша*	Moyshe	*masc. first name*
ניסן	ניסן	*Нисонъ*	Nison, Nisan	*masc. first name*
פייול	פייול	*Файвель*	Faiv[e]l'	*masc. first name*
ראובן	ראובן	*Рувинъ*	Ruvin	*masc. first name*
שמעון	שמעון	*Шимонъ*	Shimon	*masc. first name*
באשע	באשע	*Баша*	Bashe	*fem. first name*
זלאטע	זלאטע	*Злата*	Zlate	*fem. first name*
לאה	לאה	*Лея*	Leah	*fem. first name*
סימע	סימע	*Сима*	Sime	*fem. first name*
פרומע	פרומע	*Фрума*	Frume	*fem. first name*
שרה	שרה	*Сора*	Sarah, Sora	*fem. first name*
בערמאן	בערמאן	*Берманъ*	Berman	*surname*
גינזבורג	גינזבורג	*Гинзбургъ*	Ginzburg	*surname*
ווייַנשטיין	ווייַנשטיין	*Вайнштейнъ*	Vainshtein	*surname*
יודאוויטש	יודאוויטש	*Юдовичъ*	Yudovich	*surname*
זילבערשטיין	זילבערשטיין	*Зильберштейнъ*	Zilbershtein	*surname*
כראצמאן	כראצמאן	*Крацманъ*	Kratsman	*surname*
רעזניק	רעזניק	*Рѣзникъ*	Reznik	*surname*

5. Transliterating Lithuanian Names from the Cyrillic Alphabet

While Lithuanian and Russian are very different languages, there are some similarities between their basic phonetics and grammar. At one time linguists spoke of the "Balto-Slavic" subfamily of Indo-European languages, because there are significant points of comparison between the Baltic languages (Lithuanian, Latvian, and Old Prussian) and the Slavic (especially Belarusian, Russian, Ukrainian, and Polish). These days fewer linguists regard those similarities as sufficient to warrant grouping the Baltic and Slavic languages together in one subfamily. No objective observer, however, can deny that if you know quite a bit about the Slavic languages, you will find some familiar features in Lithuanian. Among these are the significance of palatalization in the language; regressive assimilation of voiced and devoiced consonants; devoicing of final consonants; and so on.

Still, Lithuanian speech features phonetic distinctions that the Cyrillic alphabet was not designed to reflect accurately. Russian spellings of Lithuanian names often ignore the finer points of Lithuanian pronunciation, especially of the vowels and diphthongs. Nonetheless, with some pointers it is not difficult to recognize the Russian spellings of most Lithuanian names.

The chart on page 1 presents its information so that one can go from Russian forms to Lithuanian. The chart below gives the same information in a format designed for transliterating in the other direction, Lithuanian to Russian. Our hope is that by studying both you will acquire enough information to recognize the names you're looking for.

This chart focuses only on letters and letter combinations that cause problems. Nothing is said about the letters *b, d, f, k, l, m, n, p, r, t, v,* and *z* because the sounds represented by these letters, their English equivalents, and their Cyrillic counterparts are similar. By focusing on the differences, we hope to help you with the letters that may give you trouble. The chart is followed by a look at some sample Russian spellings of Lithuanian names.

Lithuanian	*Cyrillic*	*Observations*
a	***а*** or ***я***	Lithuanian *a* is a short vowel, whereas *ą* is long (**not** like the Polish nasal vowel written *ą*); but normally both would be rendered **а** in Russian, unless preceded by *i-* or *j-*, in which case **я** is to be expected
ą	***а*** or ***я***	
ai	***ай*** or ***яй*** or ***е***	if transliterated mechanically, would be **аи** or **ай** or **яи** or **яй**; if transliterated phonetically, can be **е**, for example, *Telšiai* = *Тельше*
au	***ау*** or ***яу*** or ***ов***	if transliterated mechanically, would be **ау** or **яу**; if Russified, would be **ов**, for example, *Kaunas* = *Ковно*
c	***ц***	essentially the same in both languages, like *ts* in English "cats"
ch	***х***	in Lithuanian found only in words of foreign origin; pronounced like *ch* in German "Ba*ch*"; it would normally be rendered **х** in Russian
č	***ч***	essentially the same in both languages, like *ch* in English "*ch*ur*ch*"
e	***е*** or ***ѣ*** or ***э***	*e* is short, somewhat between *e* in English "b*e*t" and *a* in English "c*a*n," while *ę* is its longer, more open counterpart (it is **not** like the Polish nasal vowel written *ę*), and *ė* is like the long *a* in English "m*a*de"; in Russian, all three will normally be rendered **е**, less often **ѣ** or **э**
ę	***е*** or ***ѣ*** or ***э***	
ė	***е*** or ***ѣ*** or ***э***	

ei	***ей*** or ***ѣй***	Russian **ей** (perhaps occasionally **ѣй** or **эй**) sounds reasonably close to this Lithuanian diphthong
g	***г***	essentially the same sound in both languages, always like the *g* in English "goose," never like the *g* in "geometry"
h	***г*** or ***х***	in Lithuanian found only in words of foreign origin; we would normally expect it to be rendered as **г** in Russian, less often as **х**
i	***и*** or ***i*** or ***ы***	phonetically, Russian **ы** is the more accurate match for Lithuanian *i*, while Russian **и** more closely matches Lithuanian *y* or *į*, and you may sometimes see them used that way; but most record keepers, influenced by Polish or German, would tend to equate Lithuanian *i* automatically with Cyrillic **и** or **i**, and *y* with Cyrillic **ы**; note also that in Lithuanian spelling *i* after a consonant usually indicates palatalization—Lithuanian *ia* would usually be rendered as **я**, *ie* as **ѣ** or **е**, *io* as **іо** or **ио** or **ё**, and *iu* as **ю**
į	***и*** or ***i*** or ***ы***	
y	***и*** or ***i*** or ***ы***	
ie	***ѣ*** or ***е***	Russian **ѣ** or **е** sounds reasonably close to this Lithuanian diphthong
j	***й***	essentially the same in both languages, like English *y* in "*y*ard"; *ja* is usually rendered as **я**, *je* as **ѣ** or **е**, *jo* as **іо** or **ё**, and *ju* as **ю**
o	***о***	Lithuanian *o* will usually be rendered as **о** in Russian, unless preceded by *i-* or *j-*, in which case **іо** (less often **ио** or **ё**) would be used
š	***ш***	essentially the same sound in both languages, like *sh* in "*sh*eep"
u	***у*** or ***ю***	Lithuanian *u* is a short vowel somewhat like that in English "put," whereas *ū* and *ų* sound more like the *oo* in English "pool"; as a rule, you'd expect all three vowels, though distinct in Lithuanian, to be rendered **у** in Russian unless preceded by *i-* or *j-*, in which case **ю** is more likely to be used
ų	***у*** or ***ю***	
ū	***у*** or ***ю***	
ž	***ж***	essentially the same in both languages, like *s* in English "plea*s*ure"

In both Russian and Lithuanian, words are spelled much as they are pronounced. The Russian forms of Lithuanian names tend to be phonetically consistent with the original forms, and that generally allows us to match them with little difficulty.

There is a complicating factor, however: Lithuanian names were often Polonized before they were rendered in Russian. For a number of reasons too complicated to be discussed adequately here, Lithuanian was not the language of record for the Grand Duchy of Lithuania. In the Duchy's early days, Old White Russian (a predecessor of modern Belarusian) served as the language of law and government. After the Duchy and the Kingdom of Poland joined to become the Commonwealth of Two Nations, Polish became the language of record. Thus Slavic languages—first Old White Russian, then Polish—exercised considerable influence over the forms Lithuanian names took in records. By the time the Russian Empire seized Lithuania and much of Poland, there were often, in effect, two varieties of Lithuanian names:

1) native forms, featuring the phonetic tendencies and grammatical forms of Lithuanian

2) Polonized forms, minus the native suffixes *-as, -is, -us* and *-ys*, and with modified phonetics (especially a tendency to substitute *o* for Lithuanian *a*)

While the peasants of Lithuania went right on speaking their native language, the ruling classes tended to use Polish and Polonized forms of their names, especially in official dealings. When it became necessary to give names in Russian-language records, it was easier to convert the Polonized forms because that's what had customarily appeared in records anyway, and because those forms, with their Slavic underpinnings, were easier to spell in Russian.

Thus Lithuanian *Eismantas* usually appeared in pre-1867 legal records in the Polonized form *Ejsmont,* and that form, rather than the Lithuanian form, was the source of the Russian spelling *Эйсмонт.* Similarly, the Polonized form of Lithuanian *Giedraitis* was *Giedrojć,* and in Russian records that generally is spelled *Гедройц. Mingaila,* Polonized to *Mingajło,* shows up as *Мингайло.* Lithuanian *Gintautas* appeared as *Gintowt* in Polish, and as *Гинтовт* in Russian—note that Lithuanian *-au-* became *-ow-* in Polish, pronounced *-ov-,* and thus the Russian spelling.

Even when Lithuanian forms were the ones transliterated in the records, that form often owed something to Polish or Belarusian, because many Lithuanian names came originally from those languages. For instance, *Kazlauskas,* the most common Lithuanian surname in modern times, is a Lithuanian adaptation of Polish *Kozłowski* or Belarusian *Казлоўскі.* (Note again: Polish *-o-* matches up with Lithuanian *-a-*, Polish *-ow-* with Lithuanian *-au-*, and a suffix is added). Similarly, *Kavaliauskas* comes from *Kowalewski, Katkevičius* from *Kotkiewicz, Dembinskas* from *Dębiński,* and so on. You may even see a family's surname given in a Russian spelling of a Polonized form in one record, and in a Lithuanian-derived form in another: a *Kazlauskas* might appear in one document as *Козловский,* in another as *Казлаускас.* Transliterating the Russian spelling of the name may be the easy part: keeping straight different forms of the same name, and matching them with your ancestors, may be the hard part.

You may benefit from studying a few more examples of how Lithuanian surnames were rendered in Russian. The samples on the left are pure Lithuanian; those on the right are Lithuanian equivalents of the Polish names shown in parentheses. Or, from the point of view of ardent Lithuanian nationalists, the forms in parentheses are Polish versions of the Lithuanian ones! For comparison, Russian forms of the Polish names appear in brackets:

Balčiūnas → Бальчюнас	Arlauskas (Orłowski) → Арлаускас [Орловский]
Gaidys → Гайдис	Fedaravičius (Fedorowicz) → Федаравичюс [Федорович]
Juraitis → Юрайтис	Klimavičius (Klimowicz)→ Климавичюс [Климович]
Kairelis → Кайрелис	Mickevičius (Mickiewicz) → Мицкевичюс [Мицкевич]
Miškunas → Мишкунас	Sabaliauskas (Sobolewski) → Сабаляускас [Соболевский]
Rimša → Римша *or* Рымша	Jankauskas (Jankowski) → Янкаускас [Янковский]

6. Transliterating Polish Names from the Cyrillic Alphabet

While Polish and Russian are both Slavic languages, the differences between Polish and Russian are greater than between Belarusian or Ukrainian and Russian. In some ways Polish names were easier to convert into Russian than, say, German or Lithuanian names. That does not mean, however, that the conversion was always simple. In other words, to use our descriptions of transliteration as "mechanical" or "phonetic" (page 11), it will usually benefit us to take the phonetic approach. The chart on page 1 is helpful, and generally accurate; but (as usual) there is more to be said, and the chart beginning on page 24 clarifies much of it.

The chart on page 1 presents its information so that one can take Russian letters and see their Polish counterparts. The chart below gives the same information, and more, in a format designed for transliterating in the other direction, Polish to Russian. By studying and comparing both you should learn enough information to recognize the names you're looking for.

Polish	Cyrillic	Observations
a	*a*	Note, however, that Polish *ia* or *ja* is usually Russian **я**, not **иа** or **ia.**
ą	***он*** or ***ом***	The Polish sound, absent in Russian, has the value of *on* or *om*, depending on the consonant following it. So the usual Russian transliteration is **он** or **ом**.
b	*б*	Essentially the same sound in both languages, like *b* in English "*b*at."
c	*ц*	Essentially the same sound in both languages, *ts* in English "ca*ts*."
ć or ***ci***	*ц* or ***цъ*** or ***ци***	There is no Russian equivalent of Polish *ć* and most clerks simply transliterated it as they did *c*, with **ц**, sometimes adding **ь** if no vowel followed. *Ci* was most often rendered as **ци**, e. g., *Cibory* → *Циборы.* It is also possible that in some instances the *ć* or *ci* might be rendered as **ч** and **чи**, respectively, even though that is not correct.
ch	*x*	See **h** below.
cz	*ч*	Essentially the same sound, similar to *ch* in English "*ch*air."
d	*д*	Essentially the same sound, roughly like *d* in English "*deed*."
dź or ***dzi***	*дз* or ***дзъ*** or ***дзи***	As with *ć* and all the consonants marked with *´ (kreska)* in Polish, there is no true Russian equivalent; **дзь** or **дзи** is the usual rendering.
e	***e*** or э	The usual transcription is **e**, only rarely **э**. The Cyrillic symbol **e** is not the same as the Polish *e*, but was used for it. When Polish *e* followed the vowel *i* to form *ie*, other phonetic problems arose; depending on the consonantal environment in which it occurred, the Cyrillic version often was the now archaic vowel **ѣ** (in script, ***ѣ***). A Polish name such as *Biedno* could conceivably be written as *Биедно*, *Біедно*, *Бедно*, or *Бѣдно*, depending on the clerk.
ę	***ен*** or ***ем***	The nasal vowel *ę* has no Russian equivalent; it has the approximate sound value of *en* (or *em* when it precedes a *b* or *p*), so in Cyrillic it was usually rendered as **ен** or **ем**.
f	*ф*	Essentially the same sound, much like *f* in English "*f*ork."
g	*г*	This sound causes many problems in transcription, as the Russian symbol **г** has three sound values (see page 4). In general, Polish *h* is rendered in Russian as **г**. However the actual ***sound*** value for the Polish *h* or *ch* corresponds to the Cyrillic symbol **x**. Given all these choices and possibilities, clerks were especially non-uniform in transcribing this sound. For instance: *Godlewo* — *Годлево* (no tricks, straight transcription) *Harasimowicze* — *Гарасимовиче* (Polish *h* → as Russian **г**) *Harasimowicze* — *Харасимовиче* (Polish *h* → Russian **x**)

h	*г* or ***х***	See ***g*** above.
i	***и***	Note that in pre-1918 orthography Russian also used the letter **i** for this sound; it frequently occurs in words ending in *-ski* (-скій/ский).
j	***й***	Polish *j* should be rendered **й** only when preceding a consonant. When preceding a vowel, *j* combines with the vowel and is rendered in Cyrillic with distinct symbols, i. e., *ja* → **я**, *je* → **е** (or **ѣ**), *jo* → **ё** or **іо**, *ju* → **ю**. So Polish *Jankowo* is *Янково* in Cyrillic.
k	***к***	Essentially the same sound, like the *k* in English "*k*ind."
l	***л***	A potential problem here depends on the vowel following the **л** in Cyrillic. Since Polish *l* is classified as a soft consonant, certain spelling conventions in Russian would cause unexpected vowels (from the Polish point of view) to follow. Thus village names such as *Lachowo* or *Laskowo* may be rendered as *Ляхово* or *Лясково* instead of the more normal and conventional *Лахово* and *Ласково*. A fairly good rule of thumb is this: Polish *ł* followed by a consonant is just *л*, and *ła*, *łe*, *ło*, *łó*, *łu* and *ły* are rendered by *ла*, *ле*, *ло*, *лу*, *лу* and *лы* respectively in Russian, while Polish *l* followed by a consonant is *ль*, and *la* → *ля* or *ла*, *le* → *ле*, *li* → *ли*, *lo* → *ло*, and *lu* or *ló* → *лю*.
ł	***л***	See the note on ***l***.
m	***м***	Essentially the same sound, like the *m* in English "co*m*e."
n	***н***	Essentially the same sound, like the *n* in English "*n*urse".
ń	***нь***	When followed by a vowel, Polish *ń* becomes *ni-:* the combination *nia* is **ня**, *nie* is **не** (or **нѣ**), *ni* is **ни**, nio is **нё** or **ніо**, and *niu* is **ню**.
o	***о***	Polish *o* and Russian **о**, while different in some ways, are similar enough to be treated as the same sound.
ó	***о*** or ***у***	Polish has two symbols, *ó* and *u*, that represent the same sound (much like *oo* in "w<u>oo</u>d"), and this caused some variation in transcription. Some clerks, taking a mechanical approach, habitually transcribed the sound as Russian **о**, although it is not an accurate phonetic rendition of the Polish sound. So even though Cyrillic **у** is phonetically more accurate, one frequently sees **о**, especially in common suffixes such as *-ów* and *–ówka*. In theory they should be Cyrillic **-ув** and **-увка**, but in fact **-ов** and **-овка** are at least as common. A common root with this vowel in Polish is *gór-* (mountain), as in *Górny*, *Góra*, etc., which may be transliterated as *Гурны* or *Горны*, *Гура* or *Гора*, etc.
p	***п***	Essentially the same sound, much like *p* in English "*p*it."
r	***р***	Essentially the same sound, but not like English *r* (see page 4).
rz or ***ż***	***рж***	In most cases the sound of *rz* or *ż* (which both represent the same sound, like *s* in English "plea<u>s</u>ure") is transcribed mechanically as **рж**; but at times one may encounter simply **ж** or even **ш**, which can be phonetically more accurate in certain specific environments.

s	***с***	Polish *s* and Russian **с** are essentially the same sound, except for *ś*, which is spelled *si* when followed by a vowel (see next entry).
ś or ***si***	***с*** or ***сь*** or ***си***	As with the other *kreska* consonants, Russian does not have this sound and thus no symbol to render it accurately. The *ś* is often seen as **сь** in Cyrillic. Polish *sia* → Russian **ся**, *sie* → **се**, *si* → **си**, *sio* → **сё** or **сiо**, and *siu* or *sió* → **сю**.
ść or ***ści***	***сьц*** or ***сьци***	It is also not unheard of to see this sound combination rendered as Cyrillic **щ** or possibly even **-сть.**
sz	***ш***	Both much like English *sh*, but see note on Polish *y*, Cyrillic **ы.**
szcz	***щ***	Essentially the same sound combination, much like a combination of English *sh* and *ch*.
t	***т***	Essentially the same sound, somewhat like English *t* in "*t*ake."
u	***у***	Essentially the same sound, much like *oo* in English "t*oo*."
w	***в***	Essentially the same sound, like *v* in English "*v*ow."
y	***ы***	This vowel causes transliteration problems. In Russian, the short *i*-sound usually represented by **ы** must be spelled **и** after certain letters (notably **ч**, **ж**, and **ш**), so that it must be **чи**, not **чы**, **щи**, not **щы**, and so on. So even where Polish rules of spelling require *y* rather than *i*, Russian would tend to use **и**: thus a Polish place spelled *Czyżewo* would **usually** be rendered in Russian as *Чижево*, not *Чыжево*.
z	***з***	Essentially the same sound, like the *z* in English "*z*one."
ź or ***zi***	***з*** or ***зь*** or ***зи***	Rendered as **з** or **зь** before consonants; before vowels Polish *zia* → **зя**, *zie* → **зе**, *zio* → **зё** or **зiо**, and *ziu* or *zió* → **зю**.
ż	***ж***	Essentially the same sound, like *s* in English "plea*s*ure." See also notes on Polish *rz* and *y*.

To apply guidelines of this sort, it is helpful to have examples to work with. Here is a listing of a number of Polish surnames and spellings of them seen in Russian documents, chosen to illustrate various subtleties of phonetic translation. Note that even though Polish *–ski* sounds and is used much like Russian *–ский*, many documents mechanically transliterate the Polish suffixes *-ski*, *-cki*, and *–zki* as *–ски*, *-цки*, and *–зки*, respectively. You may see those forms, or you may see-*ский*, *-цкий*, and *-зкий:* it is best to be prepared for either eventuality.

Brzeziński[1]	*Бржезински*	*Niedźwiedzki*	*Недьзведзки*[2]
Chrzanowski	*Хржановски*	*Pietrzak*	*Петржак*
Ciemnołąski	*Цемнолонски*	*Piotrowski*	*Пиотровски*[3]
Czarnecki	*Чарнецки*	*Podgórski*	*Подгурски*
Gęsiorski	*Генсёрски* or *Генсiорски*	*Przerzecki*	*Пшежецки*[4]
Jabłoński	*Яблонски*	*Przybyszewski*	*Пшибышевски*[4]
Kwieciński	*Квецински*	*Wierzbicki*	*Вержбицки*
Leszczyński	*Лещински*	*Wrzos*	*Вржос*
Młodziejewski	*Млодзеевски*	*Zajączkowski*	*Зайончковски*

A few notes on these names:

[1] You must realize that with many names there was not just one and only one possible spelling in Russian. There were enough differences between the phonetics of Polish and Russian to allow record keepers some leeway, even if they knew both languages well and truly desired to transliterate the names accurately. Thus *Brzeziński* may appear as *Бржезински* or *Бржезиньски*, that is, with or without the letter **ь** to stand for the palatalized sound of Polish *ń*. Similarly, *Jabłoński* may be written *Яблонски* or *Яблоньски*. This "leeway" in transliteration is one reason why some documents insert Polish spellings in brackets after the Russian forms; it was one way to avoid confusion in identifying an individual Pole and thus avoid ambiguity and possible errors in enforcing laws, collecting taxes, requiring military service, etc.

[2] In fact *Недзвецки*, which is sometimes seen, matches the pronunciation of this name better. Due to regressive assimilation (page 7), the unvoiced consonants of the suffix *-ski* cause the preceding consonants *–dz-* to devoice to the sound of *-ts-*, which Poles spell *c*. Not surprisingly, we also see this name spelled *Niedźwiecki* in Polish.

[3] This name could also be spelled *Піотровски* or *Пётровски*. It is difficult to predict how a given record keeper would render the Polish combination *-io-* into Russian. Researchers are well advised to be ready to encounter **ио, іо**, or **ё**.

[4] In these forms the **ш** is a closer phonetic match to the way the name is pronounced in Polish than the renderings *Пржежецки* and *Пржибышевски*. When *prze-* and *przy-* appear at the beginning of surnames, they are actually pronounced "psheh-" and "pshy-" respectively.

7. Conclusion: Sleepless in Shidlovo

When translating a Russian-language document, it is necessary to render the transliteration of proper names in the phonetics of the appropriate language, not in English. If dealing with Germans, you need to turn the Russian symbols into their closest German equivalents; Lithuanian names should be rendered the way they'd be spelled in Lithuanian; and Polish names should be consistent with Polish orthography. Jewish names should be spelled by the values of whichever language seems appropriate in context, and may require keeping several different versions in mind; a Jewish name could easily have forms in Yiddish, German, Russian, and Polish. Determining the correct linguistic context can be a difficult job in itself—but if you wish all your hard research work to bear fruit, it is necessary. If you transliterate Cyrillic to English phonetics, the result may be a name you'll never find in a marriage register, or a village you'll never find on a map. If you turn Cyrillic *Шидлово* into its English form, *Shidlovo*, instead of Polish *Szydłowo*, there's a good chance you won't find it!

By the same token, if you decide you can't handle the translations or transliterations yourself, and you give your documents to a Russian speaker to translate into English, be **sure** he or she also speaks Polish or Lithuanian or German or Yiddish or whatever. Otherwise, once again, you may end up sleepless in "Shidlovo."

To illustrate the point, on page 28 is **Document I-1**, an excerpt from an 1880s list of members of the Jewish community in what is now Ляхавічы *(Lyakhavichy)*, Belarus. First let's consider the name of the town: in the Russian original (4th line from top, 5th word) it is *Ляховичи*. That can be transliterated by English phonetic values as *Lyakhovichi*. If you looked for that name, most sources won't have it. An exception is Avotaynu's gazetteer *Where Once We Walked (WOWW)*, which lists that spelling, giving its location as 107 km. north of Pinsk, coordinates 53º02'/26º16. *WOWW* adds (and cross-references under) these spelling variants: *Lachovici, Lachowicze, Lechovich, Lechovicz, Lechowitz, Liachovitch, Lyakhoviche*. But *WOWW* is a very specialized work, designed to help Jewish researchers find variant spellings, even outright misspellings of the names of villages and *shtetls* in central and Eastern Europe that had thriving Jewish communities before the Holocaust. It's not a book in everybody's library. If your roots are Christian rather than Jewish, you may never have heard of the book; even if you had, you might have thought it would be of no possible use to you.

Suppose you find this entry in *WOWW*. Perhaps you want to know more about the town. The area in question was long under the rule of the Polish-Lithuanian Commonwealth, so it might occur to you that Polish gazetteers would give more information. In fact the 15-volume gazetteer *Słownik geograficzny Królestwa Polskiego* (discussed at length on pages 155ff.) has a rather long article on *Lachowicze* (its Polish name), in Volume V, beginning on page 56.

But to find it, you must get the name right. You have to recognize that the Russian combination *Ля-* tells you the *L* is not the hard Polish *ł*, but the soft *l*, and thus would be rendered *La-* in Polish. (If the Polish name began with *Ła-*, the Russian rendering would be *Ла-*).

Does this matter? Yes! If you get the first letter wrong, you end up searching among entries that begin with *Ła-*, and get totally lost. Polish alphabetizes words with *ł* after *l;* in the *Słownik*, entries for *Ła-* names begin on page 565. The entry on *Lachowicze* is on page 56!

Having discussed that, let's take a look at the names of the men listed. The first line of each entry gives the man's first name and his patronymic ("son of"); his surname appears in the next line. To help you get started reading Russian, here are the first 8 names:

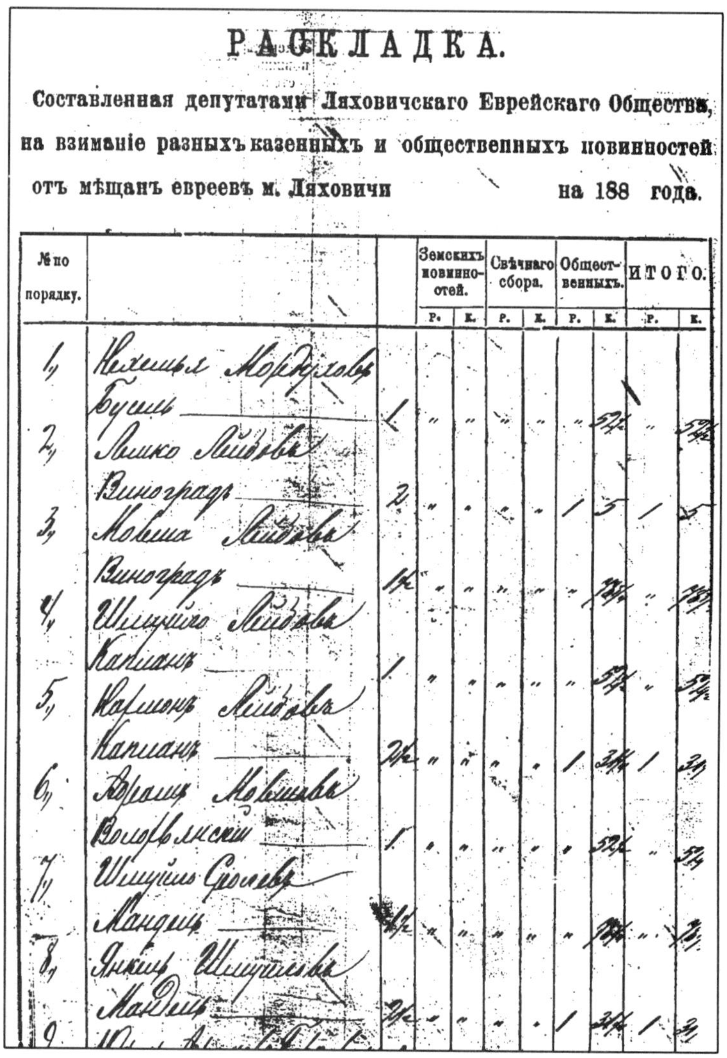
РАСКЛАДКА.

Составленная депутатами Ляховичскаго Еврейскаго Общества, на взиманіе разныхъ казенныхъ и общественныхъ повинностей отъ мѣщанъ евреевъ м. Ляховичи на 188 года.

№ по порядку.		Земскихъ повинностей. Р.	К.	Свѣчнаго сбора. Р.	К.	Общественныхъ. Р.	К.	ИТОГО. Р.	К.

1. *Нехемья Мордуховъ*
   Бусель
2. *Лемко Лейбовъ*
   Виноградъ
3. *Мовша Лейбовъ*
   Виноградъ
4. *Шмуйло Лейбовъ*
   Капланъ
5. *Нахмонъ Лейбовъ*
   Капланъ
6. *Абрамъ Мовшовъ*
   Золохвянскій
7. *Шмуйло Сролевъ*
   Мандель
8. *Янкель Шмуиловъ*
   Мандель

Now take a look at how these names would be spelled in English and Polish, going by conventional representations of those languages' phonetic values:

Russian	English	Polish
1. *Нехемья Мордуховъ Бусель*	1. *Nekhem'ya Mordukhov Busel'*	1. *Nechemja Morduchów Busel*
2. *Лемко Лейбовъ Виноградъ*	2. *Lemko Leybov Vinograd*	2. *Lemko Lejbów Winograd*
3. *Мовша Лейбовъ Виноградъ*	3. *Movsha Leybov Vinograd*	3. *Mowsza Lejbów Winograd*
4. *Шмуйло Лейбовъ Капланъ*	4. *Shmuylo Leybov Kaplan*	4. *Szmujło Lejbów Kapłan*
5. *Нахмонъ Лейбовъ Капланъ*	5. *Nakhmon Leybov Kaplan*	5. *Nachmon Lejbów Kapłan*
6. *Абрамъ Мовшовъ Золохвянскій*	6. *Abram Movshov Zolokhvyanskiy*	6. *Abram Mowszów Zołochwiański*
7. *Шмуйло Сролевъ Мандель*	7. *Shmuylo Srolev Mandel'*	7. *Szmujło Srolew Mandel*
8. *Янкель Шмуиловъ Мандель*	8. *Yankel' Shmuilov Mandel'*	8. *Jankiel Szmuilów Mandel*

Comparing the forms, you see that the differences are not enormous; most are even trivial. But every so often you notice one that could make a difference: *Vinograd* vs. *Winograd, Yankel'* vs. *Jankiel, Shmuylo* vs. *Szmujło.* Success in research has hinged on finer distinctions.

Another feature of this list worthy of attention is the format in which the **names** are given. The first name is, of course, the given name that individual went by; the last name is his surname. The middle name is what we call a **patronymic**, a name that means "son of X." In this list, the form ending in *-евъ* or *–овъ* is added to the name of the individual's father, dropping any final vowel. Such patronymics were common among peasants and merchants; in modern standard Russian, however, the patronymic is usually formed by adding the suffix *-ович [-ovich]* or *-евич [-evich]*. Name #1, *Nekhem'ya Mordukhov Busel'*, would be "Nehemiah Busel, [son] of Mordechai" if rendered in familiar English terms; *Mordukh* is a short form of the Biblical name we know as *Mordechai. Movshov* means "[son] of Movsha," a version of the name we know as *Moses; Srolev* means "[son] of Srol'," a short form from the first name *Israel.*

When you see names listed this way in Russian records — **first name + *-ev/-ov* + surname** — stop and take a good look at that middle name. Detach the suffix *–ev* or *-ov* and you have the name of the individual's father. You may have to restore a vowel that's been dropped, as in the case of *Movshov → Movsha,* or *Shmuylov → Shmuylo.* That is a small price to pay, however, to obtain information as useful as a father's name—useful if only to help keep straight individuals with the same first name.

The document itself is an assessment (раскладка) drawn up by delegates of the Lyakhovichi Jewish community for levying government and community taxes (повинностей) from Jewish townsmen of Lyakhovichi for 188_. The columns give amounts of district taxes (земскихъ повинностей), the candle tax (свѣчнаго сбора), and community taxes (общественныхъ), given in rubles (Р.) and kopeks (К.), with a total at far right (Итого).

E. RUSSIAN ALPHABETICAL ORDER

Russian indices to vital records were kept in alphabetical order—but that order is according to (what else?) the Cyrillic alphabet. As such, it can vary a great deal from what we tend to expect, conditioned as we are by our own alphabet. Below, in alphabetical order left to right, are the 37 letters of the Russian alphabet during the period before the Russian Revolution:

А а	Б б	В в	Г г	Д д	Е е	Ё ё	Ж ж	З з	И и	Й й	І і	К к
Л л	М м	Н н	О о	П п	Р р	С с	Т т	У у	Ф ф	Х х	Ц ц	Ч ч
Ш ш	Щ щ	Ъ ъ	Ы ы	Ь ь	Ѣ ѣ	Э э	Ю ю	Я я	Ѳ ѳ	Ѵ ѵ		

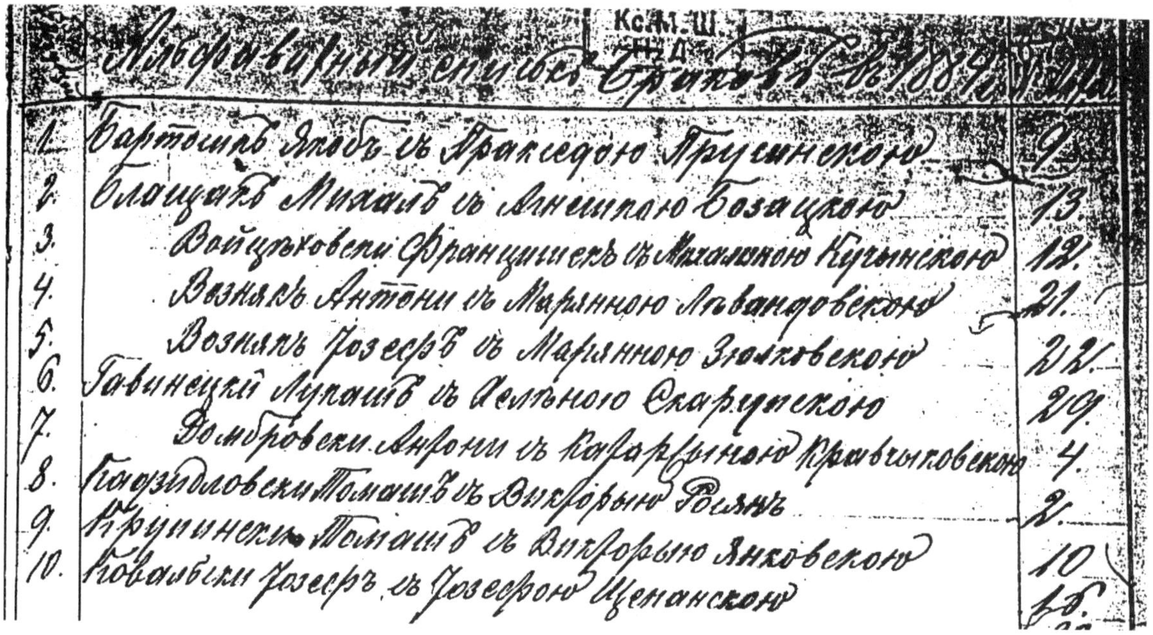

As a sample, **Document I-2: An Alphabetical Index of Marriages in 1884, Sadlno parish** is a typical alphabetical index. Here are entries 1-10 in a standardized cursive:

1.	Бартосикъ Якобъ съ Праксєдою Прусинскою	9
2.	Блацакъ Михалъ съ Агнешкою Бозацкою	13
3.	Войцѣховски Францишекъ съ Михалиною Кучынскою	12
4.	Возняк ъ Антони съ Марянною Львандовскою	21
5.	Возняк ъ Іозефъ съ Марянною Зюлковскою	22
6.	Гавинецки Лукашъ съ Хельною Скарупскою	29
7.	Домбровски Антони съ Катаржыною Кравчыковскою	4
8.	Кадзидловски Томашъ съ Викторыю Росякъ	2
9.	Крупински Томашъ съ Викторыю Янковскою	10
10.	Ковальски Іозефъ съ Іозефою Щепанскою	16

Since you probably need practice recognizing the letters, here are those same names in italic typeface, which resembles the cursive but is a little easier to recognize:

№	*Альфавитный списокъ Браковъ въ 1884 г.*	*№ Акта*
1.	*Бартосик Якобъ съ Праксед̆ою Прусинскою*	*9*
2.	*Блащакъ Михалъ съ Агнешкою Бозацкою*	*13*
3.	*Войцѣховски Францишекъ съ Михалиною Кучынскою*	*12*
4.	*Возвякъ Антони съ Марянною Лѣвандовскою*	*21*
5.	*Возякъ Іозефъ съ Марянною Зюлковскою*	*22*
6.	*Гавинецки Лукашъ съ Хелѣною Скарупскою*	*29*
7.	*Домбровски Антони съ Катаржыною Кравчыковскою*	*4*
8.	*Кадзидловски Томашъ съ Викторыю Росякъ*	*2*
9.	*Крупински Томашъ съ Викторыю Янковскою*	*10*
10.	*Ковальски Іозефъ съ Іозефою Щепанскою*	*16*

Since Sadlno is in Poland and the people mentioned in this index are Poles, it is appropriate to transliterate those names by Polish phonetic values. That produces the following list:

Serial #	*Alphabetical List of Marriages in 1884*	*Record #*
1.	*Bartosik Jakób and Prakseda Prusińska*	*9*
2.	*Błaszczak Michał and Agnieszka Bozacka*	*13*
3.	*Wojciechowski Franciszek and Michalina Kuczyńska*	*12*
4.	*Woźniak Antoni and Marjanna Lewandowska*	*21*
5.	*Woźniak Józef and Marjanna Ziółkowska*	*22*
6.	*Gawinecki Łukasz and Helena Skarupska*	*29*
7.	*Dąbrowski Antoni and Katarzyna Krawczykowska*	*4*
8.	*Kadzidłowski Tomasz and Wiktorya Rosiak*	*2*
9.	*Krupiński Tomasz and Wiktorya Jankowska*	*10*
10.	*Kowalski Józef and Józefa Szczepańska*	*16*

The following points of interest strike one in looking at the list carefully:

1. Note how the indentation goes back and forth with each successive letter of the alphabet. This is typical of indexes. The varying indentation makes it easier to keep track of changes from one letter to the next, from **А** to **Б** to **В** to **Г** to **Д**, and so on. All names beginning with the same letter are grouped together, and the overall grouping follows alphabetical order—but individual names within each group are not listed alphabetically. If this were in strict alphabetical order, *Возвякъ* (entries #4 and 5) would precede *Войцѣковски* (entry #3).

2. Record keepers often compiled these indexes at the end of the year, having waited till the last minute. They were often in a hurry, and consequently sloppy. It is not at all unusual to see various kinds of mistakes in them. While no errors are immediately apparent here, further research may uncover misspelled surnames, wrong first names, etc.

3. If you look carefully at these spellings and compare them with what we said on pages 8 and 24-26, you will see the danger of making general statements—there's always a specific instance that will make a liar of you. For instance, we said the consonant **ч** is not followed by

the vowel **ы**, but rather by **и**; yet in entry #3 there's the name *Куч**ы**нскою,* big as life. Just to prove it's no fluke, in entry #7 we see the name *Krawczykowska* spelled *Кравч**ы**ковскою* (in both cases the ending *-ою* is dictated by grammar, as we will discuss in Chapter II; the standard feminine form of these names in Polish would be *Kuczyńska* and *Krawczykowska*).

This does not mean the guidelines we gave you are worthless. As we said on page 8 regarding non-Russian names, "Record keepers generally attempted to render such names phonetically, using the Cyrillic letters or letter combinations that came closest to matching the way the names sounded. These non-Russian names often included combinations of letters and sounds not allowed in Russian, so the Cyrillic spellings may include those combinations." These names are Polish, and the discrepancies noted come from an attempt by a record keeper (probably a Polish priest who didn't speak Russian all that fluently) to render Polish sounds with Cyrillic letters. Russian names wouldn't put these sounds together—but the point is, these aren't Russian names. More often you'd see these names rendered as we indicated, *Кучинскою* and *Кравчиковскою.* The exception in this case does not invalidate the rule.

4. It is also well to note here that certain Catholic and Lutheran clergymen did **not** follow Russian alphabetical order when compiling yearly indices, but retained the alphabetical order of their native Polish or German. Perhaps it was their small way of rebelling against having to keep records in Russian, a language foreign to them. When using indices, be sure you examine them in their entirety to see if the priest who kept them was "making a political statement."

4. Finally, note the distinction between the numbers in the left column and those in the right column. The number in the left column is serial, saying in effect "In this alphabetical index, this is entry #_." The number in the right column was the number of the record itself, the number assigned as the record was drawn up. A researcher wants to request the record number (usually the one in the right column). Even when, as here, the column headings are hard to read, you can tell which is which: if the numbers are in sequential order, first 1 then 2 then 3, it's the entry number in the index, and therefore not the one that matters to you.

Find and focus on the column marked **№ Акта,** "Record #"

F. LINGUISTIC INTERFERENCE FROM OTHER LANGUAGES

Interference from English phonetic tendencies, and difficulties writing Russian-language names in the Roman alphabet, can obviously affect the forms of names and other information that show up in records. But those are not the only linguistically-related problems that can complicate a genealogist's task. Passenger lists, a primary source for researchers, can exhibit linguistic influences originating with the language spoken by European ships' officers who were charged with the completion of these forms. Many of our ancestors departed from ports such as Bremen, Hamburg, Rotterdam and Antwerp, and as such the manifests were completed by Dutch, German, French, and Flemish-speaking officers.

By and large, however, that interference is covered by the information given in Section D, Russian Forms of Proper Names. If you are having problems finding records for a particular family member, try taking into account the linguistic factors that come into play when Germans, Lithuanians, and Poles were involved. This won't always do the trick, but you may be surprised how many problems clear up once you compensate for the linguistic complications involved with tracing Eastern European roots.

II. STRUCTURE OF RUSSIAN

A. GRAMMAR

Russian, like Polish, is a member of the Slavic family of languages, which in turn is a subgroup of the much more extensive family of Indo-European languages. That family includes representatives of the Romance group, such as French and Spanish; the Germanic group, including English, German, and Dutch; the Celtic, including Irish and Welsh; the Baltic group, consisting of Old Prussian (now extinct), Lithuanian and Latvian; and others. The Slavic family of languages, in turn, is subdivided into three groups:

West Slavic — Polish, Czech, Slovak, and Lusatian, all written in the Roman alphabet
South Slavic — Serbian, Croatian, Slovenian, Bulgarian, Macedonian, all except Croatian and Slovenian written in the Cyrillic alphabet
East Slavic — Russian, Belarusian, and Ukrainian, all written in the Cyrillic alphabet

The structures, sound systems, and lexical bases of the Slavic languages are similar to some degree. It is, however, incorrect to make a blanket statement that they are "nearly the same," as significant differences do, in fact, exist in grammar, vocabulary, and structure.

Still, it is accurate to say that Russian and Polish have numerous points of communality, and we note some of them below. We do so because it may aid researchers with some knowledge of or experience with Polish, such as descendants of the many Polish Christians and Jews who emigrated from the Russian partition. Even for those not familiar with Polish, it may prove helpful to have examples in a Slavic language that uses the Roman alphabet, to compare with the Russian forms written in Cyrillic.

Both are highly inflected languages, that is, endings are added to stems of words to signal changes in meaning, as required by the exigencies of grammar. The patterns of endings added to stems is called **declension** when referring to nouns, adjectives, and pronouns.

NOUNS AND ADJECTIVES

In the declension systems of both Russian and Polish one frequently speaks of grammatical **case**. Case simply refers to the inflected form of a noun, pronoun or adjective which indicates its relationship to other words. In essence, each case has a grammatical function, such as direct object, subject of a sentence, etc. In Russian there are six cases (there are vestiges of the vocative case seen in some other Slavic languages, but they are so rare we can safely ignore the vocative). These are the cases in Russian, with indication of their most basic functions:

Nominative—subject of the sentence; this is the form of the word that appears in dictionaries or on maps. An example in English is "<u>dog</u> bites man"
Genitive—indicates possession, e. g., "dog bites <u>man's</u> leg"
Dative—indirect object, e. g., "dog gives <u>man</u> fleas"
Accusative—direct object, also used with some prepositions, e. g., "dog bites <u>man</u>"
Instrumental—instrument or means by which an action is accomplished, also used after certain prepositions, "dog bites man <u>with sharp teeth</u>"
Prepositional (also called "Locative")—place where, location; always used with a preposition, such as *в* and *на*, e. g., "dog bites man <u>in the vestibule</u>"

This means that a noun or adjective in Russian has 12 possible endings, 6 in the singular and 6 in the plural. Actually one almost never has to deal with 12 different endings—as is evident below, different cases can happen to have the same endings—but it does mean one has to be able to recognize the application of those 12 usages.

Before looking at specific case endings, it will be helpful to define a few terms one cannot avoid. One is **number**: grammatical number refers to whether a noun or adjective is used in the singular ("boy") or plural ("boys").

Another is **gender**: masculine, feminine, and neuter. Unlike English, which has "natural gender"—a noun denoting a male is masculine, a female is feminine, and if it refers to a thing, it's neuter—Russian has "grammatical" gender (like French, German, Spanish, and so forth). This means each noun in the language has a gender designation that may have no discernable connection with any inherent masculinity or femininity of the named object or concept. Thus the noun for "table," *стол*, is masculine in gender, and *стена*, "wall," is feminine, for no logical reason. Some linguists have attempted to discern rhyme and reason in gender, but invariably their explanations collapse under the weight of their own contradictions and inconsistencies. After all, why would a Russian table be masculine when a Spanish one, *mesa*, is feminine? Are Russian tables somehow more manly than Spanish ones? Most students of language find the best course is simply to accept that a noun's gender is what it is, and should be learned along with the noun's meaning. (Fortunately, most nouns referring to people tend to have the gender one would expect.)

Adjectives must agree with the nouns they modify in gender, number, and case.

Russian also has the feature known as **agreement**, which means that if the noun is masculine gender, singular number, and in the genitive case, an adjective modifying it must "agree" by taking the ending prescribed for the masculine genitive singular form. So if the expression *большой стол* (the nominative or dictionary form of "the big table") is used in a construction requiring the genitive case, it must take the form *больш**ого** стол**а*** (both the noun and adjective have masculine genitive singular endings). This may confuse someone who has little or no knowledge of the language. Think of Russian as a jigsaw puzzle where all the pieces fit into only one place to create a cohesive whole.

The **stem** of a noun, adjective, or pronoun is the base form to which endings are added. The stem of *старый*, "old," is *стар-;* the stem of *студент*, "student," is *студент*; and the stem of *стена*, "wall," is *стен-*. With practice one comes to recognize the stem of given words; for all intents and purposes, it is that part that does not change when endings are added.

As explained earlier, the term **declension** means a complete listing of the ending patterns as applied to specific nouns and adjectives. The following sample declensions illustrate the most common ending patterns; these patterns become much easier to grasp once you see them in use. Most nouns will conform to them, although of course there are always exceptions. As a rule, Russian declension is a bit simpler than Polish because it seldom includes the numerous consonant and internal vocalic stem changes that are common in that language.

Most good dictionaries give not only the nominative singular but also the genitive singular of words that feature this or other unexpected changes, so that you can recognize when the stem differs from the nominative form. To speak Russian you must be able to apply these changes correctly; but to decipher documents you need only recognize them.

SAMPLE PARADIGMS:

Masculine nouns*:* ***студент****,* "student," stem *студент,* compare Polish ***student***, "student"

Case	*Singular*	*[Polish]*	*Plural*	*[Polish]*
Nominative	*студент*	*student*	*студент**ы***	*studen**ci***
Genitive	*студент**а*** [1]	*student**a***	*студент**ов*** [1]	*student**ów***
Dative	*студент**у***	*student**owi***	*студент**ам*** [2]	*student**om***
Accusative	*студент**а*** [1]	*student**a***	*студент**ов*** [1]	*student**ów***
Instrumental	*студент**ом***	*student**em***	*студент**ами*** [2]	*student**ami***
Prepositional	*студент**е*** [3]	*studen**cie***	*студент**ах*** [2]	*student**ach***

Feminine nouns: *жена*, "wife," stem *жен-*, compare Polish ***żona****,* "wife"

Case	*Singular*	*[Polish]*	*Plural*	*[Polish]*
Nominative	*жен**а***	*żon**a***	*жен**ы***	żon***y***
Genitive	*жен**ы***	*żon**y***	*жён* [4]	żon
Dative	*жен**е***	*żon**ie***	*жен**ам*** [2]	żon***om***
Accusative	*жен**у***	*żon**ę***	*жен**ы***	żon***y***
Instrumental	*жен**ой***	*żon**ą***	*жен**ами*** [2]	żon***ami***
Prepositional	*жен**е*** [3]	*żon**ie***	*жен**ах*** [2]	żon***ach***

Neuter nouns: *место*, "place," stem *мест-*, compare Polish ***miasto****,* "town, city"

Case	*Singular*	*[Polish]*	*Plural*	*[Polish]*
Nominative	*мест**о*** [5]	*miasto*	*мест**а*** [5]	*miast**a***
Genitive	*мест**а***	*miast**a***	*мест* [4]	*miast*
Dative	*мест**у***	*miast**u***	*мест**ам*** [2]	*miast**om***
Accusative	*мест**о*** [5]	*miast**o***	*мест**а*** [5]	*miast**a***
Instrumental	*мест**ом***	*miast**em***	*мест**ами*** [2]	*miast**ami***
Prepositional	*мест**е*** [3]	*mieś**cie***	*мест**ах*** [2]	*miast**ach***

The Polish word *miasto* comes from the same Slavic root as Russian *место.* In Polish, however, that root split into *miejsce,* which means "place," while *miasto* developed in the meaning "town, city." We compare them here because, in spite of the divergent semantic development, the link between the two words is instructive.

[1] In Russian and Polish, masculine nouns denoting persons and animals have the same form in the genitive and accusative, both singular and plural. Masculine nouns denoting inanimate objects have accusative forms identical to the nominative.

[2] Nouns of all genders take the dative plural ending ***-ам***, the instrumental plural ending ***-ами***, and the prepositional plural ending ***-ах***. There are very few exceptions.

[3] The prepositional singular ending is usually ***–е*** for masculine, feminine, and neuter nouns (with some exceptions, primarily feminine nouns ending in ***–ия*** and neuter nouns ending in ***–ие***, which have ***–ии***). In pre-Revolutionary spelling, this ***–е*** was normally rendered with the character ***–ѣ*** — thus "in the city," *въ городѣ*, modern spelling *в городе.*

[4] Note that feminine and neuter nouns add no ending to the stem in the genitive plural.

[5] Neuter nouns always have the same form in the nominative and accusative, whether singular or plural.

Russian **adjectival** declension can be seen from the charts below. The adjective *новый*, "new," stem *нов-*, provides a good example:

Case	*Masculine Singular*	*Feminine Singular*	*Neuter Singular*	*Plural*
Nominative	*нов**ый***[1]	*нов**ая***	*нов**ое***	*нов**ые***
Genitive	*нов**ого***	*нов**ой***	*нов**ого***	*нов**ых***
Dative	*нов**ому***	*нов**ой***	*нов**ому***	*нов**ым***
Accusative	*нов**ый**/нов**ого***[2]	*нов**ую***	*нов**ое***	*нов**ые**/нов**ых***[2]
Instrumental	*нов**ым***	*нов**ой***	*нов**ым***	*нов**ыми***
Prepositional	*нов**ом***	*нов**ой***	*нов**ом***	*нов**ых***

[1] Some adjectives accent the last syllable of the ending, and have ***–ой*** in the nominative masculine singular, e. g., *больш**ой***, "big, large." Otherwise they follow the pattern shown above.

[2] The ending depends on whether the adjective modifies a masculine noun referring to an animate being or a thing. For animate beings the accusative singular ending is *–ого* and the plural *–ых*. For things the accusative is *-ый* in the singular, *-ые* in the plural. The accusative forms of feminine and neuter nouns, and adjectives modifying them, are not affected by the distinction between animate and inanimate.

For comparison, here is the declension in Polish of *nowy*, "new," stem *now-*:

Case	*Masculine Singular*	*Feminine Singular*	*Neuter Singular*	*Plural*
Nominative	*now**y***	*now**a***	*now**e***	*now**e***
Genitive	*now**ego***	*now**ej***	*now**ego***	*now**ych***
Dative	*now**emu***	*now**ej***	*now**emu***	*now**ym***
Accusative	*now**y**/now**ego***	*now**ą***	*now**e***	*now**e**/now**ych***
Instrumental	*now**ym***	*now**ej***	*now**ym***	*now**ymi***
Prepositional	*now**ym***	*now**ej***	*now**ym***	*now**ych***

Here is the declensional pattern for standard Russian surnames ending in *–ов* or *–ев*:

Case	*Masculine Singular*	*Feminine Singular*	*Plural*
Nominative	*Петров*	*Петров**а***	*Петров**ы***
Genitive	*Петров**а***	*Петров**ой***	*Петров**ых***
Dative	*Петров**у***	*Петров**ой***	*Петров**ым***
Accusative	*Петров**а***	*Петров**у***	*Петров**ых***
Instrumental	*Петров**ым***	*Петров**ой***	*Петров**ами***
Prepositional	*Петров**е***	*Петров**ой***	*Петров**ах***

We often see surnames, especially of ethnic Poles, of adjectival origin, ending in *–ский* (archaic *–скій*). This produces a slight difference, in that in Russian the letter *ы* cannot follow *к*. It is replaced by the letter *и* instead, as follows:

Case	*Masculine Singular*	*Feminine Singular*	*Plural*
Nominative	*Чайковск**ий***	*Чайковск**ая***	*Чайковск**ие***
Genitive	*Чайковск**ого***	*Чайковск**ой***	*Чайковск**их***
Dative	*Чайковск**ому***	*Чайковск**ой***	*Чайковск**им***
Accusative	*Чайковск**ого***	*Чайковск**ую***	*Чайковск**их***
Instrumental	*Чайковск**им***	*Чайковск**ой***	*Чайковск**ами***
Prepositional	*Чайковск**ом***	*Чайковск**ой***	*Чайковск**ах***

Other Forms of These Endings

There are several factors that can cause endings to differ from those shown in the preceding paradigms. Let us look at a few examples.

Palatalization (see page 4) affects the endings of both nouns and adjectives. If the stem ends in a palatalized consonant, the vowel of the ending comes from the "soft" list, not the "hard" list. Thus the stem of the noun *свидетель*, "witness," ends in palatalized *л*, indicated by the following "soft sign." To form the genitive singular, you add the ending *–a*, as with the noun *студент* in the noun paradigm. But the consonant's softness means that what is added is not–*a* but *–я: свидетеля*. The dative singular is *свидетелю*, not *свидетелу;* and so on.

Similarly, the stem of the adjective *средний*, "middle," ends in a palatalized *н*, as shown by the following vowel *и*. When adjectival endings are added, the vowel must reflect that palatalization. The feminine nominative singular form is not *средная* but *средняя;* the feminine accusative singular is *среднюю*, and the neuter nominative singular is *среднее*. The masculine prepositional singular is *среднем* because of the palatalized *н*; compare the ending *–ом* used when the stem ends in a non-palatalized consonant, e. g., *новом*. This explains the feminine genitive, dative, instrumental, and prepositional singular endings *средней* and *новой*.

Sometimes an ending appears with ***и*** instead of ***ы*** because using *ы* would involve a letter combination not allowed by standard Russian orthography. Thus the nominative masculine singular of the adjective *русский*, "Russian," has *–кий* , not *–кый*, because *ы* cannot follow *к* (see page 8). In other cases, however, where adding the standard endings violates no spelling rules, the forms are as expected, e. g., *русского, русскому*. The same reasoning explains *умерший* instead of *умершый* (***ы*** cannot follow ***ш***) and many other similar forms.

Some of the endings were spelled differently before the post-Revolution changes mentioned on pages 2-3. The most potentially confusing of these were as follows:

–ie = modern *–ие*	*-iй* = modern *–ий*	*-iя* = modern *–ия*
–аго = modern *-ого*	*–яго* = modern *-его*	

In general you can expect to see *i* rather than modern *и* in almost any ending where that vowel is followed by another. Thus modern *Англия*, "England," was *Англiя; присутствие*, "presence," was *присутствiе;* and so on.

Feminine instrumental singular forms of nouns and adjectives also have archaic forms with *-ою* and *-ею* instead of modern *-ой* and *–ей*. For our purposes, the difference is not significant. It is enough to be aware of it, so that you will not be baffled when you encounter it.

We have shown these paradigms with the modern spellings instead of the archaic ones, because those are what you will see in most other reference works you might consult, and we did not wish to cause confusion. Besides, once you know about the archaic characters, it is not difficult to recognize them when you see them. In analysis of sample documents we will point out archaic forms when they occur, and refer the reader back to this page.

Finally, adjectives used **predicatively**—i. e., they would be translated in English after a form of "to be"— appear in shortened forms. Thus an illiterate fellow is *неграмотный человек*, but if used in the sense "he is illiterate," the form *неграмотен* appears. A female would be described as *неграмотна*. Generally adjectives ending in *–ный* take predicative forms ending in *–ен* (masculine), *–на* (feminine), *-но* (neuter), and *-ны* (plural). The short forms of *добрый*, "kind," are *добр, добра, добро*, and *добры*. These forms are **not** declined.

The "Chopping Block"

Studying the paradigms just shown may help some. Others may find it easier to use the following "Chopping Block." The idea is to take the inflected form you've found in a document, chop off the ending, and restore any necessary nominative ending. You should be able to find the result in a dictionary. The list is not comprehensive, but has most such endings, the cases associated with them, and he corresponding nominative forms. The abbreviations for the cases are: N(ominative), G(enitive), D(ative), A(ccusative), I(nstrumental), P(repositional), *sing.* singular, *pl.* plural, *masc.* masculine, *fem.* feminine, *neut.* neuter. Forms now archaic are marked †; those differing from modern forms only by adding -ъ are indicated with *(ъ)*.

Ending	*Case(s)*	*Noun/adj.*	*Example*	*Replace with*	*Dictionary Form*
-а	G/A *masc. sing.* G *neut. sing.* N *masc. pl.* N/A *neut. pl.*	noun	*Ян**а*** *до сел**а*** *город**а*** *мест**а** († мѣста)*	*nothing* **-о** *nothing* **-о**	*Ян(ъ)* *село* *город(ъ)* *место († мѣсто)*
-аго †	G/A *masc. sing.* G *neut. sing.*	adj.	*пят**аго**, свят**аго***	**-ый** or **-ой**	*пят**ый**, свят**ой***
-ам(ъ)	D *pl.*	noun	*город**ам(ъ)*** *женщин**ам(ъ)*** *мест**ам**(† мѣстамъ)*	*nothing* **-а** **-о**	*город(ъ)* *женщина* *место († мѣсто)*
-ами	I *pl.*	noun	*внук**ами*** *рек**ами** († рѣками)* *слов**ами***	*nothing* **-а** **-о**	*внук(ъ)* *река (†рѣка)* *слово*
-ах(ъ)	P *pl.*	noun	*в акт**ах(ъ)*** *в книг**ах(ъ)*** *о слов**ах(ъ)***	*nothing* **-а** **-о**	*акт(ъ)* *книга* *слово*
-ая	N *fem. sing.*	adj.	*стар**ая***	**-ый** or **-ой**	*стар**ый***
-е † -ѣ	P *masc. sing.* P *fem. sing.* P *neut. sing.* P *masc. sing.* D/P *fem. sing.* A *neut. sing.* N *masc. pl.*	noun noun noun noun	*Петров**е** († Петровѣ)* *случа**е** († случаѣ)* *Москв**е** († Москвѣ)* *Весолов**е** († Весоловѣ)* *гост**е** († гостѣ)* *жен**е** († женѣ)* *пол**е*** *крестьян**е***	*nothing* **-й** **-а** **-о** **-ь** **-а** *no change* **-ин** († **-инъ**)	*Петров(ъ)* *случай* *Москва* *Весолово* *гость* *жена* *поле* *крестьян**ин(ъ)***
-ев(ъ)	G *masc. pl.*	noun	*Наркевич**ев(ъ)*** *евре**ев(ъ)***	*nothing* **-й**	*Наркевич(ъ)* *еврей*
-его	G/A *masc. sing.* G *neut. sing.*	adj.	*средн**его** († средняго)*	**-ий** († **-iй**)	*средн**ий** († среднiй)*
-ее	N/A *neut. sing.*	adj.	*син**ее***	**-ий** († **-iй**)	*син**ий** († синiй)*
-ей	I *fem. sing.* G *masc./fem. pl.* G/D/I/P *fem. sing.*	noun noun adj.	*недел**ей** († недѣлей)* *жител**ей*** *здешн**ей** († здѣшней)*	**-я** **-ь** **-ий** († **-iй**)	*недел**я** († недѣля)* *жител**ь*** *здешн**ий** († здѣшнiй)*
-ем	I *masc. sing.* I *neut. sing.* P *masc./neut. sing.*	noun noun adj.	*с товарищ**ем(ъ)*** *с Андре**ем(ъ)*** *настоятел**ем(ъ)*** *пол**ем(ъ)*** *син**ем(ъ)***	*nothing* **-й** **-ь** **-е** **-ий** († **-iй**)	*товарищ(ъ)* *Андрей* *настоятел**ь*** *поле* *син**ий** († синiй)*

-ему	D *masc./neut. sing.*	adj.	*среднему*	**-ий** († **-ій**)	*средний* († *средній*)
-ею †	I *fem. sing.* I *fem. sing.*	noun adj.	*девицею* († *дњвицею*) *неделею* († *недњлею*) *хорошею*	**-а** **-я** **-ий** († **-ій**)	*девица* († *дњвица*) *неделя* († *недњля*) *хороший* († *хорошій*)
-и	G *fem. sing.* N/A *masc. pl.* G/D/P *fem. sing.*	noun noun noun noun	*книги* *недели* (†*недњли*) *дожди* *случаи* *части*	**-а** **-я** **-ь** **-й** **-ь**	*книга* *неделя* († *недњля*) *дождь* *случай* *часть*
-ие († **-іе**)	N/A *pl.* N/A *neut. sing.*	adj. noun	*русские* († *русскіе*) *здание* († *зданіе*)	**-ий** († **-ій**) *no change*	*русский* († *русскій*) *здание* († *зданіе*)
-ии († **-іи**)	G/D/P *fem. sing.* P *neut. sing.*		*России* († *Россіи*) *звании* († *званіи*)	**-ия** († **-ія**) **-ие** († **-іе**)	*Россия* († *Россія*) *звание* († *званіе*)
-ий († **-ій**)	G *fem.pl.* G *neut. pl.*	noun	*фамилий* († *фамилій*) *зданий* († *зданій*)	**-ия** († **-ія**) **-ие** († **-іе**)	*фамилия* († *фамилія*) *здание* († *зданіе*)
-им(ъ)	I *sing.*, D *pl.*	adj.	*Горским(ъ)*	**-ий** († **-ій**)	*Горский* († *Горскій*)
-ими	I *pl.*	adj.	*русскими*	**-ий** († **-ій**)	*русский* († *русскій*)
-их(ъ)	G/A/P *pl.*	adj.	*здешних* († *здњшнихъ*)	**-ий** († **-ій**)	*здешний* († *здњшній*)
-ию	D *neut. sing.*	noun	*чтению* († *чтенію*)	**-ие** († **-іе**)	*чтение* († *чтеніе*)
-ия	G. *neut. sing.*	noun	*присутствия* († *-ія*)	**-ие** († **-іе**)	*присутствие* († *-іе*)
-ія †	N/A *fem./neut. pl.*	adj.	*уральскія*	**-ий** († **-іе**)	*уральский* († *-скій*)
-ов(ъ)	G/A *masc. pl.*	noun	*с Климов(ъ)*	*nothing*	*Клим(ъ)*
-ого	G/A *masc. sing.* G *neut. sing.*	adj.	*Нового Мира*	**-ый** or **–ий** or **-ой**	*Новый Мир(ъ)*
-ое	N/A *neut. sing.*	adj.	*старое*	**-ый** or **-ой**	*старый*
-ой	I *fem. sing.* G/D/P/I *fem. sing.*	noun adj.	*комнатой* *русской*	**-а** **-ый** or **–ий** or **-ой**	*комната* *русский* († *русскій*)
-ом(ъ)	I *masc. sing.* I *neut. sing.* P *masc./neut. sing.*	noun noun adj.	*сыном(ъ)* *местом* († *мњстомъ*) *большом(ъ)*	*nothing* **-о** **-ый** or **–ий** or **-ой**	*сын(ъ)* *место* († *мњсто*) *большой*
-ому	D *masc./neut. sing.*	adj.	*старому*	**-ый** or **–ий** or **-ой**	*старый*
-ою †	I *fem. sing.* I *fem. sing.*	noun adj.	*с Агатою* *новою*	**-а** **-ый** or **–ий** or **-ой**	*Агата* *новый*
-у	G *masc. sing.* D *masc. sing.* D *neut. sing.* A *fem. sing.* P *masc. sing.*	noun noun noun noun noun	*роду* *Петрову* *месту* († *мњсту*) *в Москву* *на берегу*	*nothing* *nothing* **-о** **-а** *nothing*	*род(ъ)* *Петров(ъ)* *место* († *мњсто*) *Москва* *берег(ъ)*
-ую	A *fem. sing.*	adj.	*новую*	**-ый** or **–ий** or **-ой**	*новый*
-ы	G *fem. sing.*, N *pl.* N/A *masc. pl.*	noun	*Каролины* *акты*	**-а** *nothing*	*Каролина* *акт(ъ)*
-ые	N/A pl.	adj.	*новобрачные*	**-ый** or **-ой**	*новобрачный*
-ым(ъ)	I/P *sing.*, D *pl.*	adj.	*холостым(ъ)*	**-ый** or **-ой**	*холостой*
-ыми	I *pl.*	adj.	*брачными*	**-ый** or **-ой**	*брачный*
-ых(ъ)	G/A/P *pl.*	adj.	*старых(ъ)*	**-ый** or **-ой**	*старый*
-ыя †	N/A *fem./neut. pl.*	adj.	*Снњжныя горы*	**-ый** or **-ой**	*снежный*(† *снњжный*)
-ь	G *fem. pl.*	noun	*недель* († *недњль*)	**-я**	*неделя* († *недњля*)

-ью	I *fem. sing.* I *fem. sing.*	noun	*двер**ью*** *до**черью***	*nothing* **-ь** *(delete -ер)*	*дверь* *доч**ь****
-ья	N *pl.*	noun	*брат**ья***	*nothing*	*брат(ъ)*
-ю	D *masc. sing.* D *neut. sing.* A *sing.*	noun noun noun	*настоятел**ю*** *случа**ю*** *пол**ю*** *недел**ю** († недѣл**ю**)*	**-ь** **-й** **-е** **-я**	*настоятел**ь*** *случа**й*** *пол**е*** *недел**я** († недѣл**я**)*
-юю	A *fem. sing.*	adj.	*Син**юю** Осоку*	**-яя → -ий** († **-ій**)	*Син**яя** Осока*
-я	G/A *masc./neut. sing.*	noun	*мор**я*** *евре**я*** *апрел**я** († апрѣл**я**)*	**-е** **-й** **-ь**	*мор**е*** *евре**й*** *апрел**ь** († апрѣл**ь**)*
-яго †	G/A *masc. sing.*, G *neut. sing.*	adj.	*треть**яго***	**-ий** († **-ій**)	*трет**ий** († трет**ій**)*
-ям(ъ)	D plur.	noun	*пол**ям(ъ)*** *музе**ям(ъ)*** *жител**ям(ъ)*** *недел**ям** († недѣл**ямъ**)*	**-е** **-й** **-ь** **-я**	*пол**е*** *музе**й*** *жител**ь*** *недел**я** († недѣл**я**)*
-ями	I *pl.*	noun	*мор**ями*** *геро**ями*** *читател**ями*** *стать**ями***	**-е** **-й** **-ь** **-я**	*мор**е*** *геро**й*** *читател**ь*** *стать**я***
-ях(ъ)	P *pl.*	noun	*здани**ях** († здані**яхъ**)* *поко**ях(ъ)*** *родител**ях(ъ)*** *шве**ях(ъ)***	**-е** **-й** **-ь** **-я**	*здани**е** († здані**е**)* *поко**й*** *родител**ь*** *шве**я***
-яя	N *fem. sing.*	adj.	*син**яя***	**-ий** († **-ій**)	*син**ий** († син**ій**)*

*Some feminine nouns such as *мать*, "mother," and *дочь* "daughter," add *-ер-* to the stem before adding endings. Thus *мать* is declined *мать, матери, матери, мать, матерью, матери,* in the singular, and *матери, матерей, матерям, матерей, матерями,* and *матерях* in the plural. The same pattern is true for *дочь*, except the instrumental plural is *дочерьми* instead of *дочерями*.

Comparison of the Chopping Block endings to the sample paradigms on pages 35-36 indicates that it must include a number of endings not shown in the paradigms. That's because the paradigms feature the most common patterns; there are other endings you encounter when dealing with nouns and adjectives that follow slightly different patterns. Once you factor in the effects of palatalization on pronunciation and spelling, the discrepancy isn't too great.

In the genitive plural of many feminine and neuter nouns, grammar calls for no ending to be added to the stem. To restore the nominative form, one must **add** an ending, rather than delete one:

мест → мест<u>о</u>   *женщин → женщин<u>а</u>*   *пол → пол<u>е</u>*

Other plural forms have a "fill" vowel, sometimes called an "epenthetic" vowel, either *-е* or *-о*. This is a vowel inserted between the stem and ending in some forms — usually between two consonants at the end of a word, to make the word easier to pronounce — that drops out in other forms.

полек → полка   *лавок → лавка*   *деревень → деревня*   *сестёр → сестра*

Conversely, fill vowels may have to be restored when deleting endings from nouns containing certain suffixes, especially *–ец*.

отцов (genitive plural) → *отец*   *младенца* (genitive singular) → *младенец*

The Chopping Block does not include every ending that one may encounter; there are just too many possibilities to draw up a chart that is both comprehensive and comprehensible. Here are notes on a few other declensional patterns one needs to recognize.

Two common neuter nouns with unusual patterns are *время*, "time," and *имя*, "name":

Case	Singular	Plural	Singular	Plural
Nominative	*врем**я***	*врем**ена***	*им**я***	*им**ена***
Genitive	*врем**ени***	*врем**ён***	*им**ени***	*им**ён***
Dative	*врем**ени***	*врем**енам***	*им**ени***	*им**енам***
Accusative	*врем**я***	*врем**ена***	*им**я***	*им**ена***
Instrumental	*врем**енем***	*врем**енами***	*им**енем***	*им**енами***
Prepositional	*врем**ени***	*врем**енах***	*им**ени***	*им**енах***

A pattern seen with certain common masculine nouns has *–анин* or *–янин* in the nominative singular, as seen in the nouns *крестьянин*, "peasant," and *гражданин*, "citizen." Most are normal masculine forms if you overlook that inserted *–ан- or -ян-:*

Case	Singular	Plural	Singular	Plural
Nominative	*крестьянин*	*крестьян**е***	*гражданин*	*граждан**е***
Genitive	*крестьянин**а***	*крестьян*	*гражданин**а***	*граждан*
Dative	*крестьянин**у***	*крестьян**ам***	*гражданин**у***	*граждан**ам***
Accusative	*крестьянин**а***	*крестьян*	*гражданин**а***	*граждан*
Instrumental	*крестьянин**ом***	*крестьян**ами***	*гражданин**ом***	*граждан**ами***
Prepositional	*крестьянин**е***	*крестьян**ах***	*гражданин**е***	*граждан**ах***

Two other masculine nouns that appear constantly in records are *день*, "day," and *год*, "year." These words are too important to make any mistake:

Case	Singular	Plural	Singular	Plural
Nominative	*день*	*дн**и***	*год*	*год**ы***
Genitive	*дн**я***	*дн**ей***	*год**у***	*год**ов**, лет**
Dative	*дн**ю***	*дн**ям***	*год**у***	*год**ам***
Accusative	*день*	*дн**и***	*год**а***	*год**ы***
Instrumental	*дн**ём***	*дн**ями***	*год**ом***	*год**ами***
Prepositional	*дн**е***	***днях***	*год**у***	*год**ах***

* The form *лет*, archaic *лѣтъ*, is the genitive plural of *лето*, "summer," and is used as the genitive plural of *год* with numerals (5 and higher) and other expressions of quantity. This distinction figures prominently in expressions of age, see pages 50-51.

While we could fill a book with information on the declension of Russian nouns and adjectives, two other points should be made before we move on. One is that adjectives in

Russian are often used as nouns, and thus will follow the adjectival declension patterns, even though their meaning clearly classifies them as nouns. One example is the adjective *святой*, "holy." It is used with that meaning, but it also appears with proper names in the same sense as we use "Saint." The island we call St. Helen's is called *Святой Елены [остров]* ("[island] of St. Helen") in Russian, and the St. Lawrence river is *Святого Лаврентия [река]*, "[river] of St. Lawrence." The adjective *больной* is used as a noun meaning "patient, sick person," so that "the patient's son" is *сын больного*. In form *портной* is an adjective, but it is used as a noun to mean "tailor." The masculine forms of the adjective *новобрачный*, "newly-married," are used to mean "groom"; the feminine forms are used in the meaning of "bride"; and the plural means "the newlyweds." There are many other examples.

Finally, place names in Russian come from many different sources, including nouns and adjectives. Thus there is a village *Средняя*, Srednyaya, which means literally "middle"; it is declined like any feminine adjective with a palatalized stem, so that *в Средней* means "in Srednyaya." There is a place southeast of Moscow named *Белоозерский*, an adjectival form meaning "of the white lake" and referring to a nearby lake called *Белое Озеро*, White Lake. Many other names, like *Москва*, are nouns and are declined as such (genitive *Москвы*, dative *Москве*, and so on). We also see some place names that are actually plural forms, such as *Черемушки*, south of Moscow. In form this is a plural feminine noun, from *черёмушка*, "bird cherry tree"; it is declined accordingly: genitive *Черемушек*, dative *Черемушкам*, and so on.

PRONOUNS

While we don't want to plunge into grammar too deeply, some Russian pronouns appear too often in records to ignore. Let us examine the declensions of the most important ones. First are the "personal pronouns," the equivalents of English "I," "we," "he," "she," and "it" — "you," informal *ты* and formal *вы*, is rare in records and need not concern us.

Case	*"I/me"*	*"we/us"*	*"he/him"*	*"she/her"*	*"it"*	*"they/them"*
Nominative	*я*	*мы*	*он*	*она*	*оно*	*они*
Genitive	*меня*	*нас*	*его, него**	*её, нёе**	*его, него**	*их, них**
Dative	*мне*	*нам*	*ему, нему**	*ей, ней**	*ему, нему**	*им, ним**
Accusative	*меня*	*нас*	*его, него**	*её, нёе**	*его, него**	*их, них**
Instrumental	*мной*	*нами*	*им, ним**	*ей, ней**	*им, ним**	*ими, ними**
Prepositional	*мне*	*нас*	*нём*	*ней*	*нём*	*них*

The forms marked with asterisks are used when following a preposition.

The pronouns *кто*, "who?" and *что*, "what?" and *этот*, "this," are fairly simple:

Case	*"who?"*	*"what?"*	*masc. sing.*	*fem. sing.*	*neut. sing.*	*all plural*
Nominative	*кто*	*что*	*этот*	*эта*	*это*	*эти*
Genitive	*кого*	*чего*	*этого*	*этой*	*этого*	*этих*
Dative	*кому*	*чему*	*этому*	*этой*	*этому*	*этим*
Accusative	*кого*	*что*	*этот/этого*	*эту*	*это*	*эти/этих*
Instrumental	*кем*	*чем*	*этим*	*этой*	*этим*	*этими*
Prepositional	*ком*	*чём*	*этом*	*этой*	*этом*	*этих*

When referring to an **animate being**, the accusative form is the same as the genitive.

When referring to an **inanimate object**, the accusative form is the same as the nominative.

These pronouns, too, obey the rule of thumb for the accusative shown at left. Thus *кто*, "who?" must obviously refer to a person, so the accusative-case form is the same as the genitive, *кого*. By the same logic, *что*, "what?" must have an accusative the same as the nominative, *что*. The same rule applies for the forms of *этот*. The accusative singular of *этот стол*, "this table," is *этот стол;* the accusative singular of *этот человек*, "this man," is *этого человека*, like the genitive. But the accusative of neuter *это* is *это,* like the nominative. The same holds true in the plural.

A similar pattern applies to the pronoun *тот,* "that, that one":

Case	*masc. sing.*	*fem. sing.*	*neut. sing.*	*all plural*
Nominative	*тот*	*та*	*то*	*те*
Genitive	*того*	*той*	*того*	*тех*
Dative	*тому*	*той*	*тому*	*тем*
Accusative	*тот/того*	*ту*	*то*	*те/тех*
Instrumental	*тем*	*той*	*тем*	*теми*
Prepositional	*том*	*той*	*том*	*тех*

Another pronoun often seen in records in various forms is *какой,* "what? what kind of?" This pattern also applies for *такой*, "such, such a":

Case	*Masc. sing.*	*Fem. Sing.*	*Neut. Sing.*	*Plural*
Nominative	*какой*	*какая*	*какое*	*какие*
Genitive	*какого*	*какой*	*какого*	*каких*
Dative	*какому*	*какой*	*какому*	*каким*
Accusative	*какой/какого*	*какую*	*какое*	*какие/каких*
Instrumental	*каким*	*какой*	*каким*	*какими*
Prepositional	*каком*	*какой*	*каком*	*каких*

One other pronoun we see in the records is archaic, *сей,* meaning "this." The forms most often seen (spelled with the archaic characters) are, in the masculine: nom. *сей*, gen. *сего*, dat. *сему*, acc. *сей* or *сего*, prepositional *семъ*, instrumental *симъ*; in the feminine nom. *сія,* acc. *сію;* in the neuter, nom. *cie;* and in the plural: nom. *сіи*, gen. *сихъ*. The expression *сегодня*, "today," is actually a combination of the genitive singular of *сей день*, "this day."

VERBS

The Russian verb is also highly inflected in all tenses, and is really quite complicated. Fortunately, we can simplify it a great deal because most of the records we deal with in research describe events that have already taken place. Thus we need to deal primarily with the **past tense**, which is in many ways the simplest. We may also concentrate on 3rd person forms ("he," "she," "it," "they"), as the others are rarely used in records.

Here is a sample, from the verb *читать*, "to read"—this is the so-called infinitive form, the one found in dictionaries. The stem of this verb is *чита-*, and the past tense indicator is *-л-*. So the base form to which endings will be added is *читал*. The endings to be added are as follows:

masculine: no ending = *читал*	feminine: ***-а*** = *читал**а***
neuter: ***-о*** = *читал**о***	plural (all genders): ***-и*** = *читал**и***

Here is a breakdown of the forms; for the sake of comparison, we offer the corresponding forms of the Polish verb *czytać*, also meaning "to read":

Past Tense

Person	*Russian*	*Polish*
1st singular ("I read")	*я читал* (masc.)	*czytałem* (masc.)
	я читала (fem.)	*czytałam* (fem.)
2nd singular ("you read")	*ты читал* (masc.)	*czytałeś* (masc.)
	ты читала (fem.)	*czytałaś* (fem.)
3rd singular ("he read")	*он читал* (masc.)	*on czytał* (masc.)
"she read"	*она читала* (fem.)	*ona czytała* (fem.)
"it read"	*оно читало* (neuter)	*ono czytało* (neuter)
1st plural ("we read")	*мы читали* (all genders)	*czytaliśmy* (masc.)
		czytałyśmy (fem.)
2nd plural ("you read")	*вы читали* (all genders)	*czytaliście* (masc.)
		czytałyście (fem.)
3rd plural ("they read")	*они читали* (all genders)	*oni czytali* (masc.)
		one czytały (fem.)

Present Tense

While present-tense forms do not appear as often in records as those of the past tense, it might be worthwhile to show how each language says the same thing in the present tense:

Person	*Russian*	*Polish*
1st singular ("I read")	*я читаю* (all genders)	*czytam* (all genders)
2nd singular ("you read")	*ты читаешь* (all genders)	*czytasz* (all genders)
3rd singular ("he reads")	*он читает* (masc.)	*on czyta* (masc.)
"she reads"	*она читает* (fem.)	*ona czyta* (fem.)
"it reads"	*оно читает* (neut.)	*ono czyta* (neut.)
1st plural ("we read")	*мы читаем* (all genders)	*czytamy* (all genders)
2nd plural ("you read")	*вы читаете* (all genders)	*czytacie* (all genders)
3rd plural ("they read")	*они читают* (all genders)	*czytają* (all genders)

Participles

The other verb forms one frequently encounters in records are participles, verb forms used as adjectives. English examples are "the ***beating*** heart" and "a ***broken*** heart"—the forms in bold italics are participles. That is, they're formed from verbs, but are used as adjectives to describe nouns. They can be active in voice, i. e., in the first instance (the heart is doing the beating); or they can be passive, as in the second instance (the heart has been broken).

There are a number of these in Russian, formed a variety of ways, and it would probably be counterproductive to discuss them in detail. Instead, let us simply list the more common ones and show sample forms from typical verbs, indicating how one translates them.

present active participle – distinctive suffix ***-щий***
for *объявлять: объявляющий*, "declaring, making the statement"

past active participle – distinctive suffix ***-вший***
for *прочитать*: *прочитавший*, "having read [it] aloud"
for *подписать*: *подписавший*, "having signed [it]"

past passive participle – distinctive suffixes ***–нный*** and ***-тый***
for *прочитать*: *прочитанный*, "read aloud"
for *подписать*: *подписанный*, "signed"

present active adverbial participle – distinctive suffix ***–я*** or ***–а***
for *объявлять*, "to state, declare:" *объявляя*, "(while) declaring"

Thus one who appears before the registrar to make a statement can be described as *объявляющий*, "[the one] making the statement." A witness who had signed the document might be described as *подписавший*, "having signed [it]." One who presents a newborn child to the registrar, making a statement about it, might be described as *объявляя*, "declaring." The document itself might be described as *прочитанный*, "having been read aloud," and *подписанний*, "having been signed"—or simply as *прочитан* and *подписан;* for this shortened, predicative form of adjectives, see page 37. In fact, many registry entries end by saying something along the lines of "*Актъ сей объявлящему прочитанъ и нами подписанъ*, "This document [was] read to the declarant (literally, "[the one] making the statement") and [was] signed by us." These and similar expressions are quite common in Russian records.

B. Date and Time Expressions

NUMBERS

As preceding material indicates, the inflectional changes that nouns, adjectives, and pronouns undergo can alter their forms and make them hard to find in the dictionary—which hardly seems like a fair trick to play on a researcher who is not fluent in Russian. One must learn a few basic rules and patterns in order to be able to take the inflected forms and restore the nominative forms, which one can then find in a dictionary and translate. The same is true of dates and other expressions with numbers. Before examining vital records, one must attain some familiarity with the various numerical expressions found in those records.

Numerical symbols are rarely used in vital statistics documents. As a rule, dates and ages are completely written out in words. When numerals do appear, it is usually specified that the same data must also be written in words, to avoid any possible confusion.

The following list shows cardinal numbers (e. g., one, two, three) and ordinal numbers (e. g., first, second, third) in both the nominative and genitive singular cases; the genitive singular of the ordinals is given with a masculine ending, since that's what we see most often. In a few instances, archaic spellings are given for forms one often sees in the records, simply as a reminder that those spellings appear. Note that cardinal numbers are nouns and will take nominal endings (see page 35); ordinal numbers are adjectives in form and will follow the patterns for adjectival endings (see page 36).

	Cardinal	Genitive	Ordinal	Genitive
1	*один, одна, одно*	*одного, одной*	*первый*	*первого † перваго*
2	*два, две*	*двух*	*второй*	*второго*
3	*три*	*трёх*	*третий*	*третьего †третьяго*
4	*четыре*	*четырёх*	*четвёртый*	*четвёртого*
5	*пять*	*пяти*	*пятый*	*пятого*
6	*шесть*	*шести*	*шестой*	*шестого*
7	*семь*	*семи*	*седьмой*	*седьмого*
8	*восемь*	*восьми*	*восьмой*	*восьмого*
9	*девятъ*	*девяти*	*девятый*	*девятого*
10	*десятъ*	*десяти*	*десятый*	*десятого*
11	*одиннадцать*	*одиннадцати*	*одиннадцатый*	*одиннадцатого*
12	*двенадцать*	*двенадцати*	*двенадцатый*	*двенадцатого*
13	*тринадцать*	*тринадцати*	*тринадцатый*	*тринадцатого*
14	*четырнадцать*	*четырнадцати*	*четырнадцатый*	*четырнадцатого*
15	*пятнадцать*	*пятнадцати*	*пятнадцатый*	*пятнадцатого*
16	*шестнадцать*	*шестнадцати*	*шестнадцатый*	*шестнадцатого*
17	*семнадцать*	*семнадцати*	*семнадцатый*	*семнадцатого*
18	*восемнадцать*	*восемнадцати*	*восемнадцатый*	*восемнадцатого*
19	*девятнадцать*	*девятнадцати*	*девятнадцатый*	*девятнадцатого*
20	*двадцать*	*двадцати*	*двадцатый*	*двадцатого*
21	*двадцать один*	*двадцати одного*	*двадцать первый*	*двадцать первого*
22	*двадцать два*	*двадцати двух*	*двадцать второй*	*двадцать второго*
23	*двадцать три*	*двадцати трёх*	*двадцать третий*	*двадцать третьего*
24	*двадцать четыре*	*двадцати четырёх*	*двадцать четвёртый*	*двадцать четвёртаго*
25	*двадцать пять*	*двадцати пяти*	*двадцать пятый*	*двадцать пятого*
26	*двадцать шесть*	*двадцати шести*	*двадцать шестой*	*двадцать шестого*
27	*двадцать семь*	*двадцати семи*	*двадцать седьмой*	*двадцать седьтого*
28	*двадцать восемь*	*двадцати восьми*	*двадцать восьмой*	*двадцать восьтого*
29	*двадцать девять*	*двадцати девяти*	*двадцать девятый*	*двадцать девятого*
30	*тридцать*	*тридцати*	*тридцатый*	*тридцатого*
40	*сорок*	*сорока*	*сороковой*	*сорокового*
50	*пятьдесят*	*пятидесяти*	*пятидесятый*	*пятидесятого*
60	*шестьдесят*	*шестидесяти*	*шестидесятый*	*шестидесятого*
70	*семьдесят*	*семидесяти*	*семидесятый*	*семидесятого*
80	*восемьдесят*	*восьмидесяти*	*восьмидесятый*	*восьмидесятого*
90	*девяносто*	*девяноста*	*девяностый*	*девяностого*
100	*сто*	*ста*	*сотый*	*сотого*
200	*двести*	*двухсот*	*двухсотый*	*двухсотого*
300	*триста*	*трёхсот*	*трёхсотый*	*трёхсотого*
400	*четыреста*	*четырёхсот*	*четырёхсотый*	*четырёхсотого*
500	*пятьсот*	*пятисот*	*пятисотый*	*пятисотого*
600	*шестьсот*	*шестисот*	*шестисотый*	*шестисотого*
700	*семьсот*	*семисот*	*семисотый*	*семисотого*
800	*восемьсот*	*восьмисот*	*восьмисотый*	*восьмисотого*
900	*девятьсот*	*девятисот*	*девятисотый*	*девятисотого*
1000	*тысяча*	*тысячи*	*тысячный*	*тысячного*
1400	*тысяча четыреста*	*тысячи четырёхсот*	*тысяча четырёхсотый*	*тысяча четырёхсотого*
1500	*тысяча пятьсот*	*тысячи пятисот*	*тысяча пятисотый*	*тысяча пятисотого*
1600	*тысяча шестьсот*	*тысячи шестисот*	*тысяча шестисотый*	*тысяча шестисотого*
1700	*тысяча семьсот*	*тысячи семисот*	*тысяча семисотый*	*тысяча семисотого*
1800	*тысяча восемьсот*	*тысячи восьмисот*	*тысяча восьмисотый*	*тысяча восьмисотого*
1900	*тысяча девятьсот*	*тысячи девятисот*	*тысяча девятисотый*	*тысяча девятисотого*
2000	*две тысячи*	*двух тисячи*	*двухтысячный*	*двухтысячного*

MONTHS

The months in Russian are all masculine nouns and are not usually capitalized:

январь	January	май	May	сентябрь	September
февраль	February	июнь	June	октябрь	October
март	March	июль	July	ноябрь	November
апрель	April	август	August	декабрь	December

Also potentially useful for documents dealing with Jews is this listing of the standard Russian versions of names of the months by the Hebrew calendar.

Russian	*English*	*Gregorian Calendar*	*Russian*	*English*	*Gregorian Calendar*
тевет	Tevet	December-January	тамуз *or* таммуз	Tammuz	June-July
шват	Shevat	January-February	ав	Av	July-August
адар	Adar	February-March	элул	Elul	August-September
адар II	Adar II	March-April	тишри *or* тишрей	Tishri	September-October
нисан	Nissan	March-April	хешван	Heshvan	October-November
ияр	Iyar, Iyyar	April-May	кислев	Kislev	November-December
сиван	Sivan	May-June			

DATES

Russian employs a "hundred" system for expressing years (not the "teen" system in English, e. g., "nineteen fifty-one"). Thus 1951 is expressed as *тысчя девятьсот пятьдесят первый год*, literally "the one thousand nine hundred fifty-first year."

The grammatical structure and appropriate endings necessary to express the date properly depend upon the context in which the date occurs, as well as subtle nuances in meaning the speaker may wish to convey. In vital statistics documents of the 19th and 20th centuries, the date was usually expressed with the genitive case, so we will concentrate on that usage.

In a typical vital statistics record, the date appears at least twice:

1) at the beginning of the record, indicating the date the record was drawn up,
2) the date that the birth, marriage, or death occurred (in marriage records the dates of the reading of the banns will also appear)

In the above instances, the date will appear in the genitive case, indicating the **date on which** an event occurred. A typical date—say, June 14, 1951—will have the following components:

a) an ordinal number indicating the day of the month, in the genitive case (masculine singular ending): *четырнадцатого* — the 14th
b) the month, likewise with the appropriate genitive singular ending: *июня* —of June
c) the year, in which the "one thousand nine hundred fifty" portion will be an undeclined **cardinal** number, and the final digit will be an **ordinal** number in the genitive case: *тысяча девятьсот пятьдесят первого года* — the 1,951st year

Thus the sample date will appear as follows:

14 июня 1951 г. – *четырнадцатого июня тысяча девятьсот пятьдесят первого года*

Examining how dates are used various in the context of sample documents in Chapters IV and VI will clarify their placement and use. For information on "double dates" in documents, i. e., dates by the Julian vs. Gregorian calendars, see the note on page 200.

DATES USING THE OLD CHURCH SLAVONIC ALPHABET

In an article entitled "Old Church Slavonic: Numbers, Dates, and Months," which appeared in the Winter, 1999 issue of *East European Genealogist,* (Vol. 8, #2), Matthew Bielawa described a system of recording dates one may find in documents from the 18th century and earlier in Ukraine, Belarus, and Russia. It featured use of letters from the alphabet of Old Church Slavonic (or Old Church Slavic, henceforth abbreviated as OCS) as numerals. This is not too foreign a concept; all of us are familiar with Roman numerals, a similar use of the letters of the Latin alphabet. For a detailed discussion of this phenomenon, see Mr. Bielawa's article cited above (or, at this writing, on the Internet at this address: **http://www.halgal.com/churchslavicdmy.html**). With his permission, we give a summary of his major points here.

OCS Letter	Modern Cyrillic	Numeric Value
А а	а	1
Б б	б	—
В в	в	2
Г г	г	3
Д д	д	4
Є є	е	5
Ж ж	ж	—
Ѕ ѕ	з	6
З з	з	7
И и	и	8
І і	и	10
К к	к	20
Л л	л	30
М м	м	40
Н н	н	50
О о	о	70
П п	п	80
Р р	р	100
С с	с	200
Т т	т	300
Оу ѹ	у	400
Ф ф	ф	500
Х х	х	600
Ѡ ѡ	о	800
Ц ц	ц	900
Ч ч	ч	90
Ш ш	ш	—
Щ щ	шт (щ)	—
Ъ ъ	*like* о	—
Ы ы	ы	—
Ь ь	*like* е	—
Ѣ ѣ	ие	—
Ю ю	ю	—
Ꙗ	я	—
Ѧ ѧ Ѩ ѩ	я	—
Ѫ ѫ Ѭ ѭ	у, ю	—
Ѯ ѯ	кс	60
Ѱ ѱ	пс	700
Ѳ ѳ	ф	9
Ѵ ѵ	*like* и *or* ю	400

OCS was a liturgical and literary language used first by early South Slavic scholars and monks; it influenced the development of other Slavic languages. A less archaic form, Church Slavonic, remains the liturgical language of today's Ukrainian Catholic Rite and of the Russian, Belarusian, Ukrainian, Czech, Bulgarian, and Serbian Orthodox Churches. In other words, among Slavs it played much the same role as Latin among Western Europeans.

The OCS alphabet differed from the modern Cyrillic alphabet used in Russian. The table at right shows the OCS letters, their closest equivalents in modern Russian Cyrillic, and their numerical values.

When a letter was used as a number, a mark called a *титло [titlo],* somewhat like a tilde, was to be written over it, and dots were written around it (though it is not rare to see these marks omitted). Thus 10 would be written ·і҃·. The numbers 11-19 were written backwards by our way of thinking; the letter denoting 10 follows the letters signifying 1-9:

·і҃· 10 ·аі҃· 11 ·ві҃· 12 ·гі҃· 13

Numbers 20 and higher were written in the order we would expect:

·к҃· 20 ·ка҃· 21 ·кв҃· 22 ·кг҃· 23

Entries in actual records may feature a combination of Cyrillic and Arabic numerals, sometimes even with Latin words. Thus the date "May 4, 1727" appears in one register thus:

Маꙗ днꙗ : д҃ : *1727 Anno*

The first word, **Маꙗ**, is the genitive singular of the name for the month of May (compare modern Russian мая). The second word, **днꙗ**, is an OCS word meaning "of [the] day," or as we would say it, "on [the] day" (compare modern Russian дня). The OCS text means literally "of May of day 4," i. e., "on May 4." Note the use of the Latin word *Anno* ("year")!

Also common is to see Old Church Slavonic names of the months, which differ somewhat from the modern Russian forms. For that matter, their spelling can vary from record to record, due to regionalization and a lack of standard orthography used by parish priests. Here they are given in the genitive singular, the form you would normally see in dates:

Іаннꙋарїѧ	[of] January	**Іꙋлїѧ**	[of] July
Февроуарїѧ	[of] February	**Аѵгꙋста**	[of] August
Марта	[of] March	**Септемврїѧ**	[of] September
Апріллїѧ	[of] April	**Октѡврїѧ**	[of] October
Маїѧ	[of] May	**Ноемврїѧ**	[of] November
Іꙋнїѧ	[of] June	**Декемврїѧ**	[of] December

DAYS OF THE WEEK

воскресенье, воскресенья –Sunday
понедельник, понедельника – Monday
вторник, вторника – Tuesday
среда, среды – Wednesday
четверг, четверга – Thursday
пятница, пятницы – Friday
суббота, субботы – Saturday

To say "on _day" you use the preposition **в** plus the accusative-case form: "on Sunday" is *в воскресенье*, "on Monday" is *в понедельник*, "on Tuesday" is *во вторник*, etc.

TIME

Vital records drawn up within the territory of the Russian Empire usually give the hour and time of day when the event was reported to the registrar and the record was drawn up. So a few words on expressions of time are in order.

Hour

Russian uses the following construction to express the **hour** when something occurred:

в + a cardinal number + the word *час* ("time," with the appropriate endings)

в час	at one o'clock	*в семь часов*	at seven o'clock
в два часа	at two o'clock	*в восемь часов*	at eight o'clock
в три часа	at three o'clock	*в девять часов*	at nine o'clock
в четыре часа	at four o'clock	*в десять часов*	at ten o'clock
в пять часов	at five o'clock	*в одиннадцать часов*	at eleven o'clock
в шесть часов	at six o'clock	*в двенадцать часов*	at twelve o'clock

Time of Day

вечер	evening	*полночь*	midnight
вечером	in the evening, p. m.	*по полудни*	in the afternoon
вчера	yesterday	*по полуночи*	after midnight
днём	afternoon	*сегодня*	today
ночь, ночью, ночи	night, at night, p.m.	*утро*	morning
полдень	noon	*утром*	in the morning, a.m.

Note: although they overlap to some extent, the following divisions of time of day are generally accepted:

ночь	literally "night," from midnight until about 4:00 a.m.
утро	literally "morning," from around 4:00 a.m. to about noon
день	literally "day," from noon until about 5:00 p.m.
вечер	literally "evening," from 5:00 p.m. to midnight

Thus to express the hour and time of day, one simply combines the hour expression with the appropriate time of day expression:

в три часа ночи	3:00 a.m.	*в семь часов вечера*	7:00 p.m.

The registrars of vital statistics did not always observe these distinctions strictly. The time of the day was individually interpreted, resulting in variants such as the following:

в три часа утра	3:00 a. m.	*в три часа ночи*	3:00 a. m.

Miscellaneous Expressions

year	*год*	month	*месяц*
of the present year	*текущего года*	date	*число*
day	*день*	on this date	*сего числа*

AGE

In general, age is expressed with a number plus the appropriate form of the word *год:*

1 + *год* (also 21, 31, 41, etc.)
2, 3, 4 + *года* (also 22, 32, 42, etc.)
5 and up + *лет* (archaic spelling *лѣтъ*)

Examples:

Мне двадцать один год — I am 21 years old.
Мне двадцать два года — I am 22 years old.
Мне двадцать пять лет — I am 25 years old.

Another formulation we often see in records uses a genitive expression, literally "of X years from birth":

Янъ Новакъ ... двадцати четырехъ лѣтъ отъ роду — "Jan Nowak, 24 years from birth"

In older records we often see an archaic use of the present active participle of the verbs *иметь*, "to have," and *считать*, "to count, number, reckon":

двадцать четыре лѣтъ отъ роду имѣющій — literally "having 24 years from birth"
сорокъ лѣтъ считающій, literally "40 years counting"

C. Familial Relationships

The relationships between family members of any ethnic group is basically the same. We all have grandparents, cousins, aunts, etc. However the manner of expressing these relationships varies in each language. In English, one word, "cousin," describes a relationship with the descendants of your parents' brothers and sisters. Polish, for instance, is a bit more complicated; the idea of cousin can be expressed with *cioteczny brat,* a male cousin on your mother's side, or *stryjeczna siostra,* a female cousin on the father's side.

Russian also employs a complicated system of describing relationships within the family unit. While Russian is fairly straightforward in expressing relationship between cousins, the situation becomes far more complex when dealing with in-laws. The terminology is admittedly more bothersome for English-speakers to learn; but there is an advantage in that these terms are more precise, and thus sometimes enable the researcher to establish relationships with more precision.

Enumerated below are the translations of various terms needed to understand the family relationships found in vital records. The Polish equivalents are included, in case that helps some readers better understand the terms.

	Russian	Polish
General Terms		
aunt, maternal (by blood)	*тётя*	*ciotka*
aunt, maternal (by marriage)	*тётя*	*wujna*
aunt, paternal	*тётя*	*stryjna*
brother	*брат*	*brat (rodzony)*
child	*дитя*	*dziecko*
children	*дети*	*dzieci*
cousin (male)	*двоюродный брат*	*kuzyn*
cousin (female)	*двоюродная сестра*	*kuzynka*
father	*отец*	*ojciec*
granddaughter	*внучка*	*wnuczka*
grandson	*внук*	*wnuk*
great-granddaughter	*правнучка*	*prawnuczka*
great-grandfather	*прадед*	*pradziadek*
great-grandmother	*прабабка*	*prababka*
great-grandson	*правнук*	*prawnuk*
great-great-grandfather	*прапрадед*	*prapradziadek*
great-great-grandmother	*прапрабабка*	*praprababka*
husband	*муж*	*mąż*
mother	*мать*	*matka*
nephew (sister's son)	*племянник*	*siostrzeniec*
nephew (brother's son)	*племянник*	*bratanieс*
niece (sister's daughter)	*племянница*	*bratanica*
niece (brother's daughter)	*племянница*	*siostrzenica*
parents	*родители*	*rodzice*

sister	*сестра*	*siostra*
uncle, maternal	*дядя*	*wuj*
uncle, paternal uncle	*дядя*	*stryj*
widow	*вдова*	*wdowa*
widower	*вдовец*	*wdowiec*
wife	*жена*	*żona*

In-laws

brother-in-law (sister's husband)	*зять, свояк*	*szwagier*
brother-in-law (husband's brother)	*деверь*	*szwagier*
brother-in-law (wife's brother)	*шурин*	*szwagier*
daughter-in-law	*сноха, невестка*	*synowa*
father-in-law (husband's father)	*свёкорь*	*teść*
father-in-law (wife's father)	*тесть*	*teść*
mother-in-law (husband's mother)	*свекровь*	*teściowa*
mother-in-law (wife's mother)	*тёща*	*teściowa*
sister-in-law (brother's wife)	*невестка*	*bratowa*
sister-in-law (wife's sister)	*свояченица*	*szwagierka*
sister-in-law (husband's sister)	*золовка*	*szwagierka*
son-in-law	*зять*	*zięć*

Other Terms

adopted child, foster child	*приёмыш*	*przybrane dziecko*
goddaughter	*крестница*	*chrześniaczka*
godfather	*восприемник*	*chrzestny ojciec*
godmother	*восприемница*	*chrzestna matka*
godparents	*восприемники*	*chrzestni rodzice*
godson	*крестник*	*chrześniak*
illegitimate child	*внебрачное дитя*	*dziecko nieślubne*
stepdaughter	*падчерица*	*pasierbica*
stepfather	*отчим*	*ojczym*
stepmother	*мачеха, мачиха*	*macocha*
stepson	*пасынок*	*pasierb*

D. Sample List of Occupations

What follows is a list of occupations, many taken directly from a representative sampling of vital records. The expressions used in records are often archaic and therefore hard to find in dictionaries, so we have included as many of them as possible in this list. The most extreme examples are marked with the symbol †. Other terms are not "pure" Russian but Russified versions of words in Polish or German other languages. Remember, Russian was a foreign language to many record-keepers, whose first language was, say, Polish or Yiddish or German.

You'll note that not all these terms are exactly what you'd call "occupations." Some describe nationalities or religious groups; others are names of positions of honor. But all are words you might find given to describe a person under circumstances where you'd expect a designation of occupation. That is why it seems reasonable to list them here.

The part of speech for each entry is given in parentheses. Every noun's genitive singular form and gender is indicated, e. g., (n., masc.) means "noun, masculine." In instances where the declension varies from the most common patterns, the nominative and genitive plural forms are also given. When the pre-Revolutionary spelling of a word differs significantly from the modern one, the archaic nominative singular form is also given; *нѣмецъ*, "German," is cross-referenced to the modern spelling, *немец*, where it is also given. When cross-referenced, the archaic spellings are listed according to the pre-Revolutionary alphabetical order: *i* follows *и*, and *ѣ* comes after *ь* and before *ю*. When the only difference between the archaic and modern spellings of a word is the presence of a hard sign *ъ* at the end, that form is not listed separately; the difference between, say, *муж* and *мужъ* should not confuse you too much.

Note that many masculine nouns also have a feminine form given: thus with *учитель*, "teacher," the feminine form *учительница* is also listed. In many cases the feminine form refers not to a female who worked in that occupation, but rather to the wife of a male who did. Thus *офицер* means "officer," and the feminine form is *офицерша*—but it would be virtually unheard of for a female to be an officer, especially in pre-Revolutionary Russia. In such instances *офицерша* means "officer's wife." Unless otherwise noted, these feminine forms follow the normal feminine declension: nom. sing. *учительница*, gen. sing. *учительницы*, etc., with endings as shown on pages 35 and 38-40.

Note that we give the Russian forms in "italics" rather than the normal print form given in dictionaries. This will not give you much trouble if you familiarize yourself with the print and cursive forms shown on page 1—and it will help a lot with deciphering words in handwritten documents, because the italic forms closely resemble the handwritten forms.

агроном, агронома – (n., masc.) agriculturist

администратор, администратора – (n., masc.) administrator; *администратор прихода X* – pastor of parish X

адъютант, адъютанта – (n., fem.) aide-de-camp, adjutant

акушёр, акушёра – (n., masc.) accoucheur, male midwife

акушерка, акушерки – (n., fem.) midwife

алмазник, алмазника – (n., masc.) jeweler

алмазчик, алмазчика – (n., masc.) diamond-cutter, lapidary

амбарщик, амбарщика – (n., masc.) warehouseman

англичанин, англичанина – (n., masc., nom. pl. *англичане*, gen. pl. *англичан*) Englishman; fem. *англичанка*

антрепренёр, антрепренёра – (n., masc.) manager of a theater

аптекарь, аптекаря – (n., masc.) apothecary, pharmacist; fem. *аптекарша*

армеец, армейца – (n., masc.) soldier or officer in the line

артельщик, артельщика – (n., masc.) member of an *artel*, a workmen's association; caterer of a mess; servant at an Exchange-house or other public office

арфист, арфиста – (n., masc.) harpist; fem. *арфистка*

археолог, археолога – (n., masc.) archeologist

архивариус, архивариуса – (n., masc., † *архиварiусъ*) archivist; also seen with the same meaning: † *архиварiй* and modern *архивист*

† *архидiаконъ, архидiакона* – (n., masc.) archdeacon

архиерей, архиерея – (n., masc., † *архiерей*) prelate, bishop, higher church dignitary

архитектор, архитектора – (n., masc.) architect

асессор, асессора – (n., masc., † *ассессоръ*) assessor

атаман, атамана – (n., masc.) chief, commander (especially of Cossacks, fem. *атаманша*)

бальзамировщик, бальзамировщика – (n., masc.) embalmer

барабанщик, барабанщика – (n., masc.) drummer

барочник, барочника – (n., masc.) barge-man, master of a bark

барышник, барышника – (n., masc.) jobber, forestaller (especially of horses)

баталёр, баталёра – (n., masc.) [nautical] steward

батрак, батрака – (n., masc.) journeyman, workman (among peasants)

батрачка, батрачки – (n., fem.) hired workman [female]; journeyman's wife (also seen as *батрачиха*)

батырщик, батырщика – (n., masc.) inker, printer

башмачник, башмачника – (n., masc.) shoemaker; fem. *башмачница*

бездельный – (adj., † *бездѣльный*) unemployed, idle

безземельный – (adj.) landless

белильщик, белильщика (n., masc., † *бѣлильщикъ*) bleacher, blancher, whitewasher

белошвейка, белошвейки (n., fem., † *бѣлошвейка*) seamstress

бергмейстер, бергмейстера – (n., masc.) surveyor of mines

бечевщик, бечевщика – (n., masc.) hauler, tower

библиотекарь, библиотекаря – (n., masc., † *библіотекарь*) librarian
биржевик, биржевика – (n., masc.) stockbroker, financier
благочинный, благочинного – (adj. used as a n., masc.) provost, ecclesiastical superintendent of several churches or parishes
бляхарь, бляхаря – (n., masc.) metal-plate worker
бобыль, бобыля – (n., masc.) poor, landless peasant; fem. *бобылка* or *бобылиха*
богаделенка, богаделенки – (n., fem., † *богадѣленка*) alms-woman
богемец, богемца – (n., masc.) Bohemian; fem. *богемка*
бондарь, бондаря – (n., masc.) cooper
бортник, бортника – (n., masc.) keeper of wild bee-hives
бочар, бочара – (n., masc.) cooper
брандмайор, брандмайора – (n., masc., † *брандмаіоръ*) head fireman
буггалтер → *бухгалтер*
булочник, булочника – (n., masc.) baker; fem. *булочница*
бумагопродавец, бумагопродавца – (n., masc.) paper-maker, stationer
бургомистр, бургомистра – (n., masc.) mayor; fem. *бургомистерша*
бурлак, бурлака – (n., masc.) one who worked on or hauled boats
бурмистр, бурмистра – (n., masc.) village bailiff, much like a Polish *starosta*
бухгалтер, бухгалтера – (n., masc.) accountant, bookkeeper; also sometimes seen as *буггалтер;* fem. *бухгалтерша*
буянщик, буянщика – (n., masc.) wharf-porter, laborer
бывший – (adj., † *бывшій*) former, one-time, e. g., *бывший пекарь*, former baker
бѣлильщикъ → *белильщик*
бѣлошвейка → *белошвейка*
бюргер, бюргера – (n., masc.) burgher
вабильщик, вабильщика – (n., masc.) lurer, trainer of birds
вагемейстер, вагемейстера – (n., masc.) customs-house weigher
вахмистр, вахмистра – (n., masc.) quartermaster, cavalry sergeant-major
вахтер, вахтера – (n., masc.) storekeeper; janitor, porter
ваятель, ваятеля – (n., masc.) sculptor
ведёрник, ведёрника – (n., masc.) pail-maker
венгр, венгра – (n., masc., also seen: *венгерец, венгерца*) Hungarian; fem. *венгерка*
верёвочник, верёвочника – (n., masc.) ropemaker
ветеран, ветерана – (n., masc.) veteran
ветеринар, ветеринара – (n., masc.) veterinarian
ветошник, ветошника – (n., masc.) rag-man; fem. *ветошница*
† *викарій, викарія* – (n., masc.) vicar, suffragan
винокур, винокура – (n., masc.) distiller
винопродавец, винопродавца – (n., masc.) wine merchant, wine dealer
винотогровец, виноторговца – (n., masc.) wine merchant, wine dealer
† *виночерпец, виночерпца* – (n., masc.) cupbearer; also seen as *виночерпій*
владелец, владельца – (n., masc., † *владѣлецъ*) owner, e. g. *владелец аптеки* – pharmacy owner. *владелец земли* – land-owner; fem. *владелица*
водник, водника – (n., masc.) water-transport worker
водонос, водоноса – (n., masc.) water-carrier
водопроводчик, водопроводчика – (n., masc.) plumber
возница, возницы – (n., masc.) driver, coachman
возный, возного – (adj. used as a n., masc.; in standard Russian, of, pertaining to carts); possibly a Russified version of Polish *woźny,* cart-driver, † beadle
возчик, возчика – (n., masc.) carter
войлочник, войлочника – (n., masc.) felt-maker
войт, войта – (n., masc.) Polish *wójt,* an official in charge of a district
воловщик, воловщика – (n., masc.) drover of oxen
вольноотпущенник, вольноотпущенника – (n., masc.) freedman, emancipated serf; fem. *вольно-отпущенница;* also seen: (part. used as a n.) *вольноотпущенный*, fem. *вольноотпущенная*
ворсильщик, ворсильщика – (n., masc.) carder, teaseler
воспитатель, воспитателя – (n., masc.) tutor; fem. *воспитательница*
восприемник, восприемника – (n., masc., † *воспріемникъ*) godparent, godfather; fem. *восприемница*, godmother
вотчинник, вотчинника – (n., masc.) possessor of a patrimony
вощик, вощика – (n., masc.) cart-driver, wagon-driver
врач, врача – (n., masc.) doctor
выбылой – (adj.) resigned, retired
вышивальщица, вышивальщицы – (n., fem.) embroideress
гардемарин, гардемарина – (n., masc.) midshipman
гвардеец, гвардейца – (n., masc.) soldier or officer in the guards

гвоздочник, гвоздочника – (n., masc.) maker or seller of nails
генеалог, генеалога – (n., masc.) genealogist
генерал, генерала – (n., masc.) general; *генерал-адмираль*, lord high admiral; *генерал-адъютант*, adjutant general; *генерал-аншеф* or *полный генерал*, general in chief; *генерал-губернатор*, governor general; *генерал-лейтенант*, lieutenant general; *генерал-майор*, major general; *генерал фельдмаршаль*, field marshal
геодезист, геодезиста – (n., masc.) geodesist, surveyor
геолог, геолога – (n., masc.) geologist
герцог, герцога – (n., masc.) duke (cmp. Germ. *Herzog*); fem. *герцогиня*
гетман, гетмана – (n., masc.) *hetman*, in Poland and in Ukraine a term once used for the commander in chief
гладильщик, гладильщика – (n., masc.) polisher, ironer; fem. *гладильщица*
глашатай, глашатая – (n., masc.) town-crier, public announcer of official news
гонец, гонца – (n., masc.) currier, runner
гончар, гончара – (n., masc.) potter
горничная, горничной – (adj. used as a n., fem.) chambermaid, maid-servant
горнозаводчик, горнозаводчика – (n., masc.) iron-master, iron-manufacturer
горнорабочий, горнорабочего – (adj. used as a n., masc.) miner, worker in metalworks
городничий, городничего – (adj. used as a n., masc.) provost, town bailiff
городовой, городового – (adj. used as a n., masc.) town policeman, constable
горожанин, горожанина – (n., masc., nom. pl. *горожане*, gen. pl. *горожан*) townsman; fem. *горожанка*)
горшечник, горшечника – (n., masc.) potter; fem. *горшечница*
господарь, господаря – (n., masc.) land-owner, master (cmp. Polish *gospodarz*); fem. *господарка*
гостинодворец, гостинодворца – (n., masc.) shopkeeper in a bazaar
гофмаршал, гофмаршала – (n., masc.) master of the court, knight marshal (cmp. Germ. *Hofmarschall*)
гофмейстер, гофмейстера – (n., masc.) court steward, steward of a noble's household (cmp. Germ. *Hofmeister*)
грабельщик, грабельщика – (n., masc.) raker; fem. *грабельщица*
гравёр, гравёра – (n., masc.) engraver
градоначальник, градоначальника – (n., masc.) 19th-century governor of a major city with its own administration
градоправитель, градоправителя – (n., masc.) town magistrate
гражданин, гражданина – (n., masc., nom. pl. *граждане*, gen. pl. *граждан*) citizen, burgher, freeman; fem. *гражданка*
гребенщик, гребенщика – (n., masc.) comb-maker
гренадер, гренадера – (n., masc.) grenadier
гробовщик, гробовщика – (n., masc.) coffin-maker, undertaker, gravedigger
гробокопатель, гробокопателя – (n., masc.) gravedigger
губернатор, губернатора – (n., masc.) governor; fem. *губернаторша*
гувернантка, гувернантки – (n., fem.) governess, tutoress
гувернёр, гувернёра – (n., masc.) tutor
гуртовщик, гуртовщика – (n., masc.) wholesale merchant; drover
гусар, гусара – (n., masc.) hussar
давильщик, давильщика – (n., masc.) presser, treader (of grapes)
дворецкий, дворецкого – (adj. used as a n., masc., † *дворецкій*) house steward, butler, majordomo
дворник, дворника – (n., masc.) yard-keeper, house-porter
дворянин, дворянина – (n., masc., nom. pl. *дворяне*, gen. pl. *дворян*) aristocrat; fem. *дворянка*
девица, девицы – (n., fem., † *дѣвица*) girl, maiden
декан, декана – (n., masc.) dean
делатель, делателя – (n., masc. † *дѣлатель*) maker, worker
делопроизводитель, делопроизводителя – (n., masc., † *дѣлопроизводитель*) clerk, secretary
денщик, денщика – (n., masc.) officer's servant
дернорез, дернореза – (n., masc., † *дернорѣзъ*) turf-cutter
десятник, десятника – (n., masc.) overseer, foreman
деятель, деятеля – (n., masc., † *дѣятель*) agent, promoter, activist
† *дозорщик, дозорщика* – (n., masc.) customs-house officer
доильщица, доильщицы – (n., fem.) milkmaid, one who milks cows
доимщик, доимщика – (n., masc.) collector of arrears
доктор, доктора – (n., masc., nom. pl. *доктора*) doctor; fem. *докторша*, doctor's wife, female doctor
должностной – (adj.) functionary, in office, official; *должностное лицо*, functionary

домашний – (adj.) household; *домашний учитель* – tutor, private tutor
доминиканец, доминиканца – (n., masc.) Dominican monk
домовладелец, домовладельца – (n., masc., † *домовладѣлецъ*) house-owner; fem. *домовладелица*
домовод, домовода – (n., masc.) house-keeper; fem. *домоводка*
домоправитель, домоправителя – (n., masc.) steward, house manager; fem. *домоправительница*
домостроитель, домостроителя – (n., masc.) house manager, builder; fem. *домостроительница*
домохозяин, домохозяина – (n., masc.) owner or master of a house, householder
дорожник, дорожника – (n., masc.) roadway worker; fem. *дорожница*
досмотрщик, досмотрщика – (n., masc.) searcher, inspector
доцент, доцента – (n., masc.) assistant professor
драгун, драгуна – (n., masc.) dragoon
дровокол, дровокола – (n., masc.) woodchopper
дровоносец, дровоносца – (n., masc.) carrier of wood (also seen: *дровонос*)
дровосек, дровосека – (n., masc., † *дровосѣкъ*) woodcutter
дровяник, дровяника – (n., masc.) seller of wood
дрягиль, дрягиля – (n., masc.) porter
дубильщик, дубильщика – (n., masc.) tanner
дудочник, дудочника – (n., masc.) piper
духобор, духобора – (n., masc., also seen † *духоборецъ*) Doukhobor, member of a religious sect; fem. *духоборка*
духовенство, духовенства – (n., neut.) the clergy
духовник, духовника – (n., masc.) confessor
† *дьяк, дьяка* – (n., masc.) official, clerk
дьякон, дьякона – (n., masc.) deacon
дьячок, дьячока – (n., masc.) church clerk and chanter, sexton
дѣвица → *девица*
дѣлатель → *делатель*
дѣлопроизводитель → *делопроизводитель*
дѣятель → *деятель*
еврей, еврея – (n., masc., nom. pl. *евреи*, gen. pl. *евреев*) Jew; fem. *еврейка*)
† *егермейстер, егермейстера* – (n., masc.) court master of the hunt (cmp. Germ. *Jägermeister*)
егерь, егеря – (n., masc., nom. pl. *егеря*, gen. pl. *егерей*) hunter (cmp. Germ. *Jäger*)
единоверец, единоверца – (n., masc., † *единовѣрецъ*) co-religionist, or a dissenter from the Orthodox church
ездовой, ездового – (adj. used as a n., masc., † *ѣздовой*) messenger on horseback, driver
ездок, ездока – (n., masc., † *ѣздокъ*) horseman, rider; passenger
† *екзарх* → *экзарх*
† *епархъ, епарха* – (n., masc.) eparch
епископ, епископа – (n., masc.) bishop
еретик, еретика – (n., masc.) heretic
есаул, есаула – (n., masc.) Cossack captain; assistant to a robber chief
ефрейтор, ефрейтора – (n., masc.) lance corporal (cmp. German *Gefreiter*)
жалобщик, жалобщика – (n., masc.) complainant, plaintiff
жандарм, жандарма – (n., masc.) gendarme
жезлоносец, жезлоносца – (n., masc.) crosier-bearer, mace-bearer
железнодорожник, железнодорожника – (n., masc., † *желѣзнодорожник*) railway concessionaire, railway magnate [older meanings], railway worker [modern meaning]; fem. *железнодорожница*
жена, жены – (n., fem., nom. pl. *жёны*, gen. pl. *жён*) wife
жестяник, жестяника – (n., masc.) tinsmith
живодёр, живодёра – (n., masc.) flayer, fleecer, slaughterer
† *жидъ, жида* – (n., masc.) Jew; fem. *жидовка* (please note that in modern Russian this is a very offensive slur, and *еврей* is the socially acceptable term – but in older records you may sometimes see *жидъ* used with no intention of giving offense)
жилец, жильца – (n., masc.) inhabitant; fem. *жилица*
житель, жителя – (n., masc., gen. pl. *жителей*) inhabitant; fem. *жительница*
жнец, жнеца – (n., masc., also seen: *жнея*) reaper, harvester; fem. *жница*
журналист, журналиста – (n., masc.) journalist, newspaper writer
заведующий, заведующего – († *завѣдующий*, part. of *заведывать*, to manage, administer, used as a n., masc.) manager (+ instr.)
заводитель, заводителя – (n., masc.) founder, establisher
заводчик, заводчика – (n., masc.) manufacturer, factory- or mill-owner
завѣдующій → *заведующий*
загонщик, загонщика – (n., masc.) † cattle-drover; one who beats the bushes (during a hunt)
закладчик, закладчика – (n., masc.) pawner, mortgager; fem. *закладчица*
законник, законника – (n., masc.) lawyer, jurist; fem. *законница*

законовед, законоведа – (n., masc., † *законовѣд*, also seen: *законовѣдецъ*) lawyer, jurist
законодатель, законодателя – (n., masc.) legislator, lawgiver
закройщик, закройщика – (n., masc.) cutter [of clothes]; fem. *закройщица*
закупщик, закупщика – (n., masc.) buyer, purchaser
замужняя, замужней – (adj. used as a n., fem.) married woman
заработник, заработника – (n., masc.) wage-earner
заработный – (adj.) for hire, for pay
заседатель, заседателя – (n., masc., † *засѣдатель*) assessor; *присяжный заседатель* – juror
зверолов, зверолова – (n., masc., † *звѣроловъ*) hunter
звонарь, звонаря – (n., fem.) bellringer; fem. *звонариха*, bellringer's wife
здешний – (adj., † *здѣшній*) local
зеленщик, зеленщика – (n., masc.) green-grocer
земледелец, земледельца – (n., masc., † *земледѣлецъ*) farmer
землекоп, землекопа – (n., masc.) digger (also seen: *землекопщик*)
землемер, землемера – (n., masc., † *землемѣръ*) surveyor
земляк, земляка – (n., masc.) fellow-countryman, one from the same province or village; fem. *землячка*
земский – (adj., † *земскій*) territorial; of a district
† *земской, земскаго* – (adj. used as a n.) country-clerk
зодчий, зодчего – (adj. used as a n., masc.) architect, builder
игольщик, игольщика – (n., masc.) needle-maker
игумен, игумена – (n., masc.) abbot, superior (of a monastery)
игуменья, игуменьи – (n., fem.) abbess, mother superior
иезуит, иезуита – (n., masc., † *іезуитъ*) Jesuit
иерарх, иерарха – (n., masc., † *іерархъ*) hierarch
иерей, иерея – (n., masc., † *іерей*) priest
иеродиаконъ, иеродиакона – (n., masc., † *іеродіаконъ*) deacon of an order
иеромонах, иеромонаха – (n., masc., † *іеромонахъ*) priest of an order
† *извощикъ, извощика* – (n., masc.) hired coachman (modern spelling *извозчик*)
изгнанник, изгнанника – (n., masc.) exile, outlaw; fem. *изгнанница*
издатель, издателя – (n., masc.) publisher, † editor; fem. *издательница*
иконописец, иконописца – (n., masc.) image-painter
император, императора – (n., masc.) emperor
инженер, инженера – (n., masc.) engineer
иноверец, иноверца – (n., masc., † *иновѣрецъ*) heterodox, one believing in a different religion; fem. *иноверка*
иногородец, иногородца – (n., masc.) one from a different city
иноземец, иноземца – (n., masc.) foreigner; fem. *иноземка*
† *инок, инока* – (n., masc.) monk, friar
иностранец, иностранца – (n., masc.) foreigner; fem. *иностранка*
инспектор, инспектора – (n., masc.) inspector, supervisor
интерн, интерна – (n., masc.) boarder at a boarding-school
† *иподіаконъ, иподіакона* – (n., masc.) subdeacon
искусник, искусника – (n., masc.) master, expert (*в* – in)
исповедник, исповедника – (n., masc., † *исповѣдникъ*) confessor
† *исправникъ, исправника* – (n., masc.) district police captain
истец, истца – (n., masc.) applicant, plaintive; fem. *истица*
истопник, истопника – (n., masc.) stoker, furnace-man; fem. *истопница*
іезуитъ → *иезуит*
іерархъ → *иерарх*
іерей → *иерей*
іеродіаконъ → *иеродиаконъ*
іеромонахъ → *иеромонах*
кабатчик, кабатчика - (n., masc.) tavern-keeper; fem. *кабатчица*
кавалер, кавалера – (n., masc.) knight
кавалерист, кавалериста – (n., masc.) cavalryman
кадет, кадета – (n., masc.) cadet
казак, казака – (n., masc.) Cossack
казначей, казначея – (n., masc.) treasurer, keeper of the treasury, paymaster
каменолом, каменолома – (n., masc.) quarryman
каменщик, каменщика – (n., masc.) stone mason, bricklayer
камергер, камергера – (n., masc.) chamberlain (cmp. Germ. *Kammerherr*)
камердинер, камердинера – (n., masc.) personal attendant, valet (cmp. Germ. *Kammerdiener*)
камерфрау – (n. fem., not declined) lady's maid (cmp. Germ. *Kammerfrau*)
камерфрейлина, камерфрейлины – (n. fem.) maid of honor of the bed-chamber (cmp. Germ. *Kammerfräulein*)
канатчик, канатчика – (n., masc.) rope-maker
канцелярист, канцеляриста – (n., masc.) clerk in chancery, e. g., *канцелярист суда*, court clerk

капельмейстер, капельмейстера – (n., masc.) bandleader, conductor
капитан, капитана – (n., masc.) captain
капрал, капрала – (n., masc.) corporal
каптенармус, каптенармуса – (n., masc.) master at arms
караим, караима – (n., masc.) Karaim Jew
караульщик, караульщика – (n., masc.) sentry, guard; fem. *караульщица*
каретник, каретника – (n., masc.) carriage-maker (also a coach-house)
кассир, кассира – (n., masc.) cashier
кастелян, кастеляна – (n., masc.) castellan
кастелянша, кастелянши – (n., fem.) woman in charge of linen in a hospital, rest home, etc.
каторжник, каторжника – (n., masc.) convict
кашевар, кашевара – (n., masc.) cook for a military unit, an *artel*, etc.; fem. *кашеварка*
квартирмейстер, квартирмейстера – (n., masc.) quartermaster (compare Germ. *Quartiermeister*)
келарь, келаря – (n., masc.) cellarer
кирпичник, кирпичника – (n., masc.) brick-maker
китаец, китайца – (n., masc., nom. pl. *китайцы*, gen. pl. *китайцев*) Chinese man; fem. *китаянка*
кладовщик, кладовщика – (n., masc.) store-keeper, worker in a store or warehouse
клеильщик, клеиьщика – (n., masc.) gluer, paster; fem. *клеильщица*
клеточник, клеточника – (n., masc., † *клѣточникъ*) cage-maker
ключарь, ключаря – (n., masc.) sacristan
ключник, ключника – (n., masc.) butler, steward, majordomo; fem. *ключница*, housekeeper
книгоноша, книгоноши – (n., masc.) book vendor, book hawker
книгопродавец, книгопродавца – (n., masc.) bookseller (also *книготорговец*)
княгиня, княгини – (n., fem.) princess (married); *княгиня великая* – grand duchess
княжна, княжны – (n., fem.) princess (unmarried)
князь, князя – (n., masc., nom. pl. *князья*, gen. pl. *князей*) prince; *князь великий* – grand duke
кобзарь, кобзаря – (n., masc.) player on the *kobza* (a Ukrainian stringed instrument)
ковач, ковача – (n., masc.) blacksmith
кожевник, кожевника – (n., masc.) tanner
колбасник, колбасника – (n., masc.) sausage-maker; fem. *колбасница*
колесник, колесника – (n., masc.) wheelwright, cartwright
коллежский – (adj.) collegiate; term used as the first part of the titles of several ranks of Imperial Russia's civil service, e. g., *коллежский ассессор*, collegiate assessor
колодезник, колодезника – (n., masc.) well-driller
колодник, колодника – (n., masc.) convict, prisoner; fem. *колодница*
колонист, колониста – (n., masc.) colonist, settler; fem. *колонистка*
колпачник, колпачника – (n., masc.) cap-maker
кольщик, кольщика – (n., masc.) wood-cutter, wood-splitter
командир, командира – (n., masc.) chief, commander
комендант, коменданта – (n., masc.) commandant; fem. *комендантша*
комиссар, комиссара – (n., masc., † *коммиссаръ*) commissar
кондитер, кондитера – (n., masc.) confectioner, pastry-cook
коневод, коневода – (n., masc.) horse-breeder
коновал, коновала – (n., masc.) horse-doctor, farrier
консул, консула – (n., masc.) consul
конторщик, конторщика – (n., masc.) clerk; fem. *конторщица*
конюх, конюха – (n., masc.) stable-boy, groom
корабельщик, корабельщика – (n., masc.) master of a ship, ship-builder
кораблестроитель, кораблестроителя – (n., masc.) ship-builder
корзинщик, корзинщика – (n., masc.) basket-maker
кормилец, кормильца – (n., masc.) foster-father; bread-winner
кормилица, кормилицы – (n., fem.) wet nurse, foster-mother
кормчий, кормчего – (adj. used as a n., masc.) helmsman, pilot
коробейник, коробейника – (n., masc.) mercer, haberdasher, peddler
коробочник, коробочника – (n., masc.) box-maker
корсетник, корсетника – (n., masc.) corset-maker; fem. *корсетница*
корчмарь, корчмаря – (n., masc.) innkeeper, tavern-keeper; fem. *корчмарка*
корытник, корытника – (n., masc.) trough-maker
косарь, косаря – (n., masc.) hay-maker, scytheman (also a chopper, large knife)
косец, косца – (n., masc.) hay-maker, mower, scytheman
костоправ, костоправа – (n., masc.) one who sets broken bones
котельник, котельника – (n., masc.) coppersmith, boilermaker, tinker; also *котельщик*
кочегар, кочегара – (n., masc.) stoker, fire-man (of a machine)

кошелечник, кошелечника – (n., masc.) purse-maker
кошемщик, кошемщика – (n., masc.) felt-maker
красильщик, красильщика – (n., masc.) dyer
краснодеревец, краснодеревца – (n., masc.) cabinet-maker (also *краснодеревщик*)
крахмальщик, крахмальщика – (n., masc.) starcher, starch-maker; fem. *крахмальщица*
крепостной, крепостного – (adj. used as a n., masc., † *крѣпостной*) serf , one bound to the soil; fem. *крепостная*
крестный – (adj.) of baptism; *крестная дочь*, goddaughter; *крестная мать* – godmother; *крестный отец* – godfather; *крестный сын* – godchild
крестьянин, крестьянина – (n., masc., nom. pl. *крестьяне*, gen. pl. *крестьян*) peasant, farmer; *крестьянин владеющий землей* – (land-owning) farmer
крестьянка, крестьянки – (n., fem.) (female) peasant
кровельщик, кровельщика – (n., masc.) roofer, tiler
кроильщик, кроильщика – (n., masc.) cutter (of coats and other clothes; fem. *кроильщица*
кружевник, кружевника – (n., masc.) maker or seller of lace; fem. *кружевница*
крысолов, крысолова – (n., masc.) rat-catcher
крѣпостной → *крепостной*
крючник, крючника – (n., masc.) street-porter
ксёндз, ксёндза – (n., masc.) Polish priest (from Polish *ksiądz*)
кузнец, кузнеца – (n., masc.) blacksmith; fem. *кузнечиха*, blacksmith's wife
кум, кума – (n., masc., nom. pl. *кумовья, кумьёв*) godfather, old gossip; fem. *кума*
купец, купца – (n., masc.) merchant; fem. *купчиха*
курфирст, курфирста – (n., masc.) elector (cmp. German *Kurfürst*)
курьер, клрьера – (n., masc.) courier
курятник, курятника – (n., masc.) poulterer (also means "hen-house")
кустарь, кустаря – (n., masc.) handicraftsman
кухарка, кухарки – (n., fem.) cook
кучер, кучера – (n., masc.) coachman
лабазник, лабазника – (n., masc.) corn/flour dealer
лавочник, лавочника – (n., masc.) shopkeeper; fem. *лавочница*
лакей, лакея – (n., masc.) lackey, footman
ламповщик, ламповщика – (n., masc.) lamp-maker
ландрат, ландрата – (n., masc.) member of a provincial court of justice in Livonia (cmp. German *Landrat*)
латвиец, латвийца – (n., masc., † *латвіецъ*) Latvian (fem. *латвийка*, † *латвійка*)
латыш, латыша – (n., masc., nom. pl. *латыши*, gen. pl. *латишей*) Latvian, Lett; fem. *латышка*
лейбъ-гвардеец, лейбъ-гвардейца – (n., masc.) member of the royal house guards (from Germ. *Leib-*, the prefix *лейбъ-* usually refers to someone in the service of a monarch or his court)
лейтенант, лейтенанта – (n., masc.) lieutenant
лекарь, лекаря – (n., masc., nom. pl. *лекари*, gen. pl. *лекарей*) physician
лектор, лектора – (n., masc., nom. pl. *лекторы*) lecturer at a university
ленточник, ленточника – (n., masc.) maker or seller of ribbons
лесник, лесника – (n., masc.) forester
литвин, литвина – (n., masc.) Lithuanian; fem. *литвинка*
литейщик, литейщика – (n., masc.) caster, smelter, founder
литовец, литовца – (n., masc.) Lithuanian; fem. *литовка*
ловец, ловца – (n., masc.) hunter, fowler
ловчий, ловчего – (adj. used as a n., masc., † *ловчій*) huntsman
лодочник, лодочника – (n., masc.) boatman
люстратор, люстратора – (n., masc.) controller of the revenues
лютеранин, лютеранина – (n., masc., nom. pl. *лютеране*, gen. pl. *лютеран*) Lutheran; fem. *лютеранка*
магазинщик, магазинщика – (n., masc.) owner or keeper of a storehouse (in modern Russian a *магазин* is a shop or store)
магистрат, магистрата – (n., masc.) magistrate
магнат, магната – (n., masc.) magnate
магометанин, магометанина – (n., masc., nom. pl. *магометане*, gen. pl. *магометан*) Muslim; fem. *магометанка*
майор, майора – (n., masc., † *маіоръ*) major; fem. *майорша*, major's wife
маклер, маклера – (n., masc.) broker
мальчик, мальчика – (n., masc.) boy; servant, domestic
маляр, маляра – (n., masc.) house-painter; fem. *малярша*
маркграф, маркграфа – (n., masc.) margrave (cmp. German *Markgraf*)
маркиз, маркиза – (n., masc.) marquis; fem. *маркиза, маркизы*
маркитант, маркитанта – (n., masc.) sutler, canteen-keeper; fem. *маркитантка*
маршал, маршала – (n., masc.) marshal
маслобойщик, маслобойщика – (n., masc.) oil-manufacturer

мастер, мастера – (n., masc., nom. pl. *мастера*, gen. pl. *мастеров*) foreman, master, e. g., *портной мастер*, master tailor; fem. *мастерица*
матрос, матроса – (n., masc.) sailor
махальщик, махальщика – (n., masc.) signal-man, also *махальный, махального* (adj. used as a n.)
машинист, машиниста – (n., masc.) machinist, operator, engineer
мебельщик, мебельщика – (n., masc.) maker of or dealer in furniture
меблировщик, меблировщика – (n., masc.) upholsterer
медик, медика – (n., masc.) physician; fem. *медичка*
медник, медника – (n., masc., † *мѣдникъ*) coppersmith, brazier
медовар, медовара – (n., masc.) mead-brewer
межевщик, межевщика – (n., masc.) surveyor
мельник, мельника – (n., masc.) miller; fem. *мельничиха*
меняльщик, меняльщика – (n., masc., † *мѣняльщик*) barterer; fem. *меняльщица*
метельщик, метельщика – (n., masc.) sweeper; rail-guard; fem. *метельщица*
метрдотель, метрдотеля – (n., masc.) majordomo, steward (cmp. French *maître d'hôtel*)
механик, механика – (n., masc.) mechanic
меховщик, меховщика – (n., masc., † *мѣховщикъ*) furrier
мещанин, мещанина – (n., masc., nom. pl. *мещане*, gen. pl. *мещан*, † *мѣщанинъ*) townsman, burgher (often synonymous with "merchant"; during Soviet times a contemptuous term for a narrow-minded petty bourgeois); fem. *мещанка*
милиционер, милиционера – (n., masc., † *милицiонеръ*) militia-man
министр, министра – (n., masc.) minister
мировой – (adj.) of peace; *мировой судья* – justice of the peace
митрополит, митрополита – (n., masc.) metropolitan (bishop heading an ecclesiastical province, ranking below a patriarch)
мичман, мичмана – (n., masc.) midshipman
могильщик, могильщика – (n., masc.) gravedigger, sexton
молодой – (adj.) young; used as a masc. noun, groom; used as a fem. noun, *молодая*, bride
молотильщик, молотильщика – (n., masc.) thrasher; fem. *молотильщица*
молочник, молочника – (n., masc.) milkman; fem. *молочница* (which also means "thrush, inflammation of the mouth")
монах, монаха – (n., masc.) friar, monk; fem. *монахиня*
монетчик, монетчика – (n., masc.) minter, coiner
моравец, моравца – (n., masc.) Moravian; fem. *моравка*
мореплаватель, мореплавателя – (n., masc.) navigator, seaman, seafarer; fem. *мореплавательница*
моряк, моряка – (n., masc.) seaman
мраморщик, мраморщика – (n., masc.) marble-cutter or polisher
муж, мужа – (n., masc., nom. pl. *мужья*, gen. pl. *мужей*, dat. pl. *мужьям*) husband, man
мужик, мужика – (n., masc.) peasant; fem. *мужичка, мужички*
музыкант, музыканта – (n., masc.) musician; fem. *музыкантша*
мулла, муллы – (n., masc.) mullah, Islamic clergyman
мундкох, мундкоха – (n., masc.) cook in a royal household
мундшенк, мундшенка – (n., masc.) cupbearer, butler in a royal household (cmp. Germ. *Mundschenk*)
мусорщик, мусорщика – (n., masc.) trash-hauler, dustman
мусульманин, мусульманина – (n., masc., nom. pl. *мусульмане*, gen. pl. *мусульман*) Muslim; fem. *мусульманка*
мученик, мученика – (n., masc.) martyr; fem. *мученица*
мучник, мучника – (n., masc.) dealer in meal or flour (also used in this same meaning: *мучной торговец*)
мызник, мызника – (n., masc.) farmer, tenant
мыловар, мыловара – (n., masc.) soap-maker
† *мытникъ, мытника* – (n., masc.) toll-gatherer
мѣдникъ → *медник*
мѣняльщик → *меняльщик*
мѣховщикъ → *меховщик*
мѣщанинъ → *мещанин*
мяльщик, мяльщика – (n., masc.) scutcher
мясник, мясника – (n., masc.) butcher
набойщик, набойщика – (n., masc.) (cloth-) printer
наводчик, наводчика – (n., masc.) gunner, sighter, gun layer
надзиратель, надзирателя – (n., masc.) inspector, superintendent, overseer; fem. *надзирательница*
надзорщик, надзорщика – (n., masc.) superintendent; fem. *надзорщица*
наёмник, наёмника – (n., masc.) hired hand, day laborer; fem. *наёмница*
наёмщик, наёмщика – (n., masc.) hirer, lessee, tenant, lodger

наместник, наместника – (n., masc., † *намѣстникъ*) deputy, vice-regent
наниматель, нанимателя – (n., masc.) one who hires workers or rents a house; fem. *нанимательница*
наречённый , наречённого – (part. used as a masc. n.) fiancé, bridegroom; (used as a fem. n., *наречённая, наречённой*) fiancée, bride
наследник, наследника – (n., masc., † *наслѣдникъ*) heir, successor; fem. *наследница*
наставник, наставника – (n., masc.) teacher, tutor; fem. *наставница*
настоятель, настоятеля – (n., masc.) prior, superior, arch-priest; fem. *настоятельница*, prioress
начальник, начальника – (n., masc.) head, superior, commander; fem. *начальница*
невеста, невесты – (n., fem., † *невѣста*) bride, engaged girl
невестка, невестки – (n., fem., † *невѣстка*) daughter-in-law, sister-in-law
невольник, невольника – (n., masc.) slave, bondman; fem. *невольница*
негоциант, негоцианта – (n., masc., † *негоціантъ*) merchant, trader
недойщик, недойщика – (n., masc.) one in arrears on payment (e. g., of taxes)
немец, немца – (n., masc., † *нѣмецъ*) German; fem. *немка*
неофит, неофита – (n., masc.) neophyte, convert
нищий – (adj., † *нищій*) poor, indigent; (used as a n.) beggar, pauper
новобранец, новобранца – (n., masc.) (new) recruit, one newly enlisted in the military
новобрачный – (adj.) newlywed; (used as a n., masc.) groom; *новобрачная, новобрачной* (used as a n., fem.), bride; *новобрачные* (pl.), the newlyweds
новосёл, новосёла – (n., masc.) new arrival, one who's recently moved in or settled, owner of a new house; fem. *новосёлка*
ножёвщик, ножёвщика – (n., masc.) cutler
норвежец, норвежца – (n., masc.) Norwegian; fem. *норвежка*
носильщик, носильщика – (n., masc.) bearer, carrier, porter
нотариус, нотариуса – (n., masc., † *нотаріусъ*) notary
ношатый, ношатого – (adj. used as a n., masc.) hodman, mason's assistant
нѣмецъ → *немец*
† *оберъ-*, "chief, high, grand," a prefix used in archaic German titles such as *оберъ- гофмаршалъ*, grand marshal (cmp. Germ. *Oberhofmarschall*), and *оберъ-воршнейдеръ*, gentleman-carver (Germ. *Obervorschneider*)
обозник, обозника – (n., masc.) transport driver [in the military, cmp. *обозный* and † *обозничій*, baggage master]
обойщик, обойщика – (n., masc.) upholsterer
обрезанец, обрезанца – (n., masc., † *обрѣзанецъ*) circumcised person
оброчник, оброчника – (n., masc.) peasant who pays quitrent [cmp. adj. *оброчный*, paying quitrent]
обрученник, обрученника – (n., masc.) the betrothed; fem. *обрученница*
обрѣзанецъ → *обрезанец*
обыватель, обывателя – (n., masc.) inhabitant; fem. *обывательница*
овчар, овчара – (n., masc.) shepherd, herdsman
огородник, огородника – (n., masc.) kitchen-gardener, truck farmer
однодворец, однодворца – (n., masc.) franklin, freeholder; fem. *однондворка*
оловяничник, оловняничника – (n., masc.) pewterer, tinman
опекун, опекуна – (n., masc.) guardian, tutor, trustee, warden, ward; fem. *опекунша*, governess
ополченец, ополченца – (n., masc.) militia-man
оптовщик, оптовщика – (n., masc.) wholesale dealer
оратай, оратая – (n., masc.) plowman, tiller
органист, органиста – (n., masc.) organist
ординарец, ординарца – (n., masc.) orderly
ординатор, ординатора – (n., masc.) house-surgeon, house-physician
оружейник, оружейника – (n., masc.) armorer, gunsmith
оруженосец, оруженосца – (n., masc.) armor-bearer, sword-bearer, squire
основатель, основателя – (n., masc.) founder, establisher; fem. *основательница*
остзеец, остзейца – (n., masc.) inhabitant of the "Baltic provinces"
острожник, острожника – (n., masc.) imprisoned criminal, convict; fem. *острожница*
отдатчик, отдатчика – (n., masc.) commissary of the stores
откупщик, откупщика – (n., masc.) tax-farmer, lease-holder; fem. *откупщица*
отливщик, отливщика – (n., masc.) caster, founder
отправитель, отправителя – (n., masc.) sender, dispatcher; fem. *отправительница*
отпускной – (adj.) on leave; (used as a n.) solider on leave
отпустник, отпустника – (m. masc.) soldier on leave

отпущенник, отпущенника – (n., masc.) freedman; fem. *отпущенница*
отставник, отставника – (n., masc.) retired officer
отставной – (adj.) retired, discharged, e. g., *отставной солдат*, discharged soldier
отшельник, отшельника – (n., masc.) hermit, anchorite; fem. *отшельница*
офицер, офицера – (n., masc.) officer; fem. *офицерша*, officer's wife
официант, официанта – (n., masc., † *официантъ*) house-steward, butler; [in modern Russian] waiter
охотник, окотника – (n., masc.) amateur, one who does something for the love of it; hunter, sportsman; fem. *охотница*
охранитель, охранителя – (n., masc.) keeper, guardian, custodian; fem. *охранительница*
оценщик, оценщика – (n., masc., † *оцѣнщикъ*) appraiser, estimator; fem. *оценщица*
паж, пажа – (n., masc.) page, knight's attendant, train-bearer
палач, палача – (n., masc.) executioner, hangman
пан, пана – (n., masc.) [Polish] land-owner, gentleman (cmp. Polish *pan*)
панна, панны – (n., fem.) daughter of a Polish gentleman (cmp. Polish *panna*)
пансионер, пансионера – (n., masc., † *пансіонеръ*) boarder [at a boarding school], fem. *пансионерка*
панский – (adj.,† *панскій*) mercer's; *панский ряд* – mercer's shop
панья, паньи – (n., fem.) wife of a Polish gentleman (cmp. Polish *pani*)
парикмахер, парикмахера – (n., masc.) wig-maker, hairdresser, barber; fem. *парикмахерша*
паркетчик, паркетчика – (n., masc.) one who installs parquet flooring
парусник, парусника – (n., masc.) sail-maker; sailing ship
пастор, пастора – (n., masc.) pastor; fem. *пасторша*, pastor's wife
пастух, пастуха – (n., masc.) shepherd, herdsman; fem. *пастушка*
пастырь, пастыря – (n., masc.) shepherd, herdsman; pastor
патриарх, патриарха – (n., masc., † *патріархъ*) patriarch
патронщик, патронщика – (n., masc.) cartridge-maker
пахарь, пахаря – (n., masc.) husbandman, tiller, plower
пахтальщик, пахтальщика – (n., masc.) churner; fem. *пахтальщица*
паяльщик, паяльщика – (n., masc.) solderer; fem. *паяальщица*
певец, певца – (n., masc., † *пѣвецъ*) singer, chanter; fem. *певица*, † *пѣвица*
пекарь, пекаря – (n., masc., nom. pl. *пекаря*, gen. pl. *пекарей*) baker
пеньковяз, пеньковяза – (n., masc.) hemp-binder
первосвятитель, первосвятителя – (n., masc.) primate
переводчик, переводчика – (n., masc.) translator; fem. *переводчица*
перевозчик, перевозчика – (n., masc.) ferryman
перекрест, перекреста – (n., masc.) convert to a new religion, especially a baptized Jew
переплётчик, переплётчика – (n., masc.) book-binder; fem. *переплётчица*
перепродавец, перепродавца – (n., masc.) re-seller; fem. *перепродавица*
переселенец, пшреселенца – (n., masc.) migrant, immigrant, one who moves from one place to another; fem. *переселенка*
переторговщик, переторговщика – (n., masc.) broker, retailer
песнопевец, песнопевца – (n., masc., † *пѣснопѣвецъ*) singer, chanter, psalmist
пехотинец, пехотинца – (n., masc., † *пѣхотинецъ*) foot soldier, infantryman
печатник, печатника – (n., masc.) printer
печаточник, печаточника – (n., masc.) seal-engraver
печник, печника – (n., masc.) maker or installer of stoves
пивовар, пивовара – (n., masc.) brewer
пильщик, пильщика – (n., masc.) sawyer
пирожник, пирожника – (n., masc.) pastry-cook
писарь, писаря – (n., masc., nom. pl. *писаря*, gen. pl. *писарей*) scribe, clerk
писатель, писателя – (n., masc.) writer; fem. *писательница*
писец, писца – (n., masc.) clerk, scribe
письмоводитель, письмоводителя – (n., masc.) clerk, secretary
плавильщик, плавильщика – (n., masc.) smelter, founder
† *плацъ-маіоръ, плацъ-маіора* – (n., masc.) assistant to a garrison's commandant
пленник, пленника – (n., masc., † *плѣнникъ*) captive, prisoner; fem. *пленница*
плетельщик, плетельщика – (n., masc.) plaiter, braider; fem. *плетельщица*
пломбировщик, пломбировщика – (n., masc.) one who affixes lead seals to goods
плотник, плотника – (n., masc.) carpenter

плѣнникъ → *пленник*
плющильщик, плющильщика – (n., masc.) flattener, laminator
побироха, побирохи – (n., fem.) beggar-woman (also *побирушка*)
повар, повара – (n., masc., nom. pl. *повара*, gen. pl. *поваров*) cook
поварёнок, поварёнка – (n., masc., nom. pl. *поварята*, gen. pl. *поварят*) kitchen-boy, scullion
повариха, поварихи – (n., fem.) cook
поверенный, поверенного – (adj. used as a n., masc., † *повѣренный*) trustee, attorney; *поверенный в делах* – chargé d'affaires; *присяжный поверенный* – barrister, advocate
повивальный – (adj.) relating to midwifery; *повивальная бабка* – midwife
повстанец, повстанца – (n., masc.) rebel, participant in an uprising
повѣренный → *поверенный*
погонщик, погонщика – (n., masc.) driver, drover (of cattle)
погребальщик, погребальщика – (n., masc.) grave-digger, sexton (also *погребатель*)
погребщик, погребщика – (n., masc.) wine-merchant
подвозчик, подвозчика – (n., masc.) driver of a transport
поддьяк, поддьяка – (n., masc.) sub-deacon
подёнщик, подёнщика – (n., masc.) day laborer; fem. *поддёнщица*, woman paid by the day, charwoman
подлекарь, подлекаря – (n., masc.) doctor's assistant
подмастерье, подмастерья – (n., masc., gen. pl. *подмастерьев*) apprentice, assistant to a master craftsman
подполковник, подполковника – (n., masc.) lieutenant colonel; fem. *подполковница*, lieutenant colonel's wife
подпрапорщик, подпрапорщика – (n., masc.) ensign-bearer, standard-bearer
подручный, подручного – (adj. used as a n., masc.) assistant, helper
подрядчик, подрядчика – (n., masc.) contractor
подсудимый, подсудимого – (adj. used as a n., masc.) the accused, defendant; fem. *подсудимая*
† *подъячій, подъячяго* – (adj. used as a n., masc.) clerk, copyist (16th-18th century)
позументщик, позументщика – (n., masc.) galloon-maker, lace-maker
покойник, покойника – (n., masc.) deceased person, decedent; fem. *покойница*
покупщик, покупщика – (n., masc.) buyer, purchaser; fem. *покупщица*
полесовщик, полесовщика – (n., masc., † *полѣсовщикъ*) forester, forest-ranger
политик, политика – (n., masc.) politician
полицеймейстер, полицеймейстера – (n., masc.) chief of police
полковник, полковника – (n., masc.) lieutenant; fem. *полковница*, colonel's wife
полководец, полководца – (n., masc.) general, captain, leader of an army
польский – (adj., † *польскій*) Polish
полѣсовщикъ → *полесовщик*
поляк, поляка – (n., masc., nom. pl. *поляки*, gen. pl. *поляков*) Pole; fem. *полька*
помещик, помещика – (n., masc., † *помѣщикъ*) land-owner, landlord; fem. *помещица*
помощник, помощника – (n., masc.) helper, assistant; fem. *помощница*
помѣщикъ → *помещик*
понамарь, понамаря – (n., masc.) sexton, sacristan; fem. *понамариха*
понятой, понятого – (adj. used as a n., masc.) witness; fem. *понятая*
поп, попа – (n., masc.) priest
попадья, попадьи – (n., fem.) priest's wife
попечитель, попечителя – (n., masc.) trustee, ward, warden, guardian; fem. *попечительница*
попович, поповича – (n., masc.) priest's son
поповна, поповны – (n., fem., gen. pl. *поповен*) priest's daughter
портниха, портнихи – (n., fem.) dressmaker
портной, портного – (adj. used as a n., masc.) tailor
портомой, портомоя – (n., masc.) washerman, launderer
порубщик, порубщика – (n., masc.) wood-cutter, also one who steals wood
поручик, поручика – (n., masc.) lieutenant; fem. *поручица*, lieutenant's wife
посадник, посадника – (n., masc.) mayor of certain ancient Russian free towns; fem. *посадница*
поселенец, поселенца – (n., masc.) settler, colonist; convict deported to Siberia; fem. *поселенка*
поселянин, поселянина – (n., masc., nom. pl. *поселяне*, gen. pl. *поселян*) peasant, villager; fem. *поселянка*
посланец, посланца – (n., masc.) envoy, messenger (also *посланный*)
посланник, посланника – (n., masc.) envoy, ambassador; fem. *посланница*, wife of an ambassador
послушник, послушника – (n., masc.) lay-brother, novice; fem. *послушница*
посол, посла – (n., masc.) ambassador, envoy
посредник, посредника – (n., masc.) negotiator, intermediary; fem. *посредница*

поставщик, поставщика – (n., masc.) purveyor, supplier; fem. *поставщица*
† *постельникъ, постельника* – (n., masc.) chamberlain
постоялец, постояльца – (n., masc.) lodger, tenant; fem. *постоялица*
почтальон, почтальона – (n., masc.) postman, letter-carrier
почтмейстер, почтмейстера – (n., masc.) postmaster; fem. *почтмейстерша*
правитель, правителя – (n., masc.) administrator, director; fem. *правительница*
правовед, правоведа – (n., masc., † *правовѣдъ*) jurist, legal specialist (also seen: *правоведец*, † *правовѣдецъ*)
прапорщик, прапорщика – (n., masc.) ensign; fem. *прапорщица*, ensign's wife
прасол, прасола – (n., masc.) wholesale cattle- or fish-dealer
прачка, прачки – (n., masc.) laundress, washerwoman
† *пребендарій, пребендаряго* – (adj. used as a n., masc.) prebendary (a clergyman who held an office endowed with fixed capital assets that provided a living)
предводитель, предводителя – (n., masc.) leader, chief, conductor, general; *предводитель войска* – commander in chief; *предводитель дворянства* – marshal of nobility; fem. *предводительша*, marshal's wife, or *предводительница*, conductress
предместник, предместника – (n., masc., † *предмѣстникъ*) predecessor; fem. *предместница*
председатель, председателя – (n., masc., † *предсѣдатель*) president, chairman; fem. *председательница*
представитель, представителя – (n., masc.) representative; fem. *представитеьлница*
предсѣдатель → *председатель*
преемник, преемника – (n., masc.) successor, heir; fem. *преемница*
преподаватель, преподавателя – (n., masc.) lecturer, teacher, master; fem. *преподавательница*, mistress
преступник, преступника – (n., masc.) criminal; fem. *преступница*
претендент, претендента – (n., masc.) pretender, applicant, candidate; fem. *претендентка*
привратник, привратника – (n., masc.) porter, gate-keeper; fem. *привратница*
придворный – (adj.) of the [royal or noble] court; (used as a n.) courtier
приёмыш, приёмыша – (n., masc., † *пріёмышъ*) adopted child, foster child
приказный – (adj.) of the chancellor's office; (used as a n.) clerk, scribe
приказчик, приказчика – (n., masc., also seen as *прикащик*) shop assistant; steward, bailiff [of an estate]; fem. *приказчица* or *прикащица*
приор, приора – (n., masc., † *пріоръ*) prior
прислужник, прислужника – (n., masc.) server, servant; fem. *прислужница*
присмотрщик, присмотрщика – (n., masc.) overseer, superintendent; fem. *присмотрщица*
пристав, пристава – (n., masc.) overseer, inspector; in Czarist Russia, the head of a district police force; *судебный пристав* – bailiff
присяжный, присяжного – (adj. used as a n., masc.) one who's taken an oath, especially a juror; *присяжный поверенный* – barrister, advocate
приходорасходчик, приходорасходчика – (n., masc.) cashier
прихожанин, прихожанина – (n., masc., nom. pl. *прихожане*, gen. pl. *прихожан*) parishioner; fem. *прихожанка*
причетник, причетника – (n., masc.) churchman, lowest rank of the clergy
пришелец, пришельца – (n., masc.) newcomer, stranger; fem. *пришелица*
пріёмышъ → *приёмыш*
пріоръ → *приор*
пробирер, пробирера – (n., masc.) assayer (also seen: *пробирщик*)
провизор, провизора – (n., masc.) pharmacist
провиантмейстер, провиантмейстера – (n., masc., † *провіантмейстеръ*) commissary of stores
продавец, продавца – (n., masc.) vendor, seller; fem. *продавица*
продавщик, продавщика – (n., masc.) vendor, seller; fem. *продавщица*
производитель, производителя – (n., masc.) producer, manufacturer; fem. *производительница*
прокуратура, прокуратуры – (n., fem.) prosecutor's office, prosecutors
прокурор, прокурора – (n., masc.) public prosecutor
промышленник, промышленника – (n., masc.) manufacturer
проситель, просителя – (n., masc.) petitioner; fem. *просительница*
протестант, протестанта – (n., masc.) Protestant; fem. *протестантка*
протодьякон, протодьякона – (n., masc., † *протодіаконъ*) archdeacon, first deacon

протоиерей, протоиерея – (n., masc., † *протоіерей*) archpriest
протоколист, протоколиста – (n., masc.) registrar, registrar-clerk
профессор, профессора – (n., masc., nom. pl. *профессора*) professor, teacher
пруссак, пруссака – (n., masc.) Prussian
пряничник, пряничника – (n., masc.) baker or seller of gingerbread
псаломщик, псаломщика – (n., masc.) psalm-reader, church attendant
псарь, псаря – (n., masc.) huntsman, one in charge of the hunting dogs
птицевод, птицевода – (n., masc.) breeder of birds
птицелов, птицелова – (n., masc.) bird-catcher, birder, fowler
птичник, птичника – (n., masc.) dealer in birds, one who takes care of birds
путеец, путейца – (n., masc.) railroad engineer, road-worker
путешественник, путешественника – (n., masc.) traveler; fem. *путешественница*
путник, путника – (n., masc.) traveler; fem. *путница*
пфальцграф, пфальцграфа – (n., masc.) prince palatine; fem. *пфальцграфиня*
пчеловод, пчеловода – (n., masc.) beekeeper, apiarist
пѣвецъ → *певец*
пѣснопѣвецъ → *песнопевец*
пѣхотинецъ → *пехотинец*
раб, раба – (n., masc.) slave, bondman; † *рабъ божій*, literally "slave of God," often seen on gravestones to indicate the deceased was pious; fem. *раба*
работник, работника – (n., masc.) laborer; fem. *работница*
рабочий, рабочего – (adj. used a n., masc.) worker, laborer; cmp. *работник*
раввин, раввина – (n., masc.) rabbi
разбойник, разбойника – (n., masc.) robber, cutthroat; fem. *разбойница*
разведенец, разведенца – (n., masc.) divorced man; fem. *разведёнка*
разжалованный – (part.) reduced in rank (referring to a soldier)
разносчик, разносчика – (n., masc., † *разнощикъ*) peddler; fem. *разносчица*, † *разнощица*
раскольник, раскольника – (n., masc.) schismatic; fem. *раскольница*
распильщик, распильщика – (n., masc.) sawer
расходчик, расходчика – (n., masc.) bursar, cashier; fem. *рацходщица*
ратай, ратая – (n., masc.) plowman, tiller, farmer
ратник, ратника – (n., masc.) warrior, soldier
ратоборец, ратоборца – (n., masc.) warrior, combatant
ревизор, ревизора – (n., masc.) inspector
революционер, революционера – (n., masc., † *революціонеръ*) revolutionary
регент, регента – (n., masc.) regent; precentor, chapel-master
регистратор, регистратора – (n., masc.) registrar, keeper of the register; fem. *регистраторша*
редактор, редактора – (n., masc.) editor
режиссёр, режиссёра – (n., masc.) [theater] manager
резник, резника – (n., masc., † *рѣзникъ*) butcher
резчик, резчика – (n., masc., † *рѣзчикъ*) engraver, carver
рейткнехт, рейткнехта – (n., masc.) groom (in a stable)
рекрут, рекрута – (n., masc.) recruit
ректор, ректора – (n., masc.) rector
ремесленник, ремесленника – (n., masc.) artisan, craftsman; fem. *ремесленница*
ресторатор, ресторатора – (n., masc.) restaurateur
† *ризничій, ризничяго* – (adj. used as a n., masc.) sacristan
роговщик, роговщика – (n., masc.) horn-worker
рогожник, рогожника – (n., masc.) mat-maker
родослов, родослова – (n., masc.) genealogist
рожечник, рожечника – (n., masc.) horn-player
розничный – (adj.) retail; *розничый торговец* – retailer
ростовщик, ростовщика – (n., masc.) usurer, money-lender; fem. *ростовщица*
ротмистр, ротмистра – (n., masc.) cavalry captain; fem. *ротмистрша*
рудокоп, рудокопа – (n., masc.) miner, mine-digger
ружейник, ружейника – (n., masc.) gunsmith, armorer
рукавичник, рукавичника – (n., masc.) mitten-maker
руководитель, руководителя – (n., masc.) guide, director, leader; fem. *руководительница*
рукодельник, рукодельника – (n., masc., † *рукодѣльникъ*) handicraftsman; fem. *рукодельница*
рулевой, рулевого – (adj. used as a n., masc.) helmsman
русский – (adj.) Russian
рыбак, рыбака – (n., masc.) fisherman; fem. *рыбачка*
рыбовод, рыбовода – (n., masc.) fish-breeder
рыболов, рыболова – (n., masc.) fisherman
рыбопромышленник, рыбопромышленника – (n., masc.) fishmonger (also used: *рыботорговец*)
рылейщик, рылейщика – (n., masc.) hurdy-gurdy player; fem. *рылейщица*

рыночный – (adj.) of the marketplace; *рыночная торговка* – market-woman
рыцарь, рыцаря – (n., masc.) knight
рѣзникъ → *резник*
рѣзчикъ → *резчик*
рядовой, рядового – (adj. used as a n., masc.) private, common soldier
садовник, садовника – (n., masc.) gardener; fem. *садовница*
саечник, саечника – (n., masc.) baker or seller of *сайки*, small white loaves; fem. *саечница*
самогит, самогита – (n., masc.) Samogitian, one from the lowlands of Lithuania [Lith. *žemaitis*]
сапожник, сапожника – (n., masc.) shoemaker; fem. *сапожница* or *сапожничиха*, shoemaker's wife
сафьянщик, сафьянщика – (n., masc.) tanner of Morocco leather
сборщик, сборщика – (n., masc.) collector, gatherer; *сборщик податей* – tax collector; fem. *сборщица*
сват, свата – (n., masc.) matchmaker; fem. *сваха, свахи*); also the father of one's son-in-law or daughter-in-law; fem. *сватья*
свекловод, свекловода – (n., masc.) specialist in growing sugar-beets
сверловщик, сверловщика – (n., masc.) driller, borer; also seen: *сверлильщик;* fem. *сверловщица*
светописец, светописца – (n., masc., † *свѣтописецъ*) photographer
свечник, свечника – (n., masc., † *свѣчникъ*) chandler
свидетель, свидетеля – (n., masc., † *свидѣтель*) witness; fem. *свидетельница*
свинарь, свинаря – (n., masc.) swineherd; fem. *свинарка*
свиновод, свиновода – (n., masc.) specialist in breeding swine
свинопас, свинопаса – (n., masc.) swineherd
сводчик, сводчика – (n., masc.) broker, agent, go-between
свѣтописецъ → *светописец*
свѣчникъ → *свечник*
святитель, святителя – (n., masc.) prelate, bishop
священник, священника – (n., masc.) priest (generally refers to a priest of the Orthodox Church, as opposed to a Catholic *ксёндз*, q. v.)
священноначальник, священноначальника – (n., masc.) hierarch, prelate
священнослужитель, священнослужителя – (n., masc.) priest, clergyman
сгребальщик, сгребальщика – (n., masc.) raker, shoveler; fem. *сгребальщица*
седельник, седельника – (n., masc., † *сѣдельникъ*) saddler
секретарь, секретаря – (n., masc.) secretary
сельдяник, сельдяника – (n., masc.) herring-fisher
селянин, селянина – (n., masc., nom. pl. *селяне*, gen. pl. *селян*, also seen: *сельчанин*) villager, peasant; fem. *селянка*
сенатор, сенатора – (n., masc.) senator; fem. *сенаторша*, senator's wife
сенешал, сенешала – (n., masc.) seneschal
серебряник, серебряника – (n., masc.) silversmith; also seen: *серебреник*
сержант, сержанта – (n., masc.) sergeant
сеяльщик, сеяльщика – (n., masc., † *сѣяльщикъ*) sower; fem. *сеяльщица*
сигарочник, сигарочника – (n., masc.) cigar-dealer
сигнальщик, сигнальщика – (n., masc.) signalman
сиделец, сидельца – (n., masc., † *сидѣлецъ*) shopman, barman; fem. *сиделица*
силач, силача – (n., masc.) strongman; fem. *силачка*
сирота, сироты – (n., masc. or fem.) orphan child
сказочник, сказочника – (n., masc.) story-teller; fem. *сказочница*
скитник, скитника – (n., masc.) hermit, ascetic; fem. *скитница*
скорняк, скорняка – (n., masc.) furrier
скорописец, скорописца – (n., masc.) shorthand writer
скотник, скотника – (n., masc.) drover, cattle-yard worker; fem. *скотница*
скотовод, скотовода – (n., masc.) cattle-breeder
скотопромышленник, скотопромышленника – (n., masc.) cattle-dealer
скрипач, скрипача – (n., masc.) violinist, fiddler; fem. *скрипачка*
скудельник, скудельника – (n., masc.) potter
скупщик, скупщика – (n., masc.) forestaller, one who buys things up
скуфейщик, скуфейщика – (n., masc.) maker of calottes, skullcaps
слепец, слепца – (n., masc., † *слѣпецъ*) blind person
слесарь, слесаря – (n., masc., nom. pl. *слесари* or *слесаря*, gen. pl. *слесарей*) locksmith, metal-worker; fem. *слесарша*, locksmith's wife
слобожанин, слобожанина – (n., masc., nom. pl. *слобожане*, gen. pl. *слобожан*) inhabitant of a *sloboda* [see Vocabulary, beginning p. ???]; fem. *слобожанка*
словесник, словесника – (n., masc.) humanist, man of letters
слуга, слуги – (n., masc., declined like a fem. n.) [male] servant, valet
служанка, служанки – (n., fem.) servant, maid
служивый, служивого – (adj. used as a n.) soldier, one who's been in the service

служитель, служителя – (n., masc.) servant; *служитель костела,* church sexton; *божничный служитель,* synagogue attendant
слѣпецъ → *слепец*
смолильщик, смолильщика – (n., masc.) one who works with pitch or tar
смотритель, смотрителя – (n., masc.) superintendent, overseer, warden, e. g., *смотритель Ломжинскаго Замка,* Warden of the Prison in Łomża; *смотритель дока* – dock-master; fem. *смотрительница*
сновальщик, сновальщика – (n., masc.) warper [of cloth]; fem. *сновальщица*
собственник, собственника – (n., masc.) owner; fem. *собственница*
советник, советника – (n., masc., † *совѣтникъ*) counselor, advisor, e. g., *совѣтникъ Ломжинскаго Губернскаго Правленія,* Advisor in the Łomża Provincial Government Oyce; fem. *советница*
советчик, советчика – (n., masc., *совѣтчикъ*) advisor, counselor
совладелец, совладельца – (n., masc., † *совладѣлецъ*) co-owner; fem. *совладелица*
сожитель, сожителя – (n., masc.) spouse, roommate; fem. *сожительница*
сокольник, сокольника – (n., masc.) falconer
солдат, солдата – (n., masc., gen. pl. *солдат*) soldier; *отпускный солдат,* soldier on leave; *отставоной солдат,* discharged soldier; fem. *солдатка,* soldier's wife
солевар, солевара – (n., masc.) salter
солильщик, солильщика – (n., masc.) salter, dry-salter, curer
солодовник, солодовника – (n., masc.) maltster (also seen: *солодовщик*)
соломорез, соломореза – (n., masc., † *соломорѣзъ*) straw-cutter, chaff-cutter; fem. *соломорезка*
сонаследник, сонаследника – (n., masc., † *сонаслѣдникъ*) joint heir, co-heir; fem. *сонаследница*
соопекун, соопекуна – (n., masc.) joint guardian, co-guardian
сортировщик, сортировщика – (n., masc.) sorter; fem. *сортировщица*
сосед, соседа – (n., masc., † *сосѣдъ*), nom. pl. *соседи,* gen. pl. *соседей*) neighbor
составитель, составителя – (n., masc.) writer, author, composer; fem. *составительница*
сотник, сотника – (n., masc.) commander of a Cossack squadron, or a foreman in charge of many workmen (the root of the word is *сто,* "one hundred")
спальник, спальника – (n., masc.) chamberlain of the royal bed-chamber
сплавщик, сплавщика – (n., masc.) raftsman; fem. *сплавщица*
ссудчик, ссудчика – (n., masc.) pawnbroker, lender
ссылный – (adj.) banished, transported; (used as a n.) an exile or convict banished to live in a certain area; also seen: *ссылочник,* fem. *ссылочница*
ставленник, ставленника – (n., masc.) candidate for Holy Orders; (in modern Russian) protégé, henchman
станционный – (adj., † *стантіонный*) of a station; *станционный смотритель* – stationmaster
старец, старца – (n., masc.) old man; also *старик*
старовер, старовера – (n., masc., † *старовѣръ*) Old Believer [a Russian religious sect]; fem., *староверка;* also called *старообрядец,* fem. *старообрядка*
старожил, старожила – (n., masc.) long-time resident, old-timer; fem. *старожилка*
старообрядец → *старовер*
староста, старосты – (n., masc.) bailiff, reeve (of a village); in Poland, a *starosta;* fem. *старостиха, старостихи* – wife of a *starosta*
старуха, старухи – (n., fem.) old woman
старшина, старшины – (n., masc.) head, headman, chief, foreman; *старшина присяжных,* foreman of the jury; *волостной старшина,* head of a *volost'*
старьёвщик, старьёвщика – (n., masc.) dealer in antiques or old clothes
стегальщик, стегальщика – (n., masc.) quilter; fem. *стегальщица*
стекольщик, стекольщика – (n., masc.) glassmaker; fem. *стекольщица*
степенство, степенства – (n., neut.) steadiness, staidness, sobriety; honorary title given to merchants and burghers
стипендиат, стипендиата – (n., masc., † *стипендіатъ*) student with a grant; fem. *стипендиатка*
столоначальник, столоначальника – (n., masc.) department chief, head clerk (in pre-Revolutionary Russia)
стольник, стольника – (n., masc.) dapifer at a noble's court
столяр, столяра – (n., masc.) carpenter, joiner; fem. *столяриха,* carpenter's wife
сторож, сторожа – (n., masc., nom. pl. *сторожа,* gen. pl. *сторожей*) watchman, guard; fem. *сторожиха*
стоялец, стояльца – (n., masc.) tenant, lodger; fem. *стоялица*

страж, стража – (n., masc.) guard, watchman, sentinel
стрелец, стрельца – (n., masc., † *стрѣлецъ*) archer, bowman, shot
стрелок, стрелка – (n., masc., † *стрѣлокъ*) shot, bowman
стрелочник, стрелочника – (n., masc., † *стрѣлочникъ*) pointsman, switchman [on a railroad]; fem. *стрелочница*
стремянный, стремянного – (adj. used as a n., masc.) groom, ostler
строитель, строителя – (n., masc.) builder; fem. *строительница*
струговщик, струговщика – (n., masc.) bargeman
стрѣлецъ → *стрелец*
стрѣлокъ → *стрелок*
стрѣлочникъ → *стрелочник*
стряпуха, стряпухи – (n., masc.) cook-maid
стряпчий, стряпчего – (adj. used as a n., masc. † *стряпчій*) attorney, lawyer
студент, студента – (n., masc.) student [at a college or institute of higher learning]; fem. *студентка*
судовладелец, судовладельца – (n., masc., † *судовладѣлецъ*) ship-owner
судоводитель, судоводителя – (n., masc.) navigator
судовщик, судовщика – (n., masc.) shipmaster
судомойка, судомойки – (n., fem.) scullery maid, kitchen-maid
судопромышленник, судопромышленника – (n., masc.) owner or builder of ships
судорабочий, судорабочего – (adj. used as a n., masc., † *судорабочій*) barge-worker
судостроитель, судостроителя – (n., masc.) shipbuilder
судья, судьи – (n., masc., nom. pl. *судьи*, gen. pl. *судьей*, dat. pl. *судьям*) judge
суконщик, суконщика – (n., masc.) cloth-weaver, cloth-worker
супруг, супруга – (n., masc.) spouse, husband; fem. *супруга*, wife
сучильщик, сучильщика – (n., masc.) twister; fem. *сучильщица*
счётник, счётника – (n., masc.) accountant
счетовод, счетовода – (n., masc.) bookkeeper, accountant
счётчик, счётчика – (n., masc.) one who keeps a count or tally; fem. *счётчица*
съёмщик, съёмщика – (n., masc.) surveyor, one who draws up plans; tenant
сыромятник, сыромятника – (n., masc.) leather-worker
сыщик, сыщика – (n., masc.) detective
сѣдельник → *седельник*
сѣяльщик → *сеяльщик*
табачник, табачника – (n., masc.) tobacconist; fem. *табачница*
табущик, табунщика – (n., masc.) keeper of a drove of horses
таможенник, таможенника – (n., masc.) customs official
таможенный or *таможный* – (adj.) customs; *таможенный надсмотрщик*, customs-house officer
танцмейстер, танцмейстера – (n., masc.) dancing master (cmp. Germ. *Tanzmeister*)
телеграфист, телеграфиста – (n., masc.) telegrapher; fem. *телеграфистка*
тележник, тележника – (n., masc., † *телѣжникъ*) cartwright
телохранитель, телохранителя – (n., masc., † *тѣлохранитель*) bodyguard
телѣжникъ → *тележник*
тенётчик, тенётчика – (n., masc.) net-setter
тесарь, тесаря – (n., masc.) stone-cutter
тесёмочник, тесёмочника – (n., masc.) tape-maker, ribbon-weaver; also seen: *тесёмщик*
типографщик, типографщика – (n., masc.) typographer
† *тіунъ, тіуна* – (n., masc.) bailiff
ткач, ткача – (n., masc.) weaver; fem. *ткачиха*
токарь, токаря – (n., masc., nom. pl. *токари* or *токаря*, gen. pl. *токарей*) turner, lathe operator, cabinet maker
толковник, толковника – (n., masc.) translator, interpreter
толмач, толмача – (n., masc.) translator, interpreter
торговец, торговца – (n., masc.) dealer, merchant, e. g., *торговец шелковыми товарами*, silk-merchant; fem. *торговка*
точильщик, точильщика – (n., masc.) sharpener, grinder, whetter
трактирщик, трактирщика – (n., masc.) landlord, innkeeper, publican; fem. *трактирщица*
трепальщик, трепальщика – (n., masc.) one who peels hemp, stripper; fem. *трепальщица*
† *троечникъ, троечника* – (n., masc.) keeper of a livery stable, one who leases out *troikas* (a kind of carriage drawn by a team of three horses abreast)
трубач, трубача – (n., masc.) trumpeter, horn-blower
трубник, трубника – (n., masc.) fireman
трубочист, трубочиста – (n., masc.) chimney sweep

труженик, труженика – (n., masc.) hard-working person; fem. *труженица*
тряпичник, тряпичника – (n., masc.) ragman; fem. *тряпичница*
туземец, туземца – (n., masc.) native, indigenous person, local; fem. *туземка*
тѣлохранитель → *телохранитель*
тюремник, тюремника – (n., masc.) prisoner; fem. *тюремница*
тюремщик, тюремщика – (n., masc.) jailer, warden of a prison
убийца, убийцы – (n., masc. or fem., † *убійца*) murderer, killer
углекоп, углекопа – (n., masc.) coal-miner
угольщик, угольщика – (n., masc.) charcoal-burner or dealer, coal-miner
удостоверитель, удостоверителя – (n., masc., † *удостовѣритель*) testifier, witness
укладчик, улладчика – (n., masc.) packer; fem. *укладчица*
улан, улана – (n., masc.) uhlan
униат, униата – (n., masc., † *уніат*) Uniate, term for a member of the Greek Catholic rite fem. *униатка*
унтер-офицер, унтер-офицера – (n., masc.) non-commissioned officer
упаковщиик, упаковщика – (n., masc.) packer; fem. *упаковщица*
управитель, управителя – (n., masc.) steward, manager; fem. *управительница*, specifically used in the meaning "female manager"
управительша, управительши – (n., fem.) wife of a steward
управляющий, управяющего – (part. used as a n., masc.) manager, director; used with the instr. case, e. g., *управляющий банком*, bank director, or *управляющий работами*, director of works
урождённый – (part.) born, by birth; née
уроженец, уроженца – (n., masc.) native; fem. *уроженка*
урядник, урядника – (n., masc.) village policeman; Cossack sergeant
усадебник, усадебника – (n., masc.) farmer, one who has an *усадьба*, a farmstead or country estate
услужник, услужника – (n., masc.) servant; fem. *услужница*
уставщик, уставщика – (n., masc.) head chorister
утопленник, утопленника – (n., masc.) drowned man; fem. *утопленница*
уточник, уточникя – (n., masc.) woof-layer; fem. *уточница*
ученик, ученика – (n., masc.) pupil, scholar, apprentice; fem. *ученица*
учёный, учёного – (part. of *учиться* used as a n., masc.) scholar, learned man
учитель, учителя – (n., masc., gen. pl. *учителей*) teacher; fem. *учительница*
учредитель, учредителя – (n., masc.) founder, establisher; fem. *учредительница*
фабрикант, фабриканта – (n., masc.) manufacturer, mill owner; fem. *фабрикантша*
факельщик, факельщика – (n., masc.) torch-bearer
фактор, фактора – (n., masc.) overseer, foreman of a printing office; factor; fem. *факторша*
фельдмаршал, фельдмаршала – (n., masc.) field marshal (compare Germ. *Feldmarschall*)
фельдфебель, фельдфебеля – (n., masc.) sergeant major (cmp. Germ. *Feldwebel*)
фельдшер, фельдшера – (n., masc.) surgeon's assistant (cmp. Germ. *Feldscher*); fem. *фельдшерица*
фельдъегерь, фельдъегеря – (n., masc.) courier, cabinet messenger (cmp. Germ. *Feldjäger*); fem. *фельдъегерша*
фехтмейстер, фехтмейстера – (n., masc.) fencing master (cmp. Germ. *Fechtmeister*)
фигляръ, фигляря – (n., masc.) juggler, mountebank; fem. *фиглярка*
фокусник, фокусника – (n., masc.) conjurer, juggler; fem. *фокусница*
фонтанщик, фонтанщика – (n., masc.) fountain-maker, cistern-maker
франкмасон, франкмасона – (n., masc.) freemason
францисканец, францисканца – (n., masc.) Franciscan (monk)
француз, француза – (n., masc.) Frenchman; fem. *француженка*
фрейлина, фрейлины – (n., masc.) maid of honor, attendant of a princess or queen (cmp. Germ. *Fräulein*)
фронтовик, фронтовика – (n., masc.) soldier or officer of the line
фруктовщик, фруктовщика – (n., masc.) custard or fruit vendor
фузелер, фузелера – (n., masc.) fusilier
фуилёр, фузилёра – (n., masc.) fusilier
фуражир, фуражира – (n., masc.) forager
фурлейт, фурлейта – (n., masc.) train-soldier
фурьер, фурьера – (n., masc.) quartermaster
футлярщик, футлярщика – (n., masc.) case-maker, sheath-maker
харчевник, харчевника – (n., masc.) tavern-keeper, keeper of a cook shop; fem. *харчевница*
хирург, хирурга – (n., masc.) surgeon
хитана, хитаны – (n., fem.) Gypsy woman
хлебник, клебника – (n., masc., † *хлѣбникъ*) baker; fem. *хлебница*, female baker, wife of a baker

хлебопашец, хлебопашца – (n., masc., † *хлѣбопашецъ*) farmer, plowman
хлебопёк, хлебопёка – (n., masc., † *хлѣбопёкъ*) baker (also seen: *хлебопекарь*)
хлебопродавец, хлебопродавца – (n., masc., *хлѣбопродавецъ*) corn-merchant
хлеборез, хлебореза – (n., masc., † *хлѣборѣзъ*) bread cutter
хлебороб, хлебороба – (n., masc., † *хлѣборобъ*) farmer, grain-grower
хлеботорговец, хлеботорговца – (n., masc., *хлѣботорговецъ*) grain-merchant, corn factor
хмелевод, хмелевода – (n., masc.) grower of hops
ходебщик, ходебщика – (n., masc.) peddler, hawker
хожалый, хожалого – (adj. used as a n., masc.) policeman
хожатый, хожатого – (adj. used as a n., masc.) nurse; messenger
хозяин, хозяина – (n., masc., nom. pl. *хозяева*, gen. pl. *хозяев*) master of the house, owner; husband, man; † *сельскій хозяинъ* – farmer
хозяйка, хозяйки – (n., fem.) mistress, lady of the house; housewife, housekeeper
холоп, холопа – (n., masc.) serf, bondman, thrall; fem. *холопка*
холостой – (adj., short form *холост*) unmarried, single; *холостой человек* – single man, bachelor
холостяк, холостяка – (n., masc.) bachelor
холщевник, холщевника – (n., masc.) linen-dealer
хорват, хорвата – (n., masc.) Croat (fem. *хорватка*)
хормейстер, хормейстера – (n., masc.) choirmaster
хорунжий, хорунжего – (adj. used as a n., † *хорунжій, хорунжяго*) cornet, ensign (junior officer in the Cossack cavalry, cmp. Polish *chorąży*)
храмовник, храмовника – (n., masc.) Knight Templar
хранитель, хранителя – (n., masc.) keeper, custodian; curator; fem. *хранительница*
христианин, христианина – (n., masc., nom. pl. *христиане*, gen. pl. *христиан*, † *христіанинъ*) Christian; fem. *христианка*
хромой – (adj.) lame, crippled; (used as a n.) lame man, woman
хромоножка, хромоножки – (n., fem.) cripple, lame person
художник, художника – (n., masc.) artist; fem. *художница*
цальмейстер, цальмейстера – (n., masc.) paymaster (compare German *Zahlmeister*)
царевич, царевича – (n., masc.) Czar's son, prince of the royal or imperial family
царевна, царевны – (n., fem.) Czar's daughter, royal princess
царица, царицы – (n., fem.) Czar's wife
царь, царя – (n., masc.) the Czar
цветовод, цветовода – (n., masc., † *цвѣтоводъ*) flower-gardener
цветочник, цветочника – (n., masc., † *цвѣточникъ*) florist
цейхвахтер, цейхвахтера – (n., masc.) store-keeper, gunner
цейхмейстер, цейхмейстера – (n., masc.) master-gunner (in the navy)
целовальник, целовальника – (n., masc., † *цѣловальникъ*) in 15th-17th century Russia an official who collected taxes and did other duties related to judicial and police work; tapster, barkeep; fem. *целовальница*
цензор, цензора – (n., masc.) censor
ценитель, ценителя – (n., masc., † *цѣнитель*) appraiser; fem. *ценительница*
церковник, церковника – (n., masc.) clergyman, ecclesiastic
церковноприходский – (adj., † *церковноприходскій*) parish, parochial
церковнослужитель, церковнослужителя – (n., masc.) clergyman, churchman
цесаревич, цесаревича – (n., masc.) crown-prince of Russia
цесаревна, цесаревны – (n., fem.) wife of the crown prince of Russia
цесарь, цесаря – (n., masc.) Caesar; emperor
цимбалист, цимбалиста – (n., masc., † *цымбалистъ*) cymbals-player
цирюльник, цирюльника – (n., masc., † *цырюльникъ*) barber
цыган, цыгана – (n., masc., nom. pl. *цыгане*, gen. pl. *цыган*) Gypsy; fem. *цыганка*
цымбалистъ → *цимбалист*
цыновочник, цыновочника – (n., masc.) mat-maker
цырюльникъ → *цирюльник*
цѣнитель → *ценитель*
цѣровальникъ → *целовальник*
чародей, чародея – (n., masc., *чародѣй*) magician, sorcerer; fem. *чародейка*
† *чарочник, чарочника* – (n., masc.) cupbearer at a noble's court
часовщик, часовщика – (n., masc.) watchmaker
чашник, чашника – (n., masc.) principal cupbearer (at the Czars' court)
чеботарь, чеботаря – cobbler, shoemaker, bootmaker
чеканщик, чеканщика – (n., masc.) coiner, minter; chaser, caulker

человек, человека – (n., masc., † *человѣкъ*, nom. pl. *люди*, gen. pl. *людей*) man, person
челядинец, челядинца – (n., masc.) servant, domestic; fem. *челядинка*
чемоданщик, чемоданщика – (n., masc.) trunk-maker
черепичник, черепичника – (n., masc.) tile-maker
черкес, черкеса – (n., masc.) native of Circassia; fem. *черкешенка*
чернец, чернца – (n., masc.) monk, friar
черница, черницы – (n., fem.) nun
черногорец, черногорца – (n., masc.) native of Montenegro
чернорабочий, чернорабочего – (adj. used as a n., masc., † *чернорабочій*) drudge, one doing unskilled labor
черноризец, чернориза – (n., masc.) friar, monk; fem. *черноризица*
чертёжник, чертёжника – (n., masc.) draftsman; fem. *чертёжница*
чесальщик, чесальщика – (n., masc.) carder, comber; fem. *чесальщица*
чех, чеха – (n., masc.) Czech; fem. *чешка*
чиновник, чиновника – (n., masc.) clerk, functionary; *чиновникъ Ломжинскаго Губернскаго Казначейства*, clerk in the Łomża Provincial Treasury Office; *чиновникъ по крестьянском дѣлам*, clerk in the Peasant Affairs Office; *чиновникъ таможный*, customs clerk; fem. *чиновница*
чистильщик, чистильщика – (n., masc.) cleaner, scourer, e. g. *чистильщик сапог* – bootblack; fem. *чистильщица*
чистописец, чистописца – (n., masc.) calligrapher, penman
чужеземец, чужеземца – (n., masc.) alien, foreigner; fem. *чужеземка*
чулочник, чулочника – (n., masc.) stocking-maker; fem. *чулочница*
шапочник, шапочника – (n., masc.) hatter
шарманщик, шарманщика – (n., masc.) organ-grinder
шахтёр, шахтёра – (n., masc.) miner
швед, шведа – (n., masc.) Swede; fem. *шведка*
швейцар, швейцара – (n., masc.) porter, doorkeeper
швец, швеца – (n., masc.) sewer, tailor
швея, швеи – (n., fem.) seamstress
шелковод, шелковода – (n., masc.) breeder of silkworms
шерстобой, шерстобоя – (n., masc.) wool-beater
шерсточёс, шерсточёса – (n., masc.) wool-carder
шерстяник, шерстяника – (n., masc.) worker who produces wool
шинкарь, шинкаря – (n., masc.) innkeeper, barkeeper; fem. *шинкарка*
шихтмейстер, шихтмейстера – (n., masc.) mine foreman (cmp. Germ. *Schichtmeister*)
шкипер, шкипера – (n., masc.) skipper [of a barge], shipmaster, boatswain [of a man-of-war]
школьник, школьника – (n., masc.) schoolboy; among Jews, a synagogue attendant or sexton, sometimes a title for the executive director of a Jewish community [Beider, *Dictionary of Jewish Surnames from the Russian Empire*]
школяр, школяра – (n., masc.) schoolboy; fem. *школярка*
шлифовщик, шлифовщика – (n., masc.) polisher; also seen: *шлифовальщик*; fem. *шлифовщица*
шлюзник, шлюзника – (n., masc.) lock-keeper, sluice-keeper
шляпник, шляпника – (n., masc.) hatter
шляпница, шляпницы – (n., fem.) milliner
шляпочник, шляпочника – (n., masc.) hat-maker
шляхта, шляхты – (n., fem.) [Polish] nobility (cmp. Polish *szlachta*)
шляхтич, шляхтича – (n., masc.) [Polish] nobleman (cmp. Polish *szlachcic*); fem. *шляхтянка*
шорник, шорника – (n., masc.) saddler, saddle-maker
шофёр, шофёра – (n., masc., † *шоффёръ*) chauffeur
шпион, шпиона – (n., masc., † *шпіонъ*) spy; fem. *шпионка*
шпорник, шпорника – (n., masc.) spurrier
штаб-лекарь, штаб-лекаря – (n., masc.) regimental surgeon
штаб-офицер, штаб-офицера – (n., masc.) field officer
штаб-ротмистр, штаб-ротмистра – (n., masc.) second captain (cavalry)
штабс-капитан, штабс-капитана – (n., masc.) second captain (in the military)
шталмейстер, шталмейстера – (n., masc.) equerry, master of the horse (cmp. Germ. *Stallmeister*)
штемпельмейстер, штемпельмейстера – (n., masc.) head clerk of a stamp office (cmp. Germ. *Stempelmeister*)
штопальщик, штопальщика – (n., masc.) mender of old clothes or stockings, patcher, darner ; fem. *штопальщица*
штукатур, штукатура – (n., masc.) plasterer
штурман, штурмана – (n., masc.) navigator, steersman, pilot
шулер, шулера – (n., masc., nom. pl. *шулера*) cheat, card-sharp

шульга, шульги – (n., masc. or fem.) left-handed person

щёточник, щёточника – (n., masc.) maker or seller of brushes

щитоносец, щитоносца – (n., masc.) shield-bearer, armor-bearer, squire

ѣздовой → *ездовой*

ѣздокъ → *ездок*

эквилибрист, эквилибриста – (n., masc.) equilibrist, tightrope-walker

экзарх, экзарха – (n., masc., † *екзархъ*) (n., masc.) exarch, an Eastern Orthodox bishop ranking below a patriarch

экзекутор, экзекутора – (n., masc.) usher; administrative clerk in a civil service office; fem. *экзекуторша*

экзерцирмейстер, экзерцирмейстера – (n., masc.) drill-officer (cmp. Germ. *Exerziermeister*)

эконом, эконома – (n., masc.) housekeeper, steward; fem. *экономка* or *экономша*

эльзасец, эльзяасца – (n., masc.) Alsatian; fem. *эльзаска*

эрцгерцог, эрцгергзога – (n., masc.) archduke (cmp. Germ. *Erzherzog*); fem. *эрцгерцогиня*, archduchess

эстонец, эстонца – (n., masc.) Estonian; fem. *эстонка*

ювелир, ювелира – (n., masc.) jeweler

юнга, юнги – (n., masc.) cabin boy

юнкер, юнкера – (n., masc.) military school cadet; Prussian *Junker*

юноша, юноши – (n., masc., gen. pl. *юношей*) youth, lad

юрист, юриста – (n., masc.) jurist, lawyer

языковед, языковеда – (n., masc., † *языковѣдъ*) linguist, philologist

яичник, яичника – (n., masc.) † egg-merchant; [in modern Russian] ovary

яичница, яичницы – (n., fem.) † egg-merchant, egg-merchant's wife (in modern Russian means "omelette")

ямщик, ямщика – (n., masc.) coachman, post-boy

III. LOCATING RECORDS IN AMERICA THAT LEAD BACK TO EUROPE

Before tackling the task of translating records, it is necessary to **have** the records in the first place. To obtain documents from your ancestral place of origin it is necessary to know the exact point of origin of your family. ***This is a prerequisite for any European research!*** The way you trace the family to its origin in Europe, however, is through records in America. In other words, to get there, you have to start here.

Your first task is to clean your attic and other storage places in your house, with the hope of unearthing any documents that can provide information on your family's origin, and to interview relatives who might be able to shed some light on the question. Beware of oral accounts of relatives if they themselves were not the original immigrants—family members tend to add and subtract information from stories to suit their own personal needs. For instance, your relatives may not want to admit the original immigrant was a farmer, and will give his birthplace as some larger town, so as to create the illusion that he was some sort of merchant. This might add "respectability" in their eyes, but all it does to you is send you in the wrong research direction. (Most Americans are descendants of farmers anyway, so nobody is being fooled!).

If family papers or relatives' stories do produce a birthplace, **always** corroborate this information with some reliable documentary source. Let us discuss some of those sources.

A. CHURCH RECORDS

When investigating church records created in North America, some researchers will find a wealth of geographical information on the birthplaces of their ancestors, as some clergymen—but by no means all—noted geographical information on all those they baptized, married, or buried. Most frequently such notations can be found in matrimonial registers, especially in the Roman Catholic church, because information is required as to where the parties contracting marriage were baptized. Geographical information may be exact and complete in these registers, listing the name of a village, county, province, and partition. Some entries may give a portion of this information; unfortunately, others will simply list "Russia" or leave blank the space for this information in the register. Lutheran and Eastern Orthodox registers can also contain geographical information; but as with the Catholic records, it depends on the individual clergyman's diligence and thoroughness.

When checking church records, do not fail to examine the baptismal records of the immigrants' American-born children. Clergymen sometimes noted the birthplaces of the parents. Also, do not discount parish censuses; they may contain such information, although it is less likely than in the sacramental registers.

B. CIVIL VITAL RECORDS

In most states all birth, death, and marriage records for at least the 20th century contain questions as to the birthplace of the person to whom the record pertains, or to his or her parents. Many researchers who plunge into records with high hopes of pinpointing a European birthplace find their hopes dashed when they are greeted by the words "unknown" or "unobtainable." Still, in some cases an exact birthplace will appear. Even if the information is missing in the records of your immediate family, a thorough search of the vital records of the extended family may prove fruitful; the desired information may surface on a cousin's records.

By the way, beware of bad spelling. Remember that your ancestors did not speak English, and numerous errors occurred in the writing down of information, since the clerks, as a rule, spoke no foreign languages.

C. NATURALIZATION RECORDS

The Declaration of Intention and Petition for Naturalization, filed at a court (local, state, or federal), where the immigrant applied for admission to American citizenship, may prove a veritable treasure trove of geographical information. These forms are a good place to search for a European birthplace, but some caution is in order.

Firstly, if your ancestor became a citizen before 1906, when the federal government assumed the task of naturalization and thus standardized the forms, there may be partial information, or none at all, in the documentation. Post-1906 documents do record such information, but be aware of the following cautions and limitations.

Most court clerks who collected the information for naturalization documents had no knowledge of a second language, so they often recorded place names inaccurately. If you and have difficulty locating on a map a place of birth obtained from these documents, you should consult a gazetteer to determine locations with similar spellings. It can also be worth your while to engage the assistance of a language expert, who may be able to help you arrive at a correct rendition of the name. (Chapter Five, beginning on page 115, may also aid you in this quest.) If this fails, you can always reconfirm the data by checking the ship's manifest for the vessel that brought your ancestor to America.

Another factor in naturalization records vis-à-vis geography that may lead a researcher astray is the recording of a ***general*** versus ***specific*** birthplace. For example, an applicant from a small village in the province of Grodno (today Hrodna, Belarus) may have said he came from Grodno, rather than the specific village in which he was actually born. Few officials were familiar with the names of places in eastern Europe, so those names often sounded utterly incomprehensible to them. But Vilna or Grodno, that was a different matter—those names weren't so long, and were at least somewhat more familiar. So even if an immigrant tried to say, in broken English or through a translator, "I'm from the village of Vertsyalishki, a few miles east of Grodno," to an English-speaking official it might sound like "Blah-blah-blah Grodno," and that's what he wrote down!

Naturalization papers can be located at a variety of archives. You need to check how the courts in the state that interests you disposed of these records. Also keep in mind that several courts performed naturalizations, i. e., federal, state, and local, and this jurisdictional situation could affect the disposition of the records. This means that in some states naturalizations performed in federal courts could be stored in a different archive than records created in a state court. A few examples will illustrate this state of affairs.

In Massachusetts, records from the federal courts are at a branch of the National Archives in suburban Boston, while the records created in state courts are at the Massachusetts State Archives in Boston. In Connecticut all records from all courts have been sent to the National Archives branch in Waltham, Massachusetts. In Pennsylvania county courts have retained naturalization records in the country courthouses, while records from federal courts are at the National Archives branch in Philadelphia. Each of the above examples is different in some way. The lesson here is to check all possibilities for the state in which your ancestors lived.

D. PASSENGER LISTS

Housed at the National Archives in Washington, D. C., and at various branches of the National Archives, the microfilmed copies of these lists record the vital data on all passengers entering the United States. The lists were revised and changed by the government several times during the era of great immigration. In general, the farther you go back in time, the more sparse the information; lists created in the years approaching the outbreak of World War I are the most detailed. Information given on each passenger may include:

- his or her full name
- age
- sex
- marital status
- occupation
- literacy
- citizenship (pre-World War I Polish, Lithuanian, and Ukrainian immigrants from the territory ruled by the Russian Empire will be classified as "Russian")
- race
- last permanent residence
- name of the immigrant's nearest living relative in Europe and relationship to this person
- destination in the U. S. and the name of the person to whom the passenger was going and his relationship to the passenger
- birthplace
- a physical description of the immigrant

The body of passenger lists are divided by port of arrival; thus a researcher needs to know at which port the immigrant arrived. The bulk of immigrants arrived at the Port of New York (over 22 million between 1880 and 1930), with lesser numbers at Boston (2 million), Baltimore (1.5 million), and Philadelphia (1.2 million).

Fortunately, passenger lists for New York have become much easier for researchers to study since the opening of the American Family Immigration History Center (AFIHC) Website, which allows you to search the Ellis Island database of passenger lists online. As of this writing (and presumably for the foreseeable future) this database is located at:

http://www.ellisislandrecords.org

Because of the poor legibility of some of the lists and the lack of knowledge of languages of the volunteers who transcribed them, you can expect to find many, many spelling errors. Do ***not*** view this Website as a cure-all to locate lost relatives. Some knowledge of the phonetics of your ancestors' language may prove crucial in using it effectively. You may also have to search with some degree of imagination—some researchers have reported finding S misread as L, so that people from Suwałki, Poland were listed as coming from "Luwalki!"

According to statistics given at that site, of the 27 million immigrants who came to America between 1880 and 1930—over 22 million of whom passed through Ellis Island between 1892 and 1924—some 3,300,000 were from the Russian Empire. If you don't know through which port your ancestors entered the United States, try New York first—but do not ignore the other ports.

Many of the collections of passenger lists have indexes to facilitate locating a specific passenger. Some indexes are coded by Soundex, a system that converts names to an alphanumeric code and thus bypasses some of the vagaries of spelling caused by the different orthographies of various languages; e. g., the sound by the letter *v* in English, French, Italian and Lithuanian, is written *w* in Polish and German, *в* in the Slavic languages written in the Cyrillic alphabet, and so on. American Soundex codes similar sounds by number, so that names with similar codes may be variants of the same name, just spelled in various ways. Often this can help you find even a badly mangled name. (The Daitch-Mokotoff Soundex system is somewhat better for Eastern European names, but unfortunately is not generally used for passenger list indexes.)

Even with Soundex, however, any index is sure to contain quite a few transcription and language-based errors. Human error is an ever-present reality, and researchers can't afford to ignore it. There are steps you can take, however, to help you minimize its effects.

To use indexes effectively, prepare a list of all possible ways your name could have been misspelled. Many researchers fail to find an ancestor, not because he wasn't listed—he was — but because they are not aware of certain linguistic factors that can distort name forms and confuse those unfamiliar with them.

The first rule is ***not to use an Americanized version*** of your ancestor's first name, such as "Chester," "Stanley," "Sally," or "Stella." Names entered on the passenger lists, in theory, should be properly spelled versions of your ancestor's "real" name. Thus your first task is to convert the name back into Polish, Lithuanian, Russian, or whatever language is appropriate. Unfortunately, this is not always enough.

Because our ancestors traveled to the U. S. on German, Austrian, or Russian passports, linguistic features of the German or Russian languages often crept into these official documents, influencing the spelling of their names (as well as birthplaces). In certain cases the name was translated outright, i. e., the German *Johann* was substituted for the Polish *Jan,* or Russian officials might turn Lithuanian *Jonas* (John) into *Иван* (Ivan). Even if the immigrants' passports had the correct rendition of the names, the ship's officers, who were mostly German- or Dutch-speaking, could have entered, for example, a Germanized version of the name on the passenger list. That, not the correct spelling, would then appear in the index you search through.

In addition to these linguistic features which have distinct origin in another language, the researcher must also contend with old orthography. This is not much of a factor with Russian or Ukrainian names, since those names had to be converted from the Cyrillic alphabet to the Roman alphabet, anyway, and the archaic letters ***i*** and ***ѣ*** were rendered the same as their modern counterparts, ***и*** and ***е***.

Changes in spelling trends can affect names written in the Roman alphabet, however. In modern Polish, for instance, *Maria* is the correct spelling of that first name; but at the turn of the century *Maryja* and *Marya* were common, and all these versions will be listed separately. Lithuanian names can also be a headache, because the modern Lithuanian spellings were not used much during the period of mass immigration. Lithuanian names were usually given either in Polish-influenced spellings, or as transliterations of Cyrillic versions, which in turn were based on Polish or Russian forms (see pages 21-23). Thus a Lithuanian ancestor who went by *Vaitiekus* might show up in Polish form, *Wojciech,* or Russian form, *Войтѣхъ*, rendered in English as *Voytekh*, or in some mangled hybrid.

Here is a brief sampling of some first names and reasonably legitimate variant spellings often encountered, just to give you an idea of how much variation there can be, even when outright misspelling isn't a factor. (More forms in various languages are given in the list of common first names, Christian and Jewish, in Chapter VIII, beginning on page 437):

Russian	*Polish*	*Lithuanian*	*Ukrainian*	*Variants*
Andrei	Andrzej	Andriejus	Andriy	Andreas, Andrej, Jędrzej
Frants	Franciszek	Pranciškus	Franko	Franz
Ivan	Jan	Jonas	Ivan	Johan, Johann, Iwan
Iosif	Józef	Juozapas	Yosip, Yosif	Josef, Osip, Osif, Juozas, Juzas
Yekaterina	Katarzyna	Katarina	Kateryna	Ekaterina, Kotryna, Katryna
Mikhail	Michał	Mykolas	Mykhailo	Michail, Mikhailo
Pyotr	Piotr	Petras	Petro	Pieter, Peter
Rivka	Rywka	Rivka	Ryvka	Riwka, Ryfka, Rifka
Sara	Sora	Sara, Sora	Sara, Sora	Sura, Sarah
Vikentiy	Wincenty	Vincentas	Vikent	Vincenz, Vincas

One vowel may suffice to put a person in a section of the index you'd never think to search. If, for instance, you know your ancestor's name was correctly spelled *Władysław* and don't find him, he may be there under *Wladislaw* or Vladyslav. Here are a few letter substitutions you are particularly likely to run into:

i for ***y***	Wlad***i***slaw vs. Wład***y***sław, Z***i***gmunt vs. Z***y***gmunt
c for ***k***	**C**arol vs. ***K***arol, Nicodem vs. Ni***k***odem
v for ***w***	**V**ictoria vs. ***W***iktoria, ***V***incenty vs. ***W***incenty
x for ***ks***	Feli***x*** vs. Feli***ks***, Ale***x***ander vs. Ale***ks***ander
s for ***z***	Jo***s***ef vs. Jó***z***ef, Ro***s***alia vs. Ro***z***alia
e or ***i*** or ***y*** + ***j***	Mar***yj***a vs. Mar***y***a, Salom***ej***a vs. Salom***e***a, Rozal***ij***a vs. Rozal***i***a
t for ***ł***	W***t***adys***t***aw vs. W***ł***adys***ł***aw

E. SOCIAL SECURITY

Applications for a Social Security number contain a space to provide a birthplace. If your ancestor gave complete information, chances are you will find the information here.

F. PROBATE RECORDS

While wills and inventories of estates do not generally contain geographical information, lists of surviving relatives do list their addresses, including at times siblings or other relatives in Europe.

G. MILITARY RECORDS

Did your ancestor serve in the U. S. armed forces? U. S. military records will occasionally provide an exact European birthplace. Some draft registration cards created in 1917 and including all men between the ages of 18 and 45 provide geographical information.

H. PARISH & ORGANIZATIONAL HISTORIES

Whatever their religion—Roman Catholic, Greek Catholic, Orthodox, Jewish, Protestant—most immigrants from eastern Europe took their faith seriously. When settling in a new area in North America, their first goal was often to establish a parish or other religious center, where they could be around their compatriots and share the kind of parish-centered social life they'd known in the old country. There were often publications connected with these parishes, especially histories or anniversary booklets published at various milestones in their histories. In the early part of the century they were written almost exclusively in the language of the old country, but as the century progressed they came to be issued bilingually or solely in English. Copies of many such booklets still exist among the holdings of various libraries, and they often contain biographies or other information on particularly prominent members of the parish. Thus they can be worth a close look.

I. OBITUARIES & CEMETERY INSCRIPTIONS

While it is not standard practice now, some of the earlier tombstones gave a birthplace in Europe. In most cemeteries perhaps a half dozen stones will contain this information, and you may be one of the fortunate researchers who will benefit from this information. If you have your ancestor's date of death, check his or her obituary as well as those of the whole extended family; this may lead you back to Europe. And don't forget ethnic newspapers published in the immigrant's native language! (See pages 85-88.)

J. PASSPORTS AND CONSULAR RECORDS

If your ancestor became a U. S. citizen and later journeyed back to his homeland on an American passport, an application for a U. S. passport will be on file at the U. S. State Department in Washington, listing your ancestor's birthplace and place of naturalization.

Also immigrants who came from the Russian Empire often had reason to correspond with the Russian consular offices in America, to acquire visa applications, vital records, ship arrival information, military service information, and so on. The LDS has microfilmed these Russian consular records and offers access to them through Family History Centers. The National Archives and Record Administration (NARA) also has these records on microfilm. A Soundexed index to these records was compiled by Sallyann Sack and Suzan F. Wynne, *The Russian Consular Records Index and Catalog* (New York: Garland, 1987). As of this writing more information on Russian consular records in the United States and Canada is available online: **http://pixel.cs.vt.edu/library/refs/link/usa.txt.**

K. INSURANCE AND FRATERNAL ORGANIZATION RECORDS

Immigrant groups often formed mutual benefit societies, insurance fraternals, political clubs, and so on. Such organizations typically had records of membership, payment of dues, and records of death claims. Although many of these records did not require a birthplace, some did and should be checked if all else fails. The language in which these records were kept varied; in the earlier years it was usually the language spoken by the group of people affected, e. g., Russian or Polish. As time went on and the immigrants began to be Americanized, English came to be used more and more.

It is not easy to find records for such organizations aimed primarily at Russians; for that matter, many "Russians" were actually ethnic Poles, Lithuanians, etc., and may have joined organizations founded by and for those groups. Still, some records exist for fraternal organizations designed to assist Russian immigrants. For instance, with funding from the Russian Brotherhood Organization, the Balch Institute for Ethnic Studies created a database for death claims filed with that Organization 1900-1926. The claims were written in Cyrillic, Polish, Hungarian, and English.

As of this writing the Balch Institute was merging with the Historical Society of Pennsylvania, so it is difficult to foretell exactly where to access this data; what works now might not work a year from now. Information on the Institute's Russian collection is available at this site: **http://www.balchinstitute.org/manuscript_guide/html/russian.html.**

If this information is no longer available from the Balch Institute by the time you read this, you might visit the Website of the Historical Society of Pennsylvania and try to learn more there: **http://www.hsp.org/**.

If you do good, thorough research, you may find other organizations with records that can aid you. In genealogy it is always true that the Lord helps those who help themselves!

If all of the above sources have failed, it's time to get creative: examine your ancestor's life history and ask yourself what other organization he may have dealt with, dealings that might produce a paper record. The answers may lead you toward unexpected resources:

- Was the family on public assistance during the Depression?
- Did your ancestor's long-time place of employment keep personnel records from earlier times?
- Did your ancestor have any friends who may have come from the same place?
- Did your ancestor have any dealings with the consulate of his country of origin before becoming a U. S. citizen?
- Were any news articles written about members of your family that may mention a birthplace?
- Was your ancestor mentioned in a business directory?
- If your immigrant ancestor was not a U. S. citizen, do you have his alien registration number, a number that will lead you back to a file?
- Did someone in the family fill out applications for union membership?

Only by exploring all possibilities will you find the geographical information that you need to bring you back to the point of your family's origin. That information is vital; you must have it before you even attempt to research your past in Europe. In view of all the changes in national affiliations and borders that have taken place in eastern Europe over the last two centuries, your first challenge is to figure out what country your family lived in! A family that came from "Russia" in the 19th century could have lived in what is now Lithuania, Belarus, Ukraine, Poland, and so on. That affects where records are kept.

The good news is, documents in most of the categories listed above are usually in English, and thus present no translation difficulties. The Russian-language documents you are most likely to encounter are: A. Church Records; I. Obituaries and Cemetery Inscriptions; and J. Consular Records. In Part IV we look at samples of these Russian-language records drawn up in America that may help us find information that leads us across the Atlantic to our ancestral homes.

IV. RUSSIAN-LANGUAGE RECORDS ORIGINATING IN AMERICA

A. CHURCH RECORDS: Document IV-1. Church Registry Extract

Prior to analyzing records created in Europe, researchers whose ancestors came from territory formerly ruled by the Russian Empire and followed the Orthodox religion may find records from an Orthodox church in the United States. Such records may be kept in Russian, especially if they date from the late 19th or early 20th centuries. The church registry extract on page 81, **Document IV-1**, is a sample of this type, from Holy Trinity Parish (formerly called St. Cyril and Methodius Church) in New Britain, Connecticut.

To help you ease into dealing with such records, let us repeat the information shown there with the handwritten parts given in a standardized script font that may be easier to read:

МЕТРИЧЕСКАЯ ВЫПИСЬ

Вь метрической книгѣ Русской Православной Греко-Каѳолической Церкви *Св. Кирилла и Меѳодія* в городѣ *Ню Британ* штата *Коннекѳикутъ* С. - Американскихъ Соединенныхъ Штатовъ, въ части первой, о родившихся, за 1*910* годъ, подъ № *23* записанъ слѣдующій актъ:

1910 года, мѣсяца *Августа 18* дня родил*ась*
и *1910* года, мѣсяца *Августа 23* дня крещен*а*
Меланія

Родители: *Иванъ Васильевъ Радуха — русско. под. кр. Гродненской губ. Сокольскаго уѣзда Каменской вол. д. Острово, и законная жена Его Софія Іаковлева - оба православные*

Воспріемники: *Антоній Павловъ Радуха — Каменской вол. д. Острово и Антонина Іосифова Гела-жинъ д. Острово православные*

Таинство Крещенія совершалъ: *Священникъ Константинъ Букетовъ Августа 23 дня 1910 года*

Что сія копія съ подлиннымъ актомъ вѣрна, въ томъ подписомъ и приложе-ніемъ церковной печати удостовѣряю.

New Britain Conn. мѣсяца *Aug. 16* дня *1913* г. № *—*

Настоятель, *Русской Православной Церкви*

Священникъ Конс̄танѳинъ Букетовъ

МЕТРИЧЕСКАЯ ВЫПИСЬ.

Въ метрической книгѣ Русской Православной Греко-Каѳолической Церкви Св. Кирилла и Меѳодія въ городѣ Нью Британи штата Коннектикутъ С.-Американскихъ Соединенныхъ Штатовъ, въ части первой, о родившихся, за 1910 годъ, подъ № 23 записанъ слѣдующій актъ:

1910 года, мѣсяца Августа 18 дня родилась

и 1910 года, мѣсяца Августа 23 дня крещена

Меланія

Родители: Иванъ Васильевъ Радула - русско-под. кр. Гродненской губ. Сокольскаго уѣзда, Каменской вол. д. Острово - и законная жена его Софія Яковлева-ова православные

Воспріемники: Антоній Павловъ Радула - Каменской вол. д. Острово и Антонина Іосифова Селяжинъ - д. Острово православные

Таинство Крещенія совершалъ: Священникъ Константинъ Букетовъ Августа 23 дня 1910 года

Что сія копія съ подлиннымъ актомъ вѣрна, въ томъ подписомъ и приложеніемъ церковной печати удостовѣряю.

New Britain Conn., мѣсяца Aug. 16. дня 1913 г. №

Настоятель, Русской Православной Церкви Священникъ Константинъ Букетовъ

Document IV-1: A Church Registry Extract

This document features two characters that could confuse you, including an archaic one not normally encountered in genealogical research. It is the letter ѳ, mentioned on page 3, seen here in the terms *Греко-Каѳолический*, "Greek Catholic," and in the name of the church, *Св. Кирилла и Меѳодія*, "Saints Cyril and Methodius." This letter was seldom seen outside of ecclesiastical documents. When you do see it, it can normally be traced back to Greek words with the letter θ, which tends to be rendered as "th" in English, e. g., Catholic, Methodius.

The other potentially confusing character is the letter ƒ used as a form of ꞙ, which is in turn an alternate form of the letter *m* or *m̄* (see page 9). If you look closely at Document IV-1, you will note that the priest used the forms *m* and *m̄* and ƒ at different times, with no apparent rhyme or reason to his choice.

An analysis of each segment of the record follows.

Вь метрической книгѣ Русской Православной Греко-Каѳолической Церкви *Св. Кирилла и Меѳодія* в городѣ *Ню Британи* штата *Коннектикутъ* С.-Американскихъ Соединенныхъ Штатовъ. — "In the registry book of the Russian Orthodox Greek Catholic Church of Sts. Cyril and Methodius in the city of New Britain of the state of Connecticut of the United States of North America…"

въ метрической книгѣ – literally "in the registry book," but in English it would normally be rendered "in the vital records register." Note that *книгѣ* (modern spelling *книге*) is a prepositional form of the feminine noun *книга*, "book," after the preposition *в*, "in."

Русской Православной Греко-Каѳолической Церкви – "of the Russian Orthodox Greek-Catholic Church," all in the genitive case (as suggested by the English words "of the"). The form *церкви* is genitive of the feminine noun *церковь*, "church"; the other words are adjectives modifying it, thus the singular feminine genitive adjectival ending *–ой*.

Св. Кирилла и Меѳодія – "of Sts. Cyril and Methodius."

въ городѣ Ню Британи штата Коннектикут С.-Американскихъ Соединненыхъ Штатовъ – The expression *въ городѣ* (modern spelling *в городе*) is prepositional, "in the city." "New Britain" and "Connecticut" are simply spelled phonetically in Cyrillic. In Russian "United States of America" is usually *Соединненые Штаты Америки*, but here the abbreviation *С.-* (from *северный*, "northern") specifies that we're talking of the United States of North America.

въ части первой, о родившихся, за *1910* годъ, подъ № *23* записанъ слѣдующій актъ: — "in part one, of births, for the year 1910, under No. 23, the following record is entered:"

въ части первой о родившихся – Russian registers traditionally designate baptismal records as "part one," marriage records as "part two," and death records as "part three" (in some cases part three is devoted to divorces and part four to deaths).

за 1910 годъ, подъ № 23 записанъ слѣдующій актъ – "for the year 1910, under No. 23 [is] entered the following document."

1910 года, мѣсяца *Августа 18* дня родилась и *1910* года, мѣсяца *Августа 23* дня крещена: *Меланія*. — "Melaniya was born August 18, 1910 and baptized August 23, 1910."

1910 года, мѣсяца Августа 18 дня родилась – literally "of the year 1910, of the month August, of the 18 day, was born." The form *родилась* is past tense, feminine singular, of the verb *родиться*, "to be born," so now we know the person who was born on August 18, 1910 was a female. If he were a male, the form would be *родился*.

1910 года, мѣсяца Августа 23 дня крещена: Меланія – literally "of the year 1910, of the month August, of the 23 day, [was] baptized: Melaniya." The short-form participle *крещена* is contrasted with the phrase ending *родилась* so that both can have the same subject, Melaniya; that's why both have feminine endings. We would put this "Melania was born on August 18, 1910, and baptized on August 23, 1910," but the use of declensional endings allows Russian greater flexibility in its word order.

Родители: *Иванъ Васильевъ Радуха – русско. под. кр. Гродненской губ. Сокольскаго уѣзда Каменской вол. д. Острово, и законная жена Его София Іаковлева оба православные.* — "Parents: Ivan Radukha, son of Vasily, a Russian citizen, a peasant of the Province of Grodno, county of Sokółka, district of Kamienna, village of Ostrowo, and his lawful wife Sofiya, daughter of Iakov, both Orthodox."

Родители – "parents." Standard procedure was to list the father first—first name, patronymic, and surname—followed by a statement as to his citizenship and occupation, then his place of origin, specifying province, county, district, and village. Information on the mother follows, but seldom with all those details.

Иванъ Васильевъ Радуха — "Ivan Radukha, son of Vasily." The word *Васильевъ* is what the Russians call an *отчество*, a patronymic, i. e., a name formed by adding a suffix to the name of one's father (see pages 28-29). Ivan's father was *Василій*, "Vasiliy," and the addition of the suffix *–евъ* gives *Васильевъ*. This patronymic with *–евъ* is archaic; in modern Russian the patronymic usually ends in *–ович/-евич* or *–ич*, e. g., *Василевич*. Other examples are *Иванович*, "son of Ivan"; *Ильич*, "son of Ilya," etc.

русско. под. – "Russian citizen," with *под.* short for *подданный*, "citizen, subject."

кр. – short for *крестьянинъ*, "peasant"

губ. – short for *губернія*, "province," often simply given as *gubernia* in English. Here *Гродненской губ.* means "of the province of Grodno." Note that in expressions specifying administrative subdivisions, Russian often uses adjectival forms of place names where we would use noun forms. We would say "in the province of Moscow," they say literally "in the Muscovite province." It can be tricky to determine the right place name from the adjectival form; information in Chapter V may help with this.

уѣздъ – modern spelling *уезд*, roughly equivalent to "county" in English, comparable to a *powiat* in Polish. Here *Сокольскаго уѣзда* means "of Sokółka county." Since this place is in Poland, its Polish name, Sokółka, is the appropriate one to use.

вол. – short for *волость*, "district." Here *Каменской вол.* means "of Kamienna district."

д. – short for *деревня*, "village." By the way, please note again that Russian

Main Administrative Subdivisions of the Russian Empire
(from largest to smallest)

губернія – a province, roughly comparable to a state in the U. S.

уѣздъ – a subdivision of a **губернія**, roughly comparable to a county in the U. S. or a *powiat* in Poland

волость – a subdivision of an **уѣздъ**, comprised of a number of villages (**деревни**) and settlements (**села**) and roughly comparable to a district in the U. S.

has two ways of representing a lower-case д in script or italics, either *∂* or *g*. The *∂* is considered "correct," but in records you'll see *g* often and you might as well start getting used to it. Here *g. Острово* is "village of Ostrovo" (Polish spelling *Ostrowo*).

законная жена его Софія Іаковлева – literally "lawful wife his Sofiya, daughter of Iakov"

оба православные – "both Orthodox"

NOTE ON APPROPRIATE NAME FORMS: It turns out that this family lived in what is now Polish territory, and as such may not have used the Russified versions of their names and patronymics shown above, except in a Russian-language context. The names would be rendered as "Jan (son of Wasyl) and Zofia, daughter of Jakób"; and in fact that is probably the way we should render them. As members of an ethnocultural minority in contemporary Poland, this family might well have spoken a dialect mixture of Russian, Belarusian, and Polish at home, and even used Russified names within the family unit. Outside the home and in current public documents, however, they would most likely use a standard version of the language. An analogous situation would be use of a Sicilian dialect by an Italian family at home, but use of standard Italian in all other aspects of life outside the home.

The point is simply that it can sometimes be quite difficult to determine the appropriate names to use for people in these documents. You may have no choice but to recognize that there is no one indisputably "right answer," but several, depending on context.

As for place names, it is usually advisable to use Polish forms for places now in Poland, Ukrainian forms for places in Ukraine, and so on. It can prove challenging to identify these places from their Russian names; but it usually proves necessary to do so for research purposes, so you might as well make a habit of it.

Воспріемники: *Антоній Павловъ Радуха – Каменской вол. g. Острово и Антонина Іосифова Гелажинъ g. Острово православные* — "Godparents: Antoni Raducha, son of Paweł, of the district of Kamienna, village of Ostrowo, and Antonina Giełażyn, daughter of Józef, of the village of Ostrowo, both Orthodox."

Воспріемники: Антоній Павловъ Радуха – Каменской вол. g. Острово – "Godparents: Antoni Raducha, son of Paweł, from the district of Kamienna, village of Ostrowo."

и Антонина Іосифова Гелажинъ g. Острово православные – "and Antonina Giełażyn, daughter of Józef, of the village of Ostrowo, [both] Orthodox."

Таинство Крещенія совершалъ: *Священникъ Константинъ Букетовъ Августа 23 дня 1910 года.* — "Rev. Konstantin Buketov performed the sacrament of Baptism on August 23, 1910."

Таинство Крещенія – "the sacrament of Baptism"

совершалъ – literally "performed," so that this sentence's word order is backwards, from the English-speaker's point of view: the direct object comes first, followed by the predicate, then the subject.

Священникъ – "priest" (Orthodox), or when combined with his name, as here, "Father."

Августа 23 дня 1910 года – "on the 23rd day of August, year 1910."

Что сія копія съ подлиннымъ актомъ вѣрна, въ томъ подписомъ и приложеніемъ церковной печати удостовѣряю. *New Britain Conn.* мѣсяца *Aug. 16* дня *1913* г. № –. — "I certify that this copy is faithful to the original record with my signature and the church seal. New Britain, Conn. August 16, 1913. No. _."

что сія копія съ подлиннымъ актомъ вѣрна – "That this copy is faithful to the original record." The word *что* is used many ways; here it is a conjunction. For *сія* see page 43.

въ томъ подписомъ и приложеніемъ церковной печати удосотвѣряю – literally "in this with signature and affixing of the church seal I certify." Inciently, *подписомъ* is non-standard; *подписъ* is a feminine noun, and *подписью* is what you'd normally see.

Настоятель, *Русской Православной Церкви Священникъ Константинъ Букетовъ* — "Pastor of the Russian Orthodox Church, Father Konstantin Buketov."

Настоятель – if used precisely, this term refers to a prior or arch-priest. But we often see it in records used, as here, to mean simply "pastor."

Translation – "In the registry book of the Russian Orthodox Greek Catholic Church of Sts. Cyril and Methodius in the city of New Britain of the state of Connecticut of the United States of North America, in part one, the birth register, for the year 1910, under No. 23, the following record is entered: Melaniya was born August 18, 1910 and baptized August 23, 1910. Parents: Jan Raducha, son of Wasyl, a Russian citizen, a peasant of the Province of Grodno, county of Sokółka, district of Kamienna, village of Ostrowo, and his lawful wife Zofia, daughter of Jakób, both Orthodox. Godparents: Antoni Raducha, son of Paweł, of the district of Kamienna, village of Ostrowo, and Antonina Giełażyn, daughter of Józef, of the village of Ostrowo, both Orthodox. Rev. Konstantin Buketov performed the sacrament of Baptism on August 23, 1910. I certify that this copy is faithful to the original record with my signature and the church seal. New Britain, Conn. August 16, 1913. No. _. Pastor of the Russian Orthodox Church, Father Konstantin Buketov."

B. OBITUARIES

Russian-language obituaries are not particularly intimidating, once you get past the basic problems any Russian document poses (the unfamiliar alphabet and vocabulary). The following are samples from the New York Russian-language newspaper **Новое Русское Слово** [New Russian Word]. Here is analysis of **Document IV-2**, shown at right.

14 сего июля, в гор. Монтреале, Канада
после продолжительной и тяжкой болезни,
на 78 году жизни ,тихо скончалась
МАРИЯ АНДРЕЕВНА
СЛИВИНСКАЯ
(урождённая Вишневская), по первому браку Мейер,
о чем извещают друзей покойной ее сын
АЛЕКСАНДР ГЕОРГИЕВИЧ МЕЙЕР,
ЕГО ЖЕНА, ДОЧЬ И ВНУКИ.

Document IV-2

14 сего июля – "on the 14th of this July," i. e., "this July 14th"

в гор. Монтреале, Канада – "in the city of Montreal, Canada"; *гор.* or *г.* are often used as abbreviations for some form of *город*, "city"

после продолжительной и тяжкой болезни – "after a prolonged and serious illness"

на 78 году жизни, тихо скончалась Мария Андреевна Сливинская– "in her 78th year, Mariya Slivinskaia, daughter of Andrei, died quietly"; for more on the expression *на X году жизни*, see note *на 42-ем году жизни* on page 90.

скончалась – feminine singular, past tense form of *скончаться*, "to die"; the corresponding masculine form would be *скончался.*

Мария Андреевна Сливинская – notice the standard Russian form of the name: first name, patronymic, surname. As we saw on page 83, in modern Russian the male patronymic form usually ends in *–ович, -евич,* or *–ич.* The feminine patronymic ends in *–овна* or *–евна,* so *Andreevna* means "daughter of Andrei" (*Андрей*). Note also that the feminine surname takes a feminine ending, so that an adjectival surname such as *Сливинский (Slivinskiy)* takes the usual feminine adjectival ending *–ая.* Surnames formed from nouns add *–а,* e. g., *Иванов (Ivanov)* → *Иванова (Ivanova).*

урожденная Вишневская – "nee Vishnevskaia"; *урожденная* is often used to indicate maiden names. To be perfectly accurate, the spelling is *урождённая,* but as we've said before, in standard Russian the two dots over the **е** are usually omitted.

по первому браку Мейер – "by her first marriage Meyer"

о чем извещают друзей покойной ее сын Александр Георгиевич Мейер, его жена, дочь и внуки – "of which the friends of the deceased are hereby informed by her son Aleksander Georgievich Meyer, his wife, daughter, and grandchildren."

извещают – 3rd person plural of *извещать,* "to notify, inform." The subject of this verb is *ее сын Александр Георгиевич Мейер, его жена, дочь и внуки,* "her son, Aleksander Georgievich Meyer, his wife, daughter, and grandchildren," and the direct object is *друзей покойной,* "friends of the deceased."

покойной – genitive feminine singular of the adjective *покойный,* "quiet, calm," also used to mean "the deceased [one]." That is how it is used here, so that *друзей покойной* means "friends of the deceased."

Translation – "This July 14th, in the city of Montreal, Canada, after a lengthy and serious illness, in her 78th year, Mariya Andreyevna Slivinskaya, née Vishnevskaya, by her first marriage Meyer, died quietly, of which the friends of the deceased are hereby informed by her son Aleksander Meyer, son of Georgi, his wife, daughter, and grandchildren."

ИСАЙ ШЕРР, САВВА ШЕРР С СЕМЬЕЙ

в глубоком горе извещает о безвременной кончине

дорогой сестры и тети

БЕЛЛЫ ШЕРР

Тело находится в Парк Вест Мемориал Чапел, 79 улица и Коломбус Авеню. Похороны сегодня, 19 июля, в 2 часа дня. Погребение на кладбище Одесского Землячества.

Document IV-3

Document IV-3, at left, features several more expressions of the sort you will often find in obituaries, including information on time and place of burial. It is particularly interesting because it includes English-language names of places rendered in Cyrillic.

Исай Шерр, Савва Шерр с семей – "Isai Sherr, Savva Sherr, with family"

в глубоком горе извещает о безвременной кончине – "in deep *[глубоком]* sorrow *[горе]* announce the untimely *[безвременной]* passing *[кончине]*" дорогой сестры и тети Беллы Шерр – “of [their] dear sister and aunt, Bella Sherr.”

Тело находится в Парк Вест Мемориал Чапел, 79 улица и Коломбус Авеню – “The body is to be found at Park West Memorial Chapel, 79th Street and Columbus Avenue.” While this translation is technically accurate, in English we’d more likely say something like “The remains are at…” or “The wake will take place at….”

Похороны сегодня 19 июля в 2 часа дня – “The funeral [is] today, July 19th, at two p.m.” Note the term *похороны*, “funeral, burial,” which is plural in form. For *в 2 часа дня,* “at 2 p.m.,” see the discussion of expressions of time on pages 49-50.

Погребение на кладбище Одесского Землячества – “Burial [will be] at the Odessa Society Cemetery.” The term *землячество* comes from *земляк,* “fellow countrymen, one from the same area,” so a *землячество* is an organization of people from the same area. But that’s difficult to render in English; “Odessa Society” is reasonably close without sounding awkward.

Translation – “Isai Sherr, Savva Sherr, and family, sorrowfully announce the untimely passing of their dear sister and aunt, Bella Sherr. The remains are at Park West Memorial Chapel, 79th Street and Columbus Avenue. The funeral is today, July 19th, at 2 p.m. The burial will be at the Odessa Society Cemetery.”

Let us give several more brief examples for you to practice on. We don’t provide analysis, just the sample and the translation, with an occasional note on some interesting feature.

С глубоким прискорбием извещаю о скоропостижной
смерти
МОЕЙ ДОРОГОЙ И НЕЗАБВЕННОЙ ЖЕНЫ
ИУЛИИ ЗАХАРОВНЫ МЕРЗЛЯКОВОЙ
ПОСЛЕДОВАВШЕЙ 17 СЕГО ИЮЛЯ.
Тело находится в похоронном бюро Волтера Кука, Хилсит Авеню, Джэмейка. Похороны в четверг, 20 июля, в 1 час дня.

Document IV-4 *(at right)* – “With deep sorrow I announce the sudden death of my dear unforgettable wife, Iuliya Merzliakova, daughter of Zakhar, which occurred this July 17th. The undertaker is Voltaire Cook, Hilist Avenue, Jamaica*. The funeral is Thursday, July 20th, at 1 p.m.”

*Note: *Джемейка* is a phonetic Cyrillic rendering of *Jamaica,* as in “Jamaica, Queens, New York.” It’s interesting that the name of the island of Jamaica is rendered in standard Russian as *Ямайка*, “Yamaika,” but this spelling is a phonetic rendering by Russian immigrants of the name as they heard New Yorkers pronounce it when referring to the section of Queens. It might not be “proper” Russian, but at least it helps prevent confusion between this place and the Caribbean island!

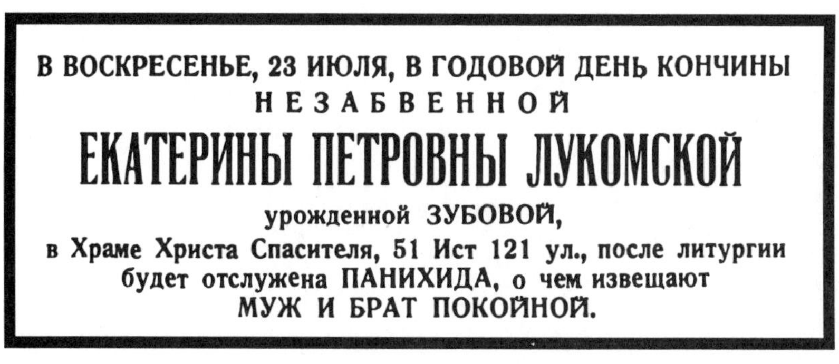
В ВОСКРЕСЕНЬЕ, 23 ИЮЛЯ, В ГОДОВОЙ ДЕНЬ КОНЧИНЫ
НЕЗАБВЕННОЙ
ЕКАТЕРИНЫ ПЕТРОВНЫ ЛУКОМСКОЙ
урожденной ЗУБОВОЙ,
в Храме Христа Спасителя, 51 Ист 121 ул., после литургии будет отслужена ПАНИХИДА, о чем извещают
МУЖ И БРАТ ПОКОЙНОЙ.

Document IV-5 *(at left)* – “On Sunday, July 23rd, the first anniversary of the passing of the unforgettable Yekaterina Lukomskaia, née Zubova, daughter of Pyotr, in the Cathedral of Christ the Savior, 51 East 121st Street, a requiem will be held after services, which is hereby announced by the husband and brother of the deceased.”

ЗАВТРА, 22 ИЮЛЯ, В ПОЛУГОДОВОЙ ДЕНЬ КОНЧИНЫ
КЛАВДИИ ДИМИТРИЕВНЫ КРАСОВСКОЙ
урожденной Препелица, вдовы последнего Председателя
Киевской Губернской Земской Управы
в 6.30 час. веч панихида в Храме Христа Спасителя, 51 Ист 121 улицо
а в воскресенье, 23 июля, после литургии панихида будет отслужена на
могиле покойной на кладбише монастыря Новое Дивеево.
о чем извещают СЫН и РОДНЫЕ.

Document IV-6 *(at left)* – "Tomorrow, July 22nd, on the six-month anniversary of the passing of Klavdiya Krakovskaia, née Prepelitsa, daughter of Dimitriy, widow of the last chairman of the Kiev Province *Zemstvo* Council, at 6:30 p.m. there will be a requiem in the Cathedral of Christ the Savior, 51 East 121st Street, and on Sunday, July 23rd, after services a requiem will be held at the grave of the deceased in the cemetery of the Monastery of Novoye Diveyevo, which is hereby announced by [her] son and relatives."

Document IV-7 *(at right)* – "On Saturday, July 29, on the second anniversary of the death of our beloved and unforgettable mother Anna Stepanovna Isayeva, a Mass for the repose of her soul will be said at 9 a.m. in the church of the Novoye Diveyevo monastery, followed at approximately 11 a.m. by a requiem at the grave of the deceased. Her daughter Elena and son-in-law Boris Mitrokin hereby inform her friends and acquaintances."

В СУББОТУ, 29 ИЮЛЯ, ВО ВТОРУЮ ГОДОВЩИНУ
смерти нашей любимой и незабвенной мамочки
АННЫ СТЕПАНОВНЫ ИСАЕВОЙ
будут отслужены: ЗАУПОКОЙНАЯ ЛИТУРГИЯ в церкви Ново-Дивеевского монастыря в 9 часов утра, а после литургии около 11 часов – ПАНИХИДА на могиле покойной, о чем извещают друзей и знакомых
дочь ЕЛЕНА и зять БОРИС МИТРОХИНЫ.

C. CEMETERY INSCRIPTIONS

Russian-American cemeteries, like those of other immigrant groups, frequently have gravestones with inscriptions in the language of the old country. These are especially valuable because the transliterated surname used by the family after immigrating to English-speaking countries may not have been totally accurate. An early ancestor's gravestone inscription in Cyrillic may be more accurate linguistically, and thus will assist you in identifying ancestors by using records created in Europe. For example, if the name as you've always seen it was spelled *Wasyleff* and you find a gravestone with the Cyrillic spelling *Васильев*, comparison of that form (which we'd render *Vasil'ev* in our alphabet) may help you find entries in records that you'd never have found looking under W-.

Of course there are other factors involved. If, for instance, the stonecutter who did the inscription knew nothing about Russian, the accuracy of the spelling he engraved could certainly suffer. Still, any form that might help you get closer to the original version of the name is potentially valuable, and worth looking for.

Please note that inscriptions on gravestones will almost always employ pre-Revolution orthography, retaining the archaic letters **ѣ** and **і** and **ъ** long after the use of those letters had been discontinued in Russia itself.

The following are several inscriptions taken from stones at the Holy Trinity Russian Orthodox Cemetery in New Britain, Connecticut. They should prove representative of inscriptions found in other Russian cemeteries in the New World.

Здѣсь почиваетъ Лаврентій Петровичъ Балдовскій
род. 29го янв. 1883 года
ум. 5го нояб. 1938 года

Здѣсь почиваетъ – a stock phrase meaning "Here rests…" Also seen is *здѣсь покоится* (or plural *покоятся*), which means the same thing.

Петрович – a patronymic (see pages 29 and 83). It tells us Lavrentiy's father was named *Пётр,* Pyotr (= English *Peter*). Female patronymics take the forms *–овна* or *-евна*, so that the daughter of a Pyotr would be called *Петровна*.

род. – this abbreviation stands for *родился* (if referring to a male) or *родилась* (for a female), and means "[he/she] was born." Note that dates are given in the genitive case, as discussed on page 47. Thus the ending ***го*** after the numerals indicates a genitive form for the day of the month, e. g., *5го* = *пятого*, "5th."

ум. – this abbreviation stands for *умер* (referring to a male) or *умерла* (for a female) and means "[he/she] died." Also frequently seen with the same meaning is *скон.*, short for *скончался* or *скончалась.*

Translation — "Here rests Lavrentiy Petrovich Baldovskiy, born 29 January 1883, died 5 November 1938."

Марія Игнатьева Груша
род. 1883 г.
ум. 12 февр. 1944 г.

Игнатьева, which we'd spell *Ignat'eva,* is a patronymic, from the first name *Игнатий,* equivalent to *Ignatius* in English. Normally we'd expect the feminine patronymic to be *Игнатьевна,* with *–евна*, not *-ева*. Perhaps the engraver omitted the *–н-* by mistake.

ум. 12 февр. – note that in this instance the genitive ending *–го* was not added to the numeral. This will vary from one stone to another. Technically this should be *12го,* but it would be an exaggeration to call this an "error"; it's more of slight deviation from standard usage.

Translation — "Mariya Grusha, daughter of Ignatiy, born 1883, died 12 February 1944." (Note, however, that if her family was of Polish descent, the Polish spelling *Grusza* would be the more appropriate version of her surname.)

Здѣсь почиваетъ Анна Степановна Панасевичъ
Грод. губ., сокольск. уѣзда, д. Ялово,
род. въ 1891 годъ
ум. 29-го сент. 1933 года
на 42емъ году жизни

Грод. губ., сокольск. уѣзда, д. Ялово – "Of Grodno province, Sokółka district, village of Jałowo." For more on these terms see the explanation on pages 83-84.

This individual, like many others in this particular cemetery, came from an area northeast of Białystok, Poland, served by the parish church in Jaczno. Since the area is now in Poland, it is proper to give the place names in Polish form, rather than in a form produced by transliterating the Russian name. Such a transliteration would result in versions you would not find on a contemporary map; but you can find Sokółka and Jałowo on good maps of that part of Poland.

Remember, in many Russian Orthodox parishes in America, the original immigrant parishioners were not always ethnic Great Russians, but descendants of Belarusian or Carpatho-Rusyn ancestors, whose first language in everyday life was not standard Russian. But since they lived in areas ruled by the Russian Empire, standard Russian was generally the *lingua franca* they were used to speaking in any formal context, especially after the Czarist government mandated use of Russian for official purposes. So you must be prepared to deal with versions of proper names (names of persons and places) in Russian form as well as in whatever language your ancestors actually spoke in everyday life.

There is not enough information provided to say for sure whether her name should be rendered Polish-style, "Anna Panasewicz, daughter of Stefan," or left as is. For that matter, *Panasiewicz* is also a feasible Polish rendering of *Панасевич*. The surname itself is of Ukrainian or Belarusian linguistic origin, meaning "son of Panas," an Eastern Slavic adaptation of the Greek name *Athanasios;* Poles seldom use this name, and when they do it is normally in the form *Atanazy*. On the other hand, the family lived in Polish territory, and may well have considered themselves Poles through and through. Sometimes numerous different versions of a person's name were equally applicable, and deciding which was "correct" is a dilemma that would baffle a Solomon!

на 42-ем году жизни – literally "in the 42nd year of life," i. e., she was in her 42nd year but had not yet completed it by celebrating her 42nd birthday. So we'd say she was 41.

Translation — "Here lies Anna Panasevich, daughter of Stepan, of Grodno province, Sokółka district, village of Jałowo, born in 1891, died 29 September 1933 in her 42nd year."

D. TERMS OFTEN FOUND IN OBITUARIES AND GRAVESTONE INSCRIPTIONS

The following are terms you are particularly likely to see in obituaries and gravestone inscriptions. It does not include most terms covered in previous vocabulary lists, with the exception of a few very basic words, because you can refer to those previous lists easily: the days of the week are on page 49; names of the months on page 47; other expressions of time on pages 49-50; family members see pages 51-52; and causes of death on pages 286-289. All these terms are also given in the master vocabulary list that comprises Chapter VII, page 358.

безвременный – (adj.) premature, untimely

болезнь, болезни – (n., fem., † *болѣзнь*) illness, disease

брак, брака – (n., masc.) marriage; *по первому браку Мейер*, by her first marriage Meyer

брат, брата – (n., masc., nom. pl. *братья*, gen. pl. *братьев*) brother; *двоюродный брат* – [male] cousin

будет → *быть*

быть – (v., irregular) to be; *будет* – [he, she, it] will be; *панихида будет отслужена* – a requiem will be said

бюро, бюро– (n., neut., not declined) office; *похоронное бюро*, undertaker's office

в – (*во* before certain consonant clusters, preposition + acc./prep., † *въ*) in[to], to

вдова, вдовы – (n., fem.) widow
вдовец, вдовца – (n., masc.) widower
веч., abbr. for *вечером*, "in the evening"
вечер, вечера – (n., masc.) evening; *вечером* – in the evening, p.m. (see page 50)
вечный – (adj., † *вѣчный*) eternal; *вечный ему покой* – [may God give] him eternal peace; *вечная память ему* – may his memory live forever
внук, внука – (n., masc.) grandson; (pl. *внуки*) grandchildren, grandsons
внучка, внучки – (n. fem.) granddaughter
вчера – (adv.) yesterday; *вчера вечером* – last evening, last night
г., abbr. for *год* ↓ or *город* ↓
герой, героя – (n., masc.) hero; *умереть смертью героя* – to die a hero's death
глубокий – (adj.) deep; *в глубоком горе* – in deep sorrow
год, года – (n., abbr. *г.*, masc., prep. sing. *годе* or *году* after *в* or *на*, nom. pl. *годы* or *года*, gen. pl. *годов* or *лет*, see pages 41 and 50) year; *текущего года* – this year; *в этом году* – this year; *в прошлом году* – last year; *на 42-ем году жизни* – in her 42nd year
годовой – (adj.) annual, one-year; *в годовой день* – on the first anniversary
годовщина, годовщины – (n., fem.) anniversary; *во вторую годовщину* – on the second anniversary
голод, голода – (n., masc.) hunger, starvation; famine; *умереть с голоду* – to die of starvation
голодный – (adj.) hungry, of hunger, famine, starvation; *умереть голодною смертью* – to starve, die of hunger
горе, горя – (n., neut.) sorrow, grief, distress; *в глубоком горе* – in deep sorrow
город, города – (n., abbr. *г.* or *гор.*, masc., nom. pl. *города*) town, city
гражданский – (adj., † *гражданскій*) civil
губерния, губернии – (n., fem., † *губернія*) *guberniya*, province
губернский – (adj., † *губернскій*) of a *губерния*, of a province, provincial
д., abbr. of *деревня* ↓
день, дня – (n., masc., see p. 41 for declension); *дня* – during the day, on such-and-such a day; *днём* – during the afternoon (see page 50)
деревня, деревни – (abbr. *д.*, n., fem., prep. sing., *деревни*, gen. pl. *деревень*) village
днём → *день*
дня → *день*
дорогой – (adj.) dear, darling; expensive (note: *дорогой* can also be the instr. sing. of the noun *дорога*, way, path)
дочь, дочери – (n., fem., instr. sing. *дочерью*, nom. pl. *дочери*, gen. pl. *дочерей*, instr. pl. *дочерьми*) daughter
друг, друга – (n., masc., nom. pl. *друзья*, gen. and acc. pl. *друзей*) friend
его – (personal and possessive pron., gen./acc. sing. of *он* and *оно*, see page 42) [of] him, [of] it; his, its
её – (personal and possessive pron., gen./acc. of *она*, see page 42) of her, of it, her, it, hers, its
ей – (personal pron., dat./instr. of *она*, see page 42) her, it, to her, to it
елеосвящение, елеосвящения – (n., neut., † *елеосвященіе*) Last Rites
ему – (personal pron., dat. of *он* and *оно*, see page 42) [to] him, [to] it
естественно – (adv.) naturally; *умереть естественно* – to die naturally
естественный – (adj.) natural; *естественная смерть* – a natural death; *умереть естественной смертью* – to die a natural death
жена, жены – (n., fem., nom. pl. *жёны*, gen. pl. *жён*) wife
жизнь, жизни – (n., fem.) life
за – (preposition): (+ instr.) behind, over, past, on the other side of, at, after, because of; (+ acc.) for, on behalf of, due to; in, within, before, at a distance of, by; *за 1910 год* – for the year 1910
завтра – (adv.) tomorrow
зараза, заразы – (n., fem.) infection, contagion
заразный – (adj.) infectious; *заразные болезни* – communicable diseases
заупокойный – (adj.) funeral, requiem, literally "for *[за]* the repose of the soul [*упокой*]" of one who has died
здесь – (adv., † *здѣсь*) here; *здѣсь почиваетъ* or *здѣсь покоится*, "here lies"
земляк, земляка – (n., masc.) fellow countryman, one who comes from the same area or village
землячество, землячества – (n., neut.) a society or association of *земляки*, people from the same area or country
земский – (adj., † *земскій*) of a *земство* (an elective district council in pre-Revolutionary Russia)
знакомый – (adj.) familiar, acquainted; (used as a n.) acquaintance, friend
зять, зятя – (n., masc., nom. pl. *зятья*, gen. pl. *зятьёв*) son-in-law; brother-in-law (sister's husband)
извещать – (v.) to notify, inform, make known; *извещает* – he informs, notifies; *извещают* – they inform, notify
кладбище, кладбища – (n., neut.) cemetery, graveyard

кончина, кончины – (n., fem.) death
костёл, костёла – (n., masc.) church (usually refers to a Polish Roman Catholic church, from Polish *kościół*, not a *церковь*, an Orthodox church)
ксёндз, ксёндза – (n., masc.) a Roman Catholic priest (from Polish *ksiądz*)
лето, лета – (n., neut., † *лѣто*) summer; in expressions of age *лет* († *лѣтъ*) means "years," see pages 41 and 50
литургия, литургии - (n., fem., † *литургія*) liturgy, mass, services
лѣтъ → *лето*
любимый – (pass. part. from *любить*, "to love") beloved
мамочка, мамочки – (n., fem.) "mom" or "mommy," an affectionate diminutive
мать, матери – (n., fem., instr. sing. *матерью*, nom. pl. *матери*, gen. pl. *матерей*) mother
месяц, месяца – (n., masc., † *мѣсяцъ*) month
муж, мужа – (n., masc., nom. pl. *мужья*, gen. pl. *мужей*, dat. pl. *мужьям*) husband
мѣсяцъ → *месяц*
на – (preposition + acc./prep.) on, upon; at, to; *на 42-ем году жизни* – in her 42nd year
насильственно – (adv.) violently; *умереть насильственно* – to die violently, by force
насильственный – (adj.) forcible, forced; *насильственная смерть* – violent death; *умереть насильственной смертью* – to die violently
находиться – (v.) to be found, be located, to be, to find oneself
незабвенный – (adj.) unforgettable, never to be forgotten
Ново-Дивеевский – (adj.) "of Novoye Diveyevo," an adjective formed from the name of a monastery
ночь, ночи – (n., fem.) night; *ночью* – at night (see page 50)
о – (*об* when the next word begins with a vowel, *обо* before certain consonant clusters, preposition + prep.) about, concerning
обедня, обедни – (n., fem., gen. pl. *обеден*, † *обѣдня*) religious service, Mass
обѣдня → *обедня*
отец, отца – (n., masc.) father
отслужена → *отслужить*
отслужить – (v.) to serve, celebrate; *панихида будет отслужена* –a requiem will be said
память, памяти – (n., fem.) memory; *в памяти* – in memory [of]; *вечная память ему* – may his memory live forever
панихида, панихиды – (n., fem.) requiem, service for the dead; *гражданская панихида* – civil funeral services; *панихида будет отслужена* – a requiem will be said
первый – (ordinal num./adj.) first; *двадцать первый* – twenty-first
по – (preposition): + dat., on, along, by, according to; *по первому браку Мейер*, by her first marriage Meyer; (+ acc.) to, up to; (+ prep.) on, after
погребение, погребения – (n., neut., † *погребеніе*) burial, interment
покоиться – (v.) to repose, rest, lie, be at rest; *здѣсь покоится* – here lies…
покой, покоя – (n., masc., nom. pl. *покои*, gen. pl. *покоев*) room; rest, repose; *вечный ему покой* – [may God give] him eternal peace
покойник, покойника – (n., masc.) the deceased [speaking of a male]
покойница, покойницы – (n., fem.) the deceased [speaking of a female]
покойный – (adj.) quiet, calm; the late, deceased (especially if used as a noun); *муж покойной* – the husband of the deceased
полугодовой – (adj.) half-year, six months; *в полугодовой день* – on the six-month anniversary
по полудни – (adv. expression) in the afternoon
после – (preposition + gen.) after
последний – (adj., † *послѣдній*) last, latest
последовавший – (adj., † *послѣдовавшій*, part. from the verb *последовать*) having occurred
похоронный – (adj.) [of a] funeral; *похоронное бюро* – undertaker's office, establishment
похороны, похорон – (n., fem. pl.) burial, funeral
почивать – (v.) to lie, be at rest; *здѣсь почиваетъ* – here lies…
почивший, почившего – (part. of *почить*, to rest, used as a noun, † *почившій*) the deceased; *семья почившего* – the family of the deceased
председатель, председателя – (n., masc., † *предсѣдатель*) president, chairman
припадок, припадка – (n., masc.) fit, attack
прискорбие, прискорбия– (n., neut., † *прискорбіе*) sorrow, regret
приход, прихода – (n., masc.) parish; also receipt, income
приходский – (adj., † *приходскій*) [of a] parish, parochial; *приходский священник* – parish priest; *приходская церковь* – parish church
продолжительный – (adj.) prolonged, lengthy
раб, раба – (n., masc.) servant; *рабъ божій* – servant of God
рана, раны – (n., fem.) wound
род., abbr. of *родился* or *родилась* or *родились* → *родиться*

родители, родителей – (n., pl.) parents
родиться – (v.) to be born; *он родился* – he was born; *она родилась* – she was born; *они родились* – they were born
родной – (adj.) one's own, full, as in the expressions *родной брат*, full brother (not a half brother); native, e. g., *родной язык*, native tongue; also used in the pl. *родные, родных*, to mean "relatives"
Россия, России – (n., fem., † *Россія*) Russia
русский – (adj.) Russian
свой – (reflexive adj.) my own, your own, our own, his own, her own, its own, their own; *своей смертью умереть* – to die a natural death
святой – (adj.) holy; (used as a n., abbr. *св.*) *святой, святого* (m.), *святая, святой* (f.) – saint
священник, священника – (n., masc.) priest (generally an Orthodox priest, as opposed to a Catholic *ксёндз*, q. v.)
сего – (gen. of *сей*) this; "on the 14th of this July," e. g., *14 сего июля*, this July 14th
сегодня – (adv.) today
семья, семьи – (n., fem., nom. pl. *семьи*, gen. pl. *семей*) family; *с семей*, with family, and family
сердечный – (adj.) of the heart; *сердечный припадок* – heart attack; *сердечная болезнь* – heart disease
сестра, сестры – (n., fem., nom. pl. *сёстры*, gen. pl. *сестёр*) sister; *двоюродная сестра* – [female] cousin
скон., abbr. for *скончался* or *скончалась* → *скончаться*
скончаться – (abbrev. *скон.*, v.) to die, pass away; *скончался* – he passed away; *скончалась* – she passed away
скоропостижно – (adv.) suddenly, unexpectedly
скоропостижный – (adj.) sudden, unexpected; *скоропостижная смерть*, sudden death
случай, случая – (n., masc.) case, incident, event, circumstance; *в случае нужды* – in case of need, if need be; *в таком случае* – in that case; *несчастный случай* – accident
смерть, смерти – (n., fem.) death; *естественная смерть* – natural death; *насильственная смерть* – violent death; *голодная смерть* – starvation; *своей смертью умереть* – to die a natural death
супруг, супруга – (n., masc.) spouse, husband
супруга, супруги – (n., fem.) spouse, wife
сын, сына – (n., masc., nom. pl. *сыновья*, gen. pl. *сыновей*) son
тело, тела – (n., neut., † *тѣло*) body
тётя, тёти – (n., fem., gen. pl. *тётей*) aunt
тихо – (adv.) quietly
тѣло → *тело*
тяжкий – (adj.) serious, grave, heavy
уезд, уезда (n., masc., † *уѣздъ*) district, a group of *volost's; уездный город*, chief town of a district
ул., abbr. for *улица*
улица, улицы – (n., fem.) street
ум., abbr. of *умер* or *умерла* or *умерли* → *умереть*
умереть – (v.; imperf. aspect *умирать*) to die (*от* + gen.) to die, e. g., *умер от раны*, he died of his wound; *умер* – he died; *умерла* – she died; *умерли* – they died; *умереть с голоду* – to die of starvation; *умереть смертью героя* – to die a hero's death; *умереть скоропостижно* – to die suddenly, unexpectedly; *умереть естественно* or *естественной смертью* – to die a natural death; *умереть насильственно* or *насильственной смертью* – to die violently; *умереть за дело* – to die for the cause
умерший – (part., † *умершій*) dead, deceased
умирать → *умереть*
умирающий – (pres. act. part. of *умирать*) dying; (used as a n.) the dying one
управа, управы – (n., fem.) board, council
урождённый – (part.) born, by birth; (used with fem. names) née
усопший – (adj., † *усопшій*) deceased, dead
утро, утра – (n., neut.) morning; *утром* – in the morning, a. m. (see page 50)
уѣздъ → *уезд*
храм, храма – (n., masc.) cathedral, temple
царство, царства – (n., neut.) kingdom; *царство ему небесное* – may the Kingdom of Heaven be his!
церковь, церкви – (n., fem.) church (usually refers to an Orthodox church, as opposed to a *костёл*, a Polish Catholic church, from Polish *kościół*)
час, часа – (n., masc.) time, hour, o'clock (see pages 49-50)

E. RUSSIAN CONSULAR RECORDS

The records of the consulate of the Russian Imperial Government in the United States were seized by the U. S. State Department in 1933, the year the U. S. recognized the Soviet Union as a nation. In 1949 the records were transferred to the custody of the National Archives.

Among the records procured were those pertaining to the activities of various Russian Imperial Consulates in the U. S. Several of the record types in this collection—namely those dealing with passports, citizenship status, and estates of deceased persons, to name but a few—are of unquestionable genealogical value.

The consulates for which records are available include Chicago (15 boxes); Honolulu (2 boxes); New York (141 boxes); Philadelphia (64 boxes); Portland (6 boxes); San Francisco (95 boxes); and Seattle (16 boxes). It is felt that these preserved boxes of materials are a mere fraction of the records, many of which were lost or destroyed over the years.

In the 1980s volunteers from the Jewish Genealogical Society of Washington, D.C., in cooperation with the National Archives, indexed these records. A name index was prepared, coded according to the **Daitch-Mokotoff Soundex System**, a method different from the Soundex used in other National Archives record groups, designed to deal better with the phonetic tendencies of the languages spoken in central and eastern Europe. This index is available in both print and microfiche format. One vendor selling the index is Avotaynu, Inc.; as of this writing, its address is Avotaynu, Inc., P. O. Box 99, Bergenfield NJ 07621, 1-800-286-8296, **http://www.avotaynu.com**. Microfilm copies of the records can be consulted by researchers at most branches of the National Archives.

Because the Russian Empire was an ethnically diverse nation, records in this collection pertain not only to Great Russians but also to Jews, Poles, Finns, Armenians, and others. Some of the material is not in Russian, but in the languages of the groups enumerated. There is also quite a bit of material, mostly correspondence, either in English or bilingually rendered in Russian and English.

Offered below are several representative document types to assist you in translating the records contained in this collection, if you are fortunate enough to locate any for your family.

1. Document IV-8: Notarized Attestation for Obtaining Traveling Papers

Document IV-8, reproduced on page 95, is an *удостовѣренiе*, a statement or attestation, sworn before a notary by a husband and father for the purpose of obtaining traveling papers for his wife and children. Here is a quick overview of what it says:

Дано сiе отъ меня нижеподписавшагося *Абрама Хачкеловича Шакера, черноховскiй мѣщанинъ*– "This [was] given by me, the undersigned Abram Khachkelovich Shaker, a townsman from Chernikhov."

временнопроживающаго въ городѣ *Филадельфiи* штата *Пеннсилванiя* Соединенныхъ Штатовъ Сѣверной Америки – "temporarily residing in the city of Philadelphia of the state of Pennsylvania of the United States of North America."

въ томъ, что о выдачѣ какъ внутренняго такъ и заграничняго паспортовъ, а равно и другихъ надлежащихъ документовъ – "for the purpose of issuing both internal and foreign passports, as well as other appropriate documents."

BERNHARD BEERGER
NOTARY PUBLIC
710 South 5th Street
PHILADELPHIA, PA., U. S. A.

БЕРНГАРДЪ БИРГЕРЪ
Публичный Нотаріусъ
На южной 5-ой улицѣ
подъ No. 710
Филадельфія, Па.

УДОСТОВѢРЕНІЕ.

Дано сіе отъ меня нижеподписавшагося Абрама Хаскелевича Шакера, Черниговскій Мѣщанинъ временнопроживающаго въ городѣ Филадельфіи штата Пенсильваніи Соединенныхъ Штатовъ Сѣверной Америки въ томъ, что о выдачѣ какъ внутренняго такъ и заграничняго паспортовъ, а равно и другихъ надлежащихъ документовъ женѣ моей Перль Мовшовнѣ съ малолѣтними дочерями Бертою Зисель Ховой и Сыномъ Мотелемъ согласно 11-ой ст. уст. Положенія о видахъ на жительство въ Россійской Имперіи а также и для выѣзда заграницу, съ моей стороны препятствій никакого рода не имѣется.

Городъ Филаделфія Февраля 20 дня (н. с.) 1911 года

Знакомъ (+) Абрамъ Хаскелевичъ Шакеръ

О собственноручной подписи вышесказаннаго Абрама Хаскелевича Шакера

а равно и о самоличности вышесказаннаго Шакера

и что онъ Абрамъ Хаскелевичъ Шакеръ

заслуживаетъ законное довѣріе

Я БЕРНГАРДЪ БИРГЕРЪ, состоящій публичнымъ Нотаріусомъ въ городѣ Филадельфіи, имѣющій свою нотаріальную контору въ собственномъ домѣ на южной 5-ой улицѣ подъ No. 710 надлежащей подписью съ приложеніемъ нотаріальной печати удостовѣряю.

Городъ Филадельфія, Февраля 20 дня (н. с.) 1911 года

Б. Биргеръ

ПУБЛИЧНЫЙ НОТАРІУСЪ

Document IV-8: Notarized Attestation for Obtaining Traveling Papers

женѣ моей, *Перлѣ Мовшовнѣ съ моими малолѣтными двумя дѣтьми дочерью Хавой и сыномъ Мотелемъ* – "to my wife, Perla Movshovna, with my two minor children, daughter Chava and son Motel."

согласно 11-ой ст. уст. Положенія о видахъ на жительство въ Россійской Имперіи а также и для выѣзда заграницу, съ моей стороны препятствіи никакого рода не имѣется – "in accordance with article 11 of the act regulating identity cards in the Russian Empire, and also for travel abroad; for my part there is no impediment of any sort."

Городъ Филаделфія *Февраля 6го* дня (н. с.) 19*11 года* – "[Dated] City of Philadelphia, February 6, 1911." Note that *(н. с.)* stands for *новаго стиля*, "of the New Style," meaning the date according to the Gregorian calendar, as used in the United States, rather than the Julian calendar, which was still in official use in Russia at this point.

/Значитъ/ Абрамъ Хачкеловичъ Шакеръ

Note that Abram Shaker signs his name in characters of the Hebrew alphabet. Under that is the word *Значитъ*, "[that] means," followed by his name as written in Cyrillic script. This is not unusual in documents dealing with Jews; often they knew how to sign their names, but only in Hebrew letters (see pages 18-20). This formula was used so that they could provide authentic signatures in their own hands, but the name could also be given in a form recognizable to those who didn't read Hebrew or Yiddish—not languages commonly mastered by Russian bureaucrats. In fact Russian regulations required giving the name in Cyrillic form, with emphasis on consistent rendering of Jewish names.

It's interesting, however, that Abram's patronymic in Russian is *Хачкеловичъ*, with the third letter clearly **ч**, which represents a *ch* sound. But his signature in Hebrew appears to read *Abram ben Khatskel Shaker,* which indicates his father's name was actually *Khatskel*—the more normal form of the name. A more accurate Cyrillic patronymic form would have been *Хацкеловичъ*, with the letter **ц** instead of **ч**. Given the Russian bureaucracy's emphasis on consistent and accurate spelling of Jewish names, this inaccuracy is puzzling. It just shows you can't afford to take anything for granted!

О собственноручной подписи *вышесказаннаго Абрама Хачкеловича Шакера* а равно и о самоличности вышесказаннаго *Шакера* и что онъ *Абрамъ Хачкеловичъ Шакеръ* заслуживаетъ законное довѣріе. – "As to the signature in his own hand of the aforesaid Abram Khachkelovich Shaker, as well as the personal identity of the aforesaid Shaker, and that he, Abram Khachkelovich Shaker, deserves the confidence of the law."

Я Бернгардъ Биргеръ, состоящій публичнымъ Нотаріусомъ въ городѣ Филадельфіи, имѣющій свою нотаріальную контору въ собственномъ домѣ на южной 5-ой улицѣ подъ No. 710 надлежащей подписью съ приложеніемъ нотаріальной печати удостовѣраю. Городъ Филадельфія, Февраля *6go* дня (н. с.) 19*11* goda. *Б. Биргеръ, Публичный Нотаріусъ.*– "...I, Bernhard Beerger, Notary Public in the city of Philadelphia, having my notarial office in my own house at 710 South 5th Street, certify with the appropriate signature and affixing of the notarial seal. City of Philadelphia, February 6, 1911. B. Beerger, Notary Public."

2. Document IV-9: A Questionnaire (Passport Application)

Document IV-9, reproduced on pages 98 and 101, is an *опросный лист*, literally "questionnaire," but in fact a passport application. A photograph usually appears in the upper left hand corner of the document. The paragraph under the photo is a statement that the Russian Consulate attests that the photo is a true likeness of the applicant. A small number of the applications in this collection are filled out in English in response to the questions posed in Russian. Most of these documents, however, feature answers in Russian as well. The terms and phrases seen here appear in many other documents and deserve a close look.

This particular application is typed, but many of the documents of this nature are not. So we have also included **Document IV-10** on pages 103-106, with the answers written in by hand, so that between the two of them you should be able to deal with either kind.

Опросный листъ – "Questionnaire"

возвращающагося въ Россію черезъ пограничный пунктъ Канада и Японія – "of one returning to Russia via the border point Canada and Japan"

возвращаться – (v.) to return; thus the present active participle, *возвращающийся*, means "returning," or used as a noun, "one returning"

Россия, России – (n., fem., † *Россія*) Russia; *в Россию* – [in]to Russia

пограничный – (adj.) border, frontier

пункт, пункта – (n., masc.) point, place, station; paragraph, item

1. Имя (если таковыхъ нѣсколько, то слѣдуетъ поименовать всѣ): Давидъ – "1. Name (if there are several, then all are to be given): David."

имя, имени – (n., neut., see page 41 for declension) first name, given name(s)

если – (conj.) if

таковый – (adj.) such, of this sort, the same; *если таковые имеют* – if any

несколько (adv., † *нѣсколько*) several; *если таковых несколько* – if there are several of these, if there are several of them

то – (conj.) as a conjunction following a clause introduced with *если*, "if," *то* is used much like "then" in English "if ... then" expressions

следует – literally "it follows," but *следует X* often means "X is to be done"

поименовать – (v.) to name, mention

все – (pron., † *всѣ*) plural nominative of *весь*, "all"

Давидъ – the first name *David*, spelled phonetically

2. Фамилія (сложныя фамиліи выписываются полностью; замужнія, разведенныя и вдовы указываютъ также свои дѣвичьи фамиліи: Мушкатъ – "Surname (compound surnames are to be written out in full; married women, divorced women, and widows provide their maiden surnames): Mushkat."

фамилия, фамилии – (n., fem., † *фамилія*) surname

сложный – (adj.) compound; the ending *–ыя* is archaic, in modern Russian this word would be spelled *сложные*, a nominative plural form modifying *фамилии*

выписывать – (v.) to extract, copy, write out; the reflexive version *выписываться* means the same thing in the passive (to be extracted, to be copied, to be written out)

Россійское Генеральное Консульство въ Нью Іоркѣ симъ удостовѣряетъ съ приложеніемъ казенной печати, что настоящая фотографическая карточка дѣйствительно изображаетъ

....

Генеральный Консулъ

ОПРОСНЫЙ ЛИСТЪ

возвращающагося въ Россію черезъ пограничный пунктъ Канада и Японія

1. Имя (если таковыхъ нѣсколько, то слѣдуетъ поименовать всѣ).	Давидъ
2. Фамилія (сложныя фамиліи выписываются полностью; замужнія, разведенныя и вдовы указываютъ также свои дѣвичьи фамиліи).	Мушкатъ
3. Званіе.	Крестьянинъ
4. Родъ занятій.	прикаэчикъ
5. Сословіе и мѣсто приписки.	Крестьянинъ Іодской вол. Вилен. губ.
6. Точное время и мѣсто рожденія.	Мая 15 дня, 1884 года.
7. Семейное положеніе (холостъ или женатъ, дѣвица, замужняя, вдова или разведенная; если есть дѣти, то ихъ имена и возрастъ).	Холоостъ
8. Отношеніе къ воинской повинности	Отбылъ

Document IV-9: A Questionnaire (Passport Application), First Page

полностью – (instr. sing. of † *полность, полности*) completely, utterly, fully, in full
замужняя – (adj.) married (said only of women, never men); (used as a n., *замужняя, замужней*, nom. pl. *замужние* † *замужныя*) married woman

разведённый – (adj.) divorced; (used as a n., masc. *разведённый, разведённого*) divorcé; (used as a fem. n., *разведённая, разведённой*) divorcée, divorced woman
вдова, вдовы – (n., fem.) widow
указывать – (v.) to indicate, point out, show, direct
свой – (refl. poss. adj.) his [own], her [own], their [own], etc.
девичий – (adj., † *дѣвичій*) maiden, virginal; *девичья фамилия* – maiden name

3. Званіе: Крестьянинъ – "Status: peasant"
звание, звания – (n., neut., † *званіе*) calling, state, station, condition
крестьянин, крестьянина – (n., masc.) peasant, farmer

4. Родъ занятій: Приказчикъ – "Nature of occupation: shop assistant" (for other possibilities see the list of terms for occupations on pages 53-72).
род, рода – (n., masc.) kind, nature, type
занятие, занятия – (n., neut., † *занятіе*) occupation, pursuit, work
приказчик, приказчика – (n., masc.) shop assistant

5. Сословіе и мѣсто приписки: Крестьянинъ Іодской вол. Вилен. губ. – "Social class and place of registration: Peasant of Iody district, Vil'na province"
сословие, сословия – (n., neut., † *сословіе*) estate, social class
место, места – (n., neut., † *мѣсто*) place
приписка, приписки – (n., fem.) registration
Іодский – (adj.) "of Iody," a place now in Belarus, in the *oblast'* of Vitsebsk, south of Braslav. In old Russian it was spelled *Іоды*, in modern Russian *Иоды*, in Belarusian *Еды*. On Polish maps it appears as *Joda*, and on Lithuanian ones as *Júodas*. This multiplicity of renditions of places names is a phenomenon the researcher must deal with when trying to locate places on a map—especially in this region of the world.

6. Точное время и мѣсто рожденія: Мая I5 дня, I884 года. – "Exact time and place of birth: May 15, 1884."
точный – (adj.) exact, precise
время, времени – (n., neut.) time
рождение, рождения – (n., neut., † *рожденіе*) birth; *место рождения* – place of birth
Мая 15 дня, 1884 года – May 15, 1884. Note the American influence on the format of the date; Russian would normally give it in the form day-month-year.

7. Семейное положеніе (холостъ или женатъ, дѣвица, замужняя, вдова или разведенная; если есть дѣти, то ихъ имена и возрастъ): Холостъ. – Marital status (single or married male, unmarried woman, married woman, widow, or divorcée; if there are children, then give their names and ages): Single.
семейный – (adj.) family, of family, domestic
положение, положения – (n., neut., † *положеніе*) situation, position; *семейное положение* – though "marital status" is not a literal translation (literally it's "family situation"), that is how we normally say the same thing in English.
холостой – (adj., short form *холост*) single, unmarried

женатый – (adj., short form *женат*) married, said only of males
девица, девицы – (n., fem., † *дѣвица*) girl, maiden, unmarried woman
замужняя, вдова, разведенная – see note to item 2, pages 98-99
есть – (verb, 3rd person plural present tense of *быть*, to be) there are
дети, детей – (n., pl., † *дѣти*) children
их – (gen. of *они*, "they") their, of them
возраст, возраста – (n., masc.) age

8. Отношеніе къ воинской повинности: `Отбылъ` – Status as to military obligation: served.
отношение, отношения – (n., neut. † *отношеніе*) attitude, relation, relationship
к – (preposition + dat., before certain consonant clusters *ко*) to, toward, for
повинность, повинности – (n., fem.) duty; *воинская повинность* – military service
отбыть – (v., conjugated like *быть* with *от-* prefixed) to serve (time); here *отбыл* means "he has served [his time in the military]." Other applications might give details such as whether he was in the reserves, the name of the unit in which he served, etc.

9. Годъ призыва на военную службу: `1914 г.` – Year called into military service: 1914.
призыв, призыва – (n., masc.) call, appeal, summons, levy
военный – (adj.) military
служба, службы – (n., fem.) service; *военная служба* – military service; *на военной службе* – in the service, in the armed forces; *призыв на военную службу* – conscription into the armed forces

10. Настоящее мѣсто жительства и съ какого времени: `Въ Штатѣ Конекдикутъ` – Present place of residence and since when: In the state of Connecticut.
настоящий – (adj., † *настоящій*) present, actual
жительство, жительства – (n., neut.) residence
какой – (adj.) what, what kind of; *с какого времени* – since what time, i. e., for how long? Note that this question is not answered.
Конекдикут – an attempt at a phonetic spelling of "Connecticut"

11. Мѣста жительства въ теченіи послѣднихъ 5 лѣтъ: `Въ Штатѣ Конекдикутъ` – Places of residence during the last 5 years: In the state of Connecticut.
течение, течения – (n., neut., † *теченіе*) current, stream, course; *в течении* – in the course of, during
последний – (adj., † *послѣдній*) last

12. Имена и мѣста жительства родителей (если родителей нѣтъ въ живыхъ, то указать гдѣ проживали въ послѣдніе годы жизни): `Не знаю гдѣ они теперь` – Parents' names and places of residence (if the parents are no longer living, then indicate where they lived during the last years of their lives): I do not know where they are now.
родители, родителей – (n., in modern Russian used only in the plural) parents
нет – (adv.) no; used with the genitive it means "are not, there are none," so that *если родителей нет* means "if there are no parents"
живой – (adj.) alive, living; *в живых* – among the living; *если родителей нет в живых* – if the parents are not alive (literally "if there are no parents among the living")

9. Годъ призыва на военную службу.	1914 г.
10. Настоящее мѣсто жительства и съ какого времени.	Въ Штатѣ Конекдикутъ
11. Мѣста жительства въ теченіи послѣднихъ 5 лѣтъ.	Въ Штатѣ Конекдикутъ
12. Имена и мѣста жительства родителей (если родителей нѣтъ въ живыхъ, то указать гдѣ проживали въ послѣдніе годы жизни).	Не знаю гдѣ они теперь
13. Религія.	Удейское
14. Національность.	Российскій гражданинъ
15. Подданство.	Бывшій Русскій подданный
16. Подданство родителей.	Тоже.
17. Если проситель перешелъ изъ иностраннаго подданства, то изъ какого и когда именно.	Не переходилъ
18. Куда именно въ Россію направляется.	Въ Москву.
19. Точное указаніе цѣли поѣздки и перечисленіе представляемыхъ въ удостовѣреніе документовъ.	Возвращаюсь на родину
20. Если имѣются въ Россіи родственники, то указать ихъ имена и мѣста жительства.	Не знаю гдѣ они теперь
21. Поѣздки заграницу въ теченіи послѣднихъ 3 лѣтъ (съ точнымъ указаніемъ времени выѣзда и возвращенія, пунктовъ переѣзда черезъ границу, цѣли поѣздки и продолжительности пребыванія въ каждомъ изъ иностранныхъ государствъ).	Никуда не ѣздилъ.

....Іюня..5..дня........191 8

(Подпись) 

Document IV-9, second page

указать – (v., perf. counterpart of *указывать*) to indicate, point, show, direct
где – (adv., † *гдѣ*) where
проживать – (v.) to live
жизнь, жизни – (n., fem.) life; *в последние годы жизни* – in the last years of [their] lives
знать – (v.) to know; *не знаю* – I do not know
теперь – (adv.) now; *не знаю, где они теперь* – I don't know where they are now

13. Религія: Удейское – Religion: Jewish.

религия, религии – (n., fem.) religion

иудейский – (adj., † *іудейскій*) Jewish; the spelling on this form, *Удейское*, is a typo, it should read *Іудейское.* Other possibilities are: *православный*, Orthodox; *римско-католический*, Roman Catholic; *греко-католический*, Greek Catholic; *лютернский*, Lutheran; and *еврейский*, another way of saying "Jewish."

14. Національность: Россійскій гражданинъ – Nationality: Russian citizen.

национальность, национальности – (n., fem., † *національность*) nationality

гражданин, гражданина – (n., masc.) citizen. Here one may see information on ethnic or religious origin, e. g., *еврей*, Jew, *поляк*, Pole, *литовец*, Lithuanian, *армянин*, Armenian, *Финн*, Finn, etc.

15. Подданство: бывшій Русскій подданный – Citizenship: former Russian citizen.

поддансво, подданства – (n., neut.) citizenship

бывший – (adj., † *бывшій*, past active participle of *быть*, to be) former, one-time

подданный, подданого – (adj. used as a n., or if used as a fem. n., *подданная, подданной*) subject, citizen

16. Подданство родителей: Тоже – Parents' citizenship: The same.

тоже – (adv.) also, here used as a short way of saying "[They are] also [Russian citizens]."

17. Если проситель перешелъ изъ иностраннаго подданства, то изъ какого и когда именно: Не переходилъ – If the petitioner changed his citizenship from a foreign one, from which one and when precisely: he has not changed it.

проситель, просителя – (n., masc.) applicant, petitioner, one who asks for something

перейти – (v., past tense *он перешел*) to cross, pass. This verb has many meanings, all connected with the idea of "to go *[идти]* over or through *[пере-]*." The usage here involves the applicant's having "crossed over" from one citizenship to another.

иностранный – (adj.) foreign, literally "of another *[иной]* country *[страна]*."

когда – (interrogative) when?

именно – (adv.) exactly, precisely

18. Куда именно въ Россію направляется: Въ Москву – Bound for where, exactly, in Russia? To Moscow.

куда – (adv.) to where?

направляться – to be bound, headed, to make one's way, direct one's steps

19. Точное указаніе цѣли поѣздки и перечисленіе представляемыхъ въ удостовѣреніе документовъ: Возвращаюсь на родину – Exact indication of the purpose of the journey, and enumeration of documents provided for certification: I am returning to my homeland.

указание, указания – (n., neut., † *указаніе*) indication

цель, цели – (n., fem., † *цѣль*) aim, goal, objective, purpose

поездка, поездки – (n., fem., † *поѣздка*) journey, trip

перечисление, перечисления – (n., neut., † *перечисленіе*) enumeration *представляемый* – (part. from the v. *представлять,* to present) presented

удостоверение, удостоверения – (n., neut., † *удостовѣреніе*) certification; *в удостоверение,* in witness (of), in certification

возвращаться – (v.) to return, come back; *возвращаюсь* – I return, am returning

родина, родины – (n., fem.) native land, homeland, motherland; *на родину* – to the motherland, to one's homeland

20. Если имѣются въ Россіи родственники, то указать ихъ имена и мѣста жительства: Не знаю гдѣ они теперь – If there are any relatives in Russia, indicate their names and places of residence: I do not know where they are now.

родственник, родственника – (n., masc.) relative

21. Поѣздки заграницу въ теченіи послѣднихъ 3 лѣтъ (съ точнымъ указаніемъ времени выѣзда и возвращенія, пунктовъ переѣзда черезъ границу, цѣли поѣздки и продолжительности пребыванія въ каждомъ изъ иностранныхъ государствъ: Никуда не ѣздилъ – Trips abroad over the last 3 years (with precise indication of the time of departure and return, border crossing points, purpose of the journey, and duration of stay in each of the foreign countries: Did not go anywhere.

выезд, выезда (n., masc., † *выѣздъ*)– departure

возвращение, возвращения – (n., neut., † *возвращеніе*) return

переезд, переезда – (n., masc., † *переѣздъ*) crossing; *пункт переезда* – crossing point

через – (preposition + acc.) across, through; (with expressions of time) in, after

граница, границы – (n., fem.) border, boundary

продолжительность, продолжительности – (n., fem.) duration

пребывание, пребывания – (n., neut., † *пребываніе*) stay, sojourn, residence

каждый – (adj.) each

государство, государства – (n., neut.) country, state, nation

никуда – (adv.) to nowhere

ездить – (v., † *ѣздить*) to travel, go; *никуда не ездил* – went nowhere

The document is dated *Июня 5 дня 1918*, June 5, 1918. The petitioner's signature *[подпись]* appears at the bottom right, *І. Мушкатъ* (I. Mushkat).

3. Document IV-10: A Handwritten Passport Application

Document IV-10, reproduced on pages 104 and 105, is exactly the same kind of questionnaire or passport application, except the responses are handwritten rather than typed. If you have occasion to deal with this sort of document, it may help you a great deal to have these two samples to study, especially when it comes to deciphering handwritten answers.

Why not see if you can decipher most of the information given in this document before you read the answers below? Here are a few words you have not encountered before:

заработок, заработка – (n., masc.) earnings, money; *уходить на заработки* – to leave to go earn a living

моряк, моряка – (n., masc.) sailor, seaman

отправиться – (v.) to set out, depart, leave; *отправиться пароходом* – to leave by ship

Россійское Генеральное Консульство въ Нью Іоркѣ симъ удостовѣряетъ съ приложеніемъ казенной печати, что настоящая фотографическая карточка дѣйствительно изображаетъ

....

Генеральный Консулъ

ОПРОСНЫЙ ЛИСТЪ

....

возвращающагося въ Россію черезъ пограничный пунктъ..................

1. Имя (если таковыхъ нѣсколько, то слѣдуетъ поименовать всѣ).	Лейба Фроимовъ
2. Фамилія (сложныя фамиліи выписываются полностью; замужнія, разведенныя и вдовы указываютъ также свои дѣвичьи фамиліи)	Меринъ
3. Званіе.	Руский Гражданинъ
4. Родъ занятій.	Морякъ
5. Сословіе и мѣсто приписки.	житель Города Радомысля, Кіевской Губерніи
6. Точное время и мѣсто рожденія.	15 Октября 1882 г. въ гор. Радомысле
7. Семейное положеніе (холостъ или женатъ, дѣвица, замужняя, вдова или разведенная; если есть дѣти, то ихъ имена и возрастъ).	"
8. Отношеніе къ воинской повинности.	отбылъ

Document IV-10 (page 1)

Here is the information contained in this application:

1. Name (if there are several of these, then all are to be given): *Leiba Froimov [Лейба Фроимовъ]*
2. Surname (compound surnames are to be written out in full; married women, divorced women, and widows provide their maiden surnames): *Merin [Меринъ]*
3. Status: *Russian citizen [Русскій гражданинъ]*

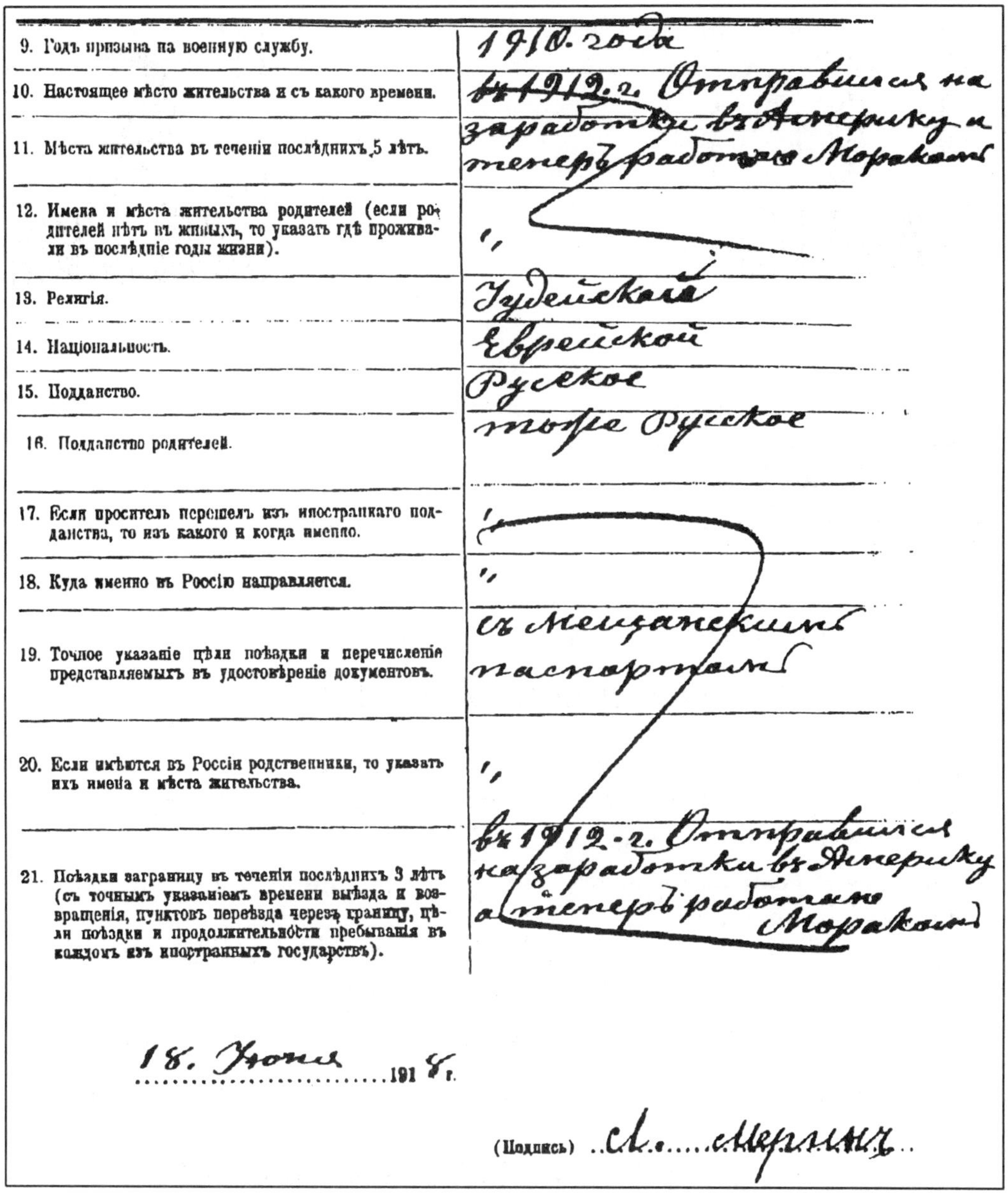

9. Годъ призыва на военную службу. — 1910 года

10. Настоящее мѣсто жительства и съ какого времени. — въ 1912 г. Отправился на заработки въ Америку и теперь работаю Морякомъ

11. Мѣста жительства въ теченіи послѣднихъ 5 лѣтъ.

12. Имена и мѣста жительства родителей (если родителей нѣтъ въ живыхъ, то указать гдѣ проживали въ послѣдніе годы жизни). — "

13. Религія. — Іудейскаго

14. Національность. — Еврейской

15. Подданство. — Руское

16. Подданство родителей. — тоже Руское

17. Если проситель перешелъ изъ иностраннаго подданства, то изъ какого и когда именно. — "

18. Куда именно въ Россію направляется. — "

19. Точное указаніе цѣли поѣздки и перечисленіе представляемыхъ въ удостовѣреніе документовъ. — съ Мещанскимъ паспортомъ

20. Если имѣются въ Россіи родственники, то указать ихъ имена и мѣста жительства. — "

21. Поѣздки заграницу въ теченіи послѣднихъ 3 лѣтъ (съ точнымъ указаніемъ времени выѣзда и возвращенія, пунктовъ переѣзда черезъ границу, цѣли поѣздки и продолжительности пребыванія въ каждомъ изъ иностранныхъ государствъ). — въ 1912 г. Отправился на заработки въ Америку а теперь работаю Морякомъ

18. Іюня 1918 г.

(Подпись)

Document IV-10 (page 2)

4. Nature of occupation: *seaman [морякъ]*
5. Social class and place of registration: *resident of the town of Radomyśl, province of Kiev [житель Города Радомысля, Кіевской Губерніи]*
6. Exact time and place of birth: *15 October 1882, in the town of Radomyśl [15. Октября 1882 г., въ гор. Радомысле]*
7. Marital status (single or married, unmarried woman, widow, or divorcée; if there are children, then give their names and ages): —.
8. Status as to military obligation: *served [отбылъ]*
9. Year called into military service: *1910 [1910 года]*
10. Present place of residence and since when: *in 1912 set out for America to earn a living, and now I work as a seaman [въ 1912 г. отправился на заработки въ Америку и теперь работаю морякомъ]*

11. Place of residence during the last 5 years: —.
12. Parents' names and places of residence (if the parents are no longer living, then indicate where they lived during the last years of their lives): —.
13. Religion: *Jewish [Iудейской]*
14. Nationality: *Hebrew [Еврейской]*
15. Citizenship: *Russian [Русское]*
16. Parents' citizenship: *Also Russian [тоже Русское]*.
17. If the petitioner changed his citizenship from a foreign one, from which one and when precisely: —
18. Bound for where, exactly, in Russia: —
19. Exact indication of the purpose of the journey, and enumeration of documents provided for certification: *with a townsman's passport [съ мещанскимъ паспортомъ]*
20. If there are any relatives in Russia, indicate their names and places of residence: —
21. Trips abroad over the last 3 years (with precise indication of the time of departure and return, border crossing points, purpose of journey, and duration of stay in each of the foreign countries: *in 1912 set out for America to earn a living, and now I work as a seaman [въ 1912 г. отправился на заработки въ Америку и теперь работаю морякомъ]*.

Note that in the previous application, every question had to have some sort of answer filled in. In this one, many of the boxes in the right column are left blank. The conscientiousness with which these papers were filled out can obviously vary from case to case.

You might hope these forms will provide considerable genealogical data, since they call for parents' names and residences, citizenship, etc. In fact, as these samples show, these hopes are often disappointed. In Document IV-9 the applicant gave no information on his parents, and didn't even know where they were. In Document IV-10, we learn only that the applicant's father was named *Froim*—item #1 asks for the applicant's name, and the answer is given in the standard Russian form with first name and patronymic: *Leiba Froimov*. Drop the suffix *-ov* and you have the first name *Froim*, a short form of *Efroim*, from Hebrew אֶפְרַיִם *'Ephrayim*.

4. Document IV-11: A Seaman's Certificate

On page 107 we see **Document IV-11**, a sample of a kind of document common in the Russian Consular collection. It features an attestation in Russian of the individual's qualifications as a professional seaman, and a portion in English that is more significant for genealogical research, because it provides personal data and a physical description.

Because the English portion is the one of primary interest to a researcher, there is no need to devote too much attention to the Russian section. This sample is reproduced here mainly to familiarize you with the appearance and format of such documents. The first paragraph in Russian states that on the basis of documents presented to establish his professional competence, he is in fact a профессiональный морякъ [professional seaman]. The second paragraph specifies what those presented documents were: a booklet from an American union *[книж. америк. юнiона]* dated 22 October 1917, No. 15357, and a statement *[удостовѣренiе]* of a notary *[нотарiуса]* regarding his discharge *[дисчаржей]*. The last paragraph requests the Consul General [Генеральное Консульство] not to refuse [не отказать] to issue a certificate for signing up for a ship [на пароходъ].

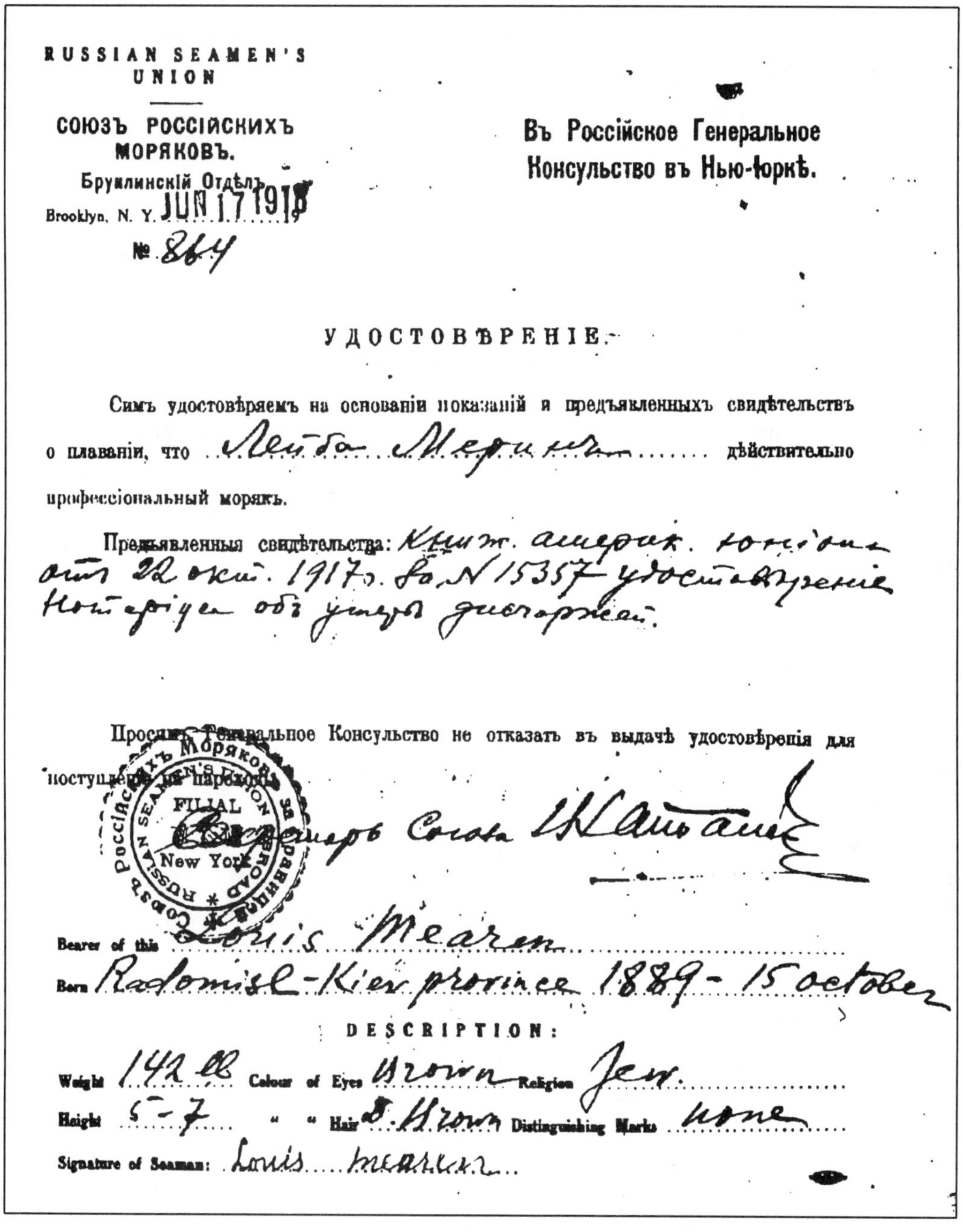

RUSSIAN SEAMEN'S UNION

СОЮЗЪ РОССІЙСКИХЪ МОРЯКОВЪ.
Бруклинскій Отдѣлъ
Brooklyn, N. Y. JUN 17 1918
№ 864

Въ Россійское Генеральное Консульство въ Нью-Іоркѣ.

УДОСТОВѢРЕНІЕ.

Симъ удостовѣряемъ на основаніи показаній и предъявленныхъ свидѣтельствъ о плаваніи, что Лейба Меринъ дѣйствительно профессіональный морякъ.

Предъявленныя свидѣтельства: Книж. америк. юніонъ от 22 окт. 1917 г. за N 15357 удостовѣреніе [illegible] объ [illegible] дисчаржей.

Просимъ Генеральное Консульство не отказать въ выдачѣ удостовѣренія для поступленія на пароходъ.

Секретарь Союза [signature]

Bearer of this Louis Mearen

Born Radomisl-Kiev province 1889 - 15 october

DESCRIPTION:

Weight 142 lb Colour of Eyes Brown Religion Jew

Height 5-7 " " Hair D. Brown Distinguishing Marks none

Signature of Seaman: Louis Mearen

Document IV-11: A Seaman's Certificate

If you're very observant you may have noticed that the subject of this document is the same person who appeared in Document IV-10. Here he is called "Louis Mearen"—he has Americanized his first name, from *Лейба (Leiba)* to *Louis,* and his Russian name *Меринъ* has been Anglicized to *Mearen.* He also somehow managed to become 7 years younger! In the previous document he was born on 15 October 188<u>2</u>; now his birthdate is 15 October 188<u>9</u>.

Even in the brief bits of Russian shown here, we see unfamiliar terms in English rendered phonetically: the word *юніонъ,* "union," and *дисчаржей,* "discharge." This mixing of Russian and English is not unusual in documents drawn up in America.

5. Document IV-12: A Request for Exemption from Military Service

The document reproduced on page 109 is typical of another kind of record found in the Consular Collection, relating to military service. This, for instance, is a request for documents proving Russian citizenship, so the petitioner can avoid serving in the American armed forces.

ШТАТЪ ПЕННСИЛЬВАНІЯ – State of Pennsylvania.

Пеннсильванія – You might notice that in Document IV-8 (page 95) this same name was spelled Пеннсилванія, but here the soft sign **ь** is inserted after -л- and before -ванія: Пеннсильванія. Rendering English names by Cyrillic phonetic values was an imprecise science at best. When in doubt, sound it out!

ГРАФСТВО ФИЛАДЕЛЬФІЯ – county of Philadelphia

Въ Россійское Консульство въ Филадельфіи, Пенна. – To the Russian Consulate in Philadephia, Penna.

ПРОШЕНІЕ – request

Я нижеподписавшійся `Владиславъ Смулка` симъ подъ присягой свидѣтельствую – "I, the undersigned Władysław Smulka, hereby certify under oath…"

нижеподписавшійся – "the undersigned," the one whose signature appears below

Владиславъ Смулка – subsequent data makes it clear the subject is a Pole, so Polish name forms are appropriate. *Władysław* is the Polish version of this first name, so that is the appropriate way to render it.

симъ – "hereby," literally "[by] this," instrumental masculine singular of the archaic pronoun *сей* (see page 43)

присяга, присяги – (n., fem.) oath; *подъ присягой* – "under oath"

свидѣтельствую – 1st personal singular, present tense, of *свидѣтельствовать*, modern spelling *свидетельствовать*, "to certify, attest"

что я уроженецъ `Деревни Комянки, Жековской Волости, Остроленскаго Уѣзда, Ломженской Губерніи` – "that I am a native of the village of Komyanki *[sic, see below]*, District of Żeków *[sic, see below]*, County of Ostrołęka, Province of Łomża."

уроженецъ, уроженца – (n., masc.) native; feminine *уроженка*

Деревни Комянки – "of the village of Komyanki." After consulting a map it was established that there is no place named *Komianki,* which would be the expected Polish version of a name rendered as *Комянки* in Russian. Research established that the village was in fact named *Kamianki* – so even if you transliterate the Russian name correctly, you are not guaranteed that the name will be right! … For the administrative divisions of *волость, уѣздъ,* and *губернія*, see the box on page 83.

Жековской Волости – "[of the] district of Żekow or Rzekow." Again, subsequent research established that the place referred to was actually Rzekuń. The Polish letter ***ż*** is pronounced the same as ***rz,*** and both can be rendered ***ж*** in Russian.

Остроленскаго Уѣзда – "County of Ostrołęka." The pronunciation of the name of the Polish city Ostrołęka would be rendered phonetically *Остроленка,* and from that was formed the adjective *остроленскій*, "of Ostrołęka."

Ломженской Губерніи – "Province of Łomża."

ШТАТЪ ПЕННСИЛЬВАНІЯ,
ГРАФСТВО ФИЛАДЕЛЬФІЯ.

Въ Россійское Консульство въ Филадельфіи, Пенна.

ПРОШЕНІЕ.

Я нижеподписавшійся, Владиславъ Смулка симъ подъ присягой свидѣтельствую, что я уроженецъ Деревни Комянки, Жековской Волости, Остроленскаго Уѣзда, Ломженской Губерни

Что я въ Америкѣ нахожусь 13 лѣтъ и что я никогда не заявлялъ своего желанія перейти въ Американское гражданство и таковыхъ Американскихъ бумагъ не имѣю.

Что призывной участокъ (Локалъ Боардъ) № ---------- города Филадельфіи, Пеннсильваніи, назначивъ мнѣ Серіалъ № ----- и Ордеръ № ----- требуетъ меня къ исполненію воинской повинности въ Американской Арміи.

На основаніи того что я Россійскій гражданинъ, никогда не заявившій своего желанія перейти въ Американское гражданство, я заявилъ о своемъ правѣ на освобожденіе, и потому долженъ представить доказательства о моемъ Россійскомъ гражданствѣ въ видѣ свидѣтельства отъ Россійскаго Консульства.

Такъ какъ я не имѣю никакихъ документовъ выданныхъ мнѣ Россійскимъ Правительствомъ въ доказательство моего Россійскаго гражданства, я къ сему прошенію присовокупляю присяжное показаніе двухъ свидѣтелей знающихъ меня изъ Россіи и свидѣтельствующихъ о моемъ Россійскомъ гражданствѣ, и прилагаю документы таковыхъ свидѣтелей.

А потому, въ виду всего вышеизложеннаго, я покорнѣйше прошу ввѣренное Вамъ Россійское Консульство мнѣ таковое свидѣтельство выдать для цѣли вышеуказанной.

Вашъ проситель Владиславъ его X знак Смулка

Адресъ: 107 Монролъ Улица, Фила. Пенна.

Мы нижеподписавшіеся, Піотръ Ружаньскій и Николай Ружанскій симъ подъ присягой, свидѣтельствуемъ, что мы и каждый изъ насъ, лично хорошо знакомы съ Владиславомъ Смулка просителемъ въ семъ прошеніи.

Что мы его знаемъ изъ Россіи и знаемъ что онъ рожденный Россійскій гражданинъ.

Въ доказательство чего, мы къ сему прилагаемъ наши Росс. Документы и подписываемся.

Николай его X знак Ружанскій

Peter Ruzanski

Подписали и присягали въ моемъ присутствіи, сего 30 дня, Января мѣсяца, 1918 года, н. ст.

L. A. Bloom

Нотаріусъ.
NOTARY PUBLIC,
Commission Expires February 19, 1921

Document IV-12: A Request for Exemption from Military Service

Что я въ Америкѣ нахожусь 13 лѣтъ и что я никогда не заявлялъ своего желанія перейти въ Американское гражданство и таковыхъ Американскихъ бумагъ не имѣю.– "That I have been in America for 13 years and that I have never declared my desire to take American citizenship and I do not possess such American papers."

я нахожусь – literally "I find myself," but often best translated "I am" or "I have been."

я никогда не заявлялъ – "I have never declared." The use of compound negatives is correct in Russian, so that this literally says "I never not have declared." The verb *заявлять* means "to declare, announce, make known."

своего желанія перейти въ Американское гражданство – literally "of my desire to pass over into American citizenship." The phrase *своего желанія* is genitive singular because the object of negated verbs is usually in that case.

таковыхъ Американскихъ бумагъ не имѣю – "such American papers I do not have." The papers referred to are surely citizenship papers.

Что призывной участокъ (Локалъ Боардъ) № --- города Филадельфіи, Пеннсильваніи, назначивъ мнѣ Серіалъ № --- и Ордеръ № --- требуетъ меня къ исполненію воинской повинности въ Американской Арміи.– "That Draft Board No. _ of the city of Philadelphia, Pennsylvania, having assigned me Serial # _ and Order No. _, requires me to fulfill my military obligation in the American Army."

призывной участокъ – "Draft Board," with "Local Board" in Cyrillic transliteration (Локалъ Боардъ) to make clear exactly what was meant. The word *призыв* means "call, levy, summons (to arms)." Note that if Władysław Smulka had received a draft notice, the appropriate blanks here would have been filled in with data.

На основаніи того что я Россійскій гражданинъ, никогда не заявившій своего желанія перейти въ Американское гражданство, я заявилъ о своемъ правѣ на освобожденіе, и потому долженъ представить доказательства о моемъ Россійскомъ гражданствѣ въ видѣ свидѣтельства от Россійскаго Консультсва – "On the basis of the fact that I am a Russian citizen and have never declared a desire to become an American citizen, I have claimed my right to be released *[i. e., from military duty]*, and therefore am obligated to present proof of my Russian citizenship in the form of a certificate from the Russian Consulate."

я заявилъ о своемъ правѣ на освобожденіе– "I claimed my right to be released." The expression *заявить право на* X can be interpreted "to claim a right to X." In this case *освобожденіе*, literally "freedom, emancipation," refers to being released from the obligation to serve in the American military.

въ видѣ свидѣтельства – "in the form of a certificate"

Такъ какъ я не имѣю никакихъ документовъ выданныхъ мнѣ Россійскимъ Правительствомъ въ доказательство моего Россійскаго гражданства, я къ сему прошенію присовокупляю присяжное показаніе двухъ свидѣтелей знающихъ меня изъ Россіи и свидѣтельствующихъ о моемъ Россійскомъ гражданствѣ, и прилагаю документы таковыхъ свидѣтелей. – "Inasmuch as I do not have any documents issued to me by the Russian Government in proof of my Russian citizenship, I am attaching the statement under oath of two witnesses who know me from Russia and attest to my Russian citizenship, and I am enclosing the documents of said witnesses."

А потому, въ виду всего вышеизложеннаго, я покорнѣйше прошу ввѣренное Вамъ Россійское Консульство мнѣ таковое свидѣтельство выдать для цѣли вышеуказанной. – "And for this reason, in view of all said above, I humbly ask the Russian Consulate entrusted to you to issue me such a certificate for the purpose indicated above ."

всего вышеизложеннаго – "of all stated above," from *весь*, "all"; *выше*, "above"; and the past passive participle of *излагать, изложить*, "to state, set forth, expound."

покорнѣйше – comparative degree of the adverb *покорно*, "humbly, submissively." In English we'd express the same thing "very humbly."

Вашъ проситель *Владиславъ [его × знакъ] Смулка* – "Your petitioner, Władysław [his × mark] Smulka."

[его × знакъ] – Note that the *x* has the word *его*, "his," over it, and the word *знакъ*, "mark," under it. So he made his mark and the notary witnessed it.

Адресъ: 107 Монролъ Улица, Фила. Пенна. – "Address: 107 Monrol St., Phila[delphia], Penn[sylvani]a."

Мы нижеподписавшіеся, Піотр Ружаньскій и Николай Ружаньскій симъ подъ присягой, свидѣтельствуемъ, что мы и каждый изъ насъ, лично хорошо знакомы съ Владиславомъ Смулка просителемъ въ семъ прошеніи. – "We, the undersigned, Piotr Różański and Mikołaj Różański, hereby certify under oath that we [together], and each of us [individually] are personally well acquainted with Władysław Smulka, the petitioner in this petition."

нижеподписавшіеся – literally "the below signing themselves," from *ниже*, "below, beneath," and the past active participle of *подписаться*, "to sign."

Что мы его знаемъ изъ Россіи и знаемъ что онъ рожденный Россійскій гражданинъ. – "That we know him from Russia and know that he is a native-born Russian citizen."

мы его знаемъ изъ Россіи – literally "We know him from Russia."

Въ доказательство чего, мы къ сему прилагаемъ нашъ Росс. Документы и подписываемся. – "In proof whereof we enclose our Russian documents and affix our signatures."

Николай [его × знакъ] Ружанскій. Peter Rozanski. – "Mikołaj Różański. Peter Różański." Mikołaj was illiterate and made his mark. Peter signed his own name, in rather cramped English penmanship.

Подписали и присягали въ моемъ присутствіи, сего 30 дня, Января мѣсяца, 1918 года, н. ст. – "[They] signed and swore their oaths in my presence, on this, the 30th day of the month of January, of the year 1918, New Style."

6. Document IV-13: A Certificate for Travel (In Place of a Passport)

When Russian citizens wished to return home but had no passport or other supporting documents to prove their citizenship, an alternate form was devised. (It is likely the bureacracy-laden Czarist government had a form for just about every life circumstance!).

Such a form is shown on page 112, with a translation on the facing page.

СИЛЫ ПАСПОРТА НЕ ИМѢЕТЪ.

М. И. Д.

РОССІЙСКОЕ
Генеральное Консульство
въ НЬЮ-ІОРКѢ

29 мая 1918 г.

No. 6193

СВИДѢТЕЛЬСТВО

на проѣздъ въ Россію.

Дано сіе Россійскимъ Генеральнымъ Консульствомъ въ Нью-Іоркѣ, съ приложеніемъ казенной печати, предъявителю заявившему, что онъ .... губерніи, ... уѣзда .... волости, гмины, деревни .... вѣроисповѣданія, и что онъ не имѣетъ установленнаго заграничнаго паспорта, и предъявивъ въ доказательство своей личности ....

Къ сему присовокупляется, что .... состоитъ въ россійскомъ подданствѣ .... и нынѣ возвращается на родину черезъ пограничный пунктъ ....

Опросный листъ .... препровождается въ .... при отношеніи отъ .... 1918 г. за No. ....

ГЕНЕРАЛЬНЫЙ КОНСУЛЪ

Симъ удостовѣряется подлинность предстоящихъ фотографій и подписи ....

ГЕН. КОНСУЛЪ

This certificate is issued by the Russian Consulate General at New York to a Russian citizen .... and is good for his returning to Russia via ....

New York, May 29th 1918

Russian Consul General

Document IV-13: A Certificate for Travel (In Place of a Passport)

M. I. D.

RUSSIAN
General Consulate
in NEW YORK

29 May 191 *8*
No. *6093*

[Photo of Abram Mlimovko, with his signature in the Hebrew alphabet. It has been stamped with the seal of the Russian General Consulate in New York]

The accuracy of this photograph and signature is hereby certified.
Abram Mlimovko

Gen. Consul
[illegible]

[Official stamps and the seal of the Russian General Consulate in New York]

IS NOT VALID AS A PASSPORT

CERTIFICATE

for travel to Russia

This was issued by the Russian General Consulate in New York, with the official seal affixed, to the bearer, who states that *he is Abram Mlimovko*

of Volyn province, of *Lutsk* county, *—* district, *gmina*, village *Kolko* *of the Jewish* religion, and that he does not have an established foreign passport, who presented as proof of [his] identity *no documents*

To which is added, that *Abram Mlimovko* is a Russian citizen *from the day of [his] birth* and now is returning to his homeland via the border crossing point *in Vladivostok*

The passport questionnaire relating to *Abram Mlimovko* is being forwarded to *Vladivostok*, with a document dated *27 June* of the year 1918, No. *2616*.

CONSUL GENERAL *[illegible]*

This certificate is issued by the Russian Consulate General at New York to a Russian citizen *Abram Mlimovko* and is good for his returning to Russia via *Japan*
New York, *May 29th* 1918

Russian Consul General *[illegible]*

Translation of Document IV-13

7. Document IV-14: A Statement Regarding Previous Employment

The Russian Consular Collection contains a great variety of records, too many to include discussion of them all here. A good number lack any significant genealogical information anyway. Let us conclude with **Document IV-14**, a statement chosen at random, as to the previous employment of a Russian subject.

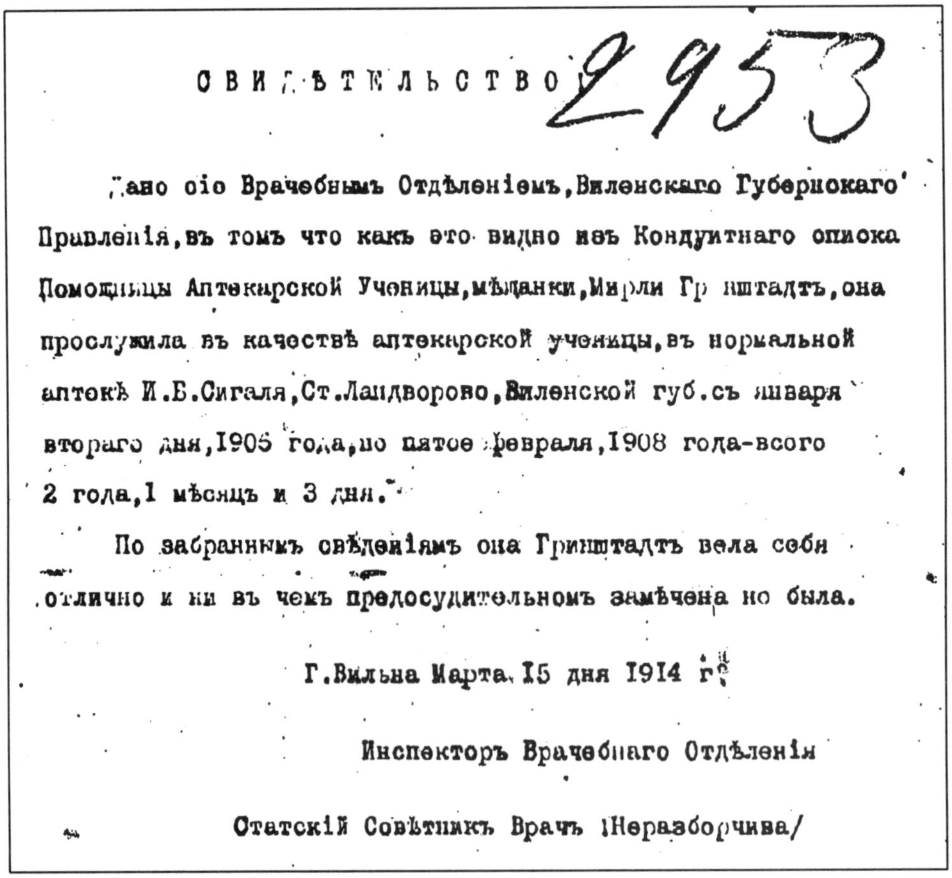

СВИДѢТЕЛЬСТВО 2953

Дано сіе Врачебнымъ Отдѣленіемъ, Виленскаго Губернскаго Правленія, въ томъ что какъ это видно изъ Кондуитнаго списка Помощницы Аптекарской Ученицы, мѣщанки, Мирли Гринштадтъ, она прослужила въ качествѣ аптекарской ученицы, въ нормальной аптекѣ И.Б.Сигаля, Ст.Ландворово, Виленской губ. съ января втораго дня, 1906 года, по пятое февраля, 1908 года-всего 2 года, 1 мѣсяцъ и 3 дня.

По забраннымъ свѣдѣніямъ она Гринштадтъ вела себя отлично и ни въ чемъ предосудительномъ замѣчена не была.

Г.Вильна Марта 15 дня 1914 г.

Инспекторъ Врачебнаго Отдѣленія

Статскій Совѣтникъ Врачъ /Неразборчива/

CERTIFICATION

This is issued by the Medical Division of the Provincial Administration of the Province of Vil'na, inasmuch as it is evident from the conduct record of Mirla Grinshtadt [Мирли Гринштадтъ], of the merchant class [мѣщанки], that she served in the capacity of a pharmaceutical apprentice in the officially registered Pharmacy of I. B. Segal in Landvarovo, Province of Vil'na, from January 2, 1906 to February 5, 1908, for a total of two years, one month, and three days. *[Landvarovo is now Lentvaris, Lithuania, about 19 km. west-southwest of Vilnius].*

According to the information gathered, she, Grinshtadt, conducted herself in an exemplary manner and that nothing deserving blame was noted.

Dated, city of Vil'na, 15 March 1914
Inspector of the Medical Divison
State Councillor, Doctor *[illegible]*

V. FINDING YOUR ANCESTRAL HOME AND ITS RECORDS

A. "I've Found It ... But Where Is it?"

As we said in the Introduction (on page *viii*), to trace your family back to the old country, you **must** have these three pieces of information for each line you trace:

- **The name of your ancestor who emigrated – not an Anglicized version, but the original name he or she went by in the old country**
- **The date of that ancestor's birth**
- **The place of that ancestor's birth**

How do you get this information? You search in the sources mentioned in Chapter Three to find the records mentioned in Chapters Three and Four. From those records you extract accurate information on your ancestor's name, place of birth, and date of birth. If the necessary records are in Russian, Chapters One, Two, and Four should help you extract that information. Once you have it, you can hope to begin locating records in the lands that were part of the Russian Empire.

A difficulty, however, soon arises in most cases: it's one thing to get the name of the town or village your ancestor came from; it's quite another to find it. English-language sources of detailed geographical information on eastern Europe and western Russia are not exactly easy to come by; sources on central and eastern Russia are even rarer.

The scarcity of such sources is due partly to our culture's focus on western Europe—hardly strange in view of the history of English-speaking lands, but a bit of a handicap when you find you need information on other parts of the world.

To some extent the paucity of English-language sources on Russian geography is also due to the political history of that country. The Soviet regime was not exactly liberal in providing any information that might have military uses. And let's face it, freely handing out detailed information on towns and villages—their location, size, industry, etc.—could be construed as making things a little too easy for potential invaders, to say nothing of enemies with nuclear missiles. At least, that's how the Soviets saw it. To them, publishing detailed information on places in the Soviet Union was tantamount to passing out secret information that should be divulged only on a need-to-know basis. And by their standards, genealogical researchers definitely did **not** need to know!

As a result, most English-language information on Russian geography comes not from Russians, but from Western academic or military sources. While reasonably accurate, it can't help but suffer from a lack of cooperation from people who actually live in Russia. Imagine trying to write anything detailed and accurate about, say, Amarillo, Texas, if you've never been there! Some errors can't help but creep in... Furthermore, you have to suspect the military may not have released all their best data for public use.

Thus if your detailed research so far has produced the breakthrough that your family came from, say, Prenai, Lithuania, your initial rapture quickly fades when you realize you haven't a clue where that is! And no one is going to walk up out of the blue and hand you a detailed map of the Prenai region. The only way you'll learn more—including where records of genealogical value for Prenai are kept—is through intelligent use of gazetteers, atlases, and similar reference works.

B. Basic Geography, and the Problems of Place Names

The Russian Empire was enormous, and as it expanded, the territories under its control changed, as did the borders of its internal administrative entities. Even the names of towns and districts changed at times. The result is, there is no way to provide a list and say "This is the composition of the Russian Empire." Any such list is inevitably oversimplified.

If you have identified your ancestral home from documents, as described in Chapters Three and Four, your first goal should be to establish in which part of the Empire it was located. Sources such as naturalization papers or passenger lists may only give very general geographic information. Before you can hope to identify a specific place you have to improve your odds somewhat by focusing on one region, rather than on the whole enormous mass of Russia. So you need to begin by grasping the outline of the Empire as a whole; identify the specific *gubernia* in which your ancestor lived; then work toward a smaller subdivision such as an *uyezd*. Only then does it make sense to start looking in gazetteers for a specific village or town.

One source that gives a reasonably good outline of the Empire as of the period of heaviest emigration, the late 19th century, is the 1902 edition of the Polish-language *Encyklopedia Powszechna of S. Orgelbrand*. The article on Russia ("Rosja," Volume XIII, pp. 51 V.) says that European Russia consisted of 49 *gubernias* or provinces and 1 region; the Kingdom of Poland consisted of 10 *gubernias;* the Duchy of Finland consisted of 8 *gubernias;* the *Кавказ* [Caucasus] consisted of 5 *gubernias,* 5 regions, and 1 district; Siberia consisted of 4 *gubernias,* 4 regions, and one peninsular district; the Central Asian part consisted of 9 regions; and there existed municipal districts of St. Petersburg, Odessa, Taganrog, Sevastopol, and Kerch-Yenikale, in which mayors or municipal chiefs played the same administrative role as a *губернаторъ* (governor) in a *gubernia.*

Provinces and regions varied in size and could be divided into *уѣзды* or *волости* or *округи*. In other words, there wasn't one uniform administrative setup that prevailed across all the Empire. As different regions came under Russian rule at different times and under different circumstances, it is no surprise that the resulting administration was a bit of a patchwork quilt, held together by the autoracy of the Tsar and the functioning of the bureaucracy. Even the lengthy discussion in the following pages can only be considered a guide; change the time-frame a few years and its details may no longer be accurate.

The Russian Empire was generally considered to consist of the following subdivisions, moving roughly (very roughly!) from west to east and from north to south:

European Russia

- the *gubernias* of the **Kingdom of Poland**: Kalisz, Kielce, Łomża, Lublin, Piotrków, Płock, Radom, Siedlce, Suwałki, and Warsaw
- **Finland**, *Финляндія*, which was ruled by the Russian Empire but had its own administrative structure and considerable autonomy
- the **Baltic** *[Балтійскія] gubernias*: *Санктъ-Петербургъ*, St. Petersburg (also called historically *Ингерманландія, Ingermanlandiya*); *Эстляндія*, Estonia; *Курляндія*, Courland [Kurland]; and *Лифляндія, Livonia* or *Livland*
- **Western Russia**, consisting of the *gubernias* of: *Ковно*, Kovno (now Kaunas, Lithuania); *Вильна*, Vil'na (now Vilnius, Lithuania; these two, along with some of the

territory in the *gubernia* of Grodna, comprised *Литва*, Polish *Litwa*, Lithuania); *Гродна*, Grodna (now Hrodna, Belarus); *Витебскъ*, Vitebsk (now Vitsebsk, Belarus); *Минскъ*, Minsk; *Могилевъ*, Mogilev (now Mahileŭ, Belarus; the last three, called collectively *Бѣлороссія*, "White Russia," comprise much of modern Belarus); *Волынь*, Volhynia (Polish name *Wołyń*); and *Подолія*, Podolia (also called "Western Ukraine"; these last two are now part of the independent nation of Ukraine)

- **Great Russia** [*Великороссія*, Polish *Wielkorosja*], 19 northern and central *gubernias* (going from west to east in north-south sweeps): *Архангельскъ*, Arkhangelsk; *Олонецъ*, Olonets; *Вологда*, Vologda; *Новгородъ*, Novgorod; *Псковъ*, Pskov; *Тверь*, Tver'; *Ярославль*, Yaroslavl'; *Кострома*, Kostroma; *Смоленскъ*, Smolensk; *Москва*, Moskva (Moscow); *Владиміръ*, Vladimir; *Нижній Новгородъ*, Nizhniy Novgorod; *Калуга*, Kaluga; *Тула*, Tula; *Рязань*, Ryazan'; *Тамбовъ*, Tambov; *Орёл*, Orel; *Курскъ*, Kursk; and *Воронежъ*, Voronezh
- **Little Russia** [*Малороссія*, Polish *Małorosja*], territory mostly in Ukraine, the *gubernias* of: *Кіевъ*, Kiev (now *Київ*); *Черниговъ*, Chernigov (now *Чернігів*); *Полтава*, Poltava; and *Харьковъ*, Khar'kov (now *Харків*)
- **South Russia**, or **New Russia**, consisting of lands now in Ukraine, on the Black Sea, or between it and the Caspian Sea, namely, the *gubernias* of *Бессарабія*, Bessarabia; *Херсонъ*, Kherson; *Екатеринославъ*, Yekaterinoslav (now *Дніпропетровськ*, *Dnipropetrovs'k*); and *Таврида*, Tavrida (comprising the Nogai steppes and the Crimean peninsula); and the Land of the Don Cossacks
- the **region of Kazan'**, *gubernias* of: *Пермь*, Perm'; *Вятка*, Viatka (now *Киров*, Kirov); *Казань*, Kazan'; *Симбирскъ*, Simbirsk (1780-1924, from 1924 on *Уляновск*, Ulyanovsk), and *Пенза*, Penza
- the **region of Астрахань**, **Astrakhan'**, consisting of the *gubernias* of: *Саратовъ*, Saratov; *Астрахань*, Astrakhan'; *Уфа*, Ufa; *Самара*, Samara (known 1935-1991 as *Куйбышев*, Kuibyshev); and *Оренбургъ*, Orenburg

Asiatic Russia

- the **Кавказ,** the **Caucasus**, consisting of: the districts of *Кубань*, Kuban'; *Терекъ*, Terek, and *Черное Море* [Black Sea]; and the *gubernias* of *Ставрополь*, Stavropol'; *Кутаисъ*, Kutais; *Тифлисъ*, Tiflis (now *Тбилиси*, Tbilisi, capital of Georgia); *Дагестанъ*, Dagestan; *Карсъ*, Kars; *Эриванъ* Erivan (now *Ереван*, the capital of Armenia); *Елисаветполь*, Yelisavetpol'; and *Баку*, Baku
- **Siberia**, consisting of the provinces of *Тобольскъ*, Tobol'sk, and *Томскъ*, Tomsk, and the districts of: *Забайкалскій* (beyond Lake Baikal); *Енисейскъ*, Yeniseysk; *Иркутскъ*, Irkutsk; *Якутія*, Yakutiya; *Приморскій* (Prymorskiy); *Амуръ*, Amur; and *Сахалинъ*, Sakhalin Island
- the districts of **Central Asia**: *Уралскій*, Urals; *Закаспийскій*, Transcaspian (literally "beyond the Caspian [Sea]"); *Тургай*, Turgai; *Сыръ-Даря*, Syr-Darya; *Акмолинскъ*, Akmolinsk; *Самаркандъ*, Samarkand; *Семипалатинскъ*, Semi-palatinsk; *Семирѣчье*, Semirech'ye; and *Фергана*, Fergana

Let us take a closer look at some of these administrative divisions and their principal subdivisions.

Russian Names of Provincial Capitals, Selected County Seats, and Other Localities

Researchers unfamiliar with the Cyrillic spellings of the names of provincial capitals and county seats will find it essential to have some source that helps them recognize these names when they see them. The following pages list a selection of those names.

The Russian Empire was huge, and comprised a great many provinces. While we don't wish to exclude anyone, it seems probable most users of this book descend from residents of the western part of the Empire, which included territories once ruled by the Grand Duchy of Lithuania and the Commonwealth of Poland and Lithuania. So those are the regions to which we will devote the most attention, and with which we will begin.

1. Kingdom of Poland (Королевство Польское *or* Царство Польское)

First let us look at the westernmost part of the Russian Empire, the ten provinces that comprised the **Kingdom of Poland**. Each *губернія* [province] and *уѣздъ* [county] bore the name of the town or city which served as its administrative center. The provinces of the Kingdom of Poland under Russian rule were those administered from, and named for, the following cities in modern Poland (moving roughly west to east, north to south): Kalisz, Płock, Warszawa, Piotrków, Radom, Kielce, Łomża, Siedlce, Lublin, and Suwałki.

Below we list each province in that order, along with the names of the county seats in that province. First we give the name of each community in Russian form, then its most common Russian adjectival form (some names had more than one). After a dash we give the Polish name of each place, then its Polish adjectival form. As we have seen and will see in sample documents, expressions we'd render in English as "province of Łomża, county of Ostrołęka" often were expressed with adjectival forms of the towns' names, not the noun forms. Thus a person may be described as an inhabitant of a village *"ломжинской губерніи, остроленскаго уѣзда"*—literally "of the Łomżan province, of the Ostrołękan county." So you need a source that gives those adjectival forms.

Please note that the Russian forms given below are the "official" ones seen in government publications. Rendering Polish names in Russian form was not an exact science, however; there was some room for variation. Thus Polish *Białystok* and its adjectival form *białostocki* generally appeared in Russian as *Бѣлостокъ* and *бѣлостокскій*. But confusion of forms was not rare; you may see an adjectival hybrid such as *бѣлостоцкій*, or *Бялостокъ* with adjectival *бялостоцкій* or *бялостокскій*. So you may occasionally encounter variations on the forms shown below. But they will almost always be very, very similar to the ones we've given—close enough that we don't think you will be too confused in the context of your research.

In any case, since we couldn't list every conceivable variation you may find without turning this list into a book by itself, we had to limit ourselves to the mainstream forms. When we noted a specific variant that was highly likely to appear, however, we inserted it in brackets for your reference.

Калишская губернія – Kalisz province

Велюнъ, велюньскій – Wieluń, wieluński
Калишъ, калишскій [калискій] – Kalisz, kaliski
Коло, кольскій - Koło, kolski
Конинъ, конинскій – Konin, koniński
Ленчицы, ленчицкій – Łęczyca, łęczycki
Слупцы, слупецкій – Słupca, słupecki
Сѣрадзъ, сѣрадзкій – Sieradz, sieradzki
Турекъ, турекскій –Turek, turecki

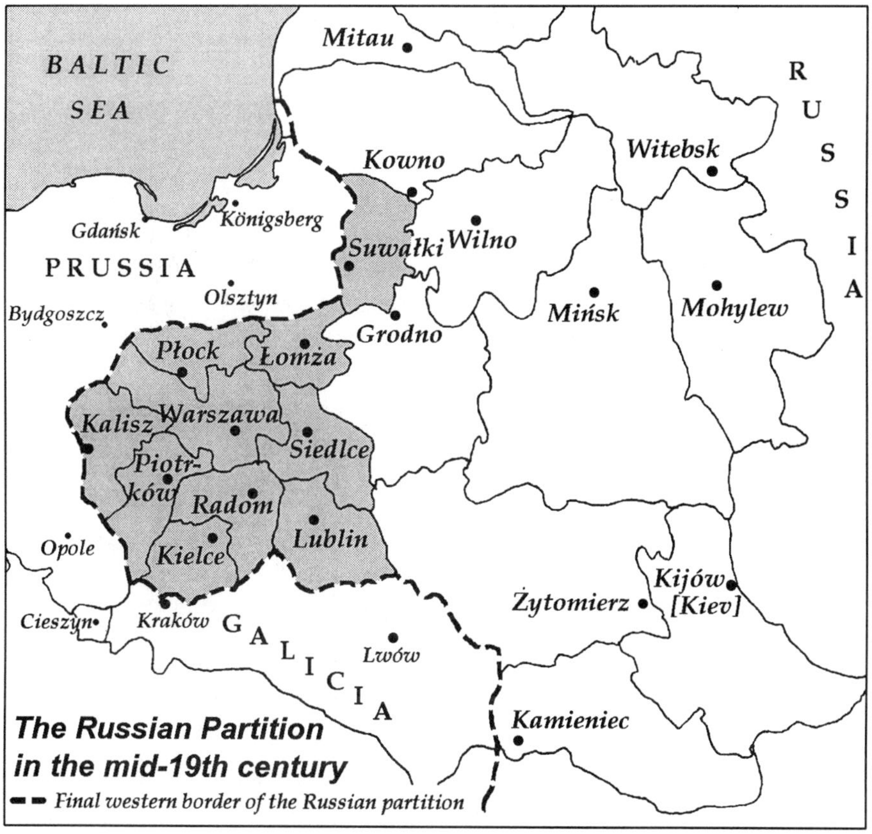

Map V-1 – The Russian Partition in the Mid-19th Century, shows the lands of the former Commonwealth of Two Nations, Poland and Lithuania, seized by the Russian Empire during the partitions in the late 18th century. The shaded areas are the 10 *gubernias* of the so-called "Congress Kingdom" of Poland; the areas to their east were once ruled by the Grand Duchy of Lithuania, and later by the Commonwealth. Officially the Congress Kingdom was autonomous, but in fact it was under strict Russian control.

Плоцкая губернія – Płock province

Липно, липновскій – Lipno, lipnowski
Млава, млавскій – Mława, mławski
Плоцкъ, плоцкій – Płock, płocki
Прасньішъ, праснышскій [пржаснкскій] – Przasnysz, przasnyski
Рыпинъ, рыпинскій – Rypin, rypiński
Серпецъ, серпецкій – Sierpc, sierpecki
Цѣхановъ, цѣхановскій – Ciechanów, ciechanowski

Варшавская губернія – Warszawa province

Блоня, блонскій – Błonie, błoński
Варшава, варшавскій – Warszawa, warszawski (English name *Warsaw*)
Влоцлавскъ, влоцлавскій – Włocławek, włocławski
Гостынинъ, гостынскій – Gostynin, gostyński
Гройцы, гроецкій – Grójec, grójecki
Кутно, кутновскій – Kutno, kutnowski
Ловичъ, ловичскій – Łowicz, łowicki
Нешава, нешавскій – Nieszawa, nieszawski
Ново-Минскъ, новоминскій – Mińsk Mazowiecki, nowomiński
Плонскъ, плонскій – Płońsk, płoński
Пултускъ, пултускій – Pułtusk, pułtuski
Радиминъ, радиминьскій – Radzymin, radzymiński
Скерневицы, скерневицкій – Skierniewice, skierniewicki
Сохачевъ, сохачевскій – Sochaczew, sochaczewski

Петроковская губернія – Piotrków province

Бендинъ, бендиньскій – Będzin, będziński
Брезины, брезинскій [Бржезины, бржезинскій] – Brzeziny, brzeziński
Ласкъ, ласкій – Łask, łaski
Лодзь, лодзинскій [лодзкій] – Łódź, łódzki
Новорадомскъ, новорадомскій – [Nowy] Radomsk, noworadomski
Петроковъ, петроковскій [Піотрковъ, піотрковскій]– Piotrków, piotrkowski
Рава, равскій – Rawa, rawski
Ченстоховъ, ченстоховскій – Częstochowa, częstochowski

Радомская губернія – Radom province

Илжа, илжецкій – Iłża, iłżecki
Козеницы, козеницкій – Kozienice, kozienicki
Конскъ, конскій – Końskie, koński *or* konecki
Опатовъ, опатовскій – Opatów, opatowski
Опочно, опоченскій – Opoczno, opoczyński
Радомъ, радомскій – Radom, radomski
Сандомиръ, сандомирскій – Sandomierz, sandomierski

Кѣлецкая губернія – Kielce province

Андреевъ, андреевскій – Jędrzejów, jędrzejowski
Влощовъ, влощовскій – Włoszczowa, włoszczowski
Кѣльцы, кѣлецкій – Kielce, kielecki
Мѣховъ, мѣховскій – Miechów, miechowski
Олькушъ, олькушскій – Olkusz, olkuski
Пинчовъ, пинчовскій – Pińczów, pińczowski
Стопница, стопницкій – Stopnica, stopnicki

Ломжинская губернія – Łomża province

Мазовецкъ [Высокіе мазовецкіе], мазовецкій – Wysokie Mazowieckie, mazowiecki
Кольно, кольненьскій – Kolno, kolneński
Ломжа, ломжинскій – Łomża, łomżyński
Маковъ, маковскій – Maków (Mazowiecki), makowski
Остроленка, остроленскій [остроленцкій] – Ostrołęka, ostrołęcki
Островъ, островскій – Ostrów (Mazowiecka), ostrowski
Щучинъ, щучинскій – Szczuczyn, szczuczyński

Сѣдлецкая губернія – Siedlce province

Бѣла, бѣльскій – Biała Podlaska, bialski [*modern* bialskopodlaski]
Венгровъ, венгровскій – Węgrów, węgrowski
Влодава, влодавскій – Włodawa, włodawski
Гарволинъ, гарволинскій – Garwolin, garwoliński
Константиновъ, константиновскій – Konstantynów, konstantynowski
Луковъ, луковскій – Łuków, łukowski
Радинь, радинскій – Radzyń [Podlaski], radzyński
Соколовъ, соколовскій – Sokołów Podlaski, sokołowski
Сѣдлецъ, сѣдлецкій – Siedlce, siedlecki

Люблинская губернія – Lublin province

Бѣлгорай, бѣлгорайскій – Biłgoraj, biłgorajski
Грубешовъ, грубешовскій – Hrubieszów, hrubieszowski
Замостье, замостскій – Zamość, zamojski
Красноставъ, красноставскій – Krasnystaw, krasnostawski
Любартовъ, любартовскій – Lubartów, lubartowski
Люблинъ, люблинскій – Lublin, lubelski
Ново-Александрія, новоалександрійскій – Nowa Aleksandryja (*now* Puławy)
Томашевъ, томашевскій – Tomaszów, tomaszowski
Холмъ, холмскій – Chełm, chełmski
Яновъ, яновскій – Janów [Lubelski], janowski

Сувалкская губернія – Suwałki province

Августовъ [Аугустовъ], августовскій [аугустовскій] – Augustów, augustowski
Владиславовъ, владиславовскій – Władysławów, władysławowski (*now* Kudirkos Naumiestis, Lithuania)
Волковышки, волковышскій – Wyłkowyszki, wyłkowyski (*now* Vilkaviškis, Lithuania)
Кальварія, кальварійскій – Kalwaryja, kalwaryjski, (*now* Kalvarija, Lithuania)
Маріамполъ, маріампольскій – *Mariampol, mariampolski*, now *Marijampolė*, Lithuania
Сейны, сейнскій – *Sejny, sejneński*
Сувалки, сувалкскій [сувальскій] – Suwałki, suwalski

Here are Russian forms you may see of names for other Polish towns in the Russian partition:

Бакаларжево – Bakałarzewo
Барглов Костельный – Bargłow Kościelny
Бѣльскъ Подласкій – Bielsk Podlaski

Васильковъ - Wasiłków
Визна - Wizna
Домброва - Dąbrowa
Гонядзъ - Goniądz
Граево [Граѣво] - Grajewo
Заблудовъ - Zabłudów
Замбровъ - Zambrów
Кнышинъ - Knyszyn
Корыцинъ - Korycin
Кржиновлога Вѣлка - Krzynowłoga Wielka
Кузьница - Kuźnica
Лапы - Łapy
Липскъ - Lipsk
Мышинецъ - Myszyniec
Радзиловъ - Radziłów
Рачки - Raczki
Рожанъ - Różan
Семятыче - Siemiatycze
Штабинъ - Sztabin
Цѣхановецъ - Ciechanowiec

2. Finland (Великое Княжество Финляндское *or* Финляндія)

For much of the last 700 years Finland was ruled by Sweden. In 1808 Russia invaded Finland. At first the invasion went well, and Czar Alexander I announced the annexation of Finland to Russia. But Finnish resistance stiffened, and ultimately the Czar decided to allow Finland to retain its constitution and civil and religious rights. So Finland achieved autonomy as a grand duchy in 1809, but formally came under Russian rule in September of that year. It remained under Russian rule, but with a considerable degree of autonomy, until after the Bolshevik Revolution. Since then it has remained independent except for a period of Soviet invasion and occupation during World War II.

According to the statistical summary of data from the 1897 Census of the Russian Empire (see pages 320-329), the Grand Duchy of Finland consisted of 8 *gubernias* (Finnish term *lääni*, modern Russian *ляни*—modern Finland is divided into 12). Both Swedish and Finnish have long been official languages in Finland, and many of the major places are known by Swedish and Finnish names.

Below for each of those provinces we give first the old adjectival Russian form (as used with the noun *губернія*, which is how you're most likely to see it in Imperial records). Next is the modern Russian name of each province, with a Roman-alphabet transliteration in brackets. That is followed by the Swedish form, then the Finnish name of the town that served as that province's administrative center.

Або-Бьернеборгская – Або [Abo]: Swedish name *Åbo-Björneborg* [Finnish *Turun-Porin*], Finnish *Turku, lääni* name *Turku-Pori* (Russian *Турку-Пори*)

Вазаская – Васа [Vasa]: called *Vaasa* by Swedes and Finns, administrative center of Vaasa *lääni*

Выборгская – Выборг [*Vyborg*]: *Vyborg*, in Russian territory, northwest of St. Petersburg; 1919-1940 it was in Finnish territory and bore the Finnish name *Viipuri*

Куопіоская – Куопио [Kuopio]: both the town and *lääni* are called *Kuopio* by Swedes and Finns

Нюландская – Усима [Usima]: Usimaa, the Finnish name of the *lääni,* also called *Uudenmaan;* the Swedish name of the *lääni* was *Nyland,* and Swedes called its capital *Helsingfors (Гельсингфорсъ),* the city we know as *Helsinki* (modern Russian *Хельсинки*)

Санктъ-Михельская – Миккели [Mikkeli]: Swedish name *St. Michel,* Finnish *Mikkeli*

Тавастгусская – Хяме [Khyame]: the Finnish name of the *lääni* was *Häme,* Swedish name *Tavastehus;* the administrative center was *Hämeenlinna* (Russian *Хяменлинна*)

Улеаборгская – Оулу [Oulu]: Swedish name *Uleåborg,* administrative center of Oulu *lääni*

The capital of Finland as a whole was *Гельсингфорсъ*, Helsingfors, which is now called Helsinki. The Finns' name for their own country is *Suomi.*

3. Baltic Provinces of the Russian Empire (not including Lithuania)

The provinces regarded as belonging to the Baltic region—also referred to sometimes as *Остзейскій край*, from *Ostsee*, the German name for the Baltic—were, from north to south, those of St. Petersburg, Estonia, Courland, and Livonia. (Many sources define the Baltic provinces as Estonia, Courland, and Livonia, with St. Petersburg province regarded as part of Russia itself.) In any case, here are the names of the provinces and *uyezdy* in archaic Russian, English transliteration, and Polish equivalents:

[Санктъ-]Петербургская губернія – St. Petersburg province (historically also called *Ингерманландія*), capital St. Petersburg

Гдовъ, гдовскій – Gdov; Polish: *Gdów, gdowski*

Луга, лужскій – Luga; Polish: *Ługa, łuski*

Новая Ладога, новоладожскій – Novaya Ladoga; Polish: *Nowa Ładoga, nowoładoski*

Петергофъ, петергофскій – Petrogof, since 1944 *Петродворец;* Polish: *Peterhof, peterhofski*

Санктъ-Петербургъ, [санктъ-]петербурскій – St. Petersburg, 1914-1924 *Петроград,* 1924-1991 *Ленинград,* 1991-present *Санкт-Петербург;* Polish: *Petersburg* or *Sankt- Peterburg, peterburski*

Царское Село, царскосельскій – Tsarskoye Selo till 1918, then *Детское Село,* since 1937 *Пушкин;* Polish: *Carskie Sioło*

Шлиссельбургъ, шлиссельбургскій – Shlissel'burg, 1611-1702 *Орешекъ,* 1702-1944 *Шлисселбургъ,* 1944-1991 *Петрокрепость,* now *Шлиссельбург* again; Polish: *Szliselburg, szliselburski*

Ямбургъ, ямбургскій – Yamburg, since 1922 called *Кингисепп, Kingisepp;* Polish: *Jamburg, jamburski*

Эстляндская губернiя – Estonia province, capital Revel' (now Tallinn)

Везенбергъ, везенбергскій – Vezenberg, now *Rakvere* (modern Russian *Раквере),* Estonia; Polish: *Wezenberg, wezenberski* or *Wirland, wirlandzki*

Вейсенштейнъ, вейсенштейнскій – Veysenshteyn, now *Paide* (*Пайде*), Estonia, ancient name *Іервенъ, Ierven* – Polish: *Weissenstejn, weissenstejński* or *Jerwen, jerweński*

Гапсаль, гапсальскій – Gapsal', now *Haapsalu,* Estonia; since 1917 its official Russian name is *Хаапсалу;* Polish: *Hapsal, hapsalski* or *wicki* or *wikski*

Ревель, ревельскій – Revel' until 1917, since then *Tallinn*; Polish *Rewel, rewelski*

Курляндская губернiя or Курляндія – Kurland (Courland) province, capital Mitava (now Jelgava)

Бауска, баускій – Bauska, Latvia; Polish: *Bowsk, bowski;* German: *Bauske*

Виндава, виндавскій – Vindava, Latvia, since 1917 *Ventspils (Вентспилс*); Polish: *Windawa, windawski;* German: *Windau*

Газенпотъ, газенпотскій – Gazenpot, Latvia, since 1917 *Aizpute* (*Айзпуте*); Polish: *Hazenpot, hazenpocki;* German: *Hasenpoth*

Гольдингенъ – Gol'dingen, Latvia, since 1917 *Kuldīga (Кулдига*); Polish: *Goldynga, goldyński,* or *Kuldyga;* German: *Goldingen*

Гробинъ, гробинскій – Grobin, now *Grobiņa,* Latvia; Polish: *Grobin, grobiński*

Иллукстъ – Ilukst, Latvia, now *Ilūkste*; Polish: *Iłukszta [Iłłukszta], iłukszciański [illukszcki]*

Митава, митавскій – Mitava, Latvia, since 1917 *Jelgava* (*Елгава*); Polish: *Mitawa, mitawski;* German: *Mitau*

Тальсенъ – Talsen, Latvia, since 1917 *Talsi (Тальси)*; Polish: *Talsen, talseński*

Туккумъ – Tukkum, Latvia, since 1917 *Tukums* (*Тукумс*); Polish: *Tukum, tukumski*

Фридрихштадтъ, фридрихштадтскій – Fridrikhshtadt, Latvia, now *Jaunjelgava (Яунелгава)* ; Polish: *Frydrychsztat, frydrychsztacki;* German *Friedrichstadt*

Лифляндская губернiя *or* **Ливонія – Livonia province**, capital Riga

Валка, валкскій – Valka, Latvia; Polish: *Walk, walcki*

Венденъ, венденскій – Venden, Latvia, since 1917 *Cēsis (Цесисъ*); Polish: *Kieś* or *Wenden, wendeński*

Верро, верроскій – Verro, Estonia, since 1917 *Võru* (*Выру*); Polish: *Werro, werroski*

Вольмаръ, вольмарскій – Vol'mar, Latvia, since 1917 *Valmiera (Валмиера*); Polish: *Wolmar*

Дерптъ, дерптскій – *Derpt*, Estonia, since 1919 *Tartu* (*Тарту;* also called *Юрьевъ*, 1893-1918); Polish: *Dorpat, dorpacki*

Перновъ or *Пернава, пернавскій* – *Pernava*, Estonia, since 1917 *Pärnu* (*Пярну*); Polish: *Parnawa, parnawski;* German *Pernau*

Рига, рижскій – *Rīga*, Latvia; Polish: *Ryga, ryski* or *rygski*

Феллинъ, феллинскій – *Fellin*, Estonia, since 1917 *Viljandi (Вильянди*); Polish: *Felin, feliński*

Юрьевъ → *Дерптъ*

Other significant towns in Estonia and Latvia

Либава – *Libava*, Latvia, since 1917 *Liepāja (Лиепая);* Polish: *Libawa* (many emigrants sailed from this port)

Нарва, нарвскій – *Narva*, Estonia

Пельтенъ, пелтенскій – *Pel'ten*, Latvia, since 1917 *Piltene (Пилтене);* Polish: *Piltyń, piltyński*

4. Lithuania (Великое Княжестао Литовское *or* Литва)

Here we concentrate on the *gubernias* covering territory now primarily in **Lithuania**, namely, *Вильна*, Vil'na (also called *Вильно*, Vil'no; now *Vilnius*) and *Ковно*, Kovno (now *Kaunas*). Remember that borders have changed frequently in this part of Europe, and from a historical perspective many other regions besides these were ruled at some point by the Grand Duchy of Lithuania. But at this point we're concentrating on those found in the modern independent nation of Lithuania (although they included territory now in Belarus). The Russian forms appear first, then the Lithuanian forms, and finally Polish noun and adjectival forms. Inasmuch as Polish was the language of record in Lithuania before Russian, many records will be in Polish, and these forms can be very helpful.

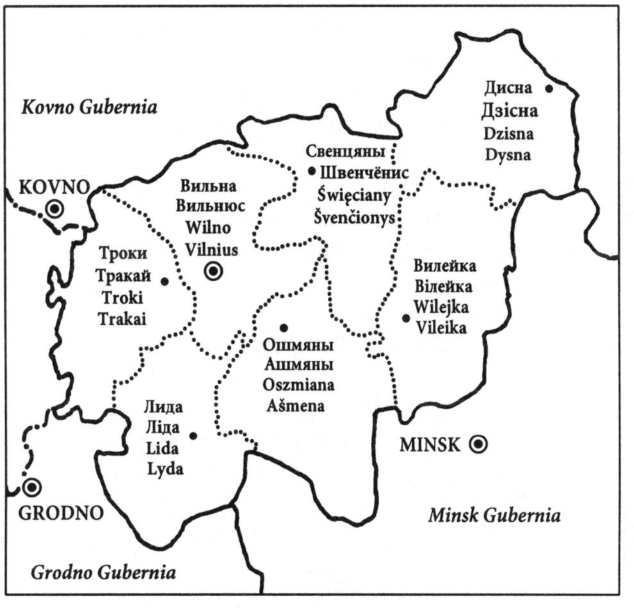

Map V-2: Counties of Vil'na Province

Map V-2, above, shows Vil'na province and its *уѣзды* or counties. For the county seats now located in the independent country of Lithuania—Trakai, Vilnius, and Švenčionys—the first name given for each is its name in pre-1918 Russian; the second is its name in modern Russian; the third is its name in Polish; and the fourth is its modern Lithuanian name. For those towns now in Belarus, the first name is pre-1918 Russian; the second is modern Belarusian; the third is Polish; and the fourth is Lithuanian. It can be helpful to know all four versions of these names!

If you wish to gain a perspective on exactly where these areas were in relationship to the other provinces of the western part of the Russian Empire, Map V-6 on page 136 should help you do so.

Виленская губернія – Vil'na province [Vilnius]

Вилейка, вилейскій – *Vileyka*, now *Вілейка*, Belarus; Polish *Wilejka, wilejski*

Вильна [Вильно], виленскій – *Vil'na* or *Vil'no*, since 1917 called *Вильнюс* in modern Russian; Lithuanian: *Vilnius;* Polish *Wilno, wileński*

Дисна, дисненскій – *Disna*, now *Дзісна*, Belarus; Polish *Dzisna, dziśnieński*

Лида, лидскій – *Lida*, now *Ліда*, Belarus; Polish *Lida, lidzki*

Ошмяны, ошмянскій – *Oshmyany*, now *Ашмяны*, Belarus; Polish *Oszmiana, oszmiański*

Свенцяны, свенцянскій – *Sventsyani*, since 1917 *Швенченис*; Lithuanian *Švenčionys;* Polish *Święciany, święciański*

Троки, трокскій [троцкій] – *Troki*, since 1917 *Тракай, Trakay;* Lithuanian: *Trakai;* Polish *Troki, trocki*

Ковенская губернія – Kovno province [Kaunas]

Вилькомиръ, вилькомирскій – *Vil'komir;* since 1917 *Укмерге;* Lithuanian: *Ukmergė;* Polish *Wilkomierz, wilkomierski*

Ковно, ковенскій – *Kovno;* since 1917 *Каунас;* Lithuanian: *Kaunas;* Polish *Kowno, kowieński*

Ново-Александровскъ, новоалександровскій – *Novo-Aleksandrovsk;* 1919-1929 *Эжеренай*, since 1929 *Зарасай;* Lithuanian: *Zarasai;* Polish *Jeziorosy*

Поневежъ, поневежскiи – *Ponevezh;* since 1917 *Паневежис;* Lithuanian: *Panevėžys;* Polish *Poniewież, poniewieski*

Россіены, россіенскій – *Rossieny;* since 1917 *Расейняй;* Lithuanian: *Raseiniai;* Polish *Ros[s]ienie, ros[s]ieński*

Тельши, тельшевскій – *Tel'shi;* since 1917 *Тельшяй;* Lithuanian: *Telšiai;* Polish *Telsze, telszewski*

Шавли, шавельскій – *Shavli;* since 1917 *Шяуляй;* Lithuanian: *Šiauliai;* Polish *Szawle, szawelski;* German: *Schaulen*

Other significant towns in Lithuania

Ворни – *Varniai*, also called *Medininkai;* Polish: *Miedniki, Worne*

Кеиданы – *Kėdainiai;* Polish: *Kiejdany*

Клаипеда – *Klaipėda;* Polish: *Klajpeda*

Мемель –Russian name for *Klaipėda* till 1923; also an old German and Russian name for the Neman River

Modern Kaliningrad Oblast', Russia

If you look carefully at a map of the Baltic States, you will notice that just west of Lithuania and north of Poland there is a small area which is marked as territory of Russia, or, on older maps, of the Soviet Union. Its capital is Kaliningrad, and in modern Russia it is an *oblast'* in its own right. The city Kaliningrad developed from a fortress founded by the Teutonic Knights in 1255; it was called *Königsberg* by the Germans, *Królewiec* by the Poles. The city and surrounding territory came under Prussian rule in the 16th century. After World War I it became the capital of the German province of East Prussia. After World War II the Soviet Union annexed the area and changed the name from *Königsberg* to *Kaliningrad.* While not part of the Russian Empire historically, it may figure in your research and you may benefit from some knowledge of the area. Some of its better known towns, and their names in various relevant languages, are:

Багратионовск – *Bagrationovsk;* till 1946 called by its German name, *Preussisch Eylau*

Гусев – *Gusev*; till 1946 called by its German name, *Gumbinnen*

Знаменск – *Znamensk;* German: *Wehlau*

Калининград, калининградский – *Kaliningrad;* Polish *Królewiec;* German: *Königsberg;* Lithuanian: *Karaliačius;* older Russian: *Кенигсбергъ* or *Кёнигсбергъ*

Неман, неманский – *Neman*, before 1946 known as *Ragnit*

Нестеров – *Nesterov*, before 1946 called by its German name, *Stalluponen*

Правдинск, правдинский – *Pravdinsk*, before 1946 called by its German name, *Friedland*

Советск – *Тильзит*, modern Russian name *Sovetsk;* German: *Tilsit;* Lithuanian: *Tilže;* Polish: *Tylża*

Черняховск, черняховский – *Chernyakhovsk*, before 1946 called by its German name, *Insterburg*

5. Belarus – old name Бѣлоруссія, now Беларусь

Next we look at provinces consisting primarily of territory now within the borders of the independent nation of Belarus: the provinces of Grodna (also called Grodno, now Hrodna), Minsk, Mogilev (now Mahileŭ), and Vitebsk (now Vitsebsk). For towns now in Belarus, the Russian noun and adjectival forms are followed by their Belarusian names, and Polish noun and adjective forms; for towns now in Poland, the Russian forms are followed only by the Polish noun and adjective forms.

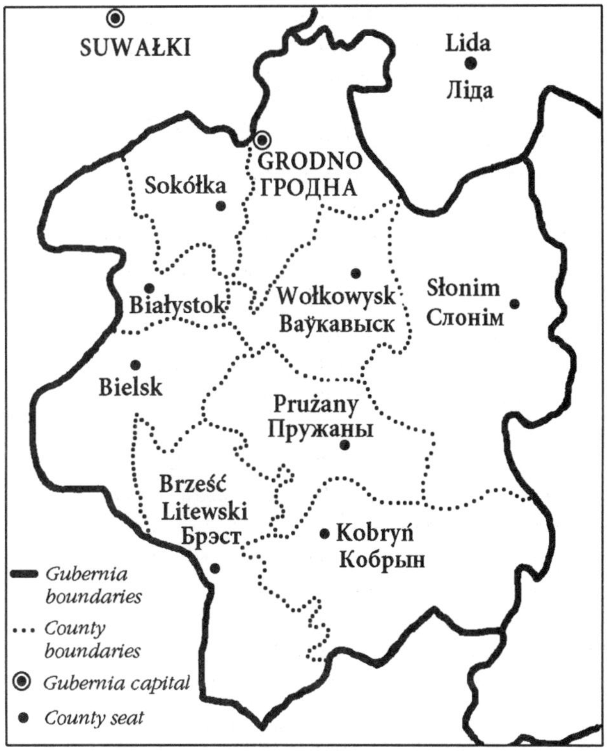

Map V-3: Counties of Grodna Province

Note: Most places in Belarus are better known to us by their Polish or Russian forms than by their Belarusian versions. But one sees attempts to use the Belarusian forms more and more often these days. It is difficult, however, to reflect in English orthography the sound of such characters as э and ў, or to represent in a comprehensible way the distinction between rendering Cyrillic *г* as *g* or *h*. Trying to decide what to call *Магілеў* is a nightmare: *Mogilev*, a transliteration of its Russian name, is best known, but in reference works you see anything from *Mahilev* to *Mohylew*.

In general, we give here the old Russian forms, followed by the modern Belarusian spellings, then the Polish forms. Most reference works you find will probably use Roman-alphabet transliterations of the Russian spellings, or the Polish versions. With the information given below, however, you can at least hope to recognize whatever version you encounter. These towns are now in Belarus unless otherwise noted.

Map V-3 shows details of the individual *уѣзды* of Grodna province. Polish names are given first, then Belarusian names for those towns now in Belarus.

Гродненская губернія – Grodna province *(now Hrodna, Belarus)*

Брестъ, брестскій – Брэст, Brest; Polish: *Brześć, brzeski;* best known in English as *Brest-Litovsk* because of a treaty signed there in 1918

Бѣлостокъ, бѣлостокскій [бѣлостоцкій] – Polish: *Białystok, białostocki* (this city is now in northeast Poland)

Бѣльскъ, бѣльскій – Polish: *Bielsk Podlaski, bielski* (now in Poland)

Волковыскъ, волковыскій – Ваўкавыск, Vaŭkavysk; Polish: *Wołkowysk, wołkowyski*

Гродна [Гродно], гродненскій – Гродна, Hrodna; Polish: *Grodno, grodzieński*

Кобринъ, кобринскій – Кобрын, Kobryn; Polish: *Kobryń, kobryński*

Пружаны, пружанскій – Пружаны, Pruzhany; Polish: *Prużany, prużański*

Слонимъ, слонимскій – Слонім, Slonim; Polish: *Słonim, słonimski*

Соколка, сокольскій – Polish: *Sokółka, sokólski* (now in Poland)

Минская губернія – Minsk province

Бобруйскъ, бобруйскій – Бабруйск, Babruysk; Polish: *Bobrujsk, bobrujski*

Борисовъ, борисовскій – Барысаў; Barysaŭ; Polish: *Borysów, borysowski*

Игуменъ, игуменскій – *Чэрвень, Chèrven'* (the Russian name *Игумен* was used before 1924); Polish: *Ihumen, ihumański*
Минскъ, минскій – *Мінск, Minsk;* Polish: *Minsk, miński*
Мозыръ, мозырскій – *Мазыр, Mazyr;* Polish: *Mozyrz, mozyrski*
Новогрудок, новогрудскій – *Навагрудак, Navahrudak;* Polish: *Nowogródek, nowogrodecki*
Пинскъ, пинскій – *Пінск, Pinsk;* Polish: *Pinsk, piński*
Рѣчица, рѣчицкій – *Рэчыца, Rèchitsa;* Polish: *Rzeczyca, rzeczycki*
Слуцкъ, слуцкій – *Слуцк, Slutsk;* Polish: *Słuck, słucki*

Могилевская губернія: Mogilev [Mahileŭ] province

[Старый] Быховъ, быховскій – *Быхаў, Bykhaй;* Polish: *[Stary] Bychów, bychowski*
Гомелъ, гомельскій – *Гомель, Homel';* Polish: *Homel, homelski*
Горки, горецкій – *Горкі, Horki;* Polish: *Horki, horecki*
Климовичи, климовицкій [климовичскій] – *Клімавічы, Klimavichy;* Polish: *Klimowicze, klimowecki*
Могилевъ, могилевскій – *Магілеў, Mahileŭ;* Polish: *Mohylew, mohylewski*
Мстиславль, мстиславскій – *Мсціслаў, Mstsislaŭ;* Polish: *Mścisław, mścisławski*
Орша, оршанскій – *Орша, Orsha;* Polish: *Orsza, orszański*
Рогачевъ, рогачевскій – *Рагачоў, Rahachoŭ;* Polish: *Rohaczew, rohaczewski*
Сенно, сенненскій – *Сянно, Syanno;* Polish: *Sien[n]o, sieński*
Чаусы, чаусскій – *Чавусы, Chavusy;* Polish: *Czausy, czausowski*
Чериковъ, чериковскій – *Чэрыкаў, Chèrykaŭ;* Polish: *Czeryków, czerykowski*

Витебская губернія – Vitebsk province

Велижъ, велижскій – *Велиж, Velizh* (in Russia); Polish: *Wieliż, wieliski*
Витебскъ, витебскій – *Віцебск, Vitsebsk;* Polish: *Witebsk, witebski*
Городокъ, городокскій – *Гарадок, Haradok;* Polish: *Horodek, horodocki*
Двинскъ, двинскій → *Динабургъ*
Динабургъ, динабургскій (1893-1917 called *Двинскъ, двинскій*) – *Daugavpils*, Latvia (modern Russian *Даугавпилс*); Polish: *Dyneburg, dyneburgski*, also *Dźwińsk, dźwiński;* German: *Dünaburg*
Дрисса, дриссенскій (now Верхнедвинск) – *Верхнядзвінск, Verkhnyadzvinsk;* Polish: *Drys[s]a, drysiński [drysieński]*
Лепелъ, лепельскій – *Лепель, Lepel';* Polish: *Lepel, lepelski*
Люцинъ, люцинскій – now *Ludza*, Latvia; Polish: *Lucyń, lucyński*
Невелъ, невельскій – *Невель, Nevel'*, Russia; Polish: *Newel, newelski*
Полоцкъ, полоцкій – *Полацк, Polatsk;* Polish: *Połock, połocki*
Рѣжица, рѣжицкій – now *Rēzekne*, Latvia (till 1893 called *Розиттенъ, Rozitten;* till 1917 *Рѣжица;* since then *Rēzekne*); Polish: *Rzeżyca, rzeżycki*
Себежъ, себежскій – *Себеж, Sebezh*, Russia; Polish: *Siebież, siebieski*

Here are the pre-Revolutionary Russian names of some other towns in Belarus, followed by English transliterations of those names. After the dash come their modern names in Belarusian, Roman-alphabet transliterations of those names, and their names in Polish, which may prove useful in looking these names up in sources such as the *Słownik Geograficzny* (see page 155):

Барановичи, Baranovichi – *Баранавічы, Baranavichy;* Polish: *Baranowicze*
Берестовица, Berestovitsa– *Бераставіца, Berastavitsa;* Polish: *Brzostowica*
Браславъ, Braslav – *Браслаў, Braslaŭ;* Polish: *Brasław*
Воложинъ, Volozhin – *Валожын, Valozhyn;* Polish: *Wołożyn*
Вороново, Voronovo – *Воранава, Voranava;* Polish: *Woronowo*
Глубокое, Glubokoye – *Глубокае, Hlubokaye;* Polish: *Głębokie*
Глускъ, Glusk – *Глуск, Hlusk;* Polish: *Hłusk*
Друя, Druya – *Друя, Druya;* Polish: *Druja*
Дятлово, Dyatlovo – *Дзятлава, Dzyatlava;* Polish: *Dziatłowo [Zdzięcioł]*

Ивье, Iv'ye – *Іўе, Iŭe;* Polish: *Iwie*
Заславль, Zaslavl' – *Заслаўе, Zaslaŭe;* Polish: *Zasław* (see note on *Изяславъ, Izyaslav,* on page 130)
Зельва, Zel'va– *Зэльва, Zel'va;* Polish: *Zelwa*
Каменецъ, Kamenets – *Камянец, Kamyanets;* Polish: *Kamieniec*
Копыль, Kopyl' – *Капыль, Kapyl';* Polish: *Kopyl*
Кореличи, Korelichi (or Кареличи, Karelichi) – *Карэлічы, Karèlichy;* Polish: *Korelicze*
Малорита, Malorita – *Маларыта, Malaryta;* Polish: *Maloryta*
Миръ, Mir – *Мір, Mir;* Polish: *Mir*
Молодечно, Molodechno – *Маладзечна, Maladzechna;* Polish: *Mołodeczno*
Мосты, Mosty – *Масты, Masty;* Polish: *Mosty*
Несвижъ, Nesvizh – *Нясвиж, Nyasvizh;* Polish: *Nieśwież*
Островецъ, Ostrovets – *Астравец, Astravets;* Polish: *Ostrowiec*
Свислочь, Svisloch – *Свіслач, Svislach;* Polish: *Swisłocz*
Сморгонь, Smorgon'– *Смаргонь, Smarhon';* Polish: *Smorgonie*

6. Ukraine (Украина)

Ukraine is a large country with a turbulent history. It has seen many changes in national affiliations, administrative divisions, the languages of the towns' names, even the names themselves; e. g., the town that used to be called *Stanisławów* by Poles is now *Івано-Франківськ (Ivano-Frankivs'k).* Depending on whether you are looking at the period when a given area was ruled by Poland, or the Austrian Empire, or the Russian Empire, or the Soviet Union, or after Ukraine gained its independence, you may find the names given in Polish, German, Russian, or Ukrainian. It would take a sizable book just to do justice to this complexity (e. g., *Ukraine: A Historical Atlas,* Paul Robert Magocsi, University of Toronto Press, 1985, revised 1987, ISBN 0-8020-3429-2); a comprehensive study is certainly beyond the scope of this book.

We have chosen to focus on the administrative divisions in force at the time of the greatest emigration from Europe to North America, from the late 19th century to the early years of the 20th century. Our experience suggests these are the ones most likely to help researchers get on the right track. But keep in mind that no one listing can possibly cover all the changes that took place over the years, and refer to detailed gazetteers and maps whenever possible (see part C of this chapter, beginning on page 140). Remember also that during the 19th century and until World War I, northern and eastern Ukraine were in the Russian Empire, while southwestern Ukraine was in the Austrian partition, comprising the eastern half of the Austrian *Kronland* ("crownland") called *Galizien* in German (in Ukrainian *Галичина,* in Russian *Галиція,* in Polish *Galicja,* in English *Galicia*).

In line with our general tendency to go from west to east, let us first take a look at those regions which were in Galicia as of the late 19th century; then the regions of "Little Russia" (as Russians categorized them); and finally those of "Southern Russia."

Territory Formerly in the Austrian Partition (Eastern Galicia), Later in the Soviet Union

The following are names of major towns in territory ruled by the Austrian Empire, not the Russian Empire, until World War I. These areas are relevant to a book on Russian research because they all came under Soviet rule at some point thereafter, so that from our perspective they were in the Soviet Union until comparatively recently. If your ancestors came from that area, we may generally expect documents relating to them and dating from the period 1945-1991 to be in Russian.

You can refer to Map V-4 on page 129 to locate some of the places listed here. Note that only the eastern half of the territory shown in that map later came under Russian rule. The places with names given only in their Polish forms (i. e., in the Roman alphabet) are in Poland and were never ruled by the Soviet Union. It is the towns with names given in Ukrainian Cyrillic forms that eventually came under Soviet rule.

The Ukrainian forms are listed below, followed by an English transliteration, then the Polish noun and adjectival forms. Russian forms are not given because, with few exceptions, they are almost identical to the Ukrainian spellings. In most cases you need only replace Ukrainian ***i*** with Russian ***u*** or ***o***, and Ukrainian ***u*** with Russian ***ы***, to get the Russian form of the name, or a spelling so close as to be easily recognizable.

Белз, Belz – Polish: *Bełz, bełzki*
Бережани, Berezhany – Polish: *Brzeżany, brzeżański*
Бібрка, Bibrka – Polish: *Bóbrka, bobrecki*
Богородчани, Bohorodchany – Polish: *Bohorodczany, bohorodczański*
Борщів, Borshchiv – Polish: *Borszczów, borszczowski*
Броди, Brody – Polish: *Brody, brodzki*
Бучач, Buchach – Polish: *Buczacz, buczacki*
Городок, Horodok – Polish: *Gródek Jagielloński, grodecki*
Городенка, Horodenka – Polish: *Horodenka, horodeński*
Гусятин, Husiatyn – Polish: *Husiatyn, husiatyński*
Добромиль, Dobromyl' – Polish: *Dobromil, dobromilski* (what was Dobromyl' district is now partly in Poland, partly in Ukraine)
Долина, Dolyna – Polish: *Dolina, doliński [doliniański]*
Дрогобич, Drohobych – Polish: *Drohobycz, drohobycki*
Жовква, Zhovkva – Polish: *Żółkiew, żółkiewski;* Russian: *Жолква*, called *Нестеров* during the Soviet era
Жидачів, Zhydachiv – Polish: *Żydaczów, żydaczowski*
Заліщики, Zalishchyky – Polish: *Zaleszczyki, zaleszczycki*
Збараж, Zbarazh – Polish: *Zbaraż, zbaraski*
Золочів, Zolochiv – Polish: *Złoczów, złoczowski*
Калуш, Kalush – Polish: *Kałusz, kałuski*
Кам'янка Бузька , Kam'yanka Buz'ka – Polish: *Kamionka Strumiłowa, kamionecki*
Коломия, Kolomyia – Polish: *Kołomyja, kołomyjski*
Косів, Kosiv – Polish: *Kosów, kosowski*
Лісько, Lis'ko; Polish: *Lisko* (also called *Lesko*), *leski* (partly in Poland, partly in Ukraine)
Львів, L'viv – Polish: *Lwów, lwowski;* Russian *Львовъ* (modern spelling *Львов*)
Мостиська, Mostys'ka – Polish: *Mościska, mościski*
Надвірна, Nadvirna – Polish: *Nadwórna, nadworniański*
Перемишль, Peremyshl' – Polish: *Przemyśl, przemyski* (part of former Przemyśl district is now in Poland, and part is in Ukraine)
Перемишляни, Peremyshlyany– Polish: *Przemyślany, przemyślański*
Підгайці, Pidhaitsi – Polish: *Podhajce, pohajecki*
Рава Руська, Rava Rus'ka – Polish: *Rawa Ruska, rawski*
Рогатин, Rohatyn – Polish: *Rohatyn, rohatyński*
Рудки, Rudky – Polish: *Rudki, rudecki*
Самбір, Sambir – Polish: *Sambor, samborski*
Скалат, Skalat –Polish: *Skałat, skałacki*
Снятин, Sniatyn – Polish: *Śniatyn, Śniatyński*
Сокаль, Sokal' – Polish: *Sokal, sokalski*
Станіславів Stanislaviv (now Івано-Франківськ, Ivano-Frankivs'k) – Polish: *Stanisławów, stanisławowski*
Старе Місто, Stare Misto – Polish: *Staremiasto, staromiejski*
Старий Самбір, Staryi Sambir – Polish: *Stary Sambor, starosamborski*
Стрий, Stryi – Polish: *Stryj, stryjski*
Тернопіль, Ternopil' – Polish: *Tarnopol, tarnopolski*
Товмач, Tovmach – Polish: *Tłumacz, tłumacki*
Теребовля, Terebovlya – Polish: *Trembowla, trembowelski*
Турка, Turka – Polish: *Turka, turczański*
Чортків, Chortkiv – Polish: *Czortków, czortkowski*
Яворів, Yavoriv– Polish: *Jaworów, jaworowski* (part of former Yavoriv district is in Poland, part in Ukraine)

Map V-4 – Galicia as of the mid-19th century, shows that part of the Polish-Lithuanian Commonwealth seized by Austria during the partitions in the late 18th century. This area, called *Galicia,* lay south of the Russian Empire and its subdivision, the Kingdom of Poland. The western half of the territory shown is now southeastern Poland. The eastern half, which is now western Ukraine, was ruled by the Austrian Empire until after World War I. It was ruled by Poland between the World Wars, then came under Soviet rule after World War II. The names of those towns are given in Polish and Ukrainian forms because both may prove helpful in your research. The Russian forms of the names are so similar to the Ukrainian ones that it seemed unnecessary to give them separately.

Ukrainian Territories in "Little Russia," "South Russia," and Western Russia

The following are provinces and *uyezdy* now in Ukraine (for the most part) but formerly part of the Russian Empire, as it existed in the late 19th century. If you look at the map on page 131, you'll see they are listed here in order from north to south, beginning in the northwest and heading eastward; but the towns within each *uyezd* are listed alphabetically. Note too that Bessarabia is included here, even though much of it is no longer in Ukraine but in Moldova. It was the southwesternmost region of the Russian Empire, however, and it seems reasonable to include it here, rather than with European Russia, which would involve suddenly jumping back southwest across the Black Sea.

Remember that one often sees conflicting spellings of Ukrainian place names on maps and in gazetteers. To some extent this is due to the vicissitudes of trying to render Ukrainian names in the Roman alphabet, which was not designed to handle its phonetics. But even Cyrillic spellings can be inconsistent. This is largely due to the confusion caused by the Russians' and Soviets' long-standing policy of "Russianizing" the Ukrainian language and "normalizing" (by Russian norms, of course) those pesky differences between Ukrainian and Russian versions of names. Thus even some reliable sources give Russian *Ровно* as the name of the town Ukrainians call *Рівне*. We have tried to give correct forms below, but in some instances even the experts are still disputing what the correct form should be!

The first form given is the old Russian spelling of the noun and adjectival forms. After the dash is the modern Ukrainian spelling, and an English transliteration; finally the Polish names are given in noun and adjectival forms. The reason we give the Polish forms is that in practice you may find Polish-language sources on these places, such as the *Słownik geograficzny Królestwa Polskiego i innych krajów słowiańskich* (see page 155) are among the most accessible and valuable ones available, especially for the period during which emigration from Eastern Europe was at its height.

Волынская губернія – Volyn' [Volhynia] province, capital Zhytomyr (or Zhitomir)

Владимиръ Волынскій, владимирскій or *владимиро-волынскій – Володимир Волиньський, Volodymyr Volyn's'kyi;* Polish: *Włodzimierz, włodzimierski*

Дубно, дубенскій – Дубно, Dubno; Polish: *Dubno, dubieński*

Житомиръ, житомирскій – Житомир, Zhytomyr; Polish: *Żytomierz, żytomierski*

Изяславъ, изяславскій [Заславль, заславскій] – Ізяслав, Izyaslav; Polish: *Zasław, zasławski* — *Note:* In modern usage Russian *Изяслав*, Ukr. *Ізяслав*, refers to this town in Khmel'nyts'kyi province of Ukraine; Russian *Заславль, Zaslavl'*, Belarusian *Заслаўе, Zaslaŭe*, refers to a town northwest of Minsk in Belarus (see page 127). But in terms of etymology and usage these two names are closely linked, and can easily be confused.

Ковель, ковельскій – Ковіль, Kovil'; Polish: *Kowel, kowelski*

Кременецъ, кременецкій – Кременець, Kremenets'; Polish: *Krzemieniec, krzemieniecki*

Луцкъ, луцкій – Луцьк, Luts'k; Polish: *Łuck, łucki*

Новоградъ-Волынскій, новоградскій – Новоград-Волиньський, Novohrad-Volyn's'kyi; Polish: *Nowograd Wołyński, nowogród-wołyński*

Овручъ, овручскій – Овруч, Ovruch; Polish: *Owrucz, owrucki*

Острогъ, острожскій – Острог, Ostroh; Polish: *Ostróg, ostrógski*

Ровно, ровенскій – Рівне, Rivne; Polish: *Równo, rowieński*

Староконстантиновъ, староконстантиновскій – Старокостянтинів, Starokostyantyniv; Polish: *Starokonstantynów, starokonstantynowski*

Map V-5 – The Pale of Settlement as of the late 19th century

The Pale of Settlement was the western part of the Russian Empire, the only part in which Jews were allowed to settle. The *gubernias* were named for the cities that served as their capitals, with four exceptions: the *gubernias* of Volyn', capital Zhitomir; Podolia, capital Kamenets-Podolskiy; Bessarabia, capital Kishinev; and Tavrida, capital Simferopol'. All names are Roman-alphabet renderings of Russian forms, e. g., *Belostok* (compare Polish *Białystok*), *Lomzha* (compare Polish *Łomża*), *Vil'na* (*Vilnius*), *Kiev* (compare Ukrainian *Київ*), etc.

Подольская губернія – Podolia province, capital Kamenets-Podol'sk

Балта, балтскій – Балта, Balta; Polish: *Bałta, bałcki*

Брацлавъ, брацлавскій – Брацлав, Bratslav; Polish: *Bracław, bracławski*

Винница, винницкій – Вінниця, Vinnytsa; Polish: *Winnica, winnicki*

Гайсинъ, гайсинскій – Гайсин, Haisyn; Polish: *Hajsyn, hajsyński*

Каменецъ Подольскій – Кам'янець Подільський, Kam'yanets Podil's'kyi; Polish: *Kamieniec Podolski, kamieniecki*

Летичевъ, летичевскій – Летичів, Letychiv; Polish: *Latyczów, latyczowski*

Литинъ, литинскій – Літин, Lityn; Polish: *Lityn, lityński*

Могилевъ Подольскій – Могилів Подільський, Mohyliv Podil's'kyi; Polish: *Mohylów Podolski*

Новая Ушица, новоушицкій – Нова Ушиця, Nova Ushytsya; Polish *Uszyca, uszycki*

Ольгополь, ольгопольскій – Ольгопіль, Ol'hopil'; Polish: *Olhopol, olhopolski*

Проскуровъ, проскуровскій – Проскурів, Proskuriv (since 1954 called *Хмельницький, Khmel'nytskyi*) – Polish: *Proskurów* or *Płoskirów, proskurowski*

Ямполь, ямпольскій – Ямпіль , Yampil'; Polish: *Jampol, jampolski*

Note: In this same region is the town of ***Чернівці***, *Chernivtsi.* Before 1940 it was the capital of the region of Bukovina, which was under the rule of the Austrian Empire until after World War I, and then was part of Romania. In 1940 that region was ceded to the Soviet Union. *Чернівці* is the Ukrainian name of this town; in German it was called *Czernowitz,* in Polish *Czerniowce,* in Romanian *Cernăuţi,* and in Russian *Черновицы, Chernovitsy* (after 1944 *Черновцы, Chernovtsy*). The other main town of Bukovina is *Хотин, Khotyn* (Polish name *Chocim*) mentioned below under Bessarabia—much of which, as we said earlier, is now part of the nation of Moldova, not Ukraine.

Бессарабская губернія – Bessarabia province, comprising most of what is now Moldova and the southern part of Odessa *oblast';* capital *Kishinev* (now *Chişinău,* Moldova)

Аккерманъ, аккерманскій – Білгород-Дністровський, Bilhorod-Dnistrovs'kyi (Ukraine); Polish: *Akkerman, akkermański,* also called *Białogród*

Бендеры, бендерскій – Tighina, Moldova; Polish: *Bendery, benderski*

Бѣльцы → Ясскяй уѣздъ

Измаил – Ізмаїл, Izmayil, Ukraine; Polish: *Izmaił, izmailski*

Кишинёвъ, кишиневскій – Chişinău, Moldova; Polish *Kiszyniów, kiszyniewski;* Ukrainian *Кишинів*

Оргѣевъ, оргѣевскій – now *Orhei,* Moldova; Polish: *Orgiejew, orgiejewski*

Сороки, сорокскій – Soroca, Moldova; Polish: *Soroki, sorocki*

Хотинъ, хотинскій – Хотин, Kotyn; Polish: *Chocim, chocimski*

Ясскій уѣздъ – the *уѣздъ* was named for the town of *Яссы,* now *Iaşi,* Moldova, Polish name *Jassy;* but the administrative center was *Бѣльцы,* now *Bălţi,* Moldova; Polish: *Bielce, bielecki*

Кіевская губернія – Kiev province, capital Kiev

Бердичевъ, бердичевскій – Бердичів, Berdychiv; Polish: *Berdyczów, berdyczowski*

Васильковъ, васильковскій – Васильків, Vasyl'kiv; Polish: *Wasylków, wasylkowski*

Звенигородка, звенигородскій – Звенигородка, Zvenyhorodka; Polish: *Zwinogródka, zwinogródzki*

Каневъ, каневскій – Канів, Kaniv; Polish: *Kaniów, kaniowski*

Кіевъ, кіевскій – Київ, Kyyiv; Polish: *Kijów, kijowski*

Липовецъ, липовецкій – Липовець, Lypovets'; Polish: *Lipowiec, lipowiecki*

Радомышль, радомышльскій – Радомишль, Radomyshl'; Polish: *Radomyśl, radomyski*

Сквира, сквирскій – Сквира, Skvyra; Polish: *Skwira, skwirski*

Таращa, таращанскій – Таращa, Tarashcha; Polish: *Taraszcza, taraszczański*

Умань, уманскій – Умань, Uman'; Polish: *Humań, humański*

Черкассы, черкасскій – Черкаси, Cherkasy; Polish: *Czerkasy, czerkaski*

Чигиринъ , чигиринскій – Чигирин, Chyhyryn; Polish: *Czehryń, czehryński*

Черниговская губернія – Chernigov province, capital Chernigov

Борзна, борзнинскій – Борзна, Borzna; Polish: *Borzna, borzneński* or *borzniański*

Глуховъ, глуховскій – Глухів, Hlukhiv; Polish: *Głuchów, głuchowski*

Городня, городнянскій – Городня, Horodnia; Polish: *Horodnia* or *Gorodnia, horodnicki*

Козелецъ, козелецкій – Козелець, Kozelets': Polish: *Kozielec, kozielecki*

Конотопъ, конотопскій – Конотоп, Konotop; Polish: *Konotop, konotopski*

Кролевецъ, кролевецкій – Кролевець, Krolevets'; Polish: Królewiec, królewiecki

Мглинъ, мглинскій – Мглин, Russia; Polish: *Mglin* or *Mhlin, mgliński*

Нежинъ, нежинскій – Ніжин, Nizhyn; Polish: *Nieżyn, nieżyński*

Новгородъ-Северскій – Новгород-Сіверський, Novhorod-Sivers'kyi; Polish: *Nowogród-Siewierski*

Новозыбковъ, новозыбковскій – Новозибков, Novozybkov, Russia; Polish: *Nowozybków, nowozybkowski*

Остеръ, остерскій [осторскій] – Остер, Oster; Polish: *Ostr* or *Ostrz, osterski*

Сосница, сосницкій – Сосниця, Sosnytsya; Polish: *Sośnica, sośnicki*

Стародубъ, стародубскій – Стародуб, Starodub, Russia; Polish: *Starodub, starodubski*

Суражъ, суражскій – Сураж, Surazh, Russia; Polish: *Suraż, suraski*

Черниговъ, черниговскій – Чернігів, Chernihiv; Polish: *Czernihów, czernihówski*

Полтавская губернія – Poltava province, capital Poltava

Гадячъ, гадячскій – Гадяч, Hadyach; Polish: *Hadziacz,hadziacki*

Золотоноша, золотоношскій – Золотоноша, Zolotonosha; Polish: *Zołotonosza, zołotonoski*

Зѣньковъ, зѣньковскій – Зіньків, Zin'kiv; Polish: *Zieńków, zieńkowski*

Кобеляки, кобелякскій – Кобеляки, Kobelyaky; Polish: *Kobielaki, kobielacki*

Константиноградъ, константиноградскій (since 1922 *Красноград*) *– Красноград, Krasnohrad;* Polish: *Konstantynogród, konstantynogradzki*

Кременчугъ, кременчугскій – Кременчук; Polish: *Kremieńczuk, kremieńczuski*

Лохвица, лохвицкій – Лохвиця, Lokhvytsya; Polish: *Łochwice, łochwicki*

Лубны, лубенскій – Лубни, Lubny; Polish: *Lubny, lubeński*

Миргородъ, миргородскій – Миргород, Myrhorod; Polish: *Mirgorod, mirgorodzki*

Переяславъ, переяславскій (since 1943 *Переяслав-Хмельницкий*) *– Переяслав-Хмельницький, Pereyaslav-Khmel'nyts'kyi;* Polish: *Perejasław, perejasławski*

Пирятинъ, пирятинскій – Пирятин, Pyryatyn; Polish: *Piratyń, piratyński*

Полтава, полтавскій – Полтава, Poltava; Polish: *Połtawa, połtawski*

Прилуки, прилукскій [прилуцкій] – Прилуки, Pryluky; Polish: *Priłuki, priłucki*

Ромны [Роменъ], роменскій – Ромни, Romny; Polish: *Romny, romeński*

Хоролъ [Хороль], хоролскій – Хорол, Khorol; Polish: *Chorol, chorolski*

Херсонская губернія – Kherson province, capital Kherson

Александрія, александрійскій – Олександрія, Oleksandriya; Polish: *Aleksandrja, aleksandryjski*

Ананьевъ – Ананьів, Anan'iv; Polish: *Ananjew, ananjewski*

Елисаветградъ, елисаветградскій – Кировоград, Kirovohrad; Polish: *Elizabetgrad, elizabetgradzki;* this city's Russian name was *Елисаветград* till 1924, then it was renamed *Зиноевск;* in 1936 it was renamed *Кирово,* and in 1939 *Кировоград;* at one time the *uyezd* capital was *Бобринецъ,* Ukr. *Бобринець*

Одесса, одесскій – Одеса, Odesa; Polish: *Odessa, odeski*

Тирасполь, тираспольскій – Tiraspol, Moldova Polish: *Tyraspol, tyraspolski*

Херсонъ, херсонскій – Херсон, Kherson; Polish *Cherson, cherskoński*

Харьковская губернія – Khar'kov province, capital Khar'kov

Ахтырка, ахтырскій – Охтирка, Okhtyrka; Polish: *Achtyrka, achtyrski*

Богодуховъ, богодуховскій – Богодухів, Bohodukhiv; Polish: *Bogoduchów, bogoduchowski* (also *Bohoduchów, bohoduchowski*)

Валки, валкскій – Валки, Valky; Polish: *Wałki, wałkowski*

Волчанскъ, волчанскій – Вовчанськ , Vovchans'k; Polish: *Wołczańsk, wołczański*

Змiевъ, змiевскiй – *Змiïв, Zmiyiv;* Polish: *Zmijew, zmijewski*
Изюмъ, изюмскiй – *Iзюм* , *Izyum;* Polish: *Izium, iziumski*
Купянскъ, купянскiй – *Куп'янськ, Kup'yans'k;* Polish: *Kupiańsk, kupiański*
Лебединъ, лебединскiй – *Лебедин, Lebedyn;* Polish: *Lebiedyn* or *Lebiedin, lebiediński* or *lebiedyński*
Старобѣльскъ , *старобѣльскiй* – *Старобiльськ, Starobil's'k;* Polish: *starobielski*
Сумы, сумскiй [суманскiй] – *Суми, Sumy;* Polish: *Sumy, sumski*
Харьковъ, харьковскiй – *Харкiв, Khar'kiv;* Polish: *Charków, charkowski*

Екатеринославская губернiя – Yekaterinoslav province, capital Yekaterinoslav

Александровскъ, александровскiй (since 1921 Запорожье) – *Олександрiвськ, Oleksandrivs'k* (since 1921 *Запорiжжя, Zaporizhzhya*); Polish: *Aleksandrowsk, aleksandrowski*
Бахмутъ, бахмутскiй (since 1924 *Артёмовск*) – *Артемiвськ, Artemivs'k;* Polish *Bachmut, bachmucki*
Верхнеднѣпровскъ, верхнеднѣпровскiй – Ukr. *Верхньоднiпровськ, Verkhn'odniprovs'k;* Polish: *Werchnie-Dnieprowsk, wierchnie-dnieprowski*
Екатеринославъ, екатеринославскiй (1796-1802 called *Новороссiйскъ*, 1802-1926 *Екатеринославъ*, 1926-present *Днепропетровск*) – *Днiпроретровськ, Dnipropetrovs'k;* Polish: *Ekaterynosław, ekaterynosławski*
Новомосковскъ, новомосковскiй – *Новомосковськ, Novomoskovs'k;* Polish: *Nowo-Moskowsk, nowo-moskiewski*
Павлоградъ, павлоградскiй – *Павлоград, Pavlohrad;* Polish: *Pawłograd, pawłogradzki* (or *Pawłogród, pawłogródzki*)
Славяносербскъ, славяносербскiй – *Слов'янсосербськ, Slov'yanoserbs'k;* Polish: *Sławianoserbsk, sławianoserbski*

[Also affiliated with this province were the municipal districts of *Ростовъ-на-Дону, Rostov-na-Donu,* and *Таганрогъ, Taganrog,* regarded as separate administrative units. They were also sometimes associated with the **Land of the Don Army**, see page 135.]

Таврическая губернiя – Tavrida province: the name given the Nogai steppes and Crimean peninsula after they were incorporated into Russia in 1783 (the Crimean peninsula is now the Republic of *Крым, Krym*), capital Simferopol'; the municipal district of *Керчъ-Еникале, Kerch-Yenikale,* was also affiliated with this province:

Алешки (since 1928 *Цюрупинск, Tsyurupinsk)* – *Олешки* (now *Цюрупинськ, Tsyurupyns'k*); Polish: *Aleszki*
Бердянскъ, бердянскiй – *Бердянськ, Berdyans'k;* Polish: *Berdiańsk, berdiański*
Евпаторiя, евпаторiйскiй – *Євпаторiя, Yevpatoriya;* Polish: *Eupatoryja, eupatoryjski*
Мелитополь, мелитопольскiй (before 1841 called *Новоалександровская Слобода, Novoaleksandrovskaya Sloboda)* – *Мелiтополь, Melitopol';* Polish: *Melitopol, melitopolski*
Перекопъ, перекопскiй – *Перекоп, Perekop;* Polish: *Perekop, perekopski*
Симферополь, симферепольскiй – *Сiмферополь, Simferopol'*, Republic of Krym (Crimea); Polish: *Symferopol, symferopolski*
Феодосiя, феодосiйскiй – *Феодосiя, Feodosiya* (Republic of Crimea); Polish *Teodozja, teodozyjski*
Ялта, ялтинскiй – *Ялта, Yalta;* Polish: *Jalta, jałtyński* or *jałcki*

The following are names of other towns in Ukraine prominent for historical reasons:

Бѣлая Церковь – *Бiла Церква, Bila Tserkva;* Polish: *Biała Cerkiew*
Галичъ, галицкiй – *Галич, Halych,* now in Ivano-Frankivs'k province, 5 km. from the ruins of the ancient town (destroyed by Mongols and Tatars in 1241) by the same name; from which the region of Galicia originally took its name*;* Polish: *Halicz, halicki*
Жолква (since 1951 *Нестеров*) – *Жовква, Zhovkva;* Polish: *Żółkiew, żółkiewski*
Лембергъ, Lemberg – *Львив; Lemberg* was the German name for the city of L'viv (see page 128). That city was normally called *Львовъ* in Russian, *Lwów* in Polish; in some historical contexts you may see this German name given in this Cyrillic spelling *Лембергъ.*
Николаевъ, николаевскiй – *Миколаïв, Mykolayiv;* Polish: *Mikołajew*

7. Great Russia

After all this, we're only now getting to "Russia" itself, the heart of the Empire. First let us deal with "Great Russia" [*Великороссія*, Polish *Wielkorosja*], which consisted of 19 central and northern *gubernias*. They are listed below in alphabetical order. In each case the Russian adjectival form is given first, followed by a transliteration in the Roman alphabet of the name of the province—usually from the town or city that served as its administrative center.

So far we've looked at the westernmost part of the Russian Empire in some detail. The rest of the Empire was so huge, and had so many subdivisions, that it is not practical to list all the administrative centers of *уѣзды* and *округи* and so forth. It would take a sizable book to do justice to that subject. And our experience is that—so far, at least—relatively few people with roots in that area are interested in genealogy; most of our readers presumably do not need that information. From this point on we list only the major administrative subdivisions. If you need more detail, you should consult a good encyclopedia or some of the gazetteers and other sources listed in Section C, beginning on page 140.

All of the provinces listed on this page are visible on the map on page 136.

Архангельская губерниія – Arkhangel'sk province
Владимірская губерниія – Vladimir province
Вологодская губерниія – Vologda province
Воронежская губерниія – Voronezh province
Калужская губерниія – Kaluga province
Костромская губерниія – Kostroma province
Курская губерниія – Kursk province
Московская губерниія – Moskva province
Нижегородская губерниія – Nizhniy Novgorod province, capital Nizhniy Novgorod
Новгородская губерниія – Novgorod province
Олонецкая губерниія – Olonets province, capital Petrozavodsk
Орловская губерниія – Orel province
Псковская губерниія – Pskov province
Рязанская губерниія – Ryazan' province
Смоленская губерниія – Smolensk province
Тамбовская губерниія – Tambov province
Тверская губерниія – Tver' province
Тульская губерниія – Tula province
Ярославская губерниія – Yaroslavl' province

8. South Russia, or "New" Russia

South Russia, or **New Russia**, consisted primarily of territory now in Ukraine, listed under that country (pages 130-134). The only part of South Russia not within the independent nation of Ukraine was **Земля войска Донского,** "Land of the Don Army," official name (1786-1870) of the Don River district (1872-1920 called the *область Войска Донского*), surrounded by the provinces of Yekaterinoslav, Khar'kov, Voronezh, Saratov, Astrakhan', Stavropol, and the Land of the Black Sea Cossacks (later Kuban').

9. The Region of Kazan', *gubernias:*

Вятская губернія, Province of Vyatka, capital Vyatka (now called *Киров, Kirov*)
Казанская губернія, Province of Kazan'
Пензенская губернія, Province of Penza
Пермская губернія, Province of Perm'
Симбирская губернія, Province of Simbirsk (now called *Ульянов, Ul'yanov*)

10. The Region of Astrakhan', *gubernias*:

Астраханская губернія, Astrakhan' province
Оренбургская губернія, Province of Orenburg, capital Orenburg
Самарская губернія, Samara province
Саратовская губернія, Saratov province
Уфимская губернія, Ufa province

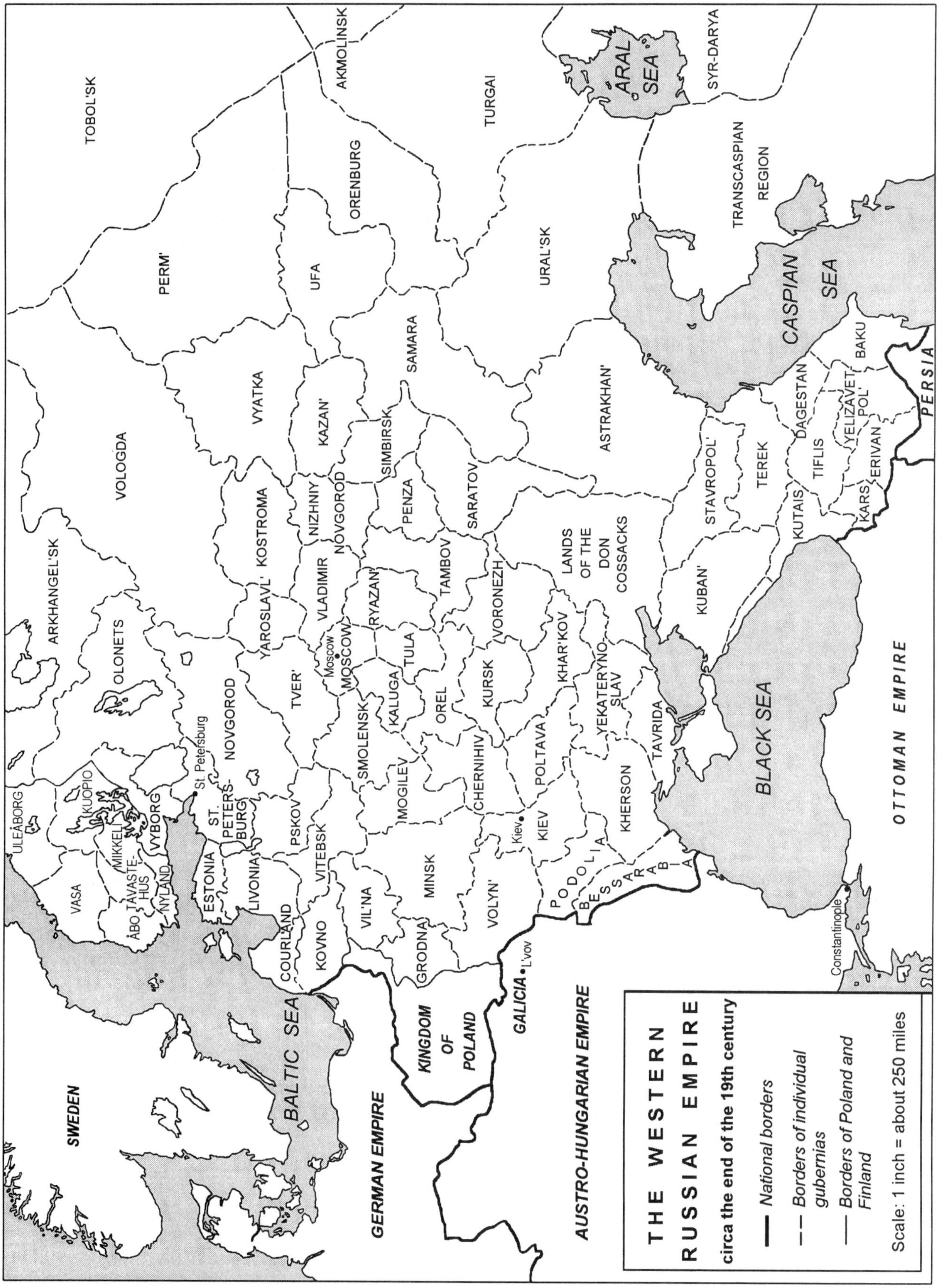

Map V-6: The Western Russian Empire as of the End of the 19th Century

11. Asiatic Russia (see maps pages 138-139)

• THE *GUBERNIAS* AND DISTRICTS OF *КАВКАЗ*, THE CAUCASUS

Бакинская губернія: province of Baku, capital *Баку, Baku,* now the capital of Azerbaijan, on the southwestern shore of the Caspian Sea

Дагестанская область: district of Dagestan, capital *Петровскъ, Petrovsk,* now *Махачкала, Makhachkala;* Dagestan is now a republic north of Azerbaijan, on the Caspian Sea

Елизаветпольская губернія: Province of Yelizavetpol', capital *Елизаветполь, Yelizavetpol',* now *Gäncä*; most of this area is now in Azerbaijan or Armenia

Карская область: the district of the ancient city of *Карсъ, Kars,* just west of Armenia, now in northeastern Turkey but under Russian rule from 1878 to 1918

Кубанская область: district of Kuban', the region of the Kuban' river (part of which was at one time called the "Black Sea Cossacks Lands"); capital *Екатеринодаръ, Yekaterinodar,* since 1920 called *Краснодар*

Кутаисская губернія: province of the city of *Кутаисъ, Kutais,* now *K'ut'aisi,* Georgia

Ставропольская губернія: Province of Stavropol', capital Stavropol'

Терская область: district of the Terek River in the northern Caucasus, including areas now in the Republics of Chechnya, Dagestan, Kabardino-Balkariya, and North Ossetia; capital *Владикавказ, Vladikavkaz*

Тифлисская губернія: Tiflis province, capital Tiflis (now *Тбилиси, Tbilisi,* Georgia)

Черноморская губернія: Black Sea province, now in the territory of *Краснодар, Krasnodar*

Эриванская губернія: Province of Erivan, capital *Эривань, Erivan* (now *Ереван*, Yerevan); this area is mostly in Armenia now, with some overlap into Azerbaijan

• THE *GUBERNIAS* AND DISTRICTS OF *СИБИРЬ*, SIBERIA

Амурская область: Amur district in far eastern Russia, capital *Благовещенскъ, Blagoveshchensk*

Енисейская губернія: province of Yeniseisk, name of a town, also of the region of the Yenisei River in central Siberia; capital *Красноярскъ, Krasnoyarsk*

Забайкальская область: Zabajkal district, i. e., "beyond [Lake] Bajkal," administrative center *Чита*, Chita, on the southern edge of the Siberian lowlands, the region called Buryatiya

Иркутская губернія: Irkutsk province, capital *Иркутскъ, Irkutsk*; the Irkutsk General-Governorship of eastern Siberia consisted of the province of Irkutsk and the territories of Yeniseisk and Yakutiya

Островъ Сахалинъ: Sakhalin island

Приморская область: Primorski district, in far eastern and northeastern Siberia; capital: *Владивостокъ, Vladivostok*

Тобольская губернія: Tobol'sk province

Томская губернія: Tomsk province

Якутская область: the district of Yakutiya, in what is now the Republic of Sakha, northeastern Siberia; capital *Якутскъ, Yakutsk*

• THE DISTRICTS OF CENTRAL ASIA

Акмолинская область: Akmolinsk district; capital *Акмолинскъ,* now *Astana,* Kazakhstan

Закаспийская область: literally "Trans-Caspian district," in central Asia

Самаркандская область: the district of Samar-kand *[Samarqand],* now in Uzbekistan

Семипалатинская область, the district of Semipalatinsk, created 1854; the town of Semipalatinsk is today Semei, Kazakhstan

Семирѣчьенсая область: the Semirech'ye district in southeast Kazakhstan

Сырдарьинская область: region on both sides of the river Syr-Darya, also the name of a city in Uzbekistan; main administrative center *Ташкентъ, Tashkent* (now *Toshkent,* Uzbekistan)

Тургайская область: the district of Turgai, named for a river in what is now central Kazakhstan; administrative center *Аркалык, Arkalyk*

Уральская область: the Ural district, capital *Уральскъ, Uralsk,* now *Oral,* Kazakhstan

Ферганская область: the district of the city of Fergana, Uzbekistan (till 1910 *Новый Маргелан, Novyi Margelan,* and 1910-1924 *Скобелев, Skobelev*)

Map V-7: Western Russia as of 2001

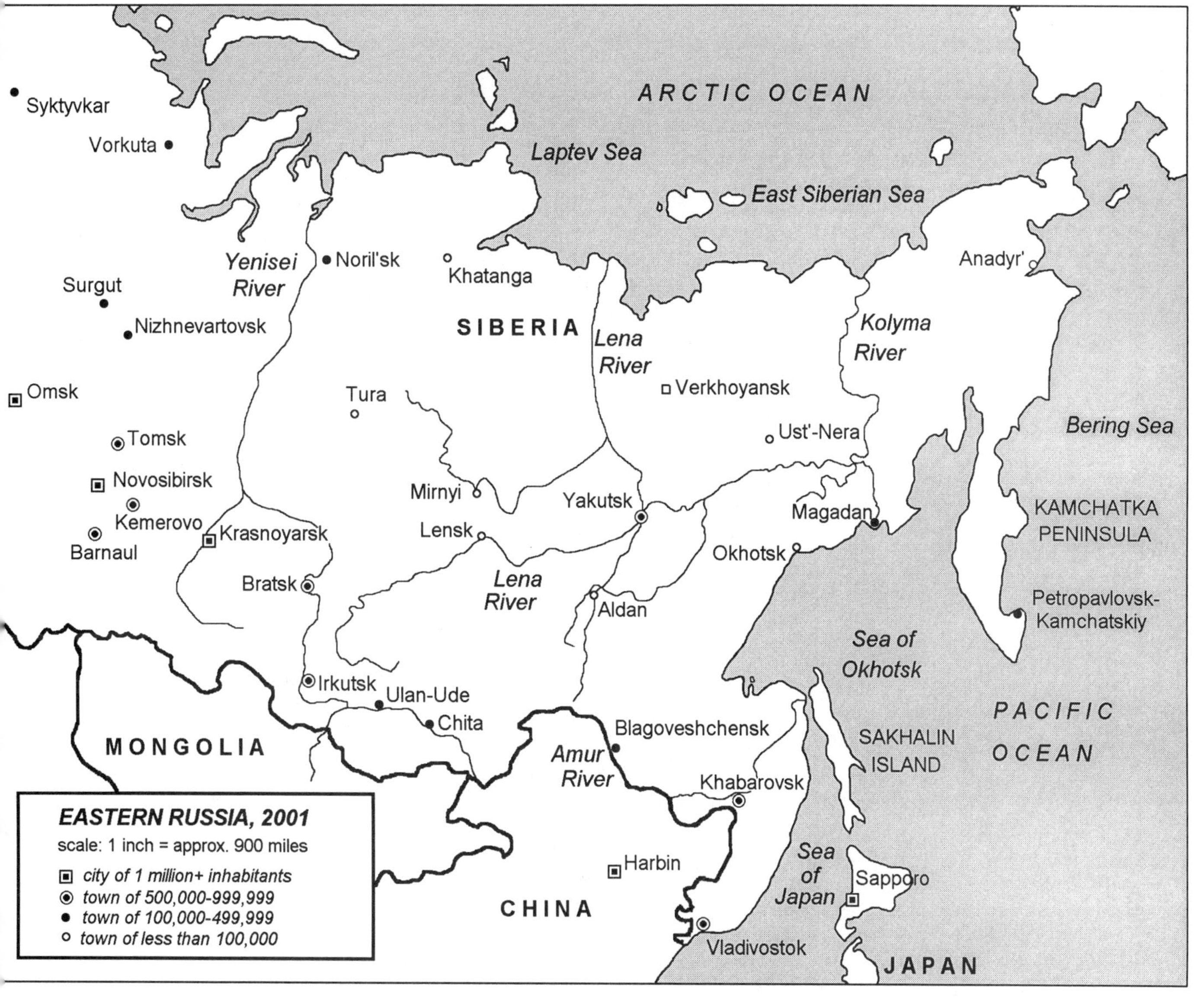

Map V-8: Eastern Russia as of 2001

12. Other Russian Geographical Names You May Encounter

Грузія, грузинскій – Georgia, since 1991 an independent republic; located between the Black Sea and the Caspian Sea

Гусевъ – Russian name of *Gumbinnen,* East Prussia

Камчатка – *Kamchatka* peninsula far eastern Russia, just west of Japan

Кишинев – *Chişinău,* Romania, see page 132

Крымъ – *Krym,* the peninsula of Crimea

Ленинград – *Leningrad,* Soviet name for the city now called (again) *St. Petersburg*

Молдавія – *Moldava,* formerly part of Romania, an independent nation since 1991

Нѣманъ – *Neman,* Russian name for the Neman river; Polish name *Niemen;* German *Memel*

Петроградъ – *Petrograd,* former name for St. Petersburg or Leningrad

Севастополь – *Sevastapol',* city on the Black Sea, now in the Republic of Crimea

Темешваръ – *Temeshvar,* an archaic Cyrillic spelling of *Timişoara,* Romania (the modern Russian spelling is *Тимишоара*)

Седмиградская Область – term for Transylvania

Червоная Русь – *Chervonaya Rus',* "Red Ruś," a term used for Ruthenia, in what is now southwestern Ukraine

C. Gazetteers for the Russian Empire

The Russian Imperial Government published provincial geographical tools which offer an in-depth statistical portrait of the population of a given province. The title of the series was ***Списки Населенныхъ мѣстъ Россійской Имперіи*** *[Spiski Naselennykh miest Rossiiskoi Imperii, Gazetteers of Populated Places of the Russian Empire]*. They are difficult to find in most North American libraries, but the Family History Library in Salt Lake City, Utah has volumes for more than 40 of Russia's *gubernias* on microfiche. A list follows)but for up-to-date information check the Library Website, **http://www.familysearch.org**):

• Published by Tsentralnyi statisticheskiy komitet Ministerstva vnutrennikh diel. Sanktpeterburg: Statisticheskii Komitet, 1861-. Gazetteer arranged by province. In Russian. 420 microfiche; 9 x 12 cm. The following volumes are on microfiche sets classified under #6002224 (note the exception for the Bessarabia index, v. 3, Bessarabia):

v. 1, Arkhangel'sk no. 1-5 (set of 5 fiche)
v. 2, Astrakhan' no. 6-8 (set of 3)
v. 3, Bessarabia, no. 9-12 (set of 4); v. 3, Bessarabia, (1 fiche), VAULT INTL Fiche 6001781
v. 6, Vladimir, no. 13-26 (set of 13)
v. 7, Vologda, no. 27-41 (set of 15)
v. 9, Voronezh, no. 42-49 (set of 8)
v. 10, Vyatka, no. 50-79 (set of 30)
v. 12, Zemlya Voyska Donskago, no. 80-85 (set of 6)
v. 13, Yekaterinoslav, no. 86-91 (set of 6)
v. 14, Kazan', no. 92-100 (set of 9)
v. 15, Kaluga, no. 101-109 (set of 9)
v. 18, Kostroma, no. 110-128 (set of 19)
v. 20, Kursk, no. 129-136 (set of 8)
v. 24, Moskva, no. 137-144 (set of 8)
v. 25, Nizhniy Novgorod, no. 145-152 (set of 8)
v. 27, Olonets, no. 153-162 (set of 10)
v. 28, Orenburg no. 163-168 (set of 6)
v. 29 Orel, no. 169-179 (set of 11)
v. 30, Penza, no. 180-184 (set of 5)
v. 31, Perm', no. 185-208 (set of 24)
v. 33, Poltava, no. 209-216 (set of 8)
v. 34, Pskov, no. 217-237 (set of 21)
v. 35, Ryazan', no. 238-243 (set of 6)
v. 36, Samara, no. 244-248 (set of 5)
v. 37, Sankt-Peterburg, no. 249-258 (set of 10)
v. 38, Saratov, no. 259-263 (set of 5)
v. 39, Simbirsk, no. 264-268 (set of 5)
v. 40, Smolensk, no. 269-289 (set of 21)
v. 41, Tavrida, no. 290-299 (set of 10)
v. 42, Tambov, no. 300-307 (set of 8)
v. 43, Tver', no. 308-321 (set of 14)
v. 44, Tula, no. 322-327 (set of 6)
v. 45, Ufa, no. 328-339 (set of 12)
v. 46, Khar'kov, no. 348-356 (set of 9)
v. 47, Kherson, no. 340-347 (set of 8)
v. 48, Chernigov, no. 357-367 (set of 11)
v. 50, Yaroslavl', no. 368-383 (set of 16)
v. 51 Yeniseisk no. 384-388 (set of 5)
v. 60, Tobol'sk, no. 389-401 (set of 13)
v. 60a, Tomsk, no. 402-411 (set of 10)
v. 65, Baku, no. 412-419 (set of 8)

Note that a number of volumes are missing. Also, the Family History Library doesn't usually provide individual microfiche from a work of this sort. If you request this work through a local Family History Center, be prepared to pay for the whole set of 420 sheets!

So what information does this series offer? Let us use as an example the directory for Poltava. The initial portion of the directory contains over 30 pages of text. The latitude and longitude of the province are provided, as well as a description of the natural and administrative provincial boundaries. The province's natural resources are also described and land-use statistics are listed. A detailed section of population statistics follows, listed by the 15 *уѣзды* (counties) which comprised the province.

Following the textual material are population figures for each county, divided alphabetically by *волость* [*volost'*]. Under each *volost'*, each village was listed with the number of male and female residents listed, as well as the distance in kilometers of the village from the county seat. The number of schools was also given, as well as the names of the churches in each city or village (presumably Orthodox).

Названіе поселеній.	Разстояніе отъ		Число жителей.		Школы.				Церкви.	Благочиническій Округъ.
	Города.	Волостного Правленія.	Мужского пола.	Женскаго пола.	Министер.	Земскихъ.	Церковно-приходскихъ.	Грамоты.		
Дытюковъ хут.	56	6	20	22	—	—	—	—	—	
Ищенковъ хут.	55	5	28	28	—	—	—	—	—	
Карпиловка село	55	15	1678	1633	гр. 1	2	—	—	Рождество-Богородичная.	V
Конюшенъ хут.	59	9	22	20	—	—	—	—	—	
Коробовщина хут.	56	7	130	126	—	—	—	—	—	
Кругляковъ хут.	56	6	20	19	—	—	—	—	—	
Кудлаевъ хут.	57	7	8	4	—	—	—	—	—	
Кузина хут.	48	6	21	26	—	—	—	—	—	
Лавренковъ хут.	56	6	72	76	—	—	—	—	—	
Макаренковъ хут.	56	7	20	28	—	—	—	—	—	
Мищенковъ хут.	58	12	9	7	—	—	—	—	—	
Молочныя Воды хут.	60	9	28	35	—	—	—	—	—	
Новоселовка хут.	65	15	79	90	—	—	—	—	—	
Онопріевъ хут.	54	4	44	46	—	—	—	—	—	
Орлявщина хут.	55	5	10	6	—	—	—	—	—	
Остапенковъ хут.	58	8	30	40	—	—	—	—	—	
Портянка хут.	52	2	82	84	—	—	—	—	—	
Спѣваковъ хут.	52	2	141	156	—	—	—	—	—	
Стрѣльцовъ хут.	57	7	8	12	—	—	—	—	—	
Трифановщина хут.	58	8	8	4	—	—	—	—	—	
Филатовъ хут.	60	15	12	12	—	—	—	—	—	
Харитоновка село	50	8	835	828	—	1	1	—	Іоанно-Предтеченская.	V
Харьковъ хут.	60	10	188	115	—	—	—	1	—	
Чернечій хут.	См. х. „Березовскій".								—	

Document V-1: Sample Page from a Russian Provincial Gazetteer

After the county listings, a master geographical alphabetical list of all localities in the province was provided. Those that were the site of a church were marked with a cross (+). Also included in the listings is a list of abbreviations, some of which are indicated below, as they will be applicable to compilations of this type for other provinces as well.

Document V-1 is a sample from this work. The column headings are as follows:

Названіе поселеній	locality name
Разстояніе отъ	distance from
Города:	town/city
Волостного правленія:	*volost'* administration
Число жителей	number of residents
Мужского пола:	of the male sex
Женскаго пола:	of the female sex
Школы	schools
Министер.:	ministerial
Земскихъ:	of the *zemstvo* [regional district]
Церковно-приходскихъ:	parochial
Грамоты:	reading and writing
Церкви	churches
Благочиническій Округъ	provost district

So the first entry on this page is for the *хутор* or farmstead of Dytiukov [Дытюковъ], 56 km. from the city and 6 km. from the local *volost'* seat, with 20 male inhabitants and 22 females, no schools or churches. Line 3 gives Karpilovka [Карпиловка] village, which does have a church, "Nativity—Mother of God" [Рождество Богородичная].

Since some of the abbreviations used in this work also appear in other reference works, it would not be a bad idea to explain them here:

Abbrev.	*Russian*	*Translation or Approximate Meaning*
у. г.	*уѣздный городъ*	*county seat*
з. г.	*заштатный городъ*	*provincial town of lesser importance*
д.	*деревня*	*village*
с.	*село*	*village*
х.	*хуторъ*	*farmstead*
псд.	*посадъ*	*settlement/suburb*
г.	*городъ*	*city, town*
слб.	*слобода*	*larger village or settlement*

Another Russian-language source of potential value to researchers is entitled and described as follows:

• ***Географическо-статистическій словарь Россійской имперіи*** *[Geografichesko-statisticheskii slovar' Rossiiskoi imperii, Geographical dictionary of Imperial Russia].* Main author: Semenov-Tian-Shanskii, Petr Petrovich, 1827-1914. Sanktpeterburg: V. Tip. Bezobrazova i komp., 1863-1885. Contents: vol. 1. A-G; vol. 2. D-K; vol. 3, L-O; vol. 4; P-S; vol. 5. T-IA. Microfilm: Tom (volume) 1 & 2 FHL INTL Film 1764206; Tom 3 & 4 FHL INTL Film 1764207; Tom 5 FHL INTL Film 1764208.

A sample page, **Document V-2**, appears at right—the beginning of the article on the town of Astrakhan', capital of the province of Astrakhan'. The virtues of this work are that it is available and contains a lot of information. Its drawback is that if you're not fluent in Russian, it is harder to decipher that information than the data in the *Списки населенных мѣстъ*, much of which is presented in columns.

Астраханъ, губ. г-дъ Астраханской губерніи.

I. Г-дъ, подъ 46°4′ с. ш. и 65°42′ в. д., на л. б. Волги, ниже отдѣленія отъ нея р. Балды, на буграхъ, между которыми протекаютъ рр. Кутумъ (соединенная съ Волгою Варвацiевымъ каналомъ), Скаржинка, Царевка и Луковка. Кремль и лучшая часть города расположены на Заячьемъ или Кремлевскомъ бугрѣ, возвышающемся надъ Волгою въ 50 ф., части же Казанская, Рождественская и предмѣстья города Солдатская слоб., Ямгурчевское, Паробичевское, Кріуша (гдѣ лучшіе сады), Армянская сл., Татарская, Безродная, Теребиловка, Зацаревка и др., расположены по берегамъ рѣчекъ и по буграмъ Ильинскому, Киселеву, Парабичеву, Казачьему, Голодному и др. Окрестности города бугристы, мѣстами покрыты болотами и озерами, почему климатъ здѣсь дѣлается лѣтомъ вреднымъ для здоровья. Полагаютъ, что на мѣстѣ Астр. въ III в. находился *Атель* или *Итиль*, древняя столица Хозаровъ. Въ исходѣ VI в. на устьѣ Волги появляется городъ *Баланіаръ*, который въ IX в. уже исчезаетъ, и наконецъ въ концѣ XIII в. монголы построили городъ *Цытрахань*, сдѣлавшійся въ XIV в. столицею царства. Во всякомъ случаѣ нынѣшняя Астрахань стоитъ не на старомъ мѣстѣ. Годъ переселенія ея на нынѣшнее мѣсто достовѣрно

Document V-2: Sample page from the *Географическо-статистическій словарь Россійской имперіи*

Of course, not everyone will wish to take on the challenge of finding and extracting information from these Russian-language works. For the Cyrillic-impaired, here is a list of selected works in the holdings of the Family History Library in languages that may seem a bit less intimidating.

GERMAN-LANGUAGE WORKS

• ***Alphabetisches Ortsverzeichnis von Russisch-Polen*** *[Gazetteer of the Russian parts of Poland]*. Herausgegeben von dem Gouvernement Königsberg i. Pr. On 1 microfilm, #0583455, Item 4. Filmed from the original in the Ev. Landeskirchenamt Bielefeld.

Unfortunately, this work is of limited use. The original publication consisted of three maps, scale 1:300,000, with an index to the location of places on those maps. But the maps are not on the microfilm, so all you get is the index—better than nothing, but without the maps it's not really all that helpful.

• ***Russisches geographisches Namenbuch*** *[Russian Book of Geographical Names]*. Max Vasmer, Ingrid Coper, ... [et al.]. Published by Max Vasmer und Herbert Bräuer. Akademie der Wissenschaften und der Literatur Mainz. Wiesbaden: O. Harrassowitz, 1964-1988. ISBN/ISSN: 3447028327; (Bd 11) 3-447-02851-5. Text in German. Place names are given primarily in the Cyrillic alphabet, with some German and Polish place names in the Roman alphabet. Arranged by Russian alphabetical order. Contents: Vol. 1, Aba-V(B)as; Vol. 2, V(B)as-Der; Vol. 3, Der-Kal; Vol. 4, Kal-Kut; Vol. 5, Kut-Mum; Vol. 6, Mum-Pet; Vol. 7, Pet-Ruia; Vol. 8. Ryb-Tap; Vol. 9. Tap-KH(X)ian; Vol. 10, TSaa-Iaiuch; Vol. 11, Ergänzungen und Nachträge — Vol. 12, Kartenband. Location: 947 E5r v. 1; FHL INTL Reference 947 E5r supp.; FHL INTL Reference 947 E5r v. 2; FHL INTL Reference 947 E5r v. 3; FHL INTL Reference 947 E5r v. 4; FHL INTL Reference 947 E5r v. 5; FHL INTL Reference 947 E5r v. 6; FHL INTL Reference 947 E5r v. 7; FHL INTL Reference 947 E5r v. 8; FHL INTL Reference 947 E5r v. 9; FHL INTL Reference 947 E5r v. 10; FHL INTL Reference 947 E5r v. 11; FHL INTL Reference 947 E5r supp. copy 2.

Since this work is not available on microfilm or microfiche, but only in book form, one would need to visit the Library in Salt Lake City to make use of it.

• ***Ortsumbenennungen und Neugründungen im Europäischen Teil der Sowjetunion: Nach dem Stand der Jahre 1910/1938/1951 mit einem Nachtrag für Ostpreußen 1953*** [Name Changes and the Establishment of Localities in the European Parts of the Soviet Union]. Meckelein, Wolfgang. Berlin: Duncker & Humbolt, 1955. Microfilmed from the original in the Library of Congress, Washington. Pages viii + 134, with maps. Call Number: 947 E5m FHL INTL Book. Also on 1 microfilm, #1187934.

ENGLISH-LANGUAGE WORKS

• ***Shtetl Finder : Jewish Communities in the 19th and Early 20th Centuries in the Pale of Settlement of Russia and Poland and in Lithuania, Latvia, Galicia, and Bukovina, with Names of Residents.*** Cohen, Chester G. Bowie, Md. : Heritage Books, Los Angeles : Periday Co., 1980, c1989. Pages iii + 145, maps. Call Number: Location 947 F24s FHL INTL Book; 947

F24s copy 2 FHL INTL Book; 947 F24s copy 3 FHL INTL Book. On microfilm: FHL US/CAN Film, 1206428, Item 4.

• ***U.S.S.R. and Certain Neighboring Areas: Official Standard Names Approved by the U.S. Board on Geographic Names.*** Authors: United States. Board on Geographic Names. 7 volumes, Washington D.C.: USGPO, 1959. Forms: book, microfilm, microfiche.

Book reference: 947 E5u; FHL INTL Book 947 E5u v. 2; FHL INTL Book 947 E5u v. 3; FHL INTL Book 947 E5u v. 4; FHL INTL Book 947 E5u v. 5; FHL INTL Book 947 E5u v. 6; FHL INTL Book 947 E5u v. 7

Film reference: v. 1 A-B: FHL INTL Film 928609; v. 2 C-J v. 3 K (1970 ed.) FHL INTL Film 928610 Items 1-2; v. 4 L-N v. 5 O-R: VAULT INTL Film 874455; v. 6 S-T v. 7 U-Z: VAULT INTL Film 874456. Also on microfiche: 121 microfiche, 11 x 15 cm: FHL INTL Fiche 6053504.

Avotaynu's *Where Once We Walked,* mentioned on page 27, can also be helpful with places in western Russia, i. e., within the Pale of Settlement (see Map V-5 on page 131). It is not available from the Family History Library on microfilm or microfiche, but it is commerically available from Avotaynu and other genealogical booksellers.

Belarus'

Geographical materials produced in Ukraine and Belarus during the Soviet era can provide information on villages long under the rule of the Grand Duchy of Lithuania, and later of the Commonwealth of Poland and Lithuania, which were officially ruled by Poland after World War I and became part of the Soviet Union after World War II.

Document V-3, at right, is an excerpt from *Краткий топономический словарь Белоруссии* [*Kratkiy toponomicheskiy slovar' Belorussii,* Brief Toponymic Dictionary of Belarus], which is etymological in nature but is still useful to the practical researcher. The name in bold is the Russian version of the place name; the Belarusian follows in parentheses. Let us take a look at a typical entry—in this case the bottom one shown.

Ереме'ичи 118

Ереме'ичи (Вераме'ічы, вар.Ераме'ічы)—с. Лидского р-на; **Ереме'евка** (Вераме'еўка)—с. Городокского р-на; **Ереме'ево** (Вераме'ева)—сс. Городокского и Россонского р-нов; **Ереме'евщина** (Вераме'еўшчына)—с. Дубровенского р-на. Названия образованы от личного имени Еремей (белорусское—Верамей) и производных от него фамилий.

Ерёмино (Яро'міна)—сс. Витебского и Гомельского р-нов; **Ере'мичи** (Ярэ'мічы)—сс. Кобринского и Кореличского р-нов. Названия, производные от фамилий Еремин, Еремич.

Ермаки' (Ермакі')—с. Молодечненского р-на; **Ермако'вка** (Ермако'ўка)—с. Кричевского р-на. Названия, производные от фамилий Ермак, Ермаков.

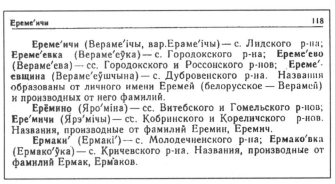

Document V-3: Sample from *Краткий топономический словарь Белоруссии*

Ермаки´—in Roman-alphabet transliteration this would be spelled *Yermakí,* with the accent on the last syllable. In Russian the accent is usually not indicated; it is shown here only because this is a reference work and is meant to indicate the correct pronunciation. The Belarusian version is pronounced essentially the same.

c. молодечненского р-на—"a village in the *raion* of Molodechno" [in Belarusian *Маладзечна*]; р-на is an abbreviation of района *[raiona],* the genitive case of район *[raion],* a Soviet administrative division; c. is an abbreviation of село, *selo,* village

Ермако´вка—*Yermakóvka;* in Belarusian it is spelled *Ермакоўка,* pronounced roughly the same (very roughly!) as the Russian name, with the accent on the third syllable

с. кричевского р-на—"a village in Krichev *raion*"

Названия, производные от фамилий Ермак, Ермаков—"[These] names derive from the surnames *Yermak* and *Yermakov.*"

The Russian and Belarusian versions of these names are almost identical. But the first entry shows that what Russians call **Еремеичи** *[Yereméichi],* Belarusians is call Верамеічы *[Veraméichy]* and sometimes Ерамеічы *[Yeraméichy].* The second entry, **Ерёмино** *[Yeryómino],* is Яромина *[Yarómina]* in Belarusian. The Russian and Belarusian forms of place names can vary just enough in pronunciation and spelling to confuse researchers. These tendencies may help you distinguish and recognize them:

Belarusian	*Russian*	*Examples (Belarusian followed by Russian)*
а	**о**	П**а**лічын vs. П**о**личин
і	**и**	Жаб**і**н vs. Жаб**и**н (the letter **i** was used in pre-Bolshevik Russian spelling, but was dropped by the Communists)
ы	**ы** *or* **и**	may be rendered as Russian **ы**, but is often **и**: Палож**ы**на vs. Полож**и**но, Жабч**ыцы** vs. Жабч**ицы**
в	–	often omitted: **Ве**рамеічы vs. **Е**ремеичи
дз	**д**	Жа**дз**ейкі vs. Жа**д**ейки
ц	**т**	Жабен**ц**яі vs. Жабен**т**ай
ў	**в**	Ермако**ў**ка vs. Ермако**в**ка
я	**е**	**Я**ромина vs. **Е**рёмино

Unfortunately, the Polish versions of the place names are not provided, and they can sometimes be relevant. The transition from the Belarusian to the Polish version is not all that difficult, however, once one grasps the following general linguistic "conversions":

Belarusian	*Polish*	*Examples (Belarusian followed by Polish)*
а	**о**	**А**гароднікі vs. **O**grodniki
ў	**w**	Адама**ў**цы vs. Adamo**w**cy
вічы	**-wicze**	Адама**вічы** vs. Adamo**wicze**
шчына	**-szczyzna**	Загор**шчына** vs. Zagor**szczyzna**

These are only a few of the most common adjustments needed, and a comprehensive phonetic analysis is not within the scope of this work. In most cases, however, the different forms of names are fairly similar ***if*** you can sound them out phonetically in one language, listen to the sounds, and then consider how those sounds are typically spelled in the other. To do this, of course, you need to become very familiar with how sounds are represented in the Cyrillic alphabet, and how Polish spellings are written in the Roman alphabet. The section on Cyrillic orthography of Polish names, pages 23-27, can help in this endeavor.

Another series of geographical references will assist researchers locating villages in territory now within Belarus. Belarus is divided into six provinces—the Belarusian term is *вобласць*—and each has its own individual listing. These volumes, published in 1981, are titled similarly (the name of the province will change, obviously), e. g., ***Слоўнік назваў населеных***

пунктаў мінскай вобласці *[Dictionary of the names of settlements in the Province of X —* in this case, of Minsk]. The volumes are all in Belarusian, with each place name given in Russian as well (see the sample, **Document V-4**, below).

Пале′ссе **204**

Пале′ссе н., -ссяя, -ссі **Полесье.** Пале′скі Полесский
в. у Будслаўскім с/с Мядзельскага р-на, у с-се «Будслаўскі».
Палёк м., -лька, -льку **Полёк.** Палёцкі Полёкский
п. у Амяльнянскім с/с Пухавіцкага р-на, у к-се імя У. І. Леніна.
Палі′к м., -ка, -ку **Палик.** Палі′цкі Паликский
в. у Майсееўшчынскім с/с Барысаўскага р-на, у с-се «Чырвонапартызанскі».
Паліка′раўка ж., -кі, -ўцы **Поликаровка.** Паліка′раўскі Поликаровский
в. у Першамайскім с/с Слуцкага р-на, у к-се «Мір».
Палі′ксаўшчына ж., -ны, -не **Поликсовщина.** Палі′ксаўшчынскі Поликсовщинский
в. у Сугваздаўскім с/с Валожынскага р-на, у к-се імя М. Ф. Гастэлы.
Палі′кшты мнл., -таў, -тах **Паликшты.** Палі′кштаўскі Паликштовский
в. у Залескім с/с Валожынскага р-на, у с-се «Залескі».
Палі′кшчына ж., -ны, -не **Паликщина.** Палі′кшчынскі Паликщинский
в. у Бабровіцкім с/с Валожынскага р-на, у к-се імя А. В. Суворава.
Па′лічнае н., -нага, -ным **Паличное.** Па′лічанскі Паличенский
в. у Сароцкім с/с Любанскага р-на, у к-се «Чырвоная змена».
Палі′чын м., -на, -не **Поличин.** Палі′чынскі Поличинский
в. у Малагарадзяціцкім с/с Любанскага р-на, ц. с-са «Калінаўка».
Палішчы′ мнл., -чоў, -чах **Полищи.** Палішчо′ўскі Полищёвский
в. да 1976 г. у Багданаўскім с/с Валожынскага р-на.
Пало′жына н., -на, -не **Положино.** Пало′жынскі Положинский
в. у Бярэзінскім с/с Бярэзінскага р-на, у с-се «Сцяг Кастрычніка».

Document V-4: ***Слоўнік назваў...вобласці***

Entries are listed alphabetically (according to Cyrillic alphabetical order, of course) and are brief. The first line gives the Belarusian version of the place name, and uses endings to indicate the declensional pattern appropriate to that name. The Russian form of the name is follows; next comes the appropriate adjectival form in Belarusian, then Russian.

The second line indicates what sort of community it is—usually в., for *вёска*, "village"—followed by the county it's in, the *раён [raion]* or district, and the name of the collective farm the locality belongs to (if applicable); *у с-се* means "in the *саўгас,*" *saŭhas,* collective farm, and *у к-се* means "in the *калгас,*" *kalhas,* another kind of collective farm (compare the Russian terms *совхоз* and *колхоз*). If the place name has been changed the "old" name appears as well. A brief bibliography can be found at the end of the volume, directing the reader to other geographical materials.

Thus in **Document V-4**, the first entry on page 204 of the volume on Minsk province is a place called Палессе [Palesse] in Belarusian. The abbreviation н. means it is a neuter noun, and it is declined according to the pattern with Пале**сся** as the genitive, Пале**ссі** as the prepositional, etc. The Russian name of the village is Полесье. The adjectival form in Belarusian is Палескі, in Russian Полесски. The second line indicates Palesse is a village in the county of Будслаў [Budslaŭ], the *раён* [district] of Мядзел [Myadzel], belonging to the "Budslaŭski" collective farm.

Similarly, the 6th entry is for Палікшты [Palikshty], in form мнл., a plural noun, genitive form Палікшт**аў** [Palikshtaŭ], prepositional Палікшт**ах** [Palikshtakh]. In Belarusian the adjectival form is Палікштаўскі. In Russian the name is Паликшты, adjectival form Паликштовский. It's a village in the county of Залессе [Zalesse], district of Валожын [Valozhyn], associated with the "Zaleski" collective farm.

Reference works of this sort typically use abbreviations to save space, and it's vital to recognize them. The abbreviations used in these volumes are:

в. – *вёска*, village
г. - *горад*, city or town
гл. – *глядзі*, see
г/с – *гарадскі Савет*, town soviet
ж. – *жаночы род*, feminine gender
з-д. – *завод*, factory
к-с – *калгас, kalhas*, collective farm
л. – *леснічоўка*, forester's lodge
л-ва – *лясніцтва*, forest district
м. – *мужчынскі род*, masculine gender
мяст. – *мястэчка*, small town
мнл. – *множналікавы назоўнік*, plural noun
н. – *ніякі род*, neuter gender
нязм. – *нязменны*, unchanging, undeclined
ням. – *нямецкі*, German
п. – *пасёлак*, settlement
п/с – *пасялковы Савет*, settlement soviet
р-д – *раз'езд*, railway shunting, siding
р-н – *раён*, region, district
р. п. – *рабочы пасёлак*, worker's settlement
с/с – *сельскі Савет*, village soviet
с-с – *саўгаз, saйhas*, collective farm
х. – *хутар*, farmstead, farm
ц. – *центр*, center
чыг. пст. – *чыгуначны паўстанак*, railroad stop
чыг. ст. – *чыгуначная станцыя*, railroad station

Capitalized abbreviations refer to *raions* or districts, so that *Бар.* refers to Baranavichi district, *Брасл.* to Braslaŭ district, *Леп.* to Lepel' district, and so on.

While these works are not exactly to be found in every library, the Resource Center of the Polish Genealogical Society of Connecticut and the Northeast (8 Lyle Rd., New Britain CT 06053-2104) has the volumes for Minsk and Hrodna provinces. Also, as we were preparing this book, Viktor Kamkin Bookstores (**http://www.kamkin.com**) was selling copies of the volumes for Brest, Vitsebsk, and Mahileŭ provinces. So they're not as impossible to find as one might think.

Two sources dealing with Belarus and available from the Family History Library are:

• ***Административно-территориальное устройство БССР: справочник в 2-х томах*** *[Administrativno-territorial'noe ustroistvo BSSR: spravochnik v 2-x tomax, Administrative Territorial Structure of the B. S. S. R. (Byelorussian Soviet Socialist Republic): Reference in Two Volumes].* Minsk: Belarus, 1985-1987. In Belarusian [according to the FHL catalog—but the title looks like it's Russian]. In book form. Volume 1 covers 1917-1941; Volume 2 1944-1980. It lists the places at each level of jurisdiction by alphabetical order. Call Number Location 947.65 E5a. FHL INTL Reference: 947.65 E5a v. 2. [Since this work is apparently not available on microfilm or microfiche, you presumably have to visit the Family History Library in Salt Lake City to consult it.]

• ***Список населенных мест Б.С.С.Р.*** *[Spisok naselennykh mest B.S.S.R. (b. Minskoi gubernii), Gazetteer of Populated Places in the B. S. S. R. (former Minsk province)].* Authors: Tsentral'noe Statisticheskoe Biuro B.S.S.R. This is a gazetteer in Russian of the Byelorussian Soviet Socialist Rupublic, pre-World War II, not including the Russian Empire *уѣздъ* of Grodna. It is a reproduction of an original published: Minsk: Beltrestpechat, 1924. 300 p. Microfilm: #2044163, Item 1. **Document V-5** on page 148 is a sample page:

The columnar headings give the following information:

№ по порядку – sequential number
Наименование волостей и населенных пунктов – names of the districts and populated localities
Род населенных пунктов – type of populated locality
Расстояние в верстах: волостн. центра | уезд. города | города Минска – distance in versts to the: district center | county seat | city of Minsk
Название ближайш. жел.-дор. станции – name of the nearest railroad station

Б. Местечки, села, деревни и прочие населенные пункты С.С.Р. Белоруссии.

Бобруйский уезд.

№№ по порядку.	Наименование волостей и населенных пунктов.	Род населенных пунктов.	Расстояние в верстах от: волости. центра.	уездн. города.	города Минска.	Название ближайш. жел.-дор. станции.	Расстояние в верст. до ближ. ж.-д. ст.	Число дворов (владений) в насел. пункте.	Наличное число жителей в насел. пункте: Мужчин.	Женщин.	Обоего пола.	Состав населения по родному языку: Белоруссы.	Великоруссы.	Украинцы.	Поляк	Евреи.	Прочие
	1. Бацевичская волость.																
1	Алексеевка	заст.	18	52	160	Бобруйск	52	12	47	46	93	93	—	—	—	—	—
2	Анатолиевка (**)	дер.	13	48	150	Бобруйск	48	14	29	39	68	42	—	—	26	—	—
3	Аполинарово	заст.	13	50	170	Бобруйск	60	9	38	37	75	57	—	—	18	—	—
4	Ачиновичи (*)	хут.	20	56	176	Бобруйск	56	2	7	8	15	15	—	—	—	—	—
5	Вацевичи	им.	1/2	35	150	Бобруйск	85	1	164	191	355	25	—	—	826	4	—
6	Вацевичи	село	—	36	150	Бобруйск	36	139	455	448	903	791	—	—	23	89	—
7	Берег-Красный	заст.	4	39	154	Бобруйск	89	3	7	6	13	13	—	—	—	—	—
8	Виордо	дер.	13	50	165	Бобруйск	50	73	272	284	556	556	—	—	—	—	—
9	Виордо	им.	13	50	165	Бобруйск	50	1	9	7	16	16	—	—	—	—	—
10	Бобовка	заст.	30	65	181	Березина	65	11	33	30	63	63	—	—	—	—	—
11	Болото-Березовое	хут.	9	30	159	Бобруйск	30	5	18	15	33	83	—	—	—	—	—
12	Борки	дер.	25	50	175	Бобруйск	50	41	125	117	242	242	—	—	—	—	—
13	Бор-Низкий	заст.	24	59	144	Бобруйск	59	6	18	23	41	41	—	—	—	—	—

Document V-5: Excerpt from *Список населенных мест Б.С.С.Р.*

Расстояние в верстах до ближ. ж.-д. ст. – distance in versts to the nearest railroad station

Число дворов (владений) в насел. пункте – number of manors (properties) in the locality

Наличное число жителей в насел. пункте | Мужчин | Женщин | Обоего пола | – number of individual residents of the locality: | Men | Women | [Total] for Both Sexes

Состав населения по родному языку: Белоруссы | Украинцы | Поляки | Евреи | Прочие – Composition of the population by native language: Belarusians | Ukrainians | Poles | Jews | Others

Abbreviations and terms used in this work include:

Бб. – Бобруйский, of Bobrusk *[uyezd]*
Бр. – Борисовский, of Borisov *[uyezd]*
буд. ж. д. – будка железной дороги, railroad service cabin, stall, booth
вин. зав.- винокуренный завод, distillery
высел. – выселок, new settlement
дер. – деревня, village
зав. – завод, plant, facility, factory
зав. лес. – завод лесопильный, sawmill
зав. пос. – заводской поселок, factory village
зав. стек. – завод стекольный, glassworks
заст. – застенок, cmp. Polish *zaścianki*, literally "[place] behind a wall," a farmstead of minor nobles who worked their own land
Иг. – Игуменский, of Igumen *[uyezd]*
им. – имение, estate
каз. стр. – казенная стража, government guard
каз. ус. – казенная усадьба, government-owned farmstead
кир. зав. – кирпичный завод, brickyard, brick works
колон. – колония, colony
лес. зав. – лесопильный завод, sawmill

лес. стр.– лесная стража, forest rangers' station
леснич. – лесничество, forest district
мельн. – мельница, mill
Мз. – Мозырский, of Mozyrsk *[uyezd] шос. ст. – шоссейная станция,* highway station
Мн. – Минский, of Minsk *[uyezd]*
однос. – односелье, single farm or settlement, one not connected with a village or estate
окол. – околица, section, neighborhood, vicinity
платф. – платформа, small railway station
пос. – посёлок, small village, settlement
почт. ст. – почтовая станция, post office
р. ж. д. or *раз. ж. д. – разъезд железной дороги,* railway station with shunting, siding
селен. – селение, settlement
село, village, settlement
Сл. – Слуцкий, of Slutsk *[uyezd]*
слоб. – слобода, large village on a highway, suburb
ст. ж. д. – станция железной дороги, railroad station
тов. or *т-во. – товарищество,* company
уроч. – урочище, plot of land, a section different from the land around it
усад. – усадьба, farmstead, country estate
фабр. – фабрика, factory
фольв. – фольварок, large manorial farmstead (mainly in Poland)
хут. – хутор, farmstead
шос. буд. – шоссейная будка, road-worker's cabin, stall, booth
м-ко. – местечко, small town

Lithuania

A source of information on communities located in the former **Grand Duchy of Lithuania** is *Indeks alfabetyczny miejscowości dawnego Wielkiego Księstwa Litewskiego* [Alphabetical Index of Localities of the Former Grand Duchy of Lithuania] by Ivan Yakovlevich Sprogis, Vilnius, 1929. It is available for loan to Family History Centers from the Family History Library in Salt Lake City on a set of 37 microfiche, #6002146.

This is an unfinished work by Sprogis, long-time director of the Wilno (Vilnius) Central Archive. It was not meant to serve as a comprehensive list of every place in Lithuania, but as an index to some 100,000 documents dealing with places in the Grand Duchy and preserved in the Wilno Archive. The first part of the Index, up through *Куяны* on page 390, is printed in Russian, as shown in the sample. The rest of the book exists only as a typed manuscript, up to *Пински,* and as a cardfile that was in the possession of the Wilno State Archive as of 1929. That cardfile has not been put in print, so the microfilm from the Family History Library includes the printed section and the typed manuscript.

As you can see from the sample, the reproduction of the printed pages is not very high quality, and the typed manuscript is even harder to read. The typed pages list places by their Russian names in Russian alphabetical order, followed by the Polish version of each name and Polish notes on the sources and their inventory data.

Document V-6 on page 150 is a sample from this work, and may give some indication of its likely value to researchers. Even if the quality of the reproduction were excellent, the book uses a variety of terms and abbreviations with which a researcher would have to familiarize himself. Let us look briefly at a few entries. The first reads as follows:

Данцелишки, фольварокъ въ упитск. пов., № 14699, л. 41–2 инв. 1670 г. 19 янв.

The name of the place is *Dantselishki,* and it is described as a *фольварокъ,* a *folwark* (from a Polish term meaning "manorial farmstead, grange"); so it was not a village or town, but a decent-sized farmstead with a manor. It was located in Upita *powiat* (from the Polish term meaning more or less "county"); *Upita* is *Upytė,* near Panevėžys, Lithuania. The reference "No. 14699, l. 41-42" is an archival entry number, item 14699, pages 41-42. The item is an *инвентарь,* an inventory of the property, dated 19 January 1670.

One would have to track down the archival collection to determine whether this document holds any information of genealogical value. Presumably the place to start asking is the Lithuanian State Historical Archives (see page 174). It is difficult to say for sure what the proper Lithuanian name of this place was. By standard orthographic conventions we would expect *Данцелишки* to be a Russian Cyrillic rendering of *Danceliškiai,* or something very similar, in Lithuanian.

The next entry reads as follows:

Данюны, село (15 ув.) им. Биржъ, въ упит. пов. № 15191, л. 516 инв. съ чиншами и повинностями, 1589 г. 15 февр.

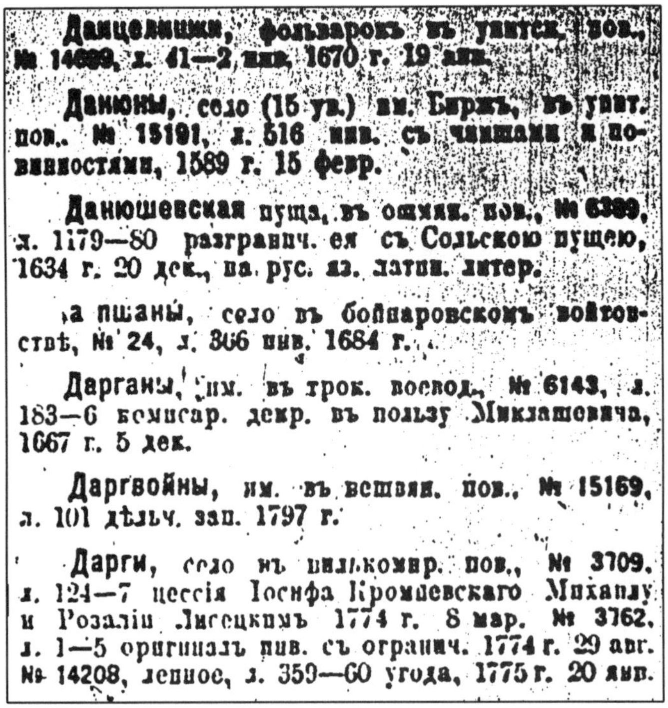

Данцелишки, фольварокъ въ упитск. пов., № 14689, л. 41—2, [illegible] 1670 г. 19 [illegible]

Данюны, село (15 ув.) им. Биржъ, въ упит. пов., № 15191, л. 516 инв. съ чиншами и повинностями, 1589 г. 15 февр.

Данюшевская пуща, въ ошмян. пов., № 6389, л. 1179—80 разгранич. ея съ Сольскою пущею, 1634 г. 20 дек., на рус. яз. латин. литер.

Дапшаны, село въ бойнаровскомъ войтовствѣ, № 24, л. 366 инв. 1684 г.

Дарганы, им. въ трок. воевод., № 6143, л. 183—6 комисар. декр. въ пользу Миклашевича, 1667 г. 5 дек.

Даргвойны, им. въ вешвян. пов., № 15169, л. 101 дѣльч. зап. 1797 г.

Дарги, село въ вилькомир. пов., № 3709. л. 124—7 цессія Іосифа Кромневскаго Михаилу и Розаліи Лисецкимъ 1774 г. 8 мар. № 3762. л. 1—5 оригиналъ инв. съ огранич. 1774 г. 29 авг. № 14208, ленное, л. 359—60 угода, 1775 г. 20 янв.

Document V-6

This translates as: "**Danyuny**, village (15 *uv.*), Birzh estate in Upita county. No. 15191, p. 516, an inventory with rents and obligations, 15 February 1589." So the archival item this entry refers to is an inventory drawn up in 1589 listing rents paid and other forms of required duties or service connected with this property. The Lithuanian name of this village is almost certainly *Daniūnai.*

The next entry is for a forest called *Данюшевская, Danyushevskaya,* in the county of Oshmyany (now Ashmyany, Belarus). Since Sprogis's work covers the territory of the old Grand Duchy of Lithuania, it will include many localities now in Belarus. The most interesting aspect of this entry is the statement that Item No. 6389, pages 1179-1180, is на рус. яз. латин. литер., "in the Russian language with Latin letters"!

The next entry translates as "**Dapshany**, village in Boynarov *vojtovstvo,* No. 24, p. 366, inventory, 1684." The term *войтовство, vojtovstvo,* refers to the area administered by a *войтъ,* Polish *wójt,* an executive official in charge of a village or group of villages.

Next comes an entry for "**Dargany**, estate in Troki [Trakai] province, No. 6143, pp. 183-6, commissar's decision in favor of Miklashevich, 5 December 1667." The abbrev. *воевод.* stands for *воеводство, voyevodstvo,* Polish *województwo,* "province."

Then comes an entry for "**Dargvoiny**, an estate in the county of Veshvyany, bequest from 1797." The Lithuanian name of this place is *Dargvainiai*, and *Veshvyany* is called *Viešvenai* in Lithuanian, *Wieszwiany* in Polish.

The entry for **Дарги**, *Dargi,* says that it was a village in the county of Vil'komir [Lith. *Ukmergė,* Polish *Wilkomierz*]. Item number 3709, pp. 124-127 is a *цессія* [a cession of property] from Iosif Kromnevskiy to Mikhail and Rozaliya Lisetski [or since these names are almost certainly Polish, from Józef Kromniewski to Michał and Rozalia Lisecki] dated 8 March 1774. Item number 3762, pp. 1-5 is the original of an *инвентарь съ ограниченіями* ["inventory with restrictions," limited inventory] dated 29 August 1774. Item number 14208, pp. 359-360, deals with an *угода* [agreement] regarding a *ленное* [feudal property] dated 20 January 1775.

Trying to use this book could be very confusing for anyone fluent in Russian, because it employs so many terms that are just Russian forms of Polish words. *Войтовство* and *воеводство* are merely Russified spellings of Polish *wójtowstwo* and *województwo;* and *угода,* mentioned in the entry for Dargi, means "gratification, pleasure" in Russian—it only means "agreement "in Polish. What kind of Russian is this?

The answer is clear when you consider the source. The documents referred to generally date from the period when these lands were part of the Grand Duchy of Lithuania, and Polish was the language of record in the Grand Duchy during that period. Sprogis was trying to remain true to his sources when he used the same Polish terms found in these primary sources, instead of substituting "proper Russian" terms that might mean some-thing slightly different. Laws requiring the exclusive use of Russian forced him to spell the terms in the Cyrillic alphabet; but they are Polish terms, nonetheless. In context, therefore, all these Polish terms make sense; but a researcher who didn't know that might have a terrible time searching Russian dictionaries for them!

The practical value of consulting this work will vary in different cases. As a rule, it will most likely prove difficult gaining access to the records cited. Once accessed, it seems unlikely they will furnish much information of genealogical value. But one never knows, as the contents of archives of the post-Soviet republics have only begun to be examined by Western eyes.

One possible benefit in using this source lies in the assistance it may provide in locating a specific community. These villages and manorial farmsteads may not appear in any other source. If nothing else, this gazetteer might prove helpful in locating Danyuny/Daniūnai, for instance. Learning that it was located in the *powiat* of Upita/Upytė may not solve all your problems, but it may be more information than you had to go on before. By the same token, referring to this work might help you establish and compare the Russian, Polish, and Lithuanian forms of place names, which can be very helpful.

Because this work was unfinished, it lacks an author's introduction and list of abbreviations, and they are sorely missed. This reminds us to offer a good piece of advice:

> *If you consult gazetteers and similar works,* ***make sure you copy the introduction and list of abbreviations for future reference!***

Reference works of this sort usually provide introductory material that defines exactly the sources consulted, the scope of the material covered, the abbreviations, and more. Having a copy of this information to study at your leisure can make an enormous difference in comprehending the entries relevant to your research.

The *Słownik geograficzny Królestwa Polskiego* (see page 155) includes information in Polish on many towns and villages in Lithuania, and may be worth consulting.

Again, perhaps not all of our readers care to attempt using a source in Russian and Polish. Perhaps they would prefer to look into an English-language gazetteer available on microfilm from the Family History Library (FHL INTL film 1573242, Item 1): the ***Gazetteer of Lithuania: Names Approved by the United States Board on Geographic Names,*** Washington, D.C.: Defense Mapping Agency, 1994, pages xvii + 476.

Ukraine

While there is no great abundance of Ukrainian gazetteers readily available in North America, there certainly are some resources one may check. Paul Robert Magocsi's *Ukraine: A Historical Atlas,* cartographer Geoffrey J. Matthews, University of Toronto Press, 1985, ISBN 0-8020-3428-4 (cloth) and 0-8020-3429-2 (paper) is valuable not only for the overview of Ukrainian history it offers, but also for its list of sources, which gives publication data on Ukrainian-language atlases, histories, and encyclopedias.

Also well worth attention are the reference works for the Russian Empire discussed on pages 140-144, namely, the volumes for regions in Ukraine. If, for instance, it proves possible to get hold of selected volumes of the massive work ***Списки Населенныхъ мѣстъ Россійской Имперіи*** (discussed on page 140), the Ukrainian researcher could learn much from the volumes covering the provinces of Bessarabia, Chernigov, Poltava, Kherson, Khar'kov, Yekaterinoslav, and Tavrida.

The Polish-language gazetteer *Słownik geograficzny Królestwa Polskiego* (page 155) and the sources cited for Galicia (pages 162 and 165-166) can also be quite helpful with places in Ukraine. The entries in the *Słownik geograficzny* for western Ukraine are particularly extensive, and of course sources for Galicia deal only with western Ukraine. But the *Słownik geograficzny* contains a number of long and informative entries for towns in eastern Ukraine as well. You may find that specific entries in this gazetteer provide you with useful background information of sufficient value to justify the effort involved in locating and translating them.

Of course, we have only listed a few of the sources available to help you locate ancestral towns and villages in Russia itself and in the territories now located within the independent nations of Lithuania, Belarus, and Ukraine. You can undoubtedly find more if you undertake a search with persistence and ingenuity. It is always a good idea to check the Family History Library catalog—either online (**http://www.familysearch.org**) or at the nearest Family History Center—to find sources we have overlooked, or ones that have been added recently. There are also booksellers that specialize in books and other materials from Russia and the former Soviet Union, such as Viktor Kamkin Bookstores (as of this writing, their Website is located at **http://www.kamkin.com**). So you should regard the information we have given in this section not as a comprehensive listing, but rather as a friendly push to get you headed in the right direction.

D. Gazetteers for the Regions of Poland Once Ruled by Russia

There are a number of Polish-language gazetteers that cover areas once in the Polish-Lithuanian Commonwealth, but more recently under Russian rule. Roughly speaking, that would be much of central and eastern Poland, all of Lithuania and Belarus, and the western half of Ukraine.

There are advantages in consulting such works, if your ancestors came from those regions. Poland has cooperated with genealogical researchers for several decades, whereas the former Soviet Union has only opened up since 1991. This means more Polish sources have been available, and have been available longer, than those dealing with Russia itself. Also, with Polish sources at least the alphabet is familiar!

Note: if you are not familiar with the partitioning of Poland in the years 1772, 1793, and 1795, as well as the changes brought about during the Napoleonic era (1795-1814), **run**, don't walk, to the nearest encyclopedia or book on European history and read about them. You have virtually no chance of making sense of what you discover otherwise.

Some of the most helpful gazetteers or geographical dictionaries give their information in a columnar format. Below are translations of the columnar headings from three of the most widely available Polish gazetteers:

Miejscowość i jej charakter	Terytorjalnie właściwe władze i urzędy oraz urządzenia komunikacyjne								
	Gmina	Powiat polityczny	Województwo	Poczta i telegraf (telefon)	Stacja kolej. z odległością km.	Najbliższa linja komunik. autobus. z odległością km.	Sąd: Grodzki	Sąd: Okręgowy	Urzędy parafjalne (rz-kat., gr-kat., wschsłow., orm.-kat., prawosł., ewang., ew.-ref.)
Bukowszczyzna, wieś	Druja	Brasław	Wil.	Druja	Druja 8		Druja	Wilno	Druja r
Bukowy Potok, przys.	Obidza	Nowy Sącz	Krak.	Jazowsko	Stary Sącz 18	Szczawnica-Stary Sącz 3	Stary Sącz	Nowy Sącz	Jazowsko
Bukowylas, wieś	Bukowylas	Środa	Pozn.	Chwalibogowo	Chwalibogowo 2	Środa-Września 2	Środa	Poznań	Murzynowo Kościelne r, Miłosław e
Buków, wieś	Buków	Kraków	Krak.	Mogilany k/Krak.	Radziszów 3	Myślenice-Kraków 25	Skawina	Kraków	Mogilany
Buków, wieś	Buków	Brzozów	Lwow.	Jasionów k/Brzozowa p Brzozów. t	Rymanów 11	Brzozów-Rymanów	Brzozów	Sanok	Trześniów

Document V-7: The 1934 *Skorowidz Miejscowości*

Locality & Its Type	*Territorial authorities and offices, as well as lines of communication*								
	District	*Political county*	*Pro vin ce*	*Post Office & Telegraph (telephone)*	*Railway Station & distance in km.*	*Nearest Bus Bus or Transportation Line, & distance in km.*	*Court: City*	*Court: Distr.*	*Parish Offices (various religions)*
Bukowszczyzna, village	Druja	Brasław	Wil.	Druja	Druja 8		Druja	Wilno	Druja r

Document V-7 is a sample from the 1934 ***Skorowidz Miejscowości Rzeczypospolitej Polski*** [Index of Localities of the Polish Republic], ed. Tadeusz Bystrzycki, 2 vols., Przemyśl: Wydawnictwo książnicy naukowej, 1934. This source is particularly valuable for finding communities within Poland's borders between World Wars I and II, but later incorporated into the Soviet Union, and now in Belarus or Lithuania or Ukraine. It is available on microfilm through the Family History Library in Salt Lake City (FHL microfilm no. 1,343,868). It can also be studied on-site at major libraries such as the New York City Public Library, and at the Archive and Resource Center of the Polish Genealogical Society of Connecticut and the Northeast (**http://www.pgsctne.org**).

SPIS MIEJSCOWOŚCI POLSKIEJ RZECZYPOSPOLITEJ LUDOWEJ

Nazwa i rodzaj miejscowości	Gromada (osiedle-osied.) (miasto-m.)	Siedziba PRN	Województwo	Poczta	Stacja, przystanek kolejowy	Urząd stanu cywilnego
Abewillów, kol.	Puszcza Mariańska	Skierniewice	Łódzkie	Wola Pękoszewska	Puszcza Mariańska	Puszcza Mariańska
Abisynia, os. m.	—	p.m. Sosnowiec	Katowickie	Sosnowiec	Sosnowiec Główny	Sosnowiec
Abisynia, kol.	Leśna Podlaska	Biała Podl.	Lubelskie	Leśna Podlaska	Mariampol p. wąsk.	Leśna Podlaska
Abisynia, kol.	Czerniczyn	Hrubieszów	Lubelskie	Czerniczyn	Metelin p.	Hrubieszów
Abisynia, kol.	Mircze	Hrubieszów	Lubelskie	Mircze	Tyszowce p. wąsk.	Mircze
Abisynia, przys.	Nieledew	Hrubieszów	Lubelskie	Nieledew	Hrubieszów wąsk.	Hrubieszów
Abisynia, kol.	Werbkowice	Hrubieszów	Lubelskie	Werbkowice	Werbkowice	Werbkowice
Abisynia, przys.	Jabłoń	Parczew	Lubelskie	Jabłoń	Milanów p.	Jabłoń
Abisynia, przys.	Perespa	Tomaszów Lub.	Lubelskie	Perespa	Koniuchy p.	Perespa
Abisynia, przys.	Tarnawatka	Tomaszów Lub.	Lubelskie	Tarnawatka	Maziły p.	Tarnawatka
Abisynia, przys.	Komarów-Osada	Tomaszów Lub.	Lubelskie	Komarów	Koniuchy p.	Komarów-Osada
Abram, os.	Czarnocin	Łódź	Łódzkie	Czarnocin	Czarnocin p.	Konstantynów Łódzki
Abramiki, kol.	Łubin Kościelny	Bielsk Podl.	Białostockie	Łubin Kościelny	Bielsk Podlaski	Bielsk Podl.
Abramowice, przys.	Szczyrzyc	Limanowa	Krakowskie	Szczyrzyc k. Limanowej	Dobra k. Limanowej	Szczyrzyc
Abramowice, os. m.	—	p.m. Lublin	Lubelskie	Głusk	Lublin	Lublin
Abramowice, wieś	Głusk	Lublin	Lubelskie	Głusk	Lublin	Głusk

Document V-8: A Sample from the 1967 *Spis Miejscowości PRL*

Name & Type of Locality	*District (settlement, town)*	*Headquarters of the People's District Council*	*Province*	*Post Office*	*Railroad Station*	*Vital Stat. Office*
Abewillów, kol.	Puszcza Mariańska	Skierniewice	Łódzkie	Wola Pękoszewska	Puszcza Mariańska	Puszcza Mariańska

Document V-8 is a sample from the 1967 ***Spis miejscowości PRL*** [List of Localities in the Polish People's Republic], which is helpful with administrative divisions as they existed after World War II but before a major reorganization in 1975. It is available from the Family History Library (the book itself is FHL Ref 943.8 E5s; on microfilm it's #844,922), and at other major research libraries.

The columnar headings mean, respectively: Name and Type of Locality; District (housing development, town); Headquarters of the PRN (People's District Council); Province; Post Office; Railroad Station; and Vital Statistics Office. Thus the first place shown, Abewillów, was classified as a *kolonia* (colony); it was in the *gromada* of Puszcza Mariańska; the nearest PRN headquarters was in Skierniewice; it was in Łódż province as of 1967; and it was served by the post office in Wola Pękoszewska, the railroad station in Puszcza Mariańska, and the Vital Statistics Office (USC) in Puszcza Mariańska.

The following abbreviations and terms are used in this work:

dziel. – dzielnica miasta, city section or quarter
kol. – kolonia, colony
m. – miasto, town
m. st. – miasto stołeczne, capital city
os. – osada, settlement, colony
osied. – osiedle, housing development
osied. m. – osiedle mieszkaniowe, residential housing development
p. – przystanek kolejowy, railroad station
p. m. – powiat miejski, municipal county
PRN – Powiatowa Rada Narodowa, People's County Council
przys. – przysiołek, hamlet, farmstead
siedziba – [county or district] seat
w. m. – miasto wyłączone z województwa, town separate from a province

Uppercase letters or numbers, e. g., A.B., I. IL., are references to hypothecary sections (i. e., real estate or mortgage records).

227 **Chmielówka – Chociczka**

Nazwa, drugi przypadek i rodzaj miejscowości	Gmina, miasto, dzielnica	Województwo	Poczta	Stacja, przystanek PKP
Chmielówka, -ki, *wieś*	Biskupiec	olsztyńskie	Kobułty	Kobułty
Chmurówka, -ki, *cz. wsi Przysietnica*	Stary Sącz	nowosądeckie	Barcice	Barcice
Chmury, Chmur, *leśn.*	Dobre Miasto	olsztyńskie	Cerkiewnik	Cerkiewnik
Chobanin*, -na, *wieś*	Wieruszów	kaliskie	Wieruszów	Pieczyska

Document V-9: *Wykaz urzędowych nazw miejscowości*

Name and Type of Locality and Form in the Genitive Singular Case	*District, City, Neighborhood*	*Province*	*Post Office*	*Railway Stop or Station*
Chmielówka, -ki, village	Biskupiec	Olsztyn	Kobułty	Kobułty
Chmurówka, -ki, *part of village Przysietnica*	Stary Sącz	Nowy Sącz	Barcice	Barcice
Chmury, Chmur, forest district	Dobre Miasto	Olsztyn	Cerkiewnik	Cerkiewnik
Chobanin, -na, village	Wieruszów	Kalisz	Wieruszów	Pieczyska

Document V-9 is a sample from ***Wykaz urzędowych nazw miejscowości w Polsce*** [List of Official Names of Localities in Poland], which is useful for information on administrative subdivisions effective 1975-1998.

Another source worth consulting in some instances is the 16-volume ***Skorowidz miejscowości rzeczypospolitej polskiej*** *[Index to Localities in the Commonwealth of Poland]*, published in 1924 in Warsaw by Glówny Urząd Statystyczny. It is based on data from the census of 1921 and gives population figures by sex, nationality, and religion, as well as totals. It is organized by *powiat* (county), with an index to localities, and includes territory now in Belarus and Lithuania. Finding it is the main problem. The Family History Library in Salt Lake City has Volumes 5 (Białystok province), 7 (parts 1 and 2, Nowogródek province, Wilno district), and 8 (Polesie) only, on microfilm #804242, Items 3-6.

The *Słownik Geograficzny Królestwa Polskiego*

While understanding the layout and contents of a gazetteer with information presented in columns is relatively easy, reading the often archaic language of a geographical dictionary can present a formidable challenge, even to individuals with a sophisticated command of the language in question. The Polish-language *Słownik geograficzny Królestwa Polskiego i innych krajów słowiańskich* [Geographical Dictionary of the Kingdom of Poland and Other Slavic Countries], published between 1880 and 1904, is a massive work, consisting of 15 volumes (but the 15th is subdivided into two thick books; so in effect there are 16 volumes). It gives historical geographic descriptions of Polish cities, towns, villages, and other physical features such as lakes, mountains, rivers, etc. But it also includes entries on many places in Lithuania, Belarus, western Ukraine, and western Russia.

Entries in the *Słownik* can range from a single line to several pages of textual material, especially for large, historically significant cities. In general, entries that go beyond brief one-line descriptions provide information on: population figures; the ethnic and religious composition of the population; the types of land division and their measures; description of physical features; mention of any industry; public offices (courts, post offices, etc.); transportation facilities (roads, railroad stations); historical highlights; schools; and the Roman and Greek Catholic parish and deanery to which the locality belongs.

In addition to description of specific communities, one may also find general descriptions of counties, provinces, even whole regions such as *Inflanty* (Polish Livonia), *Litwa* (Lithuania), etc. Most *gubernias* in western Russia, Belarus, and Ukraine are represented with entries, many of which are fairly lengthy and informative.

The *Słownik geograficzny* is available at many large libraries, including the LDS Family History Library in Salt Lake City—which means you can borrow it through local Family History Centers. As of this writing, the Polish Genealogical Society of America and Polish historian and genealogist Rafał T. Prinke were cooperating to produce a single CD-ROM disk containing the contents of the entire work, in the form of highly compressed graphic images. For more information check with the Society online at **http://www.pgsa.org**, or write to the following address: PGSA, 984 N. Milwaukee Ave., Chicago IL 60622, USA.

In using this work, as with many mentioned previously, one often encounters county, parish, and diocesan names in the form of adjectives, not the noun forms generally found on maps. It's as if we said such-and-such a place was "in the Poznanian county" instead of "in the county of Poznań." One must determine the noun form of the locality in order to find it in a gazetteer or on a map. As a rule, these adjectives are not terribly difficult to change into noun form: *powiat augustowski* is obviously "the county of Augustów," and *powiat będziński* is "the county of Będzin." For those forms that are not so easy to recognize, help is available in Daniel M. Schlyter's *A Gazetteer of Polish Adjectival Place-names,* Salt Lake City: Genealogical Library, 1980. (FHL book 943.8 E5sd; also on microfilm 1,181,581 item 4 and on microfiche no. 6,000,843).

Please note that **many, many places in Eastern Europe have the same names, or similar ones.** You can't automatically assume a place is the same as the one you're looking for because it has the same name. Try to locate a village (Russian *деревня, derevnya,* or *село, selo,* Polish *wieś*) in terms of the nearest town or city (Russian *город, gorod,* Polish *miasto*), or in terms of its *powiat* or *уѣздъ,* administrative seat.

The abbreviations and terminology in the *Słownik* can perplex even people fluent in Polish. Some terms and usages are archaic and do not conform to contemporary spelling conventions. The next few pages provide explanations of the abbreviations and terms most often encountered, or most likely to confuse researchers. Reference to this list may clarify many passages that would be otherwise incomprehensible.

A Sampling of Abbreviations and Vocabulary in the *Słownik Geograficzny*

akad. – *akademia,* academia
al. – *alias,* alias, also known as
analf. – *analfabeci,* illiterate
apt. – *apteka,* pharmacy
art. – *artykuł,* article
bagno, swamp, marsh
bernardyński, Bernardine (the Bernardine Fathers, a religious order)
bisk. – *biskup (biskupi, biskupstwo),* bishop (bishop's, bishopric)
błoto, swamp, mud
bór, forest
brz. – *brzeg,* shore (of a lake or sea), bank (of a river)
bydło, cattle
c., cent. – *cent austryacki,* Austrian cent
c. k. – *cesarsko-królewski,* royal imperial (an expression used to refer to institutions of the Austrian Emperor; German equivalent *k. u. k., kaiserlich und königlich*)
cegielnia, brickyard, brickworks

chłop, peasant
chrz. - *chrześcijanie*, Christians, or *chrześcijański*, Christian
cz. - *część*, part
czet. - *czetwiert*, from Russian *четверть*, *chetvert'*, a Russian unit of liquid measure
czynsz, rent
czyt. - *czytaj*, read, see also
d., dm. - *dom* or *domy*, homes, houses
dek. = *dekanat*, deanery (subdivision of a diocese, comprised of parishes)
dł. - *długi*, long, or *długość*, length
dł. g. - *długość geograficzna*, longitude
dolina, valley
domin. - *dominium*, domain, manor
dominikański, Dominican (adj.)
dopływ, tributary (of a river)
dr. - *drewniany*, made of wood
dr. żel. - *droga żelazna*, railway, railroad
droga bita, paved road
druk. - *drukowany*, printed
dusza, soul
dwór, manor, yard, estate
dyec. - *dyecezya*, diocese (in modern Polish spelled *diecezja*)
dym - literally "smoke," a hearth, homestead
dz., dzies. - *dziesięcina*, see **Measures of Area**
dzien. - *dziennik*, newspaper, daily
emfit. - *emfiteuza*, long-term lease of unused land (especially church property) with an obligetion to improve it
ew., ewang. - *ewangelik* or *ewangelicki*, Protestant (noun and adj. forms)
f. - *fenig pruski*, Prussian *pfennig* (coin)
fabr. - *fabryka*, factory
Ferro—refers to an archaic coordinate system measuring longitude from Ferro (now Hierro) in the Canary Islands, long the westernmost point known to Europeans, rather than from Greenwich, England; Ferro lies at about 18°W from Greenwich, so to get the right longitude for places in eastern Europe by modern standards, subtract about 18° from the so-called "Ferro longitudes"
fil. - *filia* or adj. *filialny*, branch (church)
fl. - *floren*, florin, Rhenish *złoty*
folw. - *folwark*, large manorial farmstead
fr. - *frank*, franc, or *francuski*, French
franciszkański, Franciscan (adj.)
Gal. - *Galicya* or *Galicja*, Galicia
gaz. - *gazeta*, newspaper
gimn. - *gimnazyum*, secondary school
gł. - *głęboki*, deep
gleba, soil
gm. - *gmina*, an administrative district, typically (but not always) rural and composed of several villages, although there are also *gminas* consisting of towns
góra, mountain
gorzelnia, distillery
gościniec, highway
gr. kat. - *grecko-katolicki*, Greek Catholic
granica, border, frontier; *graniczy się na*, borders on
grun. orn. - *grunt orny*, arable land
gub. - *gubernia*, from Russian *губернія*, term for a political administrative subdivision
ha. - *hektar*, hectare (see **Measures of Area**)
handel, trade, commerce; *handel zbożem*, grain trade, trade in grain
hodowla, raising, breeding, e. g., *hodowla świn i owiec*, pig and sheep raising
hr. - *hrabia*, count, or *hrabina*, countess, or *hrabstwo*, county
i i. - *i inne*, and others, et al.
incl. - *inclusive*, inclusive
inst. - *instytut*, Institute
izr. - *izraelici* or *izraelski*, Jews, Jewish
J. Ch. - *Jezus Chrystus*, Jesus Christ
j. w. - *jak wyżej*, as above
jarm. - *jarmark*, trade fair, market
jez. - *jezioro*, lake
jęz. - *język*, language
jezuicki, Jezuit (adj.)
k., kop. - *kopiejki*, kopeks
Kal. - *Kalendarz*, calendar
kapl. - *kaplica*, chapel
karczma, inn, tavern
karmelicki, Carmelite (adj.)
kasa pożyczkowa, lending institution
kat. - *katolik* or *katolicki*, Catholic
kil. - *kilometr*, kilometer
kl. - *klasa*, class, grade
kmieć, peasant
kob. - *kobiety*, women
kol. - *kolonia*, colony, settlement
kom. cel. - *komora celna*, customs office
komtur, commander of the Teutonic Knights; a *komturstwo* was the area over which he had jurisdiction
kop. - *kopiejki*, kopeks
kopalnia, mine
kośc. - *kościół*, church, or *kościelny*, of the church, ecclesiastical
kr. - *król*, king; or *krajcar*, a *Kreutzer* (Austrian unit of currency)
król. - *królewski*, royal, or *królestwo*, kingdom
Król. Pol. - *Królestwo Polskie*, Kingdom of Poland
Krzyżak, Krzyżacy, Teutonic Knight(s)

ks. - *książę*, prince, duke
kś. - *ksiądz*, priest, Father
k. u. k. - see *c. k.*
kw. - *kwadratowy*, square (meters, kilometers, and so on)
l., *ludn.* - *ludność*, populace, population
łac. - *łacina*, Latin
łąka, meadow
łan, unit of land measure, varying in different times and places—it is often used synonymously with *włóka*, q. v.
las, forest, woods
leśny, forest (adj.)
leżeć, to lie, be located
liczy, numbers, counts, e. g., *liczy 45 dm.* = numbers 45 houses
lit. - *litewski*, Lithuanian
łot. - *łotewski*, Latvian
M. - *Mały*, small, little
mad. - *madziarski*, Hungarian, Magyar
men. - *menonici*, Mennonites
męż. - *mężczyźni*, males, men
m. i. - *między innemi*, among others
mieszczanin, burgher, townsman (adj. form *mieszczański*
mil. - *milion*, million
mk. - *mieszkańcy*, inhabitants, residents
mko. - *miasteczko*, small town
Mł. - *Mały* (or a declined form of that adj.), small, little
młyn, mill
mm. - *millimetr*, millimeter
mr. - *mórg*, *morga*, morg (see **Measures of Area**)
mrk. - *marka*, mark (German currency)
msto. - *miasto*, town, city
mt. - *metr*, meter
mur. - *murowany*, made of brick or stone
n. - *nad*, above, over, on
N. - *Nowy*, new (generally used as part of a place name, e. g., Nowy Sącz)
n. p. m. - *nad powierzchnią morza*, above sea level
n. s. - *nowego stylu*, New Style (dating)
Nadw. - *Nadwiślańska (dr. ż.)*, railway on the Wisła river
nal. - *należy*, belongs to, should be
nied. - *niedaleko*, not far away (from)
niem. - *niemiecki*, German
nieużytek, barren or unused land
nizina, lowland
ob. - *obacz*, see
obejmuje, covers, encompasses, includes (from *obejmować*)
obr. - *obraz*, image, picture
obszar, area, territory
od (preposition), from, e. g., *49 w. od Trok* = 45 viorsts from Troki
odl. - *odległy*, distant, or *odległość*, distance
odn. - *odnowiony*, renewed, restored
ogr. - *ogród*, garden
okr. - *okręg*, district, a political administrative subdivision, or *okręgowy*, adjectival form of that noun
oo. - *ojcowie*, Fathers (religious), e. g., *oo. jezuici*, Jesuit Fathers
opactwo, abbey
os. - *osada*, settlement, large village
p. w. - *pod wezwaniem*, under the patronage of (refers to a church's patron saint, e. g., *kościół p. w. św. Stanisława*, "St. Stanisław's Church")
pam. - *pamiętnik*, memoir, memorial
pańszczyzna, serfdom, often used as a term for a peasant's obligation to perform labor service for his lord; corvée
par. - *parafia*, parish, or *parafialny*, parochial, of the parish
pasmo gór, mountain range
pastw. - *pastwiska*, pastureland
piasek, sand
piaszczysty, sandy (adj., e. g., soil)
płd. - *południe*, south
płn. - *północ*, north
pobl. - *pobliski* or *w pobliżu*, near
poczta, post office
pol. - *polski*, Polish, or *polityczny*, political, or *policyjny*, police
poł. - *położony*, situated, located
półw. - *półwysep*, peninsula
por. - *porównaj*, compare
pow. - *powiat*, administrative division, similar to a county or a German *Kreis*
prawosł. - *prawosławny*, Orthodox
prod. - *produkcya*, production
pryw. - *prywatny*, private
przemyśl, industry, e. g., *przemyśl naftowy*, oil industry, *przemyśl sukienniczy*, cloth industry, etc.
przepływać, flow through, over
przyl. - *przyległości*, appurtenances
przysiołek, hamlet, outlying settlement
przyst. - *przystań* or *przystanek*, harbor, port; stop, station
przyw. - *przywilej*, charter, grant
puszcza, forest
r. - *rok*, year
ref. - *reformowani (ewangelicy)*, Reformed (Protestant)
reg. - *regencya*, regency
rob. - *robotnicy*, workers, laborers

rodz. - *rodzina,* family
roln. - *rolnik* or *rolnicy,* farmer(s)
ross. - *rossyjski,-a,-e,* Russian
równina, plain
rs. - *rubel srebrny,* silver ruble
rubel, ruble
rz. or *rzk.* - *rzeka,* river
rz.-kat. - *rzymski-katolicki,* Roman Catholic
rząd. - *rządowy,* official, governmental (adj.)
s. gm. - *sąd gminny,* district court of law
s. s. - *starego stylu,* Old Style (in dates)
sąd, court of law; *sąd grodzki,* borough court; *sąd ziemski,* land court; *sąd powiatowy,* county court; *sąd gubernialny,* provincial court; *sąd wiejski,* peasants' (rural) court
saż., sąż. - *sażeń, sążeń,* see **Measures of Length**
składać się z (+ genitive case), consists of, is comprised of
sołtys, village or hamlet administrator, compare German *Schultheiß* or *Schulze*
sprzedawać, to sell
St. - *Stary,* old, or *Sanct.* - holy, St. (Latin)
st. - *stopa,* foot; *stacja,* station; *stopień,* degree
st. dr. ż. - *stacja drogi żelaznej,* railway station
st. p. - *stacja pocztowa,* post office
st. tel. - *stacja telegraficzna,* telegraph station
staroż. - *starożytny,* antique, ancient
stol. - *stolica,* capital (city)
str. - *stronica,* page
stul. - *stulecie,* century
stwo. - *starostwo,* office or property of a *starosta,* regional administrator
Ś., Św. - *Święty,* St., Saint
sz., sześc. - *sześcienny,* cubic
sz., szer. - *szeroki,* wide; or *szerokość,* width
sz. g. - *szerokość geograficzna,* latitude
szk. - *szkoła,* school
szl. - *szlachecki,* of the nobility *(szlachta)*
Szl. - *Szląsk,* Silesia (modern Polish *Śląsk,* German *Schlesien*)
szp. - *szpital,* hospital, shelter
szwedzki, Swedish
t. - *tom,* volume, or *tonna,* ton
t. n. - *tegoż nazwiska,* of the same name
tal. - *talar,* talar (unit of currency)
tartak, sawmill
tm. - *tamże,* ibid., the same place
tys. - *tysiąc,* thousand
u. gm. - *urząd gminny,* district government office
ujście, mouth (of a river), bay
um. - *umarł,* died
uniw. - *uniwersytet,* university
ur. - *urodził się,* was born, or *urodzony,* born, né (*urodzona,* née)
urząd, office, e. g., *urząd pocztowy,* post office, *urząd podatkowy,* tax office, *urząd gminy,* local government office
v. - *vel,* or, or German *von,* from, of
vol. - *volumen,* volume (Latin)
w. - *wiek,* age, century; or *wiorsta,* see **Measures of Length**
W. - *Wielki,* Great, Grand, large, big
w. a. - *waluty austriackej,* in Austrian currency
W. Ks. P. - *Wielkie Księstwo Poznańskie,* Grand Duchy of Poznań, Provinz Posen
Wiad. - *Wiadomości,* news, message, information
wiejski - village (adj.), rural
wiorsta, see **Measures of Length**
wioska - (small) village
wł. - *włóka,* see **Measures of Area**
wł., włas. - *własność,* property, usually with the genitive, e. g., *własność rodziny Mierzejewskich,* property of the Mierzejewski family
właś. - *właściwie,* actually, correctly, properly, or *właściciel,* owner
włośc. - *włościanie* or adjectival form *włościański,* peasants, peasant
włóka, see **Measures of Area**
woda, water
woj. - *województwo,* province
wójt, village chieftain
wola, a "new" settlement founded by peasants from a nearby village or by immigrants (often German), with their lord's permission and exemption from taxes or rents for a specified time
wś. - *wieś,* village; *wieś kościelna,* ecclesiastical village (i. e., Church-owned); *wieś królewska,* royal village (owned by the crown); *wieś szlachecka,* noble village (owned by nobles); *wieś włościańska,* peasant village
wsch. - *wschód,* east, or *wschodni,* eastern
wyd. - *wydanie,* edition
wym. - *wymawiaj,* pronounce as
wys. - *wysoki,* high, tall, or *wysokość,* elevation, height
wysoczyzna, highland
wyst. - *wystawiony,* exhibited, displayed, drawn up
wzgórza, hills
wzn. - *wzniesiony,* raised, elevated, or *wzniesienie,* elevation
zach. - *zachód,* west
zał. - *założony,* established, founded
zamek, castle
zaśc. - *zaścianek,* settlement of minor nobility, small village
zboże, grain
zbud. - *zbudowany,* built, constructed

złoty, gold, also a unit of currency
złr. - *złoty reński*, Rhenish *złoty*
zm. - *zmarł, zmarły*, dead, deceased

znajdować się, to be located, be found
źr. - *źródło*, source
zw. - *zwany*, called, named

Measures of Area

1 włóka pols. (nowopolska) = 30 *mórgs*
1 mórg polski = 55.9872 ars, 0.512459 *dziesiatynas*
1 dziesiatyna (dziesięcina) = 2400 sq. *sąż.*, 1.9508 new Polish *mórgs*, 109.252 ars
1 *hektar* = 100 ars (1 hectare)

1 ar. = 100 square meters
1 mórg austr. = 57.5464 ars
1 mórg pruski = 25.532 ars
1 mórg chełmiński = 56.170 ars

Measures of Length or Distance

1 łokieć polski (Polish ell) = 2 Polish *stopy*, 0.8099 *arszyn*, 0.576 meter
1 sążeń polski = 3 Polish *łokcie*
1 arszyn = 0.7111936 meter
1 sążeń = 3 *arszyns*, 7 *stóp* (feet), 2.1336 meters
1 łokieć austr. (Austrian ell) = 0.7775586 meters
1 sążeń austr. = 1.896484 meters
1 łokieć pruski (Prussian ell) = 0.66694 meters
1 stopa pruska or *reńska* (Prussian or Rhenish foot) = 0.3238535 meters

1 metr = 1.73611 Polish *łokci*
1 mila geogr. (geographic *mila*) = 7407.4074 meters, 4286.695 Polish *sążeńs*, 6.9437 *wiorstas*
1 mila polska lub ross. (Polish or Russian *mila*) = 7 *wiorstas*
1 wiorsta = 1500 *arszyns*, 1,066.7805 meters (about two-thirds of a mile)
1 kilometr = 1,000 meters
1 mila austr. (Austrian *mila*) = 7585.937 meters

Sample *Słownik Geograficzny* Entry

Translating the entry for the relatively small village of Dobrzyjałowo (**Document V-10**, below) illustrates the structure of a typical short entry in the *Słownik geograficzny*.

Dobrzyjałowo, a village and manorial farmstead in the county of Kolno, district of Rogienice. In 1877 there were 34 houses and 290 inhabitants; the parish is in the deanery of Kolno and has 3,276 parishioners. The church and parish were erected in 1425 by Stanisław of the Trzaska coat of arms; the present church [*"present," that is, as of when the* Słownik *was published*] is of stone. The properties of D. consist of the manorial farmstead in Dobrzyjałowo, as well as the villages of Dobrzyjałowo and Budy Mikołajki. [Dobrzyjałowo] is located 14 viorsts from Łomża, 20 from Kolno, 14 from Stawiski, and 3 from the main road; 55 from Czyżew; 45 from Grajewo, and 6 from the river Narew. The area of the manorial farmstead is 1,870 *mórgs*, to wit: 601 of arable land and gardens, 322 of meadows, 902 of forest, and 45 of barren or unused land and squares. There are 7 stone buildings and 15 wooden ones; [there are] two water-powered mills, deposits of peat, and ponds. A stream called the Jura flows through the property's territory. The village of Dobrzyjałowo has 64 settlements and 305 *mórgs*

> **Dobrzyjałowo**, wś i folw., pow. kolneński, gm. Rogienice. W 1827 r. było tu 34 dm. i 290 mk.; par. D. dek. kolneńskiego 3276 dusz liczy. Kościół i par. erygował 1425 r. Stanisław herbu Trzaska; obecny po 1856 r. zmurowany. Dobra D. składają się z fol. D. i wsi D. i Budy Mikołajki. Od Łomży w. 14; od Kolna w. 20; od Stawisk w. 14; od drogi bitej w. 3; od Czyżewa w. 55; od Grajewa w. 45; od rz. Narwi w. 6. Rozl. przestrzeni folw. wynosi 1870 m. a mianowicie: grunta orne i ogrody m. 601, łąk m. 322; lasu m. 902; nieużytki i place m. 45; bud. mur. 7, drew. 15; dwa młyny wodne; pokłady torfu; stawy; struga pod nazwą Jura przepływa przez territorium dóbr. Wieś D. os. 64, grun. m. 305; wś Budy Mikołajki osad 7, gruntu m. 83. Nomenklatura Jurzec, mająca około m. 6, w r. 1871 odprzedana i oddzielną księgą hypoteczną objęta.

Document V-10: A *Słownik* entry

of land; the village of Budy Mikołajki has 7 settlements, with 83 meters of land. Jurzec, having approximately 6 *mórgs* in 1871, was resold in 1871 and transferred to a separate mortgage register.

Other Polish-Language Sources

72

11. Powiat Sokółka.

1. Gmina Czarna Wieś 2. Gmina Dąbrowa 3. Gmina Janów

Miasta, Gminy, Miejscowości	Charakter miejscowości	Budynki		Ludność obecna w dniu 30 września 1921 r. (bez objętej spisem wojskowym)																
							W tej liczbie było wyznania							Podało narodowość					
		z przezn. mieszkalne	inne zamieszkałe	Ogółem	Mężczyzn	Kobiet	rzymsko-katolick.	prawo-sławn.	ewangelickiego	innego chrześc.	mojżeszowego	innego	niewiadomego	polską	białoruską	niemiecką	żydowską	inną	niewiad.
1	2	3	4	5	6	7	8	9	10	11	12	13	14	15	16	17	18	19	20
II. Gminy:																			
1. Gm. Czarna Wieś		127	–	956	460	496	777	116	7	4[a]	52	–	–	946	–	1	–	9[c]	–
1. Bukształ	nadl.	4	–	20	12	8	16	4	–	–	–	–	–	20	–	–	–	–	–
2. Bukształ	wieś	44	–	241	111	130	178	48	–	–	15	–	–	241	–	–	–	–	–
3. Czarna Wieś	st. kol.	8	–	63	30	33	61	1	1	–	–	–	–	63	–	–	–	–	–
4. Greńskie[1])	leśn.	.	.	.	.	.	.	.	.	.	.	.	.	.	.	.	.	.	.
5. Jackie Tartaki	kol.	1	–	6	3	3	6	–	–	–	–	–	–	6	–	–	–	–	–
6. Mochnacz	kol.	6	–	40	18	22	40	–	–	–	–	–	–	40	–	–	–	–	–
7. Polanki	kol.	2	–	14	7	7	14	–	–	–	–	–	–	14	–	–	–	–	–
8. Rogoziński Most	kol.	4	–	21	8	13	4	17	–	–	–	–	–	21	–	–	–	–	–
9. Rogoziński Most *	leśn.	–	–	–	–	–	–	–	–	–	–	–	–	–	–	–	–	–	–
10. Wodokaczka	nadl.	15	–	231	120	111	195	27	2	–	7	–	–	228	–	–	–	3	–
11. Wodokaczka	wieś	27	–	187	78	109	100	1	3	–	23	–	–	186	–	1	–	–	–
12. Zapieoki	wieś	16	–	133	73	60	103	18	1	4	7	–	–	127	–	–	–	6	–

Document V-11: 1921 Polish Census

While the sources discussed so far are by far the most common and frequently utilized, there are numerous other sources of information of a geographical nature on places in Poland. One is a compilation of population statistics from the 1921 Polish census, a sample of which appears above as **Document V-11**. The county *(powiat)* name appears at the top of the page, **Powiat Sokółka**, followed by an alphabetical list of all the *gminas* and subsequently by an alphabetical list of all localities in that *gmina*. The columnar headings are as follows:

1. Miasta, Gminy, Miejscowości	Cities, Districts, and Localities
2. Charakter miejscowości	Type of locality
wieś	village
leśn. (leśniczówka)	forest settlement
st. kol. (stacja kolejowa)	railroad station
nadl. (nadleśnictwo)	forest ranger's settlement
folw. (folwark)	large manorial estate
kol. (kolonia)	colony, i. e., farm settlement removed from the main village
3-4. Budynki	Buildings
3. Z przeznaczeniem mieszkalne	3. Designated as residential
4. inne zamieszkania	4. other dwellings
Ludność obecna w dniu 30 września 1921 r. (bez objętej spisem wojskowym)	Population as of September 30, 1921 (except those included in military lists)
5. ogólem	total
6. mężczyzn	of men
7. kobiet	of women

W tej liczbie było wyznania	Of that number there were of this religion
8. rzymsko-katolickiego	Roman Catholic
9. prawosławnego	Orthodox
10. ewangelickiego	Evangelical Lutheran
11. innego chrześćijańskiego	other Christian
12. mojżeszowego	Jewish
13. innego	other
14. niewiadomego	unknown

[W tej liczbie] podało narodowości	Of that number there were by nationality
15. polską	Polish
16. białoruską	Byelorussian
17. niemiecką	German
18. żydowską	Jewish
19. inną	other
20. niewiadomą	unknown

Other gazetteers were restricted to a certain region or province. **Document V-12**, below, comes from an 1897 compilation of localities in Galicia by Jan Bigo.

Nazwa miejscowości	Starostwo	Sąd powiatowy	Urzęda parafialne	Urząd pocztowy	Urząd telegraficzny	Odległość od urzędu poczt.	Odległość od urzędu telegr.	Ludność według spisu z roku 1890	Właściciel tabularny
Dobromyśl p. do Komarówki									
Dobroniów p. do Janowic									
Dobropol p. do Majdan									
Dobropole z Mateuszówką w.	Buczacz	Buczacz	ł. Wiśniowczyk g. Zarwanica	Chmielówka	Trembowla	7·58	27·0	1434	hr. Henryk Szeliski
Dobropole p. Dupliska									
Dobrosin z Łazowem w. k. P.	Żółkiew	Żółkiew	ł. Magierów g. loco	loco	loco	—	—	1483	Jan Nieczuja Urbański
Dobrostańska Wola z Grünthalem w.	Gródek	Gródek	ł. Weissenberg g. Dobrostany	Weissenberg (Białogóry)	Gródek	5·7	15·0	602	kr. Kalikst Poniński
Dobrostany z Szałapinem w.	Gródek	Gródek	ł. Weissenberg g. loco	Weissenberg	Gródek	1·37	12·0	1082	ks. Kalikst Poniński

Document V-12: Bigo's Gazetteer of Galicia

The column headings are:

1. Nazwa miejscowości — name of locality
2. Starostwo — starostwo (the area under the jurisdiction of a *starosta*, a local official)
3. Sąd powiatowy — County Court
4. Urzęda *[sic]* parafialne — Parish offices; *ł.* for Latin-rite parish, *g.* for Greek or Eastern rite; *loco* means "there, in that place, on-site" (*urzęda* is probably a misprint, since the standard nominative plural of *urząd* is *urzędy*)
5. Urząd pocztowy — Post office
6. Urząd telegraficzny — Telegraph office
7. Odległość od urzędu poczt. / telegr. — Distance from post / telegraph office
8. Ludność według spisu z roku 1890 — Population according to the 1890 census
9. Właściciel tabularny — Land-owner. Note: named here can be an individual, a clergyman (Ks. = *Ksiądz*, priest), a nobleman (hr. = *hrabia*, Count), the government (*Rząd*), or an institution (e. g., *konwent*, convent).

ORTSCHAFT MIEJSCOWOŚĆ	Kreis Powiat	Kreisteil Część powiatu	Gemeinde Gmina	Parochie Parafja	Friedensgericht Sąd pokoju	Sitz des zuständigen Bezirksgerichts Miejsce przynależnego sądu okręgowego	Polizeistation (Gendarmeriestation) Stacja policyjna (Żandarmska)	Nächste zuständige Postanstalt Najbliższe przynależne biuro pocztowe	Nächste Eisenbahnstation Najbliższa stacja kolejowa	Voll- oder Kleinbahn Kolej lub kolejka
Chruślin, Df.	Bł.-Grodzisk		Radzików	Rokitno	Błonie	Warschau	Błonie	Grodzisk	Płochocin	Vb.
Chruślin, Df.	Łowicz	Łowicz	Dąbkowice	Chruślin	Łyszkowice	Łowicz	Jamno	Łowicz	Domaniewice	„
Chrustne, Df.	Garwolin		Ryki	Ryki	Ryki	Siedlce	Ryki	Garwolin	Dęblin	„
Chrustów, Vw.	Kalisz	Kalisz	Tyniec	Borków	Tyniec	Kalisz	Kalisz	Kalisz	Kalisz	-
Chrustowo,	Włocławek	Nieszawa	Bądkowo	Bądkowo	Osięciny	Włocławek	Janowice	Włocławek	Łowiczek	Klb.
Chrustowo, Df.	Włocławek	Włocławek	Przedecz	Chodecz	Chodecz	Włocławek	Chodecz	Włocławek	Chodecz	„
Chrusty, Kol.	Kalisz	Kalisz	Strzałków	Lisków	Dobra	Kalisz	Koźminek	Turek	Radliczyce	Vb.
Chrusty, Df.	Konin	Konin	Golina	Myślibórz	Konin	Kalisz	Konin	Konin	Czarków	Klb.
Chrusty, Kol.	Konin	Konin	Golina	Myślibórz	Konin	Kalisz	Konin	Konin	Czarków	„
Chrusty, Df.	Łuków		Tuchowicz	Tuchowicz	Stanin	Siedlce	Tuchowicz	Łuków	Łuków	Vb.
Chrusty, Df.	Skierniewice	Rawa	Rawa	Rawa	Rawa	Łowicz	Rawa	Rawa	Rawa	Klb.
Chrusty, Df.	Włocławek	Nieszawa	Służewo	Służewo	Aleksandrowo	Włocławek	Służewo	Aleksandrowo	Aleksandrowo	Vb.
Chrusty Nowe, Df.	Łódź	Brzeziny	Mikołajew	Koluszki	Koluszki	Łódź	Koluszki	Brzeziny	Koluszki	„
Chrusty Stare, Df.	Łódź	Brzeziny	Mikołajew	Koluszki	Koluszki	Łódź	Koluszki	Brzeziny	Koluszki	-
Chruszczewka Szlachecka, Df.	Sokołów	Sokołów	Chruszczewka	Kossów	Kossów	Siedlce	Kossów	Sokołów	Telaki	„
Chruszczewka Włościańska, Df.	Sokołów	Sokołów	Chruszczewka	Kossów	Kossów	Siedlce	Kossów	Sokołów	Telaki	„
Chruszczewo, Gt.	Mława	Ciechanów	Nużewo	Ciechanów	Nużewo	Mława	Ciechanów	Ciechanów	Ciechanów	-

Document V-13: ***Alphabetisches Orts- und Gemeindelexikon ... Warschau***

The sample above, **Document V-13**, is from a German/Polish language compilation dating from 1917, the *Alphabetisches Orts- und Gemeindelexikon des General Gouvernement Warschau.* The eleven columnar headings read as follows:

1. Ortschaft/Miejscowość —locality
2. Kreis/Powiat — county
3. Kreisteil/Część powiatu — part of the county
4. Gemeinde/Gmina — district
5. Parochie/Parafja — parish
6. Friedensgericht/Sąd pokoju — court (literally "peace court")
7. Sitz des zuständigen Bezirksgerichts/Miejsce przynależnego sądu okręgowego — site of the District Court with jurisdiction
8. Polizeistation/Stacja policyjna — police station
9. Nächste zuständige Postanstalt/Najbliższe przynależne biuro pocztowe — nearest post office
10. Nächste Eisenbahnstation/Najbliższa stacja kolejowa — nearest train station
11. Voll- oder Kleinbahn/Kolej lub kolejka — Standard or narrow-gauge railroad

Other sources of geographical information include etymological dictionaries of place names. **Document V-14** is from a series still in progress, *Nazwy Miejscowe Polski–Historia–Pochodzenie* [Place Names of Poland –History–Origin], ed. Kazimierz Rymut, Instytut Języka Polskiego PAN, Kraków 1996. It documents the history and etymology of Polish place names and changes in those names over time. Thus in the sample at left we see that today *[dziś]* Bielnik consists of two settlements *[dwie osady]*, Bielnik Pierwszy and Bielnik Drugi (literally "First Bielnik" and "Second Bielnik"), and that they were formerly one village *[dawniej wieś]*. Next the word *elbl.* indicates that, according to the 1975-1998 arrangement of provinces, these settlements were in the province of Elbląg, and Bielnik was (were) 4 km. northwest *[płn.-zach.]*

> **Bielnik,** dziś *Bielnik Pierwszy* i *Bielnik Drugi*, dwie osady, dawniej wś, elbl., 4 km na płn.-zach. od Elbląga: *Kraffohlsdorf*, wś 1883 SG IV 579; *Bielnik — Kraffohlsdorf* 1951 Rosp 11; *Bielnik*, wś 1967 SM 59; *Bielnik Drugi, Bielnik Pierwszy, -ka -ego* 1980 WUN I 85. — Dawna n. niemiecka od n. kanału, nad którym wieś leży. Kanał *Kraffohlkanal*, dziś *Kanał Jagielloński*, wykonany w XV w., połączył rzekę Elbląg z Nogatem. N. *Bielnik* została wprowadzona urzędowo po 1945 r. *WK*
>
> **Bielny Staw** zob. **Bieliny** (3)
>
> **Bielonka,** nie istniejąca osada koło Sroczyna, pozn., gm. Kiszkowo: Seroczino, *Byelonka*, Barkowo 1550 Koz III 523. — Zapewne ze starszego **Bielanka*, z wtórną zmianą *-an-* w *-on-*, od ap. *biel*, z suf. *-anka*. Zob. wyżej *Bielanka*. *ZZ*

Document V-14

of Elbląg. The German name of the village was *Kraffohlsdorf*, mentioned in the gazetteer *Słownik Geograficzny* in volume IV on page 579 *[SG IV 579]*. The German name came from that of a canal constructed in the 15th century *[w XV w.]*, called *Kraffohlkanal*, and today *Kanal Jagielloński*, which connected the Elbląg and Nogat rivers. The name *Bielnik* became the official designation of the place as of 1945.

This is clearly going to be a valuable resource, but as of this writing only the first three volumes, covering names under A-B, C-D, and E-I, have appeared. Its one major flaw for genealogical researchers: it deals only with places within the post-World War II borders of Poland, and thus does not cover localities in Lithuania, Belarus, or Ukraine.

Guidebooks and Church Directories

Other possible sources of geographical information include **guidebooks** to specific regions and provinces, and **church directories** that give descriptions of our ancestral churches. Guidebooks can be found through searches of bibliographic databases at public or university libraries; they are not so difficult to find as you might think. The church directories are tougher—the largest collections are at the Family History Library in Salt Lake City, Utah, and at the Archives and Resource Center of the Polish Genealogical Society of Connecticut and the Northeast (8 Lyle Rd., New Britain CT 06053-2104 USA).

Document V-15 is a sample entry from a guidebook for Jedwabne, just to give an idea what sort of information these books can provide. While it is in paragraph form and thus presents the inexperienced translator with some difficulties, reference to the vocabulary for the *Słownik Geograficzny* can offer hints as to what is being discussed. Thus it is a small town *[miasteczko]* with 2,500 inhabitants, 60% Catholic and 40% Jewish; phrases such as *"w latach 1915-16"* and *"w 1917 r."* help establish the time frame of events discussed; and the second paragraph talks about the *centrum miasteczka*, "center of the town," and the *kościół*, the church. The last paragraphs mention that 8 km. to the southwest lies the village of Dobrzyjałowo, with a parish church of St. Stanisław from 1850, partly destroyed in 1915 and rebuilt in 1924. You don't have to be fluent in Polish to get at least some idea what's being said.

> **Jedwabne** (19 km), miasteczko o 2.500 mieszkańców (60% katolików. 40% żydów), położone na wzgórzu nad niewielkim strumykiem. *Restauracja* Ignacego Nowickiego przy ul. Dwornej 10. Osada powstała w początkach XVII w. przy rozległych dobrach Jedwabne, których właściciele założyli tu szereg przedsiębiorstw przemysłowych, wśród nich warsztaty tkackie. Miejscowe *targi*, odbywające się w każdą środę, ściągały coraz więcej ludności okolicznej, za czym szedł rozwój miasteczka jako centrum handlowego okolicy. W latach przedwojennych prócz warsztatów tkackich powstały tu dwie fabryki rękawiczek i kilka fabryk kapeluszy słomkowych. Niestety w latach 1915—16 miasteczko znalazło się na samej linii frontu i zostało wówczas *doszczętnie zniszczone*. Dopiero w 1917 r., rozpoczęto powoli rozbudowę miasteczka, dotychczas jeszcze niezupełnie zakończoną. W czasie wojny stary kościół drewniany i synagoga uległy zniszczeniu.
>
> Centrum miasteczka stanowi bardzo duży *Rynek*. Nad Rynkiem dominuje stojący przy nim okazały *kościół*, wykończony w 1935 r. w miejsce poprzedniego drewnianego z 1738 r. spalonego w czasie wojny. Jest to okazały budynek neobarokowy o białych ścianach z dwiema wieżami od frontu, pokryty czerwoną dachówką. Został on zbudowany według proj. arch. powiatowego inż. Piątkowskiego z Łomży. Na południe od Rynku niewielki *dworek* w starym parku.
>
> 8 km na południowy zachód leży *Dobrzyjałowo*, wieś parafialna z kościołem św. Stanisława z 1850 r. Po częściowym zniszczeniu w czasie wojny 1915 r., został on odbudowany w 1924 r.

Document V-15: Guidebook for Jedwabne

The content and quality of the church directories varies widely. Some provide extensive entries with a wealth of historical data; others amount to little more than a list of addresses.

Document V-16 is an entry for the parish of Krasnosielc, former Diocese of Płock. Here are selected phrases that appear in such entries.

patron par[afii]: patron saint of the parish

kościół paraf[ialny]: parish church building

murowany: of stone; also seen here: *ceglany,* "of brick," or *drewniany,* "of wood"

odpusty: religious processions (with the name of the Saint being honored and the date)

cmentarz przykościelny: cemetery in the churchyard; *cmentarz grzebalny:* parish cemetery

ilość mieszkańców: number of residents

miejscowości: localities, i. e., belonging to the parish. The number in parentheses gives the distance in kilometers of each village from the church. Some directories also give the number of inhabitants in each village.

archiwum: archive. Some directories give the beginning and end dates for parish registers kept at the parish level.

księgi chrztów: baptismal register; similarly, *księgi małżeństw,* marriage register, and *księgi zmarłych,* death register

proboszcz: pastor; *wikariusz,* assistant pastor

KRASNOSIELC

06-212 Krasnosielc, gm. w m., woj. ostrołęckie, tel. 33, wikariat tel. 39
PKP — Jastrząbka (17), PKS — w m.
patron par.: św. Jan Kanty
kościół paraf. p.w. św. Jana Kantego — murowany, zradiofonizowany

odpusty: św. Rocha (16 VIII), św. Jana Kantego (20 X)
nabożeństwo eucharystyczne: 9—11 XII
cmentarz przykościelny: murowana dzwonnica (2 dzwony)
cmentarz grzebalny: wystarczający, ogrodzony (0,5)
ilość mieszkańców: 5995
miejscowości: Amelin (8), Bagienice (6), Bagienice Tryłoga (6), Biernaty (4), Chłopia Łąka (3), Grabowo (8), Grądy (4), Huta (5), Józefowo (5), Kalinowo (6), Klin (5), Krasnosielc, Krasnosielc Leśny (3), Krasnosielc Nowy (1), Łazy (3), Niesułowo (8), Pach (10), Papierny Borek (6), Perzanki (8), Pieczyska (10), Pienice (4), Przyłaje (10), Przytuły (4), Raki (6), Ruzieck (10), Sielc (1), Sławki (3), Wola (5), Wola Rakowska (8), Wymysły (2), Wygoda (2)
punkty katechetyczne: Amelin, Bagienice, Grądy, Krasnosielc, Pienice, Przytuły, Raki, Wola
budynki: plebania — murowana; wikariat — murowany; organistówka — drewniana
archiwum księgi chrztów: 1808—1889; 1897—1975
księgi małżeństw: 1808—1889; 1897—1975
księgi zmarłych: 1808—1889; 1897—1975
kronika paraf.: od 1956
probszcz: ks. prał. mgr Tadeusz Goleniewski — od 1973
wikariusz: ks. Jan Lewandowski — od 1973
Dom Zgromadzenia SS. Służek NMP Niepokalanej; 06-212 Krasnosielc ul. Nadrzeczna 17

Document V-16: Sample Church Directory

Gazetteers for Former Austrian Territory

For those regions of the Commonwealth of Poland and Lithuania that Austria seized during the partitions—consisting mainly of southcentral to southeastern Poland and the western half of Ukraine—there are several sources. The *Słownik Geograficzny* (page 155) can be helpful and is certainly worth consulting.

A gazetteer devoted to the Austrian Empire itself is ***Gemeindelexikon der im Reichsrate vertretenen Königreiche und Länder*** [Gazetteer of the Crown Lands and Territories Represented in the Imperial Council], Vienna: k. u. k. Statistische Zentralkommission, 1907. It is available through the Family History Library (FHL Ref. Q 943.6; also on microfilm: Volume 9: Schlesien, film #1197927, item 2, Silesia/Slask; and Volume 10: Galizien, film #1187928 item 1 — Galicia). It is arranged by district, with an index at the end. The appendix (between text and index) lists the location of vital records offices. Most of Silesia was German territory; the part listed here is a small portion governed by Austria. The information in this work comes from the 1900 census.

PRIMARY COMMUNITY / ESTATE LIST

COMMUNITY / ESTATE (City/Town/Village/Estate	ADMIN. DISTRICT	JUDICIAL/TAX DISTRICT	CY	MAP REF.	RD	ROMAN CATHOLIC PARISH	GD	GREEK CATHOLIC PARISH	OTHER JURISDICTIONS (Evangelical, Jewish, Cadastral, etc.)
Panowice	Podhajce	Podhajce	U	R-173	L	Hnilcze [5,8,9]	S	Hnilcze [8]	Zawałów (J); Hnilcze (C)
Pantalicha[2]	Trembowla	Trembowla	U	R-110	L	Złotniki	L	Darachów	Strusów (J); Sokolniki C [31, 42]
Pantalowice	Przeworsk	Przeworsk	P	G-225	P	Pantalowice	P	Krzeczowice[15]	Kańczuga (J)
Paportno[1]	Dobromil	Dobromil	P	G-119	P	Kalwarya Pacławska	P	Paportno	
Parchacz	Sokal	Sokal	U	I-404	L	Krystynopol	P	Krystynopol	Krystynopol (J)
Parkosz	Pilzno	Pilzno	P	F-411	T	Dobrków[9]			
Partynia	Mielec	Radomyśl[15]	P	F-456	T	Zgórsko			
Parypsy	Rawa Ruska	Niemirów	U	H-374	L	Niemirów[30]	P	Szczerzec	
Paryszcze	Nadwórna	Nadwórna	U	Q-566	L	Ottynia[9]	S	Paryszcze	
Pasieczna	Stanisławów	Stanisławów	U	Q-525	L	Stanisławów[3]	S	Pasieczna (Stanisławów)[9]	
Pasieczna	Nadwórna	Nadwórna	U	Q-670	L	Nadwórna	S	Pasieczna (Nadwórna) [9]	
Pasieka Otfinowska[2]	Dąbrowa	Żabno	P	E-615	T	Otfinów			Pasieka (C)
Pasieki Zubrzyckie	Lwów	Lwów	U	I-494	L	Zubrza[9]	L	Sichów	Winniki (J)
Pasierbiec[2]	Limanowa	Limanowa	P	E-306	T	Rybie Nowe[1]			Wiśnicz Nowy (J)
Paszczyna	Ropczyce	Dębica	P	F-112	T	Lubzina			Ropczyce (J)
Paszkówka	Wadowice	Kalwarya	P	D-613	K	Pobiedr[1]			Zator (J)
Paszowa[1]	Lisko	Lisko	P	G-468	P	Tyrawa Wołoska	P	Tyrawa Wołoska	
Paszyn	Nowy Sącz	Nowy Sącz	P	E-385	T	Nowy Sącz[2]			
Pauszówka	Czortków	Czortków	U	R-206	L	Jazłowiec	S	Pauszówka	Jagielnica (J)

Document V-17: Sample from the *Genealogical Gazetteer of Galicia*

A valuable English-language work for Galician researchers is the *Genealogical Gazetteer of Galicia,* by Brian J. Lenius (sample above). The Primary Community List shows 6,300 communities and estates by their Polish names, and tells what country they are in now (Poland or Ukraine), which administrative and judicial districts served them, what Roman Catholic and/or Greek Catholic parishes they were in, where they are located in terms of a series of reference maps, etc. There is also a secondary list of 3,400 smaller places and alternate names, as well as a list of German place names for communities known to have had German inhabitants. Particularly valuable is a list of Ukrainian names for 4,052 communities, with the names given in Cyrillic spellings and Roman-alphabet transliterations, cross-referenced to the Polish names given in the Primary Community List. This work (ISBN 0-9698783-1-1) is available from the author:

Brian J. Lenius
802-11 St. Michael Rd.
Winnipeg MB R2M 2K5
CANADA

What Does All This Have to Do with RUSSIA?

It may seem as if we are complicating this whole process unnecessarily. Your ancestors came from "Russia"—why are we showing you books about Poland and Galicia and what not? To understand you must understand a little history, and Maps V-9 and V-10 may illustrate the point.

The key is that the borders of countries in eastern Europe have changed repeatedly, but national and ethnic identities have been slow to keep up with the changes. A family that has lived on the same piece of land for centuries may have had changes of citizenship forced upon them repeatedly. As an example, one of the authors is related by marriage to a family living near Alytus, Lithuania. Linguistically speaking, their surname is of Belarusian origin; but they considered themselves ethnic Poles and spoke Polish at home. Over the last three centuries they've been citizens of the Grand Duchy of Lithuania (until 1795), the Russian Empire (until 1921), the Republic of Poland (1921-1939; if they'd lived on the other side of the Neman River they'd have been in the Republic of Lithuania), the Soviet Union (1945-1991), and now independent Lithuania. Poland has ruled the area where they live for 28 years over the past three centuries, but they're "Poles" living in Lithuania—yet when a member of the family came to the United States he was described as coming from "Russia." And technically that was right; at the time, the area he came from was under Russian rule, so he was a citizen of the Russian Empire.

For that matter, many of the people with roots in the area shown as "Russian partition" in Map V-9 have been called "Poles" or referred to themselves as "Poles"—but more in the sense of "citizens of Poland as it used to be" than in the sense of "ethnic Poles." Yet the simple truth is that the eastern two-thirds of so-called "Poland" was territory of the Grand Duchy of Lithuania! The Grand Duchy was an independent nation, allied with Poland, but never ruled by it (despite the influence of Polish language and culture). When Poland was resurrected after World War I, the country's borders lay well east of their current ones, and from 1921 to 1939

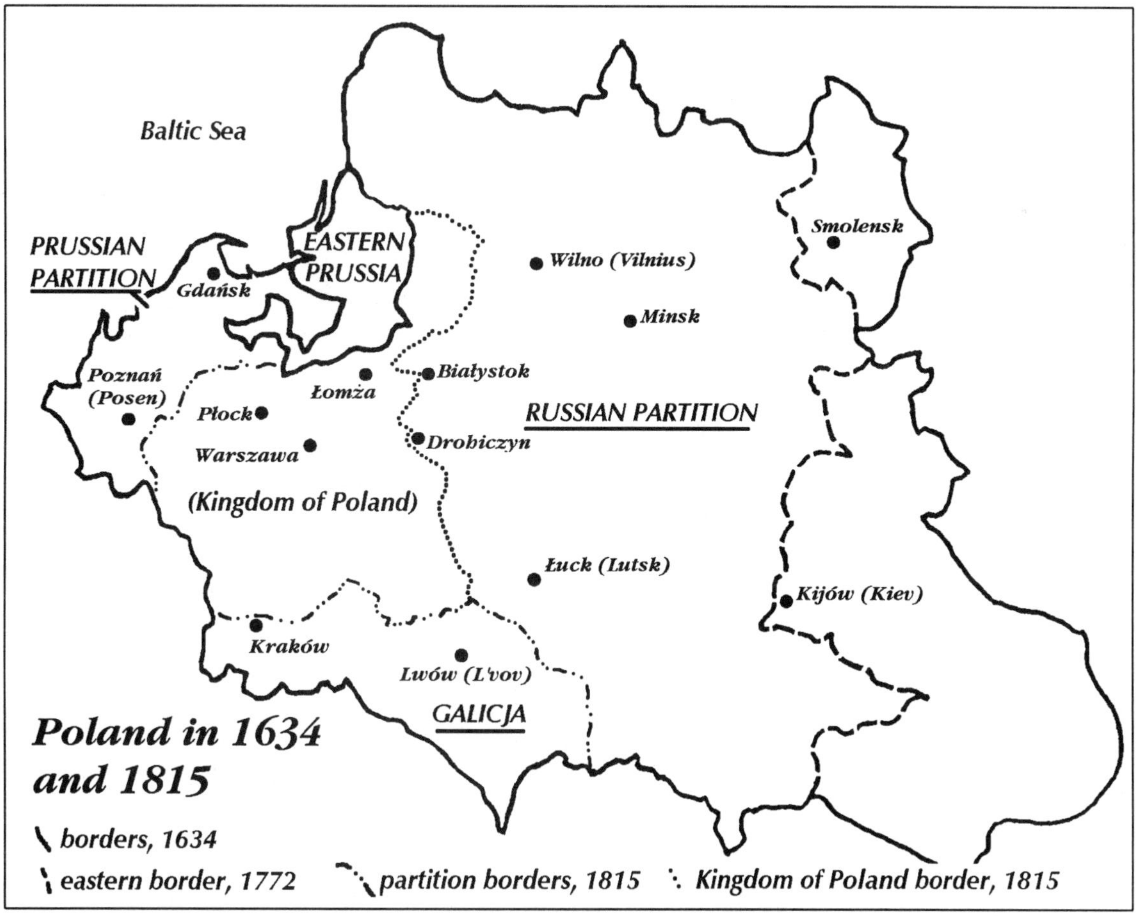

Map V-9: "Poland" (the Commonwealth of Poland and Lithuania) in 1634 and 1815

included much of the territory now comprising the nation of Lithuania—a source of great ill-will between Poles and Lithuanians.

The terms "Poland," "Lithuania," "Russia," etc., denote realities that have changed repeatedly over the years, and those terms have not always been used accurately. Saying someone's from "Russia" begs the questions, "Which Russia? When?" In general conversation, using these terms so vaguely does no great harm; but if you approach genealogical research with such sloppiness, you doom your efforts before you even start! That's why this discussion is worthwhile: it may help you determine "Which Russia? When?"

Map V-10 —Poland, 1921-1939

E. Dealing with Repositories of Records in the Former Russian Empire

Once ***sure*** of the place of origin of his or her family, the researcher's next step is to determine 1) whether any records exist for that locality, and 2) how to access them.

Here it makes a crucial difference what part of the former Russian Empire one's ancestors came from. The LDS Family History Library (FHL) has been microfilming records from Poland, for instance, since the 1970s, and has compiled an impressive collection; a researcher with Polish roots can go far in tracing his roots simply by visiting the nearest Family History Center (FHC) and making good use of its facilities.

Since the fall of the Soviet Union the FHL has made progress in microfilming records on its soil, especially in Lithuania and Ukraine. As time passes, chances are that progress will continue. In the meantime the State Archives of Lithuania, Belarus, and Ukraine have exhibited varying degrees of cooperation with researchers. Even when the FHL has not yet been able to microfilm records in relevant areas of those countries, one can put together quite a family tree by working with the State Archives of those respective countries.

For now and for the foreseeable future, however, Russia itself presents greater challenges. No small expertise is required to navigate the treacherous waters of its archival system and bureaucracy; fluency in Russian is a must. It is far more difficult for a lone researcher with no native contacts to make progress with Russian research than with Polish or Ukrainian or Lithuanian. There is a definite tendency for foreigners to be charged higher rates than natives, and payment is supposed to be in rubles, which are not exchangeable. The problem is not so much figuring out where the records are; the regional archives generally keep records from the 19th and 20th centuries, while anything older would be in federal historical archives in Moscow or St. Petersburg. It's getting at them that requires a great deal of patience and money. So far, most successful researchers owe their success to contacts in Russia, or to professionals to do the work for them.

Since circumstances for research vary greatly, depending on whether you're trying to research roots in what is today Russia or Poland or Lithuania or Belarus or Ukraine, the only sensible approach is to discuss each country separately.

1. Russia

Russia today is comprised of 89 territorial units; that is, there are a number of different administrative subdivisions, which may be classified as a *республика, respublika,* republic; an *область, oblast',* district or province; or a *край, krai,* territory. Each of these units has its own regional state archive, and a crucial step is identifying which specific one holds the records you need. That would usually involve establishing through research exactly where your ancestors lived in Russia, checking to see in which administrative unit that place is now located, and contacting that regional archive.

It seems counterproductive to list of all those addresses, since many would not be relevant to most users of this book. What's more, as rapidly as addresses can change, any list we give may already be obsolete by this time this book comes into your hands. In view of these considerations, the best suggestion is to search for an Internet Website that gives up-to-date lists. As of this writing, one such list is Rootsweb's site for Russian research:

http://www.rootsweb.com/~ruswgw/

This site has a variety of links to sites that might prove helpful, and it seems likely to remain available for the foreseeable future (something that can't be said of all Websites). You can also contact genealogical societies that serve researchers with roots in eastern Europe; if they cannot help you directly, they can surely refer you to someone who can.

As a rule we encourage researchers to do their own work, because of the satisfaction involved when they succeed, and because you can't very well expect others to bring to the search the same desire and intensity you have. Still, there's no question some people interested in tracing their roots lack the time or inclination to do it themselves. They may prefer to hire organizations and individuals who can do it for them. From a practical point of view, this can be particularly true of Russian research, since success often depends on knowledge, experience, and contacts usually possessed only by professionals. If you wish to do it yourself, by all means, go to it! If you haven't the time or desire to invest a fair amount of your energy into tracing your family, there are professionals who can help you attain the desired result—but it will cost you!

The authors are not in a position to recommend any specific organization or individual; what's more, it seems pointless putting such information into a printed book, since it can become obsolete so quickly. This information is not hard to come by, however, on the Internet and in various genealogical publications.

If you would like to test the waters, however, to see how far you can get by yourself, you will need to correspond with archives and individuals who may not be fluent in any language but Russian. Thus a Russian Letter-Writing Guide may prove essential, and such a guide follows. It will not help you produce beautiful Russian prose, but it will enable you to frame your request in Russian that your correspondent will have no trouble understanding. An added benefit of using such a guide is that it almost forces you to be concise and to the point, limiting your letter to specifics—and such letters are far more likely to receive a useful answer than longer ones that go into irrelevant details.

GUIDE TO WRITING LETTERS IN RUSSIAN

Salutation

Dear Sir (to a lay person)	Уважаемый Господин
Dear Madam	Уважаемая Госпожа
Dear Father (to a clergyman)	Святой Отец

Body

1. I am writing to you to ask for your help in seeking information on my family.	Я обращаюсь к Вам за помощью в поисках данных о своей семье.
2. I am writing a history of my family and would like to obtain some information from your	Я пишу историю моей семьи и мне хотелось бы получить информацию из Ваших книг
birth/baptism registers	рождения / крещения
marriage registers	бракосочетания
death registers	смерти

3. I am interested in the following persons. I've listed all I know about them:	Мне нужны данные о следующих людях. Я прилагаю все, что о них знаю:
name and surname	имя и фамилия
date of birth (approximate)	дата рождения (приблизительно)
place of birth	место рождения
name of father	имя отца
name of mother	имя матери
name of husband	имя мужа
name of wife	имя жены
date of marriage	дата бракосочетания
place of marriage	место бракосочетания
date of death	дата смерти
place of death	место смерти
date of emigration (approximate)	дата выезда из Европы (приблизительно)
The locality where my family lived was called __	Место, где моя семья жила, называлось __.
in Belarusian	по-белорусски
in German	по-немецки
in Polish	по-польски
in Russian	по-русски
in Ukrainian	по-украински
in Yiddish	по-еврейски
but now it may have another name.	но сейчас может иметь другое географическое название.
Religion	Вероисповедание
Orthodox	православное
Greek Catholic	греко-католическое
Lutheran	лютеранское
Jewish	еврейское
Roman Catholic	римско-католическое

Requests

4. Please check your records for the period __ to __ *[fill in appropriate numbers].*	Прошу проверять книги от __ г. до __ г.
5. Please send me an extract of the	Прошу прислать мне выписку
birth record	свидетельства о рождении
marriage record	свидетельства о бракосочетании
death record	свидетельства о смерти
6. If you do not have these records, please send me the address of the place or archive where they may be kept.	Если у Вас нет этих документов, пришлите мне, пожалуйста, адрес архива, в котором они хранятся.

7. If you do not have these records, please tell me if you think that they have been destroyed and when.	Если у Вас нет этих документов, сообщите, пожалуйста, уничтожены ли они, и когда.
8. I would like to locate any persons in your village parish town who may be members of my family have the same last name	Мне хотелось бы найти людей в Вашей деревне Вашем приходе Вашем городе которые могут быть моими родственниками имеют одну со мной фамилию
9. My ancestor's name was __ and he lived in__.	Моего предка звали __, и он жил в __.
My ancestors' names were __ and __, and they lived in __.	Моих предков звали __ и __, и они жили в __.
10. If you know of any persons with this name, please give them my letter and address, as I would like to contact them.	Если Вы знаете людей с моей фамилией, передайте им, пожалуйста, мой адрес и мое письмо, потому, что мне хочется связатьсь с ними.

Payment [for priests]

11. I am sending you a donation of $__ for your parish to thank for your help.	Высылаю Вам пожертвование для Вашего прихода в благодарность за Вашу помощь и эти данные.
Please let me know if there are any additional charges to obtain this information.	Сообщите мне, пожалуйста, надо ли платить дополнительно за получение этих данных.
I am planning to come to Europe and wish to ask your permission to search your registers in person. I will be there from __ to __.	Я собираюсь поехать в Европу и прошу разрешения просмотреть книги в Вашем архиве. Буду в Европе от __ до __.

Questions for archives

12. Please inform me of the charges to obtain the information I am seeking and how this payment may be sent to you.	Сообщите мне, пожалуйста, какова оплата за получение этих данных, которые мне нужны, и как можно будет послать Вам эту оплату.
Does your archive have Roman Catholic registers Greek Catholic registers	Напишите, пожалуйста, есть ли в Вашем архиве книги римско-католические книги греко-католические

Jewish registers	книги еврейские
Lutheran registers	книги лютеранские
for the parish in __	прихода в __
for the synagogue in __	синагоги в __
for the years __ - __	от __ г. до __ г.?
If you have no registers of this locality for the years listed, do you have any for	Если у Вас нет этих книг за эти годы, есть ли у Вас книги
an earlier period	раннего периода
a later period	позднего периода
from this parish?	из этого прихода?
Please tell me where these registers are located.	Напишите, пожалуйста, где эти книги находятся.
Does your archive have any military records for the time period __ - __?	Есть ли в Вашем архиве документы о воинской повинности от __ г. до __ г.?
for recruits	для рядовых?
for officers	для офицеров?
Does your archive have any census records for the time period __ - __ for the following locality: __?	Имеются ли в Вашем архиве переписи населения от _ г. до __ г. следующей местности: __?
Does your archive have any tax lists for the time period __ - __ for the following locality?	Есть ли в Вашем архиве налоговые списки или ревизские сказки от __ г. до __ г. следующей местности? __

Expressions of Gratitude

13. Thank you for your cooperation in helping me preserve the heritage and history of my family. I will be very grateful for any help you give me.	Благодарю Вас за помощь в поисках наследия и истории моей семьи. Я буду благодарен *[if you're a female,* благодарна*]* за любую Вашу помощь.

Closing

Sincerely yours	С уважением
My address:	Мой адрес:

Addressing the Letter

Roman Catholic parish	римско-католический приход
Greek Catholic parish	греко-католический приход
Orthodox parish	православный приход
Lutheran parish	лютеранский приход
Synagogue	еврейская синагога
Vital Statistics Office in __	ЗАГС в __ [ЗАГС = Запись актов гражданского состояния)

2. Lithuania

Lithuania is one country in which the microfilming agents working on behalf of the LDS Family History Library have been busy in recent years. Researchers with roots in Lithuania would be well advised to check the Library's catalogue, either online at **http://www.familysearch.org** or at the nearest Family History Center, to see if useful records are available. Even if actual documents are not yet microfilmed and available for loan, you may find reference works that will aid you.

For research in areas that are now within the territory of Lithuania, the most valuable resource is the Lithuanian State Historical Archives. It has copies of most vital registers up to about 1916, censuses, and many other useful sources. Its address as of this writing is:

Lietuvos Valstybinis Istorijos Archyvas
Gerosios Viltiės 10
2015 Vilnius
LITHUANIA

Experienced researchers report that the Archive's staff includes members who speak English with reasonable fluency. So you can feel free to write to the Archive in English, and look forward to replies in that language. The Archive's staff can also provide translations of documents, the originals of which are mostly in Polish or Russian. The staff members respond as promptly as possible; but please realize they have an enormous number of requests to deal with, and many months may pass before they are able to get to yours.

Portions of southwest Lithuania belonged at one time to the province of Suwałki, Poland. Some records may still be stored there; if so, the Lithuanian State Archive will say so. The address of the Suwałki archive is:

Archiwum Państwowe w Suwałkach
ul. Kościuszki 69
16-400 Suwałki
POLAND

Unfortunately there is some confusion about who has exactly which records, and you may find yourself referred back and forth before you finally track down the information you need. But if it exists, it should be at one of those two archives.

Registry information from 1916 onward is held at Lithuania's Central Civil Registry Archive and its branches. This Archive only issues certificates; it does not do genealogical research or supply hard copies of original documents. But it has branches for virtually all of Lithuania, and comparatively few gaps in its holdings. Its address, as of this writing, is:

Lietuvos Centrinis Metrikų Archyvas
K. Kalinausko g. 21
2000 Vilnius
LITHUANIA

As stated above, the staff of the Lithuanian State Historical Archives can deal with correspondence in English, so a Lithuanian Letter-Writing Guide is not necessary for corresponding with this institution. In view of that fact, it is probably advisable to write in English, so that you can express yourself accurately. But if you need to correspond with someone who does not speak English—such as potential relatives or pastors of Catholic parishes—this guide may be useful. It was originally translated by Professor Giedrius Subačius, with proofreading and help from researchers Alius Pleskačiauskas and Arleen Gould, for the Fall/Winter 2000 issue of *Protėviai,* the Journal of the Lithuanian Global Genealogical Society, and is reprinted with permission.

GUIDE TO WRITING LETTERS IN LITHUANIAN

Salutation

Dear Sir (to a lay person)	Gerbiamasis Pone *
Dear sirs	Gerbiamieji
Dear Madam	Gerbiamoji Ponia *
Dear Father (to a Catholic clergyman)	Gerbiamasis Tėve *

**Give the appropriate surname, if you know it, in the vocative case, e. g., "Dear Mr. Petraitis" = "Gerbiamasis Pone Petraiti." See the end of the guide for more on this.*

Body

Introduction

1. My name is John Petraitis I am John Petraitis.	Mano vardas John Petraitis Aš esu John Petraitis.
I live in the U. S. A. I am an American of Lithuanian descent.	Aš gyvenu JAV. Aš esu lietuvių kilmės amerikietis *[or, if you are a female,* amerikietė*].*
I'm looking for relatives in Lithuania. I am interested in the history of my family.	Aš ieškau giminių Lietuvoje. Aš domiuosi savo giminės istorija.
I am writing to you in hopes that you can assist me in gathering information on the history of my family.	Rašau Jums tikėdamasis, kad galėsite padėti man gauti informacijos apie mano giminė.
2. I am writing a history of my family and would like to obtain some information on my ancestry from your	Rašau savo giminės istoriją ir norėčiau gauti tam tikros informacijos apie savo protėvius iš Jųsū
birth/baptism registers	gimimo/krikšto įrašų
marriage registers	vedybų įrašų
death registers	mirties įrašų
3. I am interested in the following person following persons]. I've listed all the information I possess:	Aš domiuosi šiuo asmeniu [šiais asmenimis]. Išvardiju visą informaciją, kurią žinau:
name and surname	vardas ir pavardė
date of birth (approximate)	gimimo data (apytikriai)
place of birth	gimimo vieta

name of father	tėvo vardas
name of mother	motinos vardas
name of spouse	sutuoktinio vardas
name of husband/wife	vyro/žmonos vardas
date of marriage	vedybų data
place of marriage	vedybų vieta
date of death	mirties data
place of death	mirties vieta
date of emigration (approximate)	emigravimo data (apytikriai)
My mother's name is _.	Mano motina vardu _.
My father's name is _.	Mano tėvas vardu _.
His father's name is _.	Jo tėvas vardu _.
Her father's name is _.	Jos tėvas vardu _.
My grandfather [grandmother, great-grandfather/great-grandmother]	Mano senelis [senelė, prosenelis, prosenelė, proprosenelis, proprosenelė]
left Lithuania	išvyko iš Lietuvos
left for England/Scotland	išvyko į Angliją/Škotiją
left for the United States	išvyko į JAV
arrived in the United States	atvyko į JAV
in the year_ [e. g., 1910].	_ [1910] metais.
He was born in the year _.	Jis gimė _ metais.
She was born in the year _..	Ji gimė _ metais.
She was born in the district of _, in the village of _.	Ji gimė _ rajone _ kaime.
He/She/They died in the U. S. [Lithuania].	Jis/Ji/Jie mirė Juntinėse Valstijose [Lietuvoje].
The locality where my family lived was called __	Vietovė, kur mano šeima gyveno, vadinosi _
in Belarusian	baltarusiškai,
in German	vokiškai,
in Lithuanian	lietuviškai,
in Polish	lenkiškai,
in Russian	rusiškai,
in Ukrainian	ukrainietiškai,
in Yiddish	žydiškai,
but now it may have another name.	bet pavadinimas dabar gali būti pasikeitės.
Religion	Tikybos
Orthodox	provoslavų
Greek Catholic	graikų katalikų
Lutheran	liuteronų
Jewish	žydų
Roman Catholic	Romos katalikų

Requests

4. Please check your records for the period __ to __ *[fill in appropriate numbers].*

Prašyčiau pasižiūrėti Jūsų įrašus nuo ___ iki ___

5. Please send me a long-form extract of the
   birth record
   marriage record
   death record

Prašyčiau atsiųsti man ištisą ištrauką iš
gimimo įrašų
vedybų įrašų
mirties įrašų

6. If you do not have these records, please send me the address of the place or archive where they may be kept.

Jeigu Jūs neturite tokių įrašų, prašyčiau atsiųsti man adresą vietos ar archyvo kur jie gali būti laikomi.

7. If you do not have these records, please tell me if you think that they have been destroyed and when.

Jeigu Jūs neturite tokių įrašų, prašyčiau pasakyti ar Jūs manote, kad jie buvo sunaikinti ir kada.

8. I am interested in locating persons in your
   village
   parish
   town
   who
   may be members of my family (or)
   have the same last name.

Aš norėčiau surasti bet kuriuos žmones Jūsų
kaime,
parapijoje,
mieste,
kurie
galėtų būti mano giminės (ar)
turėtų tą pačią pavardę.

9. My ancestor's name was __ and he lived in__.

Mano protėvio vardas buvo ___ ir jis gyveno ___.

My ancestors' names were __ and _, and they lived in __.

Mano protėvių vardai buvo ___ ir __, ir jie gyveno___.

10. If you know of any persons with this name, please give them my letter and address, as I would like to contact them.

Jei Jūs pažįstate ką nors šiuo vardu, prašyčiau jiems duoti mano adresą ir laišką, nes labai norėčiau su jais susisiekti.

Payment [for priests]

11. I am sending you a donation of $__ for your parish and to thank for your help.

Siunčiu ___ USD auką Jūsų parapijai ir atsidėkodamas *[if you're female,* atsidėkoma*]* už Jūsų pagalbą.

Please let me know if there are any additional charges to obtain this information.

Prašyčiau pranešti man ar reikia sumokėti už ką nors papildomai, kad gaučiau šią informaciją.

I am planning to come to Europe and wish to ask your permission to search your registers in person. I will be there from __ to __.

Aš ketinu vykti į Europą ir norėčiau Jūsų paprašyti leisti peržiūrėti Jūsų bažnyčios įrašus pačiam *[if you're female,* pačiai*]*. Ten būsiu nuo … iki …

Questions for archives

12. Please inform me of the charges to obtain the information I am seeking and how this payment may be sent to you.

Prašyčiau pasakyti, kiek kainuoja įsigyti tą informaciją, kurios ieškau, ir kaip turėčiau persiųsti Jums užmokestį.

Does your archive have
- Roman Catholic registers
- Greek Catholic registers
- Jewish registers
- Lutheran registers

for the parish in __
for the synagogue in __
for the years __ - __

Ar Jūsų archyvas turi
- Romos katalikų įrašus (knygas)
- Graikų katalikų įrašus (knygas)
- Žydų įrašus (knygas)
- Liuteronų įrašus (knygas)
- __ parapijos
- __ sinagogos
- ___-___ met▯

If you do not have the registers of this locality for the years listed,
- do you have any registers for an earlier period?
- do you have any for a later period?

Jei Jūs neturite šios vietovės nurodytų metų įrašų,
- ar turite įrašų iš ankstesnio laikotarpio?
- ar turite įrašų iš vėlesnio laikotarpio?

Please tell me where these registers are located.

Prašau pasakyti, kur yra šitie įrašai.

Does your archive have any military records for the time period __ - __.
- for recruits
- for officers

Ar Jūsų archyvas turi kokių nors armijos dokumentų ____-____ laikotarpio
- rekrūtų / kareivių?
- karininkų?

Does your archive have any census records for the period __ - __ for the following locality __?

Ar Jūsų archyvas turi gyventojų surašymų dokumentų ___-___ laikotarpiui ___ vietovei?

Does your archive have any tax lists for the time period __ - __ for the following locality?

Ar Jūsų archyvas turi kokių nors mokesčių mokėtojų sąrašų ___-___ laikotarpiui ___ vietovei?

I am planning to come to Europe and wish to ask your permission to search your registers in person. I will be there from __ to __.

Aš ketinu vykti į Europą ir norėčiau Jūsų paprašyti leisti peržiūrėti Jūsų archyvo įrašus pačiam *[if you're female,* pačiai*]*. Ten būsiu nuo … iki …

Expressions of Gratitude

13. Thank you for your cooperation in helping me preserve the heritage and history of my family. I will be very grateful for any help you give me.

Dėkui Jums už pagalbą išsaugojant mano šeimos palikimą ir istoriją. Būčiau labai dėkingas *[if you're female,* dėkinga*]* už bet kokią pagalbą, kurią galėtumėte man suteikti.

I'd appreciate your response very much.	Aš būčiau labai dėkingas *[if you're female,* dėkinga*]* už Jūsų atsakymą.
I'd be very grateful for any response or help you can give me.	Aš būčiau labai dėkingas *[if you're female,* dėkinga*]* už bet kokį atsakymą ar pagalbą.
I'm looking forward to your reply [letter].	Su nekantrumu laukiu Jūsų atsakymo [laiško].

Closing

Sincerely yours	Nuoširdžiai Jūsų *[or* Su pagarba*]*
My address:	Mano adresas:

Addressing the Letter

Roman Catholic parish	Romos katalikų parapija
Greek Catholic parish	Graikų katalikų parapija
Orthodox parish	Provoslavų parapija
Lutheran parish	Liuteronų parapija
Jewish synagogue	Žydų sinagoga
Vital Statistics Office in __	Civilinės registracijos įstaiga

Note 1: there are three main endings for masculine surnames:
Petrait**is** – vocative case Petrait**i**;
Pleskačiausk**as** – vocative case Pleskačiausk**ai**;
Adamk**us** – vocative case Adamk**au**.

For feminine surnames:
Petraitien**ė** – vocative case Petraitien**e**.

Note 2: in the preceding guide we have capitalized *Jūs, Jūsų, Jums,* the Lithuanian words for "you." This is not required by grammar, but capitalizing these words in correspondence shows courtesy and respect. It certainly doesn't hurt, and might help!

3. Belarus'

Since the breakup of the Soviet Union, the Republic of Belarus' has begun to open up to Western researchers in ways that were unthinkable before 1991. The Rootsweb site on Belarusian research may provide some useful links:

http://www.rootsweb.com/~blrwgw/

For genealogical purposes the most valuable source is the National Historical Archive of the Republic of Belarus', at the following address:

Нацыянальны гисторыческі архіў Рэспублікі Беларусь
220002 Мінск
вул. Крапоткіна 55
BELARUS

As of this writing, there is an English-language Website for this archive at this address: **http://www.president.gov.by/gosarchives/EArh/E_naz_ist.htm.**

From 1922-1995 this archive was known as the Central National Historical Archive, and it was a branch of the National Archive of the Republic of Belarus'. Since 1995 it has been an independent entity, called the National Historical Archive of the Republic of Belarus'. It is the archive genealogists would want to contact first. If specific records are kept in some other institution, this Archive will refer you to the correct site.

Those fluent in Russian might want to see if they can get hold of a published guide to the Archive's holdings: *Центральный государственный исторический архив БССР в Минске. Путеводитель. [Tsentralnyi gosudarstvennyi istoricheskii arkhiv BSSR v Minske: Putevoditel'—Central National Historical Archive of the Belorussian Soviet Socialist Republic: A Directory].* Minsk, 1974, 336 pp.

The Archive staff is generally capable of conducting correspondence in English, although it may take a while to receive an answer. In practical terms it is probably best to correspond with with potential relatives or officials in English or in Russian. We advise using the Russian Letter-Writing Guide (pages 170-173) to formulate letters to anyone who is not likely to speak English.

4. Ukraine

Before 1991 and Ukrainian independence from the Soviet Union, the archival system was not generally open to foreigners, only to a select group of scholars. Even then certain collections, notably the church registers, were off limits. Before 1991, the size, availability and condition of these church registers was unknown. But with independence came a forward-looking archival administration, especially in the case of L'viv, and the beginning groundwork for genealogical research. We also learned that that the collection of church registers is extensive for the Roman Catholic, Greek Catholic, Jewish and Lutheran faiths. Note, however, that under Communist rule parish churches were generally closed or driven underground, so parishes are not significant sources of potentially useful material.

In terms of national archives, the materials of interest to genealogists are divided mainly between two central state archives. The Central State Historical Archives in L'viv (historically also called Lwów, L'vov, Lemberg, and Leopolis) has material dating from before World War II, mainly for the far western *oblast*'s of Chernivtsi, Ivano-Frankivs'k, L'viv, Rivne, Ternopil', Volyns'ka, and Zakarpats'ka, and for those formerly in the province of Galicia of the Austro-Hungarian Empire. In addition to church registers, the archives house an enormous collection of maps, land records, cadastres, educational records and other resources of importance to the genealogist.

УКРАЇНА
79008, м. Львів
пл. Соборна, 3а
Центральний Державний Історичний Архів України м. Львів
UKRAINE

Lenius's *Genealogical Gazetteer of Galicia* (see page 166) can help in determining which regions were in Galicia, what districts they were in, where records can be found, and so on.

The Central State Historical Archives in Kyiv *(Kiev, Kijów)* is responsible for materials in other *oblast's*:

> УКРАЇНА
> 03110 Київ - 110
> вул. Солом'янська 24
> Центральний Державний Історичний Архів України м. Київ
> UKRAINE

The value of these archives' holdings for Ukrainians, and for the descendants of the many Jews who once lived in Ukraine, is obvious. What might be less obvious is their value, and particularly the L'viv holdings, for ethnic Poles or Germans. Since most of the Poles and Germans living in the region of eastern Galicia and western Ukraine fall into what are today the western *oblast's* of Ukraine, the collection in the Central State Historical Archives in Lviv is of great importance. Many of our readers may be Jews, ethnic Poles, or Germans from the former Austrian crownland of Galicia. Let us cite a few remarks researcher Matthew Bielawa has written on the subject of research in the L'viv archive.

> The Lviv archives can be very receptive to the western genealogist. The value of patience, however, cannot be overemphasized. Old, unreliable institutions dating from the Soviet era are sometimes slow in reforming, such as the postal system, customer service base and general business practice. These differ greatly from what we would expect in the West. It will take time for the archivists to respond to your request. In addition to mail inquiries, the archives in Lviv are open to on-site visits by genealogists. Although not mandatory, it is best to write a letter ahead of time to the director of the archives requesting permission to use the archives. This will alert them of your arrival and perhaps give them time to gather some material for you (as was my experience). Tell them what villages you are researching and the types of documents and years in which you are interested.
>
> Upon your arrival at the archives, which are located in the impressive former Bernardine Monastery built in the beginning of the 17th century, you must ask to speak to the director. The director must first give you permission to use the resources of the archives. Once you have obtained permission, introduce yourself to the staff, who will help you use the indexes, fill out request forms, and retrieve the documents for you, which you can then study in the reading room. Again, be patient and friendly; rude and hurried behavior on your part will not yield any results. Keep in mind, this is not a day trip. After putting in your request for material, you may have to wait a day or two for the documents to be delivered to you. An index to all parish registries for Greek Catholic and Roman Catholic parishes is available. Remember that mixed marriages between Greek Catholics and Roman Catholics were very popular in many regions, so both the Greek Catholic and Roman Catholic records should be checked! If you're interested in other types of holdings, ask to see the card catalog room. The card catalog is sorted alphabetically by village. There are also other card catalogs sorted by type of document and by surname concerning people of prominence.
>
> The Family History Library is currently microfilming the large collection of the Greek Catholic Consistory. Already, at the time of the printing of this book, 35% of these parish registries have been microfilmed. Contact the FHL directly for available film numbers (which were also published in the *East European Genealogist*, Volume 9, Number 3). There is hope on the part of the archival administration that the Roman Catholic parish books will be next in line for microfilming, but this is not certain.

Some materials may be found in the various *oblast'* archives. There are 25 *oblast's*, and it seems pointless to list the addresses of them all, as subject as such information is to change. Perhaps the best practical course is to determine which of the two central state archives listed above, in L'viv and Kyiv, would hold materials for the specific area in which your ancestors lived. Write to that archive and see if it has the materials relevant to your research. If not, the staff can then direct you toward the specific *oblast'* archive appropriate for your needs. Another advantage to this approach is that the staff should (at least in theory) be able to give you reliable, up-to-date information. Various Websites list addresses, but some give conflicting data, and there is always the danger that information might be obsolete. The most reliable online source now, and for the foreseeable future, would be the Website of the Ukrainian State Archives: **http://www.scarch.kiev.ua**.

Perhaps it would not be amiss, however, to give the current addresses of five *oblast'* archives in western Ukraine, in territory formerly ruled by the Austro-Hungarian Empire. On the left is a rendering of the address in the characters of the Roman alphabet; on the right is the original Ukrainian:

State Archives of L'viv Oblast' 79008, L'viv vul. Pidval'na, 13	Державний архів Львівської області 79008, м. Львів вул. Підвальна, 13
State Archives of Ternopil' Oblast' 46001, Ternopil' vul. Sahaidachnoho, 14	Державний архів Тернопільської області 46001, м. Тернопіль вул. Сагайдачного, 14
State Archives of Ivano-Frankivs'k Oblast' 76006, Ivano-Frankivs'k vul. Sahaidachnoho, 42a	Державний архів Івано-Франківської області 76006, м. Івано-Франківськ вул. Сагайдачного, 42а
State Archives of Chernivtsi Oblast' * 58029, Chernivtsi vul. Stasiuka, 20 *formerly Bukovina	Державний архів Чернівецької області 58029, м. Чернівці вул. Стасюка, 20
State Archives of Transcarpathian Oblast' 88005 Uzhhorod vul. Minais'ka, 14a	Державний архів Закарпатської області 88005, м. Ужгород вул. Минайська, 14а

While personal visits to archives, or professional help, tend to produce the best results, one may try corresponding with these archives. The ones in Kyiv and L'viv can generally handle correspondence in English as well as Russian and Polish (and the one in L'viv can correspond in French and German); but their reply will be in Ukrainian.

Writing in English is an iffy proposition with the state and regional archives; they might or might not have staff members who can deal with it. If they don't, your letter goes to the bottom of the pile! In correspondence to these archives—or perhaps to private individuals who might be relatives or knew members of your family—writing in Ukrainian may improve the odds of a response.

Less likely to produce results are letters sent to parishes, or to the local Civil Registrar Offices (known by the acronym RAHS). Under Communist rule most parishes were closed, and their records seized and stored; if available now, they would be in official archives. So even if you get the address of a parish and happen to reach a priest who is willing to help you, chances are he does not have access to any records that would help you. (Of course, if you've tried everything else and have nothing left to lose, what harm would it do to write? The worst that can happen is your request will be ignored.)

As for the RAHS offices, Ukrainian researcher Laurence Krupnak explains that they do not respond to letters from individuals requesting documents. Their administrative policies call for them to respond only to requests submitted on the appropriate form filled out in detail, **in Ukrainian**. This requires considerable fluency, and is best done with the help of professional translators or native-speakers. These requests can be sent directly to Archives, or can be submitted through the Ukrainian Consulate. The form is online, as are instructions and more information in English, at this Website address: **http://www. ukrconsul.org/consular/english/civildocs_en.html.**

You can also write for more information to:

Ukrainian Consulate General in New York
240 East 49th Street
New York NY 10017

Just in case it might prove helpful in some instances, we wanted to include a very basic Letter-Writing Guide for Ukrainian, which follows. We wish to thank Cornelia Andrus of Brookline, Massachusetts, and Laurence Krupnak of Silver Spring, Maryland, for their help; any errors you find would have been far numerous without their assistance!

GUIDE TO WRITING LETTERS IN UKRAINIAN

Salutation

Dear Sir (to a lay person)	Шановний пане
Dear Madam	Шановна пані
Dear Sirs	Шановне панство
Dear Father (to a clergyman)	Високоповажнний Отче

Body

1. I am writing this letter to ask for your help in seeking information on my family.	Цим листом прохаю Вас допомогти мені у пошуках інформації про мою родину.
2. I am writing a history of my family and need to obtain some information from your registers [archives] of	Я пишу історію моєї родини, і мені потрібно отримати деяку інформацію з Ваших реєстрів [архівів]...
births/baptisms	народжень / хрищень
marriages	одружень
deaths	смертей
3. I would like additional information on the following persons. I've listed what I know about them:	Мені б хотілося отримати додаткову інформацію про слідуючих осіб. Подаю те, що знаю про них:

name and surname	ім'я і прізвище
date of birth (approximate)	дата народження (приблизно)
place of birth	місце народження
name of father	ім'я батька
name of mother	ім'я матері
name of husband	ім'я чоловіка
name of wife	ім'я дружини
date of marriage	дата одруження
place of marriage	мисце одруження
date of death	дата смерті
place of death	місце смерті
date of emigration (approximate)	дата еміґрації (приблизно)
[if known] passport number _, issued on _ by _.	номер паспорту ___, паспорт виданий ____ (дата) ____ (ким виданий).
The locality where my family lived was called __	Моя родина походить із місцевости яка називалася _.
in Belarusian	по-білоруськи
in German	по-німецьки
in Polish	по-польськи
in Russian	по-російськи
in Ukrainian	по-українськи
in Yiddish	мовою їдіш
(but now it may have another name).	(можливо, тепер змінилася назва).
Religion	Віросповідання
Orthodox	православна
Greek Catholic	греко-католицька
Lutheran	лютеранська
Jewish	іудаїзм
Roman Catholic	римо-католицька

Requests

4. Please check your records for the period __ to __ *[fill in appropriate numbers].*	Прошу перевірити записи від _ р. до _ р.
5. Please send me an extract [copy] of the	Був би Вам дуже вдячний, якби Ви мені надіслали витяг [копію] з...
birth record	документу, який посвідчує народження
marriage record	документу, який посвідчує одруження
death record	документу, який посвідчує смерті
6. If you do not have these records, please send me the address of the establishment	Якщо у Ваших архівах цих записів нема, будь ласка, пришліть мені адресу

or archive where they may be kept.	установи або архіва, в яких вони можуть зберігатися
7. If these records do not exist, please tell me how and when they were destroyed.	Якщо ці записи не існують, будь ласка, повідомте, як і коли їх було знищено

8. I am looking for any person in your
  village
  parish
  town
who
  may be a member of my family
  has the same last name
	Я рошукую особу у
	  Вашому селі
	  Вашій парафії
	  Вашому місті
	яка
	  може бути членом моєї родини
	  має те саме прізвище, як я.

9. My ancestor's name was __ and he lived in__.	Мій предок звався _ і жив у _.
My ancestors' names were __ and __, and they lived in __.	Мої предки звалися _ і _ і жили у _.
10. If you know of any persons with this name, please give them my letter and address, as I would like to contact them.	Якщо Вам відомий будь-хто з таким прізвищем, будь ласка, передайте йому чи їй мого листа і адресу, оскільки я би бажав із ними спілкуватися.
I am planning to come to Europe and wish to ask your permission to search your registers in person. I will be there from __ to __.	Я планую бути в Європі від ___ до ___ і прохаю Вашого дозволу особисто зайнятися пошуком у Ваших реєстрах в цей час.

Payment

11. I am sending you a donation of $__ for your church [parish] and to thank for your help.	За Вашу щиру поміч і за Вашу інформацію, висилаю Вам, Отче, $_ як пожертву на Вашу церкву [парафію].
Please let me know if there are any additional charges to look for/obtain this information [these documents].	Будь ласка, повідомте, якщо існують будь-які додаткові витрати у зв'язку з пошуком/отриманням цієї інформації [цих документів].
12. Please inform me of the charges to obtain the information [documents] I am seeking and how this payment may be sent to you.	Будь ласка, дайте мені знати які витрати пов'язані з отриманням інформації [документів], яких я шукаю, і як можна здійснити платіж.

Questions for archives

13. Does your archive have
  Roman Catholic registers
  Greek Catholic registers
  Jewish registers
	Чи Ваш архів включає
	  римо-католицькі реєстри
	  греко-католицькі реєстри
	  еврейські реєстри

Lutheran registers for the parish in __ for the synagogue in __ for the years __ - __	лютеранські реїстри від парафії у _? синаґоґи у _? між ___ і ___ роками?
If you do not have these registers for the years listed, do you have any for an earlier period a later period from this locality?	Якщо Ваш архів не включає тих реєстрів, чи Вац архів включає реєстри за попередні рокі? наступні роки? із цієї місцевости?
Please tell me where these registers are located.	Прошу повідомити, де знаходяться реєстри.
Does your archive have any military records for the time period __ - __? for recruits for officers	Чи Ваш архів включає військові документи між _ і _ роками? для рекрутів? для офіцерів?
Does your archive have any census records for the time period __ - __ for the following locality: __?	Чи Ваш архів включає переписи населення між _ і _ роками із місцевости _?
Does your archive have any tax lists for the time period __ - __ for the following locality: __?	Чи Ваш архів включає будь-які переліки платників податків в період між ___ та ___ роками із місцевості ___?

Expressions of Gratitude

14. Thank you for your help, which enables us to preserve the heritage and history of our family. I hope to receive your answer and the information as soon as possible.	Сердечно дякую за Вашу поміч. Ваша поміч дає нам можливість зберігти спадщину та історію нашої родини. Надіюся, що отримаю Вашу інформацію і відповідь у накоротшому часі.

Closing

Sincerely yours	із щирою подякою і високою пошаною до Вас,
My address:	Прошу висилати на адресу:

Addressing the Letter

Roman Catholic parish	римо-католицька парафія
Greek Catholic parish	греко-католицька парафія
Orthodox parish	православна парафія
Lutheran parish	лютеранська парафія
Jewish synagogue	синаґоґа
Baptist congregation	баптистська община

[see also the addresses of archives given on pages 180-182]

5. Poland

The archival situation in Poland is somewhat different, largely because in Poland churches were able to go on functioning and keeping records even under Communist rule. Records from the 19th-century and earlier were generally created by clergymen charged with the task of registering births, deaths, and marriages of persons residing within their jurisdiction (i. e., parish, congregation, etc.). For some periods—notably 1808 to the early 1820's—and in some areas, the Roman Catholic clergy also recorded vital data for non-Catholics living in the parish's territory. Later it became standard practice for clergy of different faiths to keep the records for their own co-religionists.

Although some Polish vital records were destroyed during the many wars fought on Poland's territory, many more survived. The first place to check is the LDS Family History Library Catalogue, available at the nearest Family History Center (FHC). The LDS has microfilmed extensive records from much of Poland (the main exception is southeastern Poland). Often a researcher will find extensive records from his family's ancestral area available for loan to the nearby FHC, where he can study them.

Only after exhausting the LDS Family History Library and all other resources available in America should one begin looking for records in present-day Poland. A researcher should check four sources to determine which records do exist, and for what time periods, as portions of the records from a given parish may today be kept in several different locations. Those sources are:

- your ancestors' parish, where the parish priest served as the Civil Registrar
- the diocesan or archdiocesan archive with jurisdiction over the ancestral parish
- the local USC [Urząd Stanu Cywilnego, Civil Registrar's office]
- the Polish State Archives system

Note that parish and diocesan archives are institutions of the Catholic Church, whereas the USC's and Polish State Archives system are civil in nature. Obvious as this distinction is, it must be kept in mind, as it can have practical consequences. For instance, Jewish or other non-Catholic researchers will seldom find Catholic parish records of any use—except for the period 1808-1825, when Jewish and other records were co-mingled in Catholic and Lutheran registers—and will want to concentrate on records kept by civil authorities or registrars of their own religion. Those records are now held primarily by civil authorities.

♦ **Parish Archives:** for those with Catholic ancestry, the ancestral parish is the best, most direct source, especially if the archive of your family's place of origin has all extant parish registers. Church directories (discussed on page 164-165) will often, but not always, list the years for which records exist at the parish level. If you happen to get hold of a cooperative priest, he may supply you with all the data available for nothing more than a moderate contribution to his parish. Correspondence with the pastor will usually have to be in Polish; Polish letter-writing guides are available from the Family History Library, as well as in Volume One of the *In Their Words* series, devoted to Polish.

In general, be as concise and accurate with your requests as possible; if the dates you provide are off by even one or two years it can make the priest go through many pages of unindexed records, looking for what you want. Also, do not ask for too much in your initial correspondence, or the sheer bulk of your request may make the priest disinclined to undertake your search. Remember, he already has a job, an important one: seeing to his parishioners' spiritual needs. It's extremely unwise to insult him by treating him like an employee!

♦ **Diocesan Archives:** researchers who encounter problems of various kinds on the parish level may find better luck at this level. Each Polish diocese has its own archive, which may contain original or duplicate copies of registers from some or all parishes in its jurisdiction. Some dioceses, such as those of Poznań and Białystok, have comprehensive and extensive collections of registers; others have few or none. If you know what parish served your ancestors, but have no luck with the parish itself, contacting the appropriate diocesan archive is worth a try. A list of addresses for these archives, current as of this writing, begins on page 189.

♦ **Vital Records Offices (USC's):** the creation of a formal Civil Registration system in Poland dates from after World War II. Before that time the local registrar, usually a clergyman, kept records of birth, death, and marriage; copies of those records were used by civil authorities for their purposes. In 1945 the Communist government created a formal system however, and demanded that the clergy turn a portion of their registers over to the state; most complied, some did not. Furthermore, Polish law dictates that civil registry records are to be kept in USC's for a period of 100 years; records older than that are to be sent on to the appropriate State Archives.

So the USC's are most valuable as a source of records from a particular time frame—mainly the late 1890s on—because these records are not available through the Family History Library (to protect the privacy of living persons, the Polish authorities only allow the filming of records more than 100 years old). Note also that the USC's have not only records from Catholic sources but for all religions, including Orthodox, Jewish, Protestant, etc. So for records within a specific time-frame (less than 100 years old) and especially for those dealing with non-Catholics who would not appear in Catholic parish registers, the local USC can be an invaluable source.

There are some 2,500 USC offices in Poland, so it is impossible to list the addresses here; but any sizable town has at least one, as do larger villages. If a village is too small to have its own USC, it will be served by the one in whatever town or village has the local *gmina* administrative offices—this information is provided in the gazetteer *Spis miejscowości PRL* (see page 154), although this material is somewhat outdated now.

A more recent source of that information is the *Ogólnopolski Spis Teleadresowy*, published in 1990; but it doesn't list which villages belong to what *gmina*—it merely lists vital records offices throughout the country. For Catholic records, the *gmina* and parish designations tend to be the same, more often than not. A fairly comprehensive list of surviving records housed at USC offices, compiled in the early 1980's, can be consulted through the Polish Genealogical Society of Connecticut and the Northeast, 8 Lyle Rd., New Britain CT 06053-2104 USA.

♦ **Polish State Archives:** Polish archival regulations require that records more than 100 years old be turned over to the State Archive system, so ***in theory*** almost all 19th-century records should be in a state archival repository.

Unfortunately, compliance with this regulation is far from uniform. The holdings of the State Archives are usually outlined in varying degrees of depth and completeness in published guides to their collections. Some state archives have large collections of records; others have minimal holdings because the records are located in any of the three previous categories of repositories, or have been lost or destroyed. Most Jewish and Protestant records are now held by the state archives. Requests for research in these records are generally coordinated by the **Naczelna Dyrekcja Archiwów Państwowych** [State Archives' Head Office] in Warsaw. For many researchers the easiest way to access civil records is through this agency (but remember, this is a civil institution; it has no control over diocesan or parish archives).

If you are going to Poland and intend to do research at an archive, you must currently **write first and get permission** from the manager of that archive. **Don't just show up** at the archive, or you may be severely disappointed. (This is good advice for dealing with any place that has records you want to search, including parish churches!).

Various Polish Genealogical Societies, as listed on pages 191-192, can help you with the addresses of individual archive addresses. You can alsoget that information from the Head Office of the State Archives at this address:

Naczelna Dyrekcja Archiwów Państwowych
ul. Długa 6
skrytka pocztowa Nr 1005
00-950 WARSZAWA
POLAND

As of this writing, its Website address is:

http://www.archiwa.gov.pl/

There is also a list of information on individual archives in English at this page:

http://www.archiwa.gov.pl/archiwa/index.eng.html

A searchable database with information on archival holdings can be found here:

http://www.archiwa.gov.pl/sezam/sezam.eng.html#info

If you need to write to **ecclesiastical archives**, there are over 40 dioceses in Poland, and the addresses and borders change from time to time; so it seems pointless to try to give all those addresses in a printed book. The following are addresses for the archives of dioceses covering territory formerly within the Russian Empire. They are current as of this writing, verified from the respective dioceses' Websites (the addresses of which are also given). But since addresses change often, it would be wise to check them if possible.

BIAŁYSTOK

Archiwum Archidiecezjalne w Białymstoku
ul. Warszawska 46
15-077 BIAŁYSTOK
POLAND
http://www.bialystok.opoka.org.pl

CZĘSTOCHOWA

Archiwum Archidiecezjalne w Częstochowie
ul. św. Barbary 41
42-200 CZĘSTOCHOWA
POLAND
http://www.adiec.czest.niedziela.pl

DROHICZYN

Archiwum diecezjalne w Drohiczynie
ul. Kościelna 10
17-312 DROHICZYN
POLAND
http://www.drohiczyn.opoka.org.pl

EŁK

Archiwum diecezjalnej w Ełku
ul. 3 Maja 10
19-300 EŁK
POLAND
http://www.diecezja.elk.pl

KALISZ

Archiwum diecezjalne w Kaliszu
ul. Widok 80-82
62-800 KALISZ
POLAND
http://www.diecezja.kalisz.pl

KIELCE

Archiwum diecezjalne w Kielcach
ul. Jana Pawła II nr. 3
25-013 KIELCE
POLAND
http://www.kielce.opoka.org.pl

ŁÓDŹ

Archiwum Archidiecezjalne w Łodzi
ul. ks. I. Skorupki 3
90-458 ŁÓDŹ
POLAND
http://www.archidiecezja.lodz.pl

ŁOMŻA

Archiwum Archidiecezjalne w Łodzi
ul. Sadowa 3
18-400 ŁOMŻA
POLAND
http://www.kuria.lomza.opoka.org.pl

ŁOWICZ

Archiwum diecezjalne w Łowiczu
Stary Rynek 20
99-400 ŁOWICZ
POLAND
http://www.diecezja.lowicz.pl

LUBLIN

Archiwum Archidiecezjalne w Lublinie
ul. Prym. Wyszyńskiego 2
20-950 LUBLIN
POLAND
http://www.kuria.lublin.pl

PŁOCK

Archiwum diecezjalne w Płocku
ul. Nowowiejskiego 2
09-400 PŁOCK
POLAND
http://www.diecezja.plock.opoka.org.pl

RADOM

Archiwum diecezjalne w Radomiu
ul. Sienkiewicza 13
26-610 RADOM
POLAND
http://www.radom.opoka.org.pl

SANDOMIERZ

Archiwum diecezjalne w Sandomierzu
ul. Mariacka 8
27-600 SANDOMIERZ
POLAND
http://www.sandomierz.opoka.org.pl

SIEDLCE

Archiwum diecezjalne w Siedlcach
ul. Piłsudskiego 62
08-110 SIEDLCE
POLAND
http://www.siedlce.opoka.org.pl

WARSZAWA

Archiwum Archidiecezjalne w Warszawie
ul. Świętojańska 8
(mailing address: ul. Kanonia 6)
00-278 WARSZAWA
POLAND
http://www.mkw.pl

also

Archiwum Kurii Metropol. w Warszawie
Oddział ksiąg metrykalnych
Pl. Grzybowski 3/5
00-115 WARSZAWA
POLAND

WARSZAWA-PRAGA

Archiwum diecezjalne Warszawsko-Praskie
ul. Floriańska 3
03-707 WARSZAWA
POLAND
http://www.diecezja.waw.pl

WŁOCŁAWEK

Archiwum diecezjalne w Włocławku
ul. Gdańska 2/4
87-800 WŁOCŁAWEK
POLAND
http://www.siedlce.opoka.org.pl

ZAMOŚĆ-LUBACZÓW

Archiwum diecezjalne Zamojsko-Lubaczowskie
ul. Hetm. J. Zamoyskiego 1
22-400 ZAMOŚĆ
POLAND
http://www.zamosc.opoka.org.pl

As of this writing, addresses of many diocesan archives, parishes, etc. are available at this site: **http://www.rootsweb.com/~polwgw/dioceses.html.**

Other Polish archives that may prove helpful include the following:

Archives of Przemysl-Warsaw Archdiocese, Greek Catholic Church
Archiwum Archidiecezji Przemysko-Warszawskiej
ul. Komisji Edukacji Narodowej 3/2
37-700 PRZEMYŚL
POLAND

Archive of Majdanek Concentration Camp
Archiwum Państwowego Muzeum na Majdanku
ul. Droga Męczenników Majdanka 67
20-325 LUBLIN
POLAND

Archive of Oświęcim [Auschwitz] Concentration Camp
Archiwum Państwowego Muzeum w Oświęciemiu-Brzezince
ul. Więźniów
32-603 OŚWIĘCIM
POLAND

Central Archive of Historical Records
Archiwum Główne Akt Dawnych
ul. Długa 7
00-263 WARSZAWA
POLAND

Jewish Historical Institute
Żydowski Instytut Historyczny
ul. Tłomackie 3/5
00-090 WARSZAWA
POLAND

Warsaw-Środmieście Vital Statistics Registrar *(with the **Zabużański Collection**, a selection of registers from territory now in western Ukraine)*
Urząd Stanu Cywilnego Warszawa-Śródmieście
Archiwum akt Zabużańskich
ul. Jezuicka 1/3
00-950 WARSZAWA
POLAND

You may also find help from the various Polish Genealogical Societies (abbreviated PGS) in America. Here is a list of some of the more established ones:

PGS of America
984 N. Milwaukee Ave.
Chicago IL 60622 USA
Publishes *Rodziny* (quarterly)
http://www.pgsa.org

PGS of California
P. O. Box 731
Midway City CA 92655-0713 USA
Publishes *PGS-California Bulletin* (quarterly)
http://www.pgsca.org

PGS of Connecticut and the Northeast
8 Lyle Rd.
New Britain CT 06053-2104 USA
Publishes *Pathways & Passages* (twice a year)
http://www.pgsctne.org

PGS of Greater Cleveland
P. O. Box 609117
Cleveland OH 44109-0117 USA
Publishes *Our Polish Ancestors* (quarterly)
http://feefhs.org/pol/frgpgsgc.html

PGS of Massachusetts
P. O. Box 381
Northampton MA 01061-0381 USA
Publishes *Biuletyn Korzenie* (twice a year)
http://feefhs.org/pol/frgpgsma.html

PGS of Michigan
c/o Burton Historical Collection
Detroit Public Library
5201 Woodward Ave.
Detroit MI 48202-4007 USA
Publishes *The Polish Eaglet* (3 issues/year)
http://www.pgsm.org

PGS of Minnesota
5768 Olson Memorial Highway
Golden Valley MN 55427 USA
Publishes *Newsletter* (quarterly)
http://www.mtn.org/mgs/branches/ polish.html

PGS of New York State
c/o 299 Barnard St.
Buffalo NY 14206-3212 USA
Publishes *PGS-NYS Searchers* (biannual)
http://www.pgsnys.org

PGS of Texas
15917 Juneau
Houston TX 77040-2155 USA
Publishes *Polish Footprints* (quarterly)
http://www.pgst.org

PGS of Wisconsin
P. O. Box 342341
Milwaukee WI 53234-2341 USA
Publishes *Korzenie* (quarterly)
http://feefhs.org/pol/frgpgswi.html

The following international societies may also be able to provide valuable assistance:

Society of Genealogists
14, Charterhouse Buildings
Goswell Rd.
London EC1M 7BA
ENGLAND
http://www.sog.org.uk/

East European Genealogical Society
P.O. Box 2536
Winnipeg MB R3C 4A7
CANADA
Publication: *East European Genealogist* (Quarterly)
http://www.eegsociety.org

Saskatchewan Genealogical Society
2nd Floor, 1870 Lorne Street
P.O. Box 1894
Regina SK S4P 3E1
CANADA
Publication: *Bulletin* (quarterly)
http://www.saskgenealogy.com/

VI. RUSSIAN-LANGUAGE RECORDS ORIGINATING IN EUROPE

A. INDEXES TO VITAL RECORDS REGISTERS

Of the records drawn up within the Russian Empire itself, the ones of most immediate interest to researchers are registers of births, marriages, and deaths. We will look at samples of those records beginning with the next section.

Let's not make the mistake of skipping a step, however. Once you've traced your ancestors in America back to their home in Europe, and once you've used the information in Chapter V to locate exactly where that place is, you can hope to locate the archive or other repository that has the documents you need. The next step is to find the actual records dealing with your relatives. To do that, you may need to be able to read the indexes to those records (assuming they exist)—not a terribly demanding task, but one that can throw you a curve or two.

We have already discussed this subject briefly on pages 30-32. But a quick look at a few more examples may help you recognize the records you want when you find them. And at the worst, it will give a little more practice reading written Cyrillic.

Document VI-1, below, is from the index to the register of births for the year 1870 in the parish of Bargłów Kościelny in Suwałki *gubernia* (as we see from the two words at the top of the stamp, Сувалкская Губернія), now in northeastern Poland. The entries are listed by sequential number, surname, the infant's name, father's name, mother's first name, her maiden name, and then the actual record number. This index is somewhat unusual in that it gives the parents' names, not just the child's; some indexes provide this kind of detail, but many are not so obliging.

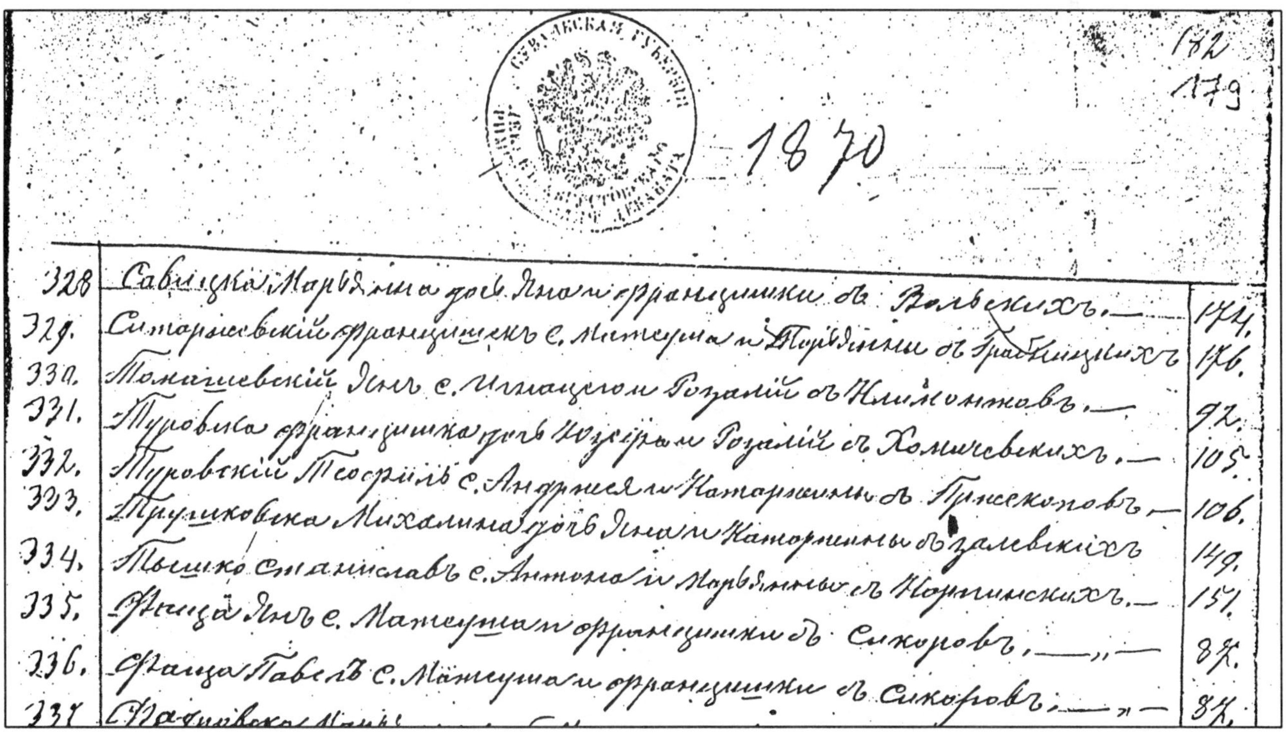

Document VI-1: Index to 1870 Births in Bargłów Kościelny, Poland

Note that the number on the left (beginning with 328) is the *№ по порядку* or "sequential number," whereas the number on the right is the actual *№ акта,* "document number." If you had only this index and needed to order the correct document from the list, it's the number on the right you need. Or you could cite both to be perfectly clear: thus for the first entry you could say you need "a copy of № 328 по порядку, № акта 174."

The first 3 entries , with translations, read as follows:

328. Савицка, Марьянна дочь Яна и Францишки съ Вольскихъ *174*
328. Sawicka, Maryanna, daughter of Jan and Franciszka née Wolska 174

329. Ситаржевскій Францишекъ с. Матеуша и Марьянны съ Грабницкихъ *176*
329. Sitarzewski, Franciszek, son of Mateusz and Maryanna née Grabnicka 176

330. Томашевскій Янъ с. Игнацего и Розалій съ Климонтовъ *92*
330. Tomaszewski Jan, son of Ignacy and Rozalia née Klimont 92

Note that for some reason this priest always wrote out the word *дочь,* "daughter," but abbreviated the word *сынъ,* "son," as *с.* Why? Who knows?

It's worth noting that in some records from Poland, one may find that record keepers did not follow the normal Russian alphabetical sequence in indexes, but rather gave the names according to Polish alphabetical order. It's possible this was a subtle protest again having to keep records in a foreign language; or perhaps it was due to the priest's unfamiliarity with Russian. Whatever the cause, it is advisable always to examine an index in its totality before using it, to familiarize yourself with the order in which the entries appear. Don't make the mistake of quitting as soon as you've gone past where you would expect the entry to appear.

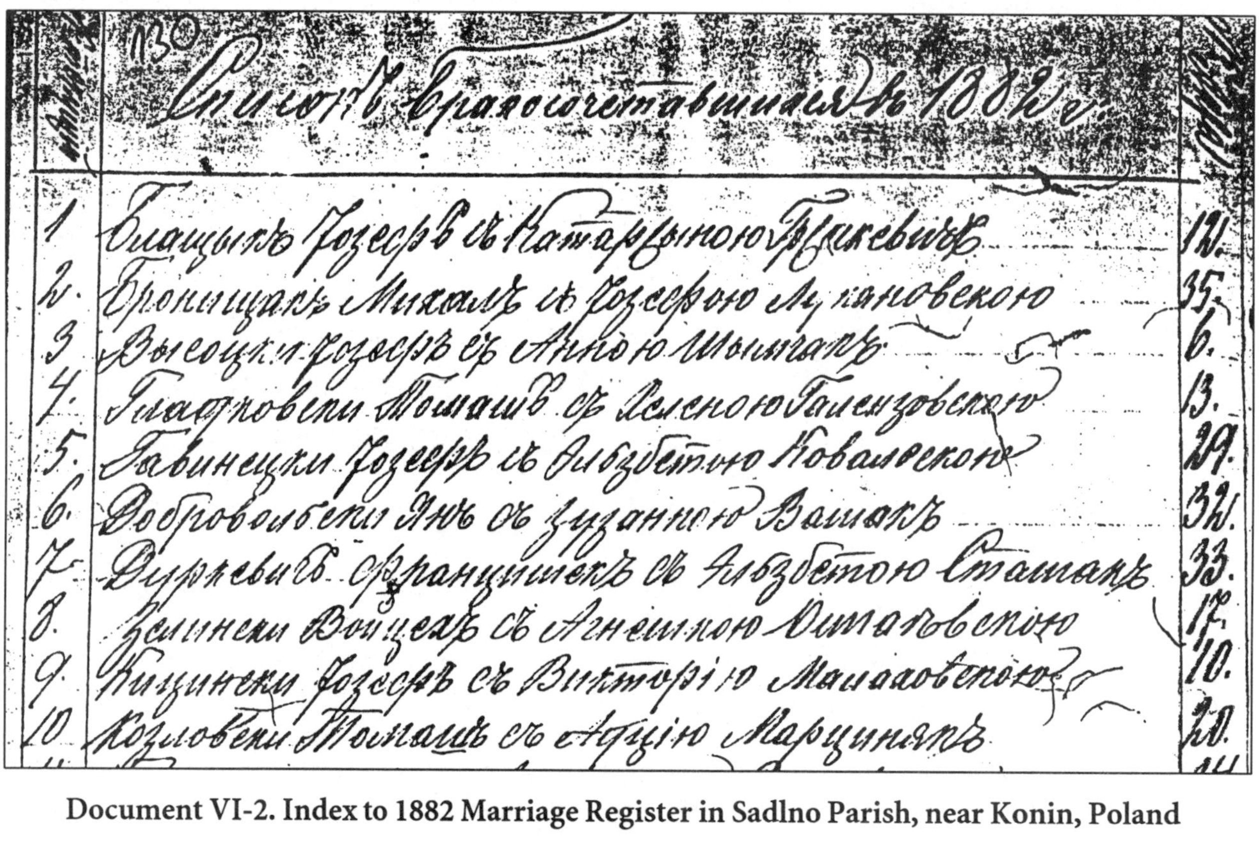

Document VI-2. Index to 1882 Marriage Register in Sadlno Parish, near Konin, Poland

For that matter, as seasoned researchers know, nothing can be counted on, including the presence of an index. Sometimes there is no index, and a page-by-page search for the desired information is the only way to find it.

Document VI-2 is a *Списокъ Бракосочетавшихся въ 1882 г.*, "List of Those Married in 1882." It shows a format common in marriage registers. Note again that the number on the left is the *№ по порядку*, the sequential number, and the number on the right is the *№ акта*, the one that matters. The entries are indexed by groom's surname, followed by his first name, the preposition *съ*, "with," and the bride's first name and maiden name (in the instrumental case after that preposition). Again, this index comes from Poland, so when we render the people's names in our alphabet we give them their Polish forms. Here are the first three entries:

1. Блащык, Iозефъ съ Катаржыною Гржакевичъ	*12*
1. Błaszczyk, Józef, to Katarzyna Grzakiewicz	12
2. Бронищакъ Михалъ съ Iозефою Лукановскою	*35*
2. Broniszczak, Michał, to Józefa Łukanowska	35
3. Высоцки Iозефъ съ Анною Шымчакъ	*6*
3. Wysocki, Józef, to Anna Szymczak	6

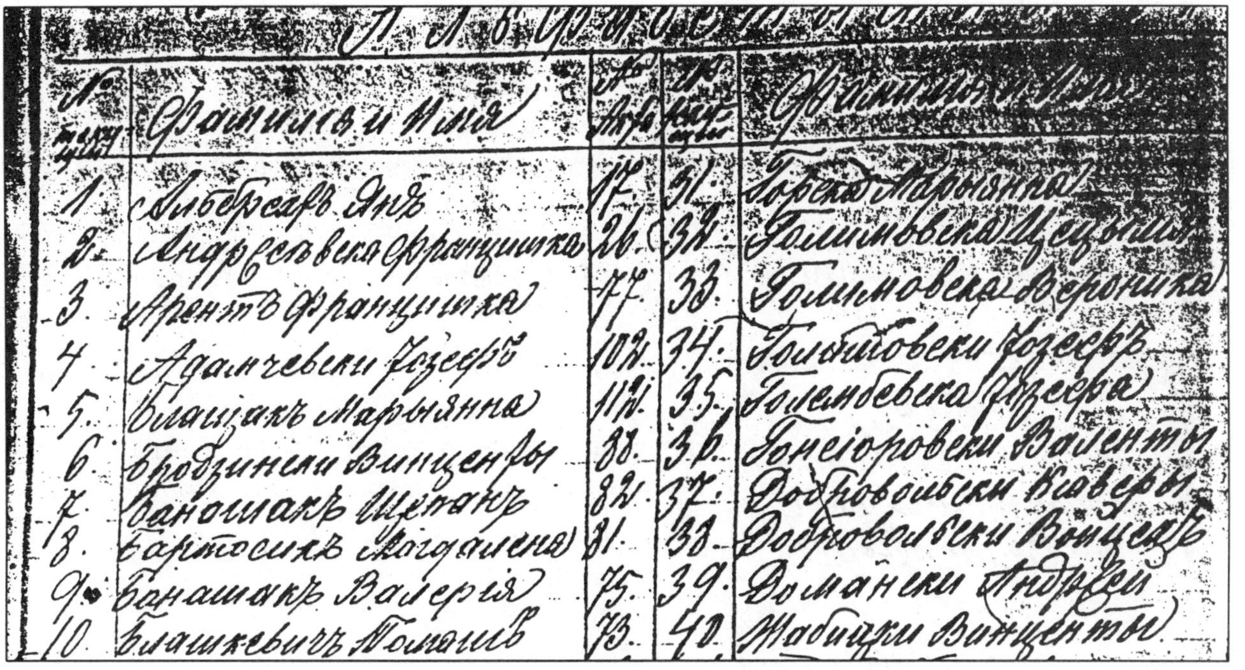

№ по пор.	Фамилія и Имя	№ Акта	№ по пор.	Фамилія и Имя
1.	Альберсаръ Янъ	17.	31.	Горека Марыянна
2.	Андржеевска Францишка	26.	32.	Голинковска Цецылия
3.	Арентъ Францишка	47.	33.	Голинковска Вероника
4.	Адамчевски Юзефъ	102.	34.	Голубковски Юзефъ
5.	Блащакъ Марыянна	112.	35.	Голембевска Юзефа
6.	Бродзинский Винценты	88.	36.	Гонсіоровски Валенты
7.	Баношакъ Щепанъ	82.	37.	Добровольски Ксаверы
8.	Бартосякъ Магдалена	81.	38.	Добровольски Войцехъ
9.	Банашакъ Валерія	75.	39.	Доманcки Андрей
10	Блашкевичъ Томашъ	73.	40.	Жабицки Винценты

Document VI-3. Index of 1882 Deaths from Sadlno Parish, near Konin, Poland

Finally, **Document VI-3** is a fairly typical register of deaths. The heading at the top of the page, cut off during reproduction, extends onto the next page: *Альфабетычный Указатель умершыхъ въ 1882 году*, "Alphabetical Index of Those Who Died in 1882." Anyone fluent in modern Russian will shudder at *альфабетычный*—obviously a phonetic spelling in Cyrillic of Polish *alfabetyczny*—instead of standard *алфавитный*, and at the misspelling *умершыхъ*, instead of *умерших*. But such errors are common in records, especially in regions where Russian was not the record keeper's first language; you might as well start getting used to them.

Here the list is formatted in two columns, each with the *№ текущій* (sequential number, meaning much the same thing as *№ по порядку* or *номеръ порядковый*) on the left, the *фамилія* (surname) and *имя* (first name—also seen: *имена*, first names) of the deceased, and the *№ Акта* (document number) on the right. In some records the heading for the column with the name of the deceased may say *Фамилія и имя Умершаго*, "Surname and First Name of the Deceased."

The first three entries in Document VI-3, with renderings in the Roman alphabet, read:

1. Альбрехтъ Янъ	*17*	1. Albrecht, Jan	17
2. Андржеѣвска Францишка	*26*	2. Andrzejewska, Franciszka	26
3. Арентъ, Францишка	*77*	3. Arent, Franciszka	77

As these examples show, the format can vary, but is usually not too hard to figure out. Even the name or title of the index can take a number of forms, as we have seen. Sometimes the title was glued to the front cover of the volume, in other cases the description of the records appears on the inside cover or on the first page. Some typical "titles" follow:

Алфавитный списокъ урожденныхъ въ _ г.	Alphabetical List of Those Born in the Year _
Выпись родившихся въ _ году	Extract of Those Born in the Year __
Списокъ урожденныхъ въ _ г.	List of Those Born in the Year _
Списокъ о *Рожденныхъ _скаго Прихода въ _ г.*	List of Those Born in _ Parish in the Year _
Списокъ браковъ въ _ г.	List of Marriages in the Year _
Списокъ бракосочетавшихся въ _ г.	List of Those Who Got Married in the Year _
Алфавитный указатель умершихъ въ _ г.	Alphabetical Register of Those Who Died in the Year_
Списокъ умершихъ въ _ году	List of Those Who Died in the Year _
Списокъ о умершихъ _скаго Прихода съ _ г.	List of Those Who Died in _ Parish from the Year _

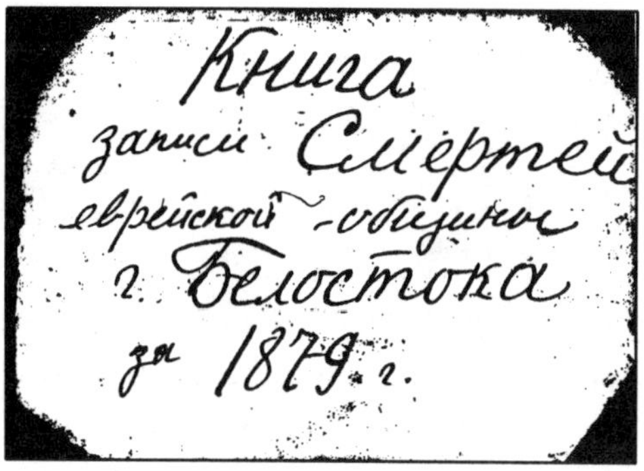
Книга
записи Смертей
еврейской общины
г. Белостока
за 1879 г.

Document VI-4

The register's title may also specify the religion of those listed in that volume, especially if it is not the dominant religion in that area. Thus the title at left, **Document VI-4**, appears on the cover of one register:

Книга
записи Смертей
еврейской общины
г. Белостока
за 1879 г.

This means "Book of entry of deaths of the Jewish community of the city of Białystok for the year 1879." (Note the Russian name of the city, *Белостокъ*, more often *Бѣлостокъ*).

If this were a register of Roman Catholics who died, we would see a declined form of *римско-католическій;* for the Orthodox church, there would be a form of *православный;* for Greek Catholics it would be *греко-католическій*, or possibly *уніатскій*, "Uniate" (but that has long been considered a derogatory term and thus is less likely to appear); and for Protestants it would be *евангелическій* or *лютеранскій*.

Obviously the wording of registers' titles and columnar headings can vary, but this is not crucial. You need only concentrate on the words delineating the **event** (birth, marriage, or death), the **place** the records are from, and the **religion**. The place name should be familiar to you if you've found the records by following the steps described in the preceding chapters. So the key words are relatively few:

актъ – record
алфавитный – alphabetical
бракъ – marriage
бракосочетавшийся – one who got married
бракосечатніе – marriage
выпись – copy, extract
греко-католическій – Greek Catholic
евангелическій – Protestant
еврейскій – Jewish
запись – entry, registration; *книга записи* – register
имя – first name; *имена* – first names
книга – book, register
лютеранскій – Lutheran
№ – abbrev. of *номеръ*
номеръ, number; *номеръ по порядку* or *порядковый* or *текущій:* sequential number, serial number
обрѣзаніе – circumcision
община – community
православный – Orthodox
приходъ – parish
римско-католическій – Roman Catholic
родившийся – born, one who was born
рождённый – born, one who was born
смерть – death
списокъ – list, register
указатель – register, index
умерший – deceased, one who died
урождённый – born, one who was born
фамилія – surname

B. RECORDS OF BIRTH, BAPTISM, OR CIRCUMCISION

1. Components of a Paragraph-Form Birth/Baptismal Record

Russian records of birth, baptism, or circumcision generally follow one of two basic formats: paragraph-form, or columnar. One cannot define precisely when and where each format was used, except to say the paragraph form was used primarily in the far western part of the Russian Empire, in the areas seized during the partitioning of the Polish-Lithuanian Commonwealth; records there began to be kept in Russian in 1868 (before that year they were in Polish or Latin). These records consist of a long paragraph, of prescribed format, laying out the facts in a specific order. The columnar records tend to predominate farther east, and generally consist of a series of questions and answers covering much the same information.

The columnar records tend to be a bit easier for researchers because at least the information is broken up into sections, and the questions in each column's heading provide helpful clues as to what you will find in that column. Records written in paragraph-form bury the pertinent information in long sentences, which cannot be deciphered without due attention to the grammatical considerations that affect the words involved. Fortunately, these records tend to follow prescribed formats, and thus we can analyze them by saying "This element comes first and should appear here; next should come this, then that." Certain **keywords** identify these elements—you should look for them carefully, as they help you break the paragraph up into something manageable.

The keywords for a paragraph-form birth record, and the facts they identify, are as follows:

I. **The Place/Date the Record Was Created** – keyword ***состоялось*** ("It happened")
II. **The Declarant/Father** – keyword ***Явился*** ("[He] appeared")
III. **The Witnesses** – keywords ***въ присутствіи*** ("in the presence of")
IV. **The Child's Gender** – keyword ***пола*** ("of the _ gender")
V. **The Child's Birth-place and Birth-date** – keyword ***родился*** ("was born")
VI. **The Mother** – keyword ***жены*** ("wife")
VII. **The Mother's Age** – keyword ***лѣтъ отъ роду*** ("years from birth")
VIII. **The Child's Name** – keyword ***имя*** ("[first] name")
IX. **The Godparents** – keyword ***воспріемниками*** ("the godparents")
X. **Record Keeper's Statement on the Witnesses' Literacy and His Signature** – keywords ***Актъ сей*** ("this document")

2. Document VI-5: A Paragraph-Form Catholic Birth Record from the Kingdom of Poland

On page 199 is a sample record, **Document VI-5**, we can analyze, emphasizing the keywords. Here is what it says in a standardized script that may be easier to read:

Кози Борекъ
№ 23.

*Состоялось въ деревнѣ Щутово шетого (девятнад-
цатого) марта тысяча девятьсотъ пятого года
въ десять часовъ утра Явился Станиславъ Заборовски
(Stanisław Zaborowski) крестьянинъ изъ Козяго Борка двадцати четырехъ лѣтъ отъ роду въ присутствіи
Яна Каминьскаго сорока трехъ и Францишка Тлуховскаго тридцати трехъ лѣтъ отъ роду обоихъ —
крестьян изъ Боруховъ и предъявилъ Намъ младенца
женскаго пола, объявляя, что онъ родился въ Козимъ
Боркѣ перваго (четырнадцатаго) марта сего года
въ десять часовъ утра отъ законной его жены Леокадіи
урожденной Тыбурской (Leokadyi z Tyburskich) двадцати лѣтъ отъ роду. Младенцу этому при святомъ
крещеніи совершенномъ сего числа дано имя Чеслава
(Czesława) воспріемниками были Францишекъ Тлуховски и Катаржина Чижевска. Актъ сей объявляющему
и свидѣтелямъ неграмотнымъ прочитанъ Нами только
подписанъ. Администраторъ прихода Щутово содержащій акты гражданскаго состоянія. (-) Кс. В. Киньски.*

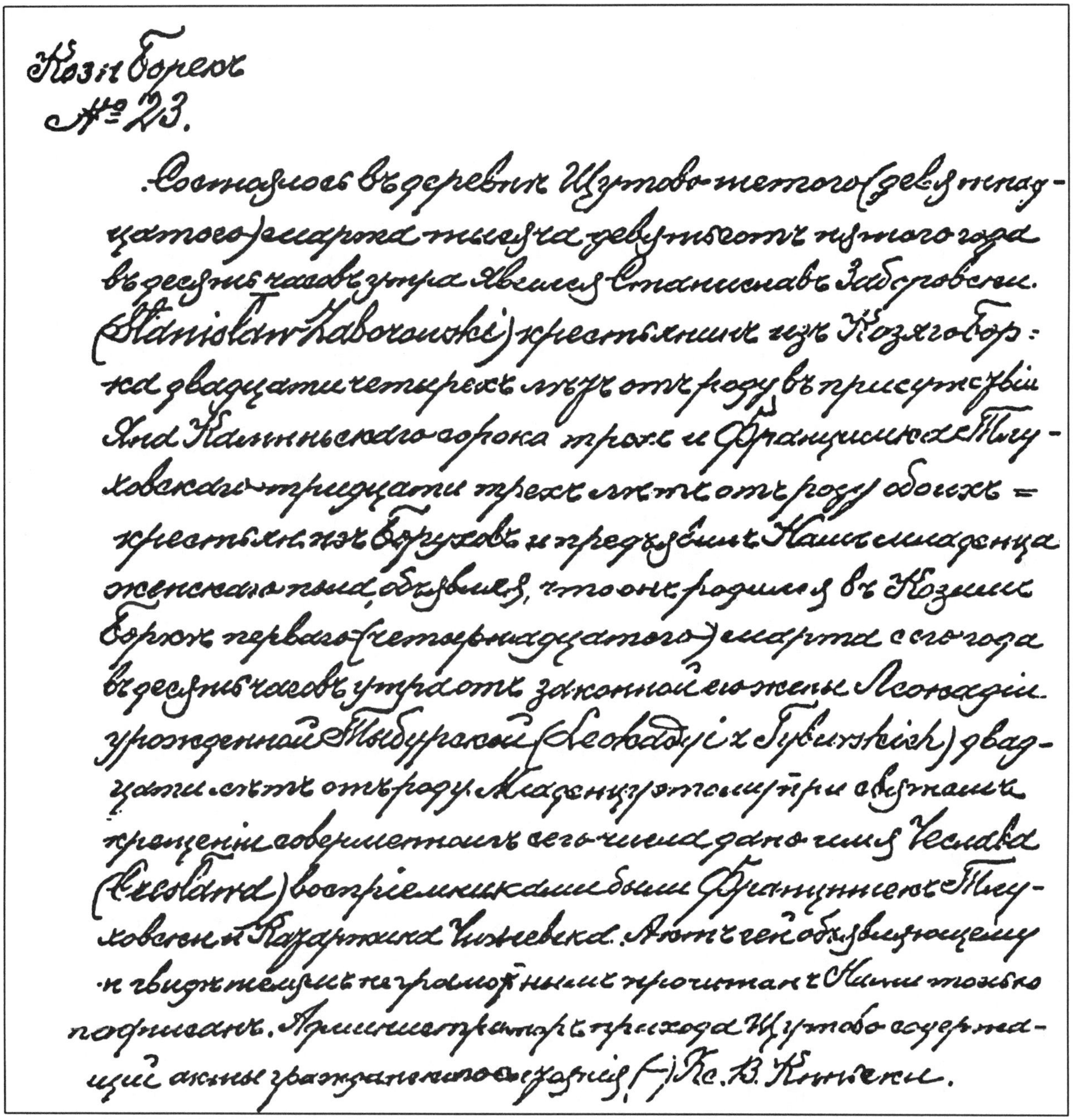
Козiнъ Борекъ
№ 23.
Состоялось въ деревнѣ Щитово третьего (девятнадцатого) марта тысяча девятьсотъ пятого года въ десять часовъ утра. Явился Станиславъ Забровски (Stanisław Zaborowski) крестьянинъ изъ Козягоборка двадцати четырехъ лѣтъ отъ роду въ присутствіи Яна Каминьского сорока трехъ и Францишка Тлуховского тридцати трехъ лѣтъ отъ роду обоихъ — крестьянъ изъ Борухова и предъявилъ Намъ младенца женскаго пола, объявивъ, что онъ родился въ Козинъ Борекъ первого (четырнадцатого) марта сего года въ десять часовъ утра отъ законной его жены Леокадіи урожденной Тыбурской (Leokadyi z Tyburskich) двадцати лѣтъ отъ роду. Младенцу этому при святомъ крещеніи совершенномъ сего числа дано имя Чеслава (Czesława) восприемниками были Францишекъ Тлуховски и Казаржина Чижевска. Актъ сей объявляющему и свидетелямъ неграмотнымъ прочитанъ Нами только подписанъ. Администраторъ прихода Щитово содержащiй акты гражданского состоянія (-) Кс. В. Кн...ски.

Document VI-5: A Paragraph-Form Catholic Birth Record from the Kingdom of Poland

First study the handwriting. Note that the priest who recorded this used two forms of the letter **з**, both the usual Russian form *з* and one like the English, *z*. He also used two forms of **т**, both the standard *m* and the variant *т*. There seems to be no real rhyme or reason to which form he used in a given instance; all we can do is note the variations and deal with them. He also likes to append a tail to the letter *я*, a quirk of which we can approve because it makes that letter easier to spot and distinguish.

Note also that he gives in parentheses the original Polish versions of the parents' and child's names—a measure prescribed in some instances to insure proper identification of the individuals involved. This, too, we can appreciate, as it makes our task easier!

Now for analysis. Since this is the first one we're looking at, we'll discuss it in some detail—but you don't have to read it all if you're not interested in the grammar. You can simply skip the analysis and concentrate on the translation.

***Состоялось** въ деревнѣ Щутово шетого/девятнадцатого марта тысяча девятьсотъ пятого года въ десять часовъ утра.*

состоялось — "it happened" (past tense, neuter, from *состояться*, "to happen, take place"). This keyword tells you the next information should be the place where the record was drawn up, then the date.

въ деревнѣ Щутово — "in the village of Szczutowo." The preposition *въ* is followed by the accusative or prepositional case; *деревнѣ* (modern spelling *деревне*) is the prepositional form of *деревня*, "village." Other possibilities here are:

въ городѣ – in the city [of]	*въ посадѣ* – in the village/settlement [of]
въ селеніи – in the settlement [of]	*въ околицѣ* – in the town, suburb

If there is a term giving the classification of the locality, the name of the place itself will generally be in the nominative; but sometimes it, too, may be in the prepositional. In some records the classification of the locality (town, village, etc.) is omitted, with only the name of the place given. In such instances the name of the town will be in the prepositional case:

въ Варшавѣ, in Warsaw *въ Домбровѣ*, in Dąbrowa *въ Ставискахъ*, in Stawiski

Since the people and places mentioned in this document are from regions of Poland taken over by the Russian Empire, proper names should be rendered in their Polish spellings.

шетого / девятнадцатого марта — "on the 6th/19th of March." The time when something happened is generally expressed with the genitive case; this means literally "of the 6th/19th of March." In Russian "sixth" is *шестой*, genitive *шестого*, but the priest who wrote up this record misspelled the word as *шетого* (as for the ending *-ого*, see the note on *второго/четырнадцатаго Декабря*, p. 217). The difference in the dates is due to the discrepancy between the **Julian calendar**, used in the Russian Empire and therefore required in records, and the **Gregorian calendar**, the standard in the West. Records in regions traditionally Russian, of course, would give only the Julian date; Russian-language records in formerly Polish and Lithuanian regions give both. Some record keepers clarified this by adding *Новаго Стиля* or *по Новому Стилю*, "New Style," after the Gregorian date. During the 19th century the Gregorian date was 12 days later than the Julian; by the 20th century the gap had grown to 13 days. When one sees double dates, the second is the one Westerners would go by.

тысяча девятьсотъ пятого года — Literally, "of [the one] thousand nine hundred and fifth year." See the section on dates (pages 47-49) for more on how the year is expressed with cardinal numbers, with the final element as an ordinal.

въ десять часов утра — "at ten o'clock in the morning."

Translation — This occurred in the village of Szczutowo on the 6th/19th of March, 1905, at 10 a.m.

Явился *Станиславъ Заборовски (Stanisław Zaborowski) крестьянинъ изъ Козяго Борка двадцати четырехъ лѣтъ отъ роду...*

явился — This keyword means "[he] appeared." It is the past tense, masculine gender, singular of the verb *явиться*, "to appear." Some records add *лично*, "in person."

Станиславъ Заборовски (Stanisław Zaborowski) — "Stanisław Zaborowski," the name of the declarant who appeared to make a statement. In records dealing with Jews the declarant's name may be preceded by the term *еврей*, "Jew." The declarant in a birth record is usually the child's father, but can be someone else. If the declarant is a female —which is rare, but it does happen—the form of the verb would be *явилась*. If the declarant (or anyone named in this type of record) had more than one first name, the phrase *двухъ именъ*, "of two names," often appears.

крестьянинъ изъ Козяго Борка — "a peasant from Kozi Borek." Generally the name of the declarant is followed by information on his occupation or social status, and his place of residence. The latter may be phrased as *имѣющій жительство въ _*, "having residence in _." The declarant may also be described as *житель*, "resident of," e. g., *житель Визны*, resident of Wizna. But the most common phrasing is with the participle *жительствующій*, "residing," which often comes **after** the name of his place of residence.

There were instances in which a declarant may have resided in a village but did extra work in a nearby town, in which case you may encounter an expression such as *жительствующій на службѣ временно въ городѣ Сувалкахъ*, "residing temporarily in Suwałki for work" (literally "on service").

двадцати четырехъ лѣтъ отъ роду — Literally "of 24 years from birth." The form *лѣтъ* (modern spelling *лет*) is used as the genitive plural of *год*, and the whole expression *двадцати четырехъ лѣтъ* is genitive. *Отъ* (modern spelling *от*) is a preposition followed by the genitive, and *роду* is the genitive of *род*, a word meaning "family, birth, origin, sort." Here are examples of other phrases indicating age:

сорокъ лѣтъ считающій, literally "forty years counting"
тридцать лѣтъ имѣющій, literally "thirty years having"

Translation — Stanisław Zaborowski appeared, a peasant from Kozi Borek, age 24...

въ присутствіи *Яна Каминьскаго сорока трехъ и Францишка Тлуховскаго тридцати трехъ лѣтъ отъ роду обоихъ крестьянъ изъ Боруховъ...*

въ присутствіи — These keywords mean "in the presence [of]"—*присутствіи* (modern spelling *присутствии*) is the prepositional case of *присутствіе*, "presence." The sense of this phrase suggests "in the presence <u>of</u>" and that explains why the names that follow are in the genitive case. Sometimes the word *свидѣтелей*, "[of the] witnesses," precedes their names; but even if it doesn't, the phrase *въ присутствіи* is a clear indication that the next names you see will be those of witnesses.

In most records from this time period the relationship between the witnesses and the child's parents is not specified. Some record keepers, however, did spell it out, e. g., *въ присутствіи брата его жены Францишка*, "in the presence of his wife's brother, Franciszek." As a rule it is a good idea to make note of the witnesses' names, as they were often relatives.

Яна Каминьскаго — "of Jan Kamiński." Note the archaic genitive ending *-аго*. The genitive singular for masculine adjectives (and *Kamiński*, though a proper name, is adjectival in form), had two variants, *-аго* and *-яго* (see page 37). Orthographic reforms in the 20th century replaced those endings with *-ого* and *-его*, respectively.

сорока трехъ — Literally, "of forty-three." Rather than repeat the word *лѣтъ* here and after Franciszek Tłuchowski's age, the word is given only there.

и Францишка Тлуховскаго тридцати трехъ лѣтъ отъ роду — "and of Franciszek Tłuchowski, 33 years from birth," or, as we'd say, "age 33."

обоихъ крестьянъ изъ Боруховъ — "both peasants from Boruchy." *Обоихъ крестьянъ* is genitive plural, as a noun phrase in opposition to "Jan Kamiński... and Franciszek Tłuchowski." *Боруховъ*, a genitive plural form in Russian (because it's preceded by a preposition, *изъ*, that requires the genitive), corresponds to *Boruchów* in Polish, and the nominative form of *Boruchów* in Polish is *Boruchy*. It's important to know this, as a search of maps for *Boruchów* will produce either no results, or misleading results.

Translation — ... in the presence of Jan Kamiński, age 43, and of Franciszek Tłuchowski, age 33, both peasants from Boruchy ...

и предъявилъ Намъ младенца женскаго ***пола****, объявляя, что онъ родился въ Козимъ Боркѣ перваго (четырнадцатаго) марта сего года въ десять часовъ утра...*

и предъявилъ Намъ — "and [he] presented to us." *Предъявилъ* (modern spelling *предъявил*) is the past tense, masculine singular form (the subject of this predicate is still "Stanisław Zaborowski"). *Нам* is the dative case of the pronoun *мы*, "we."

младенца женскаго ***пола*** — "a child of the female sex." Note the keyword ***пола***, "sex, gender," which tells us we've found the indication of the child's sex. *Младенца* is the genitive/accusative form of *младенецъ*, "baby, infant"; it's in the accusative because it is the direct object of *предъявилъ*. This noun is masculine in gender, whatever the child's sex, so subsequent references to "the child" will use the masculine pronoun *онъ*, "he," not *она*, "she," or *оно*, "it." The alternative to "of the female sex" is (obviously) "of the male sex," *мужскаго* (or the archaic form *мужескаго*) *пола*.

объявляя, что — "stating, declaring that." This is a participial form of the verb *объявлять*, "to declare, announce, make a statement." It is still Stanisław Zaborowski who is doing all the appearing, showing, and now declaring.

онъ ***родился*** *въ Козимъ Боркѣ* — "it [the child] was born in Kozi Borek." The keyword ***родился*** tells us that the child's birthplace and date of birth are about to be given. *Въ* shows location where by taking a noun in the prepositional, and *Козимъ Боркѣ* (modern spelling would be *Козим Борке*) is the prepositional form of that place name. (Actually, this form is a Polonism; the Russian adjectival prepositional ending is *-ом*).

перваго (четырнадцатаго) марта сего года — "of the 1st/14th of March of this year." *Сего* is masculine genitive singular of *сей*, an archaic pronoun meaning "this." Instead of *сего года* we frequently see *текущаго года*, "of the current year," or *прошлаго года*, "of last year"—the latter appears mainly in records created just after the beginning of a new year.

въ десять часовъ утра — "at ten o'clock in the morning."

Translation — ... and presented to us a child of the female sex, stating that it was born in Kozi Borek on the 1st/14th of March of this year at ten o'clock in the morning ...

отъ законной его ***жены*** *Леокадiи урожденной Тыбурской (Leokadyi z Tyburskich) двадцати лѣтъ отъ роду.*

отъ законной его жены Леокадiи — "of his lawful wife Leokadia." The keyword ***жены***, pointing to information on the child's mother, is the genitive form after the preposition *отъ*, which means "from, of." *Законной* is the genitive singular feminine declensional ending of the adjective *законный*, "legal, lawful," agreeing with *жены* and *Леокадiи*. Here the pronoun *его* is used as a possessive, "his, its."

урожденной Тыбурской (Leokadyi z Tyburskich) — Literally, "born Tyburska," this is one way of saying "née Tyburska." Another formulation is a Russian equivalent of the Polish expression seen here in parentheses: first name + preposition *с* or *из* + maiden name in the genitive plural: *Леокадія съ Тыбурскихъ* or *Леокадія изъ Тыбурскихъ*.

двадцати ***лѣтъ отъ роду*** — "twenty years from birth." Note that the phrase *X лѣтъ отъ роду* appears again and again in these records, used much the same as we would say "X years of age." When it comes after the keyword ***жены***, it tells you the mother's age has just been given.

Translation — ...of his lawful wife Leokadia née Tyburska, age 20.

Младенцу этому при святомъ крещенiи совершенномъ сего числа дано ***имя*** *Чеслава* (Czesława).

младенцу этому — "to this child." This is a dative masculine singular, used for an indirect object. *Этому* is the dative singular masculine of *этот*, "this" (see page 42).

при святомъ крещенiи — "at Holy Baptism." *При* is a preposition meaning "at, with, by" and takes the prepositional case, and *святомъ* (holy) *крещенiи* (baptism) are the appropriate forms of that case. The nominative of *крещенiи* is *крещенiе* (modern spelling *крещение*). Obviously for non-Christian births this whole phrase *при святомъ крещенiи совершенномъ сего числа* would be omitted or modified. In Jewish birth records we might see instead *Младенцу сему послѣ обрезанія дано* ***имя*** _, "After circumcision this child was given the name _" (see also Document VI-10, page 219).

совершенномъ сего числа — "performed on this date." *Совершенномъ* is the prepositional neuter singular case (modifying *крещенiи*) of the past passive participle from the verb *совершить*, "to perform, do, complete." The phrase *сего числа* is a genitive expression of time when, "on this date."

Although this document omits it, the name of the priest who performed the baptism and his title may follow this phrase, usually in the instrumental case (because the baptism was performed **by** the priest). Thus you may see phrases of this sort:

> *Ксендзомъ Францишкомъ Ладковскимъ въ здѣшнемъ приходскомъ костелѣ* – "by Father Franciszek Ladkowski in the local parish church"
>
> *Викарiемъ Щучинскаго прихода* – "by the assistant pastor of Szczuczyn parish"

дано имя Чеслава (Czesława) — "[was] given the name of *Czesława*." *Дано* is the neuter past passive participle from the verb *дать*, "to give." The keyword ***имя*** means "first name," it is a neuter noun (thus the neuter ending on *дано*). Of course, if the child had more than one first name, *имена*, the plural of *имя*, would appear here.

Translation — At Holy Baptism, administered on this day, this child was given the name of Czesława ...

***воспрiемниками** были Францишекъ Тлуховски и Катаржина Чижевска.*

воспрiемниками — keyword meaning "the godparents," from *воспрiемникъ* (modern spelling *восприемник*). The word is in the instrumental case (the *-ами* ending is standard instrumental plural for nouns) because the instrumental is standard when a form of the verb *быть*, "to be," is used to identify, as here: "The godparents were ..."

были — "[they] were," past tense plural of *быть*.

Францишекъ Тлуховски и Катаржина Чижевшска — "Franciszek Tłuchowski and Katarzyna Czyżewska." A phonetic transliteration would be *Frantsishek Tlukhovski* and *Katarzhina Chizhewska,* but these are Polish names and should properly be given Polish spellings, *Franciszek Tłuchowski* and *Katarzyna Czyżewska,* respectively.

If a godfather was one of the witnesses named earlier in the document, the phrase *выше упомянутый*, "above-mentioned," will proceed his name. If there was a blood relationship between the godparents, this may also be mentioned after the godparent's name, such as *и его жена*, "and his wife," or *и его сестра,* "and his sister."

Translation — The godparents were Franciszek Tłuchowski and Rozalia Czyżewska.

***Актъ сей** объявляющему и свидѣтелямъ неграмотнымъ прочитанъ Нами только подписанъ. Администраторъ прихода Щутово содержащiй акты гражданскаго состоянiя. (-) Кс. В. Киньски.*

Актъ сей — "This document." The genitive form of *сей, сего,* appeared in line 10 *(сего года)* and line 14 *(сего числа).* This keyword introduces legalese about reading the document to the witnesses and declarant, to make sure they confirm the facts are right, and getting the signatures of all concerned. Since illiteracy was fairly common, we often see various phrases explaining that the declarant and witnesses were unable to read, so the Registrar was the only one to sign the record.

объявляющему — "to the declarant." *Объявляющему* is the dative masculine singular of the present active participle *объявляющий,* "the declaring one," from the verb *объявлять*, "to declare, state." Dative constructions can generally be translated with the English prepositions "to" or "for," and the sense of this will be clear from context.

и свидѣтелямъ неграмотнымъ — "and to the illiterate witnesses." Both the noun and adjective are dative plural in form, for the same reason *объявлящему* was dative singular: as indirect objects of the verb *прочитанъ*. Sometimes the single word *присутсвующимъ*, "those present," is used as a shorter way of saying "to the declarant and witnesses."

There were several phrases used to indicate illiteracy, such as *по неграмотности*, "because of illiteracy," or *а за незнанiемъ ими грамоты*, "because of their lack of knowledge of letters." All this may seem confusing, but in fact it's not hard to figure out. If a declarant or witness could sign his/her name, it will appear along with that of the record keeper; if no other signature appears besides the record keeper's, they were illiterate and you can expect to see legalese to that effect.

прочитанъ — "[was] read," the past passive participle of the verb *прочитать,* "to read."

Нами только подписанъ — "[and] by us only signed." *Нами* is the instrumental of *мы,* "we," and *подписанъ* (from *подписать,* "to sign") is a past passive participle, like *прочитанъ.* If the witnesses were literate the phraseology here would be *Нами и ими подписанъ,* "[it was] signed by Us and them."

администраторъ прихода Щутово — "Administrator of the parish of Szczutowo."

содержащій акты гражданскаго состоянія — "the keeper of vital records," literally "The one keeping *(содержащій)* the documents *(акты)* of the civil state *(гражданскаго состоянія)*." *Содержащій* (modern spelling *содержащий*) is the present active participle of the verb *содержать*, "to keep, maintain," and *состоянiе* (modern spelling *состояние*) is a noun meaning "state, status, condition."

Кс. В. Киньски — "Rev. W. Kiński." *Кс.* is an abbreviation of *Ксёндз*, the Russian spelling of the Polish word *ksiądz*, "priest, Father."

Translation — This document was read to the declarant and illiterate witnesses and was signed by us alone. Administrator of the parish of Szczutowo and keeper of vital records. — Rev. W. Kiński.

Now let's look at a polished translation of the whole document:

Translation — This occurred in the village of Szczutowo on the 6th/19th of March, 1905, at 10 a.m. Stanisław Zaborowski appeared, a peasant from Kozi Borek, age 24, in the presence of Jan Kamiński, age 43, and of Franciszek Tłuchowski, age 33, both peasants from Boruchy, and presented to us a female child, stating that it was born in Kozi Borek on the 1st/14th of March of this year at 10 a. m. to his lawful wife Leokadia née Tyburska, age 20. At Holy Baptism, administered on this day, this child was given the name of Czesława. The godparents were Franciszek Tłuchowski and Rozalia Czyżewska. This document was read to the declarant and witnesses, who are illiterate, and was signed by us alone. Administrator of the parish of Szczutowo and keeper of vital records. — Rev. W. Kiński.

We realize this may be **way more detail** than you ever wanted to see on this subject. Actually this is a fairly superficial analysis—a really exhaustive analysis of the grammar would have been much, much longer. But we wanted to provide at least some detail for those who want it, and let those bored by grammar skip over it. In these documents every word, and every ending on those words, can have meaning; so some comment on those words and endings seemed advisable. Future records will be discussed in less detail, concentrating mainly on those elements that represent a departure from the norm, of which this document is a fairly representative example.

3. Document VI-6: Example of a Marginal Notation in a Birth Record

Document VI-6, on page 206, provides an example of an interesting practice one may encounter. It was not unusual for record keepers to make notations in the margins of original records. Some concern adoption, the legitimization of births out of wedlock, the date or place of the marriage or death of the child named in the record, and so on. We also see marginal notes correcting errors. The regulations covering record keeping said that once information was written, it could not be erased. If the registrar realized there was an error, he was to insert a symbol in the original paragraph—in many records it looks much like a backwards F—and then write a correction in the margin, with his initials.

This particular note is taken from an 1888 birth record in Nowogród. You might wish to try translating the original record yourself and compare your version to ours, on page 206. We have boxed the keywords to help you pick them out, which should make it a bit easier for you.

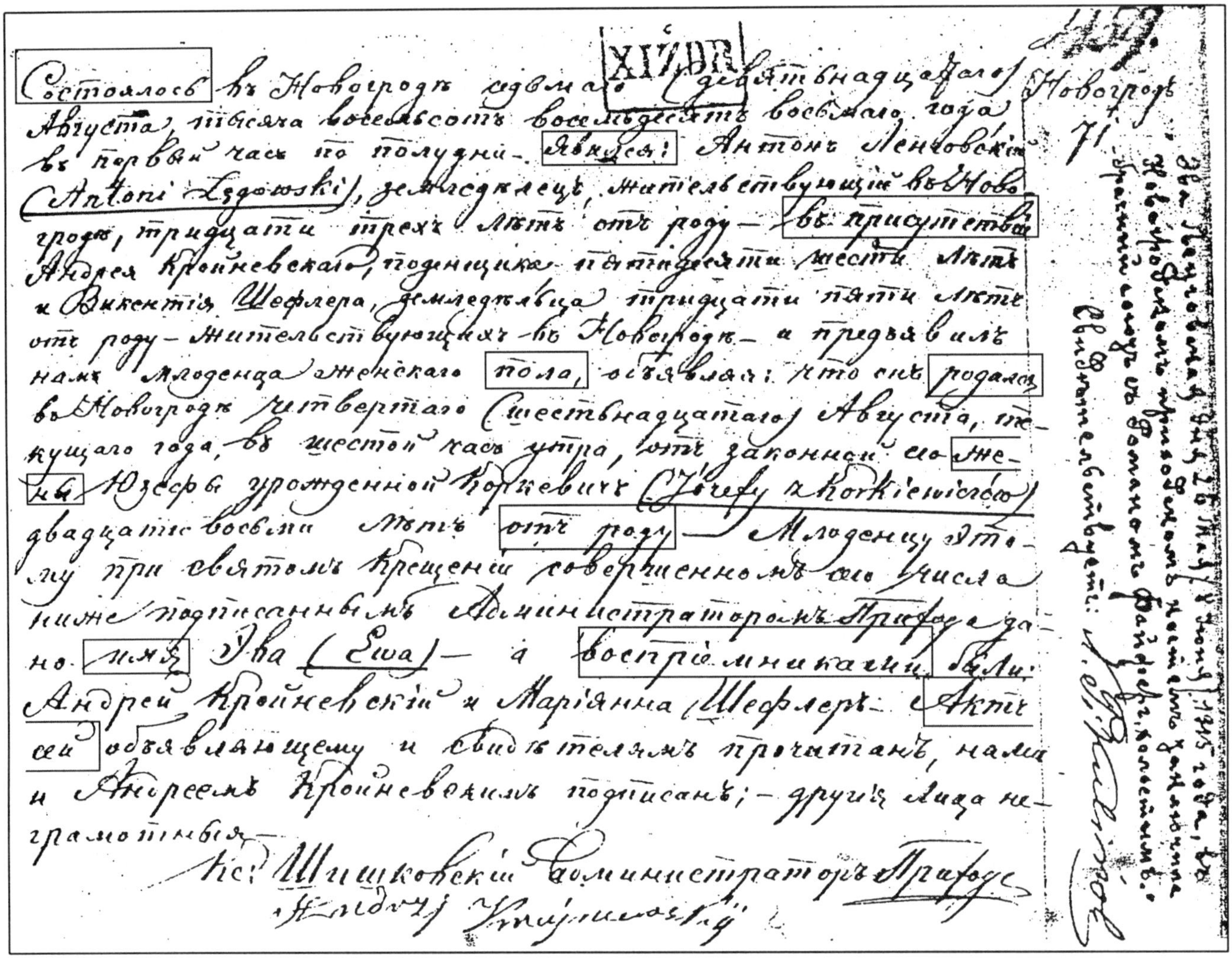

XIV/BR

Состоялось въ Новогродѣ седьмаго (девятнадцатаго) Августа, тысяча восемьсотъ восемьдесятъ восьмаго года въ первый часъ по полудни. Явился: Антонъ Ленговскій (Antoni Łęgowski), земледѣлецъ, жительствующій въ Новогродѣ, тридцати трехъ лѣтъ отъ роду — въ присутствіи Андрея Кройневскаго, поденщика пятидесяти шести лѣтъ и Викентія Шефлера, земледѣльца тридцати пяти лѣтъ отъ роду — жительствующихъ въ Новогродѣ — и предъявилъ намъ младенца женскаго пола, объявляя: что онъ родился въ Новогродѣ четвертаго (шестнадцатаго) Августа, текущаго года, въ шестомъ часу утра, отъ законной его жены Юзефы урожденной Коркевичъ (Józefy z Korkiewiczów) двадцати восьми лѣтъ отъ роду. — Младенцу этому при святомъ Крещеніи совершенномъ сего числа нижеподписаннымъ Администраторомъ Прихода дано имя Эва (Ewa) — а воспріемниками были: Андрей Кройневскій и Маріянна Шефлеръ. Актъ сей объявляющему и свидѣтелямъ прочитанъ, нами и Андреемъ Кройневскимъ подписанъ; — другія лица неграмотныя.

Кс: Шишковскій Администраторъ Прихода

Андрѣй Krujniewskÿ

Новогродъ 71

1157

Эва Ленговская дня 26 мая / 8 Іюня 1915 года, въ Новогродскомъ приходскомъ костелѣ заключила брачный союзъ съ Романомъ Файферъ, холостымъ. Свидѣтельствуетъ: X. Pikulinski

Document VI-6, Example of a Marginal Notation in a Birth Record

Here is a fairly literal translation, with the keywords highlighted in bold type:

This happened in Nowogród on the 7th (19th) of August 1888 at 1 p.m. Antoni Łęgowski **appeared**, a farmer *[земледѣлецъ]* residing in Nowogród, age 33—**in the presence of** Andrzej Krojnewski, a day-laborer *[поденщика]*, age 56, and Wincenty Szefler, a farmer *[земледѣльца]*, age 35, both living in Nowogród—and he presented to us a child of the female **sex**, stating that it **was born** in Nowogród on the 4th (16th) of August of this year at 6 a.m. to his lawful **wife** Józefa née Korkiewicz, **age** 28. At Holy Baptism, performed this day by the undersigned Parish Administrator, the child was given the **name** Ewa—the **godparents** were Andrzej Krojniewski and Marianna Szefler. **This document** was read aloud to the declarant and witnesses and was signed by us and by Andrzej Krojniewski; the other persons are illiterate. [Signed] Rev. Szyszkowski, Parish Administrator; Andrzej Krujniewskÿ.

The marginal notation says: *Эва Ленговская дня 26 мая / 8 Іюня 1915 года, въ Новогродскомъ приходскомъ костелѣ заключила брачний союзъ съ Романомъ Файферъ, холостымъ. Свидѣтельствуетъ X. Pikulinski.*

The literal translation of this is: "Ewa Łęgowska on 26 May/8 June 1915, in the Nowogród parish church, entered a marital union with Roman Fajfer, bachelor. Witnessed by Rev. Pikuliński."

Note that the Polish name *Łęgowska* had to be spelled phonetically in Russian as *Ленговская*, since Russian has no letter corresponding to the Polish nasal vowel ę (see page 24). What's unusual is that the priest Russified the name completely by adding the Russian feminine ending *-ая*. More often Polish names were simply transliterated with endings *-ски* (for masculine *-ski*) and *-ска* (for feminine *-ska*), rather than being modified with the standard Russian endings of *-скій* and *-ская*. But you will sometimes encounter this (note that the original record has *Ленговскій* and *Кройневскій*).

Also noteworthy is that the priest signed his name in Polish, *X. Pikuliński* (where X. is an abbreviation for Polish *ksiądz,* "Reverend, Father"). This, too, is a departure from the norm, but one not too uncommon.

4. Document VI-7: Another Example of a Marginal Notation in a Birth Record

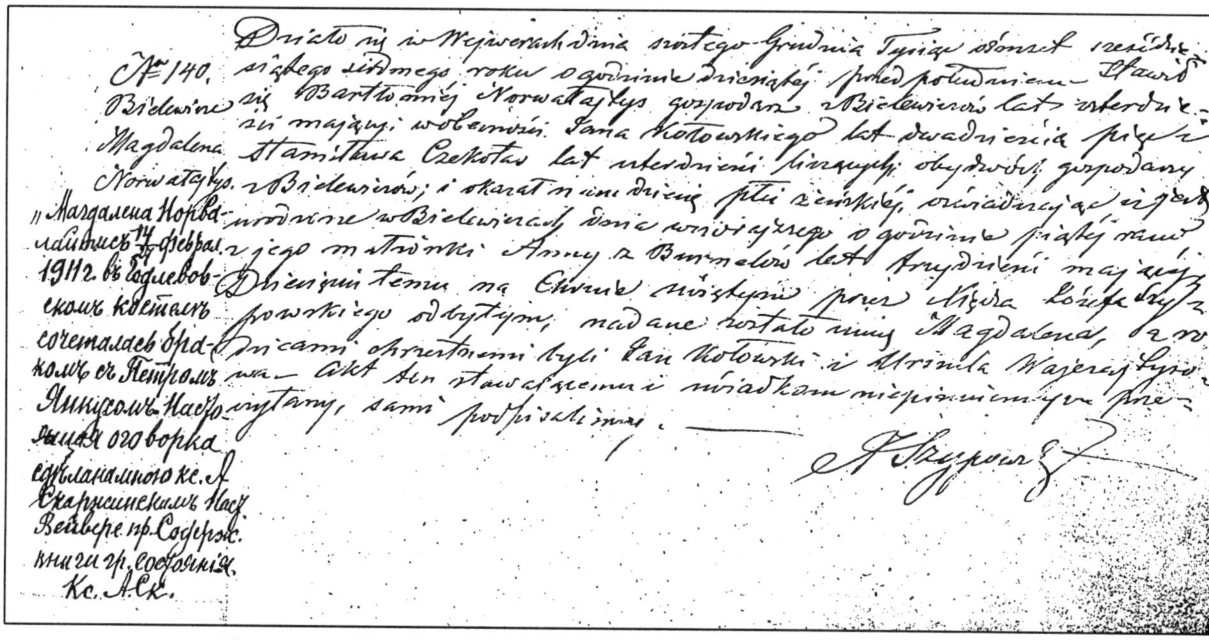

Document VI-7: Another Example of a Marginal Notation to a Birth Record

Another example of a marginal notation is **Document VI-7**, a birth record from the parish church in Veiveriai, Lithuania. This record was written in Polish, which was normal throughout the Commonwealth of Poland and Lithuania for the first half of the 19th century. In some areas, such as near Białystok, Poland, use of Russian in all records was imposed beginning in 1850. In other areas Polish was used until the unsuccessful Insurrection against the Russian Empire in 1863; after that, the use of Russian in all records was imposed as a punitive measure. This actually took effect in 1868, so that you may be paging through records from 1867, all in Polish, and turn a page to 1868, only to find everything suddenly in Russian!

Here the original record was drawn up on 6 December 1867, during the time when Polish was still used. But the marginal notation was made in 1911, after the mandatory use of Russian began. So you have a Russian notation to a Polish record.

In this record, as with any drawn up in what is now Lithuania, the question of using appropriate name forms poses some challenges. It is not too hard to recognize that *Veiveriai* was called *Wejwery* by the Poles—the names are pronounced almost identically, and differ so much in spelling only due to the different orthographic conventions of Lithuanian and Polish. But the father in this record (line 3) is called *Bartłomiej Norwałajtys*—clearly a Lithuanian surname, and therefore it is appropriate to call him *Baltramiejus Norvalaitis* (or perhaps he went by one of the short forms of that first name, *Baltras* or *Baltrus*). His wife is named as *Anna z Burnelów* (line 8), but more likely she went by the Lithuanian form of that name, *Ona Burnelis*—or, to be accurate, since we're talking about her maiden name, *Ona Burnelytė*. The standard form of the daughter's first name, *Magdalena*, is the same in Polish and Lithuanian, so that name, at least, offers no complications.

In case it is difficult to read, at right is a rendering of the Russian-language marginal notation in standardized script. In "italic" type (without hyphens or original line breaks) it would read thus:

"Магдалена Норвалайтисъ 14/27 Феврал. 1911 г. въ Годлевовскомъ костелѣ сочеталась бракомъ съ Петромъ Янкусомъ. Настоящая оговорка сдѣлана мною, кс. А. Скаржинскимъ Наст. Вейвере пр. Содерж. книги гр. состоянія. [signed] Кс. А. Ск.

This translates as: "Magdalena Norvalaitis on 14/27 February 1911 in the Garliava church was joined in marriage with Petras Jankus. This notation was made by me, Rev. A. Skaržinskas, Administrator of Veiveriai parish, Keeping the books of the Civil Register. [signed] Rev. A. Sk."

> "Магдалена Норва-
> лайтисъ 14/27 феврал.
> 1911 г. въ Годлевов-
> скомъ костелѣ
> сочеталась бра-
> комъ съ Петромъ
> Янкусомъ. Настo-
> ящая оговорка
> сдѣлана мною кс. А.
> Скаржинскимъ Наст.
> Вейвере пр. Содерж.
> книги гр. состоянія.
> Кс. А. Ск.

A few comments on the words and forms seen here:

Годлевовскомъ – this is the prepositional singular masculine form (modifying *костелѣ*, prepositional of *костелъ*, "[Roman Catholic] church") of the adjective *Годлевовскій*, "of Godlevo," the Russian name of Garliava (compare Polish *Godlewo*).

сочеталась бракомъ съ – literally "she joined herself by means of marriage with." We have already seen a noun derived from this same expression, *бракосочетаніе*, "marriage."

съ Петромъ Янкусомъ – "with Petras Jankus," the Lithuanian version of the groom's name. In Polish it would be *Piotr Jankus*, in modern Russian *Петр Янкус*.

настоящая оговорка – "this notation." In Russian *оговорка* means "a note added to something already said" as well as "reservation, stipulation, slip of the tongue."

сдѣлана мною – "[was] made by me." From the verb *сдѣлать*, "to make, do," we have *сдѣлана*, "was made." The instrumental form *мною* is archaic; in modern Russian *мной* is standard (see page 42).

Скаржинскимъ – instrumental of the surname seen in Lithuanian as *Skaržinskas*, in Polish as *Skarzyński*. It is hard to say for sure which is appropriate here, since the priest might well have been an ethnic Pole. But since the other proper names are clearly Lithuanian, consistency suggests this, too, should be given in Lithuanian form.

Наст. Вейвере пр. Содерж. книги гр. состоянія – technically a *настоятель* is a prior, father superior, or arch-priest. But sometimes, as here, it is used in the sense of "pastor, chief priest of a parish." *Вейвере* is a phonetic spelling in Cyrillic of the Lithuanian name of the village, *Veiveriai* (see pages 21-23). The phrase *Содержащій книги гражданскаго состоянія*, "[one] keeping the books of the Civil Register," is a standard title for the one who kept records for church use, which the civil government also used (see page 205). Usually this was the head of the local parish or religious community.

5. Document VI-8: A Jewish Birth Record from Russian Poland

Now that we have seen some examples of Christian birth records, **Document VI-8** on page 210 (reprinted in italic typeface on page 211 for easier reading) allows us to compare them with a record of the birth of a Jewish boy and see the similarities and differences.

Before analyzing this record, let us point out a few departures from normal spelling. In line 3, and again in line 12, *одиннадцать*, "eleven," is spelled *одинадцать*, with just one *-н-*. In line 10 *мужескаго* is a legitimate older form of *мужскаго* (modern *мужского*). Such variants need to be pointed out because otherwise you might notice them and be confused, wondering if you've made a mistake.

Here is a brief analysis, focusing on items not seen in earlier samples.

Состоялось въ посадѣ Андржеевѣ десятаго Марта тысяча восемьсотъ восемьдесятъ девятаго года въ одинадцать часовъ утра – "This happened in the settlement of Andrzejewo on March 10, 1889, at 11 a.m." The term *посадъ* was originally applied to the part of a town where the craftsmen and tradesmen lived, usually outside the town walls.

Явился лично Абрамъ Гершъ Палгонъ торговецъ сорока пяти лѣтъ въ посадѣ Андржеевѣ жительствующій –"Abram Gersz Pałgon appeared in person, a merchant, age 45, residing in the settlement of Andrzejewo." Because of Russian's tendency to turn Polish *h* into Russian *г*, it is likely his middle name was *Hersz* in Polish, which Beider says is a variant of Yiddish *hirsh*, literally "stag," a *kinnui* for *Naphthali* (Alexander Beider, *A Dictionary of Jewish Surnames in the Russian Empire,* Avotaynu, 1993, ISBN 0-9626373-3-5, p. 240).

въ присутствіи свидѣтелей Мордки Квятекъ поденщика пятидесяти лѣтъ и Ицка Шпицбергъ домовладѣльца тридцати восьми лѣтъ обоихъ въ посадѣ Андржеевѣ жительствующихъ – "in the presence of witnesses Mordka Kwiatek, a day-laborer, age 50, and Icek Szpicberg, a home-owner, age 38, both *[обоихъ]* residing in the settlement of Andrzejewo." By English phonetics the name of the second witness would be written Itsek Shpitsberg (compare German *Spitzberg*).

и предъявилъ Намъ младенца мужескаго пола – "and presented to Us a child of the male gender," i. e., "and presented to us a male child."

объявляя что онъ родился перваго Февраля тысяча восемьсотъ семьдесятъ пятаго года въ одинадцать часовъ утра – "stating that it was born on February 1, 1875, at 11 a.m." Notice the date of birth, in 1875, versus the date this record was drawn up, in 1889!

отъ законной его жены Шейны урожденной Цедекъ тридцати шести лѣтъ въ то время имѣющей – "to his lawful wife Szejna, née Cedek, age 36 at that time." In other words, she was 36 *въ то время* "at that time," when she gave birth. By English phonetics her name would be spelled Sheyna (or Sheina) Tsedek.

№ 10.

Посадъ Анджеевъ № 5.

Состоялось въ посадѣ Анджеевѣ десятаго Марта тысяча восемьсотъ восемьдесятъ девятаго года въ одинадцать часовъ утра, явился лично Абрамъ Герцъ Тамонъ торговецъ сорока пяти лѣтъ въ посадѣ Анджеевѣ жительствующій въ присутствіи свидѣтелей Мордки Квятекъ поденщика пятидесяти лѣтъ и Ицка Шпицбергъ домовладѣльца тридцати восьми лѣтъ, обоихъ въ посадѣ Анджеевѣ жительствующихъ и предъявилъ намъ младенца мужескаго пола, объявляя что онъ родился перваго Февраля тысяча восемьсотъ семьдесятъ пятаго года въ одинадцать часовъ утра отъ законной его жены Шейны урожденной Цедекъ тридцати шести лѣтъ въ то время имѣющей. Мальчику этому при религіозномъ обрядѣ совершенномъ восьмаго Февраля тысяча восемьсотъ семьдесятъ пятаго года дано имена Алтеръ-Янкель. При этомъ объявляющій заявилъ, что позднее составленіе акта онъ сдѣлалъ по той причинѣ, что незналъ до сего времени о необходимости таковаго.

Актъ сей объявляющему и свидѣтелямъ прочитанъ, нами и свидѣтелями подписанъ, такъ какъ отецъ неграмотный. Mordek Kwiatek

Ицко Шпицберг

Чиновникъ Гражданскаго Состоянія [illegible]

Document VI-8: A Jewish Birth Record from Russian Poland

Here is a rendering of the Cyrillic in "italic" type:

Посадъ Андржеево № 5.

Состоялось въ посадѣ Андржеевѣ десятаго Марта тысяча восемьсотъ восемьдесятъ девятаго года въ одинадцать часовъ утра. Явился лично Абрамъ Гершъ Палгонъ торговецъ сорока пяти лѣтъ въ посадѣ Андржеевѣ жительствующій въ присутствіи свидѣтелей Мордки Квятекъ поденщика пятидесяти лѣтъ и Ицка Шпицбергъ домовладѣльца тридцати восьми лѣтъ обоихъ въ посадѣ Андржеевѣ жительствующихъ и предъявилъ Намъ младенца мужескаго пола объявляя что онъ родился перваго Февраля тысяча восемьсотъ семьдесятъ пятаго года въ одинадцатъ часовъ утра отъ законной его жены Шейны урожденной Цедекъ тридцати шести лѣтъ въ то время имѣющей. Мальчику этому при религіозномъ обрядѣ совершенномъ восьмаго Февраля тысяча восемьсотъ семьдесятъ пятаго года дано имена Алтеръ-Янкель. При этомъ объявляющій заявилъ, что поздное составленіе акта онъ сдѣлалъ по той причинѣ, что не зналъ до сего времени о необходимости таковаго.

Актъ сей объявляющему и свидѣтелямъ прочитанъ Нами и свидѣтелями подписанъ, такъ какъ отецъ неграмотный.

Mortek Kwiatek
Ицко Шпицбергъ

Чиновникъ Гражданскаго Состоянія [? Ешевскій ?]

Мальчику этому при религіозномъ обрядѣ совершенномъ восьмаго Февраля тысяча восемьсотъ семьдесятъ пятаго года дано имена Алтеръ-Янкель – "During a religious ceremony performed on February 8, 1875, this child was given the names Alter-Jankiel." The "religious ceremony" was, of course, circumcision.

При этомъ объявляющій заявилъ, что поздное составленіе акта онъ сдѣлалъ по той причинѣ, что не зналъ до сего времени о необходимости таковаго – literally "In addition the declarant stated that he made this late drawing up of the record for this reason, that he did not know until this time about the necessity of this."

Актъ сей объявляющему и свидѣтелямъ прочитанъ Нами и свидѣтелями подписанъ, такъ какъ отецъ неграмотный. – "This document was read aloud to the declarant and witnesses and signed by Us and the witnesses, since the father is illiterate."

Translation – "This happened in the settlement of Andrzejewo on March 10, 1889, at 11 a. m. Abram Hersz Pałgon appeared in person, a merchant, age 45, residing in the suburb of Andrzejewo, and in the presence of witnesses Mordka Kwiatek, a day-laborer, age 50, and Icek Szpicberg, a home-owner, age 38, both residing in the settlement of Andrzejewo, he presented to us a male child, stating that it was born on February 1, 1875, at 11 a.m. to his lawful wife Szejna, née Cedek, age 36 at that time. During a religious ceremony performed on February 8, 1875, this child was given the name Alter-Jankiel. In addition the declarant stated that he did not have this record drawn up sooner because he did not know until now that it was necessary. This document was read aloud to the declarant and witnesses and signed by Us and the witnesses, since the father is illiterate."

6. Document VI-9: A Written Transcript of a Catholic Birth Record from Lithuania

These days researchers can hope to get photocopies of the original record drawn up when the child's father, relatives, and friends went to register his or her birth. In some cases these photocopies come from records the Family History Library has microfilmed; in others the copies were made at a parish or archive in Europe.

But it wasn't that long ago that photocopies were impossible to get, because copying machines were not available. When our parents or grandparents needed a birth or baptismal certificate—to prove their identity for some official purpose, to register children in a Catholic school, to satisfy the Church's requirements before getting married, for whatever reason—they had to write the appropriate parish or archive and request a transcript from the original record. These transcripts may not thrill us because they aren't facsimiles of the original record actually witnessed or signed by our ancestors. But they're the kind of thing you may find lying around in an attic, and they may contain information you'd never find elsewhere. They may be written by hand, or typed, on blank paper or forms—but they're always worth a close look.

Document VI-9, reproduced on page 214, is a photocopy of such a transcript. The family in question were ethnic Poles living near Alytus (Polish name *Olita*), Lithuania. At some point they needed a birth/baptismal certificate to acquire a *видъ на жительство* (residency permit). It was written by hand on a sheet of paper and stamped with the church seal and the stamp of the Troki (now Trakai) *uyezd*'s police administration, and constituted a residence permit. Later a family member had it photocopied, and it is from that photocopy that this image is reproduced. The paper has been folded and soiled, and it's hard to read. But since this is precisely the condition in which you might find such papers in an attic, practice deciphering may prove to be a useful exercise.

The words in the stamp at the top right should be read in this order:

Видъ на жительство Трокскаго уѣзднаго полицейсцкаго управленія

This translates as "Residency permit of the Troki county police administration." This does not imply that anyone was in trouble with the police. Keeping track of who was allowed to live where was a normal duty of the police, and citizens had to register so their "papers" would be in order.

The date at top right is *7 Мая 1913 г., за № 38, безсрочная* – "7 May 1913, No. 38, permanent" (in modern Russian the last word is spelled *бессрочная*).

Here is a brief analysis of this text:

Метрическая выпись изъ книги Олитскаго Р. Католическаго приходскаго Костела о родившихся за 1897 года под № 87 – A registry excerpt from the book of the Olita Roman Catholic parish church of those born for the year 1897, under No. 87.

метрическая выпись — a *выпись* is an extract or copy, and *метрический* is an adjective from *метрика*, "parish register, church register."

изъ книги Олитскаго Р. Католическаго приходскаго Костела — "from the books of the Olita Roman Catholic parish church." Olita is the Polish name of the town Lithuanians call Alytus, near Kaunas. From *приход*, parish, comes the adjective *приходский*, "of the parish, parochial." The noun *костёл* (related to the Polish term *kościół*), means "church," but especially a Roman Catholic church. Since most Russians are adherents of the Orthodox Church, the more common word for "church" in Russian, *церковь*, is associated with churches of that faith.

о родившихся за 1897 года – "of those born," from *родиться,* "to be born." Russian registers are usually divided into three sections, of which the first contains birth and baptismal records. Thus we see expressions such as *Выпись изъ метрической книги. Часть первая о родившихся за _ годъ*, "Excerpt from the church register. Part One, of births for the year _." The term *часть вторая*, "second part," refers to the register's section on marriages; and *часть третья*, "third part," is usually the death register (although in some registers the third part recorded divorces and deaths appeared in *часть четвертая,* the fourth part).

Тысяча восемьсотъ девяносто седьмаго года Октября двадцатаго дня — "On 20 October 1897"

въ Олитскомъ Римско-Католическомоъ приходскомъ Костелѣ — "in the Olita Roman Catholic parish church"

окрещено дитя по имени Вацлавъ — "a child named Wacław was baptized"

окрещено — "[was] baptized," a short form of the past passive participle of *крестить*, "to baptize," with the neuter singular ending *-o* because it refers to the neuter singular noun *дитя.*

дитя по имени – *дитя* is an archaic noun meaning "child, infant"; the expression *по имени* corresponds to English "by name, named" (from *имя*)

Настоятелемъ Ксендземъ Бенедиктемъ Біейко — "by the pastor, Rev. Benedykt Biejko"

настоятелемъ — "pastor" (see the note on this word on page 209). This noun and the priest's name are all in the instrumental case because the child was baptized **by** him.

съ совершеніемъ всѣхъ обрядовъ Таинства — "with all rites of the Sacrament performed"

Дворянъ Александра и Гелены урожденной изъ Монгиновъ Голохвастовъ законныхъ супруговъ — literally "of the nobles Aleksander and Helena née Mongin Hołochwast, married spouses"

дворянъ — "of the aristocrats," genitive plural of *дворянинъ*, "aristocrat, noble" (The analysis is continued on page 216).

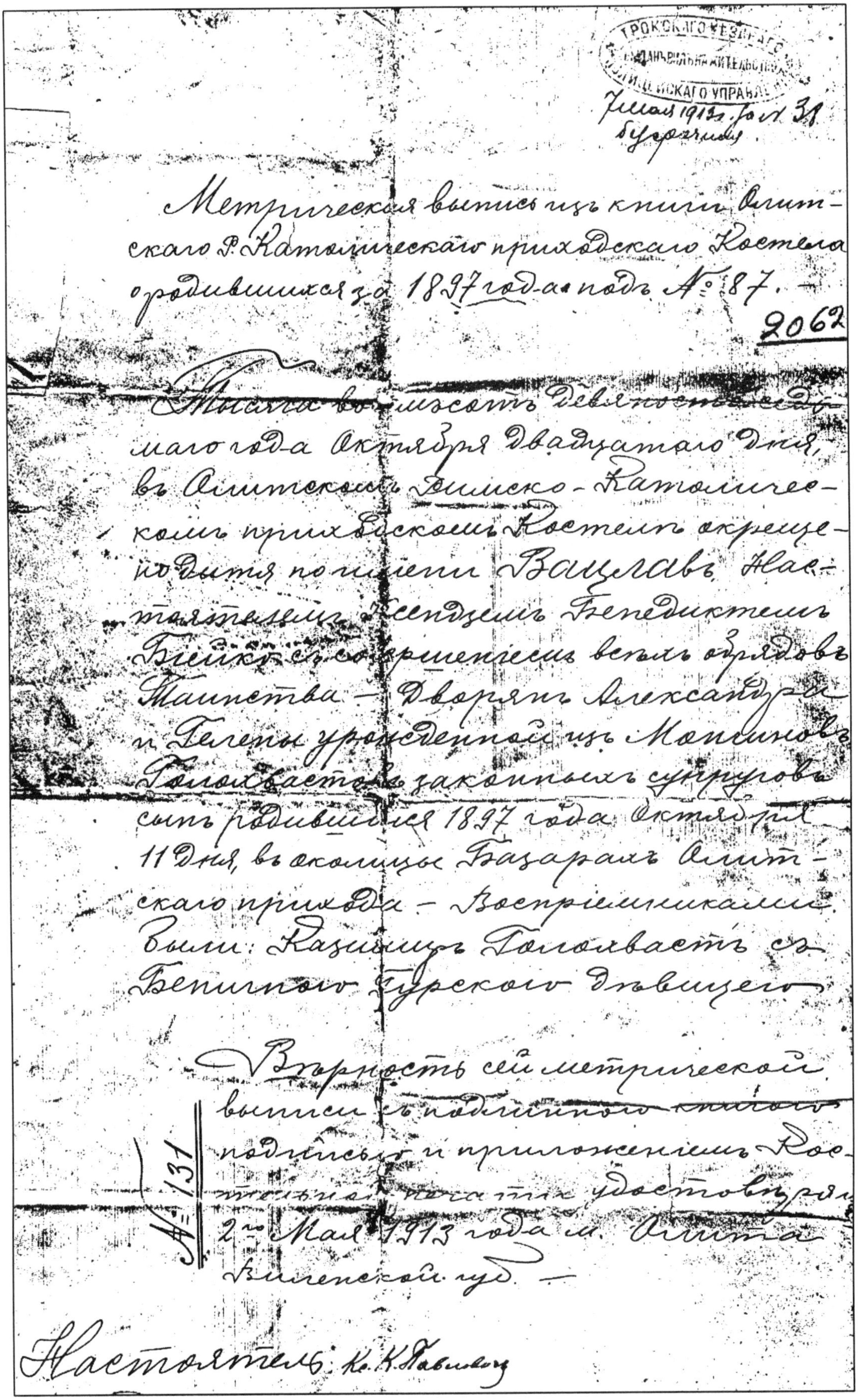
Трокскаго уѣзднаго ... полицейскаго управленія

7 июля 1913 г. за № 31

Метрическая выпись изъ книги Олитскаго Р. Католическаго приходскаго Костела
о родившихся за 1897 года подъ № 87. —

2062

Тысяча восемьсотъ девяносто седьмого года Октября двадцатаго дня,
въ Олитскомъ Римско-Католическомъ приходскомъ Костелѣ окрещено дитя по имени Вацлавъ Настоятелемъ Ксендзомъ Бенедиктомъ
Бейко съ совершеніемъ всѣхъ обрядовъ
Таинства — Дворянъ Александра
и Елены урожденной изъ Мокиновъ
Голохвастовъ законныхъ супруговъ
сынъ родившійся 1897 года Октября
11 дня, въ околицѣ Базаранъ Олитскаго прихода — Воспріемниками
были: Казимиръ Голохвастъ съ
Бенигною Гурскою дѣвицею

Вѣрность сей метрической
выписи съ подлинною [illegible]
подписью и приложеніемъ Костельной печати удостовѣряю
2го Мая 1913 года м. Олита
Виленской губ. —

№ 131

Настоятель: Кс. К. Павловичъ

Document VI-9: A Written Transcript of a Catholic Birth Record from Lithuania

Since the handwritten section is not particularly easy reading, here is a rendering in a standardized text, which may make it easier to decipher:

Метрическая выпись изъ книги Олит-
скаго Р. Католическаго приходскаго Костела
о родившихся за 1897 года под № 87.
Тысяча восемьсотъ девяносто седь-
маго года Октября двадцатаго дня,
въ Олитскомъ Римско-Католичес-
комъ приходскомъ Костелѣ окреще-
но дитя по имени Вацлавъ Нас-
тоятелемъ Ксендземъ Бенедиктемъ
Біейко съ совершеніемъ всѣхъ обрядовъ
Таинства. — Дворянъ Александра
и Гелены урожденной изъ Монгиновъ
Голохвастовъ законныхъ супруговъ
сынъ родившійся 1897 года Октября
11 дня, въ околицы Базарахъ Олит-
скаго прихода. — Воспріемниками
были: Казимиръ Голохвастъ съ
Бенигною Гурскою дѣвицею.

Вѣрность сей метрической
выписи съ подлинною книгою
No 131 подписью и приложеніемъ Кос-
тельной печати удостовѣряю
2го Мая 1913 года м. Олита
Виленской губ. —

Настоятель: Кс. К. Павловичъ

Александра и Гелены урожденной изъ Монгиновъ Голоквастовъ — Голохвастовъ is their surname, and *урожденной изъ Монгиновъ* means "born of the Mongins." *Александра, Гелены,* and *Голохвастовъ* are genitive forms because these names, along with *дворянъ*, logically follow the word *сынъ* in the next phrase. That is, the child was the son ***of the*** Hołochwasts, Aleksander and Helena née Mongin. Note that their surname could be either *Gołochwast* or *Hołochwast,* since Russian generally turned Polish *h* into *г*. From other family records, however, it's clear the family usually pronounced the name with the H-sound rather than G.

законныхъ супруговъ — literally "lawful spouses," but you could translate it by any phrase that doesn't sound awkward and conveys the essential fact that they were married.

сынъ родившійся 1897 года Октября 11 дня, въ околицы Базарахъ Олитскаго прихода — "a son born 11 October 1897 in the neighborhood of Bazary, of Olita parish"

сынъ родившийся – "a son born"

въ околицы Базарахъ – "in the neighborhood of Bazary." Russian grammar would dictate that the form be *въ околицѣ*, but it's possible the priest was thinking in Polish. In that language *w okolicy Bazarach* is correct, "in the neighborhood of Bazary"; thus the priest may have inadvertently transliterated that phrase into Russian, rendering Polish *okolicy* as *околицы*, even though that's not correct by Russian grammar. We often see instances where the record keeper's native language affected his spelling or grammar, producing incorrect Russian. Bazary was apparently a section of a settlement or a small community somewhere near Olita.

Воспріемниками были Казимиръ Голохвастъ съ Бенигною Гурскою дѣвицею — "The godparents were Kazimierz Hołochwast and Benigna Górska, a single woman."

Казимиръ Голохвастъ – since other documents prove the Hołochowasts were Poles, a Polish rendering of this name, as *Kazimierz Hołochwast,* is indicated.

съ Бенигною Гурскою дѣвицею – as indicated on page 37, the instrumental endings with *-ю* are archaic; in modern Russian this would be *с Бенигной Гурской девицей*, literally "with Benigna Górska, maiden." The *-у-* in *Гурской* is a phonetic rendering of Polish *-ó-*, and the standard spelling of this name in Polish would be *Górska,* a feminine form of the common surname *Górski.* Calling her a *дѣвица*, "maiden," simply indicates she was not married—in many records the godmother is described as "wife of so-and-so."

Вѣрность сей метрической выписи съ подлинною книгою подписью и приложеніемъ Костельной печати удостовѣряю 2 го Мая 1913 года м. Олита Виленской губ. Настоятель: Кс. К. Павловичъ — "I certify conformance of this registry copy with the original book with [my] signature and by affixing the church's seal. 2 May 1913, town of Olita, Wilno province. Pastor: Rev. K. Pawłowicz."

Вѣрность – this noun means "accuracy, conformance." A statement to this effect will appear in virtually all certificates issued by a church office or state archive. Here *вѣрность* functions as the direct object of the verb *удостовѣряю*, "I certify."

съ подлинною книгою – "with the original register." Here again the *-ю* ending is archaic, and in modern Russian this would read *с подлинной книгой*. The adjective *подлинный* means "authentic, original, real."

подписью и пріложеніемъ Костельной печати удостоверяю – here we finally get to the predicate of this sentence, *удостовѣряю*, from *удостовѣрять*, "to certify." The instrumental case is used because he certifies this copy's authenticity **by means of** his signature and affixing the church seal.

2го Мая 1913 года м. Олита Виленской губ. — here the pastor dates the certificate, 2 May 1913, in the town of Olita, in Wilno province.

Настоятель: Кс. К. Павловичъ — the term *настоятель* can be used to mean "pastor." *Кс.* is short for *Ксёндзъ*, from the Polish word *Ksiądz*, "priest, Father." *Павловичъ* transliterates as "Pavlovich," but since we have good reason to believe these people are Polish, *Pawłowicz* would be the appropriate spelling.

7. Document VI-10: A Written Transcript of a Jewish Birth Record from Russian Poland

Document V-10, reproduced on page 218, serves much the same purpose as the preceding one, but has a few interesting points of its own. It, too, is a copy or extract from the original records, but the top section is in Polish (as is the bottom section, reproduced separately on page 221). This reflects a change in borders: when the original was drawn up, the Siedlce area was part of the Russian partition of Poland and thus the record had to be in Russian; but by the time this copy was created in 1936 Siedlce was once more in independent Poland, and Polish was appropriate. So the form is in Polish, but the quotation from the records is in the language of the original. It has most of the keywords we described on page 198.

Note, too, that this form can be used for births, marriages, or deaths. The clerk simply filled in the appropriate Polish word, to go with *akt*, "record, certificate," at the end of the first printed paragraph: *urodzenia* for "birth" (or perhaps *chrztu* for "baptism"), *małżeństwa* or *ślubu* for "marriage," and *śmierci* or *zgonu* for "death."

The paragraph in Polish reads as follows: "The Civil Registrar for the Jewish faith of the town of Siedlce hereby certifies that in the Civil Registry books, under No. 237 for the year 1882, the following birth record is to be found."

Then comes the copy of the original Russian record:

Состоялось въ городѣ Сѣдлецѣ второго/четырнадцатаго Декабря тысяча восемсотъ восемдесять второго года въ десять съ половиною часовъ утра явился Зельманъ Вайншельбаумъ пятидесяти двухъ лѣтъ работникъ — "This happened in the town of Siedlce on the 2nd/14th of December 1882 at 10:30 a.m. Zelman Wajnszelbaum appeared, age 52, a worker."

второго/четырнадцатаго Декабря – as we have seen before, Russian-language records from Russian Poland generally give two dates, by the Julian calendar and then by the Gregorian calendar. We would go by the second one, here 14 December. Incidentally, you'll note that *второго* should, in theory, be the archaic form *втораго*. In several instances modern Russian spellings, and outright misspellings, sneak into this document. One would have to examine the original to be certain, but perhaps the clerk knew some Russian and slipped occasionally, writing in the modern forms instead of the archaic ones that presumably appeared in the original. For research purposes, however, this is probably insignificant—it wouldn't affect the meaning.

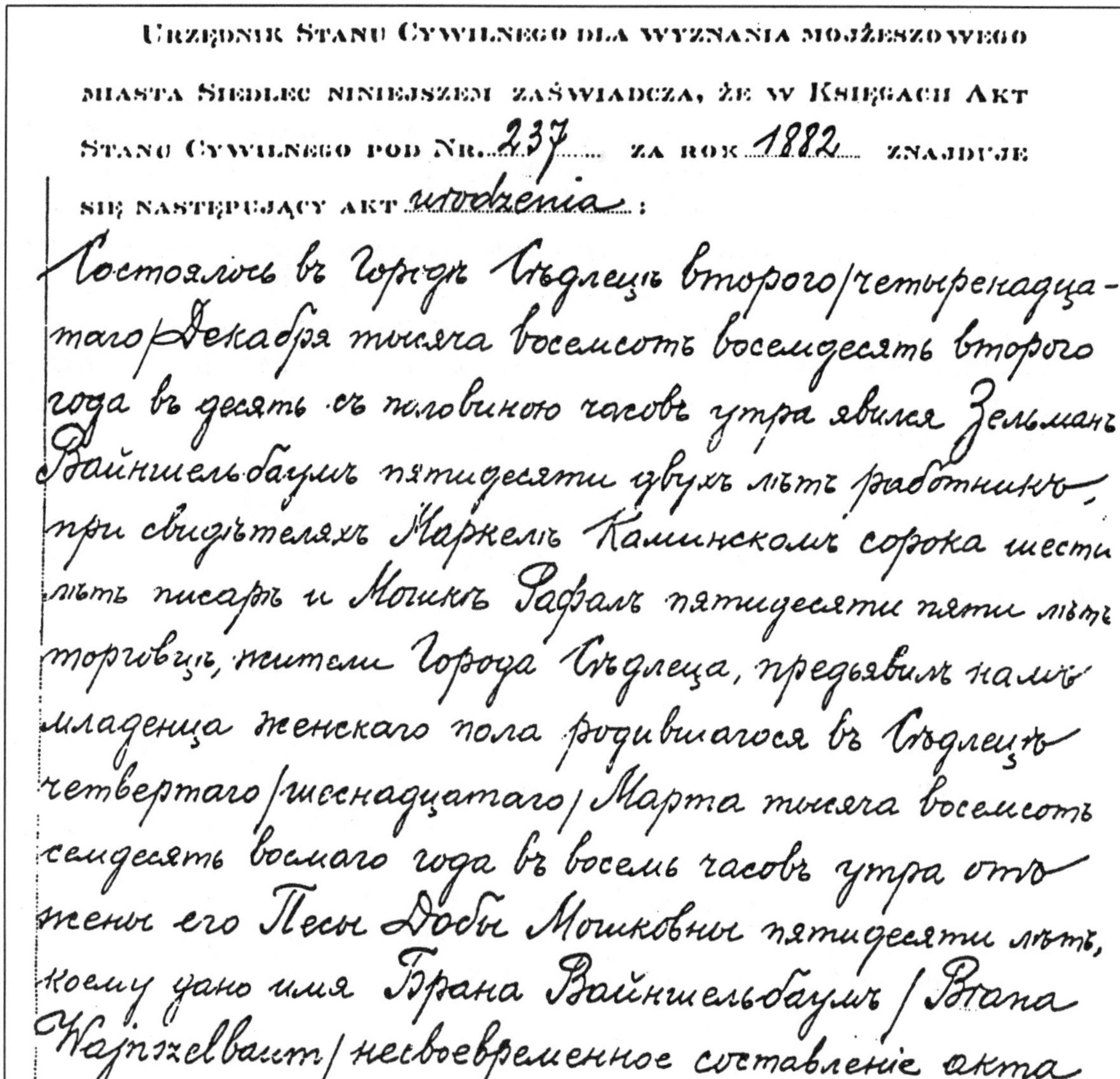

URZĘDNIK STANU CYWILNEGO DLA WYZNANIA MOJŻESZOWEGO MIASTA SIEDLEC NINIEJSZEM ZAŚWIADCZA, ŻE W KSIĘGACH AKT STANU CYWILNEGO POD NR. 237 ZA ROK 1882 ZNAJDUJE SIĘ NASTĘPUJĄCY AKT urodzenia:

Состоялось въ Городѣ Сѣдлецѣ второго/четырнадцатаго/ Декабря тысяча восемсотъ восемдесять второго года въ десять съ половиною часовъ утра явился Зельманъ Вайншельбаумъ пятидесяти двухъ лѣтъ работникъ, при свидѣтеляхъ Маркелъ Каминскомъ сорока шести лѣтъ писарь и Мошкѣ Рафалъ пятидесяти пяти лѣтъ торговцѣ, жители Города Сѣдлеца, предъявилъ намъ младенца женскаго пола родившагося въ Сѣдлецѣ четвертаго/шеснадцатаго/ Марта тысяча восемсотъ семдесять восмаго года въ восемь часовъ утра отъ жены его Песы Добы Мошковны пятидесяти лѣтъ, коему дано имя Брана Вайншельбаумъ /Brana Wajnszelbaum/ несвоевременное составленіе акта сего произошло по той причинѣ что отецъ дитяти вовремя рожденія оного находился на работѣ въ другихъ городахъ долгое время, возвратившись полагалъ что жена его сдѣлала надлежащее заявленіе о рожденіи дитяти.- Актъ сей по прочтеніи присутствующимъ нами и свидѣтелями подписанъ отецъ же писать не умѣетъ.- Содержащій Книги Гражданскаго Состоянія /-/ Podpis nieczytelny /-/ Podpis nieczytelny /-/ Podpis nieczytelny.-

Document VI-10: A Written Transcript of a Jewish Birth Record from Russian Poland

въ десять съ половиною часовъ утра — literally "at ten with a half of the morning." For information on expressions of time see pages 49-50. This record is unusual; few registrars bothered to give times accurate to half an hour!

Зельманъ Вайншельбаумъ — again the question arises of the appropriate spelling of a proper name. Since this occurred in Poland, it is likely this man went by the Polish form of his name more often than any other, so that *Zelman Wajnszelbaum* is the best way to render it. But you should be aware his surname could be spelled German-style, *Weinschelbaum,* or English-style, *Vaynshelbaum,* depending on circumstances. Beider's book on Jewish surnames in the Kingdom of Poland says it comes originally from Yiddish ווײַנשלבוים *vaynshlboym,* "cherry tree."

при свидѣтеляхъ Маркелѣ Каминскомъ сорока шести лѣтъ писарѣ и Мошкѣ Рафалѣ пятидесяти пяти лѣтъ торговцѣ жители города Сѣдлеца — "in the presence of witnesses, Markel Kamiński, age 46, a scribe, and Moszek Rafał, age 55, a merchant, residents of the town of Siedlce..."

при свидѣтеляхъ - here, instead of the standard keywords *въ присутствіи,* "in the presence of," followed by the witnesses' names in the genitive case, the clerk used a less common formulation. The preposition *при,* which requires prepositional-case endings, means basically "in, at, in the presence of"; so it's another way of saying the same thing. This explains why the witnesses' names are in the prepositional, *Маркелѣ* and *Мошкѣ,* instead of the genitive. Incidentally, the first name of the second witness could also be *Moszka* or possibly *Moszko*—it's impossible to tell which is appropriate. *Moszek, Moszka,* and *Moszko* are all diminutives of משה, the Biblical name that appears in standard Polish as *Mojżesz,* and in English as "Moses."

предъявилъ намъ младенца женскаго пола — "he presented to us a female child..."

родившагося въ Сѣдлецѣ четвертаго /шеснадцатаго/ Марта тысяча восемсотъ семдесять восмаго года въ восемь часовъ утра — "born in Siedlce on the 4th/16th of March, 1878, at 8 a. m...." Obviously there has been a delay in reporting the birth of this child, which is explained later on.

родившагося - this is a past active participle of the verb *родиться,* "to be born," and thus means "[the one] having been born." Here it's in the accusative singular because it modifies *младенца,* the direct object of the predicate *предъявилъ.* The standard keyword marking information on the child's place and date of birth is *родился,* but you can see that this means essentially the same thing.

отъ жены его Песы Добы Мошковны пятидесяти лѣтъ — "to his wife Pesa Doba, daughter of Moszek, age 50..."

коему дано имя Брана Вайншельбаумъ /Brana Wajnszelbaum/ — "to whom was given the name Brana Wajnszelbaum."

коему - this is the dative form of a relative pronoun *кой,* which means "who, which, that." If you plug this word in to replace the keywords *Младенцу этому* you'll see that this is only a slight rewording of the standard phrase telling what name the child was given.

Несвоевременное составленіе акта сего произошло по той причинѣ что отецъ дитяти вовремя рожденія онаго находился на работѣ въ другихъ городахъ долгое время, возвратившись полагалъ что жена его сдѣлала надлежащее заявленіе о рожденіи дитяти — "The late creation of this document occurred because at the time of the birth the child's father was working in other towns for a long time; after he had returned, he supposed that his wife had made the appropriate announcement of the child's birth."

несвоевременное составленіе акта сего произошло по той причинѣ – *несвоевремменый* means "unseasonable, inopportune, untimely"; but if you break it down into its components it means literally "not in its own time," and that explains the sense here: this birth was not registered at the proper time. The noun *составленіе* is from the verb *составить*, which means, among other things, "to create, write." The form *произошло* is from the verb *произойти*, "to arise from, spring from, occur." So a literal translation would be "The untimely drawing up of this act occurred for this reason." But the translation given above means the same thing and is a bit smoother.

отецъ дитяти – "the father of the child"

вовремя рожденія онаго – the form *онаго* is genitive masculine singular of the archaic pronoun *оный*, "this, that." So this means literally "at the time of the birth of that one [i. e., the child]."

находился на работѣ въ другихъ городахъ долгое время – literally "found himself at work in other cities a long time." The verb *находиться* means "to find oneself," but it is used in various expressions to mean "to be located" or simply "to be."

возвратившись – here we see a participle used adverbially to express something that requires several words in English. The past active participle of *возвратиться*, "to return, come back,"this word means literally "having returned," but in English we might also say "upon his return" or "after having returned."

полагалъ что – the verb *полагать* means literally "to put, place," but is used in some expressions to mean "suppose, think." Here it can legitimately be translated "he supposed that...."

жена его сдѣлала надлежащее заявленіе о рожденіи дитяти – *сдѣлала*, the past tense, feminine singular of the verb *сдѣлать*, means "made, did." The father assumed his wife had already made the necessary announcement *(заявленіе)* of the child's birth. The adjective *надлежащий* means "due, necessary, expedient, required."

Sometimes far less detail is given on why a document was drawn up later than it should have been. You may simply see a note such as *Актъ сей замедлилъ по винѣ отца*, "This act was delayed due to the fault of the father."

Актъ сей по прочтеніи присутствующимъ нами и свидѣтелями подписанъ отецъ же писать не умѣетъ. — "This document, after being read aloud to those present, was signed by us and by the witnesses; the father cannot write."

по прочтеніи присустсвующимъ – literally "after reading [aloud] to the [ones] present."

отецъ писать не умѣетъ – this is one of several ways of declaring that someone was illiterate; the verb *уметь* means "to know how [to do something]," so this means literally "the father does not know how to write."

Содержащій Книги Гражданскаго Состоянія — "[Signed] The Civil Registrar," literally "the one keeping the books of the Civil Register."

Podpis nieczytelny — This Polish phrase means "signature illegible." The signatures of the witnesses may have been written in the Hebrew alphabet (see pages 16-20). More likely all three signatures were simply illegible. Only a look at the original record would tell.

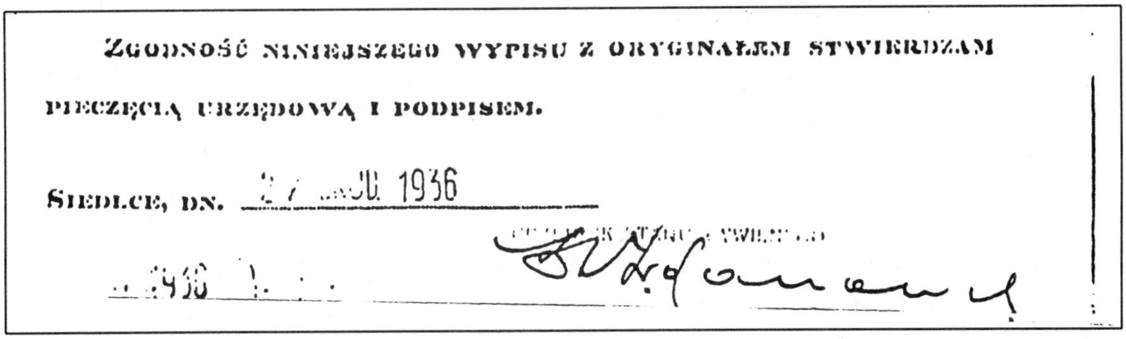
ZGODNOŚĆ NINIEJSZEGO WYPISU Z ORYGINAŁEM STWIERDZAM

PIECZĘCIĄ URZĘDOWĄ I PODPISEM.

SIEDLCE, DN. ... 1936

The section above appeared at the bottom of Document VI-10, but would not fit on page 218 without reducing the rest of that document to an undesirable extent. We include it here just for the sake of completeness. It says in Polish that the record keeper certifies the accuracy of this copy with his signature and his seal of office. It is signed "Siedlce, 27 Grud. 1936" (December 26, 1936); the signature itself is illegible, as is often true in these records.

8. Document VI-11: A Written Attestation of Determination of Age

Document VI-11 on page 222 is a slightly different kind of record. When a birth was not officially registered, a substitute birth attestation needed to be drawn up, according to strictly delineated regulations. Believe it or not, we have done a little digital enhancement on this sample—the original had a lot of "bleed-through" blotches.

The 10 lines at the upper left of the document read as follows:

Протоколъ опредѣленія возраста *Ханѣ Гершоновнѣ Кадышъ* записан*ной* въ книгѣ народонаселенія *пос. Цѣхановца подъ N. D. 8 на страницѣ* 440 — "Record of the proceedings of the determination of the age of Chana Kadysz, daughter of Gerszon, registered in the Book of Permanent Population of the town of Ciechanowiec, under [House?] Number 8, on page 440."

протоколъ – "record of proceedings, evidence"
опредѣленія – genitive of *опредѣленіе*, "determination, establishment, fixing, settling"
восраста – genitive of *возрастъ*, "age"
въ книгѣ народонаселенія – "in the Book of Permanent Population." The *книга [постояннаго] народонаселенія* was a register kept of the residents of a given locality—a valuable source of data, if the one for your ancestral community has survived. Compare Documents VI-34, pp. 299-302, and VI-49, pp. 338-341.
пос. Цѣхановца – "of the settlement of Ciechanowiec"
на страницѣ 440 – "on page 440"; *страница* is the standard term for "page"

Now, beginning at the top of the page, here is the information provided:

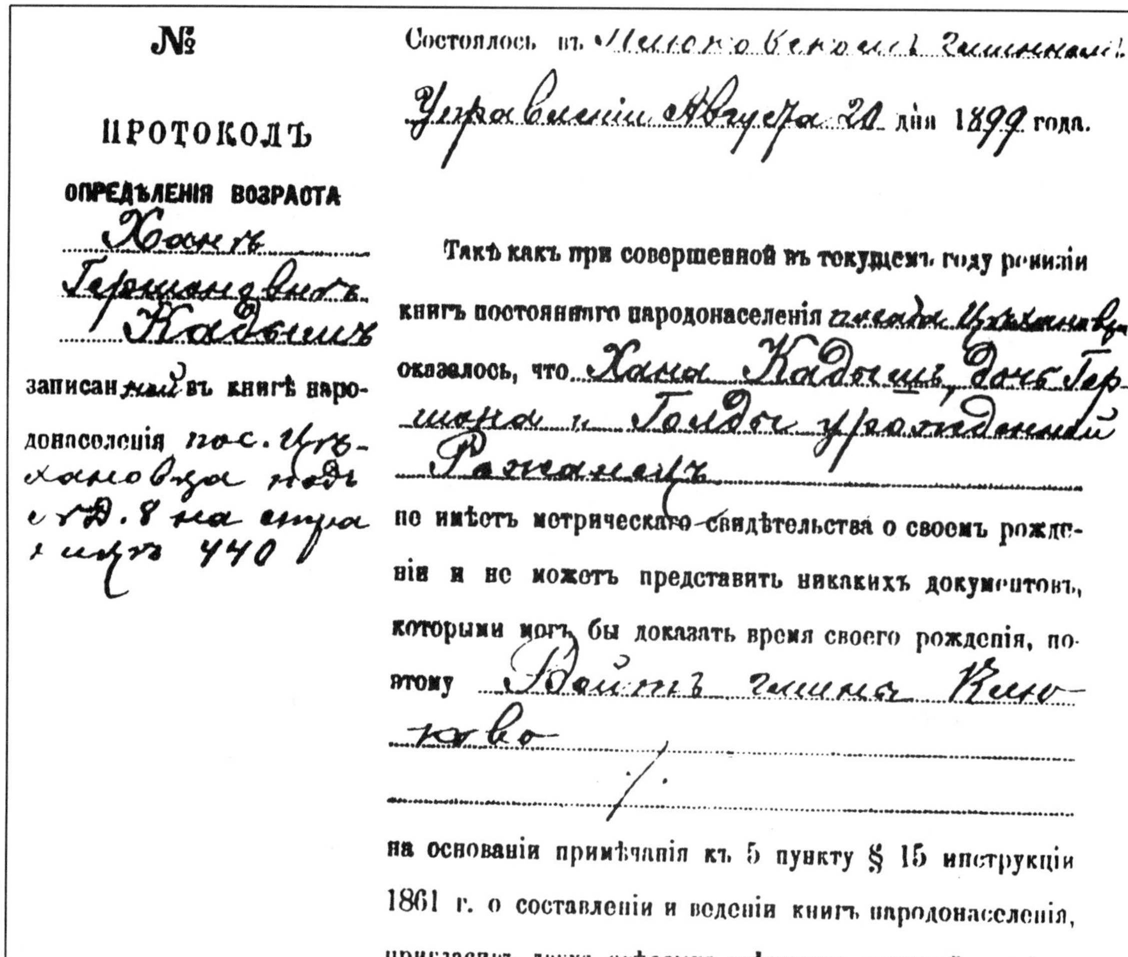

№

ПРОТОКОЛЪ

ОПРЕДѢЛЕНІЯ ВОЗРАСТА

Ханы Гершановны Кадыщъ

записанной въ книгѣ народонаселенія пос. Ицхановка подъ с.Д. 8 на странице 440

Состоялось въ Милюковскомъ Гминномъ Управленіи Августа 20 дня 1899 года.

Такъ какъ при совершенной въ текущемъ году ревизіи книгъ постояннаго народонаселенія гмина Ицхановка оказалось, что Хана Кадыщъ, дочь Гершона и Голды урожденной Рахманъ

не имѣетъ метрическаго свидѣтельства о своемъ рожденіи и не можетъ представить никакихъ документовъ, которыми могъ бы доказать время своего рожденія, поэтому Войтъ гмина Милюково

/.

на основаніи примѣчанія къ 5 пункту § 15 инструкціи 1861 г. о составленіи и веденіи книгъ народонаселенія, пригласивъ двухъ осѣдлыхъ здѣшнихъ жителей, извѣстныхъ хорошею нравственностью, именно:

1. Айзика Гонячка
2. Хаима Плошка

съ коими по личному удостовѣренію, явившаяся лично

опредѣлили

девятнадцать лѣтъ (19)

слѣдовательно родилась въ тысяча восемьсотъ во семьдесятомъ году.

При томъ призванные свидѣтели пояснили, что мѣсто рожденія Ханы Кадыщъ есть имъ извѣстно, т. е. въ пос. Ицхановка

Document VI-11: A Written Attestation of Determination of Age

Состоялось въ *Клюковскомъ Гминномъ Управленіи Августа 20* дня *1899* года — "This took place in the Klukowo District Administrative Offices on August 20, 1899."

въ Клюковскомъ Гминномъ Управленіи – а *гмина* (Polish *gmina*) was (and still is) a district, a smaller subdivision than an *уѣздъ* (Polish *powiat*), which is somewhat comparable to a county in the United States. Here we see the adjectival form *гминный*, "of a *gmina.*" *Управление* is the standard term for "administration." So this happened in the administrative office of the district of Klukowo, a village north of Ciechanowiec.

Такъ какъ при совершенной въ текущемъ году ревизіи книгъ постояннаго народонаселенія *посады Цѣхановца* оказалосъ, что... — "Inasmuch as during a review of the Books of Permanent Population for the Town of Ciechanowiec in the current year it was shown that..."

такъ какъ –literally "so how" or "so as," as a conjunction it means "since, inasmuch as."

при совершенной ... ревизіи – literally "during a conducted ... review"; *ревизія* can mean "census" (see samples of *Revizskie skazki,* pages 317-320), but it can also be used to mean "revision" or "review."

въ текущемъ году – "in the current year"

оказалось, что – the verb *оказаться* means "to show oneself, appear, prove, turn out." Often *оказалось, что* can be translated "it turned out that," but here "it was shown that" or "it became evident that" may be a bit more accurate.

Хана Кадышъ, дочь Гершона и Голды урожденной Рѣжанецъ — "Chana Kadysz, daughter of Gerszon and Golda née Reżaniec..." The second letter of the maiden name is difficult to make out; *Рожанетцъ*, Rożaniec, is also a plausible reading.

не имѣетъ метрическаго свидѣтельства о своемъ рожденіи — "does not have a registry certificate of her birth..."

не имѣет – "does not have," from the verb *иметь*, "to have, possess"; when negated, like most Russian verbs, it takes a direct object in the genitive case.

и не можетъ представить никакихъ документовъ, которыми могъ бы доказать время своего рожденія — "and cannot present any documents with which [she] could prove the time of her birth..."

не можетъ представить никакихъ документовъ — literally "cannot present no documents"; in Russian double and even triple negatives are perfectly correct.

которыми – this form is the instrumental plural of *который*, "who, which, that," used here to refer to *документовъ*, "documents by means of which."

могъ бы доказать время своего рожденія – usually documents provide a way of indicating the correct gender form of a verb for males or females, but in this instance only the masculine form *могъ бы*, "could," is given. The particle *бы* indicates the verb is in the subjunctive mood, but that subject is rather more complicated than most researchers want to deal with. Simply remember, when you see it, that *бы* means the verb is referring to something that could or might happen, or to something contrary to fact. You won't encounter it often enough in documents to be worth the trouble of discussing it at any length.

по-этому *Войтъ гмины Клюково* на основанiи примѣчанiя къ 5 пункту § 15 инструкцiи 1861 г. о составленiи и веденiи книгъ народонаселенiя, пригласивъ двухъ осѣдлыхъ здѣшнихъ жителей, извѣстныхъ хорошею нравственностью, именно: 1) *Айзыка Гонсяка* 2) *Хаима Пташка*— "for this reason the *Wójt* of the district of Klukowo, on the basis of the observations in point 5, paragraph 15 of the instructions dated 1861 regarding the establishment and conducting of the permanent population register, and having called in two permanent local residents known to be of good character, namely: 1) Ajzyk Gąsiak 2) Chaim Ptaszek..."

по-этому – a combination of the preposition *по*, which can mean "by, according to," and the dative singular masculine/neuter of *этот*, "this" (see page 42).

Войтъ –a Russian rendering of the Polish term *wójt,* the chief administrative officer of a *gmina* or district; in larger communities, the *wójt* was more or less the same as a mayor. Here the *wójt* of Klukowo district took the action prescribed by law in such cases.

на основанiи примѣчанiя къ 5 пункту § 15 инструкцiи 1861 г. о составленiи и веденiи книгъ народонаселенiя – literally "on the basis of the note to point 5, paragraph 15 of the instructions of the year 1861 on establishing and keeping books of population...."

пригласивъ двухъ осѣдлыхъ здѣшныхъ жителей – *пригласивъ* is an adverbial participle from *пригласить*, "to invite, engage, call in," and *жителей* is accusative plural of *житель*, "resident." So literally this says "having called in two *[двухъ]* permanent *[посѣдлыхъ, literally "settled"]* local *[здѣшнiхъ]* residents."

извѣстныхъ хорошею нравственностью – this phrase further describes the two permanent local residents literally as "known by means of good morality."

именно: 1) Айзыка Гонсяка 2) Хаима Пташка – *именно* means "namely, by name." The Polish forms of their names would be *Ajzyk Gąsiak* (or perhaps *Gonsiak*) and *Chaim Ptaszek.* If you pronounce *Айзыкъ* or *Ayzyk* aloud you can hear the resemblance to "Isaac," and in fact this name derives from the Biblical name which is *Isaac* in English.

съ коими по личному удостовѣренiю, явившейся лично опредѣлили — "with whom it was determined by the personal statement of the party, who appeared in person..."

съ коими – *коими* is the instrumental plural of the archaic pronoun *кой*, "who, which."

по личному удостовѣренiю – "by the personal statement." Another meaning of *по* with the dative can be "by, according to, on the basis of."

явившейся лично _ – "of the one appearing in person." The participle *явившейся* is genitive singular feminine, and is referring to Chana Kadysz.

опредѣлили – "they determined," from *опредѣлить*, "to determine, establish, define."

девятнадцать *лѣтъ (19)* слѣдовательно родилась въ тысяча восемьсотъ *восемьдесятомъ* году — "[that she is] 19 years old, and consequently was born in the year 1880"

слѣдовательно – "consequently, therefore"

При томъ признанные свидѣтели пояснили, что мѣсто рожденiя *Ханы Кадышъ* есть имъ извѣстно, т. е., въ *пос. Цѣхановцѣ*. — "At the same time the recognized witnesses explained that the place of birth of Chana Kadysz is known to them, i. e., in the town of Ciechanowiec."

пояснили – "they explained," from *пояснить*, "to clarify, explain, elucidate."

мѣсто рожденiя – "place of birth"

есть имъ извѣстно – literally "is to them known." It is rather rare to see *есть* used in this way. It means literally "is," but in modern Russian this verb is not normally expressed.

Translation — "Record of proceedings to determine the age of Chana Kadysz, the daughter of Gerszon, entered in the Population Register of the town of Ciechanowiec, under House Number 8, on page 440. This took place in the Klukowo District Administrative Offices on August 20, 1899.

"Inasmuch as during a review of the Permanent Population Register for the Town of Ciechanowiec in the current year, it was shown that Chana Kadysz, daughter of Gerszon and Golda née Reżaniec, has no registry certificate of her birth, and can present no documents with which [she] could prove the time of her birth, for this reason the *Wójt* of Klukowo district, on the basis of the observations in point 5, paragraph 15 of the instructions dated 1861 regarding establishment and keeping of the permanent population register, having called in two permanent local residents known to be of good character, namely: 1) Ajzyk Gąsiak 2) Chaim Ptaszek, established with them by personal observation of the party, who appeared in person, that she is 19 years old, and consequently was born in the year 1880. At the same time the acknowledged witnesses explained that the place of birth of Chana Kadysz is known to them, i. e., in the town of Ciechanowiec."

9. Document VI-12: A Russian Orthodox Columnar Baptismal Record

All the birth records we have seen so far were paragraph-form, either original entries in birth registers or certificates quoting such entries. The other common format consisted of columns with printed headings asking questions, which were answered with handwritten notes in the columns below each heading. These are somewhat easier to translate, but still require some familiarity with the phraseology of the questions and typical answers.

Document VI-12 is a columnar-form copy of a baptismal record from a register of a Russian Orthodox parish in Riga, Latvia. The left half appears at the top of page 226, the right half on the top of page 227. This register is printed in an archaic typeface modeled after the version of Cyrillic used in Old Church Slavonic. The letters are highly stylized, but most are easy to recognize once you have become accustomed to standard Cyrillic (see also page 48). You see ѧ used instead of modern Russian **Я**, and ѡ, based on the Greek omega ω, for **O**. The extended form of *y*, looking almost like an English numeral 8, looks a bit exotic at first glance.

The heading across the top reads: ВЫПИСЬ ИЗЪ МЕТРИЧЕСКОЙ КНИГИ, ЧАСТЬ ПЕРВАѦ, ѡ РОДИВШИХСѦ, ЗА *1905* ГОДЪ – "Extract from a Register, Part One, Of Births, for the Year 1905." As we have remarked earlier (see page 213), Russian registers are typically divided into three parts, of which the first is devoted to births.

Column 1: Счетъ родившихсѧ | Мужеска пола | Женска пола – "Birth Number | Males | Females." Entries were number sequentially as they were made, and this entry is for the 60th female born in 1905/. Note that by modern Russian grammar the indication of gender should be *мужского пола* or *женского пола*, but this is an older, more traditional way of expressing the same thing.

Column 2: Мѣсяцъ и день | рожденіѧ | крещеніѧ – "Month and day of | birth | baptism." Here the child was born on October 6th, baptized on October 16th.

Выпись изъ метрической книги, часть

Счетъ родившихся: Мужеска пола	Счетъ родившихся: Женска пола	Месяцъ и день: рожденія	Месяцъ и день: крещенія	Имена родившихся.	Званіе, имя, отчество и фамилія родителей, и какого вѣроисповѣданія.
	60.	Октября 6.	16	Софія.	Верроскій мѣщанинъ, Лифляндской губерніи, Антоній Петровъ Барановъ и законная жена его Сусанна Іосифова, - оба православнаго вѣроисповѣданія.

Document VI-12 (left side)

Column 3: Имена родивхишсѧ – “Names of those born,” here *Софія*, “Sofiya.”

Column 4: Званіе, имѧ, отчество, и фамилія родителей, и какогѡ вѣроисповѣданіѧ – “Status, first name, patronymic, and surname of the parents, and of what faith.

Верроскій мъщанинъ Лифляндской гуербніи Антоній Петровъ Барановъ и законная жена его Сусанна Іосифова, - оба православнаго въроисповъданія – “A burgher of the town of Verro, of Livonia province, Antoniy Baranov, son of Pyotr, and his lawful wife Susanna, daughter of Iosif, - both of the Orthodox faith.” *Антоній* (in Polish *Antoni,* in German *Anton*) was the son of *Pyotr/Piotr/Peter,* depending on which language proves appropriate; the surname *Baranov* suggests it might be Russian. His wife was *Susanna* or *Zuzanna,* daughter of *Joseph/ Józef/Iosif.*

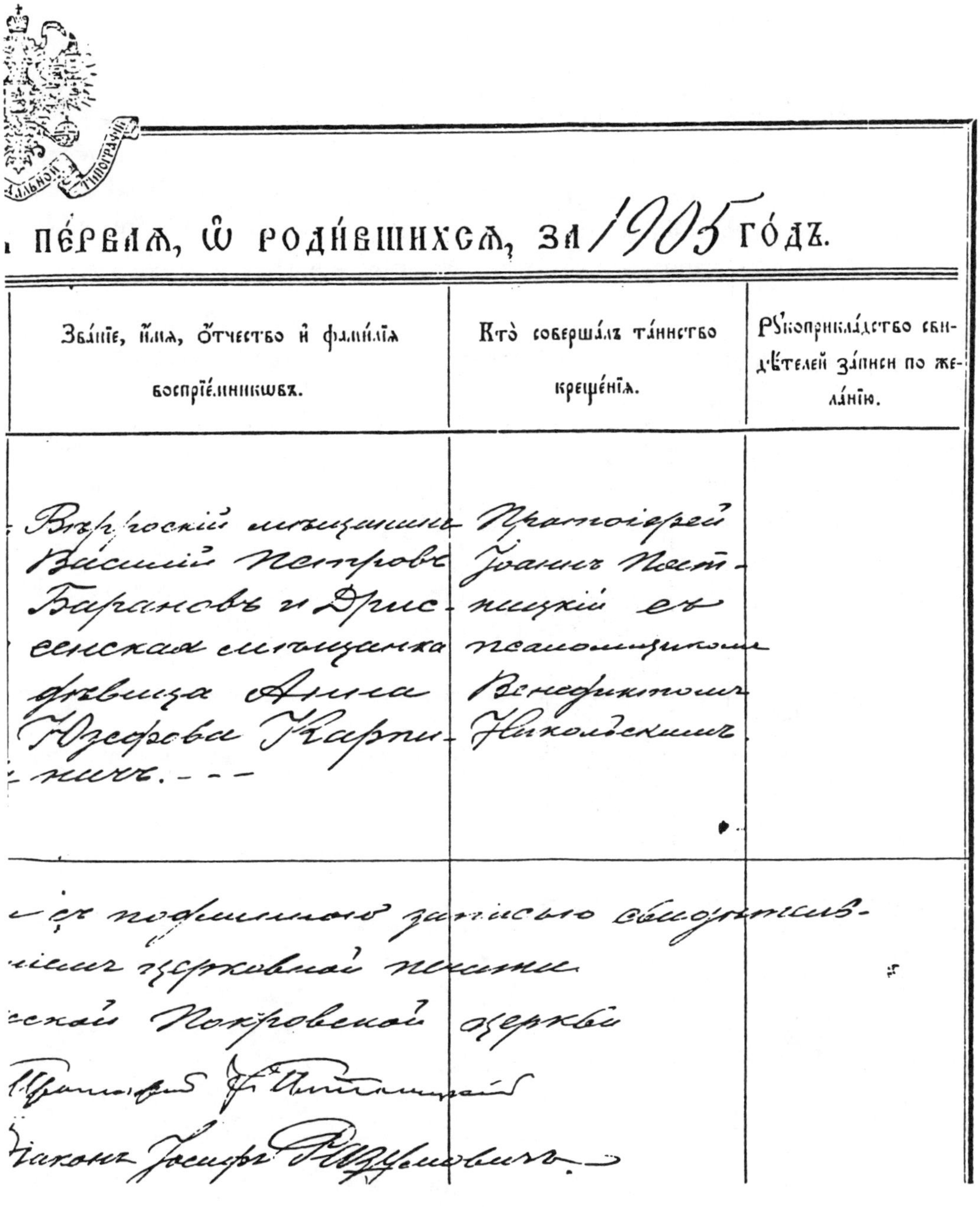

ПЕРВАЯ, О РОДИВШИХСЯ, ЗА 1905 ГОДЪ.

Званіе, имя, отчество и фамилія воспріемниковъ.	Кто совершалъ таинство крещенія.	Рукоприкладство свидѣтелей записи по желанію.
Верроскій мѣщанинъ Василій Петровъ Барановъ и Дриссенская мѣщанка дѣвица Анна Юзефова Карпиничъ.---	Протоіерей Іоаннъ Пет-ницкій съ псаломщикомъ Венедиктомъ Николаевскимъ.	

...съ подлинною записью свидѣтельствую...
...церковной ...
...ской Покровской церкви
Протоіерей І. [illegible]
Діаконъ Іосифъ [illegible]

Document VI-12 (right side)

Column 5: Званіе, имѧ, отчество, и фамилія воспріемниковъ – “Status, first name, patronymic, and surname of the godparents.”

Верроскій мѣщанинъ Василій Петровъ Барановъ и Дриссенская мѣщанка дѣвица Анна Юзефова Карпиничъ. – “A burgher of the town of Verro, Vasiliy Baranov, son of Pyotr, and a burgher of the town of Drissa, a single woman, Anna Karpinich, daughter of Juzef.” That Vasiliy has the last patronymic and surname as Antoniy suggests he may have been his brother – but only research could confirm that.

As for the godmother, she was from the town of *Дрисса, Drissa,* now *Веркхнядзвінск, Verkhnyadzvinsk,* in northwestern Belarus, just across the border from Latvia. Her father’s name *Юзеф* suggests he was a Pole, *Józef.*

Column 6: Кто совершалъ таинство крещеніѧ – “Who administered the sacrament of Baptism?”

Протоіерей Іоаннъ Пятницкій съ псаломщикомъ Венедиктомъ Никольскимъ – “Arch-priest Ioann Piatnitski, with psalmist Venedikt Nikol'skiy.” A *протоіерей* is a senior priest, and a *псаломщик* is a church attendant who reads the psalms during services and generally assists the pastor with church duties.

Column 7: Рукопридладство свидѣтелей записи по желанію – “Signature of the witnesses, comments as desired.” The witnesses apparently did not sign the register, and the priest saw no need to append any comments.

The note written across the length of the page below this entry is standard: *Вѣрность сей метрической выписи съ подлинною записью свидѣтельствуемъ подписью съ приложеніемъ церковнои печати. Рижскій Покровеной церкви* – “We certify the accuracy of this metrical copy from the original entry with our signature and by affixing the church’s seal. Riga Church of the Pokrov” [a feast commemorating the Intercession of the Blessed Mother, October 1st]. The priest’s signature is illegible; the deacon was Iosif Razumovich.

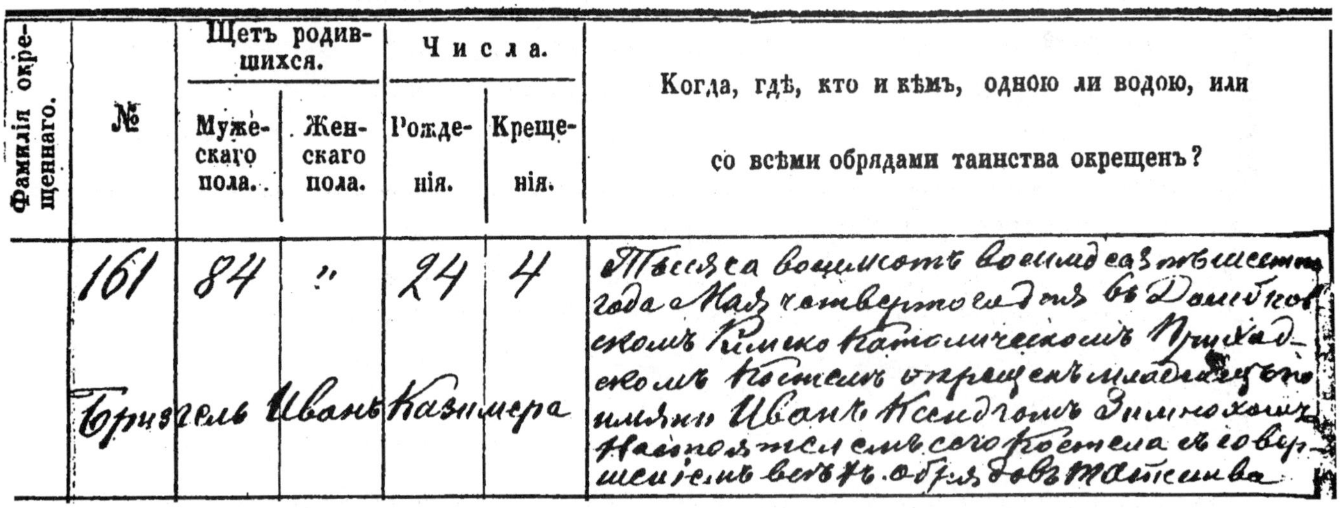

Фамилія окрещеннаго.	№	Щетъ родившихся.		Числа.		Когда, гдѣ, кто и кѣмъ, одною ли водою, или со всѣми обрядами таинства окрещенъ?
		Мужескаго пола.	Женскаго пола.	Рожденія.	Крещенія.	
	161	84	"	24	4	Тысяча восемьсотъ восемьдесятъ шестого года Мая четвертого дня въ Домбровскомъ Римско Католическомъ Приходскомъ Костелѣ окрещенъ младенецъ по имени Иванъ Ксендзомъ [illegible]
	Бризгель Иванъ Казимера					

10. Document VI-13: A Catholic Columnar Baptismal Record from Russian Poland

This columnar baptismal record is from a Catholic church in Russian Poland. It runs horizontally across two pages of the register. The right half is on page 229.

Фамилія окрещеннаго — “Surname of the one baptized.” Note that instead of filling in the space, the priest wrote the name vertically across the next few columns: *Бризгель Иванъ Казимера,* “Bryzgiel, Jan, son of Kazimierz.” In records of this sort the father’s name, in the genitive case, appears as the third element—this is not the child’s middle name!

№ *161* — Sequential # 161, i. e., the 161st birth and baptism registered in this time period.

щетъ родившихся | мужескаго пола | женскаго пола — “Number of the birth | male | female,” in this case #84 of the males. Here *щетъ* is probably a variant of *счёт.*

числа | рожденія | крещенія) — “Dates of the birth | baptism.” In this case the birth was on the 24th, the baptism on the 4th. (The month and year are specified in columns 7 and 8).

Когда, гдѣ, кто и кѣмъ, одною ли водою, или со всѣми обрядами таинства окрещенъ — "When, where, who, by whom, baptized with water alone or with all the rites of the sacrament?" Here is the answer in printed form, to make the words easier to recognize. Key elements are marked with bracketed numbers, which we have inserted (they aren't in the original text): [1] the **date of baptism**, [2] **name of the parish**, the [3] **child's first name**, and the [4] **name of the officiating priest**:

[1] Тысяча восемсотъ восемдесять шестого года Мая четвертого дня [2] въ Домбровскомъ Римско-Католическомъ Приходскомъ Костелѣ окрещенъ младенецъ по имяни [3] Иванъ, [4] Ксендзомъ Зимнохомъ настоятелемъ сего костела, съ совершініемъ всѣхъ обрядовъ Таинства.

[1] In the year 1886 on May 4th [2] in the Dąbrowa Roman Catholic parish church a child was baptized by name [3] Jan [4] by Rev. Zimnoch, the pastor of this church, with all the rites of the sacrament.

This priest didn't **transliterate** the child's first name *Jan* as *Янъ*, but **translated** it as its Russian equivalent, *Иванъ*. Also unusual is *по имяни*, instead of standard *по имени*, "by name."

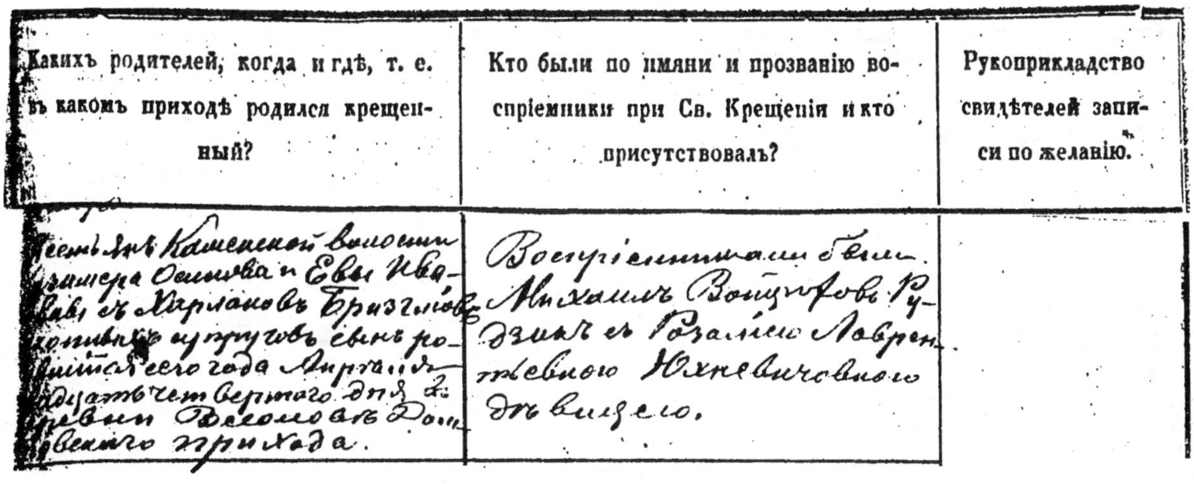

Какихъ родителей, когда и гдѣ, т. е. въ какомъ приходѣ родился крещенный?	Кто были по имяни и прозванію воспріемники при Св. Крещеніи и кто присутствовалъ?	Рукоприкладство свидѣтелей записи по желанію.
Крестьянъ Каменской волости Казимера Осипова и Евы Ивановны съ Харлановъ Бризгловъ законныхъ супруговъ сынъ родившійся сего года Априля двадцать четвертаго дня въ деревни Весолове Домбровскаго прихода.	Воспріемниками были Михаилъ Войцеховъ Рудзинскій съ Розаліею Лаврентьевною Юхневичовною дѣвицею.	

Какихъ родителей, когда и гдѣ, т. е., въ какомъ приходѣ родился крещенный? – "Of what parents, when and where, i. e., in which parish was the baptized person born?" The answers are given in this order: [1] Father's name, [2] mother's name, [3] surname, [4] date of birth, [5] place of birth:

Крестьянъ Каменской волости [1] Казимера Осипова и [2] Евы Ивановны съ Харлановъ [3] Бризгловъ законныхъ супруговъ сынъ родившійся сего года [4] Апреля двадцать четвертаго дня [5] въ деревни Весолове Домбровскаго прихода:

Of peasants of Kamienna district [1] Kazimierz, son of Józef and [2] Ewa daughter of Jan née Charłan, [3] Bryzgiel, lawful spouses, the son, born this year [4] on April the 24th day, [5] in the village of Wesołowo, Dąbrowa parish.

A smoother translation of this would be: "[He is] the son of peasants residing in the district of Kamienna, the lawfully wedded couple, the Bryzgiels: Kazimierz, son of Józef, and Ewa, daughter of Jan, née Charłan. He was born on the 24th of April of this year in the village of Wesołowo, Parish of Dąbrowa."

Кто были по имяни и прозванiю воспрiемники при Св. Крещенiи и кто присутствовалъ? — "Who were the godparents, by first name and any other name, and who was present at Holy Baptism?"

Воспрiемниками были Михаилъ Войцѣховъ Рудзикъ съ Розалiею Лаврентьевною Юхневичовною дѣвицею.	*The godparents were Michał Rudzik, son of Wojciech, and Rozalia daughter of Wawrzyniec, Juchniewicz, a maiden.*

Рукоприкладство свидѣтелей записи по желанiю: "Witnesses' signatures and any notes desired." This is the same formula we saw in the final column of Document VI-12. Here, too, neither the signature of the witnesses nor any comments are given.

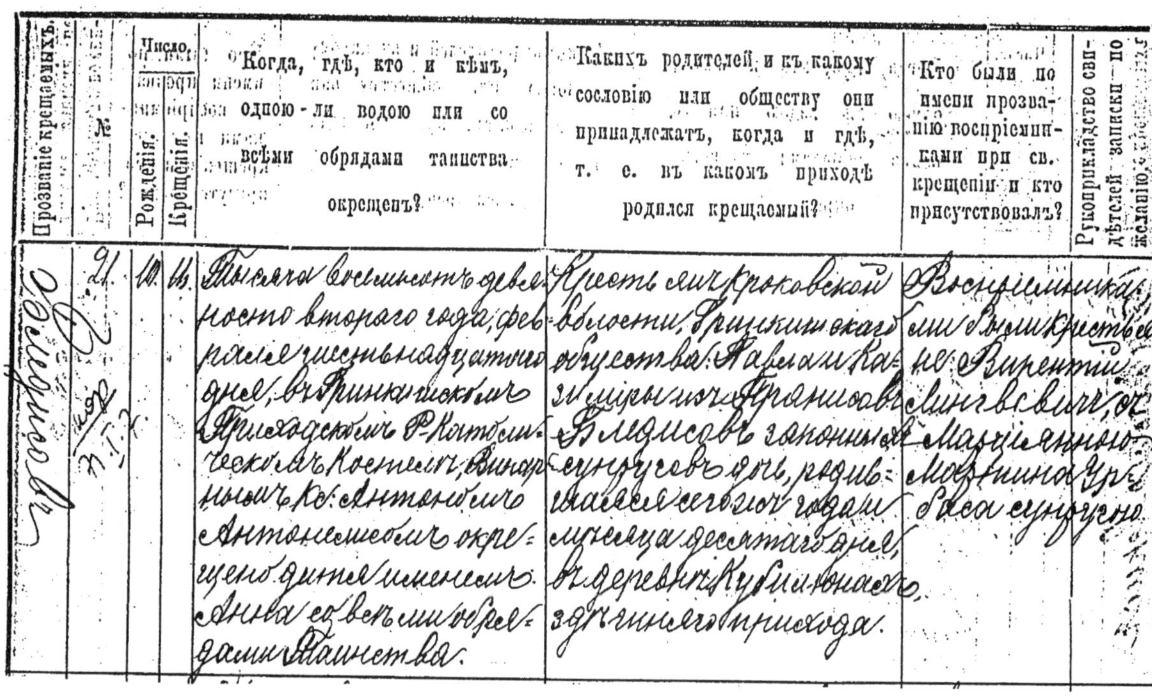

Прозванiе крещаемыхъ.	№	Число: Рожденiя.	Число: Крещенiя.	Когда, гдѣ, кто и кѣмъ, одною-ли водою или со всѣми обрядами таинства окрещенъ?	Какихъ родителей и къ какому сословiю или обществу они принадлежатъ, когда и гдѣ, т. е. въ какомъ приходѣ родился крещаемый?	Кто были по имени прозванiю воспрiемниками при св. крещенiи и кто присутствовалъ?	Рукоприкладство свидѣтелей записки по желанiю
[illegible]	21.	10.	16.	Тысяча восемьсотъ девяносто второго года, февраля шестнадцатаго дня, въ [illegible] Приходскомъ Р.-Католическомъ Костелѣ, Викарный Кс. Антоній Антоновичъ окрещено дитя именемъ Анна со всѣми обрядами Таинства.	Крестьянъ [illegible] волости, [illegible] общества: Павла Казиміровича [illegible] законныхъ супруговъ дочь, родившаяся сего года мѣсяца десятаго дня, въ деревнѣ [illegible] здѣшняго прихода.	Воспріемниками были [illegible] съ Маріянною [illegible] супругою.	

Document VI-14: A Catholic Columnar Baptismal Record from Lithuania

Document VI-14, reproduced above, is a similar record, from the baptismal register of a Roman Catholic parish in Lithuania. Since it is much like the others we've seen, we will not analyze it in depth. Instead we give a brief breakdown of each column heading and the handwritten information in each column, for comparison to the previous samples.

Прозваніе крещаемыхъ: ***Бледисовъ*** — "Surname of the ones being baptized: *Bledisov* (of the Bledises)." It is not uncommon for surnames to be listed in Russian with the ending *-ов* (*-ov*) or *-ев* (*-ev*). In fact, native Russian surnames often have that ending. For a non-Russian, however, you generally remove that ending and restore any native endings that may have been dropped before it was added. Here none were; **Bledis** is the Lithuanian form of the surname.

№: *21.* — "Number: 21," that is, entry #21 in the baptismal register. There is one slight difference between the format of this and the previous two records: this one does not number births by sex, but only gives a total for all births of both sexes.

Число Рожденія: *10* — "Date of Birth: 10." The noun **Число** refers to both **Рожденія**, "of birth," and **Крещенія**, "of baptism." The birth of this child occurred on the 10th of the month that will be specified in Column 5.

[Число] Крещенія: *16* — "Date of Baptism: 16." So the child was born on the 10th and baptized on the 16th.

Когда, гдѣ, кто и кѣмъ, одною ли водою или со всѣми обрядами таинства окрещенъ? — "Baptized when, where, who and by whom, with water alone or with all the rites of the sacrament?" The reply reads as follows, line by line:

Тысяча восемьсотъ девя-	*Of the one thousand eight hundred ninety-*
носто втораго года, фев-	*second year, of February*
раля шестьнадцатаго	*the sixteenth*
дня, въ Гринкишкомъ	*day, in Grinkiškis*
Приходскомъ Р.-Католи-	*parish R.-Catholic*
ческомъ Костелѣ. Викар-	*church, by Assistant Pastor*
нымъ Кс. Антономъ	*Rev. Anton*
Антонелисомъ окре-	*Antonelis [was] baptized*
щено дитя именемъ	*a child by name*
Анна со всѣми обря-	*Anna with all the rites*
дами Таинства.	*of the sacrament.*

Since the persons mentioned were ethnic Lithuanians, it is appropriate to change their Russianized names to Lithuanian forms. Thus the priest was Rev. Antanas Antanelis, and the baptized infant was christened Ona.

Here is a more polished rendering of this translation: "On February 16, 1892, in the Grinkiškis Roman Catholic parish church, a child named Ona was baptized by Assistant Pastor Rev. Antanas Antanelis with all the rites of the sacrament."

Какихъ родителей и къ какому сословію или обществу они принадлежатъ, когда и гдѣ, т. е. въ какомъ приходѣ родился крещаемый? — "Of what parents and to what condition or society do they belong, when and where, that is, in what parish was the baptized one born?" The "condition" referred to means more or less "social class," and "community" here is another term for an administrative district. A more polished rendering is: "Who are the parents of the one baptized, and to what class or community do they belong, and when and where, i. e., in what parish, was the baptized one born?"

The reply reads as follows, line by line:

Крестьянъ Кроковской	Of peasants of Krakės
волости, Гринкишскаго	district, Grinkiškis
общества: Павла и Ка-	community, of Pavel and
зимиры изъ Пранисовъ	Kazimira of the Pranises
Бледисовъ законныхъ	Bledis, the lawfully married
супруговъ дочь, родив-	couple, the daughter, born
шаяся сего жъ года и	the same year and
мѣсяца десятаго дня,	month of the 10th day,
въ деревнѣ Кубилюнахъ,	in the village of Kubiliūnai,
здѣшняго прихода.	of the local parish.

Again we adjust the names to reflect the Lithuanian character of the persons discussed, so *Pavel* becomes *Povilas.* "Kazimira of the Pranises" is a way of expressing her maiden name, so we adjust that to Kazimira Pranis. Polishing the translation a little, we come up with this:

"[She is the] daughter of peasants of Krakės district, Grinkiškis community, the lawfully married couple the Bledises, Povilas and Kazimira née Pranis, [and was] born this year and month on the 10th day, in the village of Kubiliūnai, of this parish."

Кто были по имени прозванію воспріемниками при св. крещеніи и кто присутствовалъ? — "Who were the godparents, by name and profession, at Holy Baptism, and who was present?"

The reply reads as follows, line by line:

Воспріемника-	The godparents
ми были крестья-	were the peasants
не Викентій	Vikentiy
Лингвевичь, съ	Lingvevich and
Марціянною	Martsiyanna,
Мартина Ур-	of Martin Urbas
баса супругою.	wife.

Once we replace the Russian names with their Lithuanian counterparts, we have: "The godparents were Vincentas Lingvevičius and Marcijona, the wife of Martynas Urbas."

Рукоприкладство свидѣтелей записки по желанію — "Signature of the witnesses, [and] comments (if desired)." Here there are no signatures or comments, and the priest used this column to include information for column 7.

That is what the document says. But when the researcher who requested the translation read this, her comments were enlightening. She said other documents prove that the first name of the mother, "Kazimira née Pranis," was really *Karolina*, and that her maiden name always appeared as *Praninskas* or *Praninskaitė,* never *Pranis.* Yet this baptismal record clearly gives her name as *Казимиры изъ Пранисовъ*, which can only be interpreted as "Kazimira née Pranis." The moral of the story is, even when you translate these records correctly, you still can't be sure the facts are right. You must check and double-check!

11. Document VI-15: A Jewish Columnar Birth Record

Document VI-15 is an interesting variation on the format we've just seen. It's a Jewish record of birth and, in the case of males, circumcision, with identical columns on left and right pages; the left page is in Russian, the right in Hebrew. We have reproduced both sides on pages 234 and 235 so that you can compare and contrast the versions in each language.

As we mentioned on pages 16-20, documents with the information entered in Russian and Hebrew can be particularly helpful because when the handwriting in Russian is difficult to decipher, the Hebrew entry may clarify it, or vice versa. For this reason, in the following analysis we will compare and contrast the entries in each language, in the hope that might help you do the same with the documents you find. We want to thank **Warren Blatt** for his insights on the Hebrew entries; any mistakes we've made in interpreting them would have been much greater without his help.

The heading at the top of each page says the same thing in Russian, **Часть I. О Родившихся**, "Part One, on Births." For the division of Russian-language registers into three parts, see the note on *o родившихся за 1897 года* on page 213.

The columnar headings are as follows:

1-2) № Женскаго | Мужскаго – Sequential birth number of the male/female sex
3) Кто совершалъ обрядъ обрѣзанія – Who performed the rite of circumcision?
4-5) Число и мѣсяцъ рожденія и обрѣзанія | Христіанскій | Еврейскій – Date and month of birth and circumcision | Christian | Jewish (i. e., date by each calendar)
6) Гдѣ родился – Where was [he/she] born?
7) Состояніе отца, имена отца и матери – Class (occupation) of the father, names of the father and mother?
8) Кто родился и какое ему или ей дано имя – Who was born, and what name was given to him or her?

The columns are the same on the Hebrew side of the register, and the same information appears for each column as on the Russian side, only written in Hebrew.

Thus the first entry on the sample page is #59 of the female births. As the child was female, no circumcision was performed, so column 3 is left blank. In columns 4-5 the first word is *Родилась*, "was born" (feminine), and the dates are 11 *Августа*, 11 August, by the Christian calendar, and *21 Ава*, 21 Av, by the Jewish calendar. Under *Гдѣ родился*, "born where," is entered *въ м. Давид-городкѣ*, "in the town of David Gorodok,"(now Давыд-Гарадок *[Davyd-Haradok]* in Belarus)—this applies to the next birth as well. In Column 7 we see this:

> *Отецъ Давид-городецкій мѣщанинъ, Зеликъ Мееровъ Рѣзникъ, мать Хая-Соша Мовшовой.*

This translates literally as: "Father, of David Gorodok a townsman, Zelik Reznik, son of Meyer, mother Khaya-Sosha, daughter of Moyshe." The term *мѣщанинъ* literally means "townsman, burgher," but in practice it was usually a synonym for "merchant, tradesman." Regarding the patronymic *Мееровъ*, "son of Meyer," see pages 28-29.

The final column is cut off somewhat by the binding, but it appears to read: *Родилась дочь и наречена Баша*, "a daughter was born and [she was] named Basha."

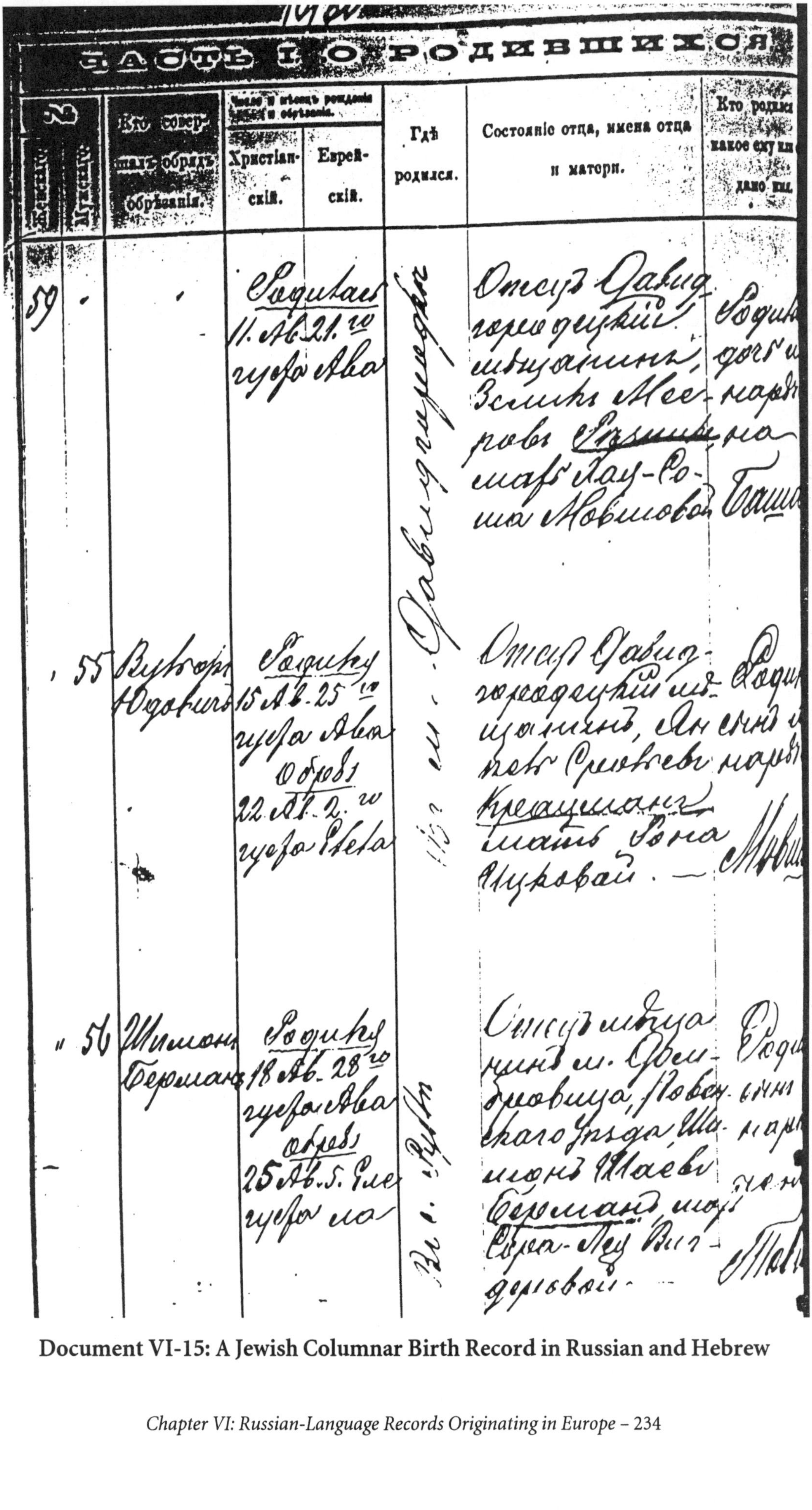

Document VI-15: A Jewish Columnar Birth Record in Russian and Hebrew

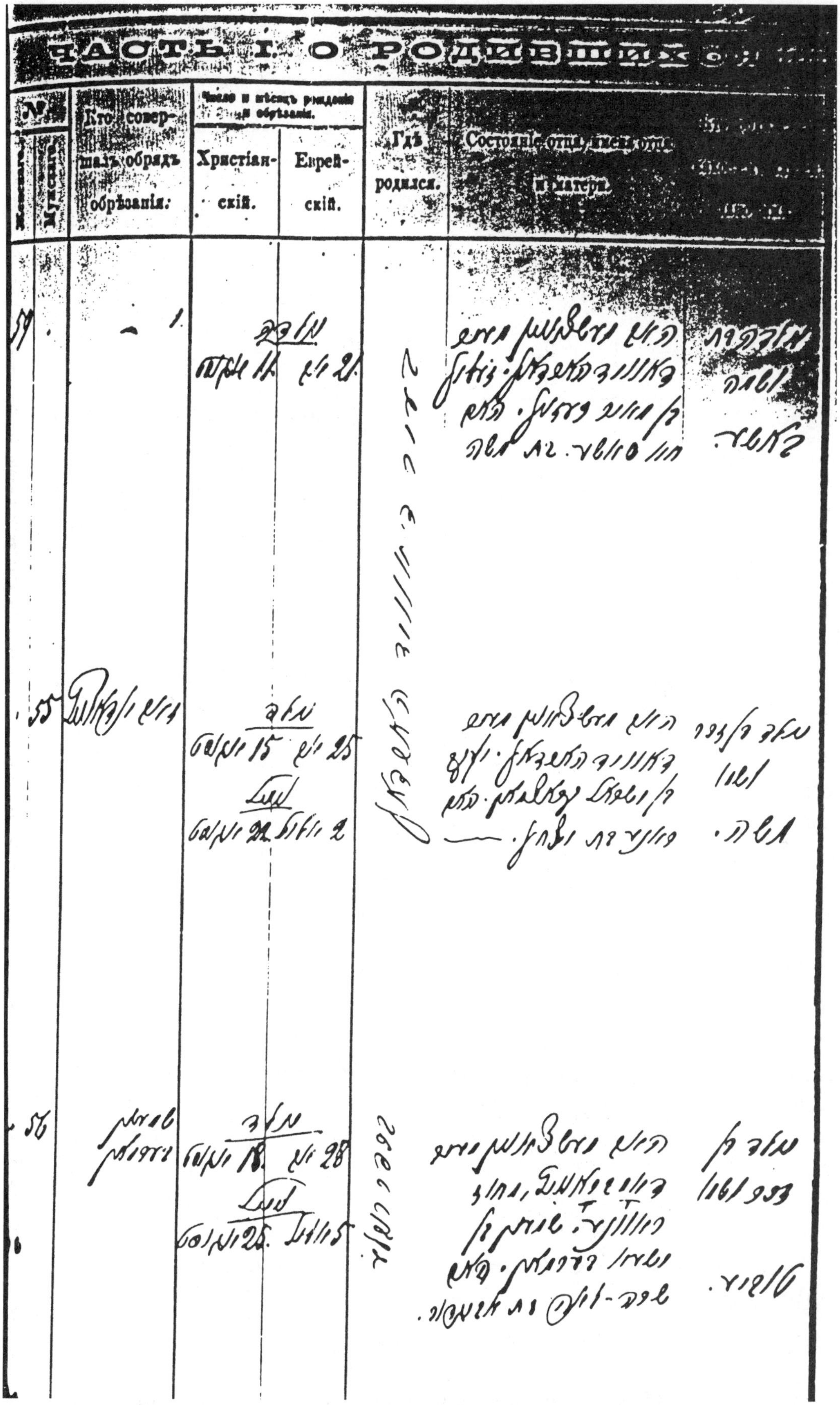

ЧАСТЬ I. О РОДИВШИХСЯ

№ Женскаго	№ Мужескаго	Кто совершалъ обрядъ обрѣзанія	Число и мѣсяцъ рожденія и обрѣзанія: Христіанскій	Еврейскій	Гдѣ родился	Состояніе отца, имена отца и матери
54						
	55					
	56					

Document VI-15 (continued)

Compare the Hebrew entry, printed below with cursive on top and the same thing in the more familiar "square" letters beneath (review pp. 18-20 for help with the Hebrew cursive, and page 47 for help with the Russian spellings of Hebrew names of the month):

59	–	–	נולדה		בעיר דאוויד הארדאק	האב מעשצאנין מעיר דאוויד הארדאק זאליק בן מאיר רעזניק. האם חיו סאשע בת משה	נולדה בת ושמה באשע
			11 אווגוסט	21 אב			

	נולדה				
59	11 אווגוסט	21 אב	בעיר דאוויד הארדאק	האב מעשצאנין מעיר דאוויד הארדאק זאליק בן מאיר רעזניק. האם חיו סאשע בת משה	נולדה בת ושמה באשע

Columns 1-3 are the same as in Russian. Columns 4-5 begin with נולדה, "was born" (feminine), and under the appropriate column are the dates אווגוסט 11, "August 11," and אב 21, "21 Av." The place of birth is בעיר דאוויד הארדאק, "in the city of David Har[o]dak." The description of the father and mother say literally "The father [is] a townsman from the town of David-Haradok, Zelik, son of Meyer, Reznik; the mother [is] Khaya Soshe, daughter of Mosheh [Moses]." The final column says literally "born a daughter, and her name [is] Bashe."

Note that the record keeper knew no exact Hebrew equivalent for Russian *мѣщанинъ*, "townsman," so he simply transliterated it into Hebrew letters as מעשצאנין, *meshtsanin*.

The mother's name is a bit of a puzzle, as we'd expect the equivalent of Russian *Хая* to be חיה, from the Hebrew word for "life," but that clearly is not the form given—it appears instead to be חיו. Perhaps it's simply a clerical error? The daughter's name, *Bashe*, is definitely a known Yiddish given name. So is *Zelik*, ultimately from the same root as German *selig*, "happy, blessed" and thought to be a Yiddish translation of the Biblical Hebrew name אשר, *Asher* or *Osher*, "happiness."

The second entry on the sample page is #55 of the male births. The name of the man who performed the circumcision is *Вульфъ Юдовичъ*, *Vul'f Yudovich*. In Columns 4-5 two dates are given, one under *Родился*, "was born," and one under *Обрѣз.*, short for *обрѣзаніе*, "circumcision." The child was born on 15 *Августа*, 15 August, by the Christian calendar, and *25 Ава*, 25 Av, by the Jewish calendar; he was circumcised on 22 August / 2 Elul. Under *Гдѣ родился*, "born where," is the same notation as for the first birth, *въ м. Давид-городкѣ*, "in the town of David Gorodok." In Column 7 we see this:

> *Отецъ Давид-городецкій мѣщанинъ, Янкель Срольевъ Крацманъ, мать Рона Ицковой.*

This translates literally as: "Father, of David Gorodok a townsman, Yankel', son of Srol', Kratsman, mother Rona, daughter of Itsko" (or possibly *Itsek*).

The final column reads: *Родился сынъ и нареченъ Мовша,* "a son was born and [he was] named Movsha" (the last letter of his name is cut off, it might also be *Movshe*).

Compare the Hebrew entry, with in both cursive and printed form:

–	55	וולף יודאוויץ	נולד אוגוסט 15 | אב 25 נמול אוגוסט 22 | אלול 2	בעיר דאוויד הארדאק	האב מעשצאנין מעיר דאוויד הארדאק יעקב בן ישראל קראצמאן. האם ראנע בת יצחק	נולד בן זכר ושמו משה

–	55	וולף יודאוויץ	נולד אוגוסט 15 | אב 25 נמול אוגוסט 22 | אלול 2	בעיר דאוויד הארדאק	האב מעשצאנין מעיר דאוויד הארדאק יעקב בן ישראל קראצמאן. האם ראנע בת יצחק	נולד בן זכר ושמו משה

The 1st and 2nd columns are the same as on the Russian side. The name of the *mohel* is given as וולף יודאוויץ, *Vul'f Yudovits.* The child was born (נולד) on the 15th of August / 25th of Av, and was circumcised (נמול) on the 22nd of August / 2nd of Elul. As with the previous entry, the place of birth was בעיר דאוויד הארדאק, "in the city of David Har[o]dak." The information on the father and mother says "The father [is] a townsman from the city of David Haradok, Yakob son of Israel Kratsman; the mother [is] Rone daughter of Itskhok." The last column says "A son was born and his name [is] Mosheh."

Note that here, as in many of these records, in Russian the first names of the father, grandfather, and son are *kinnuim* (secular names), while the Hebrew version gives their "sacred" equivalents, i. e., Hebrew יעקב *(Yakov)* instead of *Yankl,* ישראל *(Israel)* instead of *Srol',* and משה (Mosheh) instead of *Movsha.* For more on this see pages 18-20.

The date indicates that Movsha was circumcised on the 8th day after his birth. This should normally prove to be true, as that is the interval prescribed by the Law.

The third entry on the sample page is #56 of the male births. The name of the one who performed the circumcision is *Шимонъ Берманъ, Shimon Berman.* In columns 4-5 the date under *Родился,* "was born," is 18 August/28 Av; the date of *Обрѣз.,* "circumcision," is 25 August /5 Elul. Under *Гдѣ родился,* "born where" we read *въ с. Рублѣ,* "in the village of Rubel'." Column 7 provides the following information:

> *Отецъ мѣщанинъ м. Домбровица, Ровенскаго уѣзда, Шимонъ Шаевъ Берманъ, мать Сора-Лея Вигдоровой.*

This translates literally as: "The father [is] a townsman of the town of Dombrovitsa, Rovno county, Shimon Berman, son of Shaya, [and] the mother [is] Sora-Leya, daughter of Vigdor." Most likely *Dombrovitsa* is a Polonized form of this town's name (compare Polish *Dąbrowica*) and it would be better known as *Dubrovitsa.*

The final column reads: *Родился сынъ и нареченъ Тов–,* "a son was born and [he was] named Tov-"; the last part of his name is cut off, but most likely the name was *Товія,* "Toviyah," or a variant of that name, from the Biblical name known in English as "Tobias."

Compare the Hebrew entry, with cursive on top and the same thing in the more familiar square, printed letters beneath:

–	56	שמעון בערמאן	נולד 28 אב | 18 אווגוסט נמול 5 אלול | 25 אווגוסט	בכפר רובלע	האב מעשצאנין מעיר דאמבראוויץ מחוז ראוונע. שמעון בן ישעיו בערמאן. האם שרה-לאה בת אביגדור.	נולד בן זכר ושמו טוביע

–	56	שמעון בערמאן	נולד 28 אב | 18 אווגוסט נמול 5 אלול | 25 אווגוסט	בכפר רובלע	האב מעשצאנין מעיר דאמבראוויץ מחוז ראוונע. שמעון בן ישעיו בערמאן. האם שרה-לאה בת אביגדור.	נולד בן זכר ושמו טוביע

The 1st and 2nd columns are the same as on the Russian side. The name of the *mohel* is given as שמעון בערמאן, *Shimon Berman.* The child was born (נולד) on the 18th of August/ 28th of Av, and was circumcised (נמול) on the 25nd of August/ 5th of Elul. The place of birth was בכפר רובלע, "in the village of Ruble." The information on parents reads "The father [is] a townsman from the city of Dombrovits, county of Rovne, Shimon, son of Yeshay, Berman; the mother is Sora-Leya, daughter of Avigdor." The last column says "A son [male child] was born and his name [is] Tovye."

Not all Jewish registers were kept in Hebrew as well as Russian. Russian law required keeping them only in Russian—the Hebrew form is a nice extra, but not one you can count on. For more practice, **Document VI-16,** reproduced on page 239, is in Russian only.

This register is entitled Книга для записки родившихся евреевъ на 1880 годъ, "Register of Jewish Births for 1880." The page heading, Часть 1-ая о Родившихся, means "First part, of births." The columnar headings are almost the same:

- 1-2) № мужскаго | женскаго – Sequential birth number of the male/female sex?
- 3) Кто совершалъ обрядъ обрѣзанія – Who performed the rite of circumcision?
- 4-5) Число и мѣсяцъ рожденія и обрѣзанія Христіанскій | Еврейскій: Day and month of birth and circumcision | Christian | Jewish (i. e., date by each calendar)
- 6) Гдѣ родился – Where was [he/she] born?
- 7) Состоянie отца, имена отца и матери – Class (occupation) of the father, names of the father and mother?
- 8) Кто родился и какое ему или ей дано имя – Who was born, and what name was given to him or her?

The subject of the first entry was the 21st child of the female gender, born on *3 Февраля / 3 Адара* (3 February/3 Adar) *въ городѣ Бѣлостокѣ* (in the city of Białystok) to *Беръ Шлямовичъ Левинъ* (Ber Szlamowicz Lewin) and *Хане Давидовна* (Chane, daughter of Dawid), a *дочь* (daughter), named *Шейна* (*Szejna,* English spelling *Sheina*). For some reason the record keeper omitted the father's occupation.

а) Книга для записки родившихся евреевъ на 1880 годъ.

ЧАСТЬ 1-я О РОДИВШИХСЯ

№ Мужскаго	№ Женскаго	Кто совершилъ обрядъ обрѣзанія.	Число и мѣсяцъ рожденія и обрѣзанія: Христіанскій.	Число и мѣсяцъ рожденія и обрѣзанія: Еврейскій	Гдѣ родился	Состояніе отца, имена отца и матери.	Кто родился и какое ему или ей дано имя.
,	21	—"—	Февраля 3	Адара 3	Въ городѣ Бѣлостокѣ	Берь Шлемовичъ Левинъ, Хане Давидовна	Дочь Шейна
35	"	Раввинъ и Ш. Кацъ	3 10	3 10	"	Бѣлост. мѣщ. Сроель-Янкель Овсеевичъ Сегаль, Рейзель Мордуховна	Сынъ Цалель
36	"	тѣже	4 11	4 11	"	Волковыскій мѣщ. Маркусъ Боруховичъ Галлай, Гендель Янкелевна Эйнъ.	Сынъ Самуилъ

Document VI-16, Another Jewish Birth Register, from Białystok, Poland, 1880

The second entry deals with the 35th male born that year, circumcised by *Раввинъ* (the Rabbi) and *Ш. Кацъ* (Sh. Kats, presumably he assisted the rabbi), born on 3 February/3 Adar, circumcised on 10 February/10 Adar, born in the city of Białystok. His father was a *Белост. мѣщ.* (abbrev. for *Белостокскій мѣщанинъ*, "a townsman of Białystok") *Сроель-Янкель Овсеевичъ Сегаль* (Sroel-Jankiel Segal, son of Owsej) and *Рейзель Мордуховна* (Rejzel, daughter of Morduch); and the child born was a son, *Цалель* (Calel).

Note that by English phonetic and orthographic standards the son would be called *Tsalel'*, his father *Sroel'-Yankel'*, son of *Ovsei*, and his mother *Reizel'*, daughter of *Mordukh*. But since these folks lived in Poland, it seems most logical and consistent to give the Polish spellings of the names first. Also, a *мѣщанинъ* was literally a "townsman" or "burgher," but generally this description was tantamount to saying a man was a merchant.

The third entry was for the 36th male of the Jewish community of Białystok, circumcised by *тѣже*, "the same ones," in other words, the Rabbi and Sh. Kats. Born on 4 February/Adar and circumcised on 11 February/ Adar, in the city of Białystok, whose father was a townsman *Волковыскій* (of Wołkowysk), *Маркусъ Боруховичъ Галлай* (Markus Gałłaj, son of Boruch), mother *Гендель Янкелевна Эйнъ* (Gendel Ejn, daughter of Jankiel), a son, *Самуилъ* (Samuil).

12. Document VI-17: A Short-Form Birth Certificate

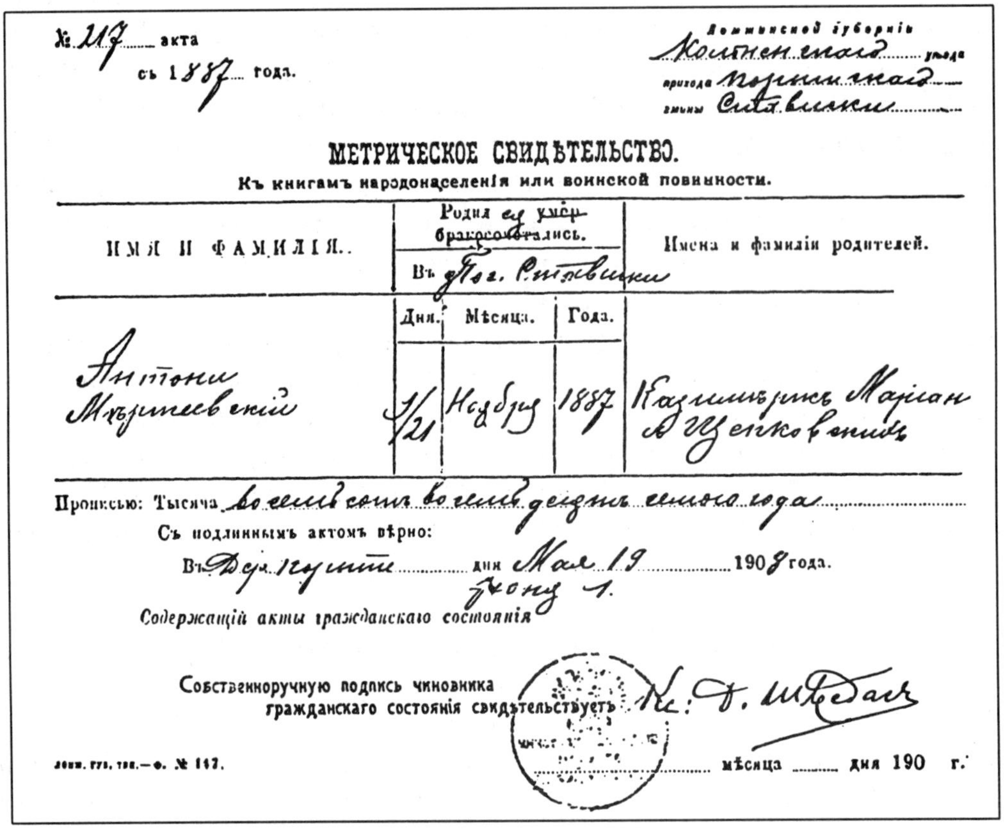

№ 217 акта
съ 1887 года.

Ломжинской губерніи
Кольненскаго уѣзда
прихода Порытскаго
гмины Стависки

МЕТРИЧЕСКОЕ СВИДѢТЕЛЬСТВО.
Къ книгамъ народонаселенія или воинской повинности.

ИМЯ И ФАМИЛІЯ.	Родил ся ~~умер~~ ~~бракосочетались~~. Въ пос. Стависки			Имена и фамиліи родителей.
	Дня.	Мѣсяца.	Года.	
Антони Мѣржеевскій	9/21	Ноября	1887	Казимѣржъ и Маріанна Щепковскихъ

Прописью: Тысяча восемьсотъ восемьдесятъ седьмого года
Съ подлиннымъ актомъ вѣрно:
Въ дер. Порыте дня Мая 19 1908 года.
Іюня 1.
Содержащій акты гражданскаго состоянія

Собственноручную подпись чиновника гражданскаго состоянія свидѣтельствуетъ [signature]

Ломж. губ. тип.—ф. № 147. мѣсяца дня 190 г.

Document VI-17: A Short-Form Birth Certificate

Record № *217*
from the year *1887*

Łomża province
Kolno county
Poryte parish
Stawiski district

REGISTRY CERTIFICATE
for population registers or military service

FIRST NAME AND SURNAME	Born ~~Died~~ ~~Was Married~~ in the *town of Stawiski*			PARENTS' FIRST NAMES AND SURNAMES
	Day	Month	Year	
Antoni Mierzejewski	*9/21*	*November*	*1887*	*Kazimierz and Marianna nee Szczepkowska*

Written out: the year one thousand *eight hundred eighty-seven*
Faithful to the original record:
In *the village of Poryte*, date *May 19th*, year 190*8*
June 1.
Civil Registrar
Certified by the signature of the Official of the Civil Registry in his own hand: *illegible*
[Official stamp] Month _ day _ year 190_

Let us end our examination of birth records with a certificate issued for official purposes, such as entry in a population register or registration for military duty. Certificates of this type resemble Documents VI-9 and VI-10 in that they were extracted from the original bound registers. The difference is that these are succinct, giving nothing but the essential facts. They may be less fascinating than the original records, but they're much easier to read!

Note that **Document VI-17**, reproduced on page 240, is an all-purpose form. It could be used for an extract from a birth, marriage, or death record. The three columns in the center of the certificate have a section saying **Родил умер бракосочетались**—"Born," "Died," and "Got Married," respectively. The clerk simply crosses out the two options that don't apply, and writes in any endings required by grammar.

At the top left it says № *217* акта съ *1887* года, "Record #217 from 1887." At top right it says *Ломжинской губерніи, Кольненскаго уѣзда, прихода порытскаго, гмины Стависки*, which means "of Łomża province, Kolno county, Poryte parish, Stawiski district."

The phrase МЕТРИЧЕСКОЕ СВИДѢТЕЛЬСТВО means "Registry Certificate," i. e., it is extracted from information in the Civil Register, which in turn came from parish records.

ИМЯ И ФАМИЛІЯ is easy enough if you've studied the previous records: "First Name and Surname." Below this is written the name *Антони Мпржеевскій*, Antoni Mierzejewski.

As stated earlier, Родил умер бракосочетались mean "was born, died, got married." The clerk crossed out the last two and added the gender-appropriate ending to Родил to created Родил*ся*, "[he] was born" (for a female he'd have added *-ась*). Below that is a space for saying where he was born/died/got married, in this case Вь *Пос. Стависки*, "in the town of Stawiski." Under Дня (Day), Мѣсяца (Month) and Года (Year) is the information *7/21 Ноября 1887*, "9/21 November 1887." The top of the number 9 did not reproduce clearly on the original, but we know it was the 9th of November because in the 19th century the Julian and Gregorian calendars were 12 days apart. (By the 20th century the gap had grown to 13 days). Thus this document, issued in 1908, is dated May 19/June 1, as we'll see below. By our reckoning the later date is correct, so Antoni Mierzejewski was born 21 November 1887.

In the third column we find Имена и фамиліи родителей, the First and Last Names of the Parents: *Казимпржъ Маріан[на] съ Щепковскихъ*, Kazimierz and Marianna née Szczepkowska (the end of Marianna's name was cut off when the document was reproduced).

Right below this it says Прописью: Тысяча *восемьсотъ восемьдесятъ семого года*, which means "Written out: the year one thousand eight hundred eighty-seven." The form *семого* is either a variant or a misspelling of standard *седьмаго*, "seventh." Records often specify that the year is to be written out in full, not just given in numbers, and in Russian *написать прописью* means to do just that.

Then comes legalese certifying the accuracy of this copy: Съ подлиннымъ актомъ вѣрно, "faithful to the original record." It is signed Въ *Дер. Порыте* дня *Мая 19,* 190*8 года*, "In the village of Poryte, May 19th, 1908." Underneath that date is written the date reckoned by the Gregorian calendar, *Іюня 1,* June 1 (13 days later than the Julian date).

It is "signed" *Содержащій акты гражданскаго состоянія*, "the Civil Registrar."

Then comes more legalese, Собственноручную подпись чиновника гражданскаго состоянія свидѣтельствуетъ, "Certified by the signature of the Official of the Civil Registry in his own hand." The actual signature of the official follows, with the seal of his office. There is a place at the bottom right for the date, but it was not filled in.

C. RECORDS OF MARRIAGE

1. Documents VI-18 and VI-19: Premarital Examination

In general the types of marriage records a researcher will encounter correspond to the kinds of birth records we examined in part B. There are paragraph-form records, columnar records, and certificates drawn up and quoting data from, or summarizing the essential facts of, the first two types. The formats vary to some extent, but on the whole once you've become familiar with the layout and terminology encountered in typical samples of each sort, you can hope to make sense of almost any marriage record you find.

There is another type of marriage record that does not correspond to any sort of birth record: a предбрачный обыскъ or premarital examination of the bride and groom. It's obvious why there is no birth counterpart: it's rather difficult to obtain statements from people before they're born!

Document VI-18, at right, is a sample title page from a volume of these *предбрачные обыски*. The original title read as follows:

КНИГА
ПРЕДБРАЧНЫХЪ ОБЫСКОВЪ
Рожаностокскаго и
Домбровскаго начинающаяся съ 1871 на листѣ 34-
Приходскаго Костела
съ мѣсяца Августа 9 дня 1864 года.

Document VI-18

> **Книга предбрачныхъ обысковъ** *Рожаностокскаго* **Приходскаго Костела съ** *мѣсяца Августа 9 дня* **18***64* **года** — "Book of premarital examinations of the Rożanystok parish church from August 9, 1864." Rożanystok is a village not far from Białystok and Dąbrowa Białostocka, in what is now northeastern Poland.

You can tell from the spacing of the lines that this was the original title. But at some point someone inserted after *Рожаностокскаго* the words *и Домбровскаго начинающая съ 1871 г. на листѣ 34,* "and of Dąbrowa, beginning with 1871 on page 34." So the volume was originally for records of premarital examination of future married couples of Rożanystok parish, beginning 9 August 1864. But because of a change of parish jurisdiction and redrawing of ecclesiastical boundaries, it began including such records for the parish church of Dąbrowa as well. This began in 1871, with the record on page 34 of the register.

A sample page from this volume, **Document VI-19**, is reproduced on page 243. The original photocopy, even after 25% reduction, was too large to fit the whole thing on one page, so the bottom fourth or so, with signatures of the future couple, is reproduced on page 246. The photocopy is obviously not very high quality, partly because ink from the preprinted sections bled from the next page onto this one. But rather than clean it up for you, we have reproduced it "warts and all," because this is the sort of copy you're likely to run into. If the photocopy you obtain is not very good, this practice may help you decipher it anyway. If it is good, after this, reading it will be a breeze!

Произведено въ Домбровѣ ...

Предбрачныя показанія отобранные при свидѣтеляхъ отъ вступающихъ въ супружескій бракъ.

Запросы:	*Отвѣты:*
1. Какое имя и прозваніе, а также какія имена Вашихъ родителей?	1. [illegible]
2. Гдѣ родились? т. е. въ какомъ именно мѣстѣ, приходѣ, Уѣздѣ и Губерніи?	2. [illegible]
3. Сколько Вамъ лѣтъ отъ роду, сходно метрическому свидѣтельству?	3. Вдовецъ 54 лѣтъ, Дѣвица 28 лѣтъ
4. Какого вѣроисповѣданія?	4. Римско-Католическаго
5. Какого происхожденія?	5. Крестьяне
6. Съ котораго времени живете въ этомъ приходѣ и гдѣ именно?	6. [illegible]
7. Не состоите-ли въ брачномъ союзѣ?	7. Вдовецъ, дѣвица
8. По добровольному-ли своему согласію намѣрены вступить въ настоящій бракъ?	8. [illegible]
9. Съ вѣдома-ли и согласія: родителей, опекуновъ или родственниковъ?	9. [illegible]
10. Не дѣлали-ли обѣтовъ цѣломудрія, а въ особенности, не учинили-ли Монашескихъ обѣтовъ?	10. Нѣтъ
11. Не обручались-ли съ другимъ лицемъ, и когда именно?	11. Нѣтъ
12. Не состоите-ли съ брачущимся лицемъ въ родствѣ и свойствѣ, плотскомъ или Духовномъ?	12. Нѣтъ

Document VI-19: A Premarital Examination from Russian Poland

At the top of the page is this heading:

Происходило въ *Домбровѣ 28 Июля 1874* **года. Предбрачныя показанія отобранные при свидѣтелямъ отъ вступающихъ въ супружескій бракъ.** — "[This] took place in Dąbrowa on 28 July 1874. Premarital depositions taken in the presence of witnesses from those entering into the state of marriage."

происходило – past tense neuter singular from the verb *происходить*, "to happen, take place." Here, as with the term we've seen before meaning the same thing, *состоялось*, (e. g., page 200), the subject "this, the following, all this," is not spelled out.

показанія – nominative plural of the neuter noun *показаніе* (modern spelling *показание*), which generally means "showing, exhibition," but in legal contexts can mean "deposition, testimony."

отобранные – past passive participle of *отобрать*, literally "to take from," but in legal context it means "to take (e. g., testimony), to hear (e. g., witnesses)." One might well ask why *отобранные* doesn't have the same archaic plural endings as the adjective *предбрачныя*, since both are used as adjectives modifying the noun *показанія*. It's a good question! But odd usages and outright grammatical errors are not particularly rare in documents of this sort, especially when they were printed and/or filled out in areas were Russian was not the first language of the population.

при свидѣтелямъ – "before witnesses" or "in the presence of witnesses."

отъ вступающихъ въ супружескій бракъ – literally "from [the ones] entering into a conjugal marriage." The verb *вступать* means "to enter into, come into." *Бракъ* means "marriage," and *супружескій* is an adjectival form derived from *супругъ*, "spouse, husband," and *супруга*, "wife."

On the left side of the page are the preprinted *запросы*, "questions," which were to be put to the couple in order to establish that they were legally entitled to marry. On the right are the handwritten *Отвѣты*, "answers." Let us examine them, since the questions are generally consistent from one form to the next, and these answers are fairly typical.

1. Какое имя и прозваніе, а также какія имена Вашихъ родителей? – 1. "What is your first name and surname, and also what are the names of your parents?"

Крестьянинъ Адамъ зак. суп. Якова и Анны съ Михаловскихъ Криштопиковъ. — A peasant, Adam, son of the Krysztopiks, Jakób and Anna née Michałowska. Note: *зак. суп.* is an abbreviation of *законныхъ супруговъ*, literally "lawful spouses."

Крестьянка Зузанна зак. суп. дочъ Ивана и Анны съ Аршиловъ Кисълюковъ. – A [female] peasant, Zuzanna, daughter of the Kiśluks, Jan and Anna née Arszyła.

2. Гдѣ родились? т. е. въ какомъ именно мѣстѣ, приходѣ, Уѣздѣ и Губерніи? – 2. "Where were you born, i. e., in which town, parish, county, and province?"

Адамъ въ д. Новабиоѕка, Зузанна въ д. Ольши, обое Домброскаго Прихода – Adam in the village of Nowa Wieś, Zuzanna in the village of Olsza, both in Dąbrowa parish.

3. Сколько Вамъ лѣтъ отъ роду, сходно метрическому свидѣтельству? – "3. How old are you, according to the registry certificate?" The phrase *сколько Вам лет* (as it's written in

modern Russian), literally "How many to you of years?" is a common way of asking "How old are you?" The adverb *сходно* means "accordingly, conformably," but here is used idiomatically in the sense of "according to, going by."

Вдовцу 54 лѣтъ – "the widower [Adam] is 54 years old." *Вдовцу* is dative singular of *вдовецъ*, "widower," so that this literally means "to the widower, 54 years."

Дѣвицѣ 28 лѣтъ – "to the maiden, 28 years." *Дѣвицѣ* is dative singular of *дѣвица*, "maiden" or "virgin," generally used in records in the sense of "single woman."

4. Какого вѣроисповѣданія? – "4. Of what faith?"

Римско-Католическаго – "Roman Catholic"

5. Какого происхожденія? – "5. Of what descent?" In other words, this is asking what social class they belong to. Besides *крестьянинъ*, "peasant," possible answers include *дворянинъ*, "noble," and *мѣщанинъ*, "burgher, townsman," i. e., in most cases a merchant or tradesman.

Крестьянинъ – "peasant."

6. Съ котораго времени живете въ этомъ приходѣ и гдѣ именно? – "6. Since when have you lived in this parish, and where, exactly?" Literally "From what time do you live..."

отъ рожденія – "since birth."

7. Не стоите-ли въ брачномъ союзѣ? – "7. Are you married?" Literally "Are you not standing in a marital union?" Besides its literal meaning of "to stand," *стоять* can mean "to be or find oneself in a certain position"; sometimes simply "to be" is the best translation. Use of *не* plus a verb and the particle *-ли* implies that a negative answer is expected, as if saying "You're not married, are you?"

Вдовецъ, дѣвица – "widower, single woman."

8. По добровольному-ли своему согласію намѣрены вступить въ настоящій бракъ? – "8. Do you intend to enter this marriage by voluntary agreement?" The adjective *добровольній* means "voluntary, of one's own will," and *намѣрены* is the plural short form of *намѣренный*, "intending, proposing."

По добровольному своему согласію – "by [my own, our own] voluntary agreement," another way of saying "Yes, we have agreed to do this of our own free will."

9. Съ вѣдома-ли и согласія: родителей, опекунов или родственниковъ? – "[Are you doing this] with the knowledge and consent of your parents, guardians, or relatives?" This is hard to translate literally. The phrase *съ вѣдома* means "with the knowledge [of]," so this question is meant to establish whether they're getting married with the knowledge and consent of whatever relative or guardian had a say in the matter.

съ вѣдома – "with the knowledge." As with the previous answer, the repetition of the key phrase without negation is tantamount to saying "Yes."

10. Не дѣлали-ли обѣтовъ цѣломудрія, а въ особенности, не учинили-ли Монашескихъ обѣтовъ? – "10. Have you made any vows [*обѣты*] of chastity, and in particular, have you made any monastic vows?" Such vows would make a person ineligible for marriage.

Нѣтъ – "No."

11. Не обручались-ли съ другомъ лицемъ, и когда именно? – "11. Have you been betrothed to any other person, and when exactly?" The verb *обручать* means "to betroth, affiance"; the reflexive form *обручаться* is used as a passive, "to be betrothed, to get engaged (to be married)." A prior promise to marry could also be an impediment, unless there was a satisfactory reason for its termination.

Нѣтъ – "No."

12. Не состоите-ли съ брачущимся лицемъ въ родствѣ и свойствѣ, плотскомъ или духовномъ? – "12. Are you and the person you're marrying kin or related in the flesh or spiritually?" The literal translation is "Are you with the marrying person in a kinship or relationship, carnal or spiritual?" At issue is whether the betrothed couple were kin or otherwise related to each other in a degree proscribed by church law.

Нѣтъ – "No."

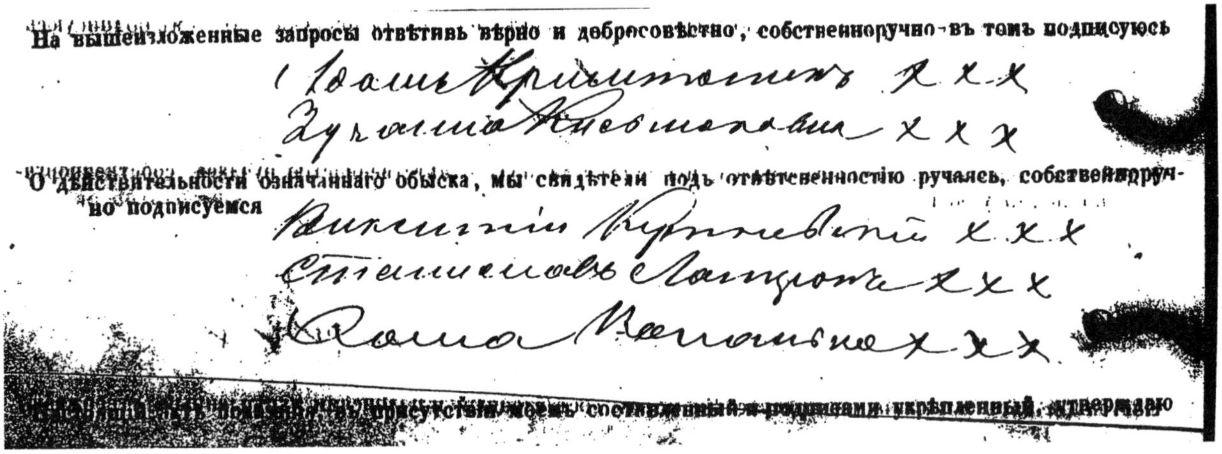
На вышеизложенные запросы отвѣтивъ вѣрно и добросовѣстно, собственноручно въ томъ подписуюсь
1 Адамъ Кристопикъ XXX
2 Зузанна Кисьлюковна XXX
О дѣйствительности означаннаго обыска, мы свидѣтели подъ отвѣтственностію ручаясь, собственноручно подписуемся
Викентій Кутневскій XXX
Станиславъ Лапцюкъ XXX
Фома Копанько XXX

The portion reproduced above appears at the bottom of Document VI-19.

На вышеизложенные запросы отвѣтивъ вѣрно и добросовѣстно, собственноручно въ томъ подписуюсь – "Having answered the above questions truthfully and conscientiously, I sign to this effect in my own hand."

1 Адамъ Кристопикъ XXX – "Adam Krysztopik" (but he just made his mark).

2 Зузанна Кисьлюковна XXX – "Zuzanna Kiśluk" (the suffix *-овна* simply indicates her maiden name; she, too, made her mark).

О дѣйствительности означаннаго обыска, мы свидѣтели подъ отвѣтственностію ручаясь, собственноручно подписуемся. – "Vouching *[ручаясь]* for the validity of the designated examination, we, the witnesses, under [our own] responsibility, sign this in our own hands."

Викентій Кутневскій XXX – "Wincenty Kutniewski XXX"

Станиславъ Лапцюкъ XXX – "Stanisław Łapciuk XXX"

Фома Копанько XXX – "Tomasz Kopańko XXX"

Note that the priest has Russified the first witness's given name, Russian *Викентій* for Polish *Wincenty*. *Станислав* is the Russian form of *Stanisław*, so the issue of Russification doesn't arise for that one. The first name of the third witness is *Фома*, the Russian version of the first name Poles use in the form *Tomasz,* in English *Thomas.* In a given record you may find that the first names were simply transliterated, e. g., Polish *Jan* → *Янъ*; or they may be translated into their Russian equivalents, Polish *Jan* → *Иванъ.*

Настоящій актъ показанія, въ присутствіи моемъ, составленній и подписями укрѣпленный, утверждаю. – "I certify *[утверждаю]* that this record of the examination was drawn up *[составленный]* and corroborated [*укрѣпленный*, literally "strengthened, fortified"] with signatures in my presence." Perhaps the priest's signature followed and was cut off on this copy. Since it looks as if the same hand made all the X's that stand for signatures, and that hand was surely the priest's, this is all legalese and just a formality.

2. Document VI-20: A Paragraph-Form Marriage Record from Russian Poland

Reproduced on page 250 is **Document VI-20**, a fairly typical paragraph-form marriage record from Russian Poland. You can see the text of this record, reprinted in italic type for easier reading, on page 251. But first let us summarize the keywords you should look for and what they tell you; then we will study this example.

I. **The Place/Date the Record Was Created** – keyword ***состоялось*** ("It happened")
II. **The Witnesses** – keywords ***свидѣтелей*** ("of the witnesses")
III. **Date of the Wedding** – keyword ***заключенъ*** ("[a marriage] was contracted")
IV. **Information on the Groom and his Parents** – keyword ***между*** ("between")
V. **Information on the Bride and Her Parents**– keyword ***а*** ("and")
VI. **The Dates of Marriage Announcements** – keywords ***Браку сему*** ("this marriage")
VII. **The Parents' Permission to Marry**– keyword ***позволеніе*** ("permission")
VIII. **Prenuptial Agreement** – keyword ***новобрачные*** ("the newlyweds")
IX. **The Officiant – *Религіозный обрядъ*** ("The religious ceremony")
X. **Signatures – *Актъ сей*** ("this document")

Since this is the first sample of this sort, we shall analyze it at some length.

Порыте. ***Состоялось*** *въ Порытомъ девятего/двадцать перваго Ноября тысяча восемьсотъ семьдесятаго года въ два часа по полудни.* – "Poryte. This happened in Poryte on the 9th/21st of November of the year 1870, at 2 p.m."

The name of this village, *Poryte,* is adjectival in Polish, and thus it has been declined like an adjective in Russian as well, with the prepositional ending *-омъ* instead of the noun ending *-ѣ*. The information on date and time should be easy to understand if you refer to the section on Date and Time Expressions, pages 45-51. In regard to the double date, see the note to *шетого/девятнадцатаго марта* on page 200. What's said in that note regarding misspellings and variant forms also applies to the incorrect ending *-его* on the word *девятего.*

Объявляемъ что въ присутствіи ***свидѣтелей*** *Францишка Паталяна пятидесяти лѣтъ и Марціана Котовскаго пятидесяти лѣтъ отъ роду крестянъ хозяевъ жительствующихъ въ Порытомъ* – "We declare that in the presence of witnesses Franciszek Patalan, age 50, and Marcyan Kotowski, age 50, peasant farmers residing in Poryte..."

объявляемъ – first person plural, present tense active form of *объявлять*, "to declare, announce." Sometimes you may see *извѣщаемъ* instead, as it means the same thing, "we declare." This is a kind of royal "we" normal in these records.

что въ присутствіи ***свидѣтелей*** – "that in the presence of witnesses." Note that "in the presence **of** witnesses" implies a relationship normally expressed with the genitive case in Russian. That's why *свидѣтелей* is the genitive plural form, and the names of the witnesses themselves, and adjectives modifying them, will also be in the genitive.

Францишка Паталяна ... и Марціяна Котовскаго ... – "[of] Franciszek Patalan ... and Marcyan Kotowski." It's important to realize that these names will be in the genitive case; for most first names of males that case has the ending *-a*, which must be removed to get the standard nominative form. This can be vital, because there is a feminine name *Franciszka* in Polish, as well as *Marcjanna*. This grammatical ending is the only thing that tells you we're talking, not about female witnesses named *Franciszka* and *Marcjanna*, but males named *Franciszek* and *Marcyan*.

пятидесяти лѣтъ ... пятидесяти лѣтъ отъ роду – if this can be believed, both witnesses were 50 years old (*отъ роду* = "from birth"). Articles have been written on the tendency to "round off" peoples' ages in these records, so it's best not to place too much confidence in the precision of such data.

крестянъ хозяевъ жительствующихъ въ Порытомъ – "peasant farmers residing in Poryte." Here *крестянъ* (which, incidentally, should be spelled *крестьянъ*), *хозяевъ*, and *жительствующихъ* are all genitive plural because they're still referring to the witnesses. In these records Russian *хозяинъ*, which can mean "master of the house, host, proprietor, owner," generally means "farmer," especially one who owned his farm.

... ***заключено*** *сего числа религіозный брачный союзъ ...* – "... on this day a religious marital union [was] contracted ..."

заключено – a neuter short form of the past passive participle of *заключить*, "to enclose, confine; to make (an alliance), close (a deal), conclude (a treaty), etc." Note that the keyword given on page 247 is ***заключенъ***, and that form is correct. This neuter construction is incorrect in Russian—but it is good Polish, the priest's native tongue. Many of the grammatical errors in this record are surely due to similar confusion.

сего числа – "on this date." If the marriage had taken place the day before the record was drawn up, the phrase would be *вчерашняго числа*, "yesterday."

... ***между*** *Францишкомъ Балдыго холостымъ сыномъ покойнаго Томаша а находящейся въ живыхъ вдовы его Гелены съ Глиньскихъ Балдыговъ крестянъ работниковъ урожденнемъ и жительствующимъ въ Порытомъ содержащимся съ работы двадцати одинъ лѣтъ отъ роду...* – "... between Franciszek Bałdyga, a bachelor, son of the late Tomasz and his widow Helena, still alive, peasant laborers; [Franciszek] was born and resides in Poryte, earning his living as a laborer, age 21 ..."

между – this keyword, which means "between," signals the beginning of information on the groom. Typically you can expect to see his name, marital status, age, and occupation; the names and occupations of his parents, and whether they are still alive; and the groom's place of birth and residence. The exact order of the information may change, and sometimes not all this is provided. But as a rule it is.

холостымъ – from the adjective *холостой*, "single, unmarried."

сыномъ покойнаго Томаша – son of the late Tomasz; *покойный* is one of several ways of saying "the late, deceased." If both parents had been deceased the form would have been genitive plural, *покойныхъ*. In some cases the word *нѣкогда*, "once, formerly," will appear before the name of a deceased individual, meaning in context "the late."

а находящейся въ живыхъ вдовы его Гелены съ Глиньскихъ Балдыговъ – literally "and of the finding herself in the living widow his, Gelena, of the Glińskis, Bałdyga." The conjunction *а* is used to say "and" when referring to two persons or things who differ in some significant way; the conjunction *и* means "and" when joining two persons or things essentially similar. Thus Tomasz is dead, **and** his widow is still among the living. Note the Russian tendency to turn Polish *h* into *г* (pages 24-25), *Helena* → *Гелена*.

супруговъ Балдыговъ – literally "the spouses the Bałdygas." This is meant to establish that Franciszek was the son of the lawfully wedded couple, the Bałdygas; but phrasing that literally in English without some awkwardness is a challenge.

крестянъ работниковъ – genitive plural forms, and thus referring to the parents of Franciszek.

урожденнемъ и жительствующимъ въ Порытомъ – "born and residing in Poryte." What's clear in Russian, but harder to make clear in English, is that we are now back to talking about Franciszek, not his parents. The endings on the participles *урожденнемъ* and *жительствующимъ* cannot refer to Tomasz and Helena; any adjectives referring to them would have to take genitive endings. Franciszek, however, was last mentioned in an instrumental form, and thus adjectives referring to him must be in that case. (For now we'll overlook the fact that *урожденнемъ* should be *урожденнымъ*. To be honest, there's a lot in this document that would make a Russian teacher cringe. But our purpose is to help you read these documents, not to grade this priest's Russian).

If the place of birth and the current residence are not the same, both locations should be provided here. If either was outside the parish boundaries—which often happened, since the wedding was usually held in the bride's home parish, and the groom could very well come from another parish—the name of that other parish would be given; perhaps also the province and county, as well. This varied from one record keeper to another; many gave only the minimum information required.

If a person named in the record was a permanent resident of one place, but was temporarily staying elsewhere (perhaps working there), you may see a phrase along the lines of *постоянный житель А, а временно проживающій въ В*, "a permanent resident of A, temporarily residing in B."

содержащимся съ работы – "supporting himself by labor" or "making a living as a laborer"; *содержаться* means "to support oneself." This, too, refers to Franciszek.

двадцати одинъ лѣтъ отъ роду – "twenty-one years old."

Before proceeding, we should explain that if the bride or groom was a widow or widower, some record keepers identify the late spouse with his or her date and place of death. Some gave full information, some only the spouse's first name or date of death. Thus you might see:

вдовою по умершимъ Осипѣ Садковскимъ восьмаго Февраля тысяча восемьсотъ восемдесятаго года – "the widow of the Osip Sadkowski, who died on 8 February 1880."

Порыте. Состоялось въ Порытомъ де
вятого/двадцать перваго/ Ноября. Тыся
ча восемьсотъ семьдесятаго года въ два ча
са пополудни Объявляемъ что въ присут
ствіи Свидѣтелей Францишка Паталяна
пятидесяти лѣтъ и Марціана Котов
скаго пятидесяти лѣтъ отъ роду Крест
янъ хозяевъ жительствующихъ въ Порытомъ. Заключено сего числа религіозный
брачный Союзъ между Францишкомъ Балды
го Холостымъ Сыномъ покойнаго Танаша
а находящейся въ живыхъ вдовы его Гелены съ
Глинскихъ Супруговъ Балдыговъ Крестянъ
работниковъ урожденнымъ и жительствующимъ
въ Порытомъ Содержащимся съ работы две
цати одинъ лѣтъ отъ роду- а Саломею Пата
ляновною дѣвицею дочерью Яна и умершей
Катаржины съ Хойновскихъ Супруговъ Паталя
новъ Крестянъ хозяевъ родавшеюся и жите
ствующею въ Порытомъ при Отцу двадцати
двухъ лѣтъ отъ роду- Браку сему предшество
вали три оглашенія публикованные въ здеш
ней Приходской Церкви двадцать пятаго Ок
тября/ шестаго Ноября/ перваго/ тринадцатаго
и восьмаго/ двадцатого Ноября текущаго года
позволеніе же присутствующихъ лично при
брачномъ Актѣ Отца невѣсты и Матери
холоста заявлено словесно. Новобрачные
объявляютъ что брачный договоръ меж
ду ими заключенъ не былъ. Религіозный
обрядъ бракосочетанія Соверши
Ксендзомъ Марціаномъ Влостовскимъ
Администраторомъ Порытскаго
Прихода- Актъ сей по прочтеніи
нами подписанъ присутствующіе объя
вляютъ что писать неумеютъ-

Document VI-20: A Paragraph-Form Marriage Record from Russian Poland

Text of Document VI-20

*Порыте. **Состоялось** въ Порытомъ де[-]*
вятего / двадцать перваго/ Ноября Тыся[-]
ча восемьсотъ семьдесятаго года, въ два ча[-]
са по полудни. Объявляемъ что въ присут[-]
*ствіи **свидѣтелей** Францишка Паталяна*
пятидесяти лѣтъ и Марціана Котов[-]
скаго пятидесяти лѣтъ отъ роду крест[-]
янъ хозяевъ жительствующихъ въ Поры[-]
*томъ **заключено** сего числа религіозный*
*брачный союзъ **между** Францишкомъ Балды[-]*
го холостымъ сыномъ покойнаго Томаша
а находящейся въ живыхъ вдовы его Гелены съ
Глиньскихъ супруговъ Балдыговъ крестянъ
работниковъ урожденнемъ и жительствующимъ
въ Порытомъ содержащимся съ работы два[-]
*цати одинъ лѣтъ отъ роду – **а** Саломею Пата[-]*
ляновною дѣвицею дочерью Яна и умершей
Катаржины съ Хойновскихъ супруговъ Паталя[-]
новъ крестянъ хозяевъ родившеюся и жите[-]
льствующею въ Порытомъ при отцу двадвать
*двухъ лѣтъ отъ роду – **Браку сему** предшество[-]*
вали три оглашенія публиклованные въ здѣш[-]
ней приходской церкви двадцать пятаго Ок[-]
тября / шестаго Ноября/ перваго / тринадцатаго
и восмаго / двадцатего Ноября текущаго года
***позоволеніе** же присутствующихъ лично при*
брачномъ Актѣ отца невѣсты и матери
*холоста заявлено словесно. **Новобрачные***
объявляютъ что брачный договоръ меж[-]
*ду ими заключенъ не былъ. **Религіозный***
***обрядъ** бракосочетанія соверш[енъ]*
Ксендзомъ Марціаномъ Влостовскимъ
Администраторомъ Порытскаго
*Прихода — **Актъ сей** по прочтеніи*
нами подписанъ присутствующіе объя[-]
вляютъ что писать не умеютъ.

Another formulation is *вдовцемъ по умершей женѣ*, "widower of his late wife," or *вдовою по умершемъ мужѣ*, "widow of her late husband." Sometimes *после*, "after," is used for *по*.

If one of the marrying parties had been married several times, the name of a preceding spouse may appear, e. g., *вдовцемъ по умершей женѣ Магдаленѣ по первому браку Рокицкой*, "a widower of his late wife Magdalena, [known as] Rokicka by her first marriage."

Yet another formulation is exemplified by this wording: *вдовцемъ по Антонинѣ изъ Колаковскихъ умершей въ деревнѣ Мосаки Годаче въ текущемъ году*, "the widower of Antonina née Kolakowska, who died in the village of Mosaki Godacze in the present year."

Or you might see simply: *сынъ Яна Бонѣцкаго и покойной его жены Магдалены Деѣвской*, "the son of Jan Boniecki and his late wife Magdalena Dejewska."

***а** Саломею Паталяновною дѣвицею дочерью Яна и умершей Катаржины съ Хойновскихъ супруговъ Паталяновъ крестянъ хозяевъ родившеюся и жительствующею въ Порытомъ при отцу двадцать двухъ лѣтъ отъ роду* – "and Salomea Patalan, single, the daughter of the lawfully wedded couple the Patalans, Jan and the late Katarzyna née Chojnowski, peasant farmers; [Salomea] was born and resides in Poryte with her father, [and is] 22 years old."

- ***а** Саломею Паталяновною дѣвицею* – "and Salomea Patalan, single." Now the same information will be given for the bride that was given for the groom.
- *дочерью Яна и умершей Катаржины съ Хойновскихъ супруговъ Паталяновъ крестянъ хозяевъ* – literally "the daughter of Jan and the late Katarzyna née Chojnowski, the spouses Palatan, peasant farmers" (and *крестянъ* should be *крестьянъ*).
- *родившеюся и жительствующею въ Порытомъ при отцу* – as the endings show, this refers to *Саломею* (Salomea), saying she was born and lives in Poryte, with her father.
- *двадцать двухъ лѣтъ отъ роду* – "22 years from birth," i. e., "age 22."

***Браку сему** предшествовали три оглашенія публиклованные въ здѣшней приходской церкви двадцать пятаго Октября / шестаго Ноября/ перваго / тринадцатаг и восмаго / двадцатего Ноября текущаго года* – "This marriage was preceded by three readings of the banns in the local parish church on the 25th of October/6th of November, and the 1st/13th and 8th/20th of November of the current year."

- ***Браку сему** предшествовали три оглашенія* – Literally "Three announcements preceded this marriage" (compare the note to the similar expression ***Бракъ этотъ***, page 257).
- *публиклованные въ здѣшней приходской церкви двадцать пятаго Октября/шестаго Ноября/ перваго/тринадцатаго и восмаго/двадцатего Ноября текущаго года* – The *оглашенія* (banns) were *публикованные* (read) in the local parish church, usually on successive Sundays. So the dates are normally 7 days apart, with the Julian dates 12 days earlier than their Gregorian equivalents (or in 20th-century records, 13 days).

***позоволеніе** же присутствующихъ лично при брачномъ Актѣ отца невѣсты и матери холоста заявлено словесно.* – "Permission was given orally by the bride's father and the groom's mother, who were present in person for the drawing up of the marriage record."

- *позволеніе* — "permission." If the bride and groom were both of age, for instance, so that no parental permission was required, this could be skipped. But as a rule some relative or guardian's permission will be mentioned. If either the bride or groom was underage, it was supposed to be mandatory.

присутствующихъ лично при брачномъ Актѣ отца невѣсты и матери холоста – literally "of those present personally at the marriage record, the father of the bride and mother of the groom."

заявлено словесно – "[was] declared orally." The adjective *словесный* means "verbal, oral, in words"; the adverb *словесно* means "by word of mouth, orally."

Новобрачные *объявляютъ что брачный договоръ между ими заключенъ не былъ.* – "The newlyweds stated that no marital agreement was made between them."

брачный договоръ – "a marital agreement." A *договоръ* (or sometimes *уговоръ*) is an agreement, contract, stipulation, etc. This sentence appears, in this form or one very similar, in virtually all marriage records. By it the newlyweds stipulate that they have made no prenuptial agreement contrary to the laws of the Church or state.

между ими заключенъ не былъ. – literally "between them was not made." For the meaning of *заключенъ* see the note on *заключено* on page 248. Incidentally, *между ими* is another grammatical error – after a preposition the form should be *ними*, not *ими*.

Религіозный обрядъ *бракосочетанія соверш[енъ] Ксендзомъ Марціаномъ Влостовскимъ Администраторомъ Порытскаго Прихода* – "The religious ceremony of marriage [was] performed by Reverend Marcyan Włostowski, administrator of Poryte parish."

Актъ сей *по прочтеніи нами подписанъ присутствующіе объявляютъ что писать не умеютъ.* – "This document, after being read aloud, was signed only by us; those present state that they do not know how to write."

нами подписанъ – literally "by us [was] signed." As shown on page 42, *нами* is the instrumental form of *мы*, "we"; the priest is still using the royal "we."

Translation – Poryte. This happened in Poryte on the 9th/21st of November, 1870, at 2 p.m. We declare that in the presence of witnesses—Franciszek Patalan, age 50, and Marcyan Kotowski, age 50, peasant farmers residing in Poryte—a religious marital union was contracted on this day between:

Franciszek Bałdyga, single, the son of the lawfully wedded couple the Bałdygas, the late Tomasz and his widow Helena née Glińska, still living, peasant laborers; Franciszek was born and resides in Poryte, earning his living as a laborer, age 21,

and **Salomea Patalan**, single, the daughter of the lawfully wedded couple the Patalans, Jan and the late Katarzyna née Chojnowski, peasant farmers; Salomea was born and resides in Poryte with her father, and is 22 years old.

This marriage was preceded by three readings of the banns proclaimed in the local parish church on the 25th of October/6th of November, and the 1st/13th and 8th/20th of November of the current year. The bride's father and the groom's mother, who were present in person for the drawing up of the marriage record, gave their permission to the marriage orally. The newlyweds stated that they had made no prenuptial agreement between them. The religious marriage ceremony was performed by Reverend Marcyan Włostowski, administrator of Poryte parish. This document, after being read aloud, was signed only by us; those present state that they do not know how to write.

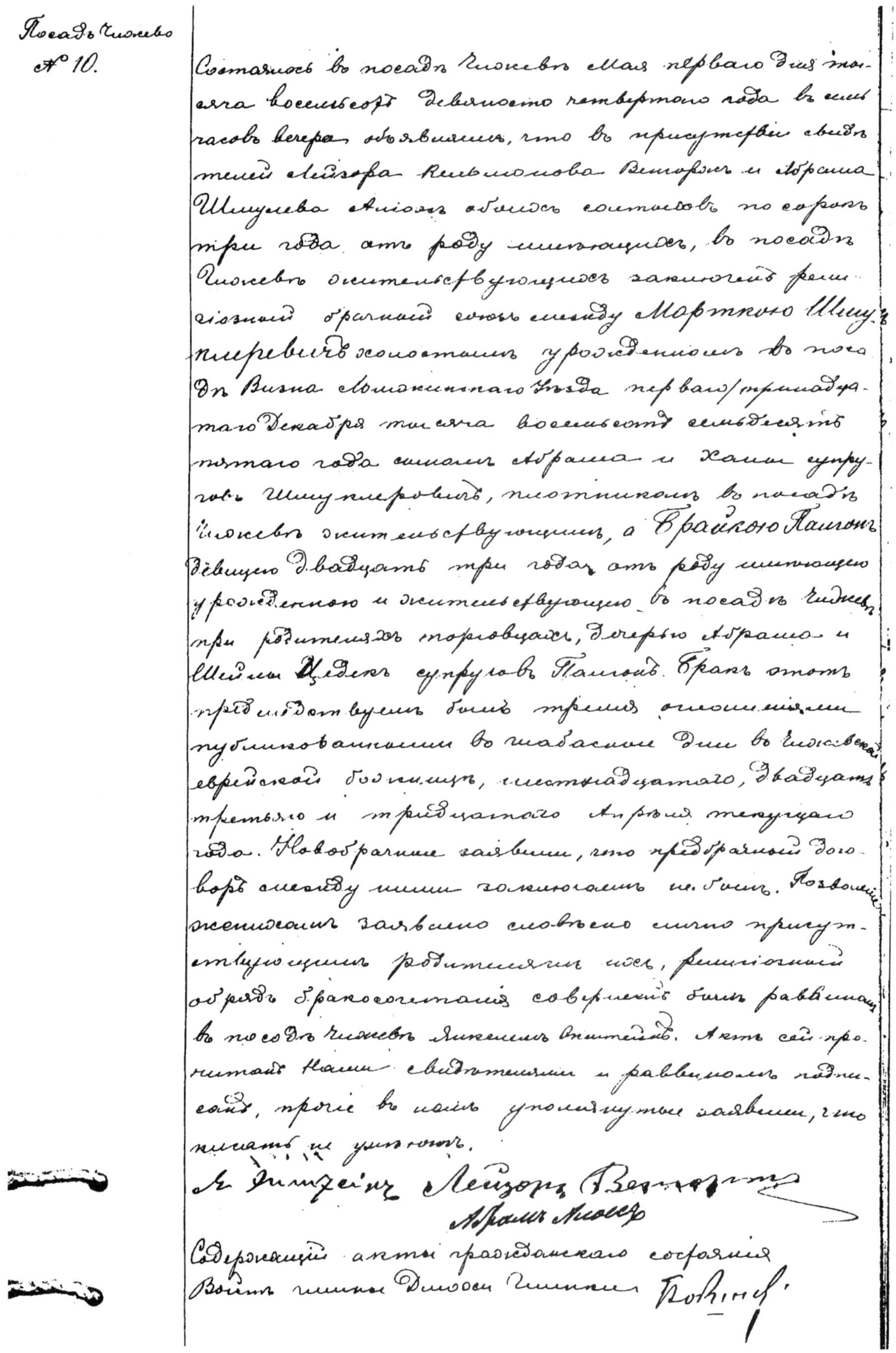

Посадъ Чижево
№ 10.

Состоялось въ посадѣ Чижевѣ Мая перваго дня тысяча восемьсотъ девяносто четвертаго года въ семь часовъ вечера. Объявляемъ, что въ присутствіи свидѣтелей Лейзора Кельмонова Ветофоза и Абрама Шмулева Аніола обоихъ совершеннолѣтнихъ по сорокъ три года отъ роду имѣющихъ, въ посадѣ Чижевѣ жительствующихъ заключенъ религіозный брачный союзъ между Мортхою Шмулкеревичемъ холостымъ урожденнымъ въ посадѣ Визна Ломжинскаго уѣзда перваго/тринадцатаго Декабря тысяча восемьсотъ семьдесятъ пятаго года сыномъ Абрама и Хаи супруговъ Шмулкеровичъ, поставщикомъ въ посадѣ Чижевѣ жительствующимъ, а Брайкою Пацонъ дѣвицею двадцать три года отъ роду имѣющею урожденною и жительствующею въ посадѣ Чижевѣ при родителяхъ торговцахъ, дочерью Абрама и Шейны Цедекъ супруговъ Пацонъ. Браку этому предшествовали были три оглашенія публикованныя въ шабасные дни въ Чижевской еврейской божницѣ, шестнадцатаго, двадцать третьяго и тридцатаго Апрѣля текущаго года. Новобрачные заявили, что предбрачный договоръ между ними заключенъ не былъ. Позволеніе заявлено словесно лично присутствующими родителями ихъ. Религіозный обрядъ бракосочетанія совершенъ былъ раввиномъ въ посадѣ Чижевѣ Янкелемъ Вайнштейномъ. Актъ сей прочитанъ нами свидѣтелями и раввиномъ подписанъ, прочіе же изъ упомянутыхъ заявили, что писать не умѣютъ.

Я. Вайнштейнъ Лейзоръ Ветофозъ
Абрамъ Аніолъ

Содержащій акты гражданскаго состоянія
Войтъ гмины Дмоховъ Чижики Pokinsk

Document VI-21: A Paragraph-Form Jewish Marriage Record from Russian Poland

3. Document VI-21: A Paragraph-Form Jewish Marriage Record from Russian Poland

Reproduced on page 254 is **Document VI-21**, a record of the marriage of a Jewish couple. It can serve a dual purpose, familiarizing Jewish researchers with specific terms and usages they are likely to encounter, while demonstrating a fair amount of consistency in format and terminology that is typical of these records, regardless of religion.

Here is the text rendered in italic type, as you may still need a bit of practice reading Russian script. The heading at the upper left says *Посадъ Чижево, №. 10,* "The village of Czyżewo, No. 10." The rest reads as follows, with keywords in boldface type:

Состоялось *въ посадѣ Чижевѣ Мая перваго дня тысяча восемьсотъ девяносто четвертаго года въ семъ часовъ вечера. Овъявляемъ, что въ присутствіи* ***свидѣ**[-]* ***телей*** *Лейзора Кельманова Веторжъ и Абрама Шмулева Аліоэсъ обоихъ солтысовъ по сорокъ три года отъ роду имѣющихъ, въ посадѣ Чижевѣ жительствующихъ* ***заключенъ*** *религіозный брачный союзъ* ***между*** *Морткою Шмуклеревичъ холостымъ урожденномъ въ посадѣ Визна Ломжинскаго уѣзда перваго/тринадцатаго Декабря тысяча восемьсотъ семьдесять пятаго года сыномъ Аврама и Ханы супруговъ Шмуклеровичъ, плотникомъ въ посадѣ Чижевѣ жительствующимъ,* ***а*** *Брайкою Палгонъ девицею двадцать три года отъ роду имѣющею урожденною и жительствующею въ посадѣ Чижевѣ при родителяхъ торговцахъ, дочерью Абрама и Шейны Цедекъ супруговъ Палгонъ.* ***Бракъ этотъ*** *предшедствуенъ былъ тремя оглошеніями публикованными въ шабасные дни въ Чижевской еврейской божницѣ, шестнадцатаго, двадцать третьяго и тридцатаго Апрѣля текущаго года.* ***Новобрачные*** *заявили, что предбрачный договоръ между ними заключенъ не былъ.* ***Позволеніе*** *женихамъ заявлено словѣсно лично присутствующимъ родителямъ ихъ.* ***Религіозный обрядъ*** *бракосочетанія совершенъ былъ раввиномъ въ посадѣ Чижевѣ Янкелемъ Эпштейнъ.* ***Актъ сей*** *прочитанъ Нами свидѣтелями и раввиномъ подписанъ, прочіе въ немъ упомянутые заявили, что писатъ не умѣютъ.*

Я. Эпштейнъ *Лейзоръ Веторжъ*
Абрамъ Алоесъ

Содержащій акты гражданскаго состоянія войтъ гмины Дмохи Глинки [signature illegible]

Состоялось *въ посадѣ Чижевѣ Мая перваго дня тысяча восемьсотъ девяносто четвертаго года въ семъ часовъ вечера.* – "This happened in the settlement of Czyżewo on May 1, 1894, at 7 o'clock in the evening."

въ посадѣ Чижевѣ – "in the settlement of Czyżewo." In the late 19th century this community was called *Czyżewo;* its current name is *Czyżew-Osada.* It's one of eight villages with hyphenated double names, of which the first is *Czyżew,* in an area some 60-70 km. southwest of Białystok in northeastern Poland. Czyżew-Osada is classified now as a *wieś,* "village," but as of the late 19th century it was classified as an *osada* or "settlement." All this illustrates the difficulty of giving a precise translation in English of a term like *посадъ,* and even of rendering place names accurately.

Овъявляемъ, что въ присутствіи ***свидѣтелей*** *Лейзора Кельманова Веторжъ и Абрама Шмулева Алиоэсъ обоихъ солтысовъ по сорокъ три года отъ роду имѣющихъ, въ посадѣ Чижевѣ жительствующихъ* – "We declare that in the presence of witnesses, Lejzor Vetorz, son of Kelman, and Abram Alioes, son of Szmul, both synagogue trustees, both 43 years of age, residing in the settlement of Czyżewo..."

Веторж ... Алиоэсъ – These names seem rather unusual, and neither appears in Alexander Beider's books on Jewish surnames in the Kingdom of Poland and the Russian Empire. The witnesses' signatures, at the end of the document, appear to read *Веторжъ, Wetorz,* and *Алоесъ, Aloes.* In such cases it is best to render the names as given in the text, but to make a note that they are questionable and to keep looking for sources that confirm or correct those versions.

по сорокъ три года отъ роду – Among its other uses, the preposition *по* (usually with the dative) in numerical expressions involving more than one person usually means "each, apiece." This says each witness was 43 years old.

солтысовъ – genitive plural of *солтысъ,* a Cyrillic rendering of Polish *sołtys,* which usually means a kind of bailiff or village administrator. It is conceivable that a Jew might be a *sołtys* in a given community, but it is unlikely there would be two men occupying this position in a small settlement. Beider's book on Jewish surnames in the Kingdom of Poland notes that *sołtys* can appear as a vernacular rendering of the Hebrew term **גבאי**, *gabbai,* a synagogue warden or trustee, collector of alms, manager of the affairs of a Hasidic rabbi. In this instance it makes good sense that these witnesses were synagogue trustees, and that seems the most plausible translation of this term.

заключенъ *религіозный брачный союзъ* – "a religious marital union was contracted..."

между *Морткою Шмуклеревичъ холостымъ урожденномъ въ посадѣ Визна Ломжинскаго уѣзда перваго/тринадцатаго Декабря тысяча восемьсотъ семьдесять пятаго года сыномъ Аврама и Ханы супруговъ Шмуклеровичъ, плотникомъ въ посадѣ Чижевѣ жительствующимъ* – "... between Mortka Szmuklerewicz, single, born in the town of Wizna, in Łomża county, on the 1st/13th of December, 1875, the son of the married couple the Szmuklerewiczes, Abram and Chana, a carpenter residing in the settlement of Czyżewo ..."

между Морткою Шмуклеревичъ – "between Mortka Szmuklerewicz." His first name might also be *Mortko,* as first names ending in *-o* are often declined like feminine nouns, and this *-ою* ending is feminine (an archaic instrumental form, modern *-ой*). *Szmuklerewicz* means "son of the lace-maker or haberdasher" (Polish *szmuklerz*).

холостымъ урожденномъ въ посадѣ Визна Ломжинскаго уѣзда перваго/тринадцатаго Декабря тысяча восемьсотъ семьдесятъ пятаго года – "single, born in the settlement of Wizna, in Łomża county, on the 1st/13th of December 1875."

сыномъ Аврама и Ханы супруговъ Шмуклеровичъ, плотникомъ въ посадѣ Чижевѣ жительствующимъ – "the son of the married couple the Szmuklerewiczes, Abram and Chana, a carpenter residing in the settlement of Czyżewo." Note that it is Mortka whose occupation is given; for all we know his father Abram may have been a carpenter, too, but the record says nothing on that score.

а *Брайкою Палгонъ девицею двадцать три года отъ роду имѣющею урожденною и жительствующею въ посадѣ Чижевѣ при родителяхъ торговцахъ, дочерью Абрама и Шейны Цедекъ супруговъ Палгонъ* – "and Brajka Pałgon, single, age 23, born and residing with her parents, merchants, in the settlement of Czyżewo, the daughter of the married couple the Pałgons, Abram and Szejna née Cedek..."

урожденною и жительствующею ... при родителяхъ торговцахъ, дочерью Абрама и Шейны Цедекъ супруговъ Палгонъ – "born and residing ... with her parents, [who are] merchants, the daughter of the Pałgons, Abram and Szejna Cedek."

Бракъ этотъ *предшедствуенъ былъ тремя оглошеніями публикованными въ шабасные дни въ Чижевской еврейской божницѣ, шестнадцатаго, двадцать третьяго и тридцатаго Апрѣля текущаго года.* – "This marriage was preceded by three readings of the banns proclaimed on the Sabbath in the Czyżewo Jewish synagogue on the 16th, 23rd, and 30th of April of this year."

Бракъ этотъ *предшедствуенъ былъ тремя оглошеніями* – "This marriage was preceded by three readings of the banns...." The formulation of the keywords here differs from what we saw in the last document, ***Браку сему***, but this is just a slightly different way of saying the same thing. In this case we have *этот*, the standard modern word for "this"; in the last document we saw the dative singular form of *сей*, an archaic word for "this" (see page 43). In this document the construction is passive, "This marriage was preceded by three readings of the banns," so ***Бракъ этотъ*** is in the nominative case; in the prior document the construction was active, "Three readings of the banns preceded this marriage." When the verb meaning "to precede," *предшествовать*, is followed by an object, that object is in the dative case, which explains the dative ***Браку сему***. The form seen here, *предшедствуенъ*, is unusual; but clearly it is a participle used to mean "[was] preceded."

публикованными въ шабасные дни въ Чижевской еврейской божницѣ – "proclaimed on days of the Sabbath in the Czyżewo Jewish synagogue." Note the expression *въ шабасные дни*, "on Sabbath days"; the form *шабашный* is also seen.

шестнадцатаго, двадцать третьяго и тридцатаго Апрѣля текущаго года – "on the 16th, 23rd, and 30th of April of this year."

Новобрачные *заявили, что предбрачный договоръ между ними заключенъ не былъ.* – "The newlyweds stated that no prenuptial agreement had been made between them."

Новобрачные *заявили, что предбрачный договоръ между ними заключенъ не былъ.* – Compare this wording to that in Document VI-20 (page 253), ***Новобрачные*** *объявляютъ что брачный договоръ между ими заключенъ не былъ.* The only differences are that here "the newlyweds stated" instead of "the newlyweds declare," and here the agreement is specified as prenuptial, *предбрачный*, not just marital, *брачный*.

Позволеніе *женихамъ заявлено словѣсно лично присутствующимъ родителямъ ихъ.* – "Permission was given the newlyweds orally by their parents, who were present in person."

Позволеніе *женихамъ заявлено словѣсно лично присутствующимъ родителямъ ихъ.* – Here, too, the differences between this and the version seen in the last document are minor. Here the parents' permission is mentioned one sentence later than in Document VI-20, and it is specifically given *женихамъ*, "to the ones marrying." There is also a non-standard usage, *присутствующимъ родителямъ*, a dative form when the sense requires instrumental, *присутствующими родителями*.

Религіозный обрядъ бракосочетанія совершенъ былъ раввиномъ въ посадѣ Чижевѣ Янкелемъ Эпштейнъ. – "The religious marriage ceremony was performed in the settlement of Czyżewo by Jankiel Epsztejn."

Актъ сей *прочитанъ Нами свидѣтелями и раввиномъ подписанъ, прочіе въ немъ упомянутые заявили, что писать не умѣютъ.* – "This document was read aloud and signed by Us, the witnesses, and the rabbi; the others mentioned in it stated that they do not know how to write."

Я. Эпштейнъ. Лейзоръ Веторжъ. Абрамъ Алоесъ. Содержащій акты гражданскаго состоянія войтъ гмины Дмохи Глинки [signature illegible] – "J. Epsztejn. Lejzor Wetorz. Abram Aloes. Civil Registrar, *Wójt* of the district of Dmochy Glinki *[signature illegible]*."

Translation – "This happened in the settlement of Czyżewo on May 1, 1894, at 7 o'clock in the evening. We declare that in the presence of witnesses, Lejzor Vetorz, son of Kelman, and Abram Alioes, son of Szmul, both synagogue trustees, both 43 years of age, residing in the settlement of Czyżewo a religious marital union was contracted between Mortka Szmuklerewicz, single, born in the town of Wizna, in Łomża county, on the 1st/13th of December, 1875, the son of the married couple the Szmuklerewiczes, Abram and Chana, a carpenter residing in the settlement of Czyżewo, and Brajka Pałgon, single, age 23, born and residing with her parents, merchants, in the settlement of Czyżewo, the daughter of the married couple the Pałgons, Abram and Szejna née Cedek. This marriage was preceded by three readings of the banns proclaimed on the Sabbath in the Czyżewo Jewish synagogue on the 16th, 23rd, and 30th of April of this year. The newlyweds stated that no prenuptial agreement had been made between them. The religious marriage ceremony was performed in the settlement of Czyżewo by Jankiel Epsztejn. This document was read aloud and signed by Us, the witnesses, and the rabbi; the others mentioned in it stated that they do not know how to write. [Signed] J. Epsztejn. Lejzor Wetorz. Abram Aloes. Civil Registrar, *Wójt* of the district of Dmochy Glinki *[signature illegible]*.

There is another sentence that may often appear in Jewish marriage records and should be explained. Not unreasonably, religious Jews felt that they were married if they underwent a Jewish religious marriage ceremony; that was what counted, not civil requirements. But in some circumstances the civil authorities did not recognize religious ceremonies as valid; such Jews were technically unwed in the eyes of the state, and any children they had were illegitimate. Later on it might prove advantageous to gain state recognition of the union and thus legitimize the children. So the parents might reluctantly comply with civil regulations regarding marriage; their attitude might be, "It doesn't really mean anything, but if it helps the kids, we'll do it." In such cases a formulation along the lines of the following, from an 1887 marriage record from Zaręby Kościelne in Poland, may appear. If so, it will usually come after the sentence beginning ***Новобрачные***, (the newlyweds' statement that they had made no prenuptial agreement):

Они заявили также, что прижитую ими	They stated also that by this marriage
до вступленія въ бракъ въ сожитію	record they acknowledge their
между собою ***дочь Двейру*** *родившуюся*	daughter Dwejra – begotten by them
въ посадѣ Чижевѣ пятнадцатаго	before their entry into marriage, during
Января тысяча восемьсотъ	their cohabitation, born in the
семьдесять седмаго года, настоящимъ	settlement of Czyżewo on the
брачнымъ актомъ ***признаютъ за***	15th of January of the year 1877 –
свою собственную *и на основаніи*	as their own, and on the basis
статьи двѣсти девяносто первой	of article 291 of the
Гражданскаго Кодекса Царства	Civil Code of the Kingdom
Польскаго, обезпечиваютъ ей	of Poland, they secure for her
состояніе и права законнаго	the status and rights of a legitimate
дитяти.	child.

The structure of this sentence is complex, taking full advantage of the freedom of word order that Russian grammar allows. After the introductory main clause *Они заявили также, что* ["They stated also that"], the first verb of the following clause is *признаютъ*, "they acknowledge," in line 7 (as printed above; in the actual record, of course, there's no telling what line this word would appear in). The direct object is *дочь Двейру*, "their daughter Dwejra," in line 3; next, logically, is the phrase *за свою собственную*, "as their own." So by registering their marriage legally, they can now recognize their daughter as legally theirs. What comes between are details on when she was begotten and when and where she was born.

The final section, stating that they hereby secure her rights under the Civil Code, is more straightforward. The last six lines are very nearly word-for-word. It's the first seven lines that may baffle researchers not fluent in Russian.

Of course there are possible variations in phrasing, conditioned by different circumstances. If it was a son begotten and born before their "civil" marriage, the word *дочь*, "daughter," in line three above would be replaced by *сына*, "son." If more than one child is affected, the word *дѣтей*, "children," would appear instead of, or as well as, *дочь* or *сына*.

This translation should help you get the gist of any such statements you see in these records. If your ancestors were Orthodox Jews, there is a real chance you will encounter something along these lines.

4. Document VI-22: A Russian Orthodox Columnar Marriage Register

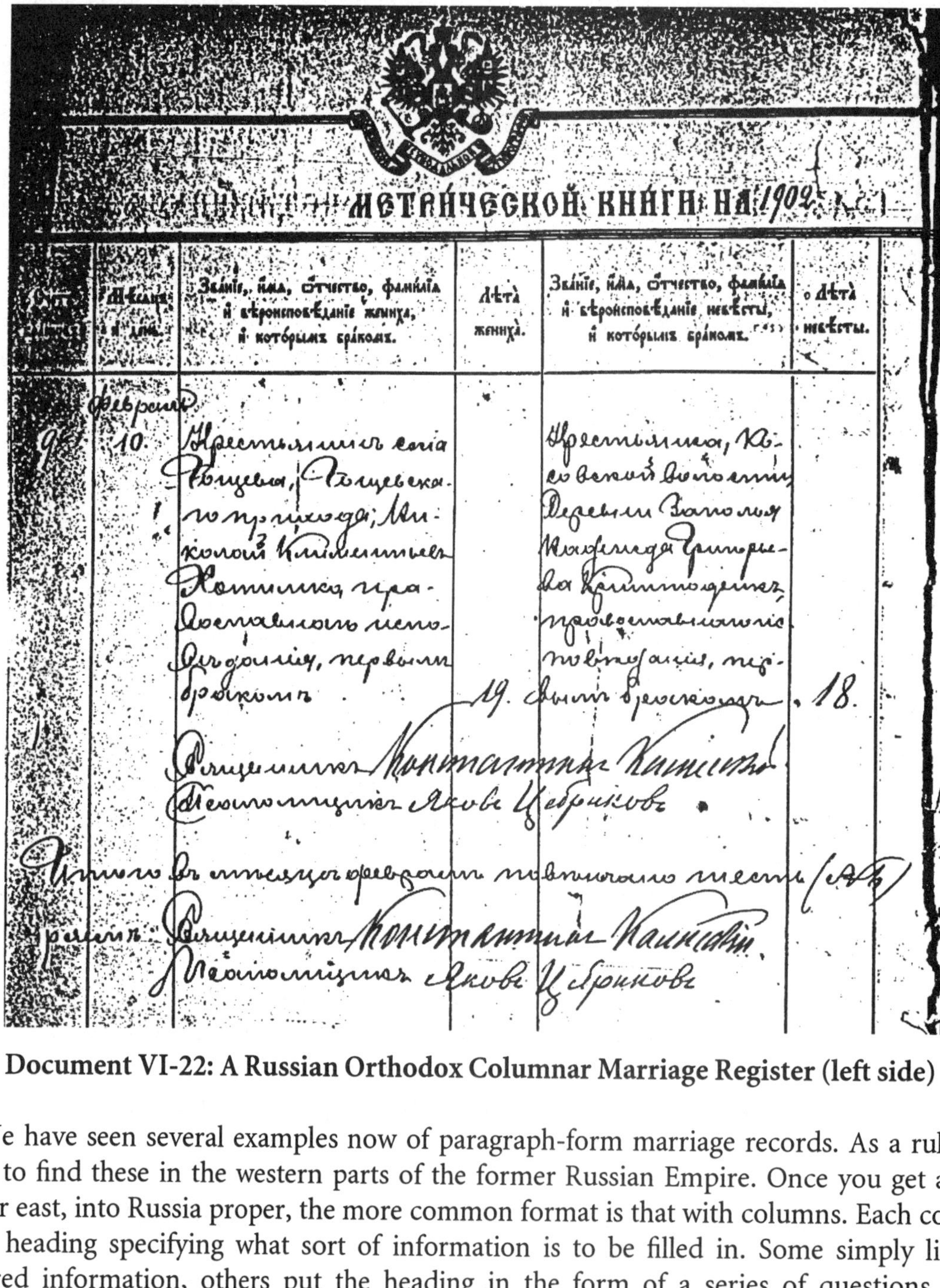
метрической книги на 1902 г.

Мѣсяцъ и день	Званіе, имя, отчество, фамилія и вѣроисповѣданіе жениха, и которымъ бракомъ.	Лѣта жениха.	Званіе, имя, отчество, фамилія и вѣроисповѣданіе невѣсты, и которымъ бракомъ.	Лѣта невѣсты.

Document VI-22: A Russian Orthodox Columnar Marriage Register (left side)

We have seen several examples now of paragraph-form marriage records. As a rule one tends to find these in the western parts of the former Russian Empire. Once you get a little farther east, into Russia proper, the more common format is that with columns. Each column has a heading specifying what sort of information is to be filled in. Some simply list the required information, others put the heading in the form of a series of questions to be answered. Either kind covers the same basic material, so that once you become familiar with a few samples, you are likely to have no great difficulty making sense of whatever variant you come across.

Document VI-22 is such a record. It's actually taken from a register of a Russian Orthodox parish in Volhynia (Polish name *Wołyń*), now in the independent nation of Ukraine. Each entry spans two facing pages; the one shown above is the left side; the right side of the same entry is reproduced on page 263.

The first thing to notice is that this register (again, like Document VI-12), uses letters of the Cyrillic alphabet as found in Old Church Slavonic (see page 48). They are highly stylized, but most are easy to recognize once you have become accustomed to standard Cyrillic. The letter ѧ is used instead of modern Russian **я**, and the letter ѡ, based on the Greek omega ω, is used for **о**. The other characters should present no real difficulties, although the extended form of *у*, looking almost like an English numeral *8*, looks a bit exotic at first glance.

The heading across the top of both pages reads:

Метрической Книги на *1902* годъ, часть вторѧ о бракосочетавшихсѧ.

This translates as "Register for 1902, Part Two, Marriages." As we have remarked earlier, Russian registers are typically divided into three parts; part one is devoted to births, part two to marriages, and part three to deaths. Thus even if we did not have the phrase о бракосочетавшихся, the simple fact that this is specified as "Part Two" would tell us it deals with marriages contracted in the parish during 1902.

Column 1: Счетъ бракѡвъ – "Marriage Number." In modern Russian this would be spelled Счет браков. Entries were number sequentially as they were made, and this is entry 9.

Column 2: Мѣсяцъ и день – "Month and day." Here: *Февраль 10,* "February 10."

Column 3: Званіе, имѧ, ѡтчество, фамилія и вѣроисповѣданіе жениха, и которымъ бракомъ – "Status, first name, patronymic, surname and faith of the groom, and which marriage" (i. e., is this his first marriage, his second, third, what?).

званіе – this noun means literally "calling," but in this context it asks for the social class *жениха,* "of the groom." The answer here is *Крестьянинъ*, "peasant."

имѧ, ѡтчество, фамилія – in modern Russian имя, отчество, и фамилия. This asks for the three standard components of a Russian's full name: the first name, patronymic (i. e., name formed from his father's name, "son of _," see pages 28-29), and surname. Here the answer reads as follows:

Крестьянинъ села Гощева, Гощевскаго прихода, Николай Климентьевъ Хотимко, православнаго исповѣданія, первымъ бракомъ – "A peasant of the village of Goshchevo, parish of Goshchevo, Nikolai Khotimko, son of Kliment, of the Orthodox faith, first marriage." *Kliment* is a Russian form of the name seen as *Clement* in English, *Klementy* in Polish. This village is now in Belarus, south of Slonim; it is called *Гощево, Goshchevo,* in Russian, and *Гошчава, Hoshchava,* in Belarusian.

вѣроисповѣданіе – this noun, in modern Russian spelled *вероисповедание,* means "faith, religion." In the answer the similar term *исповѣданіе* is used. As one would expect, he was *православнаго исповѣданія*, "of the Orthodox faith."

которымъ бракомъ – который is often used as a relative pronoun, meaning "who, which, that." It also can mean "which" (of a number of possibilities), and it is used here in that sense: which marriage was this, his first, second, etc.

Column 4: Лѣта жениха – "groom's age," literally "years of the groom. The answer is 19.

Column 5: Званіе, имѧ, ѡ тчество, фамилія и вѣроисповѣданіе невѣсты и которымъ бракомъ – "Status, first name, patronymic, surname and faith of the bride, and which marriage."

невѣсты – "of the bride." This column asks for the same information as column 3, but for the bride. The answer reads as follows:

Крестьянка Косовской волости, Деревни Заполья, Надежда Григорьева Криштофикъ, православнаго исповѣданія, первымъ бракомъ – "A peasant of Kosovo district, Zapolye village, Nadezhda Krishtofik, daughter of Grigoriy, of the Orthodox faith, first marriage." *Григорій, Grigoriy* is the standard Russian form of the name seen as *Gregory* in English, *Grzegorz* in Polish. These localities are also in Belarus, south of Slonim. The town called *Косово, Kosovo,* in Russian is called *Косава, Kosava,* in Belarusian.

Column 6: Лѣта невѣсты – "bride's age"; the answer is 18.

[The rest of the columns, on the right-hand page in the original, are reproduced on page 263.]

Column 7: Кто совершалъ таинство – "Who administered the sacrament?" The answer reads: *Священникъ Константинъ Камисскій съ псальомщикомъ Яковомъ Цебриковымъ*, "The priest (i. e., Father, Reverend) Konstantin Kamisskiy with the psalmist Yakov Tsebrikov." Note that their signatures appear at the end of the record.

Column 8: Кто были поручители? – "Who were the guarantors?" The more normal term in English, of course, would be "witnesses"; essentially, they were the people who appeared on behalf of the bride and groom. The answer to this question reads as follows:

По женихѣ: крестьяне села Гощева Стефанъ Ивановъ Порхомикъ и Феодоръ Андреевъ Юращикъ. По невѣстѣ: крестьянинъ деревни Заполья Яковъ Ивановъ Криштофикъ и крестьянинъ села Гощева Иванъ Андреевъ Юращикъ. – "For the groom: peasants of the village of Goshchevo, Stefan Porkhomik, son of Ivan, and Feodor Yurashchik, son of Andrei. For the bride: a peasant of the village of Zapolye, Yakov Krishtofik, son of Ivan, and a peasant of the village of Goshchevo, Ivan Yurashchik, son of Andrei."

Column 9: Подпись свидѣтелей записи по желанію? – "Signature of the witnesses, [and] comments as desired." The last phrase is often seen in records of various kinds, and simply means the registrar should write in any comments *по желанію*, "according to desire," i. e., as he wished. Here no signatures or comments appear, but the priest and the psalmist sign below the entry itself, at lower left, beginning in column 3 and extending to the right:

Священникъ Константинъ Камисскій – Father Konstantin Kamisskiy
Псаломщикъ Яковъ Цебриковъ – Psalmist Yakov Tsebrikov

Below this is the following notation:

Итого въ мѣсяцѣ февралѣ повѣнчало шесть (№ 6) паръ, а лицъ двѣнадцать (№ 12), что удос-

In total in the month of February there were married six (6) couples, twelve (12) individuals, which --

Almost certainly the last word, which was cut off during copying, was *удостовѣряемъ*, "we certify," since the signatures of the priest and psalmist follow.

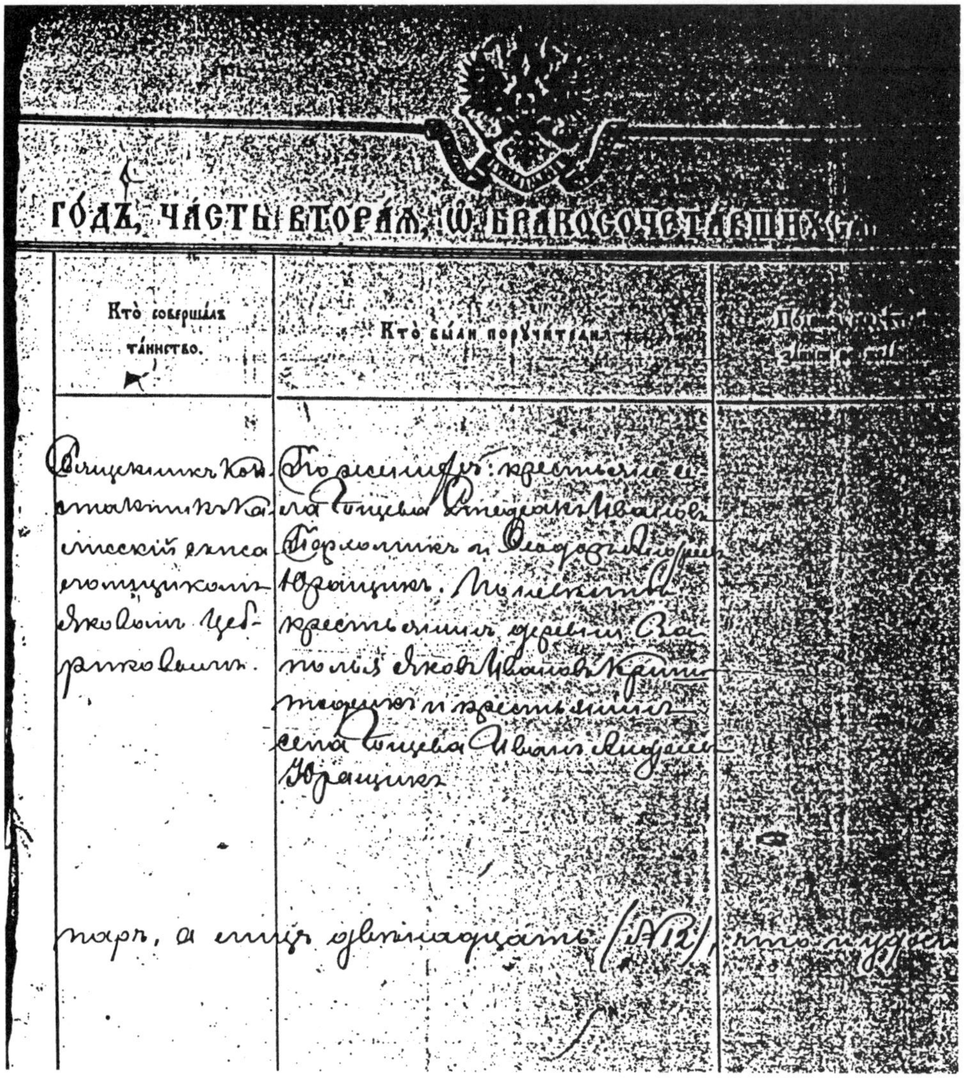

Document VI-22: A Russian Orthodox Columnar Marriage Register (right side)

5. Document VI-23: A Roman Catholic Columnar Marriage Register from Poland

Document VI-23, reproduced on page 264, represents a real challenge to the unaided researcher. The quality of the copy leaves a lot to be desired; the handwriting could be better; there are, as usual, a number of archaic words, case endings, and spellings; the wording is so tortuous that even someone fluent in Russian could have trouble putting it all together.

Furthermore, the interference of the native language is a real factor. In the western part of the Russian Empire, Russian was not the first language of most of the people; they grew up speaking Polish, Lithuanian, Belarusian, Ukrainian, etc.. When the priests filled out these records, they tried to use proper Russian; but sometimes expressions in their native languages came to mind first, and they ended up writing a kind of Russian heavily influenced by those languages. Good luck finding a dictionary that helps you with this!

If you know what should appear in a given place, however, you can hope to decipher, first one word, then another, and gradually the whole thing. So let's take a close look.

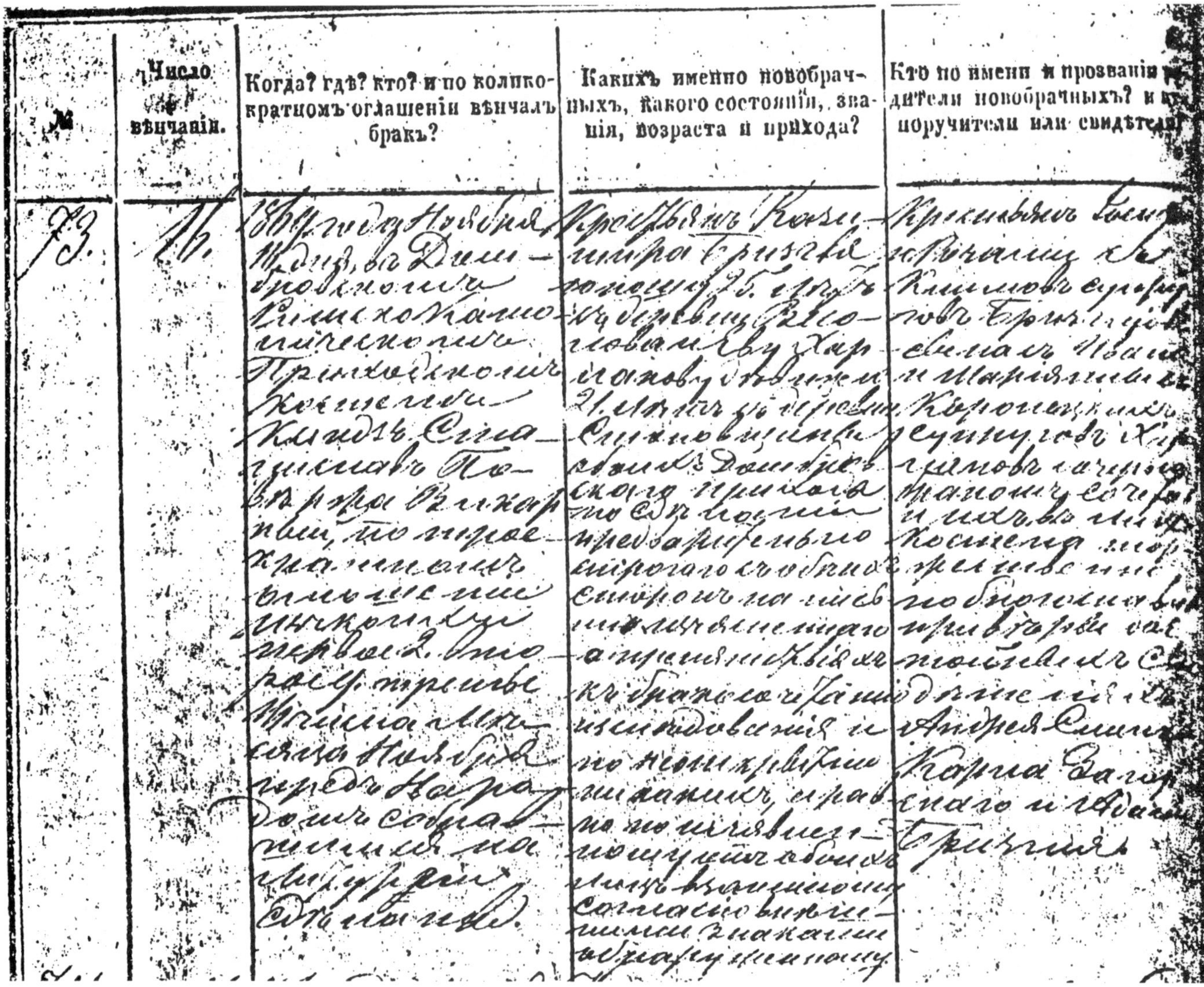

№	Число вѣнчанія.	Когда? гдѣ? кто? и по коликократномъ оглашеніи вѣнчалъ бракъ?	Какихъ именно новобрачныхъ, какого состоянія, званія, возраста и прихода?	Кто по имени и прозванію родители новобрачныхъ? и кто поручители или свидѣтели?
73.	16.			

Document VI-23: A Roman Catholic Marriage Register from Poland

Column 1: № – the record number, here 73.

Column 2: Число вѣнчанія – "Number of the marriage," here 16.

Column 3: Когда? гдѣ? кто? и по коликократномъ оглашеніи вѣнчалъ бракъ? – "When? Where? Who? And after how many readings of the banns was the marriage blessed?" The answer is long and complicated, and reads as follows:

1869 года Ноября 16 дня въ Домбровскомъ Римско-Католическомъ Приходскомъ Костелѣ Ксендзъ Станиславъ Повѣржа Викарный. По троекратномъ оглашеніи изъ коихъ первое 2. второе 9, третье 16 числа мѣсяца Ноября передъ народомъ собравшимся на литургіи сдѣланы. – "The year 1869, the 16th day of November, in the Dąbrowa Roman Catholic parish church. Rev. Stanisław Powierza, assistant pastor. After three readings of the banns, of which the first was done on the 2nd, the second on the 9th, and the third on the 16th of November, before the people assembled for the liturgy." Notice that this entry literally answers each question in the order it was asked.

73	*16*	*1869 года Ноября 16 дня въ Домбровскомъ Римско-Католическомъ Приходскомъ Костелѣ Ксендзъ Станиславъ Повѣржа Викарный. По троекратномъ оглашеніи изъ коихъ первое 2. второе 9, третье 16 числа мѣсяца Ноября передъ народомъ собравшимся на литургіи сдѣланы*	*Крестьянъ Казимира Бризгля юношу 25 лѣтъ съ деревни Весолова и Еву Харланову дѣвицей 21 лѣтъ съ деревни Смоловщизны обоихъ Домбровскаго прихода по сдѣланіи предварительно строгаго съ обѣихъ сторонъ на письмѣ изъясненнаго о препятствіяхъ къ бракосочетанію изслѣдованія и по неоткрытіи никакихъ, а равно по изъявленному имъ обоихъ лицъ, взаимному согласію внѣшнами знаками обнаруженному.*	*Крестьянъ Іосифа и Розаліи съ Климовъ супруговъ Бризгловъ сына съ Ивана и Маріянны съ Коронецкихъ супруговъ Харлановъ дочерью бракомъ сочеталъ и ихъ въ лицѣ Костела торжественно поблагословилъ при вѣры достойныхъ свидѣтелеяхъ Андрея Слинки Карла Загорскаго и Адама Бризгля.*

This handwriting is terribly difficult to read, and other similar documents we've seen are not much better. It's literally true that if you don't what words appear where, you may never be able to make them out. So we've given the text above in italic typeface, which is similar to the cursive and may enable you to familiarize yourself with the terminology, which tends to be fairly consistent from one record to the next.

Column 4: Какихъ именно новобрачныхъ, какого состоянія, званія, возраста и прихода? – "What are the names of the newlyweds, of what status, occupation, age, and parish are they?" The answer reads as follows:

> *Крестьянъ Казимира Бризгля юношу 25 лѣтъ съ деревни Весолова и Еву Харланову дѣвицей 21 лѣтъ съ деревни Смоловщизны обоихъ Домбровскаго прихода по сдѣланіи предварительно строгаго съ обѣихъ сторонъ на письмѣ изъясненнаго о препятствіяхъ къ бракосочетанію изслѣдованія и по неоткрытіи никакихъ, а равно по изъявленному имъ обоихъ лицъ, взаимному согласію внѣшнами знаками обнаруженному.* – "The peasants Kazimierz Bryzgiel, the groom, age 25, from the village of Wesołowo, and Ewa Charłan, the bride, age 21, from the village of Smołowszczyzna, both of the parish of Dąbrowa. After conducting beforehand a strict examination in writing of both parties on the impediments to marriage, and after

discovering none, and also after their expression of mutual agreement expressed by both parties by outward signs."

The grammatical structure of this response is conditioned on the fact that the question asks for the names of the newlyweds in the accusative case—i. e., the priest is responding to the question "Whom did you join in marriage?" Thus *Крестьянъ* is accusative plural, "The peasants"; and the names of the bride and groom, and all nouns and adjectives referring to them, should be in the accusative: *Казимира Бризгля юношу*, "Kazimir Brizgiel, a young man," *и Еву Харланову*, "and Eva Kharlan." Since these are Poles, it is appropriate to give the Polish versions of their names, Kazimierz Bryzgiel and Ewa Charłan." Here are notes on individual words, meanings and forms:

юношу – accusative of *юноша*, "young man, youth," used here to mean "the groom." Notice that in form it is a feminine noun, and is declined that way, even though it refers to a male! Also seen in this position is a form of the adjective *холостой*, "single."

дѣвицею – instrumental of *дѣвица*, "maiden, single woman." This usage of the instrumental seems odd; accusative *дѣвицу* is what we'd expect to see.

съ деревни Смоловщизны – "from the village of Smolowszczyzna." This village is now called *Osmołowszczyzna*, and obviously a researcher trying to find this place needs to know that. Reference to good gazetteers would be the best way to discover the change in name.

по сдѣланіи предварительно строгаго съ обѣихъ сторонъ на письмѣ изъясненнаго о препятствіяхъ къ бракосочетанію изслѣдованія и по неоткрытіи никакихъ, а равно по изъявленному имъ обоихъ лицъ, взаимному согласію внѣшнами знаками обнаруженному. – The "strict examination in writing" refers to a premarital examination like Document VI-19 on pages 242-247.

This part of the entry statement is all legalese, and of no real value to a genealogical researcher. We have spelled out and translated the Russian text solely because if you know what it says, it may provide a sample of the handwriting that will enable you to decipher difficult words in the first part of the response, which does contain useful data. Otherwise, don't waste your time deciphering it, as it doesn't tell you enough to be worth the trouble. (Incidentally, if you have a copy of Volume 1 of *In Their Words*, on Polish documents, this formulation is simply a translation into Russian of the formula used in Document VI-23, pp. 226-231, of that work.)

Column 5: Кто по имени и прозванію родители новобрачныхъ? и кто поручители или свидѣтели?– "Who, by first name and surname, are the parents of the newlyweds? And who are the guarantors or witnesses?" The answer reads as follows:

Крестьянъ Іосифа и Розаліи съ Климовъ супруговъ Бризгловъ сына съ Ивана и Маріянны съ Коронецкихъ супруговъ Харлановъ дочерью бракомъ сочеталъ и ихъ въ лицѣ Костела торжественно поблагословилъ при вѣры достойныхъ свидѣтелеяхъ Андрея Слинки Карла Загорскаго и Адама Бризгля. – "[I] united in marriage the son of the peasants, the married couple the Bryzgiels, Józef and Rozalia née Klim, with the daughter of the married couple the Charłans, Jan and Maryanna née

Koroniecka, and blessed them solemnly in the eyes of the Church before credible witnesses, Andrzej Ślinko, Karol Zagórski, and Adam Bryzgiel."

The structure of this reply is particularly difficult to unravel. The subject and verb appear in line 10 of the original, *бракомъ сочеталъ*, "[I] joined in marriage" (literally I joined by means of marriage). The direct object is *сына*, "son," the first word in line 5: "I joined in marriage the son..." Then comes the first few words of the answer, "of the peasants Józef and Rozalia née Klim, the married couple the Bryzgiels." Next comes *съ*, "with," and *дочерью*, the last word in line 9; it is followed logically by *Ивана и Маріянны съ Коронецкихъ супруговъ Харлановъ*, "of the Charłans, Jan and Maryanna née Koroniecka." So the word order as we'd put it is "I joined in marriage the son of the peasants Józef and Rozalia née Klim, the married couple the Bryzgiels, with the daughter of Jan and Maryanna née Koroniecka, the married couple the Charłans."

But if you translate it literally, what it says is: "Of the peasants Józef and Rozalia of the Klims, the spouses Bryzgiel, the son, with of Jan and Maryanna of the Koronieckis, the spouses Charłan, the daughter, I joined in marriage"! The only reason Russian can get away with this is because the grammatical endings tie everything together coherently. It makes life tough, however, for those of us who speak a language that relies far more on word order than on word endings!

Incidentally, research into this family's history established that the bride's mother's maiden name was actually *Korzeniecka*, not *Koroniecka*. Yet a close look at the document certainly seems to show that it reads:

съ Коронецкихъ

A phonetic rendering of this by English values would give *s Koronetskikh*, "of the Koronetskis," giving a maiden name of *Koronetski*, or by Polish spelling, *Koroniecki*. There seems to be no way to read it as the Russian version of "of the Korzenieckis," which would look more like this:

съ Корженецкихъ

This shows why researchers must always appreciate the need for obtaining multiple documents to compare names and establish the correct forms. No single document can be relied upon because the chances for error are too great.

As difficult as these records are to read, they can provide a lot of information. So perhaps you'll forgive us if we show you one more sample. **Document VI-24**, on page 268, deals with members of the same family as the birth record Document VI-14, on pages 230-232. It is from the area of Krakės, Lithuania. The places mentioned in it are *Бейсагола*, in Lithuanian *Baisogala; Кубилюны*, in Lithuanian *Kubiliūnai; Гринкишки*, in Lithuanian *Grinkiškis;* and *Кроки, Krakės*. The surnames of the people involved are *Бледисъ, Bledis; Піотровскій, Petrauskas; Пранинскій, Praninskas; Усевичъ, Usevičius*; and *Легечинскій, Legečinskas*.

The phrasing is very similar to that in Document VI-23, but just different enough to be a challenge. Perhaps you'd like to try your hand at deciphering it. If you need help, the translation begins just below it, and the text is given in an "italic" Cyrillic typeface on page 269. But we suggest you not peek till you've tried it without help!

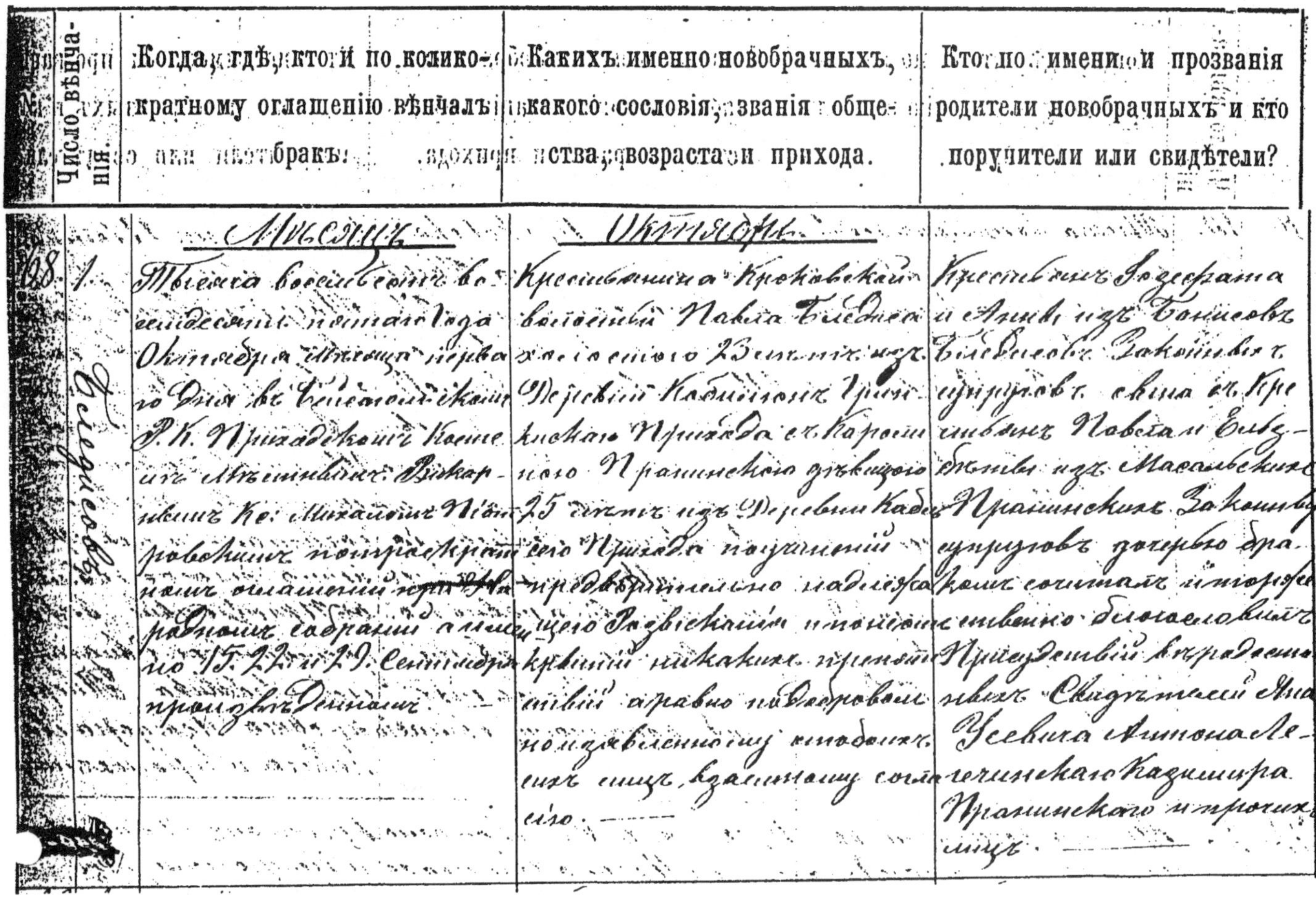

№	Число вѣнчанія.	Когда, гдѣ, кто и по коликократному оглашенію вѣнчалъ бракъ?	Какихъ именно новобрачныхъ, какого сословія, званія, общества, возраста и прихода.	Кто по имени и прозванія родители новобрачныхъ и кто поручители или свидѣтели?
		Мѣсяцъ	Октябрь	
68	1			

Document VI-24: A Roman Catholic Marriage Register from Lithuania

Column 1: № – the record number, here 68.

Column 2: Число вѣнчанія – "Date of the wedding," here on the 1st of *Мѣсяцъ Октябрь*, "the month of October."

Column 3: Когда? гдѣ? кто? и по коликократному оглашенію вѣнчалъ бракъ? – "When? Where? Who? And after how many readings of the banns was the marriage blessed?" The answer reads as follows:

> *Тысяча восемьсотъ восемдесять пятаго года Октября мѣсяца перваго дня въ Бейсагольскомъ Р.-К. Приходскомъ Костелѣ Мѣстнымъ Викарнымъ Кс. Михаиломъ Піотровскимъ по троекратномъ оглашеній при Народномъ собраніи а именно 15. 22. и 29. Сентября произвѣденномъ.* – "The year 1885, the month of October, the 1st day, in the Baisagola Roman Catholic parish church. By the local assistant pastor Rev. Mykolas Petrauskas *[or, if he was Polish, Michał Piotrowski]*. After three readings of the banns produced before the assembly of the people, to wit, on the 15th, 22nd and 29th of September."
>
> Notice that here the priest wrote the date out in longhand; he also phrases the dates of the banns slightly differently. But the wording is very similar to that in the previous sample. As for the priest's name, there's no way to know for sure whether he went by the Lithuanian form *Mykolas Petrauskas* or the Polish form *Michał Piotrowski*.

<u>*Мѣсяцъ*</u> *Тысяча восемьсотъ восемдесять пятаго года Октября мѣсяца перваго Дня въ Бейсагольскомъ Р.-К. Приходскомъ Костелѣ Мѣстнымъ Викарнымъ Кс. Михаиломъ Піотровскимъ по троекратномъ оглашеній при Народномъ собраніи а именно 15. 22. и 29. Сентября произвѣденномъ.*	<u>*Октябрь*</u> *Крестьяинна Кроковской волостьи Павла Бледиса холостаго 23 лѣтъ изъ Деревни Кабилюнъ Гринкискаго Прихода съ Каролиною Пранинскою дѣвицею 25 лѣтъ изъ Деревни Кабель сего Прихода по дѣланій предварительно надлежащею Розысканіи и по неоткрытіи никакихъ препятствій а равно по доброровольно изявленному отъ обоихъ сихъ лицъ взаимному согласію.*	*Крестьянъ Іозефата и Анны изъ Бонисовъ Бледисовъ законныхъ супруговъ сына съ Крестьянъ Павела и Ельзбѣты изъ Масальскихъ Пранинскихъ законныхъ супруговъ дочерью бракомъ сочеталъ и торжественно благословилъ Присудствій вѣродостойныхъ Свидѣтелеяхъ Яна Усевича Антона Легечинскаго Казимира Пранинскаго и прочихъ лицъ.*

Text of Columns 3-5 of Document VI-24

Column 4: Какихъ именно новобрачныхъ, какого сословія, званія, общества, возраста и прихода?– "What are the names of the newlyweds, of what status, occupation, community, age, and parish are they?" The answer reads as follows:

Крестьяинна Кроковской волостьи Павла Бледиса холостаго 23 лѣтъ изъ Деревни Кабилюнъ Гринкискаго Прихода съ Каролиною Пранинскою дѣвицею 25 лѣтъ изъ Деревни Кабель сего Прихода по дѣланій предварительно надлежащею Розысканіи и по неоткрытіи никакихъ препятствій а равно по доброровольно изявленному отъ обоихъ сихъ лицъ взаимному согласію.– "A peasant of Krakės district, Povilas Bledis, single, age 23, from the village of Kabiliūnai *[sic]*, of Grinkiškis parish, with Karolina Praninskas, a single woman, age 25, from the village of Kabliai of this parish, after conducting the required preliminary examination and after discovering no impediments, and also after a voluntarily expressed mutual consent from both these parties."

There is some slight uncertainty about two place names here. *Кабилюнъ*, literally *Kabiliun*, is almost certainly a mistake and should be *Кубилюны, Kubiliūnai*, a village between Baisagola and Grinkiškis, the site of a Roman Catholic parish church, and specifically mentioned in connection with the Bledis family in Document VI-14. Also, the bride is said to come from *Кабель*, in Baisagola parish. The most likely candidate for this place is a small village Kabliai, near Baisagola; phonetically that is consistent with the Russian form. But only actual research could confirm that it is the right spot.

Column 5: Кто по имени и прозванія родители новобрачныхъ и кто поручители или свидѣтели?– "Who, by first name and surname, are the parents of the newlyweds? And who are the guarantors or witnesses" The answer reads as follows:

Крестьянъ Іозефата и Анны изъ Бонисовъ Бледисовъ законныхъ супруговъ сына съ Крестьянъ Павела и Ельзбѣты изъ Масальскихъ Пранинскихъ законныхъ супруговъ дочерью бракомъ сочеталъ и торжественно благословилъ Присудствій вѣродостойныхъ Свидѣтелеяхъ Яна Усевича Антона Легечинскаго Казимира Пранинскаго и прочихъ лицъ. – “[I] united in marriage the son of the peasants, the married couple the Bledises, Juozapotas and Ona née Banys, with the daughter of the married couple the Praninskases, Povilas and Elzbieta née Masalskas, and blessed them solemnly in the presence of credible witnesses, Jonas Usevičius, Antanas Legečinskas, Kazimieras Praninskas, and other persons.”

6. Document VI-25: A Jewish Columnar Marriage Register from Russian Poland

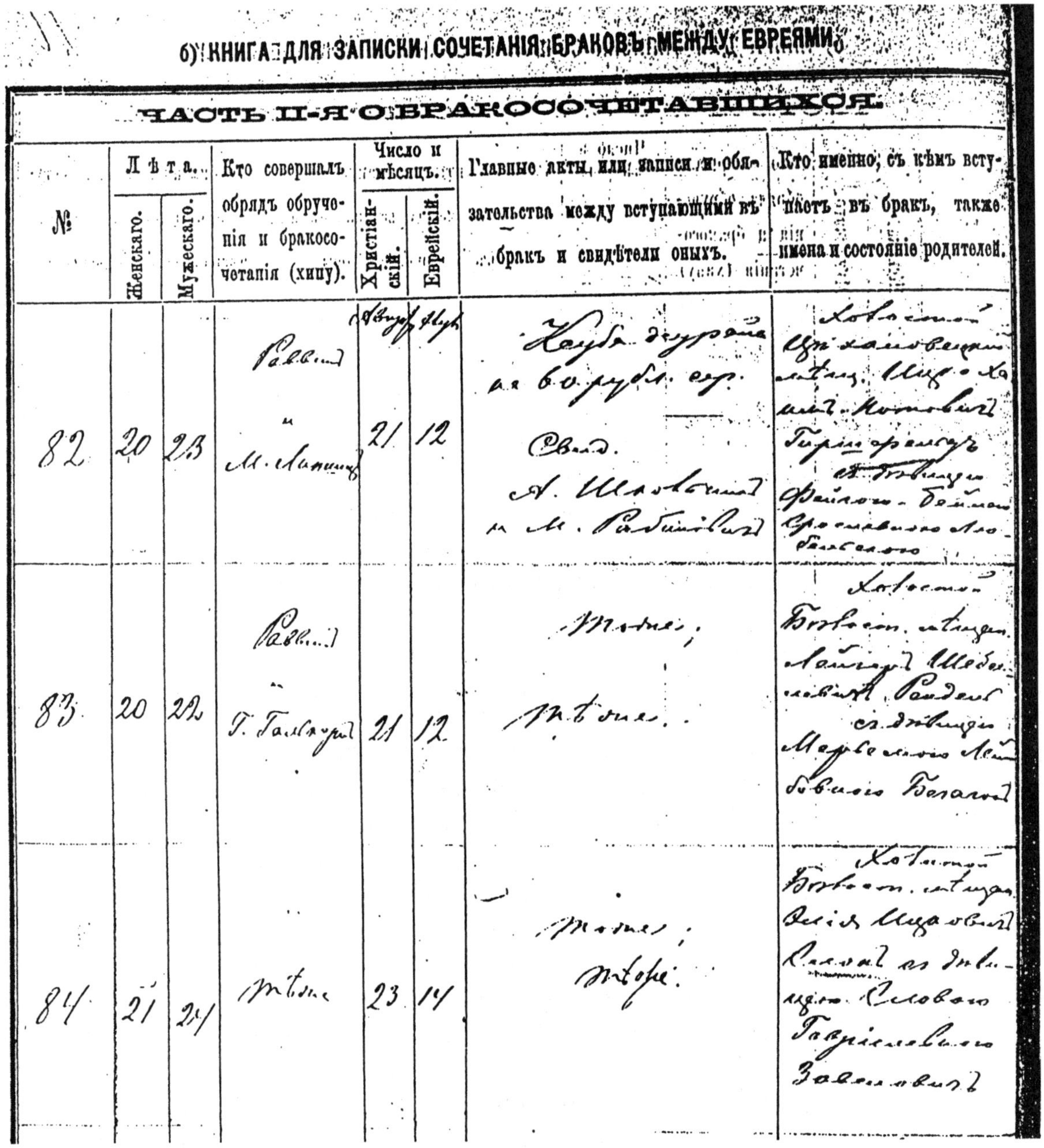

б) КНИГА ДЛЯ ЗАПИСКИ СОЧЕТАНІЯ БРАКОВЪ МЕЖДУ ЕВРЕЯМИ.

ЧАСТЬ II-я О БРАКОСОЧЕТАВШИХСЯ.

№	Лѣта. Женскаго.	Лѣта. Мужескаго.	Кто совершалъ обрядъ обручепія и бракосочетанія (хипу).	Число и мѣсяцъ. Христіанскій.	Число и мѣсяцъ. Еврейскій.	Главные акты, или записи и обязательства между вступающими въ бракъ и свидѣтели оныхъ.	Кто именно, съ кѣмъ вступаетъ въ бракъ, также имена и состояніе родителей.
82	20	23	[illegible]	21	12	[illegible]	[illegible]
83	20	22	[illegible]	21	12	[illegible]	[illegible]
84	21	24	[illegible]	23	14	[illegible]	[illegible]

Document VI-25: A Jewish Columnar Marriage Register from Russian Poland

Document VI-25 on page 270 provides an example of a Jewish columnar marriage record. As one might expect, it differs somewhat from the equivalent record for Christians, but not enormously. It also is comparable in many ways to Jewish columnar birth records, such as Documents VI-15 and VI-16, pages 233-239.

The heading at the top of the page reads:

КНИГА ДЛЯ ЗАПИСКИ СОЧЕТАНІЯ БРАКОВЪ МЕЖДУ ЕВРЕЯМИ

"Book for Registration of Marriages Contracted Between Jews"

The heading spanning all the columns reads ЧАСТЬ II-Я О БРАКОСОЧЕТАВШИХСЯ, literally "Part II, of Those Married," but better rendered as "Part II. Marriages." For the numbering of register sections, see the note to *о родившихся за 1897 года* on page 213.

The column headings, and the information supplied under them for the top entry, read as follows:

Column 1: № – the record number, here 82.

Column 2: Лѣта: Женскаго | Мужескаго – "Ages: Female | Male." In record 82, the bride was 20, the groom 23.

Column 3: Кто совершалъ обрядъ обрученія и бракосочетанія (хипу) – "Who performed the ceremony of betrothal and marriage." The name of the rabbi who officiated at the wedding appears here. In record 82, it was *Раввинъ М. Липшицъ*, "Rabbi M. Lipszyc" (typically *Lipshitz* in English). As for *хипу*, nominative *хипа*, Jewish experts we contacted suggested it is a Russified version of Hebrew **חופה**, *khupa,* the term for the wedding canopy or ceremonial cloth held over the bride and groom during the marriage ceremony, also used generally to refer to the ceremony itself. In context this seems plausible.

Column 4: Число и мѣсяцъ | Христіанскій | Еврейскій – "Day and month | Christian | Jewish," i. e., by the Christian and Jewish calendars. In entry 82 the date was *21 Августъ*, 21 August, *12 Элулъ*, 12 Elul (see page 47 for more on the Jewish calendar).

Column 5: Главные акты или записи и обязательства между вступающими въ бракъ и свидѣтели оныхъ – "Principal documents or records and commitments between the parties contracting marriage, as well as their witnesses." In entry 82 (and all other entries on the page simply say *тоже*, "the same"), the first word is clearly *Ксуба*, presumably a Russian phonetic spelling of the Ashkenazic pronunciation of the Hebrew word **כתובה**, *Ketubah,* a wedding contract specifying an amount the groom pays the bride in the event the marriage is terminated for any reason. The second word is hard to read, but appears to be *деурайса;* the whole expression is most likely a phonetic spelling of **כתובה־דאוריתא**, a marriage contract according to the Law of Moses (per Alexander Harkavy, *Yiddish-English-Hebrew Dictionary,* Schocken Books, New York, 1988, ISBN 0-8052-4027-6). The second line reads *60 рубл. ср.*, "60 silver rubles." So this would specify a wedding contract in the amount of 60 silver rubles; the fact that all the other entries copy this suggests 60 rubles represented a traditional sum for the contract in that time and place. Under *свид.*, short for *свидѣтели*, "witnesses," the names are *А. Школьникъ*, A. Szkolnik, and *М. Рабиновичъ*, M. Rabinowicz, and they, too, are cited as witnesses in the rest of the entries.

Column 6: Кто именно, съ кѣмъ вступаетъ въ бракъ, также имена и состояніе родителей – "Who, by name, is marrying whom, also the names and occupations of the parents." In entry 82 the answer is as follows:

холостой цѣхановецкій мѣщ. Ицко Хаимъ Нотовичъ Гиршфельдъ съ дѣвицею Файгой Бейлой Сролевною Любеньскою – "a single townsman of Ciechanowiec [Poland], Icko Chaim Girszfeld [or Hirszfeld], son of Nota, with a single woman, Fajga Bejla Lubeńska, daughter of Srol." Here *мѣщ.* is an abbreviation of *мѣщанинъ*, "townsman." Note that the question is phrased literally "Who by name, with whom is entering into marriage?" That's why the groom's name is given in the nominative, as the subject of the sentence; but the bride's name is in the instrumental following the preposition *съ*. The formula goes: *groom's name in the nominative* + *съ*, "with," + *the bride's name in the instrumental.*

Entry #83 says the bride was 20, the groom 22; the rabbi was Г. *Гальпернъ*, G. Gal'pern (or probably *Halpern* with typical Russian rendering *h* as *г*); the wedding took place on August 21st, Elul 12; the wedding contract and witnesses were the same (*тоже* and *тѣже*) as for entry #82; the groom was a single townsman of Białystok, Lejzor Reuben, son of Szebsel; and the bride was Mer'yem [Marjam], daughter of Lejb Begagon.

Entry #84 says the bride was 21, the groom 24; the rabbi was the same as in entry #83, G. Halpern; the wedding took place on August 23, Elul 14; the wedding contract and witnesses were the same as for the previous entries; the groom was a single townsman of Białystok, Elija Słon, son of Icko; and the bride was Słowa, daughter of Gawriel Zawelowicz.

7. Document VI-26: A Short-Form Certificate from Russian Poland

Document VI-26 on page 273 is a short-form certificate issued on the basis of information extracted from an original marriage register in northeastern Poland. Like the short-form birth certificates, such as Document VI-17 on pages 240-241, these certificates may appear in a number of slightly different forms. They are usually very easy to read, however. Since most of the terminology in this document has already been covered in analysis of the previous samples, we will simply give the translation with very little analysis.

The information at upper left tells us this is record no. 4, issued in the province of Łomża *[Ломжинская]*, county of Maków *[Маковскій]*, district of Karniewo *[Карнево]*. The place of residence [мѣсто жит.] of the bride [невѣсты] was Szwelice *[Швелице]*, and it was in the Roman Catholic parish [Рим. Кат. приходъ] of Szwelice. The information at upper right tells us this certificate was issued Для рекрутскаго на[бора] или книгъ народонаселенія, "for recruitment or population registers." Thus it could be used to establish one's identity for matters of conscription or establishing place of residence.

Свидѣтельство о бракосочетаніи – "Marriage certificate"

Выданное на основаніи метрическихъ книгъ – "Issued on the basis of vital records registers"

Сіе дано въ томъ, что *Антони Пржевлоцкій, 23* лѣтъ отъ роду, сынъ *Андржея* и *Юзефы* урожденной *Напертой* ... – "This is issued to certify that Antoni Przewłocki, age 23, son of Andrzej and Józefa née Naperta." The phrase *сіе дано въ томъ* means literally "this is given in this" (see notes to Дано сіе and въ томъ, что ..., page 94). But in this context it is legitimate to render it in English with something a bit less vague, i. e., "this is issued to certify."

заключилъ брачный союзъ – "contracted a marital union," i. e., married.

съ Матыльдою Ржепеньскою, *22* лѣтъ отъ роду, дочерью *Станислава* и *Эмиліи* урожденной *Михаловской* – "with Matylda Rzepieńska, age 22, daughter of Stanisław and Emilia née Michałowska...." Since this is phrased as "[groom] contracted a marital union **with** [bride]," the preposition *съ* is used with the instrumental case, and thus her name is in the instrumental. But *Станислава и Эмиліи урожденной Михаловской* are both in the genitive, because she is the daughter **of** those persons.

число вѣнчанія { дня *19/31 Января* Тысяча *восемьсотъ восемьдесятъ седьмого 1887* года – "The date of the marriage was the 19th/31st of January, 1887."

Съ подлиннымъ вѣрно. – "[This is] faithful to the original [record]."

въ *Швелицахъ* м-ца *октября* дня *8/21 1912* года. – "in Szwelice, *October 8/21, 1912.*" The name of the village has the prepositional plural ending *-ахъ* because this name is plural in form in Polish.

Содержащій акты Гражданскаго Состоянія *Кс. Сѣ*[illegible] – "Civil Registrar, Rev. Sie-" (the rest of his name is illegible).

Собственноручность подписи Содержащаго акты Гражданскаго Состоянія свидѣтельствуетъ. ВОЙТЪ ГМИНЫ БУРГОМИСТРЪ Г. – "The authenticity of the Civil Registrar's signature is witnessed by the District *wójt* | the town mayor."

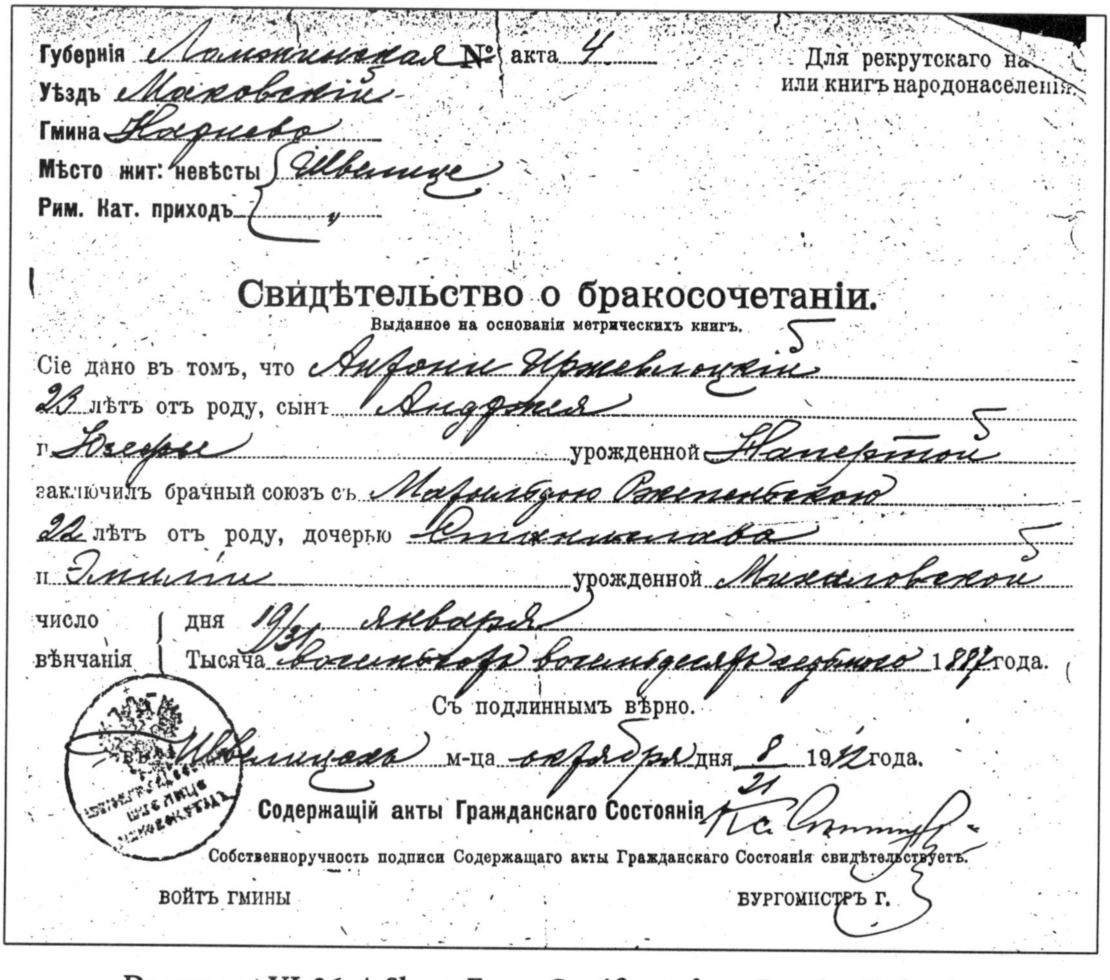

Губернія Ломжинская № акта 4 — Для рекрутскаго на... или книгъ народонаселенія

Уѣздъ Маковскій

Гмина Карнево

Мѣсто жит: невѣсты { Швелице

Рим. Кат. приходъ

Свидѣтельство о бракосочетаніи.

Выданное на основанія метрическихъ книгъ.

Сіе дано въ томъ, что Антоній Ржевницкій

23 лѣтъ отъ роду, сынъ Андрея

г Юзефы урожденной Напертой

заключилъ брачный союзъ съ Матыльдою Ржепеньскою

22 лѣтъ отъ роду, дочерью Станислава

и Эмиліи урожденной Михаловской

число { дня 19/31 января
вѣнчанія { Тысяча восемьсотъ восемьдесятъ седьмого 1887 года.

Съ подлиннымъ вѣрно.

въ Швелицахъ м-ца октября дня 8/21 1912 года.

Содержащій акты Гражданскаго Состоянія Кс. Сѣ[illegible]

Собственноручность подписи Содержащаго акты Гражданскаго Состоянія свидѣтельствуетъ.

ВОЙТЪ ГМИНЫ БУРГОМИСТРЪ Г.

Document VI-26: A Short-Form Certificate from Russian Poland

D. DEATH RECORDS

1. Document VI-27: A Paragraph-Form Death Record from Russian Poland

In general the types of death records correspond to the kinds of birth records we examined in part B and marriage records in part C. In other words, there are paragraph-form records, columnar records, and certificates drawn up and quoting data, or summarizing the essential facts of, the first two types. The formats vary in some respects, but once you're familiar with the layout and terminology encountered in the following samples, you can hope to decipher almost any death record you find. The biggest challenge is usually the cause of death, if given. That is why we provide a list of terms often seen as causes of death, beginning on page 286.

Here are the keywords you should look for and what they tell you.

I. **The Place/Date the Record Was Created** – keyword ***состоялось*** ("It happened")
II. **The Witnesses** – keywords ***явились*** ("[they] appeared")
III. **Time of Death** – keyword ***что*** ("that")
IV. **Identity of the Deceased** – keyword ***умеръ*** or ***умерла*** ("died")
V. **The Parents of the Deceased** – keywords ***сынъ*** (***сыномъ***) or ***дочь*** (***дочерью***)
VI. **Certification of Death** – keywords ***по наочномъ удостовѣреніи*** ("after eyewitness testimony")
VII. **Signature of the Clergymen and Witnesses**– ***Актъ сей*** ("this document")

If you compare these with the keywords of birth records (page 198) and marriage records (page 247) you will notice that the basic sections are similar, but death records are simpler.

Reproduced on page 275 is **Document VI-27**, a fairly typical paragraph-form death record from Russian Poland. Here is the text in italic typeface, with keywords in boldface to help you pick them out:

100. *Заскродзь.* ***Состоялось*** *въ Порытомъ восмаго/двад-*
цатаго Декабря Тысяча восемьсотъ шестьдесять
девятаго года въ восемь часовъ по полуночи. ***Яви[-]***
лись *Адам Ольшевскій шестьдесяти лѣтъ*
и Ігнацы Вѣржбицкій тридцати лѣтъ отъ
роду, крестянъ хозяевъ жительствующіе въ
Заскродзю, и объявили ***что*** *шестаго/восемнад[-]*
цатаго Декабря текущаго года въ часъ по по[-]
луночи ***умерла*** *въ Заскродзю Розалія Сѣлява*
вдова восемьдесяти лѣтъ отъ роду крестянка
работница жительствующая въ Заскродзю, ***дочерю***
умершыхъ Томаша и Марьянны супруговъ
Ходниковъ. ***По наочномъ удосотвѣреніи***
о кончинѣ Розаліи Сѣлявы. ***Актъ сей***
прочитанъ присутствующимъ пи[-]
сать неумѣющимъ и нами подписанъ
Ксендзъ Марціянъ Влостовскій Администра-
торъ Порытскаго Прихода Содержающій Акты
Гражданскаго Состоянія.

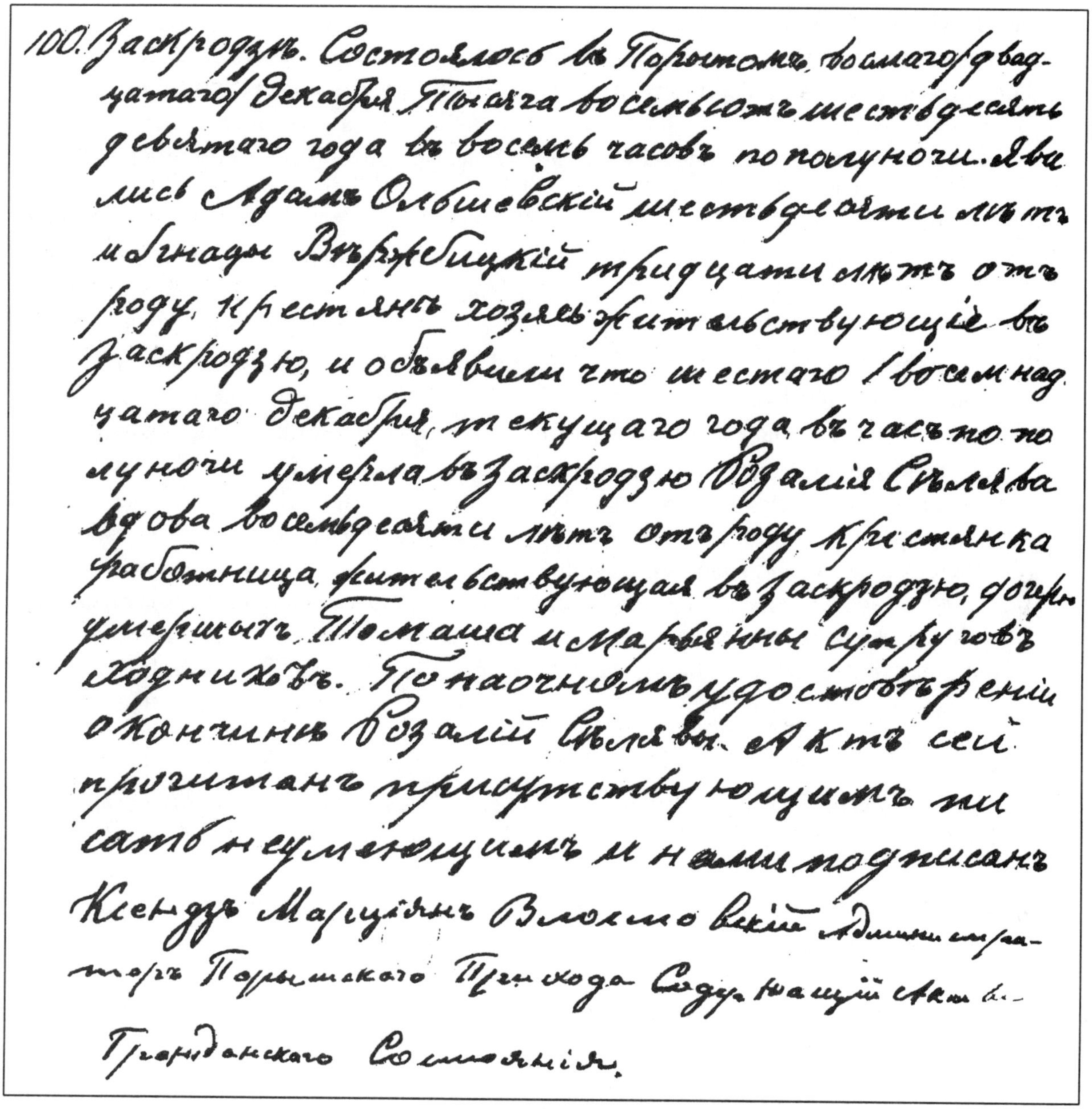

100. Заскродзѣ. Состоялось въ Порытомъ восмаго/двад-
цатаго/ Декабря Тысяча восемьсотъ шестьдесятъ
девятаго года въ восемь часовъ по полуночи. Явились Адамъ Ольшевскій шестьдесяти лѣтъ
и Игнацы Вержбицкій тридцати лѣтъ отъ
роду, крестьяне хозяева жительствующіе въ
Заскродзю, и объявили что шестаго / восемнад-
цатаго декабря, текущаго года въ часъ по полуночи умерла въ Заскродзю Розалія Сѣлява
вдова восемьдесяти лѣтъ отъ роду крестьянка
работница, жительствующая въ Заскродзю, дочь
умершихъ Томаша и Марьяны супруговъ
Ходниковъ. По наочномъ удостовѣреніи
о кончинѣ Розаліи Сѣлявы. Актъ сей
прочитанъ присутствующимъ писать неумѣющимъ и нами подписанъ
Ксендзъ Маріянъ Влосновскій Администраторъ Порытскаго Прихода Содержащій Актъ
Гражданскаго Состоянія.

Document VI-27: A Paragraph-Form Death Record from Russian Poland

Here is an analysis of the sections into which we divide such records by keywords.

Заскродзѣ. ***Состоялось*** *въ Порытомъ восмаго/двадцатаго Декабря Тысяча восемьсотъ шестьдесятъ девятаго года въ восемь часовъ по полуночи.* – "Zaskrodzie. This happened in Poryte on the 8th/20th of December 1869 at eight p.m."

Portye is the name of the village where the record was drawn up, and Zaskrodzie is where the actual death took place. The information on date and time is easy to understand if you refer to the discussion of such terms on pages 45-51. For more on the double date, see the note to *шетого / девянадцатого марта* on page 200.

Явились *Адам Ольшевскій шестьдесяти лѣтъ и Ігнацы Вѣржбицкій тридцати лѣтъ отъ роду, крестянъ хозяевъ жительствующіе въ Заскродзю...* – "Adam Olszewski, age 60, and Ignacy Wierzbicki, age 30, peasant farm-owners residing in Zaskrodzie, appeared..."

Адамъ Ольшевскій ... Ігнацы Вѣржбицкій – as we have explained in the analysis of numerous other records, since these names are clearly Polish, it is appropriate to render them in Polish form.

шестьдесяти лѣтъ ... тридцати лѣтъ – "age 60 ... age 30." The section discussing expressions of age on pages 50-51 should make this easy enough to understand. If you're starting to notice that people in these records tend to be 30 or 40 or 50 or 60, seldom 34 or 52 or 63, you are not the only one to notice this. As mentioned on page 248, at least one scholar has written an article on the tendency to "round off" ages in these records. One factor—hard as it may be for us to believe in our regimented, bureaucratized society—is that even a century ago many folks simply did not keep track of their age. They knew about how old they were; the exact number didn't matter. As a rule Europeans did not normally celebrate their birthdays (though that has changed in recent decades), and there were no forms or applications to fill out—so the question of their exact age didn't really come up all that often.

крестянъ хозяевъ жительствующіе въ Заскродзю – see page 248 for a discussion of the phrase *крестянъ хозяевъ жительствующіе въ*. The form *Заскродзю* is not proper Russian, but is due to interference of the priest's native language, Polish. In that language "in Zaskrodzie" is *w Zaskrodziu,* and the priest simply rendered that phrase phonetically in the Cyrillic alphabet.

и объявили ***что*** *шестаго/восемнадцатаго Декабря текущаго года въ часъ по полуночи ...* – "and stated that on the 6th/18th of December of this year, at 1 o'clock after midnight ..."

умерла *въ Заскродзю Розалія Сѣлява вдова восемьдесяти лѣтъ отъ роду крестянка работница жительствующая въ Заскродзю ...* – "Rozalia Sielawa died in Zaskrodzie, a widow, age 80, a peasant laborer residing in Zaskrodzie ...."

умерла – the verb here will be either the masculine form, *умеръ*, or the feminine form, *умерла*. In rare instances a record might report the deaths of more than one person, in which case *умерли*, "they died," is possible. But as a rule a separate record would have to be written up for each person who died.

крестянка работница – *крестьянка* (of which *крестянка* is a common misspelling) is the feminine form of *крестьянинъ*, "[male] peasant." And *работница* is the feminine form of *работникъ*, "worker, laborer." So Rozalia was a peasant and still working as a laborer—at the age of 80! Most likely she was retired and living with family, and did what work she could to help out. Still, there was no Social Security for peasants, and you will generally see the term *въ отставкѣ*, "retired," applied to none but members of the professional classes or the military.

дочерю *умершыхъ Томаша и Марьянны супруговъ Ходниковъ.* – "the daughter of the married couple the Chodniks, the late Tomasz and Marianna."

дочерю *умершыхъ Томаша и Марьянны супруговъ Ходниковъ* – literally "the daughter of the deceased Tomasz and Maryanna, the spouses Chodnik." Note that the mother's name is not given; this can vary from record to record. With older folks we often see very little detail, because no one still alive remembered details.

По наочномъ удосотовѣреніи о кончинѣ Розаліи Сѣлявы. – "After eyewitness testimony on the death of Rozalia Sielawa."

по наочномъ удосотвѣреніи о кончинѣ Розаліи Сѣлявы – the noun *удосотвѣреніе* means "attestation, testimony, certification," and *наочный* is an adjective meaning "eyewitness, with one's own eyes." The emphasis here is on the fact that this record was drawn up on the basis of eyewitness testimony.

The feminine noun *кончина* means "death, demise," a synonym for the more common term *смерть*. This term *кончина* is not everyday Russian, but is consistent with an elevated, archaic style. As for *наочный,* you probably won't find it in any Russian dictionary. It is a Russification of the Polish term *naoczny;* this whole phrase is modeled after one used in Polish records before use of Russian was mandated.

If the deceased was survived by a spouse, his or her name would usually appear in this part of the record. In the case of widowed individuals this type of record may also contain particulars on the deceased spouse—but as one can see from this sample, this is not always true. In rare instances the names of surviving children and their ages are provided, but this is the exception rather than the norm.

***Актъ сей** прочитанъ присутствующимъ писать неумѣющимъ и нами подписанъ. Ксендзъ Марціянъ Влостовскій Администраторъ Порытскаго Прихода Содержающій Акты Гражданскаго Состоянія.* – "This document was read to those present, who are illiterate, and signed by us. Reverend Marcyan Włostowski, Administrator of Poryte Parish, Civil Registrar." A statement of this sort comes at the end of every paragraph-form record and usually varies little from one to the next. Usually the only differences will involve instances where a witness could write and signed his name.

актъ сей прочитанъ ... и ... подписанъ – the fundamental structure of this sentence is "This document was read ... and signed," using as verbs the short forms of the past passive participles of the verbs *прочитать,* "to read (from beginning to end)" and *подписать,* "to sign."

присутствующимъ – dative plural of the present active participle of *присутствовать,* "to be present." Thus it means literally "to the ones being present," but that sounds awkward in English. "Better is "to those present."

писать неумѣющимъ – another present active participle, *неумѣющимъ,* "to those not not knowing how" + *писать,* "to write."

Translation – "Zaskrodzie. This happened in Poryte on the 8th/20th of December 1869 at 8 p. m. Adam Olszewski, age 60, and Ignacy Wierzbicki, age 30, peasant farm-owners residing in Zaskrodzie, appeared and stated that on the 6th/18th of December of this year, at 1 a. m., Rozalia Sielawa died in Zaskrodzie, a widow, age 80, a peasant laborer residing in Zaskrodzie, the daughter of the married couple the Chodniks, the late Tomasz and Marianna. After eyewitness testimony on the death of Rozalia Sielawa, this document was read to those present, who are illiterate, and signed by us. Reverend Marcyan Włostowski, Administrator of Poryte Parish, Civil Registrar."

2. Document VI-28: A Jewish Paragraph-Form Death Record from Russian Poland

Reproduced on page 279 is **Document VI-28**, another paragraph-form death record from Russian Poland. It shows that death records involving Jews seldom varied in any significant way from those for Christians. It also provides contrast with the previous sample, which dealt with the death of an elderly woman; this one deals with the death of a child.

Here's the text in a standardized cursive for comparison:

Посадъ
Андржеево
№ 3.

Тысяча восемьсотъ восемьдесятъ девятаго
года Мая тринадцатаго дня въ одинад-
цать часовъ утра. явились лично Хаимъ
Лапка шестидесяти лѣтъ и Гершко
Копыто пятидесяти девяти лѣтъ оба
сапожники въ пос. Андржеевѣ жительству-
ющіе и заявили, что вчерашняго числа
въ десять часовъ вечера въ посадѣ Ан-
држеевѣ умеръ Мошко Палонзъ полъ-
года отъ роду имѣющій сынъ нахо-
дящагося на военной службѣ Маера
и Хаи супруговъ Палонзъ, родившій-
ся въ посадѣ Зарембы-Косцѣльне и быв-
шій на выкормленіи въ посадѣ Андрже-
евѣ у Хаи суры Лапки.
По наочномъ удостовѣреніи о
кончинѣ Мошка Палонзъ, актъ
сей объявляющимъ прочитанъ, Нами
только подписанъ такъ свидѣ-
тели заявили что неграмот-
ные.
Чиновникъ Гражданскаго
Состоянія [signature illegible]

A couple of notes on the penmanship are in order. This registrar uses extensively the dashes above the letters *п̄* [п] and *т̄* [т], and under the letter *ш̲* [ш], to make them easier to distinguish. He also uses *ж* (alternate form), the alternate form of the letter *ж*, for instance, in the repeated occurrences of the village name *Андржеево*; in fact, he only uses the form *ж* once, at the beginning of *жительствующіе* at the end of line 6.

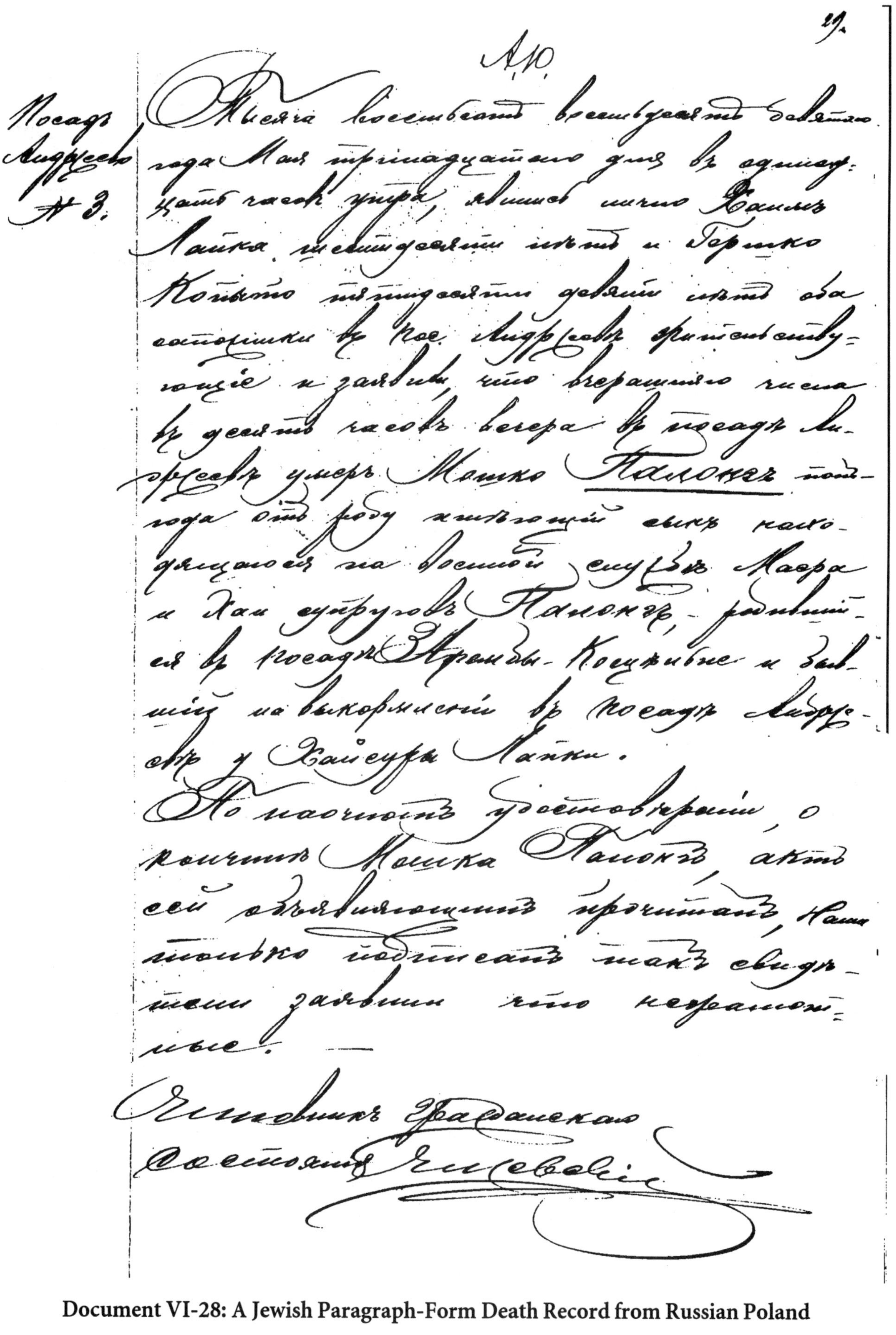

№ 10.

Посадъ Андржеевъ № 3.

Тысяча восемьсотъ восемьдесятъ девятаго года Мая тринадцатаго дня въ одиннадцать часовъ утра, явились лично Хаимъ Лайка, шестидесяти лѣтъ и Гершко Копыто пятидесяти девяти лѣтъ оба сапожники въ Пос. Андржеевѣ проживающіе и заявили, что вчерашняго числа въ десять часовъ вечера въ посадѣ Андржеевѣ умеръ Мошко Палонзъ полтора отъ роду лѣтній сынъ находящагося на военной службѣ Мафра и Хаи супруговъ Палонзъ, родившійся въ посадѣ Кренды-Косцѣльне и жившій на выкормленіи въ посадѣ Андржеевѣ у Хайсуры Лайки.

По наочномъ удостовѣреніи о кончинѣ Мошка Палонзъ, актъ сей объявляющимъ прочитанъ, нами только подписанъ такъ свидѣтели заявили что неграмотные.

Чиновникъ Гражданскаго Состоянія Чижевскій

Document VI-28: A Jewish Paragraph-Form Death Record from Russian Poland

The notation at upper left shows this was record #3, drawn up in the town of Andrzejewo.

Тысяча восемьсотъ восемьдесятъ девятаго года Мая тринадцатаго дня въ одинадцать часовъ утра. – "[This happened] in the year 1889, on the 13th day of May, at 11 o'clock in the morning." This record is unusual in that it does not begin with the usual keyword ***Состоялось*** (see page 274), but in other respects it follows the usual format.

Явились *лично Хаимъ Лапка шестидесяти лѣтъ и Гершко Копыто пятидесяти девяти лѣтъ оба сапожники въ Пос. Андржеевѣ жительствующіе и заявили* – "Chaim Lapka, age 60, and Herszko Kopyto, age 59, appeared in person, both boot-makers residing in the town of Andrzejewo, and stated..."

Явились лично – "[They] appeared in person." We often see this adverb *лично* after *явились*, emphasizing that the witnesses appeared personally.

оба сапожники – "both bootmakers." In statements giving details about two witnesses we often see various forms of *оба*, "both."

что *вчерашняго числа въ десять часовъ вечера въ Посадѣ Андржеевѣ* – "that yesterday at 10 o'clock in the evening in the town of Andrzejewo..."

вчерашняго числа – literally "on yesterday's date." Other possibilities are *сего числа*, "on this day," or an actual specification of month and day.

умеръ *Мошко Палонзъ полъ-года отъ роду имѣющій* – "Moszko Palonz died, age ½ year."

полъ-года отъ роду имѣщій – literally "having one-half year since birth." The word *полъ* is versatile, since it can mean "floor," "sex, gender," or "half." With any expression of quantity it will be used in the last meaning, and this clearly means "half a year old."

сынъ *находящагося на военной службѣ Маера и Хаи супруговъ Палонзъ, родившійся въ посадѣ Зарембы-Косцѣльне и бывшій на выкормленіи въ посадѣ Андржеевѣ у Хаи суры Лапки.* – "the son of the married couple Palonz, of Majer, who is on military service, and Chaja; he [Moszko] was born in the town of Zaręby-Kościelne and was in the town of Andrzejewo with Chaja Sura Lapka for nursing."

сынъ находящагося на военной службѣ Маера – literally "son of the finding himself in military service Majer." The verb *находиться* means literally "to find oneself," but often is best translated "to be in, to be on," and that applies in this case.

родившійся въ посадѣ Зарембы-Косцѣлне – the masculine nominative ending of the participle *родившійся* tells us it must refer back to the masculine nominative noun *сынъ*. So it was Moszko, not Majer, whose birthplace is specified as Zaręby-Kościelne.

бывшій на выкормленіи въ посадѣ Андржеевѣ у Хаи суры Лапки – this phrase is a little out of the ordinary. The participle *бывшій* is from the verb *быть*, "to be," so it means literally "being." Skipping *на выкормленіи* for a moment, *въ посадѣ Андржеевѣ* means "in the town of Andrzejewo," and *у Хаи Суры Лапки* means "with Chaja Sura Lapka" or "at Chaja Sura Lapka's house." The verb *выкармливать* means "to raise, to bring up (a child); to nurse (an infant)." In view of Moszko's age, it seems likely he was at Chaja Sura Lapka's house in Andrzejewo for nursing.

По наочномъ удостовѣреніи *о кончинѣ Мошка Палонзъ* – "After eyewitness testimony on the death of Moszko Palonz..."

***актъ сей** объявляющимъ прочитанъ, Нами только подписанъ такъ свидѣтели заявили что неграмотные. Чиновникъ Гражданскаго Состоянія.* – "This document was read aloud to the declarants and was signed by Us only, as the witnesses are illiterate. Official of the Civil Registry [signature illegible]."

Translation – "13 May 1889, at 11 a. m. Chaim Lapka, age 60, and Herszko Kopyto, age 59, appeared in person, both boot-makers residing in the town of Andrzejewo, and stated that yesterday at 10 p. m. in the town of Andrzejewo Moszko Palonz died, age ½ year, the son of the married couple Palonz, Majer, who is serving in the military, and Chaja; he was born in the town of Zaręby-Kościelne and was with Chaja Sura Lapka in the town of Andrzejewo for nursing. After eyewitness testimony on the death of Moszko Palonz. This document was read aloud to the declarants and was signed by Us only, as the witnesses are illiterate. Official of the Civil Registry *[signature illegible]*."

3. Document VI-29: A Russian Orthodox Columnar Death Record

Reproduced on page 282 is **Document VI-29**, a columnar death record. We should mention that the copy was extremely hard to read before we cleaned it up digitally—if you expect most such records to be this legible, you may be bitterly disappointed. It comes from the same register as Document VI-22 on pages 260-263, from an Orthodox church in the Volynia region of Ukraine. For the use of the letters ѧ and ѡ, see the paragraph beginning "The first thing to notice" on page 261. (The spelling *оўмер-* is archaic for modern *умер-)*.

The original document consisted of columns spread across two facing pages. This particular case was unusual because the priest used only the left-hand page for death entries. On the right-hand page, instead of filling in the requested information, he crossed out the headings and used the space to compile yearly mortality statistics for the parish. We have omitted that because you're not likely to encounter it, and even if you do, it's not hard to figure out what the columns of numbers are.

The register was not in very good condition, and given that, one may theorize that several pages are missing. The entries on the left-hand page are for the month of September, and most assuredly persons in the parish died after the last date listed, September 17, 1902.

The heading across the top of the pages (of which only the left one is shown) reads:

Метрической Книги на *1902* годъ, часть третїѧ ѡ оўмершихъ.

This translates as "Register for 1902, Part Three, Deaths." As we have remarked earlier (see page 213), Russian registers are typically divided into three parts; part one is devoted to births, part two to marriages, and part three to deaths. Thus even if we did not have the phrase о умершихъ, the fact that this is designated "Part Three" would suggest it deals with deaths in the parish during 1902. (There are, however, exceptions; see Document VI-32, page 290.)

Column 1: Счетъ оўмершихъ | Мужеска | Женска – "Death Number: Male | Female." The first entry is for #22 under "Male," so this was the 22nd male to died in the parish that year.

Column 2: Мѣсяцъ и день | смерти | погребенія – "Month and day | Death | Burial." Here the date of death was *Сентября 11*, "September 11," and he was buried on the 12th.

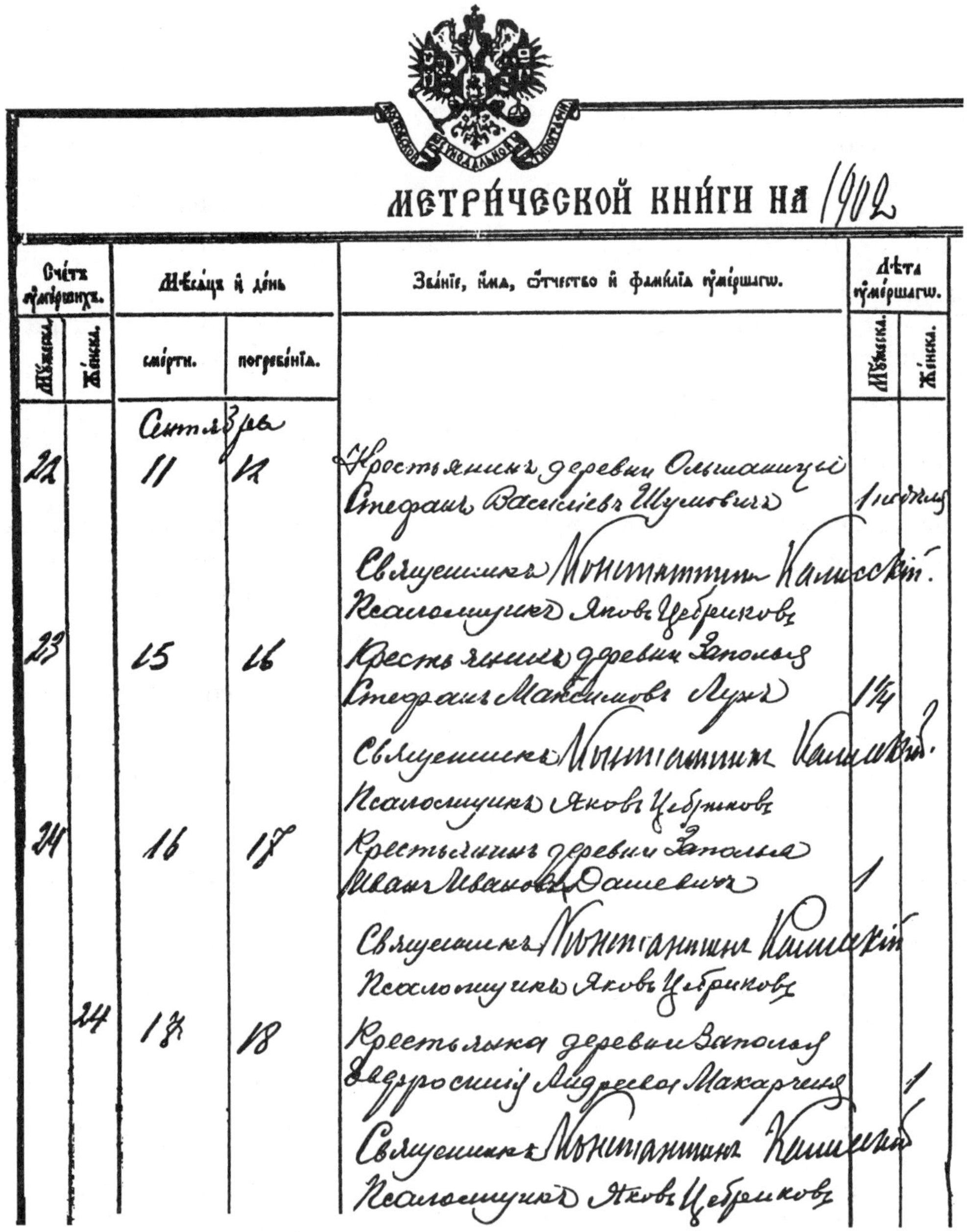

МЕТРИЧЕСКОЙ КНИГИ НА 1902

Счётъ оумершихъ		Мѣсяцъ и день		Званіе, имя, отчество и фамилія оумершагѡ.	Лѣта оумершагѡ.	
Мужеска.	Женска.	смерти.	погребенія.		Мужеска.	Женска.
		Сентябрь				
22		11	12	Крестьянинъ деревни Ольшаницы Стефанъ Василіевъ Шумовичъ Священникъ Константинъ Камисскій. Псаломщикъ Яковъ Цедриковъ	1 недѣля	
23		15	16	Крестьянинъ деревни Заполье Стефанъ Максимовъ Лухъ Священникъ Константинъ Камисскій. Псаломщикъ Яковъ Цедриковъ	1¼	
24		16	17	Крестьянинъ деревни Заполье Иванъ Ивановъ Дашевичъ Священникъ Константинъ Камисскій Псаломщикъ Яковъ Цедриковъ	1	
	24	17	18	Крестьянка деревни Заполье Евфросинія Андреева Макарчикъ Священникъ Константинъ Камисскій Псаломщикъ Яковъ Цедриковъ		1

Document VI-29: A Russian Orthodox Columnar Death Record

Column 3: Званіе, имѧ, ѡтчество, и фамилія оумершагѡ – "Status, first name, patronymic, and surname of the deceased."

званіе –literally "calling," i. e., social class—here *Крестьянинъ*, "peasant."

имѧ, ѡтчество, фамилія –the three standard components of a Russian's full name: "first name, patronymic [see page 83], and surname."

Крестьянинъ деревни Ольшаницы, Стефанъ Василіевъ Шумовичъ – "A peasant of the village of Olshanitsa, Stefan Shumovich, son of Vasiliy."

Next is a 2-line notation repeated after each entry on the page: *Священникъ Константинъ Камисскій | Псаломщикъ Яковъ Цедриковъ* – "Father Konstantin Kamisskiy, Psalmist Yakov Tsebrikov."

Column 4: Лѣта оумершагѡ | Мужеска | Женска – "age of the deceased | Male | Female." For the first entry the age is *1 недѣля*, "1 week."

Just for practice, here are the other deaths entered on the left-hand page, each followed by the signature of the priest and psalmist:

[23rd male, died the 15th, buried the 16th] Крестьянинъ деревни Заполья Стефанъ Максимовъ Лукъ, 1¼– A peasant from the village of Zapolye, Stefan Luk, son of Maksim, age 1¼

[24th male, died the 16th, buried the 17th] Крестьянинъ деревни Заполья Иванъ Ивановъ Дашевичъ, 1 – A peasant from the village of Zapolye, Ivan Dashevich, son of Ivan, age 1

[24th female, died the 17th, buried the 18th] Крестьянинка деревни Заполья Евфросинія Андреевъ Макарчикъ, 1 – A peasant from the village of Zapolye, Evfrosiniya Makarchik, daughter of Andrei, age 1

The columnar headings on the right-hand page (which we have not shown because in this case the priest crossed them out and used that page for a statistical summary), will appear in other registers and contain information. So we should mention briefly what they mean:

> ѡ чего оўмер? – "What did he die from?" (modern Russian *От чего умер?*)
> Кто исповѣдывалъ и пріобщалъ? – "Who heard his confession and gave him Communion?"
> Кто совершалъ погребеніе и гдѣ погребенъ? – "Who did the funeral and where was he buried?"

4. Document VI-30: A Catholic Columnar Death Record from Russian Poland

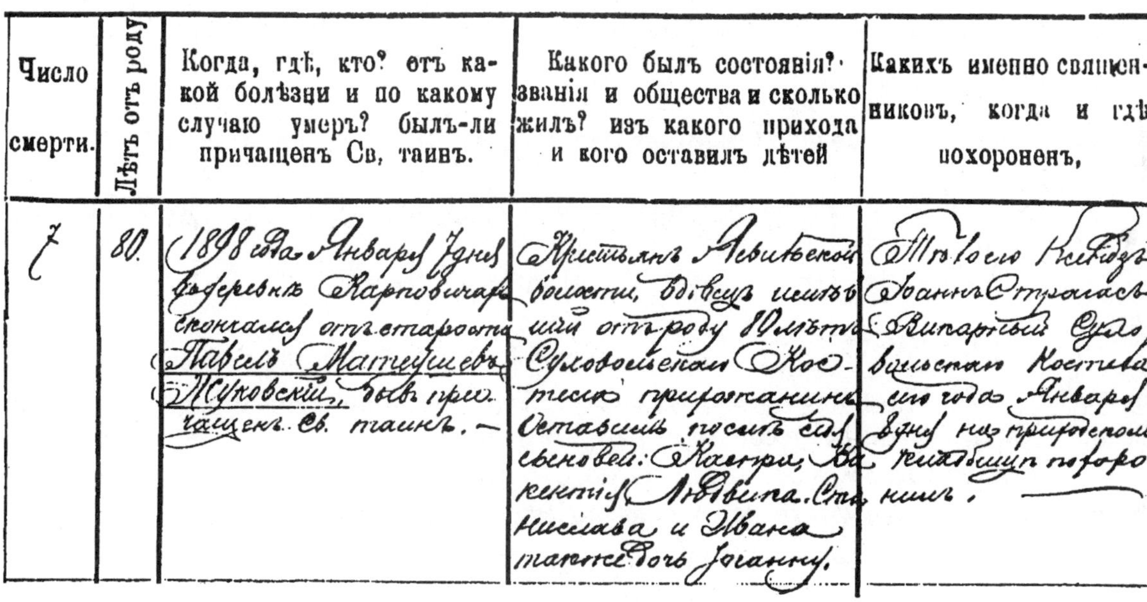

Число смерти.	Лѣтъ отъ роду	Когда, гдѣ, кто? отъ какой болѣзни и по какому случаю умеръ? былъ-ли причащенъ Св. таинъ.	Какого былъ состоянія? званія и общества и сколько жилъ? изъ какого прихода и кого оставилъ дѣтей	Какихъ именно священниковъ, когда и гдѣ похороненъ,
7	80.	1898 года Января 7 дня в деревнѣ Карповичахъ скончался отъ старости Павелъ Матеушевъ Жуковскій, былъ причащенъ Св. таинъ. —	Крестьянинъ Лебедевской волости, вдовецъ имѣвшій отъ роду 80 лѣтъ Суховольскаго Костела прихожанинъ. Оставилъ послѣ себя сыновей: Казиміра, Викентія, Людвика, Станислава и Ивана также дочь Іоанну.	Мною ксендзомъ Іоанномъ Стражасъ Викарнымъ Суховольскаго Костела сего года Января 9 дня на приходскомъ кладбищѣ похороненъ. —

Reproduced above is **Document VI-30**, a columnar-format record from a Catholic parish church in Suchowola, near Białystok in Russian Poland.

Here are the columnar headings and information written into each column, with a little brief analysis.

Число смерти: 7 — "Date of death: the 7th."
Лѣтъ отъ роду — literally "years from birth," i. e., age: 80.

Когда, гдѣ, кто? отъ какой болѣзни и по какому случаю умеръ? былъ-ли причащенъ Св. таинъ. — "Where, when, who? From what illness and in what circumstance did he die? Was he administered the Holy Sacrament [i. e., given the Last Rites]?"

1898 года Января 7 дня въ деревнѣ Карповичахъ скончался отъ старости Павелъ Матеушевъ Жуковскій. Быв. причащенъ св. таин. — "1898, January 7 in the village of Karpowicze died from old age Paweł Żukowski, son of Mateusz, the Sacrament was administered."

Какого былъ состоянія? званія и общества и сколько жилъ? изъ какого прихода и кого оставилъ дѣтей? — "What is (his/her) social status and class? How long did he live? From what parish, and what children did he leave behind?"

Крестьянъ Ясвильской волости, вдовецъ имѣвшій отъ роду 80 лѣтъ Суховольскаго Костела прихожанинъ. Оставилъ послѣ себя сыновей: Каспра, Викентія, Людвика, Станислава и Ивана также дочь Іоганну. — "A peasant of the district of Jaświły, a widower, age 80, a parishioner of the church at Suchowola. He left sons: Kasper, Wincenty, Ludwik, Stanisław, and Jan, and a daughter Joanna."

Какихъ именно священниковъ, когда и гдѣ похороненъ. — "What priests [performed the ceremony], when and where buried?"

Тѣло его Ксендзъ Іоаннъ Стралась Викарный Суховольскаго костела сего года Января 8 дня на приходскомъ кладбищѣ похороненъ. — "Reverend Jan Stralaś, assistant priest at the parish at Suchowola, buried his body on January 8 of the current year in the parish cemetery."

Note the precision of the cause of death: *отъ старости*, "of old age." This is fairly representative of the level of medical expertise in most death records—if they even mention a cause of death.

5. Document VI-31: A Jewish Columnar Death Record from Russian Poland

As **Document VI-31** shows, columnar records of Jewish deaths differ only slightly from those of Christians, and are comparable in terminology and format to columnar birth records such as Document VI-15 (pages 233-238) and marriage records such as Document VI-25 (pages 270-272).

The heading at the top of this page reads as follows: г) Книга для записки умершихъ евреевъ на 1879 года, часть IV-я о умершихъ – "Register of Jewish deaths for 1879. Part 4, Deaths." Usually deaths are recorded in part 3 of registers (see page 213). In this particular locality, however, part 3 was devoted to divorces, so deaths were recorded in part 4. (Note that this heading is preceded with the letter **г**, the 4th letter of the Russian alphabet.)

The columnar headings, and the information given under them, read as follows:

№ мужескаго | женскаго — "Number | Male | Female." Thus the first entry is for the 144th male to die in 1879.

Гдѣ умеръ и погребенъ — "Where died and buried?" All entries on this page specify the place of death as *Въ городѣ Бѣлостокъ*, "in the town of Białystok."

Число и мѣсяцъ | Христіянскій | Еврейскій – "Day and month | Christian | Jewish," i. e., give the date of death according to the Christian and Jewish calendars. The first death was *19 Іюня*, 19 June, or 10 *Тамуза*, 10 Tammuz (see page 47).

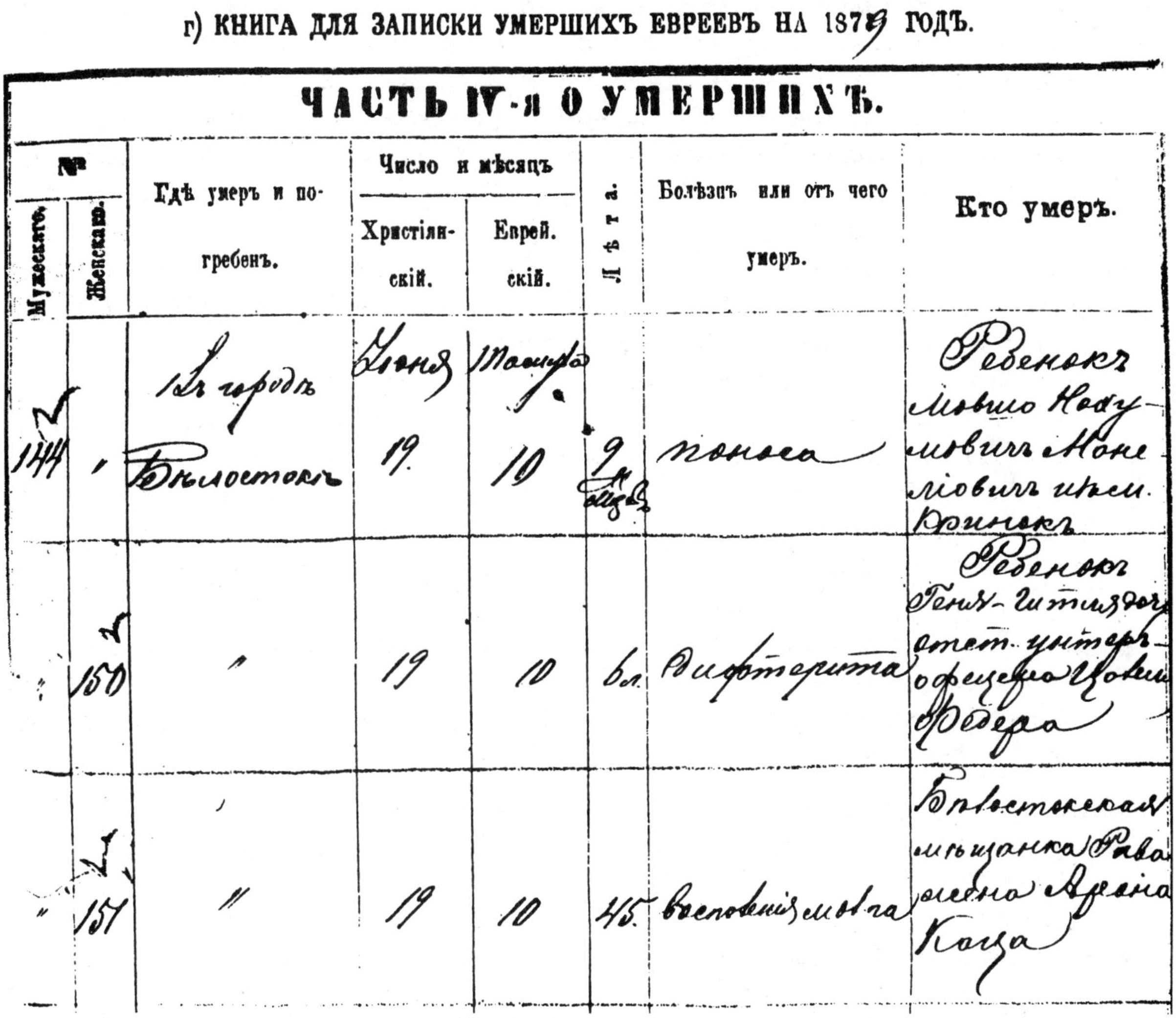

г) КНИГА ДЛЯ ЗАПИСКИ УМЕРШИХЪ ЕВРЕЕВЪ НА 1879 ГОДЪ.

ЧАСТЬ IV-я О УМЕРШИХЪ.

№ Мужескіе.	№ Женскіе.	Гдѣ умеръ и погребенъ.	Число и мѣсяцъ: Христіянскій.	Число и мѣсяцъ: Еврейскій.	Лѣта.	Болѣзнь или отъ чего умеръ.	Кто умеръ.
144		Въ городѣ Бѣлостокъ	Іюня 19	Таммуза 10	9 мѣсяцъ	поноса	Ребенокъ Мовша Нохумовичъ Монеліовичъ изъ м. Кринокъ
	150	"	19	10	6 л.	дифтерита	Ребенокъ Геня-Гитля дочь отст. унтеръ-офицера [illegible] Федера
	151	"	19	10	45	воспаленія мозга	Бѣлостокская мѣщанка [illegible] Арона Каца

Document VI-31: A Jewish Columnar Death Record from Russian Poland

Лѣта – literally "years," but we would say "age." Note that if only a number is given, it means that many years. If the age is in months it is noted, as in entry 144, *9 мѣсяцъ*. If the age is in weeks, the word *недѣль* is added.

Болѣзнъ или отъ чего умеръ – "Illness, or what he died from," i. e., cause of death. The terms given on this page are typical. No. 144 is from *поноса,* "diarrhea." The next entry shows the cause of death as *дифтерита*, "diphtheria," and the one after as *воспаленія мозга*, "inflammation of the brain." All these terms are in the genitive because they answer the question *отъ чего,* "from which," and the preposition *отъ* takes the genitive case.

кто умеръ – "who died." The first two deaths are of children, as shown by the term *ребенокъ*, "child, baby"; infant mortality was high, so you will see this term a lot. In entries where the deceased was an adult, that person's occupation, with a geographical designation, appears first. Thus entry #151 is for a *Бѣлостокская мѣщанка*, a Białystok townswoman.

The first entry reads as follows: *Ребенокъ Мовша Нохумовичъ Монеліовичъ изъ м. Кринокъ* – "a child, Mowsza Moneliowicz, son of Nochum, from the town of Krynki." The name of this town, Krynki, is plural in form, and the Russian form *Кринокъ* is genitive plural after *изъ*, "from."

The next entry reads: *Ребенокъ Геня-Гитля дочь отст. унтеръ-офицера Цалеля Федера* – "a child, Genia-Gitla, daughter of retired non-commissioned officer Calel Feder."

The third entry reads: *Бѣлостокская мѣщанка Рава, жена Арона Каца* – "Białystok townswoman Rawa, wife of Aron Kac."

The sample documents we've shown here are typical of the death records you will find during the course of your research. But we should point out that you may also see documents similar in format to those seen in part B, Birth Records, and Part C, Marriage Records. In particular, the short-form civil extract, Document VI-17 on pages 240-241, is designed so that it can be used as a form for birth, marriage, or death records. Terms appropriate for all three records are printed on the form; the registrar just crosses out those that don't apply. So if you see a short-form death certificate, it is highly likely the information given under Document VI-17 will tell you all you need to know to figure it out.

6. Terms Often Seen as Causes of Death or in Death Records

Let us end this section with a brief list of terms often seen in death records as causes of death. A cause of death isn't always given, and when one is given, it will often prove to be so vague and ill-defined as to be essentially worthless. It may even be the first or most obvious symptom of an illness, though obviously not what actually killed the deceased. In any case, when a cause of death appears, it is likely to include the following terms. Many of these terms appear in the booklet *Morbus* by Rosemary Chorzempa, available from the Polish Genealogical Society of America. Another source for terms included in this list consisted of Russian military instructions for conducting physical examinations of recruits; we thank Polish historian Michał Kopczyński, Ph. D., of the University of Warsaw, for supplying that information.

ангина, ангины – (n., fem.) quinsy, angina
аневризма, аневризмы – (n., fem.) aneurysm
атрофия, атрофии – (n., fem., † *атрофія*) atrophy
беред → *бред*
бессилие, бессилия – (n., neut. † *бессиліе*) debility
бледная немочь, бледность→ *немочь*
блѣдная немочь, блѣдность→ *немочь*
болезнь, болезни – (n., fem., † *болѣзнь*) illness, disease; *заразные болезни* – communicable diseases; *сердечная болезнь* or *болезнь сердца* – heart disease; *болезнь почек* – kidney disease
бред, бреда – (n., masc.) delirium (*беред* may be a dialect variant of this noun)
бронхит, бронхита – (n., masc.) bronchitis; *капиллярный бронхит* – capillary bronchitis
брюшина, брюшины – (n., fem.) peritoneum; *воспаление брюшины* – peritonitis
брюшной – (adj.) abdominal
бубон, бубона – (n., masc.) bubo
бубонная чума → *чума*
бугор, бугора – (n., masc.) protuberance, tubercle; *бугор лёгких* – tubercle
бугорок, бугорка – (n., masc.) tubercle, tumor; *бугорки туберкулёзные* – tubercular tumors
бугорчатка, бугорчатки – (n., fem.) tuberculosis
ветвь, ветви – (n., fem., † *вѣтвь*, gen. pl. *ветвей*) branch; *острый катар дыхательных ветвей* – severe catarrh of the respiratory passages
ветряная оспа → *оспа*
витова пляска, витовой пляски – (n., fem.) St. Vitus's Dance (also seen: *пляска Св. Витта*)
водянка, водянки or *водяная болезнь*– (n., fem.) dropsy, edema
воспаление, воспаления – (n., neut., † *воспаленіе*) inflammation, infection; *воспаление кишок* – enteritis; *воспаление лёгких* – pneumonia; *воспаление мозга* –brain fever; *воспаление суставов* – inflammation of the joints
вѣтвь → *ветвь*
вѣтряная оспа → *оспа*
гангрена, гангрены – (n., fem.) gangrene, mortification
гастрит, гастрита – (n., masc.) gastritis
гноетечение, гноетечения – (n., neut., –† *гноетеченіе*) suppuration

голод, голода – (n., masc.) hunger, starvation; famine; *умереть с голоду* – to die of starvation
голодный – (adj.) hungry, of hunger, starvation, famine; *голодная смерть* – starvation; *умереть голодной смертью* – to die of hunger, starve
горло, горла – (n., neut.) throat
гортань, гортани –(n., fem.) larynx; *круп гортани* – croup of the larynx
горячка, горячки – (n., fem.) fever
грипп, гриппа – (n., masc.) influenza
грудница, грудницы – (n., fem.) mastitis
грудной – (adj.) of the breast, chest; *грудная жаба* – angina pectoris; *грудная чахотка* – consumption
грыжа, грыжи – (n., fem.) rupture, hernia
девичья немочь → *немочь*
детский паралич → *паралич*
дизентерия, дизентерии – (n., fem., † *дисентерія*) dysentery
дифтерит, дифтерита – (n., masc.) diphtheria; also seen, *дифтерия*
дряхлость, дряхлости – (n., fem.) decrepitude, senility
дыхательный – (adj.) respiratory
дѣвичья немочь → *немочь*
дѣтскій параличъ → *паралич*
елеосвящение, елеосвящения – (n., neut., † *елеосвященіе*) Last Rites
естественно – (adv.) naturally; *умереть естественно* – to die naturally
естественный – (adj.) natural; *естественная смерть* – a natural death
жаба, жабы – (n., fem.) angina, quinsy
жар, жара – (n., masc.) fever
желтуха, желтухи – (n., fem.) jaundice
жёлтый – (adj., † *жолтый*) yellow; *жёлтая болезнь* – jaundice; *желтая лихорадка* – yellow fever
желудок, желудка – (n., masc.) stomach
желудочный – (adj.) gastric, of the stomach
жёлчная лихорадка, жёлчной лихорадки – (n., fem.) gall-sickness
жолтый → *жёлтый*
заболевание, заболевания – (n., neut., † *заболѣваніе*) disease
заражение, заражения (n., neut., † *зараженіе*) infection; *заражение крови* – blood poisoning
зараза, заразы – (n., fem.) infection, contagion
заразный – (adj.) infectious; *заразные болезни* – communicable diseases
зоб, зоба – (n., masc.) goiter, wen (struma)
золотуха, золотухи – (n., fem.) scrofula
изъявление, изъявления – (n., neut., † *изъявленіе*) ulceration
инфлуэнца, инфлуэнцы (n., fem., also seen *инфлюэнца, инфлуэнца*) influenza
катар, катара – (n., masc., † *катарръ*) catarrh
кишка, кишки – (n., fem., gen. pl. *кишок*) gut, intestine; *воспаление кишок* – enteritis
коклюш, коклюша – (n., masc.) whooping cough
колика, колики – (n., fem., often used in the plural, *колики, колик*) colic
колтун, колтуна – (n., masc.) plica
конвульсия, конвульсии – (n., fem. † *конвульсія*) convulsion
корча, корчи – (n., fem., often in the pl., *корчи, корчей*) writhing, convulsions
корь, кори – (n., fem.) measles
костоеда, костоеды – (n., fem., † *костоѣда*) caries
краснуха, краснухи – (n., fem.) German measles
кровавый – (adj.) bloody, of blood; *кровавый понос* – bloody flux; *кровавая рвота* – bloody vomiting
кровоизлияние, кровоизлияния – (n., neut., † *кровоизліяніе*) hemorrhage; *кровоизлияние в мозг* – brain hemorrhage
кровотечение, кровотечения – (n., neut., † *кровотеченіе*) hemorrhage
кровь, крови – (n., fem.) blood; *заражение крови* – blood poisoning
круп, крупа – (n., masc.) croup
лёгкое, лёгкого – (adj. used as a n., usually seen in the plural *лёгкие*, gen. *лёгких*) lung; *воспаление лёгких* – pneumonia
лёгочный – (adj.) of the lungs; *лёгочный больной* – one suffering from lung disease; *лёгочная чума* – pneumonic plague
лихорадка, лихорадки – (n., fem.) fever
малярия, малярии – (n., fem., † *малярія*) malaria
маразм, маразма – (n., masc.) marasmus, decay, weakening; *старческий маразм* – senile decay, dotage
менингит, менингита – (n., masc.) meningitis
мозг, мозга – (n., masc.) brain
насильственно – (adv.) forcibly; *умереть насильственно* – to died violently
насильственный – (adj.) forcible, forced; *насильственная смерть* – violent death
невралгия, невралгии – (n., fem., † *невралгія*) neuralgia
неврит, неврита – (n., masc.) neuritis
недостаток, недостатка – (n., masc.) insufficiency, lack (of)
недостача, недостачи – (n., fem.) insufficiency, lack of

немочь, немочи – (n., fem.) illness, sickness; *девичья* [† *дѣвичья*] *немочь* or *бледная* [† *блѣдная*] *немочь* – chlorosis, green sickness
нефрит, нефрита – (n., masc.) nephritis
одра, одры – (n., fem.) measles (actually not Russian but a Polish term you may see in records)
ожирение, ожирения – (n., neut., † *ожиреніе*) obesity
омертвелость, омертвелости – (n., fem., † *омертвѣлость*) necrosis; also seen: *омертвение* († *омертвѣніе*)
опухоль, опухоли – (n., fem.) tumor
оспа, оспы – (n., fem.) smallpox; *ветряная* [† *вѣтряная*] *оспа* – chicken pox; *телячья оспа* – cowpox; *черная оспа* – smallpox
острый – (adj.) sharp, severe
отёк, отёка – (n., masc.) edema
отравление, отравления – (n., neut. † *отравленіе*) poisoning
оўмершій → *умерший*
оўмеръ → *умереть*
падучая, падучей – (adj. used as a n.) epilepsy, falling sickness (also seen: *падучая болезнь*)
панихида, панихиды – (n., fem.) requiem, service for the dead; *гражданская панихида* – civil funeral services
паралич, паралича – (n., masc.) paralysis, palsy; *детский* († *дѣтскій*) *паралич* – infantile paralysis
пароксизм, пароксизма – (n., masc.) fit, paroxysm
печень, печени – (n., fem.) liver; *воспаление печени* – hepatitis
пищевод, пищевода – (n., masc.) esophagus (in older Russian *пищепровод* is also seen); *рак пище[про]вода* – esophageal cancer
плеврит, плеврита – (n., masc.) pleurisy
пляска Св. Витта → *витова пляска*
подагра, подагры – (n., fem.) gout, podagra
понос, поноса – (n., masc.) diarrhea
похороны, похорон – (n., fem. pl.) funeral
почка, почки – (n., fem., gen. pl. *почек*) kidney; *воспаление почек* – nephritis
припадок, припадка – (n., masc.) fit, attack; *сердечный припадок* – heart attack
проказа, проказы – (n., fem.) leprosy
простуда, простуды – (n., fem.) cold
пучеглазие, пучеглазия – (n, neut., † *пучеглазіе*) exophthalmos
пятнистый тиф → *тиф*
пятно, пятна – (n., neut.) blemish, blotch; birthmark, mole
разстройство → *расстройство*
рак, рака – (n., masc.) cancer (also means "crab"); *рак печени* – liver cancer; *рак лёгких* – lung cancer
рана, раны – (n., fem.) injury, wound; *умереть от раны* – he died of his wound
расстройство, расстройства – (n., neut., † *разстройство*) disorder; *отъ расстройства желудка* – from a stomach disorder
рахит, рахита – (n., masc.) rachitis, rickets (also seen: † *рахитизмъ*)
рахитик, рахитика – (n., masc.) one suffering from rickets
рвота, рвоты – (n., fem.) vomiting
ревматизм, ревматизма – (n., masc.) rheumatism
родильный – (adj.) relating to birth; *родильная горячка* – puerperal fever, childbed fever
родимчик, родимчика – (n., masc.) childish eclampsia, convulsions; also seen: *родимец*
родины, родин – (n., fem. pl.) childbirth
рожа, рожи – (n., fem.) erysipelas
роженица, роженицы – (n., fem.) woman giving birth, having recently given birth
рожистый – (adj.) erysipelatous; *рожистое воспаление* – erysipelas
свинуха, свинухи – (n., fem.) scrofula
свищ, свища – (n., masc.) fistula
свой – (reflexive adj.) my own, your own, our own, his own, her own, its own, their own; *своей смертью умереть* – to die a natural death
сенная лихорадка, сенной лихорадки – (n., fem.) hay fever
сердечный – (adj.) of the heart; *сердечный припадок* – heart attack; *сердечная болезнь* – heart disease
сердце, сердца – (n., neut.) heart; *болезнь сердца* – heart disease
сибирская язва → *язва*
синюха, синюхи – (n., fem.) cyanosis
скарлатина, скарлатины – (n., fem.) scarlet fever
склероз, склероза – (n., masc.) sclerosis
скончаться – (v.) to die, pass away; *он скончался* – he died; *она скончалась* – she died
скорбут, скорбута – (n., masc.) scurvy
скоропостижно – (adv.) suddenly, unexpectedly
скоропостижный – (adj.) sudden, unexpected; *скоропостижная смерть*, sudden death
слабость, слабости – (n., fem.) weakness, debility; *старческая слабость*, debility due to old age
следствие, следствия – (n., neut., † *слѣдствіе*) consequence, result; *в следствие* – as a result (of, genitive)
слезотечение, слезотечения – (n., neut., † *слезотеченіе*) epiphora

слизетечение, слизетечения – (n., neut., † *слизетеченіе*) blennorrhea
слизистый отёк, слизистого отёка – (n., masc.) myxedema
слѣдствіе → *следствие*
смерть, смерти – (n., fem.) death; *естественная смерть* – natural death; *насильственная смерть* – violent death; *голодная смерть* – starvation; *своей смертью умереть* – to die a natural death; *умереть смертью героя* – to die a hero's death
солнечный удар, солнечного удара – (n., masc.) sunstroke
спазма, спазмы – (n., fem.) spasm
старость, старости – (n., fem.) old age; *умереть от старости,* to die of old age
старческий – (adj., † *старческій*) senile
столбняк, столбняка – (n., masc.) tetanus
страдание, страдания – (n., neut. † *страданіе*) suffering, illnesss
судорога, судороги – (n., fem.) cramp, convulsion
судорожный – (adj.) convulsive
сыпной or *сыпняк* → *тиф*
тело, тела – (n., neut., † *тѣло*) body
тиф, тифа – (n., masc.) typhus; *брюшной тиф* – typhoid; *возвратный тиф* – remittent typhus; *пятнистый тиф* or *сыпной тиф*, spotted fever, typhus (also called *сыпняк*)
тифозная горячка, тифозной горячки – (n., fem.) typhoid fever (also seen: *тифозная лихорадка*)
тѣло → *тело*
туберкулёз, туберкулёза – (n., masc.) tuberculosis; *туберкулёз лёгких* – pulmonary tuberculosis
удавление, удавления – (n., neut., † *удавленіе*) strangulation; *смерть от удавления* – death by strangulation
удавленник, удавленника – (n., masc.) one who died of strangulation or hanging, at his own hand or another's; fem. *удавленница*
удар, удара – (n., masc.) stroke, attack
ум. – abbrev. of *умер* or *умерла* or *умерли* → *умереть*
умереть – (v.; † *оумеръ;* imperf. aspect *умирать*) to die (*от* + gen.) to die, e. g., *умер от раны*, he died of his wound; *умер* – he died; *умерла* – she died; *умерли* – they died; *умереть с голоду* – to die of starvation; *умереть смертью героя* – to die a hero's death; *умереть скоропостижно* – to die suddenly, unexpectedly; *умереть естественно* or *естественной смертью* – to die a natural death; *умереть насильственно* or *насильственной смертью* – to die violently; *умереть за дело* – to die for the cause
умерший – (part., † *оумершій* or *умершій*) dead, late
умирать → *умереть*
умирающий – (pres. act. part. of *умирать*) dying; (used as a n.) the dying one
уродливость, уродливости – (n., fem.) deformity
усопший – (adj., † *усопшій*) deceased, dead
утопленник, утопленника – (n., masc.) drowned man (fem. *утопленница*)
флебит, флебита – (n., masc.) phlebitis
хлороз, хлороза – (n., masc.) chlorosis
холера, холеры – (n., fem.) cholera
холерик, холерика – (n., masc.) one ill with cholera
хронический – (adj.) chronic
худосочие, худосочия – (n., neut., † *худосочіе*) cachexia, debilitation, wasting away
цепень, цепня – (n., masc., † *цѣпень*) tapeworm, taenia
цианоз, цианоза – (n., masc., † *ціанозъ*) cyanosis
цинга, цинги – (n., fem., † *цынга*) scurvy
цинготный – (adj., † *цынготный*) scorbutic
цынга → *цинга*
цынготный → *цинготный*
чахотка, чахотки – consumption, phthisis; *скоротечная чахотка* – galloping consumption
чума, чумы – (n., fem.) plague, the Black Death; *бубонная чума* – bubonic plague; *лёгочная чума* – pneumonic plague
шадра, шадры – smallpox
шок, шока – (n., masc.) shock (medical term)
экзантема, экзантемы – (n., fem.) exanthema, a skin disease
экзема, экземы – (n., fem.) eczema
эклампсия, эклампсии – (n., fem., † *эклампсія*) eclampsia
эмфизема, эмфиземы – (n., fem.) emphysema
эпилепсия, эпилепсии – (n., fem., † *эпилепсія*) epilepsy
эпилептик, эпилептика – (n., masc.) epileptic
эритема, эритемы – (n., fem.) erythema
яд, яда - (n., masc.) poison
язва, язвы – (n., fem.) ulcer; *язва желудка* – stomach ulcer; *моровая язва* – plague; *сибирская язва* – anthrax

E. MISCELLANEOUS RECORDS

The Russian Empire encompassed an enormous variety of ethnic groups, cultures, languages, and administrative setups. It would be extravagant and unrealistic to try to assemble a comprehensive collection of every possible type of document one might find in the course of Russian research. Instead, we are featuring those genealogical researchers are most likely to find, and those most likely to be helpful. We have looked closely at birth, marriage, and death records because those are the documents of most obvious genealogical value. Now let us sample other documents which our experience suggests you may find worth attention.

1. Document VI-32: A Jewish Divorce Record from Białystok

As we said on page 213, registers most often are divided into three parts, with the first consisting of birth records, the second of marriage records, and the third of death records. But in some cases we find the registers have another section, devoted to divorces. In registers with divorce records those documents generally comprise part 3, with death records relegated to part 4 (parts 1 and 2 are, as usual, devoted to birth and marriage records, respectively). Since in general Christians were forbidden to divorce until more recent times, these records will typically deal with Jews—but of course this is a generalization, and one may encounter exceptions to this rule.

Reproduced on page 291 is **Document VI-32,** a page from a divorce register for Białystok, Poland. The headings across the top of the page read as follows:

в) книга для записки разводовъ между евреями на 187<u>9</u> годъ – "v) Register for entry of divorces between Jews for the year 1879." (Note: **в** is phonetically equivalent to English **v**; but it's the third letter of the Cyrillic alphabet, and thus in a list corresponds to our "c").

ЧАСТЬ III-Я О РАЗВЕДШИХСЯ – "Part III: Divorces"

The columnar headings are as follows:

№ – Sequential number, here 8, divorce #8 in the Jewish community for the year 1879.

Лѣта | Женскаго | Мужескаго – "Age | Female | Male," here 32 and 35 respectively.

Кѣмъ совершается обрядъ разводный или халицы и кто были свидѣтелями при совершеніи онаго – "By whom was the ceremony of divorce or *ḥalitsah* performed, and who were the witnesses to its performance?" The noun *халица* is a Cyrillic phonetic rendering of Hebrew חֲלִיצָה, *ḥalitsah,* release from a levirate marriage.

Here the answer is: *Раввинъ Герцъ Гальпернъ и Янкель Крышекъ свид. Рахміель Ставискеръ и Мовша Школьникъ* – "Rabbi Herc Halpern and Jankiel Kryszek, witnesses Rachmil Stawiskier and Mowsza Szkolnik." Note that these are Polish versions of these names; English phonetic renderings of the Cyrillic spellings would be Gerts Gal'pern, Yankel' Kryshek, Rachmiel' Stavisker, and Movsha Shkol'nik.

Число и мѣсяцъ | Христіанскій | Еврейскій – "Day and month | Christian | Jewish." Here the date was *31 Октября*, 31 October, by the Christian calendar, and *26 Хешвана*, 26 Heshvan, by the Jewish (see page 47 for the Russian spellings of Jewish month names).

По какимъ причинамъ – "For what reasons." Here the entry reads *по разнымъ супружескимъ раздорамъ*, "due to various marital disagreements."

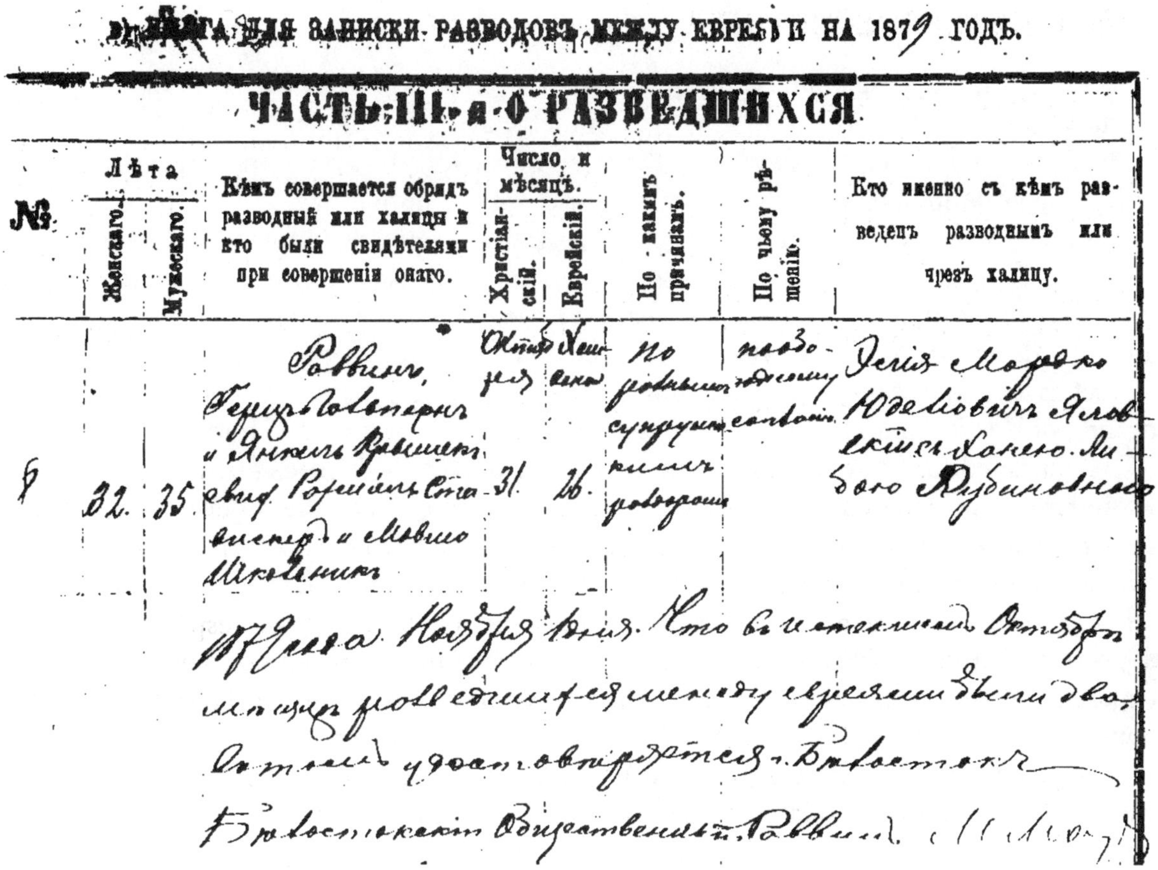

КНИГА ДЛЯ ЗАПИСКИ РАЗВОДОВЪ МЕЖДУ ЕВРЕЯМИ НА 1879 ГОДЪ.

ЧАСТЬ III-я О РАЗВЕДШИХСЯ

№	Лѣта: Женскаго	Лѣта: Мужескаго	Кѣмъ совершается обрядъ разводный или халицы и кто были свидѣтелями при совершеніи онаго.	Число и мѣсяцъ: Христіанскій	Число и мѣсяцъ: Еврейскій	По какимъ причинамъ	По чьему рѣшенію	Кто именно съ кѣмъ разведенъ разводнымъ или чрезъ халицу.
8	32.	35.	Раввинъ, [illegible]	Октября 31	[illegible] 26	[illegible]	[illegible]	[illegible]

Document VI-32: A Divorce Record

По чьему рѣшенію – "By whose decision." Here the answer reads *по обоюдному согласію*, "by mutual agreement." We may also see here phrases such as *по взаимному согласію*, "by mutual agreement," and *по желанію супруговъ*, "by the wishes of the spouses."

Кто именно съ кѣмъ разведенъ разводнымъ или чрезъ халицу – "Who, by name, is being separated from whom by divorce or by *ḥalitsah*?" Here the parties are: *Элія Мордка Юделіовичъ Яловскій съ Ханею Либою Рубиновною*, "Elija Mordka Jałowski, son of Judel, and Chana Liba, daughter of Rubin." Again, those are Polish versions of the names. English phonetic renderings of the Cyrillic spellings would be: Eliya Mordka Yalovskiy, son of Yudel', and Khana Liba, daughter of Rubin.

The handwritten paragraph below the columnar entries is just legalese. If you want to know what it says, it reads as follows:

> *1879 года Ноября 1 дня. Что въ истекшемъ Октябрѣ*
> *мѣсяцѣ разведшихся между евреями были два*
> *въ томъ удостовѣряется г. Бѣлостокъ*
> *Бѣлостокскій Общественный Раввинъ — [signature illegible]*

This translates as: "1879, November 1st. That in last October there were two divorces among the Jews is hereby certified. Town of Białystok. [Signed] the Białystok General Rabbi *[signature illegible]*."

2. Military Records: Document VI-33: Conscription Lists

As of 1874, every male subject of the Russian Empire was obligated to serve many years of military duty. Service consisted of 6 years (eventually lowered to 5) of active duty in the regular army, followed by a number of years in the reserve (запасъ) and yet more years in the militia or home guard (ополченіе); a man's eligibility did not end until the age of 40 (later 43)!

In practice, every male did not end up serving; it was possible to buy your way out of the military. Also, many young men emigrated (sometimes illegally) precisely to avoid devoting years of their life to military service. But that left large numbers of our ancestors who did serve, and records relating to their service can often be found and studied profitably.

Let us look first at documents relating to the conscription process, then proceed to records dealing with active military service, followed by service in the reserve and home guard.

A translated version of an article entitled "Russian Military Records from the Kingdom of Poland as a Source for Genealogical Research," by Professor Michał Kopczyński, a historian at the University of Warsaw, appeared in the Fall, 2001 issue of *Pathways & Passages,* the Journal of the Polish Genealogical Society of Connecticut and the Northeast. The following remarks are based on that article. A version with translation and analysis of a sample document appeared in the Winter 2002 issue of *Rodziny,* the Journal of the Polish Genealogical Society of America. We reproduce that document here as VI-33, with accompanying translation. We appreciate the respective Societies' permission to reprint this material.

The details discussed here are applicable mainly to the Kingdom of Poland, but familiarity with the format and vocabulary of these sample records should assist you in dealing with those you find, whatever part of the Empire they came from.

Every *powiat* or *уѣздъ* office kept several series of records relating to military service; from 1868 they were all in the Russian language. Those of most value to the genealogical researcher are the *księgi poborowe* (Books of Draftees), in Russian *призывной списокъ.* They were drawn up prior to the actual draft examination process, from lists of all men of draftable age in the entire county. The entries were handwritten on printed forms, so that anyone able to read Russian can hope to examine and decipher them. The individual sheets were bound into volumes, divided by *powiat* or *уѣздъ* and subdivided into district [*гмина, gmina*].

There have been instances in which the conscription lists were destroyed or lost, but lists of those who were processed and underwent physical examination may have survived. The books of those who were deemed fit to serve were called the *приёмная роспись.* These, too, were bound into cloth-covered volumes. They are not always grouped in any perceptible order; one many need to search the entire list—which in some cases may contain up to 800 individuals—with no guarantee of finding a given individual.

Other kinds of the records generated by county Commissions of Military Obligation are less useful for family history research. One type of record consists of lists of those serving in the militia *(списокъ ратникомъ ополченія),* which provide only name and surname and a reference to an entry in the conscription list. In some cases this record group contains numerous applications from draftable individuals requesting an exemption due to family circumstances, or a re-examination by the physicians. One may find an actual military booklet of the sort issued to all those who were drafted, containing personal and service information (see page 306). Sometimes photos can be found in these miscellaneous records. Looking for such materials on a specific individual, however, is like looking for a needle in a haystack.

These draft and military records are typically held by the state archives or other repositories in countries that were formerly part of the Russian Empire. You should contact them for more information. For those held by the Polish State Archives, for example, one can contact the Archives, or search online the SEZAM database on the Polish State Archives Website: **http://www.archiwa.gov.pl**.

To locate records for the period 1894-1914, enter the phrase "powinności wojskowej." For earlier records, covering 1867-1873, use the phrase "komisja konskrypcyjna." (The Polish State Archives Website has an English-language version, but you must type the phrases above **in Polish** to produce results. Do not use translations). These searches will produce a list of extant records, as well as the address of the archive where they are located and a brief description of the record series. You can then contact the archive in question to make sure they do, in fact, have the records, and arrange to get copies.

Now let's look at **Document VI-33**, a sample conscription record. These entries were made horizontally across two pages, which we reproduce here in sections. The section with columns 1-7 appears below; the other columns appear on pages 295, 296, and 298.

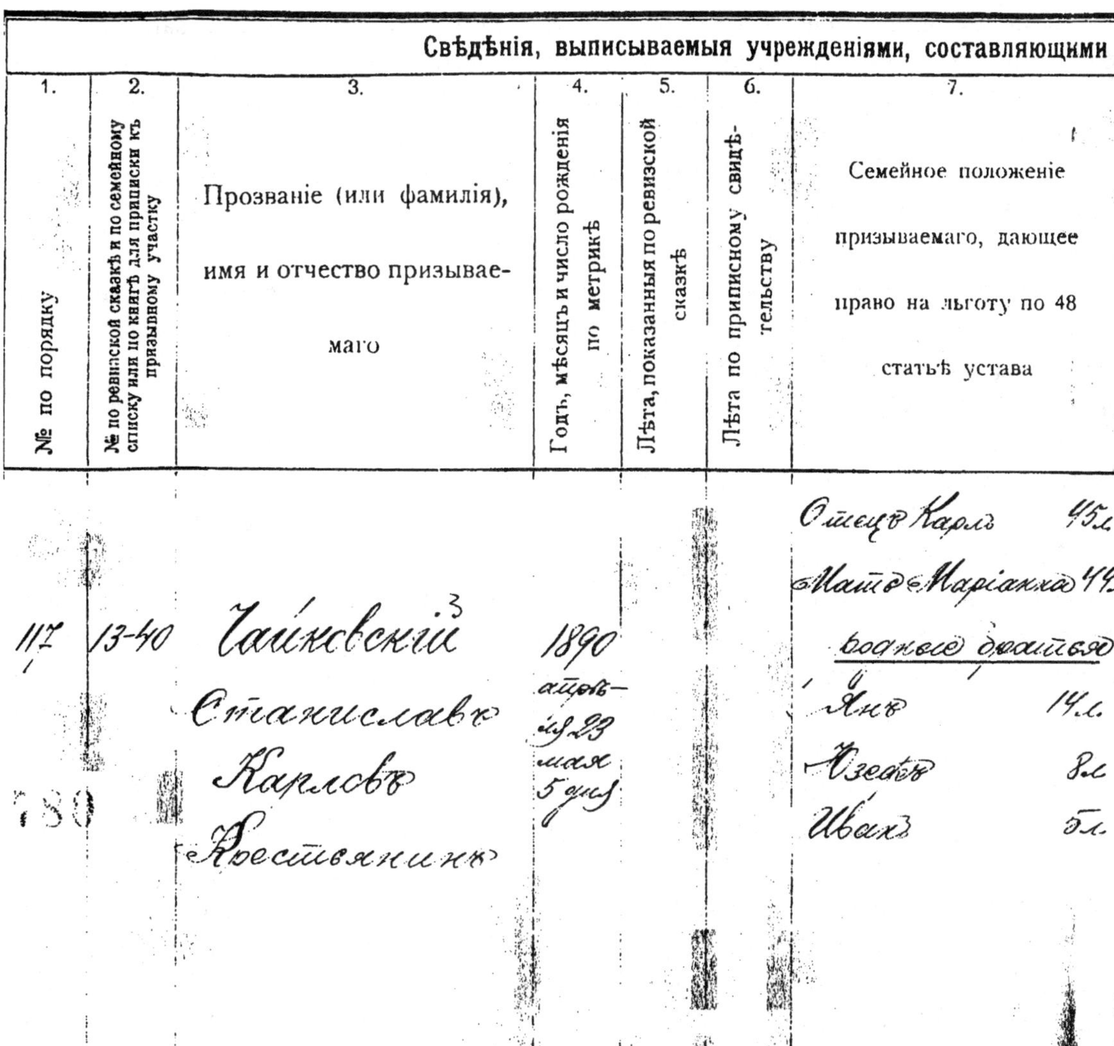

Свѣдѣнія, выписываемыя учрежденіями, составляющими

1. № по порядку	2. № по ревизской сказкѣ и по семейному списку или по книгѣ для приписки къ призывному участку	3. Прозваніе (или фамилія), имя и отчество призываемаго	4. Годъ, мѣсяцъ и число рожденія по метрикѣ	5. Лѣта, показанныя по ревизской сказкѣ	6. Лѣта по приписному свидѣтельству	7. Семейное положеніе призываемаго, дающее право на льготу по 48 статьѣ устава
117 780	13-40	Чайковскій Станиславъ Карловъ крестьянинъ	1890 апрѣля 23 мая 5 дня			Отецъ Карлъ 45 л. Мать Маріанна 44 л. родные братья Янъ 14 л. Юзефъ 8 л. Иванъ 5 л.

Document VI-33 (columns 1-7)

The heading at the top of the form reads: **Свѣдѣнія, выписываемыя учрежденіями, составляющими призывные списки** – "Information filled out by the institutions that drew up the draft lists."

Column 1: № по порядку – "Sequential number," in this case *117.*

Column 2: № по ревизской сказкѣ и по семейному списку или по книгѣ для приписки къ призывному участку – "Number per revision list (i. e., census) and family registration or per the draft enrollment register"; here, *13-40.*

Column 3: Прозваніе (или фамилія), имя и отчество призываемаго – "Surname (or family name), first name, and patronymic of the conscript [literally 'one called up']."

Here the information written in reads: *Чайковскій, Станиславъ Карловъ Крестьянинъ*, "Czajkowski, Stanisław, [son] of Karol, peasant."

Column 4: Годъ, мѣсяцъ и число рожденія по метрикѣ – "Year, month and date of birth according to the vital records certificate." Here it reads: *1890, апрѣля 23 мая 5 дня*, "1890, April 23 [Old Style]/ 5 May [New Style]."

Column 5: Лѣта, показанныя по ревизской сказкѣ – "Age shown on the revision list"; here none is given.

Column 6: Лѣта по приписному свидѣтельству – "Age per registration certificate"; here left blank.

Column 7: Семейное положеніе призываемаго, дающее право на льготу по 48 статьѣ устава – "Family situation of the conscript that entitles him to an exemption under Article 48 of the Code."

In this case the following are listed:

Отецъ Карлъ, 45 л. – "father, Karol, age 45"
Мать Маріанна 44 л. – "mother Marianna, age 44"
родные братья – "Full brothers" (i. e., not half-brothers)
Янъ, 14 л. – "Jan, age 14"
Юзефъ, 8 л. – "Józef, age 8"
Иванъ, 5 л. – "Iwan, age 5"

[Columns 8-10 appear at the top of page 295]

Column 8: 1. Какого вѣроисповѣданія призываемый; какой его родной языкъ. 2. Холостъ, вдовъ или женатъ; имѣетъ ли дѣтей и кого именно. 3. Къ какому разряду принадлежитъ по образованію, съ обозначеніемъ числа, мѣсяца, года и № свидѣтельства о томъ, и кѣмъ оно выдано. 4. Если призываемый не имѣетъ свидѣтельства объ образованіи, то знаетъ ли грамоту. 5. Занятіе, ремесло или промыселъ призываемаго. – "1. Of what religion is the conscript; what is his native language? 2. Single, widowed, or married; does he have children, and who, by name? 3. To what category does he belong in terms of education, with indication of the day, month, and year and certificate number to that effect, issued by whom? 4. If the conscript does not have an educational certificate, can he read? 5. Occupation, trade, or profession of the conscript?"

In this case answers are given to questions 1, 2, 4, and 5: 1. *Р. католическа, польскій*, "Roman Catholic, Polish." 2. *Холостъ*, "single." 4. *Неграмотенъ*, "Illiterate." 5. *Хлѣбопашецъ*, "Farmer."

призывные списки		
8.	9.	10.
1. Какого вѣроисповѣданія призываемый; какой его родной языкъ. 2. Холостъ, вдовъ или женатъ; имѣетъ ли дѣтей и кого именно. 3. Къ какому разряду принадлежитъ по образованію, съ обозначеніемъ числа, мѣсяца, года и № свидѣтельства о томъ, и кѣмъ оно выдано. 4. Если призываемый не имѣетъ свидѣтельства объ образованіи, то знаетъ ли грамоту. 5. Занятіе, ремесло или промыселъ призываемаго.	Отмѣтка о состоящихъ подъ слѣдствіемъ или судомъ и о лишенныхъ всѣхъ правъ состоянія или всѣхъ особенныхъ правъ и преимуществъ, лично и по состоянію присвоенныхъ	Если призываемый принадлежитъ къ числу лицъ, указанныхъ въ 60, 61, 63, 79, 80, 82, 83 и 84 стат. Устава то: а) къ разряду какихъ именно лицъ и б) число, мѣсяцъ, годъ и № свидѣтельства о томъ и кѣмъ оно выдано
1, Р. католическаго польскій 2, Холостъ 4, Неграмотенъ 5, Хлѣбопашецъ	Не состоитъ	Не принадлежитъ

Document VI-33 (columns 8-10)

Column 9: Отмѣтка о состоящихъ подъ слѣдствіемъ или судомъ и о лишенныхъ всѣхъ правъ состоянія или всѣхъ особенныхъ правъ и преимуществъ, лично и по состоянію присвоенныхъ. – "Notation of those under investigation of or being tried for a crime, and of those who have been deprived of all rights connected with them personally or by means of their status, or of individual rights or privileges." Here the answer is simple, *Не состоитъ*, "He is not involved," i. e., "not applicable."

Column 10: Если призываемый принадлежитъ къ числу лицъ, указанныхъ въ 60, 61, 63, 79, 80, 82, 83 и 84 стат. Устава то: а) къ разряду какихъ именно лицъ и б) число, мѣсяцъ, годъ и № свидѣтельства о томъ и кѣмъ оно выдано. – "If the conscript is among those specified under articles 60, 61, 63, 79, 80, 82, 83 and 84 of the Code, then state: a) under which category exactly, and b) the day, month, year, and number of the certificate to that effect, and by whom it was issued." Here again the answer is simple: *Не принадлежитъ*, "He does not belong [i. e., to that category]," i. e., "not applicable."

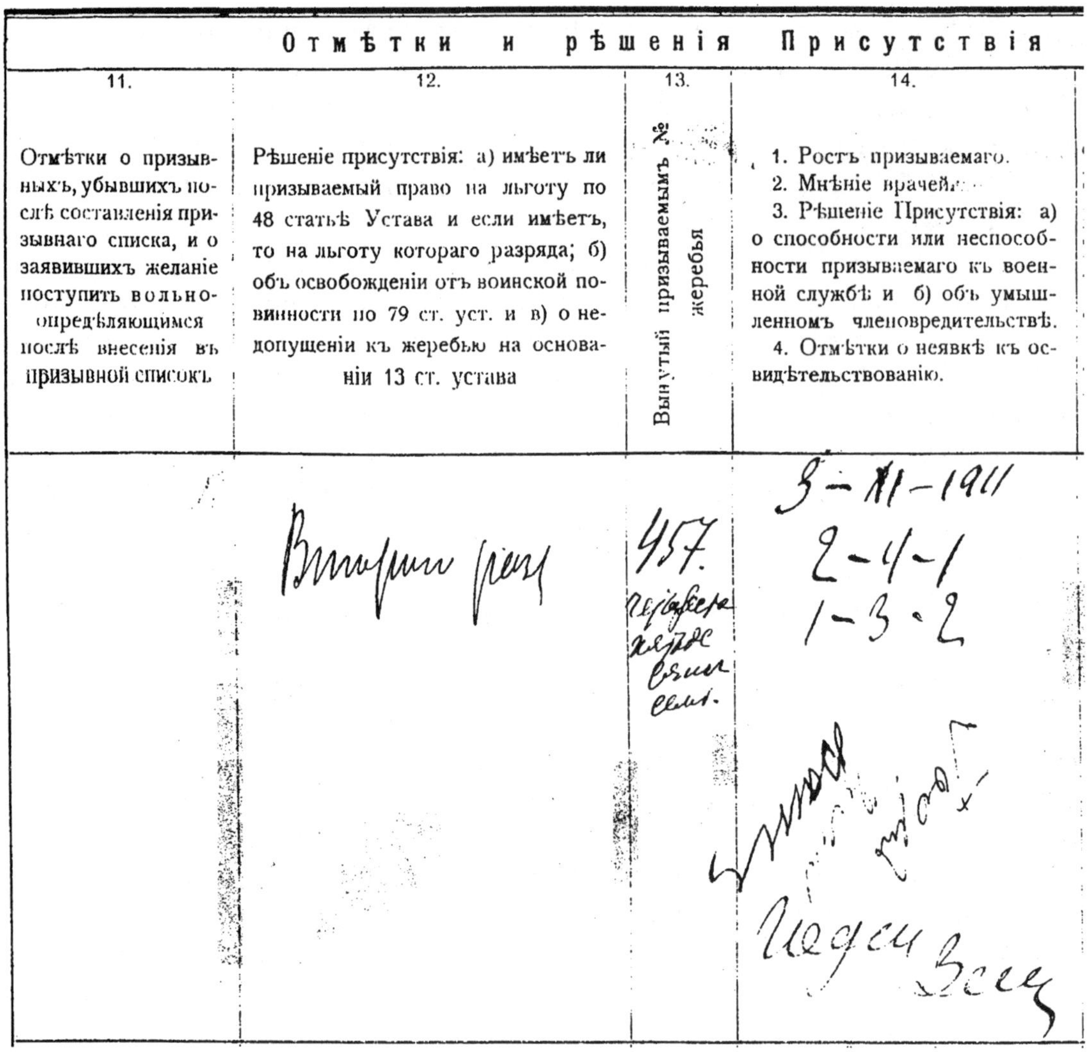

Отмѣтки и рѣшенія Присутствія			
11.	12.	13.	14.
Отмѣтки о призывныхъ, убывшихъ послѣ составленія призывнаго списка, и о заявившихъ желаніе поступить вольно-опредѣляющимся послѣ внесенія въ призывной списокъ	Рѣшеніе присутствія: а) имѣетъ ли призываемый право на льготу по 48 статьѣ Устава и если имѣетъ, то на льготу котораго разряда; б) объ освобожденіи отъ воинской повинности по 79 ст. уст. и в) о недопущеніи къ жеребью на основаніи 13 ст. устава	Вынутый призываемымъ № жеребья	1. Ростъ призываемаго. 2. Мнѣніе врачей. 3. Рѣшеніе Присутствія: а) о способности или неспособности призываемаго къ военной службѣ и б) объ умышленномъ членовредительствѣ. 4. Отмѣтки о неявкѣ къ освидѣтельствованію.
		457.	3 – XI – 1911 2 – 4 – 1 1 – 3 · 2

Document VI-33 (columns 11-14)

The heading on the right side of the page (reproduced above and on page 298) reads "**Отмѣтки и рѣшенія Присутствія по воинской повинности**, "Notes and Decisions of the Commission on Military Obligation."

Column 11: Отмѣтки о призывныхъ, убывшихъ послѣ составленія призывнаго списка, и о заявившихъ желаніе поступить вольно-опредѣляющимся послѣ внесенія въ призывной списокъ – "Notes on conscripts who departed after the draft list had been drawn up, and on those who expressed a desire to enlist as volunteers after having been enrolled in the draft list."

Here nothing was entered because none of this applied to Czajkowski.

Column 12: Рѣшеніе присутствія: а) имѣетъ ли призываемый право на льготу по 48 статьѣ Устава и если имѣетъ, то на льготу котораго разряда; б) объ освобожденіи отъ воинской повинности по 79 ст. уст. и в) о недопущенніи къ жеребью на основаніи 13 ст. устава – "Decision of the Commission: a) does the conscript have the right to a deferment per article 48 of the Code, and if he does, to a deferment of what category; b) on release from military obligation per article 79 of the code, and c) on non-admission to [the drawing of] lots on the basis of article 13 of the code."

Here the entry seems to read *Втораго разр.*, "of the second category."

Column 13: Вынутый призываемымъ № жеребья – "Lot number drawn by the conscript"

Here the lot number is *457, четыреста пятьдесятъ семь,* "457, four hundred fifty-seven."

Column 14: 1. Ростъ призываемаго. 2. Мнѣніе врачей. 3. Рѣшеніе Присутствія: а) о способности или неспособности призываемаго къ военной службѣ и б) объ умышленномъ членовредительствѣ. 4. Отмѣтки о неявкѣ къ освидѣтельствованію – "1. Conscript's height. 2. The doctors' opinion. 3. Decision of the Commission: a) on the conscript's fitness or unfitness for military service, and b) as to intentional maiming [i. e., self-mutilation to avoid military service]. 4. Notation of failure to appear for examination."

Here the date is given, *3-XI-1911,* along with some of the numerical codes that the doctors were to use according to standardized instructions, followed by signatures of the Commission members.

Column 15: 1. Рѣшенія Присутствія: а) объ отсрочкахъ для поступленія на службу; б) о назначеніи къ переосвидѣтельствованію въ Губ. Присутствіи; в) объ отправленіи въ лечебное заведеніе на испытаніе и г) о состоящихъ подъ судомъ или слѣдствіемъ. 2. Число, мѣсяцъ, годъ и № выданнаго Присутсвіемъ временнаго свидѣтельства. – "Decision of the Commission a) on deferment of reporting for service; b) on scheduling a re-examination with the Provincial authorities; c) on sending [the recruit] to a medical facility for examination, and d) on those under investigation of or on trial for a crime. 2. Day, month, year, and number of the temporary certificate issued by the Commission." None of these options applied to the decision in Czajkowski's case.

Column 16: 1. Отмѣтки: а) о принятіи на службу по жеребью; б) о принятіи на службу по жеребью съ зачисленіемъ бъ запасъ; в) объ отдачѣ на службу безъ жеребья и г) объ освобожденіи отъ службы навсегда. 2. Подъ какимъ № внесенъ въ пріемную роспись. 3. Число, мѣсяцъ, годъ и № выданнаго Присутствіемъ безсрочнаго свидѣтельства. – "1. Notes: a) on admission to the service by lot; b) on admission to the service by lot with enrollment in the reserve; c) on transfer to the service without lot; and d) on exemption from service henceforth. 2. Enrolled in the inductee register under what number. 3. The day, month, year, and number of the permanent certificate issued by the Commission." If Czajkowski had been drafted into active service, it would have been noted here (see below).

Column 17: 1. Отмѣтки: а) о зачисленіи въ ополченіе и б) объ оказавшихся по наружному осмотру неспособными носить оружіе. 2. Подъ какимъ № внесенъ въ списокъ ополченцевъ. 3. Число, мѣсяцъ, годъ и № выданнаго Присутствіемъ безсрочнаго свидѣтельства. – 1. Notes: a) on admission to the militia and b) on those who, after external examination, proved to be incapable of bearing arms. 2. Enrolled under what number in the list of members of the militia. 3. The day, month, year, and number of the permanent certificate issued by the Commission."

Here the following information is entered: *Въ ополченіе первага разряда. Свидѣтельство отъ 3 Ноября 1911 г. за № 131*: "[Enrolled] in the militia, first category. Certificate, 3 November 1911, No. 131."

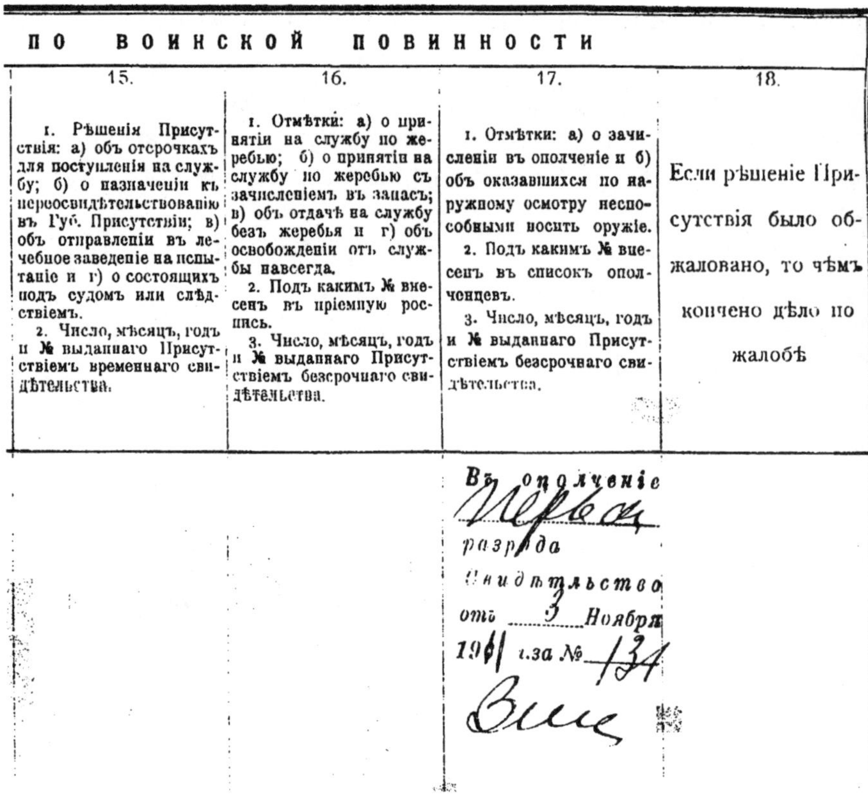

ПО ВОИНСКОЙ ПОВИННОСТИ			
15.	16.	17.	18.
1. Рѣшенія Присутствія: а) объ отсрочкахъ для поступленія на службу; б) о назначеніи къ переосвидѣтельствованію въ Губ. Присутствіи; в) объ отправленіи въ лечебное заведеніе на испытаніе и г) о состоящихъ подъ судомъ или слѣдствіемъ. 2. Число, мѣсяцъ, годъ и № выданнаго Присутствіемъ временнаго свидѣтельства.	1. Отмѣтки: а) о принятіи на службу по жеребью; б) о принятіи на службу по жеребью съ зачисленіемъ въ запасъ; в) объ отдачѣ на службу безъ жеребья и г) объ освобожденіи отъ службы навсегда. 2. Подъ какимъ № внесенъ въ пріемную роспись. 3. Число, мѣсяцъ, годъ и № выданнаго Присутствіемъ безсрочнаго свидѣтельства.	1. Отмѣтки: а) о зачисленіи въ ополченіе и б) объ оказавшихся по наружному осмотру неспособными носить оружіе. 2. Подъ какимъ № внесенъ въ списокъ ополченцевъ. 3. Число, мѣсяцъ, годъ и № выданнаго Присутствіемъ безсрочнаго свидѣтельства.	Если рѣшеніе Присутствія было обжаловано, то чѣмъ кончено дѣло по жалобѣ
		Въ ополченіе Перваго разряда Свидѣтельство отъ 3 Ноября 1911 г. за № 134	

Document VI-33 (columns 15-18)

Column 18: Если рѣшеніе Присутствія было обжаловано, то чѣмъ кончено дѣло по жалобѣ. – "If the decision of the Commission was appealed, how the matter was concluded after the appeal." (No appeal is noted).

Thus it turned out that the Commission decided Stanisław Czajkowski was entitled to a 2nd-category deferment and was enrolled in the militia or home guard.

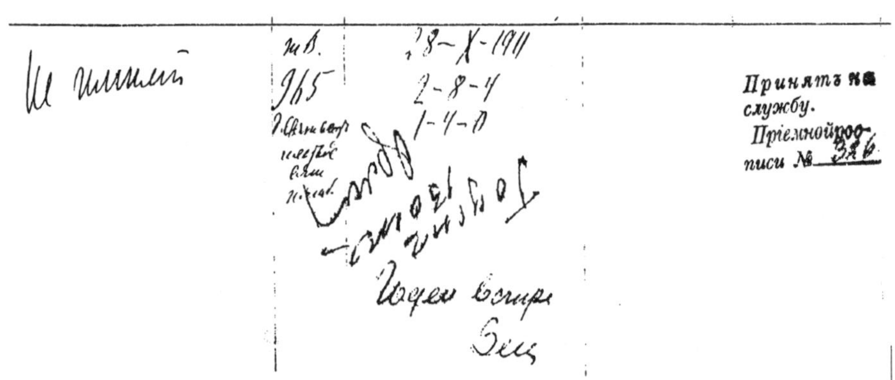

Не имѣетъ	жб. 965	28-X-1911 2-8-4 1-4-0		Принятъ на службу. Пріемной росписи № 326

By contrast, the next person listed on this page, the peasant Michał Kaczmarek, was inducted into the service. The relevant columns (12-16) are reproduced at right. In column 12, the handwritten note reads *Не имѣетъ*," "He does not have [any right to a deferment]." Column 13 shows that he drew lot #965. Column 14 gives the date, 28-X-1911, with medical codes and the signatures of the commission members. Column 15 is blank. Column 16 is stamped *Принятъ на службу. Пріемной росписи №* 326, "Accepted into the service. No. 326 in the inductee register."

Document VI-34: A List of Draftable Males from a Population Register

№ по пор.	Мужчинъ.	Женщинъ, кто онѣ урожденныя и по прежнему замужеству.	и кто урожденная мать.	Годъ.	Мѣсяцъ.	День.
1	Аронъ-Лейзоръ Хорощъ		Зельманъ и Эстера урожденная Лейбовичъ	1857	Конскрипціонная [illegible] Ломжинскаго Уѣзда октября 24 [illegible] 1874 [illegible]	
2	Зельманъ-Лейба Хорощъ		Аронъ Лейзоръ и Баша Борохъ урожденная Древенко	1890	Марта Акта №: 105	16 / 28
3	Абрамъ-Ицекъ Хорощъ		Аронъ Лейзоръ Бася-Борохъ урожденная Древенко	1895	Августа Акта №: 33	4 / 16

Вѣрность настоящей выписки съ книгой постоян[illegible]

Посадъ Задроговъ Апрѣля [illegible]

Войтъ гмины Задроговъ [illegible]

Reproduced on page 299 is the left half of **Document VI**-34, a sample page from a population register, the kind of record from which lists of draftable males were compiled. It lists those living in a locality—here, Zambrów in Łomża province—and for men, shows their status as regards military duty. The right half is reproduced on page 301.

The top part of the page was cut off when originally copied, but by comparing this with the similar Document VI-49 on page 338 we can suply the missing words in the column headings:

№ по порядку – "Sequential #"

Мужчинъ – "of men." Missing is Имя и прозванiе, so that the whole heading is "[First and last name] of men."

Женщинъ, кто онѣ урожденныя и по прежнему замужеству – "[First and last name] of women, who were they born as, and by previous marriage," i. e., for women, give their maiden and married names.

[Имена родителеи] и кто урожденная мать – The missing words mean "Names of parents." The part not cut off means literally "and who [is/was] [his/ her] born mother," in other words, "What was the mother's maiden name?"

[Время рожденія] Годъ | Мѣсяцъ | День – "[Time of birth] Year | Month | Day"

Entry #1 says of *Аронъ Лейзоръ Хорощъ*, Aron Lejzor Choroszcz, that his parents were *Зельманъ и Эстера урожденная Лейбовная*, Zelman and Estera née Lejbówna. His year of birth is given as 1854; the "month" and "year" columns are filled with the notation *Конскрипціоная Коммиссія Ломжинскаго Уѣзда октября 27 дня 1871 г. опредѣлила* "Conscription Commission of the County of Łomża, October 27 1871, determined …" The last word is illegible.

Entry #2 is for *Зельманъ Лейба Хорощъ*, Zelman Lejba Choroszcz. His parents were *Аронъ Лейзор и Баша Сора урожденная Древенко*, Aron Lejzor and Basza Sora née Drewienko. He was born March 16/28, 1890, reference Document #105. Entry #3 is for *Абрамъ Ицекъ Хорощъ*, Abram Icek Choroszcz, same parents, born August 4/16, 1895, reference birth certificate # 33.

The columns on the right half of this page are reproduced on page 301:

Мѣсто рожденія – "Place of birth"

Женатъ, замужняя или нѣтъ – "Married or not" (There are different terms in Russian for "married" when applied to males and females.)

Происхожденіе по состоянію – "Social class"

Исповѣданіе – "Religion"

Средства къ содержанію – "Means of support"

Примѣчаніе – "Note"

We see that all three of the men listed on the left side of the page (i. e., that reproduced on page 299) were born in *Посадъ Замбровъ*, the town of Zambrów. The first, Aron Lejzor Choroszcz, was *Женатъ*, married; the other two were *Холостъ*, single. All three fell into the social category of *Мѣщанинъ*, townsman or middle-class. All three were of the Jewish faith, *Іудейское*. Aron Lejzor Choroszcz was a *Работникъ*, laborer; Zelman Lejba's occupation was not given, for reasons we will discuss in a moment; and Abram Icek Choroszcz was a *Шапочникъ*, a hatter.

Мѣсто рожденія.	Женатъ, замужняя или нѣтъ.	Происхожденіе по состоянію.	Исповѣданіе.	Средства къ содержанію.	ПРИМѢЧАНІЕ. 166
Посадъ Заслдровъ	Женатъ	Мѣщанинъ	Іудейское	Работникъ	Въ 1898 году исключенъ изъ войскъ какъ выслужившій опредѣленный срокъ
Посадъ Заслдровъ	Холостъ	Мѣщанинъ	Іудейское		Въ апрѣлѣ 1911 г. къ исполненію воинской повинности не явился.-
Посадъ и гмина Заслдровъ	Холостъ	Мѣщанинъ	Іудейское	Шапочникъ	

...постоянныхъ народонаселенія свидѣтельствуютъ

...1-дня 1915 г.

Document VI-34 (right half)

The really interesting part is the last column, where notations are made. Of Aron Lejzor Choroszcz it is noted: *Въ 1898 году исключенъ изъ войска какъ выслуживиій опредѣленный срокъ*, "Excluded from the army in 1898 as having served the appointed term." So he'd served his hitch and was no longer subject to military duty.

The notation for the second entry, Zelman Lejba Choroszcz, reads as follows: *Въ призывъ 1911 г. къ исполненію воинской повинности не явился*, "In the levy of 1911 he did not report to fulfill his military duty." This may explain why his occupation was not given: having failed to report for conscription, he presumably made himself scarce, since otherwise the draft officials might have wanted to have a little talk with him. Of course he might have died, or he might have emigrated, or he might have bought his way out of serving in the military. If he had died or emigrated, however, we would expect to see a note that effect, and a reference to a death certificate or other document (compare Document VI-49, pages 338-341). Still, these records were not always cross-referenced and updated properly, so it's risky to jump to conclusions based on the absence of an explanation. From this document alone, without further information, all we can say is that he did not report for examination when summoned; we would need to find other sources to establish exactly why.

Finally, notice there is no notation for Abram Icek. As we we'll see in a moment, this document was dated April 1, 1915, and Abram Icek was born 4/16 August 1895. When this document was drawn up, then, he was not yet 21 and thus had not yet been summoned to appear for examination and conscription. He had not married yet, had not died, and had not been conscripted; so there was nothing to note about him, as of yet, and that's why the final column is blank.

The handwritten information below the third entry is of minimal research value, but it can't hurt to take a quick look at it, if only because it helps us determine when and where this document was drawn up.

Вѣрность настоящей выписки съ книгой постояннаго народонаселенія свидѣтельствуютъ – "The accuracy of this copy from the register of permanent population is attested by:"

Посадъ Замбровъ Апрѣля 1 дна 1915 г. – "town of Zambrów, April 1, 1915."

Войтъ гмины Замбровъ [signature illegible] – "*Wójt* of the *gmina* of Zambrów." A *wójt* was and is the executive officer or headman of a *gmina*, a district or township. It was standard procedure for him to be responsible for seeing that documents of this sort were drawn up, and to be responsible for their accuracy.

This clarifies the nature of this document. It is a transcript from the Zambrów *книга постояннаго народонаселенія*, "book of permanent population." This was a register kept and updated by the *wójt* or official answering to him, in which he kept track of the permanent inhabitants of a given locality. As people were born, they were entered into it. When they died or moved away, their entries were crossed out, with reference to a relevant document; males' military status was also kept current in them. We will see another example of this kind of register, Document VI-49 on page 338, illustrating some of these other kinds of notations.

Document VI-35: Certificate of Completing Training

Свидетельство

The actual text of Document VI-35 is only a small portion of the ornate certificate shown on page 303. Enlarged and reproduced at right, it reads as follows:

Свидьтельство
Дано рядовому Нахичиванской мьстной команды Болеславу Дзиковскому въ томъ, что онъ успьшно окончилъ курсъ учебной команды 261го пьхотнаго резервнаго Шемахинскаго полка.

Поведенія былъ хорошаго

Командиръ Полка
Полковникъ [illegible]
Августа 4 дня 1904 год
Полковой Адъютантъ
Штабсъ-капитанъ [illegible]

Translated, that reads literally:

CERTIFICATE

Issued to private of the Nakhichivanskiy local command Bolesław Dzikowski to the effect that he has successfully completed the course of the training command of the 261st Infantry Reserve, Shemakhinskiy Regiment.

His conduct was good.

Commander of the Regiment, Colonel *[illegible]*

August 4, 1904
Regimental Adjutant
Second Captain *[illegible]*

The underlined words are proper adjectives we could not identify with absolute certainty. But it is highly likely that *Нахичиванскій* comes from *Нахичевань, Nakhichevan.* The standard Roman-alphabet form of the name is *Naxçivan.* It is now the capital of an autonomous republic in Azerbaijan. *Шемахинскій* is almost certainly from *Шемаха, Shemakha,* now called *Şamaxi,* also in Azerbaijan. (The adjective might also refer to *Шемаха,* Shemakha, northwest of Chelyabinsk; but the Azerbaijan location seems more likely in a 1904 Russian military context).

Document VI-36: Certificate of Having Reported for Conscription

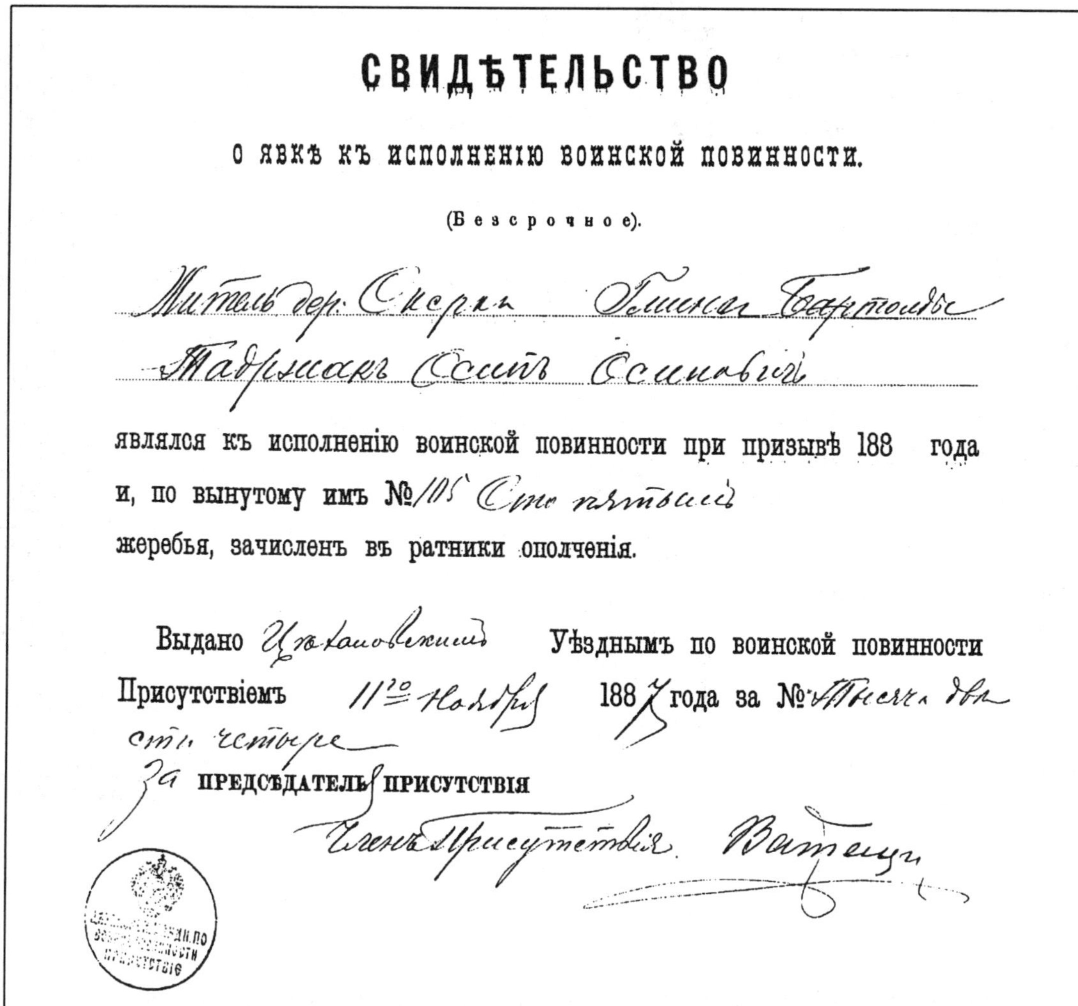

СВИДѢТЕЛЬСТВО

о явкѣ къ исполненію воинской повинности.

(Безсрочное).

Житель дер. Скерки Гмины Бартольды Тадржакъ Осипъ Осиповичъ

являлся къ исполненію воинской повинности при призывѣ 188 года и, по вынутому имъ № 105 Сто пятымъ жеребья, зачисленъ въ ратники ополченія.

Выдано Цехановскимъ Уѣзднымъ по воинской повинности Присутствіемъ 11го Ноября 1887 года за № Тысяча двѣсти четыре

За ПРЕДСѢДАТЕЛЯ ПРИСУТСТВІЯ

Членъ Присутствія

Once called up for examination by the local Conscription Commission, a man might be classified fit for duty and thus immediately draftable, physically or otherwise unfit for duty; or entitled to deferment due to family considerations. If determined fit for duty, he drew lots to determine his draft priority number, which determined the order by which he'd be called to active service in the regular army, or assigned to the militia or home guard. But the first step was that the subject responded to the summons; it was standard procedure of the authorities to check any male's status in this regard. The above document, issued to prove the bearer had done so, is a *свидѣтельство* о *явкѣ къ исполненію воинской повинности*, "certificate of appearance to fulfill military obligation." It had no restricted period of validity (Безсрочное).

Житель дер. Скерки Гмины Бартольды Тадржак Осипъ Осиповичъ – "Inhabitant of the village of Skierki, district of Bartołdy, Tadrzak, Józef, son of Józef." Note that for some reason his Polish name, *Józef,* has been translated to the Russian form *Осипъ*, rather than simply transliterated as *Юзефъ*.

являлся къ исполненію воинской повинности при призывѣ 188_ года и, по вынутому имъ № *105 Сто пятымъ* жеребья, зачисленъ въ ратники ополченія – "appeared to fulfill his military duty during the conscription of 188_ and, after having drawn lot # 105, was enlisted among the soldiers of the militia." A few of these terms are rare and seldom found in modern dictionaries:

призывъ – "conscription, summons, call"
вынутый – "drawn," from *вынуть*, "to draw" (lots)
жеребей or *жеребій* or *жеребьё* – archaic variants of modern *жребий*, "lot, fortune"
зачисленъ – "enrolled, entered into a list," from *зачислить*
ратникъ – "warrior, soldier"
ополченіе – "militia, home guard" i. e., military personnel not serving in the regular army and/or too old to serve in the *запасъ*, the reserve

Выдано *Цѣхановскимъ* Уѣзднымъ по воинской повинности Присутствіемъ *11го ноября* 1887 года за № *тысяча двѣсти четыре*. – "Issued by the Ciechanów County Commission on Military Obligation 11 November 1887 as No. 1204."

присутствие – "commission." The standard meaning of this word is "presence," as *в присутствии свидетелей*, "in the presence of witnesses." It was also used for provincial or district draft boards meeting formally to act in an official capacity.

За Предсѣдателья присусвія: *Членъ Присутсвія [illegible]* – "For the president of the commission: Member of the commission _."

Document VI-37: Military Discharge Booklet

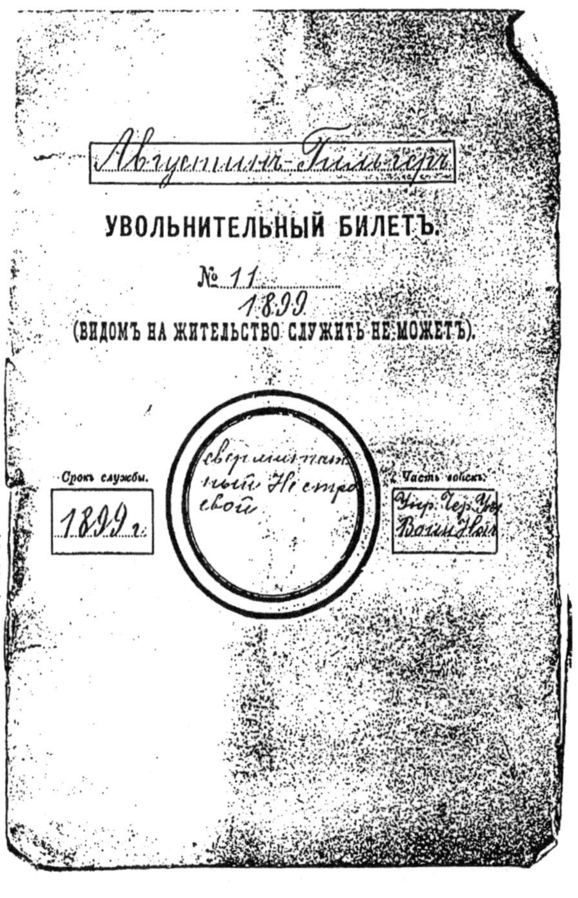

Let us now look at selected portions of a *увольнительный билетъ*, "discharge booklet," which typically contained 24 pages detailing an individual's service. Most discharged men were rank and file foot soldiers who saw no combat, so the pages relating to such activities will not be translated. Also omitted were several pages of tedious regulations, pages set aside for details on campaigns, leaves, and when and where to report if recalled to active duty. We concentrate here on the pages of each booklet that give personal data.

At right is the cover page, with the soldier's name, *Августинъ Гильгеръ*, Avgustin Gil'ger, given in the box on top of the page. This is **Увольнительный Билетъ №** *11/1899*, "Discharge Document #11/1899." The sentence **Видомъ на жительство служить не можетъ**, standard on these documents, means "Can not serve as an identity document." The Срокъ службы, "term of service," is given as 1899. His часть войскъ, "military unit," was *Упр. Чер.*

Уѣз. Воин. Нач., "Cherepovets County Military Command" (as we'll see on the next page). The phrase within the double circle, *сверхштатный Нестроевой*, means "supernumerary, out of the ranks."

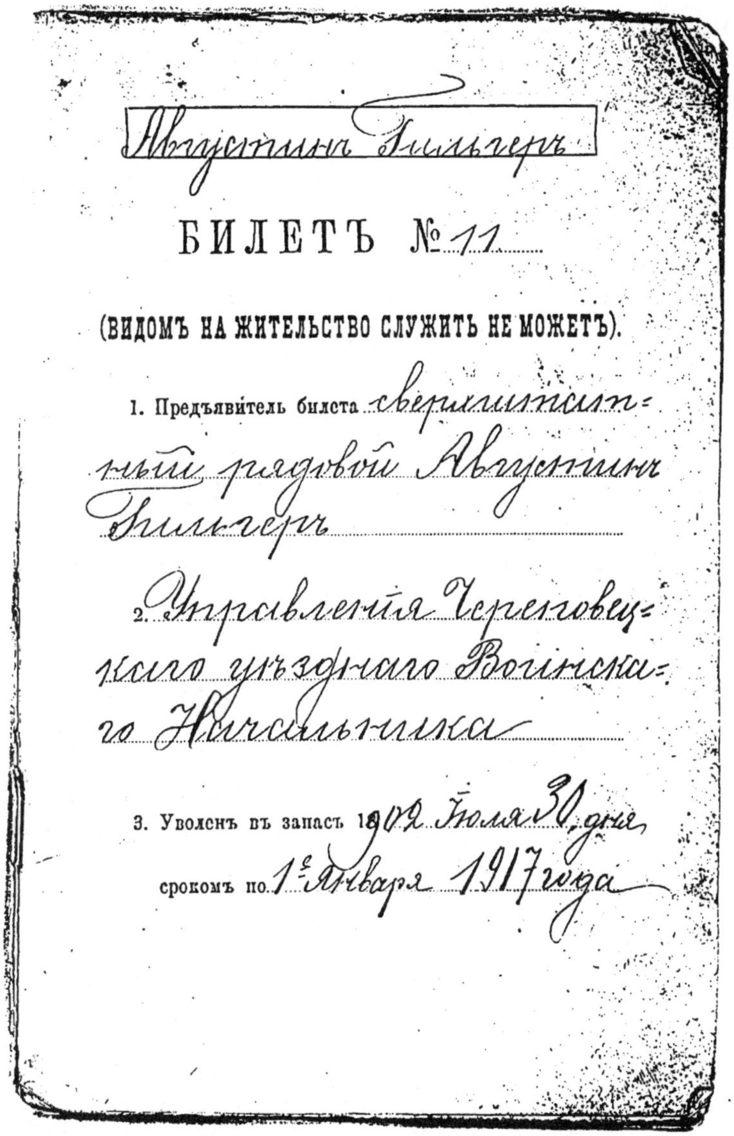

Августинъ Гильгеръ

БИЛЕТЪ № 11

(ВИДОМЪ НА ЖИТЕЛЬСТВО СЛУЖИТЬ НЕ МОЖЕТЪ).

1. Предъявитель билета сверхштатный рядовой Августинъ Гильгеръ

2. Управленія Череповецкаго уѣзднаго Воинскаго Начальника

3. Уволенъ въ запасъ 1902 Іюля 30 дня

срокомъ по 1е Января 1917 года

The first page of the booklet is reproduced at left, at approximately 75% of full size. Note that it gives the bearer's full name in the box at the top; the information is repeated that this is Discharge No. 11, and that it may not be used as an identity document.

Item 1 identifies the Предъявитель билета (bearer of the document) as *сверхштатный рядовой Августинъ Гильгеръ*, supernumerary private Avgustin Gil'ger—which, incidentally, is a Russified form of his name; he usually was called Augustyn Hilger.

Item 2 identifies his military unit, writing out in full the information that was abbreviated on the cover: *Управленія Череповецкаго уѣзднаго Воинскаго Начальника*, Office of the Cherepovets County Military Commander.

Item 3 explains that he was Уволенъ въ запасъ (discharged to the reserves) *1902 Іюля 30 дня* (30 July 1902) срокомъ по *1е Января 1917 года* (for a term to 1 January 1917).

Page 2, reproduced on page 308, has been cropped and reduced somewhat, so as to fit available space without making it more difficult to read. Note that it shows the soldier's first name in the box at the top of the page, while his surname appears in the box at the top of the facing page, page 3. This pattern repeats through the rest of the booklet.

Item 4 says that Hilger was На службу принятъ *Волковишскимъ уѣзднымъ* присутствіемъ (accepted into the service by the Wołkowyszki county board), по пріемному формулярному списку за № *11* (according to service list #11) 18*98* года *Октября 16* дня (16 October 1898); начало службы считается съ 18*99* г. *Января 1* дня (the beginning of service is reckoned as dating from January 1, 1899).

Item 5 states: 5. Въ походахъ: *Не былъ*, "In campaigns: he was not." In other words, he participated in no military campaigns. If he had, details would appear in this space.

Some discharge documents may also contain the following entries:

a) Раненъ? "Wounded?" The usual response to this will be *Не былъ*, "he was not." Of course, if he was injured in battle, details will be given in this space.

b) Въ дѣлахъ противъ непріятеля, "[Was he] in any actions against the enemy?" Again, the usual response will be *Не былъ*, "he was not." But if he did take part in actual combat, details will be provided in this space.

Item 6 reads: Знаки отличія: *Не имѣетъ*, "Decorations: he does not have [any]."

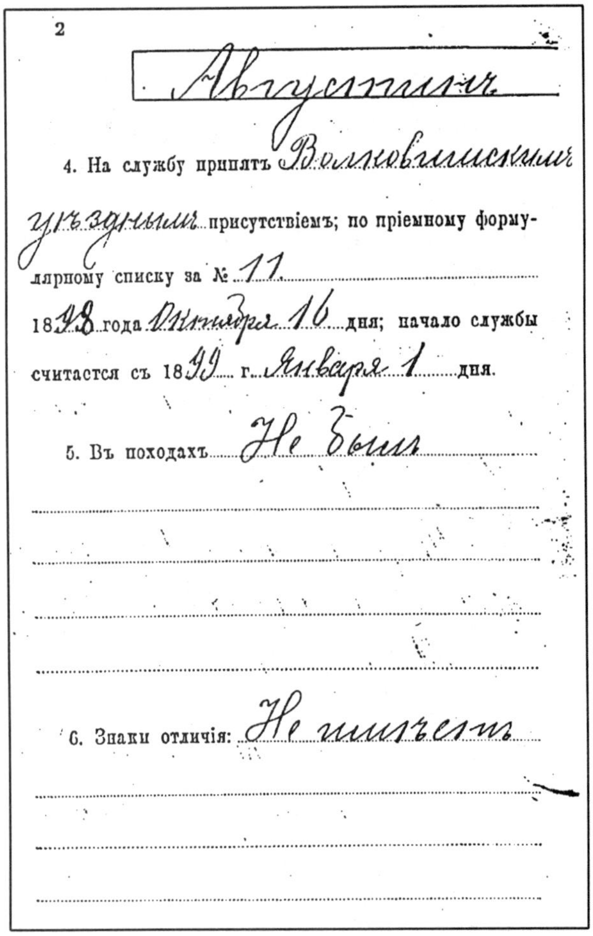
2

4. На службу принятъ Волковыйскимъ уѣзднымъ присутствіемъ; по пріемному формулярному списку за № 11 18 98 года Октября 16 дня; начало службы считается съ 18 99 г. Января 1 дня.

5. Въ походахъ Не былъ

6. Знаки отличія: Не имѣетъ

Reproduced below, cropped and reduced, is page 3 of the booklet.

Item 7 reads: По успѣхамъ въ строевомъ образованіи, можетъ ли быть назначенъ въ кадры запасныхъ войскъ? "After successful active service training, can he be assigned to the cadre of reserve troops?" The answer: *Не можетъ*, "He cannot."

Item 8 calls for Состоя на службѣ обучался, "During tenure in the service he was trained in _." Nothing is specified in this case. Sometimes specific military skills may be listed here, e. g., *саперному дѣлу,* combat engineer training. In other cases skills applicable to his civilian life may be listed, e. g., "shoemaker."

Item 9 asks Какія знаетъ мастерства, "What mastery skills does he have?" Nothing is listed.

Item 10 says Въ алфавитѣ, принадлежащемъ части войскъ, записанъ подъ № _, "In the alphabetical list regarding military unit, he is listed under #." Here this is left blank.

Item 11 calls for his age, Отъ роду лѣтъ (literally "Years from birth"). The answer is

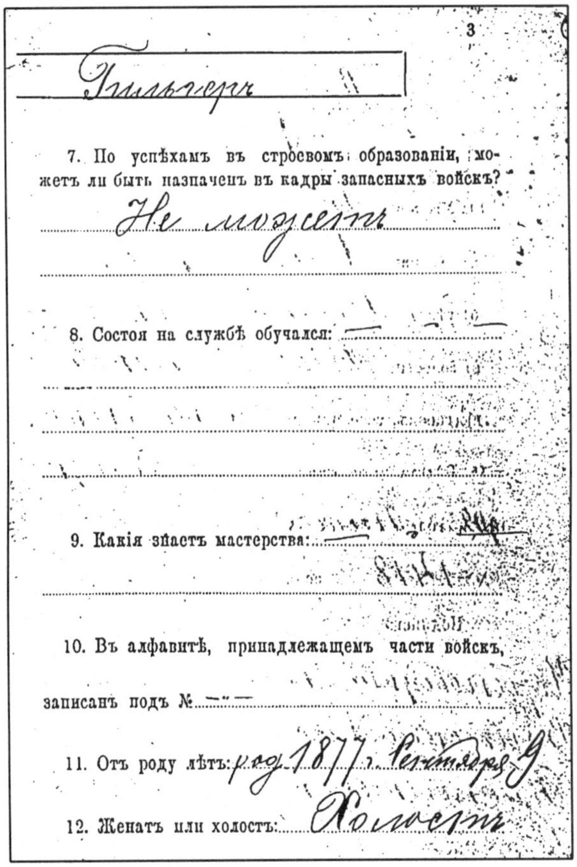
3

7. По успѣхамъ въ строевомъ образованіи, можетъ ли быть назначенъ въ кадры запасныхъ войскъ? Не можетъ

8. Состоя на службѣ обучался:

9. Какія знаетъ мастерства:

10. Въ алфавитѣ, принадлежащемъ части войскъ, записанъ подъ №

11. Отъ роду лѣтъ: род. 1877 г. Сентября 9

12. Женатъ или холостъ: Холостъ

род. 1877 г. Сентября 9, "born 1877, September 9." At this point some discharge booklets may word this differently, e. g., Время рожденія ("time of birth") or Возрастъ ("age").

Item 12 asks Женатъ или холостъ, "Married or single?" The answer here is *Холостъ*, "single."

Reproduced at right is page 4, at 75%, with no cropping, because we wanted to preserve the information given at the bottom, which spreads across the whole page.

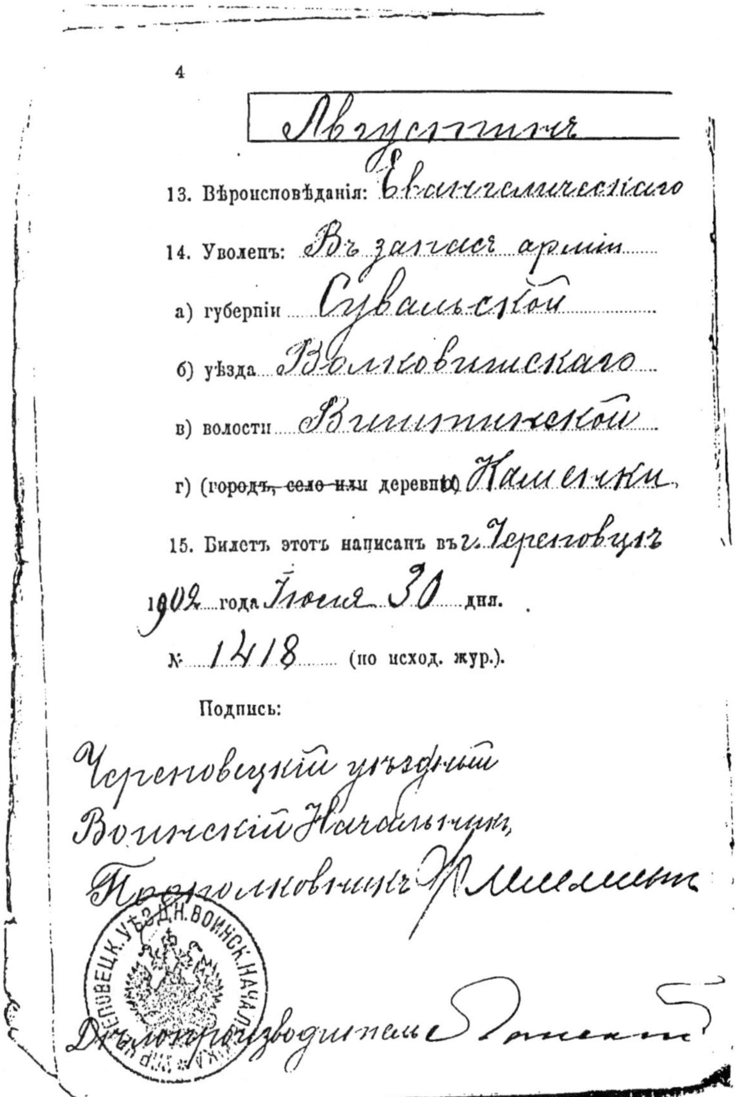
4

Августина

13. Вѣроисповѣданія: Евангелическаго

14. Уволенъ: Въ запасъ арміи

а) губерніи Сувальской

б) уѣзда Волковишскаго

в) волости Виштинской

г) (~~городъ, село или~~ деревню) Каменки

15. Билетъ этотъ написанъ въ г. Череповцѣ

1902 года Іюля 30 дня.

№ 1418 (по исход. жур.).

Подпись:

Череповецкій уѣздный Воинскій Начальникъ, Подполковникъ

Дѣлопроизводитель

Item 13 asks for the bearer's Вѣроисповѣданія, "Religion." The answer in this instance is *Евангелическаго*, "Evangelical [Lutheran]." Some papers also ask here for Сословіе, "social class," to which the answer is typically *крестьянское*, "peasant," or *мѣщанское*, "middle class." Also seen may be a space for грамотность, "literacy." Replies to this can vary from *грамотный*, "literate," or *неграмотный*, "illiterate," to an indication of number of years of schooling completed, often abbreviated, for instance, *3 кл.*, "3 grades."

Item 14 reads Уволенъ, "Discharged," in this case *Въ запасъ арміи*, "to the army reserves," with subheadings for the details on the place to which he was discharged:

а) губерніи *Сувальской*, "Province: Suwałki"
б) уѣзда: *Волковишскаго*, "County: Wyłkowyszki" (now Vilkaviškis, Lithuania)
в) волости: *Виштинской*, "District: Wisztyniec" (now Vištytis, Lithuania)
г) ~~городъ, село или~~ деревн~~ю~~*и*: *Каменки*, "town or village: Kamionka." Note that *село* and *деревня* both mean essentially the same thing, "village." The official filling out the papers was to cross out whichever option did not apply, in this case leaving деревню, "village"; he crossed out the ending –ю and wrote in –*и*.

Item 15 reads Билетъ этотъ написанъ въ г. *Череповцѣ 1902* года *Іюля 30* дня, № *1418* (по исход. жур.) – "This document was written in Cherepovets on 30 July 1902, No. 1418 (in the book of departure papers)." Note that Cherepovets, in Novgorod *gubernia*, is called

Czerepowiec in Polish, which may have been this individual's mother tongue. So that form of the name might appear in some contexts (though not in official papers—from 1868 on only Russian was allowed in official documents). The abbreviation по исход. жур. stands for по исходящему журналу, a register keeping track of departure papers issued.

The Подпись, "signature," is followed by the signatures of two officials: *Череповецкій уѣздный Воинскій Начальникъ, Подполковникъ [illegible]*, "Cherepovets County Military Commander, Colonel *[illegible]*, and *Дѣлопроизводитель [illegible]*, Clerk *[illegible]*." The document is also stamped with the seal of the Cherepovets County Military Commander.

Document VI-37 is a reasonably good example of the sort of thing you see in military discharge papers, and gives a good idea which pages bear information useful to your research. Researcher Sharon Allen submitted a similar set of papers for her ancestor Tadeusz Bubulis alias Lukoshus, son of Mateusz (surely in Lithuanian he was Tadas Bubulis alias Lukošius). These papers give some idea what we're missing if we don't look at the other pages (which we have **not** reproduced here). For instance, page 5 is filled with instructions on what was to happen if the bearer was recalled to active duty and brought along his own boots (with bootlegs not shorter than 9 *vershoks*), usable linen, and how much he was to be paid per item for having brought them along so that he didn't have to be supplied with them. Not exactly prime research material!

Similarly, pages 10 and 11 were designated for Священническія надписи и отмѣтка объ убыли, "Comments by priests on [his] loss," and were empty.

Pages 12-17 were specified for Надписи о временныхъ отлучкахъ и возвращеніи изъ оныхъ, "Notes on temporary absences and return from them," and were also empty.

Page 19 was set aside for Отмѣтка о бытности на службѣ по вольному найму: а) на желѣзныхъ дорогахъ; б) по почтово-телеграфному вѣдомству и в) на коммерческихъ судахъ, "Notation on voluntary service a) on railroads, b) under postal-telegraphic jurisdiction, and c) in commercial courts." No comments appeared.

Page 20 was for Отмѣтка о бытности въ учебныхъ сборахъ, "Notation on presence at training assemblies." Nothing was entered here, either.

Page 21 reads: По призывѣ на службу явился въ: _. Отмѣтка, дѣлаемая Управленіемъ уѣзднаго воинскаго Начальника, *(штемпелемъ черной краски)* по призывѣ на дѣйствительную службу (см. форму прик. по в. в. 1876 г. № 205). This translates, "Upon summons to duty, reported on _. Notation made by the County Military Commander's Office (stamped in black ink) after summons to active duty (see order form per 1876, No. 205)."

Page 22 is blank. Page 23 calls for entry of the year his term of service began and his number in the alphabetized list of district and police institutions. On the left is a vertical line with the notation По этой линіи листокъ отрѣзывается или отр-ется [there is a gash in the original document] въ волостномъ или полицейскомъ управленіи во время призыва на дѣйствительную службу, "To be cut off along this line in the office of district or police administration at the time of summons to active duty." Page 24 is blank.

There was also an envelope that went along with this booklet, marked: Въ семъ конвертѣ хранится послужной листъ вынимаемый въ управленіи уѣзднаго воинскаго начальника, при призывѣ на службу, "In this envelope is to be kept the service record, to be removed in the office of the County Military Commander upon summons to duty."

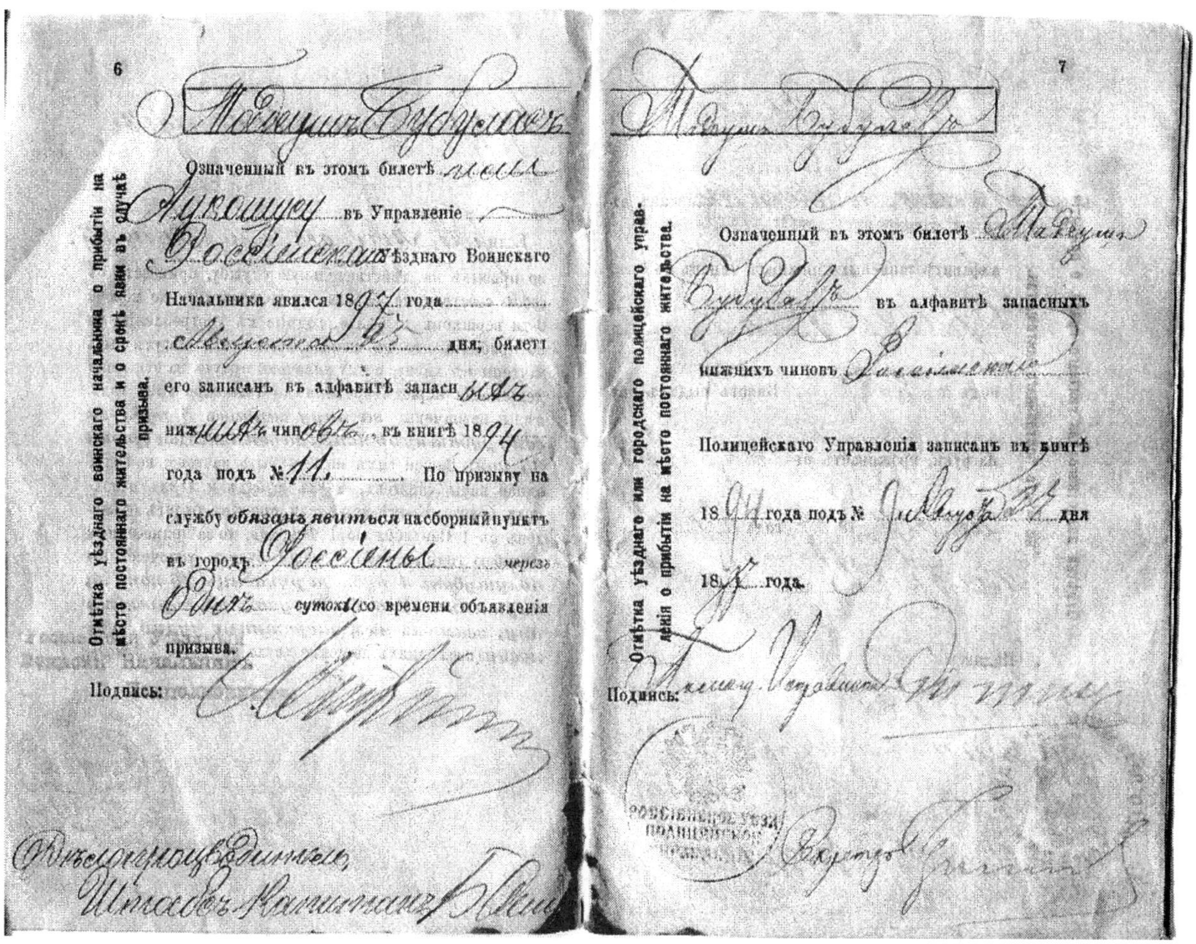

6

Означенный въ этомъ билетѣ ... въ Управленіе ... Уѣзднаго Воинскаго Начальника явился 18... года ... дня; билетъ его записанъ въ алфавитѣ запасн... ниж... чин..., въ книгѣ 18... года подъ № ... По призыву на службу *обязанъ явиться* на сборный пунктъ въ городѣ ... *черезъ* ... *сутокъ* со времени объявленія призыва.

Подпись:

Отмѣтка уѣзднаго воинскаго начальника о прибытіи на мѣсто постояннаго жительства и о срокѣ явки въ случаѣ призыва.

7

Означенный въ этомъ билетѣ ... въ алфавитѣ запасныхъ нижнихъ чиновъ ... Полицейскаго Управленія записанъ въ книгѣ 18... года подъ № ... дня 18... года.

Подпись:

Отмѣтка уѣзднаго или городскаго полицейскаго управленія о прибытіи на мѣсто постояннаго жительства.

Document VI-38A: Details from another Discharge Booklet

Page 6, reproduced as **Document VI-38A** above, features some potentially useful details. At left Отмѣтка уѣзднаго воинскаго начальника о прибытіи на мѣсто постояннаго жительства и о срокѣ явки въ случаѣ призыва calls for the "County Military Commander's notation of his arrival in his place of permanent residence and of the period for reporting in case of a call-up." The main text reads:

Тадеушъ Бубуласъ

Означенный въ этомъ Билетѣ *или Лукошусу* въ Управленіе — *Россіенскаго* Уѣзднаго Воинскаго Начальника явился 18*97* года *Августа 25* дня; билетъ его записанъ въ алфавитѣ запасн*ныхъ* ниж*нихъ* чин*овъ*, въ книгѣ 18*94* года подъ № *11*. По призыву на службу ***обязанъ явиться*** на сборный пунктъ въ городѣ *Россіены* *черезъ* *однѣ* *сутоки* со времени объявленія прызива. Подпись __

Tadeusz Bubulas

Designated in this document, *alias Lukošius*, reported in at the Office of the *Rossieny* County Military Commander on 1897, August 25; his discharge was registered in the alphabetical list of reserves of the rank and file, in the book 1894 under No. *11*. Upon call-up to active service he is to report to the assembly point in the town of *Rossieny* within *one 24-hour* period of the time the call-up is announced. Signature _

This document establishes that Bubulis (on some pages clearly written *Бубулисъ*, *Bubulis*, but on others *Бубуласъ*, *Bubulas*) reported to the County Military Commander's Office in the county seat of Rossieny (now Raseiniai, Lithuania) on 25 August 1897. This, and any subsequent notes as to his moving—or, for that matter, the lack of any such notations—could be very helpful in establishing his whereabouts during a given period.

Page 7 is for the registration of his reporting in at the уѣзднаго или городскаго полицейскаго управленія, "office of the county or town police." Most of the details are the same, but in this case he is registered in the book of 1894 under no. 9, on 27 August 1897. Both on pages 6 and 7 the signatures are of officials and are more or less illegible.

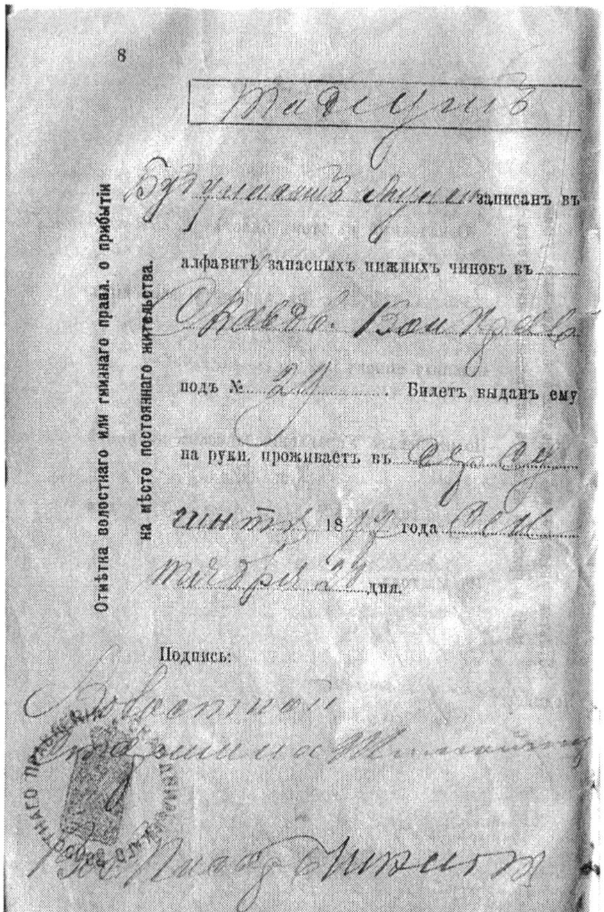
8

Отмѣтка волостнаго или гминнаго правл. о прибытіи на мѣсто постояннаго жительства.

записанъ въ алфавитѣ запасныхъ нижнихъ чиновъ въ ... подъ № ... Билетъ выданъ ему на руки, проживаетъ въ ... 18... года ... дня.

Подпись:

Page 8 from the same booklet is reproduced at right as **Document VI-38B**. It, too, provides a couple of useful details. In this case it features an Отмѣтка волостнаго или гминнаго правл. о прибытіи на мѣсто постояннаго жительства, "notation of the district administration of the bearer's arrival at his place of permanent residence." The first two lines are the same old stuff about his being registered in the alphabetical list of the reserves rank and file, but line three says this happened in *Скавдв. Вол. Прав.*, the "Skavd. District Offices." By peeking at the seal at the bottom left of the page we make out the stamp is of the Скавдвильскаго Волостнаго Правленія, and thus we determine that the name of the place is something like *Skavdvil* in Russian. Reference to the gazetteer *Słownik geograficzny* described in Chapter Five (pages 155ff.) establishes that a place called *Skaudwile* by Poles was a *gmina* seat in Raseiniai county. A look at a good map shows there is a Skaudvilė not far from Raseiniai, in about the right place. So Skaudvilė is presumably the district seat referred to, where Bubulis/ Lukošius was entered in the local register under No. 29.

The rest of the text says: Билетъ выданъ ему на руки, проживаетъ въ *дер. Сугинты* 18*97* года *Сентября 27* дня, "The booklet was issued to him; he resides in the village of Suginty, 27 September 1897." The *Słownik geograficzny* establishes that there was a Suginty not far from Skaudvilė; Lithuanians call it Sugintai.

Thus in the middle of these mind-numbing, repetitive notations of trivial bureaucratic details, one can, with a bit of help, find a bit of information that can prove priceless in research. Buried deep in this document is a fairly precise determination of where Tadas Bubulis settled down to live after he'd finished active duty and been transferred to the reserves!

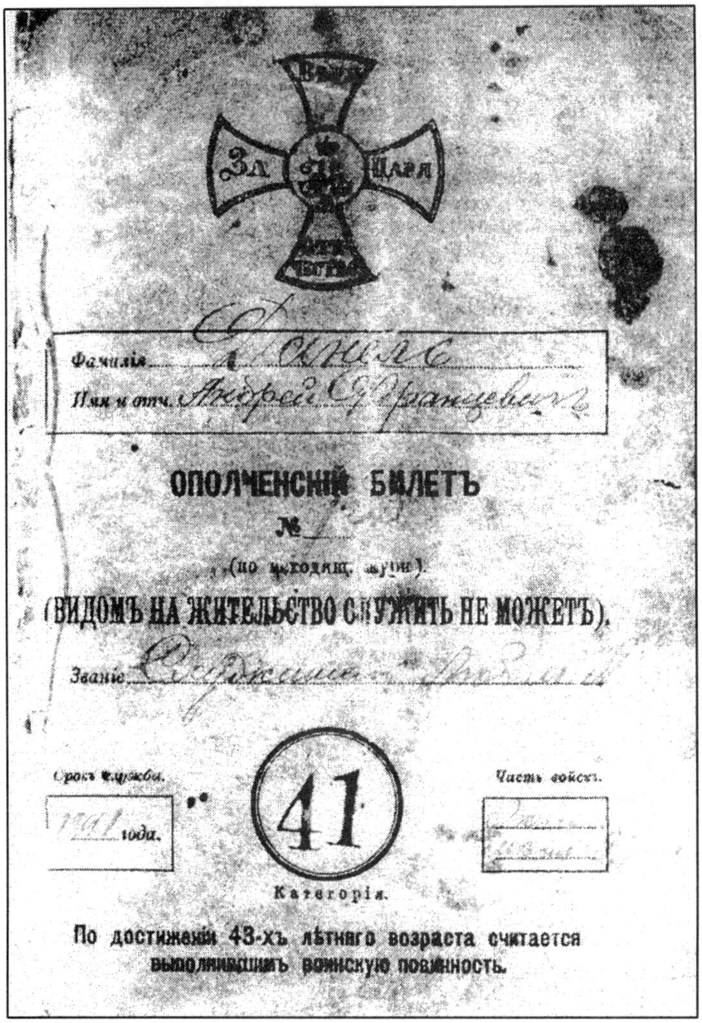

Фамилія Данель
Имя и отч. Андрей Францевичъ
ОПОЛЧЕНСКІЙ БИЛЕТЪ
№
(ВИДОМЪ НА ЖИТЕЛЬСТВО СЛУЖИТЬ НЕ МОЖЕТЪ).
Званіе
Срокъ службы.
1891 года.
41
Категорія.
Часть войскъ.
По достиженіи 43-хъ лѣтняго возраста считается выполнившимъ воинскую повинность.

Document VI-39: A "Militia Ticket"

Let us look briefly at one more such document, since they are records one often finds in attics, scrapbooks, and other places where old papers are stored.

Document VI-39 is called an Ополченскій билетъ, or "Militia ticket," but serves much the same purpose as the previous documents. The cover page, reproduced at left, gives the bearer's surname, *Данель,* in Polish *Daniel;* his first name was *Андрей,* in Polish *Andrzej.* His patronymic was *Францевичъ,* "son of Frants," so his father would have been called *Franciszek* or a variant of that name (e. g., *Franc*). His званіе or occupation was *служитель,* "servant." His term of service began in 1891; his military unit is illegible (but is spelled out on the next page). The notation at the bottom, По достиженіи 43-хъ лѣтняго возраста считается выполнившимъ воинскую повинность, means "Upon having reached the age of 43 he will be regarded as having fulfilled his military obligation."

The inside cover and first page are shown (reduced) on page 314. The key information on the inside cover was that: 1) he was enrolled in the militia soldiers of the 1st category, from the reserve, until 31 December 1912; 2) in case the militia was called up he was obligated to report to the county seat nearest his residence, and he had *трое сутокъ,* three days, to settle domestic affairs before reporting; 3) if he moved to a new residence within the same county in which he was registered, more than 50 versts away or for more than 14 days, he was to report this to the local district office or to the police officials in charge of maintaining the register. The papers were issued in Lublin in 1909, by the Lublin County Military Commander's office.

Page 1 establishes that he was *Андрей Данель,* Andrzej Daniel (using the Polish form of this name since he was a Pole), and this was militia discharge record No. 240, which could not be used as an identity document. Item 1 identifies the bearer was a servant, Andrzej Daniel, son of Franciszek. Item 2 says he was *Люблинскаго мѣстнаго военнаго лазарета,* "of the Lublin local military infirmary." Item 3 says he was discharged to the reserve on 9 January 1895, and his term of service ran to 1 January 1909.

On page 2, item 4 says he was inducted into the service by the Janów County board, registered as No. 460 on the service list, on 9 November 1890; his term of service was consider-

1) Зачисленъ въ ратники ополченія I разряда, изъ запаса до 31-го Декабря 19.. г.

2) Въ случаѣ призыва ополченія обязанъ явиться въ ближайшій къ мѣсту жительства уѣздный городъ. На устройство домашнихъ дѣлъ дается *трое сутокъ.*

3) При перемѣнѣ мѣста жительства внѣ предѣловъ уѣзда, въ которомъ состоитъ на учетѣ, на разстояніи далѣе 50 вер. или на срокъ свыше 14 дней, обязанъ заявить о семъ мѣстному волостному правленію или чинамъ полиціи, ведущимъ учетъ.

Данъ въ городѣ .... 190.. г.

.... *Уѣздный*

Воинскій начальникъ,

Нейшин

Дѣлопроизводитель ....

№ ....

(исх. журн.).

Андрей Даниль

БИЛЕТЪ № 240

(ВИДОМЪ НА ЖИТЕЛЬСТВО СЛУЖИТЬ НЕ МОЖЕТЪ).

1. Предъявитель билета служитель Андрей Францевичъ Даниль

2. Людвинскаго мѣстнаго военнаго лазарета

3. Уволенъ въ запасъ 1895 г. Января 9 дн. срокомъ по 1° Января 1909 года

2

Андрей Даниль

4. На службу принятъ Яновскимъ Уѣзднымъ присутствіемъ; по пріемному формулярному списку за № 440

1890 года Ноября 9 дня; начало службы считается съ 1891 г. Январь 1 дня

5. Въ походахъ не былъ

6. Знаки отличія: не имѣетъ

3

7. По успѣхамъ въ строевомъ образованіи, можетъ ли быть назначенъ въ кадры запасныхъ войскъ? ....

8. Состоя на службѣ обучался: ....

9. Какія знаетъ мастерства: Конюхъ

10. Въ алфавитѣ, принадлежащемъ части войскъ, записанъ подъ № 7

11. Отъ роду лѣтъ: 25

12. Женатъ или холостъ: Холостъ

Document VI-39: A Discharge to the Militia

ed as having commenced on 1 January 1891. Item 5 says he participated in no campaigns; item 6 says he has no decorations. Items 7 and 8 are left blank. Item 9 says he knows the skill of working as a *Конюхъ*, "groom, stablehand." Item 10 says he was enrolled in the alphabetical list of his unit under No. 7. Item 11 says he was 25 years old. Item 12 says he was *Холостъ*, "single."

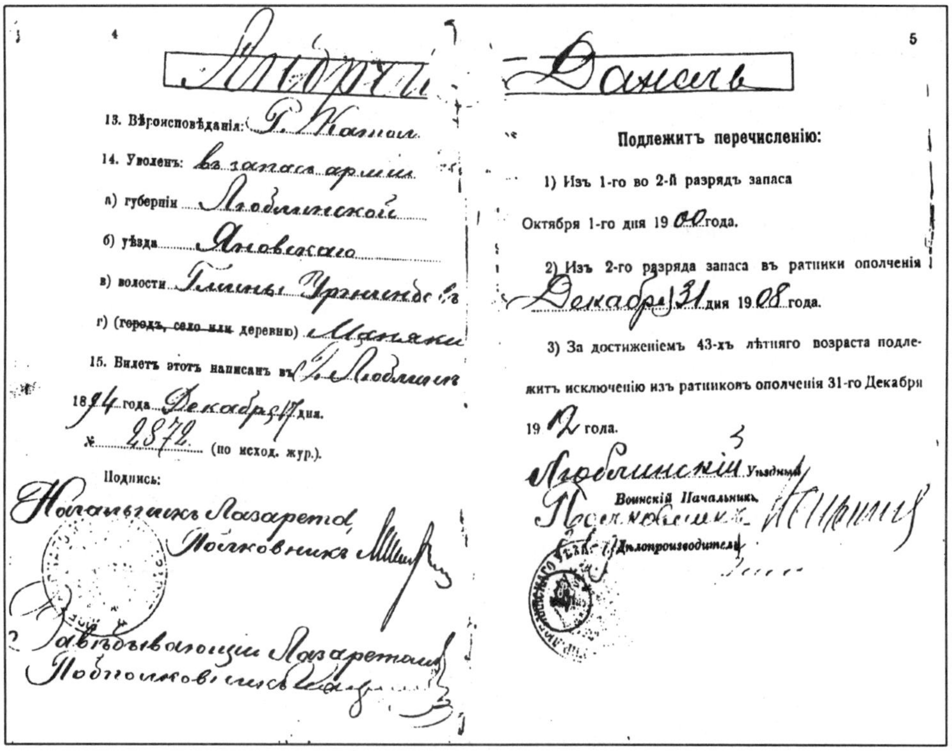
4

13. Вѣроисповѣданія: Р. Катол.

14. Уволенъ: въ запасъ арміи

а) губерніи Люблинской

б) уѣзда Яновскаго

в) волости

г) (городъ, село или деревню)

15. Билетъ этотъ написанъ въ г. Люблинѣ

1894 года Декабря 17 дня.

№ 2872 (по исход. жур.).

Подпись:

5

Подлежитъ перечисленію:

1) Изъ 1-го во 2-й разрядъ запаса

Октября 1-го дня 1900 года.

2) Изъ 2-го разряда запаса въ ратники ополченія

Декабря 31 дня 1908 года.

3) За достиженіемъ 43-хъ лѣтняго возраста подлежитъ исключенію изъ ратниковъ ополченія 31-го Декабря 1912 года.

Люблинскій Уѣздный Воинскій Начальникъ.

Дѣлопроизводитель

→

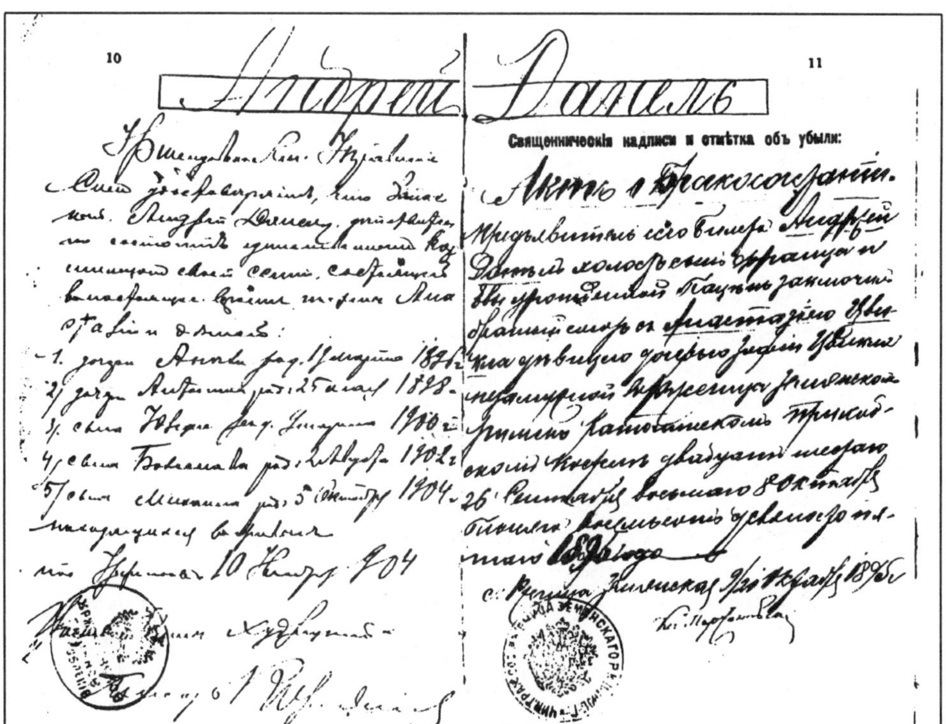
10

11

Священническія надписи и отмѣтка объ убыли:

Актъ о бракосочетаніи.

Pages 4-5 and 10-11 are reproduced (in reduced size) on page 315. On page 4, item 13 says the bearer was of the Roman Catholic faith. Item 14 says he was discharged to the reserve in губерніи *Люблинской* (the province of Lublin), уѣзда *Яновскаго* (county of Janów), *Гмины Урждндовъ* (district of Urzędów), деревню *Маняки* village of Maniaki (now called Moniaki). Item 15 says these papers were issued in the town of Lublin on 7 December 1894, No. 2372 in the book of departure papers. They were signed by the *Начальникъ Лазарета* (Infirmary Superintendent), *Полковникъ* (Colonel) *[illegible]*, and the *Завѣдывающій Лазаретомъ* (Infirmary Administrator), *Подполковникъ* (Lt. Colonel) *[illegible]*.

Page 5 says Подлежитъ перечисленію (he will be subject to transfer) from the 1st category of the reserve to the 2nd on 1 October 1900, and from the 2nd category of the reserve to the militia on 31 December 1908. On reaching the age of 43 he will be subject to exemption from the reserve on 31 December 1912. It is signed by the Lublin County Military Commander, Colonel *[illegible]*, and the Clerk *[illegible]*.

The notes on page 10 are difficult to read, but valuable because about halfway down (at the end of the line the arrow is pointing to) we can make out *жены Анастасіи и дѣтей*, "of wife Anastazja and children," followed by a list of names and birthdates of daughters and sons:

1. дочери Анѣли род. 13 марта 1896 г.	1. daughter Aniela, born 13 March 1896
2. дочери Анотонины род. 25 мая 1898 г.	2. daughter Antonina, born 25 May 1898
3. сына Јозефа род. 9 марта 1900 г.	3. son Józef, born 7 March 1900
4. сына Болеслава род. 2 Августа 1902 г.	4. son Bolesław, born 2 August 1902
5. сына Михаила род. 4 Октября 1904 г.	5. son Michał, born 4 October 1904

These children are described as *находящихся въ живыхъ*, "among the living," as of 10 November 1904. So it's possible there were others who died before 1904; but at least this list tells the members of the family alive as of the end of that year.

On page 11 we have Священническія надписи и отмѣтка о убыли, "Priests' inscriptions and notes on losses." This page is often blank, but not in this case. Instead we see written in an *Актъ о Бракосочетаніи*, "Marriage Record"! Fortunately the handwriting on this page is a bit clearer than on page 10 and we can make out the wording:

Предъявитель сего Билета Андржей Данѣль холостъ сынъ Франца и Евы урожденной Пацѣкъ заключилъ брачный союзъ съ Анастазіею Цвикла дѣвицею дочерью Зофіи Цвикла незамужной въ Ржечица землянской римско Католическомъ приходскомъ костелѣ двадцать шестаго 26 Сентября восьмаго 8 Октября тысяча восемьсотъ девяносто пятаго 1895 года.

The bearer of these papers, Andrzej Daniel, single, the son of Franciszek and Ewa née Paciek, contracted a marital union with Anastazja Ćwikla, single, the daughter of Zofia Ćwikla, unmarried, in the Rzeczyca Ziemiańska Roman Catholic parish church on the twenty-sixth 26th of September eighth 8th of October of the one thousand eight hundred ninety fifth year 1895.

This may seem like a lot of space to devote to military records; but we believe it's justified. Men had to carry these records with them as long as they lived in the Russian Empire, and often brought them along when they emigrated. So these are the sort of records you're particularly likely to find—and they can give you a lot of facts to work with!

3. Document VI-40: *Revizskie Skazki* [Revision Lists]

A valuable source of information, and one that has become more available to researchers in recent years, is the so-called *Ревизская Сказка, Revizskaia skazka* (some use the spelling *Ревижская*) or as it is generally called in English, "Revision List." These were essentially lists of taxpayers, encompassing most social classes. Since the majority of the population paid taxes of some sort, these documents are, for all practical purposes, the equivalents of census returns. Ten such lists were compiled at irregular intervals from 1719 to 1858.

Because these were Russian Imperial documents, the earlier lists do not cover any territory populated by an appreciable number of ethnic Poles or Lithuanians. Thus researchers looking for traces of Polish or Lithuanian ancestors need only be concerned with materials compiled after the partitions (i. e., 1811, 1815/1816, 1833-1835, 1850, and 1857-1858). The territory covered by the Kingdom of Poland (the so-called *Kongresówka* or "Congress Kingdom") was not included in these lists, inasmuch as that Kingdom was treated officially as an autonomous entity affiliated with, but not part of, the Russian Empire (a pretense that grew more and more absurd as time passed). Thus the revision lists will prove of value to those who trace their roots to officially recognized subdivisions of the Russian Empire, territory east of the Congress Kingdom (*gubernias* such as Minsk and Grodno, for instance).

Records were kept at the *gubernia* level, in the *казенная палата* (Treasury office) for that province. They were further subdivided by *уѣздъ* (county) and ultimately by town or village. It is thus of vital importance that you accurately define the geographical location of your ancestral village. Keep in mind that place names repeat in various counties and provinces, so you must be sure of the geographical data in your possession. If it is vague or ambiguous you will need to consult supplementary documents here in North America and locate the place in a gazetteer (using the sources mentioned in Chapter V).

In addition to the geographical subdivisions as enumerated above, the records were further subdivided by social class or category. The principal social classes included:

1) *крестьяне*, "peasants," further subdivided into such categories as *помѣщичіе крестьяне*, "estate peasants," *государственные крестьяне*, "state peasants," *удѣльные крестьяне*, "appanaged peasants" (attached to lands given by the sovereign for the maintenance of a member of the ruling family), and so on;
2) city dwellers, including *мѣщане*, literally "townsmen" but also meaning "merchant class, middle class"
3) *шляхта*, "nobility." Many ethnic Poles were in this category due to the settlement patterns in the *Kresy* or eastern borderlands (as the Poles called them). Poles were frequently landowners in the regions east of Poland's current borders,
d) others, including *евреи*, "Jews," and *иностранцы*, "foreigners."

The information was recorded on preprinted column-format forms in Russian or Polish. The languages were sometimes mixed on some forms, e. g., a Russian printed form could have information written in Polish, and vice versa. At times the entire form (both the printed material and the handwritten entries in the columns) was in Russian but with notations on the bottom of the page in Polish. It can be helpful to be familiar with both languages when using these lists; Volume I of *In Their Words* can help you with Polish versions of these lists.

Males and females were listed on separate pages.

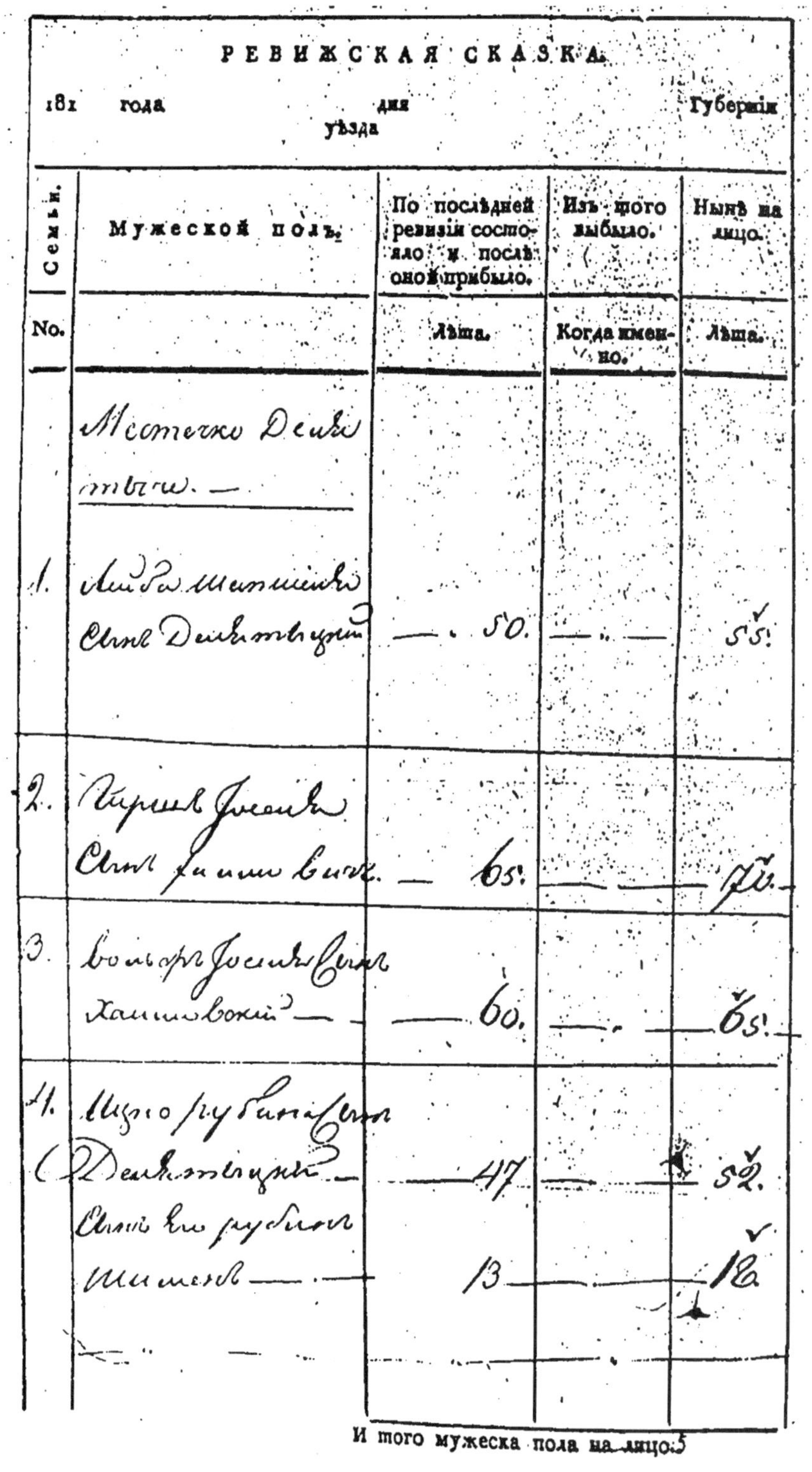

РЕВИЖСКАЯ СКАЗКА.

181 года для Губерніи
уѣзда

Семьи No.	Мужеской полъ.	По послѣдней ревизіи состояло и послѣ оной прибыло. Лѣта.	Изъ того выбыло. Когда именно.	Нынѣ на лицо. Лѣта.
	Местечко Делятыче.			
1.	Лейба Шапшеля Сынъ Делятыцкій	50.		55.
2.	[illegible]	65.		70.
3.	[illegible]	60.		65.
4.	[illegible]	47		52.
	[illegible]	13		18.

И того мужеска пола на лицо: 5

Document VI-40, left half, for males

The page of sample **Document VI-40** dealing with males is printed at left, to familiarize you with its layout and help you make out the relevant data:

181 _ года _ для _ Губерніи _ уѣзда _ – "181 _ year_ for _ province _ county." The clerk who filled out this form did not provide this information. Instead under column 2, above the first entry, he wrote in *Местечко Делятыче,* "town of Deliatyche."

Column 1: **Семьи №** – "family #." Each family was given a sequential number.

Column 2: **Мужеской Полъ** – "Male sex." All the males in the household are listed. In household #1 the only male resident was: *Лейба Шапшеля Сынъ Делятыцкій,* "Leyba Deliatytskiy, Shapshel's son."

Column 3: **По послѣдней ревизіи состояло и послѣ оной прибыло | Лѣта**– "Age according to the previous revision list and whether [he] arrived since then." Leyba was 50 when the last list was compiled.

Column 4: **Изъ того выбыло | Когда именно** – "Of those who have departed [i. e., by moving away or by death) | Exactly when." For entry #1 nothing is filled in, which suggests Leyba was there when the last revision list was compiled. If he had died, his year of death would be indicated here.

Column 5: **Нынѣ на лицо | Лѣта** – "Current age by person, in years." Leyba was 55 when this list was compiled.

At the bottom of the page, **И того мужеска пола на лицо: 5** means "Total of persons of the male sex: 5."

At right is the corresponding page for females. The column headings are slightly different:

181 _ года _ для _ Губерніи _ уѣзда _ – "181 _ year_ for _ province _ county." As on the page for males, the clerk just wrote *Местечко Делятыче*, "town of Deliatyche."

Column 1: **Семьи №** – "family #." The sequential number here would correspond to that established for the household on the male page.

Column 2: **Женской Полъ** – "Female sex." All the females in the household are listed. In #1 they were: *Жена Его Ханна*, "His wife [i. e., Leyba's] Khanna"; and *Дочери: 1. Товба, 2. Сора*, "Daughters: 1. Tovba, 2. Sora."

Column 3: **Во временной отлучкѣ | Съ котораго времени** – "Has this person been gone in the interim, and since when?" Nothing is entered.

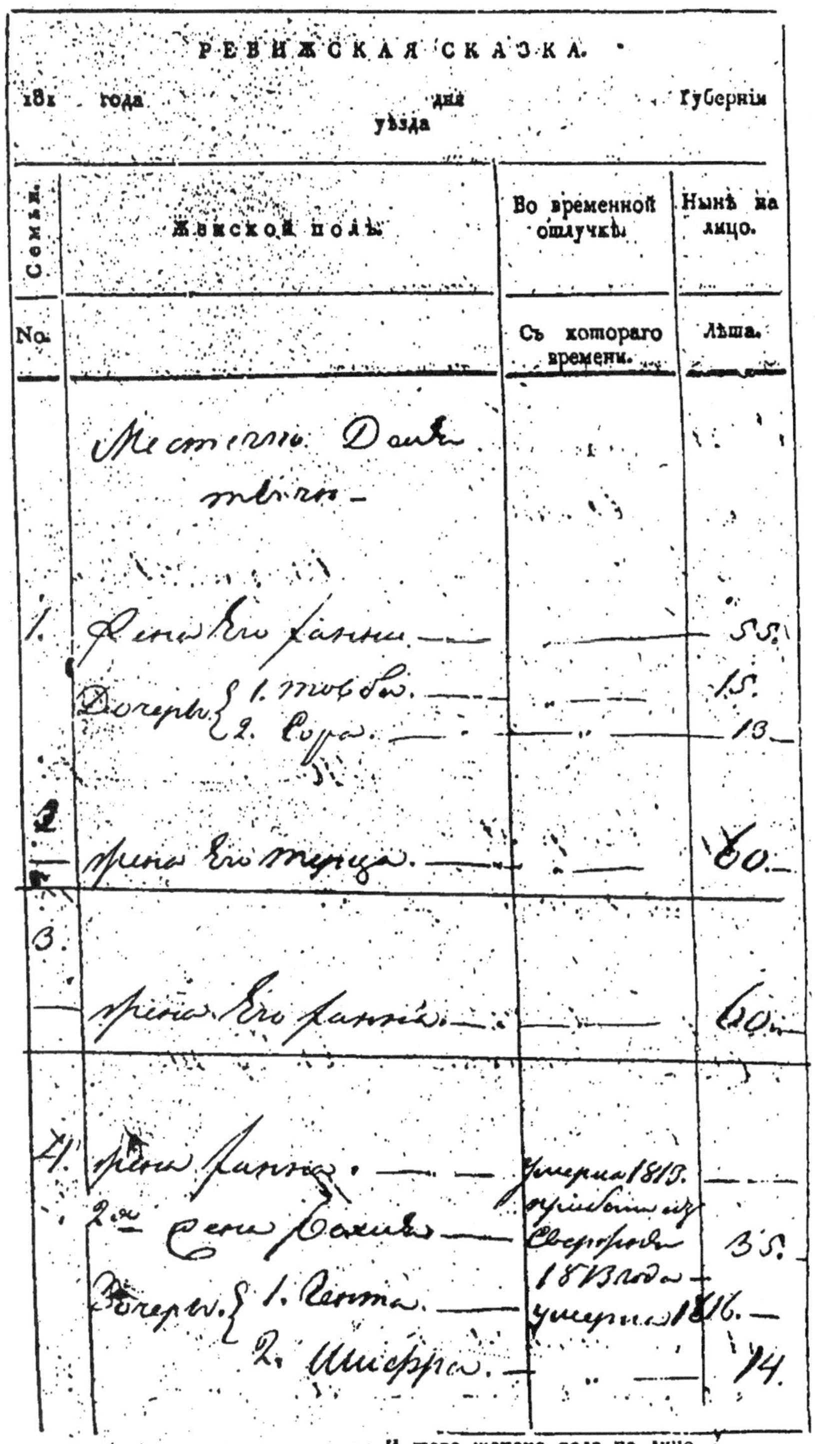

РЕВИЖСКАЯ СКАЗКА.

18 _ года _ для _ Губерніи _ уѣзда _

Семьи №	Женской полъ	Во временной отлучкѣ / Съ котораго времени	Нынѣ на лицо / Лѣта
	Местечко Делятыче		
1.	Жена Его Ханна		55
	Дочери 1. Товба		15
	2. Сора		13
2	Жена Его [illegible]		60
3.	Жена Его Ханна		60
4.	Жена Ханна	умерла 1813	
	2я Жена [illegible]	прибыла из [illegible] 1813 года	35
	Дочери 1. [illegible]	умерла 1816	
	2. [illegible]		14

И того женска пола на лицо.

Document VI-40, right half, for females

Column 4: **Нынѣ на лицо | Лѣта** – "Current age, in years." Khanna was 55, Tovba was 15, and Sora was 13.

At the bottom of the page, **И того женска пола на лицо:** 7 means "Total of persons of the female sex: 7."

(Incidentally, in a Polish-language context these persons' names would be Lejba Delatycki, son of Szapszel, his wife Channa, and daughters Towba and Sora.)

For the other entries on these pages, the data given can be summarized as follows:

2. *Гиршъ Јоселя Сынъ Хаимовичъ,* Girsh Khaimovich, son of Yosel', was 65 when the last list was compiled, and 70 when the current one was drawn up. His wife *Терца,* Tertsa, was 60 as of this list's compilation. (The Polish forms of these names would be Hirsz Chaimowicz, son of Josel, and his wife Terca).

3. *Вольфъ Јоселя Сынъ Хаимовскій,* Vol'f Khaimovskiy, son of Yosel', was 60 / 65, and his wife *Ханна,* Khanna, was 60. Only more research could determine whether Girsh was truly the son of Yosel' Khaimovich and Vol'f the son of Yosel' Khaimovskiy, or if both were the son of the same man and the clerk erroneously wrote the surname two different ways (Khaimovich vs. Khaimovskiy). (In Polish the names would be Wolf Chaimowski, son of Josel, and his wife Channa or Chana.)

4. *Ицко Рубина Сынъ Делятыцкій,* Itsko Deliatytskiy, son of Rubin, age 47 / 52; *Сынъ Его Рубинъ Шименъ,* his son Rubin Shimen, age 13 / 18; *жена Ханна умерла 1813,* his (Itsko's) wife Khanna, died 1813; *2 я жена Рохля, прыбыла из Сверження 1813 года,* [Itsko's] "2nd wife Rokhlya, came from Sverzhen' in 1813," age 35 when this list was compiled; and their *Дочери,* daughters: *Гента, умерла 1816,* "Genta, died 1816," and *Шифра,* Shifra, age 14 when this list was compiled. (The Polish forms of these names would be Icko Delatycki, his son Rubin Szymen, his first wife Channa, his second wife Rochla, his first daughter Genta, and his second one Szyfra. We keep giving Polish forms because in some instances one might find materials on these people in that language, and it's useful to see how the forms of the names differ in these two languages.)

4. Returns from the 1897 Russian National Census

We said on page 317 that "Revision lists" serve much the same function as census returns. In fact, the Russian Empire conducted only one national census, in 1897. A particularly good article on this census, and on the history of similar types of records, entitled "The Russian National Census of 1897," was written by Thomas K. Edlund and appeared in the Fall 2000 issue of *Avotaynu.* Much of what we say here is based on that article, and we advise those who wish to obtain a good overview to find a copy and read it (see **http://www.avotaynu.com**).

The idea of the 1897 census was to give a statistical overview of the entire Empire as of one day, 9 February 1897, with data on all residents, regardless of their social class or tax status. Previous enumerations (such as the revision lists) had focused on taxpayers; this census was intended to provide the government with accurate data on the whole population.

It was a massive undertaking, and ten years after the data was gathered, officials were still hard at work analyzing it and publishing summaries. Those summaries are of little use to genealogists, however. It's the actual returns that would interest us. Some of those were destroyed after the central commission tabulated them for statistical purposes. This led many to think all the returns were destroyed, a notion more readily accepted because for a long time the returns that survived were difficult to find and get hold of.

That is gradually changing. As of this writing, only returns from the provinces of Tobol'sk and Vyatka have been microfilmed and are beginning to show up in the LDS Family History Library catalog. But Edlund confirms having seen returns from many other areas, including the province of Grodno, those covering what are now Lithuania and Latvia, Ryazan' province, the cities of St. Petersburg and Yekaterinoslav, and so forth. As time passes, surviving returns from the areas most likely to interest Western genealogical researchers should become available. Let us familiarize you with their format, terminology, and typical contents, so that as they become accessible, you will have some guidance in making out what they say.

Different forms were used on the basis of where the people enumerated resided:

- Переписной Листъ **Форма А** [Census Sheet, Form A] was used for peasant households residing on agricultural property
- Переписной Листъ **Форма Б** [Form B] covered people living on landed estates
- Переписной Листъ **Форма В** [Form V] was used for enumerating urban populations (note that **В** is the third letter of the Cyrillic alphabet, so by our terminology it would be "Form C"; but to avoid confusion we'll call it Form V.)
- A separate form entitled **Воинская Перечневая Вѣдомость** (Military Summary Form) was used for the military.
- One called **Общая Перечневая Вѣдомость** (General Summary Form) was used for boarding students, clergy, wards of charitable organizations; and so on.

Each form was accompanied by a sheet of instructions and a two-page questionnaire on which data for individuals was entered. Edlund says over 30 million forms were completed. The returns were kept at the local administration headquarters, but copies were sent on to the central commission in charge of the overall census. The term for the census itself was Первая Всеобщая Перепись Населенія Россійской Имперіи, the First General Census of the Population of the Russian Empire.

Notes on the LDS Family History Library Website (at **http://www.familysearch.org**) for returns from both Tobol'sk and Viatka provinces explain that returns are for each community in those provinces, and are arranged by street and city district (часть), or by house number (in the case of Tobol'sk province).

The first three forms listed (A, B, and V) were very similar, differing only slightly in terminology. A look at a sample of one will illustrate the organizational methodology. Thus **VI-41**, reproduced on page 322, is a sample of Form A, for peasant households on agricultural property. A translation is given on page 323, formatted for easy comparison with the original.

Document VI-42, on pages 324 and 325 with translations appearing directly below each sample, illustrates the actual returns filled out for these three forms.

The questionnaire used with the form for military personnel is somewhat different. A sample of it appears as Document VI-43 on page 326, with an attempt to translate the information it contains, as best we can read it, on pages 327. A sample of the two-page return for this form is shown as Document VI-44 on pages 328 and 329. All the words are listed in the vocabulary (Chapter VII), it's just a matter of reading them correctly and interpreting them according to context. You should only need a little help to do so.

Edlund's article suggests that column 8 of the return illustrated on page 324 (or column 7 of the return on page 328) deserves special attention because certain classes of people—including Jews and peasants, before and after their emancipation—were required to register at specific localities for purposes of taxation and conscription. These localities may or may not have been where they actually lived, so one must exercise caution in drawing conclusions from that data. Still, that information may prove valuable, since members of these classes could not move about the Empire without internal passports or special papers issued periodically by a local Council of Elders or similar authority (compare Document VI-52, page 348).

Безплатно.

№ Листа [redacted]

ПЕРВАЯ ВСЕОБЩАЯ ПЕРЕПИСЬ

населенія Россійской Имперіи,

на основаніи ВЫСОЧАЙШЕ УТВЕРЖДЕННАГО ПОЛОЖЕНІЯ 5 Іюня 1895 года.

Губернія или область: Рязанская	ПЕРЕПИСНОЙ ЛИСТЪ ФОРМА А.	Уѣздъ или округъ: Данковский

Переписной участ. № 2 Счетный участ. № 3

Станъ № 2 или полицейскій участокъ № —

(Подчеркнуть подлежащее названіе и проставить №)

Волость, гмина, станица или соотвѣтствующее имъ дѣленіе Ивановская

Сельское общество или соотвѣтствующее ему дѣленіе Рождественское

Село, деревня или другое поселеніе на земляхъ сельскаго общества (прописать подробно какого рода поселеніе и его названіе). Село Рождественское

Имя, отчество и фамилія хозяина двора Макар Федоров Анофрин

Хозяинъ живетъ въ собственномъ-ли дворѣ? да или на квартирѣ въ чужомъ дворѣ?

Сколько во дворѣ жилыхъ строеній? 2

Изъ чего каждое строеніе построено.	Чѣмъ крыто.	Изъ чего каждое строеніе построено.	Чѣмъ крыто.
1 Изъ кирпича	Деревом	6	
2 Изъ дерева	Соломой	7	
3		8	
4		9	
5		10	

Примѣчаніе. Эти свѣдѣнія относятся къ цѣлому двору и заполняются только въ случаѣ, если хозяинъ живетъ въ своемъ дворѣ или занимаетъ весь чужой дворъ. Если-же во дворѣ живетъ нѣсколько хозяйствъ, то на переписныхъ листахъ каждаго изъ нихъ эта табличка оставляется безъ заполненія, а свѣдѣнія о числѣ жилыхъ строеній во дворѣ проставляются на отдѣльномъ переписномъ листѣ, на которомъ вмѣстѣ съ тѣмъ дѣлается подсчетъ по всему двору; въ этотъ листъ вкладываются переписные листы отдѣльныхъ хозяйствъ двора, какъ въ обложку.

Подсчетъ населенія въ день, къ которому пріурочена перепись.

Всего наличнаго населенія.		Постоянно живущаго здѣсь населенія.		Въ числѣ наличнаго населенія было лицъ некрестьян. сословій.		Приписаннаго здѣсь крестьянскаго населенія.	
Здѣсь проставляется итогъ всѣхъ тѣхъ лицъ (мужчинъ и женщинъ отдѣльно), противъ которыхъ въ 10-й графѣ проведена черта, а также тѣхъ, противъ коихъ отмѣчено «врем. преб.» и «врем. преб. со знакомъ V».		Сюда вносится общее число всѣхъ тѣхъ лицъ (мужчинъ и женщинъ отдѣльно), противъ которыхъ въ 9-й графѣ отмѣчено «здѣсь».		Здѣсь проставляется (изъ графы 6-й) общее число всѣхъ лицъ некрестьянскихъ сословій (мужчинъ и женщинъ отдѣльно), противъ которыхъ въ графѣ 10-й проведена черта, а также тѣхъ, противъ коихъ отмѣчено «врем преб.» и «врем. преб. со знакомъ V».		Сюда вносится общее число всѣхъ лицъ (мужчинъ и женщинъ отдѣльно), противъ которыхъ въ графѣ 6-й отмѣчено «здѣсь» и «здѣсь въ волости».	
М.	Ж.	М.	Ж.	М.	Ж.	М.	Ж.
4	4	5	3	1	—	3	3

Document VI-41: Census Form A

No charge

Sheet Number 21

FIRST GENERAL CENSUS
OF THE POPULATION OF THE RUSSIAN EMPIRE
ON THE BASIS OF AN ORDER ISSUED 5 JUNE 1895 BY THE SUPREME AUTHORITY

Gubernia or oblast': *Ryazan*	CENSUS SHEET FORM A	Uyezd or okrug: *Dankov*

Census section No. 2, Account section No. 3
District No. 2 or police station No. –
(Underline the appropriate one and give the number)

Volost', Gmina, Stanitsa, or corresponding subdivision: *Ivanov*

Village society or corresponding subdivision: *Rozhdestvenskoe*

Village or other settlement on the grounds of the village society
(Write out what kind of settlement it is and its name)
village of Rozhdestvenskoe

First name, patronymic, and surname of the manor's landowner *Makar Fedorov Anokhin.*

Does the landowner live in his manor? *Yes* or in an apartment at someone else's manor?

How many inhabitable buildings are there on the manor grounds? 2

What is each made of?	*Covered with what?*	*What is each made of?*	*Covered with what?*
1 *Of brick*	*Wood*	6	
2 *Of wood*	*Straw*	7	
3		8	
4		9	
5		10	

Notes: [not translated]

Tally of the population on the day for which the census was designated

Total population present		Population living here permanently		Of those present, the number of persons who were not of the peasant class		Number of the peasant population assigned here	
Write here the total of all persons (male and female separately) *etc.*		Enter here the total number of all persons (male and female separately) for whom in column 9 "here" was entered		Enter here the total number (from column 6) of all non-peasants (male and female separately) … *etc.*		Enter here the total number of all persons (male and female separately) for whom in column 8 "here" and "to the *volost'* here" was entered	
Male	Female	Male	Female	Male	Female	Male	Female
4	4	5	3	1	—	3	3

Translation of Document VI-41

1	2	3	4	5	6	7	8
ФАМИЛІЯ, (прозвище), ИМЯ и ОТЧЕСТВО или ИМЕНА, если ихъ нѣсколько. Отмѣтка о тѣхъ, кто окажется: слѣпымъ на оба глаза, нѣмымъ, глухонѣмымъ или умалишеннымъ.	Полъ. М-мужской. Ж-женскій.	Какъ записанный приходится главѣ хозяйства и главѣ своей семьи.	Сколько минуло лѣтъ или мѣсяцевъ отъ роду.	Холостъ, женатъ, вдовъ или разведенъ.	Сословіе, состояніе или званіе.	Родился-ли ЗДѢСЬ, а если не здѣсь, то гдѣ именно? (Губернія, уѣздъ, городъ).	Приписанъ-ли ЗДѢСЬ, а если не здѣсь, то гдѣ именно? (для лицъ, обязанныхъ припиской).
1 Домнинъ Степанъ Андреевъ.	М.	хозяинъ.	64.	ж.	крест. инъ госуд.	здѣсь	здѣсь
2 Домнина Глафира Ефимова.	ж	жена.	61.	ж.	крест. ка госуд.	здѣсь	здѣсь
3 Домнинъ Петръ Степановъ.	М.	сынъ.	32.	х.	крест. инъ госуд.	здѣсь	здѣсь
4 Домнина Анна Степанова.	ж.	дочь.	18.	д.	крест. ка госуд.	здѣсь.	здѣсь

1	2	3	4	5	6	7	8
SURNAME, (last name), FIRST NAME and PATRONYMIC or FIRST NAMES, if there are several. Note those who turn out to be blind in both eyes, mute, deaf and dumb, or insane.	Sex M- male F- Female	How this person is related to the head of the household and head of his/her family	Age in years and months	Single, married, widowed, divorced	Class, estate, or occupation	Born HERE? and if not, where exactly? (gubernia, uyezd, and town)	Registered HERE? If not, where exactly? (for those obligated to register
1. Domnin Stepan [son] of Andrei	*M*	*Head*	*64*	*m*	*peasant, govern.*	*here*	*here*
2. Domnina Glafira [dau.] of Yefim	*F*	*wife*	*61*	*m*	*peasant, govern.*	*here*	*here*
3. Domnin Pyotr [son] of Stepan	*M*	*son*	*32*	*s*	*peasant, govern.*	*here*	*here*
4. Domnina Anna [dau.] of Stepan	*F*	*daughter*	*18*	*s*	*peasant, govern.*	*here*	*here*

Document VI-42, A Sample Return for Forms A, B, and V, and Translation

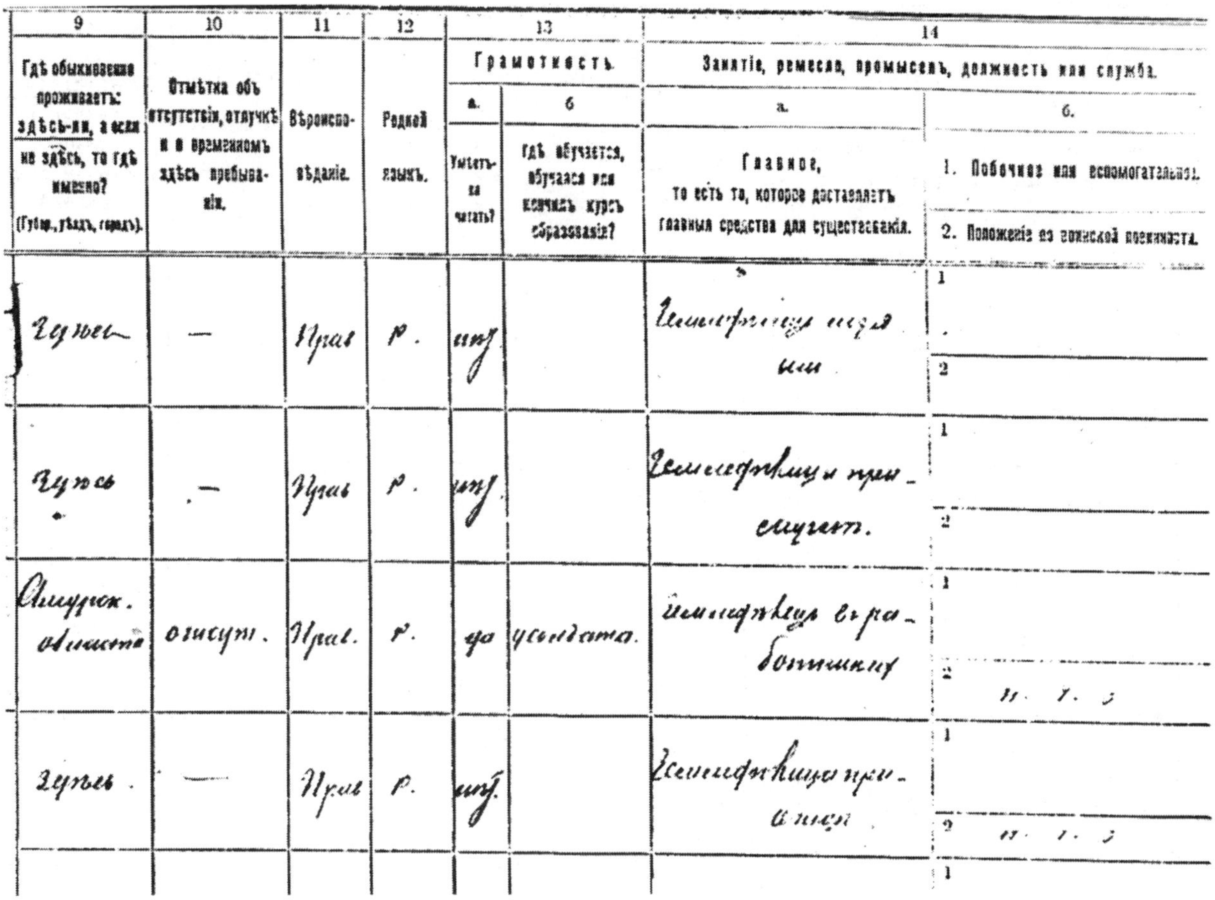

9	10	11	12	13		14	
Гдѣ обыкновенно проживаетъ: здѣсь-ли, а если не здѣсь, то гдѣ именно? (Губ., уѣздъ, городъ).	Отмѣтка объ отсутствіи, отлучкѣ и о временномъ здѣсь пребываніи.	Вѣроисповѣданіе.	Родной языкъ.	Грамотность. а. Умѣетъ-ли читать?	б. Гдѣ обучается, обучался или кончилъ курсъ образованія?	Занятіе, ремесло, промыселъ, должность или служба. а. Главное, то есть то, которое доставляетъ главныя средства для существованія.	б. 1. Побочное или вспомогательное. 2. Положеніе по воинской повинности.
здесь	—	Прав	р.	нет		Земледелица с мужем	1 2
здесь	—	Прав	р.	нет		Земледелица при мужем	1 2
Амурск. область	отсут.	Прав.	р.	да	у солдата	земледелец в работниках	1 2 н. т. з.
здесь	—	Прав	р.	нет		Земледелица при отце	1 2 н. т. з.

9	10	11	12	13		14	
Where does he usually live? HERE? If not, where exactly (province, county, city)	Notes about absence and temporary residence here	Faith	Native tongue	Education		Profession, craft, business, office or service	
				a. Can he read?	b. Where is he studying or had studied or graduated?	a) Main profession, i. e., that which is his chief source of income	b) 1. Side-line or subsidiary business 2. Military status
here	—	*Orth*	*R*	*no*		*farmer*	
here	—	*Orth*	*R*	*no*		*farmer with her husband*	
Amur oblast'	*absent*	*Orth*	*R*	*yes*	*with a soldier*	*farmer in workers*	
here	—	*Orth*	*R*	*no*		*farmer with her father*	

Document VI-42 and Translation (continued)

№ Листа 95

ПЕРВАЯ ВСЕОБЩАЯ ПЕРЕПИСЬ

населенія Россійской Имперіи,

на основаніи ВЫСОЧАЙШЕ УТВЕРЖДЕННАГО ПОЛОЖЕНІЯ 5 Іюня 1895 года.

Губернія или область: Тобольская	ВОИНСКАЯ ПЕРЕЧНЕВАЯ ВѢДОМОСТЬ.	Уѣздъ или округъ: Тобольскій

Перечень нижнихъ чиновъ, состоящихъ на дѣйствительной службѣ въ *(прописать названіе воинской части)* 1-й ротѣ Тобольскаго Резервнаго Пѣхотнаго баталіона,

ОБОЗНАЧИТЬ ДЛЯ ВОИНСКИХЪ ЧАСТЕЙ:

а) квартирующихъ въ городахъ:

Городъ (посадъ, мѣстечко) Тобольскъ

Городская часть 1

Участокъ (кварталъ) —

Пригородъ (предмѣстье) —

Улица (площадь) Большая Петропавловская

Домъ № 17

б) квартирующихъ внѣ городовъ:

Станъ ...

Волость, гмина, станица или соотвѣтствующее имъ дѣленіе *(если воинская часть расположена въ селеніи)* ...

Село, деревня или поселокъ *(прописать подробно названіе и родъ поселка)* ...

Переписной участокъ № 1.

Воинская часть расквартирована { въ казенной казармѣ? да. / или въ частномъ домѣ казарменнымъ порядкомъ? нѣтъ / или на квартирахъ у обывателей? нѣтъ } *писать да или нѣтъ.*

Если расквартирована въ казармахъ или казарменнымъ порядкомъ, то занимаетъ-ли { только часть дома? нѣтъ / или весь домъ? да. }

Если занимаетъ *весь домъ*, то отмѣтить: сколько на дворовомъ мѣстѣ жилыхъ строеній?

	Изъ чего каждое строеніе построено.	Чѣмъ крыто.		Изъ чего каждое строеніе построено.	Чѣмъ крыто.
1	деревянное	желѣзомъ	6		
2			7		
3			8		
4			9		
5			10		

Примѣчаніе. Если воинская часть занимаетъ только *часть дома*, то эта таблица оставляется безъ заполненія; требуемыя-же свѣдѣнія о жилыхъ строеніяхъ прописываются на переписномъ листѣ, который долженъ служить обложкой для всѣхъ перечневыхъ вѣдомостей и переписныхъ листовъ по *всему дому* (см. ст. 9 «Наставленія городскимъ счетчикамъ»).

Подсчетъ нижнихъ чиновъ въ день, къ которому пріурочена перепись.

Состояло на лицо (всего наличнаго населенія).	Состояло по списку (постоянно живущаго здѣсь населенія).	Въ числѣ нижнихъ чиновъ, состоящихъ на лицо (наличное населеніе), было лицъ некрестьянскихъ сословій.
Въ этой графѣ проставляется общій итогъ нижнихъ чиновъ, записанныхъ въ вѣдомость, кромѣ тѣхъ, о коихъ въ 12-й графѣ вѣдомости сдѣланы *отмѣтки объ отсутствіи.*	Въ этой графѣ проставляется итогъ всѣхъ нижнихъ чиновъ, *состоящихъ по списку* означенной воинской части (не исключая имѣющихъ отмѣтки въ 12-й графѣ вѣдомости), но безъ *прикомандированныхъ* къ ней *изъ другихъ* частей.	Въ этой графѣ проставляется общее число нижнихъ чиновъ, показанныхъ въ 1-й графѣ состоящими на лицо, за исключеніемъ изъ него лицъ *крестьянскихъ* сословій (по отмѣткамъ въ 5-й графѣ вѣдомости).
Число нижнихъ чиновъ.	Число нижнихъ чиновъ.	Число нижнихъ чиновъ.
139	148	18

Подпись командира роты, эскадрона, команды и т. п. (должность, чинъ и фамилія) Вр. Командующій 1-й ротой Капитанъ Кандаратъ

Document VI-43: Military Census Form

Sheet Number 25

FIRST GENERAL CENSUS
OF THE POPULATION OF THE RUSSIAN EMPIRE
ON THE BASIS OF AN ORDER ISSUED 5 JUNE 1895 BY THE SUPREME AUTHORITY

Gubernia or oblast': *Tobol'sk*	MILITARY SUMMARY FORM	Uyezd or okrug: *Tobol'sk*

Summary of the rank and file in active service in (write in full the name of the military unit)

1st company of the Tobol'sk Reserve Infantry Battalion,

FOR MILITARY UNITS, DESIGNATE:

a) Those quartered in towns

Town (village, small town): *Tobol'sk*
Town district: *1*
Section (quarter): —
Suburb (outskirt): —
Street (square) *Bol'shaia Petropavolov.*
House # *17*

b) Those quartered outside of towns:

Police District:
District, township, *stanitsa* or corresponding division:
(if the military unit is dispersed throughout the settlement)

Village or settlement *(write in full the settlement's name and type)*

Census Section No. *1*

Is the military unit quartered
in official barracks? *Yes*
or in a private home in barrack order? *No*
or in apartments with citizens? *No*

If quartered in barracks or in barrack order, then does it occupy
only one part of the house? *No*
the whole house? *Yes*

Write Yes or No

If it occupies the whole house, then note: how many inhabitable buildings are there on the grounds? ....

What is each made of?	*Covered with what?*	*What is each made of?*	*Covered with what?*
1 *Wooden*	*???*	6	
2		7	
3		8	
4		9	
5		10	

Notes: [not translated]

Subcount of the rank and file on the day for which the census was designated

Total of persons present	Total registered (those living here permanently)	Of the rank and file present, were there any of non-peasant descent?
139	*148*	*18*

Signature of the Commander of the Company, Squadron, Command, etc. (duty, rank, and surname) [illegible]

Translation of Document VI-43

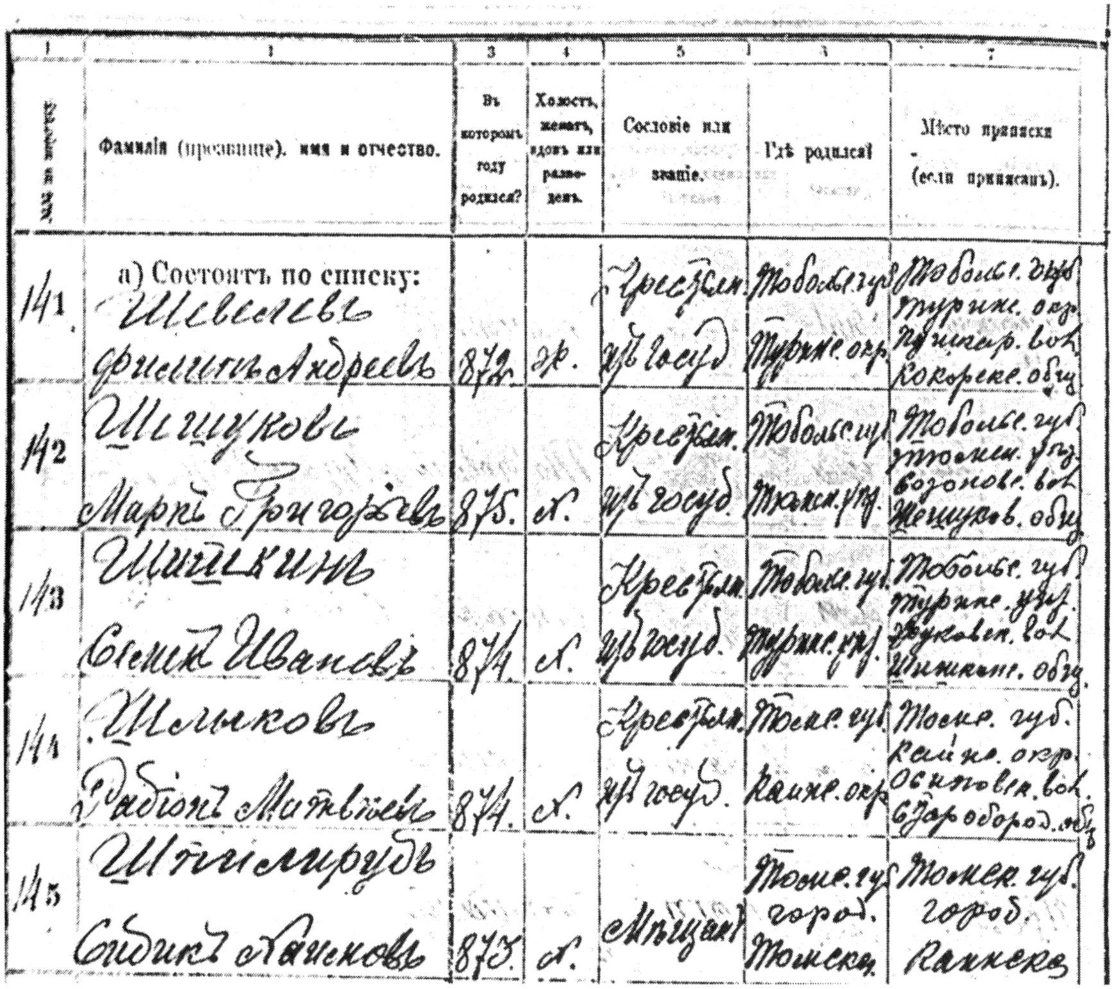

№№ по пор.	Фамилія (прозвище), имя и отчество.	Въ которомъ году родился?	Холостъ, женатъ, вдовъ или разведенъ.	Сословіе или званіе.	Гдѣ родился?	Мѣсто приписки (если приписанъ).
	а) Состоятъ по списку:					
141	Шешелевъ Филиппъ Андреевъ	872	ж.	Крестьян. изъ госуд.	Тобольск. губ. Туринск. окр.	Тобольск. губ. Туринск. окр. [illegible] вол. Кокоревск. общ.
142	Шещуковъ Маркъ Григорьевъ	875	ж.	Крестьян. изъ госуд.	Тобольск. губ. Тюмен. у.	Тобольск. губ. Тюмен. у. [illegible] вол. [illegible] общ.
143	Шипкинъ Семенъ Ивановъ	874	ж.	Крестьян. изъ госуд.	Тобольск. губ. Туринск. у.	Тобольск. губ. Туринск. у. [illegible] вол. Шипкин. общ.
144	Шмыковъ Родіонъ Матвѣевъ	874	ж.	Крестьян. изъ госуд.	Томск. губ. Каинск. окр.	Томск. губ. Каинск. окр. Осиповск. вол. [illegible] общ.
145	[illegible]	873	ж.	Мѣщанинъ	Томск. губ. город Томскъ	Томск. губ. город Каинскъ

Document VI-44: Questionnaire for Military Census Form (first page)

Above we see the first of two pages of a sample questionnaire filled out to accompany the Military Census Form just examined. There are a total of 12 columns, 7 shown on this page and 5 on page 329. The columnar headings are:

1) №№ по порядку – Entry number (in sequential order)
2) Фамилія (прозвище), имя и отчество – Surname (last name), first name and patronymic
3) Въ которомъ году родился? – In what year was he born?
4) Холостъ, женатъ, вдовъ, или разведенъ – Single, married, widower, or divorced?
5) Сословіе или званіе – Social class or rank
6) Гдѣ родился? – Where was he born?
7) Мѣсто приписки (если приписанъ) – Place of registration (if registered)
8) Вѣроисповѣданіе – Religion
9) Родной языкъ – native tongue
10) Грамотность | а) Умѣетъ-ли читать? | б) Гдѣ обучается, обучался или кончилъ курсъ образованi? – Education: a) Can he read? B) Where is he studying, or where did he study or graduate?

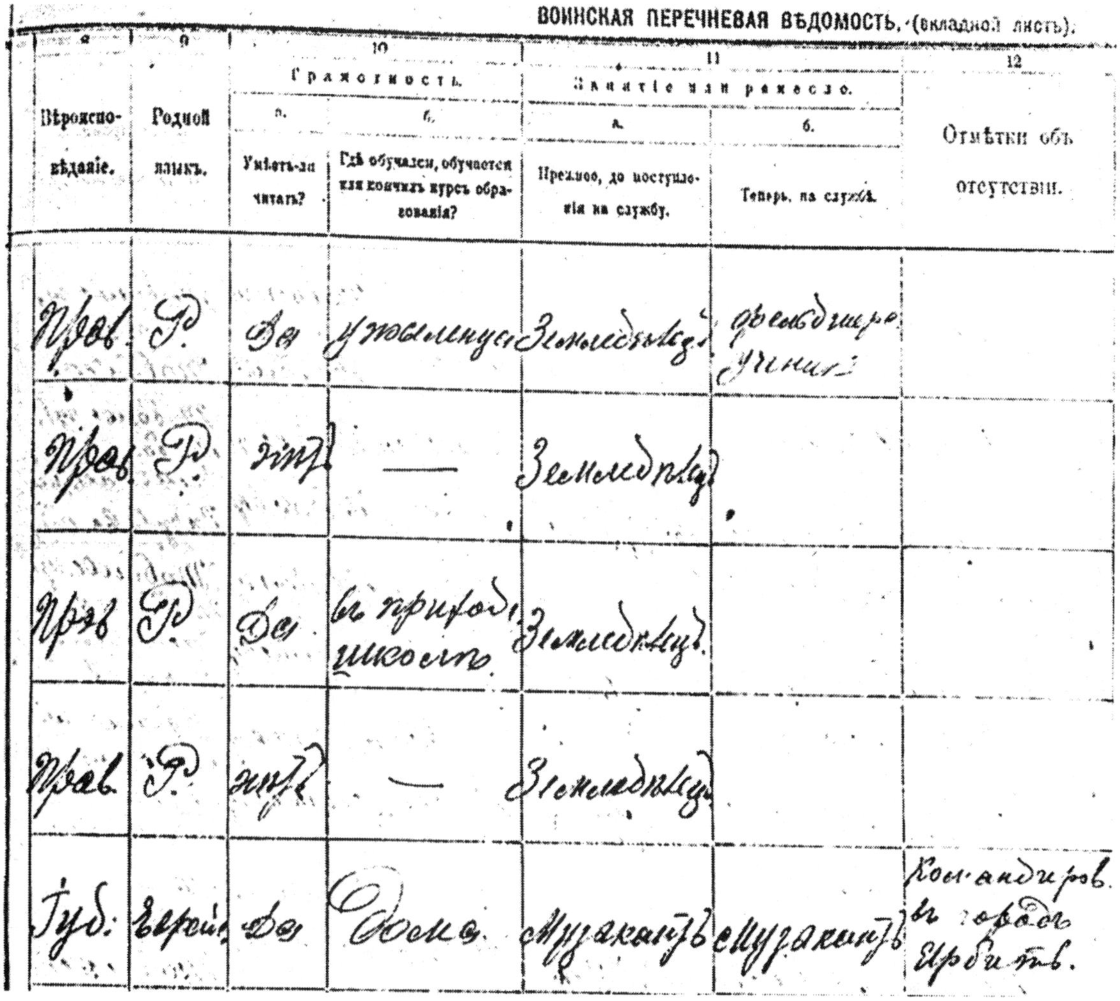

ВОИНСКАЯ ПЕРЕЧНЕВАЯ ВѢДОМОСТЬ. (вкладной листъ).

8	9	10		11		12
		Грамотность.		Занятіе или ремесло.		
Вѣроисповѣданіе.	Родной языкъ.	а. Умѣетъ-ли читать?	б. Гдѣ обучался, обучается или кончилъ курсъ образованія?	а. Прежнее, до поступленія на службу.	б. Теперь, на службѣ.	Отмѣтки объ отсутствіи.
Прав.	Р.	Да	у псаломщика	Земледѣлецъ	фельдшерскій ученикъ	
Прав.	Р.	нѣтъ	—	Земледѣлецъ		
Прав.	Р.	Да	въ приход. школѣ	Земледѣлецъ		
Прав.	Р.	нѣтъ	—	Земледѣлецъ		
Іуд.	Еврейс.	Да	Дома	Музыкантъ	Музыкантъ	Командиров. въ городъ Ирбитъ.

Document VI-44 (second page)

11) Занятіе или ремесло | а) Прежнее, до поступленія на службу | б) Теперь, на службѣ – Profession or handicraft: a) Previously, before entering the service; b) Now, while in the service

12) Отмѣтки объ отсутсвіи – Notes regarding absence.

There is some fascinating information to be found here. Note, for instance, that of the five soldiers enumerated on these pages, #141, Filip Shevelev, son of Andrei, was the oldest (born 1872) and the only one married (column 4). Three of the five could read (column 10a). All but one was a *крестьян. изъ госуд.*, a peasant attached to a government-owned estate (column 5)—the exception was #145, Sadik Shpilirud, son of Khaim, classified as *Мѣщан.*, "townsman" or "middle-class." As his name and class might suggest, he was noted as being of the Jewish faith (column 8, *Іуд.*) instead of Orthodox (*Прав.*), and his native tongue was given as *Еврейс.*, "Jewish," instead of the Russian the others spoke. He was also a *Музыкантъ*, "musician" (column 11a), while the others were classified as *Земледѣлецъ*, "farmer." In column 12 we see he was *Командиров. въ городъ Ирбить*, "dispatched to the town of Irbit'."

Of course, for genealogical research columns 6 and 7 are the real payoff. We see all these men were born and registered either in Tobol'sk or Tomsk province, in counties such as Turinsk, Kainsk, Tyumen'.

5. Document VI-45: А Легитимаціонная Книжка (Identification Booklet)

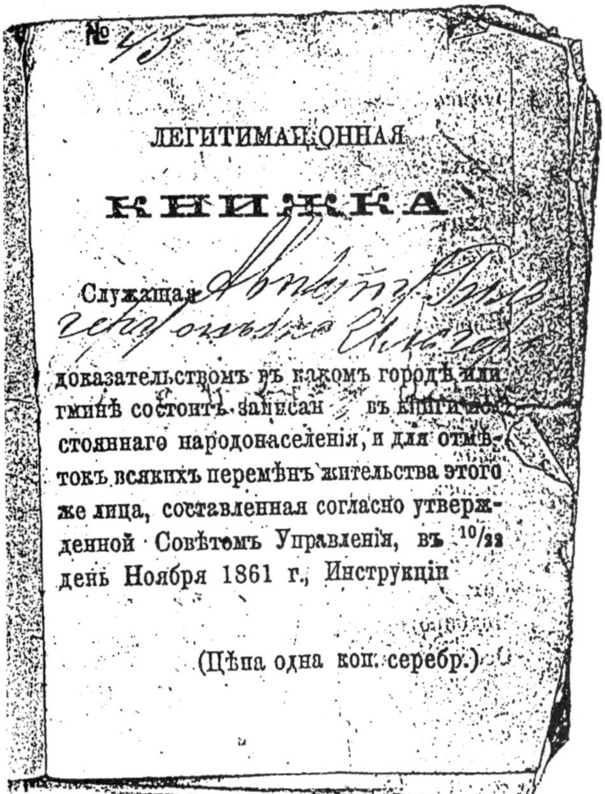
№ 43

ЛЕГИТИМАЦІОННАЯ

КНИЖКА

Служащая Августу Гильгеру онъже Ильгеръ

доказательствомъ въ какомъ городѣ или гминѣ состоитъ записан въ книги постояннаго народонаселенія, и для отмѣтокъ всякихъ перемѣнъ жительства этого же лица, составленная согласно утвержденной Совѣтомъ Управленія, въ 10/22 день Ноября 1861 г., Инструкціи

(Цѣна одна коп. серебр.)

The Russian government required all its citizens to carry a **Легитимаціонная Книжка**, identification booklet. Most of its pages were full of endless rules and regulations, but the first few contain valuable genealogical data. Let us look at three pages from a sample booklet.

On page 1, at left, Служающая *Августу Гильгеру онъже Ильгеръ* means literally "serving August Hilger, also known as Ilger." The participle служающая has the feminine ending –ая because it refers to the feminine noun *книжка*. The verb *служить* takes an object in the dative case, which explains the *–у* ending of *Августу Гильгеру* (compare Augustyn Hilger in Document VI-37, on page 306).

The rest of the text on this page says this document is proof of the bearer's compliance with all residency registration requirements, etc.

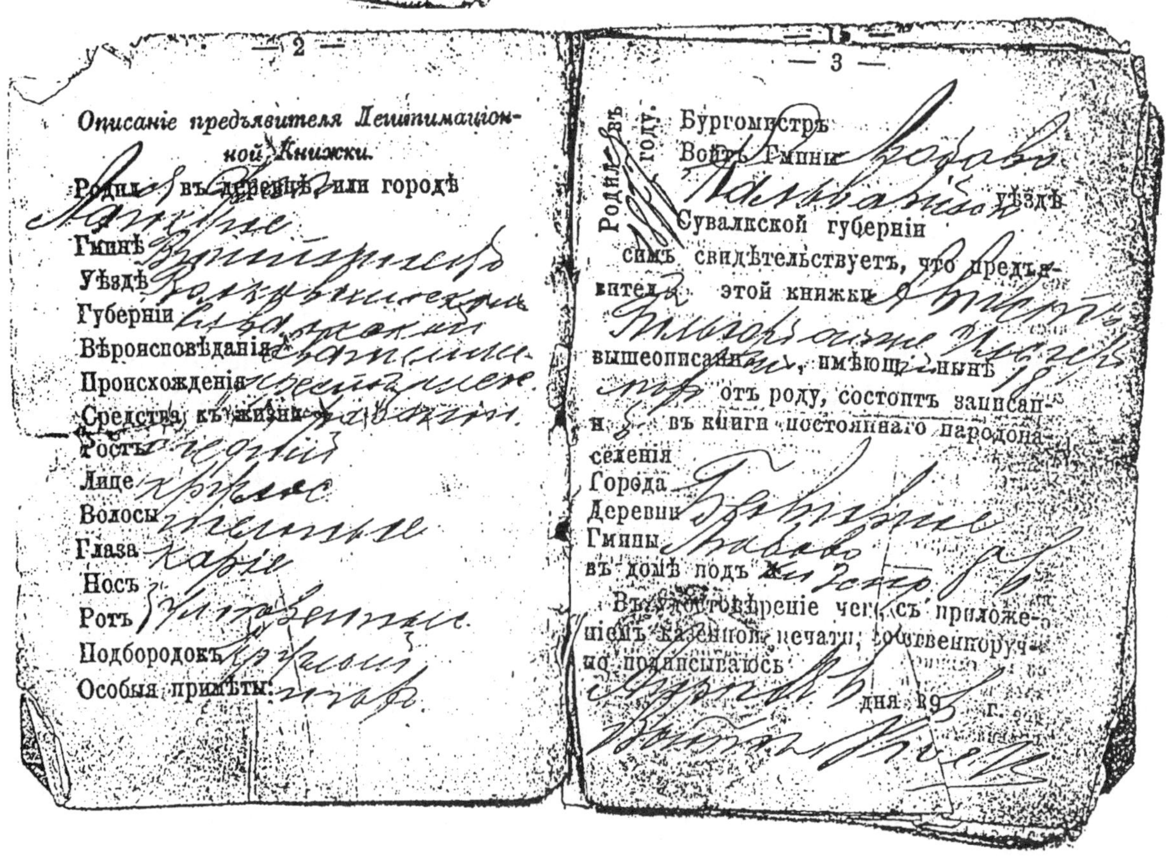
— 2 —

Описаніе предъявителя Легитимаціонной Книжки.

Родился въ деревнѣ, или городѣ

Гминѣ

Уѣздѣ

Губерніи

Вѣроисповѣданія

Происхожденія

Средства къ жизни

Ростъ

Лице

Волосы

Глаза каріе

Носъ

Ротъ

Подбородокъ

Особыя примѣты:

— 3 —

Родился въ ... году.

Бургомистръ

Войтъ Гмины

Уѣздѣ

Сувалкской губерніи

симъ свидѣтельствуетъ, что предъявитель этой книжки

вышеописанный, имѣющій ... отъ роду, состоитъ записанъ въ книги постояннаго народонаселенія

Города

Деревни

Гмины

въ домѣ подъ №

Въ удостовѣреніе чего съ приложеніемъ казенной печати, собственноручно подписываюсь

дня ... г.

– 2 –	– 3 –
Description of the bearer of this Identity Booklet. Born in the ~~village or~~ town of *Łankupa* Gmina: *Wysztyniec* County: *Wyłkowyszki [*see note below]* Province: *Suwałki* Religion: *Evangelical Lutheran* Social class: *peasant* Means of support: *laborer* Height: *medium* Face: *oval* Hair: *dark* Eyes: *brown* Nose: *normal* Mouth: *normal* Chin: *round* Distinguishing marks: *none*	Born in *1877* The Mayor The Administrator of the Gmina of *Lubowo* County: *Kalwaria* Province: *Suwałki* hereby certifies that the bearer of this booklet *August Hilger aka Ilger* described above, *18* years of age, has been entered in the Permanent Population Register of the settlement of the town of the village *Bawirsze* Gmina: *Lubowo* in house number *3*, page *86* In witness whereof I affix my signature and my seal of office [*illegible*]

Above is a translation of the information contained on pages 2 and 3 of the booklet, which provides details that are, at the least, interesting, and at best priceless. Let's look briefly at what's written here and at some alternatives you may see:

Родил*ся* въ деревнѣ или въ городѣ – "Born in the village or in the town." The official filling out the information was supposed to add the correct ending to Родил, either *–ся* for a male or *–ась* for a female. He was also supposed to cross out either the word for "village" or for "town," whichever did not apply. Here the town is *въ … Ланкупе*, a village called Łankupa in Polish. Named next is the gmina, *Выштынецъ*, Wisztyniec (now Vištytis, Lithuania); the *уѣздъ* or county, *Волковишкимъ*, Wyłkowyszki*; then the *губернiа* or province, *Сувалкской*, Suwałki. Obviously these details would vary from place to place; information in Chapter V should help you decipher whatever locations are specified here.

*The names of Volkovyshki (Polish name Wyłkowyszki), in Suwałki *gubernia*, now Vilkaviškis, Lithuania, and Volkovysk (Polish Wołkowysk), in Grodno province and now Vaŭkavysk, Belarus, are very similar and were often confused. This is surely the former.

Вѣроисповѣданія: *Евангелич.* – Religion: Evangelical." Other possibilities here (which may be abbreviated, as this is), are forms of: *iудейскій* or *еврейскій*, Jewish; *православный*, Orthodox; *римско-католическій*, Roman Catholic; *греко-католическій*, Greek Catholic; *лютеранскій*, Lutheran; and *мусульманскій* or *магометанскій*, Muslim.

Происхожденія: *крестьянск.* – "Social class: peasant." Some booklets use состоянія or сословія instead of происхожденія, which is literally "descent"; but in every case, what's being asked for is the bearer's social class. Usually the answer is *крестьянскаго*, "peasant," but also seen are *мѣщанскаго*, "middle class," and *дворянскаго*, "noble."

Средства къ жизни: *работ.* – "Means of support: laborer." Also seen for "means of support" is способъ жизни. A term for an occupation will usually be given here (see Chapter Two, pages 52-72). If the bearer was young and living at home, you may see a phrase such as *при родителяхъ*, "with his/her parents," or *при матери*, "with his/her mother."
Ростъ: *среднiй* – "Height: medium." Most of the terms usually seen in these physical descriptions are included in the Vocabulary (Chapter VII); see also pages 344-345.
Лице: *круглое* – "Face: oval"
Волосы: *темные* – "Hair: dark"
Глаза: *карiе* – "Eyes: brown"
Носъ: *умѣренный* – "Nose: normal"
Ротъ: *умѣренный* – "Mouth: normal"
Подбородокъ: *круглiй* – "Chin: round"
Особыя примѣты: *нѣтъ* – "Distinguishing marks: none"

On page 3 at upper left the bearer's date of birth is given, in this case 1877. The rest of the page consists of a statement by the mayor of the town and/or the *wójt* (administrator) of the local *gmina* affirming that the bearer is properly registered. Here it is the *wójt* of the district of Suwałki province with *Любово,* Lubowo (now Liubavas, Lithuania) as its seat who affirms that August Hilger aka Ilger, the person described above, age 18, has been duly registered in the Permanent Population Register for the village of *Бавирше*, Bawirsze, Lubowo district, in house #3, page 26.

6. Notarial Documents: Document VI-46: A Notarized Deed of Sale

Notarial documents, while not always abundant in personal data, may shed light on property owned by our ancestors; and knowing an ancestor owned property can open many research doors. **Document VI-46**, reproduced on page 333, is a short-form deed of sale from the province of Grodno. Since both italic print and handwritten information appears in this document, we use the italic Cyrillic font for the former and a script font for the latter.

Гродненскiй Нотарiусъ Георгий Николаевичъ Гордынскiй – "Notary of Grodno, Georgiy Nikolayevich Gordynskiy"
Ноября 30 дня *1905 г.* № *195* – "30 November 1905, No. 195"
г. Гродна – "city of Grodna"
Его Высокородiю Г[осподину] старшему Нотарiусу Гродненскаго Окружнаго Суда – "To His Honor the Senior Notary of the Grodno District Court"
На основанiи 80 ст. полож. о нотар. части, доношу, что 28-го Ноября сего года совершен у меня – "On the basis of regulations on page 80 in the section on Notaries, I report that on November 28th of this year [there was] executed by me …."
купчая крѣпость на проданное крестьянкою Анною Станиславовною Зильберовичъ – "a title deed to [ownership] sold by the peasant Anna Zilberowicz, daughter of Stanisław …"
крестьянину Григорiю Иванову Пауку право на половину недвижимаго имущества – "to Grzegorz Pauk, son of Jan, for half the real property" …
расположеннаго при селенiи Кально, Сокольскаго уѣзда – "situated near the village of Kalno, county of Sokółka"

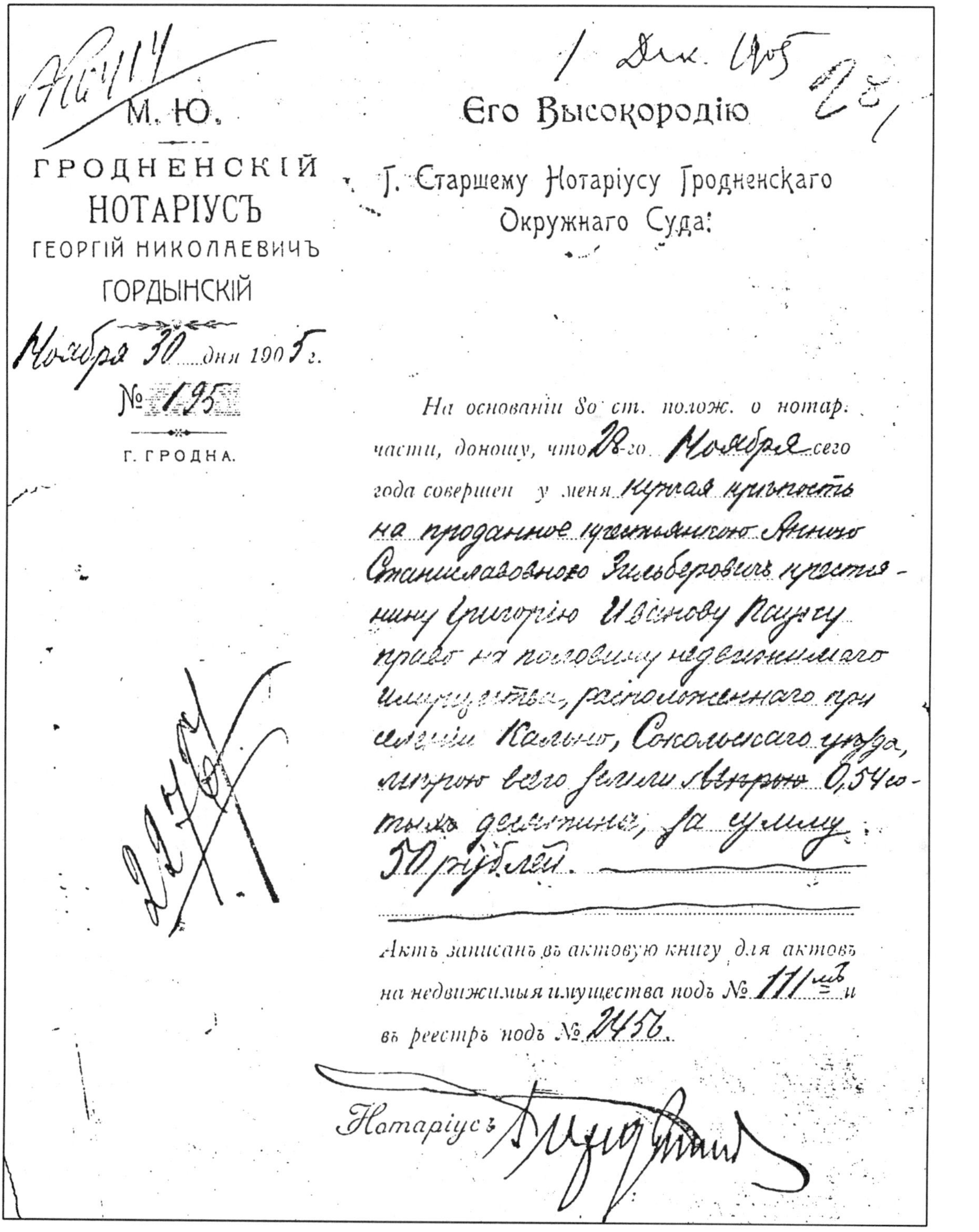
М. Ю.
ГРОДНЕНСКІЙ
НОТАРІУСЪ
ГЕОРГІЙ НИКОЛАЕВИЧЪ
ГОРДЫНСКІЙ
Ноября 30 дня 1905 г.
№ 195
г. Гродна.

Его Высокородію
Г. Старшему Нотаріусу Гродненскаго
Окружнаго Суда:

На основаніи 80 ст. полож. о нотар. части, доношу, что 28-го Ноября сего года совершен у меня купчая крепость на проданное крестьянкою Анною Станиславовною Зильберовичъ крестьянину Григорію [illegible] право на половину недвижимаго имущества, расположеннаго при селеніи [illegible], Сокольскаго уѣзда, мѣрою всего земли 0,54 сотыхъ десятины, за сумму 50 рублей.

Актъ записанъ въ актовую книгу для актовъ на недвижимыя имущества подъ № 111 и въ реестръ подъ № 2456.

Нотаріусъ [illegible]

Document VI-46: Notarized Deed of Sale

мѣрою всего земли 0.54 сотныхъ десятины, за сумму 50 рублей – "the measure of the whole being 0.54 of a *desyatina* of land, for the sum of 50 rubles."

Актъ записанъ въ актовую книгу для актовъ на недвижимыя имущества подъ № 111ᵐᵒ и въ реестръ подъ № 2456. Нотаріусъ [illegible] – "This document was entered into the real property records as No. 111 and in the register as No. 2456. Notary *[illegible]*."

Document VI-47: A Bilingual Notarized Document

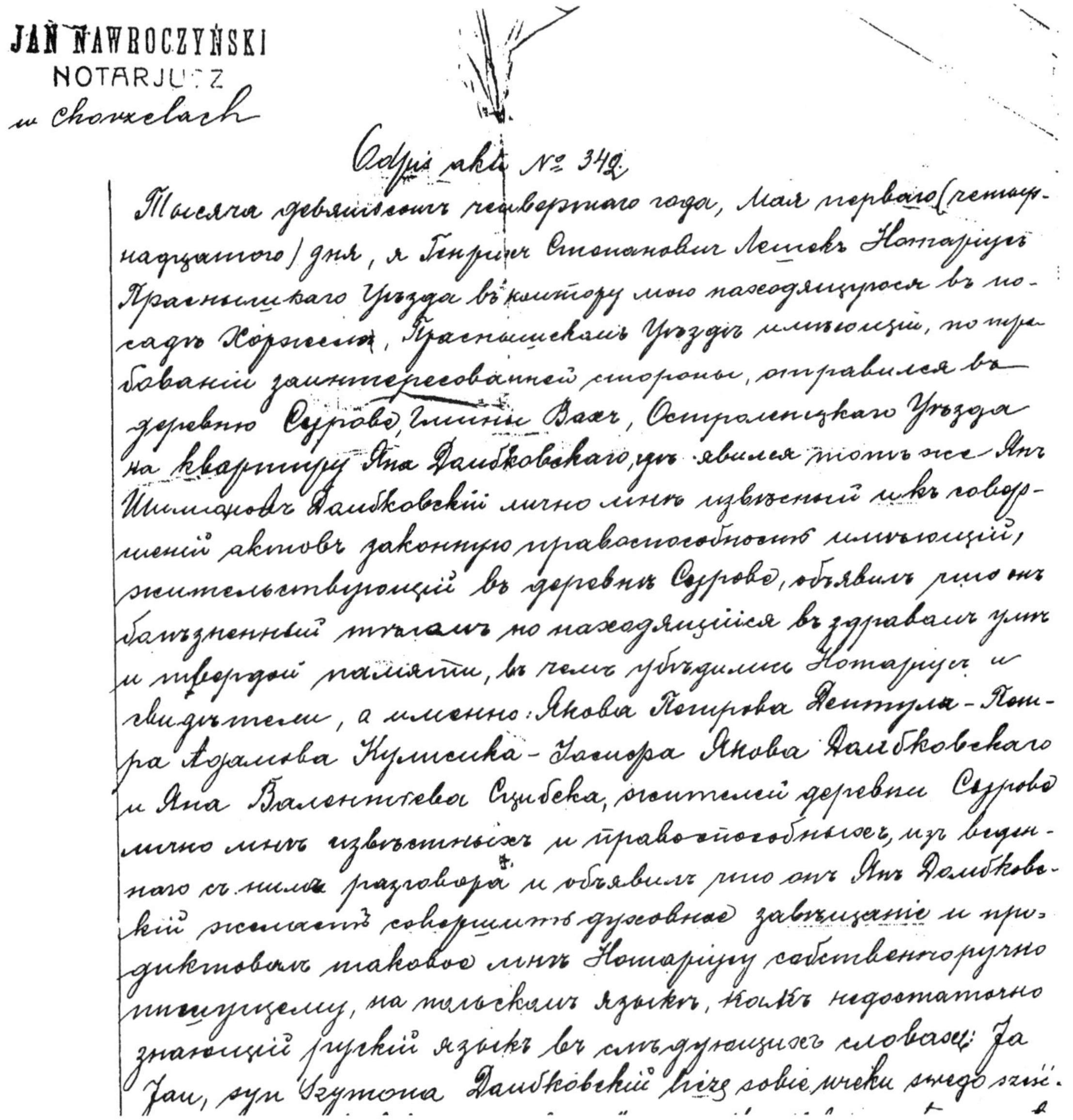

JAN NAWROCZYŃSKI
NOTARJUSZ
w Chorzelach

Odpis aktu № 342.

Тысяча девятьсотъ четвертаго года, Мая перваго (четырнадцатаго) дня, я Генрихъ Степановичъ Лешевъ Нотаріусъ
Прасныщскаго Уѣзда въ контору мою находящуюся въ посадѣ Хоржели, Прасныщскаго Уѣзда имѣющій, по тре-
бованій заинтересованной стороны, отправился въ
деревню Сурово, гмины Вахъ, Остроленскаго Уѣзда
на квартиру Яна Дамбковскаго, гдѣ явился тотъ же Янъ
Шимоновъ Дамбковскій лично мнѣ извѣстный и къ совер-
шеній актовъ законную правоспособность имѣющій,
жительствующій въ деревнѣ Сурово, объявилъ что онъ
болѣзненный тѣломъ но находящійся въ здравомъ умѣ
и твердой памяти, въ чемъ убѣдились Нотаріусъ и
свидѣтели, а именно: Якова Петрова Пентуля - Петра Адамова Кулесика - Гаспара Якова Дамбковскаго
и Яна Валентіева Сцибека, жителей деревни Сурово
лично мнѣ извѣстныхъ и правоспособныхъ, изъ веденнаго съ нимъ разговора и объявилъ что онъ Янъ Дамбковскій желаетъ совершить духовное завѣщаніе и продиктовалъ таковое мнѣ Нотаріусу собственноручно
пишущему, на польскомъ языкѣ, какъ недостаточно
знающій русскій языкъ въ слѣдующихъ словахъ: Ja
Jan, syn Szymona Дамбковскій leżę sobie, wręku swego zmi.

Notaries in Europe held responsibilities well beyond those of an American Notary Public. They performed tasks relating to land purchases, financial agreements, and other matters handled normally by attorneys in the United States. Document VI-47, reproduced above, gives us another sample of the kind of thing notaries handled. It is an unusual document because much of the text in Russian, as required by law, but then, near the bottom of the portion shown above, it mixes in a statement in Polish (for reasons explained in the text).

The original document is several pages long. We have reproduced only part of the first, as that should be enough to familiarize you with the format and terminology generally encountered in this sort of record. Nor will we analyze it extensively: a straight translation should suffice for our purposes. Note, incidentally, that the writer (whose first language was surely Polish) made several errors in Russian spelling and word choice, at least one of which is (unintentionally) rather comical!

The document begins in Polish, with the notary's name in the upper left hand corner, "Jan Nawroczyński, Notary in Chorzele," and centered at the top *Odpis aktu No. 342,* "A copy of Document #342." Then the Russian text begins:

Тысяча девятьсотъ четвертаго года, Мая перваго (четырнадцатаго) дня – "In the year 1904, on the 1st (14th) of May …"

я Генрихъ Степановичь Лешекъ Нотаріусъ Праснышкаго Уѣзда въ контору мою находящуюся въ посадѣ Хоржелѣ, Праснышскомъ уѣздѣ имѣющій – "I, Henryk Leszek, son of Stepan, Notary of Przasnysz County, in my office located in the village of Chorzele …"

по требованіи заинтересованней стороны, отравился въ деревню Сурове, Гмины Вахъ, Остроленцкаго Уѣзда – "on the request of the interested party, [I] went to the village of Surowe, in the District of Wach, County of Ostrołęka…" Note that *отравился* is surely an error—it means "I poisoned myself"! Surely he meant *от**п**равился*, "I set off, went to."

Note also that the most common Russian adjectival form of the name of the town Ostrołęka is *остроленскій*, but this writer transcribed the Polish version, *ostrołęcki,* phonetically into Russian as *остроленцкій*. In dealing with this sort of "cross-lingual contamination," which is common in areas where cultures and languages clashed, it is very helpful to acquire some knowledge of both languages, if possible!

на квартиру Яна Домбковскаго, гдѣ явился тотъ же Янъ Шимоновъ Домбковскій лично мнѣ извѣстный – "to the quarters of Jan Dąbkowski, where that same Jan Dąbkowski, son of Szymon, personally known to me, appeared …"

и къ совершеніи актовъ законную правоспособность имѣющій – "and who possesses the legal capacity to make such documents"

жительствующій въ деревнѣ Сурове, объявилъ что онъ болѣзненный тѣломъ но находящіися въ здравомъ умѣ и твердой памяти, въ чемъ убѣдились Нотаріусъ и свидѣтели … – "and resides in the village of Surowe, declared that he is sickly in body but finds himself healthy in mind and of a strong memory, of which the notary and witnesses convinced themselves …"

а именно: Якова Петрова Дептула – Петра Адамова Кулисика – Іосифа Янова Домбковскаго и Яна Валентіева Сцибека, жителей деревни Сурове лично мнѣ извѣстныхъ и правоспособныхъ изъ веденнаго съ ними разговора – "to wit: Jakób Deptuła, son of Adam; Piotr Kulisik, son of Adam; Józef Dąbkowski, son of Jan; and Jan Ścibek, son of Walenty; residents of the village of Surowe, personally known to me and legally competent as the result of a conversation conducted with them …" The names prove these gentlemen were Poles, and it is worth noting that Poles do not generally use patronymics the way Russians do. The only reason all these "son of" expressions appear here is because the Russian culture and language were forced upon Poles and Lithuanians during this period.

и объявилъ, что онъ Янъ Домбковскій желаетъ совершить духовное завѣщаніе и продиктовалъ таковое мнѣ Нотаріусу собственноручно пишущему на польскомъ языкѣ, какъ недостаточно знающій рускій языкъ въ слѣдующихъ словахъ – "and [he] stated that he, Jan Dąbkowski, wishes to execute a last will and testament and dictated same to me, the Notary, writing it with my own hand in the Polish language, since he does not know Russian sufficiently, in the following words."

The rest of the text is mainly in Polish—albeit with Russian words interspersed, for reasons that are not entirely clear—and for the most part enumerates monetary distribution. As such it is unlikely to prove enlightening to people who bought this book, after all, for help with Russian! But we hope this sampling of the format and terminology often seen in notarial records will help you to make sense of any you happen to encounter during your research.

7. Document VI-48: A Catholic Church's Register of Easter Communicants

Reproduced on page 337, **Document VI-48** is a fragment from a Roman Catholic church's Книга о исповѣдающихся и причащающихся, literally "Book of those making their Confession and taking Communion"—or to use older terminology, "Register of Those Having Fulfilled their Easter Duty." Catholics were obliged to confess and take Holy Communion at least once a year, on Easter Sunday; even if they were Catholics in name only, this was one religious duty few dared ignore. Thus in villages where the overwhelming majority of the population belonged to the Roman Catholic Church, these documents are, in effect, substitute census records.

Here is a brief analysis and translation of the information given:

Column Headings

Число дворовъ – "number of the households"

№ | Мужеск. | Женск. – "Number | Male | Female"

Деревня Веселово – "village of Wesołowo." The priest has used this space to specify that he is listing parishioners in the village of Wesołowo. It's interesting that the priest has modified the Polish name somewhat, rendering it in Russian as if it were *Wesełowo* and putting a stroke over the Russian *л*, like that over Polish cursive *ł*.

Лѣта | Мужеск. | Женск. – "Age | Male | Female"

Показанія дѣйствія | Кто были у исповѣди и Св. Причастія | Кто исповѣдались токмо а не причащались | Которые у исповѣди не были. – "Statement of action | Who went to Confession and received Holy Communion | Who went to Confession but did not take Communion | Those who did not go to Confession."

The information written in under these columns is generally not too difficult to understand. Each household was given a number, and that shows up in column 1. Then each person is designated by a sequential number, with a separate count for males and females; that number appears in columns 2-3. The 4th column gives the names of the individuals. Column 5 or 6 lists their ages, again separated by gender. Columns 7, 8, and 9 classify them as to whether they confessed and took Communion, confessed but did not take Communion, or did not go to confession. The entries in column 7 are usually *б.*, short for *былъ/была*, "he/she was."

Column 4, under *Деревня Веселово*, is where the priest wrote in the names of his parishioners. What's somewhat unusual, for a priest in a Polish parish, is that he rendered their first names in Russian form, rather than spelling their Polish forms phonetically in the Cyrillic alphabet. Thus the first person listed, *Иванъ Андрушкѣвичъ*, was almost certainly called Jan Andruszkiewicz; *Jan* in Cyrillic would be *Янъ;* but the priest gave his first name in Russian form as *Иванъ*. Jan's son *Викентій* would be called *Wincenty* by Poles. But the name of his second son, *Анджей,* reflects the Polish form *Andrzej,* rather than standard Russian *Андрей.* So there is a lot of inconsistency here, and that is not so unusual.

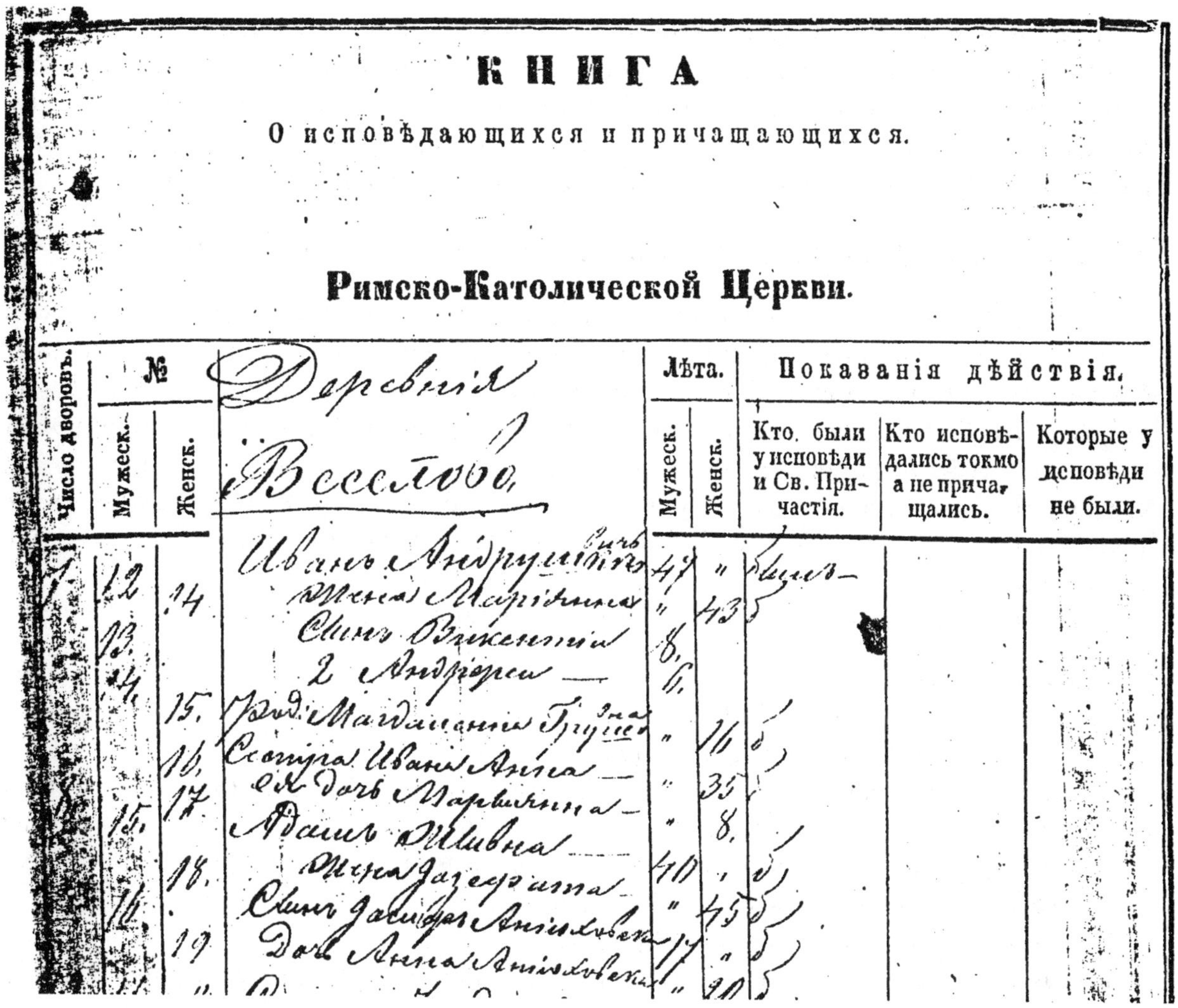

КНИГА

О исповѣдающихся и причащающихся.

Римско-Католической Церкви.

Число дворовъ.	№ Мужеск.	№ Женск.	Деревня Веселово	Лѣта. Мужеск.	Лѣта. Женск.	Показанія дѣйствія. Кто были у исповѣди и Св. Причастія.	Кто исповѣдались токмо а не причащались.	Которые у исповѣди не были.

Document VI-48: A Roman Catholic Church Register of Easter Communicants

Generally the head of the house is entered first, followed by his wife, then his sons in descending order of age, then daughters, also in descending order by age, and then relatives, tenants, or servants. Sometimes the relationship is specified with a term such as *братъ*, brother, or *сестра*, sister. In many cases all that's given is *род.*, for *родственникъ*, "relative."

Thus family #7 consisted of:

№ 12, Иванъ Андрушкѣвичъ, Jan Andruszkiewicz, male #12, age 47
№ 14, жена Марiянна, his wife Maryjanna, female #14, age 43
№ 13, сынъ Викентiй, son Wincenty, male #13, age 8
№ 14, 2 Андржей, 2nd son Andrzej, male #14, age 6
№ 15, род. Магдаленна Грушевна, relative Magdalena Gruszewna, female # 15, age 16
№ 16, сестра Ивана Анна, female #16, Anna, sister of Jan, age 35
№ 17, ея дочь Марыянна, female #17, Maryanna, her daughter, age 8

Jan and Maryjanna went to Confession and took Communion, as indicated by the entry *былъ* for Jan and the abbreviation *б.* for Maryjanna. Nothing is noted for Wincenty and Andrzej, presumably because they were too young to take these sacraments.

8. Document VI-49: A Population Register

№ дома. / № по порядку.	ИМЯ И ПРОЗВАНІЕ. МУЖЧИНЫ.	ИМЯ И ПРОЗВАНІЕ. ЖЕНЩИНЫ, кто урожденная и по первому замужеству.	Имена родителей и кто урождена мать.	Время рожденія. Число.	Время рожденія. Мѣсяцъ.	Время рожденія. Годъ.	Мѣсто рожденія.
86 / 1	Бурштайнъ Фришель		Мошекъ и Бинда Ента урожденная Фрельдонъ	14	Ноября	1877	Города Згержъ
2		Бурштайнъ Ента урожденная Гершонъ	Шмуель и Лая урожденная Млынарчевская	18/25	Октября	1883	Дер. Юзефово Гмины Шрота Долина Брезинскаго уѣзда
3	Бурштайнъ Давидъ Маеръ		Фришель и Ента урожденная Гершонъ	12/25	Сентября	1903	гор. Брезины
4		Бурштайнъ Райзля-Сында	Фришель и Ента урожденная Гершонъ	2/15	февраля	1906	Брезины
5		Бурштайнъ Рывка	Фришель и Ента урожденная Гершонъ	18/31	Января	1909	Брезины
6		Bursztajn Estera Fryda	Fiszel i Yenta z Gerszonów	3	Sierpnia	1910	Brzeziny
7		Bursztajn Masza	Fiszel i Yenta z Gerszonów	12	październik	1912	Brzeziny
8		Bursztajn Dobrysz	Fiszel i Yenta z Gerszonów	20	grudnia	1914	Brzeziny

Sample courtesy of Fay Bussgang

Reproduced above and on page 340 are two pages from the Register of Permanent Population for Brzeziny, a county seat east of Łódź in what is now central Poland. These registers can be sources of enormous value, as they were used to record circumstances under which residents came to a given locality—by birth, moving in, whatever—and left—by moving away, dying, etc. We have already seen one sample of these registers in Document VI-34 beginning on page 299, shown there to use how authorities kept track of males' military status. These samples—facing pages from the register, showing information on 8 individuals—demonstrate other things these books can tell us.

One thing you notice quickly is that entries 1-5 are in Russian, 6-8 in Polish. That's because the first 5 entries date from the period 1868-1918 when this area was ruled by Russia, when Russian was the required official language. The last three come from the period after World War I, when Poland was reborn and documents were kept in Polish.

You also notice that all these entries are crossed out. This was done as individuals no longer resided in the locality in question; in some cases they died, in others they moved away.

Here is a quick translation of the data provided in these first 8 columns:

House #	FIRST AND LAST NAME		Parents' Names and mother's maiden name	Time of birth [i. e. Date of Birth]			Place of Birth
Seq. #	MEN	WOMEN maiden name and name by previous marriages		Day	Month	Year	
1	*Bursztajn Fiszel*		*Moszek & Hinda Jenta née Feldon*	*14*	*November*	*1877*	*town of Zgierz*
2		*Bursztajn Jenta née Gerszon*	*Szyme and Laja née Młynarzewska*	*13/25*	*October*	*1883*	*village Józefów, gmina Mroga Dolna, county Brzeziny*
3	*Bursztajn Dawid Majer*		*Fiszel and Jenta née Gerszon*	*12/25*	*September*	*1903*	*town of Brzeziny*
4		*Bursztajn Rajzla-Hinda*	*Fiszel and Jenta née Gerszon*	*2/15*	*February*	*1906*	*town of Brzeziny*
5		*Bursztajn Rywka*	*Fiszel and Jenta née Gerszon*	*18/31*	*January*	*1909*	*town of Brzeziny*
6		*Bursztajn Estera Fajga*	*Fiszel and Jenta née Gerszon*	*3*	*August*	*1910*	*Brzeziny*
7		*Bursztajn Masza*	*Fiszel and Jenta née Gerszon*	*12*	*October*	*1912*	*Brzeziny*
8		*Bursztajn Dobrysz*	*Fiszel and Jenta née Gerszon*	*20*	*December*	*1914*	*Brzeziny*

Since the people and places involved were all in Poland, we print proper names above in their Polish spellings (a rendering of the Cyrillic spellings by English phonetic values would be, for instance, Fishel' and Yenta). The place names are also given in their Polish versions, but note that Zgierz is spelled *Згержъ* in Russian, and Brzeziny is *Брезины*.

The double dates given for Jenta Bursztajn and her first three children are due to the Russian system of giving dates by Old Style, then New Style (see page 200).

Now for the facing page, with columns 9-14 for these entries.

Женатъ, замужняя или нѣтъ.	Происхожденіе.	Вѣроисповѣданіе.	Средства къ содержанію.	Мѣсто прежняго жительства.	ПРИМѢЧАНІЕ. (Здѣсь записываются всѣ происшедшія съ жителями перемѣны какъ-то: смерть, переселеніе, переходъ въ другой домъ и т. п., согласно ст. 15-ой).
Женатъ	мѣщанское	еврейское	портной	№ 86 Стр. 767	Въ призывъ 1899 года уволенъ на всегда отъ военной службы по неспособности. Бургомистръ [illegible] [illegible] 1914 r. Burmistrz
Замужняя	мѣщанское	еврейское	при мужѣ	№ 86	[illegible] 1920 r. [illegible] Burmistrz
Холостъ	мѣщанское	еврейское	при родителяхъ	№ 86.	Умеръ въ гор. Брезинахъ 20 марта / 2 Апрѣля 1904 года. Бургомистръ [illegible]
дѣвица	мѣщанское	еврейское	при родителяхъ	—	[illegible] Burmistrz
дѣвица	мѣщанское	еврейское	при родителяхъ	—	
panna	mieszczańskie	mojżeszowe	przy rodzicach	—	
panna	mieszczańskie	mojżeszowe	przy rodzicach	—	
panna	mieszczańskie	mojżeszowe	przy rodzicach	—	

Sample courtesy of Fay Bussgang

Document VI-49, page 2

Married or not	Descent [i. e., social class]	Religion	Means of support	Previous residence	**NOTES** (Enter here all changes that occur with residents, such as death, moving away, moving to another house, etc., as per. Statute 15)
Married	*Townsman [i. e., middle class]*	*Jewish*	*Tailor*	*№ 86 p. 767*	*In the call-up of 1899 he was released from all military service due to unfitness. Mayor [illegible]. He died in the village of Słupia, county of Skierniewice, in 1914. Mayor.*
Married	*Townsman*	*Jewish*	*with her husband*	*№ 86*	*Per notice No. 294, gmina Niesułków, Brzeziny county, dated 6 August 1920, she moved in with her husband Szmul Josiek Arbuz. Mayor.*
Single	*Townsman*	*Jewish*	*with his parents*	*№ 86*	*Died in the town of Brzeziny, 20 March / 2 April 1904. Mayor [illegible]*
Single	*Townsman*	*Jewish*	*with her parents*		*All crossed out, went with their mother to Niesułków gmina, Brzeziny county. Mayor [illegible]*
Single	*Townsman*	*Jewish*	*with her parents*		
Single	*Townsman*	*Jewish*	*with her parents*		
Single	*Townsman*	*Jewish*	*with her parents*		
Single	*Townsman*	*Jewish*	*with her parents*		

Column 13, "Previous residence," suggests that Fiszel and Jenta had apparently moved to Brzeziny from elsewhere, as referred to on page 767 of the register. Their son Dawid was born in Brzeziny, but apparently he, too, was involved in the move described in that entry.

The main point, however, is that the last column explains why all these entries are crossed out. The father, Fiszel, died in 1914. His widow remarried and in 1920 went to live with her new husband, Szmul Josiek Arbuz, in Niesułków district, Brzeziny county. Fiszel and Jenta's son Dawid Majer had already died in Brzeziny in 1894. The girls all went to live with their mother when she remarried and moved. So one way or another, they had all left Brzeziny.

Do you see why these population registers are well worth the effort it takes to find them? In Russian they are called *книги постояннаго народонаселенія* (or *жительства*); in Polish they have been called at various times *księgi ludności, księgi kontroli ruchu ludności, rejestry mieszkania, księgi meldunkowe, karty meldunkowe,* and so on. For more on this subject see Fay Bussgang's article "Books of Residents *(Księgi Ludności)* and Other Books of Registration" in the *Kielce-Radom SIG Journal,* Volume 4, Number 3, and the articles by Julian and Fay Bussgang in *Avotaynu,* Vol. 16, No. 3 (Fall 2000), pp. 12-14.

9. Passports: Document VI-50, Long-Form Passport Booklet

Passports can provide a wealth of family history information. Many of the Russian passports from the great era of immigration—frequently green, dark red, black or blue in color—resembled the modern passport. They contained typically three to four pages of personal data, with numerous pages devoted to government regulations.

There were two types of the so-called Паспортная Книжка, or booklet-form passport. One, which we have chosen to call the "short form," gave very basic data and was far less extensive than the "long form" version. **Document VI-50**, below and on the next few pages, is an example of the long-form passport.

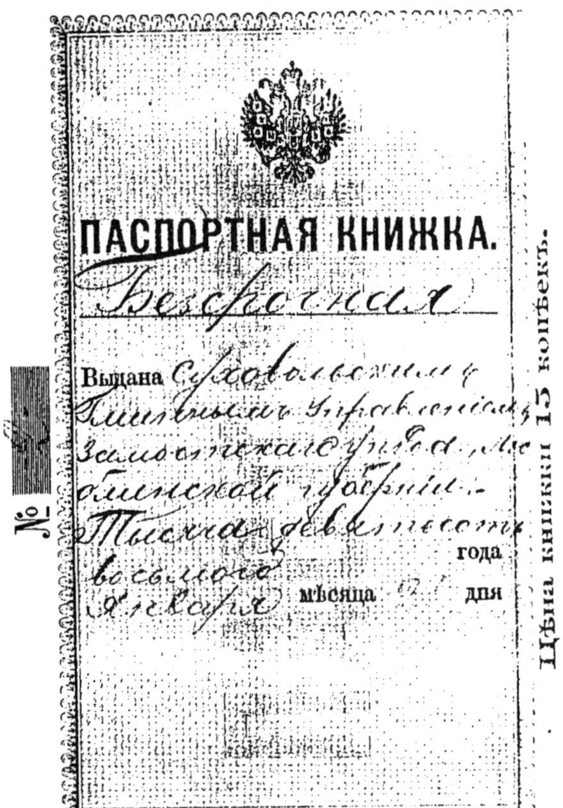
№

ПАСПОРТНАЯ КНИЖКА.

Безсрочная

Выдана Суховольскимъ Гминнымъ Управленiемъ Замостскаго уѣзда, Люблинской губернiи. Тысяча девятьсотъ восьмого года Января мѣсяца дня

Цѣна книжки 15 копѣекъ.

Паспортная Книжка – Passport Booklet

Безсрочная – "termless," that is, no fixed *срокъ* or period of validity.

Выдана *суховольскимъ Гминнымъ Управленіемъ Замостскаго уѣзда, Люблинской губерніи. Тысяча девятьсотъ восьмого* года *Января* мѣсяца *8* дня – "Issued by the Suchowola District Administrative Office of Zamość County, Province of Lublin, 28 January 1908."

The information following Выдана will usually appear in this order:

1. The name of the *волость* (*volost'*) or *гмина* (*gmina*), both meaning "district"
2. The name of the *уѣздъ* (county)
3. The name of the *губернія* (province)
4. The date (year, month, day)

Sometimes the first name, patronymic, and surname of the bearer will appear in the space on the bottom of the page. In this case, however, that information appears on page 2.

On the booklet's second page (reproduced on page 343) we have the following:

1. Владѣлецъ книжки: 1. Имя, отчество, фамилія: *Бартломей Фіялекъ* – "Bearer's name: 1. First name, patronymic, surname: Bartłomiej Fijałek." Since he was clearly a Pole, we're giving his name in the standard Polish form, which is what he surely went by when not dealing with Russian bureaucracies. The patronymic is not given here; for more information on that, and especially as it applies to Poles, who, unlike Russians, didn't normally use a patronymic as part of their standard name, see pages 28-29, 83, and 86.
2. Званіе: *Крестьянское* – "Class: peasant." The term *званіе* can mean several things: "title, rank, occupation." But in documents it, or *сословіе* or *происхожденіе*, usually calls for information on the bearer's social class.

3. Время рожденія или возрастъ: *24 Іюля / 5 Августа 1877 г.*– "Time of birth or age: 24 July / 5 August 1877." For more on the double date see page 200.

Page 3 provides the following information:

4. Вѣроисповѣданіе: *Римско-Католическое* – "Religion: Roman Catholic." Other possibilities here (which may be abbreviated), are: *іудейское* or *еврейское*, Jewish; *православное*, Orthodox; *греко-католическое*, Greek Catholic; *лютеранское*, Lutheran; and *мусульманское* or *магометанское*, Muslim.
5. Мѣсто постояннаго жительства: *Дер. Гутковъ, Гмины Суховоля, Замостскаго уъзда, Люблинской губернія. N дома 47 стр. 944.* – "Place of permanent residence: Village of Gutków, district of Suchowola, county of Zamość, province of Lublin. House # 47, page 944." The reference here is to the *Книга постояннаго жительства*, Permanent Population Register, a sample of which we just saw in Document VI-49. In other words, this information was copied from page 944 of that register, from the entry for house # 47.

Состоитъ ли или состоялъ ли въ бракѣ: *Состоитъ* – "Is he, or has he been, married? He is." The verb *состоять* can be translated several ways; in the expressions *состоитъ въ бракъ* and *состоитъ на службъ* it is best translated simply "is": "He is married" and "He is in the service."

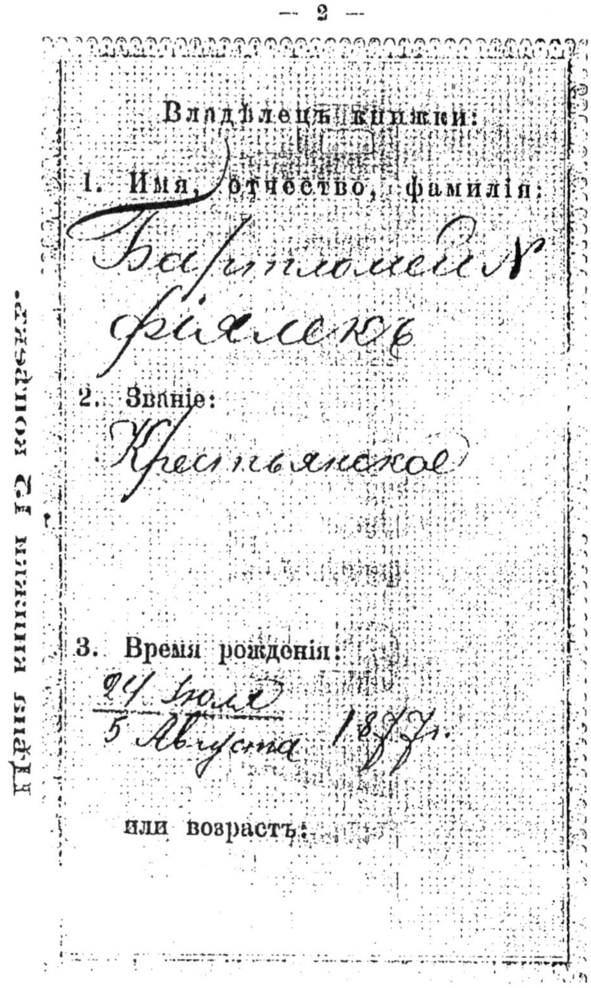
— 2 —

Владѣлецъ книжки:

1. Имя, отчество, фамилія:
Бартломей Фіялекъ

2. Званіе:
Крестьянское

3. Время рожденія:
24 Іюля / 5 Августа 1877 г.

или возрастъ:

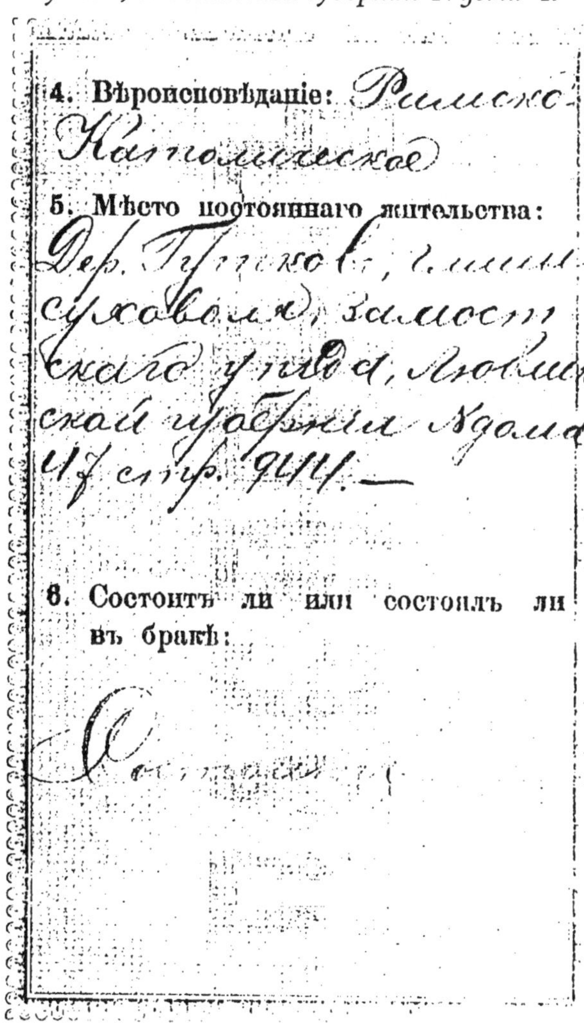
4. Вѣроисповѣданіе: Римско-Католическое

5. Мѣсто постояннаго жительства:
Дер. Гутковъ, гмины Суховоля, Замостскаго уѣзда, Люблинской губерніи N дома 47 стр. 944.—

6. Состоитъ ли или состоялъ ли въ бракѣ:
Состоитъ

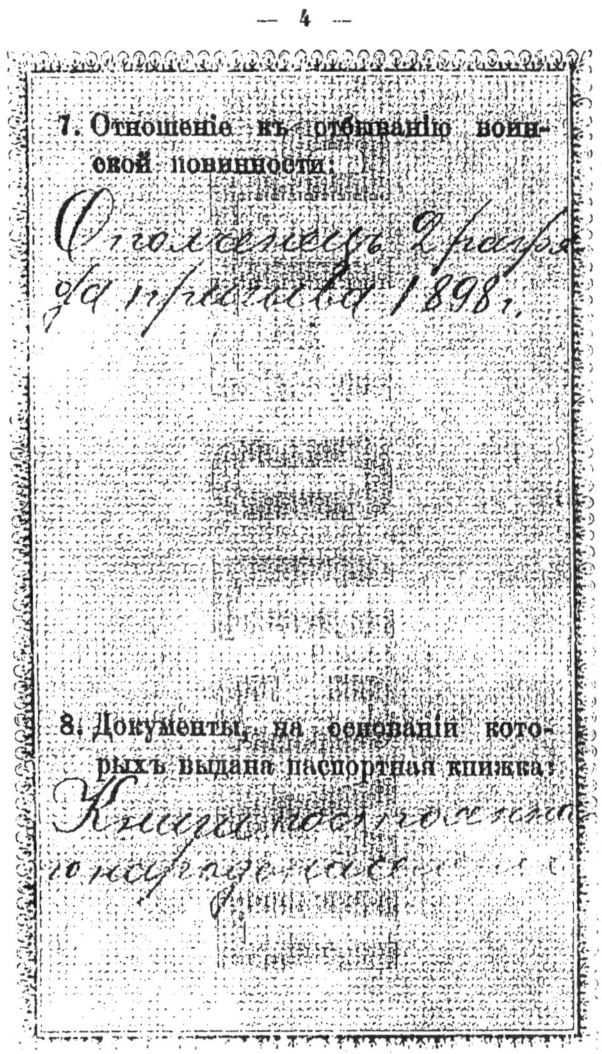

— 4 —

7. Отношеніе къ отбыванію воинской повинности:

Ополченецъ 2 разряда призыва 1898 г.

8. Документы, на основаніи которыхъ выдана паспортная книжка:

Книги постояннаго народонаселенія

Page 5 in this particular booklet was blank, but in other passports may list more documents providing information repeated in the passport.

Page 6 shows the following:

9. Подпись владѣльца книжки: *Bartłomi Fijałek* – "Signature of the bearer of this booklet: Bartłomi Fijałek." If he could not write, officials usually would write here *Неграмотный* or *неграмотенъ*, "illiterate."

Если владѣлецъ книжки неграмотенъ, то его примѣты – "If the bearer of this booklet is illiterate, then his description." In this case Fijałek could sign his name; but it was not rare for individuals to be illiterate, and thus a description may be given here.

Ростъ – "Height." Here you might see such terms as *малый,* "small"; *низкій,* "short"; *средній,* "medium"; and *высокій,* "tall."

Here is the information given on page 4:

7. Отношеніе къ отбыванію воинской повинности: *Ополченецъ 2 разряда призыва 1898 г.* – "Relationship to fulfillment of military service: Member of the Home Guard, second category, draft of 1898." An *ополченецъ* was one assigned to the *ополченіе,* militia or home guard. For more see the documents discussed on pages 292-316.

8. Документы, на основаніи которыхъ выдана паспортная книжка: *Книги постояннаго народонаселенія* – "Documents on the basis of which the passport booklet was issued: Permanent Population Registers."

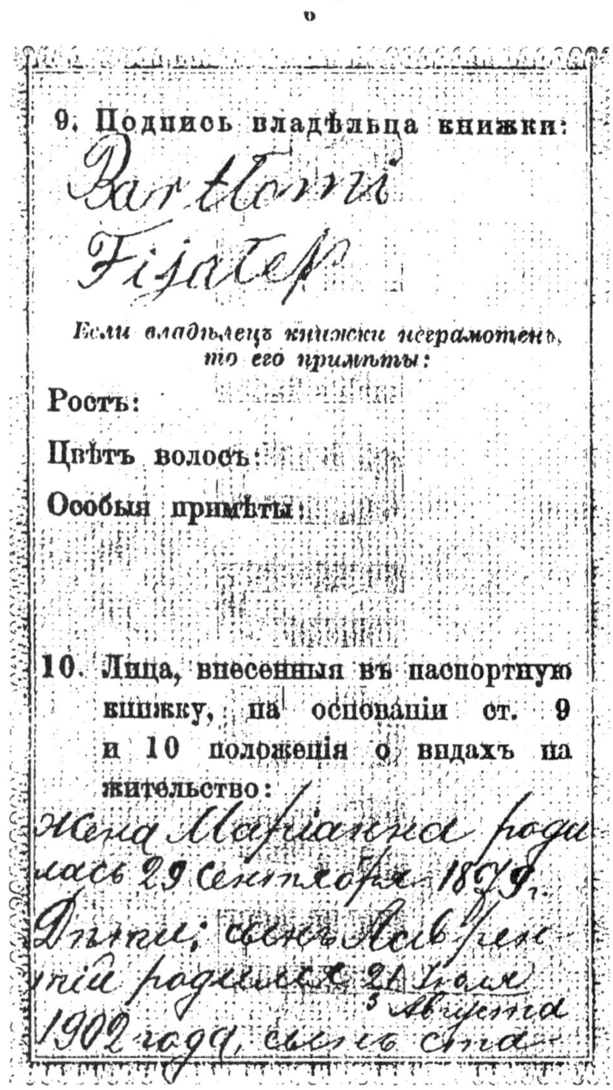

6

9. Подпись владѣльца книжки:

Bartłomi Fijałek

Если владѣлецъ книжки неграмотенъ, то его примѣты:

Ростъ:

Цвѣтъ волосъ:

Особыя примѣты:

10. Лица, внесенныя въ паспортную книжку, на основаніи ст. 9 и 10 положенія о видахъ на жительство:

Жена Марianna родилась 29 Сентября 1879 г.

Цвѣтъ волосъ – "Hair color." You might see here:

бѣлокурый – blond	*бѣлый* – white	*съ просѣдью* – graying
рыжий – red	*русый* – light brown	*светлый* – light
серый – grey	*темный* – dark	

Особыя примѣты – "Distinguishing marks."

— 7 —
1905 г. и сынъ
16/29 Августа

Item 10 fills the rest of page 6 and part of page 7, which is reproduced here:

10. Лица внесенныя въ паспортную книжку, на основанiи ст. 9 и 10 положенiя о видахъ на жительство: *Жена Марiанна родилась 29 Сентября 1879 г. Дѣти: сынъ Лаврентiй родился 21 Iюля / 5 Августа 1902 года, сынъ Станиславъ род. 9/22 Апрѣля 1905 г. и сынъ Iоаннъ род. 16/29 Августа 1907 г.* – "Persons entered into the passport booklet on the basis of statutes 9 and 10 of the regulation on identity papers: Wife Marianna was born 29 September 1879. Children: son Wawrzyniec was born 21 July/5 August 1902, son Stanisław was born the 9th/22nd of April 1905, and son Jan was born the 16th/29th of August 1907."

A couple of points here need clarification. The legalese about statute this and that obscures the simple import of this paragraph: it calls for listing the persons traveling with the passport bearer. As might be expected, his wife and children (*дѣти*) are listed here.

Note also that the official who filled out the passport Russified the childrens' Polish names. He could have simply spelled them phonetically by Cyrillic values—many officials did—and thus entered *Wawrzyniec* (the Polish version of "Lawrence," believe it or not!) as *Вавржинецъ*. Instead he converted it into the Russian version of Lawrence, *Лаврентiй*. Similarly, he changed Polish *Jan* into *Iоаннъ*, an Old Church Slavonic-based form (usually in Russian this name would be *Иванъ, Ivan*). *Stanisław* was not changed radically because it exists in almost exactly the same form in Russian, *Станиславъ*. You can see why it might be vital in researching this family to grasp this point: if you're looking for a Wawrzyniec Fijałek, you might sail right past this data and never recognize its significance!

Document VI-51: A Sample of the "Short-Form" Booklet Passport

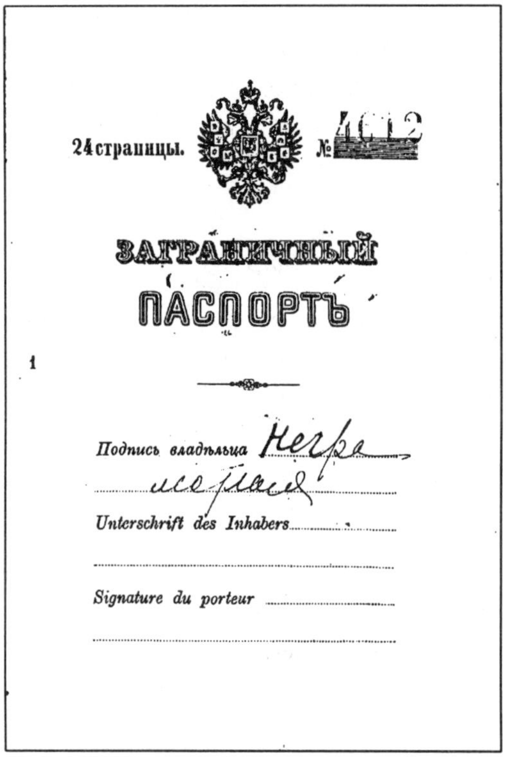
24 страницы. № 1612

ЗАГРАНИЧНЫЙ ПАСПОРТЪ

1

Подпись владѣльца Неграмотная

Unterschrift des Inhabers

Signature du porteur

As we said on page 342, there was a "short form" type of passport booklet that gave very basic data and was far less extensive than the "long form" version. Some of these were trilingual, in Russian, French, and German. Document VI-51 is an example; the first page appears at left:

24 страницы № 1612

ЗАГРАНИЧНЫЙ
ПАСПОРТЪ

Подпись владѣльца Неграмотная – "Signature of the bearer: Illiterate." The adjective *неграмотная* has the feminine ending *–ая* because the bearer in this case is a female.

Unterschrift des Inhabers, Signature du porteur — "Signature of the bearer" (in German and French)

Предъявитель сего

во свидѣтельство чего и для свободнаго

2

3

проѣзда данъ сей паспортъ съ приложеніемъ печати. Въ г. Гродне

Ноября 7 дня 191 года.

За Гродненскаго Губернатора

Вице-Губернаторъ

За Правителя Канцеляріи

The significant information on Page 2 is contained in this paragraph:

Предъявитель сего Скидельская мѣщанка Либа Роха Аронова-Шимелева Виницкая 30 лѣтъ съ дѣтьми: Машкою, 7 л. и Симою 6 л. отправляется за границу." – "The bearer of this [document], the middle-class woman of Skidel, Liba Rokha Vinitskaia, daughter of Aron-Shimel, age 30, with children Mashka, age 7, and Sima, age 6, is headed abroad."

This is followed by stamped information that is virtually illegible (except for the handwritten word *пятнадцать*, "fifteen").

At the bottom of page 2, and continuing onto page 3, is this information:

Во свидѣтельство чего и для свобонаго проѣзда данъ сей паспортъ съ приложеніемъ печати. Въ г. Гроднѣ, Ноября 7 дня 1912 года. – "In certification whereof and for free passage this passport is issued, stamped with the seal. In the town of Grodno, November 7, 1912."

This is signed *За Гродненскаго Губернатора, Вице-Губернаторъ*, "For the Governor of Grodno province, the Vice-Governor, *[signature illegible]*," and *За Правителя Канцеляріи*, "For the Directory of the Chancellory, *[signature illegible]*."

Pages 4 and 5 of this booklet are interesting in that they repeat the same information just given, but in German (on page 4) and French (page 5). There is no need to analyze or translate them here, but if you encounter a booklet of this sort, these pages can be very helpful. Any information that is difficult to make out in Russian can be compared with the same information in German and French, which should be a lot easier to decipher.

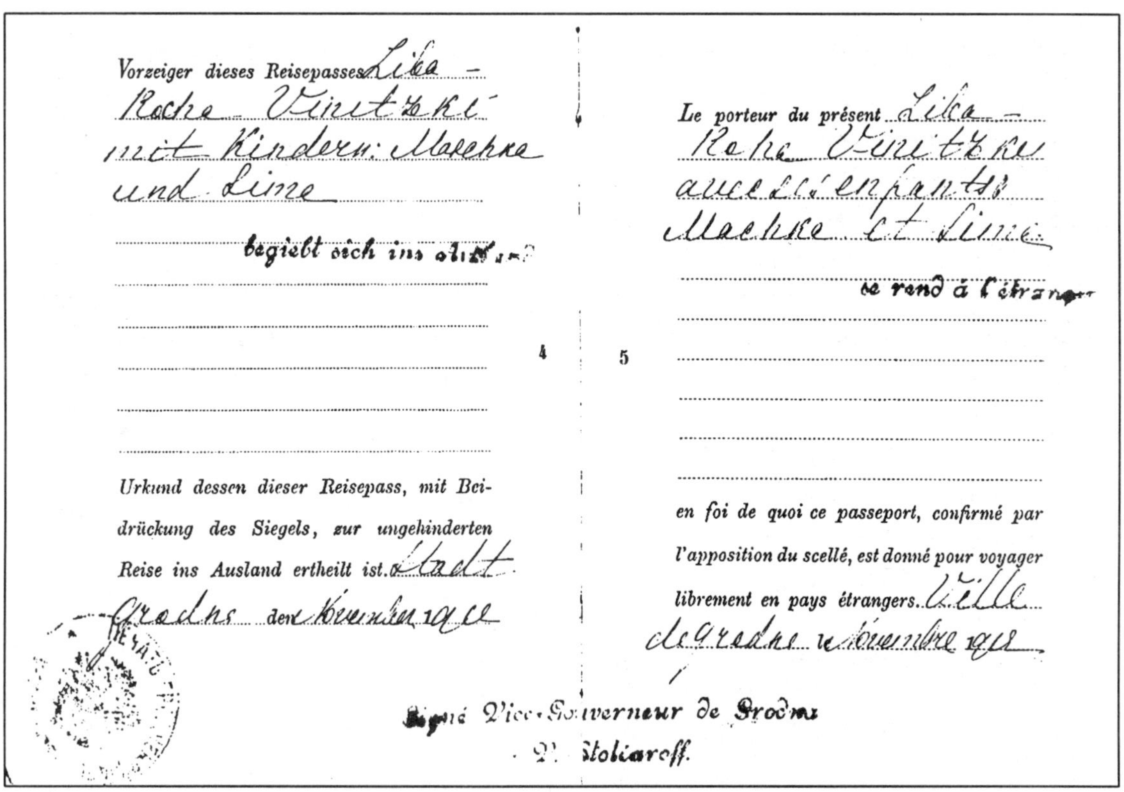
Vorzeiger dieses Reisepasses Liba – Roche Vinitzki mit Kindern: Maschke und Sime

begiebt sich ins Ausland

Urkund dessen dieser Reisepass, mit Beidrückung des Siegels, zur ungehinderten Reise ins Ausland ertheilt ist. Stadt Grodno den [illegible]

4

5

Le porteur du présent Liba – Roche Vinitzki avec ses enfants Maschke et Sime

se rend à l'étranger

en foi de quoi ce passeport, confirmé par l'apposition du scellé, est donné pour voyager librement en pays étrangers. Ville de Grodno [illegible]

Signé Vice-Gouverneur de Grodno

[illegible] Stoliaroff.

Document VI-52: A Single-Sheet Russian Passport

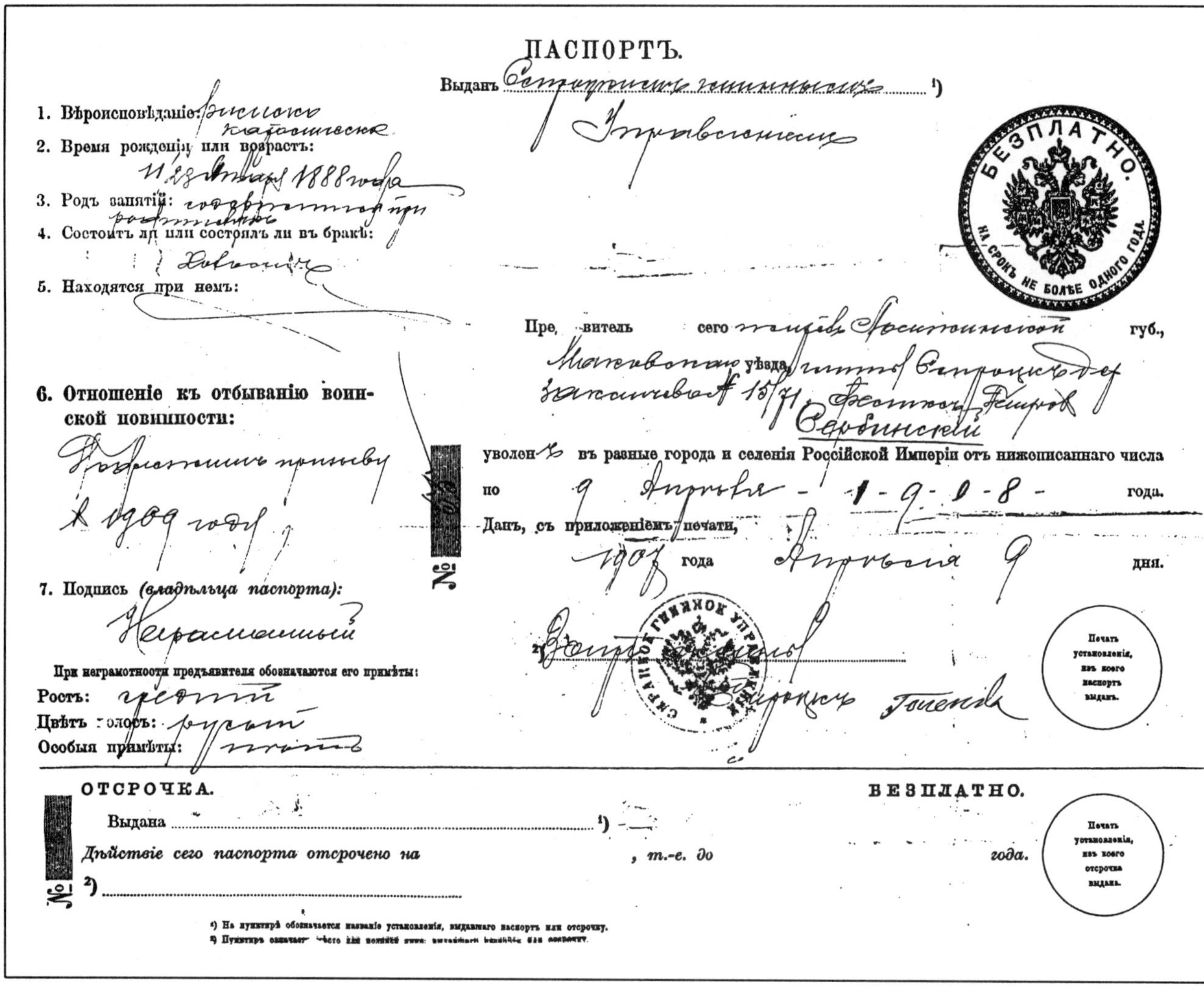

ПАСПОРТЪ.

Выданъ ¹)

1. Вѣроисповѣданіе:
2. Время рожденія или возрастъ:
3. Родъ занятій:
4. Состоитъ ли или состоялъ ли въ бракѣ:
5. Находятся при немъ:
6. Отношеніе къ отбыванію воинской повинности:
7. Подпись *(владѣльца паспорта):*

При неграмотности предъявителя обозначаются его примѣты:

Ростъ:

Цвѣтъ волосъ:

Особыя примѣты:

БЕЗПЛАТНО. НА СРОКЪ НЕ БОЛѢЕ ОДНОГО ГОДА.

Предъявитель сего губ., уѣзда,

уволенъ въ разные города и селенія Россійской Имперіи отъ нижеписаннаго числа

по года.

Данъ, съ приложеніемъ печати,

года дня.

Печать установленія, изъ коего паспортъ выданъ.

ОТСРОЧКА.

Выдана ¹)

Дѣйствіе сего паспорта отсрочено на , т.-е. до года.

²)

БЕЗПЛАТНО.

Печать установленія, изъ коего отсрочка выдана.

¹) На пунктирѣ обозначается названіе установленія, выдавшаго паспортъ или отсрочку.

Reproduced above is an example of a single-sheet passport used for travel within the Empire. The lines at the top of the sheet read: ПАСПОРТЪ Выданъ *Смроцкимъ гминнымъ Управленіемъ* – "Passport issued by the Administration of Smrock District." Below and to the right is the stamp showing the fee for this kind of document, in this case Безплатно, "no fee," and its validity на срокъ не болѣе одного года, "for a term of no more than one year."

Left Column:

1. Вѣроисповѣданіе: *римско католическое* –"Religion: Roman Catholic" (see pp. 331 and 343 for other answers)
2. Время рожденія или возрастъ: *11/23 Января 1888 года* – "Date of birth or age: 11/23 January 1888"
3. Родъ занятій: *содержится при родителяхъ* – "Occupation: lives with his parents."
4. Состоитъ ли или состоялъ ли въ бракѣ: *Холостъ* – "Is he or has he been married: Single." If he were married the answer would generally be either *Состоитъ,* "he is [married]," or *Женатъ,* "married."
5. Находятся при немъ – "Accompanied by [literally, "are found with him]."

6. Отношеніе къ отбыванію воинской повинности: *Подлежитъ призыву въ 1909 году* – "Relationship as to fulfillment of military service: Subject to 1909 draft."
7. Подпись (владѣльца паспорта): *Неграмотный* – "Signature (of passport bearer: Illiterate."

При неграмотности предъявителя обозначаются его примѣты – "In the event of the bearer's illiteracy, his description is to be given."

Ростъ: *средній* – "Height: medium"

Цвѣтъ волосъ: *русый* – "Color of hair: light brown"

Особыя примѣты: *нѣтъ* – "Distinguishing marks: none"

If the bearer had been able to write his name, his signature would have appeared above. Since he could not, a description is given instead. Compare item 9 on page 344. In fact, it's a good idea to contrast the contents of this sheet with that of Document VI-50, as this is just a condensed version of booklet-style passports and uses similar phrases.

Right Column (beginning just below the Безплатно stamp):

Предъявитель сего *житель Ломжинской* губ., *Маковскаго* уѣзда *гмины Смроцкъ дер. Закличево No. 15/74 Феликсъ Петровъ Сербинскій* – "The bearer of this [document], a resident of Łomża province, Maków county, Smrock district, village of Zakliczewo, No. 15/74, Feliks Sierbiński, son of Piotr …."

уволенъ въ разные города и селенія Россійской Имперіи отъ нижеписаннаго числа – "is free [to travel] into the various cities and villages of the Russian Empire as of the date written below … "

по *9 Апрѣля 1908* года – "up to 9 April 1908."

Данъ, съ приложеніемъ печати, *1907* года *Апрѣля 9* дня. – "Issued, with seal affixed, April 9, 1907." Often you see the year spelled out here in words as well as in numbers.

Войтъ Гмины Смороцкъ [illegible] – "Smrock District Administrator [?]. Different authorities could issue these passports; in a rural area, as here, the *wójt* in charge of the *gmina* would normally be the one whose signature appears. Another example we have seen was issued by the *Ровенскій Мѣщанъ Управа,* "Rovno Council of Townsmen"; it was signed by the *Предсѣдатель Управы,* "Council President," and a *Членъ Управы,* "Council member." Obviously that sort of document would only be issued in a town.

At the bottom of the page space is provided for information on any delay or deferment in the time when this document would take effect:

ОТСРОЧКА. Выдана _ 1)_. *Дѣйствіе сего паспорта отсрочена на _, т. е. до _.* 2. _ — "Deferment. Issued _ 1) _. The taking effect of this passport is deferred for _, that is, until _.2. _ ."

No deferment was involved here, so this is all left blank.

The two circular spaces at lower right are for the seal or stamp of the institutions issuing the passport (the upper of the two) and the deferment (the lower one).

Document VI-53: Another Example of a Single-Sheet Russian Passport

Document VI-53, at right, is a variation on the same theme.

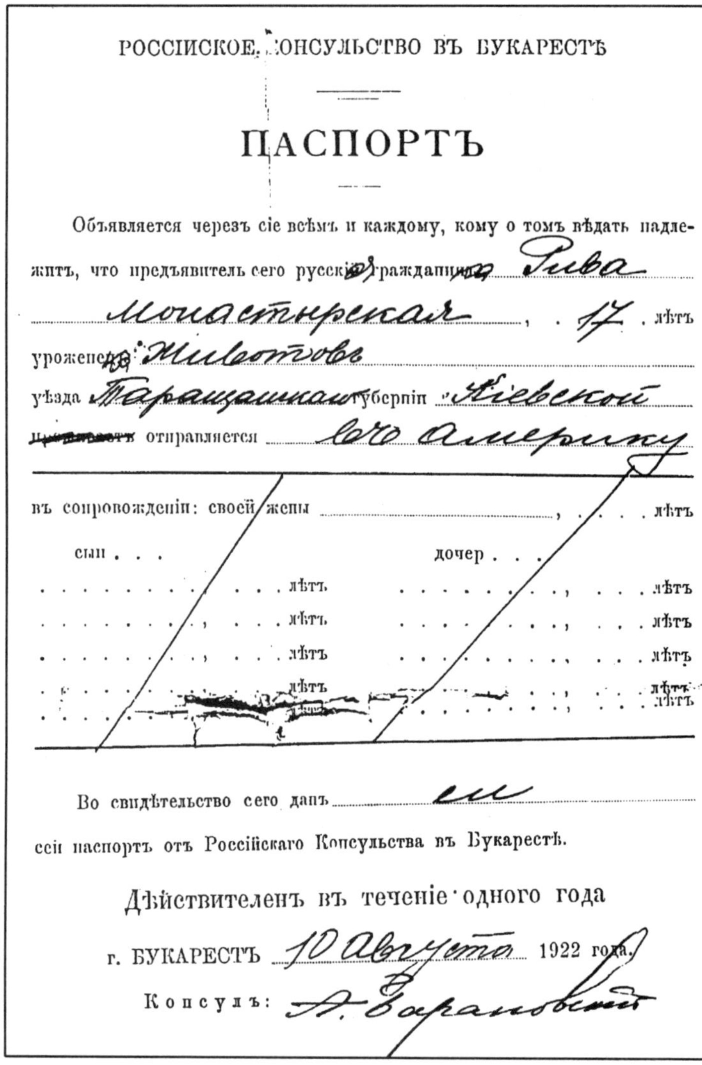

РОССИСКОЕ КОНСУЛЬСТВО ВЪ БУКАРЕСТѢ

ПАСПОРТЪ

Объявляется черезъ сіе всѣмъ и каждому, кому о томъ вѣдать надлежитъ, что предъявитель сего русская гражданка Рива Монастырская, 17 лѣтъ

уроженка Животовъ

уѣзда Таращанскаго губерніи Кіевской

отправляется въ Америку

въ сопровожденіи: своей жены ..., ... лѣтъ

сын ... дочер ...

... лѣтъ ... лѣтъ

... лѣтъ ... лѣтъ

... лѣтъ ... лѣтъ

... лѣтъ ... лѣтъ

Во свидѣтельство сего данъ ей

сей паспортъ отъ Россійскаго Консульства въ Букарестѣ.

Дѣйствителенъ въ теченіе одного года

г. БУКАРЕСТЪ 10 Августа 1922 года.

Консулъ: А. Барановскій

РОССІЙСКОЕ КОНСУЛЬСТВО ВЪ БУКАРЕСТѢ – "Russian Consulate in Bucharest"

Объявляется черезъ сіе всѣмъ и каждому, кому о томъ вѣдать надлежатъ – " It is announced hereby to any and all who need to know of this ..." This phrase is used much as we say "To whom it may concern" in English.

что предъявитель сего русск*ая* граждан*ка* *Рива Монастырская, 17* лѣтъ урожен*ка* *Животовъ* уѣзда *Таращанскаго* губерніи *Кіевской* – "that the bearer of this, Russian citizen Riva Monastyrskaya, age 17, a native of Zhivotov, district of Tarashcha, province of Kiev ..." Note that the form was printed up in the expectation that the bearers would normally be males. The official who filled this out crossed out the masculine endings on the words *русскій* (Russian), *гражданинъ* (citizen) and *уроженецъ* (native) and replaced them with the applicable feminine endings, thus: *русская*, *гражданка*, and *уроженка*.

отправляется *въ Америку* – "is leaving for America ..."

въ сопровожденіи: своей жены_, _ лѣтъ – "in the company of [accompanied by] his wife _, age _." Space is also left for filling in the names and ages of any son or daughter who might be going with the bearer. Note that the words сын... and дочер... lack grammatical endings. Here again, the official filling out the paperwork was supposed to write in the appropriate endings.

Во свидѣтельство сего данъ *ей* сей паспортъ отъ Россійскаго Консульства въ Букарестѣ – "In certification of which this passport was given *her* by the Russian Consulate in Bucharest."

Дѣйствителенъ въ теченіе одного года – "Valid for the course of one year."

г. Букарестъ *10 Августа* 1922 года – "city of Bucharest, 10 August 1922."

Консулъ: *А. Барановскій*. "Consul: A. Baranovskiy."

Document VI-54: A 28-Day Identification Document

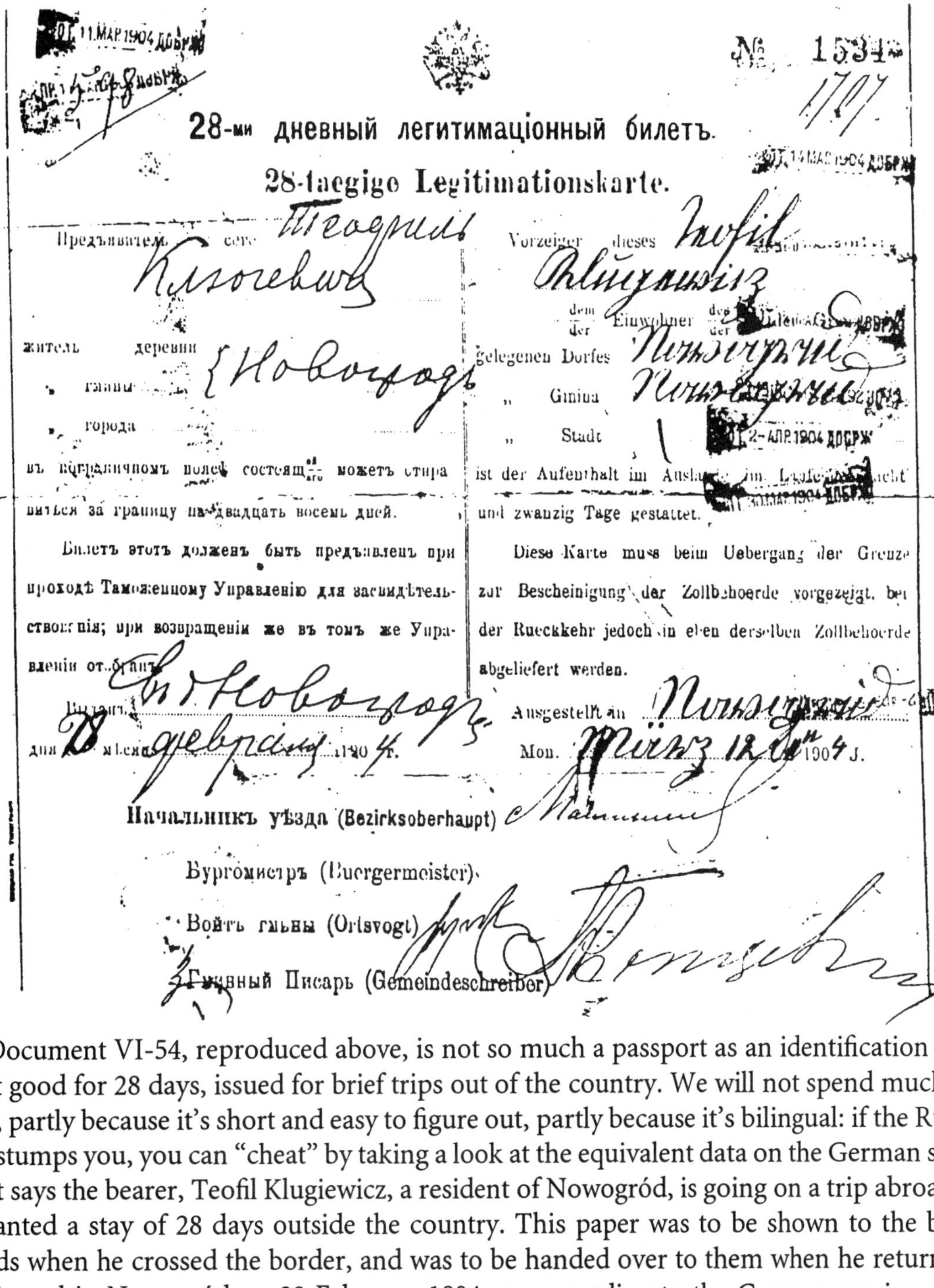

№ 1534

1707

28-ми дневный легитимаціонный билетъ.

28-taegige Legitimationskarte.

Предъявитель сего Теофилъ Клюгевичъ житель деревни, гмины, города Новогродъ въ пограничномъ полосѣ состоящ... можетъ отправиться за границу на двадцать восемь дней.

Билетъ этотъ долженъ быть предъявленъ при проходѣ Таможенному Управленію для засвидѣтельствованія; при возвращеніи же въ томъ же Управленіи отданъ.

Выданъ въ Новогродѣ дня 28 мѣсяца февраля 1904 г.

Vorzeiger dieses Teofil Klugiewicz dem/der Einwohner des/der gelegenen Dorfes, Gmina, Stadt ist der Aufenthalt im Auslande im Laufe acht und zwanzig Tage gestattet.

Diese Karte muss beim Uebergang der Grenze zur Bescheinigung der Zollbehoerde vorgezeigt, bei der Rueckkehr jedoch in eben derselben Zollbehoerde abgeliefert werden.

Ausgestellt in ... Mon. März 12 1904 J.

Начальникъ уѣзда (Bezirksoberhaupt)

Бургомистръ (Buergermeister)

Войтъ гмины (Ortsvogt)

Гминный Писарь (Gemeindeschreiber)

Document VI-54, reproduced above, is not so much a passport as an identification document good for 28 days, issued for brief trips out of the country. We will not spend much time on it, partly because it's short and easy to figure out, partly because it's bilingual: if the Russian part stumps you, you can "cheat" by taking a look at the equivalent data on the German side.

It says the bearer, Teofil Klugiewicz, a resident of Nowogród, is going on a trip abroad and is granted a stay of 28 days outside the country. This paper was to be shown to the border guards when he crossed the border, and was to be handed over to them when he returned. It was issued in Nowogród on 28 February 1904, or, according to the German version, on 12 March 1904. (Why the difference? If you don't know by now, here's a clue: look at page 200).

The document was to be signed by the Начальникъ уѣзда, County Administrator; or the Бургомистръ, Mayor; or the Войтъ гмины (District Administrator) and the Гминный Писарь, District Clerk. Which officials signed it would depend on whether you applied for it in a town, the *уѣздъ* administration offices, or the office of the local *гмина*.

Губ. Петроковская.—Уѣздъ Лодзинскій.

Управа Старшинъ ремесленнаго цеховаго общества Пекарей въ гор. Лодзи.

На основаніи 49 Ст. постановленія б. Намѣстника въ Царствѣ Польскомъ отъ 31 Декабря 1816 г. (Дн. Зак. т. 4) выдаетъ настоящій аттестатъ приписанному къ ремесленному цеховому обществу Пекарей въ Гор. Лодзи въ качествѣ ученика, постоянному жителю Гмины Малянов Губерніи Калиской 19 лѣтъ въ томъ, что на засѣданіи Старшинъ, состоявшемся 28/11 Іюня Іюля 1900 г послѣ производства испытанія, онъ Болеславъ Дзиковскій оказалъ знаніе Пекарскаго ремесла и потому произведенъ въ подмастерья сего ремесла.

Гор. Лодзь Іюня Іюля 28/12 дня 1900 года.

Старшина.
Станиславъ Виднер

Подстаршина.
Рудольфъ Шилле

Цеховой Ассесоръ.

Assessor cech.

Document VI-55: A Guild Membership Certificate

10. Document VI-55: A Guild Membership Certificate

The document reproduced on page 352 is from a large, ornate certificate in Russian and Polish; the Russian section is shown here. It was issued by the Управленіе Старшинъ Общества *Подмастеровъ пекарей* Города *Лодзи*, Office of Elders of the Assembly of Bakers' Apprentices of the City of Łódź, Poland. While not bristling with genealogical information, it is fascinating in its own right; if you find such a certificate in your family papers, you'd want to know what it is! And it just might give you clues that would prove helpful in your research, by telling you where an ancestor was registered as a member. (The Polish part of this certificate appeared as Document VI-42 in the Polish volume of *In Their Words.*

Губ. Петроковская – Уѣздъ Лодзинскій. – "Province of Piotrków. County of Łódź."

Управа Старшинъ ремесленнаго цеховаго общества Пекарей въ гор. Лодзи – "The Council of Elders of the Craft Guild Assembly of Bakers of the city of Łódź"

На основаніи 49 ст. постановленія б. Намѣстника въ Царствѣ Польскомъ отъ 31 Декабря 1816 г. (Дн. Зак. т. 4) – "on the basis of article 49 of the ruling of the former Viceroy in the Kingdom of Poland from 31 December 1816 (*Dn. Zak.*, Vol. 4)." *Дн. Зак.* is presumably an abbreviation of *Дневникъ законовъ* (Journal of Laws) or some similar title of a publication containing legal rulings. There was such a publication, called *Dziennik Praw* in Polish, issued from 1807 to 1871 and containing laws for the Kingdom of Poland; context suggests that might be what this refers to.

выдаетъ настоящій аттестатъ приписанному къ ремесленному цеховому обществу Пекарей въ Гор. Лодзи въ качествѣ ученика – "this certificate is issued to the one entered into the trade guild assembly of bakers in the town of Łódź in the capacity of apprentice..." The one **to whom** the certificate is issued will be named later.

постоянному жителю Гмины Маляновъ Губерніи Калиской 19 лѣтъ въ томъ – "permanent resident of the district of Malanów, Province of Kalisz, age 19, to this effect"

что на засѣданіи Старшинъ, состоявшемся 28/11 Іюня/Іюля 1900 г. – "that at the meeting of the Elders that took place on 28 June / 11 July 1900"

послѣ производства испытанія, онъ Болеславъ Дзиковскій оказалъ знаніе Пекарскаго ремесла и потому произведенъ въ ***подмастерья*** *сего ремесла* – "after being tested, he, Bolesław Dzikowski, demonstrated his knowledge of the baker's craft and for this reason has been promoted to apprentice of the craft."

Гор. Лодзь Іюня / Іюля 29/12 дня 1900 года – "City of Łódź, June / July 29 / 12 1900."

Старшина: Станиславъ Виднеръ – "Elder: Stanisław Widner"

Цеховой Ассесоръ Архиваріусъ Магистрата г. Лодзи [illegible]: "Guild Assessor, Archivist of the Magistracy of the city of Łódź" [illegible]

Подстаршина: Рудольфъ Шиле – "Assistant Elder: Rudolf Schiele" [This spelling is taken from his signature in Roman-alphabet characters on the Polish half of the certificate, of which a portion is visible to the right of the Russian section. The name and spelling *Schiele* are German, which is not unusual; Germans tended to be well represented in guilds and professional organizations, both in Poland and Russia.]

№ 3061

СВИДѢТЕЛЬСТВО.

По указу **ЕГО ИМПЕРАТОРСКАГО ВЕЛИЧЕСТВА**, дано сіе изъ Департамента Герольдіи Правительствующаго Сената Іосифу Михайловичу Божичко, родившемуся десятаго Сентября тысяча восемьсотъ девяностаго года, въ томъ, что опредѣленіемъ Правительствующаго Сената 19 Октября 1906 года онъ признанъ въ потомственномъ дворянскомъ достоинствѣ, съ правомъ на внесеніе въ дворянскую родословную книгу въ шестую часть оной. Установленныя пошлины за свидѣтельство представлены.

С.-Петербургъ, Ноября „20„ дня 1906 года.

Герольдмейстеръ

Ис. об. Оберъ-Секретаря

Помощникъ Оберъ-Секретаря

Document VI-56: A Certificate of Nobility

11. Document VI-56: A Certificate of Nobility

Reproduced on page 354 is a **Свидѣтельство** [certificate] stating that an individual has demonstrated his descent from nobility to the satisfaction of the Russian Empire's Department of Heraldry. Only a comparatively small percentage of people living under Russian rule were noble, of course. Still, the numbers were larger in Poland, Lithuania, Belarus and Ukraine than for most western European countries; so odds are good that at some point in your family tree you'll find a connection to nobility. In fact, as you trace your ancestry back farther and farther, it becomes a virtual certainty a noble will show up somewhere. This can be great news because records on nobility tend to be more plentiful, and go back farther, than those for commoners. So if you find a certificate of this sort in old family papers, the information it contains could be a great help in your research.

It's fairly short and to the point:

По указу ЕГО ИМПЕРАТОРСКАГО ВЕЛИЧЕСТВА, дано сіе изъ Департамента Герольдіи Правительствующаго Сената – "By decree of His Imperial Majesty, this [certificate] is issued from the Department of the Herald of the Ruling Senate ..." There are several terms here you will see often in Russian official documents:

указ – "order, decree"; this term produced the English word "ukase," defined as "a proclamation of a Czar having the force of law in imperial Russia."

Его Императорское Величество – "His Imperial Majesty"

Департаментъ Герольдіи – "Department of Heraldry." The term *департаментъ*, from French *département*, often appears as the name of a branch of the government. The Department of Heraldry was charged with oversight of matters concerning the nobility, including the determination of who did and did not have a right to be considered noble.

Правительствующій Сенатъ – "the Ruling Senate." While the Czar's autocratic power was absolute, many official documents were issued by branches of the Ruling Senate, which in turn carried out the Czar's edicts.

Іосифу Михайлову Божичко, родившемуся десятаго Сентября тысяча восемьсотъ девяностаго года – "To Józef Bożyczko, son of Michał, born 10 September 1890 ..."

въ томъ, что опредѣленіемъ Правительствующаго Сената 19 Октября 1906 года онъ пРзинанъ въ потомственномъ дворянскомъ достоинствѣ – "to the effect that by a determination of the Ruling Senate on 19 October 1906 he is recognized in his hereditary noble rank ..."

съ правомъ на внесеніе въ дворянскую родословную книгу въ шестую часть оной – "with the right to be entered into the genealogical register of the nobility in its sixth section."

Установленныя пошлины за свидѣтельство представлены – "The established fees for this certificate have been presented."

С.-Петербургъ, Ноября 20 дня 1906 года – "St. Petersburg, November 20, 1906."

Герольдмейстеръ – "Master Herald" *[signature illegible]*

Оберъ-Секретарь – "Chief Secretary"

Помощникъ Оберъ-Секретаря – "Assistant to the Chief Secretary"

12. Document VI-57: A Personal Letter

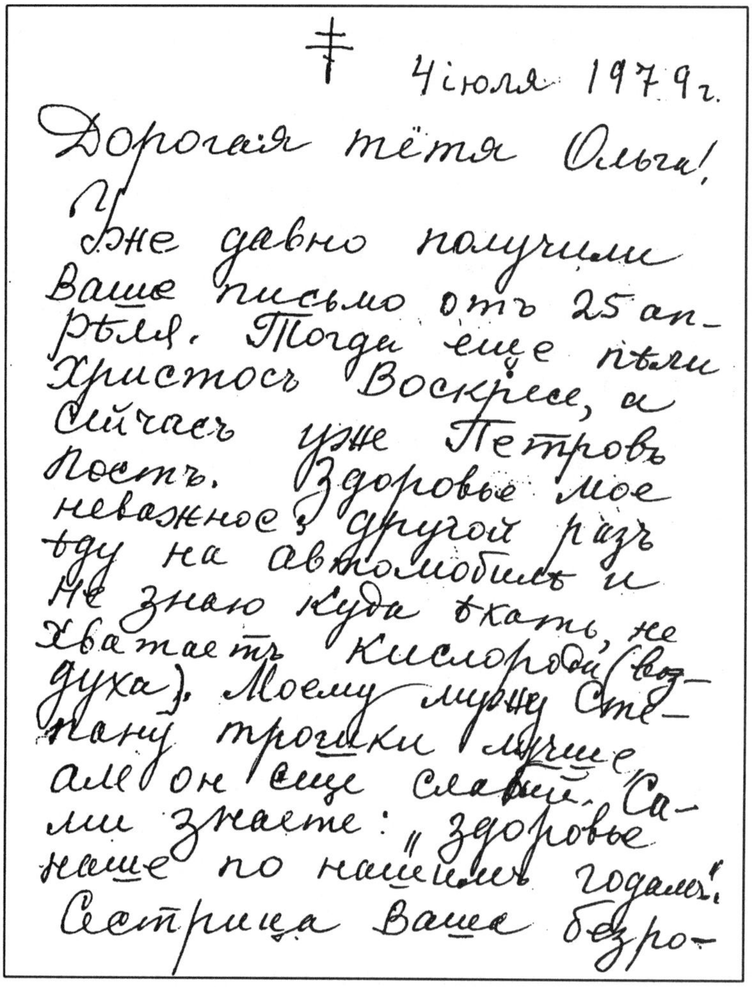
† 4 іюля 1979 г.
Дорогая тётя Ольга!
Уже давно получили
Ваше письмо отъ 25 ап-
рѣля. Тогда еще пѣли
Христосъ Воскресе, а
Сейчасъ уже Петровъ
Постъ. Здоровье мое
неважное: другой разъ
ѣду на автомобилѣ и
Не знаю куда ѣхать, не
хватаетъ кислороду (воз-
духа). Моему мужу Сте-
пану трошки лучше,
але он еще слабый. Са-
ми знаете: „здоровье
наше по нашимъ годамъ".
Сестрица Ваша безро-

Reproduced at left is a page from one of the most frustrating family papers we deal with: personal letters! At times they are wholly devoid of genealogical information, and yet sometimes they are virtual treasure troves. It is very difficult for someone not fluent in a language to make sense of such letters, but in case you wish to try, here are a few things worth keeping in mind as you deal with them.

Firstly, in the earlier decades of the 20th century, the world's population did not possess formal education to the extent we take for granted today. Many of our ancestors had at most basic and rudimentary writing skills. The letters they wrote tend to contain numerous dialect expressions, archaic terms, and obscure references to events and things with which we have little or no familiarity.

What's more, the orthography and grammar frequently deviate from the standard proscriptive grammar of the language. The spelling is often phonetic—if you know the language and pronounce the words out loud you can hear them and make allowances; but you will never find them in a dictionary spelled that way. Furthermore, letters written in the U. S. by European-born family members often contain English words that have been adapted to Russian phonetic spelling, e. g., *Мои чилдренята засиковали,* "My children have gotten sick." If you don't speak the language, you can't imagine how awful that sounds to someone used to "proper" Russian! But this "Ruslish" is quite typical of immigrants.

Since all letters are unique to themselves, it isn't possible to "teach" you how to read them; they are all different, and it's only the sameness of documents that lets you focus on the repetition and comprehend it by comparison. Plus you never know what surprises you'll find. The letter above, written in 1979, **still** uses the archaic pre-Revolution characters ***і*** and ***ѣ***!

If you do find an old letter with an address, chances are you won't be able to use the address. Your family may still be in the same place it has been in for hundreds of years, but to reach them you need to "modernize" the address by determining what province—or even what country!—it's in now. Some of the sources discussed in Chapter V may be able to assist you with this.

Some suggestions are:

1) Keep an eye open for dates and other standardized information that may be easy to spot. It does wonders for your morale just to find anything you recognize—it helps you feel the task before you may not be hopeless, after all!

2) Try to write in advance the Cyrillic forms of names of persons and places you know may be mentioned. If you know an uncle was named Kirill and lived near Minsk, you can use the alphabet chart on page 1 to see that these names are spelled *Кирилл* and *Минск* in Russian, and that might help you recognize them.

3) Look for terms describing family relationships, such as *сестра,* "sister;" *тётя,* "aunt"; *сын,* "son"; and others seen on pages 51-52. Letters from relatives will most likely include such terms, perhaps along with personal names; if you can spot them, it might help you decipher some facts that will help you.

These tips might assist you. Still, unless you have enormous patience and a real gift for languages, you will probably find correspondence too difficult to decipher. If so, you will have little choice but to retain the services of a translator.

13. Other Documents

There are, of course, a great many other documents you may encounter. A book that attempted to include a sample of every possible document one might find in the territory of the Russian Empire would be even more huge and expensive than this one! We've tried to include the kinds of documents that our experience suggests you will need to deal with.

Of course, with any luck more and more records will become available to researchers. Many, such as telephone directories or lists of voters, require little more than familiarity with the Cyrillic alphabet and practice reading the handwriting. We hope this book has provided numerous opportunities for you to acquire both.

Other records are becoming available, but will be of little practical use until they are indexed. For instance, many researchers are interested in *Губернскiе Вѣдомости, Gubernskie Vedomosti,* governmental newspapers published in *gubernias* and *oblast's* all over the Russian Empire, primarily between 1838 and the Revolution. They contained governors' orders and regulations, information on taxes, and other official information. They also printed a wide range of other articles and information of a non-official nature. They are fascinating historical documents, and contain information potentially quite valuable for genealogical researchers.

The problem is that so far only certain ones have been indexed. Without an index, it would be enormously difficult to find information on given individuals. If you are interested in learning more, as of this writing, Norman Ross Publishing is the main source of *Vedomosti* in America, offering them on microfilm reels. This Website address has more information:

http://www.nross.com/slavic/slav16.htm

In any case, we believe and hope this book has offered you the chance to familiarize yourself with the alphabet, format, and basic terminology necessary to help you make sense of almost any Russian-language document you come across. We wish you the best of luck with your research!

VII. VOCABULARY

To put it briefly, what follows is a list of the terms you are most likely to see in records, with the meanings and in the forms you are most likely to encounter. Please note that **in many instances** these forms or meanings differ from standard modern usage. But we took them terms from actual documents we have seen, so whether they're "correct" or not is a moot point—they are the kind of thing you will actually run into! In fact, the less "correct" a spelling or usage is, the more reason it should be included here. Any dictionary can provide you with standard words and spellings; it's the archaic or unusual forms you'll need the most help with.

The basic format of each entry is illustrated by this sample:

① Австрия, Австрии ② *Австрия, Австрии* – ③ (n., fem., † *Австрія*) ④ Austria

These are: ① the nominative singular and genitive singular forms in standard type; ② the same forms in "italic" type; ③ the part of speech (noun, adjective, adverb, etc.), followed by gender if it's a noun, and then, if the pre-Revolutionary spelling was significantly different, the symbol † with that spelling; finally ④ the English translation. Thus this entry shows that Австрия is the nominative singular of this word, Австрии the genitive singular, and those forms look like *Австрия* and *Австрии* in italics and script; it's a feminine noun, spelled *Австрія* before the Communist Revolution; and it's equivalent to "Austria" in English. If the term can be used in more than one meaning, representative examples follow; but we tried not to stray too far from what you will actually see in records.

For a verb only the infinitive is given as item ①. If a particular conjugated form is especially likely to appear in your documents, or for some reason offers a challenge, it is mentioned as part of item ④. By the same token, only the standard nominative masculine singular form of adjectives is given in item ①, with short or archaic forms given as part of item ③. This may sound complicated, but we think you'll find it's pretty intuitive and will quickly grasp it.

We have given the forms in standard and italic type because both versions can be helpful. Either may appear in reference works and printed material; the italic forms are particularly useful because they closely resemble handwriting. We thought it would help you to have them available so you can compare them with any illegible word, whether in print or script, that may pop up in the documents you're trying to decipher.

We pondered long and hard over whether to give these words in their modern spellings or in the archaic ones used before the Revolution. As you can see from the sample documents, most sources you find will feature the archaic spellings, so those are perhaps the ones you will have to deal with most often. On the other hand, anything printed in Russian since the Revolution will feature modern spellings. That includes most grammars and dictionaries! So if you want to use any other reference work to supplement this one, the modern spellings are the ones you'll need, to find the words you're looking for.

That's why this list gives words first in modern spelling, with the symbol † to indicate archaic forms, and with cross-references under those forms. The changes are usually not too difficult to make sense of, so long as someone alerts you that the word in question was once spelled differently. Thus when a word ends with the letter **ъ**, you can usually just ignore that letter; for archaic **ѣ** substitute **е**, for **і** substitute modern **и**. For more on these changes, see pages 1-3. If you keep these few points in mind, archaic spellings should cause you no trouble.

One other spelling note: we indicate **ё** here when it occurs, because technically that's correct. But be advised that in most Russian-language material this letter is not distinguished from plain **е**. For researchers' purposes it's probably best to simply ignore the difference between **ё** and **е**; but we have indicated it, to aid those who wish to use this work as an aid to serious study of the Russian language.

In a list of this sort, it is vital to save space by abbreviating terms repeated constantly. Here are the abbreviations used in the vocabulary:

Symbols and Abbreviations

abbr. – abbreviation
acc. – accusative case
adj. – adjective
adv. – adverb, adverbial
cmp. – compare
conj. – conjunction
dat. – dative case
demonstr. – demonstrative
dim. – diminutive
e. g. – for example
fem. – feminine
gen. – genitive case
Germ. – German
i. e. – that is
imperf. – imperfective *
instr. – instrumental case
interr. – interrogative
Lith. – Lithuanian
masc. – masculine
mil. – military
n. – noun
neut. – neuter
nom. – nominative case
num. – numeral
p. – page
part. – participle
perf. – perfective *
pl. – plural
poss. – possessive
prep. – preposition *or* prepositional case
pron. – pronoun
q. v. – see which
refl. – reflexive
rel. – relative
sing. – singular
Ukr. – Ukrainian
v. – verb
† – archaic form
№ – number, No.
+ gen. – takes the genitive case
+ dat. – takes the dative case
+ acc. – takes the accusative case
+ instr. – takes the instrumental case
+ prep. – takes the prepositional case
↑ – see above
↓ – see below

*The whole subject of perfective and imperfective verbs is one that baffles many English-speakers. We've tried not to give it too much attention, as mastering this grammatical feature is not essential to the level of comprehension required for genealogical research. Let's say simply that in Russian (and in the Slavic languages in general) most verbs come in two forms that are similar, e. g., *подписывать* vs. *подписать*, *выдавать* vs. *выдать*, *получать* vs. *получить*. One is called the imperfective aspect, the other the perfective aspect; in the samples just given, the first of each pair is imperfective, the second its perfective counterpart. In some instances there is a perfective with no imperfective counterpart, or vice versa. In others the two forms are quite different, but perceived as related; thus *брать* is the imperfective of the verb meaning "to take," whereas *взять* is regarded as the perfective.

These verb pairs mean more or less the same thing, but the imperfective implies that the action was ongoing or continual in nature; the perfective implies that it was done, once, and over with. This explanation is greatly oversimplified, but that is the essential difference.

If you are not prepared to invest a lot of effort into studying this matter at length, that's about all you need to know. Of course to achieve any degree of fluency in Russian, you must master this feature of the language. But in the context of genealogical records the distinction is seldom important enough to require your attention. We mention it only because you might notice that some verbs seem to have two forms that mean the same thing, and that might confuse you. We hope this brief explanation will satisfy your curiosity without distracting you needlessly.

A LIST OF TERMS ENCOUNTERED FREQUENTLY IN RECORDS

а *а* – (conj.) and

Ав, Ава *Ав, Ава* – (n., masc.) Av, the name of a month in the Jewish calendar (see page 47)

август, августа *август, августа* – (n., masc.) August

Августовъ, Августова *Августовъ, Августова* – (n., masc., also *Аугустовъ*) town of Augustów, Poland (see page 120); *августовский* – (also you may see † *аугустовскій*) of Augustów

Австрия, Австрии *Австрия, Австрии* – (n., fem., † *Австрія*) Austria

агроном, агронома *агроном, агронома* – (n., masc.) agriculturist, farmer

Адар, Адара *Адар, Адара* – (n., masc.) Adar, a month in the Jewish calendar (see page 47)

административный *административный* – (adj.) administrative

администратор, администратора *администратор, администратора* – (n., masc.) administrator; *администра-тор прихода X* –pastor of parish X

адрес, адреса *адрес, адреса* – (n., masc.) address; *по слѣдующему адресу* – to the following address

адъютант, адъютанта *адъютант, адъютанта* – (n., fem.) aide-de-camp, adjutant

азбука, азбуки *азбука, азбуки* – (n., fem.) alphabet

азбучный *азбучный* – (adj.) alphabetical

Азия, Азии *Азия, Азии* – (n., fem., † *Азія*) Asia

Азовское море, Азовского моря *Азовское море, Азовского моря* – (n., neut.) Sea of Azov

† Аккерман, Аккермана *Аккерман, Аккермана* – (n., masc.) town now called Bilhorod-Dnistrovs'kyi, Ukraine (see page 132); *аккерманскій* – (adj.) of Akkerman

акт, акта *акт, акта* – (n., masc.) act; document; (pl.) *акты, актов* – records (papers)

актовый *актовый* – (adj.) of records; *актовая бумага* – stamped paper (valid for official documents)

акушёр, акушёра *акушёр, акушёра* – (n., masc.) accoucheur, male midwife

акушерка, акушерки *акушерка, акушерки* – (n., fem.) midwife

Александрия, Александрии *Александрія, Александріи* – (n., fem., † *Александрія*) Russian name of the town of Oleksandriya, Ukraine (see page 133); *александрийский* – (adj.) of Aleksandriya/Oleksandriya

Александровск, Александровска *Александровск, Александровска* – (n., masc.) Russian name of the Ukrainian town now called Zaporizhzhya (see page 134); *александровский* – (adj.) of Aleksandrovsk/ Zaporizhzhya

† Алешки, Алешек *Алешки, Алешек* – (n., pl.) Russian name of Tsyurupins'k, Ukraine (see page 134)

алмазник, алмазника *алмазник, алмазника* – (n., masc.) jeweler

алмазчик, алмазчика *алмазчик, алмазчика* – (n., masc.) diamond-cutter, lapidary

алфавит, алфавита *алфавит, алфавита* – (n., masc.) alphabet; alphabetical list

алфавитный *алфавитный* – (adj.) alphabetical

альфабетычный *альфабетычный* – (adj.) a Polonism, obviously a phonetic rendering of Polish *alfabetyczny;* standard Russian would be *алфавитный* or *азбучный*

амбарщик, амбарщика *амбарщик, амбарщика* – (n., masc.) warehouseman

Америка, Америки *Америка, Америки* – (n., fem.) America

Ананьев, Ананьева *Ананьев, Ананьева* – (n., masc.) town of Ananiv, Ukraine (see page 133); *ананьевский* – (adj.) of Anan'ev/Ananiv

ангина, ангины *ангина, ангины* – (n., fem.) quinsy, angina

англичанин, англичанина *англичанин, англичанина* – (n., masc., nom. pl. *англичане*, gen. pl. *англичан*) Englishman (fem. *англичанка*)

Англия, Англии *Англия, Англии* – (n., fem., † *Англія*) England

† Андреевъ, Андреева *Андреевъ, Андреева* – (n., masc.) town of Jędrzejów, Poland (see page 120); *андреевскій* – of Jędrzejów

аневризма, аневризмы *аневризма, аневризмы* – (n., fem.) aneurysm

антрепренёр, антрепренёра *антрепренёр, антрепренёра* – (n., masc.) manager of a theater

апрель, апреля *апрель, апреля* – (n., masc., † *апрѣль*) April

аптека, аптеки *аптека, аптеки* – (n., fem.) pharmacy

аптекарский *аптекарский* – (adj., † *аптекарскій*) pharmaceutical

аптекарь, аптекаря *аптекарь, аптекаря* – (n., masc.) apothecary, pharmacist (fem. *аптекарша*)

Аральское море, Аральского моря *Аральское море, Аральского моря* – (n., neut.) Aral Sea

армеец, армейца *армеец, армейца* – (n., masc.) soldier or officer in the line

Армения, Армении *Армения, Армении* – (n., fem., † *Арменія*) Armenia

армия, армии *армия, армии* – (n., fem., † *армія*) army

армянин, армянина *армянин, армянина* – (n., masc., nom. pl. *армяне*, gen. pl. *армян*) Armenian (fem. *армянка*)

армянский *армянский* – (adj., † *армянскій*) Armenian

артельщик, артельщика *артельщик, артельщика* – (n., masc.) member of an *artel*, a workmen's

association; caterer of a mess; servant at an Exchange-house or other public office
арфист, арфиста *арфист, арфиста* – (n., masc.) harpist (fem. *арфистка*)
Архангельск, Архангельска *Архангельск, Архангельска* – (n., masc.) Arkhangel'sk, name of a town in Russia; *архангельскій* – of Arkhangel'sk
археолог, археолога *археолог, археолога* – (n., masc.) archeologist
архив, архива *архив, архива* – (n., masc.) archive
архивариус, архивариуса *архивариус, архивариуса* – (n., masc., † *архиваріусъ*) archivist; also seen with the same meaning: † *архиварій* and modern *архивист*
† архидіаконъ, архидіакона *архидіаконъ, архидіакона* – (n., masc.) archdeacon
архиерей, архиерея *архиерей, архиерея* – (n., masc., † *архіерей*) prelate, bishop, higher church dignitary
архитектор, архитектора *архитектор, архитектора* – (n., masc.) architect
асессор, асессора *асессор, асессора* – (n., masc., † *ассессоръ*) assessor
Астрахань, Астрахани *Астрахань, Астрахани* – (n., fem.) Astrakhan', town and region in Russia (see page 135); *астраханский* – of Astrakhan'
атаман, атамана *атаман, атамана* – (n., masc.) chief, commander (especially of Cossacks, fem. *атаманша*)
атрофия, атрофии *атрофия, атрофии* – (n., fem., † *атрофія*) atrophy
аттестат, аттестата *аттестат, аттестата* – (n., masc.) certificate
Аугустовъ *Аугустовъ* → Августовъ *Августовъ*
Ахтырка, Ахтырки *Ахтырка, Ахтырки* – (n., fem.) town of Okhtyrka, Ukraine (see page 133); *ахтырский* – of Akhtyrka/Okhtyrka
б. *б.* → бывший *бывший*
бабушка, бабушки *бабушка, бабушки* – (n., fem.) grandmother
Балта, Балты *Балта, Балты* – (n., fem.) town of Balta, Ukraine (see page 132); *балтский* – (adj.) of Balta
Балтийское Море, Балтийского Моря *Балтийское Море, Балтийского Моря* – (n., neut., † *Балтійское Море*) Baltic Sea
бальзамировщик, бальзамировщика *бальзамировщик, бальзамировщика* – (n., masc.) embalmer
банкир, банкира *банкир, банкира* – (n., masc.) banker
барабанщик, барабанщика *барабанщик, барабанщика* – (n., masc.) drummer
Барановичи, Баранович *Барановичи, Баранович* – (n.) Baranavichy, Belarus' (see page 126); *барановичский* – (adj.) of Baranovichy/ Baranavichy
барочник, барочника *барочник, барочника* – (n., masc.) barge-man, master of a bark
барышник, барышника *барышник, барышника* – (n., masc.) jobber, forestaller (especially of horses)
баталёр, баталёра *баталёр, баталёра* – (n., masc.) [nautical] steward
батальон, батальона *батальон, батальона* – (n., masc.) battalion
батрак, батрака *батрак, батрака* – (n., masc.) journeyman, workman (among peasants)
батрачка, батрачки *батрачка, батрачки* – (n., fem.) hired workman [female]; journeyman's wife (also seen as *батрачиха*)
батырщик, батырщика *батырщик, батырщика* – (n., masc.) inker, printer
Бахмут, Бахмута *Бахмут, Бахмута* – (n., masc.) town now called Artemivs'k, Ukraine (see page 134); *бахмутский* – (adj.) of Bakhmut/ Artemivs'k
башмачник, башмачника *башмачник, башмачника* – (n., masc.) shoemaker (fem. *башмачница*)
без *без* – (prep. + gen.) without; *безъ жеребья* – without (drawing) lots
безвременный *безвременный* – (adj.) premature, untimely
бездельный *бездельный* – (adj., † *бездѣльный*) unemployed, idle
безземельный *безземельный* – (adj.) landless
безплатно *безплатно* – (adv.) free of charge, without payment
безсрочный *безсрочный* → бессрочный *бессрочный*
Белая Церковь, Белой Церкви *Белая Церковь, Белой Церкви* – (n., fem., † *Бѣлая Церковь*) town of Bila Tserkva, Ukraine (see page 134); *белоцерковскій* – (adj.) of Belaya Tserkov'/Bila Tserkva
Белград, Белграда *Белград, Белграда* – (n., masc., † *Бѣлградъ*) Belgrade
белильщик, белильщика *белильщик, белильщика* (n., masc., † *бѣлильщикъ*) bleacher, blancher, whitewasher
Белое море, Белого моря *Белое море, Белого моря* – (n., neut., † *Бѣлое море*) White Sea
белокурый *белокурый* – (adj., † *бѣлокурый*) light-haired, blond
Белорус, Белоруса *Белорус, Белоруса* – (n., masc., † *Бѣлорусъ*) Belarusian (fem., *белоруска*)
Белоруссия, Белоруссии *Белоруссия, Белоруссии* – (n., fem., † *Бѣлоруссія*) now called Беларусь, Belarus'
белорусский *белорусский* – (adj., † *бѣлорусскій*) Belarusian
Белосток, Белостока *Белосток, Белостока* – (n., masc., † *Бѣлостокъ*) Białystok (city in north-eastern Poland); † *бѣлостокскій* – of Białystok
белошвейка, белошвейки *белошвейка, белошвейки* (n., fem., † *бѣлошвейка*) seamstress

белый *белый* – (adj., † *бѣлый*) white
бельский *бельский* – (adj., † *бѣльскій*) referring to any of a number of towns and villages with names such as Biała, Bielsk, etc.
Бендеры *Бендеры* – (n.) Russian name of Tighina, Moldova (see page 132); *бендерский* – (adj.) of Bendery/Tighina
бергмейстер, бергмейстера *бергмейстер, бергмейстера* – (n., masc.) surveyor of mines
Бердичев, Бердичева *Бердичев, Бердичева* – (n., masc.) town of Berdychiv, Ukraine (see page 132); *бердичевский* – (adj.) of Berdychiv
Бердянск, Бердянска *Бердянск, Бердянска* – (n., masc.) town of Berdyans'k, Ukraine (see page 134); *бердянский* – (adj.) of Berdyansk
берег, берега *берег, берега* – (n., masc., nom. pl. *берега*, gen. pl. *берегов*) shore, [river] bank
Берестовица, Берестовицы *Берестовица, Берестовицы* – (n.) Russian name of the town of Berastavitsa, Belarus' (see page 126); *берестовицкий* – (adj.) of Berestovitsa/Berastavitsa
Бессарабия, Бессарабии *Бессарабия, Бессарабии* – (n., fem., † *Бессарабія*) Bessarabia (see page 132); *бессарабский* – (adj.) of Bessarabia
бессилие, бессилия *бессилие, бессилия* – (n., neut. † *бессиліе*) debility
бессрочный *бессрочный* – (adj., † *безсрочный*) termless, indefinite (i. e., without fixed expiration date), permanent
бечевщик, бечевщика *бечевщик, бечевщика* – (n., masc.) hauler, tower
библиотекарь, библиотекаря *библиотекарь, библиотекаря* – (n., masc., † *библіотекарь*) librarian
билет, билета *билет, билета* – (n., masc.) billet, card, note; *увольнительный билетъ* – discharge booklet, discharge papers; *отпускной билетъ* – furlough
биржевик, биржевика *биржевик, биржевика* – (n., masc.) stockbroker, financier
благодарить *благодарить* – (v.) to thank
благодарность, благодарности *благодарность, благодарности* – (n., fem.) gratitude, appreciation
благодарный *благодарный* – (adj.) grateful
† благочинническій *благочинническій* – (adj.) of, relating to a *благочинный* ↓
благославить *благославить* – (v.) to bless, give one's blessing; (if referring to a wedding) to bless the union, unite in matrimony
благочинный, благочинного *благочинный, благочинного* – (adj. used as a n., masc.) provost, ecclesiastical superintendent
бледный *бледный* – (adj., † *блѣдный*) pale, pallid; *бледная немочь* – chlorosis, green sickness
ближайший *ближайший* – (adj.) nearest
Блоня, Блони *Блоня, Блони* – (n., fem.) town of Błonie, Poland (see page 119); *блонский* – of Błonie
блѣдный *блѣдный* → бледный *бледный*
бляхарь, бляхаря *бляхарь, бляхаря* – (n., masc.) metal-plate worker
Бобринец, Бобринца *Бобринец, Бобринца* – (n., masc.) town of Bobrynets', Ukraine (see page 133); *бобринецкий* – (adj.) of Bobrinets'/ Bobrynets'
Бобруйск, Бобруйска *Бобруйск, Бобруйска* – (n., masc.) town of Babruysk, Belarus' (see page 125); *бобруйский* – (adj.) of Bobruysk/Babruysk
бобыль, бобыля *бобыль, бобыля* – (n., masc.) poor, landless peasant (fem. *бобылка* or *бобылиха)*
богаделенка, богаделенки *богаделенка, богаделенки* – (n., fem., † *богадѣленка*) alms-woman
богемец, богемца *богемец, богемца* – (n., masc.) Bohemian (fem. *богемка*)
Богодухов, Богодухова *Богодухов, Богодухова* – (n., masc.) town of Bohodukhiv, Ukraine (see page 133); *богодуховский* – (adj.) of Bohodukhiv
божница, божницы *божница, божницы* – (n., fem.) synagogue (a Polonism, compare Polish *bóżnica;* in standard Russia a *божница* is an icon display-case
Болгария, Болгарии *Болгария, Болгарии* – (n., fem., † *Болгарія*) Bulgaria
более *более* – (adv., † *болѣе*) more; *не болѣе одного года* – no more than a year
болезненный *болезненный* – (adj., † *болѣзненный*) sickly, unhealthy
болезнь, болезни *болезнь, болезни* – (n., fem., † *болѣзнь*) illness, disease; *заразные болезни* – communicable diseases; *сердечная болезнь* or *болезнь сердца* – heart disease; *болезнь почек* – kidney disease
больница, больницы *больница, больницы* – (n., fem.) hospital
больной *больной* – (adj.) ill, sick; (used as a n.) patient, sick person
большой *большой* – (adj.) big, great, large
болѣе *болѣе* → более *более*
болѣзнь *болѣзнь* → болезнь *болезнь*
бондарь, бондаря *бондарь, бондаря* – (n., masc.) cooper
Борзна, Борзны *Борзна, Борзны* – (n., fem.) town of Borzna, Ukraine (see page 133)
Борисов, Борисова *Борисов, Борисова* – (n., masc.) town of Barysaŭ, Belarus' (see page 125); *борисовский* – (adj.) of Borisov/Barysaŭ
борода, бороды *борода, бороды* – (n., fem.) beard
бортник, бортника *бортник, бортника* – (n., masc.) keeper of wild bee-hives
бочар, бочара *бочар, бочара* – (n., masc.) cooper
бояться *бояться* – (v.) to fear, be afraid of

брак, брака *брак, брака* – (n., masc.) marriage; *по первому браку Мейер*, by her first marriage Meyer; *вступающій въ супружескій бракъ* – [one] entering into a conjugal marriage; *состоит ли или состоялъ ли въ бракѣ* – is he, or has he been, married?

бракосочетавшийся *бракосочетавшийся* – (part.) marrying; *о бракосочетавшихся* – of those marrying, of marriages

бракосочетание, бракосочетания *бракосочетание, бракосочетания* – (n., neut., † *бракосочетаніе*) marriage; *книга бракосочетания* – marriage register

бракосочетаться *бракосочетаться* – (v.) to get married; *бракосочетались* – [they] got married

брандмайор, брандмайора *брандмайор, брандмайора* – (n., masc., † *брандмаіоръ*) head fireman

Браслав, Браслава *Браслав, Браслава* – (n.) town of Braslaŭ, Belarus' (see page 126); *браславский* – (adj.) of Braslav/ Braslaŭ

брат, брата *брат, брата* – (n., masc., nom. pl. *братья*, gen. pl. *братьев*) brother; *двоюродный брат* – [male] cousin

братаниха, братанихи *братаниха, братанихи* – (n., fem.) the wife of your first cousin

братаница, братаницы *братаница, братаницы* – (n., fem.) niece, brother's daughter

братанник, братанника *братанник, братанника* – (n., masc.) male cousin

братова, братовы *братова, братовы* – (n., fem.) your brother's wife

братыч, братыча *братыч, братыча* – (n., masc.) son of your brother

Брацлав, Брацлава *Брацлав, Брацлава* – (n., masc.) Bratslav, Ukraine (see page 132); *брацлавский* – (adj.) of Bratslav

брачный *брачный* – (adj.) of marriage, marital; *брачный союз* – a marital union, marriage

брачущийся *брачущийся* – (part. from the rare archaic verb *брачиться*, † *брачущійся*) [the one] getting married

бред, бреда *бред, бреда* – (n., masc.) delirium

† Брест-Литовскъ *Брест-Литовскъ* – (n., masc.) Brest-Litovsk (see page 125); *брестский* – (adj.) of Brest

бронхит, бронхита *бронхит, бронхита* – (n., masc.) bronchitis; *капиллярный бронхит* – capillary bronchitis

брюшина, брюшины *брюшина, брюшины* – (n., fem.) peritoneum; *воспаление брюшины* – peritonitis

брюшной *брюшной* – (adj.) abdominal

бубон, бубона *бубон, бубона* – (n., masc.) bubo

бубонная чума *бубонная чума* → чума *чума*

Буг, Буга *Буг, Буга* – (n., masc.) Bug [river]

буггалтер *буггалтер* → бухгалтер *бухгалтер*

бугор, бугора *бугор, бугора* – (n., masc.) protuberance, tubercle; *бугор лёгких* – tubercle

бугорок, бугорка *бугорок, бугорка* – (n., masc.) tubercle, tumor; *бугорки туберкулёзные* – tubercular tumors

бугорчатка, бугорчатки *бугорчатка, бугорчатки* – (n., fem.) tuberculosis

будет, буду *будет, буду* → быть *быть*

будка, будки *будка, будки* –(n., fem.) sentry-box, cabin, shed; *будка железной дроги* – railway service cabin, or railroad sentry box; *шоссейная будка* – road-worker's cabin or booth

булочник, булочника *булочник, булочника* – (n., masc.) baker (fem. *булочница*)

бумага, бумаги *бумага, бумаги* (n., fem.) paper; *гербовая бумага* – stamped paper, paper with a seal on which official documents were to be printed or filled out, with the cost varying by usage; *таковыхъ Американскихъ бумагъ не имѣю* – I do not have American papers for this

бумагопродавец, бумагопродавца *бумагопродавец, бумагопродавца* – (n., masc.) stationer

бургомистр, бургомистра *бургомистр, бургомистра* – (n., masc.) mayor (fem. *бургомистерша*)

бурлак, бурлака *бурлак, бурлака* – (n., masc.) one who worked on or hauled boats

бурмистр, бурмистра *бурмистр, бурмистра* – (n., masc.) village bailiff (cmp. Polish *starosta*)

бухгалтер, бухгалтера *бухгалтер, бухгалтера* – (n., masc.) accountant, bookkeeper; also sometimes seen as *буггалтер* (fem. *бухгалтерша*)

буянщик, буянщика *буянщик, буянщика* – (n., masc.) wharf-porter, laborer

бы *бы* – (particle indicating conditional or subjunctive mode); *мне хотелось бы* – I would like to

бывший *бывший* – (adj., † *бывшій*, abbr. *б.*) former, one-time, e. g., *бывший пекарь*, former baker

бытность, бытности *бытность, бытности* – (n., fem.) stay, sojourn; presence

быть *быть* – (v., irregular) to be; *будет* – [he, she, it] will be; *панихида будет отслужена* – a requiem will be said; *буду в Европе* – I will be in Europe; *был* – he was; *были* – they were

Быхов, Быхова *Быхов, Быхова* – (n., masc.) town of Bykhaŭ, Belarus' (see page 126); *быховский* – of Bychov/Bykhaŭ

† Бѣла, Бѣлы *Бѣла, Бѣлы* – (n., fem.) town of Biała Podlaska, Poland (see page 120)

† Бѣлгорай, Бѣлгорая *Бѣлгорай, Бѣлгорая* – (n., masc.) town of Biłgoraj, Poland (see page 120); *бѣлгорайскій* – of Biłgoraj

Бѣлградъ *Бѣлградъ* → Белград *Белград*
бѣлильщикъ *бѣлильщикъ* → белильщик *белильщик*
Бѣлое море *Бѣлое море* → Белое море *Белое море*
вѣлокурый *бѣлокурый* → белокурый *белокурый*
Бѣлоруссія *Бѣлоруссія* → Белоруссия *Белоруссия*
бѣлорусскій *бѣлорусскій* → белорусский *белорусский*
Бѣлостокъ *Бѣлостокъ* → Белосток *Белосток*
бѣлошвейка *бѣлошвейка* → белошвейка *белошвейка*
бѣлый *бѣлый* → белый *белый*
† Бѣльскъ, Бѣльска *Бѣльскъ, Бѣльска* – (n., masc.) town of Bielsk Podlaski, Poland (see page 125); *бѣльскій* – of Bielsk (can also refer to other places with similar names, e. g., Бѣла, q. v.)
† Бѣльцы *Бѣльцы* – (n.) Russian name of Bălţi, Moldova (see page 132); † *бѣлецкій* – (adj.) of Bălţi
бюргер, бюргера *бюргер, бюргера* – (n., masc.) burgher
бюро *бюро* – (n., neut., not declined) office
в *в* – (*во* before certain consonant clusters, preposition + acc./prep., † *въ*) in, into, to; *в том, что* – in this [purpose], that… (i. e., for this purpose); *во всёмъ* – in toto, completely
вабильщик, вабильщика *вабильщик, вабильщика* – (n., masc.) lurer, trainer of birds
вагемейстер, вагемейстера *вагемейстер, вагемейстера* – (n., masc.) customs-house weigher
Валахия, Валахии *Валахия, Валахии* – (n., fem., † *Валахія*) Wallachia (region of southeast Romania)
Валки, Валок *Валки, Валок* – (n., pl.) town of Valky, Ukraine (see page 133); *валкский* – (adj.) of Valky
Вам *Вам*, Вами *Вами* → Вы *Вы*
Варшава, Варшавы *Варшава, Варшавы* – (n., fem.) Warsaw; *варшавский* – of Warsaw
Вас *Вас* → Вы *Вы*
Васильков, Василькова *Васильков, Василькова* – (n., masc.) town of Vasyl'kiv, Ukraine (see page 132); *васильковский* – (adj.) of Vasyl'kov/ Vasyl'kiv
вахмистр, вахмистра *вахмистр, вахмистра* – (n., masc.) quartermaster, cavalry sergeant-major
вахтер, вахтера *вахтер, вахтера* – (n., masc.) storekeeper; janitor, porter
Ваш *Ваш* – (poss. pron. from *Вы*) your[s]
ваятель, ваятеля *ваятель, ваятеля* – (n., masc.) sculptor
вверенный *вверенный* – (part. from *вверить*, † *ввѣренный*) entrusted
вверить *вверить* – (v., † *ввѣрить*) to entrust
вдова, вдовы *вдова, вдовы* – (n., fem.) widow; *вдова по* – widow of
вдовец, вдовца *вдовец, вдовца* – (n., masc.) widower
ведать *ведать* – (v., † *вѣдать*) to know
ведение, ведения *ведение, ведения* – (n., neut., † *веденіе*) leading, conducting; keeping (of books)
ведёрник, ведёрника *ведёрник, ведёрника* – (n., masc.) pail-maker
ведённый *ведённый* – (part. from *вести*) led, conducted, held
ведомо *ведомо* – (adv., † *вѣдомо*) really, indeed (*used mainly in the expression съ вѣдома – with the knowledge [of]*)
ведомость, ведомости *ведомость, ведомости* – (n., fem., † *вѣдомость*) list, roll, account, form; (pl.) *ведомости* – newspaper, gazette
ведомство, ведомства *ведомство, ведомства* – (n., neut., † *вѣдомство*) department, jurisdiction
ведущий *ведущий* – (part. from *вести*, † *ведущій*) leading, managing, conducting, keeping (books)
вексель, вексселя *вексель, вексселя* – (n., masc.) bill or letter of exchange; *вексельный курс* – rate of [currency] exchange
вёл *вёл*, вела *вела* → вести *вести*
Велиж, Велижа *Велиж, Велижа* – (n.) town of Velizh, Russia (see page 126); *велижский* – (adj.) of Velizh
великий *великий* – (adj., † *великій*) great, large; *великий дядя* – brother of your grandparent; *великая матка* – sister of your grandparent
† Великороссія, Великороссии *Великороссія, Великороссии* – (n., fem.) Great Russia (see page 135)
величество, величества *величество, величества* – (n., neut.) majesty; used in titles such as *Его Императорское Величество*, His Imperial Majesty
† Велюнъ, Велюна *Велюнъ, Велюна* – (n., masc.) town of Wieluń (see page 118); *велюньскій* – (adj.) of Wieluń
Вена, Вены *Вена, Вены* – (n., fem.) Vienna
венгр, венгра *венгр, венгра* – (n., masc., also seen: *венгерец, венгерца*) Hungarian (fem. *венгерка*)
Венгрия, Венгрии *Венгрия, Венгрии* – (n., fem., † *Венгрія*) Hungary
† Венгровъ, Венгрова *Венгровъ, Венгрова* – (n., masc.) town of Węgrów, Poland (see page 120); *венгровскій* – of Węgrów
венчание, венчания *венчание, венчания* – (n., neut., † *вѣнчаніе*) wedding
венчать *венчать* – (v., † *вѣнчать*) to marry (i. e., unite the bride and groom in matrimony), bless the marriage
вер. *вер.* → верста *верста*
вера, веры *вера, веры* (n., fem., † *вѣра*) faith; *магометанская вера* – Islam, the Islamic faith
верёвочник, верёвочника *верёвочник, верёвочника* – (n., masc.) ropemaker
верно *верно* – (adv., † *вѣрно*) truthfully, faithfully; *съ подлиннымъ вѣрно* – faithful to the original
верность, верности *верность, верности* – (n., fem., † *вѣрность*) fidelity, conformance, faithfulness, accuracy

верный *верный* – (adj., † *вѣрный*) faithful; *сія копія съ подлиннымъ актомъ вѣрна* – this copy [is] faithful to the original document
верoдостойный *верoдостойный* – (adj., † *вѣродостойный*) worthy of belief, credible
вероисповедание, вероисповедания *вероисповедание, вероисповедания* – (n., neut., † *вѣроисповѣданіе*) faith, religion
Верхнеднепровск, Верхнеднепровска *Верхнеднепровск, Верхнеднепровска* – (n., masc., † *Верхнеднѣпровскъ*) town of Verkhn'odniprovs'k, Ukraine (see page 134)
верста, версты *верста, версты* – (n., fem., abbr. *вер.*) verst, measure of distance, about two-thirds of a mile or 1.06 km
вершок, вершка *вершок, вершка* – (n., masc.) unit of measurement, approximately 1.75 inches or 4.4 centimeters
вести *вести* – (v., past tense masc. *вёл*, fem. *вела*) to lead, conduct, keep (books or accounts); *она вел себя отлично* – to behave in an excellent manner
весь *весь* – (pron., fem. nom. *вся*, neut. sing. *всё*, pl. nom. *все*, † *всѣ*, gen. pl. *всех*, † *всѣхъ*) all; *всё* – everything; *всего* – of all, of everything (can also mean "in all, for a total of"); *всѣмъ и каждому* – to all and to each; *во всёмъ* completely
ветвь, ветви *ветвь, ветви* – (n., fem., † *вѣтвь*, gen. pl. *ветвей*) branch; *острый катар дыхательных ветвей* – severe catarrh of the respiratory passages
ветеран, ветерана *ветеран, ветерана* – (n., masc.) veteran
ветеринар, ветеринара *ветеринар, ветеринара* – (n., masc.) veterinarian
ветошник, ветошника *ветошник, ветошника* – (n., masc.) rag-man (fem. *ветошница*)
ветряная оспа *ветряная оспа* → оспа *оспа*
веч. *веч.*, abbr. for *вечером* → *вечер*
вечер, вечера *вечер, вечера* – (n., masc.) evening; *вечером* – in the evening, p.m. (see page 50)
вечный *вечный* – (adj., † *вѣчный*) eternal; *вечный ему покой* – [may God give] him eternal peace; *вечная память ему* – may his memory live forever
вещь, вещи *вещь, вещи* – (n., fem.) thing, object; (pl.) goods, luggage
взаимный *взаимный* – (adj.) reciprocal, mutual
вид, вида *вид, вида* – (n., masc.) face, view, sight; official identification document; *вид на жительство* — residency permit, identity card; *в виде свидетельства* – in the form of a certificate; *въ виду всего вышеизложеннаго* – in view of everything said above
видеть *видеть* – (v., † *видѣть*) to see
видный *видный* – (adj.) evident, apparent; *видно* – it is evident, it is apparent
† викарій, викарія *викарій, викарія* – (n., masc.) vicar, suffragan
викарный *викарный* – (adj.) of a vicar; (used as a n.) assistant pastor
Вилейка, Вилейки *Вилейка, Вилейки* – (n., fem.) town of Vileika, Belarus' (see page 123); *вилейский* – (adj.) of Vileika
виленский *виленский* – (adj., † *виленскій*) of Vil'no/Vil'na/Vilnius → Вильно *Вильна*
† Вилькомиръ, Вилкомира *Вилькомиръ, Вилкомира* – (n., masc.) Russian name of the town of Ukmergė, Lithuania (see page 124); *вилькомирский* – (adj.) of Vilkomir/Ukmergė
Вильна, Вильны *Вильна, Вильны* – (n., fem., also † *Вильно*) Vilnius, Lithuania (see page 123); *виленский* – (adj.) of Vilnius
вина, вины *вина, вины* – (n., fem.) fault, blame, guilt; *по винѣ отца* – due to the father's fault (i. e., the father was to blame)
Винница, Винницы *Винница, Винницы* – (n., fem.) Vinnitsa, Ukraine (see page 132); *винницкий* – (adj.) of Vinnitsa
винокур, винокура *винокур, винокура* – (n., masc.) distiller
винокуренный *винокуренный* – (adj.) of a distillery or distiller; *винокуренный завод* – distillery
винопродавец, винопродавца *винопродавец, винопродавца* – (n., masc.) wine merchant or dealer
винотогровец, виноторговца *винотогровец, виноторговца* – (n., masc.) wine merchant, wine dealer
† виночерпец, виночерпца *виночерпец, виночерпца* – (n., masc.) cupbearer; also seen as *виночерпій*
Висла, Вислы *Висла, Вислы* – (n., fem.) Vistula [river]
Витебск, Витебска *Витебск, Витебска* – (n., masc.) name of the town of Vitebsk, now in Belarus' (see page 126); *витебский* – (adj.) of Vitebsk
витова пляска, витовой пляски *витова пляска, витовой пляски* – (n., fem.) St. Vitus's Dance (also seen: *пляска Св. Вита*)
вице-губернатор, вице-губернатора *вице-губернатор, вице-губернатора* – (n., masc.) vice-governor
вклад, вклада *вклад, вклада* – (n., masc.) deposit
вкладывание, вкладывания *вкладывание, вкладывания* – (n., neut., † *вкладываніе*) inserting, putting in or on
включать *включать* – (v.) to include
включая *включая* – (part. from *включать*) including, inclusive
владелец, владельца *владелец, владельца* – (n., masc., † *владѣлецъ*) owner, e. g. *владелец аптеки* – pharmacy owner (fem. *владелица*); *владелец земли* – land-owner

владельческий *владельческий* – (adj., † *владѣльческій*) proprietor's, owner's
Владимир, Владимира *Владимир, Владимира* – (n., masc.) Vladimir, name of a town in Russia (see page 135); *владимирский* – of Vladimir
Владимир-Волынский, Владимира-Волынского *Владимир-Волынский, Владимира-Волынского* – (n., masc.) Vladimir, name of a town in the Volhynia region of Ukraine (see page 130)
† Владиславовъ, Владиславова *Владиславовъ, Владиславова* – (n., masc.) town of Władysławów, Poland (see page 120); *владиславовскій* – (adj.) of Władysławów
владѣльческій *владѣльческій* → владельческий *владельческий*
Влодава, Влодавы *Влодава, Влодавы* – (n., fem.) town of Włodawa, Poland (see page 120); *влодавский* – (adj.) of Włodawa
Влоцлавек, Влоцлавка *Влоцлавек, Влоцлавка* – (n., masc., † *Влоцлавскъ*) town of Włocławek, Poland (see page 119); *влоцлавский* – (adj.) of Włocławek
† Влощовъ, Влощова *Влощовъ, Влощова* – (n., masc.) town of Włoszczowa, Poland (see page 120); *влощовскій* – (adj.) of Włoszczowa
вне *вне* – (prep. + gen., † *внѣ*) outside of
внебрачный *внебрачный* – (adj., † *внѣбрачный*) outside of marriage; *внебрачное дитя* – illegitimate child
внесение, внесения *внесение, внесения* – (n., neut., † *внесеніе*) entry, enrollment
внесённый *внесённый* – (part. from *внести*, to enroll, enlist) enrolled, enlisted, entered
внешний *внешний* – (adj., † *внѣшній*) external, outward
вноситься *вноситься* – (v.) to be entered, inserted
внук, внука *внук, внука* – (n., masc.) grandson, or the son of a nephew or niece; (pl. *внуки, внуков*) grandsons, grandchilddren
внука, внуки *внука, внуки* – (n. fem.) granddaughter, or the daughter of a nephew or niece
внутренний *внутренний* (adj., † *внутренній*, also *внутренный*) internal, interior, inner
внучатый *внучатый* – (adj., also seen as *внучатный*) adjective describing relatives three or more generations removed
внучка, внучки *внучка, внучки* – (n., fem.) granddaughter
внѣ *внѣ* → вне *вне*
внѣбрачный *внѣбрачный* → внебрачный *внебрачный*
внѣшній *внѣшній* → внешний *внешний*
вобласць *вобласць* – Belarusian term, equivalent to Russian область, q. v.
во *во* – в *в*
вода, воды *вода, воды* – (n., fem.) water; *одною ли водою* – with water only?
водка, водка *водка, водка* – (n., fem.) vodka
водник, водника *водник, водника* – (n., masc.) water-transport worker
водонос, водоноса *водонос, водоноса* – (n., masc.) water-carrier
водопроводчик, водопроводчика *водопроводчик, водопроводчика* – (n., masc.) plumber
водянка, водянки *водянка, водянки* or водяная болезнь *водяная болезнь* – (n., fem.) dropsy, edema
воеводство, воеводства *воеводство, воеводства* – (n., neut.) province, voivodeship (cmp. Polish *województwo*)
военный *военный* – (adj.) military
возвратившись *возвратившись* – (part. from *возвратиться*) having returned, upon his return
возвратиться *возвратиться* – (v.) to return, come back
возвращаться *возвращаться* – (v.) to return; *возвращаюсь* – I return, am returning; *возвращается на родину* – he is returning to his homeland
возвращающийся *возвращающийся* – (part. from *возвращаться*] returning; (used as a noun) the one returning; *возвращающагося въ Россію* – of one returning to Russia
возвращение, возвращения *возвращение, возвращения* – (n., neut., † *возвращеніе*) return
возница, возницы *возница, возницы* – (n., masc.) driver, coachman
возный, возного *возный, возного* – (adj. used as a n., masc.) possibly a Russified version of Polish *woźny*, cart-driver, † beadle
возраст, возраста *возраст, возраста* – (n., masc.) age; *в возрасте 15 лет* – age 15
возчик, возчика *возчик, возчика* – (n., masc.) carter
воинский *воинский* – (adj., † *воинскій*) military
войлочник, войлочника *войлочник, войлочника* – (n., masc.) felt-maker
войско, войска *войско, войска* – (n., neut.) army; *Земля войска Донского* – Land of the Don Army (see page 135)
войт, войта *войт, войта* – (n., masc.) Polish *wójt*, an administrative official in charge of a *gmina* or district
войтовсвто, войтовства *войтовсвто, войтовства* – (n., neut.) the office or jurisdiction or property of a *войт* ↑
вол. *вол.* → волость *волость*
Волга, Волги *Волга, Волги* – (n., fem.) Volga [river]
Волковыск, Волковыска *Волковыск, Волковыска* – (n., masc.) town of Vaŭkovysk, Belarus' (see page

125); *волковыский* – (adj.) of Volkovysk/ Vaŭkovysk

† Волковышки, Волковышокъ *Волковышки, Волковышокъ* – (n., pl.) town of Wyłkowyszki, now Vilkaviškis, Lithuania (see page 120); *волковышскій* – (adj.) of Wyłkowyszki

воловщик, воловщика *воловщик, воловщика* – (n., masc.) drover of oxen

Вологда, Вологды *Вологда, Вологды* – (n., fem.) Vologda, town in Russia (see page 135); вологодский *вологодский* – (adj., † *вологодскій*) of Vologda

Воложин, Воложин *Воложин, Воложина* – (n.) town of Valozhyn, Belarus' (see page 126); *воложинский* – (adj.) of Volozhin/Valozhyn

волос, волоса – (n., masc.) hair (a single hair; when referring to a person's hair collectively, the plural is used: *волосы*, gen. pl. *волос*)

волостный *волостный* – (adj.) of, from, pertaining to a *volost'*, see волость ↓

волость, волости *волость, волости* – (n., fem., abbr. *вол.*) district (see page 83)

Волчанск, Волчанска *Волчанск, Волчанска* – (n., masc.) town of Vovchansk, Ukraine (see page 134); *волчанский* – (adj.) of Vovchansk

волынский *волынский* – (adj., † *волынскій*) of Volhynia ↓

Волынь, Волыни *Волынь, Волыни* – (n., fem.) Volyn', region of Ukraine (see page 130)

вольнонаёмный *вольнонаёмный* – (adj.) free to hire out on one's accord (as opposed to serfs or slaves)

вольноопределяющийся *вольноопределяющийся* – (part. from *вольно*, freely, + *определяться*, to take a position; † *вольноопредѣляющійся*) volunteer for military service among the rank and file

вольноотпущенник, вольноотпущенника *вольноотпущенник, вольноотпущенника* – (n., masc.) freedman, emancipated serf (fem. *вольноотпущенница*); also seen: (part. used as a n.) *вольноотпущенный*, fem. *вольноотпущенная*

вольный *вольный* – (adj.) free, voluntary

Воронеж, Воронежа *Воронеж, Воронежа* – (n., masc.) Voronezh, name of a town in Russia (see page 135); *воронежский* – of Voronezh

Вороново, Воронова *Вороново, Воронова* – (n., neut.) town of Voranava, Belarus' (see page 126); *вороновский* – (adj.) of Voronovo/Voranava

ворсильщик, ворсильщика *ворсильщик, ворсильщика* – (n., masc.) carder, teaseler

восемнадцатый *восемнадцатый* – (ordinal num./adj.) eighteenth

восемнадцать, восемнадцати *восемнадцать, восемнадцати* – (num.) eighteen

восемь, восьми *восемь, восьми* – (num.) eight

восемьдесят, восьмидесяти *восемьдесят, восьмидесяти* – (num.) eighty; *восемьдесят один* – eighty-one; *восемьдесят первый* – eighty-first

восемьсот, восьмисот *восемьсот, восьмисот* – (num.) eight hundred

воскресенье, воскресенья *воскресенье, воскресенья* – (n., neut.) Sunday; *в воскресенье* – on Sunday; *по воскресеньям* – on Sundays, every Sunday

воспаление, воспаления *воспаление, воспаления* – (n., neut., † *воспаленіе*) inflammation, infection; *воспаление кишок* – enteritis; *воспаление лёгких* – pneumonia; *воспаление мозга* –brain fever; *воспаление суставов* – inflammation of the joints

воспитатель, воспитателя *воспитатель, воспитателя* – (n., masc.) tutor (fem. *воспитательница*)

восприемник, восприемника *восприемник, восприемника* – (n., masc., † *воспріемникъ*) godparent, godfather; *восприемники* – godparents

восприемница, восприемницы *восприемница, восприемницы* – (n., fem. † *воспріемница*) godmother

восьмидесятый *восьмидесятый* – (ordinal num./adj.) eightieth

восьмисотый *восьмисотый* – (ordinal num./adj.) eight hundredth

восьмой *восьмой* – (ordinal num./adj.) eighth

вотчинник, вотчинника *вотчинник, вотчинника* – (n., masc.) possessor of a patrimony

† вотчинный *вотчинный* – (adj.) patrimonial; *вотчинное управленіе* – provincial registrar's office

вощик, вощика *вощик, вощика* – (n., masc.) cart-driver, wagon-driver

врач, врача *врач, врача* – (n., masc.) doctor

временно *временно* – (adv.) temporarily, for a time; *временнопроживающий* – temporarily residing

временный *временный* – (adj.) temporary

время, времени *время, времени* – (n., neut., see page 41 for declension) time; *время рождения* – time (i. e., date) of birth; *с какого времени* or *с которого времени* – since what time, i. e., for how long?; *со времени* – from the time [of]; *в то время* – at that time; *во время* – in time, at the time

вручённый *неврученный* – (part., from *вручить*) delivered, handed over

вручить *вручить* – (v.) to deliver, hand over

все, всё *все, всё*, всего *всего* → весь *весь*

вскормленник, вскормленника *вскормленник, вскормленника* – (n., masc.) foster-son (fem. *вскормленница*, foster-daughter)

вспомогательный *вспомогательный* – (adj.) subsidiary, auxiliary

вступать *вступать* – (v.) to enter, come into; *съ кьмъ вступаетъ въ бракъ* – is marrying whom?

вступающий *вступающий* – (part. from *вступать*, † *вступающій*) entering; *отъ вступающихъ въ супружескій бракъ* – from those entering into a conjugal marriage
вступить *вступить* – (v., perf. counterpart of *вступать*) to enter, come into; *вступить в брак* – to enter into marriage, get married
вступление, вступления *вступление, вступления* – (n., neut., † *вступленіе*) entering; *до вступленія въ бракъ* – before their entering into marriage
всѣ *всѣ* or *всѣхъ* or вся *вся* → весь *весь*
всякий *всякий* – (adj., † *всякій*) all sorts of, every kind of
вторник, вторника *вторник, вторника* – (n., masc.) Tuesday; *во вторник* – on Tuesday; *по вторникам* – on Tuesdays, every Tuesday
второй *второй* – (ordinal num./adj.) second; *часть вторая* – second part (of parish registers, for marriages)
вчера *вчера* – (adv.) yesterday; *вчера вечером* – last evening, last night
вчерашний *вчерашний* – (adj., † *вчерашній*) of yesterday; *вчерашняго числа* – yesterday
Вы *Вы* – (pron., gen., acc. and prep. *Вас*, dat. *Вам*, instr. *Вами*) you (polite form)
выбылой *выбылой* – (adj.) resigned, retired
выбыть *выбыть* – (v.) to retire, leave
выводная, выводной *выводная, выводной* – (adj. used as a n., fem.) marriage permit for peasant girls marrying in another village
выводное, выводного *выводное, выводного* – (adj. used as a n., neut.) the fee for the *выводная* permit
выдавать *выдавать* – (v., imperf. counterpart of *выдать*) to issue, give out
выданный *выданный* – (part. from *выдать*) issued, published, given out; *кѣмъ оно выдано* – by whom was it issued?
выдать *выдать* – (v.) to issue
выдача, выдачи *выдача, выдачи* – (n., fem.) issuing, issuance
выезд выезда *выезд выезда* – (n., masc., † *выѣздъ*) exit, departure; *дата выезда* – date of departure
выкормление, выкормления *выкормление, выкормления* – (n., neut., † *выкормленіе*) nursing, feeding, raising (a child); *на выкормленіи* – for nursing, raising
вымерлый *вымерлый* – (adj.) extinct, died out (e. g., a family)
вынимаемый *вынимаемый* – (part. from *вынимать*, to take out) to take out
вынутый *вынутый* – (part. from *вынуть*, to draw, take out) drawn (as of lots)
выписка, выписки *выписка, выписки* – (n., fem.) extract, copy, summary
выписываемый *выписываемый* – (part. from *выписывать*) filled out, written out
выписывать *выписывать* – (v.) to extract, copy, write out
выписываться *выписываться* – (v., refl.) to be extracted, copied, written out
выпись, выписи *выпись, выписи* – (n., fem.) extract, copy
выполнивший *выполнивший* – (part. from *выполнить*; † *выполнившій*) having fulfilled, performed
выполнить *выполнить* – (v.) to fulfill, perform
выселок, выселка *выселок, выселка* – (n., masc.) new settlement of colonists, formed by splitting off from an old settlement
высланный *высланный* – (part. from *выслать*) sent
выслать *выслать* – (v.) to send off
выслуживший *выслуживший* – (part. from *выслужить*, to serve one's term, † *выслужившій*) having served
высокий *высокий* – (adj., † *высокій*) tall, high
Высокоблагородие, Высокоблагородия *Высокоблагородие, Высокоблагородия* – (n., neut., † *Высокоблагородіе*) used in titles, e. g., *ваше Высокоблагородие*, Your Honor, Your Worship
Высокопревосходительство, Высокопревосходительства *Высокопревосходительство, Высокопревосходительства* – (n., neut.) used in titles, e. g., *ваше Высокопревосходительство*, Your Excellency
Высокопреосвященство, Высокопреосвященства *Высокопреосвященство, Высокопреосвященства* – (n., neut.) used in titles, e. g., *Высокопреосвященство*, Eminence
Высокопреосвященный *Высокопреосвященный* – (adj.) Most Eminent (used in titles)
Высокопреподобие, Высокопреподобия *Высокопреподобие, Высокопреподобия* – (n., neut., † *Высокопреподобіе*) Reverence (used in titles)
Высокопреподобный *Высокопреподобный* – (adj.) Right Reverend (used in titles)
Высокородие, Высокородия *Высокородие, Высокородия* – (n., neut., † *Высокородіе*) Right Honorable (used in titles)
высочайше *высочайше* – (adv.) at the highest level (used typically of decrees confirmed by the Emperor)
высылать *высылать* – (v.) to send
высылка, высылки *высылка, высылки* – (n., fem.) transfer, sending; *высилка денег* – money transfer
выше *выше* – (adv.) above
вышеизложенный *вышеизложенный* – (part. from *изложить*, to set forth + *выше*, above) aforesaid

вышеозначенный *вышеозначенный* – (part. from *означить*, to designate, + *выше*, above) above designated
вышеописанный *вышеописанный* – (part. from *выше*, above + *описать*, to describe) described above
вышесказанный, вышесказанный *вышесказанный, вышесказанный* – (adj.) aforesaid, above-mentioned
вышеуказанный *вышеуказанный* – (part. from *указать*, to indicate, + *выше*, above) aforesaid, indicated above
вышеупомянутый *вышеупомянутый* – (part. from *упомянуть*, to mention, + *выше*, above) aforementioned, aforesaid
вышивальщица, вышивальщицы *вышивальщица, вышивальщицы* – (n., fem.) embroideress
выѣздъ *выѣздъ* → выезд *выезд*
вѣдомо *вѣдомо* → ведомо *ведомо*
вѣдомость *вѣдомость* → ведомость *ведомость*
вѣдомство *вѣдомство* → ведомство *ведомство*
вѣнчаніе *вѣнчаніе* → венчание *венчание*
вѣнчать *вѣнчать* → венчать *венчать*
вѣра *вѣра* → вера *вера*
вѣрно *вѣрно* → верно *верно*
вѣрность *вѣрность* → верность *верность*
вѣрный *вѣрный* → верный *верный*
вѣродостойный *вѣродостойный* → вèродостойный *веродостойный*
вѣроисповѣданіе *вѣроисповѣданіе* → вероисповедание *вероисповедание*
вѣтвь *вѣтвь* → ветвь *ветвь*
вѣтряная оспа *вѣтряная оспа* → оспа *оспа*
Вятка, Вятки *Вятка, Вятки* – (n., fem.) Vyatka, name of a town in Russia (see page 135); *вятский* – (adj.) of Vyatka
г. *г.* → год *год* or город *город*
Гадяч, Гадяча *Гадяч, Гадяча* – (n., masc.) town of Hadyach, Ukraine (see page 133); *гадячский* – (adj.) of Gadyach/Hadyach
Гайсин, Гайсина *Гайсин, Гайсина* – (n., masc.) town of Haisyn, Ukraine (see page 132); *гайсинский* – (adj.) of Haisyn
Галиция, Галиции *Галиция, Галиции* – (n., fem., † *Галиція*) Galicia (Austrian partition)
Галич, Галича *Галич, Галича* – (n., masc.) town of Halych, Ukraine, see page 134); *галицкий* – (adj.) of Halych
Гамбург, Гамбурга *Гамбург, Гамбурга* – (n., masc.) Hamburg
гангрена, гангрены *гангрена, гангрены* – (n., fem.) gangrene, mortification
Гарволин, Гарволина *Гарволин, Гарволина* – (n., masc.) town of Garwolin, Poland (see page 120); *гарволинский* – (adj.) of Garwolin
гардемарин, гардемарина *гардемарин, гардемарина* – (n., masc.) midshipman
гастрит, гастрита *гастрит, гастрита* – (n., masc.) gastritis
гвардеец, гвардейца *гвардеец, гвардейца* – (n., masc.) soldier or officer in the guards
гвоздочник, гвоздочника *гвоздочник, гвоздочника* – (n., masc.) maker or seller of nails
Гданьск, Гданьска *Гданьск, Гданьска* – (n., masc.) Gdańsk, Poland
где *где* – (adv., † *гдѣ*) where
генеалог, генеалога *генеалог, генеалога* – (n., masc.) genealogist
генерал, генерала *генерал, генерала* – (n., masc.) general; *генерал-адмиралъ*, lord high admiral; *генерал-адъютант*, adjutant general; *генерал-аншеф* or *полный генерал*, general in chief; *генерал-губернатор*, governor general; *генерал-лейтенант*, lieutenant general; *генерал-майор*, major general; *генерал фельдмаршалъ*, field marshal
генеральный *генеральный* – (adj.) general
географический *географический* – (adj., † *географическій*) geographical
геодезист, геодезиста *геодезист, геодезиста* – (n., masc.) geodesist, surveyor
геолог, геолога *геолог, геолога* – (n., masc.) geologist
гербовник, гербовника *гербовник, гербовника* – (n., masc.) armorial, book of heraldry
гербовой *гербовой* – (adj., accented on the first syllable) stamped, with a seal; (accented on the second syllable) armorial; *гербовая бумага*, see бумага
герой, героя *герой, героя* – (n., masc.) hero; *умереть смертью героя* – to die a hero's death
† герольдмейстеръ, герольдмейстера *герольдмейстеръ, герольдмейстера* – (n., masc.) Master Herald
герцог, герцога *герцог, герцога* – (n., masc.) duke [cmp. Germ. *Herzog;* fem. *герцогиня*]
гетман, гетмана *гетман, гетмана* – (n., masc.) *hetman*, in Poland and in Ukraine a term once used for the commander in chief of the army
глава, главы *глава, главы* – (n., fem.) head (literally and figuratively)
главный *главный* – (adj.) chief, main, principal
гладильщик, гладильщика *гладильщик, гладильщика* – (n., masc.) polisher, ironer; fem. *гладильщица*
глаз, глаза *глаз, глаза* – (n., masc.; nom. pl. *глаза*, gen. pl. *глаз*) eye
глашатай, глашатая *глашатай, глашатая* – (n., masc.) town-crier, public announcer of official news

глубокий *глубокий* – (adj.) deep; *в глубоком горе* – in deep sorrow
Глубокое, Глубокого *Глубокое, Глубокого* – (n., neut.) town of Hlubokaye, Belarus' (see page 126)
Глуск, Глуска *Глуск, Глуска* – (n., masc.) town of Hlusk, Belarus' (see page 126); *глуский* – (adj.) of Glusk/Hlusk
Глухов, Глухова *Глухов, Глухова* – (n., masc.) Russian name of the town of Hlukhiv, Ukraine (see page 133)
глухой *глухой* – (adj.) deaf; dull, dark
глухонемой *глухонемой* – (adj., † *глухонѣмой*) deaf and dumb
гмина, гмины *гмина, гмины* – (n., fem.) district (compare Polish *gmina*)
гминный *гминный* – (adj.) of a гмина ↑
гноетечение, гноетечения *гноетечение, гноетечения* – (n., neut., –† *гноетеченіе*) suppuration
год, года *год, года* – (n., abbr. *г.*, masc., prep. sing. *годе* or *году* after *в* or *на*, nom. pl. *годы* or *года*, gen. pl. *годов* or *лет*, see pages 41 and 50) year; *текущего года* – this year; *в этом году* – this year; *в прошлом году* – last year; *на 42-ем году жизни* – in her 42nd year; *за 1910 год* – for the year 1910; *за эти годы* – for these years
годовой *годовой* – (adj.) annual, one-year; *в годовой день* – on the first anniversary
годовщина, годовщины *годовщина, годовщины* – (n., fem.) anniversary; *во вторую годовщину* – on the second anniversary
голод, голода *голод, голода* – (n., masc.) hunger, starvation; famine; *умереть с голоду* – to die of starvation
голодный *голодный* – (adj.) hungry, of hunger, starvation, famine; *голодная смерть* – starvation; *умереть голодною смертью* – to die of hunger, starve
Гомель, Гомеля *Гомель, Гомеля* – (n., masc.) town of Homel', Belarus' (see page 126); *гомельский* – of Gomel'/Homel'
гонец, гонца *гонец, гонца* – (n., masc.) currier, runner
гончар, гончара *гончар, гончара* – (n., masc.) potter
гор. *гор.* → город *город*
горе, горя *горе, горя* – (n., neut.) sorrow, grief, distress; *в глубоком горе* – in deep sorrow
Горки, Горок *Горки, Горок* – (n.) town of Horki, Belarus' (see page 126); *горецкий* – (adj.) of Gorki/Horki
горло, горла *горло, горла* – (n., neut.) throat
горничная, горничной *горничная, горничной* – (adj. used as a n., fem.) chambermaid, maid-servant
горнозаводчик, горнозаводчика *горнозаводчик, горнозаводчика* – (n., masc.) iron-master, iron-manufacturer
горнорабочий, горнорабочего *горнорабочий, горнорабочего* – (adj. used as a n., masc.) miner, worker in metalworks
город, города *город, города* – (n., abbr. *г.* or *гор.*, masc., nom. pl. *города*) town, city
городничий, городничего *городничий, городничего* – (adj. used as a n., masc.) provost, town bailiff
Городня, Городни *Городня, Городни* – (n., fem.) town of Horodnya, Ukraine (see page 133); *городнянский* – (adj.) of Gorodnya/Horodnya
городовой, городового *городовой, городового* – (adj. used as a n., masc.) town policeman, constable
Городок, Городка *Городок, Городка* – (n., masc.) Russian name of the town of Haradok, Belarus' (see page 126); *городокский* – (adj.) of Gorodok/Haradok
городской *городской* – (adj.) of a town
горожанин, горожанина *горожанин, горожанина* – (n., masc., nom. pl. *горожане*, gen. pl. *горожан*) townsman (fem. *горожанка*)
гортань, гортани *гортань, гортани* –(n., fem.) larynx; *круп гортани* – croup of the larynx
горшечник, горшечника *горшечник, горшечника* – (n., masc.) potter (fem. *горшечница*)
горячка, горячки *горячка, горячки* – (n., fem.) fever
господарь, господаря *господарь, господаря* – (n., masc.) land-owner, master [cmp. Polish *gospodarz*]
господин, господина *господин, господина* – (n., masc., nom. pl. *господа*, gen. pl. *господ*) lord, master, gentleman; (in titles and greetings) Mister, Sir
госпожа, госпожи *госпожа, госпожи* – (n., fem.) lady, mistress; (in titles and greetings) Madam, Mrs.
гостинодворец, гостинодворца *гостинодворец, гостинодворца* – (n., masc.) shopkeeper in a bazaar
Гостынин, Гостынина *Гостынин, Гостынина* – (n., masc.) town of Gostynin, Poland (see page 119); *гостынский* – of Gostynin
гость, гостья *гость, гостья* – (n., masc., nom. pl. *гости*, gen. pl. *гостей*) visitor, guest
государственный *государственный* – (adj.) national, of the state
государство, государства *государство, государства* – (n., neut.) country, state, nation
государь, государя *государь, государя* – (n., masc.) sovereign, monarch; *милостивый государъ* – Dear Sir (salutation in a letter)
гофмаршал, гофмаршала *гофмаршал, гофмаршала* – (n., masc.) master of the court, knight marshal [cmp. Germ. *Hofmarschall*]
гофмейстер, гофмейстера *гофмейстер, гофмейстера* – (n., masc.) court steward, steward of a noble's household [cmp. Germ. *Hofmeister*]

грабельщик, грабельщика *грабельщик, грабельщика* – (n., masc.) raker (fem. *грабельщица*)
гравёр, гравёра *гравёр, гравёра* – (n., masc.) engraver
градоначальник, градоначальника *градоначальник, градоначальника* – (n., masc.) 19th century governor of a major city with its own administration
градоправитель, градоправителя *градоправитель, градоправителя* – (n., masc.) town magistrate
гражданин, гражданина *гражданин, гражданина* – (n., masc., nom. pl. *граждане*, gen. pl. *граждан*, see page 41 for declension) citizen, burgher, freeman (fem. *гражданка*)
гражданский *гражданский* – (adj., † *гражданскій*) civil; *гражданское состояние* – Civil Registry
гражданство, гражданства *гражданство, гражданства* – (n., neut.) citizenship; *перейти въ Американское гражданство* – to change [my] citizenship to American
грамота, грамоты *грамота, грамоты* – (n., fem.) reading and writing, literacy; edict, decree, charter; letter, bill; *за незнаніемъ ими грамоты* – due to their not knowing how to read and write
грамотность, грамотности *грамотность, грамотности* – (n., fem.) literacy
граница границы *граница границы* – (n., fem.) border, boundary; *за границу* or *заграницу* – (destined, headed) beyond the border, abroad; *за границей* – (located) beyond the border, abroad; *через границу* – across the border
графство, графства *графство, графства* – (n., neut.) literally "county, earldom"(*графъ* – count, earl)
гребенщик, гребенщика *гребенщик, гребенщика* – (n., masc.) comb-maker
греко-католический *греко-католический* – (adj., † *греко-каѳолическій*) Greek Catholic
гренадер, гренадера *гренадер, гренадера* – (n., masc.) grenadier
грипп, гриппа *грипп, гриппа* – (n., masc.) influenza
гробовщик, гробовщика *гробовщик, гробовщика* – (n., masc.) coffin-maker, undertaker, gravedigger
гробокопатель, гробокопателя *гробокопатель, гробокопателя* – (n., masc.) gravedigger
Гродно, Гродна *Гродно, Гродна* – (n., neut. , also † *Гродна*, Grodna) Grodno, now Hrodna, a city in Belarus' (see page 125); *гродненский* – of Grodno
† Гройцы, Гроецъ *Гройцы, Гроецъ* – (n., pl.) town of Grójec, Poland (see page 119); *гроецкий* – of Grójec
† Грубешовъ, Грубешова *Грубешовъ, Грубешова* – (n., masc.) town of Hrubieszów, Poland (see page 120); *грубешовскій* – of Hrubieszów
грудница, грудницы *грудница, грудницы* – (n., fem.) mastitis
грудной *грудной* – (adj.) of the breast, chest; *грудная жаба* – angina pectoris; *грудная хачотка* – consumption
Грузия, Грузии *Грузия, Грузии* – (n., fem., † *Грузія*) Georgia (region in the Caucasus, not the U. S. state)
грыжа, грыжи *грыжа, грыжи* – (n., fem.) rupture, hernia
губ. *губ.* → губерния *губерния*
губернатор, губернатора *губернатор, губернатора* – (n., masc.) governor (fem. *губернаторша*)
губерния, губернии *губерния, губернии* – (n., fem., † *губернія*, abbr. *губ.*) *gubernia*, province (see page 83)
губернский *губернский* – (adj., † *губернскій*) of a *губерния*, of a province, provincial
гувернантка, гувернантки *гувернантка, гувернантки* – (n., fem.) governess, tutoress
гувернёр, гувернёра *гувернёр, гувернёра* – (n., masc.) tutor
гуртовщик, гуртовщика *гуртовщик, гуртовщика* – (n., masc.) wholesale merchant; drover
гусар, гусара *гусар, гусара* – (n., masc.) hussar
д., *д.* or *g.* → деревня *деревня* or дом *дом*
давильщик, давильщика *давильщик, давильщика* – (n., masc.) presser, treader (of grapes)
далее *далее* – (adv., † *далѣе*) farther than
далеко *далеко* – (adv.) far
дальше *дальше* – (adv.) farther
данный *данный* – (part. from *дать*, short forms: masc. *дан* or † *данъ*, fem. *дана*, neut. *дано*) given, issued; (pl.) *данные, данных* – information, data
Данциг, Данцига *Данциг, Данцига* – (n., masc.) Danzig (now Gdańsk, Poland)
дата, даты *дата, даты* – (n., fem.) date; *дата рождения* – date of birth
дать *дать* – (v.) to give, issue
дающий *дающий* – (part. from *давать*, to give; † *дающій*) giving; *дающее право на льготу* – entitling [him] to an exemption
два, двух *два, двух* – (num., masc./neut., dat. *двум*, instr. *двумя*, prep. *двух*) two
двадцатый *двадцатый* – (ordinal num./adj.) twentieth (see page 46)
двадцать, двадцати *двадцать, двадцати* – (num.) twenty; *двадцать один* – twenty-one; *двадцать два* – twenty-two, etc.; *двадцать первый* – twenty-first (see page 46)
две, двух *две, двух* – († *двѣ*, num., fem., dat. *двум*, instr. *двумя*, prep. *двух*) two
двенадцатый *двенадцатый* – (ordinal num./adj., † *двѣнадцатый*) twelfth
двенадцать, двенадцати *двенадцать, двенадцати* – (num., † *двѣнадцать*) twelve
дверь, двери *дверь, двери* – (n., fem.) door

двести, двухсот *двести, двухсот* – (num., † *двѣсти*) two hundred

две тысячи, двух тысячи *две тысячи, двух тысячи* – (num., † *двѣ тысячи*) two thousand

Двина, Двины *Двина, Двины* – (n., fem.) Dvina [river]

† Двинскъ, Двинска *Двинскъ, Двинска* – (n., masc.) old Russian name of Daugavpils, Latvia (see page 126); *двинскій* – of Dvinsk/Daugavpils

двоекратный *двоекратный* – (adj.) twofold, done twice

двор, двора *двор, двора* – (n., masc.) court, courtyard, manor, household

дворецкий, дворецкого *дворецкий, дворецкого* – (adj. used as a n., masc., † *дворецкій*) house steward, butler, majordomo

дворник, дворника *дворник, дворника* – (n., masc.) yard-keeper, house-porter

дворовый *дворовый* – (adj.) of a house, of a manor; (used as a n.) menial, manor serf

дворянин, дворянина *дворянин, дворянина* – (n., masc., nom. pl. *дворяне*, gen. pl. *дворян*) aristocrat

дворянский *дворянский* – (adj., † *дворянскій*) noble, aristocratic

двоюродный *двоюродный* – (adj.) used in terms *двоюродный брат*, [male] cousin, and *двоюродная сестра*, [female] cousin

двум, двумя, двух *двум, двумя, двух* → два *два* or две *две*

двухсотый *двухсотый* – (ordinal num./adj.) two hundredth

двухтысячный *двухтысячный* – (ordinal num./adj.) two thousandth; *в двухтысячном году* – in the year 2000; *в две тысячи первом году* – in the year 2001

двѣ *двѣ* → две *две*

двѣнадцатый *двѣнадцатый* → двенадцатый *двенадцатый*

двѣнадцать *двѣнадцать* → двенадцать *двенадцать*

двѣсти *двѣсти* → двести *двести*

деверь, деверя *деверь, деверя* – (n., masc., nom. pl. *деверья*, gen. pl. *деверей*) brother-in-law (husband's brother)

девица, девицы *девица, девицы* – (n., fem., † *дѣвица*) girl, maiden, young unmarried woman

девичий *девичий* – (adj., † *дѣвичій*) maiden, virginal; *девичья фамилия* – maiden name; *девичья немочь* – chlorosis, green sickness

девяносто, девяноста *девяносто, девяноста* – (num.) ninety; *девяносто один* – ninety-one; *девяносто первый* – ninety-first, etc. (see page 46)

девяностый *девяностый* – (ordinal num./adj.) ninetieth

девятисотый *девятисотый* – (ordinal num./adj.) nine hundredth

девятнадцатый *девятнадцатый* – (ordinal num./adj.) nineteenth

девятнадцать, девятнадцати *девятнадцать, девятнадцати* – (num.) nineteen

девятый *девятый* – (ordinal num./adj.) ninth

девять, девяти *девять, девяти* – (num.) nine

девятьсот, девятисот *девятьсот, девятисот* – (num.) nine hundred

дед, деда *дед, деда* – (n., masc., dim. *дедушка*, † *дѣдъ*) grandfather

дедич, дедича *дедич, дедича* – (n., masc.) a direct descendant of your grandfather

дедка, дедки *дедка, дедки* – (n., fem.) an aunt by marriage to an uncle

дедовщина, дедовщины *дедовщина* , *дедовщины* – (n., fem., † *дѣдовщина*) inheritance from a grandfather

действие, действия *действие, действия* – (n., neut., † *дѣйствіе*) action, effect

действительность, действительности *действительность, действительности* – (n., fem., † *дѣйствительность*) validity, authenticity

действительный *действительный* – (adj., † *дѣйствительный*) active, effective, valid, in force

декабрь, декабря *декабрь, декабря* – (n., masc.) December

декан, декана *декан, декана* – (n., masc.) dean

делаемый *делаемый* – (part. from *делать*, † *дѣлаемый*) made, done

делание, делания *делание, делания* – (n., neut., † *дѣланіе*) making, doing, executing

делатель, делателя *делатель, делателя* – (n., masc. † *дѣлатель*) maker, worker

делать *делать* – (v., † *дѣлать*) to make, do; *не дѣлали-ли обѣтовъ цѣломудрія* – have you made any vows of chastity?

деление, деления *деление, деления* – (n., neut., † *дѣленіе*) dividing, division

дело, дела дело, *дела* – (n., neut., † *дѣло*) affair, matter, case, action; *чѣмъ кончено дѣло* – how did the matter end?

делопроизводитель, делопроизводителя *делопроизводитель, делопроизводителя* – (n., masc., † *дѣлопроизводитель*) clerk, secretary

денщик, денщика *денщик, денщика* – (n., masc.) officer's servant

день, дня *день, дня* – (n., masc., see page 41 and 50); *дня* – during the day, on such-and-such a day; *днём* – during the afternoon

деньги, денег *деньги, денег* – (n., fem. pl.) money

департамент, департамента *департамент, департамента* – (n., masc.) department

дер. *дер.* → деревня *деревня*

деревня, деревни *деревня, деревни* – (abbr. *д.* or *дер.*, n., fem., gen. pl. *деревень*) village
дерево, дерева *дерево, дерева* – (n., neut., nom. pl. *деревья*, gen. pl. *деревьев*) wood
деревянный *деревянный* – (adj.) wooden
дернорез, дернореза *дернорез, дернореза* – (n., masc., † *дерноръзъ*) turf-cutter
десятина, десятины *десятина, десятины* – (n., fem.) one-tenth; tithe; also a measure of area = about 1.09 hectares
десятник, десятника *десятник, десятника* – (n., masc.) overseer, foreman
десятый *десятый* – (ordinal num./adj.) tenth
десять, десяти *десять, десяти* – (num.) ten
дети, детей *дети, детей* (n., masc. pl., † *дъти*) babies, children; *если есть дъти* – if there are children; *съ моими дътьми* – with my children, and my children
детский *детский* – (adj., † *дътскій*) of children, infantile; *детский паралич* – infantile paralysis
дешёвый *дешёвый* – (adj.) cheap
деятель, деятеля *деятель, деятеля* – (n., masc., † *дъятель*) agent, promoter, activist
дизентерия, дизентерии *дизентерия, дизентерии* – (n., fem., † *дисентерія*) dysentery
Дисна, Дисны *Дисна, Дисны* – (n., fem.) town of Disna, Belarus' (see page 124); *disненский* – (adj.) of Disna
дитя, дитяти *дитя, дитяти* – (n., neut., for pl. forms see *дети*) baby, child
дифтерит, дифтерита *дифтерит, дифтерита* – (n., masc.) diphtheria; also seen, *дифтерия*
для *для* – (prep. + gen.) for
дневник, дневника *дневник, дневника* – (n., masc.) journal, diary, day-book
дневной *дневной*– (adj., † *дневный*) days', thus *28-ми дневный* – 28-day
днём *днём* → день *день*
Днепр, Днепра *Днепр, Днепра* – (n., masc., † *Днъпръ*) Dniepr [river]
Днестр, Днестра *Днестр, Днестра* – (n., masc., † *Днъстръ*) Dniestr [river]
дня *дня* → день *день*
до *до* – (prep. + gen.) up to, until, before; *до сего времени* – until this time, before now
добровольно *добровольно* – (adv.) voluntarily, of one's own free will
добровольный *добровольный* – (adj.) voluntary, of one's own will
добросовестно *добросовестно* – (adv., † *добросовъстно*) conscientiously, scrupulously
добрый *добрый* – (adj.) good, kind
доверие, доверия *доверие, доверия* – (n., neut., † *довъріе*) confidence, trust
доверенность, доверенности *доверенность, доверенности* – (n., fem., † *довъренность*) trust, confidence; power of attorney; commission
доверенный *доверенный* – (adj. used as a n., † *довъренный*) proxy, agent, trustee
договор, договора *договор, договора* – (n., masc.) agreement, covenant, pact; *договор между ими заключенъ не былъ* – no agreement was made between them
дождь, дождья *дождь, дождья* – (n., masc., nom. pl. *дожди*, gen. pl. *дождей*) rain
† дозорщик, дозорщика *дозорщик, дозорщика* – (n., masc.) customs-house officer
доильщица, доильщицы *доильщица, доильщицы* – (n., fem.) milkmaid, one who milks
доимщик, доимщика *доимщик, доимщика* – (n., masc.) collector of arrears
доказательство, доказательства *доказательство, доказательства* – (n., neut.) proof, evidence; *в докозательство своей личности* – as proof of his identity
доказать *доказать* – (v.) to prove
доктор, доктора *доктор, доктора* – (n., masc., nom. pl. *доктора*) doctor (fem. *докторша*, doctor's wife, female doctor)
документ, документа *документ, документа* – (n., masc.) document
долгий *долгий* – (adj., † *долгій*) long
должен *должен* – (adj., short form of *должный*) – must, obligated; *[я] должен представить доказателства* – [I] must produce proof; *билетъ этотъ долженъ быть предъявленъ* – this document is to be presented
должностной *должностной* – (adj.) functionary, in office, official; *должностное лицо*, functionary, person in an official capacity
должность, должности *должность, должности* – (n., fem.) duty, employment, function, situation
должный *должный* – (adj.) due, owing; (in expressions with *должен, должна* and *должно*) [I, you, he/she] must
доллар, доллара *доллар, доллара* – (n., masc.) dollar
дом дома *дом дома* – (n., masc.) house
домашний *домашний* – (adj., † *домашній*) household; *домашний учитель* – tutor, private tutor; *на устройство домашнихъ дълъ* – for settling household affairs
доминиканец, доминиканца *доминиканец, доминиканца* – (n., masc.) Dominican monk
домовладелец, домовладельца *домовладелец, домовладельца* – (n., masc., † *домовладълецъ*) house-owner (fem. *домовладелица*)
домовод, домовода *домовод, домовода* – (n., masc.) house-keeper (fem. *домоводка*)

домоправитель, домоправителя *домоправитель, домоправителя* – (n., masc.) steward, house manager (fem. *домоправительница*)
домостроитель, домостроителя *домостроитель, домостроителя* – (n., masc.) good manager, house manager; house builder (fem. *домостроительница*)
домохозяин, домохозяина *домохозяин, домохозяина* – (n., masc., see *хозяин* for declensional forms) owner or master of a house, householder
Донец, Донца *Донец, Донца* – (n., masc.) Donets [river]
доносить *доносить* – (v.) to report; *доношу* – I report
дополнительно *дополнительно* – (adv.) in addition, additionally, more
дорога, дороги *дорога, дороги* – (n., fem.) road, path, way; *железная дорога* – railway
дорогой *дорогой* – (adj.) dear, darling; expensive (note: *дорогой* can also be the instr. sing. of the noun *дорога* ↑)
дорожник, дорожника *дорожник, дорожника* – (n., masc.) roadway worker (fem. *дорожница*)
досмотрщик, досмотрщика *досмотрщик, досмотрщика* – (n., masc.) searcher, inspector
достижение, достижения *достижение, достижения* – (n., neut., † *достиженіе*) reaching, attaining; *за достиженіемъ 43-хъ лѣтняго возраста* – after attaining the age of 43
достовлять *достовлять* – (v.) to furnish, provide
достоинство, достоинства *достоинство, достоинства* – (n., neut.) dignity, merit
достойный *достойный* – (adj.) worthy, deserving
доцент, доцента *доцент, доцента* – (n., masc.) assistant professor
дочь, дочери *дочь, дочери* – (n., fem., instr. sing. *дочерью*, nom. pl. *дочери*, gen. pl. *дочерей*, instr. pl. *дочерьми*) daughter
драгун, драгуна *драгун, драгуна* – (n., masc.) dragoon
† Дрисса, Дриссы *Дрисса, Дриссы* – (n., fem.) town now called Verkhnyadzvinsk, Belarus' (see page 126); *дриссенскій* – of Drissa
дровокол, дровокола *дровокол, дровокола* – (n., masc.) woodchopper
дровоносец, дровоносца *дровоносец, дровоносца* – (n., masc.) carrier of wood (also seen: *дровонос*)
дровосек, дровосека *дровосек, дровосека* – (n., masc., † *дровосѣкъ*) wood-cutter
дровяник, дровяника *дровяник, дровяника* – (n., masc.) one who sells wood
Дрогичин, Дрогичина *Дрогичин, Дрогичина* – (n., masc.) town of Drohiczyn, Poland; *дрогичинский* – (adj.) of Drohiczyn
друг, друга *друг, друга* – (n., masc., nom. pl. *друзья*, gen. and acc. pl. *друзей*) friend
другой *другой* – (adj.) other, another
друзья *друзья*, друзей *друзей* → друг *друг*
Друя, Друи *Друя, Друи* – (n.) town of Druya, Belarus' (see page 126); *друйский* – (adj.) of Druya
дрягиль, дрягиля *дрягиль, дрягиля* – (n., masc.) porter
дряхлость, дряхлости *дряхлость, дряхлости* – (n., fem.) decrepitude, senility
дубильщик, дубильщика *дубильщик, дубильщика* – (n., masc.) tanner
Дубно, Дубна *Дубно, Дубна* – (n., neut.) town of Dubno, Ukraine (see page 130); *дубенский* – of Dubno
дуга, дуги *дуга, дуги* – (n., fem.) arch, bow
дудочник, дудочника *дудочник, дудочника* – (n., masc.) piper
Дунай, Дуная *Дунай, Дуная* – (n., masc.) Danube [river]
духобор, духобора *духобор, духобора* – (n., masc., also seen † *духоборецъ*) Doukhobor, member of a religious sect (fem. *духоборка*)
духовенство, духовенства *духовенство, духовенства* – (n., neut.) collective noun, "the clergy"
духовный *духовный* – (adj.) spiritual; ecclesiastical; *духовное завѣщаніе* – last will and testament
духовник, духовника *духовник, духовника* – (n., masc.) confessor
дщериц, дщерица *дщериц, дщерица* – (n., masc.) nephew, child of your aunt
дщерша, дщерши *дщерша, дщерши* – (n., fem.) niece, child of your aunt
дыхательный *дыхательный* – respiratory
† дьяк, дьяка *дьяк, дьяка* – (n., masc.) official, clerk
дьякон, дьякона *дьякон, дьякона* – (n., masc.) deacon
дьячок, дьячока *дьячок, дьячока* – (n., masc.) church clerk and chanter, sexton
дѣвица *дѣвица* → девица *девица*
дѣвичій *дѣвичій* → девичий *девичий*
дѣдъ *дѣдъ* → дед *дед*
дѣдовщина *дѣдовщина* → дедовщина *дедовщина*
дѣйствительность *дѣйствительность* → действительность *действительность*
дѣйствительный *дѣйствительный* → действительный *действительный*
дѣйствіе *дѣйствіе* → действие *действие*
дѣланіе *дѣланіе* → делание *делание*
дѣлатель *дѣлатель* → делатель *делатель*
дѣлать *дѣлать* → делать *делать*
дѣленіе *дѣленіе* → деление *деление*
дѣло *дѣло* → дело *дело*
дѣлопроизводитель *дѣлопроизводитель* → делопроизводитель *делопроизводитель*
дѣти *дѣти* → дети *дети*
дѣтскій *дѣтскій* → детский *детский*

дѣятель *дѣятель* → деятель *деятель*
дюйм, дюйма *дюйм, дюйма* – (n., masc.) inch
дядя, дяди *дядя, дяди* – (n., masc., gen. pl. *дядей*) uncle; diminutives include *дяденька, дядюшка* and *дядька,* which can also mean "under-tutor"; *великий дядя* – brother of your grandmother or grandfather; *малый дядя* – brother of your father or mother
Дятлово, Дятлова *Дятлово, Дятлова* – (n., neut.) town of Dzyatlava, Belarus' (see page 126); *дятловский* – of Dyatlovo/Dzyatlava
евангелический *евангелический* – (adj., † *евангелическій*) Evangelical Lutheran, Protestant
Евпатория, Евпатории *Евпатория, Евпатории* – (n., fem., † *Евпаторія*) town of Yevpatoriya, Ukraine (see page 134); *евпаторийский* – (adj.) of Yevpatoriya
еврей, еврея *еврей, еврея* – (n., masc., nom. pl. *евреи*, gen. pl. *евреев*) Jew (fem. *еврейка*)
еврейский *еврейский* – (adj., † *еврейскій*) Jewish; Yiddish (when referring to language)
Европа, Европы *Европа, Европы* – (n., fem.) Europe
† егермейстер, егермейстера *егермейстер, егермейстера* – (n., masc.) court master of the hunt [cmp. Germ. *Jägermeister*]
егерский *егерский* – (adj., † *егерскій*) of hunters; *егерскій полкъ* – regiment of chasseurs
егерь, егеря *егерь, егеря* – (n., masc., nom. pl. *егеря*, gen. pl. *егерей*) hunter [cmp. Germ. *Jäger*]
его *его* – (personal and poss. pron., gen./acc. sing. of *он* and *оно*, see page 42) of him, of it; him, it; his, its
единоверец, единоверца *единоверец, единоверца* – (n., masc., † *единовѣрецъ*) co-religionist; also a dissenter from the Orthodox church
единокровный *единокровный* – (adj.) consanguineous; *единокровный брат*, half brother
единственный *единственный* – (adj.) single, sole, only
её *её* – (personal and poss. pron., gen./acc. of *она*, see page 42) of her, of it, her, it, hers, its
ежедневный *ежедневный* – (adj.) daily, every day
ездить *ездить* – (v., † *ѣздить*) to travel, go; *никуда не ездил* – went nowhere
ездовой, ездового *ездовой, ездового* – (adj. used as a n., masc., † *ѣздовой*) messenger on horseback, driver (in a battery)
ездок, ездока *ездок, ездока* – (n., masc., † *ѣздокъ*) horseman, rider; passenger
ей *ей* – (personal pron., dat./instr. of *она*, see page 42) her, it, to her, to it
Екатеринослав, Екатеринослава *Екатеринослав, Екатеринослава* – (n., masc.) town now called Dnipropetrovs'k, Ukraine (see page 134); *екатеринославский* – of Yekaterinoslav
† екзарх *екзарх* → экзарх *экзарх*
елеосвящение, елеосвящения *елеосвящение, елеосвящения* – (n., neut., † *елеосвященіе*) Extreme Unction, last rites
Елизаветполь, Елизаветполя *Елизаветполь, Елизаветполя* – (n., masc., also spelled *Елисаветполь*) Yelizavetpol', name of a town in Azerbaijan (see page 137); *елизаветпольский* – of Yelizavetpol'
† Елисаветград, Елисаветграда *Елисаветград, Елисаветграда* – (n., masc.) town now called Kirovohrad, Ukraine (see page 133); *елисаветградский* – of Elisavetgrad/Kirovohrad
Елисаветполь *Елисаветполь* → Елизаветполь *Елизаветполь*
ему *ему* – (personal pron., dat. of *он* and *оно*, see page 42) [to] him, [to] it
Енисей, Енисея *Енисей, Енисея* – (n., masc.) Yenisei [river]
енисейский *енисейский* – (adj., † *енисейскій*) of the Yenisei region , especially Yeniseisk *gubernia* (see page 137)
† епархъ, епарха *епархъ, епарха* – (n., masc.) eparch
епископ, епископа *епископ, епископа* – (n., masc.) bishop
Ереван *Ереван* → Эриванъ *Эриванъ*
еретик, еретика *еретик, еретика* – (n., masc.) heretic
есаул, есаула *есаул, есаула* – (n., masc.) Cossack captain; assistant to a robber chief
если *если* – (conj.) if
естественно *естественно* – (adv.) naturally; *умереть естественно* – to die naturally
естественный *естественный* – (adj.) natural; *естественная смерть* – a natural death; *умереть естественной смертью* – to die a natural death
есть *есть* – (verb, 3rd person plural present tense of *быть*, to be) there are; *есть ли X в Вашем архиве* – is/are there X in your archive?
ефрейтор, ефрейтора *ефрейтор, ефрейтора* – (n., masc.) lance corporal [cmp. German *Gefreiter*]
ею *ею* – (personal pron., † form of *ей*, instr. of *она*) her, it
ж *ж* → же *же*
жаба, жабы *жаба, жабы* – (n., fem.) angina, quinsy
жалоба, жалобы *жалоба, жалобы* – (n., fem.) complaint, appeal; *по жалобѣ* – after the appeal
жалобщик, жалобщика *жалобщик, жалобщика* – (n., masc.) complainant, plaintiff
жандарм, жандарма *жандарм, жандарма* – (n., masc.) gendarme
жар, жара *жар, жара* – (n., masc.) fever
ж-д. *ж-д.* → железнодорожный *железнодорожный*
же *же* – (adverb, also sometimes simply *ж*, † *жъ*) the same, e. g., *сего жъ года*, that same year; *в то же время* – at the same time

жезлоносец, жезлоносца *жезлоносец, жезлоносца* – (n., masc.) crosier-bearer, mace-bearer
желание, желания *желание, желания* – (n., neut., † *желаніе*) desire; *по желанію* – as desired; *по желанію супруговъ* – by the wishes of the spouses
желать *желать* – (v.) to wish, desire
жел.-дор. *жел.-дор.* → железнодоржный *железнодорожный*
железная дорога, железной дороги *железная дорога, железной дороги* – (n., fem., *желѣзная дорога*) railroad
железнодорожник, железнодорожника *железнодорожник, железнодорожника* – (n., masc., † *желѣзнодорожник*) railway concessionaire, railway magnate [older meanings], railway worker [modern meaning] (fem. *железнодорожница*)
железнодорожный *железнодорожный* – (adj., abbr. *ж-д.* or *жел.-дор.*, † *желѣзнодорожный*) railroad, of the railroad
желтуха, желтухи *желтуха, желтухи* – (n., fem.) jaundice
жёлтый *жёлтый* – (adj., † *жолтый*) yellow; *жёлтая болезнь* – jaundice; *желтая лихорадка* – yellow fever
желудок, желудка *желудок, желудка* – (n., masc.) stomach
желудочный *желудочный* – (adj.) of the stomach; *желудочное заболевание* – gastric disease
жёлчная лихорадка, жёлчной лихорадки *жёлчная лихорадка, жёлчной лихорадки* – (n., fem.) gall-sickness
желѣзнодорожный *желѣзнодорожный* → железнодорожный *железнодорожный*
жена, жены *жена, жены* – (n., fem., nom. pl. *жёны*, gen. pl. *жён*) wife
женатый *женатый* – (adj., short form *женат*) married (said only of males)
жених, жениха *жених, жениха* – (n., masc.) bridegroom, betrothed; eligible bachelor
женский *женский* – (adj., † *женскій*) of a woman, female; † *женска пола* – of the female gender
женщина, женщины *женщина, женщины* – (n., fem.) woman
жеребью *жеребью* or жеребья *жеребья* → жребий *жребий*
жестяник, жестяника *жестяник, жестяника* – (n., masc.) tinsmith
живёт *живёт* or живёте *живёте* → жить *жить*
живодёр, живодёра *живодёр, живодёра* – (n., masc.) flayer, fleecer, slaughterer
живой *живой* – (adj.) alive, living; *если родителей нѣтъ въ живыхъ* – if there are no parents among the living, i. e., if the parents are no longer alive; *находящійся въ живыхъ* – still alive, still among the living
живущий *живющий* – (part. from *жить*; † *живущій*) living
† жидъ, жида *жидъ, жида* – (n., masc.) Jew (fem. *жидовка*). **Please note**: in modern Russian this word is a very offensive slur; *еврей* is the socially acceptable term. But in older records you may see *жидъ* used with no intention of giving offense, influenced perhaps by Polish *Żyd* and Lithuanian *žydas,* which in those languages are normal and acceptable words for "Jew."
жизнь, жизни *жизнь, жизни* – (n., fem.) life; *средства къ жизни* – means of support
жилец, жильца *жилец, жильца* – (n., masc.) inhabitant (fem. *жилица*)
жилой *жилой* – (adj.) habitable; *жилое строение* – habitable structure
житель, жителя *житель, жителя* – (n., masc., gen. pl. *жителей*) inhabitant, resident (fem. *жительница*); *постоянный житель* – permanent resident
жительство, жительства *жительство, жительства* – (n., neut.) residence, stay
жительствующий *жительствующий* – (part. from *жительствовать*, to reside, † *жительствующій*) residing
Житомир, Житомира *Житомир, Житомира* – (n., masc.) Zhytomyr, Ukraine (see page 130)
жить *жить* – (v.) to live; *съ котораго времени живете въ этомъ приходѣ* – how long have you lived in this parish
жнец, жнеца *жнец, жнеца* – (n., masc., also seen: *жнея*) reaper, harvester (fem. *жница*)
жолтый *жолтый* → жёлтый *жёлтый*
жребий, жребия *жребий, жребия*– (n., masc., † *жребій* or *жеребій* or *жеребьё*) lot, drawing of lots; *по жеребью* – by lot
журнал, журнала *журнал, журнала* – (n., masc.) journal, day-book, log
журналист, журналиста *журналист, журналиста* – (n., masc.) journalist, newspaper writer
за *за* – (prep.: + instr.) behind, over, past, on the other side of, at, after, because of; (+ acc.) for, on behalf of, due to; in, within, before, at a distance of, by; *за 1910 год* – for the year 1910
забайкальский *забайкальский* – (adj., † *забайкальскій*) of the region beyond Lake Baikal in Asiatic Russia (see page 137)
заболевание, заболевания *заболевание, заболевания* – (n., neut., † *заболѣваніе*) disease
забранный *забранный* – (part. from *забрать*) gathered, collected, assembled
забрать *забрать* – (v.) to gather, collect

заведение, заведения *заведение, заведения* – (n., neut., † *заведенie*) facility
заведующий, заведующего *заведующий, заведующего* – († *завѣдующий*, part. of *заведовать*, to manage, administer, used as a n., masc.) manager (+ instr.)
заведывающий, заведывающего *заведывающий, заведывающего* – († *завѣдывающий*, part. of *заведывать*, to manage, administer, used as a n., masc.) administrator, manager (+ instr.)
завет, завета *завет, завета* (n., masc., † *завѣтъ*) covenant, law; *Ветхий Завет*, the Old Testament; *Новый Завет*, the New Testament
завещание, завещания *завещание, завещания* – (n., neut., † *завѣшанie*) order; testament, will (also *духовное завещание*); *умереть без завещания* – to die intestate
завещатель, завещателя *завещатель, завещателя* – (n., masc., † *завѣщатель*) testator
завод, завода *завод, завода* – (n., masc.) works, plant, factory, facility
заводитель, заводителя *заводитель, заводителя* – (n., masc.) founder, establisher
заводчик, заводчика *заводчик, заводчика* – (n., masc.) manufacturer, factory- or mill-owner
завтра *завтра* – (adv.) tomorrow
завѣдующiй *завѣдующiй* → заведующий *заведующий*
завѣдывающiй *завѣдывающiй* → заведывающий *заведывающий*
завѣщанie *завѣщанie* → завещание *завещание*
загонщик, загонщика *загонщик, загонщика* – (n., masc.) † cattle-drover; one who beats the bushes (during a hunt)
заграницу *заграницу* → граница *граница*
заграничный *заграничный* – (adj.) foreign; *заграничный паспорт* – passport for traveling abroad (as opposed to the internal passports all citizens were required to carry)
заём, займа *заём, займа* – (n., masc.) borrowing, loan; *актъ займа ссуды* – document of taking out a loan
заёмщик, заёмщика *заёмщик, заёмщика* – (n., masc.) borrower (fem. *заёмщица*)
заинтересованный *заинтересованный* – (part. from *заинтересовать*, to interest) interested, concerned, involved
заказной *заказной* – (adj.) registered; *заказное письмо* – registered letter
закаспийский *закаспийский* – (adj., † *закаспiйскiй*) of the area beyond the Caspian Sea (see page 137)
закладчик, закладчика *закладчик, закладчика* – (n., masc.) pawner, mortgager (fem. *закладчица*)
заключённый *заключённый* – (part. from *заключить*) [was] contracted, concluded
заключить *заключить* – (v.) to conclude, close; *заключила брачный союзъ съ* – contracted a marital union with (i. e., married)
закон, закона *закон, закона* – (n., masc.) law; religion
законник, законника *законник, законника* – (n., masc.) lawyer, jurist (fem. *законница*)
законный *законный* – (adj.) legal, lawful; *законная жена* – lawful wedded wife; *законное дитя* – legitimate child
законовед, законоведа *законовед, законоведа* – (n., masc., † *законовѣд*, also seen: *законовѣдецъ*) lawyer, jurist
законодатель, законодателя *законодатель, законодателя* – (n., masc.) legislator, lawgiver
законченный *законченный* – (part. from *закончить*, to finish) [was] finished, concluded
закройщик, закройщика *закройщик, закройщика* – (n., masc.) cutter [of clothes] (fem. *закройщица*)
закупщик, закупщика *закупщик, закупщика* – (n., masc.) buyer, purchaser (fem. *закупщица*)
залог, залога *залог, залога* – (n., masc.) security, guarantee; pledge, pawn
замедлить *замедлить* – (v.) to linger, delay, be tardy
замеченный *замеченный* – (part. from *замечить*, † *замѣченный*) noted, observed
заметить *заметить* – (v., † *замѣтить*) to note, observe
Замосць, Замосця *Замосць, Замосця* – (n., masc., † *Замостье*) town of Zamość, Poland (see page 120); *замосцьский* – († *замостскiй*) of Zamość
замужество, замужества *замужество, замужества* – (n., neut.) marriage (used only of women)
замужняя, замужней *замужняя, замужней* – (adj. used as a n., fem.) married woman
занимать *занимать* – (v.) to occupy
занятие, занятия *занятие, занятия* – (n., neut., † *занятie*) occupation, pursuit, work
занятой *занятой* – (adj.) busy, occupied
запас, запаса *запас, запаса* – (n., masc.) provision, stock, reserve; (military) reserves
запасный *запасный* – (adj.) reserve
записанный *записанный* – (part. from *записать*) entered, written down
записать *записать* – (v.) to enter, write down; *записан* – entered, written down
записка, записки *записка, записки* – (n., fem.) note
записываться *записываться* – (v.) to be written in, inscribed
запись, записи *запись, записи* – (n., fem.) writing, entry in a register or roll
запрос, запроса *запрос, запроса* – (n.) inquiry, question, demand
заработник, заработника *заработник, заработника* – (n., masc.) wage-earner

заработный *заработный* – (adj.) for hire, for pay
заработок, заработка *заработок, заработка* – (n., masc.) earnings, money; *уходить на заработки* – to leave to go earn a living
заражение, заражения *заражение, заражения* (n., neut., † *зараженіе*) infection; *заражение крови* – blood poisoning
зараза, заразы *зараза, заразы* – (n., fem.) infection, contagion
заразный *заразный* – (adj.) infectious; *заразные болезни* – communicable diseases
засвидетельствование, засвидетельствования *засвидетельствование, засвидетельствования* – (n., neut., † *засвидѣтельствованіе*) authentication
заседание, заседания *заседание, заседания* – (n., neut., † *засѣданіе*) session, sitting
заседатель, заседателя *заседатель, заседателя* – (n., masc., † *засѣдатель*) assessor; *присяжный заседатель* – juror
Заславль, Заславля *Заславль, Заславля* – (n., masc.) town of Zaslaŭe, Belarus' (see page 127); *заславский* – (adj.) of Zaslavl'/ Zaslaŭe
заслуживать *заслуживать* – (v.) to deserve, earn, merit
заст. *заст.* → застенок *застенок*
застенок, застенка *застенок, застенка* (n., masc. † *застѣнокъ*) "[place] behind a wall," in a Polish or Belarusian context a farmstead of minor nobles who worked their own land (compare Polish *zaścianek*); in a purely Russian context, a term for "torture chamber"
застрахованный *застрахованный* – (part. from *застраховать*, to insure) insured
засѣданіе *засѣданіе* → заседание, *заседание*
засѣдатель *засѣдатель* → заседатель, *заседатель*
заупокойный *заупокойный* – (adj.) for the repose of the soul, e. g., *литургия заупокойная*, a Mass for the repose of the soul [of]
зачисление, зачисления *зачисление, зачисления* – (n., neut., † *зачисленіе*) enrollment, registration
зачисленный *зачисленный* – (part., from *зачислить*) enlisted, enrolled, entered
зачислить *зачислить* – (v.) to enlist, enroll (e. g., in a regiment); to enter (e. g., make an entry in a register or account)
заштатный *заштатный* – (adj.) supernumerary; † *заштатный городъ* – a town within an *uyezd* that was not its administrative center
заявить *заявить* – (v., perf. counterpart of *заявлять*) to declare, state; *я заявилъ о своемъ правѣ на освобожденіе* – I claimed my right to be released
заявивший *заявивший* – (part., from *заявить*, † *заявившій*) having declared, stated; (used as a n.) the one[s] having stated, having declared; *никогда не заявившій своего желанія* – having never declared a desire
заявление, заявления *заявление, заявления* – (n., neut., † *заявленіе*) deposition, statement, testimony
заявленный *заявленный* – (part. from *заявить*) stated, declared; *позволеніе заявлено словесно* – permission was given orally
заявлять *заявлять* – (v.) to declare, announce, make known; *я никогда не заявлялъ* – I have never declared
звание, звания *звание, звания* – (n., neut., † *званіе*) calling, state, estate, condition
звать *звать* – (v.) to call, name; *моего предка звали X* – my ancestor's name was X
Звенигородка, Звенигородки *Звенигородка, Звенигородки* – (n., fem.) town of Zvenyhorodka, Ukraine (see page 132); *звенигородский* – (adj.) of Zvenyhorodka
зверолов, зверолова *зверолов, зверолова* – (n., masc., † *звѣроловъ*) hunter
звонарь, звонаря *звонарь, звонаря* – (n., fem.) bellringer (fem. *звонариха*, bellringer's wife)
здание, здания *здание, здания* – (n., neut., † *зданіе*) building, edifice
здесь *здесь* – (adv., † *здѣсь*) here; *здѣсь почиваетъ* or *здѣсь покоится*, "here lies"
здешний *здешний* – (adj., † *здѣшній*) local, from here; *здѣшный житель* – local resident; *здѣшные земледѣльцы* – local farmers
здоровый *здоровый* – (adj.) healthy
здравый *здравый* – (adj.) sound, sane
здѣсь *здѣсь* → здесь *здесь*
здѣшний *здѣшний* → здешний *здѣшний*
зеленщик, зеленщика *зеленщик зеленщика* – (n., masc.) green-grocer
Зельва, Зельвы *Зельва, Зельвы* – (n., fem.) town of Zel'va, Belarus' (see page 127); *зельвинский* – (adj.) of Zel'va
земледелец, земледельца *земледелец, земледельца* – (n., masc., † *земледѣлецъ*) farmer
землекоп, землекопа *землекоп, землекопа* – (n., masc.) digger (also seen: *землекопщик*)
землемер, землемера *землемер, землемера* – (n., masc., † *землемѣръ*) surveyor
земля, земли *земля, земли* – (n., fem.) land, district; *Земля войска Донского* – Land of the Don Army
земляк, земляка *земляк, земляка* – (n., masc.) fellow countryman, one who comes from the same area or village (fem. *землячка*)
землячество, землячества *землячество, землячества* – (n., neut.) a society or association of *земляки*, people from the same area or country

земский *земский* – (adj., † *земскій*) of a *земство*
† земской, земскаго *земской, земскаго* – (adj. used as a n.) country-clerk
земство, земства *земство, земства* – (n., neut.) elective district council in pre-Revolutionary Russia
Змиев, Змиева *Змиев, Змиева* – (n., masc., † *Зміевъ*) town of Zmiyiv, Ukraine (see page 134); *змиевский* – (adj.) of Zmiyev/Zmiyiv
знак, знака *знак, знака* – (n., masc.) sign, mark, token; *его знак* – his mark (made by one who can't sign his name); *знак отличия* – (military) decoration, medal
знакомый *знакомый* – (adj.) familiar, acquainted (*с* – with); (used as a n.) acquaintance, friend
знание, знания *знание, знания* – (n., neut., † *знаніе*) knowledge, skill
знать, знати *знать, знати* – (n., fem.) nobles, gentry
знать *знать* – (v.) to know; *я знаю* – I know; *он знает* – he knows; *мы знаем* – we know; *не знаю* – I don't know; *если Вы знаете* – if you know
значить *значить* – (v.) to mean; for *значитъ* with a signature in Hebrew letters, see page 96
знающий *знающий* – (part. from *знать*, † *знающій*) knowing; *показаніе двухъ свидѣтелей знающихъ меня* – the statement of two people knowing me (i. e., who know me)
зоб, зоба *зоб, зоба* – (n., masc.) goiter, wen
зодчий, зодчего *зодчий, зодчего* – (adj. used as a n., masc.) architect, builder
золовка, золовки *золовка, золовки* – (n., fem.) sister-in-law (husband's sister)
Золотоноша, Золотоноши *Золотоноша, Золотоноши* – (n., fem.) town of Zolotonosha, Ukraine (see page 133); *золотоношенский* – (adj.) of Zolotonosha
золотуха, золотухи *золотуха, золотухи* – (n., fem.) scrofula, struma
† Зѣньковъ, Зѣнькова *Зѣньковъ, Зѣнькова* – (n., masc.) town of Zin'kiv, Ukraine (see page 133); † *зѣньковскій* – (adj.) of Zin'kiv
зять, зятя *зять, зятя* – (n., masc., nom. pl. *зятья*, gen. pl. *зятьёв*) son-in-law; brother-in-law (sister's husband)
и *и* – (conj.) and; *и так далее* († *и такъ далѣе*) and so on, etc.; *и тому подобное* – and the like
Ивье, Ивья *Ивье, Ивья* – (n., neut.) town of Iŭe, Belarus' (see page 126); *ивьевский* – (adj.) of Iv'ye/Iŭe
игольщик, игольщика *игольщик, игольщика* – (n., masc.) needle-maker
игумен, игумена *игумен, игумена* – (n., masc.) abbot, superior (of a monastery)
† Игуменъ, Игумена *Игуменъ, Игумена* – (n., masc.) former Russian name of the town of Chèrven', Belarus' (see page 126); *игуменскій* – (adj.) of Igumen/Chèrven'
игуменья, игуменьи *игуменья, игуменьи* – (n., fem.) abbess, mother superior
идея, идеи *идея, идеи* – (n., fem.) idea
иезуит, иезуита *иезуит, иезуита* – (n., masc., † *іезуитъ*) Jesuit
иерарх, иерарха *иерарх, иерарха* – (n., masc., † *іерархъ*) hierarch
иерей, иерея *иерей, иерея* – (n., masc., † *іерей*) priest
иеродиаконъ, иеродиакона *иеродиаконъ, иеродиакона* – (n., masc., † *іеродіаконъ*) deacon of an order
иеромонах, иеромонаха *иеромонах, иеромонаха* – (n., masc., † *іеромонахъ*) priest of an order
Иерусалим, Иерусалима *Иерусалим, Иерусалима* – (n., masc., † *Іерусалимъ*) Jerusalem
из *из* – (*изо* before certain consonant clusters, prep. + gen.) from, out of
изба, избы *изба, избы* – (n., fem.) peasant's house, hut, cottage
избиратель, избирателя *избиратель, избирателя* – (n., masc.) elector (fem. *избирательница*); *список избирателей* – poll-book
известный *известный* – (adj., † *извѣстный*) – known, well-known; *мѣсто есть имъ извѣстно* – the place is known to them; *известно, что* – it is well known that …
извещать *извещать* – (v., † *извѣщать*) to notify, inform, make known; *извещает* – he informs, notifies; *извещают* – they inform, notify
† извощикъ, извощика *извощикъ, извощика* – (n., masc.) carrier, hired coachman (modern spelling *извозчик*)
извѣстный *извѣстный* → известный *известный*
извѣщать *извѣщать* → извещать *извещать*
изгнанник, изгнанника *изгнанник, изгнанника* – (n., masc.) exile, outlaw (fem. *изгнанница*)
издатель, издателя *издатель, издателя* – (n., masc.) publisher, † editor (fem. *издательница*)
Измаил, Измаила *Измаил, Измаила* – (n., masc.) town of Izmayil, Ukraine (see page 132); *измаильский* – (adj.) of Izmail/Izmayil
изслѣдованіе *изслѣдованіе* → исследование *исследование*
изъявление, изъявления *изъявление, изъявления* – (n., neut., † *изъявленіе*) ulceration; testimony
изъявленный *изъявленный* – (part. from *изъявить*, to express) expressed, stated
изъяснённый *изъяснённый* – (part. from *изъяснить*, to explain) explained, expounded
Изюм, Изюма *Изюм, Изюма* – (n., masc.) town of Izyum, Ukraine (see page 134); *изюмский* – (adj.) of Izyum

Изяслав, Изяслава *Изяслав, Изяслава* – (n., masc.) town of Izyaslav, Ukraine (see page 130); *изяславский* – (adj.) of Izyaslav
иконописец, иконописца *иконописец, иконописца* – (n., masc.) image-painter
† Илжа, Илжи *Илжа, Илжи* – (n., fem.) town of Iłża, Poland (see page 120); *илжецкій* – of Iłża
или *или* – (conj.) or
им *им* – (personal pron., instr. sing. of *он* and *оно*, dat. of *они*, see page 42) him, it, them
имевший *имевший* – (part. from *иметь*, to have, † *имѣвшій*) having had; *имѣвшій отъ роду 80 лѣтъ* – at the age of 80
имена *имена*, имени *имени* → имя *имя*
именинник, именинника *именинник, именинника* – (n., masc.) one celebrating his name-day (fem. *именинница*)
имение, имения *имение, имения* – (n., neut., † *имѣніе*) estate, landed property
именно *именно* – (adv.) exactly; to wit, namely
иметь *иметь* – (v., † *имѣть*) to have; *не имѣю* – I do not have; *двадцать четыре лѣтъ отъ роду имѣющій* — literally "having 24 years from birth," i. e., 24 years old; *имѣетъ ли дѣтей* – does he/she have children?
иметься *иметься* – (v., † *имѣться*) to be, to exist; *не имѣется* – there is no, there is not (literally "does not have itself"); *если имѣются въ Россіи родственники* – if there are relatives in Russia
имеющий *имеющий* – (part. of *иметь*, † *имѣющій*) having, possessing; *полъ-года отъ роду имѣющій* – 6 months old
ими *ими* – (personal pron., instr. of *они*, see page 42) them
император, императора *император, императора* – (n., masc.) emperor
императорский *императорский* – (adj., † *императорскій*) imperial
империя империи *империя империи* – (n., fem., † *имперія*) empire
имущество, имущества *имущество, имущества* – (n., neut.) property, goods, chattels; *они никакого уговора о имуществѣ между собою не заключили* – they had made no agreement between themselves regarding property
имѣвшій *имѣвшій* → имевший *имевший*
имѣніе *имѣніе* → имение *имение*
имѣющій *имѣющій* → имеющий *имеющий*
имя, имени *имя, имени* – (n., neut., see page 41 for declension) first name; *по имени Вацлавъ* – Wacław by name; *окрещено дитя именемъ Анна* – the child was christened Anna
инвентарь, инвентаря *инвентарь, инвентаря* – (n., masc.) inventory
† Ингерманландія, Ингерманландіи *Ингерманландія, Ингерманландіи* – (n., fem.) archaic name for the area around St. Petersburg (see page 122)
инженер, инженера *инженер, инженера* – (n., masc.) engineer
иноверец, иноверца *иноверец, иноверца* – (n., masc., † *иновѣрецъ*) heterodox, one believing in a different religion (fem. *иноверка*)
иногородец, иногородца *иногородец, иногородца* – (n., masc.) one from a different city
иноземец, иноземца *иноземец, иноземца* – (n., masc.) foreigner (fem. *иноземка*)
† инок, инока *инок, инока* – (n., masc.) monk, friar
иностранец, иностранца *иностранец, иностранца* – (n., masc.) foreigner (fem. *иностранка*)
иностранный *иностранный* – (adj.) foreign; *Министерство Иностранныхъ Дѣлъ* – Ministry of Foreign Affairs
инспектор, инспектора *инспектор, инспектора* – (n., masc.) inspector, supervisor
инструкция, инструкции *инструкция, инструкции* – (n., fem., † *инструкція*) instruction, order; paragraph (a specific point in a regulation)
интерн, интерна *интерн, интерна* – (n., masc.) † boarder at a boarding-school; intern (doctor)
инфлуэнца, инфлуэнцы *инфлуэнца, инфлуэнцы* (n., fem., also seen *инфлюэнца, инфлуэнца*) influenza
Инфлянты *Инфлянты* → Ливония *Ливония*
информация, информации *информация, информации* – (n., fem., † *информація*) information
† иподіаконъ, иподіакона *иподіаконъ, иподіакона* – (n., masc.) subdeacon
Иркутск, Иркутска *Иркутск, Иркутска* – (n., masc.) Irkutsk, name of a town and a region in Siberia (see page 137); *иркутский* – of Irkutsk
исключённый *исключённый* – (part. from *исключить*, to exclude) excluded
искусник, искусника *искусник, искусника* – (n., masc.) master, expert (*в* – in)
искусство, искусства *искусство, искусства* – (n., neut.) art, skill
исповедание, исповедания *исповедание, исповедания* – (n., neut., † *исповѣданіе*) religion, faith; confession
исповедаться *исповедаться* – (v., † *исповѣдаться*) to be confessed
исповедающийся *исповедающийся* – (part. from *исповедаться*, to confess; † *исповѣдающій*) making Confession
исповедник, исповедника *исповедник, исповедника* – (n., masc., † *исповѣдникъ*) confessor
исповедывать *исповедывать* – (v., † *исповѣдывать*) to hear confession, shrive

исповедь, исповеди *исповедь, исповеди* – (n., fem., † *исповѣдь*) confession (to a priest)
исполнение, исполнения *исполнение, исполнения* – (n., neut., † *исполненіе*) fulfillment; *требуетъ меня къ исполненію воинской повинности* – requires me to fulfill [my] military obligation; *явился къ исполненію воиннской повинности* – reported to fulfill his military duty
† исправникъ, исправника *исправникъ, исправника* – (n., masc.) district police captain
испытание, испытания *испытание, испытания* – (n., neut., † *испытаніе*) examination, testing
исследование, исследования *исследование, исследования* – (n., neut., † *изслѣдованіе*) investigation, inquiry
истёкший *истёкший* – (part. from *истечь*, to flow out, elapse; † *истёкшій*) past, last, expired; *въ истекшемъ Октябрѣ* – in last October
истец, истца *истец, истца* – (n., masc.) applicant, plaintiff (fem. *истица*)
истопник, истопника *истопник, истопника* – (n., masc.) stoker, furnace-man (fem. *истопница*)
исторический *исторический* – (adj., † *историческій*) historical
история, истории *история, истории* – (n., fem., † *исторія*) history
исходящий *исходящий* – (part. from *исходить*, to go out; † *исхчодящій*) departing, of departures
и. т. д. *и. т. д.* – (abbr. for *и так далее*) and so on, etc.
и т. п. *и т. п.* – (abbr. for *и тому подобное*) and the like
итого *итого* – (adv.) in total, for a total of
итогъ, итога *итогъ, итога* – (n., masc.) total; *въ итогѣ* – in total, in all
иудейский *иудейский* – (adj., † *іудейскій*) Jewish
их *их* – (personal and poss. pron., gen./acc. of *они*, see p. 42) them; their, of them
июль, июля *июль, июля* – (n., masc., † *іюль*) July
июнь, июня *июнь, июня* – (n., masc., † *іюнь*) June
Ияр, Ияра *Ияр, Ияра* – (n., masc., † *Іяръ*) Iyar, a month in the Jewish calendar (see page 47)
іезуитъ *іезуитъ* → иезуит *иезуит*
іерархъ *іерархъ* → иерарх *иерарх*
іерей *іерей* → иерей *иерей*
іеродіаконъ *іеродіаконъ* → иеродиаконъ *иеродиаконъ*
іеромонахъ *іеромонахъ* → иеромонах *иеромонах*
іудейскій *іудейскій* → иудейский *иудейский*
іюль *іюль* → июль *июль*
іюнь *іюнь* → июнь *июнь*
к *к* – (prep. + dat., before certain consonant clusters *ко*) to, toward, for
кабатчик, кабатчика *кабатчик, кабатчика* - (n., masc.) tavern-keeper (fem. *кабатчица*)
кавалер, кавалера *кавалер, кавалера* – (n., masc.) knight
кавалерист, кавалериста *кавалерист, кавалериста* – (n., masc.) cavalryman
Кавказ, Кавказа *Кавказ, Кавказа* – (n., masc.) the Caucasus; *на Кавказе* – in the Caucasus
кагал, кагала *кагал, кагала* – (n., masc.) *kahal*, an autonomous Jewish administration
кадастр, кадастра *кадастр, кадастра* – (n., masc.) cadastre, official statement of the quantity and value of real property
кадет, кадета *кадет, кадета* – (n., masc.) cadet
кадры, кадров *кадры, кадров* – (n., masc., pl.) cadre, list of officers, regiment staff
каждый *каждый* – (adj.) each; *каждый из нас* – each of us
казак, казака *казак, казака* – (n., masc.) Cossack
Казань, Казани *Казань, Казани* – (n., fem.) Kazan', name of a town and region (see page 135); *казанский* – of Kazan'
казарма, казармы *казарма, казармы* – (n., fem.) barracks
казарменный *казарменный* – (adj.) of, like barracks
казённый *казённый* – (adj.) of the crown, fiscal; *казённая палата* – the *gubernia* institution in charge of taxation and finances
казначей, казначея *казначей, казначея* – (n., masc.) treasurer, keeper of the treasury, paymaster
казначейство, казначейства *казначейство, казначейства* – (n., neut.) treasury, exchequer
как *как* – (adv., † *какъ*) how, in what manner; *как ... так и* – both ... and; (conj.) when
каков *каков* – (interr. pron.) what sort of? what [is]
какой *какой* – (pron., see declension on p. 43) what? what kind of?; some kind of; which; *какое ему дано имя* – what name was given him?
калгас *калгас* – Belarusian term, equivalent to Russian колхоз, q. v.
Калининград, Калининграда *Калининград, Калининграда* – (n., masc.) Russian name for the city Poles call *Królewiec* († *Королевецъ*), Germans *Königsberg* († *Кёнигсбергъ*), Lithuanians *Karaliaučius* (see page 124)
Калиш, Калиша *Калиш, Калиша* – (n., masc.) Kalisz, Poland (see page 118); *калишский* – of Kalisz
Калуга, Калуги *Калуга, Калуги* – (n., fem.) Kaluga, name of a town in Russia (see page 135); *калужский* – of Kaluga
Кальвария, Калвьарии *Кальвария, Кальварии* – (n., fem., † *Кальварія*) Kalvarija, Lithuania (see page 120); † *кальварійскій* – of Kalwaryja
Каменец, Каменца *Каменец Каменца* – (n., masc.) town of Kamyanets, Belarus' (see page 127); *каменецкий* – (adj.) of Kamenets/Kamyanets

Каменец-Подольский, Каменца-Подольского *Каменец-Подольский, Каменца-Подольского* – (n., masc.) town of Kam'yanets Podil's'kyi, Ukraine (see page 132)
каменолом, каменолома *каменолом, каменолома* – (n., masc.) quarryman
каменщик, каменщика *каменщик, каменщика* – (n., masc.) stone mason, bricklayer
камергер, камергера *камергер, камергера* – (n., masc.) chamberlain [cmp. Germ. *Kammerherr*]
камердинер, камердинера *камердинер, камердинера* – (n., masc.) personal attendant, valet [cmp. Germ. *Kammerdiener*]
камерфрау *камерфрау* – (n. fem., not declined) lady's maid [cmp. Germ. *Kammerfrau*]
камерфрейлина, камерфрейлины *камерфрейлина, камерфрейлины* – (n. fem.) maid of honor of the bed-chamber [cmp. Germ. *Kammerfräulein*]
кампания, кампании *кампания, кампании* – (n., fem., † *кампанія*) campaign
канатчик, канатчика *канатчик, канатчика* – (n., masc.) rope-maker
Канев, Канева *Канев, Канева* – (n., masc.) town of Kaniv, Ukraine (see page 132); *каневский* – (adj.) of Kanev
канцелярист, канцеляриста *канцелярист, канцеляриста* – (n., masc.) clerk in chancery, e. g., *канцелярист суда*, court clerk
канцелярия, канцелярии *канцелярия, канцелярии* – (n., fem., † *канцелярія*) chancellory, chancery
капельмейстер, капельмейстера *капельмейстер, капельмейстера* – (n., masc.) bandleader, conductor [cmp. German *Kappelmeister*]
капитан, капитана *капитан, капитана* – (n., masc.) captain
капрал, капрала *капрал, капрала* – (n., masc.) corporal
каптенармус, каптенармуса *каптенармус, каптенармуса* – (n., masc.) master at arms
караим, караима *караим, караима* – (n., masc.) Karaim Jew (fem. *караимка*)
караульщик, караульщика *караульщик, караульщика* – (n., masc.) sentry, guard (fem. *караульщица*)
Кареличи *Кареличи* → Кореличи *Кореличи*
каретник, каретника *каретник, каретника* – (n., masc.) carriage-maker (also a coach-house)
Карпаты, Карпат *Карпаты, Карпат* – (n., fem. pl.) the Carpathian mountains, also *Карпатские горы*
карий *карий* – (adj., † *карій*) brown, hazel
кассация, кассации *кассация, кассации* – (n., fem., † *кассація*) cassation, an appeal of a judicial verdict; sometimes refers to the government's seizure of church property
Каспийское море, Каспийского моря *Каспийское море, Каспийского моря* – (n., neut., † *Каспійское море*) Caspian Sea
касса, кассы *касса, кассы* – (n., fem.) cash, cash-office; bank
кассир, кассира *кассир, кассира* – (n., masc.) cashier
кассовый *кассовый* – (adj.) of cash, of banks
кастелян, кастеляна *кастелян, кастеляна* – (n., masc.) castellan
кастелянша, кастелянши *кастелянша, кастелянши* – (n., fem.) woman in charge of linen in a hospital, rest home, etc.
катар, катара *катар, катара* – (n., masc., † *катарръ*) catarrh
каторжник, каторжника *каторжник, каторжника* – (n., masc.) convict
качество, качества *качество, качества* – (n., neut.) quality, property; capacity, position; *в качестве* – in the capacity (of), in the position (of), as
кашевар, кашевара *кашевар, кашевара* – (n., masc.) cook for a military unit, an *artel*, etc. (fem. *кашеварка*)
квартал, квартала *квартал, квартала* – (n., masc.) quarter, block (in a town)
квартира, квартиры *квартира, квартиры* – (n., fem.) apartment; (mil.) quarters
квартирмейстер, квартирмейстера *квартирмейстер, квартирмейстера* – (n., masc.) quartermaster [cmp. Germ. *Quartiermeister*]
квартирующий *квартирующий* – (part. from *квартировать*, to be billeted; † *квартирующій*) quartered, billeted
квитанция, квитанции *квитанция, квитанции* – (n., fem., † *квитанція*) receipt
келарь, келаря *келарь, келаря* – (n., masc.) cellarer (one responsible for stocking food and drink)
Кёльн, Кёльна *Кёльн, Кёльна* – (n., masc.) Cologne, Germany [German name *Köln*]
Кельце, Келец *Кельце, Келец* – (n., pl., † *Кѣльцы*) town of Kielce, Poland (see page 120); *келецкий* – († *кѣлецкій*) of Kielce
кем *кем* – (pron., instr. of *кто*, see page 42) who?
Кёнигсбергъ → Калининград
Киев, Киева *Киев, Киева* – (n., masc., † *Кіевъ*) Kiev, now Kyiv, Ukraine (see page 132); *киевский* – (adj., † *кіевскій*) of Kiev
Киргизия, Киргизии *Киргизия, Киргизии* – (n., fem., † *Киргизія*) Kirghizia
кирпич, кирпича *кирпич, кирпича* – (n., masc.) brick; *из кирпича* – of brick
кирпичник, кирпичника *кирпичник, кирпичника* – (n., masc.) brick-maker
кирпичный *кирпичный* – (adj.) of brick; *кирпичный завод* – brickyard

Кислев, Кислева *Кислев, Кислева* – (n., masc.) Kislev, the name of a month in the Jewish calendar (see page 47)
китаец, китайца *китаец, китайца* – (n., masc., nom. pl. *китайцы*, gen. pl. *китайцев*) Chinese man (fem. *китаянка*)
Китай, Китая *Китай, Китая* – (n., masc.) China
Кишинёв, Кишинева *Кишинёв, Кишинева* – (n., masc.) Russian name of the town of Chişinău, Moldova (see page 132); *кишиневский* – (adj.) of Kishinev/Chişinău
кишка, кишки *кишка, кишки* – (n., fem., gen. pl. *кишок*) gut, intestine; *воспаление кишок* – enteritis
Кіевъ *Кіевъ* → Киёв *Киёв*
кладбище, кладбища *кладбище, кладбища* – (n., neut.) cemetery, graveyard
кладовщик, кладовщика *кладовщик, кладовщика* – (n., masc.) worker in a store or warehouse
Клайпеда, Клайпеды *Клайпеда, Клайпеды* – (n., fem.) Klaipėda [city in Lithuania]
клеильщик, клеиьщика *клеильщик, клеиьщика* – (n., masc.) gluer, paster (fem. *клеильщица*)
клеточник, клеточника *клеточник, клеточника* – (n., masc., † *клѣточникъ*) cage-maker
Климовичи, Климович *Климовичи, Климович* – (n., pl.) town of Klimavichy, Belarus' (see page 126); *климовичский* – (adj.) of Klimovichi/ Klimavichy
ключарь, ключаря *ключарь, ключаря* – (n., masc.) sacristan
ключник, ключника *ключник, ключника* – (n., masc.) butler, steward, majordomo
ключница, ключницы *ключница, ключницы* – (n., fem.) housekeeper
книга, книги *книга, книги* – (n., fem.) book; *метрическая книга* – registry book, vital records register; *книга записи смертей* – death register; *книга для приписки къ призывному участку* – draft enrollment register
книгоноша, книгоноши *книгоноша, книгоноши* – (n., masc.) book vendor, book hawker
книгопродавец, книгопродавца *книгопродавец, книгопродавца* – (n., masc.) bookseller (also *книготорговец*)
книжка, книжки *книжка, книжки* – (n., fem.) booklet
княгиня, княгини *княгиня, княгини* – (n., fem.) princess (married); *княгиня великая* – grand duchess
княжна, княжны *княжна, княжны* – (n., fem.) princess (unmarried)
князь, князя *князь, князя* – (n., masc., nom. pl. *князья*, gen. pl. *князей*) prince; *князь великий* – grand duke
ко *ко* → к *к*
Кобеляки, Кобеляк *Кобеляки, Кобеляк* – (n., pl.) town of Kobelyaky, Ukraine (see page 133); *кобелякский* – (adj.) of Kobelyaki
кобзарь, кобзаря *кобзарь, кобзаря* – (n., masc.) one who plays the *kobza* (a Ukrainian stringed instrument)
Кобрин, Кобрина *Кобрин, Кобрина* – (n., masc.) town of Kobryn, Belarus' (see page 125); *кобринский* – (adj.) of Kobrin/Kobrin
ковач, ковача *ковач, ковача* – (n., masc.) blacksmith
Ковель, Ковеля *Ковель, Ковеля* – (n., masc.) town of Kovil', Ukraine (see page 130); *ковельский* – (adj.) of Kovel'/Kovil'
† Ковно, Ковна *Ковно, Ковна* – (n., neut.) city of Kaunas city in Lithuania (see page 124); *ковенскій* – of Kovno
когда *когда* – (conj., interr.) when
кого *кого* – (pron., gen./acc. of *кто*, see page 42) who? whom?
кодекс, кодекса *кодекс, кодекса* – (n., masc.) code, codex; *Гражданскій Кодекс Царства Польскаго* – Civil Code of the Kingdom of Poland
кожевник, кожевника *кожевник, кожевника* – (n., masc.) tanner
Козелец, Козельца *Козелец, Козельца* – (n., masc.) town of Kozelets', Ukraine (see page 133); *козелецкий* – (adj.) of Kozelets'
† Козеницы, Козеницъ *Козеницы, Козеницъ* – (n., pl.) town of Kozienice, Poland (see page 120); *козеницкій* – of Kozienice
† кой *кой* – (pron.) who, which, that (fem. *коя*, neut. *кое*); *коему* – to whom
коклюш, коклюша *коклюш, коклюша* – (n., masc.) whooping cough
колбасник, колбасника *колбасник, колбасника* – (n., masc.) sausage-maker (fem. *колбасница*)
колесник, колесника *колесник, колесника* – (n., masc.) wheelwright, cartwright
колика, колики *колика, колики* – (n., fem., often used in the plural, *колики, колик*) colic
кoликократный *коликократный* – (adj.) how many, how many times?
коллежский *коллежский* – (adj.) collegiate; term used as the first part of the titles of several ranks of Imperial Russia's civil service, e. g., *коллежский ассессор*, collegiate assessor
Коло, Кола *Коло, Кола* – (n., neut.) town of Koło, Poland (see page 118); *кольскій* – of Koło
колодезник, колодезника *колодезник, колодезника* – (n., masc.) well-driller
колодник, колодника *колодник, колодника* – (n., masc.) convict, prisoner (fem. *колодница*)
колонист, колониста *колонист, колониста* – (n., masc.) colonist, settler (fem. *колонистка*)

колония, колонии *колония, колонии* – (n., fem., † *колонія*) colony
колпачник, колпачника *колпачник, колпачника* – (n., masc.) cap-maker
колтун, колтуна *колтун, колтуна* – (n., masc.) plica
колхоз, колхоза *колхоз, колхоза* – (n., masc.) Soviet collective farm
Кольно, Кольна *Кольно, Кольна* – (n., neut.) town of Kolno, Poland (see page 120); *кольненский* – of Kolno
кольщик, кольщика *кольщик, кольщика* – (n., masc.) wood-cutter, wood-splitter
ком *ком* – (pron., prep. of *кто*, see p. 42) who? whom?
команда, команды *команда, команды* – (n., fem.) detachment; command
командир, командира *командир, командира* – (n., masc.) chief, commander
командированный *командированный* – (part. from *командировать*, to detach, dispatch) dispatched, detached
комендант, коменданта *комендант, коменданта* – (n., masc.) commandant (fem. *комендантша*, wife of a commandant)
комиссар, комиссара *комиссар, комиссара* – (n., masc., † *коммиссаръ*) commissar
коммерческий *коммерческий* – (adj., † *коммерческій*) commercial
коммиссия, коммиссии *коммиссия, коммиссии* – (n., fem., † *коммиссія*) commission, committee
комната, комнаты *комната, комнаты* – (n., fem.) room
кому *кому* – (pron., dat. of *кто*, see page 42) whom? to whom?
конверт, конверта *конверт, конверта* – (n., masc.) envelope
конвульсия, конвульсии *конвульсия, конвульсии* – (n., fem. † *конвульсія*) convulsion
кондитер, кондитера *кондитер, кондитера* – (n., masc.) confectioner, pastry-cook
кондуитный *кондуитный* – (adj.) of conduct; *кондуитный список* –a list of conduct, record of conduct
коневод, коневода *коневод, коневода* – (n., masc.) horse-breeder
Конин, Конина *Конин, Конина* – (n., masc.) town of Konin, Poland (see page 118); *конинский* – of Konin
коновал, коновала *коновал, коновала* – (n., masc.) horse-doctor, farrier
Конотоп, Конотопа *Конотоп, Конотопа* – (n., masc.) town of Konotop, Ukraine (see page 133); *конотопский* – (adj.) of Konotop
конскрипционный *конскрипционный* – (adj., † *конскрипціонный*) of conscription
† Конскъ, Конска *Конскъ, Конска* – (n., masc.) Końskie, Poland (see page 120); *конскій* – of Końskie
Константинов, Константинова *Константинов, Константинова* – (n., masc.) town of Konstantynów, Poland (see page 120); *константиновский* – of Konstantynów
† Константиноград, Константинограда *Константиноград, Константинограда* – (n., masc.) town now called Krasnohrad, Ukraine (see page 133)
Константинополь, Константинополя *Константинополь, Константинополя* – (n., masc.) Constantinople
консул, консула *консул, консула* – (n., masc.) consul
консульство, консульства *консульство, консульства* – (n., neut.) consulate
контора, конторы *контора, конторы* – (n., fem.) office
конторщик, конторщика *конторщик, конторщика* – (n., masc.) clerk (fem. *конторщица*)
конченный *конченный* – (part. from *кончить*) ended, finished, concluded
кончина, кончины *кончина, кончины* – (n., fem.) death, passing
кончить *кончить* – (v.) to finish, end, conclude
конюх, конюха *конюх, конюха* – (n., masc.) stable-boy, groom, ostler
копейка, копейки *копейка, копейки* – (n., fem.) kopek (= 1/100th of a ruble)
Копыль, Копыля *Копыль, Копыля* – (n., masc.) town of Kapyl', Belarus' (see page 127); *копыльский* – (adj.) of Kopyl'/Kapyl'
корабельщик, корабельщика *корабельщик, корабельщика* – (n., masc.) master of a ship, ship-builder
кораблестроитель, кораблестроителя *кораблестроитель, кораблестроителя* – (n., masc.) ship-builder
Кореличи, Корелич *Кореличи, Корелич* – (n., pl., also *Кареличи*) town of Karèlichy, Belarus' (see page 127); *кореличский* – of Korelichi/Karèlichy
корзинщик, корзинщика *корзинщик, корзинщика* – (n., masc.) basket-maker
кормилец, кормильца *кормилец, кормильца* – (n., masc.) foster-father; bread-winner
кормилица, кормилицы *кормилица, кормилицы* – (n., fem.) wet nurse, foster-mother
кормчий, кормчего *кормчий, кормчего* – (adj. used as a n., masc.) helmsman, pilot
коробейник, коробейника *коробейник, коробейника* – (n., masc.) mercer, haberdasher, peddler
коробочник, коробочника *коробочник, коробочника* – (n., masc.) box-maker

Королевство Польское, Королевства Польского *Королевство Польское, Королевства Польского* – (n., neut.) the Kingdom of Poland, until 1867 the name of the eastern and central sections of Poland seized by the Russian Empire during the Partitions
корсетник, корсетника *корсетник, корсетника* – (n., masc.) corset-maker (fem. *корсетница*)
корча, корчи *корча, корчи* – (n., fem., often in the pl., *корчи, корчей*) writhing, convulsions
корчмарь, корчмаря *корчмарь, корчмаря* – (n., masc.) innkeeper, tavern-keeper (fem. *корчмарка*)
корытник, корытника *корытник, корытника* – (n., masc.) trough-maker
корь, кори *корь, кори* – (n., fem.) measles
косарь, косаря *косарь, косаря* – (n., masc.) hay-maker, scytheman (also a chopper, large knife)
косец, косца *косец, косца* – (n., masc.) hay-maker, mower, scytheman
костёл, костёла *костёл, костёла* – (n., masc.) church (from Polish *kościół*, usually a Polish Roman Catholic church; compare *церковь*)
костоеда, костоеды *костоеда, костоеды* – (n., fem., † *костоѣда*) caries
костоправ, костоправа *костоправ, костоправа* – (n., masc.) one who sets broken bones
Кострома, Костромы *Кострома, Костромы* – (n., masc.) Kostroma, town in Russia (see page 135); *костромский* – (adj.) of Kostroma
котельник, котельника *котельник, котельника* – (n., masc.) coppersmith, boilermaker, tinker; also *котельщик*
который *который* – (rel. pron. and adj.) who, which, that; *въ которомъ году родился?* – in what year was he born?
кочегар, кочегара *кочегар, кочегара* – (n., masc.) stoker, fire-man (of a machine)
кошелечник, кошелечника *кошелечник, кошелечника* – (n., masc.) purse-maker
кошемщик, кошемщика *кошемщик, кошемщика* – (n., masc.) felt-maker
коя → кой
кр. → крестьянин
край, края *край, края* – (n., masc.) territory, land, country; edge
Краков, Кракова *Краков, Кракова* – (n., masc.) city of Kraków, Poland
красильщик, красильщика *красильщик, красильщика* – (n., masc.) dyer
краска, краски *краска, краски* – (n., fem.) color, dye
краснодеревец, краснодеревца *краснодеревец, краснодеревца* – (n., masc.) cabinet-maker (also *краснодеревщик*)
† Красноставъ, Красностава *Красноставъ, Красностава* – (n., masc.) town of Krasnystaw, Poland (see page 120); *красноставскій* – of Krasnystaw
краснуха, краснухи *краснуха, краснухи* – (n., fem.) German measles
красный *красный* – (adj.) red
краткий *краткий* – (adj., † *краткій*) short, brief
крахмальщик, крахмальщика *крахмальщик, крахмальщика* – (n., masc.) starcher, starch-maker (fem. *крахмальщица*)
Кременец, Кременца *Кременец, Кременца* – (n., masc.) town of Kremenets, Ukraine (see page 130); *кременецкий* – (adj.) of Kremenets
Кременчуг, Кременчуга *Кременчуг, Кременчуга* – (n., masc.) town of Kremenchuk, Ukraine (see page 133); *кременчугский* – (adj.) of Kremenchuk
крепостной, крепостного *крепостной, крепостного* – (adj. used as a n., masc., † *крѣпостной*) serf, one bound to the soil (fem. *крепостная*)
крепость, крепости *крепость, крепости* (n., fem., † *крѣпость*) firmness, vigor; stronghold; *купчая крѣпость* – deed of sale
крестить *крестить* – (v.) to baptize
крестник, крестника *крестник, крестника* – (n., masc.) godson
крестница, крестницы *крестница, крестницы* – (n., fem.) goddaughter
крестный *крестный* – (adj.) of baptism; *крестная дочь*, goddaughter; *крестная мать* – godmother; *крестный отец* – godfather; *крестный сын* – godchild
крестьянин, крестьянина *крестьянин, крестьянина* – (n., masc., nom. pl. *крестьяне*, gen. pl. *крестьян*, see page 41 for declension) peasant, farmer; *крестьянин владеющий землей* – (landowning) farmer
крестьянка, крестьянки *крестьянка, крестьянки* – (n., fem.) (female) peasant
крещаемый *крещаемый* – (part. from † *крещать*, to baptize) baptized
крещение, крещения *крещение, крещения* – (n., neut., † *крещеніе*) baptism; *книга крещенія* – baptismal register; *число крещенія* – date of baptism
крещённый *крещённый* – (part. from *крестить*, short form *крещен*) christened, baptized
кровавый *кровавый* – (adj.) bloody, of blood; *кровавый понос* – bloody flux; *кровавая рвота* – bloody vomiting
кровельщик, кровельщика *кровельщик, кровельщика* – (n., masc.) roofer, tiler
кровоизлияние, кровоизлияния *кровоизлияние, кровоизлияния* – (n., neut., † *кровоизліяніе*) hemorrhage; *кровоизлияние в мозг* – brain hemorrhage

кровотечение, кровотечения *кровотечение, кровотечения* – (n., neut., † *кровотеченіе*) hemorrhage
кровь, крови *кровь, крови* – (n., fem.) blood; *заражение крови* – blood poisoning
кроильщик, кроильщика *кроильщик, кроильщика* – (n., masc.) cutter (of coats and other clothes; fem. *кроильщица*)
Кролевец, Кролевца *Кролевец, Кролевца* – (n., masc.) town of Krolevets', Ukraine (see page 133); *кролевецкий* – (adj.) of Krolevets'
круглолицый *круглолицый* – (adj.) round-faced
круглый *круглый* – (adj.) round, circular
кружевник, кружевника *кружевник, кружевника* – (n., masc.) maker or seller of lace (fem. *кружевница*)
круп, крупа *круп, крупа* – (n., masc.) croup
Крым, Крыма *Крым, Крыма* – (n., masc.) Crimea; *в Крыму* – in Crimea
крысолов, крысолова *крысолов, крысолова* – (n., masc.) rat-catcher
крытый *крытый* – (part. from *крыть*, to cover) covered, roofed; *чѣмъ крыто* – covered or roofed with what?; *крытый соломой* – with a thatched roof
крыша, крыши *крыша, крыши* – (n., fem.) roof
крѣпостной *крѣпостной* → крепостной *крепостной*
крѣпость *крѣпость* → крепость *крепость*
крючник, крючника *крючник, крючника* – (n., masc.) street-porter
Кс. *Кс.* → ксёндз *ксёндз*
ксёндз, ксёндза *ксёндз, ксёндза* – (n., masc., abbr. *Кс.*) a Roman Catholic priest (from Polish *ksiądz*)
ксуба, ксубы *ксуба, ксубы* – (n., fem.) a *ketubah* (see page 271)
кто *кто* – (pron., for declension see page 42; † instr. sing. *кѣмъ*) who?
Кубань, Кубани *Кубань, Кубанази* – (n., fem.) Kuban', name of a region in Asiatic Russia (see page 137); *кубанский* – of Kuban'
куда *куда* – (adv., interr.) to where?
кузнец, кузнеца *кузнец, кузнеца* – (n., masc.) blacksmith (fem. *кузнечиха*, blacksmith's wife)
Куйбышев, Куйбышева *Куйбышев, Куйбышева* – (n., masc.) Kuibyshev
кум, кума *кум, кума* – (n., masc., nom. pl. *кумовья, кумьёв*) godfather, old gossip (fem. *кума*)
купец, купца *купец, купца* – (n., masc.) merchant (fem. *купчиха*, merchant's wife, or female merchant)
купчая, купчей *купчая, купчей* – (adj. used as a n., fem.) deed of purchase; also used: *купчая крѣпость*
Купянск, Купянска *Купянск, Купянска* – (n., masc.) town of Kup'yansk, Ukraine (see page 134); *купянский* – (adj.) of Kupyansk
Курляндия, Курляндии *Курляндия, Курляндии* – (n., fem., † *Курляндія*) Courland
курс, курса *курс, курса* – (n., masc.) course; exchange rate; *по курсу дня* – at the exchange rate of the day
Курск, Курска *Курск, Курска* – (n., masc.) Kursk, name of a town in Russia (see page 135); *курский* – of Kursk
курфирст, курфирста *курфирст, курфирста* – (n., masc.) elector [cmp. German *Kurfürst*]
курьер, курьера *курьер, курьера* – (n., masc.) courier, messenger
курятник, курятника *курятник, курятника* – (n., masc.) poulterer; hen-house, hen-coop
кустарь, кустаря *кустарь, кустаря* – (n., masc.) handicraftsman
Кутно, Кутна *Кутно, Кутна* – (n., neut.) town of Kutno, Poland (see page 119); *кутновский* – of Kutno
кухарка, кухарки *кухарка, кухарки* – (n., fem.) cook
кучер, кучера *кучер, кучера* – (n., masc.) coachman
Кѣльцы *Кѣльцы* → Кельце *Кельце*
кѣмъ *кѣмъ* → кто *кто*
л. л. → лето *лето*
лабазник, лабазника *лабазник, лабазника* – (n., masc.) dealer in corn or flour
лавка, лавки *лавка, лавки* – (n., fem., gen. pl. *лавок*) bench; shop
лавочник, лавочника *лавочник, лавочника* – (n., masc.) shopkeeper (fem. *лавочница*)
лазарет, лазарета *лазарет, лазарета* – (n., masc.) infirmary
лакей, лакея *лакей, лакея* – (n., masc.) lackey, footman, man-servant
ламповщик, ламповщика *ламповщик, ламповщика* – (n., masc.) lamp-maker
ландвер, ландвера *ландвер, ландвера* – (n., masc.) provincial militia, reserve [cmp. German *Landwehr*]
ландрат, ландрата *ландрат, ландрата* – (n., masc.) member of a provincial court of justice in Livonia [cmp. German *Landrat*]
латвиец, латвийца *латвиец, латвийца* – (n., masc., † *латвіецъ*) Latvian (fem. *латвийка*, † *латвійка*)
латвийский *латвийский* – (adj., † *латвійскіий*) Latvian
Латвия, Латвии *Латвия, Латвии* – (n., fem., † *Латвія*) Latvia
латыш, латыша *латыш, латыша* – (n., masc., nom. pl. *латыши*, gen. pl. *латишей*) Latvian, Lett (fem. *латышка*)

Лебедин, Лебедина *Лебедин, Лебедина* – (n., masc.) town of Lebedyn, Ukraine (see page 134); *лебединский* – (adj.) of Lebedin/Lebedyn

† легитимаціонный *легитимаціонный* – (adj.) for identification; *легитимаціонная книжка* – identification booklet

лёгкое, лёгкого *лёгкое, лёгкого* – (adj. used as a n., usually seen in the plural *лёгкие*, gen. *лёгких*) lung; *воспаление лёгких* – pneumonia

лёгочный *лёгочный* – (adj.) of the lungs; *лёгочный больной* – one suffering from lung disease; *лёгочная чума* – pneumonic plague

лежать *лежать* – (v.) to lie, repose

лейбъ-гвардеец, лейбъ-гвардейца *лейбъ-гвардеец, лейбъ-гвардейца* – (n., masc.) member of the royal house guards (from Germ. *Leib-*, the prefix *лейбъ-* usually refers to someone in the service of a monarch or his court)

Лейпциг, Лейпзига *Лейпциг, Лейпзига* – (n., masc.) Leipzig, Germany

лейтенант, лейтенанта *лейтенант, лейтенанта* – (n., masc.) lieutenant

лекарь, лекаря *лекарь, лекаря* – (n., masc., nom. pl. *лекари*, gen. pl. *лекарей*) physician

лектор, лектора *лектор, лектора* – (n., masc., nom. pl. *лекторы*) lecturer at a university

Лембергъ *Лембергъ* → Львов *Львов*

Лена, Лены *Лена, Лены* – (n., fem.) Lena [river]

Ленинград, Ленинграда *Ленинград, Ленинграда* – (n., masc.) Leningrad

ленный *ленный* – (adj.) feudal

ленточник, ленточника *ленточник, ленточника* – (n., masc.) maker or seller of ribbons

† Ленчицы, Ленчицъ *Ленчицы, Ленчицъ* – (n., pl.) archaic Russian name of the town of Łęczyca, Poland (see page 118); *ленчицкій* – of Łęczyca

Лепель, Лепеля *Лепель, Лепеля* – (n., masc.) town of Lepel', Belarus' (see page 126); *лепельский* – (adj.) of Lepel'

лесник, лесника *лесник, лесника* – (n., masc., † *лѣсникъ*) forester

лесничество, лесничества *лесничество, лесничества* – (n., neut., † *лѣсничество*) forest district

лесной *лесной* – (adj., † *лѣсной*) of the woods, of the forest; *лесная стража* –forest rangers' station

лесопильный *лесопильный* – (adj., † *лѣсопильный*) of sawing; *лесопильный завод* – sawmill

Летичев, Летичева *Летичев, Летичева* – (n., masc.) Russian name of the town of Letychiv, Ukraine (see page 132); *летичевский* – (adj.) of Letichev/Letychiv

летний *летний* – (adj., † *лѣтній*) of summer, years; *по достиженіи 43-лѣтняго возраста* – after reaching the age of 43

лето, лета *лето, лета* – (n., neut., † *лѣто*, abbr. *л.*) summer; in expressions of age *лет* († *лѣтъ*) means "years," see pages 41 and 50; *лѣтъ отъ роду* – years from birth (i. e., age)

лечебный *лечебный* – (adj.) of medicine, medical

ли *ли* – (interrogative particle, usually indicates a question and added to the key word of the question; if translated, it usually is rendered "whether, if"); *уничтожены ли они* – have they been destroyed?

Ливония, Ливонии *Ливония, Ливонии* – (n., fem., † *Ливонія*) Livonia, a region of southern Estonia and northern Latvia (also called † *Лифляндія*, cmp. the German name *Livland*, and Polish *Inflanty*, Russian *Инфлянты*)

Лида, Лиды *Лида, Лиды* – (n., fem.) town of Lida, Belarus' (see page 124); *лидский* – (adj.) of Lida

линия, линии *линия, линии* – (n., fem., † *линія*) line

Липно, Липна *Липно, Липна* – (n., neut.) Lipno, Poland (see page 119); *липновский* – (adj.) of Lipno

Липовец, Липовца *Липовец, Липовца* – (n., masc.) town of Lypovets', Ukraine (see page 132); *липовецкий* – (adj.) of Lipovets/Lypovets'

лист, листа *лист, листа* – (n., masc.; nom. pl. *листы*) letter; sheet of paper, page; *опросный листъ* – questionnaire

листок, листка *листок, листка* – (n., masc.) leaflet; leaf

Литва, Литвы *Литва, Литвы* – (n., fem.) Lithuania

литвин, литвина *литвин, литвина* – (n., masc.) Lithuanian (fem. *литвинка*)

литейщик, литейщика *литейщик, литейщика* – (n., masc.) caster, smelter, founder

Литин, Литина *Литин, Литина* – (n., masc.) town of Lityn, Ukraine (see page 132); *литинский* – (adj.) of Litin/Lityn

литовец, литовца *литовец, литовца* – (n., masc.) Lithuanian (fem. *литовка*)

литургия, литургии *литургия, литургии* - (n., fem., † *литургія*) liturgy, mass, services; *передъ народомъ собравшимся на литургіи* – before the people assembled for services

Лифляндія *Лифляндія* → Ливония *Ливония*

лихорадка, лихорадки *лихорадка, лихорадки* – (n., fem.) fever

лицо, лица *лицо, лица* – (n., neut., † *лице*) face, countenance; person; *другія лица неграмотныя* – the other persons being illiterate; *въ лицѣ Костела* – in the eyes of the Church

лично *лично* – (adv.) personally, in person

личность, личности *личность, личности* – (n., fem.) identity

личный *личный* – (adj.) personal, individual

лишённый *лишённый* – (part. from *лишить*, to deprive) deprived; *лишённый всѣхъ правъ* – deprived of all rights
ловец, ловца *ловец, ловца* – (n., masc.) hunter, fowler
Лович, Ловича *Лович, Ловича* – (n., masc.) town of Łowicz, Poland (see page 119); *ловичский* – of Łowicz
ловкость, ловкости *ловкость, ловкости* – (n., fem.) dexterity, skill
ловчий, ловчего *ловчий, ловчего* – (adj. used as a n., masc., † *ловчій*) huntsman
лодочник, лодочника *лодочник, лодочника* – (n., masc.) boatman
Ломжа, Ломжи *Ломжа, Ломжи* – (n., fem.) town of Łomża, Poland (see page 120); *ломжинский* (also † *ломженскій*) of Łomża, Poland
Лохвица, Лохвицы *Лохвица, Лохвицы* – (n., fem.) town of Lokhvytsya, Ukraine (see page 133); *лохвицкий* – (adj.) of Lokhvitsa/Lokhvytsya
Лубны, Лубнов *Лубны, Лубнов* – (n., pl.) town of Lubny, Ukraine (see page 133); *лубенский* – (adj.) of Lubny
† Луковъ, Лукова *Луковъ, Лукова* – (n., masc.) archaic Russian name of the town of Łuków, Poland (see page 120); *луковскій* – of Łuków
Луцк, Луцка *Луцк, Луцка* – (n., masc.) town of Luts'k, Ukraine (see page 130); *луцкий* – (adj.) of Luts'k
Львов, Львова *Львов, Львова* – (n., masc.) town of L'vov [Polish name *Lwów*, Ukr. name *Львів*, Germ. *Lemberg* († *Лембергъ*)]; *львовский* – (adj.) of L'vov
льгота, льготы *льгота, льготы* – (n., fem.) exemption; *право на льготу* – the right to an exemption
лѣсникъ *лѣсникъ* → лесник *лесник*
лѣсничество *лѣсничество* → лесничество *лесничество*
лѣсной *лѣсной* → лесной *лесной*
лѣсопильный *лѣсопильный* → лесопильный *лесопильный*
лѣтній *лѣтній* → летний *летний*
лѣтъ *лѣтъ* → лето *лето*
† Любартовъ, Любартова *Любартовъ, Любартова* – (n., masc.) town of Lubartów, Poland (see page 120); *любартовскій* – of Lubartów
любимый *любимый* – (part. from *любить* ↓) beloved
любить *любить* – (v.) to love
Люблин, Люблина *Люблин, Люблина* – (n., masc.) Lublin, Poland (see page 120); *люблинский* – (adj.) of Lublin
любой *любой* – (adj.) any, any and all, every
люди, людей *люди, людей* – (masc. pl.) people
люстратор, люстратора *люстратор, люстратора* – (n., masc.) controller of the revenues
лютеранин, лютеранина *лютеранин, лютеранина* – (n., masc., nom. pl. *лютеране*, gen. pl. *лютеран*) Lutheran (fem. *лютеранка*)
лютеранский *лютеранский* – (adj., † *лютеранскій*) Lutheran
† Люцинъ, Люцина *Люцинъ, Люцина* – (n., masc.) town now called Ludza, Latvia (see page 126); *люцинский* – (adj.) of Liutsin/Ludza
ляни *ляни* – (n., Cyrillic spelling of the Finnish term *lääni*) term for a province in Finland
магазинщик, магазинщика *магазинщик, магазинщика* – (n., masc.) owner or keeper of a storehouse (in modern Russian a *магазин* is a shop or store)
магистрат, магистрата *магистрат, магистрата* – (n., masc.) magistrate
магнат, магната *магнат, магната* – (n., masc.) magnate
магометанин, магометанина *магометанин, магометанина* – (n., masc., nom. pl. *магометане*, gen. pl. *магометан*) Muslim (fem. *магометанка*)
магометанский *магометанский* – (adj.) Islamic, Muslim
† Мазовецкъ, Мазовецка *Мазовецкъ, Мазовецка* – (n., masc.) town of Wysokie Mazowieckie, Poland (see page 120); *мазовецкій* – of Wysokie Mazowieckie
Мазовия, Мазовии *Мазовия, Мазовии* – (n., fem., † *Мазовія*) Mazovia [region in northeastern Poland, Polish name *Mazowsze*]
май, мая *май, мая* – (n., masc.) May
майор, майора *майор, майора* – (n., masc., † *маіоръ*) major (fem. *майорша*, major's wife)
маклер, маклера *маклер, маклера* – (n., masc.) broker
† Маковъ, Макова *Маковъ, Макова* – (n., masc.) town of Maków Mazowiecki, Poland (see page 120); *маковскій* – of Maków
малолетка, малолетки *малолетка, малолетки* – (n., masc. or fem., († *малолѣтка*) child under the age of 14; also *малолеток, малолетка* († *малолѣтокъ*)
малолетний *малолетний* – (adj., † *малолѣтній*) minor, underage
Малорита, Малориты *Малорита, Малориты* – (n., fem.) town of Malaryta, Belarus' (see page 127); *малоритский* – (adj.) of Malorita/Malaryta
Малороссия, Малороссии *Малороссия, Малороссии* – (n., fem., † *Малороссія*) Little Russia (term sometimes used for Ruthenia or Ukraine – but not by Ukrainians or Rusyns!)
малый *малый* – (adj.) small; *малый дядя* – a brother of your father or mother; *малая матка* – sister of your father or mother

мальчик, мальчика *мальчик, мальчика* – (n., masc.) boy; servant, domestic
маляр, маляра *маляр, маляра* – (n., masc.) house-painter
малярия, малярии *малярия, малярии* – (n., fem., † *малярія*) malaria
мамочка, мамочки *мамочка, мамочки* – (n., fem.) mommy (but in Russian it doesn't sound out-of-place in instances where "mommy" might in English
маразм, маразма *маразм, маразма* – (n., masc.) marasmus, decay, weakening; *старческий маразм* – senile decay, dotage
Мариямполе, Мариямполя *Мариямполе, Мариямполя* – (n., neut., † *Маріамполь*) town of Mariampol, now Marijampolė, Lithuania (see page 120); † *маріампольскій* – of Mariampol
маркграф, маркграфа *маркграф, маркграфа* – (n., masc.) margrave
маркиз, маркиза *маркиз, маркиза* – (n., masc.) marquis (fem. *маркиза, маркизы*)
маркитант, маркитанта *маркитант, маркитанта* – (n., masc.) sutler, canteen-keeper (fem. *маркитантка*)
март, марта *март, марта* – (n., masc.) March
маршал, маршала *маршал, маршала* – (n., masc.) marshal
маслобойщик, маслобойщика *маслобойщик, маслобойщика* – (n., masc.) oil-manufacturer
мастер, мастера *мастер, мастера* – (n., masc., nom. pl. *мастера*, gen. pl. *мастеров*) foreman, master, e. g., *портной мастер*, master tailor (fem. *мастерица*)
мастерство, мастерства *мастерство, мастерства* – (n., neut.) mastery, skill
матка, матки *матка, матки* – (n., fem.) mother; *великая матка* – sister of your grandfather or grandmother; *малая матка* – sister of your father or mother
матрос, матроса *матрос, матроса* – (n., masc.) sailor
мать, матери *мать, матери* – (n., fem., instr. sing. *матерью*, nom. pl. *матери*, gen. pl. *матерей*) mother
махальщик, махальщика *махальщик, махальщика* – (n., masc.) signal-man, also *махальный, махального* (adj. used as a n.)
мачеха, мачехи *мачеха, мачехи* – (n., fem.) stepmother (also *мачиха, мачихи*)
машина, машины *машина, машины* – (n., fem.) machine, engine
машинист, машиниста *машинист, машиниста* – (n., masc.) machinist, operator, engineer
машинка, машинки *машинка, машинки* – (n., fem.) [small] machine
Мглин, Мглина *Мглин, Мглина* – (n., fem.) town of Mglin, Russia (see page 133); *мглинский* – (adj.) of Mglin
мебельщик, мебельщика *мебельщик, мебельщика* – (n., masc.) maker of or dealer in furniture
меблировщик, меблировщика *меблировщик, меблировщика* – (n., masc.) upholsterer
медаль, медали *медаль, медали* – (n., fem.) medal
медик, медика *медик, медика* – (n., masc.) physician (fem. *медичка*)
† Медіоланъ, Медіолана *Медіоланъ, Медіолана* – (n., masc.) archaic name for Milan, Italy
медник, медника *медник, медника* – (n., masc., † *мѣдникъ*) coppersmith, brazier
медовар, медовара *медовар, медовара* – (n., masc.) mead-brewer
между *между* – (prep. + inst.) between, among
межевщик, межевщика *межевщик, межевщика* – (n., masc.) surveyor
Мелитополь, Мелитополя *Мелитополь, Мелитополя* – (n., masc.) town of Melitopol', Ukraine (see page 134), *мелитопольский* – (adj.) of Melitopol'
мельник, мельника *мельник, мельника* – (n., masc.) miller (fem. *мельничиха*)
мельница, мельницы *мельница, мельницы* – (n., fem.) mill
менингит, менингита *менингит, менингита* – (n., masc.) meningitis
меня *меня* – (personal pron., gen./acc. of *я*, see page 42) me
меняльщик, меняльщика *меняльщик, меняльщика* – (n., masc., † *мѣняльщикъ*) barterer (fem. *меняльщица*)
мера, меры *мера, меры* – (n., fem., † *мѣра*) measure
местечко, местечка *местечко, местечка* – (n., neut. † *мѣстечко*) small town, borough (cmp. Polish *miasteczko*)
местность, местности *местность, местности* – (n., fem., † *мѣстность*) locality
местный *местный* – (adj., † *мѣстный*) local, of this place
место, места *место, места* – (n., neut., † *мѣсто*) place; *место жительства* – place of residence; *место приписки* – registration place (i. e., locality where officially registered as a resident); *место рождения* – place of birth
местожителсво, местожительства *местожителсво, местожительства* – (n., neut., † *мѣстожительство*) residence; *по местожительству* – by residence (i. e., resident of)
месяц, месяца *месяц, месяца* – (n., masc., † *мѣсяцъ*) month; *м-ца* – (abbr. = *месяца*) in the month of

метельщик, метельщика *метельщик, метельщика* – (n., masc.) sweeper; rail-guard (fem. *метельщица*)

метрдотель, метрдотеля *метрдотель, метрдотеля* – (n., masc.) majordomo, steward [cmp. French *maître d'hôtel*]

метрика, метрики *метрика, метрики* – (n., fem.) parish register, registry; *по метрикѣ* – according to the register (or registry certificate)

метрический *метрический* – (adj., † *метрическій*) of the parish registers; *метрическая книга* – parish register, vital records register

механик, механика *механик, механика* – (n., masc.) mechanic

меховщик, меховщика *меховщик, меховщика* – (n., masc., † *мѣховщикъ*) furrier

мечетный *мечетный* – (adj.) of a mosque; *печать мечетная* – the mosque's seal

мечеть, мечети *мечеть, мечети* – (n., fem.) mosque

мещанин, мещанина *мещанин, мещанина* – (n., masc., nom. pl. *мещане*, gen. pl. *мещан*, † *мѣщанинъ*) townsman, burgher [during Soviet times a contemptuous term for a narrow-minded petty bourgeois] (fem. *мещанка*)

мещанский *мещанский* – (adj., † *мѣщанскій*) of a townsman

М. И. Д. – (abbr. for *Министерство иностраныхъ дѣлъ*) Ministry of Foreign Affairs

милиционер, милиционера *милиционер, милиционера* – (n., masc., † *милиціонеръ*) militia-man

милостивый *милостивый* – (adj.) favorable, gracious; *милостивый государъ* – Dear Sir

министерство, министерства *министерство, министерства* – (n., neut.) ministry

министр, министра *министр, министра* – (n., masc.) minister

Минск, Минска *Минск, Минска* – (n., masc.) Minsk, Belarus' (see page 125-126); *минский* – of Minsk

минуть *минуть* – (v.) to pass, elapse; *сколько минуло лѣтъ отъ роду* – how many years have elapsed since birth? (i. e., how old is he/she?)

Мир, Мира *Мир, Мира* – (n., masc.) town of Mir, Belarus' (see page 127)

Миргород, Миргорода *Миргород, Миргорода* – (n., masc.) town of Myrhorod, Ukraine (see page 133); *миргородский* – (adj.) of Mirgorod/ Myrhorod

мировой *мировой* – (adj.) of peace; *мировой судья* – justice of the peace

митрополит, митрополита *митрополит, митрополита* – (n., masc.) metropolitan, bishop heading an ecclesiastical province, ranking below a patriarch

мичман, мичмана *мичман, мичмана* – (n., masc.) midshipman

Млава, Млавы *Млава, Млавы* – (n., fem.) town of Mława, Poland (see page 119); *млавский* – of Mława

младенец, младенца *младенец, младенца* – (n., masc.) infant, child, baby

мне *мне* – (pron., † *мнѣ*, dat./prep. of *я*, see page 42) me, to me

мнение, мнения *мнение, мнения* – (n., neut., † *мнѣніе*) opinion

многоуважаемый *многоуважаемый* – (adj.) literally "much respected," used mainly in the salutation of letters where English uses "Dear"

мной *мной* – (pron., † *мною*, instr. of *я*, see page 42) me

мнѣ *мнѣ* → мне *мне*

мог, могла, могли, могут *мог, могла, могли могут* → мочь *мочь*

могила, могилы *могила, могилы* – (n., fem.) grave, tomb

Могилев, Могилева *Могилев, Могилева* – (n., masc.) the city of Mogilev, now Mahileŭ, Belarus' (see page 126); *могилевский* – of Mogilev

Могилев-Подольский, Могилева-Подольского *Могилев-Подольский, Могилева-Подольского* – (n., masc.) the town of Mohyliv Podil's'kyi, Ukraine (see page 132)

могильщик, могильщика *могильщик, могильщика* – (n., masc.) gravedigger, sexton

может *может* → мочь *мочь*

можно – (verb form) it is possible, one can; *как можно будет послать оплату* – how can one send payment?

мозг, мозга *мозг, мозга* – (n., masc.) brain

Мозырь, Мозыря *Мозырь, Мозыря* – (n., masc.) town of Mazyr, Belarus' (see page 126); *мозырский* – (adj.) of Mozyr'/Mazyr

мой *мой* – (poss. pron.) my; *женѣ моей* – to my wife; *съ моими дѣтьми* – with my children, and my children

молдаванин, молдаванина *молдаванин, молдаванина* – (n., masc., nom. pl. *молдаване*, gen. pl. *молдаван*) Moldavian (fem. *молдаванка*)

Молдавия, Молдавии *Молдавия, Молдавии* – (n., fem., † *Молдавія*) Moldavia

молебствие, молебствия *молебствие, молебствия* (n., neut., † *молебствіе*) public prayer, church service; *собраннымъ на молебствѣ людямъ* – to the people assembled for services

Молодечно, Молодечна *Молодечно, Молодечна* – (n., neut.) Russian name of the town of Maladzechna, Belarus' (see page 127); *молодечненский* – (adj.) of Maladzechna

молодой *молодой* – (adj.) young; used as a masc. noun, groom; used as a fem. noun, *молодая*, bride

молотильщик, молотильщика *молотильщик, молотильщика* – (n., masc.) thrasher (fem. *молотильщица*)
молочник, молочника *молочник, молочника* – (n., masc.) milkman (fem. *молочница*, which also means "thrush, inflammation of the mouth")
монах, монаха *монах, монаха* – (n., masc.) friar, monk (fem. *монахиня*)
монашеский *монашеский* – (adj., † *монашескій*) monastic, of monks
монетчик, монетчика *монетчик, монетчика* – (n., masc.) minter, coiner
моравец, моравца *моравец, моравца* – (n., masc.) Moravian (fem. *моравка*)
Моравия, Моравии *Моравия, Моравии* – (n., fem., † *Моравія*) Moravia
морг, морга *морг, морга* – (n., masc.) morgue; † a unit of measurement, see *mórg*, age 160
море, моря *море, моря* – (n., neut., nom. pl. *моря*, gen. pl. *морей*) sea
мореплаватель, мореплавателя *мореплаватель, мореплавателя* – (n., masc.) navigator, seaman, seafarer (fem. *мореплавательница*)
моряк, моряка *моряк, моряка* – (n., masc.) seaman
Москва, Москвы *Москва, Москвы* – (n., fem.) Moscow (see page 135); *московский* – of Moscow
Мосты, Мостов *Мосты, Мостов* – (n., pl.) town of Masty, Belarus' (see page 127); *мостовский* – (adj.) of Mosty/Masty
мочь *мочь* – (v.) to be able to, may; *сейчас может иметь другое название* – now it may have another name; *люди, которые могут быть моими родственниками* – people who may be my relatives; *не можетъ* – cannot
мраморщик, мраморщика *мраморщик, мраморщика* – (n., masc.) marble-cutter or polisher
Мстиславль, Мстиславля *Мстиславль, Мстиславля* – (n., masc.) town of Mstsislaŭ, Belarus' (see page 126); *мстиславльский* – of Mstsislaŭ
муж, мужа *муж, мужа* – (n., masc., nom. pl. *мужья*, gen. pl. *мужей*, dat. pl. *мужьям*) husband
† мужескій *мужескій* – (adj.) male, masculine (in modern Russian *мужской* is used instead, but in records of genealogical interest you may see either *мужескій* or *мужской*); *мужескаго пола* – of the male gender; † *мужеска пола* – of the male gender
мужик, мужика *мужик, мужика* – (n., masc.) peasant (fem. *мужичка, мужички*)
мужской *мужской* – (adj.) male, masculine (see note under мужескій); *мужскаго пола* – of the male gender
мужчина, мужчины – (n., masc. in gender but declined as if it were fem.) man
музей, музея *музей, музея* – (n., masc.) museum
музыкант, музыканта *музыкант, музыканта* – (n., masc.) musician (fem. *музыкантша*)
мулла, муллы *мулла, муллы* – (n., masc.) mullah, Islamic clergyman
мундкох, мундкоха *мундкох, мундкоха* – (n., masc.) cook in a royal household
мундшенк, мундшенка *мундшенк, мундшенка* – (n., masc.) cupbearer, butler in a royal household [cmp. Germ. *Mundschenk*]
мусорщик, мусорщика *мусорщик, мусорщика* – (n., masc.) trash-hauler, dustman
мусульманин, мусульманина *мусульманин, мусульманина* – (n., masc., nom. pl. *мусульмане*, gen. pl. *мусульман*) Muslim (fem. *мусульманка*)
мусульманский *мусульманский* – (adj., † *мусульманскій*) Muslim
мученик, мученика *мученик, мученика* – (n., masc.) martyr (fem. *мученица*)
мучник, мучника *мучник, мучника* – (n., masc.) dealer in meal or flour (also *мучной торговец*)
м-ца *м-ца* → месяц *месяц*
мы *мы* – (personal pron., see page 42) we
мызник, мызника *мызник, мызника* – (n., masc.) farmer, tenant
мыловар, мыловара *мыловар, мыловара* – (n., masc.) soap-maker
† мытникъ, мытника *мытникъ, мытника* – (n., masc.) toll-gatherer
мѣдникъ *мѣдникъ* → медник *медник*
мѣняльщик *мѣняльщик* → меняльщик *меняльщик*
мѣра *мѣра* → мера *мера*
мѣстный *мѣстный* → местный *местный*
мѣсто *мѣсто* → место *место*
мѣсяцъ *мѣсяцъ* → месяц *месяц*
мѣховщикъ *мѣховщикъ* → меховщик *меховщик*
† Мѣховъ, Мѣхова *Мѣховъ, Мѣхова* – (n., masc.) town of Miechów, Poland (see page 120); *мѣховскій* – of Miechów
мѣщанинъ *мѣщанинъ* → мещанин *мещанин*
мѣщанскій *мѣщанскій* → мещанский мещанский
Мюнхен, Мюнхена *Мюнхен, Мюнхена* – (n., masc.) Russian name of the town of Munich, Germany [cmp. German name *München*]
мяльщик, мяльщика *мяльщик, мяльщика* – (n., masc.) scutcher
мясник, мясника *мясник, мясника* – (n., masc.) butcher
№ → номер *номер*
на *на* – (prep. + acc./prep.) on, upon; at, to; *на 42-ем году жизни* – in her 42nd year; *на польскомъ языкѣ* – in Polish
набойщик, набойщика *набойщик, набойщика* – (n., masc.) (cloth-) printer

набор, набора *набор, набора* – (n., masc.) assembling, collection; *рекрутскій наборъ* – recruiting, recruitment; *наборъ войскъ* – levy
наводчик, наводчика *наводчик, наводчика* – (n., masc.) gunner, sighter, gun layer
навсегда *навсегда* – (adv.) forever
надеяться *надеяться* – (v.) to hope
надзиратель, надзирателя *надзиратель, надзирателя* – (n., masc.) inspector, superintendent, overseer (fem. *надзирательница*)
надзорщик, надзорщика *надзорщик, надзорщика* – (n., masc.) superintendent (fem. *надзорщица*)
надлежать *надлежать* – (v.) to be necessary; *всѣмъ и каждому, кому о томъ вѣдать надлежитъ* – to each and every one who needs to know of this (used much like English "to whom it may concern")
надлежащий *надлежащий* – (adj.) due, expedient, necessary, required, appropriate
надо *надо* – (particle, indicates necessity) *мне надо* – I must; *надо ли платить дополнительно* – is it necessary to pay more?
надпись, надписи *надпись, надписи* – (n., fem.) inscription, writing
наём, найма *наём, найма* – (n., masc.) hire, rent; *по найму* – in service
наёмник, наёмника *наёмник, наёмника* – (n., masc.) hired hand, day laborer (fem. *наёмница*)
наёмщик, наёмщика *наёмщик, наёмщика* – (n., masc.) hirer, lessee, tenant, lodger
название, названия *название, названия* – (n., neut., † *названіе*) name
назначаться *назначаться* – (v.) to be set, designated
назначение, назначения *назначение, назначения* – (n., neut., † *назначеніе*) designation, appointment
назначенный *назначенный* – (part. from *назначить*) assigned, designated
назначить *назначить* – (v.) to designate, assign, allot; *назначив мнѣ Серіалъ №* – having assigned to me Serial #
называться *называться* – (v.) to be called, be named
наименование, наименования *наименование, наименования* –(n., neut., † *наименованіе*) naming, designation, denomination
найма *найма* or найму *найму* → наём *наём*
найти *найти* – (v.) to find
наличный *наличный* – (adj.) ready (cash); effective, actual; *наличное число жителей* – number of actual residents (those actually there in person)
налог, налога *налог, налога* – (n., masc.) tax, duty; *поголовный налог* – poll tax, income-tax, tax per person
налоговый *налоговый* – (adj.) tax; *налоговые списки* – tax lists
нам *нам* – (personal pron., dat. of *мы*, see page 42) (to) us
намеренный *намеренный* – (adj., † *намѣренный*) intentional; *намѣрены вступить въ бракъ* – do you intend to enter into marriage
наместник, наместника *наместник, наместника* – (n., masc., † *намѣстникъ*) deputy, vice-regent
нами *нами* – (personal pron., instr. of *мы*, see page 42) us
намѣстникъ *намѣстникъ* → наместник *наместник*
наниматель, нанимателя *наниматель, нанимателя* – (n., masc.) one who hires workers or rents a house (fem. *нанимательница*)
наочный *наочный* – (adj.) eyewitness, visual, with one's own eyes (probably a Polonism, from Polish *naoczny*)
написанный *написанный* – (part. from *написать*, to write) written
написать *написать* – (v.) to write; *напишите, пожалуйста* – please write
направляться *направляться* – to be bound, headed, to make one's way, direct one's steps
наречение, наречения *наречение, наречения* – (n., neut., † *нареченіе*) naming, designation
наречённый , наречённого *наречённый , наречённого* – (part. from *наречь*, to name, designate) named, designated; *родилась дочь и наречена Баша* – a daughter was born and named Basha; (part. used as a masc. n.) fiancé, bridegroom; (used as a fem. n., *наречённая, наречённой*) fiancée, bride
народ, народа *народ, народа* – (n., masc.) people, nation, folk
народонаселение, народонаселения *народонаселение, народонаселения* – (n., neut., † *народонаселеніе*) population; *книга постояннаго народонаселенія* – Book of Permanent Population
наружный *наружный* – (adj.) external, outward
нас *нас* – (personal pron., gen./acc./prep. of *мы*, see page 42) us
население, населения *население, населения* – (n., neut., † *населеніе*) population
населённый *населённый* – (part. from *населить*, to populate) people, populated, inhabited
насильственно *насильственно* – (adv.); violently, by force; *умереть насильственно* – to die violently
насильственный *насильственный* – (adj.) forcible, forced; *насильственная смерть* – violent death; *умереть насильственной смертью* – to die violently
наследие, наследия *наследие, наследия* – (n., neut., † *наслѣдіе*) inheritance, heritage
наследник, наследника*наследник, наследника* – (n., masc., † *наслѣдникъ*) heir, successor (fem. *наследница*)

наследственный *наследственный* – (adj., † *наслѣдственный*) of inheritance, hereditary
наставник, наставника *наставник, наставника* – (n., masc.) teacher, tutor (fem. *наставница*)
настоятель, настоятеля *настоятель, настоятеля* – (n., masc.) prior, superior, arch-priest; sometimes used for the pastor of a parish (fem. *настоятельница*, prioress)
настоящий *настощий* – (part., † *настоящій*) present, actual, real, genuine; [the one] under discussion; *настоящого года* – of/in the current year; *настоящим* –by means of the present [document], hereby
находиться *находиться* – (v.) to be found, be located, to be, to find oneself; *тело находится в Парк Вест Мемориал Чапел* – the body is at Park West Memorial Chapel (i. e., that's where the wake is being held); *я нахожусь* – literally "I find myself," i. e., I am, have been; *находился на работѣ въ другихъ городахъ* – was at work in other towns
находящийся *находящийся* – (part. from *находиться*, † *находящійся*) finding oneself, located; *находящійся въ живыхъ* – still alive, still among the living; *сын находящагося на военной службѣ Маера* – son of Majer, who is on military service
национальность национальности *национальность национальности* – (n., fem., † *національность*) nationality
начало, начала *начало, начала* – (n., neut.) beginning; principle
начальник, начальника *начальник, начальника* – (n., masc.) head, superior, commander (fem. *начальница*)
начатый *начатый* – (part. from *начать*, to begin) begun
начинать *начинать* – (v.) to begin; *начиная* – beginning (*с* – with)
наш *наш* – (poss. pron.) our, ours; *для нашихъ дѣтей* – for our children
не *не* – (adv.) not; *не имеѣтся* – there is not
Нева, Невы *Нева, Невы* – (n., fem.) Neva [river]
Невель, Невеля *Невель, Невеля* – (n., masc.) Nevel', Russia (see page 126); *невельский* – (adj.) of Nevel'
невеста, невесты *невеста, невесты* – (n., fem., † *невѣста*) bride, engaged girl
невестка, невестки *невестка, невестки* – (n., fem., † *невѣстка*) daughter-in-law, sister-in-law (brother's wife)
невольник, невольника *невольник, невольника* – (n., masc.) slave, bondman (fem. *невольница*)
невралгия, невралгии *невралгия, невралгии* – (n., fem., † *невралгія*) neuralgia
неврит, неврита *неврит, неврита* – (n., masc.) neuritis
неврученный *неврученный* – (part., from *не*, not, + *вручить*, to deliver) not delivered, not handed over
невѣста *невѣста* → невеста *невеста*
него *него* – (pron., gen./acc. sing. of *он*, and *оно*, see page 42) him, it
негоциант, негоцианта *негоциант, негоцианта* – (n., masc., † *негоціантъ*) merchant, trader
неграмотность, неграмотности *неграмотность, неграмотности* – (n., fem.) illiteracy; *по неграмотности* – due to illiteracy
неграмотный *неграмотный* – (adj., short forms *неграмотен, неграмотна*) illiterate
недвижимость, недвижимости *недвижимость, недвижимости* – (n., fem.) real estate
недвижимый *недвижимый* – (adj.) immovable, real; *невдижимое имущество* – real estate, real property
неделя, недели *неделя, недели* – (n., fem., † *недѣля*) week
недойщик, недойщика *недойщик, недойщика* – (n., masc.) one in arrears on payment (e. g., of taxes)
недопущение, недопущения *недопущение, недопущения* – (n., neut., † *недопущеніе*) non-admission
недостаток, недостатка *недостаток, недостатка* – (n., masc.) insufficiency, lack (of)
недостаточно *недостаточно* – (adv.) insufficiently, not enough
недостача, недостачи *недостача, недостачи* – (n., fem.) insufficiency, lack of
незабвенный *незабвенный* – (adj.) unforgettable, never to be forgotten
незаконнорождённый *незаконнорождённый* – (adj.) illegitimate, born outside wedlock
незаконный *незаконный* – (adj.) illegitimate, illegal
неё *неё* – (personal pron., gen./acc. of *она*, see page 42) her, it
Нежин, Нежина *Нежин, Нежина* – (n., masc.) town of Nezhyn, Ukraine (see page 133); *нежинский* – (adj.) of Nezhin/Nezhyn
незабвенный *незабвенный* – (adj.) unforgettable, never to be forgotten
незнание, незнания *незнание, незнания* – (n., neut., † *незнаніе*) not knowing, ignorance; *за незнаніемъ ими грамоты* – because of their not knowing how to read and write
ней *ней* – (personal pron., dat./instr./prep. of *она*, see page 42) her, it, to her, to it
неизвестный *неизвестный* – (adj., † *неизвѣстный*) unknown, uncertain
некогда *некогда* – (adv., † *нѣкогда*) formerly, at one time; (with the names of persons) the late, the deceased
некрестьянский *некрестьянский* – (adj., † *некрестьянскій*) non-peasant

нём *нём* – (pron., prep. sing. of *он* and *оно*, see page 42) him, it
Неман, Немана *Неман, Немана* – (n., masc., † *Нѣманъ*) Nieman river
немец, немца *немец, немца* – (n., masc., † *нѣмецъ*) German (fem. *немка*)
немецкий *немецкий* – (adj., † *нѣмецкій*) German
немного *немного* – (adv.) some, a little, somewhat
немочь, немочи *немочь, немочи* – (n., fem.) illness, sickness, disease; *девичья немочь* or *бледная немочь* – chlorosis, green sickness
нему *нему* – (pron., dat. sing. of *он* and *оно*, see page 42) him, it
немой *немой* – (adj., † *нѣмой*) mute
необходимость, необходимости *необходимость, необходимости* – (n., fem.) necessity
неоткрытие, неоткрытия *неоткрытие, неоткрытия* – (n., neut., † *неоткрытіе*) non-discovery, failure to find; *по неоткрытіи никакихъ* – after failing to find any
неофит, неофита *неофит, неофита* – (n., masc.) neophyte, new religious convert
неприятель, неприятеля *неприятель, неприятеля* – (n., masc., † *непріятель*) foe, enemy
Несвиж Несвижа, *Несвиж, Несвижа* – (n., masc.) Russian name of the town of Nyasvizh, Belarus' (see page 127); *несвижский* – (adj.) of Nesvizh/ Nyasvizh
несвоевременый *несвоевременый* – (adj.) late, untimely, at the wrong time
несколько *несколько* – (pron., † *нѣсколько*) some, a few, several; *если таковых несколько* or *если ихъ нѣсколько* – if there are several of these, if there are several of them
неспособность, неспособности *неспособность, неспособности* – (n., fem.) unsuitability, unfitness (*к* – for)
неспособный *неспособный*– (adj.) unsuitable, unfit (*к* – for)
нестроевой *нестроевой* – (adj.) out of the ranks
нет *нет* – (adv., † *нѣтъ*) no; there is not, there is no; *если родителей нѣтъ въ живыхъ* – if there are no parents among the living, i. e., if no parents are alive; *если у Вас нет этих документов* – if you do not have these documents
неумеющий *неумеющий* – (part. from *не*, not + *уметь,* to be able to, † *неумѣющій*) unable to
нефрит, нефрита *нефрит, нефрита* – (n., masc.) nephritis
Нешава, Нешавы *Нешава, Нешавы* – (n., fem.) town of Nieszawa, Poland (see page 119); *нешавский* – of Nieszawa
нею *нею* – (personal pron., † form of *ней*, instr. of *она*) her, it
неявка, неявки *неявка, неявки* – (n., fem.) non-appearance; *неявка к освидѣтельствованію* – failure to appear for examination (for military service)
нижегородский *нижегородский* → Нижний Новгород *Нижний Новгород*
нижеписанний *нижеписаный* – (part. from *ниже*, below + *писать*, to write) written below; *отъ нижеписаннаго числа* – from the date written below
нижеподписавший *нижеподписавший* – (part. from *подписать*, to sign, plus *ниже*, below), † *нижеподписавшій*) the undersigned, the one whose signature appears below (*нижеподписавшийся* means the same thing)
нижний *нижний* – (adj.. † *нижній*) lower, inferior; *нижніе чины* – rank and file
Нижний Новгород, Нижнего Новгорода *Нижний Новгород, Нижнего Новгорода* – (n., masc., † *Нижній Новгородъ*) Nizhniy Novgorod, name of a town in Russia (see page 135); *нижегородский* – of Nizhniy Novgorod
низкий *низкий* – (adj., † низкій) short
никакой *никакой* – (adj., declined like *какой*, see page 43) none, not any, not any kind of
никогда *никогда* – (adv.) never
никуда *никуда* – (adv.) to nowhere
ним *ним* – (personal pron., instr. of *он* and *оно*, dat. of *они*, see p. 42) him, it, them
ними *ними* – (personal pron., instr. of *они*, see p. 42) them
Нисан, Нисана *Нисан, Нисана*– (n., masc.) Nissan, the name of a month in the Jewish calendar (see page 47)
них *них* – (personal pron., gen./acc./prep. of *они*, see p. 42) them
нищий *нищий* – (adj., † *нищій*) poor, indigent; (used as a n.) beggar, pauper
но *но* – (conj.) but
Новая Ушица, Новой Ушицы *Новая Ушица, Новой Ушицы* – (n., fem.) town of Nova Ushytsya, Ukraine (see page 132); *новоушицкий* – of Nova Ushytsya
Новгород, Новгорода *Новгород, Новгорода* – (n., masc.) Novgorod, town in Russia; *новгородский* – of Novgorod
Новгород-Северский, Новгорода-Северского *Новгород-Северский, Новгорода-Северского* – (n., masc.) town of Novhorod-Sivers'kyi, Ukraine (see page 133)
† Ново-Александрія, Ново-Александріи *Ново-Александрія, Ново-Александріи* – (n., fem.) town of Puławy, Poland (see page 120); *новоалександрійскій* – of Puławy

† Ново-Александровскъ, Ново-Александровска *Ново-Александровскъ, Ново-Александровска* – (n., masc.) town of Zarasai, Lithuania (see page 124); *новоалександровскій* – of Zarasai
новобранец, новобранца *новобранец, новобранца* – (n., masc.) (new) recruit, one newly enlisted in the military
новобрачный *новобрачный* – (adj.) newlywed; (used as a n., masc.) groom; *новобрачная, новобрачной* (used as a n., fem.), bride; *новобрачные* (pl.), the newlyweds
Новоград-Волынский, Новограда-Волынского *Новоград-Волынский, Новограда-Волынского* – (n., masc.) town of Novohrad-Volyn's'kyi, Ukraine (see page 130)
Новогрудок, Новогрудка *Новогрудок, Новогрудка* – (n., masc.) town of Navahrudak, Belarus' (see page 126); *новогрудский* – (adj.) of Novogrudok/ Navahrudak
Новое Дивеево, Нового Дивеева *Новое Дивеево, Нового Дивеева* – (n., neut.) the name of a famous Russian monastery in New York
Новозыбков, Новозыбкова *Новозыбков, Новозыбкова* – (n., masc.) town of Novozybkov, Russia (see page 133); *новозыбковский* – (adj.) of Novozybkov
† Ново-Минскъ, Ново-Минска *Ново-Минскъ, Ново-Минска* – (n., masc.) town of Mińsk Mazowiecki, Poland (see page 119); *новоминскій* – of Mińsk Mazowiecki
Новомосковск, Новомосковска *Новомосковск, Новомосковска* – (n., masc.) town of Nowomoskovs'k, Ukraine (see page 134); *новомосковский* – (adj.) of Novomoskovs'k
новосёл, новосёла *новосёл, новосёла* – (n., masc.) new arrival, one who's recently moved in or settled, owner of a new house (fem. *новосёлка*)
нововступивший *нововступивший* – (part., † *нововступившій*) the one having newly entered, e. g., *нововступившіе въ законный бракъ* – the ones who have newly entered into a marital union, i. e., newlyweds
новый *новый* – (adj.) new; *нового стиля*, (abbr. *н. с.*) New Style (in dating, i. e., by the Gregorian calendar)
ножёвщик, ножёвщика *ножёвщик, ножёвщика* – (n., masc.) cutler
номер, номера *номер, номера* – (n., masc., abbr. №) number
Норвегия, Норвегии *Норвегия, Норвегии* – (n., masc., † *Норвегія*) Norway
норвежец, норвежца *норвежец, норвежца* – (n., masc.) Norwegian (fem. *норвежка*)
нормальный *нормальный* – (adj.) normal
нос, носа *нос, носа* – (n., masc.) nose
носильщик, носильщика *носильщик, носильщика* – (n., masc.) bearer, carrier, porter
носить *носить* – (v.) to carry, bear
нотариальный *нотариальный* – (adj., † *нотаріальный*) of a notary, notarial
нотариус, нотариуса *нотариус, нотариуса* – (n., masc., † *нотаріусъ*) notary
ношатый, ношатого *ношатый, ношатого* – (adj. used as a n., masc.) hodman, mason's assistant
ночь, ночи *ночь, ночи* – (n., fem.) night; *ночью* – at night (see page 50)
ноябрь, ноября *ноябрь, ноября* – (n., masc.) November
нравственность, нравственности *нравственность, нравственности* – (n., fem.) morality, moral character
Н. С. → новый *новый*
нужный *нужный* – (adj.) necessary, needful; *мне нужны данные* – I need information; *которые мне нужны* – which I need
нумерация, нумерации *нумерация, нумерации* – (n., fem., † *нумерація*) numeration, numbering
нынешний *нынешний* – (adj., † *нынѣшній*) of today
нынѣ *нынѣ* – (adv.) now, presently
нѣкогда *нѣкогда* → некогда *некогда*
Нѣманъ *Нѣманъ* → Неман *Неман*
нѣмецкій *нѣмецкій* → немецкий *немецкий*
нѣмецъ *нѣмецъ* → немец *немец*
нѣмой *нѣмой* → немой *немой*
нѣсколько *нѣсколько* → несколько *несколько*
нѣтъ *нѣтъ* → нет *нет*
Нью-Йорк, Нью-Йорка *Нью-Йорк, Нью-Йорка* – (n., masc., † *Нью-Іоркъ*) New York
о *о* – (*об* when the next word begins with a vowel, *обо* before certain consonant clusters, preposition + prep.) about, concerning
оба, обоих *оба, обоих* – (adj., masc. pl.) both
обе, обеих *обе, обеих* – (adj., fem. pl., † *обѣ*) both
обедня, обедни *обедня, обедни* – (n., fem., gen. pl. *обеден*, † *обѣдня*) religious service, Mass
обезпечение *обезпеченіе* → обеспечение *обеспечение*
обезпечивать *обезпечивать* → обеспечивать *обеспечивать*
† оберъ- *оберъ-*, "chief, high, grand," a prefix used in archaic German titles such as *оберъ-гофмаршалъ*, grand marshal [cmp. Germ. *Oberhofmarschall*], and *оберъ-воршнейдеръ*, gentleman-carver [Germ. *Obervorschneider*]
обеспечение, обеспечения *обеспечение, обеспечения* – (n., neut., † *обезпеченіе*) bail, security, guarantee; warrant, warranty
обеспечивать *обеспечивать* – (v., † *обезпечивать*) to secure, guarantee

обет, обета *обет, обета* – (n., masc., † *обѣтъ*) promise, vow
обжалованный *обжалованный* – (part. from *обжаловать*, to lodge a complaint, to appeal) appealed
областной *областной* – (adj.) of an *oblast'* (see *область*)
область, области *область, области* – (n., fem., nom. pl. *области*, gen. pl. *областей*) an *oblast'*, regional administrative district
обложение, обложения *обложение, обложения* – (n., neut., † *обложенiе*) assessment, taxation
обнаруженный *обнаруженный* – (part. from *обнаружить*, to display, uncover) expressed, displayed, shown; *взаимному согласiю внѣшнами знаками обнаруженному* – mutual consent expressed by outward signs
обо *обо* → о *о*
обозначение, обозначения *обозначение, обозначения* – (n., neut., † *обозначенiе*) indication, designation
обозначить *обозначить* – (v.) to designate
обозначиться *обозначиться* – (v.) to be designated, listed; *обозначаются его примѣты* – his description is given
обозник, обозника *обозник, обозника* – (n., masc.) transport driver [in the mili-tary, cmp. *обозный* and † *обозничiй*, baggage master]
обоихъ *обоихъ* → оба *оба*
обойщик, обойщика *обойщик, обойщика* – (n., masc.) upholsterer
обоюдный *обоюдный* – (adj.) mutual
образование, образования *образование, образования* – (n., neut., † *образованiе*) education, training; formation
обращаться *обращаться* – (v.) to turn, apply, write to *(к)*
обрезанец, обрезанца *обрезанец, обрезанца* – (n., masc., † *обрѣзанецъ*) circumcised person
обрезание, обрезания *обрезание, обрезания* – (n., neut., † *обрѣзанiе*) circumcision
оброчник, оброчника *оброчник, оброчника* – (n., masc.) peasant who pays quitrent [cmp. adj. *оброчный*, paying quitrent]
обручаться *обручаться* – (v.) to be betrothed, get engaged; *не обручались-ли съ другомъ лицемъ* – have you ever been engaged to another person?
обручение, обручения *обручение, обручения* – (n., neut., † *обрученiе*) betrothal
обрученник, обрученника *обрученник, обрученника* – (n., masc.) the betrothed (fem. *обрученница*)
обрѣзанецъ *обрѣзанецъ* → обрезанец *обрезанец*
обрѣзание *обрѣзание* → обрезание *обрезание*
обряд, обряда *обряд, обряда* – (n., masc.) ceremony; rite; *свадебный обряд* – marriage ceremony; *по обряду магометанской веры* – in accordance with the rite of the Islamic faith; *при религiозномъ обрядѣ* – during a religious ceremony
обучаться *обучаться* – (v.) to study, go through a course, be trained
общественный *общественный* – (adj.) of a society, company, district; common, general, public
общество, общества *общество, общества* – (n., neut.) society, company; community, district
общий *общий* – (adj., † *общiй*) general, common
община, общины *община, общины* – (n., fem.) community, parish, township
объявить *объявить* – (v., perf. counterpart to *объявлять*) to announce, state, declare, make a statement; *объявили* – they declared, stated
объявление, объявления *объявление, объявления* – (n., neut. † *объявленiе*) announcing, announcement
объявлять *объявлять* – (v.) to announce, declare, make a statement; *объявляя*, declaring, stating
объявляться *объявляться* – (v.) to be announced, declared; *объявляется черезъ сiе:* it is hereby declared
объявляющий *объявляющий* – (part., † *объявляющiй*) making a statement; (often used as a n.) declarant
объявляя *объявляя* – (adv. part. from *объявлять*) declaring, stating
обыватель, обывателя *обыватель, обывателя* – (n., masc.) inhabitant (fem. *обывательница*)
обыкновенно *обыкновенно* – (adv.) normally, usually
обыск, обыска *обыск, обыска* – (n., masc.) examination, search, perquisition
обѣ *обѣ* → обе *обе*
обѣдня *обѣдня* → обедня *обедня*
обѣтъ *обѣтъ* → обет *обет*
обязанный *обязанный* – (part. from *обязать*, to obligate) obligated, required
обязываться *обязываться* – (v.) to obligate oneself, owe; to be obligated
Овруч, Овруча *Овруч, Овруча* – (n., masc.) town of Ovruch, Ukraine (see page 130); *овручский* – (adj.) of Ovruch
овчар, овчара *овчар, овчара* – (n., masc.) shepherd, herdsman
оглашение, оглашения *оглашение, оглашения* – (n., neut., † *оглашенiе*) readings of the banns
оговорка, оговорки *оговорка, оговорки* – (n., fem.) reserve, clause, limitation
огородник, огородника *огородник, огородника* – (n., masc.) kitchen-gardener, truck farmer
ограничение, ограничения *ограничение, ограничения* – (n., neut., † *ограниченiе*) restriction, limitation

одеваться *одеваться* – (v., † *одѣваться*) to dress oneself, get dressed
Одесса, Одессы *Одесса, Одессы* – (n., fem.) town of Odesa, Ukraine (see page 133); *одесский* – (adj.) of Odessa
один, одного *один, одного* – (num., masc.) one; *имеют одну со мной фамилию* – they have the same surname I have; *одною ли водю* – with water alone?
одиннадцатый *одиннадцатый* – (ordinal num./adj.) eleventh
одиннадцать, одиннадцати *одиннадцать, одиннадцати* – (num.) eleven
одна, одной *одна, одной* – (num., fem., † fem. pl. *однѣ*) one
одно, одного *одно, одного* – (num., neut.) one
однодворец, однодворца *однодворец, однодворца* – (n., masc.) franklin, freeholder (fem. *однондворка*)
однородный *однородный* – (adj.) having the same father
односелье, односелья *односелье, односелья* – (n., neut.) single farm or settlement, not part of a village or estate
одноутробный *одноутробный* – (adj.) having the same mother
однѣ *однѣ* → одна *одна*
ожирение, ожирения *ожирение, ожирения* – (n., neut., † *ожиренiе*) obesity
означанный *означанный* – (part. from *означать*, to mark, designate) marked, designated
означенный *означенный* – (part. from *означить*) marked, designated
означить *означить* – (v.) to designate, mark, note, betoken, signify
Ока, Оки *Ока, Оки* – (n., fem.) Oka [river]
оказавшийся *оказавшийся* – (part. from *оказаться*; † *оказавшiйся*) having turned out [to be], proved [to be]
оказать *оказать* – (v.) to prove, show
оказаться *оказаться* – (v.) to prove, turn out to be; *на срок, какой ей окажется нужнымъ* – for whatever period turns out to be necessary for her; *оказалось, что* – it turned out that …
окладная книга, окладной книги *окладная книга, окладной книги* – (n., fem.) tax-book
околица, околицы *околица, околицы* – (n., fem.) section, neighborhood, vicinity; outskirts of a village
оконченный *оконченный* – (part. from *окончить*) done, finished, completed
окончить *окончить* – (v.) to finish, complete
окрещённый *окрещённый* – (part. from *окрестить*, to baptize) baptized; (used as a noun) the one baptized; *окрещено дитя* – a child [was] baptized
округ, округа *округ, округа* – (n., masc.) district, *okrug*
окружный *окружный* – (adj.) of a district (*okrug*); *окружный город* – town that served as the administrative center of an *округ*
октябрь, октября *октябрь, октября* – (n., masc.) October
оловяничник, оловняничника *оловяничник, оловняничника* – (n., masc.) pewterer, tinman
Олонец, Олонца *Олонец, Олонца* – (n., masc.) Olonets, a town in Russia (see page 135); *олонецкий* – of Olonets
Ольгополь, Ольгополя *Ольгополь, Ольгополя* – (n., masc.) Russian name of the town of Ol'hopil', Ukraine (see page 132); *ольгопольский* – (adj.) of Ol'gopol'/ Ol'hopil'
Олькуш, Олькуша *Олькуш, Олькуша* – (n., masc.) town of Olkusz, Poland (see page 120); *олькушский* – of Olkusz
омертвелость, омертвелости *омертвелость, омертвелости* – (n., fem., † *омертвѣлость*) necrosis; also seen: *омертвение* († *омертвѣнiе*)
он *он* – (personal pron., see p. 42) he
она *она* – (personal pron., see p. 42) she
† онаго *онаго* → оный *оный*
они *они* – (personal pron., see p. 42) they
оно *оно* – (personal pron., see p. 42) it
† оный *оный* – (pron.) this, that; *во время рожденiя онаго* – at the time of the latter's birth; *послѣ оной* – after that
† оныхъ *оныхъ* – (personal pron., † for modern *них*, see page 42) them
† онѣ *онѣ* (personal pron.) they (used to refer to more than one female)
† Опатовъ, Опатова *Опатовъ, Опатова* – (n., masc.) town of Opatów, Poland (see page 120); *опатовскiй* – of Opatów
опекун, опекуна *опекун, опекуна* – (n., masc.) guardian, tutor, trustee, warden, ward (fem. *опекунша*, governess)
описание, описания *описание, описания* – (n., neut., † *описанiе*) description
описанный *описанный* – (part. from *описать*) described
описать *описать* – (v.) to describe
опись, описи *опись, описи* – (n., fem.) inventory; *оцѣночная опись* – appraisal inventory
оплата, оплаты *оплата, оплаты* – (n., fem.) payment, charge; *какова оплата з получение этих данных* – what is the charge for obtaining this information?
ополченец, ополченца *ополченец, ополченца* – (n., masc.) militia-man, one serving in the militia or home guard
ополчение, ополчения *ополчение, ополчения* – (n., neut., † *ополченiе*) militia, home guard

ополченский *ополченский* – (adj., † *ополченскій*) of the militia, home guard
Опочно, Опочна *Опочно, Опочна* – (n., neut.) town of Opoczno, Poland (see page 120); *опоченский* – of Opoczno
определение, определения *определение, определения* – (n., neut., † *опредѣленіе*) determining, establishing
определённый *определённый* – (part. from *определить;* † *опредѣлённый*) determined, appointed, established
определить *определить* – (v., † *опредѣлить*) to determine, establish
опросный *опросный* – (adj.) interrogatory; *опросный лист* – questionnaire
оптовщик, оптовщика *оптовщик, оптовщика* – (n., masc.) wholesale dealer
опухоль, опухоли *опухоль, опухоли* – (n., fem.) tumor
оратай, оратая *оратай, оратая* – (n., masc.) plowman, tiller
органист, органиста *органист, органиста* – (n., masc.) organist
† Оргѣевъ, Оргѣева *Оргѣевъ, Оргѣева* – (n., masc.) Russian name of Orhei, Moldova (see page 132); *оргеевский* – (adj., † *оргѣевскій*) of Orgeev/Orhei
ординарец, ординарца *ординарец, ординарца* – (n., masc.) orderly
ординатор, ординатора *ординатор, ординатора* – (n., masc.) house-surgeon, house-physician
Орёл, Орла *Орёл, Орла* – (n., masc.) Orel, Russia (see page 135); *орловский* – (adj.) of Orel
Оренбург, Оренбурга *Оренбург, Оренбурга* – (n., masc.) Orenburg, Russia (see page 135); *оренбургский* – of Orenburg
оружейник, оружейника *оружейник, оружейника* – (n., masc.) armorer, gunsmith
оруженосец, оруженосца *оруженосец, оруженосца* – (n., masc.) armor-bearer, sword-bearer, squire
оружие, оружия *оружие, оружия* – (n., neut., † *оружіе*) arms, weapon
Орша, Орши *Орша, Орши* – (n., fem.) town of Orsha, Belarus' (see page 126); *оршанский* – (adj.) of Orsha
освидетельствование, освидетельствования *освидетельствование, освидетельствования* – (n., neut., † *освидѣтельствованіе*) examination
освобождение, освобождения *освобождение, освобождения* – (n., neut., † *освобожденіе*) deliverance, liberation, release; *освобожденіе отъ воинской повинности* – deferment from military service
оседлый *оседлый* – (adj., † *осѣдлый*) settled
осмотр, остмотра *осмотр, остмотра* – (n., masc.) examination, inspection
основание основания *основание основания* – (n., neut., † *основаніе*) basis; *на основании того, что ...* – on the basis of the fact that ...
основатель, основателя *основатель, основателя* – (n., masc.) founder, establisher (fem. *основательница*)
особенность, особенности *особенность, особенности* – (n., fem.) separateness, peculiarity; *в особенности* – particularly, in particular, especially
особенный *особенный* – (adj.) separate, private, particular, special
особый *особый* – (adj.) particular, special; *особыя примѣты* – distinguishing marks
оспа, оспы *оспа, оспы* – (n., fem.) smallpox; *ветряная* [† *вѣтряная*] *оспа* – chicken pox; *телячья оспа* – cowpox; *черная оспа* – smallpox
оспопрививание, оспопрививания *оспопрививание, оспопрививания* – (n., neut.) vaccination
оставить *оставить* – (v.) to leave behind, abandon, be survived by
Остер, Остра *Остер, Остра* – (n., masc.) town of Oster, Ukraine (see page 133); *остерский* – (adj.) of Oster
остзеец, остзейца *остзеец, остзейца* – (n., masc.) inhabitant of the "Baltic provinces" [cmp. *Ostsee*, "East Sea," German name for the Baltic]
† остзейскій *остзейскій* – (adj.) of the Baltic (of the *Ostsee*, see остзеец ↑); *остзейскій край* – term for the Baltic provinces (see page 122)
остров, острова *остров, острова* – (n., masc.) island
Остров, Острова *Остров, Острова* – (n., masc.) town Ostrów Mazowiecka, Poland (see page 120); *островский* – of Ostrów
Островец, Островца *Островец, Островца* – (n., masc.) town of Astravets, Belarus' (see page 127); *островецкий* – of Ostrovets/Astravets
Острог, Острога *Острог, Острога* – (n., masc.) town of Ostroh, Ukraine (see page 130); *острожский* – (adj.) of Ostrog/Ostroh
острожник, острожника *острожник, острожника* – (n., masc.) imprisoned criminal, convict (fem. *острожница*)
Остроленка, Остроленки *Остроленка, Остроленки* – (n., fem.) tOstrołęka, Poland (see page 120); *остроленкский* (or † *остроленцкій*) – of Ostrołęka
острый *острый* – (adj.) sharp, severe
от *от* – (*omo* before certain consonant clusters, † *отъ*, prep. + gen.) from, of; *от меня* – from me, by me; *отъ чего умеръ* – what did he died of?; *X лет от роду* – X years from birth, X years old
отбывание, отбывания *отбывание, отбывания* – (n., neut., † *отбываніе*) fulfillment; *отношеніе къ*

отбыванію воинской повинности – status as regards completion of military service

отбыть *отбыть* – (v., conjugated like *быть* with *от-* prefixed) to serve (time), e. g., in regard to questions on military service *отбылъ* means "he has served [his time]"

ответ, ответа *ответ, ответа* – (n., masc., † *отвѣтъ*) answer, reply

ответив *ответив* – (adv. part. from *ответить*, † *отвѣтивъ*) having answered, responded

ответить *ответить* – (v., † *отвѣтить*) to answer

ответственность, ответственности *ответственность, ответственности* – (n., fem., † *отвѣтственность*) responsibility, accountability

отдатчик, отдатчика *отдатчик, отдатчика* – (n., masc.) commissary of the stores

отдача, отдачи *отдача, отдачи* – (n., fem.) admission, enrollment

отдел, отдела *отдел, отдела* – (n., masc., † *отдѣлъ*) division, section

отделение, отделения *отделение, отделения* – (n., neut., † *отдѣленіе*) division; *Врачебное Отдѣленіе* – Medical Division

отдельно *отдельно* – (adv., † *отдѣльно*) separately, individually

отдельный *отдельный* – (adj., † *отдѣльный*) separate, apart, individual

отёк, отёка *отёк, отёка* – (n., masc.) edema

отец, отца *отец, отца* – (n., masc.) father

открывать *открывать* – (v.) to open

открываться *открываться* – (v.) to open, be opened

откуда *откуда* – (adv.) from where, whence

откупщик, откупщика *откупщик, откупщика* – (n., masc.) tax-farmer, lease-holder (fem. *откупщица*)

отливщик, отливщика *отливщик, отливщика* – (n., masc.) caster, founder

отличие, отличия *отличие, отличия* – (n., neut., † *отличіе*) medal, decoration

отлично *отлично* – (adv.) in an excellent or outstanding manner

отлучка, отлучки *отлучка, отлучки* – (n., fem.) absence

отметить *отметить* – (v., † *отмѣтить*) to note down

отметка, отметки *отметка, отметки* – (n., fem., † *отмѣтка*) notation

относительно *относительно* – (adv.) in regard to

относиться *относиться* – (v.) to refer (*к* – to), have to do with

отношение, отношения *отношение, отношения* – (n., neut. † *отношеніе*) attitude, relation, relationship; report; *при отношеніи* – with a report, official document

ото *ото* → от *от*

отобранный *отобранный* – (part. from *отобрать*) taken away

отобрать *отобрать* – (v.) to take away, choose, select; *отобрать показанія* – to take depositions

отправитель, отправителя *отправитель, отправителя* – (n., masc.) sender, dispatcher, remitter (fem. *отправительница*)

отправиться *отправиться* – (v.) to set out, depart, leave; *отправиться пароходом* – to set out by steamship

отправление, отправления *отправление, отправления* – (n., neut., † *отправленіе*) forwarding, sending; administration, function

отправляться *отправляться* – (v., imperf. counterpart of *отправиться*) to set out, be headed; *отправляется за границу* – is headed abroad

отпускной *отпускной* – (adj.) on leave; (used as a n.) solider on leave (also seen: *отпустник*); *отпускной билетъ* – ticket of leave, furlough

отпущенник, отпущенника *отпущенник, отпущенника* – (n., masc.) freedman (fem. *отпущенница*)

отравление, отравления *отравление, отравления* – (n., neut. † *отравленіе*) poisoning

отрез, отреза *отрез, отреза* – (n., masc., † *отрѣзъ*) cutting; *линія отрѣза* – cutting line (i. e., "cut here")

отрезываться отрезываться – (v., † *отрѣзываться*) to cut off

отслужена *отслужена* → отслужить *отслужить*

отслужить *отслужить* – (v.) to serve, celebrate (services); *панихида будет отслужена* –a requiem will be said

отсроченный *отсроченный* – (part. from *отсрочить*, to adjourn, delay) deferred, postponed

отсрочка, отсрочки *отсрочка, отсрочки* – (n., fem.) deferment

отст. *отст.* – abbr. for отставной *отставной*, q. v.

отставник, отставника *отставник, отставника* – (n., masc.) retired officer

отставной *отставной* – (adj.) retired, discharged, e. g., *отставной солдат*, discharged soldier

отсут. *отсут.* → отсутствующий *отсутствующий*

отсутствие, отсутствия *отсутствие, отсутствия* – (n., neut., † *отсутствіе*) absence

отсутствующий *отсутствующий* – (abbr. *отсут.*, part. from *отсутствовать*, to be absent; † *отсутствующій*) absent, missing, away

отца *отца* → отец *отец*

Отче наш *отче наш* – the Lord's Prayer, "Our Father"

отчество, отчества *отчество, отчества* – (n., neut.) patronymic (name meaning "son of," thus *Иванович*, *Ivanovich*, "son of Ivan")

отчизна, отчизны *отчизна, отчизны* – (n., fem.) fatherland
отчим, отчима *отчим, отчима* – (n., masc.) stepfather; father-in-law
отчинник, отчинника *отчинник, отчинника* – (n., masc.) son, male descendant
отчиц, отчица *отчиц, отчица* – (n., masc.) son, male descendant
отшельник, отшельника *отшельник, отшельника* – (n., masc.) hermit, anchorite (fem. *отшельница*)
отъ *отъ* → от *от*
оўмершій *оўмершій* → умерший *умерший*
оўмеръ *оўмеръ* → умереть *умереть*
офицер, офицера *офицер, офицера* – (n., masc.) officer; fem. *офицерша*, officer's wife)
официант, официанта *официант, официанта* – (n., masc., † *официантъ*) house-steward, butler; [in modern Russian] waiter
охотник, окотника *охотник, окотника* – (n., masc.) amateur, one who does something for the love of it; hunter, sportsman (fem. *охотница*)
охранитель, охранителя *охранитель, охранителя* – (n., masc.) keeper, guardian, custodian (fem. *охранительница*)
оценка, оценки *оценка, оценки* – (n., fem., † *оцѣнка*) appraisal, estimate
оценочный *оценочный* – (adj., † *оцѣночный*) of estimation, appraisal
оценщик, оценщика *оценщик, оценщика* – (n., masc., † *оцѣнщикъ*) appraiser, estimator (fem. *оценщица*)
очерк, очерка *очерк, очерка* – (n., masc.) outline, description, sketch
Ошмяны, Ошмян *Ошмяны, Ошмян* – (n., pl.) town of Oshmyany (see page 124); *ошмянский* – (adj.) of Oshmyany
Павлоград, Павлограда *Павлоград, Павлограда* – (n., masc.) town of Pavlohrad, Ukraine (see page 134); *павлоградский* – (adj.) of Pavlohrad
падучая, падучей *падучая, падучей* – (adj. used as a n.) epilepsy, falling sickness (also seen: *падучая болезнь*)
падчерица, падчерицы *падчерица, падчерицы* – (n., fem.) stepdaughter
паж, пажа *паж, пажа* – (n., masc.) page
палата, палаты *палата, палаты* – (n., fem.) chamber, tribunal; house; ward; *казённая палата* – treasury office, the court of exchequer
палач, палача *палач, палача* – (n., masc.) executioner, hangman
память, памяти *память, памяти* – (n., fem.) memory; *в памяти* – in memory [of]; *вечная память ему* – may his memory live forever; *твердой памяти* – of sound memory
пан, пана *пан, пана* – (n., masc.) [Polish] land-owner, gentleman [cmp. Polish *pan*]
панихида, панихиды *панихида, панихиды* – (n., fem.) requiem, service for the dead; *гражданская панихида* – civil funeral services; *панихида будет отслужена* – a requiem will be said
панна, панны *панна, панны* – (n., fem.) daughter of a Polish gentleman [cmp. Polish *panna*]
пансионер, пансионера *пансионер, пансионера* – (n., masc., † *пансіонеръ*) boarder [at a boarding school], fem. *пансионерка*
панский *панский* – (adj.,† *панскій*) mercer's; *панский ряд* – mercer's shop; *панские товары* – linens and such goods
панья, паньи *панья, паньи* – (n., fem.) wife of a Polish gentleman [cmp. Polish *pani*]
паралич, паралича *паралич, паралича* – (n., masc.) paralysis, palsy; *детский* († *дѣтскій*) *паралич* – infantile paralysis
Париж, Парижа *Париж, Парижа* – (n., masc.) Russian name of Paris, France
парикмахер, парикмахера *парикмахер, парикмахера* – (n., masc.) wig-maker, hairdresser, barber (fem. *парикмахерша*)
паркетчик, паркетчика *паркетчик, паркетчика* – (n., masc.) one who installs parquet flooring
пароксизм, пароксизма *пароксизм, пароксизма* – (n., masc.) fit, paroxysm
пароход парохода *пароход парохода* – (n., masc.) steamship
парусник, парусника *парусник, парусника* – (n., masc.) sail-maker; sailing ship
паспорт паспорта *паспорт паспорта* – (n., masc.) passport
паспортный *паспортный* – (adj.) passport; *паспортная книжка* – booklet-form passport
пассажир, пассажира *пассажир, пассажира* – (n., masc.) passenger
пастор, пастора *пастор, пастора* – (n., masc.) pastor (fem. *пасторша*, pastor's wife)
пастух, пастуха *пастух, пастуха* – (n., masc.) shepherd, herdsman (fem. *пастушка*)
пастырь, пастыря *пастырь, пастыря* – (n., masc.) shepherd, herdsman; pastor
пасха, пасхи *пасха, пасхи* – (n., fem.) Passover (among Jews); Easter (among Christians)
пасынок, пасынка *пасынок, пасынка* – (n., masc.) stepson
патриарх, патриарха *патриарх, патриарха* – (n., masc., † *патріархъ*) patriarch
патронщик, патронщика *патронщик, патронщика* – (n., masc.) cartridge-maker
пахарь, пахаря *пахарь, пахаря* – (n., masc.) husbandman, tiller, plower

пахтальщик, пахтальщика *пахтальщик, пахтальщика* – (n., masc.) churner (fem. *пахтальщица*)
паяльщик, паяльщика *паяльщик, паяльщика* – (n., masc.) solderer (fem. *паяальщица*)
певец, певца *певец, певца* – (n., masc., † *пѣвецъ*) singer, chanter (fem. *певица*, † *пѣвица*)
пейс, пейса *пейс, пейса* – (n., masc.) ringlets worn by Jews, usually used in the pl., *пейсы*
пекарь, пекаря *пекарь, пекаря* – (n., masc., nom. pl. *пекаря*, gen. pl. *пекарей*) baker
Пенза, Пензы *Пенза, Пензы* – (n., fem.) Penza, name of a town in Russia (see page 135); *пензенский* – (adj.) of Penza
пеньковяз, пеньковяза *пеньковяз, пеньковяза* – (n., masc.) hemp-binder
первенец, первенца *первенец, первенца* – (n., masc.) firstborn
первосвятитель, первосвятителя *первосвятитель, первосвятителя* – (n., masc.) primate
первый *первый* – (ordinal num./adj.) first; *двадцать первый* – twenty-first; *по первому браку Меер*, by her first marriage Meyer; *часть первая* – first part (of a parish register, recording births); *во-первых* – in the first place, firstly
переводчик, переводчика *переводчик, переводчика* – (n., masc.) translator (fem. *переводчица*)
перевозчик, перевозчика *перевозчик, перевозчика* – (n., masc.) ferryman
перед *перед* – (prep. + instr.) before, in front of
передать *передать* – (v.) to give, pass on; *передайте им, пожалуйста, мой адрес* – please give them my address
переезд, переезда *переезд, переезда* – (n., masc., † *переѣздъ*) crossing; *пункт переезда* – crossing point
перейти *перейти* – (v., past tense *он перешел*) to cross, pass over or through, change (from one thing to another); *перейти въ Американское гражданство* – to change [my] citizenship to American
Перекоп, Перекопа *Перекоп, Перекопа* – (n., masc.) town of Perekop, Ukraine (see page 134); *перекопский* – (adj.) of Perekop
перекрест, перекреста *перекрест, перекреста* – (n., masc.) convert to a new religion, especially a baptized Jew
перемена, перемены *перемена, перемены* – (n., fem., † *перемѣна*) change
переосвидетельствование, переосвидетельствования *переосвидетельствование, переосвидетельствования* – (n., neut., † *переосвидѣтельствованіе*) re-examination
переписной *переписной* – (adj.) of a census; *переписной лист* – census form
перепись, переписи *перепись, переписи* – (n., fem.) census, inventory, catalog; *перепись населения* – census
переплётчик, переплётчика *переплётчик, переплётчика* – (n., masc.) book-binder (fem. *переплётчица*)
перепродавец, перепродавца *перепродавец, перепродавца* – (n., masc.) re-seller (fem. *перепродавица*)
переселенец, пшреселенца *переселенец, пшреселенца* – (n., masc.) migrant, immigrant, one who moves from one place to another (fem. *переселенка*)
переселение, переселения *переселение, переселения* – (n., neut., † *переселеніе*) emigration, moving
пересылка, пересылки *пересылка, пересылки* – (n., fem.) remittance, transfer (e. g., of money)
пересылочный *пересылочный* – (adj.) sent over, forwarded, relating to transfer; *включая пересылочные расходы* – including transfer expenses
переторговщик, переторговщика *переторговщик, переторговщика* – (n., masc.) broker, retailer
переулок, переулка *переулок, переулка* – (n., masc.) by-street, lane, alley
переход, перехода *переход, перехода* – (n., masc.) passage, move, march
переходить *переходить* – (v., past tense *он переходил*) to cross, pass, change
перечень, перечня *перечень, перечня* – (n., masc.) summary, list, inventory
перечисление, перечисления *перечисление, перечисления* – (n., neut., † *перечисленіе*) enumeration; transfer; *подлежитъ перечисленію* – is subject to transfer
перечневой *перечневой* – (adj.) summary, succinct
переѣздъ *переѣздъ* → переезд *переезд*
Переяслав, Переяслава *Переяслав, Переяслава* – (n., masc.) town of Pereyaslav-Khmel'nytsk'yi, Ukraine (see page 133); *переяславский* – (adj.) of Pereyaslav
период, периода *период, периода* – (n., masc.) period
Пермь, Перми *Пермь, Перми* – (n., fem.) Perm', name of a town in Russia (see page 135); *пермский* – of Perm'
песнопевец, песнопевца *песнопевец, песнопевца* – (n., masc., † *пѣснопѣвецъ*) singer, chanter, psalmist
Петркув-Трыбунальски *Петркув-Трыбунальски* – (n., masc., † *Петроковъ*) town of Piotrków Trybunalski, Poland (see page 119); *петркувский* – († *петроковскій*) of Piotrków
Петроградъ *Петроградъ* → Санктъ-Петербургъ *Санктъ-Петербургъ*
Петроковъ *Петроковъ* → Петркув-Трыбунальски *Петркув-Трыбунальски*

пехота, пехоты *пехота, пехоты* – (n., fem., † *пѣхота*) infantry
пехотинец, пехотинца *пехотинец, пехотинца* – (n., masc., † *пѣхотинецъ*) foot soldier, infantryman
пехотный *пехотный* – (adj., † *пѣхотный*) of the infantry
печатник, печатника *печатник, печатника* – (n., masc.) printer
печаточник, печаточника *печаточник, печаточника* – (n., masc.) seal-engraver
печать, печати *печать, печати* – (n., fem.) seal, stamp
печень, печени *печень, печени* – (n., fem.) liver; *воспаление печени* – hepatitis
печник, печника *печник, печника* – (n., masc.) maker or installer of stoves
пивовар, пивовара *пивовар, пивовара* – (n., masc.) brewer
пильщик, пильщика *пильщик, пильщика* – (n., masc.) sawyer
Пинск, Пинска *Пинск, Пинска* – (n., masc.) town of Pinsk, Belarus' (see page 126); *пинский* – (adj.) of Pinsk
† Пинчовъ, Пинчова *Пинчовъ, Пинчова* – (n., masc.) archaic Russian name of the town of Pińczów, Poland (see page 120); *пинчовскій* or *пиньчовскій* – of Pińczów
пирожник, пирожника *пирожник, пирожника* – (n., masc.) pastry-cook
Пирятин, Пирятина *Пирятин, Пирятина* – (n., masc.) town of Piryatyn, Ukraine (see page 133); *пирятинский* – (adj.) of Piryatin
писарь, писаря *писарь, писаря* – (n., masc., nom. pl. *писаря*, gen. pl. *писарей*) scribe, clerk
писатель, писателя *писатель, писателя* – (n., masc.) writer (fem. *писательница*)
писать *писать* – (v.) to write; *я пишу* – I am writing
писаться *писаться* – (v.) to be written; *пишется* – is written, is to be written
писец, писца *писец, писца* – (n., masc.) clerk, scribe
писцовый *писцовый* – (adj.) of writers, of scribes; † *писцовыя книги* – cadasters, land survey books
письменно *письменно* – (adv.) in writing
письменный *письменный* – (adj.) writing-, written;
письмо, письма *письмо, письма* – (n., neut.) letter; *на письмѣ* – in writing; *въ заказномъ письмѣ* – in a registered letter
письмоводитель, письмоводителя *письмоводитель, письмоводителя* – (n., masc.) clerk, secretary
питомец, питомца *питомец, питомца* – (n., masc.) foster-child (fem. *питомица*)
пишу *пишу* → писать *писать*
пишущий *пишущий* – (part. from *писать;* † *пишущій*) writing; *пишущая машинка* – typewriter
пищевод, пищевода *пищевод, пищевода* – (n., masc.) esophagus (in older Russian *пищепровод* is also seen); *рак пище[про]вода* – esophageal cancer
плавильщик, плавильщика *плавильщик, плавильщика* – (n., masc.) smelter, founder
платёж, платёжа *платёж, платёжа* – (n., masc.) payment
платить *платить* – (v.) to pay
платформа, платформы *платформа, платформы* – (n., fem.) small railway station
† плацъ-маіоръ, плацъ-маіора *плацъ-маіоръ, плацъ-маіора* – (n., masc.) assistant to a garrison's commandant
плеврит, плеврита *плеврит, плеврита* – (n., masc.) pleurisy
племянник, племянника *племянник, племянника* – (n., masc.) nephew
племянница, племянницы *племянница, племянницы* – (n., fem.) niece
племяш, племяша *племяш, племяша* – (n., masc.) male relative
пленник, пленника *пленник, пленника* – (n., masc., † *плѣнникъ*) captive, prisoner (fem. *пленница*)
плетельщик, плетельщика *плетельщик, плетельщика* – (n., masc.) plaiter, braider (fem. *плетельщица*)
пломбировщик, пломбировщика *пломбировщик, пломбировщика* – (n., masc.) one who affixes lead seals to goods
Плоньск, Плоньска *Плоньск, Плоньска* – (n., masc., † *Плонскъ*) town of Płońsk, Poland (see page 119); *плонский* or *плоньский* – (adj.) of Płońsk
плотник, плотника *плотник, плотника* – (n., masc.) carpenter
плотский *плотский* – (adj., † *плотскій*) carnal, of the flesh
Плоцк, Плоцка *Плоцк, Плоцка* – (n., masc.) town of Płock, Poland (see page 119); *плоцкий* – (adj.) of Płock
площадь, площади *площадь, площади* – (n., fem.) public square, market-place
плѣнникъ *плѣнникъ* → пленник *пленник*
плющильщик, плющильщика *плющильщик, плющильщика* – (n., masc.) flattener, laminator
пляска Св. Вита *пляска Св. Вита* → витова пляска *витова пляска*
по *по* – (prep. + dat.): on, along, by, according to; *по-этому,* for this reason; *по первому браку Мейер,* by her first marriage Meyer; *по имени* – by name, named; *по сорокъ три года* – each 43 years old; (+ acc.) to, up to; (+ prep.) on, after; *по 9 Апрѣля 1908 года* – up to April 9, 1908
побироха, побирохи *побироха, побирохи* – (n., fem.) beggar-woman (also *побирушка*)

поблагославить *поблагославить* – (v.) to bless, give one's blessing; (if referring to a wedding) to bless the union, unite in matrimony

побочный *побочный* – (adj.) accessory, indirect, collateral

повар, повара *повар, повара* – (n., masc., nom. pl. *повара*, gen. pl. *поваров*) cook

поварёнок, поварёнка *поварёнок, поварёнка* – (n., masc., nom. pl. *поварята*, gen. pl. *поварят*) kitchen-boy, scullion

повариха, поварихи *повариха, поварихи* – (n., fem.) [female] cook

поведение, поводения *поведение, поводения* – (n., neut., † *поведенiе*) conduct, behavior

поверенный, поверенного *поверенный, поверенного* – (adj. used as a n., masc., † *повѣренный*) trustee, attorney; *поверенный в делах* – chargé d'affaires; *присяжный поверенный* – barrister, advocate

повивальный *повивальный* – (adj.) relating to midwifery; *повивальная бабка* – midwife

повинность, повинности *повинность, повинности* – (n., fem.) duty; tax; *воинская повинность* – military service, obligetion to serve in the military

повстанец, повстанца *повстанец, повстанца* – (n., masc.) rebel, participant in an uprising

повѣренный *повѣренный* → поверенный *поверенный*

погасить *погасить* – (v.) to liquidate, pay off (e. g., a debt)

поголовный *поголовный* – (adj.) per head, per capita; *поголовная подать* – poll tax

погонщик, погонщика *погонщик, погонщика* – (n., masc.) driver, drover (of cattle)

пограничный *пограничный* – (adj.) border, of the border, frontier

погребальщик, погребальщика *погребальщик, погребальщика* – (n., masc.) grave-digger, sexton (also *погребатель*)

погребание, погребания *погребание, погребания* – (n., neut., † *погребанiе*) burial, interment

погребение, погребения *погребение, погребения* – (n., neut., † *погребенiе*) burial, interment

погребённый *погребённый* – (part. from *погрести*, to bury) buried; *гдѣ погребенъ* – where [was he] buried?

погребщик, погребщика *погребщик, погребщика* – (n., masc.) wine-merchant

под *под* – (prep. + acc. or instr.) under; at hand; near; *под № X* – at # X, under # X

подагра, подагры *подагра, подагры* – (n., fem.) gout, podagra

подать, подати *подать, подати* (n., fem.) tax, tribute

подбородок, подбородка *подбородок, подбородка* – (n., masc.) chin

подвозчик, подвозчика *подвозчик, подвозчика* – (n., masc.) driver of a transport

подворный *подворный* – (adj.) referring to an inventory of the goods belonging to a specific household, used for tax assessment

подданство, подданства *подданство, подданства* – (n., neut.) citizenship

подданный *подданный* – (part., masc., used as a noun) subject (fem. *подданная*)

поддьяк, поддьяка *поддьяк, поддьяка* – (n., masc.) sub-deacon

подёнщик, подёнщика *подёнщик, подёнщика* – (n., masc.) day laborer (fem. *поддёнщица*, woman paid by the day, charwoman)

подлежать *подлежать* – (v.) to be subject to, liable to, in the jurisdiction of

подлежащий *подлежащий* – (part. from *подлежать;* † *подлежащiй*) applicable, relevant, competent

подлекарь, подлекаря *подлекарь, подлекаря* – (n., masc.) doctor's assistant

подлинный *подлинный* – (adj.) authentic, original

Подляхия, Подляхии *Подляхия, Подляхии* – (n., fem., † *Подляхiя*) Podlachia, the region of east central Poland called *Podlasie* by the Poles

подмастерье, подмастерья *подмастерье, подмастерья* – (n., masc., gen. pl. *подмастерьев*) apprentice, assistant to a master craftsman

Подолия, Подолии *Подолия, Подолии* – (n., fem., † *Подолiя*) the region of Podolia in Ukraine, also called *подольская губернiя*

подольский *подольский* – (adj., † *подольскiй*) of Podolia

подписание, подписания *подписание, подписания* – (n., neut., † *подписанiе*) signature

подписанный *подписанный* – (part. from *подписать*, to sign) signed

подписать *подписать* – (v.) to sign (a paper, a document), sign up for, subscribe; *подписаться* – to affix one's signature, sign one's name

подписомъ *подписомъ* – with signature, by means of a signature (see page 85; *подпись* is a fem. noun, so we'd normally expect this to be *подписью*)

подписываться *подписываться* – (v., refl., imperfective counterpart of *подписаться*) to sign, sign one's name, subscribe

подпись, подписи *подпись, подписи* – (n., fem.) signature; *надлежащей подписью* – with the required signature

подполковник, подполковника *подполковник, подполковника* – (n., masc.) lieutenant colonel (fem. *подполковница*, lieutenant colonel's wife)

подпрапорщик, подпрапорщика *подпрапорщик, подпрапорщика* – (n., masc.) ensign-bearer, standard-bearer

подробно *подробно* – (adv.) in detail, at length; *прописать подробно* – write out in full
подросток, подростка *подросток, подростка* – (n., masc.) teen, youth
подручный, подручного *подручный, подручного* – (adj. used as a n., masc.) assistant, helper
подрядчик, подрядчика *подрядчик, подрядчика* – (n., masc.) contractor
подстаршина, подстаршины *подстаршина, подстаршины* – (n., masc. but declined as if fem.) assistant elder
подсудимый, подсудимого *подсудимый, подсудимого* – (adj. used as a n., masc.) the accused, defendant (fem. *подсудимая*)
подсчёт, посчёта *подсчёт, посчёта* – (n., masc.) calculation; poll, tally
подушный *подушный* – (adj.) by head, per person; *подушная подать*, a tax per head
подчеркнуть *подчеркнуть* – (v.) to underline
подчиняться *подчиняться* – (v.) to submit, abide by
† подъячій, подъячяго *подъячій, подъячяго* – (adj. used as a n., masc.) clerk, copyist (16th-18th century)
поездка, поездки *поездка, поездки* – (n., fem., † *поѣздка*) journey, trip
пожалуйста *пожалуйста* – (adv.) please
пожертвование, пожертвования *пожертвование, пожертвования* – (n., neut., † *пожертвованіе*) offering, donation, sacrifice
позволение, позволения *позволение, позволения* – (n., neut., † *позволеніе*) permission
поздний *поздний* – (adj., † *поздній*) late
Познань, Познани *Познань, Познани* – (n., fem.) Poznań, Poland
позументщик, позументщика *позументщик, позументщика* – (n., masc.) galloon-maker, lace-maker
поименовать *поименовать* – (v.) to name, mention
поиск, поиска *поиск, поиска* – (n., masc.) search, quest
показание, показания *показание, показания* – (n., neut., † *показаніе*) deposition, statement; *присяжное показаніе* – sworn deposition, statement under oath
показанный *показанный* – (part. from *показать*, to show) shown
покоиться *покоиться* – (v.) to repose, rest, lie; *здѣсь покоится* – here lies…
покой, покоя *покой, покоя* – (n., masc., nom. pl. *покои*, gen. pl. *покоев*) room; rest, repose; *вечный ему покой* – [may God give] him eternal peace
покойник, покойника *покойник, покойника* – (n., masc.) the deceased [speaking of a male]
покойница, покойницы *покойница, покойницы* – (n., fem.) the deceased [speaking of a female]
покойный *покойный* – (adj.) quiet, calm; the late, deceased (especially if used as a noun); *муж покойной* – the husband of the deceased
покорнейше *покорнейше* – (adv., † *покорнѣйше*) very humbly
покупка, покупки *покупка, покупки* – (n., fem.) purchase
покупщик, покупщика *покупщик, покупщика* – (n., masc.) buyer, purchaser (fem. *покупщица*)
пол, пола *пол, пола* – (n., masc.) gender, sex; floor; *женскаго пола* – of the female gender
пол- *пол-* – (prefix) half; *полгода* – half a year, six months
полагать *полагать* – (v.) to put, place; to suppose
полдень, полдня *or* полудня *полдень, полдня* or *полудня* – (n., masc.) noon, midday; south; *до полудня* – before midday, a.m.; *по полудни* – afternoon, p. m.
поле, поля *поле, поля* – (n., neut., nom. pl. *поля*, gen. pl. *полей*) field
полесовщик, полесовщика *полесовщик, полесовщика* – (n., masc., † *полѣсовщикъ*) forester, forest-ranger
политик, политика *политик, политика* – (n., masc.) politician
полицеймейстер, полицеймейстера *полицеймейстер, полицеймейстера* – (n., masc.) chief of police
полицейский *полицейский* – (adj., † *полицейскій*) police, of police
полк, полка *полк, полка* – (n., masc.) regiment
полка, полки *полка, полки* – (n., fem., gen. pl. *полек*) shelf
полковник, полковника *полковник, полковника* – (n., masc.) lieutenant (fem. *полковница*, colonel's wife)
полководец, полководца *полководец, полководца* – (n., masc.) general, captain, leader of an army
полковой *полковой* – (adj.) regimental
полнородный *полнородный* – (adj.) having the same mother and father
полностью *полностью* – (instr. sing. of † *полность, полности*) completely, utterly, fully, in full
полночь, полночи *or* полуночи *полночь, полночи* or *полуночи* – (n., fem.) midnight; north; *по полуночи* – after midnight (see page 50)
полный *полный* – (adj.) full
половина, половины *половина, половины* – (n., fem.) half; *въ десять съ половиною часовъ утра* – at 10:30 a.m.
положение, положения *положение, положения* – (n., neut., *положеніе*) position, situation; condition, state; statute, article, regulation; *семейное положение* – family situation

положенный *положенный* – (part. from *положить*, to place) placed, positioned
Полоцк, Полоцка *Полоцк, Полоцка* – (n., masc.) town of Polatsk, Belarus' (see page 126); *полоцкий* – (adj.) of Polotsk/Polatsk
Полтава, Полтавы *Полтава, Полтавы* – (n., fem.) town of Poltava, Ukraine (see page 133); *полтавский* – (adj.) of Poltava
полугодовой *полугодовой* – (adj.) half-year, six months; *в полугодовой день* – on the six-month anniversary
полудня *полудня* or полудни *полудни* → полдень *полдень*
полугодовой *полугодовой* – (adj.) semiannual
полуночи *полуночи* → полночь *полночь*
получаемый *получаемый* – (part. from *получать*) received
получать *получать* – (v., imperf. counterpart of *получить*) to receive
получаться *получаться* – (v.) to be received, obtained; *ссуда получается заёмщикомъ* – the loan is being granted to the borrower
получение, получения *получение, получения* – (n., neut., † *полученiе*) receiving, obtaining
полученный *полученный* – (part. from *получить*) received
получить *получить* – (v.) to receive
полька *полька* → поляк *поляк*
польский *польский* – (adj., † *польскiй*) Polish
Польша, Польши *Польша, Польши* – (n., fem.) Poland
полѣсовщикъ *полѣсовщикъ* → полесовщик *полесовщик*
поляк, поляка *поляк, поляка* – (n., masc., nom. pl. *поляки*, gen. pl. *поляков*) Pole (fem. *полька*)
Померания, Померании *Померания, Померании* – (n., fem., † *Померанiя*) Pomerania
помещик, помещика *помещик, помещика* – (n., masc., † *помѣщикъ*) land-owner, landlord (fem. *помещица*)
помещичий *помещичий* – (adj., † *помѣщичiй*) of an estate
помощник, помощника *помощник, помощника* – (n., masc.) helper, assistant (fem. *помощница*)
помощь, помощи *помощь, помощи* – (n., fem.) help, aid, assistance
помѣщикъ *помѣщикъ* → помещик *помещик*
помѣщичiй *помѣщичiй* → помещичий *помещичий*
понамарь, понамаря *понамарь, понамаря* – (n., masc.) sexton, sacristan (fem. *понамариха*)
† Поневежъ, Поневежа *Поневежъ, Поневежа* – (n., masc.) Russian name of the town of Panevėžys, Lithuania (see page 124); *поневежскiй* – of Panevėžys
понедельник, понедельника *понедельник, понедельника* – (n., masc., † *понѣдельник*) Monday; *в понедельник* – on Monday; *по понедельникам* – on Mondays, every Monday
понос, поноса *понос, поноса* – (n., masc.) diarrhea
понятой, понятого *понятой, понятого* – (adj. used as a n., masc.) witness (fem. *понятая*)
поп, попа *поп, попа* – (n., masc.) priest
попадья, попадьи *попадья, попадьи* – (n., fem.) priest's wife
попечитель, попечителя *попечитель, попечителя* – (n., masc.) trustee, ward, warden, guardian (fem. *попечительница*)
попович, поповича *попович, поповича* – (n., masc.) priest's son
поповна, поповны *поповна, поповны* – (n., fem., gen. pl. *поповен*) priest's daughter
по полудни *по полудни* → полдень *полдень*
портниха, портнихи *портниха, портнихи* – (n., fem.) dressmaker
портной, портного *портной, портного* – (adj. used as a n., masc.) tailor
портомой, портомоя *портомой, портомоя* – (n., masc.) washerman, launderer
порубщик, порубщика *порубщик, порубщика* – (n., masc.) wood-cutter, also one who steals wood
поручик, поручика *поручик, поручика* – (n., masc.) lieutenant (fem. *поручица*, lieutenant's wife)
поручитель, поручителя *поручитель, поручителя* – (n., masc.) guarantor
порядковый *порядковый* – (adj.) ordinal
порядок, порядка *порядок, порядка* – (n., masc.) order; *№ по порядку* – number by [sequential] order
посад, посада *посад, посада* – (n., masc.) originally the part of a town where the craftsmen and tradesmen lived, usually outside the town walls; in more modern usage, a kind of suburb, except "suburb" in modern English has such a different connotation that it doesn't work to translate *посад* as "suburb"
посадник, посадника *посадник, посадника* – (n., masc.) mayor of certain ancient Russian free towns (fem. *посадница*)
поселенец, поселенца *поселенец, поселенца* – (n., masc.) settler, colonist; convict deported to Siberia (fem. *поселенка*)
поселение, поселения *поселение, поселения* – (n., neut., † *поселенiе*) settlement, colony
посёлок, посёлка *посёлок, посёлка* – (n., masc.) small village or settlement
поселянин, поселянина *поселянин, поселянина* – (n., masc., nom. pl. *поселяне*, gen. pl. *поселян*) peasant, villager (fem. *поселянка*)
посланец, посланца *посланец, посланца* – (n., masc.) envoy, messenger (also *посланный*)

посланник, посланника *посланник, посланника* – (n., masc.) envoy, ambassador (fem. *посланница*, wife of an ambassador)
послать *послать* – (v.) to send
после *после* – (prep. + gen., † *послѣ*) after
последний *последний* – (adj., † *послѣдний*) last, latest
последовавший *последовавший* – (adj., † *послѣдовавшій*, part. from the verb *последовать*) having occurred
послужной *послужной* – (adj.) [of] service; *послужной листъ* – service record
послушник, послушника *послушник, послушника* – (n., masc.) lay-brother, novice (fem. *послушница*)
послѣ *послѣ* → после *после*
послѣднiй *послѣднiй* → последний *последний*
послѣдовавшiй *послѣдовавшiй* → последовавший *последовавший*
посол, посла *посол, посла* – (n., masc.) ambassador, envoy
посредник, посредника *посредник, посредника* – (n., masc.) negotiator, intermediary (fem. *посредница*)
поставщик, поставщика *поставщик, поставщика* – (n., masc.) purveyor, supplier (fem. *поставщица*)
постановление, постановления *постановление, постановления* – (n., neut., † *постановленіе*) ruling, decision, regulation
† постельникъ, постельника *постельникъ, постельника* – (n., masc.) chamberlain
постоялец, постояльца *постоялец, постояльца* – (n., masc.) lodger, tenant (fem. *постоялица*)
постоянный *постоянный* – (adj.) constant, continual, permanent; *постоянный житель* – permanent resident; *мѣсто постояннаго жительства* – place of permanent residence
построенный *построенный* – (part. from *построить*, to build) constructed, built
постройка, постройки *постройка, постройки* – (n., fem.) construction, building
поступить *поступить* – (v.) to act, behave; to enter, enlist
поступление, поступления *поступление, поступления* – (n., neut., † *поступленіе*) entrance, enlistment; *поступление на службу* – reporting for service
потомок, потомка *потомок, потомка* – (n., masc.) descendant, offspring
потомственный *потомственный* – (adj.) hereditary
потому *потому* – (adv.) for that reason
потому, что *потому, что* – (conj.) because
поход, похода *поход, похода* – (n., masc.) march, campaign, expedition
похороненный *похороненный* – (part. from *похоронить*, to bury) buried; *гдѣ похороненъ* – where was he buried?
похоронный *похоронный* – (adj.) [of a] funeral; *похоронное бюро* – undertaker's office, establishment
похороны, похорон *похороны, похорон* – (n., fem. pl. dat. *похоронам*) burial, funeral
почивать *почивать* – (v.) to lie, be at rest; *здѣсь почиваетъ* – here lies…
почивший, почившего *почивший, почившего* – (part. of *почить*, to rest, used as a noun, † *почившій*) the deceased; *семья почившего* – the family of the deceased
почка, почки *почка, почки* – (n., fem., gen. pl. *почек*) kidney; *воспаление почек* – nephritis
почтальон, почтальона *почтальон, почтальона* – (n., masc.) postman, letter-carrier
почтение, почтения *почтение, почтения* – (n., neut., † *почтеніе*) respect, regard
почтмейстер, почтмейстера *почтмейстер, почтмейстера* – (n., masc.) postmaster (fem. *почтмейстерша*)
почтовый *почтовый* – (adj.) post, postal; *почтовая станция* – post office
пошлина, пошлины *пошлина, пошлины* – (n., fem.) duty, toll, tax, fee
поѣздка *поѣздка* → поездка *поездка*
по-этому *по-этому* – (adv. phrase) for this reason, in this way
пояснить *пояснить* – (v.) to explain, clarify
пра- *пра-* – a prefix meaning the same as "great-" in English "great-grandfather"
прабабка, прабабки *прабабка, прабабки* – (n., fem.) great-grandmother, also seen: *прабабушка, прабабушки*
правило, правила *правило, правила* – (n., neut.) rule
правитель, правителя *правитель, правителя* – (n., masc.) administrator, ruler, director (fem. *правительница*)
правительственный *правительственный* – (adj.) governmental
правительство, правительства *правительство, правительства* – (n., neut.) government, administration; *не имѣю документовъ выданныхъ мнѣ Россійскимъ правительствомъ* – I do not have[any] documents issued to me by the Russian government
† правительствующiй *правительствующiй* – (adj.) ruling; *правительствующiй сенатъ*, the Ruling Senate
правление, правления *правление, правления* – (n., neut., † *правленiе*) administration
правнук, правнука *правнук, правнука* – (n., masc.) great-grandson
правнучка, правнучки *правнучка, правнучки* – (n., fem.) great-granddaughter

право, права *право, права* – (n., neut.) law, right

правовед, правоведа *правовед, правоведа* – (n., masc., † *правовѣдъ*) jurist, legal specialist (also seen: *правоведец*, † *правовѣдецъ*)

православный *православный* – (adj.) Orthodox (religion)

правоспособность, правоспособности *правоспособность, правоспособности* – (n., fem.) [legal] capacity, ability

правоспособный *правоспособный* – (adj.) [legally] capable, able

правый *правый* – (adj.) right (as opposed to left, also in the sense of correct, upright, innocent)

Прага, Праги *Прага, Праги* – (n., fem.) Prague

прадед, прадеда *прадед, прадеда* – (n., masc., † *прадѣдъ*) great-grandfather, also seen: *прадедушка, прадедушки*

прапорщик, прапорщика *прапорщик, прапорщика* – (n., masc.) ensign (fem. *прапорщица*, ensign's wife)

прапрабабка, прапрабабки *прапрабабка, прапрабабки* – (n., fem.) great-great-grandmother, also seen: *прапрабабушка, прапрабабушки*

прапрадед, прапрадеда *прапрадед, прапрадеда* – (n., masc., † *прапрадѣдъ*) great-great-grandfather, also seen: *прапрадедушка, прапрадедушки*

прапращур, прапращура *прапращур, прапращура* – (n., masc.) great-great-grandfather's grandfather

† Прасньшъ, Прасныша *Прасньшъ, Прасныша* – (n., masc., may also appear as *Пржаснышъ*) town of Przasnysz, Poland (see page 119); *прасньшскій* or *пржаснаскій*– (adj.) of Przasnysz

прасол, прасола *прасол, прасола* – (n., masc.) wholesale cattle- or fish-dealer

прачка, прачки *прачка, прачки* – (n., masc.) laundress, washerwoman

пращур, пращура *пращур, пращура* – (n., masc.) great-great-grandfather's father

† пребендарій, пребендаряго *пребендарій, пребендаряго* – (adj. used as a n., masc.) prebendary (holder of a benefice or prebend)

пребывание, пребывания *пребывание, пребывания* – (n., neut., † *пребываніе*) stay, sojourn, residence

превосходительство, превосходительства *превосходительство, превосходительства* – (n., neut.) Excellency (used in titles, *Ваше Превосходительство*, Your Excellency)

предбрачный *предбрачный* – (adj.) premarital; *предбрачный договор* – prenuptial agreement

предварительно *предварительно* – (adv.) beforehand, as a preliminary

предводитель, предводителя *предводитель, предводителя* – (n., masc.) leader, chief, conductor, general; *предводитель войска* – commander in chief; *предводитель дворянства* – marshal of nobility (fem. *предводительша*, marshal's wife, or *предводительница*, conductress)

предел, предела *предел, предела* – (n., masc., † *предѣлъ*) limit, end, bound; *в пределах* – within, within the borders of, within the confines of

предместник, предместника *предместник, предместника* – (n., masc., † *предмѣстникъ*) predecessor (fem. *предместница*)

предместье, предместья – (n., neut., † *предмѣстье*) settlement just outside a town, suburb

предок, предка *предок, предка* – (n., masc.) ancestor

предосудительный *предосудительный* – (adj.) reprehensible, culpable

председатель, председателя *председатель, председателя* – (n., masc., † *предсѣдатель*) president, chairman (fem. *председательница*)

представитель, представителя *представитель, представителя* – (n., masc.) representative (fem. *представитеьлница*)

представить *представить* – (v.) to present, offer, produce

представленный *представленный* – (part. from *представить*) presented

представляемый *представляемый* – (part. from *представлять*, to present) presented, produced

представлять *представлять* – (v., imperf. counterpart of *представить*) to present, offer, produce

представляя *представляя* – (part. from *представлять*, to present) presenting

предсѣдатель *предсѣдатель* → председатель *председатель*

предшествуенный *предшествуенный* – (part. from *предшествовать*) preceded

предшествовать *предшествовать* – (v.) to precede, go before (followed by an object in the dative case)

предъявивший *предъявивший* – (part. from *предъявить*, † *предъявившій*) having produced, presented; (used as a n.) the one having produced

предъявитель, предъявителя *предъявитель, предъявителя* – (n., masc.) bearer, presenter

предъявить *предъявить* – (v.) to show, produce, present

предьявленный *предъявленный* – (part. from *предъявить*) produced, presented

преемник, преемника *преемник, преемника* – (n., masc.) successor, heir (fem. *преемница*)

прежний *прежний* – (adj., † *прежній*) previous, prior

преимущество, преимущества *преимущество, преимущества* – (n., neut.) privilege, prerogative

† Прейсишъ-Ейлау *Прейсишъ-Ейлау* – (n., masc.) the town in East Prussia called *Preussisch-Eylau* by Germans, *Bagrationovsk* by Russians

† прентъ, прента *прентъ, прента* – (n., masc.) a *pręt*, Polish unit of measure of length
преображение, преображения *преображение, преображения* – (n., neut., † *преображеніе*) transformation; *Преображение Господне* – the Lord's Transfiguration
преосвященство, преосвященства *преосвященство, преосвященства* – (n., neut.) Eminence, Grace (used in titles)
преподаватель, преподавателя *преподаватель, преподавателя* – (n., masc.) lecturer, teacher, master (fem. *преподавательница*, mistress)
препровождать *препровождать* – (v.) to forward, expedite, send
препровождаться *препровождаться* – (v.) to be sent, forwarded; *препровождается* – is being sent, forwarded
препятствие, препятствия *препятствие, препятствия* – (n., neut., † *препятствіе*) impediment, obstacle; *о препятствіязъ къ бракосочетанію* – about impediments to marriage
преступник, преступника *преступник, преступника* – (n., masc.) criminal (fem. *преступница*)
претендент, претендента *претендент, претендента* – (n., masc.) pretender, applicant, candidate (fem. *претендентка*)
Пржаснышъ *Пржаснышъ* → Праснышъ *Праснышъ*
при *при* – (prep. + prepositional) near, at, by, on; *при мнѣ* – before me, in my presence; *при мужемъ* – with [her] husband; *при семъ* – herewith, with this; *при томъ* – at that time; *при этомъ* – during this, on this occasion; *находятся при немъ* – are accompanying him, with him; *жительствующая при отцу* – living with her father
приблизительно *приблизительно* – (adv.) approximately
прибытие, прибытия *прибытие, прибытия* – (n., neut., † *прибытіе*) arrival
прибыть *прибыть* – (v.) to arrive, come
привенчанный *привенчанный* – (adj.) describing descent from the same set of parents but *before* they were married
привислинский *привислинский* – (adj., † *привислинскій*) on the Vistula River; *привислинскій край* – official name of the 10 *gubernias* of the Kingdom of Poland (1867-1917)
привратник, привратника *привратник, привратника* – (n., masc.) porter, gate-keeper (fem. *привратница*)
пригласив *пригласив* – (adv. part. from *пригласить*) have invited, called in
пригласить *пригласить* – (v.) to invite, engage, call in
пригород, пригорода *пригород, пригорода* – (n., masc.) suburb, settlement outside a town
пригородный *пригородный* – (adj.) of a пригород ↑, suburban
придворный *придворный* – (adj.) of the [royal or noble] court; (used as a n.) courtier
приёмный *приёмный* – (adj., † *пріёмный*) of reception; *пріёмная роспись* – list of draftees deemed fit to serve (page 292); *пріёмный отецъ* – foster-father
приёмыш, приёмыша *приёмыш, приёмыша* – (n., masc., † *пріёмышъ*) adopted child, foster child
прижитый *прижитый* – (part. from *прижить*, to beget) begotten
призванный *призванный* – (part. from *призвать*, to summon, call up) summoned, called up
признанный *признанный* – (part. from *признать*) acknowledged, recognized
признать *признать* – (v.) to acknowledge, recognize; *признаютъ за свою собственную* – they recognize as their own
признаться *признаться* – (v.) to be recognized, acknowledged
призыв, призыва *призыв, призыва* – (n., masc.) call, levy, conscription, draft; *призыв на военную службу* – conscripttion into the armed forces
призываемый *призываемый* – (part. from *призывать*, to summon, call up) called up; (used as a n.) the conscript, draftee
призывной *призывной* – (adj., also seen in the form *призывный*) conscription, draft; *призывной участокъ* – "Draft Board"; *призывный список* – conscription list, book of draftees; (used as a n.) conscript, draftee
приказный *приказный* – (adj.) of the chancellor's office; (used as a n.) clerk, scribe
приказчик, приказчика *приказчик, приказчика* – (n., masc., also seen as *прикащик*) shop assistant; steward, bailiff [of an estate] (fem. *приказчица* or *прикащица*)
прилагать *прилагать* – (v.) to apply, add, enclose; *я прилагаю* – I am adding, enclosing
приложение, приложения – (n., neut., † *приложеніе*) placing, affixing; *приложеніемъ церковной печати* – by the affixing of the church seal; *съ приложе-ніемъ казенной печати* – with affixation of the crown seal
Прилуки, Прилук *Прилуки, Прилук* – (n.) town of Pryluky, Ukraine (see page 133); *прилукский* – (adj., also *прилуцкий*) of Pryluky
примета, приметы *примета, приметы* – (n., fem., † *примѣта*) sign, token, mark; (pl.) description; *особыя примѣты* – distinguishing marks
примечание, примечания *примечание, примечания* – (n., neut., † *примѣчаніе*) remark, observation, note

приморский *приморский* – (adj., † *приморскій*) maritime, by the seaside; *Приморская область* – a region of far eastern Russia, of which Vladivostok is the administrative center (see page 137)
примѣта *примѣта* → примета *примета*
примѣчаніе *примѣчаніе* → примечание *примечание*
принадлежащий *принадлежащий* – (part. from *принадлежать*) belonging to, regarding
принадлежать *принадлежать* – (v.) to belong (*к* – to)
принадлежность, принадлежности *принадлежность, принадлежности* – (n., fem.) appurtenance (right, privilege, or property considered incident to the principal property for purposes such as passage of title, conveyance, or inheritance)
принятие, принятия *принятие, принятия* – (n., neut., † *принятіе*) acceptance, admission
принятый *принятый* – (part. from *принять*) accepted; *принятъ на службу* – inducted into the service
принять *принять* – (v.) to accept
приобретённый *приобретённый* – (part. from *приобрести*, to acquire, obtain; † *пріобрѣтённый*) acquired, gotten, obtained
приобщать *приобщать* – (v., † *пріобщать*) to unite; to give Communion
приор, приора *приор, приора* – (n., masc., † *пріоръ*) prior
припадок, припадка *припадок, припадка* – (n., masc.) fit, attack; *сердечный припадок* – heart attack
приписанный *приписанный* – (part. from *приписать*, to register) registered; *приписанъ-ли здѣсь* – is he registered here?
приписка, приписки *приписка, приписки* – (n., fem.) registration
приписной *приписной* – (adj.) of registration
припятствие припятствия *припятствие припятствия* – (n., neut., † *припятствіе*) obstacle, impediment
природный *природный* – (adj.) natural, by birth, e. g., *природный дворянин*, a noble by birth
присвоенный *присвоенный* – (part. from *присвоить*, to appropriate to oneself) assigned, attached, usurped
присёлок, присёлка *присёлок, присёлка* – (n., masc.) hamlet, small village
прискорбие, прискорбия *прискорбие, прискорбия*– (n., neut., † *прискорбіе*) sorrow, regret
прислать *прислать* – (v.) to send; *пришлите мне, пожалуйста* – please send me
прислужник, прислужника *прислужник, прислужника* – (n., masc.) server, servant (fem. *прислужница*)
присмотрщик, присмотрщика *присмотрщик, присмотрщика* – (n., masc.) overseer, superintendent (fem. *присмотрщица*)
присовокуплять *присовокуплять*– (v.) to attach; *присовокупляю къ сему прошенію* – I am attaching to this petition; *къ сему присовокупляется* –in addition to this (literally "it is added to this, attached to this")
присоединившийся *присоединившийся* – (part. from *присоединить*, to join, come into; † *присоединившійся*) having joined
пристав, пристава *пристав, пристава* – (n., masc.) overseer, inspector; in Czarist Russia, the head of a district police force; *судебный пристав* – bailiff
присутствие, присутствия *присутствие, присутствия* – (n., neut., † *присутствіе*) presence; (especially capitalized) draft commission, draft board; *в моим присутствии* – in my presence
присутствовать *присутствовать* – (v.) to be present; *кто присутствовалъ* – who was present?
присутствующий *присутствующий* – (part. from *присутствовать*, to be present, † *присутствующій*) the one[s] present
присяга, присяги *присяга, присяги* – (n., fem.) oath; *подъ присягой* – under oath
присягать *присягать* – (v.) to swear, take an oath
присяжный, присяжного *присяжный, присяжного* – (adj. used as a n., masc.) one who's taken an oath, especially a juror, juryman; *присяжный поверенный* – barrister, advocate; *присяжное показаніе* – sworn statement, statement under oath
приход, прихода *приход, прихода* – (n., masc.) parish; receipt, income; *сумма записана на приходъ* – the sum was entered as a credit
приходиться *приходиться* – (v.) to fit, fall due, cost, be related to; *какъ приходится главѣ хозяйства* – how is he/she related to the head of the household?
приходорасходчик, приходорасходчика *приходорасходчик, приходорасходчика* – (n., masc.) cashier
приходский *приходский* – (adj., † *приходскій*) [of a] parish, parochial; *приходский священник* – parish priest; *приходская церковь* – parish church
прихожанин, прихожанина *прихожанин, прихожанина* – (n., masc., nom. pl. *прихожане*, gen. pl. *прихожан*) parishioner (fem. *прихожанка*)
причастие, причастия *причастие, причастия* – (n., neut., † *причастіе*) Communion, Eucharist
причастить *причастить* – (v.) to administer Communion
причащаться *причащаться* – (v.) to take Communion

причащающийся *причащающийся* – (part. from *причащаться*, † *причащающійся*) receiving Communion
причащённый *причащённый* – (part. from *причастить*) given Communion; administered the Sacrament
причетник, причетника *причетник, причетника* – (n., masc.) churchman, lowest rank of the clergy
причина, причины *причина, причины* – (n., fem.) reason, cause; *по той причинѣ, что...* because, for this reason; *по какимъ причинамъ* – for what reasons
пришелец, пришельца *пришелец, пришельца* – (n., masc.) newcomer, stranger (fem. *пришелица*)
пришлите *пришлите* → прислать *прислать*
пріёмный *пріёмный* → приёмный *приёмный*
пріёмышъ *пріёмышъ* → приёмыш *приёмыш*
пріобрѣтённый *пріобрѣтённый*) → приобретённый *приобретённый*
пріобщать *пріобщать* → приобщать *приобщать*
пріоръ *пріоръ* → приор *приор*
пробирер, пробирера *пробирер, пробирера* – (n., masc.) assayer (also seen: *пробирщик*)
проверять *проверять* – (v., *провѣрять*) to examine, check, verify
провизор, провизора *провизор, провизора* – (n., masc.) pharmacist
провиантмейстер, провиантмейстера *провиантмейстер, провиантмейстера* – (n., masc., † *провіантмейстеръ*) commissary of stores
продавец, продавца *продавец, продавца* – (n., masc.) vendor, seller (fem. *продавица*)
продавщик, продавщика *продавщик, продавщика* – (n., masc.) vendor, seller (fem. *продавщица*)
продажа, продажи *продажа, продажи* – (n., fem.) sale
проданный *проданный* – (part. from *продать*, to sell) sold
продиктовать *продиктовать* – (v.) to dictate
продолговатый *продолговатый* – (adj.) oblong, elongated (e. g., face)
продолжительность, продолжительности *продолжительность, продолжительности* – (n., fem.) duration
продолжительный *продолжительный* – (adj.) prolonged, lengthy
проезд, проезда *проезд, проезда* – (n., masc., † *проѣздъ*) passage, passing; *свидѣтельство на проѣздъ въ Россію* – certificate for passage into Russia
проживать *проживать* – (v.) to live
прозвание, прозвания *прозвание, прозвания* – (n., neut., † *прозваніе*) surname
произведённый *произведённый* – (part. from *произвести*, to produce, promote) promoted
производитель, производителя *производитель, производителя* – (n., masc.) producer, manufacturer (fem. *производительница*)
производство, производства *производство, производства* – (n., neut.) promotion; production
произосшло *произосшло* → происходить *происходить*
происходить *происходить* – (v.) to arise, result from, be caused by; *происходило* – [this] happened, took place; *произошло* – it happened, was caused by
происходший *происходший* – (adj., † *происходшій*) past; *происходшаго года* – last year
происхождение, происхождения *происхождение, происхождения* – (n., neut., † *происхожденіе*) origin, source, descent; social class; *он немцем по происхождению*, he is a German by descent; *немецкого происхождения* – of German extraction
происшедший *происшедший* – (part. from *произойти*, to happen; † *происшедшій*) having occurred
проказа, проказы *проказа, проказы* – (n., fem.) leprosy
прокуратура, прокуратуры *прокуратура, прокуратуры* – (n., fem.) prosecutor's office, prosecutors
прокурор, прокурора *прокурор, прокурора* – (n., masc.) public prosecutor
промысел, промысла *промысел, промысла* – (n., masc.) business, trade, profession
промышленник, промышленника *промышленник, промышленника* – (n., masc.) manufacturer
прописать прописать – (v.) to write out; *прописать подробно* – write out in full
пропись, прописи *пропись, прописи* – (n., fem.) copy-book, [*написать*] *прописью* – to write out in full, spell out
прорез, прореза *прорез, прореза* – (n., masc., † *прорѣзъ*) cutting, opening
проседь, проседи *проседь, проседи* – (n., fem., † *просѣдь*) some gray hair, graying; *съ просѣдью* – graying
проситель, просителя *проситель, просителя* – (n., masc.) petitioner (fem. *просительница*)
просить *просить* – (v.) to ask, request; *я прошу* – I ask, I request (often used much as we use "Please")
Проскуров, Проскурова *Проскуров, Проскурова* – (n., masc.) town now called Khmel'nytskyi, Ukraine (see page 132); *просуровский* – (adj.) of Proskurov/Khmel'nytskyi
прослужить *прослужить* – (v.) to serve; *прослужить въ качестве* – to serve in the position of
просмотреть *просмотреть* – (v., † *просмотрѣть*) to look over, inspect
проставить *проставить* – (v.) to write down, fill in

пространство, пространства *пространство, пространства* – (n., neut.) space, expanse
простуда, простуды *простуда, простуды* – (n., fem.) cold
просѣдь *просѣдь* → проседь *проседь*
протестант, протестанта *протестант, протестанта* – (n., masc.) Protestant (fem. *протестантка*)
против *против* – (prep. + gen.) against
протодьякон, протодьякона *протодьякон, протодьякона* – (n., masc., † *протодіаконъ*) archdeacon, first deacon
протоиерей, протоиерея *протоиерей, протоиерея* – (n., masc., † *протоіерей*) archpriest, senior priest
протокол, протокола *протокол, протокола* – (n., masc.) register, record; protocol
протоколист, протоколиста *протоколист, протоколиста* – (n., masc.) registrar, registrar-clerk
профессор, профессора *профессор, профессора* – (n., masc., nom. pl. *профессора*) professor, teacher
проход, прохода *проход, прохода* – (n., masc.) passage
процессия, процессии *процессия, процессии* – (n., fem., † *процессія*) procession
прочий *прочий* – (adj., † *прочій*) other, the rest, remaining
прочитанный *прочитанный* – (part., short form *прочитан*) read aloud
прочитать *прочитать* – (v.) to read, read aloud
прочтение, прочтения *прочтение, прочтения* – (n., neut., † *прочтеніе*) reading something all the way through, especially aloud; *по прочтеніи:* after being read aloud
прошение, прошения *прошение, прошения* – (n., † *прошеніе*) request, petition
прошу *прошу* → просить *просить*
проѣздъ *проѣздъ* → проезд *проезд*
Пружаны, Пружан *Пружаны, Пружан* – (n., pl.) town of Pruzhany in Belarus' (see page 125); *пружанский* – (adj.) of Pruzhany
пруссак, пруссака *пруссак, пруссака* – (n., masc.) Prussian
Пруссия, Пруссии *Пруссия, Пруссии* – (n., fem., † *Пруссія*) Prussia
прямой *прямой* – (adj.) straight, direct, true, upright
пряничник, пряничника *пряничник, пряничника* – (n., masc.) baker or seller of gingerbread
псаломщик, псаломщика *псаломщик, псаломщика* – (n., masc.) psalm-reader, church attendant
псарь, псаря *псарь, псаря* – (n., masc.) huntsman, one in charge of the hunting dogs
Псков, Пскова *Псков, Пскова* – (n., masc.) Pskov, name of a town in Russia (see page 135); *псковский* – (adj.) of Pskov
птицевод, птицевода *птицевод, птицевода* – (n., masc.) breeder of birds
птицелов, птицелова *птицелов, птицелова* – (n., masc.) bird-catcher, birder, fowler
птичник, птичника *птичник, птичника* – (n., masc.) dealer in birds, one who takes care of birds
публикованный *публикованный* – (part. from *публиковать*) published, announced, proclaimed
публиковать *публиковать* – (v.) to publish, announce, proclaim
публичный *публичный* – (adj.) public
Пултуск, Пултуска *Пултуск, Пултуска* – (n., masc.) town of Pułtusk, Poland (see page 119); *пултуский* – (adj.) of Pułtusk
пункт пункта *пункт пункта* – (n., masc.) point, spot; article, clause; *пограничный пункт* – border point (place where one crosses the border)
путеводитель, путеводителя *путеводитель, путеводителя* – (n., masc.) directory, guide
путеец, путейца *путеец, путейца* – (n., masc.) railroad engineer, road-worker
путешественник, путешественника *путешественник, путешественника* – (n., masc.) traveler (fem. *путешественница*)
путник, путника *путник, путника* – (n., masc.) traveler (fem. *путница*)
пучеглазие, пучеглазия *пучеглазие, пучеглазия* – (n, neut., † *пучеглазіе*) exophthalmos
пфальцграф, пфальцграфа *пфальцграф, пфальцграфа* – (n., masc.) prince palatine (fem. *пфальцграфиня*)
пчеловод, пчеловода *пчеловод, пчеловода* – (n., masc.) beekeeper, apiarist
пѣвецъ *пѣвецъ* → певец *певец*
пѣснопѣвецъ *пѣснопѣвецъ* → песнопевец *песнопевец*
пѣхота *пѣхота* → пехота *пехота*
пѣхотинецъ *пѣхотинецъ* → пехотинец *пехотинец*
пѣхотный *пѣхотный* → пехотный *пехотный*
пятидесятый *пятидесятый* – (ordinal num./adj.) fiftieth
пятисотый *пятисотый* – (ordinal num./adj.) five hundredth
пятнадцатый *пятнадцатый* – (ordinal num./adj.) fifteenth
пятнадцать, пятнадцати *пятнадцать, пятнадцати* – (num.) fifteen
пятнистый тиф *пятнистый тиф* → тиф *тиф*
пятница, пятницы *пятница, пятницы* – (n., fem.) Friday; *в пятницу* – on Friday; *по пятницам* – on Fridays, every Friday
пятно, пятна *пятно, пятна* – (n., neut.) blemish, blotch; birthmark, mole
пятый *пятый* – (ordinal num./adj.) fifth

пять, пяти *пять, пяти* – (num.) five
пятьдесят, пятидесяти *пятьдесят, пятидесяти* – (num.) fifty; *пятьдесят один* – fifty-one, etc.; *пятьдесят первый* – fifty-first, etc. (see page 46)
пятьсот, пятисот *пятьсот, пятисот* – (num.) five hundred
раб, раба *раб, раба* – (n., masc.) slave, bondman (fem. *раба*); † *рабъ божій*, literally "slave of God," often on gravestones to indicate the deceased was pious
работать *работать* – (v.) to work; *работает моряком* – he works as a seaman
работник, работника *работник, работника* – (n., masc.) laborer (fem. *работница*)
рабочий, рабочего *рабочий, рабочего* – (adj. used a n., masc.) worker, laborer; cmp. *работник*
Рава, Равы *Рава, Равы* – (n., fem.) town of Rawa, Poland (see page 119); *равский* – of Rawa
раввин, раввина *раввин, раввина* – (n., masc.) rabbi
равно *равно* – (adv.) equally, as well as
равный *равный* – (adj.) equal, even
† Радиминъ, Радимина *Радиминъ, Радимина* – (n., masc.) town of Radzymin, Poland (see page 119); *радиминьскій* – of Radzymin
† Радинъ, Радина *Радинъ, Радина* – (n., masc.) town of Radzyń, Poland (see page 120); *радинскій* – of Radzyń
Радом, Радома *Радом, Радома* – (n., masc.) town of Radom, Poland (see page 120); *радомский* – of Radom
Радомышль, Радомышля *Радомышль, Радомышля* – (n., masc.) town of Radomyshl', Ukraine (see page 132); *радомышльский* – (adj.) of Radomyshl'
раён *раён* – Belarusian term, equivalent to Russian район, q. v.
раз, раза – (n., masc.) blow, stroke; time, occurrence; *всякій разъ* – every time, always; *в первый раз* – the first time; *ни разу* – not once; *разом* – together
разбойник, разбойника *разбойник, разбойника* – (n., masc.) robber, cutthroat (fem. *разбойница*)
разборчивый *разборчивый* – (adj.) discerning, discriminative; (of handwriting) legible
разведенец, разведенца *разведенец, разведенца* – (n., masc.) divorced man (fem. *разведёнка*)
разведённый *разведённый* – (adj.) divorced (short forms *разведен*, masc., and *разведена*, fem.); (used as a n., masc. *разведённый, разведённого*) divorcé; (used as a fem. n., *разведённая, разведённой*) divorcée, divorced woman
разведшийся *разведшийся* (part. from imperf. *разводиться*, perf. *развестись*, to get a divorce; † *разведшійся*) having been divorced; *часть 3-я о разведшихся* – Register Part III: Divorces
развод, развода *развод, развода* – (n., masc.) divorce; distribution, division, separation
разводный *разводный* – (adj.) of divorce; *обрядъ разводный* – the divorce ceremony
разговор, разговора *разговор, разговора* – (n., masc.) conversation
раздор, раздора *раздор, раздора* – (n., masc.) dissension, strife, disagreement
разжалованный *разжалованный* – (part.) reduced in rank (referring to a soldier)
размер, размера *размер, размера* – (n., masc., † *размѣръ*) dimension, scale; *ссуду въ размѣрѣ 300 рублей* – a loan for the amount of 300 rubles
разносчик, разносчика *разносчик, разносчика* – (n., masc., † *разнощикъ*) peddler (fem. *разносчица*, † *разнощица*)
разный *разный* – (adj.) different, various
разр. *разр.* → разряд *разряд*
разрешать *разрешать* – (v., † *разрѣшать*) to permit; *разрѣшаю* – I give permission
разрешение, разрешения *разрешение, разрешения* – (n., neut., † *разрѣшеніе*) permission
разряд, разряда *разряд, разряда* – (n., masc., abbr. *разр.*) category
разрѣшеніе *разрѣшеніе* → разрешение *разрешение*
разстояніе *разстояніе* → расстояние *расстояние*
разстройство *разстройство* → расстройство *расстройство*
разъезд, разъезда *разъезд, разъезда* – (n., masc.) departure, setting out (of many people); (pl.) *разъезды пути* – shunting, siding; *разъезд железной дороги* – railway station with shunting
район, района *район, района* – (n., masc.) region, district; a Soviet administrative subdivision
рак, рака *рак, рака* – (n., masc.) cancer; crab; *рак печени* – liver cancer; *рак лёгких* – lung cancer
рана, раны *рана, раны* – (n., fem.) injury, wound; *умереть от раны* – he died of his wound
раненый *раненый* – (part. from *ранить*, to wound) wounded
ранный *ранный* – (adj.) early
расквартированный *расквартированный* – (part. from *расквартировать*, to quarter, billet) quartered
раскладка, раскладки *раскладка, раскладки* – (n., fem.) assessment (of taxes)
раскольник, раскольника *раскольник, раскольника* – (n., masc.) schismatic, dissenter (fem. *раскольница*)
распильщик, распильщика *распильщик, распильщика* – (n., masc.) sawer
расположенный *расположенный* – (part. from *расположить*, to place, distribute) located, placed, billeted
расстояние, расстояния *расстояние, расстояния* – (n., neut., † *разстояніе*) distance (*от* – from)

расстройство, расстройства *расстройство, расстройства* – (n., neut., † *разстройство*) disorder; *отъ расстройства желудка* – from a stomach disorder
расход, расхода *расход, расхода* – (n., masc.) expense, outlay; *пересылочные расходы* – including transfer expenses
расходчик, расходчика *расходчик, расходчика* – (n., masc.) bursar, cashier (fem. *рацходщица*)
ратай, ратая *ратай, ратая* – (n., masc.) plowman, tiller, farmer
ратник, ратника *ратник, ратника* – (n., masc.) warrior, soldier
ратоборец, ратоборца *ратоборец, ратоборца* – (n., masc.) warrior, combatant
ратуша, ратуши *ратуша, ратуши* – (n., fem.) town hall, guild hall
рахит, рахита *рахит, рахита* – (n., masc.) rachitis, rickets (also seen: † *рахитизмъ*)
рахитик, рахитика *рахитик, рахитика* – (n., masc.) one suffering from rickets
рвота, рвоты *рвота, рвоты* – (n., fem.) vomiting
ребёнок, ребёнка *ребёнок, ребёнка* – (n., masc., nom. pl. *дети*, gen. pl. *детей*) baby, child
ревижский *ревижский* → ревизский *ревизский*
ревизия, ревизии *ревизия, ревизии* – (n., fem., † *ревизія*) census; revision
ревизор, ревизора *ревизор, ревизора* – (n., masc.) inspector
ревизский *ревизский* – (adj., † *ревизскій;* also sometimes seen as *ревижский*) of the census, of the tax rolls; *ревизская душа* – a person subject to taxation; *ревизская сказка* – a list of taxable persons
ревматизм, ревматизма *ревматизм, ревматизма* – (n., masc.) rheumatism
революционер, революционера *революционер, революционера* – (n., masc., † *революціонеръ*) revolutionary
регент, регента *регент, регента* – (n., masc.) regent; precentor, chapel-master
регистратор, регистратора *регистратор, регистратора* – (n., masc.) registrar, keeper of the register (fem. *регистраторша*)
редактор, редактора *редактор, редактора* – (n., masc.) editor
реестр, реестра *реестр, реестра* – (n., masc.) register
режиссёр, режиссёра *режиссёр, режиссёра* – (n., masc.) [theater] manager
Режица, Режицы *Режица, Режицы* – (n., fem., † *Рѣжица*) Russian name of the town now called Rēzekne, Latvia (see page 126); † *рѣжицкій* – of Rēzekne
резервный *резервный* – (adj.) of the reserves (military)
резник, резника *резник, резника* – (n., masc., † *рѣзникъ*) butcher
резчик, резчика *резчик, резчика* – (n., masc., † *рѣзчикъ*) engraver, carver
Рейн, Рейна *Рейн, Рейна* – (n., masc.) Rhine [river]
рейткнехт, рейткнехта *рейткнехт, рейткнехта* – (n., masc.) groom (in a stable)
река, реки *река, реки* – (n., fem., † *рѣка*) river
рекрут, рекрута *рекрут, рекрута* – (n., masc.) recruit
рекрутский *рекрутский* – (adj., † *рекрутскій*) of recruiting or recruits
ректор, ректора *ректор, ректора* – (n., masc.) rector
религиозный *религиозный* – (adj., † *религіозный*) religious
религия, религии *религия, религии* – (n., fem., † *религія*) religion
ремесленник, ремесленника *ремесленник, ремесленника* – (n., masc.) artisan, craftsman (fem. *ремесленница*)
ремесленный *ремесленный* – (adj.) of trade
ремесло, ремесла *ремесло, ремесла* – (n., neut., nom. pl. *ремёсла*, gen. pl. *ремёсел*) trade, profession, handicraft
республика, республики *республика, республики* – (n., fem.) republic
ресторатор, ресторатора *ресторатор, ресторатора* – (n., masc.) restaurateur
Речица, Речицы *Речица, Речицы* – (n., fem., † *Рѣчица*) town of Rèchitsa, Belarus' (see page 126); † *рѣчицкій* – (adj.) of Rèchitsa
решение, решения *решение, решения* – (n., neut., † *рѣшеніе*) decision; *по чьему рѣшенію* – by whose decision?
Рига, Риги *Рига, Риги* – (n., fem.) town of Riga, Latvia; *рижский* – (adj.) of Riga
† ризничій, ризничяго *ризничій, ризничяго* – (adj. used as a n., masc.) sacristan
Рим, Рима *Рим, Рима* – (n., masc.) Rome; *римский* – (adj.) of Rome, Roman
римско-католический *римско-католический* – (adj., † *римско-католическій*) Roman Catholic
ровенский *ровенский* → Ровно *Ровно*
ровесник, ровесника *ровесник, ровесника* – (n., masc.) person of the same age, e. g., *они ровесники*, "they are the same age" (fem. *ровесница*)
Ровно, Ровна *Ровно, Ровна* – (n., neut.) town of Rivne, Ukraine (see page 130); *ровенский* – of Rovno
Рогачёв, Рогачева *Рогачев, Рогачева* – (n., masc.) town of Rahachoŭ, Belarus' (see page 126); *рогачевский* – of Rogachev/ Rahachoŭ
роговщик, роговщика *роговщик, роговщика* – (n., masc.) horn-worker
рогожник, рогожника *рогожник, рогожника* – (n., masc.) mat-maker

род, рода *род, рода* – (n., masc., gen. sing. form *роду* sometimes used) race, family, birth; kind, nature, type; *никакого рода* – of no kind, of no sort; *X лет от роду* – X years from birth, X years old; *роды, родов* – (pl.) childbirth, e. g., *преждевременные роды,* premature birth

род., *род.*, abbr. of *родился* or *родилась* or *родились* → родиться *родиться*

родившийся *родившийся* – (part. of *родиться*, † *родившійся*) having been born; *о родившихся* – of those born, of births

родильный *родильный* – (adj.) relating to birth; *родильная горячка* – puerperal (childbed) fever

родился *родился* → родиться *родиться*

родимчик, родимчика *родимчик, родимчика* – (n., masc.) childish eclampsia, convulsions; also seen: *родимец*

родина, родины *родина, родины* – (n., fem.) native land; *возвращается на родину* – he is returning to his homeland

родины, родин *родины, родин* – (n., fem. pl.) childbirth, delivery

† родитель, родителя *родитель, родителя* – (n., masc.) father (fem. *родительница*); no longer used in the singular, but the plural, *родители, родителей*, is the standard term for "parents"

родиться *родиться* – (v.) to be born; *он родился* – he was born; *она родилась* – she was born; *они родились* – they were born

родной *родной* – (adj.) one's own, full, as in the expressions *родной брат*, full brother (not a half brother); native, e. g., *родной язык*, native tongue, *по родному языку*, by native tongue; also used in the pl. *родные, родных*, to mean "relatives"

родовой *родовой* – (adj.) of birth, patrimonial, ancestral; *родовые потуги* – labor contractions

родом *родом* – (adv., originally the instr. singular of *род*) by birth, e. g., *он родом немец*, "he is a German by birth," or *он родом из Москвы*, "he is a native of Moscow"

родослов, родослова *родослов, родослова* – (n., masc.) genealogist

† родословіе, родословія *родословіе, родословія* – (n., neut.) genealogy

родословная, родословной *родословная, родословной* – (adj. used as a n., fem.) genealogy, pedigree

родословный *родословный* – (adj.) genealogical; *родословное дерево* – family tree; *родословная книга* – genealogical register

родственник, родственника *родственник, родственника* – (n., masc.) relative (fem. *родственница*)

родство, родства *родство, родства* – (n., neut.) kindred, affinity; *не состоите-ли съ брачущимся лицемъ въ родствѣ* – are you related to the person you're marrying?

роду, роды *роду, роды* → род *род*

рожа, рожи *рожа, рожи* – (n., fem.) erysipelas

рождение, рождения *рождение, рождения* – (n., neut., † *рожденіе*) birth; *время рождения* – time (i. e., date) of birth; *день рождения* – birthday; *место рождения* – birthplace; *книга рождения* – birth register; *число рождения* – date of birth

рождённый *рождённый* – (part. from *родиться*) born, native-born

Рождество Христово, Рождества Христова *Рождество Христово, Рождества Христова* – (n., masc.) Christmas

роженица, роженицы *роженица, роженицы* – (n., fem.) woman giving birth, or one who recently gave birth

рожечник, рожечника *рожечник, рожечника* – (n., masc.) horn-player

рожистый *рожистый* – (adj.) erysipelatous; *рожистое воспаление* – erysipelas

розничный *розничный* – (adj.) retail; *розничый торговец* – retailer

розыскание, розыскания *розыскание, розыскания* – (n., neut., † *розысканіе*) inquiry, questioning, examination

Ромны, Ромнов *Ромны, Ромнов* – (n., pl.) town of Romny, Ukraine (see page 133); *роменский* – (adj.) of Romny

роспись, росписи *роспись, росписи* – (n., fem.) list, catalog, inventory; *государственная роспись* – government rent-roll; [in modern Russian] painting; *пріёмная роспись* – list of draftees found fit to serve (see page 292)

российский *российский* – (adj., † *россійскій*) Russian (archaic)

Россия, России *Россия, России* – (n., fem., † *Россія*) Russia

† Россиены, Россіенъ *Россіены, Россіенъ* – (n.) Russian name of the town that is now Raseiniai, Lithuania (see page 124); *россіенскій* – (adj.) of Rossieny/Raseiniai

рост, роста *рост, роста* – (n., masc.) stature, size, height

Ростов-на-Дону, Ростова-на-Дону *Ростов-на-Дону, Ростова-на-Дону* – (n., masc.) town of Rostov on the Don, Russia (see page 134); *ростовский* – (adj.) of Rostov

ростовщик, ростовщика *ростовщик, ростовщика* – (n., masc.) usurer, money-lender (fem. *ростовщица*)

рот, рта *рот, рта* – (n., masc., dat. *рту*) mouth

рота, роты *рота, роты* – (n., fem.) [military] company

ротмистр, ротмистра *ротмистр, ротмистра* – (n., masc.) cavalry captain (fem. *ротмистрша*, wife of a cavalry captain)
рта *рта* or рту *рту* → рот *рот*
рубль, рубля *рубль, рубля* – (n., masc.) ruble
рудокоп, рудокопа *рудокоп, рудокопа* – (n., masc.) miner, mine-digger
ружейник, ружейника *ружейник, ружейника* – (n., masc.) gunsmith, armorer
рука, руки *рука, руки* – (n., fem.) hand
рукавичник, рукавичника *рукавичник, рукавичника* – (n., masc.) mitten-maker
руководитель, руководителя *руководитель, руководителя* – (n., masc.) guide, director, leader, instructor (fem. *руководительница*)
рукодельник, рукодельника *рукодельник, рукодельника* – (n., masc., † *рукодѣльникъ*) handicraftsman (fem. *рукодельница*)
рукоприкладство, рукоприкладства *рукоприкладство, рукоприкладства* – (n., neut.) signature
рулевой, рулевого *рулевой, рулевого* – (adj. used as a n., masc.) helmsman
русский *русский* – (adj., † *русскій*) Russian
русый *русый* – (adj.) light brown
ручаться *ручаться* – (v.) to answer for, vouch
ручаясь *ручаясь* – (adv. part. from *ручаться*) vouching (*о* – for)
рыбак, рыбака *рыбак, рыбака* – (n., masc.) fisherman (fem. *рыбачка*)
рыбовод, рыбовода *рыбовод, рыбовода* – (n., masc.) fish-breeder
рыболов, рыболова *рыболов, рыболова* – (n., masc.) fisherman
рыбопромышленник, рыбопромышленника *рыбопромышленник, рыбопромышленника* – (n., masc.) fishmonger (also used: *рыботорговец*)
рыжий *рыжий* – (adj., † *рыжій*) red-haired
рылейщик, рылейщика *рылейщик, рылейщика* – (n., masc.) hurdy-gurdy player (fem. *рылейщица*)
рыночный *рыночный* – (adj.) of the marketplace; *рыночная торговка* – market-woman
Рыпин, Рыпина *Рыпин, Рыпина* – (n., masc.) town of Rypin, Poland (see page 119); *рыпинский* – (adj.) of Rypin
рыцарь, рыцаря *рыцарь, рыцаря* – (n., masc.) knight
Рѣжица *Рѣжица* → Режица *Режица*
рѣзникъ *рѣзникъ* → резник *резник*
рѣзчикъ *рѣзчикъ* → резчик *резчик*
рѣка *рѣка* → река *река*
Рѣчица *Рѣчица* → Речица *Речица*
рѣшеніе *рѣшеніе* → решение *решение*
рядовой, рядового *рядовой, рядового* – (adj. used as a n., masc.) private, common soldier
Рязань, Рязани *Рязань, Рязани* – (n., fem.) Ryazan', Russia (see page 135); *рязанский* – of Ryazan'
с *с* – (prep., † *съ*, + instr.) with, in the company of; (+ gen.) from; *с ... по ...* – (with dates) from ... to ...; *со мной* – with me
С.-Американский *С.-Американский* – (adj.) North American
С. С. *С. С.* – abbrev. for *Старый Стиль*, Old Style (in dating, i. e., by the Julian calendar)
садовник, садовника *садовник, садовника* – (n., masc.) gardener (fem. *садовница*)
саечник, саечника *саечник, саечника* – (n., masc.) baker or seller of *сайки*, small white loaves (fem. *саечница*)
сажень, сажени *сажень, сажени* – (n., fem., nom. pl. *сажени*, gen. pl. *саженей*) a sagene, a measure of linear distance, = 7 feet or 2.13 meters
Самара, Самары *Самара, Самары* – (n., fem.) Samara, name of a town in Russia (see page 135); *самарский* – (adj.) of Samara
Самарканд, Самарканда *Самарканд, Самарканда* – (n., masc.) name of a town in Uzbekistan (see page 137); *самаркандский* – (adj.) of Samarkand
самогит, самогита *самогит, самогита* – (n., masc.) Samogitian, one from the lowlands of Lithuania [Lith. *žemaitis*]
самоличность, самоличности *самоличность, самоличности* – (n., fem.) personality, personal identity
Сандомеж, Сандомежа *Сандомеж, Сандомежа* – (n., masc., † *Сандомиръ*) Russian name of the town of Sandomierz, Poland (see page 120); *сандомежский* († *сандомирскій*) – of Sandomierz
† Санктъ-Петербургъ, Санктъ-Петербурга *Санктъ-Петербургъ, Санктъ-Петербурга* – (n., masc.) city of St. Petersburg (called *Петроград*, Petrograd 1914-1924, and *Ленинград*, Leningrad, 1924-1991, since 1991 once more *Санкт-Петербург*)
сапёр, сапёра *сапёр, сапёра* – (n., masc.) sapper
сапёрный *сапёрный* – (adj.) sapper's, of a sapper
сапожник, сапожника *сапожник, сапожника* – (n., masc.) shoemaker (fem. *сапожница* or *сапожничиха*, shoemaker's wife)
Саратов, Саратова *Саратов, Саратова* – (n., masc.) Saratov, name of a town in Russia (see page 135); *саратовский* – of Saratov
саўгас *саўгас* – Belarusian term, equivalent to Russian совхоз, q. v.
сафьянщик, сафьянщика *сафьянщик, сафьянщика* – (n., masc.) tanner of Morocco leather
сберегательный *сберегательный* – (adj.) of savings; *сберегательная касса* – savings bank
сбор, сбора *сбор, сбора* – (n., masc.) assembly, meeting; harvest; roll call; tax, duty

сборный *сборный* – (adj.) of meeting, assembly; *сборный пунктъ* or *сборное мѣсто* – assembly point, meeting place
сборщик, сборщика *сборщик, сборщика* – (n., masc.) collector, gatherer (fem. *сборщица*); *сборщик податей* – tax collector
св. *св.* → святой *святой*
свадьба, свадьбы *свадьба, свáдьбы* – (n., fem., gen. pl. *свадеб*) wedding, nuptials
сват, свата *сват, свата* – (n., masc.) matchmaker (fem. *сваха, свахи*); father of son-in-law or daughter-in-law (fem. *сватья*)
сведение, сведения *сведение, сведения* – (n., neut., † *свѣдѣніе*) information, knowledge; learning
свежий *свежий* – (adj., † *свѣжій*) fresh
свекловод, свекловода *свекловод, свекловода* – (n., masc.) specialist in growing sugar-beets
свёкор, свёкра *свёкор, свёкра* – (n., masc.) father-in-law (husband's father)
свекровь, свекрови *свекровь, свекрови* – (n., fem.) mother-in-law (husband's mother)
† Свенцяны, Свенцян *Свенцяны, Свенцян* – (n.) town of Święcany, now Švenčionys, Lithuania (see page 124); *свенцянскій* – (adj.) of Sventsiany/Švenčionys
сверловщик, сверловщика *сверловщик, сверловщика* – (n., masc.) driller, borer; also seen: *сверлильщик* (fem. *сверловщица*)
сверх *сверх* – (prep. + gen.) over, above, besides
сверхштатный *сверхштатный* – (adj.) supernumerary
свет, света *свет, света* – (n., masc., † *свѣтъ*) light; world
светловолосый *светловолосый* – (adj., † *свѣтловолосый*) having light-colored hair
светлость, светлости *светлость, светлости* – (n., fem., † *свѣтлость*) lightness, brightness; [in titles] Highness, Serene Highness
светлый *светлый* – (adj., † *свѣтлый*) light
светописец, светописца *светописец, светописца* – (n., masc., † *свѣтописецъ*) photographer
свечник, свечника *свечник, свечника* – (n., masc., † *свѣчникъ*) chandler
свечной *свечной* – (adj., † *свѣчной*) of candles; *свѣчной сборъ* – candle tax
свидетель, свидетеля *свидетель, свидетеля* – (n., masc., † *свидѣтель*) witness (fem. *свидетельница*); *при свидѣтелямъ* – before witnesses
свидетельство, свидетельства *свидетельство, свидетельства* – (n., neut., † *свидѣтельство*) certificate; *в виде свидетельства* – in the form of a certificate; *свидетельство о рождении* – birth record, birth certificate; *сходно метрическому свидѣтельству* – according to a registry certificate
свидетельствовать *свидетельствовать* – (v., † *свидѣтельствовать*) to certify, attest; *свидетельствую* – I attest; *свидѣтельствуетъ* – [he/she] attests
свидетельствующий *свидетельствующий* – (part. from *свидетельствовать*, † *свидѣтельсвующій*) attesting, stating
свинарь, свинаря *свинарь, свинаря* – (n., masc.) swineherd (fem. *свинарка*)
свиновод, свиновода *свиновод, свиновода* – (n., masc.) specialist in breeding swine
свинопас, свинопаса *свинопас, свинопаса* – (n., masc.) swineherd
свинуха, свинухи *свинуха, свинухи* – (n., fem.) scrofula
Свислочь, Свислочи *Свислочь, Свислочи* – (n., fem.) Russian name of the town of Svislach, Belarus' (see page 127); *свислочский* – (adj.) of Svisloch', Svislash
свищ, свища *свищ, свища* – (n., masc.) fistula
свободный *свободный* – (adj.) free, unrestricted
сводный *сводный* – (adj.) descent from various parents; *сводные* – stepbrothers and stepsisters
сводчик, сводчика *сводчик, сводчика* – (n., masc.) broker, agent, go-between
своеручный *своеручный* – (adj.) written with one's own hand
свой *свой* – (reflexive adj.) my own, your own, our own, his own, her own, its own, their own; *своей смертью умереть* – to die a natural death
свойственник, свойственника *свойственник, свойственника* – (n., masc.) relative by marriage (fem. *свойственница*)
свойство, свойства *свойство, свойства* – (n., neut.) relationship, alliance
свояк, свояка *свояк, свояка* – (n., masc.) brother-in-law (husband of the wife's sister)
свояченица, свояченицы *свояченица, свояченицы* – (n., fem.) sister-in-law (wife's sister)
свыше *свыше* – (prep. + gen.) above, beyond; (adv.) from above; over
свѣдѣніе *свѣдѣніе* → сведение *сведение*
свѣжій *свѣжій* → свежий *свежий*
свѣтловолсый *свѣтловолсый* → светловолосый *светловолосый*
свѣтлость *свѣтлость* → светлость *светлость*
свѣтлый *свѣтлый* → светлый *светлый*
свѣтописецъ *свѣтописецъ* → светописец *светописец*
свѣтъ *свѣтъ* → свет *свет*
свѣчникъ *свѣчникъ* → свечник *свечник*
свѣчной *свѣчной* → свечной *свечной*
связаться *связаться* – (v.) to communicate, get in touch (*с* – with)

святитель, святителя *святитель, святителя* – (n., masc.) prelate, bishop

святой *святой* – (adj.) holy; *при святомъ крещеніи* – at Holy Baptism; (used as a n., abbr. *св.*) *святой, святого* (masc.), *святая, святой* (fem.) – saint

† Святѣйшество, Святѣйшества *Святѣйшество, Святѣйшества* – (n., neut.) Holiness [in titles]

священник, священника *священник, священника* – (n., masc.) priest (generally an Orthodox priest, as opposed to a Catholic *ксёндз*, q. v.)

священнический *священнический* – (adj., † *священническій*) of priest[s]

священноначальник, священноначальника *священноначальник, священноначальника* – (n., masc.) hierarch, prelate

священнослужитель, священнослужителя *священнослужитель, священнослужителя* – (n., masc.) priest, clergyman

сгребальщик, сгребальщика *сгребальщик, сгребальщика* – (n., masc.) raker, shoveler (fem. *сгребальщица*)

сделание, сделания *сделание, сделания* – (n., neut., † *сдѣланіе*) making, doing

сделанный *сделанный* – (part. from *сделать*, † *сдѣланный*) done, made; *сдѣлана мною* – [was] made by me

сделать *сделать* – (v., † *сдѣлать*) to make, do

Себежа, Себежа *Себеж, Себежа* – (n., masc.) town of Sebezh, Russia (see page 126); *себежский* – (adj.) of Sebezh

себя *себя* – (refl. pron.; dat. *себе*, † *себѣ*, instr. *собой* or *собою*) himself, herself; *для себя* – for herself

северный *северный* – (adj., *сѣверный*) northern; *Северная Америка* – North America

сего *сего* → сей *сей*

сегодня *сегодня* – (adv.) today

сегодняшний *сегодняшний* – (adj., † *сегодняшній*) of today; *съ сегодняшняго числа* – from today's date

седельник, седельника *седельник, седельника* – (n., masc., † *сѣдельникъ*) saddler

Седльце, Седльца *Седльце, Седльца* – (n., neut., † *Сѣдлецъ*) town of Siedlce, Poland (see page 120); *седлецкий* – († *сѣдлецкій*) of Siedlce

седьмой *седьмой* – (ordinal num./adj.) seventh

† сей *сей* – (pron., see page 43) this; *14 сего июля*, this July 14th; *сія копія* – this copy; *симъ* – by this, hereby; *до сего времени* – till now, hitherto; *сего жъ года* – in this same year; *сего числа* – on this date; *до сихъ поръ* – till now

сейм, сейма *сейм, сейма* – (n., masc.) parliament, legislative body, diet [cmp. Polish *Sejm*]

† Сейны, Сейн *Сейны, Сейн* – (n., pl.) Russian name of the town of Sejny, Poland (see page 120); *сейнскій* – of Sejny

сейчас *сейчас* – (adv.) now

секретарь, секретаря *секретарь, секретаря* – (n., masc.) secretary

селение, селения *селение, селения* – (n., neut., † *селеніе*) village, settlement

село, села *село, села* – (n., neut., nom. pl. *сёла*, gen. pl. *сёл*) village

сельдяник, сельдяника *сельдяник, сельдяника* – (n., masc.) herring-fisher

сельский *сельский* – (adj., † *сельскій*) rural, of a village, country

селянин, селянина *селянин, селянина* – (n., masc., nom. pl. *селяне*, gen. pl. *селян*, also seen: *сельчанин*) villager, peasant (fem. *селянка*)

семей *семей* → семья *семья*

семейный *семейный* – (adj.) family, of family, domestic; *по семейному списку* – by family registration; *семейное положеніе* – family situation

семидесятый *семидесятый* – (ordinal num./adj.) seventieth

Семипалатинск, Семипалатинска *Семипалатинск, Семипалатинска* – (n., masc.) name of a town in Kazakhstan, now Semei (see page 137); *семипалатинский* – of Semipalatinsk

Семиречье, Семиречья *Семиречье, Семиречья* – (n., neut., † *Семирѣчье*) Semirech'ye, a region of Kazakhstan (see page 137); *семиреченский* – of Semirechye

семисотый *семисотый* – (ordinal num./adj.) seven hundredth

семнадцатый *семнадцатый* – (ordinal num./adj.) seventeenth

семнадцать, семнадцати *семнадцать, семнадцати* – (num.) seventeen

семъ *семъ*, сему, *сему* → *сей*

семь, *семь* семи, *семи* – (num.) seven

семьдесят, семидесяти *семьдесят, семидесяти* – (num.) seventy; *семьдесят один* – seventy-one; *семьдесят первый* – seventy-first

семьсот, семисот *семьсот, семисот* – (num.) seven hundred

семья, семьи *семья, семьи* – (n., fem., nom. pl. *семьи*, gen. pl. *семей*) family; *с семей*, with family, and family

сенат, сената *сенат, сената* – (n., masc.) Senate

сенатор, сенатора *сенатор, сенатора* – (n., masc.) senator (fem. *сенаторша*, senator's wife)

сенешал, сенешала *сенешал, сенешала* – (n., masc.) seneschal

Сенно, Сенна *Сенно, Сенна* – (n., neut.) town of Syanno, Belarus' (see page 126); *сенненский* – of Senno/Syanno

сенной *сенной* – (adj., † *сѣнной*) of hay; *сенная лихорадка* – (n., fem.) hay fever сентябрь, сентября *сентябрь, сентября* – (n., masc.) September

сердечный *сердечный* – (adj.) of the heart; *сердечный припадок* – heart attack; *сердечная болезнь* – heart disease

Серадз, Серадза *Серадз, Серадза* – (n., masc., † *Сѣрадзъ*) Sieradz, town in Poland (see page 118); *серадзский* († *сѣрадзскій*) of Sieradz

сердце, сердца *сердце, сердца* – (n., neut.) heart

серебряник, серебряника *серебряник, серебряника* – (n., masc.) silversmith; also seen: *серебреник*

сержант, сержанта *сержант, сержанта* – (n., masc.) sergeant

† Серпецъ, Серпца *Серпецъ, Серпца* – (n., masc.) town of Sierpc, Poland (se page 119); *серпецкий* – of Sierpc

серый *серый* – (adj., † *сѣрый*) gray (e. g., eyes, hair)

сестра, сестры *сестра, сестры* – (n., fem., nom. pl. *сёстры*, gen. pl. *сестёр*) sister; *двоюродная сестра* – [female] cousin

сестренич, сестренича *сестренич, сестренича* – (n., masc.) the son of your mother's or father's sister

сестренница, сестринницы *сестренница, сестринницы* – (n., fem.) female cousin, the daughter of your mother's or father's sister

сестренка, сестренки *сестренка, сестренки* – (n., fem.) sister

сестрина, сестрины *сестрина, сестрины* – (n., fem.) female cousin

сестричка, сестрички *сестричка, сестрички* – (n., fem.) female cousin

сеяльщик, сеяльщика *сеяльщик, сеяльщика* – (n., masc., † *сѣяльщикъ*) sower (fem. *сеяльщица*)

сибирская язва *сибирская язва* → язва *язва*

Сибирь, Сибири *Сибирь, Сибири* – (n., fem.) Siberia

Сиван, Сивана *Сиван, Сивана* – (n., masc.) Sivan, a month in the Jewish calendar (see page 47)

сигарочник, сигарочника *сигарочник, сигарочника* – (n., masc.) cigar-dealer

сигнальщик, сигнальщика *сигнальщик, сигнальщика* – (n., masc.) signalman

сиделец, сидельца *сиделец, сидельца* – (n., masc., † *сидѣлецъ*) shopman, barman (fem. *сиделица*)

сила, силы *сила, силы* – (n., fem.) strength, power, force; *силы паспорта не имѣетъ* – is not valid as a passport

силач, силача *силач, силача* – (n., masc.) strongman (fem. *силачка*)

Силезия, Силезии *Силезия, Силезии* – (n., fem., † *Силезія*) Silesia [region of southwestern Poland called *Schlesien* by Germans and *Śląsk* by Poles]

Симбирск, Симбирска *Симбирск, Симбирска* – (n., masc.) Simbirsk, name of a town in Russia (see page 135); *симбирский* – of Simbirsk

Симферополь, Симферополя *Симферополь, Симферополя* – (n., masc.) town of Simferopol', Crimea (see page 134); *симферопольский* – (adj.) of Simferopol'

симъ *симъ* → сей *сей*

синагога, синагоги *синагога, синагоги* – (n., fem.) synagogue

синий *синий* – (adj., † *синній*) dark blue

синюха, синюхи *синюха, синюхи* – (n., fem.) cyanosis

сирота, сироты *сирота, сироты* – (n., masc. or fem.) orphan child

сихъ *сихъ* → сей *сей*

сіе, *сіе or* сію, *сію or* сіи, *сіи or* сія, *сія* → сей *сей*

† Сіятельный *Сіятельный* or Сіятельнѣйшій *Сіятельнѣйшій* – (adj.) Illustrious, Most Excellent (used in titles)

† Сіятельство, Сіятельства *Сіятельство, Сіятельства* – (n., neut.) Excellence, Excellency (used in titles for princes or counts)

сказанный *сказанный* – (part. from *сказать*, to say, tell) said

сказка, сказки *сказка, сказки* – (n., fem.) tale, story; deposition; *ревизская сказка* – revision list

сказочник, сказочника *сказочник, сказочника* – (n., masc.) story-teller (fem. *сказочница*)

скарлатина, скарлатины *скарлатина, скарлатины* – (n., fem.) scarlet fever

Сквира, Сквиры *Сквира, Сквиры* – (n., fem.) Skvyra, Ukraine (see page 132); *сквирский* – (adj.) of Skvira/Skvyra

Скерневице, Скерневиц – (n., pl., † *Скерневицы*) town of Skierniewice, Poland (see page 119); *скерневицкий* – of Skierniewice

скитник, скитника *скитник, скитника* – (n., masc.) hermit, ascetic (fem. *скитница*)

склероз, склероза *склероз, склероза* – (n., masc.) sclerosis

сколько *сколько* – (interr.) how much, how many; *сколько Вамъ лѣтъ* – how old are you?

скон. *скон.* → скончаться *скончаться*

скончаться *скончаться* – (v.) to die, pass away; *скончался* (abbr. *скон.*) – he passed away; *скончалась* (abbr. *скон.*) – she passed away

скорбут, скорбута *скорбут, скорбута* – (n., masc.) scurvy

скорняк, скорняка *скорняк, скорняка* – (n., masc.) furrier

скорописец, скорописца *скорописец, скорописца* – (n., masc.) shorthand writer

скоропостижно *скоропостижно* – (adv.) suddenly, unexpectedly

скоропостижный *скоропостижный* – (adj.) sudden, unexpected; *скоропостижная смерть*, sudden death

скорый *скорый* – (adj.) fast, quick, swift
скотник, скотника *скотник, скотника* – (n., masc.) drover, cattle-yard worker (fem. *скотница*)
скотовод, скотовода *скотовод, скотовода* – (n., masc.) cattle-breeder
скотопромышленник, скотопромышленника *скотопромышленник, ското-промышленника* – (n., masc.) cattle-dealer
скрипач, скрипача *скрипач, скрипача* – (n., masc.) violinist, fiddler (fem. *скрипачка*)
скудельник, скудельника *скудельник, скудельника* – (n., masc.) potter
скупщик, скупщика *скупщик, скупщика* – (n., masc.) forestaller, one who buys things up
скуфейщик, скуфейщика *скуфейщик, скуфейщика* – (n., masc.) maker of calottes, skullcaps
слабость, слабости *слабость, слабости* – (n., fem.) weakness; *старческая слабость,* debility due to old age
Славяносербск, Славяносербска *Славяносербск, Славяносербска* – (n., masc.) town of Slov'yano-serbs'k, Ukraine (see page 134); *славяносербский* – (adj.) of Slavyanoserbsk/Slov'yanoserbs'k
следовательно *следовательно* – (adv., † *слѣдовательно*) consequently
следовать *следовать* – (v., † *слѣдовать*) to follow, go after, be bound; (in impersonal constructions) to be supposed to, ought, be necessary; *слѣдуетъ поименовать всѣ* – all are to be named; *слѣдуетъ упомянуть номеръ шифкарты* – the ticket number is to be mentioned
следствие, следствия *следствие, следствия* – (n., neut., † *слѣдствiе*) consequence, result; *в следствие* – as a result (of, genitive); *подъ слѣдствiемъ* – under investigation
следующий *следующiй* – (part., † *слѣдующiй*] following
слезотечение, слезотечения *слезотечение, слезотечения* – (n., neut., † *слезотеченiе*) epiphora
слепец, слепца *слепец, слепца* – (n., masc., † *слѣпецъ*) blind person
слепой *слепой* – (adj., † *слѣпой*) blind
слесарь, слесаря *слесарь, слесаря* – (n., masc., nom. pl. *слесари* or *слесаря,* gen. pl. *слесарей*) locksmith, metal-worker (fem. *слесарша,* locksmith's wife)
слизетечение, слизетечения *слизетечение, слизетечения* – (n., neut., † *слизетеченiе*) blennorrhea
слизистый отёк, слизистого отёка *слизистый отёк, слизистого отёка* – (n., masc.) myxedema
слобода, слободы *слобода, слободы* – (n., fem.) a *sloboda:* before the emancipation of the serfs, a large village populated by non-serfs; in more modern usage, a large village on the high-road; a suburb, outskirts of a town
слобожанин, слобожанина *слобожанин, слобожанина* – (n., masc., nom. pl. *слобожане,* gen. pl. *слобожан*) inhabitant of a *sloboda,* q. v. (fem. *слобожанка*)
словарь, словаря *словарь, словаря* – (n., masc.) dictionary
словесник, словесника *словесник, словесника* – (n., masc.) humanist, man of letters
словесно *словесно* (adv., sometimes † *словѣсно*) orally, by word of mouth
слово, слова *слово, слова* – (n., neut.) word
словѣсно *словѣсно* → словесно *словесно*
сложный *сложный* – (adj.) compound, complex, complicated; *сложная фамилия* – compound surname
Слоним, Слонима *Слоним, Слонима* – (n., masc.) town of Slonim, Belarus' (see page 125); *слонимский* – (adj.) of Slonim
слуга, слуги *слуга, слуги* – (n., masc., declined like a fem. n.) [male] servant, valet
служанка, служанки *служанка, служанки* – (n., fem.) [female] servant, maid
служащий *служащий* – (part. from *служить;* † *служащiй*) serving; (used as a pl. n.) office clerks
служба, службы *служба, службы* – (n., fem.) service; *военная служба* – military service; *на военной службе* – in the service, in the armed forces; *призыв на военную службу* – conscription into the armed forces; *на службѣ* – in service, for work; *на службу* – into the service
служивый, служивого *служивый, служивого* – (adj. used as a n.) soldier, one who's been in the service
служитель, служителя *служитель, служителя* – (n., masc.) servant; *служитель костела,* church sexton; *божничный служитель,* synagogue attendant
служить *служить* – (v.) to serve; *видомъ на жительство служить не можетъ* – cannot serve as an identity document
Слупца, Слупцы *Слупца, Слупцы* – (n., fem., † *Слупцы, Цлупецъ*) town of Słupca, Poland (see page 118); *слупецкий* – of Słupca
Слуцк, Слуцка *Слуцк, Слуцка* – (n., masc.) Slutsk, Belarus' (see page 126); *слуцкий* – (adj.) of Slutsk
случай, случая *случай, случая* – (n., masc.) case, incident, event, circumstance; *в случае нужды* – in case of need, if need be; *в таком случае* – in that case; *несчастный случай* – accident; *по какому случаю* – under what circumstances
слѣдовательно *слѣдовательно* → следовательно *следовательно*
слѣдовать *слѣдовать* → следовать *следовать*

слѣдствіе *слѣдствіе* → следствие *следствие*
слѣдующій *слѣдующій* → следующий *следующий*
слѣпецъ *слѣпецъ* → слепец *слепец*
слѣпой *слѣпой* → слепой *слепой*
смерть, смерти *смерть, смерти* – (n., fem.) death; *естественная смерть* – natural death; *насильственная смерть* – violent death; *голодная смерть* – starvation; *своей смертью умереть* – to die a natural death; *книга смертеи* – death register; *дата смерти* – date of death
Смоленск, Смоленска *Смоленск, Смоленска* – (n., masc.) Smolensk, name of a town in Russia (see page 135); *смоленский* – (adj.) of Smolensk
смолильщик, смолильщика *смолильщик, смолильщика* – (n., masc.) one who works with pitch or tar
Сморгонь, Сморгони *Сморгонь, Сморгони* – (n., fem.) town of Smarhon', Belarus' (see page 127); *сморгонский* – (adj.) of Smorgon'/Smarhon'
смотритель, смотрителя *смотритель, смотрителя* – (n., masc.) superintendent, overseer, warden, e. g., *смотритель Ломжинскаго Замка*, Warden of the Prison in Łomża; *смотритель дока* – dock-master (fem. *смотрительница*)
снежный *снежный* – (adj., † *снѣжный*) snowy
сновальщик, сновальщика *сновальщик, сновальщика* – (n., masc.) warper [of cloth] (fem. *сновальщица*)
сноха, снохи *сноха, снохи* – (n., fem.) daughter-in-law
сношенница, сношенницы *сношенница, сношенницы* – (n., fem.) wife of your husband's brother
снѣжный *снѣжный* → снежный *снежный*
со *со* → с *с*
собираться *собираться* – (v.) to gather, assemble, prepare, make oneself ready; *я собираюсь поехать в Европу* – I'm planning to come to Europe
собой *собой* or собою *собою* → себя *себя*
собравшийся *собравшийся* – (part. from *собраться*, † *собравшійся*) gathered, assembled
собранный *собранный* – (part.) gathered, assembled; *собраннымъ на молебствѣ людямъ* – to the people assembled for services
собраться *собраться* – (v.) to gather, assemble
собственник, собвственника *собственник, собственника* – (n., masc.) owner (fem. *собственница*)
собственноручно *собственноручно* – (adv.) in [his] own hand
собственноручность, собственноручности *собственноручность, собственноручности* – (n., fem.) authenticity [of a signature]
собственноручный *собственноручный* – (adj.) autographic, in [his] own hand
собственный *собственный* – (adj.) one's own (my own, your own, his own, etc.)
совершать *совершать* – (v.) to complete, accomplish, perform, administer
совершаться *совершаться* – (v.) to be performed, administered; *кѣмъ совершается обрядъ разводный* – by whom is the divorce performed?
совершение, совершения *совершение, совершения* – (n., neut., † *совершеніе*) performance, completion, execution; *съ совершеніемъ всѣхъ обрядовъ Таинства* – with performance of all rites of the Sacrament
совершённый *совершенный* – (part. from *совершить*) performed, done, completed
совершить *совершить* – (v.) to complete, accomplish, perform, administer
совет, совета *совет, совета* – (n., masc., † *совѣтъ*) council, advice; council-board; (in post-Revolutionary usage) Soviet
советник, советника *советник, советника* – (n., masc., † *совѣтникъ*) counselor, advisor, e. g., *совѣтникъ Ломжинскаго Губернскаго Правленія*, Advisor in the Łomża Provincial Government Office (fem. *советница*); *Статскій Совѣтникъ* – State Councillor
советчик, советчика *советчик, советчика* – (n., masc., *совѣтчикъ*) advisor, counselor
совладелец, совладельца *совладелец, совладельца* – (n., masc., † *совладѣлецъ*) co-owner (fem. *совладелица*)
совхоз, совхоза *совхоз, совхоза* – (n., masc.) a Soviet collective farm
совѣтъ *совѣтъ* → совет *совет*
совѣтникъ *совѣтникъ* → советник *советник*
согласие, согласия *согласие, согласия* – (n., neut., † *согласіе*) harmony, understanding, agreement; *по обоюдному согласію* – by mutual consent
согласно *согласно* – (adv.) harmoniously; (prep. + dat.) in agreement with, in compliance with
содержание, содержания *содержание, содержания* – (n., neut., † *содержаніе*) support, keeping, maintenance; *средства къ содержанію* – means of support, livelihood
содержать *содержать* – (v.) to keep, keep up, maintain, support
содержаться *содержаться* – (v.) to maintain oneself, support oneself; *содержится при родителямъ* – he/she lives with his/her parents
содержащий *содержащий* – (part. from *содержать*, † *содержащій*) maintaining, keeping; *Содержащій акты гражданскаго состоянія* – Civil Registrar
содержащийся *содержащийся* – (part. from *содержаться*, to support oneself, † *содержащійся*) supporting himself/ herself, earning his/her living

Соединённые Штаты Америки, Соединённых Штатов Америки *Соединённые Штаты Америки, Соединённых Штатов Америки* – (n., masc. pl., abbr. *США*) United States of America

сожитель, сожителя *сожитель, сожителя* – (n., masc.) spouse, roommate (fem. *сожительница*)

сожитие, сожития *сожитие, сожития* – (n., neut., † *сожитіе*) cohabitation, living together

† Соколка, Соколки *Соколка, Соколки* – (n., fem.) town of Sokółka, Poland (see page 125); † *сокольскій* – (adj.) of Sokółka

† Соколовъ, Соколова *Соколовъ, Соколова* – (n., masc.) town of Sokołów Podlaski, Poland (see page 120); *соколовскій* – (adj.) of Sokołów Podlaski

сокольник, сокольника *сокольник, сокольника* – (n., masc.) falconer

солдат, солдата *солдат, солдата* – (n., masc., gen. pl. *солдат*) soldier; *отпускный солдат*, soldier on leave; *отставоной солдат*, discharged soldier (fem. *солдатка*, soldier's wife)

солевар, солевара *солевар, солевара* – (n., masc.) salt-maker, salter

солильщик, солильщика *солильщик, солильщика* – (n., masc.) salter, dry-salter, curer

солнечный удар, солнечного удара *солнечный удар, солнечного удара* – (n., masc.) sunstroke

солодовник, солодовника *солодовник, солодовника* – (n., masc.) maltster (also seen: *солодовщик*)

солома, соломы *солома, соломы* – (n., fem.) straw; *крытый соломой* – with a thatched roof

соломорез, соломореза *соломорез, соломореза* – (n., masc., † *соломорѣзъ*) straw-cutter, chaff-cutter (fem. *соломорезка*)

солтыс, солтыса *солтыс, солтыса* – (n., masc.) in Polish *sołtys*, a village administrator, or among Jews a synagogue trustee (see page 256)

сонаследник, сонаследника *сонаследник, сонаследника* – (n., masc., † *сонаслѣдникъ*) joint heir, co-heir (fem. *сонаследница*)

сообщать *сообщать* – (v.) to tell, communicate, inform, *сообщите мне, пожалуйста* – please inform me

соопекун, соопекуна *соопекун, соопекуна* – (n., masc.) joint guardian, co-guardian

соответствующий *соответствующий* – (part. from *соотвествовать*, to correspond, conform, be in line with) † *соотвѣтствующій*) corresponding

сопровождение, сопровожения *сопровождение, сопровожения* – (n., neut., † *сопровожденіе*) accompanyment; *въ сопровожденіи своей жены* – accompanied by his wife

сорок, сорока *сорок, сорока* – (num.) forty; *сорок один* –forty-one, etc.; *сорок первый* – forty-first, etc. (see page 46)

† Сороки, Сорок *Сороки, Сорок* – (n., pl.) Russian name of the town of Soroca, Moldova (see page 132); † *сорокскій* – (adj.) of Soroka/ Soroca

сороковой *сороковой* – (ordinal num./adj.) fortieth

сортировщик, сортировщика *сортировщик, сортировщика* – (n., masc.) sorter (fem. *сортировщица*)

сосед, соседа *сосед, соседа* – (n., masc., † *сосѣдъ*), nom. pl. *соседи*, gen. pl. *соседей*) neighbor (fem. *соседка*)

сословие, сословия *сословие, сословия* – (n., neut., † *сословіе*) estate, social class

Сосница, Сосницы *Сосница, Сосницы* – (n., fem.) Russian nameo f the town of Sosnytsya, Ukraine (see page 133); *сосницкий* – (adj.) of Sosnytsya

состав, состава *состав, состава* – (n., masc.) composition, structure, formation

составитель, составителя *составитель, составителя* – (n., masc.) writer, author (fem. *составительница*)

составление, составления *составление, составления* – (n., neut., † *составленіе*) composing, drawing up, writing

составленный *составленный* – (part. from *составить*, to compose, write) composed, written, drawn up

составляющий *составляющий* – (part. from составлять, † *составляющій*) comprising, amounting to; drawing up, writing up

состоя *состоя* – (adv. part. from *состоять*) while being; *состоя на службѣ* – while [being] in the service

состоявшийся *состоявшийся* – (part. from *состояться*; † *состоявшійся*) having happened, having taken place

состоялось *состоялось* → состояться *состояться*

состояние, состояния *состояние, состояния* – (n., neut., † *состояніе*) state, condition, circumstances, occupation; *гражданское состояние* – Civil Registry

состоять *состоять* – (v.)to be composed of, made of; to consist of; to be attached, to be (often best left untranslated, or rendered as a form of "to be"); *X состоитъ въ россійскомъ подданствѣ* – X is a Russian citizen; *состоит ли или состоялъ ли въ бракѣ* – is he, or has he been, married?

состояться *состояться* – (v.) to take place, happen; *состоялось* – [this] happened, took place

состоящий *состоящий* – (part. of *состоять*, † *состоящій*) being, consisting; *состоящій публичнымъ Нотаріусомъ* – being a public notary; *состоящимъ изъ* – consisting of

сосѣдъ *сосѣдъ* → сосед *сосед*

сотник, сотника *сотник, сотника* – (n., masc.) commander of a Cossack squad-ron, or a foreman

in charge of many workmen (the root of the word is *сто*, "one hundred")
сотый *сотый* – (ordinal num./adj.) hundredth
соха, сохи *соха, сохи* – (n., fem.) a kind of primitive plow; † a unit of land measurement, the basis for ancient tax assessment
Сохачев, Сохачева *Сохачев, Сохачева* – (n., masc.) Russian name of the town of Sochaczew, Poland (see page 119); *сохачевский* – of Sochaczew
сочетание браком, сочетания браком *сочетание браком, сочетания браком* – (n., neut., † *сочетаніе бракомъ*) the contracting of marriage, marriage
сочетать бракомъ *сочетать бракомъ*– (v.) to join in marriage
сочетаться *сочетаться* – (v.) to get married, join in marriage; *сочеталась бракомъ* – she got married, was joined in marriage (*съ* – with)
союз, союза *союз, союза* – (n., masc.) union; *брачный союз* – marital union, marriage
Союз Советских Социалистических Республик, Союза ... *Союз Советских Социалистических Республик, Союза* ... – (n., masc., abbrev. *СССР*) Union of Soviet Socialist Republics, U.S.S.R.
спазма, спазмы *спазма, спазмы* – (n., fem.) spasm
† спальник, спальника *спальник, спальника* – (n., masc.) chamberlain of the royal bed-chamber
спаситель, спасителя *спаситель, спасителя* – (n., masc.) savior
список, списка *список, списка* – (n., masc.) list, register, roll; *кондуитный список* –a list of conduct, record of conduct; *призывной список* – conscription list, books of draftees; *списокъ ратникомъ ополченія* – list of those serving in the militia (see page 292)
сплавщик, сплавщика *сплавщик, сплавщика* – (n., masc.) raftsman (fem. *сплавщица*)
способ, способа *способ, способа* – (n., masc.) means, way, mode; *способ жизни* – means of support
способность, способности *способность, способности* – (n., fem.) capacity, ability, fitness (*к* – for)
справка, справки *справка, справки* – (n., fem.) inquiry, information
справочник, справочника *справочник, справочника* – (n., masc.) reference work
среда, среды *среда, среды* – (n., fem.) Wednesday; *в среду* – on Wednesday; *по средам* – on Wednesday, every Wednesday
средний *средний* – (adj., † *среднiй*) middle, medium
средство, средства *средство, средства* – (n., neut.) means; *срества къ жизни* – means of support
срок срока *срок срока* – (n., masc.) term, period, date; *на срок* – for a term, for a period [of]; *срокъ службы* – term of service
ссуда, ссуды *ссуда, ссуды* – (n., fem.) loan
ссудо-сберегательный *ссудо-сберегательный* – (adj.) savings and loan, e. g., *ссудо-сберегательная касса* – savings and loan bank
ссудчик, ссудчика *ссудчик, ссудчика* – (n., masc.) pawnbroker, lender
ссылный *ссылный* – (adj.) banished, transported; (used as a n.) an exile or convict banished to a certain area; also seen: *ссылочник*, fem. *ссылочница*
ставленник, ставленника *ставленник, ставленника* – (n., masc.) candidate for Holy Orders; (in modern Russian) protégé, henchman
Ставрополь, Ставрополя *Ставрополь, Ставрополя* – (n., masc.) Stavropol', name of a town in Russia (see page 137); *ставропольский* – (adj.) of Stavropol'
стан, стана *стан, стана* – (n., masc.) stature, size; camp; police district
станица, станицы *станица, станицы* – (n., fem.) sizable village in Cossack lands; † flock
станционный *станционный* – (adj., † *стантіонный*) of a station; *станционный смотритель* – stationmaster
станция, станции *станция, станции* – (n., fem. † *станція*) station; *почтовая станція* – post office, postal station; *железнодорожная станция* – railroad station; *шосеейная станция* – highway station
старец, старца *старец, старца* – (n., masc.) old man; also *старик*
Старобельск, Старобельска *Старобельск, Старобельска* – (n., masc., † *Старобѣльскъ*) town of Starobil's'k, Ukraine (see page 134); *старобельский* – of Starobil's'k
старовер, старовера *старовер, старовера* – (n., masc., † *старовѣръ*) Old Believer [a Russian religious sect] (fem., *староверка*); also called *старообрядец* (fem. *старообрядка*)
Стародуб, Стародуба *Стародуб, Стародуба* – (n., masc.) town of Starodub, Russia (see page 133); *стародубский* – (adj.) of Starodub
старожил, старожила *старожил, старожила* – (n., masc.) long-time resident, old-timer (fem. *старожилка*)
Староконстантинов, Староконстантинова *Староконстантинов, Староконстантинова* – (n., masc.) town of Starokostyantyniv, Ukraine (see page 130); *староконстантиновский* – (adj.) of Starokonstantinov/Starokostyantyniv
старообрядец *старообрядец* → *старовер*
† Старый Быхов, Стараго Быхова *Старый Быхов, Стараго Быхова* – (n., masc.) town of Bykhaŭ, Belarus' (see page 126); *старобыховскій* – of Stary Bychov/Bykhaŭ

староста, старосты *староста, старосты* – (n., masc.) bailiff, reeve (of a village); in Poland, a *starosta;* fem. *старостиха, старостихи* – wife of a *starosta*
старость, старости *старость, старости* – (n., fem.) old age; *умереть от старости,* to die of old age
старуха, старухи *старуха, старухи* – (n., fem.) old woman
старческий *старческий* – (adj., † *старческій*) senile; of an old man
старший *старший* – (adj., † *старшій*) senior, older (in the sense of "senior" also seen as *старшой*)
старшина, старшины *старшина, старшины* – (n., masc. but declined as if fem.) head, headman, chief, foreman; *старшина присяжных,* foreman of the jury; *волостной старшина,* head of a *volost'*
старшой *старшой* → старший *старший*
старый *старый* – (adj.) old; *старый стиль,* Old Style (in dating, i. e., by the Julian calendar)
старьёвщик, старьёвщика *старьёвщик, старьёвщика* – (n., masc.) dealer in antiques or old clothes
статский *статский* – (adj., † *статскій*) state, of the state
статья, статьи *статья, статьи* – (n., fem., nom. pl. *статьи,* gen. pl. *статей*) article
стегальщик, стегальщика *стегальщик, стегальщика* – (n., masc.) quilter (fem. *стегальщица*)
стекольный *стекольный* – (adj.) of glass; *стекольный завод* – glassworks
стекольщик, стекольщика *стекольщик, стекольщика* – (n., masc.) glassmaker (fem. *стекольщица*)
стена, стены *стена, стены* – (n. fem., † *стѣна*) wall
степенство, степенства *степенство, степенства* – (n., neut.) steadiness, staidness, sobriety; honorary title given to merchants and burghers
ст. ж. д. *ст. ж. д.* – (abbr.) *станция железной дороги,* railroad station
стиль, стиля *стиль, стиля* – (n., masc.) style; *нового стиля* or *по новому стилю,* New Style (by the Gregorian calendar); *старого стиля* or *по старому стилю,* Old Style (by the Julian calendar)
стипендиат, стипендиата *стипендиат, стипендиата* – (n., masc., † *стипендіатъ*) student with a grant (fem. *стипендиатка*)
сто, ста *сто, ста* – (num.) hundred
стоите *стоите* → стоять *стоять*
стоить *стоить* – (v.) to cost; to deserve, be worth; *что стоитъ* – which costs
стол, стола *стол, стола* – (n., masc.) table
столбняк, столбняка *столбняк, столбняка* – (n., masc.) tetanus
столетие, столетия *столетие, столетия* – (n., neut., † *столѣтіе*) century
столоначальник, столоначальника *столоначальник, столоначальника* – (n., masc.) department chief, head clerk (in pre-Revolutionary Russia)
стольник, стольника *стольник, стольника* – (n., masc.) dapifer at a noble's court
столяр, столяра *столяр, столяра* – (n., masc.) carpenter, joiner (fem. *столяриха,* carpenter's wife)
Стопница, Стопницы *Стопница, Стопницы* – (n., fem.) town of Stopnica, Poland (see page 120); *стопницкий* – of Stopnica
сторож, сторожа *сторож, сторожа* – (n., masc., nom. pl. *сторожа,* gen. pl. *сторожей*) watchman, guard (fem. *сторожиха*)
сторожка, сторожки *сторожка, сторожки* – (n., fem.) sentry-box
сторона стороны *сторона стороны* – (n., fem.) side; *с моей стороны* – for my part, on my part; *съ обоихъ сторонъ* – on both sides, of both parties; *по требованіи заинтересованней стороны* – at the demand of the interested party
стоялец, стояльца *стоялец, стояльца* – (n., masc.) tenant, lodger (fem. *стоялица*)
стоять *стоять* – (v.) to stand; to be, to be or find oneself (in certain situation); *не стоите-ли въ брачномъ союзѣ* – are you married? (literally "do you not stand in a marital union?")
страдание, страдания *страдание, страдания* – (n., neut. † *страданіе*) suffering, illnesss
страж, стража *страж, стража* – (n., masc.) guard, watchman, sentinel
стража, стражи *стража, стражи* – (n., fem.) guard, watch
стрелец, стрельца *стрелец, стрельца* – (n., masc., † *стрѣлецъ*) archer, bowman, shot
стрелок, стрелка *стрелок, стрелка* – (n., masc., † *стрѣлокъ*) shot, bowman
стрелочник, стрелочника *стрелочник, стрелочника* – (n., masc., † *стрѣлочникъ*) pointsman, switchman [on a railroad] (fem. *стрелочница*)
стремянный, стремянного *стремянный, стремянного* – (adj. used as a n., masc.) groom, ostler
строгий *строгий* – (adj., † *строгій*) strict
строевой *строевой* – (adj.) front-line, of active service
строение, строения *строение, строения* – (n., neut., † *строеніе*) structure, building
строитель, строителя *строитель, строителя* – (n., masc.) builder (fem. *строительница*)
струговщик, струговщика *струговщик, струговщика* – (n., masc.) bargeman
стрѣлецъ *стрѣлецъ* → стрелец *стрелец*
стрѣлокъ *стрѣлокъ* → стрелок *стрелок*
стрѣлочникъ *стрѣлочникъ* → стрелочник *стрелочник*

стряпуха, стряпухи *стряпуха, стряпухи* – (n., masc.) cook-maid

стряпчий, стряпчего *стряпчий, стряпчего* – (adj. used as a n., masc. † *стряпчій*) attorney, lawyer

студент, студента *студент, студента* – (n., masc.) student [at a college or institute of higher learning] (fem. *студентка*)

стѣна *стѣна* → стена *стена*

суббота, субботы *суббота, субботы* – (n., fem.) Saturday; *в субботу* – on Saturday; *по субботам* – on Saturdays, every Saturday

субботний *субботний* – (adj. , also *суботний*, † *субботній*) of Saturday

Сувалки, Сувалк *Сувалки, Сувалк* – (n., pl.) Russian name of the town of Suwałki, Poland (see page 120); *сувалкский* – (also † *сувалскій*) of Suwałki

сувалкский *сувалкский* – (adj., *сувалкскій*, also sometimes † *сувальскій* (a Polonism)

суд, суда *суд, суда* – (n., masc.) tribunal, court, judgment; *подъ судомъ* – on trial, being tried

судовладелец, судовладельца *судовладелец, судовладельца* – (n., masc., † *судовладѣлецъ*) ship-owner

судоводитель, судоводителя *судоводитель, судоводителя* – (n., masc.) navigator

судовщик, судовщика *судовщик, судовщика* – (n., masc.) shipmaster

судомойка, судомойки *судомойка, судомойки* – (n., fem.) scullery maid, kitchen-maid

судопромышленник, судопромышленника *судопромышленник, судопромышленника* – (n., masc.) owner or builder of ships

судорабочий, судорабочего *судорабочий, судорабочего* – (adj. used as a n., masc., † *судорабочій*) workman on a barge

судорога, судороги *судорога, судороги* – (n., fem.) cramp, convulsion

судорожный *судорожный* – (adj.) convulsive

судостроитель, судостроителя *судостроитель, судостроителя* – (n., masc.) shipbuilder

судья, судьи *судья, судьи* – (n., masc., nom. pl. *судьи*, gen. pl. *судьей*, dat. pl. *судьям*) judge

суконщик, суконщика *суконщик, суконщика* – (n., masc.) cloth-weaver, cloth-worker

сумма, суммы *сумма, суммы* – (n., fem.) sum, total

Сумы, Сум *Сумы, Сум* – (n., pl.) name of the town of Sumy, Ukraine (see page 134); *сумский* – (adj.) of Sumy

супруг, супруга *супруг, супруга* – (n., masc.) spouse, husband

супруга, супруги *супруга, супруги* – (n., fem.) spouse, wife

супружеский *супружеский* – (adj., † *супружескій*) conjugal, marital

супружество, супружества *супружество, супружества* (n., neut.) marriage, matrimony

Сураж, Суража *Сураж, Суража* – (n., masc.) town of Surazh, Russia (see page 133); *суражский* – (adj.) of Surazh

сутки, суток *сутки, суток* – (n., fem. pl.) 24 hours; *черезъ однѣ сутки* – within 24 hours; *трое суток* – three days

сучильщик, сучильщика *сучильщик, сучильщика* – (n., masc.) twister (fem. *сучильщица*)

существование, существования *существование, существования* – (n., neut., † *существованіе*) existence, being; *средства для существованія* – living, means of existence

сходно *сходно* – (adv.) accordingly, likely; according to

счёт, счёта *счёт, счёта* – (n., masc., perhaps sometimes *щетъ*) account, counting, number

счётник, счётника *счётник, счётника* – (n., masc.) accountant

счётный *счётный* – (adj.) of accounting, counting

счетовод, счетовода *счетовод, счетовода* – (n., masc.) bookkeeper, accountant

счётчик, счётчика *счётчик, счётчика* – (n., masc.) one who keeps a count or tally (fem. *счётчица*)

считать *считать* – (v.) to reckon, figure, count, consider

считаться *считаться* – (v.) to be reckoned, figured, counted, considered

считающий *считающий* – (part. from *считать*, † *считающій*) counting, reckoning, figuring; *сорокъ лѣтъ считающій*, literally "40 years counting," i. e., 40 years old

считая *считая* – (adv. part. from *считать*) counting, reckoning, considering

С.Ш.А. *С.Ш.А.* – (abbr.) U.S.A. (see Соединённые Штаты Америки)

съ *съ* → s *с*

съёмщик, съёмщика *съёмщик, съёмщика* – (n., masc.) surveyor, one who draws up plans; tenant

сын, сына *сын, сына* – (n., masc., nom. pl. *сыновья*, gen. pl. *сыновей*) son; *сын крестный* – godson

сыпной *сыпной* or сыпняк *сыпняк* → тиф *тиф*

Сырдарья, Сырдарьи *Сырдарья, Сырдарьи* – (n., fem.) Syrdarya, name of a town and river in Uzbekistan (see page 137); *сырдарьинский* – of Syr-Darya

сыромятник, сыромятника *сыромятник, сыромятника* – (n., masc.) leather-worker

сыщик, сыщика *сыщик, сыщика* – (n., masc.) detective

сѣверный *сѣверный* → северный *северный*

сѣдельник *сѣдельник* → седельник *седельник*

Сѣдлецъ *Сѣдлецъ* → Седльце *Седльце*

сѣнной *сѣнной* → сенной *сенной*

Сѣрадзъ *Сѣрадзъ* → Серадз *Серадз*
сѣрый *сѣрый* → серый *серый*
сѣяльщик *сѣяльщик* → сеяльщик *сеяльщик*
та *та* → тот *тот*
табачник, табачника *табачник, табачника* – (n., masc.) tobacconist (fem. *табачница*)
табущик, табунщика *табущик, табунщика* – (n., masc.) keeper of a drove of horses
† таврическій *таврическій* – (adj.) of Tavrida, a province in what is now Ukraine
Таганрог, Таганрога *Таганрог, Таганрога* – (n., masc.) town of Taganrog, Russia (see page 134); *таганрогский* – (adj.) of Taganrog
таинство, таинства *таинство, таинства* – (n., neut., abbr. *таинъ.*) sacrament
таинъ. *таинъ.* → таинство *таинство*
так *так* – (adv.) so, thus, in that way; *так как* – since, inasmuch as
также *также* – (adv.) too, likewise
таковый *таковый* – (adj.) such, of this sort, the same; *если таковые имеют* – if any; *не знал о необходимости таковаго* – he did not know about the necessity of this
такой *такой* – (pron., for declension see page 43) such, such a
Таллин, Таллина *Таллин, Таллина* – (n., masc.) Tallinn [capital of Estonia]
там *там* – (adv.) there
Тамбов, Тамбова *Тамбов, Тамбова* – (n., masc.) Tambov, name of a town in Russia (see page 135); *тамбовский* – of Tambov
Таммуз *Таммуз* → Тамуз *Тамуз*
таможенник, таможенника *таможенник, таможенника* – (n., masc.) customs official
таможенный *таможенный* or таможный *таможный* – (adj.) customs; *таможенный надсмотрщик*, customs-house officer
Тамуз, Тамуза *Тамуз, Тамуза* – (n., masc.) Tammuz, a month in the Jewish calendar (see page 47)
танцмейстер, танцмейстера *танц-мейстер, танцмейстера* – (n., masc.) dancing master [cmp. Germ. *Tanzmeister*]
Таращa, Таращи *Тараща, Таращи* – (n., fem.) town of Tarashcha, Ukraine (see page 132); *таращанский* – (adj.) of Tarashcha
твёрдый *твёрдый* – firm, hard, solid, sound
Тверь, Твери *Тверь, Твери* – (n., fem.) Tver', name of a town in Russia (see page 135); *тверской* – of Tver'
т. е. *т. е.* (abbr. of *то есть*) – that is, i. e.
те *те* → тот *тот*
тебе *тебе* – (pron., dative of *ты*, † *тебѣ*) to you
тебя *тебя* – (pron., accusative of *ты*) you
Тевет Тевета *Тевет Тевета* – (n., masc.) Tevet, a month in the Jewish calendar (see page 47)
текущий *текущий* – (part. from *течь*, to flow, run, † *текущій*) current; *текущего года* – this year, during the the current year
телеграфист, телеграфиста *телеграфист, телеграфиста* – (n., masc.) telegrapher (fem. *телеграфистка*)
телеграфный *телеграфный* – (adj.) of telegraphs
тележник, тележника *тележник, тележника* – (n., masc., † *телѣжникъ*) cartwright
тело, тела *тело, тела* – (n., neut., † *тѣло*) body; *болѣзненный тѣломъ* – sickly in body
телохранитель, телохранителя *телохранитель, телохранителя* – (n., masc., † *тѣлохранитель*) bodyguard
† Тельши, Тельш *Тельши, Тельш* – (n., pl.) town of Telšiai, Lithuania (see page 124); *тельшевскій* – (adj.) of Tel'she/ Telšiai
телѣжникъ *телѣжникъ* → тележник *тележник*
тем, теми *тем, теми* († *тѣм, тѣми*) → тот *тот*
тёмный *тёмный* – (adj.) dark
тенётчик, тенётчика *тенётчик, тенётчика* – (n., masc.) net-setter
теперь *теперь* – (adv.) now
территориальный *территориальный* – (adj.) territorial
тесарь, тесаря *тесарь, тесаря* – (n., masc.) stone-cutter
тесёмочник, тесёмочника *тесёмочник, тесёмочника* – (n., masc.) tape-maker, ribbon-weaver; also seen: *тесёмщик*
тесть, тестя *тесть, тестя* – (n., masc.) father-in-law (wife's father)
тётка, тётки *тётка, тётки* – (n., fem.) aunt
тётя, тёти *тётя, тёти* – (n., fem., gen. pl. *тётей*) aunt
течение, течения *течение, течения* – (n., neut., † *теченіе*) current, stream, course; *в течении* – in the course of, during; *въ теченіе одного года* – for the course of one year, for one year
тёща, тёщи *тёща, тёщи* – (n., fem.) mother-in-law (wife's mother)
тех *тех* → тот *тот*
типографщик, типографщика *типографщик, типографщика* – (n., masc.) typographer
Тирасполь, Тирасполя *Тирасполь, Тирасполя* – (n.) town of Tiraspol', Moldova (see page 133); *тираспольский* – (adj.) of Tiraspol'
тиф, тифа *тиф, тифа* – (n., masc.) typhus; *брюшной тиф* – typhoid; *возвратный тиф* – remittent typhus; *пятнистый тиф* or *сыпной тиф*, spotted fever, typhus (also called *сыпняк*)
Тифлис, Тифлиса *Тифлис, Тифлиса* – (n., masc.) Tiflis, name of a town now called Tbilisi, Georgia (see page 137); *тифлисский* – of Tiflis

тифозная горячка, тифозной горячки *тифозная горячка, тифозной горячки* – (n., fem.) typhoid fever (also seen: *тифозная лихорадка*)
тихо *тихо* – (adv.) quietly
Тишри *Тишри* (n., not declined, also called *Тишрей*) Tishri, the name of a month in the Jewish calendar (see page 47)
† тіунъ, тіуна *тіунъ, тіуна* – (n., masc.) bailiff
ткач, ткача *ткач, ткача* – (n., masc.) weaver (fem. *ткачиха*)
то *то* → тот *том*
то *то* – (conj.) then; *если … то* – if … then
тобой *тобой* or † тобою *тобою* – (pron., instr. of *ты*) you
Тобольск, Тобольска *Тобольск, Тобольска* – (n., masc.) Tobol'sk, name of a town in Siberia (see page 137); *тобольский* – of Tobol'sk
товарищ, товарища *товарищ, товарища* – (n., masc.) comrade, companion
товарищество, товарищества *товарищество, товарищества* – (n., neut.) company, society, association, partnership
того *того* → тот *том*
то есть *то есть* – (abbr. *т. е.*) that is, i. e.
тоже *тоже* – (adv.) also, the same
той, том, тому *той, том, тому* → тот *том*
токарь, токаря *токарь, токаря* – (n., masc., nom. pl. *токари* or *токаря*, gen. pl. *токарей*) turner, lathe operator, cabinet maker
токмо *токмо* – (adv.) only
толковник, толковника *толковник, толковника* – (n., masc.) translator, interpreter
толмач, толмача *толмач, толмача* – (n., masc.) translator, interpreter
только *только* – (adv.) only; *Нами только подписанъ* – [it] was signed only by Us
том *том* → тот *том*
том, тома *том, тома* – (n., masc.) volume
Томашув, Томашува *Томашув, Томашува* – (n., masc., † *Томашевъ*) Russian name of the town of Tomaszów, Poland; † *томашевскій* – of Tomaszów
Томск, Томска *Томск, Томска* – (n., masc.) Tomsk, name of a town in Siberia (see page 137); *томский* – of Tomsk
тому *тому* → тот *том*
топонимический *топонимический* – (adj.) toponymic
торговец, торговца *торговец, торговца* – (n., masc.) dealer, merchant, e. g., *торговец шелковыми товарами*, silk-merchant (fem. *торговка*)
торжественно *торжественно* – (adv.) solemnly
Торунь, Торуня *Торунь, Торуня* – (n., masc.) Toruń, Poland, called *Thorn* [† *Торнъ*] by Germans
тот *том* – (demonstr. pron., for declension see page 43) that, that one; *тотъ же* – the same one; *тѣже* – the same ones; *тѣмъ* – with this, thereby
точильщик, точильщика *точильщик, точильщика* – (n., masc.) sharpener, grinder, whetter
точный *точный* – (adj.) exact, precise
трактирщик, трактирщика *трактирщик, трактирщика* – (n., masc.) landlord, innkeeper, publican (fem. *трактирщица*)
требование, требования *требование, требования* – (n., neut., *требованіе*) demand, request
требовать *требовать* – (v.) to demand, require; *требуетъ* – demands, requires
трепальщик, трепальщика *трепальщик, трепальщика* – (n., masc.) one who peels hemp, stripper (fem. *трепальщица*)
третий *третий* – (ordinal num./adj., † *третій*) third; *часть третья* – third part (of registers, either of deaths or, sometimes, divorces)
трёхсотый *трёхсотый* – (ordinal num./adj.) three hundredth
три, трёх *три, трёх* – (num.) three
тридцатый *тридцатый* – (ordinal num./adj.) thirtieth
тридцать, тридцати *тридцать, тридцати* – (num.) thirty; *тридцать один* – thirty-one, etc.; *тридцать первый* – thirty-first, etc.
тринадцатый *тринадцатый* – (ordinal num./adj.) thirteenth
тринадцать, тринадцати *тринадцать, тринадцати* – (num.) thirteen
триста, трёхсот *триста, трёхсот* – (num.) three hundred
трое *трое* – (num.) three; *трое суток* – three days
троекратный *троекратный* – (adj.) threefold, done three times
† троечникъ, троечника *троечникъ, троечника* – (n., masc.) keeper of a livery stable, one who leases out *troikas* (carriages drawn by a team of three horses)
тройца, тройцы *тройца, тройцы* – (n., fem.) Trinity
† Троки, Трок *Троки, Трок* – (n.) town of Troki, now Trakai, Lithuania (see page 124); *трокский* – (adj., also † *троцкій*) o f Troki/Trakai
трубач, трубача *трубач, трубача* – (n., masc.) trumpeter, horn-blower
трубник, трубника *трубник, трубника* – (n., masc.) fireman
трубочист, трубочиста *трубочист, трубочиста* – (n., masc.) chimney sweep
труженик, труженика *труженик, труженика* – (n., masc.) hard-working person (fem. *труженица*)
тряпичник, тряпичника *тряпичник, тряпичника* – (n., masc.) ragman (fem. *тряпичница*)
ту *ту* → тот *том*

туберкулёз, туберкулёза *туберкулёз, туберкулёза* – (n., masc.) tuberculosis; *туберкулёз лёгких* – pulmonary tuberculosis

туземец, туземца *туземец, туземца* – (n., masc.) native, indigenous person, local (fem. *туземка*)

Тула, Тулы *Тула, Тулы* – (n., fem.) Tula, name of a town in Russia (see page 135); *тульский* – of Tula

Тургай, Тургая *Тургай, Тургая* – (n., masc.) Turgai, name of a river in Kazakhstan (see page 137); *тургайский* – of Turgai

† Турекъ, Турка *Турекъ, Турка* – (n., masc.) town of Turek, Poland (see page 118); *турекскій* – of Turek

Турция, Турции *Турция, Турции* – (n., fem., † *Турція*) Turkey

тысяча, тысячи *тысяча, тысячи* – (num.) thousand; *две тысячи* – two thousand; *тысяча четыреста* – 1,400 (see page 46)

тысячный *тысячный* – (ordinal num./adj.) thousandth

тѣже *тѣже* → тот *тот*

тѣло *тѣло* → тело *тело*

тѣлохранитель *тѣлохранитель* → телохранитель *телохранитель*

† тѣмъ *тѣмъ* or тѣми *тѣми* or тѣхъ *тѣхъ* → тот *тот*

тюремник, тюремника *тюремник, тюремника* – (n., masc.) prisoner (fem. *тюремница*)

тюремщик, тюремщика *тюремщик, тюремщика* – (n., masc.) jailer, warden of a prison

тягло, тягла *тягло, тягла* – (n., neut.) a household, a married couple with a certain amount of land on which a certain amount of tax is to be paid; the tax itself

тяжкий *тяжкий* – (adj., † *тяжкій*) grave, serious, grievous, heavy

тятя, тяти *тятя, тяти* – (n., masc.) daddy

у *у* – (prep. with gen.) at, with, at the house of, e. g., *у Хаи Суры* – at Chaja Sura's, with Chaja Sura

убедиться *убедиться* – (v., † *убѣдиться)* to convince oneself, to satisfy oneself (*в* – of); *въ чемъ убѣдились Нотаріусъ и свидѣтели* – of which the notary and witnesses convinced themselves

убийца, убийцы *убийца, убийцы* – (n., masc. or fem., † *убійца*) murderer, killer

убывший *убывший* – (part. from *убыть*, to decrease, diminish, wane; † *убывшій*) gone away, departed, lost

убыль, убыли *убыль, убыли* – (n., fem.) loss (i. e., loss of troops), decline in number or quality

убѣдиться *убѣдиться* → убедиться *убедиться*

уважаемый *уважаемый* – (adj.) honored, respected; *Уважаемый Господин* – Dear Sir

уважение, уважения *уважение, уважения* – (n., neut., † *уваженіе*) esteem, respect; *с уважением* – sincerely yours, respectfully yours

уволенный *уволенный* – (part. from *уволить*) released, discharged; *уволенъ въ запасъ* – discharged to the reserves; *уволенъ въ разные города* – is free [to travel] to various towns

уволить *уволить* – (v.) to release, discharge; *уволить въ отпускъ* – to furlough, give a leave of absence; *уволить въ запасъ* – to discharge to the reserve; *уволить въ отставку* – to pension off, superannuate; *уволить отъ должности* – to discharge

увольнение, увольнения *увольнение, увольнения* – (n., neut., † *увольненіе*) leave, discharge

увольнительный *увольнительный* – (adj.) release, discharge; *увольнительный билетъ* – discharge papers

углекоп, углекопа *углекоп, углекопа* – (n., masc.) coalminer

уговор, уговора *уговор, уговора* – (n., masc.) agreement, stipulation; *они никакого уговора о имуществѣ между собою не заключили* – they had made no agreement between themselves regarding property

угольщик, угольщика *угольщик, угольщика* – (n., masc.) charcoal-burner, coalminer, charcoal-dealer

удавление, удавления *удавление, удавления* – (n., neut., † *удавленіе*) strangulation; *цмерть от удавления* – death by strangulation

удавленник, удавленника *удавленник, удавленника* – (n., masc.) one who died of strangulation or hanging, at his own hand or another's (fem. *удавленница*)

удар, удара *удар, удара* – (n., masc.) stroke, attack

удельный *удельный* – (adj., † *удѣльный*) appanaged (see page 317)

удостоверение, удостоверения *удостоверение, удостоверения* – (n., neut., † *удостовѣреніе*) evidence, testimony, statement, attestation; *в удостоверение,* in witness (of), in certification; *по наочномъ удостовѣреніи* – after eyewitness testimony

удостоверитель, удостоверителя *удостоверитель, удостоверителя* – (n., masc., † *удостовѣритель*) testifier, witness

удостоверять *удостоверять* – (v., † *удостовѣрять*) to certify

удостоверяться *удостоверяться* – (v., † *удостовѣряться*) to be certified

удочеренная *удочеренная* – (adj.) adoptive, referring to a female

удѣльный *удѣльный* → удельный *удельный*

уезд, уезда *уезд, уезда* (n., masc., † *уѣздъ*) district, a subdivision of a *губерния* (see page 83); *уездный город*, chief town of a district
уездный *уездный* – (adj., † *уѣздный*) of an *uyezd; уѣздный городъ* – a town that was the administrative center of an *uyezd*
указ, указа *указ, указа* – (n., masc.) edict, decree, ukase, *по указу* – by decree
указание, указания *указание, указания* – (n., neut., † *указанiе*) indication
указанный *указанный* – (part. from *указать*) indicated, specified, listed
указатель, указателя *указатель, указателя* – (n., masc.) index
указать *указать* – (v., perf. counterpart of *указывать*) to indicate, point out, show, direct
указывать *указывать* – (v.) to indicate, point out, show, direct
укладчик, улладчика *укладчик, улладчика* – (n., masc.) packer (fem. *укладчица*)
Украина, Украины *Украина, Украины* – (n., fem.) Ukraine; *на Украине* – in Ukraine
Украинец, Украинца *Украинец, Украинца* – (n., masc.) Ukrainian (fem. *Украинка*)
украинский *украинский* – (adj., † *украинскiй*) Ukrainian
укреплённый *укреплённый* – (part. from *укреплить*, to strengthen, fortify; † *укрѣплённый*) strengthened, fortified, (figuratively) corroborated
ул. *ул.* → улица *улица*
улан, улана *улан, улана* – (n., masc.) uhlan
улица, улицы *улица, улицы* – (n., fem., abbr. *ул.*) street
улучшение, улучшения *улучшение, улучшения* – (n., neut., † *улучшенiе*) improvement
ум, ума *ум, ума* – (n., masc.) mind; *находящiйся въ здравомъ умѣ* – of sound mind, mentally healthy
ум. *ум.* – abbrev. of *умер* or *умерла* or *умерли* → *умереть*
умалишённый *умалишённый* – (adj.) insane, mad
Умань, Уманя *Умань, Уманя* – (n., masc.) town of Uman', Ukraine (see page 132); *уманский* – (adj.) of Uman'
умеренный *умеренный* – (adj., † *умѣренный*) moderate, temperate; medium (i. e., not too big, not too small)
умереть *умереть* – (v.; † *оумеръ;* imperf. aspect *умирать*) to die (*от* + gen.) to die, e. g., *умер от раны*, he died of his wound; *умер* – he died; *умерла* – she died; *умерли* – they died; *умереть с голоду* – to die of starvation; *умереть смертью героя* – to die a hero's death; *умереть скоропостижно* – to die suddenly, unexpectedly; *умереть естественно* or *естественной смертью* – to die a natural death; *умереть насильственно* or *насильственной смертью* – to die violently; *умереть за дело* – to die for the cause
умерший *умерший* – (part., † *оумершiй* or *умершiй*) dead, deceased; о *умершихъ* – of the dead, of deaths
уметь *уметь* – (v., † *умѣть*) to be able to, know how to; can; *писать не умѣетъ* – does not know how to write, can't write
умирать *умирать* → *умереть*
умирающий *умирающий* – (part. of *умирать*) dying; (used as a n.) the dying one
умышленный *умышленный* – (adj.) intentional, premeditated
умѣренный *умѣренный* → умеренный *умеренный*
умѣть *умѣть* → уметь *уметь*
униат, униата *униат, униата* – (n., masc., † *унiатъ*) Uniate, old term for a member of the Greek Catholic rite (it came to be regarded as derogatory; (fem. *униатка*)
уничтожить *уничтожить* – (v.) to destroy; *уничтожены ли они* – if they have been destroyed
унтер-офицер, унтер-офицера *унтер-офицер, унтер-офицера* – (n., masc.) non-commissioned officer
унция, унции *унция, унции* – (n., fem., † *унцiя*) ounce
упаковщиик, упаковщика *упаковщиик, упаковщика* – (n., masc.) packer (fem. *упаковщица*)
уплачивать *уплачивать* – (v.) to pay
упомянутый *упомянутый* – (part. from *упомянуть*, to mention) mentioned, named above
употребить *употребить* – (v.) to use
управа, управы *управа, управы* – (n., fem.) board, council
управитель, управителя *управитель, управителя* – (n., masc.) steward, manager; fem. *управительница* (i. e., a female steward or manager)
управительша, управительши *управительша, управительши* – (n., fem.) wife of a steward
управление, управления *управление, управления* – (n., neut., † *управленiе*) administration, direction; office
управляющий, управяющего *управляющий, управяющего* – (part. used as a n., masc.) manager, director; used with the instr. case, e. g., *управляющий банком*, bank director, or *управляющий работами*, director of works
Урал, Урала *Урал, Урала* – (n., masc.) Ural region; *уральские горы*, the Ural Mountains; *на Урале* – in the Urals
уральский *уральский* – (adj., † *уральскiй*) of the Urals (see page 137)
уродливость, уродливости *уродливость, уродливости* – (n., fem.) deformity

урождённый *урождённый* – (part.) born, by birth; (used with fem. names) née
уроженец, уроженца *уроженец, уроженца* – (n., masc.) native (fem. *уроженка*)
урочище, урочища *урочище, урочища* – (n., neut.) plot of land, a section different from the land around it
урядник, урядника *урядник, урядника* – (n., masc.) village policeman; Cossack sergeant
усадебник, усадебника *усадебник, усадебника* – (n., masc.) farmer, one who has an *усадьба* ↓ (fem. *усадебница*)
усадьба, усадьбы *усадьба, усадьбы* – (n., fem.) farmstead, country estate
условие, условия *условие, условия* – (n., neut., † *условіе*) term, clause, condition
услужник, услужника *услужник, услужника* – (n., masc.) servant (fem. *услужница*)
усовершенствовавшийся *усовершенствовавшийся* – (part. from *усовершенствоваться*, to improve oneself, perfect oneself; † *усовершенство-вавшійся*) having improved, perfected
усопший *усопший* – (adj., † *усопшій*) deceased, dead
Успение, Успения *Успение, Успения* – (n., neut., † *Успеніе*) Assumption of the Blessed Virgin
успех, успеха *успех, успеха* – (n., masc., † *успѣхъ*) success
успешно *успешно* – (adv., † *успѣшно*) successfully
устав устава *устав устава* – (n., masc.) statute, regulation, code
уставщик, уставщика *уставщик, уставщика* – (n., masc.) head chorister
установить *установить* – (v.) to place, establish
установленный *установленный* – (part. from *установить*) established, prescribed
устройство, устройства *устройство, устройства* – (n., neut.) structure; *на устройство домашнихъ дѣлъ дается трое сутокъ* – three days will be given for settling household affairs
усыновлённый *усыновлённый* – (adj.) adoptive, referring to a male
утверждать *утверждать* – (v.) to certify
утверждённый *утверждённый* – (part. from *утвердить*, to decree, confirm) decreed; *высочайше утверждённый* – decreed at the highest level (i. e., by His Imperial Majesty)
утопленник, утопленника *утопленник, утопленника* – (n., masc.) drowned man (fem. *утопленница*)
уточник, уточникя *уточник, уточникя* – (n., masc.) woof-layer (fem. *уточница*)
утро, утра *утро, утра* – (n., neut.) morning; *утром* – in the morning, a. m. (see page 50)
Уфа, Уфы *Уфа, Уфы* – (n., fem.) Ufa, name of a town in Russia (see page 135); *уфимский* – of Ufa
уходить *уходить* – (v.) to leave, go away; *уходить на заработки* – to leave to go earn a living
участок, участка *участок, участка* – (n., masc.) plot, parcel, section, district; *призывной участок* – Draft Board
учебный *учебный* – (adj.) of education, training
ученик, ученика *ученик, ученика* – (n., masc.) pupil, scholar, apprentice (fem. *ученица*)
учёный, учёного *учёный, учёного* – (part. of *учиться* used as a n., masc.) scholar, learned man
учёт, учёта *учёт, учёта* – (n., masc.) accounting, registration
учинить *учинить* – (v.) to make, do, perpetrate
учитель, учителя *учитель, учителя* – (n., masc., gen. pl. *учителей*) teacher (fem. *учительница*)
учредитель, учредителя *учредитель, учредителя* – (n., masc.) founder, establisher (fem. *учредительница*)
учреждение, учреждения *учреждение, учреждения* – (n., neut., † *учрежденіе*) institution, foundation, establishment
уѣздъ *уѣздъ* → уезд *уезд*
фабрика, фабрики *фабрика, фабрики* – (n., fem.) factory
фабрикант, фабриканта *фабрикант, фабриканта* – (n., masc.) manufacturer, mill owner (fem. *фабрикантша*)
фабричный *фабричный* – (adj.) of a factory
факельщик, факельщика *факельщик, факельщика* – (n., masc.) torch-bearer
фактор, фактора *фактор, фактора* – (n., masc.) overseer, foreman of a printing office; factor (fem. *факторша*)
фамилия, фамилии *фамилия, фамилии* – (n., fem., † *фамилія*) surname
февраль, февраля *февраль, февраля* – (n., masc.) February
фельдмаршал, фельдмаршала *фельдмаршал, фельдмаршала* – (n., masc.) field marshal [cmp. Germ. *Feldmarschall*]
фельдфебель, фельдфебеля *фельдфебель, фельдфебеля* – (n., masc.) sergeant major [cmp. Germ. *Feldwebel*]
фельдшер, фельдшера фельдшер, *фельдшера* – (n., masc.) surgeon's assistant [cmp. Germ. *Feldscher*] (fem. *фельдшерица*)
фельдъегерь, фельдъегеря *фельдъегерь, фельдъегеря* – (n., masc.) courier, cabinet messenger [cmp. Germ. *Feldjäger*] (fem. *фельдъегерша*)
Феодосия, Феодосии *Феодосия, Феодосии* – (n., fem., † *Феодосія*) town of Feodosiya, Crimea (see page 134); *феодисийский* – (adj.) of Feodosiya
фехтмейстер, фехтмейстера *фехт-мейстер, фехтмейстера* – (n., masc.) fencing master

фиглярь, фигляря *фиглярь, фигляря* – (n., masc.) juggler, mountebank (fem. *фиглярка*)
Финляндия, Финляндии *Финляндия, Финляндии* – (n., fem., † *Финляндія*) Finland
флебит, флебита *флебит, флебита* – (n., masc.) phlebitis
фокусник, фокусника *фокусник, фокусника* – (n., masc.) conjurer, juggler (fem. *фокусница*)
фольварк, фольварка *фольварк, фольварка* – (n., masc., also † *фольварокъ*) a *folwark* [manorial farmstead in Poland]
фонтанщик, фонтанщика *фонтанщик, фонтанщика* – (n., masc.) fountain-maker, cistern-maker
форма, формы *форма, формы* – (n., fem.) form
формулярный *формулярный* – (adj.) of a service list
франкмасон, франкмасона *франкмасон, франкмасона* – (n., masc.) freemason
францисканец, францисканца *францисканец, францисканца* – (n., masc.) Franciscan (monk)
Франция, Франции *Франция, Франции* – (n., fem., † *Франція*) France
француз, француза *француз, француза* – (n., masc.) Frenchman (fem. *француженка*)
фрейлина, фрейлины *фрейлина, фрейлины* – (n., masc.) maid of honor, attendant of a princess or queen [cmp. Germ. *Fräulein*]
фронтовик, фронтовика *фронтовик, фронтовика* – (n., masc.) soldier or officer of the line
фруктовщик, фруктовщика *фруктовщик, фруктовщика* – (n., masc.) custard or fruit vendor
фузилёр, фузилёра *фузилёр, фузилёра* – (n., masc.) fusilier (also seen: *фузелер, фузелера*)
фуражир, фуражира *фуражир, фуражира* – (n., masc.) forager
фурлейт, фурлейта *фурлейт, фурлейта* – (n., masc.) train-soldier
фурьер, фурьера *фурьер, фурьера* – (n., masc.) quartermaster
футлярщик, футлярщика *футлярщик, футлярщика* – (n., masc.) case-maker, sheath-maker
халица, халицы *халица, халицы* – (n., fem.) a *ḥalitsah*, Jewish divorce ceremony (see page 290)
Харбин, Харбина *Харбин, Харбина* – (n., masc.) Harbin [city in northeast China]
харчевник, харчевника *харчевник, харчевника* – (n., masc.) tavern-keeper, keeper of a cook shop (fem. *харчевница*)
Харьков, Харькова *Харьков, Харькова* – (n., masc.) Russian name of the town of Kharkiv, Ukraine (see page 134); *харьковский* – (adj.) of Khar'kov/Kharkiv
Хелм, Хелма *Хелм, Хелма* – (n., masc., † *Холмъ*) town of Chełm, Poland (see page 120); *хелмский* – (adj., † *холмскій*) of Chełm
Херсон, Херсона *Херсон, Херсона* – (n., masc.) town of Kherson, Ukraine (see page 133)
Хешван, Хешвана *Хешван, Хешвана* – (n., masc.) Heshvan, the name of a month in the Jewish calendar (see page 47)
хипа, хипы *хипа, хипы* – (n., fem.) [Jewish] wedding ceremony (see page 271)
хирург, хирурга *хирург, хирурга* – (n., masc.) surgeon
хитана, хитаны *хитана, хитаны* – (n., fem.) Gypsy woman
хлебник, клебника *хлебник, клебника* – (n., masc., † *хлѣбникъ*) baker (fem. *хлебница*, female baker, wife of a baker)
хлебопашец, хлебопашца *хлебопашец, хлебопашца* – (n., masc., † *хлѣбопашецъ*) farmer, plowman
хлебопёк, хлебопёка *хлебопёк, хлебопёка* – (n., masc., † *хлѣбопёкъ*) baker (also seen: *хлебопекарь*)
хлебопродавец, хлебопродавца *хлебопродавец, хлебопродавца* – (n., masc., *хлѣбопродавецъ*) corn-merchant
хлеборез, хлебореза *хлеборез, хлебореза* – (n., masc., † *хлѣборѣзъ*) bread cutter
хлебороб, хлебороба *хлебороб, хлебороба* – (n., masc., † *хлѣборобъ*) farmer, grain-grower
хлеботорговец, хлеботорговца *хлебо-торговец, хлеботорговца* – (n., masc., *хлѣботорговецъ*) grain-merchant, corn factor
хлороз, хлороза *хлороз, хлороза* – (n., masc.) chlorosis
хмелевод, хмелевода *хмелевод, хмелевода* – (n., masc.) grower of hops
ходебщик, ходебщика *ходебщик, ходебщика* – (n., masc.) peddler, hawker
хожалый, хожалого *хожалый, хожалого* – (adj. used as a n., masc.) policeman
хожатый, хожатого *хожатый, хожатого* – (adj. used as a n., masc.) nurse; messenger
хозяин, хозяина *хозяин, хозяина* – (n., masc., nom. pl. *хозяева*, gen. pl. *хозяев*) master of the house, owner; husband, man; † *сельскій хозяинъ* – farmer
хозяйка, хозяйки *хозяйка, хозяйки* – (n., fem.) mistress, lady of the house; housewife, housekeeper
хояйство, хозяйства *хояйство, хозяйства* – (n., neut.) household
холера, холеры *холера, холеры* – (n., fem.) cholera
холерик, холерика *холерик, холерика* – (n., masc.) one ill with cholera; temperamental, choleric person
Холмъ *Холмъ* → Хелм *Хелм*
холоп, холопа *холоп, холопа* – (n., masc.) serf, bondman, thrall (fem. *холопка*)

холост, холоста *холост, холоста* – (n., masc.) single man, bachelor
холостой *холостой* – (adj., short form *холост*) unmarried, single; *холостой человек* – single man, bachelor
холостяк, холостяка *холостяк, холостяка* – (n., masc.) bachelor
холщевник, холщевника *холщевник, холщевника* – (n., masc.) linen-dealer
хорват, хорвата *хорват, хорвата* – (n., masc.) Croat (fem. *хорватка*)
хормейстер, хормейстера *хормейстер, хормейстера* – (n., masc.) choirmaster
Хорол, Хорола *Хорол, Хорола* – (n., masc.) town of Khorol, Ukraine (see page 133); *хорольский* – (adj.) of Khorol
хороший *хороший* – (adj., short forms *хорош*, masc., and *хороша*, fem., † *хорошій*) good
хорошо *хорошо* – (adv.) well
хорунжий, хорунжего *хорунжий, хорунжего* – (adj. used as a n., † *хорунжій, хорунжяго*) cornet, ensign [junior officer in the Cossack cavalry, cmp. Polish *chorąży*]
хотеть *хотеть* – (v., † *хотѣть*) to desire, want; *мне хотелось бы* – I would like to
Хотин, Хотина *Хотин, Хотина* – (n., masc.) town of Khotyn, Ukraine (see page 132); *хотинский* – (adj.) of Khotyn
храм, храма *храм, храма* – (n., masc.) cathedral, temple
храмовник, храмовника *храмовник, храмовника* – (n., masc.) Knight Templar
хранитель, хранителя *хранитель, хранителя* – (n., masc.) keeper, custodian; curator (fem. *хранительница*)
храниться *храниться* – (v.) to be kept, preserved
христианин, христианина *христианин, христианина* – (n., masc., nom. pl. *христиане*, gen. pl. *христиан*, † *христіанинъ*) Christian (fem. *христианка*)
христианский *христианский* – (adj., † *христіанскій*) Christian
Христос, Христоса *Христос, Христоса* – (n., masc.) Christ; *Христов* – (adj. short form) of Christ
хромой *хромой* – (adj.) lame, crippled; (used as a n.) lame man, woman
хромоножка, хромоножки *хромоножка, хромоножки* – (n., fem.) cripple, lame person
хронический *хронический* – (adj.) chronic
худение, худения *худение, худения* – (n., neut., † *худѣніе*) emaciation
художник, художника *художник, художника* – (n., masc.) artist (fem. *художница*)
худой *худой* – (adj.) bad, ill, wretched
худосочие, худосочия *худосочие, худосочия* – (n., neut., † *худосочіе*) cachexia, debilitation, wasting away
хутор, хутора *хутор, хутора* – (n., masc.) isolated farmstead; in southern Russia and Ukraine, a small peasant settlement
цальмейстер, цальмейстера *цальмейстер, цальмейстера* – (n., masc.) paymaster [cmp. Germ. *Zahlmeister*]
царевич, царевича *царевич, царевича* – (n., masc.) Czar's son, prince of the royal or imperial family
царевна, царевны *царевна, царевны* – (n., fem.) Czar's daughter, royal princess
царица, царицы *царица, царицы* – (n., fem.) Czar's wife
царство, царства *царство, царства* – (n., neut.) kingdom; *царство ему небесное* – may the Kingdom of Heaven be his!; *Царство Польское* – a name for the Kingdom of Poland, also called *Королевство Польское*
царь, царя *царь, царя* – (n., masc.) the Czar
цвет, цвета *цвет, цвета* – (n., masc., † *цвѣтъ*) color; flower
цветовод, цветовода *цветовод, цветовода* – (n., masc., † *цвѣтоводъ*) flower-gardener
цветочник, цветочника *цветочник, цветочника* – (n., masc., † *цвѣточникъ*) florist
цейхвахтер, цейхвахтера *цейхвахтер, цейхвахтера* – (n., masc.) store-keeper, gunner
цейхмейстер, цейхмейстера *цейхмейстер, цейхмейстера* – (n., masc.) (naval) master-gunner
целовальник, целовальника *целовальник, целовальника* – (n., masc., † *цѣловальникъ*) in 15th-17th century Russia an official who collected taxes and did other duties related to judicial and police work; tapster, barkeep (fem. *целовальница*)
целомудрие, целомудрия *целомудрие, целомудрия* – (n., fem., † *цѣломудріе*) chastity
целый *целый* – (adj., † *цѣлый*) whole, entire; safe and sound
цель, цели *цель, цели* – (n., fem., † *цѣль*) aim, goal, objective, purpose
цена, цены *цена, цены* – (n., fem., † *цѣна*) price, cost, value
цензор, цензора *цензор, цензора* – (n., masc.) censor
ценитель, ценителя *ценитель, ценителя* – (n., masc., † *цѣнитель*) appraiser (fem. *ценительница*)
цент, цента *цент, цента* – (n., masc.) cent
центнер, центнера *центнер, центнера* – (n., masc.) a quintal, a hundredweight (100 kilograms)
центр, центра *центр, центра* – (n., masc.) center
центральный *центральный* – (adj.) central
цепень, цепня *цепень, цепня* – (n., masc., † *цѣпень*) tapeworm, taenia

церковник, церковника *церковник, церковника* – (n., masc.) clergyman, ecclesiastic
церковноприходский *церковноприходский* – (adj., † *церковноприходскій*) parish, parochial
церковнославянский *церковнославянский* – (adj.) Old Church Slavonic
церковнослужитель, церковнослужителя *церковнослужитель, церковнослужителя* – (n., masc.) clergyman, churchman
церковный *церковный* – (adj.) of a church, of the church's
церковь, церкви *церковь, церкви* – (n., fem.) church (usually refers to an Orthodox church, as opposed to a *костёл*, a Polish Catholic church)
цесаревич, цесаревича *цесаревич, цесаревича* – (n., masc.) crown-prince of Russia
цесаревна, цесаревны *цесаревна, цесаревны* – (n., fem.) wife of the crown prince of Russia
цесарь, цесаря *цесарь, цесаря* – (n., masc.) Caesar; emperor
цессия, цессии *цессия, цессии* – (n., fem., † *цессія*) cession
Цеханув, Цеханува *Цеханув, Цеханува* – (n., masc., † *Цѣхановъ*) town of Ciechanów, Poland (see page 119); *цеханувский* († *цѣхановскій*) – of Ciechanowiec
цеховой *цеховой* – (adj.) of a guild or corporation
цианоз, цианоза *цианоз, цианоза* – (n., masc., † *ціанозъ*) cyanosis
цимбалист, цимбалиста *цимбалист, цимбалиста* – (n., masc., † *цымбалистъ*) cymbals-player
цинга, цинги *цинга, цинги* – (n., fem., † *цынга*) scurvy
цинготный *цинготный* – (adj., † *цынготный*) scorbutic
цирюльник, цирюльника *цирюльник, цирюльника* – (n., masc., † *цырюльникъ*) barber
цыган, цыгана *цыган, цыгана* – (n., masc., nom. pl. *цыгане*, gen. pl. *цыган*) Gypsy (fem. *цыганка*)
цымбалистъ *цымбалистъ* → цимбалист *цимбалист*
цынга *цынга* → цингацинга
цынготный *цынготный* → цинготный *цинготный*
цыновочник, цыновочника *цыновочник, цыновочника* – (n., masc.) mat-maker
цырюльникъ *цырюльникъ* → цирюльник *цирюльник*
цѣловальникъ *цѣловальникъ* → целовальник *целовальник*
цѣломудріе *цѣломудріе* → целомудрие *целомудрие*
цѣлый *цѣлый* → целый *целый*
цѣль *цѣль* → цель *цель*
цѣна *цѣна* → цена *цена*
цѣнитель *цѣнитель* → ценитель *ценитель*
цѣпень *цѣпень* → цепень *цепень*
Цѣхановъ *Цѣхановъ* → Цеханув *Цеханув*

Цюрих, Цюриха *Цюрих, Цюриха* – (n., masc.) Zürich, Switzerland
чародей, чародея *чародей, чародея* – (n., masc., *чародѣй*) magician, sorcerer (fem. *чародейка*)
† чарочник, чарочника *чарочник, чарочника* – (n., masc.) cupbearer at a noble's court
час, часа *час, часа* – (n., masc.) time, hour, o'clock (see pages 49-50); *в десять часов* – at ten o'clock
часовщик, часовщика *часовщик, часовщика* – (n., masc.) watchmaker
частный *частный* – (adj.) partial; private, e. g., *частный дом* – private home
часть, части *часть, части* – (n., fem., nom. pl. *части*, gen. pl. *частей*) part; section, district (of a town or community); department; *часть первая* (of church registers) birth register; *часть вторая*, the marriage register; *часть третья*, the death register (or, in some cases, the divorce register, in which case the death register is *часть четвёртая*, the fourth part) ; *часть воискъ* – military unit; *во всѣ части свѣта* – to all parts of the world
Чаусы, Чаусов *Чаусы, Чаусов* – (n., pl.) town of Chavusy, Belarus' (see page 126); *чаусский* or *чауский* – of Chausy/ Chavusy
чахотка, чахотки *чахотка, чахотки* – consumption, phthisis; *скоротечная чахотка* – galloping consumption
чашник, чашника *чашник, чашника* – (n., masc.) principal cupbearer (at the Czars' court)
чеботарь, чеботаря *чеботарь, чеботаря* – cobbler, shoemaker, bootmaker
чего *чего* – (demonstr. pron./adj., gen. of *что*, see page 42) of what?; of that
чей *чей* – (interr. pron.; fem. sing. *чья*, neut. *чьё*, pl. *чьи*) whose?
чеканщик, чеканщика *чеканщик, чеканщика* – (n., masc.) coiner, minter; chaser, caulker
человек, человека *человек, человека* – (n., masc., † *человѣкъ*, nom. pl. *люди*, gen. pl. *людей*) man, person
челядинец, челядинца*челядинец, челядинца* – (n., masc.) servant, domestic (fem. *челядинка*)
чем *чем* – (demonstr. pron./adj., instr. of *что*, see page 42) what?; that
чём *чём* – (demonstr. pron./adj., prep. of *что*, see page 42) what?; that
чемоданщик, чемоданщика *чемоданщик, чемоданщика* – (n., masc.) trunk-maker
чему *чему* – (demonstr. pron./adj., dat. of *что*, see page 42) what?; that
Ченстохова, Ченстоховы *Ченстохова, Ченстоховы* – (n., fem., † *Ченстоховъ*) town of Częstochowa, Poland (see page 119); *ченстоховский* – of Częstochowa

через *через* – (also *чрез*, prep. + acc.) over, across, through, by; (with expressions of time) in, after
черепичник, черепичника *черепичник, черепичника* – (n., masc.) tile-maker
Чериков, Черикова *Чериков, Черикова* – (n., masc.) town of Chèrikaŭ, Belarus' (see page 126); *чериковский* – (adj.) of Cherikov/Chèrikaŭ
Черкассы, Черкасс *Черкассы, Черкасс* – (n.) town of Cherkasy, Ukraine (see page 132); *черкасский* – (adj.) of Cherkasy
черкес, черкеса *черкес, черкеса* – (n., masc.) native of Circassia (fem. *черкешенка*)
чернец, чернца *чернец, чернца* – (n., masc.) monk, friar
Чернигов, Чернигова *Чернигов, Чернигова* – (n., masc.) town of Chernihiv, Ukraine (see page 133); *черниговский* – (adj.) of Chernigov/ Chernihiv
черница, черницы *черница, черницы* – (n., fem.) nun
Черновицы, Черновиц *Черновицы, Черновиц* – (n., pl.) Russian name of the town of Chernivtsi, Ukraine (see page 132); *черновицкий* – (adj.) of Chernovitsy/Chernivtsi
черногорец, черногорца *черногорец, черногорца* – (n., masc.) native of Montenegro
Черногория, Черногории *Черногория, Черногории* – (n., fem., † *Черногорія*) Montenegro
Чёрное море, Чёрного моря *Чёрное море, Чёрного моря* – (n., neut.) Black Sea
черноморский *черноморский* – (adj., † *черномоскій*) of the Black Sea, especially referring to a region of the Caucasus (see page 137)
черноокий *черноокий* – (adj., † *черноокій*) dark-eyed
чернорабочий, чернорабочего *черно-рабочий, чернорабочего* – (adj. used as a n., masc., † *чернорабочій*) drudge, one doing unskilled labor
черноризец, черноризца *черноризец, черноризца* – (n., masc.) friar, monk (fem. *черноризица*)
чёрный *чёрный* – (adj.) black, dark
чертёжник, чертёжника *чертёжник, чертёжника* – (n., masc.) draftsman (fem. *чертёжница*)
чесальщик, чесальщика *чесальщик, чесальщика* – (n., masc.) carder, comber (fem. *чесальщица*)
четверг, четверга *четверг, четверга* – (n., masc.) Thursday; *в четверг* – on Thursday; *по четвергам* – on Thursday, every Thursday
четвёртый *четвёртый* – (ordinal num./adj.) fourth
четверть, четверти *четверть, четверти* – (n., fem., nom. pl. *четверти*, gen. pl. *четвертей*) quarter, one fourth; a measure of grain, about 8 bushels
четыре, четырёх *четыре, четырёх* – (num.) four
четыреста, четырёхсот *четыреста, четырёхсот* – (num.) four hundred
четырёхсотый *четырёхсотый* – (ordinal num./adj.) four hundredth
четырнадцатый *четырнадцатый* – (ordinal num./adj.) fourteenth
четырнадцать, четырнадцати *четырнадцать, четырнадцати* – (num.) fourteen
чех, чеха *чех, чеха* – (n., masc.) Czech, Bohemian (fem. *чешка*)
Чигирин, Чигирина *Чигирин, Чигирина* – (n., masc.) town of Chyhyryn, Ukraine (se page 132); *чигиринский* – (adj.) of Chigirin/Chyhyryn
Чикаго *Чикаго* – (n., not declined) Chicago
чин, чина *чин, чина* – (n., masc.) rank; *нижніе чины* – rank and file
чиновник, чиновника *чиновник, чиновника* – (n., masc.) clerk, functionary (fem. *чиновница*); *чиновникъ Ломжинскаго Губернскаго Казначейства*, clerk in the Łomża Provincial Treasury Office; *чиновникъ таможный*, customs clerk; *чиновникъ по крестьянском дѣлам*, clerk in the Peasant Affairs Office
чинш, чинша *чинш, чинша* – (n., masc.) rent on a farm [in Poland, cmp. Polish *czynsz*]
число, числа *число, числа* – (n., neut., nom. pl. *числа*, gen. pl. *чисел*) number, quantity; date; *сего числа* – on this date; *въ томъ числѣ* – [included] in that number
чистильщик, чистильщика *чистильщик, чистильщика* – (n., masc.) cleaner, scourer, e. g. *чистильщик сапог* – bootblack (fem. *чистильщица*)
чистописец, чистописца *чистописец, чистописца* – (n., masc.) calligrapher, penman
читатель, читателя *читатель, читателя* – (n., masc.) reader (fem. *читательница*)
читать *читать* – (v.) to read
член, члена *член, члена* – (n., masc.) member, limb (referring to a body part)
членовредительство, членовредительство *членовредительство, членовредительство* – (n., neut.) maiming, mutilation
чрез *чрез* → через *через*
чтение, чтения *чтение, чтения* – (n., neut., † *чтеніе*) reading, lecture
что *что* – (demonstr. pron., for declension see page 42) what?; that, which; (conj.) that; *чѣмъ кончено дѣло* – how did the matter end?
чужеземец, чужеземца *чужеземец, чужеземца* – (n., masc.) alien, foreigner (fem. *чужеземка*)
чулочник, чулочника *чулочник, чулочника* – (n., masc.) stocking-maker (fem. *чулочница*)
чума, чумы *чума, чумы* – (n., fem.) plague, the Black Death; *бубонная чума* – bubonic plague; *лёгочная чума* – pneumonic plague
чьё *чьё* or чьи *чьи* or чья *чья* → чей *чей*
чѣмъ *чѣмъ* → что *что*

шабасный *шабасный* – (adj.) of the Sabbath (cmp. *шабашный*, of the day of rest); *въ шабасные дни* – on days of the Sabbath
† Шавли, Шавель *Шавли, Шавель* – (n., pl.) Russian name of Šiauliai, Lithuania (see page 124); *шавельскій* – (adj.) of Shavli/ Šiauliai
шадра, шадры *шадра, шадры* – (n., fem.) smallpox
шапочник, шапочника *шапочник, шапочника* – (n., masc.) hatter
шарманщик, шарманщика *шарманщик, шарманщика* – (n., masc.) organ-grinder
шахтёр, шахтёра *шахтёр, шахтёра* – (n., masc.) miner
Шват, Швата *Шват, Швата* – (n., masc.) Shevat, a month in the Jewish calendar (see page 47)
швед, шведа *швед, шведа* – (n., masc.) Swede (fem. *шведка*)
шведский *шведский* – (adj., † *шведскій*) Swedish
швейцар, швейцара *швейцар, швейцара* – (n., masc.) porter, doorkeeper
Швейцария, Швейцарии *Швейцария, Швейцарии* – (n., fem., † *Швейцарія*) Switzerland
швец, швеца *швец, швеца* – (n., masc.) sewer, tailor
Швеция, Швеции *Швеция, Швеции* – (n., fem., † *Швеція*) Sweden
швея, швеи *швея, швеи* – (n., fem.) seamstress
шелковод, шелковода *шелковод, шелковода* – (n., masc.) breeder of silkworms
шерстобой, шерстобоя *шерстобой, шерстобоя* – (n., masc.) wool-beater
шерсточёс, шерсточёса *шерсточёс, шерсточёса* – (n., masc.) wool-carder
шерстяник, шерстяника *шерстяник, шерстяника* – (n., masc.) worker who produces wool
шестидесятый *шестидесятый* – (ordinal num./adj.) sixtieth
шестисотый *шестисотый* – (ordinal num./adj.) six hundredth
шестнадцатый *шестнадцатый* – (ordinal num./adj.) sixteenth
шестнадцать, шестнадцати *шестнад-цать, шестнадцати* – (num.) sixteen
шестой *шестой* – (ordinal num./adj.) sixth
шесть, шести *шесть, шести* – (num.) six
шестьдесят, шестидесяти *шестьдесят, шестидесяти* – (num.) sixty; *шестьдесят один* – sixty-one; *шестьдесят первый* – sixty-first
шестьсот, шестисот *шестьсот, шестисот* – (num.) six hundred
шинкарь, шинкаря *шинкарь, шинкаря* – (n., masc.) innkeeper, barkeeper (fem. *шинкарка*)
широконосый *широконосый* – (adj.) broad-nosed
широта, широты *широта, широты* – (n., fem.) latitude; breadth
шифкарта, шифкарты *шифкарта, шифкарты* – (n., fem.) ship ticket
шихтмейстер, шихтмейстера *шихт-мейстер, шихтмейстера* – (n., masc.) mine foreman [cmp. Germ. *Schichtmeister*]
шкипер, шкипера *шкипер, шкипера* – (n., masc.) skipper [of a barge], shipmaster, boatswain [of a man-of-war]
школа, школы *школа, школы* – (n., fem.) school
школьник, школьника *школьник, школьника* – (n., masc.) schoolboy; among Jews, a synagogue attendant or sexton, also sometimes a title for the executive director of a Jewish community [Beider, *Dictionary of Jewish Surnames from the Russian Empire*]
школяр, школяра *школяр, школяра* – (n., masc.) schoolboy (fem. *школярка*)
шлифовщик, шлифовщика *шлифовщик, шлифовщика* – (n., masc.) polisher (fem. *шлифовщица*); also seen: *шлифовальщик*
шлюзник, шлюзника *шлюзник, шлюзника* – (n., masc.) lock-keeper, sluice-keeper
шляпник, шляпника *шляпник, шляпника* – (n., masc.) hatter
шляпница, шляпницы *шляпница, шляпницы* – (n., fem.) milliner
шляпочник, шляпочника *шляпочник, шляпочника* – (n., masc.) hat-maker
шляхта, шляхты *шляхта, шляхты* – (n., fem.) [Polish] nobility (Polish *szlachta*)
шляхтич, шляхтича *шляхтич, шляхтича* – (n., masc.) [Polish] nobleman (cmp. Polish *szlachcic*), fem. *шляхтянка*
шок, шока *шок, шока* – (n., masc.) shock (medical term)
шорник, шорника *шорник, шорника* – (n., masc.) saddler, saddle-maker
шоссе *шоссе* – (n., neut., not declined) highway, roadway
шоссейный *шоссейный* – (adj.) of a highway, roadway
шофёр, шофёра *шофёр, шофёра* – (n., masc., † *шоффёръ*) chauffeur
шпион, шпиона *шпион, шпиона* – (n., masc., † *шпіонъ*) spy (fem. *шпионка*)
шпорник, шпорника *шпорник, шпорника* – (n., masc.) spurrier
штаб-лекарь, штаб-лекаря *штаб-лекарь, штаб-лекаря* – (n., masc.) regimental surgeon
штаб-офицер, штаб-офицера *штаб-офицер, штаб-офицера* – (n., masc.) field officer
штаб-ротмистр *штаб-ротмистр* → штабс-ротмистр *штабс-ротмистр*
штабс-капитан, штабс-капитана *штабс-капитан, штабс-капитана* – (n., masc.) second captain

штабс-ротмистр *штабс-ротмистр* штабс-ротмистра *штабс-ротмистра* – (n., masc.) second captain of cavalry
шталмейстер, шталмейстера *штал-мейстер, шталмейстера* – (n., masc.) equerry, master of the horse [cmp. Germ. *Stallmeister*]
штат, штата *штат, штата* – (n., masc.) state; *Соединённые Штаты* – United States
штемпель, штемпеля *штемпель, штемпеля* – (n., masc.) stamp
штемпельмейстер, штемпельмейстера *штемпельмейстер, штемпель-мейстера* – (n., masc.) head clerk of a stamp office [cmp. Germ. *Stempelmeister*]
штопальщик, штопальщика *штопальщик, штопальщика* – (n., masc.) mender of old clothes or stockings, patcher, darner (fem. *штопальщица*)
штрафованный *штрафованный* – (part. from *штрафовать*, to fine) fined
штукатур, штукатура *штукатур, штукатура* – (n., masc.) plasterer
штурман, штурмана *штурман, штурмана* – (n., masc.) navigator, steersman, pilot
шулер, шулера *шулер, шулера* – (n., masc., nom. pl. *шулера*) cheat, card-sharp
шульга, шульги *шульга, шульги* – (n., masc. or fem.) left-handed person
шурин, шурина *шурин, шурина* – (n., masc., nom. pl. sometimes *шурья*) brother-in-law (wife's brother)
щедриноватый *щедриноватый* – (adj.) pock-marked
щетъ *щетъ* → счёт *счёт*
щёточник, щёточника *щёточник, щёточника* – (n., masc.) maker or seller of brushes
щитоносец, щитоносца *щитоносец, щитоносца* – (n., masc.) shield-bearer, armor-bearer, squire
Щучин, Щучина *Щучин, Щучина* – (n., masc.) town of Szczuczyn, Poland (see page 120), or Shchuchin, Belarus'; *щучинский* – (adj.) of Szczuczyn or Shchuchin
ѣздить *ѣздить* → ездить *ездить*
ѣздовой *ѣздовой* → ездовой *ездовой*
ѣздокъ *ѣздокъ* → ездок *ездок*
эквилибрист, эквилибриста *эквилибрист, эквилибриста* – (n., masc.) equilibrist, tightrope-walker
экзантема, экзантемы *экзантема, экзантемы* – (n., fem.) exanthema, a skin disease
экзарх, экзарха *экзарх, экзарха* – (n., masc., † *екзархъ*) (n., masc.) exarch, an Eastern Orthodox bishop ranking below a patriarch
экзекутор, экзекутора *экзекутор, экзекутора* – (n., masc.) usher; administrative clerk in a civil service office (fem. *экзекуторша*)
экзема, экземы *экзема, экземы* – (n., fem.) eczema
экзерцирмейстер, экзерцирмейстера *экзерцирмейстер, экзерцирмейстера* – (n., masc.) drill-officer [cmp. Germ. *Exerziermeister*]
эклампсия, эклампсии *эклампсия, эклампсии* – (n., fem., † *эклампсія*) eclampsia
эконом, эконома *эконом, эконома* – (n., masc.) housekeeper, steward (fem. *экономка* or *экономша*)
экстракт, экстракта *экстракт, экстракта* – (n., masc.) extract
Элул, Элула *Элул, Элула* – (n., masc.) Elul, name of a month in the Hebrew calendar (see page 47)
Эльба, Эльбы *Эльба, Эльбы* – (n., fem.) Elbe [river]
эльзасец, эльзасца *эльзасец, эльзасца* – (n., masc.) Alsatian (fem. *эльзаска*)
эмфизема, эмфиземы *эмфизема, эмфиземы* – (n., fem.) emphysema
эпилепсия, эпилепсии *эпилепсия, эпилепсии* – (n., fem., † *эпилепсія*) epilepsy
эпилептик, эпилептика *эпилептик, эпилептика* – (n., masc.) epileptic
† Эриванъ, Эривана *Эриванъ, Эривана* – (n., masc.) archaic name of the Armenian capital, now *Ереван*; *эриванскій* – of Erevan
эритема, эритемы *эритема, эритемы* – (n., fem.) erythema
эрцгерцог, эрцгергзога *эрцгерцог, эрцгергзога* – (n., masc.) archduke [cmp. Germ. *Erzherzog*] (fem. *эрцгерцогиня*, archduchess)
эскадрон, эскадрона *эскадрон, эскадрона* – (n., masc.) squadron
Эстляндія, *Эстляндія* → Эстония *Эстония*
эстонец, эстонца *эстонец, эстонца* – (n., masc.) Estonian (fem. *эстонка*)
Эстония, Эстонии *Эстония, Эстонии* – (n., fem., † *Эстонія*) Estonia (also called † *Эстляндія*)
этот *этот* – (demonstr. pron., for declension see page 42) this
ювелир, ювелира *ювелир, ювелира* – (n., masc.) jeweler
юг, юга *юг, юга* – (n., masc.) south; *юго-восток* – southeast; *юго-запад* – southwest
южный *южный* – (adj.) southern, south
юлианский *юлианский* – (adj., † *юліанскій*) Julian
юнга, юнги *юнга, юнги* – (n., masc.) cabin boy
юнкер, юнкера *юнкер, юнкера* – (n., masc.) military school cadet; Prussian junker [cmp. Germ. *Junker*]
юноша, юноши *юноша, юноши* – (n., masc., gen. pl. *юношей*) youth, lad
юный *южный* – (adj.) youthful, young
юрист, юриста *юрист, юриста* – (n., masc.) jurist, lawyer
я *я* – (personal pron., see page 42) I

явившийся *явившийся* – (part., from *явиться*, † *явившійся*) the one appearing

явиться *явиться* – (v.) to appear, to report; *явился* – [he] appeared, reported; *явились* – they appeared, reported

явка, явки *явка, явки* – (n., fem.) appearance, reporting in

яд, яда *яд, яда* - (n., masc.) poison

язва, язвы *язва, язвы* – (n., fem.) ulcer; *язва желудка* – stomach ulcer; *моровая язва* – plague; *сибирская язва* – anthrax

язык, языка *язык, языка* – (n., masc.) language; *по родному языку* – by native language

языковед, языковеда *языковед, языковеда* – (n., masc., † *языковѣдъ*) linguist, philologist

яичник, яичника *яичник, яичника* – (n., masc.) † egg-merchant; [in modern Russian] ovary

яичница, яичницыяичница, *яичница, яичницы* – (n., fem.) † egg-merchant, egg-merchant's wife; [in modern Russian] omelette

Якутия, Якутии *Якутия, Якутии* – (n., fem., † *Якутія*) region in Siberia (see page 137); *якутский* - of Yakutia

Ялта, Ялты *Ялта, Ялты* – (n. fem.) Yalta (see page 134); *ялтинский* – (adj.) of Yalta

Ямполь, Ямполя *Ямполь, Ямполя* – (n., masc.) town of Yampil', Ukraine (see page 132)

ямщик, ямщика *ямщик, ямщика* – (n., masc.) coachman

январь, января *январь, января* – (abbr. *янв.*, n., masc.) January

† Яновъ, Янова *Яновъ, Янова* – (n., masc.) town of Janów Lubelski, Poland (see page 120); *яновскій* – (adj.) of Janów

Ярослав, Ярослава *Ярослав, Ярослава* – (n., masc.) Jarosław, Poland

Ярославль, Ярославля *Ярославль, Ярославля* – (n., masc.) Yaroslavl', Russia (northeast of Moscow, see page 135); *ярославский* – (adj.) of Yaroslavl'

Яссы, Ясс *Яссы, Ясс* – (n., pl.) town of Iaşi, Moldova (see page 132); *ясский* – (adj.) of Iassy/Iaşi

VIII. AN INDEX OF FIRST NAMES

The following is a list of the first names most often seen in Russian-language documents encountered during the course of genealogical research. As such, it includes, in addition to native Russian names, Ukrainian names, and Russified forms of Jewish names and of names borne by ethnic Germans, Lithuanians, Poles, and Ukrainians—because those are names we encounter during research.

It does not, of course, include every Russian name, only the ones our experience suggests you're most likely to see and, perhaps, find unfamiliar. We've focused on names found in the western, European part of the Russian Empire, because most of the people we've dealt with had roots in that part of the Empire. Names of other origins tend to be rendered phonetically in the Cyrillic alphabet; so that if your names do not appear here, we hope the information we've given in Chapter One will still enable you to reconstruct their likely Russian spellings and recognize them when you encounter them.

In each entry the standard Russian spelling of the name is given in boldface type, both in print and italic form; we give both because the print forms are the ones most often seen in reference works you may use to supplement this book, but the italic forms resemble the handwritten versions you're most likely to encounter in actual records. Common variations you may see are given in some cases as well. These are followed by symbols to indicate gender, ♂ for masculine and ♀ for feminine. Next comes a brief indication of each name's linguistic origin, followed by its equivalent, if any, in other languages relevant to Russian research—usually English, Latin, Lithuanian, and Polish. If the form of the name in Ukrainian differs significantly from its spelling in Russian, we give that as well. Each entry ends with a listing of name days, if any, associated with that name in the Roman Catholic, Greek Catholic, and Russian Orthodox Churches, whenever we could find that information.

Feminine Forms

Many, many masculine names have feminine counterparts formed simply by adding *-a*. We have not tried to list all of those—only the ones that, in our experience, are most common. Incidentally, some of these feminine names ending in *-a* happen to be much more common than the corresponding masculine form; we have tried to note the most prominent examples.

Keeping these masculine and feminine names straight can be a problem, because most Russian masculine names form genitive and accusative forms by adding *-a*—so they look just like feminines. In such instances the grammatical points discussed on pages 33-45 are vital. If you read that a man was *сын Станислава и Болеславы*, you might easily be misled into thinking Stanisława was his mother, when in fact that is the name of the father; the mother is Bolesława. Only knowing how the endings differentiate forms will save you from error.

Linguistic and Ethnic Origins

The indications of linguistic origin are, of necessity, brief and generalized. To supply even a little detail on this subject for a decent sampling of names would require a full-sized book. Most names borne by readers of this book can be categorized as Germanic, Greek, Hebrew, Latin, Lithuanian, Romance, or Slavic in origin. (Please note, "Germanic" does not mean "German"! German is just one of many languages, including English, that developed from a common "Germanic" predecessor.)

The names identified as "Slavic" are ones used in similar forms in several Slavic languages, not just Russian. Many of the names associated primarily with the Eastern Slavs—Belarusians, Russians, and Ukrainians—derived originally from Greek via the Orthodox Church, and are quite unfamiliar to those of us with cultural ties to Western Europe, with its historical links to the Church of Rome and Latin.

Note that some names are categorized as "Hebrew," and others are "Jewish." The former refers to Biblical names that were Hebrew in origin, but later came to be used by Christians. Those names categorized as "Jewish" were ones Jews tended to use exclusively. While some were German or Slavic in origin, many came from the same Hebrew roots as the Christian versions, and differed from them in some way that made them more readily identifiable as Jewish. For instance, the Hebrew name שְׁלֹמֹה *Šlōmōh* came to be used by Christians in the forms *Salomon, Solomon,* etc. Jews of Eastern Europe often used the forms *Shloma* or *Shlama.* Christians turned Hebrew שְׁמוּאֵל *Šmū'ēl* into *Samuel;* Jews favored *Shmul.* There were Jews named *Salomon* or *Samuel,* but the forms *Shloma* or *Shmul* are more distinctively Jewish, and perhaps a bit less familiar to many English-speakers.

Jewish names are a rich field of study, on which whole books have been written. We cannot begin to do justice to them in a brief appendix. We have tried to give some basic information on the ones we've run into most often. But for detailed information on this subject, you would do well to consult a work devoted solely to Jewish names. In many cases we were guided by the analysis of Alexander Beider in his books *Dictionary of Jewish Surnames from the Russian Empire* and *Dictionary of Jewish Surnames from the Kingdom of Poland,* both published by Avotaynu, Inc. While no one is infallible when it comes to names, Beider's work is usually quite reliable.

Name Equivalents

In regard to name equivalents, please note that names printed in parentheses and marked with an asterisk, e. g., *(Stanley*)*, are ***not true equivalents*** of the names under which they are listed. *Lottie* is mentioned as an English "equivalent" of *Владислава,* Polish *Władysława,* but bears an asterisk, because these two names actually have nothing to do with each other, except for an accidental similarity in sound. We felt we had to mention these so-called "equivalents" because immigrants often changed their original names to them. English-speakers had so much trouble pronouncing Eastern European names that immigrants found many good, practical reasons to adopt "less foreign" names. There were no rules to this game; they could go by whatever name they liked, and often chose English names totally unlike the ones they were christened with. But researchers see certain correlations, and we felt we ought to point out such correlations, because they might sometimes help researchers make a connection. Please don't be misled, however: many of the names identified as "Slavic" in our list have no true equivalent in English, and it's potentially disastrous to make the mistake of assuming they do. ***If no English equivalent is given, there is none.***

Name Days

We have provided name days whenever possible because they can prove helpful in research. Children were often named after the saint on whose feast days they were baptized; so when other data is lacking, a name day may provide at least an approximation of an ancestor's date of birth.

Note that most days are associated with more than one saint, and there can be many saints with the same name; there are 170 name days for saints named *Иван*, for instance! Furthermore, different countries, and different parts of the same country, may venerate specific saints. So there can be no one standard, invariable list of name days applicable everywhere. The best we can do is list the most common name days as they are generally recognized.

For names used primarily by Russians, the Orthodox name days given here, marked with the sumbol ‡, are taken from information in *Словарь русских личных имен*, A. N. Tikhonov, L. Z. Boyarinova, and A. G. Ryzhova, Moscow: Shkola-Press, 1995, ISBN 5-88527-108-9, supplemented by information from another book with the same title by N. A. Petrovskiy (Moskva: Russkie slovari, 1996, ISBN 5-89216-003-3).

Name days as recognized *na Rusi,* "in Ruthenia," (for instance, by Greek Catholics) are marked with the symbol Ω and are taken from *Chronologia Polska,* ed. Bronisław Włodarski, Warszawa: 1957, Państwowe Wydawnictwo Naukowe. As one would expect, the Russian and Ukrainian name days usually overlap. Note that they are dated by the Julian calendar traditionally used by the Orthodox Churches; during the 19th century the Gregorian date was 12 days later than the Julian; during the 20th century the gap was 13 days. Thus for Russians the name day for *Савелий,* Saveliy, has traditionally fallen on June 17th; but by our reckoning it was on June 30th during the 20th century, June 29th during the 19th, and so on.

You cannot, however, always rely on that gap between the calendars. Roman Catholics celebrate the feast of St. Andrew the Apostle on November 30th—and so do Russians and Ukrainians! Apparently with some of the most prominent and universally recognized saints their name days were firmly set as falling on such and such a date, and that persisted through schism and turmoil. So a 12- or 13-day gap between name days on these two calendars is not absolutely reliable. But you will encounter one often enough that it is best to be prepared for it.

Roman Catholics living under Russian rule were almost always Poles or Lithuanians, so for Roman Catholic name days we relied primarily on information in *Księga naszych imion,* by J. Bubak, Wrocław-Warszawa-Kraków, 1993, supplemented in some cases with information from *Księga imion,* Bogdan Kupis *et al.*, Książka i Wiedza 1975. Feast days as recognized by the Roman Catholic Church are marked with the symbol ⊕.

When sources allowed us to identify a name with one major saint and a specific day—for instance, St. Andrew the Apostle and November 30—we gave that day and omitted all the days associated with various other St. Andrews. This is regrettable, as we generally prefer to give as much information as possible, and let you decide which is relevant. But the alternative is to devote space we don't have to a list that may only confuse you. If you want the details on which name day is associated with a specific saint—this Andrew rather than that one, St. John of the Cross rather than the Apostle John—you will need to consult a specialized work anyway.

Obviously there will be no saint's feast day for names associated primarily with Jews, unless the same name was also in common use among Christians.

Name Variants, Diminutives, Alternate Forms, etc.

Names cross-referenced to others with an arrow, e. g., *Адальберт* → **Альберт**, are either equivalents or variations of the names referenced. Thus *Адальберт* is a variation of the name *Альберт.* In some entries they are mentioned explicitly, especially if they are equivalents in another language. If they are diminutives or affectionate short forms—of which there are a plethora in the Slavic languages and in Yiddish—they may not be explicitly listed, but they can be regarded as variants of the name indicated. If you'd like more information, see one of the works cited in the Bibliography.

Alphabetical Order

Names are listed in this index in Russian alphabetical order, not that an English-speaker might expect. This may seem cruel, but the truth is, if you're going to get anywhere with Russian-language documents you have to start dealing with the language on its own terms. Trying to "Anglicize" it doesn't work well—you must "think Russian," at least to some extent. Part of adjusting to "thinking Russian" is getting used to the alphabet. In the long run, we think you'll do better if you plunge in and start coping with Russian alphabetical order.

Note, too, that we have tried to make this index fairly compact and easy to use, without utterly sacrificing accuracy. This affects the listing of names. If you're looking for *Танхель*, you will scan down the list till you come to any entry beginning *Тан-*. That will lead you to the entry for *Танхум*, of which *Танхель* is a hypocoristic form (i. e., a form of a name used as an endearment, such as "Annie" for "Anne," or "Ted" for "Theodore," in English). So we have listed *Танхель* under *Танхум*, and not given a separate cross reference, because that cross-reference would have appeared in the list directly above the name to which it refers. If you're looking for one, you're sure to find the other.

In other words, if looking for a separate cross-reference to a variant or diminutive of a specific name would lead you right to the main entry under which that variant is listed, why bother taking precious space to state the obvious? So as you scan this list for names, keep your eyes open! If you don't spot the specific name you're looking for, try the nearest entry for a name beginning with the same letters.

Summary

As we said earlier, this appendix cannot begin to do justice to the wealth of names encountered in research; that would require several thick volumes dedicated to the subject. We can only hope to provide a little information that will help you recognize and deal with the names you're most likely to encounter. That is what we try to do in the following pages.

Abbreviations and Symbols

These are the abbreviations and symbols used in the list:

(*) not a true equivalent	cmp. - compare	dim. - diminutive form
→ see this name, variant of	etc. - there are more like this	Eng. - English
< from	E. Slav. - Eastern Slavic	Lat. - Latin
⊕ nameday, Roman Catholic	Lith. - Lithuanian	Russ. - Russian
‡ nameday, Orthodox Church	Ω nameday, Greek Catholic	Ukr. - Ukrainian

ALPHABETICAL LIST OF SELECTED FIRST NAMES

А а

Аарон ***Аарон***, also *Арон* – ♂ Hebrew; Jewish diminutives include *Орель* and *Орка*. Eng. *Aaron*. ‡ 20 Jul.

Абакум → **Аввакум**

Абель ***Абель*** –♂ Hebrew, Eng. *Abel*.

Абрам → **Аврам**

Аввакум ***Аввакум***, also *Абакумъ* – ♂ Hebr. (Bibl. prophet *Habakkuk*). Ukr. *Абакум, Авакум*. ⊕ 15 Jan. ‡ 6 Jul, 2 Dec.

Август ***Август***, also *Аугуст* – ♂ Latin. Lat./Eng. *Augustus*, Lith. *Augustas*. ⊕ 3 Aug, 31 Oct.

Августа ***Августа*** – ♀ of **Август**. Eng./Lat. *Augusta*, Lith. *Augusta, Augustė*. ⊕ 27 Mar, 3 Aug, 31 Oct. ‡ 24 Nov.

Августин ***Августин*** – ♂ Latin. Eng. *Augustine*, Lat. *Augustinus*, Pol. *Augustyn*. ⊕ 28 Jan, 29 Apr, 28 May, 28 Aug. ‡ 15 Jun.

Августина ***Августина*** – ♀ of **Августинъ**. Eng./Lat./Lith. *Augustina*. ⊕ 9 Sep.

Авдей ***Авдей***, also *Авдий, Овадия*, † *Авдій, Авдњй, Овадія* – ♂ Hebr. Eng. *Obadiah*, Pol. *Abdiasz*, Ukr. *Овдій*. ‡ 31 Mar, 5 Sep, 19 Nov.

Авдоким → **Евдоким**

Авдотья → **Евдокия**

Авель ***Авель*** – ♂ Hebrew. ‡ 2 Jan.

Аверкий ***Аверкий*** – ♂ Latin. Ukr. *Аверкий, Авер'ян, Оверкій*. Ω 22 Oct. ‡ 22 Oct, etc.

Авив ***Авив*** –♂ Hebrew. Ω 15 Nov. ‡ 28 Nov, etc.

Авива ***Авива*** – ♀ of **Авив**.

Авигдор ***Авигдор*** –♂ Jewish, variant *Вигдор*.

Авксентий ***Авксентий***, also *Аксён* – ♂ Greek. Lat. *Auxentius*, Ukr. *Оксентій, Оксент*. ‡ 14 Feb, 18 Apr, 12 Jun, 13 Dec.

Авраам, Авраамий → **Аврам**

Аврам ***Аврам***, also *Абрам, Авраам, Авраамий, Авром, Аврум* – ♂ Hebrew. Eng. *Abraham*, Lith. *Abraomas, Abromas*, Ukr. *Аврам, Абрам,Оврам*. Ω 5 Feb, 29 Oct. ‡ 4 Feb, 29 Oct, etc.

Аврелия ***Аврелия***, † *Аврелія* – ♀ Latin. ⊕ 15 Oct.

Аврора ***Аврора*** – ♀ Latin.

Аврум → **Аврам**

Авсей → **Евсевий**

Агап ***Агап*** – ♂ Greek. Ukr. *Агапій*. Ω 18 Feb, 19 Mar, 19 Aug. ‡ 19 Aug, etc.

Агапит ***Агапит***, also † *Агапид* – ♂ Greek. Ukr. *Агапіт*. Ω & ‡ 17 Apr.

Агапия ***Агапия*** – ♀ Greek. Ukr. *Агапія*. Ω & ‡ 16 Apr.

Агапон → **Агафон**

Агата → **Агафия**

Агафия ***Агафия***, also *Агафья* – ♀ Greek. Eng. *Agatha*, Lith. *Agata*, Pol. *Agata [Агата]*, Ukr. *Агафія*. Ω 5 Feb. ‡ 5 Feb, 28 Dec.

Агафонъ ***Агафонъ***, † *Агавонъ* – ♂ Greek. Ukr. *Агафон, Агапон, Гапон*. Ω 21 Feb. ‡ 20 Feb, 2 Mar, 28 Aug.

Агафья → **Агафія**

Аггей ***Аггей*** † *Аггій, Аггњй* – ♂ from Hebrew *Haggai*. Ω & ‡ 16 Dec.

Аглай ***Аглай*** – ♂ Greek. ‡ 9 Mar.

Аглая ***Аглая*** – ♀ of **Аглай**. ‡ 19 Dec.

Агнесса ***Агнесса*** – ♀ Greek. Eng. *Agnes*, Lith. *Agnetė*, Pol. *Agnieszka [Агнешка]*, Ukr. *Агнеса*. ⊕ 21 Jan.

Агриппина ***Агриппина*** – ♀ Latin. Ω & ‡ 23 Jun.

Адальберт → **Альберт**

Адам ***Адам*** – ♂ Hebrew. Eng./Pol. *Adam*, Lith. *Adomas*. ⊕ 6 Apr, 24 Dec.

Аделаида ***Аделаида*** – ♀ Germanic. Eng. *Adelaide*, Lat. *Adelheidis, Adelais*, Pol. *Adelajda*, Ukr. *Аделаїда*. ⊕ 5 Feb, 11 Jun, 16 Dec.

Адольф ***Адольф*** – ♀ Germanic. Eng. *Adolph*, Lith. *Adolfas*. ⊕ 13 Feb, 17 Apr, 16 Dec.

Адриан ***Адриан***, also *Андриан*, † *Адріянъ* – ♂ Eng. *Adrian*, Ukr. *Адріан, Андріан, Андріян*. Ω & ‡ 26 Aug.

Азарій ***Азарий***, also *Азария*, † *Азарій, Азарія* – ♂ Hebrew. Ukr. *Азар, Азарій*. Ω 17 Dec. ‡ 3 Feb, 17 Dec.

Азриель ***Азриель*** † *Азріель* – ♂ Jewish.

Айзик, Айзык → **Исаакий**

Акакій ***Акакій***– ♂ Greek. Ω & ‡ 17 Apr, 7 & 19 May.

Акива → **Яков**

Акилина ***Акилина***, also *Акулина, Кулина* – ♀ Latin *Aquilina*. ‡ 7 Apr, 13 Jun.

Аким → **Иаким**

Аксель ***Аксель*** – ♂ Jewish, origin unclear.

Аксён → **Авксентий**

Акулина → **Акилина**

Александр ***Александр*** – ♂ Greek. Variants used by Jews included *Зандель, Зандер, Сандор, Санка, Сендер, Сендор*, and *Шандор*. The standard Russian dim. form is *Саша*. Eng./Lat. *Alexander*, Lith. *Aleksandras*, Pol. *Aleksander*, Ukr. *Олександр*. ⊕ 3 May. ‡ 16 Mar, 20 Apr, etc.

Александра ***Александра*** – ♀ of **Александр**. Ukr. *Олександра*. ⊕ 18 Mar, 18 May. Ω 21 Apr. ‡ 18 & 20 Mar, 23 Apr, 18 May, 6 Nov.

Алексей ***Алексей*** † *Алексњй* – ♂ Greek; standard Russian dim. *Алёша*. Eng. *Alexis*, Lat. *Alexius*, Lith. *Aleksys, Aleksius*, Pol. *Aleksy*, Ukr. *Олексій, Олекса*. ⊕ 17 Jul. Ω & ‡ 17 Mar.

Алойзий *Алойзий* –♂ Latin. Eng./Lat. *Aloysius*, Lith. *Alojzas*, Pol. *Alojzy*. ⊕ 21 Jun.

Алтер *Алтер* – ♂ Jewish, variant *Альтер*.

Альберт *Альберт*, also *Адальберт* or *Альбрехт* [rare] – ♂ Germanic; cmp. **Войтех**. Eng. *Albert*, Lat. *Albertus, Adalbertus*, Lith. *Albertas, Albrechtas*, Pol. *Albert, Wojciech*. ⊕ 18 Feb, 7 Aug, 21 Nov.

Альбин *Альбин* – ♂ Latin. Eng./Pol. *Albin*, Lat. *Albinus*, Lith. *Albinas*. Ukr. *Альбін*. ⊕ 1 Mar.

Альбина *Альбина* – ♀ of **Альбин**. Ukr. *Альбіна*. ⊕ 16 Dec.

Альбрехт → **Альберт**

Альтер → **Алтер**

Альфонс *Альфонс* – ♂ Germanic. Eng. *Alphonse*, Lat. *Alfonsus, Alphonsus*, Lith. *Alfonsas*, Pol. *Alfons*. ⊕ 1 Jun, 27 Jul, 1 & 16 Aug, 19 Sep, 30 & 31 Oct.

Амадей *Амадей* – ♂ Latin. Eng./Lat. *Amadeus*. ⊕ 28 Jan, 30 Mar, 10 Aug.

Амалия *Амалия* –♀ Germanic; Eng. *Amelia*, Lat./Lith. *Amalia*, Pol. *Amelia*. ⊕ 30 Mar, 20 Apr, 10 Jul, 7 Oct.

Амвросий *Амвросий*, also *Амбросий* – ♂ Greek. Eng. *Ambrose*, Lith. *Ambraziejus*, Pol. *Ambroży*, Ukr. *Амвросій, Амбросій, Амбрось*. ⊕ 7 Dec. Ω 7 Dec. ‡ 10 Oct, 7 Dec.

Амелфа → **Мамелфа**

Амос *Амос* – ♂ Hebrew. Eng. *Amos*. ⊕ 28 Jun. Ω & ‡ 15 Jun.

Ананий *Ананий* – ♂ Hebrew. Eng. *Ananias*, Ukr. *Ананій, Анань*. ⊕ 17 Jan, 14 Oct. Ω 27 Jan, 1 Oct, 1 & 17 Dec. ‡ 4 & 26 Jan, 1 Oct, 17 Dec.

Анастасий *Анастасий*, also *Настас, Настасий* – ♂ Greek. Eng./Lat. *Anastasius*, Lith. *Anastazas*, Pol. *Anastazy*, Ukr. *Анастас, Анастасій, Настас*. ⊕ 22 Jan, 11 Jun. Ω 22 Jan. ‡ 8 & 21 & 22 Jan, etc.

Анастасия, *Анастасия*, also *Настасия, Настасья* – ♀ of **Анастасий**. Eng. *Anastasia, Stacey*, Lat. *Anastasia*, Lith. *Anastazija*, Pol. *Anastazja*, Ukr. *Анастасія, Настасія, Настя*. ⊕ 15 Apr, 25 Dec. Ω 29 Oct, 22 Dec. ‡ 10 Mar, 29 Oct, 22 Dec

Анатолий *Анатолий* – ♂ Greek. Eng. *Anatole*, Lat. *Anatolius*, Lith. *Anatolijus*, Pol. *Anatol*, Ukr. *Анатолій, Анатоль*. ⊕ 3 Jun, 20 Nov. ‡ 23 Apr, 3 Jul, 28 Aug, 28 Sep, 20 Nov, etc.

Ангела *Ангела* –♀ Latin. Eng./Lat. *Angela*, Lith. *Anelė*, Pol. *Aniela [Анеля, Анюля]*. ⊕ 4 & 27 Jan, 28 & 30 Mar, 1 & 31 May, 10 & 21 Jul, 7 Oct, 18 & 20 & 30 Nov.

Ангелина *Ангелина* – ♀ Italian. Eng. *Angelina, Angeline*, Ukr. *Ангеліна*. ⊕ 29 Apr, 15 Jun, 15 & 21 Jul. ‡ 1 Jul, 10 Dec.

Андрей *Андрей* – ♂ Greek; standard Russian dim. *Андрюша*. Eng. *Andrew*, Lat. *Andreas*, Lith. *Andriejus*, Polish *Andrzej [Анджей], Jędrzej [Енджей]*, Ukr. *Андрій*. ⊕ & Ω & ‡ 30 Nov.

Анджей → **Андрей**

Андриан, Андріян → **Адриан**

Андрій → **Андрей**

Андроник *Андроник* – ♂ Greek. Ukr. *Андроник, Андрон*. Ω 22 Feb, 17 May, 12 Oct, 20 Oct. ‡ 4 Jan, 17 May, 13 Jun, 30 Jul, 9 & 12 Oct.

Андрюша → **Андрей**

Анеля → **Ангела**

Аникий *Аникий* – ♂ Greek. Ukr. *Оникій*. Ω & ‡ 4 Nov.

Аникита *Аникита* – ♂ Greek. Ω 12 Aug. ‡ 12 Aug, 7 Nov.

Анисий *Анисий* – ♂ Greek. ‡ 5 Mar.

Анисим → **Онисим**

Анисья *Анисья* – ♀ of **Анисий**. Ω & ‡ 30 Dec

Анна *Анна* – ♀ Hebrew; Jews often preferred the form *Хана [Ханна]* and variants from it such as *Гендель* and *Геня*. Eng. *Ann, Anna, Anne*, Lat. *Anna*, Lith. *Ona*, Ukr. *Анна, Ганна*. ⊕ 9 Jun, 26 Jul. Ω & ‡ 3 Feb, 25 Jul, 9 Sep, 9 Dec.

Антип *Антип* – ♂ Greek. Ω & ‡ 11 Apr.

Антон *Антон*, † *Антоній* – ♂ Latin. Eng. *Anthony*, Lat. *Antonius*, Lith. *Antanas*, Pol. *Antoni [Антони]*, Ukr. *Антін, Антон, Антоній*. ⊕ 13 Jun. Ω & ‡ 17 Jan, 12 Feb, etc.

Антонин *Антонин* – ♂ Latin. Ukr. *Антонін*. Ω 23 Oct. ‡ 22 Oct, 7 & 13 Nov, etc.

Антонина *Антонина* – ♀ of **Антон** or **Антонин**. Ukr. *Антоніна*. ⊕ 1 Mar, 3 May, 12 Jun, 27 Oct. Ω 10 Jun. ‡ 1 Mar, 10 & 13 Jun.

Антония *Антония* – ♀ of **Антон**. Eng. *Antonia, Antoinette*, Lith. *Antanina, Antanė, Antonija*, Pol. *Antonia*, Ukr. *Антонія*. ⊕ 1 Mar, 3 May, 12 Jun, 27 Oct.

Анфим *Анфрим* – ♂ Greek. Ω & ‡ 3 Sep.

Анфиноген → **Афиноген**

Анфиса *Анфиса* – ♀ Greek. Ukr. *Анфіса*. ‡ 12 Apr, 27 Jul, 22 & 27 Aug, 8 Dec.

Аншель *Аншель* – ♂ Jewish.

Анюля → **Ангела**

Аполлинарий *Аполлинарий* – ♂ Latin. Lat. *Apollinaris*, Lith. *Apolinaras*, Pol. *Apolinary*, Ukr. *Аполлінарій*. Ω 5 Jan. ‡ 23 Jul.

Аполлинария *Аполлинария* – ♀ of **Аполлинарий**. Ω & ‡ 5 Jan.

Аполлон *Аполлон*, † *Аполоній* – ⊕ 10 Apr, 18 Apr. Ω & ‡ 14 Dec.

Аполлония *Аполлония* – ♀ of **Аполлон**. Eng. *Apollonia, (Pearl*)*, Lat. *Apollonia*, Lith. *Apolonija, Apolė*, Pol. *Apolonia*, Ukr. *Аполлонія*. ⊕ 9 Feb.

Ардалион *Ардалион* – ♂ Latin. Ukr. *Ардаліон*. ‡ 27 Apr.

Арест ***Арест*** – ♂ Greek. Ω 10 Nov, 13 Dec.
Ариель ***Ариель*** † *Аріель* – ♂ Jewish.
Арий ***Арий*** – ♂ Hebrew. ‡ 5 Jun.
Аркадий ***Аркадий*** – ♂ Greek. Eng./Lat. *Arcadius*, Lith. *Arkadijus, Arkadas*, Pol. *Arkadiusz*, Ukr. *Аркадій*. ⊕ 12 Jan, 13 Nov. ‡ 26 Jan, 6 Mar, 14 Aug, 18 Sep, 13 Dec.
Арнольд ***Арнольд*** – ♂ Germanic; also used is the variant *Арнгольд*. ⊕ 19 Feb, 18 Jul, 9 Oct.
Арон → **Аарон**
Арсений ***Арсений***, also *Арсен*, † *Арсеній* – ♂ Greek. Eng. *Arsenio*, Lat. *Arsenius*, Lith. *Arsenijas*, Pol. *Arseniusz*, Ukr. *Арсен, Арсеній*. ⊕ 19 Jul, 30 Oct. Ω & ‡ 8 May.
Артемий ***Артемий*** –♂ Greek. Lat. *Artemius*, Pol. *Artemiusz*, Ukr. *Артем, Артемій, Артемон*. ⊕ 2 Nov, etc. Ω & ‡ 20 Oct.
Архипп ***Архипп*** – ♂ Greek. Ukr. *Архип*. Ω 19 Feb. ‡ 4 Jan, 19 Feb, 19 Jun, 6 Sep, 22 Nov.
Арье ***Арье*** – ♂ Jewish.
Асна → **Оснас**
Астахий → **Евстахий**
Аугуст → **Август**
Афанасий ***Афанасий*** † *Аѳанасій* – ♂ Greek *Athanasios*. Eng./Lat. *Athanasius*, Lith. *Atanazas*, Pol. *Atanazy*, Ukr. *Атанас, Атанасій, Опанас, Панас, Танас, Танасій*. ⊕ 2 May, 5 Jul, 15 Jul. Ω 18 Jan, 22 Feb, 2 May, 4 May, 23 Jun. ‡ 18 Jan, 22 Feb, 2 May, 22 Aug, 5 & 12 Sep, 24 Oct., etc.
Афанасия ***Афанасия*** – ♀ of **Афанасий**. Ukr. *Афанасія*. ‡ 31 Jan, 12 Apr, 9 Oct, 6 Nov.
Афиноген ***Афиноген*** † *Анфиноген* – ♂ Greek. Ukr. *Афіноген*. Ω 7 Dec. ‡ 16 Jul.
Афросинья → **Ефросиния**
Ахилл ***Ахилл*** – ♂ Greek *Achilles*. Ukr. *Ахіллій, Ахіла*. ⊕ 12 May. ‡ 15 May, 28 Aug.
Ашер → **Ошер**

Б б

Базилій → **Василий**
Бальбина ***Бальбина*** – ♀ Latin. Eng./Pol. *Balbina*. ⊕ 11 & 31 Mar, 2 Dec.
Барбара → **Варвара**
Бартломей, Бартоломій → **Варфоломей**
Барух ***Барух***, also *Борух* – ♂ primarily Jewish.
Басилій → **Василий**
Басшева ***Басшева*** – ♀ Jewish; variants include *Баша, Шева, Шейва, Шейвель*. Eng. *Bathsheba*.
Бася ***Бася*** – ♀ Jewish; may be a variant of **Басшева**.
Баша → **Басшева**
Беатриса ***Беатриса*** – ♀ Latin. ⊕ 29 Jul.
Бейла ***Бейла*** – ♀ Jewish.
Бейнус ***Бейнус*** – ♂ Jewish.
Бейрах, ***Бейрах*** – ♂ Jewish.
Белла ***Белла*** – ♀ Latin.
Бенедикт → **Венедикт**
Бенигна ***Бенигна*** – ♀ Latin. Eng./Lat./Pol. *Benigna*, Lith. *Benigna, Benyna*. ⊕ 20 Jun.
Бенцион ***Бенцион***, also *Бенцян*, † *Бенціонъ* or *Бенціянъ* – ♂ Jewish ("son of Zion").
Бенямин → **Вениамин**
Бер ***Бер*** – ♂ Jewish, with dim. such as *Берек, Берель, Берко, Берля, Берман*, etc.
Бернард ***Бернард***, also *Бернгард* – ♂ Germanic. Eng./Pol. *Bernard*, Lat. *Bernardus*, Lith. *Bernardas*. ⊕ 20 May, 15 Jun, 2 Jul, 4 Dec.
Берта ***Берта*** – ♀ Germanic. Eng. *Bertha*, Pol. *Berta*.
Бесель ***Бесель*** – ♀ Jewish; variants include *Песа, Песель, Песка, Песля*, and *Песя*.
Бецалель ***Бецалель*** – ♂ Jewish; variants include *Цалель* and *Цаля*.
Бина ***Бина*** – ♀ Jewish; variants include *Бинка*.
Бинямин → **Вениамин**
Блажей → **Влас**
Блума ***Блума*** – ♀ Jewish; variants include *Блюма* and *Блюмка*.
Богдан ***Богдан*** – ♂ Slavic. Lat./Lith. *Bogdanus*, Pol. *Bogdan*. ⊕ 6 Feb, 19 Mar, 17 Jul, 10 & 31 Aug, 2 Sep. ‡ (considered same as **Федот**).
Богдана ***Богдана*** – ♀ of **Богдан**. ⊕ 6 Feb, 6 Nov.
Богумил ***Богумил*** – ♂ Slavic. Lat. *Bogumilus*, Lith. *Bogumilas*, Pol. *Bogumił*. ⊕ 10 Jun.
Богумила Богумила – ♀ of **Богумил.** Lat. *Bohumila*, Pol. *Bogumiła*. ⊕ 10 Jun, 20 Dec.
Богуслав ***Богуслав*** – ♂ Slavic. Lat. *Boguslaus*, Pol. *Bogusław*. ⊕ 29 Apr, 18 Dec.
Богуслава ***Богуслава*** – ♀ of **Богуслав.** Lat. *Bogusla[v]a*, Pol. *Bogusław*. ⊕ 29 May.
Божена ***Божена*** – ♀ Slavic. Cz. *Božena*. Pol. *Bożena*. ⊕ 13 Mar.
Болеслав ***Болеслав*** – ♂ Slavic. Lat. *Boleslaus*, Lith. *Boleslovas*, Pol. *Bolesław*. ⊕ 19 Aug.
Болеслава, ***Болеслава*** – ♀ Slavic. Lat. *Bolesla[v]a*, Pol. *Bolesława*. ⊕ 19 Aug.
Бона ***Бона*** – ♀ often Jewish, but not exclusively; variants include *Буна* and *Буня*. ⊕ 14 & 29 May.
Бонифатий → **Вонифатий**
Боримир ***Боримир*** – ♂ Slavic.
Борис ***Борис*** – ♂ origin uncertain. Eng. *Boris*, Pol. *Borys*. ⊕ 2 May. Ω & ‡ 2 May, 24 Jul.
Борислав ***Борислав*** – ♂ Slavic. ⊕ 19 Jun.
Борух → **Барух**
Боян ***Боян*** – ♂ Slavic. ⊕ 5 Sep. ‡ 28 Mar.
Брайна, Брайндель, Брана, Брейна → **Бройна**
Бригида ***Бригида*** – ♀ Celtic. Eng. *Bridget*, Lat. *Brigida*, Lith. *Brigita, Brigė, Gita*, Pol. *Brygida*. ⊕ 1 Feb, 23 Jul.

Бройна ***Бройна***– ♀ Jewish, variants include *Брайна, Брайндел, Брана, Брейна, Брона, Рона, Ронка, Роня*, etc.

Бронислав ***Бронислав*** – ♂ Slavic. Lat. *Bronislaus*, Lith. *Bronislovas, Bronys*, Pol. *Bronisław*, Ukr. *Бронiслав*. ⊕ 1 Sep.

Бронислава ***Бронислава*** – ♀ Slavic. Lat. *Bronislaa, Bronislava*, Lith. *Bronislova, Bronė*, Pol. *Bronisława*, Ukr. *Бронiслава*. ⊕ 1 Sep.

Броха ***Броха*** – ♀ Jewish, variants include *Бруха*.

Буна, Буня → **Бона**

Буним ***Буним*** –♂ Jewish.

В в

Вавила ***Вавила*** also *Вавула* – ♂ Greek. Ukr. *Вавило, Вавил*. Ω 4 Sep. ‡ 24 Jan, 4 Sep.

Вавржинец, Вавржынец → **Лаврентий**

Вадим ***Вадим*** – ♂ Russian. ‡ 9 Apr.

Валентин ***Валентин*** – ♂ Latin. Eng. *Valentine*, Lat. Valentinus, Lith. *Valentinas, Valentas*, Pol. *Walenty*. Ukr. *Валентин, Валентiй, Валент*. ⊕ 14 Feb. ‡ 24 Apr, 6 & 30 Jul.

Валентина ***Валентина*** – ♀ of **Валентин**. Eng. *Valentine*, Lat./ Lith. *Valentina*, Pol. *Walentyna*. ⊕ 25 Jul. ‡ 10 Feb, 16 Jul.

Валериан ***Валериан***, also *Валерьян*, † *Валерiанъ* – ♂ Latin. Eng. *Valerian*, Lat. *Valerianus*, Lith. *Valerijonas, Valius*, Pol. *Walerian*, Ukr. *Валер'ян, Валерiан*. ⊕ 29 Jan, 14 Apr. ‡ 21 Jan, 1 Jun, 13 Sep, 22 Nov.

Валерий ***Валерий*** also *Валер*, † *Валерiй* – ♂ Latin. Lat. *Valerius*, Lith. *Valerijus, Valeras*, Pol. *Walery*, Ukr. *Валерiй*. ⊕ 29 Jan, 14 Apr, 15 Dec. ‡ 9 Mar, 7 Nov.

Валерия, ***Валерия*** – ♀ of **Валерий**. Eng. *Valerie*, Lat. *Valeria*, Lith. *Valerija*, Pol. *Waleria*, Ukr. *Валерiя*. ⊕ 28 Apr, 5 Jun, 9 Dec.

Валтасар ***Валтасар*** – ♂ Babylonian. Eng. *Balthasar*, Lat. *Balt[h]assar*, Lith. *Baltazaras*, Pol. *Baltazar*. ⊕ 6 Jan.

Вальтер ***Вальтер*** – ♂ Germanic. Eng. *Walter*, Latin *Gualterus, Waltherus*, Lith. *Valteris*. ⊕ 2 May, 5 Jun.

Ванда ***Ванда*** – ♀ Polish. Eng./Pol. *Wanda*, Lith. *Vanda*. ⊕ 23 Jun.

Варвара ***Варвара***, also *Барбара* – ♀ Greek. Eng./ Lat./Pol. *Barbara*, Lith. *Barbora*. ⊕ & Ω & ‡ 4 Dec.

Варлаам ***Варлаам*** also *Варлам, Варламий* – ♂ origin unclear. Ukr. *Варлам, Орлам*. Ω 16 Nov. ‡ 19 Jun, 28 Sep, 6 & 19 Nov.

Варнава ***Варнава*** – ♂ Aramaic. Eng. *Barnabas, Barnaby*, Lat./Lith. *Barnabas*, Pol. *Barnaba*. ⊕ 11 Jun. Ω 11 Jun, 24 Aug.

Варфоломей ***Варфоломей*** also *Вахрамей* † *Варѳоломей* – ♂ Aramaic. Eng. *Bartholomew*, Lat. *Bartholomeus*, Lith. *Baltramiejus, Baltras, Baltrus*, Pol. *Bartłomiej [Бартломей]*, Ukr. *Варфоломiй, Бартоломiй*. ⊕ 24 Aug, 11 Nov. Ω 11 Jun, 24 Aug. ‡ 22 Apr, 11 & 30 Jun, 25 Aug.

Василий ***Василий***, sometimes † *Басилiй* – ♂ Greek. Eng. *Basil*, Lat. *Basilius*, Lith. *Bazilijus, Baziliejus*, Pol. *Bazyli [Базилiй]*, Ukr. *Василь*. ⊕ 2 Jan, 14 & 20 May, 14 Jun, 1 Oct. Ω 1 & 2 Jan, 27 Feb, 7 & 22 & 24 Mar, 12 & 26 Apr, 22 May. ‡ 1 Jan, etc.

Васса ***Васса*** – ♀ origin unclear. ‡ 21 Aug.

Вахрамей → **Варфоломей**

Вацлав ***Вацлав***, also *Венцеслав, Вяцеслав* and *Вячеслав* – ♂ Slavic. Eng. *Wenceslaus*, Lat. *Venceslaus*, Lith. *Vaclovas, Vacys, Vacius*, Pol. *Wacław, Więcesław*, Ukr. *Вацлав, В'ячеслав*. ⊕ & Ω & ‡ 28 Sep.

Вацлава ***Вацлава***, also *Венцеслава, Вячеслава* – ♀ of **Вацлав**. Latin *Venceslava*, Lith. *Vaclova, Vaclava*, Pol. *Wacława*. ⊕ 28 Sep.

Векла → **Фёкла**

Велвель → **Вольф**

Венантий ***Венантий*** – ♂ Latin. Lat. *Venantius*, Lith. *Venancijus, Venantas*, Pol. *Wenancjusz*. ⊕ 1 Apr, 14 Dec.

Вендимиан ***Вендимиан*** – ♂ Latin. Ω & ‡ 1 Feb.

Венедикт ***Венедикт***, also *Бенедикт* and *Венедей* – ♂ Latin. Eng. *Benedict*, Lat. *Benedictus*, Lith. *Benediktas*, Pol. *Benedykt*. ⊕ 16 Apr, 11 Jul. Ω 27 Mar. ‡ 14 Mar.

Венедикта ***Венедикта*** – ♀ of **Венедикт**. Eng./Lat. *Benedicta*, Lith. *Benedikta*, Pol. *Benedykta*. ⊕ 6 May, 2 Jul.

Венедим ***Венедим*** – ♂ Latin. Ω & ‡ 18 May.

Вениамин ***Вениамин***, also *Бенямин, Бинямин, Веньямин, Венямин* – ♂ Hebrew; often Jewish, but not exclusively. Eng. *Benjamin*, Ukr. *Венiамiн*. ⊕ 3 Mar, 19 Dec. ‡ 14 Jan, 31 Mar, 28 Aug, 13 Oct.

Венцеслав → **Вацлав**

Венцеслава → **Вацлава**

Вера ***Вера***, † *Вѣра* – ♀ Latin. Eng./Lat. *Vera*, Ukr. *Вiра*. ⊕ 30 Sep. ‡ 17 Sep.

Веремiй → **Еремий**

Вереника **Вереника** – ♀ Greek. Eng. *Bernice*, Lat. *Berenice*, Pol. *Berenika*. ⊕ 20 Apr.

Вероника ***Вероника*** – ♀ Greek. Eng./Lat. *Veronica*, Lith. *Veronika*, Pol. *Weronika*, Ukr. *Веронiка*. ⊕ 13 Jan, 4 Feb, 17 May, 9 Jul. ‡ 12 Jul.

Вигдор → **Авигдор**

Викентий *Викентий*, † *Викентiй* – ♂ Latin. Eng. *Vincent*, Lat. *Vincentius*, Lith. *Vincentas, Vincas*, Pol. *Wincenty*, Ukr. *Вiкент, Вiкентiй*. ⊕ 22 Jan, 8 Mar, 19 Jul. Ω & ‡ 11 Nov.

Викентия ***Викентия***, † *Викентія* – ♀ of *Викентий*. Eng./Lat. *Vincentia*, Lith. *Vincenta*, Pol. *Wincentyna*. ⊕ 7 May.

Виктор ***Виктор*** also *Викторий* – ♂ Latin; sometimes used by Jews. Eng. *Victor*, Lat. *Victor*, *Victorius*, Lith. *Viktoras*, Pol. *Wiktor*, Ukr. *Віктор*. ⊕ 28 Jul. Ω & ‡11 Nov.

Виктория ***Виктория*** – ♀ Latin. Eng./Lat. *Victoria*, Lith. *Viktorija*, Pol. *Wiktoria*, Ukr. *Вікторія*. ⊕ 20 May, 23 Dec.

Вильгельм ***Вильгельм*** – ♂ Germanic. Eng. *William*, *Will*, *Willie*, *Bill*, Lat. *Guilelmus*, Lith. *Vilhelmas*, *Vilimas*, *Vilius*, Pol. *Wilhelm*. ⊕ 25 Jun.

Вильгельмина ***Вильгельмина*** – ♀ of **Вильгельм**. Eng. *Wilhelmina*, *Willa*, *Wilma*, Lat. *Wilhelmina*, Lith. *Vilhelma*, *Vilhelmina*, Pol. *Wilhelmina*. ⊕ 26 May, 25 Oct.

Виргиния ***Виргиния*** – ♀ Latin. Eng./Lat. *Virginia*, Lith. *Virginija*, Pol. *Wirginia*, Ukr. *Віргінія*. ⊕ 8 Aug.

Виссарион ***Виссарион*** – ♂ Greek. Ukr. *Віссаріон*. ‡ 6 Jun.

Вит ***Вит*** –♂ Latin. Eng. *Guy*, Latin *Vitus*, Lith. *Vitas*, Pol. *Wit*. ⊕ 15 Jun. Ω 15 Jun.

Вита ***Вита*** – ♀ primarily Jewish, but can be ♀ of **Вит**. Ukr. *Віта*.

Виталий ***Виталий***, † *Виталій* – ♂ Latin. Lat. *Vitalis*, Lith. *Vitalis*, *Vitalius*, Pol. *Witalis*, Ukr. *Віталій*. ⊕ 20 Oct. ‡ 25 Jan, 22 & 28 Apr.

Витольд *Витольд* – ♂ Lithuanian or Germanic. Eng. *Vitold*, Latin *Witoldus*, Lith. *Vytautas*, Pol. *Witold*, Ukr. *Вітольд*. ⊕ 15 Jun, 12 Oct, 12 Nov.

Вікент, *Вікентій* → **Викентий**

Віктор → **Виктор**

Вікторія → **Виктория**

Віра → **Вера**

Віргінія → **Виргиния**

Віссаріон → **Виссарион**

Віталій → **Виталий**

Владимир ***Владимир***, † *Владиміръ* – ♂ Slavic. Eng. *Vladimir*, Lat. *Vladimirus*, *Vlodimirus*, Lith. *Vladimiras*, Pol. *Włodzimierz*, Ukr. *Володимир*. ⊕ 16 Jan, 25 Sep. ‡ 22 May, 25 Jul, 4 Oct.

Владислав ***Владислав*** – ♂ Slavic. Eng. *Ladislas*, Lat. *Vladislaus*, *Ladislaus*, Lith. *Vladislovas*, Pol. *Władysław*. ⊕ 27 Jun, 25 Sep. ‡ 24 Sep.

Владислава ***Владислава*** – ♀ of **Владислав**. Lat. *Vladisla[v]a*, *Ladisla[v]a*, Eng. *(Lottie*)*, Lith. *Vladislova*, *Vladislava*, Pol. *Władysława*. ⊕ 27 Jun, 25 Sep.

Влас ***Влас***, also *Власий* † *Власій* – ♂ Latin. Eng. *Blaise*, Lat. *Blasius*, Lith. *Blažiejus*, *Blažys*, Pol. *Błażej [Блажей]*, Ukr. *Влас*, *Улас*, *Власій*. ⊕ 3 Feb. Ω 11 Feb, 31 Mar. ‡ 3 & 11 Feb.

Войтех ***Войтех*** † *Войтѣхъ* – ♂ regarded as Slavic equivalent of **Альберт**, but rare in Russian; it's usually a Russified form of Polish *Wojciech*. Eng. *Adalbert*, *Albert*, Lat. *Adalbertus*, Lith. *Vaitiekus*, *Vaitkus*, *Adalbertas*, Pol. *Wojciech*. ⊕ 23 Apr.

Володимир → **Владимир**

Волько → **Вольф**

Вольф ***Вольф***, also *Вульф* – ♂ Jewish; variants include *Велвель* and *Волько*.

Вонифатий ***Вонифатий***, also *Бонифатий* – ♂ Latin. Eng. *Boniface*, Lat. *Bonifatius*, Lith. *Bonifacijus*, *Bonifacas*, Pol. *Bonifacy*, Ukr. *Воніфатій*, *Боніфатій*, *Боніфат*. ⊕ 14 May, 5 Jun. ‡ 19 Dec.

Всеволод ***Всеволод*** – ♂ Russian. ‡ 11 Feb, 22 Apr, 27 Nov.

Вульф → **Вольф**

Вѣра → **Вера**

Вяцеслав, *Вячеслав*, *В'ячеслав* → **Вацлав**

Гг

Гавел ***Гавел*** – ♂ Latin. Eng. *Gall*, Lat. *Gallus*, Pol. *Gaweł*, Ukr. *Гаваил*, *Гавел*. ⊕ 16 Oct.

Гавриил ***Гавриил***, † *Гавріилъ*, also *Гавриел*, *Гаврил*, *Гавриило*. – ♂ Hebrew, used by Christians and Jews. Eng./Lat. *Gabriel*, Lith. *Gabrielius*, *Gabrys*, Pol. *Gabriel*, *Gabryel*, Ukr. *Гаврило*. ⊕ 27 Feb, 16 & 24 Mar, 29 Sep, 19 Oct. Ω & ‡ 26 Mar, 12 Jul, 8 Nov.

Гадас ***Гадас***, also *Годес* – ♀ Jewish (cmp. *Hadassah*).

Галактион ***Галактион*** – ♂ Greek. Ukr. *Галактіон*. Ω 5 Nov. ‡ 12 Jan, 22 Jun, 24 Sep, 5 Nov.

Галина ***Галина*** – ♀ Greek. In some cases a Russification of Polish *Halina*, in others a variation of *Helena* or some similar name. ⊕ 1 Jul. ‡ 10 Mar, 16 Apr.

Ганна → **Анна**

Гапон → **Агафон**

Гарасим → **Герасим**

Гарцел ***Гарцел*** – ♂ Jewish.

Гдаля → **Гедалья**

Гедалья ***Гедалья***, also *Гдаля* – ♂ Jewish.

Гедеон ***Гедеон*** – ♂ Hebrew. Eng. *Gideon*, Lat. *Gedeon*, Lith. *Gedeonas*, Pol. *Gedeon*. ⊕ 28 Mar, 10 Oct.

Гелена ***Гелена*** – ♀ Greek; this will usually be either Ukr. *Гелена* or a Russification of Polish *Helena*, since the standard Russian form of this name is **Елена** (short form *Лена*).

Гелий – ♂ Latin. ‡ 4 Jul.

Гельман ***Гельман***, also *Ильман*, *Эльман* – ♂ Jewish.

Гендель → **Анна** and **Ханох**

Гензель ***Гензель*** – ♂ Jewish; variants include *Геншель*. Pol. *Henszel*, *Henzel*.

Геннадий ***Геннадий*** – ♂ Greek. Ukr. *Геннадій.* ‡ 23 Jan, 9 Feb, 23 May, 31 Aug, 4 Dec.

Геновефа ***Геновефа*** – ♀ Romance. Eng. *Genevieve (Jeanette, Jennifer*),* Lat. *Genovefa,* Lith. *Genovaitė,* Pol. *Genowefa.* ⊕ 3 Jan.

Генриетта ***Генриетта*** – ♀ French; Eng. *Henrietta, Harriet,* Lith. *Henrieta,* Pol. *Henryka.* ⊕ 16 Mar.

Генрих ***Генрих*** – ♂ Germanic (cmp. *Heinrich*). Eng. *Henry,* Latin *Henricus,* Lith. *Henrikas, Enrikas,* Pol. *Henryk,* Ukr. *Генріх.* ⊕ 19 Jan, 19 Feb, 2 Mar, 10 Jun, 15 Jul.

Гента → **Ентель**

Геншель → **Гензель**

Геня → **Анна** or **Геновефа**

Георгий, ***Георгий*** – ♂ Greek, an alternate form of the name Russians generally use in the form **Юрий**, q. v. Cz. *Jiří,* Eng. *George, (Jerry*),* Lat. *Georgius,* Lith. *Jurgis, Juris, Juras,* Pol. *Jerzy,* Ukr. *Георгій.* ⊕ 23 Apr. Ω & ‡ 23 Apr.

Геракл ***Геракл*** – ♂ Greek (cmp. *Heracles*). Ukr. *Гераклій, Геракл.*

Герасим ***Герасим*** – ♂ Greek. Lat. *Gerasimus,* Ukr. *Гарасим, Герасим.* Ω 4 Mar. ‡ 24 & 29 Jan, 4 Mar, 1 May.

Гервасий ***Гервасий,*** † *Гервасій* – ♂ Latin. Ukr. *Гервасій.* Ω 14 Oct.

Герман ***Герман*** – ♂ from Latin *germanus,* but can also be a Russified form of Germanic *Herman.* Eng. *Herman,* Latin *Hermannus,* Lith. *Hermanas, Ermonas.* ⊕ 7 Apr, 24 Sep. Ω & ‡ 12 May.

Гертруда ***Гертруда*** – ♀ Germanic. Eng. *Gertrude,* Lat. *Gertrudis,* Lith. *Gertrūda, Gendruta,* Pol. *Gertruda.* ⊕ 17 Mar, 16 Nov.

Герц ***Герц*** – ♂ Jewish (*Herts* or *Herc*).

Герш ***Герш,*** also *Гершель, Гершко* – ♂ Jewish. Pol. *Hersz, Herszel, Herszko,* etc.

Гершель → **Герш**

Гершен → **Гершон**

Гершко → **Герш**

Гершон ***Гершон,*** also *Гершен* – ♂ Jewish.

Гилель ***Гилель*** –♂ Jewish (cmp. *Hillel*).

Гильдегарда ***Гильдегарда*** – ♀ Germanic. Eng. *Hildegarde,* Lat. *Hildegardis,* Lith. *Hildegarda.* ⊕ 30 Apr, 17 Sep.

Гинда, ***Гинда,*** also *Гиндель* – ♀ Jewish *(Hinda).*

Гирш ***Гирш*** – ♂ Jewish.

Гита, Гитель, Гитка, Гитля → **Гута**

Глафира ***Глафира*** – ♀ Greek. Ukr. *Глафіра.* ‡ 26 Apr.

Глеб ***Глеб,*** † *Глѣбъ* – ♂ Norse. Ukr. *Гліб.* ‡ 2 May, 20 Jun, 24 Jul, 5 Sep.

Гликерий ***Гликерий,*** also † *Глукерій* – ♂ Greek. Ukr. *Гликерій.* Ω 13 May. ‡ 28 Dec.

Гликерия ***Гликерия,*** † *Лукерья* – ♀ of **Гликерий**. Ukr. *Гликерія, Лукерія.* ‡ 13 May, 22 Oct.

Гліб → **Глеб**

Глукерій → **Гликерий**

Глѣбъ → **Глеб**

Гнат → **Игнатий**

Говсей, Говсѣй → **Ишия**

Годес → **Гадас**

Гольда ***Гольда*** – ♀ Jewish.

Гонората ***Гонората*** – ♀ Latin. Lat./Lith. *Honorata,* Pol. *Honorata.* ⊕ 16 Jan, 22 Feb.

Гордей ***Гордей*** – ♂ Greek. Ukr. *Гордій.* Ω & ‡3 Jan.

Готлиб ***Готлиб*** – ♂ Germanic. Germ. *Gottlieb,* Pol. *Gotlib.*

Готфрид ***Готфрид*** – ♂ Germanic. Eng. *Godfrey, GeoVrey, JeVrey,* Latin *Godefridus, Gottfridus,* Lith. *Gotfridas,* Pol. *Gotfryd.* ⊕ 8 Nov.

Гошко → **Ишия**

Григорий ***Григорий*** – ♂ Greek. Eng. *Gregory,* Latin *Gregorius,* Lith. *Grigalius, Grigalis,* Pol. *Grzegorz,* Ukr. *Григорій, Григір, Грицько.* ⊕ 12 Mar, 9 & 25 May, 17 Nov. Ω 5 & 10 & 25 Jan, 30 Sep, 17 & 20 & 24 Nov. ‡ 12 Mar, 25 Jan, 30 Sep, etc.

Грина → **Груна**

Грицько → **Григорий**

Груна ***Груна,*** also *Грина* – ♀ Jewish.

Гурий ***Гурий*** – ♂ Hebrew. Ukr. *Гурій.* Ω 15 Nov. ‡ 20 Jun, 1 Aug, 4 Oct, 15 Nov, 5 Dec.

Густав ***Густав*** – ♂ Scandinavian. Eng. *Gustave,* Lat. *Gustavus,* Lith. *Gustavas,* Pol. *Gustaw.* ⊕ 2 Aug.

Гута ***Гута,*** also *Гита, Гитель, Гитка, Гитля, Гутка, Гутля* – ♀ Jewish.

Гутка, Гутля → **Гута**

Гутманъ ***Гутманъ*** – ♂ Jewish.

Д д

Давид ***Давид*** – ♂ Hebrew, often, but not always, Jewish; Jewish variants include *Довид* and *Тевель.* Eng./Lat. *David,* Lith. *Dovydas, Dovas,* Pol. *Dawid.* ⊕ 15 Jul, 17 Sep, 29 Dec. Ω 26 Jun. ‡ 26 Dec, 7 May, 26 Jun, 6 Sep, etc.

Дамасий ***Дамасий*** – ♂ Greek; Latin *Damasus,* Lith. *Damazas,* Pol. *Damazy.* ⊕ 27 Nov, 11 Dec.

Даміан → **Демьян**

Даниил ***Даниил,*** also *Данило,* † *Даніилъ, Даніель* – ♂ Hebrew. Eng./Lat./Pol. *Daniel,* Lith. *Danielius, Danis, Danys,* Ukr. *Данило.* ⊕ 16 Feb, 11 Dec. ‡ 16 Feb, 10 Jul, 11 & 17 Dec, etc.

Данута ***Данута*** – ♀ Lithuanian; Lith. *Danutė,* Pol. *Danuta.* ⊕ 24 Jun, 1 Oct.

Дарий ***Дарий*** – ♂ Persian; Eng./Lat. *Darius,* Lith. *Darijus,* Pol. *Dariusz,* Ukr. *Дарій.* ⊕ 25 Oct, 19 Dec.

Дарья ***Дарья***, † *Дарія* – ♀ of **Дарий**. Eng./Lat. *Daria*, Lith. *Darija*, Pol. *Daria*, Ukr. *Дарія*, *Дарина*, *Дар'я*, *Одарка*. ⊕ 22 Sep, 25 Oct. ‡ 19 Mar.

Двейра, *Двойра* → **Дебора**

Дебора ***Дебора***, also *Девора* – ♀ Hebrew. Jews often used the forms *Двойра* and *Двейра*. Eng. *Deborah*, *Debra*, Lat./Lith. *Debora*. ⊕ 24 Apr.

Девора → **Дебора**

Дементий ***Дементий***, also *Дометий* – ♂ Latin. Ukr. *Дементій*, *Дометій*. Ω 7 Aug. ‡ 8 Mar, 7 Aug.

Демид ***Демид***, † *Діомидъ* – ♂ Greek. Latin *Diomedes*, Lith. *Diomedas*, *Medas*, Pol. *Demid*. Ω 16 Aug. ‡ 3 Jul, 16 Aug.

Демьян ***Демьян*** † *Даміанъ* – ♂ Greek. Eng. *Damon*, *Damian*, Lat. *Damianus*, Lith. *Damijonas*, Pol. *Damian*, Ukr. *Дем'ян*. 23 Feb, 27 Sep. ⊕ 23 Feb, 27 Sep. Ω & ‡ 1 Jul, 17 Oct, 1 Nov.

Денис ***Денис***, also *Денисий*, † *Діонисій* – ♂ Greek. Eng. *Dennis*, Lat. *Dionysius*, Lith. *Dionizas*, *Dionyzas*, *Denys*, Pol. *Dionizy*. ⊕ 9 Oct, 26 Dec. Ω & ‡ 15 Mar, 18 May, 3 & 23 Oct.

Денисия ***Денисия*** – ♀ of **Денис**. Eng. *Denise*, Lat. *Dionysia*, Lith. *Dionizija*, Pol. *Dioniza*, Ukr. *Денисія*. ⊕ 15 May, 6 Dec.

Дина ***Дина*** – ♀ primarily Jewish, but not exclusively.

Дишель → **Душка**

Діна → **Дина**

Діонисій → **Денис**

Дмитрий ***Дмитрий***, † *Дмитрій* – ♂ Greek. Eng./Lat. *Demetrius*, Lith. *Demetrijus*, *Demetras*, Pol. *Dymitr*, Ukr. *Дмитро*, *Дмитріан*. ⊕ 9 Apr, 21 Sep, 26 Oct. Ω 23 Jun, 26 Oct. ‡ Oct. 26, etc.

Добра ***Добра*** – ♀ Jewish; variants include *Доба*, *Добрушка*, and *Добка*.

Доброслав ***Доброслав*** – ♂ Slavic. ⊕ 10 Jan.

Дов → **Дойв**

Довид → **Давид**

Дойвъ ***Дойв***, also *Дов* – ♂ Jewish.

Дометий → **Дементий**

Доминик ***Доминик*** – ♂ Latin. Eng. *Dominic*, Lat. *Dominicus*, Lith. *Dominykas*, *Domininkas*, *Domas*, Pol. *Dominik*. ⊕ 9 Apr, 4 Aug, 14 Oct, 5 Nov.

Доминика ***Доминика*** – ♀ of **Доминик**. Eng./Lat. *Dominica*, Lith. *Dominyka*, Ukr. *Домініка*. ⊕ 6 Jun, 4 Aug.

Домитилла ***Домитилла***, also *Домицела* – ♀ Latin. Eng./Lat. *Domitilla*, Lith. *Domicelė*, *Domicė*, Pol. *Domicela*. ⊕ 12 May.

Домна ***Домна*** – ♀ Latin. Ukr. *Домна*, *Домаха*. ‡ 3 Sep, 28 Dec.

Дона ***Дона***, also *Доня* – ♀ Jewish.

Донат ***Доната*** – ♂ Latin. Lat. *Donatus*, Lith. *Donatas*, Pol. *Donat*. ⊕ 17 Feb, 7 Apr, 21 May, 7 Aug, 5 Oct. ‡ 30 Apr, 4 Sep.

Доната ***Доната*** – ♀ of **Донат**; Lat./Lith./Pol. *Donata*.

Доня → **Дона**

Дорофей ***Дорофей*** – ♂ Greek. Lat. *Dorotheus*, Lith. *Dorotėjas*, *Dorotėjus*, Pol. *Doroteusz*, Ukr. *Дорофій*, *Дорош*. ⊕ 6 Jun. Ω 6 Jun. ‡ 5 Jun, 3 & 16 Sep, 7 Nov, 28 Dec.

Дорофея ***Дорофея*** – ♀ Greek. Eng. *Dorothy*, *Dolly*, *Dotty*, Lat. *Dorothea*, Lith. *Dorotėja*, *Darata*, Pol. *Dorota*, Ukr. *Дорофея*, *Доротея*. ⊕ & ‡ 6 Feb.

Дульца ***Дульца*** – ♀ Jewish; variants include *Тельцель* and *Тольца*.

Дуня ***Дуня*** – ♀, sometimes a Russian short form of **Евдокия**, sometimes a Jewish affectionate form from **Дина**.

Душка ***Душка*** – ♀ Jewish; variants included *Дишель*, *Дышель*.

Дышель → **Душка**

Е е

Ева ***Ева*** – ♀ Hebrew, used by Christians and Jews, but Jews often used *Хава* (Polish *Chawa*) as closer to the original Hebrew form of the name. Eng. *Eve*, Lat. *Eva*, Lith. *Ieva*, *Ievė*, *Jieva*, Pol. *Ewa [Эва]*, Ukr. *Єва*. ⊕ 14 Mar, 24 Dec.

Евгений ***Евгений***, also *Евген*, † *Еугеній* – ♂ Greek. Eng. *Eugene*, *Gene*, Lat. *Eugenius*, Lith. *Eugenijus*, Pol. *Eugeniusz*, Ukr. *Євген*, *Євгеній*. ⊕ 4 Jan, 4 Mar, 2 Jun, 8 & 13 Jul, 6 Sep, 13 Nov, 30 Dec. Ω 7 Mar, 13 & 24 Dec. ‡ 21 Jan, 12 & 19 Feb, 7 Mar, 7 Nov, 13 Dec.

Евгения ***Евгения***, † *Евгенія* – ♀ of **Евгений**. Eng./Lat. *Eugenia*, Lith. *Eugenija*, *Augenė*, *Augė*, Pol. *Eugenia*, Ukr. *Євгенія*. ⊕ 7 Feb, 16 Sep, 25 Dec. ‡ 24 Dec.

Евграф ***Евграф***, † *Еуграфъ* – ♂ E. Slav. from Greek. Ukr. *Євграф*. Ω & ‡10 Dec.

Евдоким ***Евдоким***, also *Авдоким*, † *Еудокимъ* – ♂ Greek. Ukr. *Євдоким*, *Явдоким*. ‡ 31 Jul.

Евдокия ***Евдокия***, also *Автдотья*, short forms include *Дуня* – Greek. Ukr. *Євдокія*. Ω 1 Mar, 4 Aug. ‡ 1 Mar, 4 Aug, 17 May, 7 Jul.

Евель → **Иоиль**

Евзор → **Ойзер**

Евлалий ***Евлалий*** – ♂ E. Slav. from Greek. Ukr. *Євлампій*. ‡ 30 Aug.

Евлалия ***Евлалия*** – ♀ of **Евлалий**. Eng. *Eulalia*, Latin *Eulalia*, Lith. *Eulalija*, Ukr. *Євлалія*. ⊕ 12 Feb, 10 Dec. ‡ 10 Dec, etc.

Евлампий ***Евлампий*** – ♂ E. Slav. from Greek. Ukr. *Євлампій*. ‡ 5 Mar, 3 Jul, 10 Oct.

Евлампия, ***Евлампия*** – ♀ of **Евлампий**. Ukr. *Євлампія*. Ω & ‡10 Oct.

Евна → **Иона**

Евпатий ***Евпатий,*** † *Еупатій* – ♂ E. Slav. from Greek. Ω 16 Nov.

Евпраксия ***Евпраксия*** – ♀ E. Slav. from Greek. Ukr. *Євпраксія.* Ω 25 Jul. ‡ 12 Jan, 25 Jul, 16 Oct.

Евсевий ***Евсевий,*** also *Авсей, Евсей, Овсей* – ♂ Greek (but *Овсей* can also be Jewish, from a form of **Ишия**). Eng./Lat. *Eusebius,* Lith. *Euzebijus,* Pol. *Euzebiusz,* Ukr. *Євсевій, Євсей, Овсій.* ⊕ 20 Jan, 22 Jun, 17 Aug, 16 Dec. Ω & ‡ 22 Jun.

Евстафий ***Евстафий*** – ♂ Greek. Ukr. *Євстафій.* Ω & ‡ 21 Feb, 28 Jul, 20 Sep.

Евстахий ***Евстахий,*** also *Астахий, Остап.* – ♂ Greek. Eng. *Eustace,* Lat. *Eustachius,* Lith. *Eustachijus, Eustakas,* Pol. *Eustachy,* Ukr. *Євстахій, Остап.* ⊕ 29 Mar, 16 Jul, 8 & 20 Sep, 12 Oct, 10 Dec.

Евтихий ***Евтихий,*** † *Еутихій* – ♂ Greek. Ukr. *Євтихій, Євтух.* Ω & ‡ 6 Apr, 28 May, 24 Aug.

Евфалия ***Евфалия*** – ♀ E. Slav. from Greek. Lith. *Eutalija,* Pol. *Eufalia.* ‡ 2 Mar.

Евфимій → **Ефим**

Евфросинія → **Ефросиния**

Егор, ***Егор*** – ♂ E. Slav., variation of **Григорий,** q. v. Ukr. *Єгор.*

Едидия, Едидія, Едыдия, Едыдья → **Иедидия**

Езекия ***Езекия*** † *Езекія* – ♂ Hebrew. ‡ 28 Aug.

Екатерина ***Екатерина*** – ♀ E. Slav. from Greek. Eng. *Catherine, Kathleen,* Latin *Catharina, Catherina,* Lith. *Katarina, Kotryna, Katryna,* Pol. *Katarzyna (Катаржина, Катаржына),* Ukr. *Катерина.* ⊕ 30 Apr, 25 Nov, 31 Dec, etc. Ω 25 Nov. ‡ 24 Nov.

Еким → **Иаким**

Екусель → **Кусель**

Елена ***Елена*** – ♀ Greek. Eng. *Helen,* Lat. *Helena,* Lith. *Elena, Alena,* Pol. *Helena.* Ukr. *Олена, Гелена.* ⊕ 2 Mar, 23 Apr, 22 May, 31 Jul, 18 Aug. Ω 21 May. ‡ 21 & 26 May, 11 Jul, 30 Oct.

Елеферий ***Елеферий,*** † *Елеуферій* – ♂ Greek. Ω 4 Aug, 15 Dec. ‡ 4 & 8 Aug, 3 Oct, 15 Dec.

Елизавета ***Елизавета,*** † *Елизавеѳа* – ♀ Hebrew. Eng. *Elizabeth, Bess, Beth, Betsy, Betty,* Lat. *Elisabeth,* Lith. *Elzbieta, Elžbieta,* Pol. *Elżbieta [Елжбета, Ельзбѣта],* Ukr. *Єлизавета.* ⊕ 18 Jun, 4 & 8 Jul, 14 Sep, 21 Oct, 19 Nov. ‡ 24 Apr, 5 Sep, 22 Oct.

Елизар ***Елизар,*** † *Елеазар* – ♂ Hebrew. Ukr. *Єлизар.* ‡ 13 Jan, 1 Aug.

Елисей ***Елисей,*** † *Іелисей* – ♂ Hebrew. Eng. *Elisha,* Latin *Eliseus,* Pol. *Elizeusz,* Ukr. *Єлисей, Ялисей.* ⊕ 14 Jun. Ω 24 Jun. ‡ 14 Jun, 23 Oct.

Елля → **Илья**

Ельзбѣта → **Елизавета**

Емельян ***Емельян,*** also *Эмилиан,* † *Емиліянъ* – ♂ Latin. Eng. *Emilian,* Latin *Aemilianus,* Lith. *Emilijonas, Emilas,* Pol. *Emilian,* Ukr. *Омелян, Омелько.* ⊕ 5 Jan, 18 Jul, 8 Aug, 11 Oct., 6 Dec. Ω & ‡ 18 Jul, 8 Aug.

Ентель ***Ентель*** – ♂ Jewish; variants include *Ента, Гента.* Eng. *Yenta, Yentel,* Pol. *Jenta, Jentel.*

Епифан ***Епифан*** – ♂ E. Slav. from Greek. Ukr. *Єпіфан.* Ω 12 May. ‡ 12 May, 7 Sep.

Еразм → **Эразм**

Еремей ***Еремей,*** also *Иеремия,* † *Іеремія, Ермія* – ♂ Hebrew. Eng. *Jeremiah, Jeremy, (Jerry*),* Lat. *Jeremias,* Lith. *Jeremijas,* Pol. *Jeremiasz,* Ukr. *Єремія, Ярема, Веремій.* ⊕ 16 Feb, 1 May, 6 Dec. Ω & ‡ 1 May.

Ермолай ***Ермолай*** – ♂ Greek. Lat. *Hermolaus,* Ukr. *Єрмолай, Ярмолай.* Ω 13 Jan, 26 Jul. ‡ 26 Jul.

Ермія → **Еремей**

Естер, Есфирь → **Эсфирь**

Еу-: *archaic spellings for names now beginning* ***Ев*** .

Ефим ***Ефим,*** also *Ефимий,* † *Евфимій, Еуфимій* – ♂ E. Slav. from Greek. Lat. *Euphemius,* Pol. *Eufemiusz,* Ukr. *Юхим, Єфим.* ⊕ 20 Mar, 16 Sep. Ω 20 Jan, 1 Apr, 11 & 28 Jul, 16 Sep, 27 Dec. ‡ 4 & 20 Jan, 1 & 18 Apr, 4 Jul, 28 Aug, 15 Oct, etc.

Ефимия ***Ефимия*** – ♀ of **Ефим.** Eng./Lat. *Euphemia,* Lith. *Eufemija,* Pol. *Eufemia,* Ukr. *Євимія, Юхимія.* ⊕ 19 Jan, 20 Mar, 16 Sep. ‡ 20 Mar, 11 Jul, 16 Sep.

Ефрем ***Ефрем,*** also *Эфраим, Охрим* – ♂ Hebrew; Jews tended to use the forms *Эфроим, Фроим* and *Фреймель.* Eng./Lat. *Ephraim,* Pol. *Efrem,* Ukr. *Охрім, Єфрем.* Ω 28 Jan. ‡ 28 Jan, 7 Mar, 16 May, 8 & 11 & 15 Jun, 30 Aug, 26 Sep.

Ефросиния ***Ефросиния,*** also *Афросинья,* † *Евфросинія* – ♀ E. Slav. from Greek. Eng./Lat. *Euphrosyne,* Lith, *Eufrozina,* Pol. *Eufrozyna.* Ukr. *Єфросинія, Фросина.* ⊕ 1 & 11 Jan. Ω 25 Sep. ‡ 25 Sep, 6 Nov, etc.

Ехель → **Иохель**

Є is a letter used in Ukrainian much as ***E*** *is in Russian. For any name beginning with* ***Є-****, try the equivalent spelling with* ***E-****. That should give you the Russian form, or something very close to it.*

Ж ж

Желислав ***Желислав*** – ♂ Slavic. Pol. *Żelisław.* ⊕ 21 Apr.

З з

Завель → **Савелий**

Закхей ***Закхей*** – ♂ Hebrew. Eng. *Zacchaeus,* Lat. *Zachaeus,* Lith. *Zacheušas,* Pol. *Zacheusz.* ⊕ 15 Mar, 6 Sep, 5 Nov. ‡ 2 Jan, 20 Apr, 18 Nov.

Залкинд ***Залкинд***, also *Зелкинд* – ♂ Jewish.
Залман, Зальман, Зальмон → **Соломон**
Зандель, Зандер → **Александр**
Захар ***Захар***, † *Захарій, Захарья, Захарія* – ♂ Hebrew; Jews often used such forms as *Зхарья* and *Схарія*. Eng. *Zachary, Zachariah*, Lat. *Zacharias, Zacharius*, Lith. *Zacharijas, Zakarijas*, Pol. *Zachariasz*. ⊕ 15 Mar, 6 Sep, 5 Nov. Ω 8 & 21 Feb, 5 Sep. ‡ 8 Feb, 24 Mar, 28 Aug, 5 Sep, 5 Dec.
Здзислав ***Здзислав*** – ♂ Slavic (mainly Polish, unheard of among Russians). Pol. *Zdzisław*. ⊕ 29 Jan, 28 Nov.
Зеев ***Зеев*** – ♂ Jewish; variants include *Зев, Зевель, Зейв, Зейвель*, and *Зив*.
Зелиг ***Зелиг***, also *Зелик* – ♂ Jewish.
Зелка → **Зельда**
Зелкинд → **Залкинд**
Зельда ***Зельда***, also *Зелка* – ♀ Jewish. Eng. *Zelda*.
Зельман → **Соломон**
Зенон ***Зенон***, † *Зинонъ* – ♂ Greek. Eng./Lat. *Zeno*, Lith. *Zenonas, Zenas, Zenis, Zenius*, Pol. *Zenon*. Ω 10 Apr. ‡ 10 & 28 Apr, 22 Jun, 3 & 6 Sep, etc.
Зефирин ***Зефирин*** – ♂ Latin. Eng./Lat. *Zephyrinus*, Lith. *Zefyrinas, Zefirinas*, Pol. *Zefiryn*. ⊕ 26 Aug.
Зив → **Зев**
Зигфрид ***Зигфрид***, also *Зыгфрыд* – ♂ Germanic *Siegfried*. Eng. *Sigfried*, Lat. *Sigfridus*, Lith. *Zigfridas*, Pol. *Zygfryd*. ⊕ 15 Feb, 22 Aug.
Зигмунд ***Зигмунд***, also *Зыгмунд* – ♂ Polish < Germanic *Sigmund;* Eng. *Sigmund*, Lat. *Sigismundus*, Lith. *Sigismundas, Zigmantas*, Pol. *Zygmunt*, Ukr. *Сигізмунд*. ⊕ 2 May.
Зимель, Зимля → **Семён**
Зина ***Зина*** – ♀ Christian and Jewish. ‡ 17 Jan, 5 Jul, 4 Aug, 10 Oct.
Зинаида ***Зинаида*** – ♀ E. Slav. from Greek. Lith./Pol. *Zinaida*. Ukr. *Зінаїда*. ‡ 11 Oct.
Зиндель → **Зундель**
Зиновий ***Зиновий*** – ♂ E. Slav. from Greek. Eng./ Lat. *Zenobius*, Lith. *Zenobijus*, Pol. *Zenobiusz*, Ukr. *Зіновій*. ⊕ 20 Feb, 24 Dec. ‡ 30 Oct.
Зиновия ***Зиновия*** – ♀ of **Зиновий**. Eng./Lat./Pol. *Zenobia*, Lith. *Zenobija*, Ukr. *Зіновія*. ⊕ 20 Feb, 24 Dec. ‡ 30 Oct.
Зиса, Зисель, Зиска, Зисля → **Зуса** and **Зускинд** and **Зусман**
Зискинд → **Зускинд**
Зисман → **Зусман**
Злата ***Злата***, also *Златка* – ♀ often Jewish, but not exclusively. ‡ 12 Oct.
Зорах ***Зорах***, also *Зорох* – ♂ Jewish.
Зосима ***Зосима***, also *Зосим*, † *Изосима* – ♂ E. Slav. from Greek. Lat. *Zosimus*, Pol. *Zosim*, Ukr. *Зосим*. Ω 21 Jan, 4 & 29 Apr. ‡ 4 & 17 Apr, etc.
София, Софія → **Софья**
Зоя ***Зоя*** – ♀ Greek. ‡ 13 Feb, 2 May, 18 Dec.
Зузанна → **Сусанна**
Зундель ***Зундель*** – ♂ Jewish; variants include *Зиндель* and *Зуня*.
Зуса ***Зуса*** – ♀ Jewish; variants include *Зиса, Зиска, Зисля, Зуска, Зусля, Зуся*, etc.
Зуска → **Зуса** and **Зускинд** and **Зусман**
Зускинд ***Зускинд*** – ♂ Jewish, cmp. Germ. *Süßkind;* variants include *Зиса, Зисель, Зискинд, Зуска, Зысель, Зышель, Зышко*, etc.
Зусля → **Зуса** and **Зускинд** and **Зусман**
Зусман ***Зусман*** – ♂ Jewish, also *Зиса, Зисель, Зисман, Зуска, Зусьман, Зышель, Зышко*, etc.
Зуся → **Зуса** and **Зускинд** and **Зусман**
Зхарья → **Захар**
Зыгфрыд → **Зигфрид**
Зыгмунд → **Зигмунд**
Зымель → **Семён**
Зысель, Зышель, Зышко → **Зуса** and **Зускинд** and **Зусман**
Зысля → **Зуса** and **Зускинд** and **Зусман**
Зышель, Зышко → **Зускинд** and **Зусман**

И и

Иаким ***Иаким***, † *Іоакимъ* or *Іоахимъ* – ♂ Hebrew; variants include *Аким, Еким, Яким*, etc. Eng./Pol. *Joachim*, Lat. *Joachim, Joachimus*, Lith. *Joakimas, Jakimas, Jokimas*, Ukr. *Яким*. ⊕ 26 Jul, 16 Aug. Ω & ‡ 9 Sep.
Иакинф ***Иакинф***, also *Акинф, Акинфий*, † *Іакинѳъ*. – Greek. Eng. *Hyacinth*, *(Jack*)*, Latin *Hyacinthus*, Lith. *Hiacintas, Jacintas*, Pol. *Jacenty, Jacek [Яценты, Яцек]*. ⊕ 10 Feb, 16 Mar, 3 & 17 Jul, 11 Sep. Ω & ‡ 3 & 18 Jul.
Иаков → **Яков**
Ив ***Ив*** – ♂ Germanic. Latin *Ivo*, Eng. *Ives*, Lith. *Ivas*, Pol. *Iwo*. ⊕ 19 & 20 May.
Иван ***Иван***, † *Іоаннъ* – ♂ Hebrew; standard Russian dim. *Ваня*. Eng. *John, Jack*, Latin *Joannes, Johannes*, Lith. *Jonas, Jasius*. Pol. *Jan [Ян]*, Ukr. *Іван*. [numerous name-days in all churches].
Иванна ***Иванна***, † *Иоанна, Іоанна, Іоганна* – ♀ of **Иван**. Eng. *Jane, Joan*, Lat. *Joanna, Johanna*, Lith. *Joana*, Pol. *Joanna*, Ukr. *Іванна*. ⊕ 2 & 4 Feb, 1 Mar, etc. ‡ 27 Jun.
Игнатий ***Игнатий***, † *Игнатій* – ♂ Latin. Eng./Lat. *Ignatius*, Lith. *Ignacijus, Ignotas, Ignacas, Ignasius*, Pol. *Ignacy [Игнацы]*, Ukr. *Ігнат, Ігнатій, Гнат*. ⊕ 1 Feb, 31 Jul, 17 Oct. Ω & ‡ 29 Jan, 23 Oct, 20 Dec.
Игор ***Игор*** – ♂ E. Slav. from Scandinavian. Eng. *Igor*, Lith. *Ingvaras*, Ukr. *Ігор*. ‡ 5 Jun, 19 Sep.

Ида ***Ида***, also *Идка, Итка* – ♀ Christian and Jewish. Eng./Lat./Lith./Pol. *Ida*. ⊕ 13 Apr, 4 Sep.

Идель → **Иуда**

Идка → **Ида**

Иегуда → **Иуда**

Иедидия, Иедидия, † *Іедидія* – ♂ Jewish; variants include *Едидія, Едидья, Едыдія, Едыдья, Иодидия*. Eng. *Jedidiah*.

Иезекииль ***Иезекииль***, † *Іезекіиль* – ♂ Hebrew, Jews tended to prefer *Хаскель* and *Хацкель*. Eng./Lat. *Ezechiel*, Lith. *Ezekielis*. ⊕ 10 Apr. ‡ 21 Jul.

Иеремия → **Еремей**

Иероним ***Иероним***, † *Іеронимъ* – ♂ Greek. Eng. *Jerome (Harry*, Jerry*)*, Lat. *Hieronymus*, Lith. *Jeronimas*, Pol. *Hieronim*, Ukr. *Ієронім*. ⊕ 8 Feb, 20 Jul, 30 Sep. ‡ 15 Jun.

Изаакъ → **Исаакий**

Изабелла ***Изабелла*** – ♀ Spanish. Eng. *Isabel, Isabella, Isabelle*, Latin *Isabella*, Lith. *Izabelė, Zabelė*, Pol. *Izabela*. ⊕ 22 Feb, 16 Mar, 14 Jul, 3 Sep, etc.

Измаил ***Измаил***, † *Исмаилъ* – ♂ Hebrew. Ukr. *Ізмаїл*. Ω & ‡ 17 Jun.

Изосима → **Зосима**

Израиль ***Израиль*** – ♂ usually Jewish (= *Israel*). variants include *Иссер, Сроель, Сроль, Сруль*.

Иисус ***Иисус*** – ♂ Hebrew (from the same Hebrew name as Eng. *Jesus*). Ukr. *Ісус*. ‡ 6 Mar, 1 Sep.

Иларий ***Иларий*** – ♂ Greek. Eng. *Hilary, Hillary*, Latin *Hilarius*, Lith. *Hilaras, Hilarijus, Ilarijus*, Pol. *Hilary*, Ukr. *Іларій*. ⊕ 14 Jan, 13 Feb, 16 Mar, 5 May, 21 Oct. Ω & ‡ 12 Jul.

Иларион ***Иларион***, † *Іларіонъ* – ♂ Greek. Ukr. *Іларіон*. Ω 4 May, 21 Oct. ‡ 28 Mar, 6 May, 6 Jun, 28 Aug, 21 Oct, 19 Nov.

Илиодор ***Илиодор*** – ♂ Greek. Latin *Heliodorus*, Lith. *Heliodoras*, Ukr. *Іліодор*. ⊕ 22 Apr. ‡ 28 Mar, 28 Sep, 19 Nov.

Ильман → **Гельман**

Илья ***Илья***, also *Элия*, † *Элія* – ♂ Hebrew. Jews tended to use this name in forms such as *Елля* and † *Элія*. Eng. *Elijah, Elias*, Lat. *Elias*, Lith. *Elijas, Eliošius*, Pol. *Eliasz*, Ukr. *Ілля*. ⊕ 16 Feb, 17 Apr, 20 Jul. Ω 12 Jan, 20 Jul, 19 Dec. ‡ 8 & 14 Jan, 20 Jul, 19 Dec, etc.

Иннокентий ***Иннокентий*** – ♂ Latin. Eng. *Innocent*, Lat. *Innocens, Innocentius*, Lith. *Inocentas*, Pol. *Inocenty*, Ukr. *Інокентій*. ⊕ 17 Apr, 22 Jun, 28 Jul, 13 Aug. ‡ 9 Feb, 19 & 31 Mar, 6 Jul, 23 Sep, 26 Nov.

Иоаким, Иоахимъ → **Иаким**

Иоан → **Иван**

Иоанна → **Иванна**

Иов ***Иов***, † *Іовъ* – ♂ Hebrew. English *Job*, Lith. *Jobas*, Pol. *Hiob*, Ukr. *Іов, Йов [Iov, Yov]*. ⊕ 10 May. Ω & ‡ 6 May.

Иоиль ***Иоиль***, also *Евель, Иовель, Иоель*, † *Іоель, Іовель* – ♂ Jewish (cmp. *Joel*). Eng. *Joel*, Lat. *Ioel*. Ω & ‡ 19 Oct.

Иойна → **Иона**

Иоланта ***Иоланта*** – ♀ origin unclear. Eng. *Iolanthe, Yolande, Jolantha, Iolanta, Violante*, Lith. *Jolanta*, Latin *Jolanta*, Pol. *Jolanta*. Ukr. *Іоланта*. ⊕ 15 Jun, 15 Sep.

Иона ***Иона*** † *Іона*– ♂ Hebrew; Jews often used forms such as *Евна, Иойна* († *Іойна*), and *Явна*. Eng. *Jonah, Jonas*, Lat. *Ionas, Jonas*, Lith. *Jonas, Jonošius*, Pol. *Jonasz*, Ukr. *Іона, Йона, Івон*. ⊕ 22 Sep. Ω & ‡ 28 Mar, 22 Sep.

Иосафат ***Иосафат*** – ♂ Hebrew. Eng. *Josaphat, Jehoshaphat*, Lat. *Iosaphat, Josaphat*, Lith. *Juozapotas, Juozapatas*, Pol. *Józefat, Józafat [Позефат, Юзефат, Юзафат]*, Ukr. *Йосафат, Осафат, Сафат*. ⊕ 12 Nov.

Иосель ***Иосель*** † *Іосель* – ♂ Jewish, cmp. **Иосиф**. Pol. *Josel*.

Иосип → **Иосиф**

Иосиф ***Иосиф***, also *Иосип, Осип*, † *Іосифъ, Іосипъ* – ♂ Hebrew. Eng. *Joseph*, Lat. *Josephus*, Lith. *Juozapas, Jūzupas, Juozas*, Pol. *Józef [Юзеф, Іозеф]*, Ukr. *Йосип, Осип, Юзеф*. –⊕ 19 Mar, 1 May, 18 Sep, 14 Nov. Ω 26 Jan, 4 Apr, 3 Nov. ‡ 4 Jan, 31 Mar, 4 Apr, 11 May, 3 Nov, etc.

Иохвед ***Иохвед*** – ♀ Jewish. Eng. *Jochabed*, Lat. *Iochabed*.

Иохель ***Иохель***, † *Іохель* – ♂ Jewish; variants include *Ехель, Хиль*, and *Яхель*.

Ипатий ***Ипатий***, also *Ипат*, † *Ипатій* – ♂ E. Slav. from Greek. Lat. *Hipatius*, Pol. *Hipacy*, Ukr. *Іпат, Іпатій*. ⊕ 17 Jun, 14 Nov. Ω 17 & 18 Jun. ‡ 31 Mar, 3 & 18 Jun, 21 Sep, 20 Nov, etc.

Ипполит ***Ипполит***, † *Пополитъ* – ♂ Greek. Eng. *Hippolyt*, Lat. *Hippolytus, Ippolytus*, Lith. *Ipolitas*, Pol. *Hipolit*, Ukr. *Іполит*. ⊕ 3 Feb, 13 Aug. Ω 30 Jun, 10 Aug. ‡ 30 Jan, 13 Aug.

Ираклий ***Ираклий*** † *Ираклій* – ♂ Greek. Eng. *Heracles, Hercules*, Ukr. *Іраклій*. ‡ 9 Mar, 18 May, 22 Oct.

Ирина ***Ирина*** – ♀ Greek. Eng. *Irene*, Latin *Irene, Irena*, Lith./Pol. *Irena*, Ukr. *Ірина, Орина*. ⊕ 3 Apr, 20 Oct. Ω 2 & 16 Apr, 5 May. ‡ 16 Apr, 5 May, 18 Sep.

Иринарх ***Иринарх*** – ♂ Greek. Ω 28 Nov.

Ириний ***Ириний***, also *Ириней* – ♂ Greek. Eng./Lat. *Irenaeus*, Lith. *Irenėjas, Ireniejus*, Pol. *Ireneusz*, Ukr. *Іриній*. ⊕ 25 Mar, 28 Jun, 23 Aug.

Исаакий ***Исаакий***, also *Исаак*, † *Исакій, Изаакъ* – ♂ Hebrew. Jews often used such forms as *Айзик, Айзык*, and *Ицхок*, and from the latter *Ицек, Ицко, Ицык*, etc. Eng./Lat. *Isaac*, Lith. *Izaokas*,

Pol. *Izaak*, Ukr. *Ісак*, *Сакій*. Ω & ‡ 21 Apr, 30 May, 3 Aug, 21 Sep.

Исаия ***Исаия*** also *Исай* – ♂ Hebrew; Jews tended to prefer the forms *Ишая* and *Шая*. Eng. *Isaiah*, Lat. *Isaias*, Lith. *Izaijas*, *Jezajas*, *Izajas*, *Izajus*, Pol. *Izajasz*, Ukr. *Ісай*. ⊕ 16 Feb, 6 Jul. Ω 9 May. ‡ 14 Jan, 16 Feb, 9 & 15 & 23 May, 28 Sep.

Исидор ***Исидор***, also *Сидор* – ♂ Greek. Eng. *Isidore*, Lat. *Isidorus*, Lith. *Izidorius*, *Dzidorius*, *Zidorius*, Pol. *Izydor*, Ukr. *Сидір*. ⊕ 15 Jan, 5 Feb, 4 Apr, 15 May, 14 Dec. Ω 4 Feb, 14 May. ‡ 8 Jan, 4 Feb, 7 & 14 & 23 May, 6 Jul.

Исмаил → **Измаил**

Исраель → **Израиль**

Иссахар ***Иссахар*** – ♂ Hebrew, including variants *Сахар* and *Сохор* used mainly by Jews. Lat. *Issachar*, Pol. *Izachar*.

Иссер → **Израиль**

Итка → **Ида**

Иуда ***Иуда*** – ♂ often Jewish, but not exclusively; Jewish variants include *Идель*, *Иегуда* († *Іегуда*), *Юдель*, *Юдка*, *Ютка*. Eng. *Judah*, *Judas*, Lat. *Iuda*, *Juda*. ‡ 19 & 30 Jun, 21 Aug.

Иудифь → **Юдифь**

Иулиан → **Юлиан**

Иулиания → **Юлиания**

Иулий → **Юлий**

Иулия → **Юлия**

Иуст → **Юст**

Иустин → **Юстин**

Иустина → **Юстина**

Ицек, *Ицко*, *Ицхок*, *Ицык* → **Исаакий**

Ишая → **Исаия**

Ишия ***Ишия***, † *Ишія* – ♂ Hebrew, short for *Иегошуа* or *Иегошія*, from Hebrew *Yᵉhōshūʿa* (cmp. Eng. *Joshua*). Among the many Jewish variants from this name or its original long form are *Говсѣй*, *Гошко*, *Овсей*, *Овшія*, *Шия*, and *Шийка*. Pol. *Gowsiej*, *Goszko*, *Jozue*, *Szyja*, etc.

Й й

Йов → **Иов**

Йона → **Иона**

Йосафат → **Иосафат**

Йосип → **Иосиф**

І і

Іаковъ → **Яков**

Іван → **Иван**

Іванна → **Иванна**

Івон → **Иона**

Ігнат, *Ігнатій* → **Игнатий**

Ігор → **Игор**

Іегуда → **Иуда**

Іедидия, *Іедидья* → **Иедидия**

Іекусіель → **Кусель**

Іелисей → **Елисей**

Іеремія → **Еремей**

Іеронімъ, *Ієроним* → **Иероним**

Іларій → **Иларий**

Іларіон → **Иларион**

Іліодор → **Илиодор**

Ілля → **Илья**

Інокентій → **Иннокентий**

Іоакимъ → **Иаким**

Іоанна → **Иванна**

Іоаннъ → **Иван**

Іовъ → **Иов**

Іовель, *Іоель* → **Иоиль**

Іоганна → **Иванна**

Іодидия → **Иедидия**

Іозеф → **Иосиф**

Іозефат → **Иосафат**

Іона → **Иона**

Іосель → **Иосель**

Іохель → **Иохель**

Іпат, *Іпатій* → **Ипатий**

Іполит → **Ипполит**

Іраклій → **Ираклий**

Ірина → **Ирина**

Іриній → **Ириний**

Ісай → **Исай**

Ісак → **Исаакий**

Ісус → **Иисус**

Іуліанъ → **Юлиан**

Іуліана → **Юлиания**

Іустина → **Юстина**

Іустинъ → **Юстин**

Іустъ → **Юст**

Іяковъ → **Яков**

К к

Кадиш ***Кадиш***, also *Кадыш* – ♂ Jewish.

Каем ***Каем*** – ♂ Jewish.

Казимир ***Казимир*** – ♂ Slavic, mainly Polish. Eng. *Casimir*, (*Charles**, *Casey**), Lat. *Casimirus*, Lith. *Kazimieras*, *Kazys*, Pol. *Kazimierz [Казимерж]*. ⊕ & Ω 4 Mar.

Казимира ***Казимира*** – ♀ of **Казимир**. Lat. *Casimira*, Lith. *Kazimiera*, Pol. *Kazimiera*.⊕ 4 Mar.

Калерия ***Калерия*** – ♀ Latin. Ukr. *Калерія*. ‡ 7 Jun.

Калина ***Калина*** – ♀ of **Каллиник**.

Каллиник ***Каллиник***, also *Калина*, † *Калиньникъ* – ♂ E. Slav. from Greek. Ukr. *Каленик*, *Калина*. Ω 29 Jul, 23 Aug. ‡ 24 May, 29 Jul, 23 Aug, etc.

Каллист ***Каллист*** – ♂ Greek. Lat. *Callistus, Callixtus,* Lith. *Kalikstas, Kalistas,* Pol. *Kalikst,* Ukr. *Калiст.* ⊕ 14 Oct. ‡6 Mar.

Каллистрат ***Каллистрат*** – ♂ Greek. Ukr. *Калiстрат.* Ω & ‡ 27 Sep.

Кальман ***Кальман***, also *Кальмон, Кельман* – ♂ Jewish, originally from Hebrew *Kalonymos,* Russian form *Клейнимес.*

Камилла ***Камилла*** – ♀ Latin Eng. *Camille,* Lat. *Camilla,* Lith. *Kamilė,* Pol. *Kamilla,* Ukr. *Камiла.* ⊕ 31 May, 16 Sep.

Капитон ***Капитон*** – ♂ Latin. Ukr. *Капiтон.* Ω 22 Dec. ‡ 7 Mar, 24 Jul, 12 Aug.

Карл ***Карл*** – ♂ Germanic. Eng. *Charles, Karl, Carl,* Latin *Carolus,* Lith. *Karolis, Karalius,* Pol. *Karol.* Ukr. *Карл, Карло.* ⊕ 4 Jun, 4 Nov.

Каролина ***Каролина*** – ♀ Romance. Eng. *Caroline,* Lith. *Karolina,* Lat. *Carolina,* Pol. *Karolina,* Ukr. *Каролiна.* ⊕ 9 May, 5 Jul, 4 Nov. ‡ 20 May.

Карп ***Карп*** – ♂ Greek. Ukr. *Карпо.* ⊕ 25 May, 13 Oct. ‡ 4 Jan, 26 May, 13 Oct.

Карпель ***Карпель***, also *Корпель* – ♂ Jewish.

Каспер ***Каспер*** – ♂ Persian (?). Eng. *Jasper, Casper,* Lat. *Gasparus, Casparus,* Lith. *Kasparas, Gasparas,* Pol. *Kacper, Kasper.* ⊕ 6 Jan.

Касрель ***Касрель***, also † *Касрiель* – ♂ Jewish.

Касьян ***Касьян***, † *Кассiанъ* – ♂ Latin. Eng. *Cassian,* Lat. *Cassianus,* Lith. *Kasijonas, Kasijus,* Pol. *Kasjan,* Ukr. *Касян.* ⊕ 13 Aug, 3 Dec. ‡ 29 Feb, 16 & 21 & 23 May, 15 Jun, 28 Aug, 28 Sep.

Катаржина, Катаржына, Катерина → **Екатерина**

Кельман → **Кальман**

Келестин ***Келестин***, also *Целестин* – ♂ Latin. Eng. *Celestine,* Lat. *Coelestinus, Caelestinus,* Lith. *Celestinas,* Pol. *Celestyn.* ⊕ 6 Apr, 19 May, 27 Jul. ‡ 8 Apr.

Келестина ***Келестина***, also *Целестина* – ♀ of **Келестин**. Eng. *Celestine,* Lat. *Caelestina,* Lith. *Celestina,* Pol. *Celestyna.* ⊕ 6 Apr.

Кесарий ***Кесарий***, also *Цезарь,* † *Кесарь* – ♂ Latin. Eng. *Caesar,* Lat. *Caesar, Caesarius,* Lith. *Cezarijus, Cezaris,* Pol. *Cezary,* Ukr. *Кесар.* ⊕ 27 Jul. Ω 8 Dec. ‡ 7 Oct, 1 Nov, 8 Dec.

Киприан ***Киприан***, also *Куприан,* † *Кюпрiянъ* – ♂ Latin. Eng. *Cyprian,* Latin *Cyprianus,* Lith. *Kiprijonas, Kipras,* Pol. *Cyprian,* Ukr. *Купрiян, Купер'ян, Купрiй.* ⊕ 16 & 26 Sep. Ω & ‡ 10 Mar, 2 Oct.

Кир ***Кир***, † *Кюръ* – ♂ E. Slav. from Greek. Ω 31 Jan. ‡ 31 Jan, 28 Jun.

Кирилл ***Кирилл***, † *Кюрилъ* – ♂ Greek. Eng. *Cyril,* Latin *Cyrillus,* Lith. *Kirilas,* Pol. *Cyryl,* Ukr. *Кирило.* ⊕ 18 Mar, 27 Jun. Ω & ‡ 18 & 29 Mar, 13 Apr, 9 & 27 Jun, 6 Sep.

Кифа ***Кифа*** – ♂ Aramaic. Ω 28 Jun, 8 Dec. ‡ 30 Mar, 8 Dec.

Кiндрат → **Кондратий**

Клавдий ***Клавдий***, † *Клавдiй* – ♂ Latin. Eng. *Claude,* Lat. *Claudius,* Lith. *Klaudijus,* Pol. *Klaudiusz,* Ukr. *Клавдiй.* ⊕ 15 Feb, 26 Apr, 6 Jun, 8 Sep. ‡ 31 Jan, 9 & 10 & 19 Mar, 3 & 7 Jun, 11 Aug, 29 Oct, 18 Dec.

Клавдия ***Клавдия***, † *Клавдiя* – ♀ of **Клавдий**. Eng./Lat. *Claudia,* Lith. *Klaudija,* Pol. *Klaudia,* Ukr. *Клавдiя.* ⊕ 20 Mar, 7 Aug. ‡ 20 Mar, 18 May, 6 Nov, 24 Dec.

Клара ***Клара*** – ♀ Latin. Eng./Lat. *Clara,* Lith., Pol. *Klara.* ⊕ 7 Apr, 12 & 18 Aug.

Клементина ***Клементина*** – ♀ of **Климент**. Eng. *Clementine,* Lat. *Clementina,* Lith. *Klementina, Klema, Klemė,* Pol. *Klementyna.* ⊕ 8 Sep.

Клеоник ***Клеоник*** – ♂ Greek. Ω & ‡ 3 Mar.

Климент ***Климент***, also *Клим, Климентий* – ♂ Latin. Eng. *Clement,* Lat. *Clemens,* Lith. *Klemensas, Klementas, Klemas,* Pol. *Klemens.* ♂ Latin. ⊕ 23 Jan, 13 Feb, 15 Mar, 23 Nov. Ω 23 Jan, 27 May, 25 Nov. ‡ 4 & 23 Jan, 22 Apr, 4 May, 27 Jul, 10 Sep, 25 Nov.

Кодратъ → **Кондратий**

Козьма → **Кузьма**

Колев ***Колев*** – ♂ Jewish name, cmp. Eng. *Caleb.*

Кондратий ***Кондратий***, † *Кодратъ* – ♂ Greek or Latin. Ukr. *Кiндрат.* Ω 10 Mar, 21 Apr, 21 Sep. ‡ 4 Jan, 10 Mar, 15 & 21 Apr, 21 Sep.

Конон ***Конон*** – ♂ Greek when used by Christians, also a Jewish name from **Эльханан**. Ω & ‡ 6 Mar.

Константин ***Константин***, † *Костянтинъ* – ♂ Latin. Eng. *Constantine,* Lat. *Constantius,* Lith. *Konstantas, Kastantas, Konstantinas,* Pol. *Konstanty,* Ukr. *Костянтин.* ⊕ 11 Mar, 29 Jul, 26 Aug, 30 Nov. Ω 21 May, 23 Oct. ‡ 21 May, 5 Jun, 29 Jul, 2 Oct, 26 Dec, etc.

Констанция ***Констанция*** – ♀ Latin. Eng. *Constance,* Lat. *Constantia,* Lith. *Konstancija, Kastancija,* Pol. *Konstancja,* Ukr. *Констанцiя.* ⊕ 18 Feb, 17 Jul, 19 Sep.

Копель → **Яков**

Корнелия ***Корнелия*** – ♀ of **Корнилий**. Eng. *Cornelia,* Lat. *Cornelia,* Lith. *Kornelija,* Pol. *Kornelia,* Ukr. *Корнелiя.* ⊕ 31 Mar, 16 Sep.

Корнилий **Корнилий** – ♂ Latin. Eng. *Cornell, Cornelius,* Lat. *Cornelius,* Lith. *Kornelijus, Kornelis,* Pol. *Kornel,* Ukr. *Корнелiй, Корнило, Корнилiй.* ⊕ 16 Sep. Ω 13 Sep, 20 Oct. ‡ 20 Feb, 19 May, 22 Jul, 13 Sep.

Корпель → **Карпель**

Костянтинъ → **Константин**

Крейна, Крейндель → **Кройна**

Кристина → **Христина**

Кройна ***Кройна*** – ♀ Jewish, variants include *Крона, Крейна, Крейндель, Рона, Роня,* etc.

Ксаверий ***Ксаверий*** – ♂ Romance. Eng. *Xavier,* Lat. *Xaverius,* Lith. *Ksaveras,* Pol. *Ksawery.* Ukr. *Ксаверій.* ⊕ 31 Jan, 3 Dec.

Ксения ***Ксения*** – ♀ Greek. Eng. *Xenia,* Pol. *Ksenia,* Ukr. *Ксенія, Оксана.* ⊕ 16 Apr. ‡ 24 Jan.

Ксенофонт ***Ксенофонт*** – ♂ Greek. Ω 26 Jun. ‡ 26 Jan, 28 Jun.

Кузьма ***Кузьма,*** also *Козьма* – ♂ Greek, Eng. *Cosmo,* Lat. *Cosmas,* Lith. *Kozmas,* Pol. *Kosma.* ⊕ 26 Sep. Ω & ‡ 18 Apr, 1 Jul, 17 Oct, 1 Nov.

Кулина → **Акилина**

Кунегунда ***Кунегунда*** – ♀ Germanic (rare among Russians). Hung. *Kunigunda, Kinga,* Lat. *Cunegundis,* Lith. *Kunigunda,* Pol. *Kunegunda.* ⊕ 3 Mar, 24 Jul.

Куприан, Купріян → **Киприан**

Кусель ***Кусель*** – ♂ Jewish, from Hebrew *Yekusiel († Іекусіель),* variants include *Кушель.*

Кюр → **Кир**

Кюрилъ → **Кирилл**

Л л

Лавр ***Лавр*** – ♂ Latin. Ukr. *Лавро.* ‡ 18 Aug.

Лаврентий ***Лаврентий,*** † *Лаврентій, Лаурентій* – ♂ Latin. Eng. *Lawrence, Larry,* Lat. *Laurentius,* Lith. *Laurencijus, Laurentas,* Pol. *Wawrzyniec [Вавржинец, Вавржынец],* Ukr. *Лаврентій, Лаврін.* ⊕ 10 Aug, etc. ⊕ 21 Jul, 10 Aug, 5 Sep Ω 10 Aug. ‡ 23 Jan, 16 May, 10 & 28 Aug, etc.

Лазарь ***Лазарь*** – ♂ Hebrew; Jewish forms include *Лайзер, Лейзер, Лейзор,* and † *Эліезеръ.* Eng./ Lat. *Lazarus,* Lith. *Lozorius,* Pol. *Łazarz,* Ukr. *Лазар.* ⊕ 17 Dec. Ω 17 Mar, 4 May, 17 Oct. ‡ 8 & 17 Mar, 15 Jun, 17 Jul, 17 Oct, 7 & 17 Nov.

Лайб → **Лейб**

Лайзер → **Лазар**

Лапидус ***Лапидус*** – ♂ Jewish.

Лариса ***Лариса*** – ♀ Greek. ⊕ 5 Sep. ‡ 26 Mar.

Лахман ***Лахман*** – ♂ Jewish.

Лая → **Лея**

Леб → **Лейб**

Лев ***Лев*** – ♂ Greek or Slavic, used by Christians and Jews; variants include *Левко.* ⊕ 11 May. Ω & ‡ 18 & 20 & 21 Feb.

Левин ***Левин*** – ♂ Jewish.

Левко → **Лев**

Лейб ***Лейб*** – ♂ Jewish, variants include *Лайб, Леб, Лейба, Лейбуш.*

Лейви ***Лейви*** – ♂ Jewish *(Levi).*

Лейзер, Лейзор → **Лазарь**

Лейка → **Лея**

Лейма → **Леман**

Леман ***Леман*** – ♂ Jewish, cmp. German *Lehmann;* variants include *Лейма.*

Лемель ***Лемель*** – ♂ Jewish; variants include *Лемка* and *Лемко.*

Лемко → **Лемель**

Лена → **Гелена**

Леокадия ***Леокадия*** – ♀ Greek. Eng. *Leocadia, (Lydia*, Lucie*),* Lat. *Laocadia,* Lith. *Leokadija,* Pol. *Leokadia,* Ukr. *Леокадія.* ⊕ 9 Dec. ‡ 9 Nov.

Леон ***Леон*** – ♂ Greek or Latin, a Romance equivalent to Slavic **Лев**, q. v. Eng. *Leo, Leon, Lionel,* Lat. *Leo,* Lith. *Leonas, Levas,* Pol. *Leon.* ⊕ 11 & 19 Apr, 12 Jun, 3 & 17 Jul, 10 Nov.

Леонард ***Леонард*** – ♂ Germanic (rare among Russians). Eng./Pol. *Leonard,* Lat. *Leonardus,* Lith. *Leonardas.* ⊕ 30 Mar, 6 & 26 Nov.

Леонид ***Леонид*** – ♂ Greek. Eng./Lith. *Leonidas,* Lat. *Leonides,* Pol. *Leonid,* Ukr. *Леонід.* ⊕ 15 & 22 Apr. Ω 16 Apr. ‡ 10 Mar, 16 Apr, 5 Jun, etc.

Леонтий ***Леонтий,*** † *Леонтъ* – ♂ Greek. Ukr. *Леонт, Леонтій.* Ω 18 Feb, 18 Jun, 30 Dec. ‡ 22 Jan, 9 Mar, 24 Apr, 18 Jun, 10 Jul, 28 Aug, etc.

Леонтина ***Леонтина*** –♀ of **Леонтий**. Eng. *Leontine, Leontyne,* Lith. *Leontina,* Pol. *Leontyna.* ⊕ 22 Mar.

Леопольд ***Леопольд*** – ♂ Germanic (rare among Russians). Eng. *Leopold,* Latin *Leopoldus,* Lith. *Leopoldas, Poldas,* Pol. *Leopold.* ⊕ 15 Nov.

Лешек ***Лешек*** – ♂ Polish *Leszek* (used almost exclusively by Poles). ⊕ 3 Jun.

Лея ***Лея*** – ♀ Jewish or Christian, variants include *Лая, Лейка* and *Лия.* Eng. *Leah,* Ukr. *Лія.*

Либа ***Либа*** – ♀ Jewish.

Либер ***Либер*** – ♂ Jewish.

Либман ***Либман*** – ♂ Jewish; variants include *Липман, Липка, Липко,* etc.

Ливерий ***Ливерий*** – ♂ Latin. ‡ 27 Aug.

Ливия ***Ливия*** – ♀ Latin. Eng./Lat. *Livia,* Lith. *Livija,* Pol. *Liwia. Ливия.* ⊕ 14 Dec. ‡ 25 Jun.

Лидия **Лидия** – ♀ Greek. Eng./Lat. *Lydia,* Lith. *Lidija, Lida,* Pol. *Lidia,* Ukr. *Лідія.* ⊕ 27 Mar, 3 Aug. ‡ 23 Mar.

Ликерия → **Глигерия**

Лилия ***Лилия,*** also *Лилиана* – ♀ Latin. Eng. *Lily, Lillian,* Lat. *Liliana,* Lith. *Lilija, Lilijana, Lijana,* Pol. *Lilianna,* Ukr. *Ліліана, Ліліяна.* ⊕ 14 Feb, 30 Apr, 27 Jul, 4 Sep, 19 Nov.

Лин ***Лин*** – ♂ Greek. Ω 4 Nov. ‡ 4 Jan, 11 Mar, 5 Nov.

Лина ***Лина*** – ♀ Jewish or Christian; dim. *Линка.*

Липка, Липко, Липман → **Либман**

Литман ***Литман*** – ♂ Jewish, may be a variant of **Либман.**

Лия, Лія → **Лея**

Логвин → **Лонгин**

Лонгин ***Лонгин***, † *Логинъ* – ♂ Latin. Eng. *Longin*, Lat. *Longinus*, Lith. *Lionginas*, *Longinas*, Ukr. *Логвин*. ⊕ 15 Mar. Ω & ‡ 16 Oct.

Луїза → **Людвига**

Лука ***Лука*** – ♂ Greek. Eng. *Lucas*, *Luke*, Lat. *Lucas*, Lith. *Lukošius*, *Lukas*, Pol. *Łukasz [Лукаш]*. ⊕ 18 Oct, 11 Dec. Ω 18 Oct. ‡ 4 Jan, 18 Oct, etc.

Лукерья, *Лукерія* → **Гликерия**

Лукий ***Лукий*** – ♂ Latin. Eng./Lat. *Lucius*, Lith. *Liucijus*, *Lucijus*, Pol. *Lucjusz*, Ukr. *Лукій*. ⊕ 8 & 24 Feb, 4 Mar, 3 Dec. ‡ 4 Jan, 10 Sep.

Лукия, *Лукія* → **Люция**

Лукиян, *Лукіян* → **Лукьян**

Лукреция ***Лукреция*** – ♀ Latin. Eng./Lat. *Lucretia*, Lith. *Lukrecija*, *Liukrecija*, Pol. *Lukrecja*.⊕ 7 Jun, 9 Jul, 11 Aug.

Лукьян ***Лукьян***, also *Люциан*, † *Лукіянъ*, *Люціанъ* – ♂ Latin. Eng. *Lucian*, Lat. *Lucianus*, Lith. *Liucijonas*, Pol. *Lucjan*, Ukr. *Лук'ян*. ⊕ 7 Jan, 11 Feb, 13 Jun, 26 Oct. Ω & ‡ 3 Jun, 15 Oct.

Люба ***Люба*** – ♀ Jewish.

Любобь ***Любобь***, also *Любава* – ♀ Slavic, "love." Ukr. *Любава*, *Любов*. ‡ 17 Sep.

Любомир ***Любомир*** – ♂ Slavic. Lat. *Lubomirus*. ⊕ 20 Feb, 21 Mar, 1 May, 28 Jun, 31 Jul, 20 Nov.

Любомира ***Любомира*** – ♀ of **Любомир**. ⊕ 23 Aug.

Людвиг ***Людвиг***, also *Людвик* – ♂ Germanic. Eng. *Louis*, *Lewis*, Lat. *Ludovicus*, *Lodovicus*, Lith. *Liudvikas*, Pol. *Ludwik*. ⊕ 25 Aug.

Людвига ***Людвига***, also *Людвика* – ♀ of **Людвиг**. Eng. *Louisa*, *Louise*, Lat. *Ludovica*, *Lodovica*, Lith. *Liudvika*, Pol. *Ludwika*, Ukr. *Луїза*, *Людвіга*. ⊕ 15 Mar.

Людмила ***Людмила*** – ♀ Slavic. Eng. *Ludmilla*, Lith. *Liudmila*, *Liudmilė*, Pol. *Ludmiła*. ⊕ & ‡ 16 Sep.

Людомир ***Людомир*** – ♂ Slavic. ⊕ 10 Nov.

Люциан, *Люціянъ* → **Лукьян**

Люция ***Люция***, also *Лукия* – ♀ Latin. Eng. *Lucy*, *Lucia*, *Lucie*, Lat. *Lucia*, Lith. *Liucija*, *Lucija*, *Liucė*, Pol. *Łucja*, Ukr. *Лукія*, *Люція*. ⊕ 25 Mar, 25 Jun, 9 Jul, 16 Sep, 13 Dec. ‡ 6 Jul, 13 Dec.

М м

Мавра ***Мавра*** – ♀ Greek. ‡ 3 May, 31 Oct.

Маврикий ***Маврикий***, † *Маврикій* – ♂ Latin. Eng. *Maurice*, *Morris*, Lat. *Mauritius*, Lith. *Mauricijus*, Pol. *Maurycy*, Ukr. *Маврикій*. ⊕ 22 Sep. ‡ 10 Jul, 22 Feb.

Магдалина ***Магдалина*** – ♀ Aramaic. Eng. *Magdalene*, *Madeline*, Lat./Lith. *Magdalena*, Pol. *Magdalena*, Ukr. *Магдалина*, *Магдалена*. ⊕ 25 May, 22 Jul. Ω 4 May, 22 Jul.

Маер → **Меер**

Макар ***Макар***, † *Макарій* – ♂ Greek. Eng. *Macaire*, Lat. *Macarius*, Lith. *Makaras*, Pol. *Makary*. ⊕ 2 & 15 Jan, 28 Feb, 10 Mar, 10 Apr, 12 Aug, 20 Dec. Ω 19 Jan, 19 Dec. ‡ 19 Jan, 23 Nov, etc.

Макрина ***Макрина*** – ♀ Latin. Ukr. *Мокрина*. ‡ 19 Jul.

Максим ***Максим*** – ♂ Latin. Eng. *Max*, *Maxim*, Latin *Maximus*, Lith. *Maksimas*, Pol. *Maksym*. ⊕ 8 Jun, 13 Aug, 12 Oct. Ω & ‡ 21 Jan, 19 Feb, 10 Apr, 14 May, 13 Aug.

Максимиан ***Максимиан***, † *Максиміанъ* – ♂ Latin. Ω 23 Oct. ‡ 21 Apr, 7 Nov.

Максимилиан ***Максимилиан***, also *Максимильян* –♂ Latin. Eng. *Maximilian*, Lat. *Maximilianus*, Lith. *Maksimilijonas*, Pol. *Maksymilian*, Ukr. *Максиміліан*. ⊕ 14 & 25 Aug, 12 Oct, 27 Nov. ‡ 4 Aug, 22 Oct.

Малахий ***Малахий***, † *Малахій*, *Малафей* – ♂ Hebrew. Eng. *Malachi*, Lat. *Malachias*, Pol. *Malachiasz*. ⊕ 14 Jan, 3 Nov. Ω & ‡ 3 Jan.

Малгоржата ***Малгоржата*** – ♀ Cyrillic phonetic version of Polish *Małgorzata*, see **Маргарита**.

Малка ***Малка*** – ♀ Jewish.

Малкиель ***Малкиель***, † *Малкіель* – ♂ Jewish; variants include dim. *Малко*.

Мальвина ***Мальвина*** – ♀ Germanic. Eng./Lith. *Malvina*, Pol. *Malwina*, Ukr. *Мальвіна*. ⊕ 4 Jul.

Мамелфа ***Мамелфа***, also *Амелфа* – ♀ origin unclear. Ω & ‡ 5 Oct.

Ман ***Ман*** – ♂ Jewish, variants include *Мана*, *Манко*, *Мандель*, *Манель*, and *Мендель*.

Манаше → **Менаше**

Мандель, *Манель*, *Манко* → **Ман**

Мануил ***Мануил***, † *Мануило* – ♂ Hebrew, variants include *Эммануил* and *Эмануель*. The long forms *Эмануель* and *Эммануил* are also seen. Eng./Lat. *Emmanuel*, Lith. *Emanuelis*, Pol. *Emanuel*, Ukr. *Мануїл*, *Мануйло*. ⊕ 26 Mar, 10 Jul. Ω 17 Jun. ‡ 22 Jan, 27 Mar, 17 Jun.

Маргарита ***Маргарита*** – ♀ Greek. Eng. *Margaret*, *Marjorie*, *Margot*, Lat. *Margareta*, *Margarita*, Lith. *Margarita*, *Magryta*, *Grėta*, Pol. *Małgorzata*. ⊕ 18 Jan, 22 Feb, 10 Jun, 13 Jul, 16 Oct. ‡ 17 Jul, 1 Sep.

Марголис ***Марголис*** – ♀ Jewish < Hebrew, "pearl"; variants include *Марголя*, *Маргулис*, *Маргуля*.

Мариам ***Мариам***, also *Марьям* – ♀ Hebrew, from the same origin as "Mary," cmp. **Мариамна**, **Мария** and **Мириам**. Variants include *Машка*.

Мариамна ***Мариамна*** – ♀ Hebrew, cmp. **Мариам**. ‡ 17 Feb, 30 Sep.

Мариан ***Мариан***, also *Марьян* – ♂ Latin. Eng. *Marion*, Lat. *Marianus*, Lith. *Marijonas*, Pol. *Marian*, Ukr. *Маріан*, *Мар'ян*. ⊕ 20 Apr, 6 May. ‡ 19 & 29 Mar, 10 Dec.

Марианна ***Марианна***, † *Маріанна*, also *Марьяна* and *Мариана* – ♀ of **Мариан**. Eng. *Marion, Marian, Marianna, Marianne, Maryanne*, Lith. *Marijona, Marijonė*, Pol. *Marianna [Маріанна, Маріянна, Марыянна, Марянна, Марьянна]*. ⊕ 17 Feb, 26 May, 2 Jun, 8 Sep.

Марина ***Марина*** – ♀ Latin. Eng./Lat./Lith./Pol. *Marina*. ⊕ 3 Mar. Ω 17 Jul. ‡ 28 Feb, 17 Jul.

Мария ***Мария***, also *Марья* – ♀ Hebrew. Eng. *Mary*, Lat./Pol. *Maria*, Lith. *Marija, Marė, Maria, Marytė*, Ukr. *Марія*. ⊕ *[numerous]*. Ω & ‡ 1 Apr, etc.

Маріянна → **Марианна**

Марк ***Марк*** – ♂ Latin. Eng. *Mark*, Lat. *Marcus*, Lith. *Morkus, Markas*, Pol. *Marek*, Ukr. *Марко*. ⊕ 24 Mar, 25 Apr, 18 Jun, 7 Oct, 22 Nov. Ω 29 Mar, 25 Apr, 20 Oct, 22 Nov. ‡ 4 Jan, 25 Apr, 27 Sep, 30 Oct, etc.

Маркелл ***Маркелл*** – ♂ Latin. Eng./Lat. *Marcellus*, Lith. *Marcelijus, Marcys*, Pol. *Marceli*, Ukr. *Маркел, Маркело*. ⊕ 16 Jan, 19 Feb, 10 Mar, 26 Apr, 17 Jul. Ω 25 Feb, 14 Aug, 29 Dec. ‡ 9 Feb, 7 Jun, 14 Aug, 29 Dec, etc.

Маркеллина ***Маркеллина*** – ♀ of **Маркелл**. Eng./Lat. *Marcella*, Lith. *Marcelija*, Pol. *Marcela [Марцелла, Марцеллина]*. ⊕ 31 Jan.

Маркель → **Маркус**

Маркиан ***Маркиан***, also *Маркиян, Мартьян, Мартиан*, † *Маркіянъ, Мартіанъ* – ♂ Latin. Eng. *Martian*, Lat. *Martianus*, Lith. *Marcijonas*, Pol. *Marcjan, Marcyan [Марціанъ, Марціянъ]*, Ukr. *Маркіян*. ⊕ 4 Jan, 17 Jun. Ω 9 & 27 Feb, 5 Jun, 25 & 30 Oct. ‡ 10 & 18 Jan, 5 Jun, 13 Jul, 9 Aug, 25 & 30 Oct, 2 Nov.

Марко → **Марк** and **Маркус**

Маркус ***Маркус*** – ♂ Jewish, from Latin *Marcus;* variants include *Маркель, Марко*, and *Меркель*.

Марта → **Марфа**

Мартиан → **Маркиан**

Мартин ***Мартин*** – ♂ Latin. Eng. *Martin*, Lat. *Martinus*, Lith. *Martynas, Marčius, Merčius*, Pol. *Marcin [Марцин]*. ⊕ 13 Apr, 8 & 24 Oct, 11 Nov, 7 & 29 Dec. Ω 13 Apr, 7 Dec. ‡ 14 Apr, 27 Jun, 12 Oct.

Мартиниан ***Мартиниан*** – ♂ Latin. Ω 13 Feb, 23 Oct. ‡ 12 Jan, 13 Feb, 11 Apr, 4 Aug, 7 & 22 Oct.

Мартьян → **Маркиан**

Марфа ***Марфа***, also *Марта* – ♀ Aramaic. Eng./Lat. *Martha*, Lith. *Morta, Marta*, Pol. *Marta*. ⊕ 19 Jan, 22 Feb, 21 Jun, 29 Jul. Ω 5 Jul, 1 Sep. ‡ 6 Feb, 4 & 9 & 23 Jun, 1 Sep, 8 Nov.

Марцелла, Марцеллина → **Маркеллина**

Марциан, Марціанъ, Марціянъ → **Маркиан**

Марциана ***Марциана***, or *Марцяна* – ♀, Cyrillic spelling of Latin *Marciana*, Lith. *Marcijona*, Pol. *Marcianna [Марціянна]* or *Marcjanna [Марцянна]*. ⊕ 9 Jan.

Марцин → **Мартин**

Марья → **Мария**

Марьям → **Мариам**

Марьянна, Марыянна, Марянна → **Марианна**

Машка → **Мариам**

Матвей ***Матвей*** – ♂ Hebrew, † *Матѳѣй, Матфѣй, Матфій*. Eng. *Matthew*, Lat. *Matthaeus*, Lith. *Motiejus*, Pol. *Mateusz [Матеуш]* or *Maciej*, Ukr. *Матвій*. ⊕ 21 Sep. Ω 9 Aug, 16 Nov. ‡ 30 Jun, 9 Aug, 5 Oct, 16 Nov.

Матильда ***Матильда*** – ♀ Germanic. Eng./Lith. *Matilda*, Lat. *Mathildis*, Pol. *Matylda [Матыльда]*. ⊕ 14 Mar.

Матис ***Матис*** – ♂ Jewish (usually), variants include *Матус, Матушь*.

Матрона ***Матрона*** – ♀ Latin. Ukr. *Мотрона*. Ω 9 Nov. ‡ 27 Mar, 9 Nov.

Матыльда → **Матильда**

Меер ***Меер*** – ♂ Jewish, variants include *Маер*.

Мейлах ***Мейлах*** – ♂ Jewish < Hebrew *'Elīmelekh*, usually *Элимелах* in Russian; variants include *Мелах, Мелих, Мейлих*.

Мелания ***Мелания***, † *Меланія* – ♀ Greek. Eng. *Melanie*, Lat./Pol. *Melania*, Lith. *Melanija*, Ukr. *Меланія, Мелана*. ⊕ & Ω & ‡ 31 Dec.

Мелетий ***Мелетий*** – † *Мелетій* – ♂ Greek. Ω & ‡ 12 Feb, 24 May, 21 Sep.

Мелитина ***Мелитина*** – ♀ Greek. Eng. *Melissa*, Lith. *Melita*, Pol. *Melisa*. ⊕ 10 Mar, 15 Sep. ‡ 16 Sep.

Мелих → **Мейлах**

Мелхиор ***Мелхиор*** – ♂ Hebrew. Eng./Lat./Pol. *Melchior*, Lith. *Melchioras, Melkijoras*. ⊕ 6 Jan, 7 Jul, 28 Sep.

Мемнон ***Мемнон*** – ♂ Greek. Ω 29 Apr. ‡ 12 May, 2 Sep, 29 Dec.

Менахем ***Менахем***, also *Менахим, Монахем* – ♂ Jewish. Eng. *Menahem*, Lat. *Manahem*.

Менаше ***Менаше***, also *Манаше, Менашь* – ♂ Jewish (compare *Manasseh* in English).

Мендель → **Ман**

Менуха ***Менуха*** – ♀ Jewish; variants include *Мнуха* and *Нуха*. Polish: *Menucha*.

Меркель → **Маркус**

Меркурий ***Меркурий***, † *Меркурій* – ♂ Greek. Ω 25 Nov. ‡ 7 & 28 Aug, 28 Sep, 4 & 24 Nov.

Методій → **Мефодий**

Мешель → **Мешулом** and **Мишель**

Мешулом ***Мешулом*** – ♂ Jewish, variants include *Мешель*.

Мефодий ***Мефодий***, also *Нефёд*, † *Мефодій, Меѳодій* – ♂ Greek. Eng./Lat. *Methodius*, Lith. *Metodijus*, Pol. *Metody*, Ukr. *Мефодій, Методій*.

⊕ 14 Feb, 11 May. Ω 22 Feb, 13 May, 14 & 20 Jun. ‡ 6 Apr, 11 May, 4 & 14 & 20 Jun.

Мечислав ***Мечислав*** – ♂ Slavic. Lat. *Mecislaus,* Lith. *Mečislovas, Mečislavas, Mečys, Mečius,* Pol. *Mieczysław.* ⊕ 1 Jan.

Мечислава ***Мечислава*** – ♀ of **Мечислав.** Lat. *Mecisla[v]a,* Pol. *Mieczysława.* ⊕ 1 Jan.

Микита → **Никита**

Микифор → **Никифор**

Микодим → **Никодим**

Микола, Миколай → **Николай**

Милан ***Милан*** – ♂ Slavic.

Милослав ***Милослав*** – ♂ Slavic. Pol. *Miłosław.* ⊕ 3 Aug, 18 Dec.

Мина ***Мина*** – ♀ Germanic, often (but not always) Jewish; Jewish variants include *Минда, Миндля, Минка, Минца.* Ω 11 Nov, 10 Dec. ‡ 24 Nov, 23 Dec, etc.

Минодора ***Минодора*** – ♀ Greek. Ω 10 Sep. ‡ 23 Sep.

Мириам ***Мириам*** – ♀ Hebrew, usually Jewish (cmp. English *Miriam*); variants include *Мирель, Мирля.*

Мирон ***Мирон*** – ♂ Greek. Eng. *Myron,* Lat. *Myro,* Pol. *Miron.* ⊕ 17 Aug, 10 Dec. Ω & ‡ 8 & 17 Aug.

Мирослав ***Мирослав*** – ♂ Slavic. Lat. *Miroslaus,* Lith. *Miroslavas,* Pol. *Mirosław.* ⊕ 26 Feb.

Мирослава ***Мирослава*** – ♀ of **Мирослав.** ⊕ 26 Feb.

Митрофан ***Митрофан*** – ♂ Greek. Ω 4 Jun. ‡ 4 & 23 Jun, 7 Aug, 23 Nov.

Михаил ***Михаил*** – ♂ Hebrew; Jews often used such forms as *Михель, Михно, Мишка,* etc.—the standard Russian dim. is *Миша.* Eng. *Michael,* Lat. *Michael,* Lith. *Mykolas, Mikolas, Mikelis, Mikola, Mikas,* Pol. *Michał [Михал],* Ukr. *Михайло.* ⊕ 29 Sep. Ω & ‡ 23 May, 6 Sep, 8 Nov.

Михайлина ***Михайлина*** – ♀ of **Михаил.** French *Micheline,* Lat. *Michaela,* Lith. *Mikalina, Michalina,* Pol. *Michalina.* ⊕ 19 Jun, 29 Sep.

Михал, Михель, Михно → **Михаил**

Мишель ***Мишель*** – ♂ often Jewish < **Мешулом,** but can also be a variant of **Михаил.**

Мнуха → **Менуха**

Мовша, Мовше → **Моисей**

Модель → **Мордехай**

Модест ***Модест*** –♂ Latin. Lat. *Modestus,* Lith. *Modestas,* Pol. *Modest.* ⊕ 17 Dec. Ω 15 Jun. ‡ 15 Jun, 18 Dec.

Моисей ***Моисей,*** also *Мойсей* – ♂ Hebrew. Often Jewish, but until the 18th century used also by Christians; variants primarily associated with Jews include *Мовша, Мовше, Моско, Моша, Мошек, Мошель,* and *Мошко.* Eng. *Moses,* Lat. *Moyses,* Lith. *Mozė,* Pol. *Mojżesz [Мойжеш].* Ukr. *Мусій, Мойсей.* ⊕ 4 Nov. Ω 28 Aug, 3 Sep. ‡ 28 Aug, 4 Sep, etc.

Мокрина → **Макрина**

Монахем → **Менахем**

Моника ***Моника*** – ♀ origin unclear. Eng./Lat. *Monica,* Lith./Pol. *Monika.* ⊕ 4 May.

Мониш ***Мониш*** – ♂ Jewish, variants include *Монис, Монус, Монуш,* etc.

Мордехай ***Мордехай,*** also *Мордхай* – ♂ Hebrew name (cmp. Eng. *Mordechai)* associated primarily with Jews; its many variants include *Модель, Мордух, Мордка, Мордко, Мортек, Мортка, Мотель,* and *Мотко*

Моско → **Моисей**

Мотель, Мотко → **Мордехай**

Мотрона → **Матрона**

Моша, Мошек, Мошель, Мошко → **Моисей**

Мстислав ***Мстислав*** – ♂ Slavic. Lat. *Mstislaus,* Pol. *Mścisław.* ⊕ 8 Jan. ‡ 15 Apr, 14 & 23 Jun.

Мусій → **Моисей**

Мушка ***Мушка*** – ♀ Jewish.

Н н

Надежда ***Надежда*** – ♀ Russian ("hope"). Eng. *Hope, Nadine,* Latin *Spes,* Lith. *Viltė,* Pol. *Nadzieja,* Ukr. *Надія.* ⊕ 30 Sep. ‡ 17 Sep.

Назар ***Назар,*** † *Назарій* – ♂ Hebrew. Lat. *Nazarius,* Lith. *Nazaras,* Pol. *Nazar,* Ukr. *Назар, Назарій.* Ω & ‡ 14 Oct.

Наркисс ***Наркисс,*** also *Нарсисс, Нарцисс* – ♂ Greek. Eng./Lat. *Narcissus,* Lith. *Narcyzas, Narcizas,* Pol. *Narcyz,* Ukr. *Наркис, Нарцис.* ⊕ 18 Mar, 17 Sep, 29 Oct. Ω 31 Oct. ‡ 4 Jan, 31 Oct.

Настас, Настасий → **Анастасий**

Настасия, Настасья → **Анастасия**

Наталия ***Наталия,*** also *Наталья,* dim. *Наташа* – ♀ Latin. Eng. *Natalie, Noelle,* Lat./Pol. *Natalia,* Lith. *Natalija, Natalė,* Ukr. *Наталія.* ⊕ 27 Jul, 26 Aug, 1 Dec. Ω & ‡ 26 Aug.

Натан ***Натан*** – ♂ Hebrew; as a Jewish name, it usually took the form *Носон,* with variants such as *Носек, Носель,* and *Носен.* Eng. *Nathan.*

Наум ***Наум*** – ♂ Hebrew; also used by Jews in the forms *Нахум* and *Нохум.* Eng./Lat. *Nahum,* Pol. *Naum.* Ω 1 Dec. ‡ 20 Jun, 27 Jul, 1 Dec.

Нафанаил ***Нафанаил*** – ♂ Hebrew. Eng. *Nathanael.* Ω 22 Apr. ‡ 22 Apr, 28 Oct, 27 Nov.

Нафтали ***Нафтали*** – ♂ Jewish, variants include *Нафтель* and *Нафтоль.* Eng. *Naftali.*

Нахама → **Нехама**

Нахля → **Нахман** and **Нехама**

Нахман ***Нахман*** – ♂ Jewish, variants include *Нахля, Нахмон,* and *Нохмон.*

Нахум → **Наум**

Невах, Невель → **Ноах**

Несанель *Несанель* – ♂ Jewish, cmp. Eng. *Nathanael;* variants include *Сана, Санель,* and *Санко.*

Нестор *Нестор* – ♂ Greek. Eng./Pol. *Nestor,* Ukr. *Нестір.* ⊕ 26 Feb, 8 Sep. Ω & ‡ 28 Feb, 27 Oct.

Нефёд → **Мефодий**

Нехама *Нехама* – ♀ Jewish, variants include *Нахама* and *Нахля.*

Нехемия *Нехемия,* *Нехемья,* † *Нехемія* – ♂ Jewish; variants include *Хемель* and *Хемка.*

Никандр *Никандр* – ♂ Greek. Ω & ‡ 5 Jun, 4 Nov.

Никита *Никита* – ♂ Greek. Lith. *Nicetas,* Pol. *Mikita,* Ukr. *Микита.* Ω & ‡ 20 Mar, 3 Apr, 15 Sep.

Никифор *Никифор,* also *Микифор* – ♂ Greek. Lat. *Nicephorus,* Lith. *Nikiforas, Nikiporas,* Pol. *Nicefor,* Ukr. *Никифор, Ничишр.* ⊕ 9 Feb, 1 Mar. Ω & ‡ 9 Feb, 13 Mar, 4 May, 2 Jun, 23 Oct.

Никін → **Никон**

Никодим *Никодим* – ♂ Greek. Eng./Lat. *Nicodemus,* Lith. *Nikodemas,* Pol. *Nikodem,* Ukr. *Никодим, Микодим.* ⊕ 3 Aug, 15 Sep. ‡ 3 Jul, 2 Aug, 31 Oct.

Николай *Николай,* also *Никола* and *Миколай* – ♂ Greek. Eng. *Nicholas,* Lat. *Nicolaus,* Lith. *Mikalojus, Nikalojus, Nikelis,* Pol. *Mikołaj,* Ukr. *Микола.* ⊕ 6 Dec. Ω 4 & 6 & 16 Dec, etc. ‡ 3 & 4 Feb, 9 Mar, 9 May, 6 Dec, etc.

Никон *Никон* – ♂ Greek. Ukr. *Никін, Никон.* Ω 23 Mar ‡ 23 Mar, 24 Jun, 28 Sep, 7 Nov, 11 Dec.

Нил *Нил* – ♂ apparently from the name of the river Nile. Ω 12 Nov. ‡ 7 Apr, 27 May, 12 Nov, 7 Dec.

Нисан, Нисель, Нисин → **Нисон**

Нисифор → **Онисифор**

Нисон *Нисон* – ♂ Jewish; variants include *Нисан, Нисель., Нисин,* etc.

Ничишр → **Никифор**

Ноах *Ноах* – ♂ Hebrew; variants used by Jews include *Невах, Невель,* and *Новах.* Eng. *Noah,* Lith. *Nojus.*

Новах → **Ноах**

Нонна *Нонна* – ♀ Latin *Nonna.* ⊕ 14 Jan. ‡ 5 Aug.

Норберт *Норберт* – ♂ Germanic. Eng. *Norbert,* Latin *Norbertus,* Lith. *Norbertas.* ⊕ 6 Jun.

Носек, Носел, Носон → **Натан**

Нота *Нота* – ♂ Jewish, variants include *Нотель, Нотка, Нута,* and *Нутка.*

Нохмон → **Нахман**

Нохум → **Наум**

Нута, Нутка → **Нота**

Нуха → **Менуха**

О о

Овадія, Овдій → **Авдей**

Оверкій → **Аверкий**

Овзер → **Ойзер**

Оврам → **Аврам**

Овсей → **Евсевий** and **Ишия**

Овшія → **Ишия**

Ойзер *Ойзер* – ♂ Jewish; variants include *Евзор* and *Овзер.*

Оксана → **Ксения**

Оксент, Оксентій → **Авксентий**

Октавиан *Октавиан* – ♂ Latin. Eng. *Octavian,* Lat. *Octavianus,* Lith. *Oktavijonas,* Pol. *Oktawian.* ⊕ 6 Aug, 23 Dec.

Октавий *Октавий* – ♂ Latin. Eng./Lat. *Octavius,* Lith. *Oktavijus, Oktavas,* Pol. *Oktawiusz.* ⊕ 20 Nov.

Октавия *Октавия* – ♀ of **Октавий**. Eng./Lat. *Octavia,* Lith. *Oktavija,* Pol. *Oktawia.* ⊕ 16 Mar.

Олег *Олег* – ♂ Norse. ‡ 20 Sep.

Олекса, Олексій → **Алексей**

Олександр → **Александр**

Олександра → **Александра**

Олена → **Елена**

Оливия *Оливия,* † *Оливія* – ♀ Latin. Eng. *Olive,* Lat. *Olivia,* Lith. *Olivija,* Pol. *Oliwia.* ⊕ 5 Mar.

Олимпиан *Олимпиан,* also *Олимп, Олимпий,* † *Олимпіянъ* – ♂ Greek. Ukr. *Олімп, Олімпій, Олімпіан.* Ω 8 Aug. ‡ 30 Jul, 2 Aug.

Олимпия *Олимпия* – ♀ of **Олимпиан**. Eng./Lat./ Pol. *Olympia,* Lith. *Olimpija,* Ukr. *Олімпіада, Олімпія.* ⊕ 25 Jul, 17 Dec. Ω & ‡ 25 Jul.

Ольга *Ольга* – ♀ Norse. Eng./Lat. *Olga.* ‡ 11 Jul.

Ольгерд *Ольгерд* – ♂ Lithuanian. Latin *Olgerdus,* Lith. *Algirdas,* Pol. *Olgierd.* ⊕ 11 Feb.

Оляна → **Юлиания**

Омелько, Омелян → **Емельян**

Оникій → **Аникий**

Онисий *Онисий* – ♂ Greek. Ukr. *Онисій, Онисько.* ‡ 5 Mar.

Онисим *Онисим,* also *Анисим* – ♂ Greek; Lat. *Onesimus,* Ukr. *Онисим, Онисько.* Ω 15 Feb. ‡ 4 Jan, 15 Feb, 10 May, 14 Jul, etc.

Онисифор *Онисифор,* also *Нисифор* – ♂ Greek. Ω 16 Jul, 8 Dec. ‡ 4 Jan, 9 Nov, 2 & 8 Dec, etc.

Онисько → **Онисій**

Онопрій, Онупрій → **Онуфрий**

Онуфрий *Онуфрий* – ♂ Greek; Lat. *Onuphrius,* Lith. *Anupras,* Pol. *Onufry,* Ukr. *Онопрій, Онупрій, Онуфрій.* ⊕ 12 Jun. Ω 12 Jun. ‡ 12 Jun, 21 Jul, 28 Sep.

Опанас → **Афанасий**

Орель → **Аарон**

Орест *Орест* – ♂ Greek. Ω & ‡ 10 Nov, 13 Dec.

Орина → **Ирина**

Орка → **Аарон**

Орлам → **Варлаам**

Осафат → **Иосафат**

Осип → **Иосиф**

Осия ***Осия***, † *Осія* – ♂ Hebrew (compare English *Hosea*). Ω & ‡ 17 Oct.

Оскар ***Оскар*** – ♂ Germanic. Eng. *Oscar*, Lat. *Anscharius, Ansgarius*, Lith. *Oskaras, Anskaras*. ⊕ 3 Feb.

Оснас ***Оснас*** – ♀ Jewish; also seen as *Асна*.

Остап → **Евстахий**

Ошер ***Ошер*** – ♂ Jewish, variants include *Ашер, Усер*, and *Ушер*.

Охрим, Охрім → **Ефрем**

Ошер ***Ошер***, also *Ашер*– ♂ Jewish.

П п

Павел ***Павел*** – ♂ Latin. Eng. *Paul*, Lat. *Paulus*, Lith. *Povilas, Paulius, Povilis*, Pol. *Paweł*, Ukr. *Павло*. ⊕ 25 Jan, 6 Feb, 28 Apr, 29 Jun. Ω 15 & 24 Jan, 18 & 28 May, 29 Jun, 17 Aug, 4 Oct, 6 Nov. ‡ 29 Jun, 22 Oct, 23 Dec, etc.

Павла ***Павла*** – ♀ of **Павел**. Eng./Lat. *Paula*, Lith. *Paulė*. ‡ 10 Feb, 3 Jun.

Павлина ***Павлина*** – ♀ Latin, ultimately from *Paulus* (**Павел**). Eng. *Pauline*, Lat./ Pol. *Paulina*, Lith. *Paulina, Povilina*. ⊕ 26 Jan.

Павло → **Павел**

Памфил ***Памфил***, also *Памфилий, Панфил* – ♂ Greek. Lat. *Pamphilus*, Ukr. *Памфіл, Панфіл*. Ω 16 Feb. ‡ 16 Feb, 12 Aug.

Панас → **Афанасий**

Панкратий ***Панкратий***, also *Панкрат* – ♂ Greek. Eng. *Pancras*, Lat. *Pancratius*, Lith. *Pankracijus*, Pol. *Pankracy*, Ukr. *Панкрат, Панкратій*. ⊕ 12 May. Ω & ‡ 9 Feb, 9 Jul.

Панталеимон ***Панталеймон*** – ♂ Greek. Pol. *Pantalejmon*. Ω & ‡ 27 Jul.

Панфил, Панфіл → **Памфил**

Параска, Параскева, Парасковья → **Прасковья**

Пармен ***Пармен*** – ♂ Greek. Ω 2 Mar. ‡ 4 Jan, 28 Jul.

Парфён ***Парфён***, also *Парфений*, † *Парѳеній* – ♂ Greek. Lat. *Partenius*, Pol. *Parfien*, Ukr. *Парфен, Парфеній, Парфентій, Пархім, Пархом, Партен*. Ω 7 Feb. ‡ 7 Feb, 23 Jul.

Патапій → **Потап**

Патрикий ***Патрикий*** – ♂ Greek. Eng. *Patrick*, Lat. *Patricius*. ⊕ 17 Mar. Ω 19 May. ‡ 20 Mar, 19 May, 23 Jun.

Пафнутий ***Пафнутий*** – ♂ Greek. Lat. *Paphnutius*, Pol. *Pafnucy*. ⊕ 21 Mar, 11 Sep. Ω 19 Apr, 25 Sep. ‡ 15 Feb, 19 Apr, 1 May, 28 Aug, 25 Sep.

Пейсах ***Пейсах*** – ♂ Jewish; variants include *Песель*.

Пелагея ***Пелагея*** – ♀ Greek. Eng./Lat. *Pelagia*, Lith. *Pelagija, Pelaga*, Pol. *Pelagia*, Ukr. *Пелагія*. ⊕ 8 Oct. Ω 4 & 6 May, 8 Oct. ‡ 4 May, 7 & 8 Oct.

Перель → **Перла**

Перец ***Перец*** – ♂ Jewish. Eng. *Perez*.

Перла ***Перла*** – ♀ German or Yiddish; used by Christians but more often by Jews, especially in the forms *Перля* and *Перель*.

Песель → **Бесель** and **Пейсах**

Песа, Песка, Песля, Песя → **Бесель**

Пётр ***Пётр*** – ♂ Greek. Eng. *Peter*, Lat. *Petrus*, Lith. *Petras*, Pol. *Piotr*, Ukr. *Петро*. ⊕ 29 Jun. Ω 29 Jun, etc. ‡ 4 & 16 Jan, etc.

Петронилла ***Петронилла*** – ♀ Latin. Eng. *Parnel*, Lat. *Petronella*, Lith. *Petronėlė*, Pol. *Petronela*, Ukr. *Петрунеля*. ⊕ 31 May. ‡ 29 Sep, 8 Oct.

Пилип → **Филипп**

Пимен ***Пимен*** – ♂ Greek. Ukr. *Пимін, Пимон*. ‡ 8 May, 2 & 27 & 28 Aug, 28 Sep.

Пинка → **Пиня**

Пинкус, Пинхас, Пинхос → **Финеес**

Пиня ***Пиня***, dim. *Пинка* – ♀ Jewish.

Пионий ***Пионий***, † *Піоній* – ♂ Greek. Ω & ‡ 11 Mar.

Піотр → **Пётр**

Поликарп ***Поликарп*** – ♂ Greek. Eng. *Polycarp*, Lat. *Polycarpus*, Lith. *Polikarpas*, Pol. *Polikarp*, Ukr. *Полікарп*. ⊕ 26 Jan. Ω 23 Feb, 2 Apr. ‡ 23 Feb, 2 Apr, 24 Jul, 28 Sep, 23 Dec.

Порфирий ***Порфирий*** – ♂ Greek. Ukr. *Порфир, Порфирій*. Ω 10 & 26 Feb, 4 Nov. ‡ 10 & 16 & 26 Feb, 15 Sep, 9 & 24 Nov.

Потап ***Потап***, † *Патапій* – ♂ Greek. Ω & ‡ 8 Dec.

Пракседа ***Пракседа*** – ♀ Greek. Lat. *Praxedes*. ⊕ 21 Jul.

Прасковья ***Прасковья***, also *Парасковья* – ♀ Greek. Ukr. *Парасковія, Параскева, Параска*. Ω 28 Oct. ‡ 20 Mar, 26 Jul, 14 & 28 Oct.

Приск ***Приск*** – ♂ Latin. Ω 7 Dec. ‡ 9 Mar, 21 Sep, 1 Oct.

Прокопий ***Прокопий***, also *Прокоп, Прокофий*, † *Прокофій, Прокопій* – ♂ Greek. Eng. *Procop*, Lat. *Procopius*, Pol. *Prokop*, Ukr. *Прокіп, Прокопій*. ⊕ 25 Mar. Ω & ‡ 27 Feb, 8 Jul, 22 Nov.

Протасий ***Протасий***, † *Протасій* – ♂ Greek. Eng. *Protase*, Lat. *Protasius*, Lith. *Protazijus, Protazas*, Pol. *Protazy*, Ukr. *Протас*. Ω & ‡ 14 Oct.

Прохор ***Прохор*** – ♂ Greek. Lat. *Prochorus*, Pol. *Prochor*. ‡ 4 & 15 Jan, 10 Feb, 23 Jun, 28 Jul, 28 Sep.

Пульхерия ***Пульхерия***, † *Пульхерія* – ♀ Latin. Lat. *Pulcheria*, Lith. *Pulcherija, Pulkerija*, Ukr. *Пульхерія*. ‡ 10 Sep.

Р р

Радивон → **Родион**

Радимир ***Радомир***, also *Радомир* – ♂ Slavic.

Радислав ***Радислав***, also *Радослав* – ♂ Slavic. Pol. *Radosław*.

Раиса ***Раиса*** – ♀ Greek. ‡ 5 Sep.
Райза, Райзля → **Роза**
Райка → **Райха**
Райха ***Райха*** – ♀ Jewish, variants include *Райка, Райхель, Райхля,* etc.
Рафаил ***Рафаил*** – ♂ Hebrew. Eng./Lat. *Raphael,* Lith. *Rapolas, Rapalas,* Pol. *Rafał,* Ukr. *Рафаїл.* ⊕ 24 Oct. ‡ 8 Nov.
Рахиль ***Рахиль*** – ♀ Hebrew; forms used by Jews include *Рашел, Роха, Рохель, Рохля,* and *Рухля.* Eng. *Rachel, Raquel,* Lat. *Rachel,* Lith. *Rachelė,* Pol. *Rachela,* Ukr. *Рахіль, Рахіля.* ⊕ 30 Sep.
Рахмиель ***Рахмиель,*** † *Рахміель* – ♂ Jewish.
Рашел → **Рахиль**
Ребекка ***Ребекка*** – ♀ Hebrew, but Jews tended to prefer the form *Ривка* and its variants, including *Рива, Рывка, Рывля, Рыша,* and *Рышка.* Eng. *Rebecca,* Pol. *Rebeka, Rywka.* ⊕ 9 Mar. ‡ 23 Sep.
Регина ***Регина*** – ♀ Latin. Eng./Lat. *Regina,* Ukr. *Регіна.* ⊕ 17 Mar, 22 Aug, 7 Sep.
Рейза, Рейсель, Рейзля → **Роза**
Рейна ***Рейна*** – ♀ Jewish.
Ремигий ***Ремигий*** – ♂ Latin. Eng. *Remy,* Lat. *Remigius,* Lith. *Remigijus,* Pol. *Remigiusz.* ⊕ 1 Oct.
Рената ***Рената*** – ♀ Latin. Eng. *Renée,* Latin/Lith. *Renata.* ⊕ 12 Nov.
Рива, Ривка → **Ребекка**
Рика ***Рика*** – ♀ Jewish, variants include *Рикель* and *Рикля.*
Роберт ***Роберт*** – ♂ Germanic. Eng. *Robert,* Lat. *Robertus,* Lith. *Robertas.* ⊕ 17 Sep.
Рода ***Рода*** – ♀ Jewish, variants include *Родель, Родка, Рудель, Рудка,* etc.
Родион ***Родион,*** also *Родивон,* † *Родіонъ* – ♂ Greek. Ukr. *Родіон, Радивон.* Ω 28 Mar, 8 Apr, 10 Nov. ‡ 4 Jan, 10 Nov.
Роза ***Роза*** – ♀ Latin; Jews tended to use *Ройза* and forms derived from it, including *Райза, Райзля, Рейза, Рейзель,* etc. Eng. *Rose, Rosa,* Lat. *Rosa,* Lith. *Rožė,* Pol. *Róża.* ⊕ 6 Mar, 23 Aug, 4 Sep.
Розалия ***Розалия,*** † *Розалія* – ♀ Romance. Eng. *Rosalie, Rosalia,* Lat. *Rosalia,* Lith. *Rozalija,* Pol. *Rozalia,* Ukr. *Розалія, Рузалія.* ⊕ 4 Sep.
Ройза → **Роза**
Роксана ***Роксана*** – ♀ Persian. Eng. *Roxanne,* Pol. *Roksana.* ⊕ 20 Mar, 13 Dec.
Роман ***Роман*** – ♂ Latin. Eng./Pol. *Roman,* Lat. *Romanus,* Lith. *Romanas, Romas.* ⊕ 28 Feb, 9 Aug, 18 Nov. Ω 16 Mar, 1 Oct, 18 Nov. ‡ 29 Jan, 10 Aug, 18 & 19 Nov, 1 Oct, etc.
Рона, Ронка, Роня → **Бройна** and **Кройна**
Ростислав ***Ростислав*** – ♂ Slavic. Pol. *Rościsław.* ⊕ 17 Jan. ‡ 14 Mar.
Рох ***Рох*** – ♂ German. Eng. *Roch,* Lat. *Rochus,* Lith. *Rokas,* Pol. *Roch.* ⊕ 16 Aug.
Роха, Рохель, Рохля → **Рахиль**
Рубин → **Рувим**
Рувим ***Рувим*** – ♂ mainly Jewish; variants include *Рубин* and *Рувин.* Eng. *Reuben,* Lat. *Ruben.*
Рудель, Рудка → **Рода**
Руслан ***Руслан*** – ♂ Turkish.
Рухама ***Рухама*** – ♀ Jewish. Pol. *Ruchama.*
Рухля → **Рахиль**
Руфин ***Руфин*** – ♂ Latin. Lat. *Rufinus,* Lith. *Rufinas, Rufas.* ⊕ 14 Jun. ‡ 23 Mar, 20 Apr, 19 Jul.
Руфь ***Руфь*** – ♀ Hebrew. Eng./Lat. *Ruth,* Lith. *Rūta.* ⊕ 1 Sep.
Рывка, Рывля, Рышка → **Ребекка**
Рюрик ***Рюрик*** – ♂ Norse. Eng. *Roderick,* Lat. *Rodericus,* Lith. *Rodrigas, Ruderikas.* ⊕ 13 Mar.

С с

Сабина ***Сабина*** – ♀ Latin. Eng. *Sabine, Sabina,* Lat. *Sabina,* Lith. *Sabina, Sabinė,* Ukr. *Савіна.* ⊕ 29 Aug, 27 Oct, 30 Dec.
Сава → **Савва**
Саватій → **Савватий**
Савва ***Савва*** – ♂ Aramaic. Ukr. *Сава, Савка.* ⊕ 5 Dec. Ω 15 & 24 Apr, 5 Dec. ‡ 12 Jan, 8 Feb, 2 Mar, 15 & 24 Apr, 27 Jul, 3 & 5 Dec, etc.
Савватий ***Савватий,*** † *Савватій* – ♂ Hebrew; Jews tended to use the forms *Шабсай, Шапсель, Шапшель, Шебшель, Шепсель,* etc. Eng. *Shabbethai,* Ukr. *Саватій.* Ω 19 Sep. ‡ 2 Mar, 8 Aug, 19 & 27 & 28 Sep.
Савелий ***Савелий*** – ♂ Hebrew; Jews tended to use *Завель, Шавель, Шауль, Шоель,* etc. Eng./Latin *Saul,* Lith. *Saulius,* Pol. *Saul, Szaul, Szaweł, Szojel,* Ukr. *Савелій.* ⊕ 25 Feb. Ω & ‡ 17 Jun.
Савин ***Савин*** – ♂ Latin. Ω 12 Mar.
Савіна → **Сабина**
Садок ***Садок,*** also *Садох* – ♂ Hebrew; Jews tended to use the forms *Цадак, Цадык,* and *Цодик.* Ω & ‡ 20 Feb, 19 Oct.
Сакій → **Исаакий**
Салівон → **Селиван**
Саломея ***Саломея,*** also *Соломея* – ♀ Hebrew. Eng. *Salome,* Lat. *Salomea,* Lith. *Salomėja, Saliomė,* Pol. *Salomea,* Ukr. *Соломія, Саломея.* ‡ 3 Apr.
Саломон → **Соломон**
Самійло → **Самуил**
Самсон ***Самсон*** – ♂ Hebrew (cmp. English *Samson*); Jews tended to prefer the forms *Шимсон, Шимшон, Шимшель,* etc. Ω & ‡ 27 Jun.
Самуил ***Самуил,*** also *Самойла,* † *Самойло* – ♂ Hebrew (cmp. English *Samuel*); Jews tended to

prefer the forms *Смуль, Шмуль, Шмуиль, Шмуйло, Шмулька, Шмулько,* etc. Eng./Lat. *Samuel,* Lith. *Samuelis,* Ukr. *Самійло.* ⊕ 20 Aug. Ω 20 Aug. ‡ 16 Feb, 20 Aug, 9 Dec.

Сана → **Александр** and **Несанель**

Сандор → **Александр**

Санель → **Несанель**

Санка, Санко → **Александр** and **Несанель**

Сарра *Сарра* – ♀ Hebrew; Jews used such forms as *Серка, Сора, Соша, Сура, Цира, Цирель, Цирля, Цыра, Шора.* Eng. *Sarah, Sara,* Lat./Lith. *Sara,* Ukr. *Сара.* ⊕ 19 Jan, 13 Jul, 9 Oct.

Сафат → **Иосафат**

Сахар → **Иссахар**

Саша → **Александр**

Светлана *Светлана* – ♀ Slavic. Ukr. *Світлана.* ‡ 13 Feb, 20 Mar.

Светозар *Светозар* – ♂ Slavic. Ukr. *Світозар.*

Світлана → **Светлана**

Свирид → **Спиридон**

Святополк *Святополк* – ♂ Slavic. Pol. *Świętosław.*

Святослав *Святослав* – ♂ Slavic. Pol. *Świętopełk.* ‡ 29 Jun, 14 Oct.

Севастьян *Севастьян*, † *Севастіанъ* – ♂ Greek. Eng. *Sebastian,* Lat. *Sebastianus,* Lith. *Sebastijonas,* Pol. *Sebastian,* Ukr. *Севастян, Севастіан, Себастіян.* ⊕ 20 Jan. Ω 18 Dec. ‡ 26 Feb, 20 & 23 Mar, 18 Dec.

Северин *Северин* – ♂ Latin. Eng. *Severin,* Lat. *Severinus,* Lith. *Severinas,* Pol. *Seweryn,* Ukr. *Северин, Север'ян.* ⊕ 8 Jan, 19 Nov. ‡ 4 Jun.

Сезон → **Созонт**

Селиван *Селиван*, or *Сильван* – ♂ Latin. Eng. *Silas,* Lat. *Silvanus,* Lith. *Silvanas,* Pol. *Sylwan,* Ukr. *Саливон, Селіфан.* ⊕ 18 Feb, 10 Jul. Ω 6 Feb, 4 May. ‡ 4 & 25 & 29 Jan, 4 May, 10 & 30 Jul, 14 Oct.

Семён *Семён*, † *Симеон, Семеон* – ♂ Hebrew, this name tends to overlap with the Eng. usages of *Simon* and *Simeon,* and it can be quite difficult to tell these names apart. Jews tended to use such forms as *Зимель, Зимля, Зымель, Симон, Шиме, Шимель, Шимен, Шимон,* etc. Eng./Lat. *Simeon* and *Simon,* Lith. *Simeonas, Simas, Simanas, Simonas,* Pol. *Szymon, Symeon,* Ukr. *Семен, Симон.* ⊕ 5 Jan, 16 May, 1 Jun, 18 Jul, 8 & 28 Oct. Ω 3 Feb, 14 & 17 & 27 Apr, 24 May, 21 Jul, 1 & 18 Sep. ‡ 4 Jan, 27 Apr, 12 Sep, etc.

Сендер, Сендор → **Александр**

Серапион *Серапион*, † *Серапіонъ* – ♂ Greek. Ω 24 May. ‡ 24 May, 12 Jul, etc.

Серафим *Серафим* – ♂ Hebrew. Lat. *Seraphinus,* Lith. *Serapinas, Serafinas,* Pol. *Serafin.* ⊕ 12 & 29 Oct. ‡ 2 Jan, 19 Jul.

Серафима *Серафима* – ♀ of **Серафим**. Eng./Lat. *Seraphina,* Lith. *Serapina, Serafina,* Pol. *Serafina.* ⊕ 8 Sep. ‡ 29 Jul.

Серватий *Серватий* – ♂ Latin. Lat. *Servatius,* Lith. *Servacijus,* Pol. *Serwacy.* ⊕ 13 May.

Сергей *Сергей*, † *Сергій* – ♂ Latin. Eng. *Serge,* Latin *Sergius,* Lith. *Sergijus,* Pol. *Sergiusz,* Ukr. *Сергій.* ⊕ 7 Oct. Ω 13 May, 7 Oct. ‡ 14 Jan, 20 Mar, 19 May, 23 & 28 Jun, 5 Jul, 11 & 25 & 28 Sep, 7 Oct.

Серка → **Сарра**

Сигізмунд → **Зигмунд**

Сидония *Сидония*, † *Сидонія* – ♀ Latin. Lat. *Sidonia,* Lith. *Sidona,* Pol. *Sydonia.* ⊕ 6 & 23 Jun.

Сидір, Сидор → **Исидор**

Сикст *Сикст* – ♂ Greek-Latin. Eng./Lat. *Sixtus,* Lith. *Sikstas,* Pol. *Sykstus.* ⊕ 5 Aug. ‡ 10 Aug.

Сильвестр *Сильвестр*, † *Селивестр* – ♂ Latin. Eng. *Silvester, Sylvester,* Lat. *Silvester,* Lith. *Silvestras,* Pol. *Sylwester.* ⊕ 31 Dec. Ω 2 Jan. ‡ 3 Jan, 23 Apr, 23 May, 28 Sep.

Сильван → **Селиван**

Сильвия *Сильвия* – ♀ Latin. Eng. *Sylvia,* Lat. *Silvia,* Lith. *Silvija,* Pol. *Sylwia,* Ukr. *Сільвія.* ⊕ 29 Sep, 3 Nov.

Сима, Симка → **Симха**

Симеон, Симон → **Семён**

Симха *Симха*, dim. *Сима, Симка* – ♀ or ♂ Jewish. Beider says *Симха* or *Шимха* was generally used for males, *Сима, Симка* or *Сыма* for females (variants: *Цимха, Цимель*). Pol. *Symcha, Syma.*

Сільвія → **Сильвия**

Слава *Слава* – ♀ Slavic, also used by Jews, including variants *Славка, Слова.*

Славомир *Славомир* – ♂ Slavic. Pol. *Sławomir.* ⊕ 17 May.

Слова → **Слава**

Смуль → **Самуил**

Созонт *Созонт*, also *Созон, Созонтий* – ♂ Greek. Ukr. *Созонт, Созон, Сезон.* Ω 7 Sep. ‡ 7 Jun, 20 Aug, 20 Sep.

Сократ *Сократ*, also *Сократий* – ♂ Greek. Ω 23 Oct. ‡ 4 May, 3 Nov, 11 Dec.

Соломея, Соломія → **Саломея**

Соломон *Соломон*, or *Саломон* – ♂ Hebrew, cmp. Eng. *Solomon;* Jews preferred various forms, including *Залман, Зальман, Зальмон, Зельман, Шліома, Шлома, Шлойма, Шляма, Шолом, Шулим.* Eng. *Solomon,* Lat. *Salomon,* Lith. *Saliamonas, Salomonas.* ⊕ 28 Sep. ‡ 23 Jan.

Соня → **Софья**

Сопрон → **Софрон**

Сора → **Сарра**

Сосанна → **Сусанна**

Сосипатр *Сосипатр* – ♂ Greek. Ω 28 Apr, 10 Nov. ‡ 4 Jan, 28 Apr, 10 Nov.

София, Софiя → **Софья**

Софоний *Софоний*, also *Софон*, † *Софонія* – ♂ Hebrew. Ω & ‡ 3 Dec.

Софрон *Софрон*, also *Сопрон*, † *Софроній* – ♂ Greek. Ω 11 Mar, 8 Dec. ‡ 11 & 30 Mar, 11 May, 23 & 30 Jun, 28 Aug, 9 Dec.

Софья *Софья*, also *София*, † *Софія*, dim. *Соня* – ♀ Greek. Eng. *Sophie, Sophia, Sophy,* Lat. *Sophia,* Lith. *Sofija, Zofija, Zopija, Zosė,* Pol. *Zofia [Зофия, Зофія],* Ukr. *Софія.* ⊕ 15 May, 30 Sep. Ω 17 Sep. ‡ 23 Jul, 17 & 18 Sep, 16 Dec.

Сохор → **Иссахар**

Соша → **Сарра**

Спиридон *Спиридон*, also *Свирид, Спиридоний,* † *Спюридонъ* – ♂ Greek. Ukr. *Свирид, Свиридон, Спиридон.* Ω 12 Dec. ‡ 28 Sep, 31 Oct, 12 Dec.

Сроель, Сроль, Сруль → **Израиль**

Станислав *Станислав* – ♂ Slavic. Eng. *Stanislaus, (Stanley*),* Latin *Stanislaus,* Lith. *Stanislovas, Stanys, Stasys, Stasius, Stonys,* Pol. *Stanisław,* Ukr. *Станіслав, Стасій.* ⊕ 8 May, 13 Nov.

Станислава *Станислава* – ♀ of **Станислав**. Eng. *(Stella*),* Latin *Stanisla[v]a,* Lith. *Stanislova, Stanislava, Stasė,* Pol. *Stanisława,* Ukr. *Станіслава.* ⊕ 8 May, 13 Nov.

Стасій → **Станислав**

Стахий *Стахий*, † *Стахій* – ♂ Greek. Ω 31 Oct. ‡ 4 Jan, 31 Oct.

Степан *Степан*, † *Стефанъ* – ♂ Greek. Eng. *Stephen, Steven,* Lat. *Stephanus,* Lith. *Steponas,* Pol. *Stefan, Szczepan,* Ukr. *Степан, Стефан.* ⊕ 2 & 16 Aug, Dec 26. Ω 13 Jan, 26 Feb, 31 Mar, 2 Aug, 28 Oct, 22 & 28 Nov, 27 Dec. ‡ 4 Jan, 2 Aug, 15 Sep, 27 Dec, etc.

Стефания *Стефания*, also *Степанида* – ♀ of **Степан**. Eng. *Stephanie,* Lat. *Stephan[i]a,* Lith. *Stefanija, Stepanija,* Pol. *Stefania,* Ukr. *Степанида, Степанія, Стефанія.* ⊕ 18 Sep. ‡ 11 Nov.

Сура → **Сарра**

Сусанна *Сусанна*, † *Сосанна* – ♀ Hebrew; Jews tended to prefer forms such as *Шошана, Шоса, Шушана,* etc. Eng. *Susan, Susanna, Suzanne,* Lat. *Susanna,* Lith. *Zūzana, Zūzanė, Zuzė, Zūzė,* Pol. *Zuzanna [Зузанна].* ⊕ 24 May, 11 Aug, 20 Sep. Ω 15 Dec. ‡ 24 May, 6 Jun, 11 Aug.

Схария → **Захар**

Сыма → **Симха**

Тт

Таврион *Таврион*, † *Тавріонъ* – ♂ Latin. ‡ 7 Nov.

Тадей, Тадеуш → **Фаддей**

Таисия *Таисия*, also *Таисья* – ♀ Greek. Ukr. *Таїсія, Таїса.* ‡ 10 May, 8 Oct.

Тамара *Тамара* – ♀ Hebrew; Jewish variants include *Тамарка, Тема, Темка, Темерель.* Eng. *Tamara.* ⊕ 25 Mar. ‡ 1 Mar.

Танас, Танасій → **Афанасий**

Танхум *Танхум* – ♂ Jewish; variants include *Танель, Танхель, Танфель,* etc.

Таня → **Татьяна**

Тарас *Тарас*, also *Тарасий*, † *Тарасій* – ♂ Greek; Eng. *Taras,* Lat. *Tharasius.* Ω & ‡ 25 Feb.

Татьяна *Татьяна*, † *Татіяна* – ♀ Latin, short forms include *Таня, Татя.* Eng./Lat. *Tatiana,* Ukr. *Тетяна.* ⊕ 3 Jun. Ω & ‡ 12 Jan.

Тауба *Тауба* – ♀ Jewish; variants include *Товба, Тойба,* and *Тоуба.*

Тевель → **Давид** and **Товий**

Тейвъ → **Тов**

Текла, Текля → **Фёкла**

Тельцель → **Дульца**

Тема, Темка, Темерель → **Тамара**

Теодор → **Фёдор**

Теофан → **Феофан**

Теофиль, Теофіль → **Феофил**

Теофіла → **Феофила**

Телесфор *Телесфор* – ♂ Greek (rare among Russians). Eng./Latin *Telesphorus,* Lith. *Telesforas,* Pol. *Telesfor.* ⊕ 5 Jan.

Тереза *Тереза*, † *Терезія* – ♀ Greek. Eng. *Teresa, Theresa,* Lat. *Teresia,* Lith. *Teresė.* ⊕ 1 & 3 & 15 Oct.

Терентий *Терентий*, † *Терентій* – ♂ Latin. Ukr. *Терентій.* Ω 10 Apr, 20 Oct, 10 Nov. ‡ 13 Mar, 10 Apr, 21 Jun, 28 Oct.

Терца → **Тирца**

Тетяна → **Татьяна**

Тиберий *Тиберий* – ♂ Latin. Eng./Lat. *Tiberius,* Lith. *Tiberijus,* Pol. *Tyberiusz.* ⊕ 11 Aug, 10 Nov.

Тила *Тила* – ♀ Germanic or Hebrew; variants include *Тилка, Тилька,* and *Тильча.*

Тилимон → **Филимон**

Тимон *Тимон* – ♂ Greek; Eng./Lat. *Timon,* Lith. *Timonas,* Pol. *Tymon,* Ukr. *Тимон.* ⊕ 28 Sep. Ω & ‡ 31 Dec.

Тимофей *Тимофей*, † *Тимовей* – ♂ Greek. Eng. *Timothy,* Lat. *Timotheus,* Lith. *Timotiejus, Timas,* Pol. *Tymoteusz,* Ukr. *Тимофій.* ⊕ 24 Jan, 21 May, 22 Aug, 19 Dec. Ω 22 Jan, 21 Feb, 22 Apr, 3 May, 10 Jun, 19 Aug, 31 Dec. ‡ 4 & 22 & 24 Jan, 21 Feb, 3 & 20 May, 10 Jun, 19 Aug, 19 Dec.

Тирца *Тирца* – ♀ Jewish; variants include *Терца* (?) *Тирцель* and *Тирча.* Eng. *Tirzah,* Pol. *Tyrca.*

Тит *Тит* – ♂ Latin. Eng./Lat. *Titus,* Lith. *Titas,* Pol. *Tytus.* ⊕ 4 & 26 Jan, 6 Feb. Ω 2 Apr, 25 Aug. ‡ 4 Jan, 27 Feb, 2 Apr, 25 & 28 Aug, 28 Sep.

Тихон ***Тихон*** – ♂ Greek.Ukr. *Тихін, Тихон.* Ω 16 Jun. ‡ 16 & 26 Jun, 13 Aug.
Тов ***Тов*** – ♂ Jewish, variants include *Тейв* and *Тойв.*
Товба → **Тауба**
Товий ***Товий***, † *Товія* – ♂ Hebrew; variants used by Jews include *Тевель, Товія, Тувія, Тувля,* etc. Eng. *Tobias, Tobiah, Toby,* Lat. *Tobias,* Lith. *Tobijas,* Pol. *Tobiasz.* ⊕ 2 Sep.
Тода, Тодор, Тодрес → **Фёдор**
Тодос, Тодосій → **Феодосій**
Тодося → **Феодосия**
Тойба → **Тауба**
Тойв → **Тов**
Тольца → **Дульца**
Тома, Томаш → **Фома**
Тоуба → **Тауба**
Трайтель ***Трайтель***, also *Трайтля* – ♂ Jewish.
Трифон ***Трифон***, also *Трифан* – ♂ Greek. Lat. *Trypho,* Pol. *Tryfon.* Ω 1 Feb. ‡ 1 Feb, 19 Apr, 8 Oct, 15 Dec.
Трофим ***Трофим*** – ♂ Greek. Lat. *Trophimus,* Pol. *Trofim,* Ukr. *Трохим.* Ω 15 Apr, 23 Jul, 19 Sep. ‡ 4 Jan, 16 & 18 Mar, 15 Apr, 23 Jul, 19 Sep.
Трохим → **Трофим**
Тувія, Тувля → **Товий**

У у

Узиель ***Узиель***, † *Узіель* – ♂ Jewish.
Улас → **Влас**
Уліян, Улян → **Юлиан**
Уляна → **Юлиания**
Урбан ***Урбан***, † *Урванъ* – ♂ Latin. Eng. *Urban,* Lat. *Urbanus,* Lith. *Urbonas, Urbas.* Ω & ‡ 31 Oct.
Ури ***Ури*** – ♂ Jewish; dim. forms include *Урко* and *Юрко.*
Урия ***Урия***, † *Урія* – ♂ Hebrew; Jewish variants include *Урко* and *Юрко.* Eng. *Uriah,* Lat. *Urias,* Pol. *Uriasz.*
Урсула ***Урсула*** – ♀ Latin. Eng. *Ursula,* Lat. *Ursula,* Lith. *Uršulė, Uršė,* Pol. *Urszula [Уршуля].* ⊕ 21 Oct.
Усер → **Ошер**
Устим, Устин → **Юстин**
Устина → **Юстина**
Ушер → **Ошер**

Ф ф

Фабиан ***Фабиан*** – ♂ Latin. Eng. *Fabian,* Lat. *Fabianus,* Lith. *Fabijonas, Pabijonas.* ⊕ 20 Jan.
Фавст → **Фауст**
Фаддей ***Фаддей***, also *Фадей* – ♂ Aramaic. Eng. *Thaddeus,* Lat. *Thaddaeus,* Lith. *Tadas,* Pol. *Tadeusz [Тадеуш],* Ukr. *Тадей, Фадей.* ⊕ 28 Oct. Ω 20 Aug. ‡ 4 Jan, 7 May, 21 Aug, 29 Dec, etc.
Фаина ***Фаина*** – ♀ Greek. Ukr. *Фаїна.* ‡ 18 May.
Файвус ***Файвус*** – ♂ Jewish, variants include *Файвель, Файвуш,* and *Фейвель.*
Файга, Файгель → **Фойгель**
Файтель ***Файтель*** – ♂ Jewish; variants include *Файтля.*
Фалалей ***Фалалей***, † *Фалелњй* – ♂ Greek. Ω 28 Feb, 20 May. ‡ 27 Feb, 20 May.
Фальк ***Фальк*** – ♂ Jewish.
Фауст ***Фауст***, also *Фавст* – ♂ Latin. Ω 24 May, 3 Aug. ‡ 24 Apr, 24 May, 3 Aug, 6 Sep, 4 Oct.

***Фе** : many of these names beginning with **Фе-** had archaic spellings with **Ѳе-**. It seems superfluous to make a note of all of them, however, as you will probably seldom encounter them. Also, many names beginning **Фео-** have variants with simply **Фе-** and vice versa. **Фео-** usually corresponds to English* Theo- *in Greek-derived names.]*

Феврония ***Феврония***, also *Хавронья,* † *Февронія* – ♀ Latin or Greek. Lat./Pol. *Febronia.* Ω & ‡ 25 Jun.
Фёдор ***Фёдор***, also *Феодор, Теодор,* † *Ѳедоръ* – ♂ Greek; Jewish variants of this name include *Тода* and *Тодрес.* Eng. *Theodore,* Lat. *Theodorus,* Lith. *Teodoras, Tevadorius,* Pol. *Teodor,* Ukr. *Федір, Теодор, Тодор.* ⊕ Ω ‡ *[numerous].*
Федора → **Феодора**
Федос, Федосій → **Феодосий**
Федосия, Федосія, Федося → **Феодосия**
Федот ***Федот***, also *Федотий,* † *Феодотъ* – ♂ Greek. Ukr. *Федот.* Ω 19 Feb, 2 Mar, 18 May, 17 Jun. ‡ 19 Feb, 2 Mar, 29 Apr, 8 & 18 May, 7 Jun, 4 Jul, 2 & 15 Sep, 7 Nov.
Федул → **Феодул**
Фейвель → **Файвус**
Фейга, Фейге, Фейгель → **Фойгель**
Фёкла ***Фёкла***, † *Ѳекла* – ♀ Greek. Eng. *Thecla, Tecla, Thekla,* Lat. *Thecla,* Lith. *Teklė,* Pol. *Tekla,* Ukr. *Текля, Векла.* ⊕ 23 Sep. Ω 19 Aug, 24 Sep. ‡ 6 & 9 Jun, 19 Aug, 24 Sep, 20 Nov.
Феликс ***Феликс*** – ♂ Latin. Eng./Lat. *Felix,* Lith. *Peliksas, Feliksas,* Pol. *Feliks,* Ukr. *Фелікс.* ⊕ 14 Jan, 1 Mar, 21 Apr, 30 May, 11 Jun, 12 Jul, 11 Sep, 6 & 20 Nov, 20 Dec. ‡ 25 Jan, 18 Apr, 6 Jul.
Фелиция ***Фелиция***, † *Феліція* – ♀ Latin. Eng. *Felicia (Phyllis*),* Lat. *Felicia,* Lith. *Felicija,* Polish *Felicja.* ⊕ 24 Jan, 27 Apr. ‡ 1 Feb.
Фелициан ***Фелициан***, † *Феліціанъ* – ♂ Latin. Eng. *Felician,* Lat. *Felicianus,* Lith. *Felicijonas,* Pol. *Felicjan.* ⊕ 24 Jan, 9 Jun, 29 Oct.
Фемистокл ***Фемистокл*** – ♂ Greek. ‡ 21 Dec.

Феодор → **Фёдор**

Феодора *Феодора*, also *Федора* – ♀ of **Фёдор**. Eng./Lat. *Theodora*, Lith. *Teodora, Tevadorė*, Pol. *Teodora*, Ukr. *Федора, Тодора.* ⊕ 28 Apr, 17 Sep. Ω 5 Apr, 11 Sep, 14 Nov, 30 Dec. ‡ 11 Feb, 10 Mar, 5 & 16 Apr, 27 May, 16 Aug, 11 Sep, 14 Nov, 30 Dec.

Феодосий *Феодосий*, also *Федос* – ♂ Greek. Eng./ Lat. *Theodosius*, Lith. *Teodosijus*, Pol. *Teodozjusz*, Ukr. *Феодосій, Федос, Федосій, Тодос, Тодосій.* ⊕ 11 Jan, 3 May, 25 Oct. Ω 8 Feb, 3 & 31 May, 8 Aug. ‡ 11 & 28 Jan, 5 Feb, 3 May, 23 Jun, 14 & 28 Aug, 2 & 9 Sep.

Феодосия *Феодосия*, also *Федосия*, † *Феодосія* – ♀ of **Феодосий**. Eng./Lat. *Theodosia*, Lith. *Teodosija*, Pol. *Teodozja*, Ukr. *Феодосія, Федосія, Федося, Тодося.* ⊕ 2 Apr, 29 May. Ω 3 Apr, 29 May, 18 Jul. ‡ 20 Mar, 3 apr, 29 May, 23 Jun.

Феодот → **Федот**

Феодул *Феодул*, also *Федул* – ♂ Greek. Ω & ‡ 14 Jan, 4 Apr.

Феоктист *Феоктист* – ♂ Greek. ‡ 4 & 23 Jan, 6 Aug, 3 Sep, 2 Oct, 23 Dec.

Феофан *Феофан* – ♂ Greek. Ukr. *Феофан, Теофан.* Ω 12 Mar, 11 Oct. ‡ 10 Jan, 12 Mar, 10 Jun, 9 & 22 & 28 & 29 Sep, 11 Oct.

Феофания *Феофания*, † *Феофанія* – ♀ of **Феофан**. Ukr. *Феофанія.* Ω & ‡ 16 Dec.

Феофил *Феофил* – ♂ Greek. Eng./Lat. *Theophilus*, Lith. *Teofilis, Teofilas, Topylis*, Pol. *Teofil [Теофиль, Теофіль]*, Ukr. *Феофіл, Теофіл.* ⊕ 30 Jan, 27 Apr, 2 & 13 Oct. Ω & ‡ 8 Jan, etc.

Феофила *Феофила* – ♀ of **Феофил**. Eng./Lat. *Theophila*, Lith. *Teofilija, Teofilė, Topylė*, Pol. *Teofila [Теофиля]*, Ukr. *Феофіла, Теофіла.* ⊕ & ‡ 28 Dec.

Ферапонт *Ферапонт* – ♂ Greek. Ω 25 & 26 May. ‡ 25 & 27 May, 12 Dec..

Филимон *Филимон* – ♂ Greek. Ukr. *Филимон, Тилимон.* Ω 19 Feb, 22 Nov, 14 Dec. ‡ 4 Jan, 19 Feb, 29 Apr, 22 Nov, 14 Dec.

Филипп *Филипп* – ♂ Greek. Eng. *Philip*, Lat. *Phillipus*, Lith. *Pilypas*, Pol. *Filip*, Ukr. *Пилип.* ⊕ 11 Apr, 6 & 26 May, 6 Jun, 10 Jul, 23 Aug, 13 & 20 Oct. Ω 28 Mar, 10 & 11 Oct, 14 Nov. ‡ 4 Jan, 30 Jun, 11 Oct, 14 Nov, etc.

Финеес *Финеес* – ♂ Hebrew; Jews tended to use the forms *Пинкус, Пинхас, Пинхос*, etc. Eng. *Phineas*, Lat. *Phinees*, Polish *Finees.* ‡ 12 Mar.

Фирс *Фирс* – ♂ Greek. Ukr. *Фірс.* ‡ 17 Aug, 14 Dec.

Фишель *Фишель* – ♂ Jewish, variants include *Фисель, Фишка, Фишль, Фишля.*

Флавий *Флавий*, † *Флавій* – ♂ Latin. Ukr. *Флавіан, Флавій.* ‡ 9 Mar.

Флор *Флор* – ♂ Latin. Ω & ‡ 18 Aug, 18 Dec.

Флориан *Флориан* – ♂ Latin. Eng. *Florian*, Lat. *Florianus*, Lith. *Florijonas*, Pol. *Florian*, Ukr. *Флоріан.* ⊕ 4 May, 5 Nov, 17 Dec.

Фойгель *Фойгель* – ♀ Jewish, variants include *Файга, Файгель, Фейга, Фейге, Фейгель*, etc.

Фока *Фока* – ♂ Greek. Ω & ‡ 22 Jul, 22 Sep.

Фома *Фома*, also *Хома*, † *Θома* – ♂ Aramaic. Eng./Lat. *Thomas*, Lith. *Tomas*, Pol. *Tomasz [Томаш]*, Ukr. *Хома, Тома.* ⊕ 7 Mar, 3 Jul, 22 Sep, 30 Dec. Ω 19 Mar, 7 Jul, 6 Oct. ‡ 21 Mar, 24 Apr, 30 Jun, 7 Jul, 6 Oct, 1 Nov, 10 Dec.

Франко → **Франц**

Франц *Франц* – ♂ Latin. Eng. *Francis, Frank*, Lat. *Franciscus*, Lith. *Franas, Pranciškus, Pranas, Pranys*, Pol. *Franciszek [Францишек]*, Ukr. *Франко.* ⊕ 24 Jan, 2 Apr, 4 Jun, 3 & 4 Oct, 3 Dec.

Францишка *Францишка* – ♀ of **Франц**. Eng. *Frances*, Lat. *Francisca*, Lith. *Pranciška, Pranė*, Pol. *Franciszka [Францишка]*, Ukr. *Франка.* ⊕ 9 Mar, 22 Dec.

Фрейда *Фрейда* – ♀ Jewish, variants include *Фрейдка, Фрейдель, Фрейдля, Фрида, Фридель, Фридка.*

Фреймель → **Ефрем**

Фридель → **Фрейда** and **Фридман**

Фридка → **Фрейда**

Фридман *Фридман* – ♂ Jewish, hypocoristic form *Фридель* (which can also be a feminine form of **Фрейда**).

Фридрих *Фридрих* – ♂ Germanic. Eng. *Frederick*, Lat. *Fridericus*, Lith. *Fridrikas, Pridrikis, Pol. Fryderyk*, Ukr. *Фрідріх.* ⊕ 5 Mar, 8 May, 18 Jul, 30 Nov.

Фроим → **Ефрем**

Фросина → **Ефросиния**

Фрума *Фрума* – ♀ Jewish.

Хх

Хава → **Ева**

Хавронья → **Феврония**

Хайка, Хайла → **Хая**

Хаим *Хаим*, also *Хайм* – ♂ Jewish. Eng. *Chaim.*

Хайцель → **Хая**

Хана → **Анна**

Ханан → **Эльханан**

Ханна → **Анна**

Ханох *Ханох*– ♂ Jewish; variants include *Хенох, Энох, Гендель*, etc. Eng. *Enoch.*

Харитон *Харитон* – ♂ Greek. Ukr. *Харитон, Харитін.* ⊕ 1 Jun, 28 Sep. Ω & ‡ 1 Jun, 28 Sep.

Харлампій *Харлампий*, † *Харлампій* – ♂ Greek. Ukr. *Харламп.* Ω & ‡ 10 Feb.

Хаскель, Хацкель, Хачкель → **Иезекииль**

Хая ***Хая***– ♀ Jewish; variants include *Хайка, Хайцель,* and *Хайла.*

Хелена ***Хелена,*** also *Хелъна* – ♀ Greek; variant of **Елена** (influenced by Polish *Helena*).

Хемель, Хемка → **Нехемия**

Хенох → **Ханох**

Хиль → **Иохель**

Хома → **Фома**

Хона, Хонон → **Эльханон**

Христиан ***Христиан,*** † *Христіанъ* – ♂ Greek. Eng. *Christian,* Lat. *Christianus,* Lith. *Kristijonas, Kriščius,* Pol. *Krystian,* Ukr. *Християн.* ⊕ 4 Dec. ‡ 24 May.

Христина ***Христина,*** also *Кристина* – ♀ Greek. Eng. *Christine,* Lat. *Christina,* Lith. *Kristina,* Pol. *Krystyna.* ⊕ 13 Mar, 24 Jul. Ω 24 Jul. ‡ 6 Feb, 13 May, 18 May, 23 Jun, 24 Jul.

Христофор ***Христофор*** – ♂ Greek. Eng. *Christopher,* Lat. *Christophorus, Christoferus,* Lith. *Kristoforas, Kristupas,* Pol. *Krzysztof.* ⊕ 2 Mar, 25 Jul. Ω 19 Apr. ‡ 19 Apr, 9 May, 30 Aug.

Ц ц

Цадок, Цадык → **Садок**

Цалель, Цаля → **Бецалель**

Цви ***Цви*** – ♂ Jewish. Pol. *Cwi.*

Цезарь → **Кесарий**

Целестин → **Келестин**

Целестина → **Келестина**

Цецилия ***Цецилия,*** † *Цецилія* – ♀ Latin. Eng. *Cecilia,* Lat. *Caecilia,* Lith. *Cecilija, Cecilė,* Pol. *Cecylia,* Ukr. *Цецілія.* ⊕ & ‡ 22 Nov.

Цейтель ***Цейтель,*** also *Цейтля* – ♀ Jewish.

Цемах ***Цемах*** – ♂ Jewish; variant *Цемель.*

Цива ***Цива*** – ♀ Jewish; variants include *Цивья, Цивка,* and *Цивля.* Pol. *Cywia.*

Циля ***Циля*** – ♀ mainly (but not exclusively) used by Jews, from a short form of **Цецилия.**

Цимель, Цимха → **Симха**

Цина ***Цина*** – ♀ Jewish; variants include *Цинка.*

Ципора ***Ципора*** – ♀ Jewish; variants include *Цина, Ципка, Ципра,* and *Цыпа.* Eng. *Zipporah,* Pol. *Cypora.* Russ. *Ципора, Цыпа, Ципа.*

Цира, Цирель, Цирля → **Сарра**

Цодик → **Садок**

Цыпа → **Ципора**

Цыра → **Сарра**

Ч ч

Чарна ***Чарна*** – ♀ Jewish. Pol. *Czarna.*

Чеслав ***Чеслав*** – ♂ Slavic. Eng. *Ceslas (Chester*),* Lat. *Ceslaus,* Lith. *Česlovas,* Pol. *Czesław.* ⊕ 17 & 20 Jul.

Чеслава ***Чеслава*** – ♀ of **Чеслав.** Latin *Ceslava, Ceslaa,* Lith. *Česlova,* Pol. *Czesława.* ⊕ 12 Jan.

Ш ш

Шабсай → **Савватий**

Шавель → **Савелий**

Шайна, Шайндля → **Шейна**

Шандор → **Александр**

Шапсель, Шапшель → **Савватий**

Шауль → **Савелий**

Шахна ***Шахна,*** or *Шахно* – ♂ Jewish. Pol. *Szachna.*

Шая → **Исаия**

Шебшель → **Савватий**

Шева → **Басшева**

Шевах ***Шевах*** – ♂ Jewish; variants include *Шевель, Шевля, Шейвель.* Pol. *Szewach, Szewel.*

Шейва, Шейвель → **Басшева**

Шейна ***Шейна*** – ♀ Jewish; variants include *Шайна, Шайндля, Шейндель, Шейндля, Шейнка, Шенка,* etc. Pol. *Szajna, Szajndla, Szejndel,* etc.

Шепсель → **Савватий**

Шефтель ***Шефтель*** – ♂ Jewish. Pol. *Szeftel.*

Шийка → **Ишия**

Шиме, Шимель, Шимен, Шимон → **Семён**

Шимсон → **Самсон**

Шимха → **Симха**

Шимшель, Шимшон → **Самсон**

Шифель, Шифка → **Шифра**

Шифра ***Шифра*** – ♀ Jewish; variants include *Шифель, Шифка, Шифрель.* Eng. *Shifra, Shiphrah,* Latin *Sephora,* Polish *Sefora, Szyfra.*

Шия, Шія → **Ишия**

Шліома, Шлойма, Шлома, Шляма → **Соломон**

Шмарья ***Шмарья*** – ♂ Jewish, variants include *Шмерель* and *Шмерко.* Eng. *Shemariah.* Pol. *Szmaria, Szmerel, Szmerko.*

Шмая ***Шмая*** – ♂ Jewish. Pol. *Szmaja.*

Шмерель, Шмерко → **Шмарья**

Шмуил, Шмуйло, Шмуль, Шмулька → **Самуил**

Шоель → **Савелий**

Шолом → **Соломон**

Шора → **Сарра**

Шоса, Шошана → **Сусанна**

Шпринца ***Шпринца*** – ♀ Jewish; variants include *Шпринцель.* Pol. *Szprynca.*

Шулим → **Соломон**

Шушана, Шушанка → **Сусанна**

Э э

Эва → **Ева**

Эгидий ***Эгидий,*** † *Егидій* – ♂ Greek. Eng. *Giles,* Lat. *Aegidius,* Lith. *Egidijus,* Pol. *Idzi.* ⊕ 23 Apr, 1 Sep.

Эзра ***Эзра*** – ♂ Hebrew. Eng. *Esdras, Ezra,* Latin *Esdras,* Pol. *Ezdrasz.*

Элеонора ***Элеонора*** – ♀ origin unclear. Eng. *Eleanor, Leonore, Nora,* Lat. *Eleanora,* Lith. *Eleanora, Leonora,* Pol. *Eleonora.* ⊕ 12 & 21 Feb, 11 Jul, 19 Dec.

Эліезеръ → **Лазарь**

Элимелах → **Мейлах**

Элия, Элія → **Илья**

Эльвира ***Эльвира*** – ♀ Spanish. Eng./Lat. *Elvira,* Lith. *Elvyra,* Pol. *Elwira.* ⊕ 25 Aug, 21 Nov.

Эльман → **Гельман**

Эльханан ***Эльханан*** – ♂ Jewish; variants include *Ханан* and *Хонон.*

Эмилиан → **Емельян**

Эмилий Эмилий, † *Емиліан, Эмилій* – ♂ Latin; Eng. *Emil,* Latin *Aemilius,* Lith. *Emilijus, Emilis,* Pol. *Emil.* ⊕ 10 Mar, 22 May, 25 Jun. ‡ 8 Jan, 7 Mar, 18 Jul, 8 & 18 Aug.

Эмилия Эмилия – ♀ of **Эмилий**. Eng. *Emily,* Latin *Aemilia,* Lith. *Emilija, Emilė,* Pol. *Emilia.* ⊕ 23 May, 5 & 30 Jun, 24 Aug. ‡ 1 Jan.

Эмма ***Эмма*** – ♀ Germanic. Eng./Lat. *Emma,* Lith. *Ema,* Pol. *Emma.* ⊕ 8 & 19 Apr, 29 Jun, 24 Nov, 3 Dec. ‡ 4 Jun, 23 Jul.

Эммануил, Эмануель → **Мануил**

Энох → **Ханох**

Эразм ***Эразм***, † *Еразм* – ♂ Greek. Eng. *Erasmus, Elmo,* Lat. *Erasmus,* Lith. *Erazmas, Razmas,* Pol. *Erazm.* ⊕ 2 Jun, 25 Nov. ‡ 25 Feb, 4 & 10 May, 18 Jun, 3 Jul, 28 Sep.

Эраст ***Эраст*** – ♂ Greek. ‡ 4 Jan, 10 Nov.

Эсфирь ***Эсфирь***, also *Эстер,* † *Есфирь, Эсѳирь* – ♀ Hebrew from Persian. Eng. *Esther, Hester,* Lat. *Esthera, Hestera,* Lith./Pol. *Estera [Эстера],* Ukr. *Есфір, Естер.* ⊕ 19 Dec.

Эта ***Эта*** – ♀ can be Christian, but is often a Jewish short form of **Эсфирь**, with variants including *Этка, Этля.*

Эфраимъ, Эфроимъ → **Ефрем**

Ю ю

Юда, Юдель, Юдка, Ютка → **Иуда**

Юдифь ***Юдифь***, or *Иудифь,* † *Іудифь, Юдиѳь* – ♀ Hebrew. Eng. *Judith, Judy,* Latin *Judith, Juditha,* Lith. *Judita,* Pol. *Judyta.* ⊕ 6 May, 14 Nov, 22 Dec.

Юзафат → **Иосафат**

Юзеф → **Иосиф**

Юзефа ***Юзефа*** – ♀ from *Józefa,* Polish fem. form of **Иосиф**. Eng./Lat. *Josepha,* Lith. *Juozapa,* Pol. *Józefa,* Ukr. *Юзефа.* ⊕ 14 Feb, 19 Mar, 3 Oct.

Юзефат → **Иосафат**

Юзефина ***Юзефина*** – ♀ from *Józef,* Polish form of **Иосиф**. Eng. *Josephine, Josephina,* Lith. *Juozapina.* Pol. *Józefina.* ⊕ 12 & 19 Mar.

Юлиан ***Юлиан***, also *Иулиан,* † *Іуліанъ* – ♂ Latin. Eng. *Julian,* Lat. *Julianus,* Lith. *Julijonas,* Pol. *Julian,* Ukr. *Юліан, Уліян.* ⊕ 9 Jan. Ω & ‡ 6 Feb, 16 Mar, 21 Jun, etc.

Юлиания ***Юлиания***, also *Иулианна,* † *Іуліана* – ♀ of **Юлиан**. Eng. *Julianna, Gilian,* Lat. *Juliana,* Lith. *Julijona, Ulijona,* Pol. *Julianna,* Ukr. *Уляна, Оляна.* ⊕ 16 Feb, 19 Jun. Ω 6 Feb, 17 Aug, 21 Dec. ‡ 2 Jan, 4 & 20 Mar, 22 Jun, 6 Jul, 17 Aug, 1 Nov, 21 Dec.

Юлий ***Юлий***, also *Иулий* – ♂ Latin. Eng. *Julius,* Lith. *Julijus,* Pol. *Juliusz,* Ukr. *Юлій.* ‡ 21 Jun.

Юлия ***Юлия***, also *Иулия,* † *Іулія, Юлія* – ♀ of **Юлий**. Eng./Lat./Pol. *Julia.* ‡ 18 May, 16 Jul.

Юрий ***Юрий*** † *Юрій,* dim. *Юрко.* –♂ Slavic, cmp. **Георгий**. Ukr. *Юрій, Юрко.* ‡ 4 Feb.

Юрко → **Ури** and **Урия** and **Юрий**

Юст ***Юст***, also *Иуст,* † *Іустъ* – ♂ Latin. Ω 20 Oct. ‡ 4 Jan, 14 Jul, 30 Oct.

Юстин ***Юстин***, also *Устин,* † *Іустинъ* – ♂ Latin. Eng. *Justin,* Latin *Justinus,* Lith. *Justinas,* Pol. *Justyn,* Ukr. *Устим, Устин, Юстим, Юстин.* ⊕ 14 Apr. Ω 1 Jun, 14 Nov. ‡ 1 Jun.

Юстина ***Юстина***, also *Устина,* † *Іустина* – ♀ of **Юстин**. Eng. *Justine,* Lith. *Justina,* Pol. *Justyna,* Ukr. *Устина, Юстина.* ⊕ 12 Mar, 26 Sep. Ω & ‡ 2 Oct.

Юхим → **Ефим**

Ютка, Юшко → **Иуда**

Я я

Явдоким → **Евдоким**

Явна → **Иона**

Ядвига ***Ядвига*** – ♀ Germanic. Eng. *Hedvig,* Latin *Hedvigis,* Lith. *Jadvyga,* Pol. *Jadwiga,* Ukr. *Ядвіга.* ⊕ 17 Jul, 16 Oct. ‡ 16 Oct.

Якель → **Яков**

Якер → **Якир**

Яким → **Иаким**

Якир ***Якир*** – ♂ Jewish; variants include *Якер* and *Якира.*

Яків → **Яков**

Яков ***Яков***, also *Иаков,* † *Іаковъ, Іяковъ* – ♂ Hebrew. Jews also used forms such as *Акива, Копель, Якель, Якуш,* etc. Eng. *Jacob, James, Jake,* Latin *Jacobus,* Lith. *Jokubas, Jakubas,* Pol. *Jakób, Jakub [Якоб, Якуб],* Ukr. *Яків.* ⊕ 25 Jul. Ω & ‡ 13 Jan, 4 & 21 Mar, 30 Apr, 9 & 23 Oct, 15 & 27 Nov.

Ялисей → **Елисей**

Ян → **Иван**

Янкель ***Янкель*** – ♂ Jewish, actually began as a hypocoristic form of Yiddish *Yankev,* from *Ya'akov* (cmp. **Яков**). Eng. *Yankel.* Pol. *Jankiel.*

Янина ***Янина*** – ♀ Slavic equivalent of "Jane." Eng. *Jane,* Lith. *Janina, Janė,* Pol. *Janina.*

Ярема → **Еремей**

Ярмолай → **Ермолай**

Яромир ***Яромир*** – ♂ Slavic. Pol. *Jaromir.*

Ярополк ***Ярополк*** – ♂ Slavic. Pol. *Jaropełk.* ⊕ 18 Jan. ‡ 22 Nov.

Ярослав ***Ярослав*** – ♂ Slavic; Pol. *Jarosław.* ⊕ 21 Jan, 25 Apr, 7 Jun.

Яцек, Яценты → **Иакинф**

Яхелъ → **Ехиель**

Яха → **Яхна**

Яхель → **Иохель**

Яхля → **Яхна**

Яхна ***Яхна*** – ♂ Jewish; variants include *Яха* and *Яхля.* Pol. *Jachna.*

IX. ACKNOWLEDGEMENTS AND BIBLIOGRAPHY

In the course of researching and writing this book, we asked for and received permission from many researchers to use their documents as samples to illustrate various points. To all who gave their permission—including many whose documents we did not end up using—we wish to express our sincere thanks. It seems only proper to give their names and thank them publicly, and a list follows. Only documents from individual researchers are acknowledged below. Those documents not listed came from libraries or other repositories—mainly the Archives and Resource Center of the Polish Genealogical Society of Connecticut and the Northeast—or from the personal papers of the authors.

I-1, p. 28: Gary Palgon, Atlanta GA
I-2, p. 30: Mrs. S. Kasuk, Lockport IL
IV-1, p. 80: Kathleen Stott, Middletown CT
V-17, p.166: Brian Lenius, Manitoba
VI-2, p. 194: Mrs. S. Kasuk, Lockport IL
VI-3, p. 195: Mrs. S. Kasuk, Lockport IL
VI-7, p. 207, Bill Succolosky, Sterling VA
VI-8, p. 210, Gary Palgon, Atlanta GA
VI-9, p. 214: Tom Hollowak, Baltimore MD
VI-14, p. 230: Arleen Gould, Glenview IL
VI-15, p. 234-235: Don Szumowski, Washington, D. C.
VI-21, p. 254, Gary Palgon, Atlanta GA
VI-22 , p. 260 and 263: Matthew Bielawa, Stratford CT
VI-24, p. 268, Arleen Gould, Glenview IL
VI-28, p. 279, Gary Palgon, Atlanta GA
VI-30, p. 283: Dr. Edward Zukowski, Chesterfield MO
VI-33, pp. 293, 295, 296, 298: Michał Kopczyński, Warsaw
VI-34, pp. 299-300: Morris Spector, Hamden CT
VI-35, pp. 303-304: Wanda Mead Campbell, Binghamton NY
VI-38, pp. 311-312: Sharon Allen, Derry, NH
VI-39, pp. 313-315: Chester Daniels, Rochester NY
VI-41, p. 322: Thomas K. Edlund, Salt Lake City UT
VI-42, pp. 324-325: Thomas K. Edlund, Salt Lake City UT
VI-43, p. 326: Thomas K. Edlund, Salt Lake City UT
VI-44, pp. 328-329: Thomas K. Edlund, Salt Lake City UT
VI-47, p. 334: Rose Bernhardt, West Hartford CT
VI-49, pp. 338 and 340: Fay Bussgang, Boston MA
VI-54, p. 351:Esther Klugiewicz, Erie PA
VI-55, p. 352: Wanda M. Campbell, Binghamton NY
VI-57, p. 356: Kathleen Stott, Middletown CT

The maps in Chapter V were prepared by the authors. They were scanned from sources in the public domain and then modified with reference to a number of published works (which are cited in the Bibliography). Maps V-1, V-2, V-3, V-4, and V-9 were originally prepared for publication in *Pathways & Passages*, the Journal of the Polish Genealogical Society of Connecticut and the Northeast. They are reprinted with permission. Maps V-5, V-6, V-7, V-8, and V-10 were prepared by the authors for the *In Their Words* series.

A number of persons with special expertise aided us with their advice and consultation, and we wish to express particular thanks to them. They include: **Matthew Bielawa**, Vice President of the Polish Genealogical Society of Connecticut and the Northeast, for proofreading, offering advice on Ukrainian sources, and letting us use his article on Old Church Slavonic alphabet in dates; **Thomas K. Edlund**, for permission to use the reproductions and analyses from his *Avotaynu* article on the 1897 Russian Imperial Census; **Michał Kopczyński**, Ph.D., of the University of Warsaw, for assistance with materials on conscription and terms for diseases; **Rafał Prinke** for obtaining copies of several rare reference works; **Laurence Krupnak** for informed and constructive criticism of our Ukrainian Letter-Writing Guide; and **Zachary Baker, Yankiel Salant**, and **Warren Blatt** for valuable assistance with information on Jewish names and spelling in Hebrew and Yiddish. Any mistakes we've made on those subjects are our fault and made despite, not because of, the generous assistance of these experts.

BIBLIOGRAPHY

It would be nice if we could pretend this is the only book you need for research, but of course that's nonsense. Listed below are a number of publications we have used and learned from, which you, too, may wish to consult. We have also included some titles we have written, in the belief you may find them worth a look.

Aleksandrow, A. *Полный русско-англійскій словарь: Complete Russian-English Dictionary*. 4th edition Polyglotte G.m.b.h, Berlin (no date given). Special thanks to **Kathleen LaBudie-Szakall**, who graciously bought a copy and donated it to the authors!

Beider, Alexander. *A Dictionary of Jewish Surnames from the Russian Empire*. Avotaynu, Inc., Teaneck, NJ: 1993. ISBN 0-0626373-3-5. Beider's dictionary deals with Jewish surnames, telling where each name was most common in the Russian Empire and discussing their derivations. We used it primarily to help with Jewish first names in Chapter VIII. Available from Avotaynu, Inc., P. O. Box 99, Bergenfield NJ 07621 USA, **www.avotaynu.com**.

Bubak, Józef. *Księga naszych imion* [Book of Our First Names]. Ossolineum, Wrocław-Warszawa-Kraków: 1993. This Polish-language work provides information on the derivations and forms of the given names of Polish Christians. It gives equivalents of those names in various languages, including Russian, and was quite helpful in preparing Chapter VIII.

Chorzempa, Rosemary A. *Morbus — Why and How Our Ancestors Died*. Polish Genealogical Society of America, Chicago IL: 1991. The terms found in this booklet are those seen most often as causes of death in 18th- and 19th-century Europe and America. An appendix lists common terms found as causes of death in German, Latin, Polish, and Russian. Available from the Polish Genealogical Society of America, 984 N. Milwaukee Ave., Chicago IL 60622 USA, **www.pgsa.org**.

Dal', Vladimir, *Толковый словарь живого великорусского языка в 4-ах томах*. Terra-Kinzhniy Klub, Moskva: 1998. ISBN: 5-300-01627-6. This reprint of Vladimir Dal's classic dictionary of the Russian language was a great help with obscure and archaic terms we encountered during research.

Harkavy, Alexander. *Yiddish-English-Hebrew Dictionary*, Schocken Books, New York, 1988, ISBN 0-8052-4027-6. It assisted us with several Yiddish and Hebrew terms we encountered.

Hoffman, William F., and Helon, George W. *First Names of the Polish Commonwealth: Origins & Meanings*. Polish Genealogical Society of America, Chicago IL: 1998. ISBN 0-924207-06-X. Available from the PGSA, 984 N. Milwaukee Ave., Chicago IL 60622 USA, **www.pgsa.org**.

Kopczyński, Michał. "Russian Military Records from the Kingdom of Poland as a Source for Genealogical Research." *Rodziny, The Journal of the Polish Genealogical Society of America*. Winter 2002, Vol. XXV, No. 1. Pages 7-14. This is an expanded version of an article under the same title published in the Fall 2001 issue of *Pathways & Passages*, the official publication of the Polish Genealogical Society of Connecticut and the Northeast. Also of interest is his article "Is Old Age Not a Joy? The Elderly in Villages of the Kujawy Region at the End of the 18th Century," in the May 1998 issue of *Rodziny*, in which he discusses the "rounding off" of ages in vital records.

Lenius, Brian J. *Genealogical Gazetteer of Galicia*. Available from the author, Brian J. Lenius, 802-11 St. Michael Rd., Winnipeg Manitoba R2M 2K5, Canada. If you're doing genealogical research in the region of Galicia, you need to consult this book.

Magocsi, Paul Robert. *Historical Atlas of East Central Europe*, revised and expanded edition, University of Washington Press, Seattle, 2002. ISBN 0-295-98146-6. This historical atlas provides well-made maps in color and with explanatory text to lead the reader through the maze of border changes and shifts of territorial government in eastern Europe.

Magocsi, Paul Robert. Matthews, Geoffrey J., cartographer. *Ukraine: A Historical Atlas*. University of Toronto Press, 1985. ISBN 0-8020-3429-2. Its color maps and succinct commentary help the reader grasp the complex and turbulent history of Ukraine.

Mokotoff, Gary. Sack, Sally Amdur, Ph.D. *Where Once We Walked: A Guide to the Jewish Communities Destroyed in the Holocaust.* Avotaynu, Inc. Teaneck, NJ: 2002. ISBN 1-886223-15-7. Revised and updated in 2002, this reference allows one to locate over 20,00 small central and eastern European towns and villages. Their encoding and listing by the Daitch-Mokotoff Soundex system facilitates finding the correct spelling when all you have is a mangled form of the name. Available from Avotaynu, Inc., P. O. Box 99, Bergenfield NJ 07621 USA, **www.avotaynu.com**.

Orgelbrand, S. *Encyklopedia Powszechna z ilustracjami i mapami.* Towarzystwo S. Orgelbranda Synów. Warszawa: 1904. We used this well-known Polish reference work, published within territory ruled by the Russian Empire and passed by Imperial censors, as a source of information for the composition of that Empire as it existed before the Revolution.

Schlyter, Daniel M. *Essentials in Polish Genealogical Research.* Polish Genealogical Society of America, Chicago IL: 1993. This brief booklet serves as an introduction to Polish research, which can prove useful for research in much of the western Russian Empire. It provides particularly useful guidance in using the resources of the Family History Library in Salt Lake City (through local Family History Centers) to solve the problems that typically frustrate beginners. Available from the Polish Genealogical Society of America, 984 N. Milwaukee Ave., Chicago IL 60622 USA, **www.pgsa.org**.

Shea, Jonathan D. *Russian Language Documents from Russian Poland: A Translation Manual for Genealogists.* Genun Publishers, Orem UT: 1989. ISBN 0-912811-05-6. This book is very helpful, but has long been out of print. The present volume of *In Their Words* is intended to serve as an updated and expanded version of this work.

Shea, Jonathan D.; Hoffman, William F. *Following the Paper Trail: A Multilingual Translation Guide.* Avotaynu, Inc., Teaneck, NJ. ISBN 0-9626373-4-3. *Paper Trail* uses much the same approach as this book to analyze documents in 13 European languages, including German, Latin, Polish, and Russian. Of course, dealing with 13 languages, it does not go into the same depth for Russian records that is possible in this book, which concentrates on only one language. Available from Avotaynu, Inc., P. O. Box 99, Bergenfield NJ 07621 USA, **www.avotaynu.com**.

Shea, Jonathan D.; Hoffman, William F. *In Their Words: A Genealogist's Translation Guide to Polish, German, Latin, and Russian Documents. Volume 1: Polish.* Language & Lineage Press, New Britain CT. ISBN 0-9631579-4-9, **www.langline.com**.

Sulimierski, Filip; Chlebowski, Bronisław; Walewski, Władysław. *Słownik geograficzny Królestwa Polskiego i innych krajów słowiańskich* [Geographical Dictionary of the Kingdom of Poland and Other Slavic Lands]. Warszawa: Nakładem Władysława Walewskiego, 1880-1902. See pp. 155ff.

Tikhonov, A. N.; Boyarinova, L. Z.; Ryzhkova, A. G. *Словарь русских личных имен* [Dictionary of Russian Personal Names]. Shkola-Press, Moscow: 1995. ISBN 5-88527-108-9.

Thode, Ernest. *German-English Genealogical Dictionary.* Genealogical Publishing Company, Inc., Baltimore: 1992. ISBN 0-8063-1342-0. Obviously this work is primarily useful for German research, but there are a number of terms listed that can be useful in Russian research as well.

Weiner, Miriam. *Jewish Roots in Poland: Pages from the Past and Archival Inventories.* Routes to Roots Foundation, Secaucus NJ: 1997. ISBN 0-96565-080-4. This beautifully-produced work contains massive amounts of information helpful to anyone, but especially Jews, wishing to research their roots in Poland; it contains maps, color photos, and an index of records pertinent to Jewish research from the Polish State Archives. It is available from Routes to Roots Foundation, P. O. Box 1376, Secaucus NJ 07066-1376, **www.rtrfoundation.org**.

Weiner, Miriam. *Jewish Roots in Ukraine and Moldova: Pages from the Past and Archival Inventories.* Routes to Roots Foundation, Secaucus NJ, and YIVO Institute for Jewish Research, New York NY: 1999. ISBN 0-965608-1-2. Perhaps even more impressive than the earlier volume for Poland, this massive book gives the same kind of extensive information helpful for people with roots in Ukraine and Moldova—but of course especially for Jews. It is available from Routes to Roots Foundation, P. O. Box 1376, Secaucus NJ 07066-1376, **www.rtrfoundation.org**.

X. INDEX

The page numbers indicated are those where each subject is mentioned. Page numbers printed in *italics* refer to information found on maps or in their captions. Page numbers printed in ***bold italics*** refer to passages where terms are defined, or to the most comprehensive discussion of the subject. In regard to place names mentioned, please remember that few place names are unique; there may be other towns or villages that have the same names as the ones discussed here. Place names are given primarily in their current forms, with older versions given as cross-references.

ą (Polish letter): 11, 24
abbreviations (Russian and Belarusian): 89, 146, 148, 151
abbreviations (Polish): 154, 156
Åbo-Björneborg, Finland: 121, *136*
accented syllables: 5-6, 8, 36, 144, 145
accuracy of records and record copies: 75, 96, 107, 108, 216, 221, 228, 232, 241, 248, 267
accusative case: ***33***, 35-36, 200, 266
active (voice): 44, 257
adjectival forms of place names: 83, 118, 121, 123, 146, 156, 208
adjectives: ***33-40***, 45
administrative divisions, Russia: ***83***, 169
Administrativno-territorial'noe ustroistvo BSSR: 147
adoption: 205
AGAD → Archiwum Główne Akt Dawnych
age, expressions for: 41, ***50-51***, 90, 198, 201, 203, 224, 245, 248, 256, 276, 280, 282, 283, 285, 290, 294, 318, 319, 343, 348
ages, "rounding off": 248, 276, 468
agreement of adjectives with nouns: ***34***
Akhtyrka → Okhtyrka
Akkerman → Bilhorod-Dnistrovs'kyi
Akmolinsk → Astana
Aldan, Russia: *139*
Aleksandrivs'k → Zaporizhzhya
Aleksandriya → Oleksandrivka
Aleksandrow, A.: 468
Aleshki → Tsyurupyns'k
Alexander I, Czar: 121
alien registration number: 79
Allen, Sharon: 310, 467
alphabet, Cyrillic: ***1***
Alphabetical Index of Localities of the Former Grand Duchy of Lithuania: 149
alphabetical order in Russian: ***30***, 53, 146, 149, 194, 195, 290, 443
Alphabetisches Orts- und Gemeindelexikon des General Gouvernement Warschau (1917): 163
Alytus, Lithuania (Polish *Olita*): 167, 212, 213
American Family Immigration History Center: 75
Americanized names: 76, 107
Amur district, Russia: 117, 137, *139*
Anadyr', Russia: *139*
Anan'iv, Ukraine (Russian *Ананьев*): *131*, 133
Andrzejewo, Poland: 280
Anglicized versions of Russian names: ***12-14***
animate beings: 35, 36, 43
Ankara, Turkey: *138*
anniversary commemorations: 88
Antwerp: 32
apostrophe in Roman-alphabet spelling of Russian names 3
Arabic names: 8, 11
Aral Sea: *136, 138*
Aramaic: 19
archaic spellings: 1-3, 6, ***8***, 24, 35, 36, 37, 45, 53, 76, 82, 97, 202, 208, 212, 216, 217, 225, 260, 281, 358
archaic terms: 43, 52, 202, 220, 257, 358
archdiocesan archives → diocesan archives
Archiwum Główne Akt Dawnych: 191
Archiwum Państwowe → Polish State Archives
area, measures of: 160
Arkalyk → Arqalyq
Arkhangel'sk, Russia: 117, 135, *136, 138*, 140
Armenia: 117, 137, *138*
Armenian names: 11
Armenians: 94
Arqalyq (Russian *Аркалык*), Kazakhstan: 137
Artemivs'k, Ukraine (old Russian *Бахмутъ*): *131*, 134
Ashgabat, Turkmenistan (formerly *Асхабад*): *138*
Ashmiany, Belarus: *123*, 124, *131*, 150
Asian Russia: 116
assimilation (phonetic) → regressive assimilation
assistant rabbi: 239
Askhabad → Ashgabat
Astana, Kazakhstan (formerly *Акмолинскъ*): 117, *136*, 137, *138*
Astrakhan', Russia: 117, 135, *136, 138*, 140, 142
Atyraū, Kazakhstan (formerly *Гурьев*): *138*
Augustów, Poland: 120, 156
Auschwitz → Oświęcim
Austrian Empire: 127, 129, *136*, 156, 165, 180, 182
Austrian partition → Galicia
authenticity of documents: 216, 221, 273
Avotaynu, Inc.: 16, 27, 94, 144, 209, 320, 341, 441, 468, 469
Azerbaijan: 137, *138*
Azov, Sea of: *131*

Babruysk, Belarus': 125, *131*, 148
Baikal, Lake: 117, 137
Baisagola, Lithuania: 267, 268
Bakałarzewo, Poland: 120
Baker, Zachary M.: 19, 467
Bakhmut → Artemivs'k
Baku, Azerbaijan: 117, *136*, 137, *138*, 140
Balch Institute: 79
Balta, Ukraine: *131*, 132
Bălţi, Moldova (old Russian *Бѣльцы*, Polish *Bielce*): *131*, 132
Baltic languages: 21, 33
Baltic provinces: 116, ***122-123***
Baltimore passenger arrival lists: 75
banns: 247, 252, 257, 264, 268
baptismal records → birth records
Baranovichi, Belarus': 126, 147, *168*
Barents Sea: *138*
Bargłów Kościelny: 120, 193
Barisaŭ, Belarus' (Russian *Борисов*): 125, *131*, 148
Barnaul, Russia: *139*
Bartołdy, Poland: 305
Bazary, Lithuania: 216
Będzin, Poland: 119, 156
Beider, Alexander: 16, 209, 219, 256, 441, 468
Belarus' (old Russian *Бѣлороссія*): viii, 48, 117, 123, ***125***, 144-149, 150, 152, 153, 155, 169, 179-180, 355
Belarusian language: 1, 2, 22, 33, 84, 144-147
Belarusians: 90, 441
Belorossiya → Belarus'
Belostok → Białystok
Bel'tsy → Bălţi
Bendery → Tighina
Berdychiv, Ukraine (Russian *Бердичев*, Polish *Berdyczów*): *131*, 132
Berdyans'k, Crimea: *131*, 134
Berezhany, Ukraine (Polish *Brzeżany*): 128, *129*
Berezniki, Russia: *138*
Bering Sea: *139*
Bernardine Monastery, L'viv: 181
Bernhardt, Rose: 467
Bessarabia, Ukraine: 117, *131*, ***132***, *136*, 140, 152
Biała Cerkiew → Bila Tserkva
Biała Podlaska, Poland: 120
Białystok, Poland (old Russian *Бѣлостокъ*): 90, *125*, 125, *131*, 155, *167*, *168*, 188, 189, 196, 238, 242, 256, 283, 291
Bielawa, Matthew: 48, 181, 467
Bielce → Bălţi
Bielnik: 163
Bielsko-Biała: *129 [shows Biała]*
Bielsk Podlaski, Poland: 120, *125*, 125, *131*
Bigo, Jan: 162
Bila Tserkva, Ukraine: 134
Biłgoraj, Poland: 120
Bilhorod Dnistrovs'kyi, Ukraine (old Russian *Аккерманъ*): *131*, 132
birth certificate: 240-241, 244
birth, date of: 198, 202, 225, 233, 276, 294, 300, 309
birth indexes: 194, 196
birthplace: 74, 202, 233
birth records: 194, ***197-241***
birth, time of: 198
Biuletyn Korzenie: 191
Black Sea: 117, 130, *131*, *136*, 137
Blagoveshchensk, Russia: *139*
Blatt, Warren: 233, 467
Błonie, Poland: 119
boarding students: 321
Board on Geographic Names: 144
Bobruysk → Babruysk
Bobrynets', Ukraine: 133
Bogodukhov → Bohodukhiv
Bohodukhiv, Ukraine (Russian *Богодухов*): *131*, 133
Bolshevik Revolution → Russian Revolution
Books of Residence: 341
Borisov → Barisaŭ
Borzna, Ukraine: *131*, 133
Boston passenger arrival lists: 75
Boyarinova, L. Z.: 442, 469
Braslaŭ, Belarus': 147
Bratsk, Russia: *139*
Bratslav, Ukraine: *131*, 132
Bräuer, Herbert: 143
Bremen: 32
Brest(-Litovsk): *125*, 125, *131*, *138*, 147, *168*
bride: 195, 247, 249, 252, 262, 265
Brody, Ukraine: 128, *129*, *168*
Bryansk, Russia: *138*
Brześć Litewski → Brest(-Litovsk)
Brzeżany → Berezhany
Brzeziny, Poland: 119, 338
B.S.S.R. → Byelorussian Soviet Socialist Republic
Bubak, Józef: 442, 468
Buchach, Ukraine: 128, *129*
Bucharest, Romania: 350
Budy Mikołajki: 160
Bug River: *168*
Bukovina (Polish *Bukowina*): *129*, *131*, 182
Bulgarian language: 1, 33
burgher → townsman
burial, place and date of: 281, 284
Buryatiya, Russia: 137
business directories → directories, business
Bussgang, Fay: 338, 340, 341, 467
Bussgang, Julian: 341
Bydgoszcz (German name *Bromberg*): *119*, *168*
Byelorussian Soviet Socialist Republic: 147 (*see* Belarus')

Bykhaŭ (Russian *[Старый] Быхов*), Belarus': 126, *131*
Bystrzycki, Tadeusz: 153
ć (Polish letter): 11
calendar: ***200***, 217, 233, 284, 290
Campbell, Wanda M.: 467
candle tax: 29
cardinal numbers: ***45***, 56
Carpatho-Rusyns: 90
case (grammatical): 33
Caspian Sea: 117, *136*, 137
Caucasus → Kavkaz
Celtic languages: 33
cemetery inscriptions: 78, ***88-93***
census, Austrian (1890): 162
census, Austrian (1900): 166
census, Polish (1921): 161
census, Russian: 317, ***320-329***, 467
Central Archive of Historical Records (Poland): 191
Central National Historical Archive: 180
Central National Historical Archive of the Belorussian Soviet Socialist Republic: A Directory: 180
Central State Historical Archives in L'viv and Kyiv: 180, 181, 182
Cernăuţi → Chernivtsy
certification of death: 274, 277
certification of professional competence: 106-107, 353
Charków → Kharkiv
Chavusy, Belarus' (Russian *Чауссы*): 126, *131*
Chechnya: 137
Chełm, Poland: 120, *168*
Chełmno, Poland: *168*
Chelyabinsk, Russia: *138*
Cherepovets, Russia: 307, 309, 310
Cherikaŭ, Belarus' (Russian *Чериков*):126, *131*
Cherkasy, Ukraine (Russian *Черкассы*, Polish *Czerkasy*): *131*, 132, *138*
Cherkessk, Russia: *138*
Chernihiv, Ukraine (Russian name *Чернигов*, Polish *Czernihów*): 117, *131*, ***133***, *136*, *138*, 140, 152
Chernivtsi, Ukraine: (Russian *Черновицы*, Romanian *Cernăuţi*, Polish *Czerniowce*): *129*, *131*, 132, 180, 182
Chernomorskaia *gubernia*: 137
Cherson → Kherson
chetvert': 157
Chicago, Illinois: 94
Chigirin → Chyhyryn
China: *139*
Chişinău, Moldova (Russian *Кишинёв*): *131*, 131, 132, *138*, 139
Chita, Russia: 137, *139*
Chlebowski, Bronisław: 469
Chojnice, Poland: *168*
Chopping Block: ***38-40***
Chorol → Khorol
Chorzempa, Rosemary A.: 286, 468
Chocim → Khotyn
Chorzele, Poland: 335
Chronologia Polska: 442
church attendant: 228, 262, 282
church directories: 164-165, 187
church records: 73, ***80-85***, 180, 213
church seal → parish seal
Church Slavonic: 48
Chyhyryn, Ukraine (Russian *Чигирин*, Polish *Czehryń*): *131*, 132
Ciechanów, Poland: 119, *168*, 306
Ciechanowiec, Poland: 121, 221, 223
Cieszyn, Poland: *119*, *168*
circumcision: 197, 203, 211, 233, 236, 237
citizenship: 75, 102, 108
city-dwellers → townsman
Civil Code: 259
civil registrars: 182, 187, 205, 208, 209, 221, 241
civil vital records in America: 73-74
clergy: 32, 321
Cohen, Chester G.: 143
collective farms: 146
columnar format records: 197, ***225-239***, 242, ***260-272***, ***281-286***
Commonwealth of Two Nations, Poland and Lithuania: 14, 22, 117, 119, 129, 153, 165, *167*, 197, 207
Communion (Catholic sacrament): 336-337
Communists: 180, 182, 187, 188
Complete Russian-English Dictionary: 468
concentration camp records: 191
Confession (Catholic sacrament): 336-337
Congress Kingdom → Kingdom of Poland
Connecticut court records: 74
conscription (draft): 110, 272, 292-298, 305-306, 467
consonants, Russian: **4**, 7, 14, 17
consular records: 78, 79, ***94-114***
conversion of Slavs to Christianity 2
Coper, Ingrid: 143
Courland (*Kurland, Kurlandiya*): 116, ***122***, *131*, *136*
courts, county (U. S.) 74
courts, federal (U. S.) 74
courts, Polish: 162, 163
courts, state (U. S.): 74
craftsmen: 209
Crimea → Krym
criminal record or investigation: 295
Croatian language: 33
cursive → handwriting
Cyril, St.: 2
Cyrillic alphabet: ***1-32***, 33, 145, 151, 225, 260, 357
Czech language: 33
Czehryń → Chyhyryn

Czerepowiec → Cherepovets
Czerkasy → Cherkasy
Czernihów → Chernihiv
Czerniowce → Chernivtsi
Częstochowa, Poland: 119, 189
Czyżew, Poland: 160, 256, 259
Dąbrowa [Białostocka], Poland: 121, 229, 242, 244, 264
Dagestan, Russia: 117, *136*, 137
Daitch-Mokotoff Soundex System: ***94***, 469
Dal', Vladimir: 468
Daniels, Chester: 467
Daniūnai, Lithuania: 150, 151
Danzig → Gdańsk
Dargvainai, Lithuania: 150
date of wedding: 247, 268
date of death → death, date of
dates, double: ***200***, 217, 275
dates, expressing: ***47-49***, 198, 200, 228, 342, 351
dative case: ***33***, 35-36, 202, 203, 204, 257, 277
Daugavpils, Latvia (Russian *Двинскъ* and *Динабургъ*): 126, *131*
Davyd-Haradok, Belarus' (Russian *Давид Городок*): 233-237
days of the week, Russian names for: ***49***
death benefits and claims: 78
death, cause of: 283, 285, ***286-289***, 468
death certificates: 286, 302
death, date of: 274, 280, 281, 283
death indexes and records: 195-196, ***274-289***, 341
death, place of: 274, 284
"deceased," expressions meaning: 196, 249, 252, 276
declarant: 198, 201
Declaration of Intention → naturalization records
declensions: 33, ***34***, 146
deed to property: 332-333
Defense Mapping Agency: 151
deferment of military service: 296, 298, 305
description, physical → physical description
Department of Heraldry: 355
Depression: 79
devoicing → voiced consonants vs. voiceless
diacritical marks: 4, 8
dialect influences on spelling: 15
Dictionary of Ashkenazic Given Names: Their Origins, Structure, Pronunciation, and Migrations: 16
Dictionary of Jewish Surnames from the Kingdom of Poland: 441
Dictionary of Jewish Surnames from the Russian Empire: 16, 209, 441, 468
Dinaburg → Daugavpils
diocesan archives (Poland): 187, 188, 189-191
diphthongs, German: 14-15
diphthongs, Lithuanian: 21-22
diphthongs, Yiddish: 17-18
directories, business: 79
directories, provincial: 140-141
discharge papers (military): ***306-312***, 313
Disna, Belarus': 124, *131*
distance, measures of: 160
divorce records: 82, 284, 290-291
Dniestr river: *129, 168*
Dnipropetrovs'k, Ukraine (former Russian name *Екатеринослав*): 117, *131*, ***134***, 135, *136*, 140, 152, 320
Dobromyl', Ukraine: 128, *129*
Dobrzyjałowo: 160, 164
Dolyna, Ukraine: 128, *129*
Don Army, Land of: 117, 135, *136*
Don Cossacks: 117
Don River: 135
Dorpat → Tartu, Estonia
double dates → dates, double
double first names: 201
draft (military) → conscription
Drissa → Verkhnyadzvinsk
Drohiczyn, Poland: *167*, 189
Drohobych, Ukraine: 128, *129*
Dubno, Ukraine: 130, *131*
Dushanbe, Tajikistan: *138*
Dutch language: 32, 76
Dvinsk → Daugavpils
Dytiukov: 142
Działowo → Dzyatlava
Dziennik Praw: 353
Dzisna → Disna
Dzyatlava, Belarus': 126
ё (Russian vowel): ***8***, 14
ę (Polish letter): 11, 24, 207
East European Genealogical Society: 192
East European Genealogist: 48, 181, 192
East Prussia: *131, 167, 168*
Easter duty: 336
Eastern Slavs: 441
East Siberian Sea: *139*
ecclesiastical archives (Poland): 189-191
Edlund, Thomas K.: 320, 321, 467
education → schools
Elbląg, Poland: 164, *168*
Elista, Russia: *138*
Ełk, Poland: *168*, 190
Ellis Island: 75
employment records: 79, 114
Encyklopedia Powszechna S. Orgelbranda: 116, 469
endings (on words): ***34-45***
English language: 2, 182, 440
epenthetic vowel → fill vowel
equivalents of names: ***441***
Erivan → Yerevan

errors, correction: 205
Essentials in Polish Genealogical Research: 469
estates: 94, 99, 317, 321, 324, 329
Estonia (Russian *Эстляндія*): 116, ***122, 136***
European Russia: 116, 130
-ev or *-evich* suffix: 29, 83
-evna suffix: 86
exemption from military service: 108-111
eyewitness testimony on death: 277
Family History Centers: 78, 140, 149, 152, 169, 187
Family History Library, Salt Lake City, Utah: ix, 140, 143, 144, 147, 149, 151, 152, 153, 154, 155, 156, 164, 165, 169, 174, 181, 187, 188, 212, 320, 321, 469
family relationships: ***51-52***, 357
father's absence: 201, 220
father's name, age, occupation: 83, 198, 201, 229, 257
Feldblyum, Boris: 16
feminine forms of nouns: 53, 276, 350
feminine forms of verbs: 44, 82, 86, 89, 201, 223, 241, 276, 331
feminine gender: ***34***, 35-36
Feodosiya, Crimea: *131*
Fergana, Uzbekistan: 117
Ferro, longitude measured from: 157
fill vowel: ***40-41***
Finland (formerly the Duchy of Finland): 116, ***121***, *138*
Finns: 94, 121
first names: 198, 203, ***440-466***, 468 (*see also* Jewish first names)
First Names of the Polish Commonwealth: Origins & Meanings: 468
Flemish language: 32
Following the Paper Trail: A Multilingual Translation Guide: 469
fraternal organizations: 78
French (language): 32, 182
funeral ceremonies: 87
g vs. *h:* 6, 14, 17
gabbai: 256
Gadyach → Hadyach
Galicia (German *Galizien*): ***127-128***, *129*, 134, *136*, 152, 162, 165-166, 180, 181, 468
Gäncä, Azerbaijan (formerly *Елизаветполь*): 117, *136*, 137, *138*
Garliava, Lithuania (Polish *Godlewo*): 208
Garwolin, Poland: 120
Gaisin → Haisyn
Gazetteer of the Crown Lands and Territories Represented in the Imperial Council: 165
Gazetteer of Galicia: 162
Gazetteer of Lithuania: Names Approved by the United States Board on Geographic Names: 151
Gazetteer of Polish Adjectival Place-Names: 156
Gazetteer of Populated Places in the B. S. S. R.: 147
gazetteers: 74, ***140-166***
Gdańsk, Poland (German name *Danzig*): *119, 167, 168*
Gemindelexikon der im Reichsrate vertretenen Königreiche und Länder: 165
gender (grammatical): ***34***, 358
gender, expressions indicating: 198, 202, 225, 290, 318, 319, 336
Genealogical Gazetteer of Galicia: 166, 180, 468
genitive case: **33**, 34-36, 47, 110, 200, 201, 202, 216, 223, 248, 249, 285, 358, 440
Genun Publishers: viii, 469
Geograficheskо-statisticheskii slovar' Rossiiskoi imperii: 142
geographical considerations: ***115-193***
Geographical Dictionary of the Kingdom of Poland and Other Slavic Countries: 155
Georgia: 117, 137, 139
German Empire: *136*
German-English Genealogical Dictionary: 469
German language: 182
German-language books on the Russian Empire: 143
German partition: *167*
German names, Russified: 11, ***14-16***, 353, 440
Germanic languages: 33, 440
Germanized names: 32, 76
German records: 181
Germany: 14
Glazov, Russia: *138*
Głuchów *or* Glukhov → Hlukhiv
gmina: 161, 188, 223, 292, 302, 312, 331, 332, 341, 342, 349, 351
Gniezno, Poland: *168*
Godlewo → Garliava
godparents: 84, 198, 204, 206, 227, 230
Gomel' → Homel'
Goniądz, Poland: 121
Gorbachev: 13
Gorki → Horki
Gorodnya → Horodnya
Gorodok → Haradok, Belarus' *and* Horodok, Ukraine
Gostynin, Poland: 119
Goshchevo → Hoshchava
Gould, Arleen: 175, 467
Grajewo, Poland: 121, 160
grammar, Russian: ***33-51***
Grand Duchy of Lithuania → Lithuania
gravestones → cemetery inscriptions
Great Russia: 117, 135
Greek Catholic archdiocese: 191
Greek Catholics: 82, 155, 166, 180, 181, 196, 440, 442
Greek language: 2, 3, 261, 440, 441
Gregorian calendar: 96, **200**, 217, 241, 252, 294, 339, 442
Grinkiškis, Lithuania: 231, 267, 269
Gródek Jagielloński → Horodok

Grodno → Hrodna
Grójec, Poland: 119, *168*
gromada: 154
groom: 195, 247, ***248***, 261, 265, 266
Grudziądz, Poland: *168*
Gruziya → Georgia
gubernia: ***83***, 116, 118, 121, 131, 140, 156, 317, 331, 342
Gubernskie Vedomosti: 357
guidebooks: 164
guilds: 352-353
Gumbinnen, East Prussia: 139
Gur'yev → Atyraū
Gusev → Gumbinnen
guttural: 14
h vs. *g*: 6, 14, 17, 209, 216, 249, 272
Hadyach, Ukraine (Russian *Гадяч*): *131,* 133
ḥalitsah: 290, 291
Halych, Ukraine (Polish *Halicz*): *129,* 134
Hamburg: 32
Häme, Finland: 121
handwriting, Russian: ***8-10***, 53, 199, 278, 358
handwriting, samples printed for better legibility: 30-31, 80, 194, 195, 196, 198, 208, 211, 215, 236-238, 251, 255, 269, 274, 278
Haradok, Belarus' (Russian *Городок*): 126, *131*
Harbin, China: *139*
Harkavy, Alexander: 271, 468
Harrassowitz, O.: 143
Haisyn, Ukraine (Russian *Гайсин*): *131,* 132
head of household: 337
Hebrew alphabet: 2, ***18-20***, 96, 221, 467
Hebrew language: 233-238, 440
Hebrew names of months: ***47***
Hebrew personal names: ***18-20***, 441
Helon, George W.: 467
Helsinki, Finland (Swedish *Helsingfors*): 121, *138*
Heritage Books: 143
Hierro: 157
Historical Atlas of East Central Europe: 468
Historical Society of Pennsylvania: 79
Hlukhiv, Ukraine (Russian *Глухов*, Polish *Głuchów*): *131,* 133
Hoffman, William F.: 468
Hollowak, Thomas: 467
Holocaust: 28
Homel', Belarus: 126, *131, 138*
Honolulu, Hawaii, U.S.A.: 94
Horki, Belarus': 126, *131*
Horodenka, Ukraine: 128, *129*
Horodnya, Ukraine (Russian *Городня*): *131,* 133
Horodok, Ukraine (Polish *Gródek Jagielloński*): 128, *129*
Hoshchava, Belarus' (Russian *Гощево*): 261
house number: 343
Hrodna, Belarus (Russian *Гродно* or *Гродна*, Polish *Grodno*): 74, 117, *119, 123, 125,* ***125***, *131, 136,* 147, *168,* 317, 320, 331, 332, 347
Hrubieszów, Poland: 120
Humań → Uman'
Husiatyn, Ukraine: 128, *129*
hypocoristic names: 443
Iaşi, Moldova (Russian *Яссы*): *131,* 132
identification papers: 96, 306, 313, ***330-332***, 351
Ihumen, Belarus' (Russian name *Игумен*): 126, *131,* 148
illegitimate → legitimacy
illiteracy → literacy, statements regarding
illness, expressions for: 285, ***286-289***, 467
Iłża: 120
impediment to marriage: 245-246, 265
inanimate objects: 43
Indeks alfabetyczny miejscowości dawnego Wielkiego Księstwa Litewskiego: 149
indexes to vital records: 193-197
Index of Localities of the Polish Republic: 153
Indo-European family of languages: 33
induction into the military: 298
Inflanty → Livonia
Inowrocław, Poland: *168*
inscriptions on graves → cemetery inscriptions
instrumental case: ***33-43***, 195, 203, 204, 213, 217, 249, 272, 273
Instytut Języka Polskiego PAN: 164
insurance death claim records: 78
In Their Words series: 187, 266, 317, 467
Iody, Belarus: 99
Irkutsk (town and province): 117, 137, *139*
Istanbul, Turkey: *138*
"italic" forms of Russian letters: 10, 53, 332, 358
Iŭe, Belarus' (Russian *Ивье*, Polish *Iwie*): 127
Ivano-Frankivs'k (old Polish name *Stanisławów*): 127, 128, *129, 168,* 180, 182
Izhevsk, Russia: *138*
Izmayil, Ukraine (Russian *Измаил*): *131,* 132
Izyaslav, Ukraine: 130, *131*
Izyum, Ukraine: *131,* 134
Jaczno, Poland: 90
Jamaica: 87
Jampol → Yampil'
Janów Lubelski, Poland: 120, 316
Japan: *139*
Jarosław, Poland: *129, 168*
Jasło: *129, 168*
Jassy → Iaşi
Jaświły, Poland: 284
Jaworów → Yavoriv
Jędrzejów, Poland (old Russian name *Андреевъ*): 120
Jedwabne: 164
Jelgava, Latvia (formerly *Mitau, Mitava*): *119,* 122

Jewish calendar: 233, 271, 284
Jewish communities: 143, 196, 239
Jewish first names: ***18-20***, 219
Jewish Genealogical Society of Washington, D.C.: 94
Jewish Historical Institute: 131
Jewish months, Russian names of: ***47***, 233, 290
Jewish names, Russified: ***16-20***, 27, 201, 209, 224, 236, 441, 467
Jewish records (including sample documents): 94-96, 97-103, 103-106, 106-107, 111-113, 114, 180, 181, 187, 188, 189, 196, 209-212, 217-221, 221-225, 233-239, 255-259, 270-272, 278-281, 284-286, 290-291, 299-302, 318-320, 329, 338-341, 346-347
Jewish Roots in Poland: 19, 469
Jewish Roots in Ukraine and Moldova: 469
Jewish surnames: 17, 20, 219, 468
Jews and so-called "illegitimacy": 259
Jews as a social class: 317
Jeziorosy → Zarasai
Julian calendar: 96, ***200***, 217, 241, 252, 294, 339, 442
Kabardino-Balkariya: 137
Kabliai, Lithuania: 269
Kainsk, Russia: 329
Kaliningrad, Russia: *119*, ***124***, *168*
Kalisz, Poland: 118, *119*, *168*, 190, 353
Kaluga, Russia: 117, 135, *136*, *138*, 140
Kalush, Ukraine: 128, *129*
Kalvarija, Lithuania: 120
Kamchatka peninsula: *139*, 139
Kamieniec Podolski → Kam'yanets Podil's'kyi
Kamkin Bookstores: 147, 152
Kam'yanets' Podil's'kyi, Ukraine (Polish name *Kamieniec Podolski*): *119*, *131*, 131
Kam'yanka-Buz'ka (Polish *Kamionka Strumiłowa*): 128
Kamyshin, Russia: *138*
Kaniv, Ukraine (Russian *Канев*, Polish *Kaniów*): *131*, 132
Kara Sea: *138*
Karaliaučius → Kaliningrad
Karniewo, Poland: 272
Karpilovka: 142
Karpowicze, Poland: 284
Kars, Turkey: 117, *136*, 137, *138*
karty meldunkowe: 341
Kasuk, Mrs. S.: 467
Katowice, Poland: *168*
Kaunas, Lithuania (Polish *Kowno*, Russian *Ковно*): 116, *119*, 123, 124, *131*, *136*, *168*
Kavkaz (Caucasus): 116, 117, ***137***
Kazakhstan: 137, *138*
Kazan', Russia: 117, 135, *136*, *138*, 140
Kel'tsy → Kielce
Kemerovo, Russia: *139*
Kerch-Yenikale, Russia: 116, *131*, 134
ketubah: 271
keywords, birth records: 197, ***198***
keywords, death records: ***274***
keywords, marriage records: ***247***, 280
Khabarovsk, Russia: *139*
Kharkiv, Ukraine (Russian name *Харьков*, Polish *Charków*): 117, *131*, ***133***, 135, *136*, *138*, 140, 152
Khatanga, Russia: *139*
Kherson, Ukraine: 117, *131*, ***133***, *136*, 140, 152
Khmel'nyts'kyi, Ukraine (old Russian *Проскуровъ*): *131*, 132
Khorol, Ukraine (Polish *Chorol*): *131*, 133
Khotyn, Ukraine (Russian: *Хотин*, Polish *Chocim*): *131*, 132
khupa: 271
Kielce, Poland (old Russian name *Кѣльцы*): 120, *168*, 190
Kielce-Radom SIG Journal: 341
Kiev, Kijów → Kyiv
Kingdom of Poland: 22, 116, ***118-121***, 129, *136*, *167*, 198, 292, 317, 353
kinnui (secular or vernacular name): 19, 237
Kirov (Russia, formerly *Вятка*): 117, 135, *136*, *138*, 140, 320
Kirovohrad, Ukraine (old Russian *Елисаветградъ*): *131*, 133
Kishinev → Chişinău
Klimavichy, Belarus' (Russian *Климовичи*) 126, *131*
Klugiewicz, Esther: 467
Klukowo, Poland: 223, 224
Knyszyn, Poland: 121
Kobelyaki, Ukraine: *131*, 133
Kobryn, Belarus: *125*, 125, *131*
Kolno, Poland: 120, 160, 241
Koło, Poland: 118
Kolomyia, Ukraine: 128, *129*
Kolyma river: *139*
Kongresówka → Kingdom of Poland
Königsberg → Kaliningrad
Konin, Poland: 118, 194, 195
Konotop, Ukraine: *131*, 133
Końskie, Poland: 120
Konstantinograd → Krasnohrad
Konstantynów, Poland: 120
Kopczyński, Michał: 286, 292, 467, 468
kopeks: 29
Korycin, Poland: 121
Korzenie: 192
Kosava, Belarus': 262
Kosiv, Ukraine: 128, *129*
Kostroma, Russia: 117, 135, *136*, 140
Koszalin (German name *Köslin*): *168*
Kovil', Ukraine (Russian *Ковель*, Polish *Kowel*): 130, *168*
Kovno *or* Kowno → Kaunas

Kowel → Kovil'
Kozelets', Ukraine: *131*, 133
Kozienice, Poland: 120
Kraffohlsdorf: 164
krai: 169
Krakės, Lithuania: 232, 267
Kraków, Poland: *119, 167, 168*
Krasnodar, Russia (formerly *Екатеринодар*): 137, *138*
Krasnystaw, Poland: 120
Krasnohrad, Ukraine (Russian *Константиноград*): *131*, 133
Krasnosielc, Poland: 165
Krasnoyarsk, Russia: *139*
Kratkiy toponomicheskiy slovar' Belorussii: 144
Kremenchuk, Ukraine (Russian *Кременчуг*): *131*, 133
Kremenets', Belarus': 130, *131*
Krichev, Belarus': 145
Krolevets', Ukraine (Polish *Królewiec*): *131*, 133
Królewiec → Kaliningrad *or* Krolevets'
Krosno, Poland: *129*
Krupnak, Laurence: 183, 467
Krym (Crimea): 117, 134, 139
Krzynowłoga Wielka, Poland: 121
Księga imion: 442
Księga naszych imion: 442, 468
księgi ludności: 341
ksuba → ketubah
Kuban', Russia: 117, 135, *136*, 137
Kubiliūnai, Lithuania: 232, 267, 269
Kudirkos Naumiestis, Lithuania: 120
Kulisher, Iser: 17
Kuopio, Finland: 121, *136q*
Kupisz, Bogdan: 442
Kup'yans'k, Ukraine: *131*, 134
Kurgan, Russia: 138
Kurland, Kurlandiya → Courland
Kursk, Russia: 117, 135, *136, 138*, 140
K'utais'i, Georgia: 117, *136*
Kutno, Poland: 119, *168*
Kuźnica, Poland: 121
Kyiv, Ukraine (Russian *Киев*, Polish *Kijów*): 117, *119, 131*, ***132***, *136, 138, 167*, 180, 182, 350
lääni: 121
LaBudie-Szakall, Kathleen: 468
Łańcut, Poland: *129*
land divisions: 155
Land of the Black Sea Cossacks: 135, 137
Land of the Don Cossacks: 117, 135, *136*, 140
Laptev Sea: *139*
Łapy, Poland: 121
Łask, Poland: 119
Last Rites: 284
Latin: 48, 197, 440, 441
Latvia: 320
Latvian language: 21, 33
Latyczów → Letychiv
Law of Moses: 237, 271
LDS (Church of Jesus Christ of Latter-Day Saints): 78
Lebedyn, Ukraine: *131*, 134
Łęczyca, Poland: 118
legal capacity: 335
legitimacy: 205, 259
Lemberg → L'viv
Lena river: *139*
length, measures of: 160
Leningrad, Russia: 139
Lenius, Brian J.: 166, 180, 467, 468
Lensk, Russia: *139*
Leopolis → L'viv
Lepel', Belarus: 126, *131*, 146
Lesko, Poland (also called *Lisko*): *129*
Leszno, Poland: *168*
Letter-Writing Guide (Lithuanian): 175-179
Letter-Writing Guide (Russian): 170-173
Letter-Writing Guide (Ukrainian): 183-186
letters, personal: 356
Letychiv, Ukraine (Russian: *Летичев*): *131*, 132
levirate marriage: 290
Libava, Latvia → Liepāja, Latvia
Library of Congress: 143
Lida, Belarus': *123*, 124, *125, 131, 168*
Liepāja, Latvia (also called *Libava*): 123
Lietuva → Lithuania
Lietuvos Centrinis Metrikų Archyvas: 174
Lietuvos Valstybinis Istorijos Archyvas: 174
Liflyandiya → Livonia
Limanowa, Poland: *129*
Lipetsk, Russia: *138*
Lipno, Poland: 119
Lipovets *or* Lipowiec → Lypovets'
Lipsk, Poland: 121
Lisko → Lesko
List of Localities in the Polish People's Republic: 154
List of Official Names of Localities in Poland: 155
literacy, statements regarding: 198, 204, 220, 258, 309, 344, 346, 349
Lithuania (Lithuanian *Lietuva*, Russian *Литва*, Polish *Litwa*): viii, 14, 21-23, 117, 119, ***123-124***, 144, 149-151, 152, 153, 155, 156, 167, *168*, 169, 174, 200, 207, 208, 317, 320, 355, 442
Lithuanian language: 1, 21-23, 33, 169, 208, 440
Lithuanian Letter-Writing Guide: 175-179
Lithuanian names: 8, 11, ***21-23***, 76-77, 208, 231, 268, 310, 440
Lithuanian State Historical Archive: 150, 174
Lithuania's Central Civil Registry Archive: 174
Little Russia: 117, 127, 130
Litva → Lietuva

Lityn, Ukraine (Russian *Литин*): *131*, 132
Liubavas, Lithuania: 332
Livonia: 116, *131*, ***122***, *136*, 156, 226
locative case → prepositional case
Łódź, Poland: 119, *168*, 190, 338, 353
Lokhvytsya, Ukraine (Russian *Лохвица*): *131*, 133
Łomża, Poland: 108, *119*, 120, *131*, 160, *167*, *168*, 190, 257, 272, 300, 349
lots, drawing of (conscription): 297, 306
Łowicz, Poland: 119, 190
Lubaczów, Poland: 191
Lubartów, Poland: 120
Lublin, Poland: *119*, 120, *168*, 190, 313, 316, 342-343
Lubny, Ukraine: *131*, 133
Ludza, Latvia (Russian *Люцинъ*): 126, *131*
Łuków, Poland: 120
Lusatian language: 33
Lutherans: 32, 73, 180, 309
Lutsk, Ukraine (Polish *Łuck*): 113, 130, *131*, *167*, *168*
L'viv (Russian *Львов*, Polish *Lwów*, Ukr. *Львів*, Latin *Leopolis;* German *Lemberg*): *119*, 128, *129*, 134, *138*, *167*, *168*, 180, 182
Lyakhavichy, Belarus' (Polish *Lachowicze*): 27-28
Lypovets', Ukraine (Russian *Липовец*, Polish *Lipowiec*): *131*, 132
Lyutsin → Ludza
Macedonian language: 1, 33
Magadan, Russia: *139*
Magocsi, Paul Robert: 127, 152, 468
Mahileŭ, Belarus (Russian name *Могилев*): 117, *119*, 125, ***126***, *131*, *136*, 147
maiden names: 203, 208, 232, 300
Majdanek concentration camp: 191
Makhachalka, Dagestan (formerly *Петровск*): 137, *138*
Maków Mazowiecki, Poland: 120, 272, 349
Maladzechna, Belarus' (Russian *Молодечно*): 144
maps: 119, 123, 125, 129, 131, 136, 138, 139, 167, 168
marginal notations in records: 206-209
Marijampolė, Lithuania: 120
marital status: 99, 300, 328, 343, 348
marriage certificate: 272-273
marriage indexes: 195, 196
marriage information added to baptismal records: 205-208
marriage, usually held in bride's parish: 249
marriage records: 195, ***242-273***, 316
marriage, religious vs. civil: 259
marriages, first, second, etc.: 86, 252
married names: 300
masculine gender: ***34***, 35-36
Massachusetts federal court records: 74
Matthews, Geoffrey J.: 152
Maykop, Russia: *138*
Mazyr, Belarus': 126, *131*, 149
measures of area, length, distance: 160
"mechanical" transliteration ***11***, 21, 23
Meckelein, Wolfgang: 143
Melitopol', Crimea: *131*, 134
Memel → Neman
memorial notices (on the anniversary of a death): 88
merchant class: 317
Methodius: 2
Mezen', Russia: *138*
Mglin, Russia: *131*, 133
middle class → townsman
Miechów, Poland (old Russian name *Мѣховъ*): 120
Mikkeli, Finland: 121
military records and service: 77, 100, 108-111, 241, 280, ***292-316***, 321, 341, 344, 349
military training: 303-304, 308
militia (military home guard): 292, 297, 305, 313, 316, 344
minor children: 96
Minsk, Belarus (Russian name *Минск*, Polish name *Mińsk*): 116, *119*, *123*, **125**, *131*, *136*, *138*, 146, 147, 149, *167*, *168*, 317
Mińsk Mazowiecki, Poland: 119
Mirgorod → Myrhorod
Mirnyi, Russia: *139*
misspellings: 88, 96, 195, 209, 200, 217, 244, 252, 334
Mitau *or* Mitava → Jelgava
Mława, Poland: 119
Mogilev → Mahileŭ
Mogilev Podol'skiy → Mohyliv Podil's'kyi
mohel: 236
Mohylew → Mahileŭ
Mohyliv Podil's'kyi, Ukraine (Russian *Могилев Подольский*): *131*, 132
Mokotoff, Gary: 469
Moldova: 130, 139
Molodechno → Maladzechna
Mongolia: *139*
months, Old Church Slavonic names of: ***49***
months, Russian names of: ***47***
months of the Jewish calendar: ***47***
Moravia 2
Morbus: How and Why Our Ancestors Died: 286, 468
mórg (Polish measurement of surface area): 160
mortality statistics: 281
Moskva, Russia (English name *Moscow*): 117, 135, *138*, 140, 169
mother's name, age, etc.: 203, 229
moving → relocation
Mozyr' → Mazyr
Mstsislaŭ, Belarus' (Russian *Мстиславль*): 126, *131*
Murmansk, Russia: *138*
mutual benefit societies: 78
Myadzel, Belarus': 146

Mykolayiv, Ukraine (Russian *Николаев*): 134
Myrhorod, Ukraine (Russian *Миргород*): *131*, 133
Myszyniec, Poland: 121
ń (Polish letter): 11, 27
Naczelna Dyrekcja Archiwów Państwowych: 189
Nadvirna, Ukraine (Polish *Nadwórna*): 128, *129*
Nakhichevan → Naxçivan
Nal'chik, Russia: *138*
Name Changes and the Establishment of Localities in the European Parts of the Soviet Union: 143
name days: ***441-442***
name of deceased: 274, 276, 280, 282, 284, 285
names, Americanized: viii, 76
names, first: 10-29, 77
names, Polish vs. Belarusian: 145
names, Polish vs. Russian → Russified names
name variations, diminutives, etc.: 442-443
Napoleonic era: 153
Narew river: 160, *168*
National Archive of the Republic of Belarus': 180
National Archives (U. S.): 75, 94
National Archives and Record Administration (NARA) 78
National Historical Archive of the Republic of Belarus': 179-180
nationality (ethnic affiliation): 102
naturalization records: ***74-75***
Navahrudak, Belarus' (Russian *Новогрудокъ*): 126, *131*, 155, *168*
Naxçivan, Azerbaijan: 304
Nazwy miejscowe Polski: 163-164
negatives, multiple: 110, 223
Neman river: 124, 139, 167, *168*
Nesterov → Zhovkva
neuter gender: ***34***, 35-36
Nevel', Russia: 126, *131*
New Britain, CT: 80, 88
New Russia: 117, 130, 135
newspapers: 79
New Style (dating) → Gregorian calendar
New York City: 94
New York City Public Library: 153
New York passenger lists: 75
Nezhin → Nizhyn
Niemen → Neman
Niesułków, Poland: 341
Nieszawa, Poland: 119
Nikolayev → Mykolayiv
Nikopol', Ukraine: *138*
Nizhnevartovsk, Russia: *138, 139*
Nizhny Novgorod, Russia: 117, 135, *136, 138*, 140
Nizhyn, Ukraine (Russian *Нежин*): *131*, 133
nobles: 213, 245, 317, 331, 355
Nogai steppes: 117, 134
Noginsk, Russia: *138*
nominative case: ***33***, 34-36, 200, 257, 358, 440
Noril'sk, Russia: *138, 139*
Norman Ross Publishing: 357
North America: 82
North Ossetia: 137
Norway: *138*
notaries and notarized documents: 96, ***332-336***
notations added to documents: 205, 302
nouns: ***33-42***
Nova Ushitsya, Ukraine (Russian *Новая Ушица*): *131*, 132
Novaya Zemlya, Russia: *138*
Novgorod, Russia: 117, 135, *136, 138*, 309
Novhorod-Sivers'kyi, Ukraine (Russian *Новгород Северский*): *131*, 133
Novo-Aleksandrovsk → Zarasai
Novohrad-Volyn's'kyi, Ukraine: 130, *131*
Novominsk → Mińsk Mazowiecki
Novomoskovs'k, Ukraine: *131*, 134
Novorossiysk → Dnipropetrovs'k
Novosibirsk, Russia: *139*
Novotroitsk, Russia: *138*
Novoye Diveyevo: 88
Novoye Russkoye Slovo (Russian newspaper): 85
Novozybkov, Russia: *131*, 133
Novyi Margelan → Fergana
Nowa Aleksandryja → Puławy, Poland
Nowogród, Poland: 206, 351
Nowogródek → Navahrudak
Nowy Radomsk, Poland: 119
Nowy Sącz, Poland: *129, 168*
number (grammatical): ***34***
numbering of records: 32, 194-196, 228, 231, 271, 284, 290, 300, 318, 319, 328, 336
numerals: 45, ***46***
Nyland, Finland: 121, *136*
ó (Polish letter): 11
obituaries: 78, ***85-88***, 90-93
objections to marriage → impediments to marriage
oblast': 124, 169, 182
occupations: ***52-72***, 75, 201, 257, 329, 332
Odes[s]a, Ukraine: 116, *131*, 133, *138*
Ogólnopolski Spis Teleadresowy: 188
Okotsk, Russia: *139*
Okhtyrka, Ukraine (Russian *Ахтырка*): *131*, 133
Old Church Slavonic (alphabet): ***48***, 225, 261, 281, 467
Old Church Slavonic (language): 2, 345
Old Prussian (language): 21, 33
Old Style (dating) → Julian calendar
Old White Russian (language): 22
Oleksandriya, Ukraine (old Russian *Александрія*): *131*, 133
Oleksandrivs'k → Zaporizhzhya

Oleshki → Tsyurupyns'k
Ol'hopol', Ukraine (Russian *Ольгополь*): *131*, 132
Olita → Alytus
Olkusz, Poland: 120
Olonets, Russia: 117, 135, *136*, 140
Olsztyn, Poland: *119, 168*
Omsk, Russia: *138, 139*
Opatów, Poland: 120
Opoczno, Poland: 120
Opole, Poland: *119*
Oral (formerly *Уральскъ*): *136*, 137, *138*
ordinal numbers: ***45***, 46, 200
Orel, Russia: 117, 135, *136, 138*, 140
Orenburg: 117, 135, *136, 138*, 140
organizational histories: 78
Orgeev → Orhei
Orgelbrand → *Encyklopedia Powszechna S. Orgelbranda*
Orhei, Moldova (old Russian *Оргѣевъ*): *131*, 132
Orsha, Belarus': 126, *131*
Orthodox churches (i. e., Russian Orthodox): 48, 73, 80, 140, 188, 196, 213, 226, 281, 329, 440, 441, 442
orthography, Russian: 2, ***8***
Ortsumbenennungen und Neugründungen im Europäischen Teil der Sowjetunion: Nach dem Stand der Jahre 1910/1938/1951 mit einem Nachtrag für Ostpreußen 1953: 143
Oshmiany → Ashmiany, Belarus'
Osmołowszczyzna, Poland: 265
Oster, Ukraine: *131*, 133
Ostroh, Ukraine (Russian *Острог*): 130, *131*
Ostrołęka, Poland: 108, 120, 335
Ostrów Mazowiecka, Poland: 120
Ostsee: 122
Oświęcim, Poland (German name *Auschwitz*): 191
Oszmiana → Ashmiany, Belarus'
Ottoman Empire: *136*
Oulu, Finland: 121, *138*
Our Polish Ancestors: 191
-ov or *-ovich* suffix: 29, 83
-ovna suffix: 86
Ovruch, Ukraine: 130, *131*
palatalization: 3, ***4-5***, 13, 21, 37
Pale of Settlement: *131*, 143, 144
Palgon, Gary: 467
Panevėžys, Lithuania: 124, *131*
paradigms of noun and adjective declensions: ***35-36***
paragraph-form records: ***197-225***, 242, ***247-259***, ***274-281***
parental consent to marriage: 245, 252, 258
parents of conscripts: 294
parents of the deceased: 274
parents of the newlyweds: 244, 247, 266, 269
parish histories: 78
parish seal: 212, 216, 228
"part one, part two, part three, part four" of Russian registers: 82, ***213***, 225, 261, 271, 281, 284, 290
participles: ***44-45***, 51, 78, 83, 97, 203, 204, 205, 213, 220, 224, 244, 248, 277, 280
partitions of Poland and Lithuania: 14, 153, 217
passenger lists → ship passenger lists
passive voice: 44, 97, 257
passports and passport applications: 97-106, 111-113, 321, ***342-351***
past tense: ***43-44***, 200, 202, 244
pastors: 85, 209 (*see also* registrars for vital records)
paternity, acknowledging: 259
Pathways & Passages: 191, 292, 467, 468
patronymic: ***28-29***, 83, 86, 89, 226, 227, 228, 261, 282, 313, 335, 342
Pavlohrad, Ukraine (Russian *Павлоград*): *131*, 134
peasants, categories of: 317
Pechora, Russia: *138*
Pennsylvania court records: 74-75
Penza, Russia: 117, 135, *136, 138*, 140
Perekop, Crimea: *131*, 134
Peremyshlyany, Ukraine (Polish name *Przemyślany*): 128, *129*
Pereyaslav-Khmel'nyts'kyi, Ukraine: *131*, 133
Periday Co.: 143
Perm', Russia: 117, 135, *136, 138*, 140
permanent population → population registers
personnel records: 79
Petition for Naturalization → naturalization records
Persian names: 8
Petrograd → St. Petersburg
Petrokov → Piotrków Trybunalski, Poland
Petropavlovsk-Kamchatskiy, Russia: *139*
Petrovsk → Makhachalka
Petrovskiy, N. A.: 442
Petrozavodsk, Russia: *138*
PGS-NY Searchers: 192
Philadelphia: 94
Philadelphia passenger arrival lists: 75
phonetic spelling: 6, 7, ***10-29***, 108, 145, 209, 239, 290, 291
phonetic transliteration: ***11***, 23, 204
photocopies of records: 212
physical description: 297, 332, 344-345, 349
physical examination: 292, 297
Pidhaitsi, Ukraine (Polish *Podhajce*): 128
Piła, Poland: *168*
Pilzno, Poland: *129*
Pinsk, Belarus': 126, *131, 168*
Pińczów, Poland: 12
Piotrków Trybunalski (old Russian name: *Петроковъ*): *119*, 119, *168*
Piryatin → Pyryatyn
place names, forms of: 202

place of birth → birthplace
place of death → death, place of
place of marriage: 205
place where a document was drawn up: 198, 200, 247, 274
Pleskačiuaskas, Alius: 175
Płock, Poland: *119*, 119, 165, *167*, *168*, 190
Płońsk, Poland: 119
plural (number): ***34***
Podhajce → Pidhaitsi
Podolia province (old Russian name *Подолія*, Polish name *Podole*): 117, *131*, 131, ***132***, *136*
Pokrov, feast of: 228
Poland: viii, 14 (see also: Kingdom of Poland), 129, 169, 200, 355
Poland, 1634 and 1815: *167*
Poland, 1921-1939: *168*
Polatsk, Belarus' (Russian *Полоцк*): 126
Poles: 94, 167, 181, 317, 442
Polesie: 155, *168*
police: 212, 310, 312, 313
Polish Eaglet: 192
Polish Footprints: 192
Polish Genealogical Society of America: 156, 191, 286, 292, 468, 469
Polish Genealogical Society of California: 191
Polish Genealogical Society of Connecticut & the Northeast: 147, 153, 164, 188, 191, 292, 467, 468
Polish Genealogical Society of Greater Cleveland: 191
Polish Genealogical Society of Massachusetts: 191
Polish Genealogical Society of Michigan: 192
Polish Genealogical Society of Minnesota: 192
Polish Genealogical Society of New York State: 192
Polish Genealogical Society of Texas: 192
Polish Genealogical Society of Wisconsin: 192
Polish language: 1, 2, 6, 22, 23, 33-36, 51, 84, 197, 207, 335-336, 339, 440
Polish letter-writing guides: 187
Polish names (or Polish forms of names): 8, 11, ***23-27***, 31, 36, 145, 149, 150, 195, 199, 200, 204, 207, 208, 216, 217, 219, 224, 237, 239, 268, 276, 440
Polish records: 187-189
Polish spellings of Jewish names: 29, 290, 291, 319, 320, 339
Polish State Archives: 174, 187, 188-189, 293, 469
political clubs: 78
Polonism: 194, 202, 248, 276, 277, 336
Polonization of Lithuanian names: 22-23
Polotsk → Polatsk
Poltava, Ukraine: 117, ***133***, *136*, 140-141, 152
Pomerania (German *Pommern*, Polish *Pomorze*): *168*
Pommern *or* Pomorze → Pomerania
Ponevezh *or* Poniewież → Panevėžys
population records and statistics: 140-142, 147, 155, 161, 162, 320
population registers: 221, 224, 241, 272, ***300-302***, ***338-341***, 343, 344
port of arrival: 75
ports of departure: 32
Portland: 94
Poryte, Poland (near Łomża): 241, 247, 275
Posen → Poznań
powiat: 83, 155, 158, 161, 223, 292
Poznań, Poland (German name *Posen*): *167*, *168*, 188
predicate adjectives: ***37***
premarital announcements → banns
premarital examinations: 242, ***243-247***
prenuptial agreements: 247, 253
Prenai, Lithuania: 115
prepositional case: ***33***, 35-36, 200, 202, 203, 208, 219, 273
present tense: ***44***
priests: 183, 187, 203, 205, 207, 209, 217, 228, 262, 284
Priluki → Pryluky
Primorskaia oblast': 117, 137
Prinke, Rafał T.: 156, 442, 467
privacy concerns: 188
probate records: 77
professional researchers: 169, 170, 182, 183
pronouns: ***42-43***
pronunciation, Russian: ***4-7***
property ownership: 151
Proskurov → Khmel'nits'kyi
Protestants: 78, 188, 189, 196, 309
Protėviai: 175
provinces of Poland → *województwo*
Prussia: 124
Prussian partition → German partition
Pruzhany, Belarus': *125*, 125, *131*
Pryluky, Ukraine (Russian *Прилуки*): *131*, 133
Przasnysz, Poland: 119, 335
Przemyśl, Poland: 128, *129*, *168*, 191
Przemyślany → Peremyshlyany
psalmist → church attendant
Pskov, Russia: 117, 135, *136*, *138*, 140
Puławy, Poland (once called *Nowa Aleksandryja*): 120
Pułtusk, Poland: 119
Puszcza Mariańska: 154
Pyryatyn, Ukraine (Russian *Пирятин*): *131*, 133
rabbis: 239, 256, 271, 291
Raczki, Poland: 121
Radom, Poland: *119*, 120, *168*, 190
Radomyshl', Ukraine (Russian *Радомышль*, Polish *Radomyśl*): 78, *131*, 132
Radziłów, Poland: 121
Radzymin, Poland: 119
Radzyń Podlaski, Poland: 120

Rahachoŭ, Belarus' (Russian *Рогачев*): 126, *131*
RAHS: 182, 183
railroad station: 147, 154, 155, 163
raion: 144, 146
Raseiniai, Lithuania (old Russian *Россиены*): 124, *131*, 311, 312
Rava Rus'ka, Ukraine: 128, *129*
Rawa Mazowiecka, Poland: 119
Rèchitsa, Belarus': 126, *131*
record number → numbering of records
"Red Russia": 139
regional archives: 169, 182
registers, parts one, two, three, and four: 82, ***213***
registrars for vital records → civil registrars
registration for taxation and conscription: 321, 328
regressive assimilation (phonetic): ***7***, 21, 27
relationships, family: ***51-52***
religion: 102, 261, 300, 309, 328, 331, 343
relocation: ***339-341***
remarks added to documents: 206-209
replacements for destroyed documents: 221
Republic of Poland: 167
requiem: 87-88
reserves (military): 292, 297, 307, 309, 313, 316
residence, place of: 100, 105, 201, 221, 312, 343
residency permit: 212
retirement: 276, 286
Revel' → Tallinn
Revision Lists: 294, ***317-320***
Rēzekne, Latvia (Russian *Рѣжица*): 126, *131*
Rezhitsa → Rēzekne
Riga, Latvia: 122, *131, 138*, 225
Rivne, Ukraine (Russian *Ровно*, Polish *Równo*): 130, *131, 168*, 180
Rodziny (journal of the Polish Genealogical Society of America): 192, 292, 468
Rogachev → Rahachoŭ
Rogienice, Poland: 160
Roman alphabet: 7, 12, 33, 144, 166, 182
Roman Catholic Church, members and clergy: 32, 73, 155, 181, 187, 196, 213, 336, 442
Roman numerals: 48
Romance languages: 33, 440
Romny, Ukraine: *131*, 133
Rootsweb: 169, 179
Rosien[n]y → Raseiniai
Rostov-na-Donu: 134, *138*
Rotterdam: 32
Routes to Roots Foundation: 469
Rovno, Równo → Rivne
Różan, Poland: 121
Różanystok, Poland: 242
Rubel', Belarus': 237
rubles: 29, 169
Russian alphabet → Cyrillic alphabet
Russian Book of Geographical Names: 143
Russian Brotherhood Organization: 79
Russian Consular Records: ***94-114***
Russian Consular Records Index and Catalog: 78
Russian Empire: viii, 8, 49, 76, 94, 116, 117, 124, 127, 129, 130, 131, 152, 155, 166-168, 169, 189, 193, 197, 200, 207, 260, 292, 293, 316, 317, 320, 349, 468, 469
Russian-Jewish Given Names: Their Origins and Variants: 16
Russian Jews: 17, 94
Russian Language Documents from Russian Poland: A Translation Manual for Genealogists: viii, 469
Russian Letter-Writing Guide: 170-173
Russian names: 12-14, 29, 76, 83, 208, 282, 328, ***440-462***
Russian national census of 1897: ***320-329***
Russian Orthodox parishes: 82, 90, 225, 260
Russian partition of Poland and Lithuania: 14, 33, *167*
Russian Revolution: 1, 2, 3, 17, 30, 37, 53, 121
Russified names: ***10-32***, 84, 231, 246, 261, 304, 335, 336, 342, 345, 353
Russisches geographisches Namenbuch: 143
Ruthenia: 442
Rymut, Kazimierz: 163
Ryazan', Russia: 117, 135, *136, 138*, 140, 320
Rypin, Poland: 119
Ryzhkova, A. G.: 442, 469
Rzeczyca Ziemiańska, Poland: 316
Rzekuń, Poland: 108
Rzeszów, Poland: *129, 168*
ś (Polish letter): 11
Sabbath: 257
Sack, Sallyann Amdur: 78, 469
sacrament: 84, 228, 229, 262
"sacred name," Jews: 19-20, 237
Sadlno (Poland) parish: 30-31, 194, 195
saints' names: 442
Sakha, Republic of: 137
Sakhalin Island: 117, 137, *139*
Salant, Yankl (Jeffrey): 19, 467
Salt Lake City, Utah: 140, 143, 155, 164, 469
Şamaxi, Azerbaijan: 304
Samara, Russia: 117, 135, *136, 138*, 140
Samarkand, Uzbekistan: 117, 137
Sambir, Ukraine: 128, *129*
San Francisco, California: 94
San River: *129*
Sandomierz, Poland (old Russian name *Сандомиръ*): 120, *129, 168*, 190
Sankt-Petersburg → St. Petersburg
Sanok, Poland: *129*
Sapporo, Japan: *139*
Saratov, Russia: 117, 135, *136, 138*, 140
Saskatchewan Genealogical Society: 192

Schlyter, Daniel M.: 156, 469
schools: 140, 141, 156, 328
schwa: 6
script, Russian → handwriting
Sea of Japan: *139*
seaman: 106
Seattle, Washington: 94
Sebezh, Russia: 126, *131*
Sedmigradskaia district: 139
Sejny, Poland: 120
Semenov-Tian-Shanskii, Petr Petrovich: 142
Semei, Kazakhstan (formerly *Семипалатинскъ*): 117, 137
Semipalatinsk → Semey
Semirech'ye district: 117, 137
Senno → Syanno
Serbian language: 1, 33
Serov, Russia: *138*
Sevastopol: 116, 139
sex → gender
Sezam: 293
Shea, Jonathan D.: viii, 469
Shemakha → Şamaxi
shem ha-kodesh → "sacred name," Jews
ship passenger lists: 32, ***75-77***
short forms of adjectives: ***37***, 45, 83
shtetl: 28
Shtetl Finder: Jewish Communities in the 19th and Early 20th Centuries in the Pale of Settlement of Russia and Poland and in Lithuania, Latvia, Galicia, and Bukovina, with Names of Residents: 143
Šiauliai, Lithuania (Russian *Шавли*): 124, *131*
Siberia: 116, 117, ***137***, *139*
Siedlce, Poland (old Russian name *Сѣдлецъ*): *119*, 120, *168*, 190, 217, 221
Siemiatycze, Poland: 121
Sieradz, Poland: 118
Sierpc, Poland: 119
signatures, or making one's mark: 18-19, 96, 111, 241, 246, 247, 256, 258, 262, 282, 310, 344, 346, 349
Silesia, Poland: *168*
Simbirsk → Ul'yanov
Simferopol', Crimea: *131*, 131, 134, *138*
singular (number): ***34***
Skalat, Ukraine: 128
Skaudvilė, Lithuania: 312
-ski: 36
Skidel, Belarus': 347
Skierki, Poland: 305
Skierniewice: 119, 154
Skobelev → Fergana
Skorowidz miejscowości Rzeczpospolitej Polski: 153
Skvyra, Ukraine (Russian *Сквира*, Polish *Skwira*): *131*, 132
Slavic languages 1, 2, 4, 21, 33, 440, 441
Slavyanoserbsk → Slov'yanoserbs'k
Slonim, Belarus': *125*, 125, *131*, 261, 262
Sloŭnik nazvaŭ naselenykh punktaŭ minskaŭ voblastsy: 146
Slovak language: 33
Slovar' russkikh lichnykh imyon: 442, 469
Slovenian language: 33
Slov'yanoserbs'k, Ukraine (Russian *Славяносербск*): *131*, 134
Słownik geograficzny Królestwa Polskiego i innych krajów słowiańskich: 28, 126, 151, 152, ***155-161***, 164, 165, 312, 469
Słupca, Poland: 118
Słupsk (German name *Stolp*): *168*
Slutsk, Belarus': 126, *131*, 149
Smarhon', Belarus': 127
Smolensk, Russia: 117, 135, *136*, 140, *167*
Smrock, Poland: 348, 349
Sniatyn, Ukraine: 128, *129*
Sochaczew, Poland: 119
social class: 105, 201, 231, 261, 282, 284, 300, 309, 328, 331, 342
Social Security: 77
Society of Genealogists: 192
Sokal', Ukraine: 128
Sokółka, Poland: *125*, 125, *131*, 332
Sokołów Podlaski, Poland: 120
Solikamsk, Russia: *138*
sołtys: 256
"son of" → patronymic
Soroca, Moldova (Russian *Сороки*): *131*, 132
Soroki → Soroca
Sosnytsya, Ukraine (Russian *Сосница*): *131*, 133
Soundex: ***76***, 78
South Russia: 117, 127, 130, 135
South Slavic: 48
Sovetsk, Russia: 124
Soviet Union: 8, 124, 127, 152, 153, 167, *168*, 169, 180, 181
Spector, Morris: 467
spelling, standard: 1-32, 37, 130 (*see also* archaic spellings)
Spis miejscowości PRL: 154, 188
Spisok naselennykh mest B.S.S.R.: 147
Spisok naselennykh miest Rossiiskoi Imperii: 140, 152
Sprogis, Ivan Yakovlevich: 149, 151
Stanisławów → Ivano-Frankivs'k
Starobil's'k, Ukraine (old Russian *Старобѣльскъ*): *131*, 134
Starodub, Russia: *131*, 133
Starokostyantyniv, Ukraine (Russian *Старо-константинов*): 130, *131*
starostwo: 162

Stary Bykhov → Bykhaŭ
State Archives' Head Office (Poland): 189
State Archives of Belarus: 169
State Archives of Lithuania: 169
State Archives of Ukraine: 169
Stavropol', Russia: 117, 135, *136*, 137
Stawiski, Poland: 160, 241
stem (part of a word to which endings are added): ***34***
St. Michel, Finland: 121, *136*
Stockholm, Sweden: *138*
Stopnica, Poland: 120
Stott, Kathleen: 467
St. Petersburg: 116, ***122***, *136*, *138*, 140, 169, 320
Stryi, Ukraine: 128, *129*, *168*
Subačius, Giedrius: 175
subjunctive mood: 223
substitute documents → replacements for destroyed documents
Succolosky, Bill: 467
suffixes: 34-45
Sugintai, Lithuania: 312
Sulimierski, Filip: 469
Sumy, Ukraine: *131*, 134
Suomi → Finland
Surazh, Russia: *131*, 133
Surgut, Russia: *138*, *139*
surnames, Russian, declensions: ***36***
surnames, variants: 2, 6
Surowe, Poland: 335
Suwałki, Poland: *119*, 120, *125*, *168*, 174, 193, 309, 331
Švenčionys, Lithuania (Polish *Święciany*): *123*, 123, 124, *131*
Sweden: 121, *136*, *138*
Święciany → Švenčionys, Lithuania
Syanno, Belarus' (Russian *Сенно*): 126, *131*
Syktyvkar, Russia: *138*, *139*
Syr-Darya: 117, *136*, 137
Szawle → Šiauliai
Szczuczyn, Poland: 120
Szląsk → Silesia
Sztabin, Poland: 121
Szumowski, Don: 467
Szwelice, Poland: 272
Taganrog, Russia: 116, 134
Tallinn, Estonia: 122, *138*
Tambov, Russia: 117, 135, *136*, 140
Tarashcha, Ukraine: *131*, 132, 350
Tarnopol → Ternopil'
Tartu, Estonia: 123, *138*
Tashkent → Toshkent
Tavastehus, Finland: 121, *136*
Tavrida province: 117, *131*, 131, ***134***, *136*, 140, 152
taxation: 29, 320 (*see also* Revision Lists)
Tbilisi, Georgia (formerly *Тифлисъ*): 117, *136*, 137, *138*
Tehran, Iran: *138*
Telšiai, Lithuania (Russian *Тельши*): 124, *131*
Temeshvar → Timişoara
Terebovlya, Ukraine (Polish *Trembowla*): 128, *129*
Terek (river and district), Russia: 117, *136*, 137
Ternopil', Ukraine (Polish *Tarnopol*): 128, *129*, *168*, 180, 182
Teutonic Knights: 157
Thode, Ernst: 469
Tiflis → Tbilisi
Tighina, Moldova (old Russian *Бендеры*, Polish *Bendery*): *131*, 132
Tikhonov, A. N.: 442, 469
Tilsit → Sovetsk
Timişoara, Romania (old Russian *Темешваръ*): 139
Tiraspol, Moldova: *131*, 133
time, expressing: ***49-50***, 219
time of death: 274
Tobol'sk, Russia: 117, *136*, 137, 140, 320, 329
Tolkovyi slovar' zhivogo velikorusskogo yazyka v 4 tomakh: 468
Tomaszów Lubelski, Poland: 120
tombstone inscriptions → cemetery inscriptions
Tomsk (town and province): 117, 137, *139*, 140, 329
Torah: 19
Toruń, Poland: *168*
Toshkent, Uzbekistan (formerly *Ташкент*): 137, *138*
townsman (or "burgher" or "city-dweller" or "middle-class person" as a translation of Russian *мѣщанинъ*): 226, 227, 233, 236, 239, 272, 285, 300, 317, 329, 331, 341, 347
tradesmen: 209, 245
Trakai, Lithuania (Russian *Троки*): *123*, 123, 124, *131*, 150, 212
Transcarpathian region → Zakarpats'ka oblast'
Transcaspian Region: *136*
transcripts: 212, 217-221
transliteration vs. translation: ***10-12***, 21
Transylvania: 139
traveling papers: 94, 111-113, 321, 348-349, 351
Treasury Office (Russian Empire): 317
Trembowla → Terebovlya
Troki → Trakai, Lithuania
Tsyurupyns'k, Crimea (former Russian name *Алешки*): *131*, 134
Tula, Russia: 117, 135, *136*, 140
Tura, Russia: *139*
Turek, Poland: 118
Turgai: 117, *136*, 137
Turinsk, Russia: 329
Turka, Ukraine: 128, *129*
Turkish names: 8
Turku, Finland: 121
Turun-Porin, Finland: 121

Tver', Russia: 117, 135, *136, 138*, 140
two first names: 201
Tyumen', Russia: 329
uezd → *uyezd*
Ufa, Russia: 117, 135, *136, 138*, 140
Ukhta, Russia: *138*
Ukmergė, Lithuania (old Russian: *Вилькомиръ*): 124, *131*, 150
Ukraine: viii, 48, 117, ***127-134***, 135, 152, 153, 155, 169, 180-186, 260, 355, 468, 469
Ukraine: A Historical Atlas, 127, 152, 468
Ukrainian Catholic rite: 48
Ukrainian Consulate: 183
Ukrainian language: 1, 2, 33, 130, 169, 182
Ukrainian Letter-Writing Guide: 183-186
Ukrainian personal names: 76, 440
Ukrainian place names: 128, *129*, 166
Ukrainian State Archives: 182
Ulan-Ude, Russia: *139*
Uleåborg, Finland: 121, *136*
Ul'yanov, Russia (formerly called *Симбирск*): 117, 135, *136, 138*, 140
Uman', Ukraine (Polish *Humań*): *131*, 132
umlauted vowels (German) 15-16
Uniates: 196
union membership: 79, 107
United States of America: 82
University of Toronto Press: 152
Upytė, Lithuania: 149, 150, 151
uppercase letters: 3, 8
Urals: 117
Urals'k → Oral
USC (Urząd Stanu Cywilnego): 154, 187, 188
Usimaa, Finland: 121
U.S.S.R. → Soviet Union
U.S.S.R. and Certain Neighboring Areas: Official Standard Names Approved by the U.S. Board on Geographic Names: 144
Ust'-Nera, Russia: *139*
Uudenmaan, Finland: 121
uyezd [old Russian *уѣздъ*]: 83, 116, 118, 123, 125, 130, 140, 156, 223, 292, 311, 312, 317, 331, 342, 351
Uzbekistan: 137, *138*
Vaasa, Finland: 121, *136*
Valky, Ukraine (Polish *Wałki*): *131*, 133
Valozhyn, Belarus': 146
Varshava → Warszawa, Poland
Vasa → Vaasa
Vasmer, Max: 143
Vasyl'kiv, Ukraine (Russian *Васильков*, Polish *Wasylków*): *131*, 132
Vaŭkavysk, Belarus': *125*, 125, *131*, 307, 331
Veiveriai, Lithuania: 207, 208
Velizh, Russia: 126, *131*
verbs: ***43-45***, 359
Verkhn'odniprovs'k, Ukraine: *131*, 134
Verkhnyadzvinsk, Belarus' (old Russian *Дрисса*): 126, *131*, 227
Verkhoyansk, Russia: *139*
Verro, Estonia: 122, 226, 227
Viešvenai, Lithuania: 150
Viipuri, Finland: 121
Vileika, Belarus': *123*, 123, *131*
Vilkaviškis, Lithuania (Polish *Wyłkowyszki*): 120, 309, 331
Vilkomir → Ukmergė
villages: 83, 141, 142, 144, 146, 151, 156, 256, 309, 317
Vilnius, Lithuania: (Russian *Вильна* or *Вильно*, Polish *Wilno*): 116, *119, 123*, 123, *131, 136, 138*, 149, 155, *167, 168*, 216
Vistula → Wisła River
Vištytis, Lithuania (old Russian *Вынштынецъ*, Polish *Wisztyniec*): 309, 331
Vitsebsk, Belarus' (Russian name *Витебск*, Polish name *Witebsk*): 117, 125, ***126***, *131, 136*, 147
Vladikavkaz: 137
Vladimir, Russia: 117, 135, *136*, 140
Vladimir Volynskiy → Volodymyr Volyn's'kyi
Vladislavov → Kudirkos Naumiestis
Vladivostok, Russia: 137, *139*
voiced consonants vs. voiceless: 7, 12, 13, 14, 21
vocative case: 33
Volchan'sk → Vovchan'sk
Volgodonsk, Russia: *138*
Volgograd, Russia: *138*
Volhynia → Volyn'
Volkovyshki → Vilkaviškis
Volkovysk → Vaŭkavysk
Volodymyr Volyn's'kyi, Ukraine (Russian *Владиміръ*): 130, *131*
Vologda, Russia: 117, 135, *136, 138*, 140
Volyn' province (Russian name *Волынь*, English name *Volhynia*, Polish name *Wołyń*): 113, 116, ***130***, *131*, 131, *136, 168*, 180, 260, 281
volost': 83, 113, 140, 141, 312, 342
volunteers for military service: 296
Vorkuta, Russia: *138, 139*
Voronezh, Russia: 117, 135, *136, 138*, 140
Võru, Estonia → Verro, Estonia
Vovchan'sk, Ukraine (Russian *Волчаньск*), Polish *Wołczańsk*): *131*, 133
vowels, Russian: ***5-6***, 17
Vyatka → Kirov
Vyborg, Finland: 121, *136, 138*
Wach, Poland: 335
Walewski, Władysław: 469
Wałki → Valky
Waltham, Massachusetts: 74

Warszawa, Poland (English name *Warsaw*, Russian *Варшава*): *119*, 119, *167*, *168*, 189, 190, 191
Wasiłków, Poland: 120
Wasylków → Vasyl'kiv
wedding contract: 271
Weiner, Miriam: 19, 469
Węgrów, Poland: 120
Wejwery → Veiveriai
Western Russia: 116
West Prussia: *168*
Where Once We Walked: 27-28, 144, 469
White Russia → Belarus'
widow: 245, 249, 252
widower: 245, 252
Wieliczka: *129*
Wielkie Księstwo Litewskie → Lithuania
Wieluń: 118
wife: 198, 203, 244, 316, 345
Wilejka → Vileika, Belarus'
Wilkomierz → Ukmergė
wills: 334-335
Wilno → Vilnius
Wisła River (English *Vistula*): *129*, *168*
Wisztyniec → Vištytis
Witebsk → Vitsebsk
witnesses: 111, 198, 201, 219, 228, 246, 247, 248, 266, 271, 274, 280, 290, 335
Wizna, Poland: 120, 257
Władysławów → Kudirkos Naumiestis
Włocławek, Poland: 119, 190
Włodarski, Bronisław: 442
Włodawa, Poland: 120
Włoszczowa, Poland (old Russian name *Влощовъ*]: 120
województwo: 150
wójt: 150, 224, 302, 332, 351
Wola Pękoszewska: 154
Wołczańsk → Vovchan'sk
Wołkowysk → Vaŭkovysk
Wołyń → Volyn'
women's names in documents: 20
word order: 259, 267
World War II, border shifts: 129, 153, 154
wounded in battle: 308
Wrocław, Poland: *168*
Wykaz urzędowych nazw miejscowości w Polsce: 155
Wyłkowyszki → Vilkaviškis
Wynne, Suzan F.: 78
Wysokie Mazowieckie, Poland: 120
Yakutiya: 117, 137
Yakutsk, Russia: *139*
Yalta, Crimea: *131*, 134
Yampil', Ukraine (Russian *Ямполь*): *131*, 132
Yaroslavl', Russia: 117, 135, *136*, *138*, 140
Yassy → Iaşi
Yavoriv, Ukraine (Polish *Jaworów*): 128, *129*
year, expressing: 47, 49, 200, 202, 223, 241, 328
Yekaterinburg, Russia: *138*
Yekaterinodar → Krasnodar
Yekaterinoslav → Dnipropetrovs'k
Yelisavetgrad → Kirovohrad
Yelisavetpol' → Gäncä
Yenisei river: *139*
Yeniseisk (town and province): 117, 137, 140
Yerevan, Armenia (formerly *Эриванъ*): 117, *136*, 137, *138*
Yevpatoriya, Crimea: *131*, 134
Yeysk, Russia: *138*
Yiddish: 17-20, 27, 96, 467
Yiddish alphabet → Hebrew alphabet
Yiddish-English Hebrew Dictionary: 271, 468
ź (Polish letter): 11
ż (Polish letter): 11, 13
Zabaikal'skaia district: 137
Zabłudów, Poland: 121
Zabużański Collection: 191
Zakarpats'ka oblast' (Ukraine): 180, 182
Zakaspiyskaia district: 137
Zambrów, Poland (near Łomża): 121, 300
Zamość, Poland: 120, *129*, *168*, 191, 342-343
Zaporizhzhya, Ukraine (Russian *Александровск*, formerly *Oleksandrivs'k*: *131*, 134, *138*
Zarasai, Lithuania (, Polish *Jeziorosy*, Russian *Ново-Александровскъ*): 124, *131*
Zaręby Kościelne, Poland: 259, 280
Zaskrodzie, Poland: 275
Zdzięcioł → Dzyatlava
Zemlya voyska Donskago → Land of the Don Cossacks
zemstvo: 141
Zen'kov → Zin'kiv
Zhovkva, Ukraine (old Russian *Жолква*, later *Нестеров*, Polish *Żołkiew*): 128, *129*, 134
Zhytomyr, Ukraine (Polish *Żytomierz*, Russian *Житомир*): *119*, 130, *131*
Zin'kiv, Ukraine (old Russian *Зѣньковъ*, Polish *Zienków*: *131*, 133
Zmiyiv, Ukraine (old Russian *Змiевъ*): *131*, 134
Zolochiv, Ukraine (Polish *Złoczów*): 128, *129*
Żółkiew → Zhovkva
Zolotonosha, Ukraine: *131*, 133
Zukowski, Dr. Edward: 467
Zvenyhorodka, Ukraine (Russian *Звенигородка*, Polish *Zwinigródka*): *131*, 132
Żydowski Instytut Historyczny: 191
Żytomierz → Zhytomyr